TO THE INSTRUCTOR

WileyPLUS is built around the activities you perform

Prepare & Present

Create outstanding class presentations using a wealth of resources, such as PowerPoint™ slides, interactive simulations, and more. Plus you can easily upload any materials you have created into your course, and combine them with the resources contained in *WileyPLUS*.

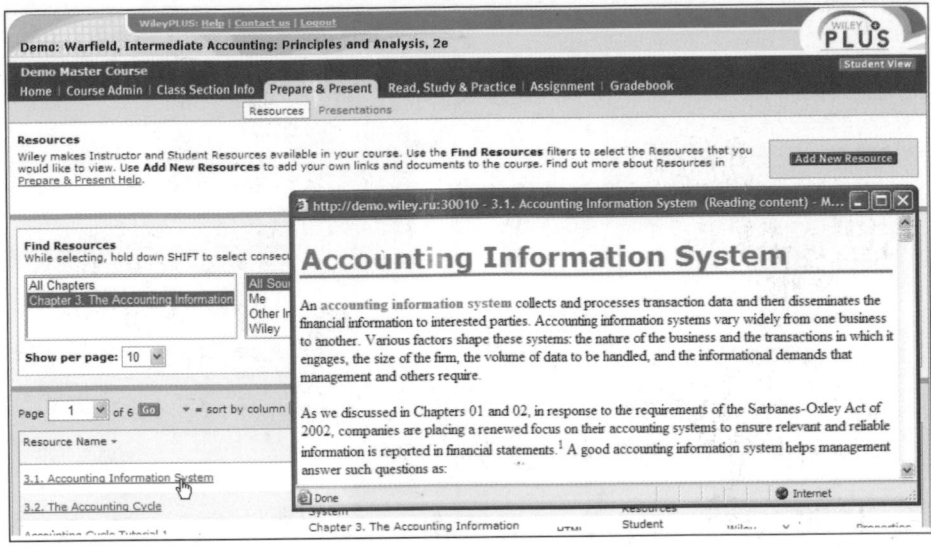

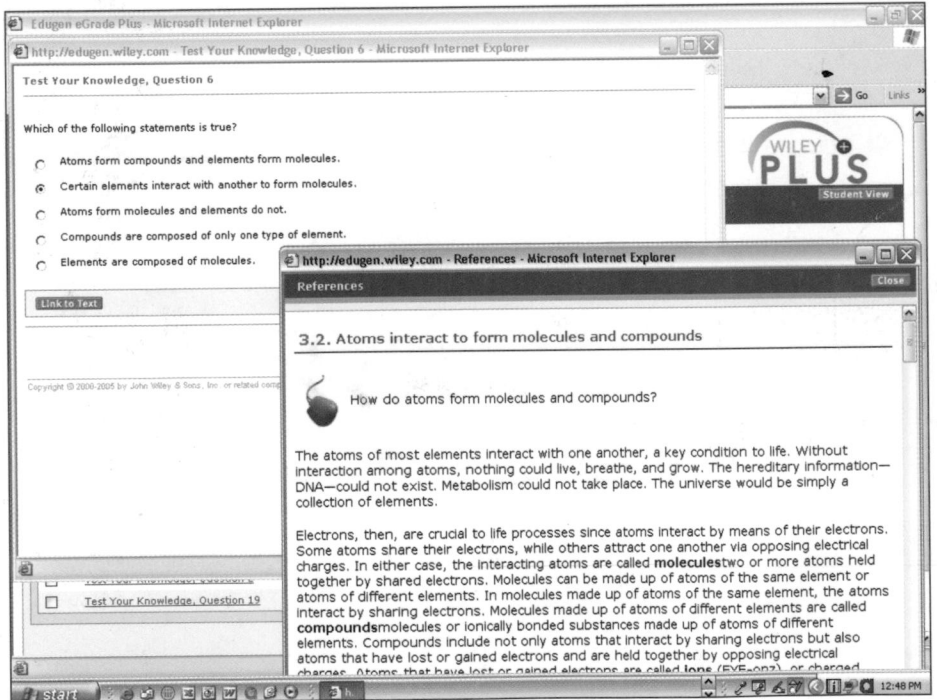

Create Assignments

Automate the assigning and grading of homework or quizzes by using the provided question banks, or by writing your own. Student results will be automatically graded and recorded in your gradebook. *WileyPLUS* also links homework problems to relevant sections of the online text, hints, or solutions—context-sensitive help where students need it most!

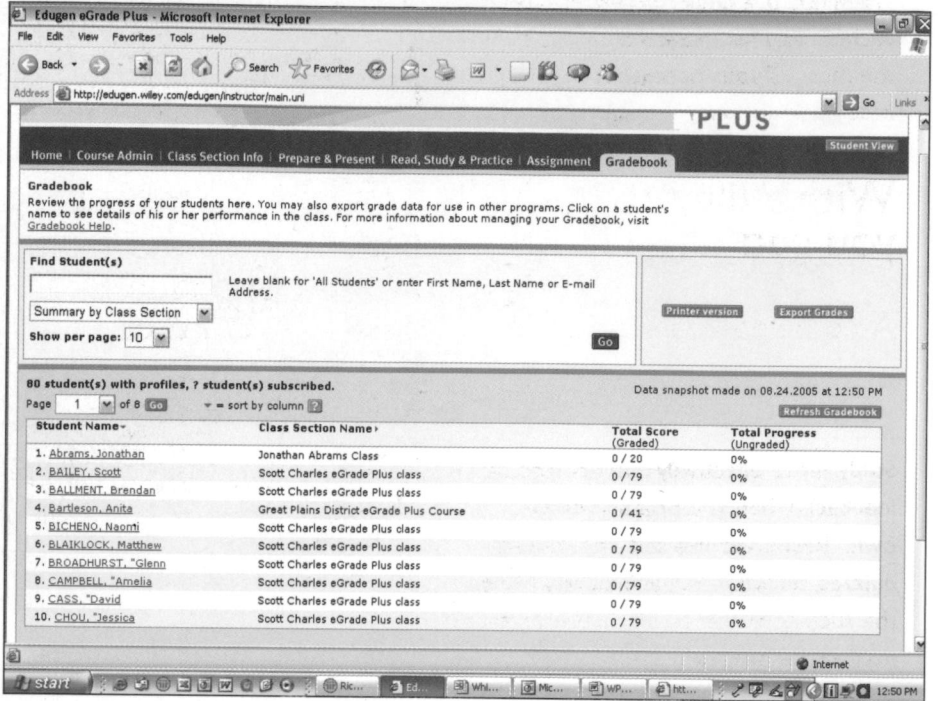

TO THE STUDENT

You have the potential to make a difference!

WileyPLUS is a powerful online system packed with features to help you make the most of your potential, and get the best grade you can!

With Wiley**PLUS** you get:

A complete online version of your text and other study resources

Study more effectively and get instant feedback when you practice on your own. Resources like self-assessment quizzes, tutorials, and animations bring the subject matter to life, and help you master the material.

Problem-solving help, instant grading, and feedback on your homework and quizzes

You can keep all of your assigned work in one location, making it easy for you to stay on task. Plus, many homework problems contain direct links to the relevant portion of your text to help you deal with problem-solving obstacles at the moment they come up.

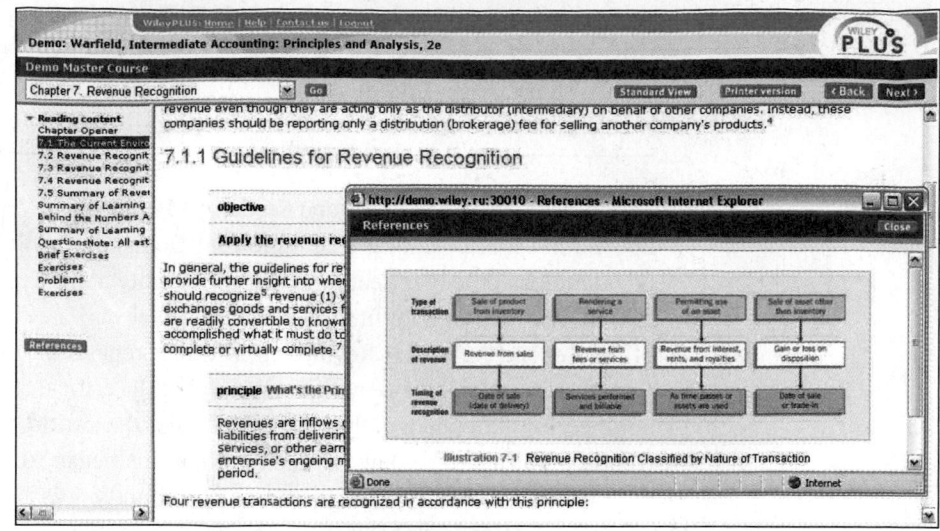

The ability to track your progress and grades throughout the term.

A personal gradebook allows you to monitor your results from past assignments at any time. You'll always know exactly where you stand.

If your instructor uses *WileyPLUS*, you will receive a URL for your class. If not, your instructor can get more information about *WileyPLUS* by visiting www.wileyplus.com
or
by viewing a *WileyPLUS* demo at www.wileyplus.com/experience

---

"It has been a great help, and I believe it has helped me to achieve a better grade."

Michael Morris, *Columbia Basin College*

74% of students surveyed said it helped them get a better grade. *

*Based on a fall 2006 survey of 519 accounting student users of *WileyPLUS*

BICENTENNIAL
1807
⊕WILEY
2007
BICENTENNIAL

THE WILEY BICENTENNIAL—KNOWLEDGE FOR GENERATIONS

*E*ach generation has its unique needs and aspirations. When Charles Wiley first opened his small printing shop in lower Manhattan in 1807, it was a generation of boundless potential searching for an identity. And we were there, helping to define a new American literary tradition. Over half a century later, in the midst of the Second Industrial Revolution, it was a generation focused on building the future. Once again, we were there, supplying the critical scientific, technical, and engineering knowledge that helped frame the world. Throughout the 20th Century, and into the new millennium, nations began to reach out beyond their own borders and a new international community was born. Wiley was there, expanding its operations around the world to enable a global exchange of ideas, opinions, and know-how.

For 200 years, Wiley has been an integral part of each generation's journey, enabling the flow of information and understanding necessary to meet their needs and fulfill their aspirations. Today, bold new technologies are changing the way we live and learn. Wiley will be there, providing you the must-have knowledge you need to imagine new worlds, new possibilities, and new opportunities.

Generations come and go, but you can always count on Wiley to provide you the knowledge you need, when and where you need it!

WILLIAM J. PESCE
PRESIDENT AND CHIEF EXECUTIVE OFFICER

PETER BOOTH WILEY
CHAIRMAN OF THE BOARD

SECOND EDITION

INTERMEDIATE ACCOUNTING:
PRINCIPLES AND ANALYSIS

TERRY D. WARFIELD, Ph.D.

Associate Professor
Director, Andersen Center for Financial Reporting and Control
University of Wisconsin
Madison, Wisconsin

JERRY J. WEYGANDT, Ph.D., C.P.A.

Arthur Andersen Alumni Professor of Accounting
University of Wisconsin
Madison, Wisconsin

DONALD E. KIESO, Ph.D., C.P.A.

KPMG Emeritus Professor of Accounting
Northern Illinois University
DeKalb, Illinois

BICENTENNIAL
1807
WILEY
2007
BICENTENNIAL

JOHN WILEY & SONS, Inc.

Dedicated to our wives,

Mary, Enid, and Donna,

and to our children, Andrew, Lauren, and Katie;

Matt, Erin, and Lia; and Douglas and Debra

EXECUTIVE PUBLISHER *Donald Fowley*
EXECUTIVE EDITOR *Christopher DeJohn*
SENIOR MARKETING MANAGER *Julia Flohr*
PROJECT EDITOR *Ed Brislin*
DEVELOPMENT EDITOR *Ann Torbert*
EDITORIAL ASSISTANT *Kathryn Fraser*
DESIGN DIRECTOR *Harry Nolan*
SENIOR DESIGNER *Madelyn Lesure*
SENIOR PRODUCTION EDITOR *Patricia McFadden*
SENIOR ILLUSTRATION EDITOR *Elle Wagner*
SENIOR PHOTO EDITOR *Anna Melhorn*
SENIOR MEDIA EDITOR *Allison Morris*
OUTSIDE PROJECT MANAGEMENT *Ingrao Associates*
COVER IMAGE *Gavin Hellier/Image Bank/Getty Images*

This book was set in Times Roman by Aptara and printed and bound by R. R. Donnelley, Jefferson City, MO.
The cover was printed by R. R. Donnelley, Jefferson City, MO.

This book is printed on acid free paper. ∞

To order books or for customer service, please call 1-800-CALL WILEY (225-5945).

ISBN-13   978 0471737933

Printed in the United States of America

10 9 8 7 6 5 4 3 2 1

Terry D. Warfield, Ph.D., is associate professor of accounting at the University of Wisconsin—Madison. He received a B.S. and M.B.A. from Indiana University and a Ph.D. in accounting from the University of Iowa. Professor Warfield's area of expertise is financial reporting, and prior to his academic career, he worked for five years in the banking industry. He served as the Academic Accounting Fellow in the Office of the Chief Accountant at the U.S. Securities and Exchange Commission in Washington, D.C. from 1995–1996. Professor Warfield's primary research interests concern financial accounting standards and disclosure policies. He has published scholarly articles in *The Accounting Review, Journal of Accounting and Economics, Research in Accounting Regulation, Review of Accounting Studies,* and *Accounting Horizons*, and he has served on the editorial boards of *The Accounting Review, Accounting Horizons,* and *Issues in Accounting Education.* He has served as president of the Financial Accounting and Reporting Section, the Financial Accounting Standards Committee of the American Accounting Association (Chair 1995–1996), the AAA-FASB Research Conference Committee and the AAA Regulation Committee, and is a member of the Financial Accounting Standards Advisory Council to the FASB. Professor Warfield has received teaching awards at both the University of Iowa and the University of Wisconsin, and he was named to the Teaching Academy at the University of Wisconsin in 1995. Professor Warfield has developed and published several case studies based on his research for use in accounting classes. These cases have been selected for the AICPA Professor-Practitioner Case Development Program and have been published in *Issues in Accounting Education.*

Jerry J. Weygandt, Ph.D., C.P.A., is Arthur Andersen Alumni Professor of Accounting at the University of Wisconsin—Madison. He Holds a Ph.D. in accounting from the University of Illinois. Articles by Professor Weygandt have appeared in the *Accounting Review, Journal of Accounting Research, Accounting Horizons, Journal of Accountancy*, and other academic and professional journals. These articles have examined such financial reporting issues as accounting for price-level adjustments, pensions, convertible securities, stock option contracts, and interim reports. Professor Weygandt is author of other accounting and financial reporting books and is a member of the American Accounting Association, the American Institute of Certified Public Accountants, and the Wisconsin Society of Certified Public Accountants. He has served on numerous committees of the American Accounting Association and as a member of the editorial board of the *Accounting Review*; he also has served as President and Secretary-Treasurer of the American Accounting Association. In addition, he has been actively involved with the American Institute of Certified Public Accountants and has been a member of the Accounting Standards Executive Committee (AcSEC) of that organization. He has served on the FASB task force that examined the reporting issues related to accounting for income taxes and as a trustee of the Financial Accounting Foundation. Professor Weygandt has received the Chancellor's Award for Excellence in Teaching and the Beta Gamma Sigma Dean's Teaching Award. He is on the board of directors of M & I Bank of Southern Wisconsin. He is the recipient of the Wisconsin Institute of CPA's Outstanding Educator's Award and the Lifetime Achievement Award. In 2001 he received the American Accounting Association's Outstanding Accounting Educator Award.

Donald E. Kieso, Ph.D., C.P.A., received his bachelor's degree from Aurora University and his doctorate in accounting from the University of Illinois. He has served as chairman of the Department of Accountancy and is currently the KPMG Emeritus Professor of Accounting at Northern Illinois University. He has public accounting experience with Price Waterhouse & Co. (San Francisco and Chicago) and Arthur Andersen & Co. (Chicago) and research experience with the Research Division of the American Institute of Certified Public Accountants (New York). He has done postdoctorate work as a Visiting Scholar at the University of California at Berkeley and is a

v

recipient of NIU's Teaching Excellence Award and four Golden Apple Teaching Awards. Professor Kieso is the author of other accounting and business books and is a member of the American Accounting Association, the American Institute of Certified Public Accountants, and the Illinois CPA Society. He has served as a member of the Board of Directors of the Illinois CPA Society, the AACSB's Accounting Accreditation Committees, the State of Illinois Comptroller's Commission, as Secretary-Treasurer of the Federation of Schools of Accountancy, and as Secretary-Treasurer of the American Accounting Association. Professor Kieso served as a charter member of the national Accounting Education Change Commission. He is the recipient of the Outstanding Accounting Educator Award from the Illinois CPA Society, the FSA's Joseph A. Silvoso Award of Merit, and the NIU Foundation's Humanitarian Award for Service to Higher Education.

Intermediate Accounting: Principles and Analysis, Second Edition, provides a solid foundation for instructors whose goal is to help accounting students build an understanding of the principles, concepts, and methods of financial accounting and reporting. To that end, we address the following key themes that users have identified as important in their intermediate accounting courses.

- *Go "beyond the numbers"*

The importance of accounting to the capital market and the business community in general has never been more important. In *Intermediate Accounting, Second Edition,* boxed stories entitled "What Do the Numbers Mean?" convey the excitement and ever-changing nature of accounting, highlighting its importance. We have found that when introduced to the issues involved in the financial reporting of real companies, students genuinely enjoy the subject area.

- *"What's the principle?"*

An important instructional objective in *Intermediate Accounting, Second Edition,* is to reinforce students' understanding of the principles and concepts that are fundamental to financial reporting. Most students quickly forget procedural details, but they can internalize principles and concepts that will serve as important cornerstones for decision making throughout their careers. Concepts are especially important in a world in which the details are frequently changing. Furthermore, a conceptual orientation is consistent with the evolving orientation toward principles-based, as opposed to rules-based, accounting standards.

- *Active learning—"Try it out!"*

Students learn best when they are actively engaged. An overriding pedagogical approach for the book is to provide students opportunities for active learning. Each chapter contains strategically placed "Try it out!"exercises (with worked-out solutions) that give added opportunities for active learning.

- *"You need to decide"*

All business people and accounting professionals must make decisions. Decision making involves critical evaluation and analysis of information. A new review exercise in each chapter, titled "Accounting, Analysis, Principles," helps students evaluate and analyze information from the chapter. They review the accounting introduced in the chapter ("Accounting"), consider how the information provided by the accounting is useful to investors and creditors ("Analysis"), and reflect on how the accounting is related to accounting principles and concepts ("Principles"). Such exercises, reinforced with end-of-chapter homework activities, give students the practice they will need to build decision-making skills using the accounting concepts and procedures they are learning.

- *"What can you do?"*

Students need to develop competencies that will be useful in their careers. As described above, the book provides multiple opportunities for students to develop the critical thinking and analysis skills that will be the backbone of career competency. In addition, explicit writing components in end-of-chapter assignments require students to practice communication skills. Other assignments for use by students working in groups help develop facility in group problem solving, a skill useful in the working world.

In addition, for those students who will eventually sit for the CPA exam, we offer *interactive* integrative problems at the book's companion website that mirror the new computerized exam. Finally, each chapter also contains stand-alone financial accounting research cases using the Financial Accounting Research System (FARS) database.

BOOK RATIONALE AND ORGANIZATION

Some instructors have expressed a desire for a slightly different type of book for the intermediate accounting course. They asked for something that would enable them to have more time to develop various professional competencies, such as analysis and communication skills, and to place more emphasis on applying accounting concepts in various settings, such as in oral and written presentations and with introduction of more technology and other enhancements. Still others have expressed a need for a book that will better help students cope with the complexity and rigor of the intermediate course. *Intermediate Accounting: Principles and Analysis, Second Edition,* is intended to address those stated needs.

With 18 chapters, this book meets the needs of various audiences. Instructors who intend to use the textbook over two semesters can enhance the book with additional readings, cases, exercises, or other professional-competency activities. Instructors who wish to cover the book in a single semester can do so, by omitting some subject material, but still have complete treatment of the topics covered. Because the book provides the core concepts that must be covered in intermediate accounting, instructors can use this textbook in graduate, masters, and MBA courses. The 18-chapter book also provides additional flexibility to instructors who are interested in teaching a corporate reporting course. For an overview of the chapter sequence, see the Brief Contents list on page xxi.

The underlying theme around which each chapter is based is to learn the accounting for various transactions (accounting), to use the accounting in various decision-making contexts (analysis), and to develop understanding of the concepts or principles underlying the accounting treatment (principles).

Organization

The book's organization offers an integrated framework in which to study the essential concepts of intermediate accounting. The first two chapters discuss the standard-setting process, starting with the institutional structure and following with the conceptual framework. A review of the accounting process then follows in Chapter 3, as a refresher on basic understanding of the recording process, which is intended to bring all students up to the same level.

The next three chapters address the three major financial statements—the balance sheet, the income statement, and (in a separate chapter) the statement of cash flows. Revenue recognition is moved up in the "batting order" (relative to its position in Kieso, *Intermediate Accounting, Twelfth Edition)* and appears next, as Chapter 7. Chapters 6 and 7 represent a change from the first edition, where cash flows and revenue recognition were covered in a single chapter (Chapter 6). Separation of these important topics into two chapters makes possible a more complete discussion of the statement of cash flows and income measurement concepts that are important to subsequent chapter topics.

What then follows, in Chapters 8 through 14, is a discussion of the basic issues related to cash and receivables, inventories, plant assets, intangible assets, liabilities, stockholders' equity, and investments. Following these basic-issues chapters are chapters (Chapters 15 through 17) on the important topics of income taxes, compensation (including pensions and stock options), and leases. We complete the chapter-length coverage with discussion in Chapter 18 of other reporting and disclosure issues, including accounting changes and earnings per share.

Two end-of-book appendices address time value of money concepts and applications (Appendix A) and reporting cash flows (Appendix B). Another seven appendices dealing with more specialized accounting topics are available at the book's companion website. See the Brief Contents on page xxi for the complete list of online appendices.

Throughout all chapters, we balance discussion of concepts and applications so that these elements are mutually reinforcing. In addition, we focus discussion on explaining the rationale behind business transactions before addressing the accounting and reporting for those activities.

Distinctive Content Areas

The following are the distinctive content areas of the book.

Separate Chapters on Cash Flows and Revenue Recognition

Many users requested earlier discussion of the statement of cash flows and revenue recognition. *Intermediate Accounting, Second Edition,* provides us the opportunity to address both these desires. In Chapter 6, we present a substantive discussion of the cash flow statement. We transition from the discussion of cash flows in Chapter 6 to revenue recognition in Chapter 7 with its accrual concepts, to provide a perspective on the use of various performance measurements. Given that many companies report pro-forma earnings numbers that range from cash flow per share to earnings before interest and taxes, the logic of discussing cash flow and revenue recognition in sequence seemed appropriate.

Chapter on Compensation

Intermediate Accounting, Second Edition, features a chapter on compensation, including the topics of payroll, stock options, and pensions. The content in the area is very similar to the treatment in Kieso, *Intermediate Accounting, Twelfth Edition.*

Combined Chapters

One differentiating feature of Warfield, *Intermediate Accounting, Second Edition,* is that it *combines* selected chapters that in Kieso, *Intermediate Accounting, Twelfth Edition,* are separate chapters. We carefully planned and executed this combination of related topics, which makes possible a textbook that can be covered in a single semester, in order to provide adequate topic coverage for the second course in financial reporting. The combined chapters are as follows.

Inventories

Kieso, *Intermediate Accounting, Twelfth Edition,* covers inventories in two chapters because of the many complexities associated with the topic. In order to distill coverage of inventories to one chapter, Warfield, *Intermediate Accounting, Second Edition,* omits certain topics related to managerial accounting. In addition, online appendices discuss specialized industry topics like the retail inventory method, but still permit adequate discussion of the key concepts related to inventories in the chapter.

Property, Plant, and Equipment

Warfield, *Intermediate Accounting, Second Edition,* combines two chapters—Property, Plant, and Equipment, and Depreciation—from the longer book. In order to achieve a single chapter of manageable length, we streamlined discussions related to interest capitalization and special depreciation methods. We moved the important topic of impairments to the intangibles chapter, so that this subject can be discussed fully in one place. The subject matter related to depletion appears in an online appendix.

Liabilities

For Warfield, *Intermediate Accounting, Second Edition,* we streamlined and rewrote the two chapters on liabilities for presentation in a single chapter on this topic.

OTHER FEATURES

Intermediate Accounting: Principles and Analysis, Second Edition, is packaged with many pedagogical tools to help students learn more effectively and to help instructors respond to the changing needs of the course. We developed the following pedagogical features based on extensive reviews, focus groups, interactions with intermediate accounting instructors and students, and our own experiences with the intermediate accounting course.

Textbook Features

Chapter-Opening Vignettes

We have updated or added new chapter-opening stories to provide a real-world context that helps motivate student interest in the chapter topic.

"What Do the Numbers Mean?" Boxes

As described earlier, *What Do the Numbers Mean?* boxes help students think about the real-world consequences of accounting. In this edition of the book, we have added critical thinking questions (*Beyond the Numbers*) at the end of each box. These questions encourage students to stretch their thinking about the boxed story and to relate it to underlying accounting topics and concepts. Guideline answers at the end of the chapter provide immediately available feedback to students' efforts.

What do the numbers mean?   **You Have to Step Back**

Should the accounting profession have principles-based standards or rules-based standards? Critics of the profession today say that over the past three decades, standard-setters have moved away from broad accounting principles aimed at ensuring that companies' financial statements are fairly presented.

Instead, these critics say, standard-setters have moved toward drafting voluminous rules that, if technically followed in "check-box" fashion, may shield auditors and companies from legal liability. That has resulted in companies creating complex capital structures that comply with GAAP but hide billions of dollars of debt and other obligations. To add fuel to the fire, the chief accountant of the enforcement division of the SEC recently noted, "One can violate SEC laws and still comply with GAAP."

In short, what he is saying is that it is not enough just to check the boxes. You then have to step back and determine whether the *overall impression* created by GAAP financial statements fairly portrays the underlying economics of the company. It is a tough standard, but one that auditors and corporate management should strive to achieve.

Sources: Adapted from S. Liesman, "SEC Accounting Cop's Warning: Playing by the Rules May Not Head Off Fraud Issues," *Wall Street Journal* (February 12, 2002), p. C7. See also "Study Pursuant to Section 108(d) of the Sarbanes-Oxley Act of 2002 on the Adoption by the United States Financial Reporting System of a Principles-Based Accounting System," *SEC* (July 25, 2003).

Beyond the Numbers

Do you believe that standard-setters should issue principle-based standards or rule-based standards?

WHAT'S THE PRINCIPLE?

Providing a supplemental schedule with expense detail helps meet the objectives of the *full disclosure principle.*

"What's the Principle?"

These marginal notes relate topics covered within each chapter back to the conceptual principles introduced in the beginning of the book. This continual reinforcement of the essential concepts and principles illustrates how the concepts are applied in practice and helps students understand the *why*, as well as the *how*.

"Try It Out" Exercises

New in the Second Edition, strategically placed *Try It Out* exercises, with accompanying solutions, engage students in active learning as they work their way through a chapter.

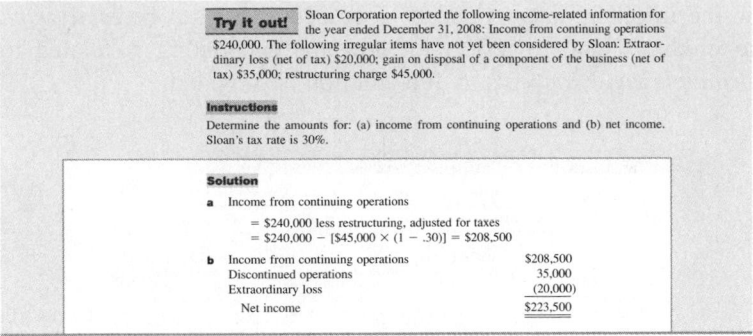

"Convergence Corners"

Accounting is going global, led by the FASB and the IASB who are working on an ambitious convergence project to result in one set of high-quality accounting standards. Students need to be informed of this important project. Thus, each chapter of the second edition contains a single-page discussion, called **Convergence Corner**, of the international accounting issues related to the chapter topics.

Each Convergence Corner consists of four sections: (1) An introduction which typically lists the current international pronouncements related to the chapter topic; (2) "Relevant Facts," which explains similarities and differences of U.S. GAAP and international standards (referred to as iGAAP); (3) "About the Numbers," which provides an example of application of iGAAP (in many cases, using real international companies); and (4) "On the Horizon," which discusses the convergence progress and plans related to that topic.

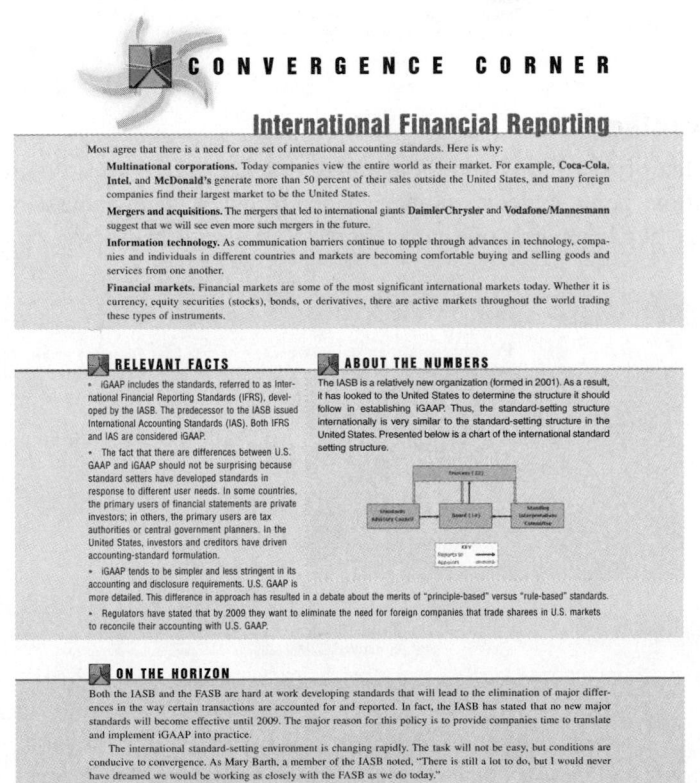

"Accounting, Analysis, Principles" Review

Also new in the Second Edition, the *Accounting, Analysis, Principles* review exercise, as the first feature of the chapter-review apparatus, summarizes the three important elements of each chapter. It helps students to review the *accounting* introduced in the chapter, to consider how the information provided by the accounting can be *analyzed and used* by investors and creditors, and to reflect on how the accounting is related to *underlying accounting principles and concepts*. A full solution is provided.

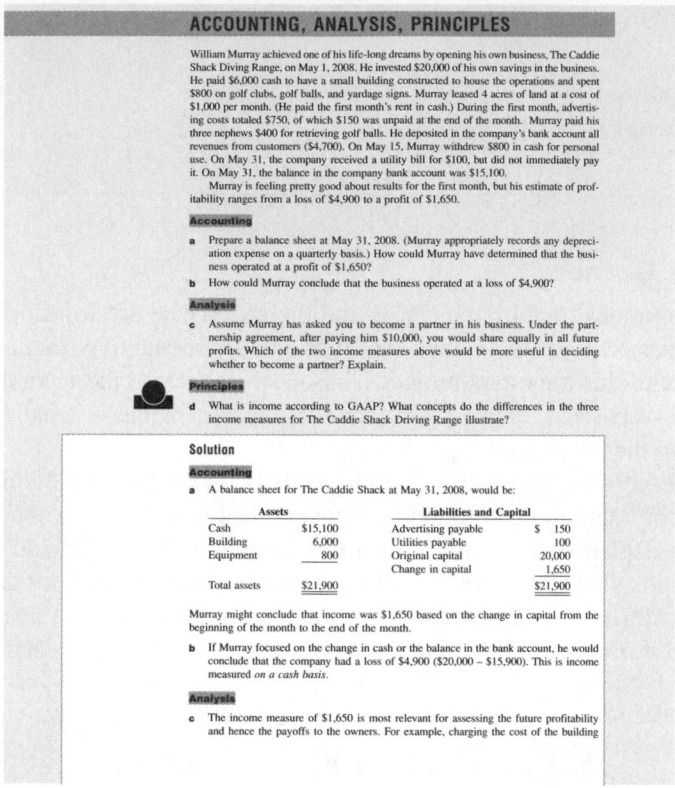

Review Exercise

Following the list of *Key Terms* and the *Summary of Learning Objectives*, a *Review Exercise*, with solution, gives students another chance to check their understanding of chapter concepts before they begin end-of-chapter homework assignments.

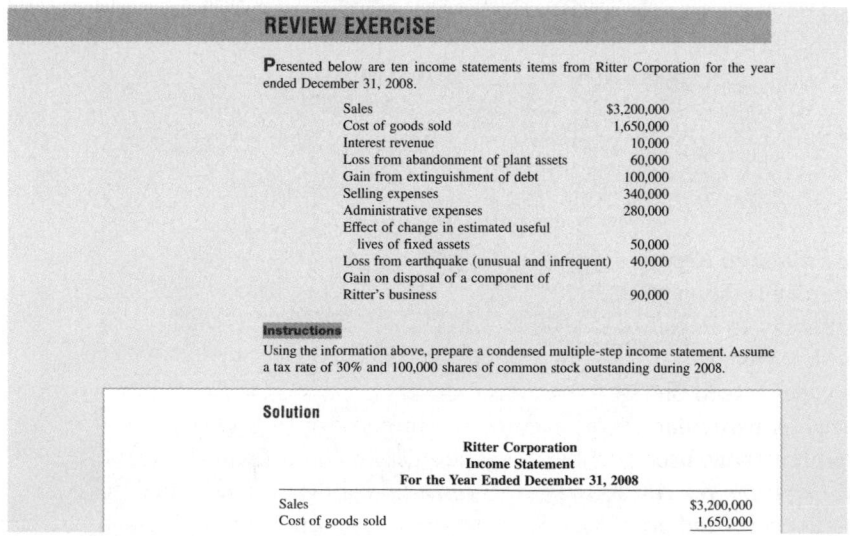

Questions, Brief Exercises, Exercises, and Problems

A full complement of homework materials of varying lengths and difficulty levels gives instructors a wide variety of class-tested and time-proven materials from which to make assignment selections. Numerous exercises and problems are adapted from professional exams, to give students practice in the type of materials they will encounter in these testing situations. Special icons identify problems that are good for group work or for writing assignments. Homework materials that can be solved using the Excel Problems supplement are identified by a spreadsheet icon. In addition, end-of-chapter Brief Exercises, Exercises, and Problems are now classified by learning objective.

Exercises

E2-1 **(Qualitative Characteristics)** *SFAC No. 2* identifies the qualitative characteristics that make accounting information useful. Presented below are a number of questions related to these qualitative characteristics and underlying constraints.

(LO 4, 8)

(a) What is the quality of information that enables users to confirm or correct prior expectations?
(b) Identify the two overall or pervasive constraints developed in *SFAC No. 2*.

We have carefully chosen all homework materials to reflect key chapter content and have triple-checked them for accuracy. Also, new in this edition, we have added a set of Additional Exercises, which are available at the book's companion website. These additional materials give instructors an alternate set of exercises to assign.

 **See the book's website, at www.wiley.com/college/warfield, for additional exercises.**

"Accounting in Action" Section

The *Accounting in Action* section at the end of each chapter groups problems that require students to apply their accounting knowledge while expanding student competencies in analysis and decision-making contexts.

Included in the *Accounting in Action* section are three sub-sections: *Financial Reporting and Analysis, Concepts for Analysis,* and *Professional Tools.* Homework materials in each sub-section are as follows.

ACCOUNTING IN ACTION

Financial Reporting and Analysis

P&G

■ **Financial Reporting Issues: The Procter & Gamble Company**

AIA3-1 The financial statements of **Procter & Gamble (P&G)** can be accessed at the book's website.

Instructions

Refer to P&G's financial statements and the accompanying notes to answer the following questions.

(a) What were P&G's total assets at June 30, 2006? At June 30, 2005?
(b) How much cash (and cash equivalents) did P&G have on June 30, 2006?
(c) What were P&G's research and development costs in 2004? In 2006?
(d) What were P&G's revenues in 2004? In 2006?

The *Financial Reporting and Analysis* section includes a *Financial Reporting Problem* (focused in this edition on Procter & Gamble), *Comparative Analysis* (comparing The Coca-Cola Company to PepsiCo, Inc.), *Financial Statement Analysis Cases* (using a variety of real-world companies), and in some chapters, an *International Reporting Case.* The international cases, based on real companies, are designed to illustrate international accounting differences. A particular emphasis is on the implications of these differences for analysis, which reinforces the user orientation of the *Accounting in Action* elements.

The *Concepts for Analysis* section contains numerous conceptual cases that focus on reporting concepts and principles. Many of these cases are adapted from professional exams.

Students entering the accounting profession must demonstrate not only accounting knowledge but also the ability to apply that knowledge and to use the tools that are used in practice to solve accounting problems. To address these new demands, the *Professional Tools* section in the Second Edition includes one or more *Ethical Decision Making* cases, *Financial Accounting Research* (FARs) exercises, and an online *Professional Simulation.*

Professional Tools

■ Ethical Decision Making

AIA4-11 **(Presentation of Property, Plant, and Equipment)** Andrea Pafko, corporate comptroller for Nicholson Industries, is trying to decide how to present "Property, plant, and equipment" in the balance sheet. She realizes that the statement of cash flows will show that the company made a significant investment in purchasing new equipment this year, but overall she knows the company's plant assets are rather old. She feels that she can disclose one figure titled "Property, plant, and equipment, net of depreciation," and the result will be a low figure. However, it will not disclose the age of the assets. If she chooses to show the cost less accumulated depreciation, the age of the assets will be apparent. She proposes the following.

The FARs exercises require students to use the Financial Accounting Research System (FARS) database to perform accounting research of the authoritative literature. This skill is increasingly required in the professional workplace and is tested on the computerized CPA exam, so students will experience long-term benefits from the practice they get doing these exercises as part of the intermediate accounting course.

The *Accounting in Action* section concludes by referring students to the book's companion website where they can purchase a *Professional Simulation* related to the chapter content. This exercise provides students with an interactive integrative context in which to apply the concepts introduced in the chapter. The exercises are patterned after the computerized CPA exam that tests a candidate's ability to read, digest, research, and respond to both a numeric problem and a short-answer essay, and they expand on the professional competency elements that students will need to apply their accounting knowledge in the professional workplace. (For more on developing professional competencies, see the next section, *Gateway to the Profession* Portal.)

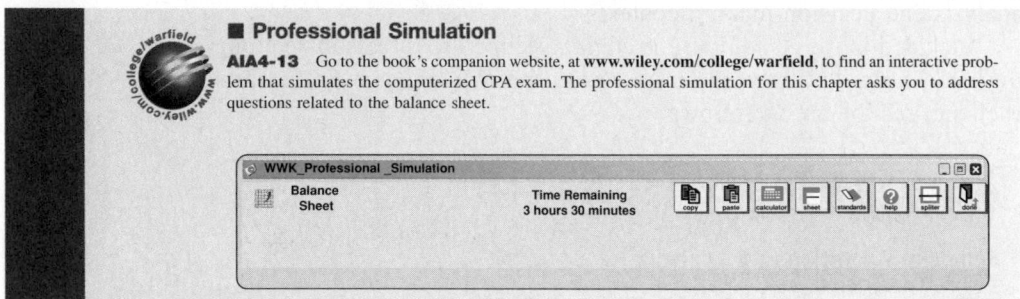

■ Professional Simulation

AIA4-13 Go to the book's companion website, at **www.wiley.com/college/warfield**, to find an interactive problem that simulates the computerized CPA exam. The professional simulation for this chapter asks you to address questions related to the balance sheet.

Gateway to the Profession Portal

The *Gateway to the Profession* supplement to the textbook content is an electronic gateway at the book's companion website (*www.wiley.com/college/warfield*), to a comprehensive set of additional materials. These materials include: the *Professional Simulation* exercises; a database of annual reports of real companies; professional-competency tools on writing, group work, and ethics; discussion of additional topics not included in the printed textbook; and student tutorials, self-tests, and a comprehensive glossary. The *Gateway to the Profession* portal enables instructors to enrich and custom-design course content using easy-to-access materials.

In addition to the material available via the *Gateway to the Profession* portal, *WileyPLUS* offers students a suite of online homework, with access to an online version of the text. All Brief Exercises, Exercises, and select Problems are available within *WileyPLUS*. Instructor resources include a wealth of presentation and preparation tools, easy-to-navigate assignment and assessment tools, and a complete system to administer and manage your course.

Supplementary Materials

Accompanying this textbook is an improved and expanded package of student learning aids and instructor teaching aids. The *Gateway to the Profession* portal provides expanded materials, as discussed above, including *WileyPLUS*, whose resources can help you prepare class presentations, create assignments, offer help to students, and track student progress. Other teaching and learning aids to supplement the textbook are described below.

Instructor Teaching Aids

The following teaching aids are available to support instructors using Warfield, *Intermediate Accounting: Principles and Analysis, Second Edition.*

Instructor's Manual

The online *Instructor's Manual* is designed to assist professors in preparing lectures and assignments. It contains chapter reviews, study objectives for each chapter, sample syllabi, lecture outlines, and printed teaching transparency masters. Each chapter also provides quizzing exercises, a Bloom's taxonomy table, and much more.

Solutions Manual

The *Solutions Manual* provides answers to all end-of-chapter Questions, Brief Exercises, Exercises, Problems, and Accounting in Action materials. Classification tables categorize solutions by topic, and the new solutions manual also categorizes solutions by textbook learning objective. The estimated time to complete exercises, problems, and cases is provided. Print is large and bold for easy readability in lecture settings.

Test Bank

The Second Edition Test Bank contains over 500 new testing questions. Exercises, problems, true/false, multiple choice, and conceptual short-answer questions help instructors test students' knowledge and communication skills. The Test Bank is designed to allow instructors to tailor examinations according to study objectives, learning skills, and content. The Test Bank provides a final exam in addition to chapter tests, achievement tests, and comprehensive tests.

Computerized Test Bank

This easy-to-use program allows instructors to create multiple versions of the same test. This computerized test bank also has authoring capabilities and randomizing functions.

Solutions Transparencies

These acetate transparencies contain solutions to textbook end-of-chapter material (brief exercises, exercises, problems, and Accounting in Action materials). The transparencies contain large, bold type for classroom presentation.

PowerPoint™ Presentations

The PowerPoint™ presentations are designed to enhance classroom presentation of chapter topics and examples by emphasizing the key concepts in each chapter. The Second Edition templates have a new design with review questions and many examples illustrating textbook content. Available for download from the companion website or in CD format.

Teaching Transparencies

These four-color acetates provide illustrations of key concepts for classroom viewing.

Checklist of Key Figures

Available for download from the website or the Instructor's Resources CD (IR-CD), the check figures are partial and complete answers (not solutions) to select end-of-chapter materials.

Instructor's Resource CD (IR-CD)

This CD-ROM contains the Instructor's Manual, Solutions Manual, Test Bank, teaching transparencies, text art, computerized test bank, PowerPoint™ presentations, Excel Workbook solutions, and check figures.

Companion Website

At *www.wiley.com/college/warfield,* the book's companion website offers a wealth of content and teaching aids.

Solutions to Rockford Practice Set

This supplement provides solutions to the *Rockford Practice Set,* which is available in print form or electronically on a CD-ROM.

Solutions to Excel Workbook Templates

Available for download from the website, these are solutions to the Excel problem templates discussed in the Warfield, *Intermediate Accounting Excel Workbook.*

Course Management Resources

Course content cartridges are available from both WebCT and Blackboard to support this textbook.

Student Learning Aids

Working Papers

The working papers are printed templates that can help students correctly format their textbook accounting solutions. Working paper templates are available for all end-of-chapter Brief Exercises, Exercises, and Problems.

Excel Working Papers

An electronic version of the printed working papers, these Excel-formatted templates help students properly format and present end-of-chapter textbook solutions.

Problem-Solving Survival Guide, with Excel Working Papers

This study guide provides exercises and problems that will develop students' problem-solving skills in intermediate accounting. Accompanying the *Problem-Solving Survival Guide* is a CD containing the Excel working papers.

Rockford Corporation: An Accounting Practice Set

This revised practice set has been designed as a student review and update of the accounting cycle and the preparation of financial statements.

Rockford Corporation: A Computerized Accounting Practice Set

This computerized practice set is a general ledger software version of the printed practice set. The *new* computerized Rockford Practice Set is available on CD-ROM.

Excel Workbook and Templates

This workbook contains Excel templates that help students complete selected end-of-chapter exercises and problems identified by a spreadsheet icon in the margin of the main text. A useful introduction to Excel, this package details how students can work with preprogrammed spreadsheets, and it explains to students how they can design their own spreadsheets.

Web Quizzing

The Web Quizzes are online true/false and multiple-choice quizzes with grading and feedback. They can be found at the book's companion website at http://www.wiley.com/college/warfield.

Acknowledgments

We thank the users of the First Edition and the many instructors who contributed to the revision through their comments and instructive criticism. Special thanks are extended to the focus group participants and the primary reviewers of and contributors to our Second Edition manuscript.

Markus J. Ahrens
St. Louis Community College

June Aono
University of Hawaii–West Oahu

Lisa Bostick
University of Tampa

Greg Brookins
Santa Monica College

Laura Delaune
Louisiana State University

Lynda Dennis
University of Central Florida

Edmond d'Ouville
Indiana University Northwest

Claire Eckstein
CUNY–Baruch

Robert Eskew
Purdue University

Dave Farber
Michigan State University

Clyde Galbraith
West Chester University

Ellen Goldberg
Northern Virginia Community College

Marty Gosman
Quinnipiac College

Konrad Gunderson
Missouri Western University

Julia Higgs
Florida Atlantic University

Geoffrey Horlick
St. Francis College

Allen Hunt
Southern Illinois University

Marilyn Hunt
University of Central Florida

Cynthia Jeffrey
Iowa State University

Mary Jo Jones
Eastern University

Art Joy
University of South Florida

Celina Jozci
University of South Florida

Lisa Koonce
University of Texas at Austin

Christopher Kwak
DeAnza College

Doug Laufer
The Metropolitan State College of Denver

Timothy Lindquist
University of Northern Iowa

Barbara Lippincott
University of Tampa

Gary Luoma
University of Southern California

Matt Magilke
University of Utah

Bob Rouse
College of Charleston

Daphne Main
University of New Orleans

Tim Shea
University of Wisconsin–Madison

R. D. Nair
University of Wisconsin–Madison

Jerry Siebel
University of South Florida

Ed Nathan
University of Houston

Douglas Smith
Samford University

Hugo Nurnberg
CUNY–Baruch

Karen Squires
University of Tampa

Ann O'Brien
University of Wisconsin–Madison

Gary Taylor
University of Alabama

Anne Oppegard
Augustana College, SD

Lynn Thomas
Kansas State University

Alee Phillips
University of Kansas

Tom Tierney
University of Wisconsin–Madison

Marlene Plumlee
University of Utah

Bruce Wampler
Louisiana State University–Shreveport

Wing Poon
Montclair State University

David Weiner
University of San Francisco

Jay Price
Utah State University

Ken Winter
University of Wisconsin–LaCrosse

Paul (Jep) Robertson
Henderson State University

Wanda Wong
Chabot College

Larry Roman
Cuyahoga Community College

Steve Zeff
Rice University

In addition, we thank the following colleagues who contributed to development or production of the book:

Gateway to the Profession Portal and FARS Cases

Michelle Ephraim
Worcester Polytechnic Institute

Jeremy Kunicki
Walgreens

Erick Frederickson
Madison, Wisconsin

Andrew Prewitt
KPMG, Chicago

Jason Hart
Grant Thornton, Milwaukee

Jeff Seymour
KPMG, Minneapolis

Kayla Hasz
Deloitte, Chicago

Matt Sullivan
Deloitte & Touche, Milwaukee

Chad Hilgenberg
KPMG, Minneapolis

Jen Vaughn
PricewaterhouseCoopers, Chicago

Kelly Krieg
E & Y, Milwaukee

Erin Viel
PricewaterhouseCoopers, Milwaukee

Ancillary Authors, Contributors, Proofers, and Accuracy Checkers

Mary Ann Benson

Margaret Blais
Rhode Island College

John C. Borke
University of Wisconsin–Platteville

Jack Cathey
University of North Carolina–Charlotte

Betty Connor
University of Colorado at Denver

Robert Derstine
Villanova University

Gregory Dold
Southwestern College

Terry Elliott
Morehead State University

Jim Emig
Villanova University

Larry Falcetto
Emporia State University

Tom Forehand
State University of New York–New Paltz

Rosemary Fullerton
Utah State University

Clyde Galbraith
West Chester University

Edwin Hackleman
Delta Software

Coby Harmon
University of California, Santa Barbara

Wayne Higley
Buena Vista University

Debra R. Hopkins
Northern Illinois University

Judi Hora
University of San Diego

Marilyn F. Hunt
University of Central Florida

Douglas W. Kieso
Aurora University

Mark Kohlbeck
Florida Atlantic University

Jennifer Laudermilch
PricewaterhouseCoopers

Ann Martin
University of Colorado at Denver

Barbara Muller
Arizona State University

Don Newell
Delta Software

Tom Noland
University of Houston

Anne Oppegard
Augustana College

Yvonne Phong
Borough of Manhattan Community College

Paul (Jep) Robertson
Henderson State University

Rex A. Schildhouse
Miranar College

Alice Sineath
Forsyth Technical Community College

Dick D. Wasson
Southwestern College, San Diego University

Bernie Wienrich
Linderwood University

WileyPLUS Developers and Reviewers

Laura McNally
University of Maryland, University College

Jan Mardon
Green River Community College

James Mraz

Melanie Yon

Perspectives and "From Classroom to Career" Interviews

Stuart Weiss
Stuart Weiss Business Writing, Inc., Portland, Oregon

Practicing Accountants and Business Executives

From the fields of corporate and public accounting, we owe thanks to the following practitioners for their technical advice and for consenting to interviews.

Ron Bernard
NFL Enterprises

Mike Crooch
FASB

Tracy Golden
Deloitte & Touche

John Gribble
PricewaterhouseCoopers

Darien Griffin
S.C. Johnson & Son Wax

Michael Lehman
Sun Microsystems, Inc.

Tom Linsmeier
FASB

Michele Lippert
Evoke.com

Sue McGrath
Vision Capital Management

David Miniken
Sweeney Conrad

Robert Sack
University of Virginia

Clare Schulte
Deloitte & Touche

Willie Sutton
*Mutual Community Savings Bank,
Durham, NC*

Lynn Turner
Glass, Lewis, LLP

Gary Valenzuela
Yahoo!

Rachel Woods
PricewaterhouseCoopers

Arthur Wyatt
The University of Illinois–Urbana

In addition, we appreciate the exemplary support and professional commitment given us by the editorial, marketing, production, and design staffs of John Wiley & Sons, including the following: Chris DeJohn, Mark Bonadeo, Amy Scholz, Julia Flohr, Ed Brislin, Allie Morris, Kathryn Fraser, Trish McFadden, Maddy Lesure, Anna Melhorn, and Dorothy Sinclair. Thanks to Ann Torbert for her editorial assistance in pulling together the various pieces of the manuscript. Thanks, too, to Suzanne Ingrao for her production work, to Steve Ingle for his indexing, to the management and staff, particularly Jane Shifflet, at Aptara for their work on the textbook, and to Kim Nichols and the management and staff at Elm Street Publishing Services for their work on the solutions manual.

We also appreciate the cooperation of the American Institute of Certified Public Accountants and the Financial Accounting Standards Board in permitting us to quote from their pronouncements. We thank The Procter & Gamble Company, The Coca-Cola Company, and PepsiCo, Inc. for permitting us to use their 2006 annual reports for our specimen financial statements. We also acknowledge permission from the American Institute of Certified Public Accountants, the Institute of Management Accountants, and the Institute of Internal Auditors to adapt and use material from the Uniform CPA Examinations, the CMA Examinations, and the CIA Examination, respectively.

If this book helps teachers instill in their students an understanding of the accounting for various transactions, prepares students to use this accounting in various decision-making situations, and helps students understand the basic concepts and principles involved in financial accounting and reporting, then we will have attained our objective.

We will appreciate suggestions and comments from users of this book. You can send comments to us by email at *AccountingAuthors@yahoo.com.*

Terry D. Warfield
Madison, Wisconsin

Jerry J. Weygandt
Madison, Wisconsin

Donald E. Kieso
Somonauk Illinois

BRIEF CONTENTS

CONTENTS

CHAPTER 1

FINANCIAL ACCOUNTING AND ACCOUNTING STANDARDS

The Size of the New York Phone Book, if Necessary

Enron, **Global Crossing**, **Kmart**, **WorldCom**, **Williams Cos.**, and **Xerox** are all companies that the Securities and Exchange Commission (SEC) recently scrutinized because of accounting issues. Share prices of all these companies have declined substantially. Investors punish any company whose quality of earnings is in doubt.

The unfortunate part of accounting scandals is that we all pay. For example, Enron's market capitalization totaled $80 billion before disclosure of its accounting irregularities. Today, it is bankrupt. Employees lost their pension money and investors their savings. Further, the entire stock market caught "Enronitis," a distrust of accounting that has led to substantial declines in the overall stock market. At one point, at least 10 congressional committees were inquiring into corporate governance issues, and Congress introduced over 30 Enron-related bills that addressed matters such as regulation of derivative securities, auditor–client conflicts, and development of an oversight body to regulate the accounting profession.

Companies have also taken steps to respond to the many investor concerns about the completeness and reliability of the accounting numbers. Many companies now expand the financial disclosures in their annual reports. For example, **General Electric**'s CEO Jeffrey Immelt stated, "I want people to think about GE as we think of GE—as a transparent company." He noted that GE's annual report will be "the size of New York City's phone book, if necessary" to provide the information needed to help investors and creditors make the proper investing decisions.

We believe that meaningful reform will come out of these recent investigations into sloppy or fraudulent accounting. Although many consider the United States to have the finest financial reporting system in the world, we must do better. As former chair of the FASB Ed Jenkins remarked recently, "If anything positive results . . . it may be that [these accounting issues] serve as an indelible reminder to all that transparent financial reporting does matter and that lack of transparency imposes significant costs on all who participate [in our markets]."

2

Preview of Chapter 1

As our opening story indicates, companies must provide relevant and reliable information so that our capital markets work efficiently. *This chapter explains the environment of financial reporting and the many factors affecting it, as follows.*

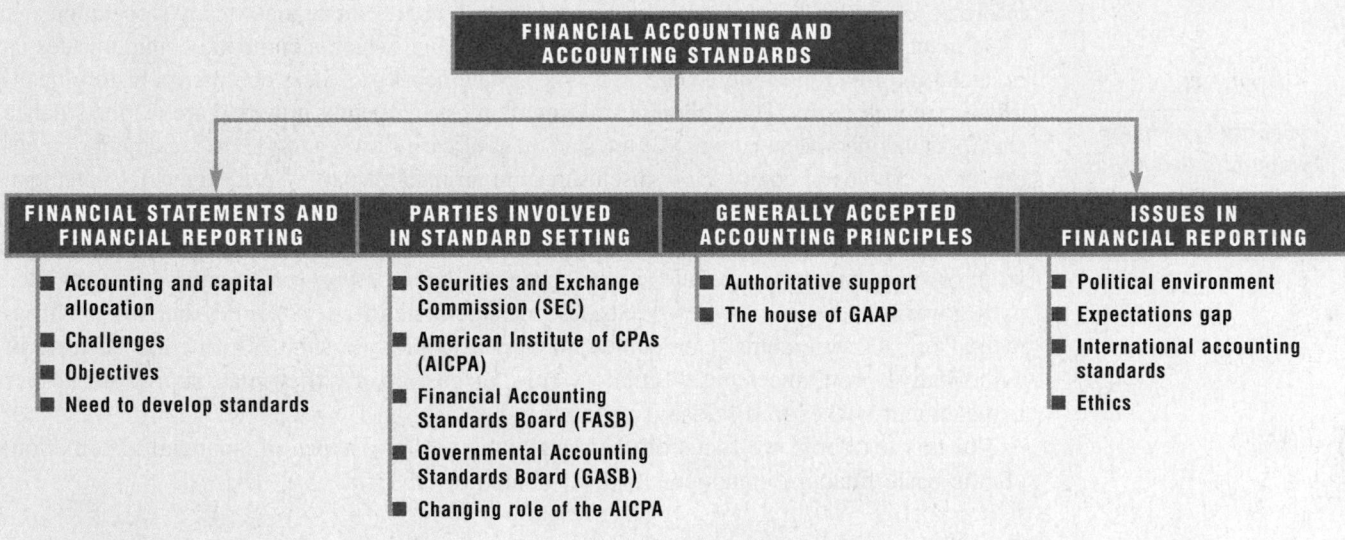

FINANCIAL ACCOUNTING AND ACCOUNTING STANDARDS

FINANCIAL STATEMENTS AND FINANCIAL REPORTING	PARTIES INVOLVED IN STANDARD SETTING	GENERALLY ACCEPTED ACCOUNTING PRINCIPLES	ISSUES IN FINANCIAL REPORTING
■ Accounting and capital allocation ■ Challenges ■ Objectives ■ Need to develop standards	■ Securities and Exchange Commission (SEC) ■ American Institute of CPAs (AICPA) ■ Financial Accounting Standards Board (FASB) ■ Governmental Accounting Standards Board (GASB) ■ Changing role of the AICPA	■ Authoritative support ■ The house of GAAP	■ Political environment ■ Expectations gap ■ International accounting standards ■ Ethics

Learning Objectives

After studying this chapter, you should be able to:

1. Identify the major financial statements and other means of financial reporting.
2. Explain how accounting assists in the efficient use of scarce resources.
3. Describe some of the challenges facing accounting.
4. Identify the objectives of financial reporting.
5. Explain the need for accounting standards.
6. Identify the major policy-setting bodies and their role in the standard-setting process.
7. Explain the meaning of generally accepted accounting principles.
8. Describe the impact of user groups on the standard-setting process.
9. Understand issues related to ethics and financial accounting.

Inside Chapter 1

■ **What Do the Numbers Mean?**

"It's not the economy anymore, stupid" (p. 5)

You have to step back (p. 15)

The economic consequences of goodwill (p. 17)

■ **What's the Principle?** (pp. 5, 6, 16, 19)

■ **Convergence Corner** (p. 20)

■ **Accounting, Analysis, Principles** (p. 21)

Identify and discuss two major entities involved in standard setting,

Indicate reasons for increase in financial information in annual reports.

Identify concepts and principles related to the expansion of financial reporting.

The essential characteristics of accounting are: (1) the identification, measurement, and communication of financial information about (2) economic entities to (3) interested parties. **Financial accounting** is the process that culminates in the preparation of financial reports on the enterprise for use by both internal and external parties. Users of these financial reports include investors, creditors, managers, unions, and government agencies. In contrast, **managerial accounting** is the process of identifying, measuring, analyzing, and communicating financial information needed by management to plan, control, and evaluate a company's operations.

OBJECTIVE 1

Identify the major financial statements and other means of financial reporting.

Financial statements are the principal means through which a company communicates its financial information to those outside it. These statements provide a company's history quantified in money terms. The **financial statements** most frequently provided are (1) the balance sheet, (2) the income statement, (3) the statement of cash flows, and (4) the statement of owners' or stockholders' equity. Note disclosures are an integral part of each financial statement.

Some financial information is better provided, or can be provided only, by means of **financial reporting** other than formal financial statements. Examples include the president's letter or supplementary schedules in the corporate annual report, prospectuses, reports filed with government agencies, news releases, management's forecasts, and social or environmental impact statements. Companies may need to provide such information because of authoritative pronouncement, regulatory rule, or custom. Or they may supply it because management wishes to disclose it voluntarily.

In this textbook, we focus on the development of two types of financial information: (1) the basic financial statements and (2) related disclosures.

Accounting and Capital Allocation

OBJECTIVE 2

Explain how accounting assists in the efficient use of scarce resources.

Resources are limited. As a result, people try to conserve them and ensure that they are used effectively. Efficient use of resources often determines whether a business thrives. This fact places a substantial burden on the accounting profession.

Accountants must measure performance accurately and fairly on a timely basis, so that the right managers and companies are able to attract investment capital. For example, relevant and reliable financial information allows investors and creditors to compare the income and assets employed by such companies as **IBM**, **McDonald's**, **Microsoft**, and **Ford**. Because these users can assess the relative return and risks associated with investment opportunities, they channel resources more effectively. Illustration 1-1 shows how this process of capital allocation works.

Illustration 1-1
Capital Allocation
Process

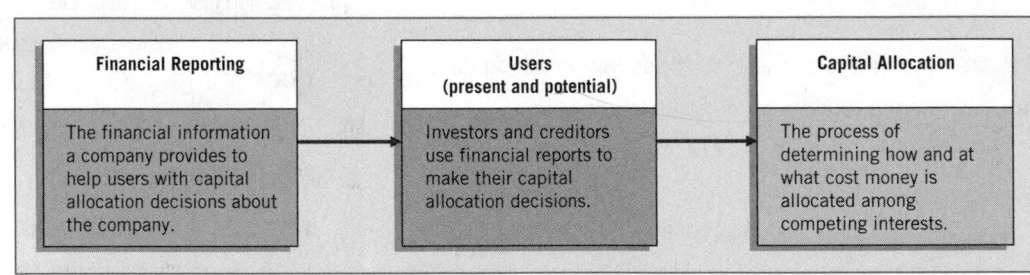

Financial Reporting	Users (present and potential)	Capital Allocation
The financial information a company provides to help users with capital allocation decisions about the company.	Investors and creditors use financial reports to make their capital allocation decisions.	The process of determining how and at what cost money is allocated among competing interests.

An effective process of capital allocation is critical to a healthy economy. It promotes productivity, encourages innovation, and provides an efficient and liquid market for buying and selling securities and obtaining and granting credit.[1] As we indicated in our opening story, unreliable and irrelevant information leads to poor capital allocation, which adversely affects the securities markets.

[1]AICPA Special Committee on Financial Reporting, "Improving Business Reporting—A Customer Focus," *Journal of Accountancy*, Supplement (October 1994).

It's not the economy anymore. It's the accounting. That's what many investors seem to be saying these days. As indicated in our opening story, even the slightest hint of any accounting irregularity at a company leads to a subsequent pounding of the company's stock price. For example, recent editions of the *Wall Street Journal* had the following headlines related to accounting and its effects on the economy.

- Stocks take a beating as accounting woes spread beyond **Enron**.
- Once hot **Krispy Kreme** ousts its CEO amid accounting woes.
- **Nortel** unveils new accounting flubs.
- Accounting woes at **AIG** take their toll on insurers' shares.
- Bank stocks fall as investors take issue with **PNC**'s accounting.

It now has become clear that investors must trust the accounting numbers or they will abandon the market and put their resources elsewhere. With investor uncertainty, the cost of capital increases for companies who need additional resources. In short, relevant and reliable financial information is necessary for markets to be efficient.

Beyond the Numbers

Explain the difference between relevance and reliability. Why are these concepts important in reporting financial information?

The Challenges Facing Financial Accounting

Much is right about financial reporting in the United States. We presently have the most liquid, deep, secure, and efficient public capital markets of any country at any time in history. One reason for this success is that our financial statements and related disclosures capture and organize financial information in a relevant and reliable fashion. However, much still needs to be done. For example, if we move to the year 2020 and look back at financial reporting today, we might read the following:

OBJECTIVE **3**
Describe some of the challenges facing accounting.

- **Nonfinancial Measurements.** Financial reports failed to provide some key performance measures widely used by management, such as customer satisfaction indexes, backlog information, and reject rates on goods purchased.
- **Forward-looking Information.** Financial reports failed to provide forward-looking information needed by present and potential investors and creditors. One individual noted that financial statements in 2005 should have started with the phrase, "Once upon a time," to signify their use of historical cost and accumulation of past events.
- **Soft Assets.** Financial reports focused on hard assets (inventory, plant assets) but failed to provide much information about a company's soft assets (intangibles). The best assets are often intangible. Consider **Microsoft**'s know-how and market dominance, **Dell**'s unique marketing setup and well-trained employees, and **J. Crew**'s brand image.
- **Timeliness.** Companies only prepared financial statements quarterly, and provided audited financials annually. Little to no real-time financial statement information was available.

WHAT'S THE PRINCIPLE?
Relevance and *reliability* are the two primary qualities that make accounting information useful for decision making. Discussions in the "What's the Principle?" boxes throughout the text highlight the essential idea or principle that you will want to remember about the topic being studied.

We believe each of these challenges must be met for the accounting profession to provide the type of information needed for an efficient capital allocation process. We are confident that changes will occur, based on these positive signs:

- Already some companies voluntarily disclose information deemed relevant to investors. Often such information is nonfinancial. For example, regional banking companies, such as **BankOne Corp.**, **Fifth Third Bancorp**, and **Sun Trust Banks**, now include data on loan growth, credit quality, fee income, operating efficiency, capital management, and management strategy.

- Initially, companies used the World Wide Web to provide limited financial data. Now most companies publish their annual reports in several formats on the Web. The most innovative companies offer sections of their annual reports in a format that the user can readily manipulate, such as in an Excel spreadsheet format. Companies also format their financial reports using extensible business reporting language (XBRL), which permits quicker and lower cost access to companies' financial information.

- More accounting standards now require the recording or disclosing of fair value information. For example, companies either record investments in stocks and bonds, debt obligations, and derivatives at fair value or companies show information related to fair values in the notes to the financial statements.

Changes in these directions will enhance the relevance of financial reporting and provide useful information to financial statement readers.

Objectives of Financial Reporting

To establish a foundation for financial accounting and reporting, the accounting profession identified a set of **objectives of financial reporting by business enterprises**. Financial reporting should provide information that:

OBJECTIVE 4

Identify the objectives of financial reporting.

1 Is useful to present and potential investors and creditors and other users **in making rational investment, credit, and similar decisions**. The information should be comprehensible to those who have a **reasonable understanding** of business and economic activities and are willing to study the information with reasonable diligence.

2 Helps present and potential investors, creditors, and other users **assess the amounts, timing, and uncertainty of prospective cash receipts** from dividends or interest and the proceeds from the sale, redemption, or maturity of securities or loans. Since investors' and creditors' cash flows are related to enterprise cash flows, financial reporting should provide information to help investors, creditors, and others assess the amounts, timing, and uncertainty of prospective net cash inflows to the related enterprise.

3 **Clearly portrays the economic resources of an enterprise, the claims to those resources** (obligations of the enterprise to transfer resources to other entities and owners' equity), and the effects of transactions, events, and circumstances that change its resources and claims to those resources.[2]

In brief, the objectives of financial reporting are to provide information that is (1) useful in investment and credit decisions, (2) useful in assessing cash flow prospects, and (3) about company resources, claims to those resources, and changes in them.

The emphasis on "assessing cash flow prospects" does not mean that the cash basis is preferred over the accrual basis of accounting. That is not the case. Information based on **accrual accounting generally better indicates a company's present and continuing ability to generate favorable cash flows** than does information limited to the financial effects of cash receipts and payments.[3]

Recall from your first accounting course the objective of **accrual-basis accounting**: It ensures that a company records events that change its financial statements in the periods in which the events occur, rather than only in the periods in which it receives or pays cash. Using the accrual basis to determine net income means that a company recognizes revenues when it earns them rather than when it

---

[2]"Objectives of Financial Reporting by Business Enterprises," *Statement of Financial Accounting Concepts No. 1* (Stamford, Conn.: FASB, November 1978), pars. 5–8.

[3]*SFAC No. 1*, p. iv. As used here, *cash flow* means "cash generated and used in operations." The term *cash flows* also frequently means cash obtained by borrowing and used to repay borrowing, cash used for investments in resources and obtained from the disposal of investments, and cash contributed by or distributed to owners.

receives cash. Similarly, it recognizes expenses when it incurs them rather than when it pays them. Under accrual accounting, a company generally recognizes revenues when it makes sales. The company can then relate the revenues to the economic environment of the period in which they occurred. Over the long run, trends in revenues and expenses are generally more meaningful than trends in cash receipts and disbursements.

The Need to Develop Standards

The main controversy in setting accounting standards is, "Whose rules should we play by, and what should they be?" The answer is not immediately clear. Users of financial accounting statements have both coinciding and conflicting needs for information of various types. To meet these needs, and to satisfy the fiduciary[4] reporting responsibility of management, companies prepare a single set of **general-purpose financial statements**. Users expect these statements to present fairly, clearly, and completely the company's financial operations.

The accounting profession has attempted to develop a set of standards that are generally accepted and universally practiced. Otherwise, each enterprise would have to develop its own standards. Further, readers of financial statements would have to familiarize themselves with every company's peculiar accounting and reporting practices. It would be almost impossible to prepare statements that could be compared.

This common set of standards and procedures is called **generally accepted accounting principles (GAAP)**. The term "generally accepted" means either that an authoritative accounting rule-making body has established a principle of reporting in a given area or that over time a given practice has been accepted as appropriate because of its universal application.[5] Although principles and practices continue to provoke both debate and criticism, most members of the financial community recognize them as the standards that over time have proven to be most useful. We present a more extensive discussion of what constitutes GAAP later in this chapter.

> **OBJECTIVE 5**
> **Explain the need for accounting standards.**

PARTIES INVOLVED IN STANDARD SETTING

Four organizations are instrumental in the development of financial accounting standards (GAAP) in the United States:

1   Securities and Exchange Commission (SEC)
2   American Institute of Certified Public Accountants (AICPA)
3   Financial Accounting Standards Board (FASB)
4   Government Accounting Standards Board (GASB)

> **OBJECTIVE 6**
> **Identify the major policy-setting bodies and their role in the standard-setting process.**

Securities and Exchange Commission (SEC)

External financial reporting and auditing developed in tandem with the growth of the industrial economy and its capital markets. However, when the stock market crashed in 1929 and the nation's economy plunged into the Great Depression, there were calls for increased government regulation of business generally, and especially financial institutions and the stock market.

As a result of these events, the federal government established the **Securities and Exchange Commission (SEC)** to help develop and standardize financial information presented to stockholders. The SEC is a federal agency. It administers the Securities

> **INTERNATIONAL INSIGHT**
>
> The International Organization of Securities Commissions (IOSCO), established in 1987, consists of more than 100 securities regulatory agencies or securities exchanges from all over the world. Collectively, its members represent a substantial proportion of the world's capital markets. The SEC is a member of IOSCO.

---

[4]Management's fiduciary responsibility is to manage assets with care and trust.

[5]The terms *principles* and *standards* are used interchangeably in practice and throughout this textbook.

Exchange Act of 1934 and several other acts. Most companies that issue securities to the public or are listed on a stock exchange are required to file audited financial statements with the SEC. In addition, the SEC has broad powers to prescribe, in whatever detail it desires, the accounting practices and standards to be employed by companies that fall within its jurisdiction. The SEC currently exercises oversight over 12,000 companies that are listed on the major exchanges (e.g., the New York Stock Exchange and the Nasdaq).

Public/Private Partnership

At the time the SEC was created, no group—public or private—issued accounting standards. The SEC encouraged the creation of a private standard-setting body because it believed that the private sector had the appropriate resources and talent to achieve this daunting task. As a result, accounting standards have developed in the private sector either through the American Institute of Certified Public Accountants (AICPA) or the Financial Accounting Standards Board (FASB).

The SEC has affirmed its support for the FASB by indicating that financial statements conforming to standards set by the FASB are presumed to have substantial authoritative support. In short, the **SEC requires registrants to adhere to GAAP**. In addition, the SEC indicated in its reports to Congress that "it continues to believe that the initiative for establishing and improving accounting standards should remain in the private sector, subject to Commission oversight."

SEC Oversight

The SEC's partnership with the private sector works well. The SEC acts with remarkable restraint in the area of developing accounting standards. Generally, **the SEC relies on the FASB to develop accounting standards**.

The SEC's involvement in the development of accounting standards varies. In some cases, the SEC rejects a standard proposed by the private sector. In other cases, the SEC prods the private sector into taking quicker action on certain reporting problems, such as accounting for investments in debt and equity securities and the reporting of derivative instruments. In still other situations, the SEC communicates problems to the FASB, responds to FASB exposure drafts, and provides the FASB with counsel and advice upon request.

The SEC's mandate is to establish accounting principles. The private sector, therefore, must listen carefully to the views of the SEC. In some sense the private sector is the formulator and the implementor of the standards.[6] However, when the private sector fails to address accounting problems as quickly as the SEC would like, the partnership between the SEC and the private sector can be strained. This occurred in the recent deliberations on the accounting for business combinations and intangible assets, and concerns over the accounting for off-balance sheet special-purpose entities, highlighted in the failure of **Enron**.

Enforcement

As we indicated earlier, companies listed on a stock exchange must submit their financial statements to the SEC. If the SEC believes that an accounting or disclosure irregularity exists regarding the form or content of the financial statements, it sends a deficiency letter to the company. Companies usually resolve these deficiency letters quickly. However, if disagreement continues, the SEC may issue a "stop order," which prevents the registrant from issuing or trading securities on the exchanges. The Department of Justice may also file

---

[6]One writer described the relationship of the FASB and SEC and the development of financial reporting standards using the analogy of a pearl. The pearl (a financial reporting standard) "is formed by the reaction of certain oysters (FASB) to an irritant (the SEC)—usually a grain of sand—that becomes embedded inside the shell. The oyster coats this grain with layers of nacre, and ultimately a pearl is formed. The pearl is a joint result of the irritant (SEC) and oyster (FASB); without both, it cannot be created." John C. Burton, "Government Regulation of Accounting and Information," *Journal of Accountancy* (June 1982).

criminal charges for violations of certain laws. The SEC process, private sector initiatives, and civil and criminal litigation help to ensure the integrity of financial reporting for public companies.

American Institute of Certified Public Accountants (AICPA)

The **American Institute of Certified Public Accountants (AICPA)**, which is the national professional organization of practicing Certified Public Accountants (CPAs), has been an important contributor to the development of GAAP. Various committees and boards established since the founding of the AICPA have contributed to this effort.

Committee on Accounting Procedure

At the urging of the SEC, the AICPA appointed the Committee on Accounting Procedure in 1939. The **Committee on Accounting Procedure (CAP)**, composed of practicing CPAs, issued 51 **Accounting Research Bulletins** during the years 1939 to 1959. These bulletins dealt with a variety of accounting problems. But this problem-by-problem approach failed to provide the needed structured body of accounting principles. In response, in 1959 the AICPA created the Accounting Principles Board.

Accounting Principles Board

The major purposes of the **Accounting Principles Board (APB)** were to (1) advance the written expression of accounting principles, (2) determine appropriate practices, and (3) narrow the areas of difference and inconsistency in practice. To achieve these objectives, the APB's mission was twofold: to develop an overall conceptual framework to assist in the resolution of problems as they become evident and to substantively research individual issues before the AICPA issued pronouncements. The Board's 18 to 21 members, selected primarily from public accounting, also included representatives from industry and academia. The Board's official pronouncements, called **APB Opinions**, were intended to be based mainly on research studies and be supported by reasons and analysis. Between its inception in 1959 and its dissolution in 1973, the APB issued 31 opinions.

Unfortunately, the APB came under fire early, charged with lack of productivity and failing to act promptly to correct alleged accounting abuses. Later the APB tackled numerous thorny accounting issues, only to meet a buzz saw of opposition from industry and CPA firms. It also ran into occasional governmental interference. In 1971 the accounting profession's leaders, anxious to avoid governmental rule-making, appointed a Study Group on Establishment of Accounting Principles. Commonly known as the **Wheat Committee** for its chair Francis Wheat, this group examined the organization and operation of the APB and determined the necessary changes to attain better results. The Study Group submitted its recommendations to the AICPA Council in the spring of 1972. The AICPA Council adopted the recommendations in total, and implemented them by early 1973.

Financial Accounting Standards Board (FASB)

The Wheat Committee's recommendations resulted in the demise of the APB and the creation of a new standard-setting structure composed of three organizations—the Financial Accounting Foundation (FAF), the Financial Accounting Standards Board (FASB), and the Financial Accounting Standards Advisory Council (FASAC). The **Financial Accounting Foundation** selects the members of the FASB and the Advisory Council, funds their activities, and generally oversees the FASB's activities.

The major operating organization in this three-part structure is the **Financial Accounting Standards Board (FASB)**. Its mission is to establish and improve standards of financial accounting and reporting for the guidance and education of the public, which includes issuers, auditors, and users of financial information. The expectations of success

---

INTERNATIONAL INSIGHT

Nations also differ in the degree to which they developed national standards and consistent accounting practices. One indicator of the level of a nation's accounting is the nature of the accounting profession within the country. For example, the Netherlands, the U.K., Canada, and the U.S. established professional accounting bodies in the nineteenth century. In contrast, Hong Kong, Singapore, and Korea established similar bodies only in the last half century.

and support for the new FASB relied on several significant differences between it and its predecessor, the APB:

1 Smaller Membership. The FASB consists of seven members, replacing the relatively large 18-member APB.

2 Full-time, Remunerated Membership. FASB members are well-paid, full-time members appointed for renewable 5-year terms. The APB members volunteered their part-time work.

3 Greater Autonomy. The APB was a senior committee of the AICPA. The FASB is not part of any single professional organization. It is appointed by and answerable only to the Financial Accounting Foundation.

4 Increased Independence. APB members retained their private positions with firms, companies, or institutions. FASB members must sever all such ties.

5 Broader Representation. All APB members were required to be CPAs and members of the AICPA. Currently, it is not necessary to be a CPA to be a member of the FASB.

In addition to research help from its own staff, the FASB relies on the expertise of various task force groups formed for various projects and on the **Financial Accounting Standards Advisory Council (FASAC)**. FASAC consults with the FASB on major policy and technical issues and also helps select task force members.

Due Process

In establishing financial accounting standards, the FASB relies on two basic premises: (1) The FASB should be responsive to the needs and viewpoints of the entire economic community, not just the public accounting profession. (2) It should operate in full view of the public through a **"due process"** system that gives interested persons ample opportunity to make their views known. To ensure the achievement of these goals, the FASB follows specific steps to develop a typical FASB Statement of Financial Accounting Standards, as Illustration 1-2 shows.

Illustration 1-2
The Due Process System of the FASB

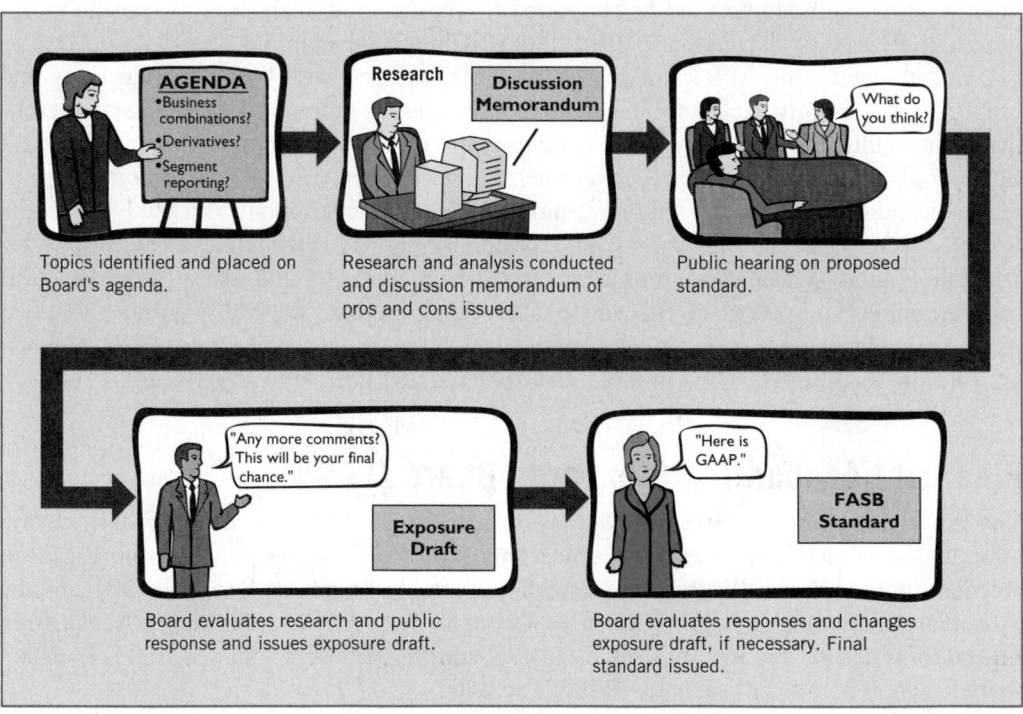

Topics identified and placed on Board's agenda.

Research and analysis conducted and discussion memorandum of pros and cons issued.

Public hearing on proposed standard.

Board evaluates research and public response and issues exposure draft.

Board evaluates responses and changes exposure draft, if necessary. Final standard issued.

The passage of a new **Statement of Financial Accounting Standards** requires the support of four of the seven Board members. FASB Statements are considered GAAP and thereby binding in practice. All ARBs and APB Opinions implemented by 1973 (when the FASB formed) continue to be effective until amended or superseded by FASB pronouncements. In recognition of possible misconceptions of the term "principles," the FASB uses the term **financial accounting standards** in its pronouncements.

Types of Pronouncements

The FASB issues three major types of pronouncements:

1 Standards, Interpretations, and Staff Positions.

2 Financial Accounting Concepts.

3 Emerging Issues Task Force Statements.

Standards, Interpretation, and Staff Positions. Financial accounting **standards** is-sued by the FASB are considered generally accepted accounting principles. In addition, the FASB also issues **FASB interpretations** that modify or extend existing standards. Inter-pretations have the same authority, and require the same votes for passage, as standards. The APB also issued interpretations of APB Opinions. Both types of interpretations are now considered authoritative for purposes of determining GAAP. Finally, the FASB issues staff positions, which provide interpretive guidance and also minor amendments to standards and interpretations. These staff positions have the same authority as standards and interpretations. The Board also has issued FASB Technical Bulletins, which provide timely guidance on selected issues; staff positions are now used in lieu of technical bulletins. Since replacing the APB, the FASB has issued 159 standards, 48 interpretations, and over 40 staff posi-tions. (See list at the back of the book.)

Financial Accounting Concepts. As part of a long-range effort to move away from the problem-by-problem approach, the FASB in November 1978 issued the first in a series of **Statements of Financial Accounting Concepts** as part of its conceptual framework proj-ect. (See list at the back of the book.) The series sets forth fundamental objectives and con-cepts that the Board uses in developing future standards of financial accounting and reporting. The Board intends to form a cohesive set of interrelated concepts—a conceptual framework—that will serve as tools for solving existing and emerging problems in a con-sistent manner. Unlike a Statement of Financial Accounting Standards, **a Statement of Financial Accounting Concepts does not establish GAAP.** Concepts statements, how-ever, pass through the same due process system (discussion memo, public hearing, expo-sure draft, etc.) as do standards statements.

Emerging Issues Task Force Statements. In 1984 the FASB created the **Emerging Issues Task Force (EITF)**. The EITF is comprised of representatives from CPA firms and financial statement preparers. Observers from the SEC and AICPA also attend EITF meet-ings. The purpose of the task force is to reach a consensus on how to account for new and unusual financial transactions that may potentially create differing financial reporting prac-tices. Examples include accounting for pension plan terminations, revenue from barter trans-actions by Internet companies, and excessive amounts paid to takeover specialists. The EITF also provided timely guidance for the reporting of the losses arising from the terrorist at-tacks on the World Trade Center on September 11, 2001.

We cannot overestimate the importance of the EITF. In one year, for example, the task force examined 61 emerging financial reporting issues and arrived at a consensus on approximately 75 percent of them. The FASB reviews and approves all EITF consensuses. And the SEC indi-cated that it will view consensus solutions as preferred accounting. Further, it requires persua-sive justification for departing from them.

The EITF helps the FASB in many ways. For example, emerging issues often attract pub-lic attention. If not resolved quickly, they can lead to financial crises and scandal. They can also undercut public confidence in current reporting practices. The next step, possible governmental intervention, would threaten the continuance of standard setting in the private sector. The EITF identifies controversial accounting problems as they arise. The EITF determines whether it can quickly resolve them, or whether to involve the FASB in solving them. In essence, it becomes a "problem filter" for the FASB. Thus, the FASB will hopefully work on more pervasive long-term problems, while the EITF deals with short-term emerging issues.

Governmental Accounting Standards Board (GASB)

Financial statements prepared by state and local governments are not comparable with financial reports prepared by private business organizations. The lack of comparability was highlighted in the 1970s when a number of large cities such as New York and Cleveland faced potential bankruptcy. As result, the **Governmental Accounting Standards Board (GASB)** came into being.

The operational structure of the GASB is similar to that of the FASB. That is, it has an advisory council called the Governmental Accounting Standards Advisory Council (GASAC), and has its own technical staff and task forces to assist its work.

The creation of the GASB was controversial. Many believe that there should be only one standard-setting body—the FASB. It was hoped that dividing standard-setting between the GASB, which deals with state and local government reporting, and the FASB, which addresses reporting for all other entities, would not lead to conflict. Since we are primarily concerned with financial reports prepared by profit-seeking organizations, this textbook focuses on standards issued by the FASB. Illustration 1-3 shows the current formal organizational structure for the development of financial reporting standards.

Illustration 1-3
Organizational Structure for Setting Accounting Standards

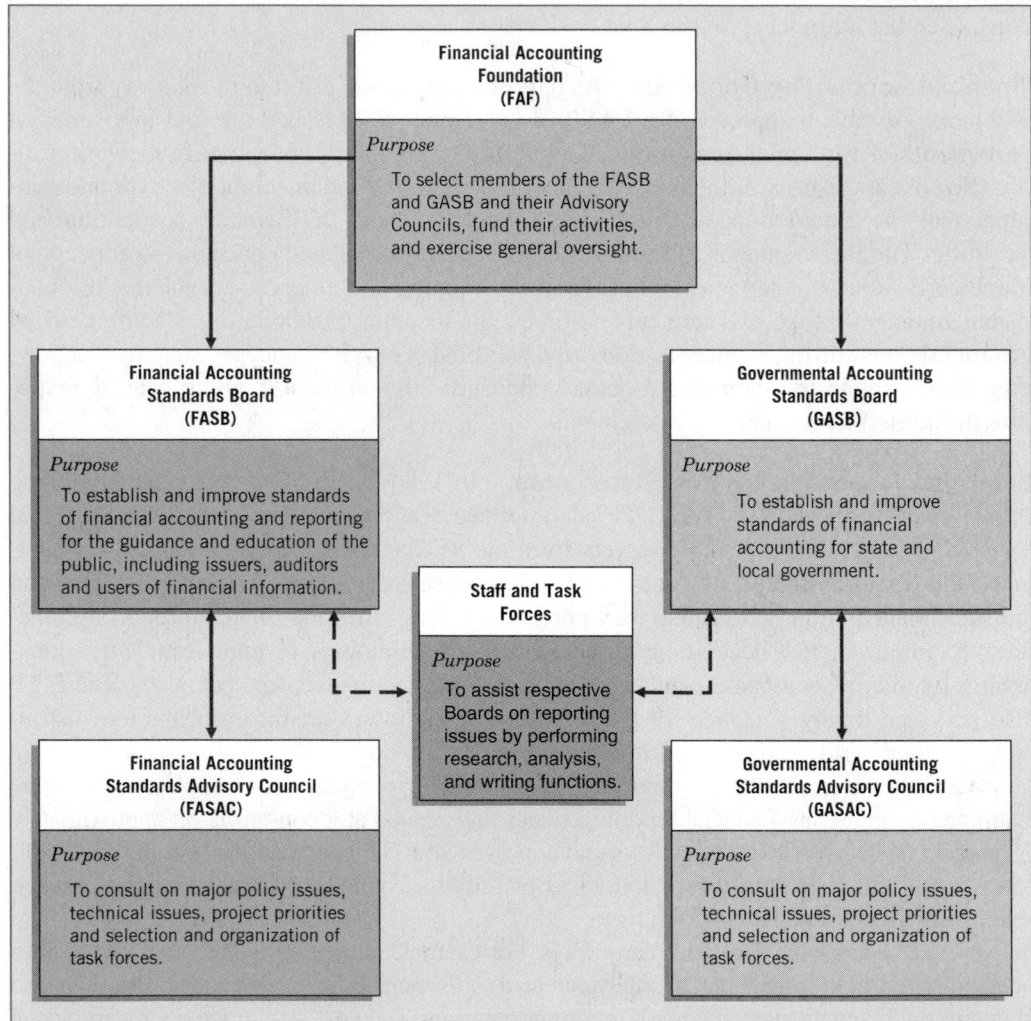

Changing Role of the AICPA

For several decades the AICPA provided leadership in developing accounting principles and rules. More than any other organization, it regulated the accounting profession, and developed and enforced accounting practice. When the FASB replaced the Accounting Principles Board, the AICPA established the **Accounting Standards Executive Committee (AcSEC)** as the committee authorized to speak for the AICPA in the area of financial accounting and reporting. It does so through various written communications:

Audit and Accounting Guides summarize the accounting practices of specific industries and provide specific guidance on matters not addressed by the FASB. Examples are accounting for casinos, airlines, colleges and universities, banks, insurance companies, and many others.

Statements of Position (SOP) provide guidance on financial reporting topics until the FASB sets standards on the issue in question. SOPs may update, revise, and clarify audit and accounting guides or provide free-standing guidance.

Practice Bulletins indicate AcSEC's views on narrow financial reporting issues not considered by the FASB.

Recently, the role of the AICPA in standard-setting has diminished. The FASB and the AICPA agree that, after a transition period, the AICPA and AcSEC no longer will issue authoritative accounting guidance for public companies. Furthermore, while the AICPA has been the leader in developing auditing standards through its **Auditing Standards Board**, the Sarbanes-Oxley Act of 2002 requires the Public Company Accounting Oversight Board to oversee the development of auditing standards. The AICPA will continue to develop and grade the CPA examination, which is administered in all 50 states.

Try it out!   Presented below is a list of acronyms common in accounting. Identify the term for which each acronym stands and provide a brief discussion.

a	FASB	e	FAF
b	SOP	f	ARB
c	APB	g	CAP
d	SEC	h	CPA

Solution

a   **FASB**. Financial Accounting Standards Board. The primary body which currently establishes and improves financial accounting and reporting standards for the guidance of issuers, auditors, users, and others.

b   **SOP**. Statements of Position. Statements issued by the AICPA (through the Accounting Standards Executive Committee of its Accounting Standards Division) which are generally devoted to emerging problems not addressed by the FASB or the SEC.

c   **APB**. Accounting Principles Board. A committee of public accountants, industry accountants, and academicians which issued 31 Opinions between 1959 and 1973. The APB replaced the CAP and was itself replaced by the FASB. Its opinions, unless superseded, remain a primary source of GAAP.

d   **SEC**. Securities and Exchange Commission. An independent regulatory agency of the U.S. government which administers the Securities Acts of 1933 and 1934 and other acts.

e   **FAF**. Financial Accounting Foundation. An organization whose purpose is to select members of the FASB and its Advisory Councils, fund their activities, and exercise general oversight.

f **ARB**. Accounting Research Bulletins. Official pronouncements of the Committee on Accounting Procedure which, unless superseded, remain a primary source of GAAP.

g **CAP**. Committee on Accounting Procedure. A committee of practicing CPAs which issued 51 Accounting Research Bulletins between 1939 and 1959 and is a predecessor of the FASB.

h **CPA**. Certified Public Accountant. An accountant who has fulfilled certain educational and experience requirements and passed a rigorous examination. Most CPAs offer auditing, tax, and management consulting services to the general public.

GENERALLY ACCEPTED ACCOUNTING PRINCIPLES

<table>
<tr><td>OBJECTIVE 7

Explain the meaning of generally accepted accounting principles.</td></tr>
</table>

Generally accepted accounting principles (GAAP) have substantial authoritative support. The AICPA's Code of Professional Conduct requires that members prepare financial statements in accordance with GAAP. Specifically, Rule 203 of this Code prohibits a member from expressing an unqualified opinion on financial statements that contain a material departure from generally accepted accounting principles.

The FASB is working on a standard, "The Hierarchy of Generally Accepted Accounting Principles," that defines the meaning of generally accepted accounting principles. This standard identifies the sources of accounting principles and the framework for selecting the principles to be used in the preparation of financial statements. The standard categorizes the major sources of GAAP as follows: **FASB Standards, Interpretations, and Staff Positions; APB Opinions;** and **AICPA Accounting Research Bulletins**.[7]

Often, however, a specific accounting transaction occurs that these documents do not cover. In this case, companies must use other authoritative literature. Major examples include AICPA Industry Audit and Accounting Guides and Statements of Position. The recognized professional bodies provide substantial authoritative support to these documents. Why? Because these professional bodies vote their issuance only after giving interested and affected parties the opportunity to react to exposure drafts and respond at public hearings. If these pronouncements lack guidance, companies may then consider other sources. Illustration 1-4 presents the hierarchy of these sources.[8] If the accounting treatment of an event is not specified by a Category A pronouncement, then Categories B through D should be investigated. If there is a conflict between pronouncements in B through D, companies should follow the higher category. For example, B is higher than C.

If none of these pronouncements addresses the event, companies seek support from other accounting literature. Examples include FASB Concepts Statements, International Accounting Standards, and accounting articles.[9]

---

[7]The auditing literature presented the GAAP hierarchy prior to the issuance of this standard. The FASB decided that the GAAP hierarchy should be directed specifically to the company because it is the company (not the auditor) that is responsible for selecting the accounting principles for financial statements. As a result, the GAAP hierarchy should reside in the accounting literature, not the auditing literature. "The Hierarchy of Generally Accepted Accounting Principles," *Proposed Statement of Financial Accounting Standards* (Norwalk, Conn.: FASB, April 28, 2005.)

[8]See for example, Douglas Sauter, "Remodeling the House of GAAP," *Journal of Accountancy* (July 1991), pp. 30–37.

[9]A reasonable question to ask is, "Why is one set of documents more authoritative than others?" There are two explanations. First, at the time the AICPA or FASB developed a standard, the SEC recognized these organizations as the appropriate body to establish accounting principles. Second, in most cases, a document is more authoritative if, before the document is issued, its contents are (a) debated in a public forum, (b) exposed in writing to the public for comment, and (c) approved by the Board.

Existing GAAP comprises over 2,000 pronouncements. Recently the FASB has started a project to codify all these pronouncements into one major document. Everything in this document will be considered authoritative. Any material excluded would be considered non-authoritative.

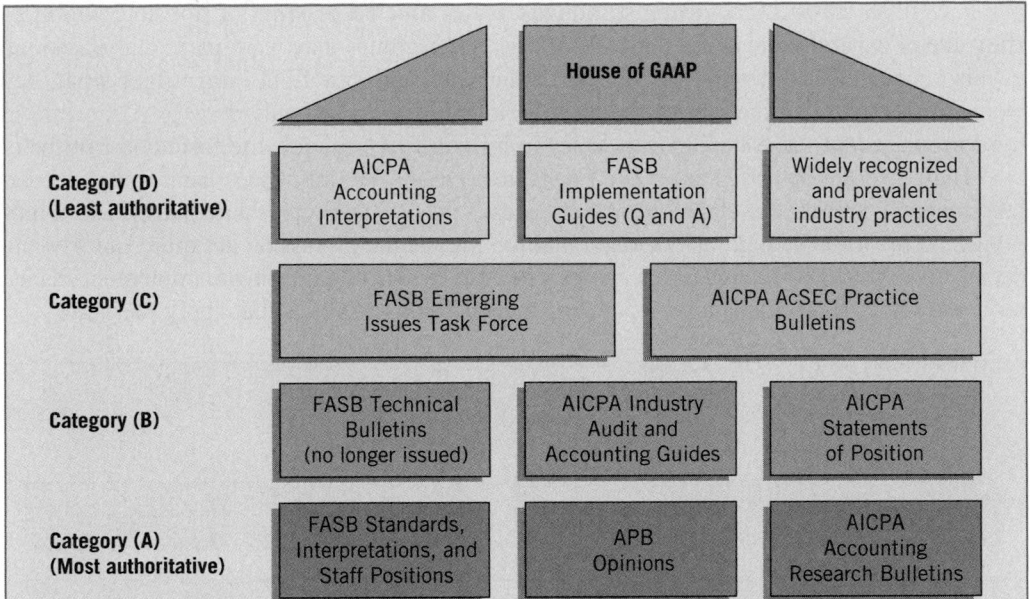

Illustration 1-4
The House of GAAP

What do the numbers mean? You Have to Step Back

Should the accounting profession have principles-based standards or rules-based standards? Critics of the profession today say that over the past three decades, standard-setters have moved away from broad accounting principles aimed at ensuring that companies' financial statements are fairly presented.

Instead, these critics say, standard-setters have moved toward drafting voluminous rules that, if technically followed in "check-box" fashion, may shield auditors and companies from legal liability. That has resulted in companies creating complex capital structures that comply with GAAP but hide billions of dollars of debt and other obligations. To add fuel to the fire, the chief accountant of the enforcement division of the SEC recently noted, "One can violate SEC laws and still comply with GAAP."

In short, what he is saying is that it is not enough just to check the boxes. You then have to step back and determine whether the *overall impression* created by GAAP financial statements fairly portrays the underlying economics of the company. It is a tough standard, but one that auditors and corporate management should strive to achieve.

Sources: Adapted from S. Liesman, "SEC Accounting Cop's Warning: Playing by the Rules May Not Head Off Fraud Issues," *Wall Street Journal* (February 12, 2002), p. C7. See also "Study Pursuant to Section 108(d) of the Sarbanes-Oxley Act of 2002 on the Adoption by the United States Financial Reporting System of a Principles-Based Accounting System," *SEC* (July 25, 2003).

Beyond the Numbers

Do you believe that standard-setters should issue principle-based standards or rule-based standards?

ISSUES IN FINANCIAL REPORTING

Since the implementation of an accounting standard may affect many interests, much discussion often occurs about who should develop these standards and to whom they should apply. We discuss some of the major issues below.

Standard Setting in a Political Environment

User groups are possibly the most powerful force influencing the development of accounting standards. User groups consist of those most interested in or affected by accounting standards, rules, and procedures. Like lobbyists in our state and national capitals, user groups play a significant role. **Accounting standards are as much a product of political action as they are of careful logic or empirical findings.** User groups may want particular economic events accounted for or reported in a particular way, and they fight hard to get what they want. They know that the most effective way to influence the standards is to participate in the formulation of these standards or to try to influence or persuade the formulator of them.

These user groups often target the FASB, to pressure it to influence changes in the existing standards and the development of new ones.[10] In fact, these pressures have been multiplying. Some influential groups demand that the accounting profession act more quickly and decisively to solve its problems. Other groups resist such action, preferring to implement change more slowly, if at all. Illustration 1-5 shows the various user groups that apply pressure.

OBJECTIVE 8

Describe the impact of user groups on the standard-setting process.

Illustration 1-5
User Groups that Influence the Formulation of Accounting Standards

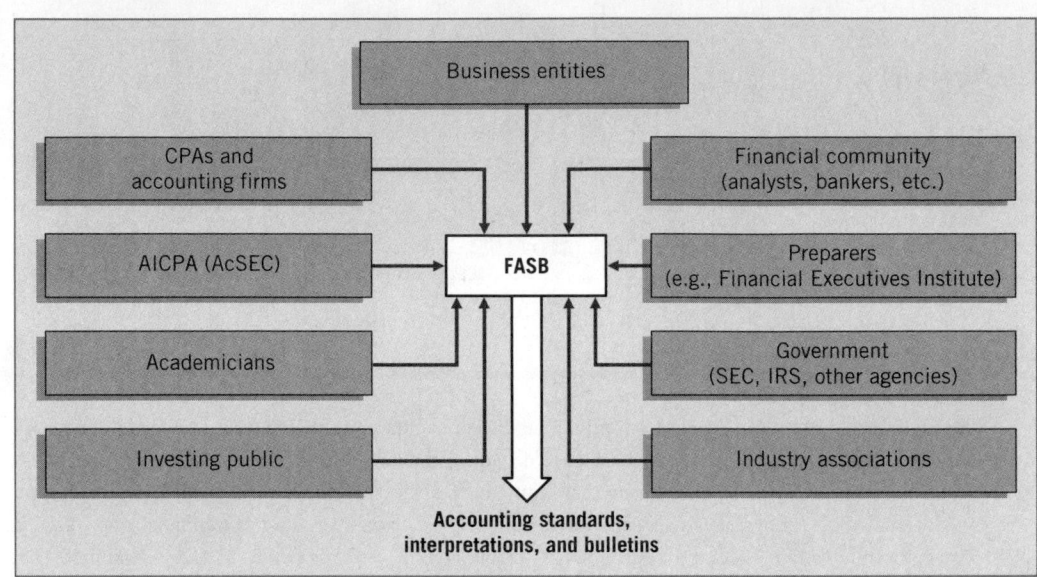

Should there be politics in setting standards for financial accounting and reporting? Why not? We have politics at home; at school; at the fraternity, sorority, and dormitory; at the office; at church, temple, and mosque. Politics is everywhere. Standard setting is part of the real world, and it cannot escape politics and political pressures.

That is not to say that politics in standard setting is a negative force. Considering the **economic consequences**[11] of many accounting standards, special interest groups should vocalize their reactions to proposed standards. What the Board should *not* do is issue pronouncements that are primarily politically motivated. While paying attention to its constituencies, the Board should base its standards on sound research and a conceptual framework that has its foundation in economic reality.

WHAT'S THE PRINCIPLE?

Financial information should be *neutral*; that is, a company should not select information to favor one set of interested parties over another.

The Expectations Gap

Accounting scandals at companies like **Enron**, **Cendant**, **Sunbeam**, **Rite-Aid**, **Xerox**, and **WorldCom** have attracted the attention of Congress. In 2002, it enacted legislation—the **Sarbanes-Oxley Act**. The new law increases the resources for the SEC to combat fraud and

---

[10]FASB board members acknowledged that they undertook many of the Board's projects, such as "Accounting for Contingencies," "Accounting for Pensions," "Statement of Cash Flows," and "Accounting for Derivatives," due to political pressure.

[11]*Economic consequences* means the impact of accounting reports on the wealth positions of issuers and users of financial information, and the decision-making behavior resulting from that impact. The resulting behavior of these individuals and groups could have detrimental financial effects on the providers of the financial information. See Stephen A. Zeff, "The Rise of 'Economic Consequences'," *Journal of Accountancy* (December 1978), pp. 56–63. We extend appreciation to Professor Zeff for his insights on this chapter.

<u>**What do the numbers mean?**</u>   **The Economic Consequences of Goodwill**

Investors generally ignore an accounting change, except when it substantially affects net income. Recently issued goodwill rules are one such change. Under previous GAAP, companies with goodwill charged it to revenues over time. Under new rules, companies no longer have to write off this cost. The effect on the bottom line for some companies is substantial. For example, assuming no goodwill amortization, **International Paper** estimates an income increase of 21 percent, **Johnson Controls** 16 percent, and **Pepsi Bottling Group** 30 percent.

Some believe this change will increase their stock's attractiveness. Others argue that it should have no effect because the write-off is a mere bookkeeping charge. Still others argue that the change has no effect on cash flows, but that investors will perceive the company to be more profitable, and therefore a good buy in the marketplace. In short, the numbers have consequences.

Beyond the Numbers

What is meant by the phrase *economic consequences of accounting standards?* Identify some accounting issue, other than accounting for goodwill, that would have economic consequences.

---

curb poor reporting practices.[12] And the SEC has increased its policing efforts, approving new auditor independence rules and materiality guidelines for financial reporting. In addition, the Sarbanes-Oxley Act introduces sweeping changes to the institutional structure of the accounting profession. The following are some of the key provisions of the legislation.

- Establishes an oversight board, the **Public Company Accounting Oversight Board (PCAOB)**, for accounting practices. The PCAOB has oversight and enforcement authority and establishes auditing, quality control, and independence standards and rules.

- Implements stronger independence rules for auditors. Audit partners, for example, are required to rotate every five years and auditors are prohibited from offering certain types of consulting services to corporate clients.

- Requires CEOs and CFOs to personally certify that financial statements and disclosures are accurate and complete and requires CEOs and CFOs to forfeit bonuses and profits when there is an accounting restatement.

- Requires audit committees to be comprised of independent members and members with financial expertise.

- Requires codes of ethics for senior financial officers.

In addition, Section 404 of the Sarbanes-Oxley Act requires public companies to attest to the effectiveness of their internal controls over financial reporting. **Internal controls** are a system of checks and balances designed to prevent and detect fraud and errors. Most companies have these systems in place, but many have never completely documented them. Companies are finding that it is a costly process but perhaps badly needed. Already intense examination of internal controls has found lingering problems in the way companies operate. Recently, 424 companies reported deficiencies in internal control.[13] Many problems involved closing the books, revenue recognition deficiencies, reconciling accounts, or dealing with inventory. **SunTrust Bank**, for example, fired three officers after discovering errors in how the company calculates its allowance for bad debts. **Visteon**, a car parts supplier, said it found problems recording and managing receivables from its largest customer, **Ford Motor**.

Will these changes be enough? The **expectations gap**—what the public thinks accountants *should* do and what accountants think they *can* do—is difficult to close.

---

[12]*Sarbanes-Oxley Act of 2002,* H. R. Rep. No. 107-610 (2002).

[13]Leah Townsend, "Internal Control Deficiency Disclosures—Interim Alert," *Yellow Card—Interim Trend Alert* (April 12, 2005), Glass, Lewis & Co., LLC.

Due to the number of fraudulent reporting cases, some question whether the profession is doing enough. Although the profession can argue rightfully that accounting cannot be responsible for every financial catastrophe, it must strive to meet the needs of society. However, efforts to meet these needs will become more costly to society. The development of a highly transparent, clear, and reliable system will require considerable resources.

International Accounting Standards

Former Secretary of the Treasury Lawrence Summers indicated that the single most important innovation shaping the capital markets was the idea of generally accepted accounting principles. He went on to say that we need something similar internationally.

We believe that the Secretary is right. Relevant and reliable financial information is a necessity for viable capital markets. Unfortunately, companies outside the United States often prepare financial statements using standards different from U.S. GAAP. As a result, international companies such as **Coca-Cola**, **Microsoft**, and **IBM** have to develop financial information in different ways. Beyond the additional costs these companies incur, users of the financial statements often must understand at least two sets of GAAP. (Understanding one set is hard enough!) It is not surprising therefore that there is a growing demand for one set of high-quality international standards.

Presently, there are two sets of standards accepted for international use—U.S. GAAP and the international standards, also known as **iGAAP**, issued by the London-based **International Accounting Standards Board (IASB)**. As you will learn, there are many similarities between U.S. and IASB standards.

U.S. companies that list overseas are still permitted to use U.S. GAAP. Conversely foreign companies listed on our exchanges are required to reconcile their financial information to U.S. GAAP. The reason for the reconciliation is that U.S. GAAP is more extensive and detailed than iGAAP.

Already over 100 countries use iGAAP, and the European Union now requires all listed companies in Europe (over 7,000 companies) to use it. The FASB and the IASB are now working hard to find common ground related to existing and proposed standards. Both parties recognize that global markets will best be served if only one set of GAAP is used. Convergence of U.S. GAAP with international standards now appears to be a real possibility. For example, in 2002 the FASB and the IASB formalized their commitment to the convergence of U.S. GAAP and iGAAP by issuing a memorandum of understanding (often referred to as the Norwalk agreement). The two boards agreed to use their best efforts to:

- make their existing financial reporting standards fully compatible as soon as practicable, and
- coordinate their future work programs to ensure that once achieved, compatibility is maintained.

As a result of this agreement, the two boards identified a number of short-term and long-term projects that would lead to convergence. For example, one short-term project was for the FASB to issue a standard that permits a fair value option for financial instruments. This standard was issued in 2007, and now the FASB and the IASB follow the same accounting in this area. Conversely, the IASB is presently working on a standard related to borrowing costs, in an effort to make it consistent with U.S. standards. Long-term convergence projects relate to such issues as revenue recognition, the conceptual framework, and research and development costs.

In addition, the SEC and European regulators have pledged by 2009 to recognize each other's standards for listing on the various world stock market exchanges. As a result, costly reconciliation requirements will be eliminated and, it is hoped, lead to greater comparability and transparency.

Because convergence is such an important issue, we provide in each chapter of this textbook a summary page on international accounting called **Convergence Corner**. This feature will help you understand the changes that are taking place in the financial reporting area as we move to one set of international financial reporting standards.

Ethics in the Environment of Financial Accounting

Robert Sack, a noted commentator on the subject of accounting ethics, observed, "Based on my experience, new graduates tend to be idealistic . . . thank goodness for that! Still it is very dangerous to think that your armor is all in place and say to yourself, 'I would have never given in to that.' The pressures don't explode on us; they build, and we often don't recognize them until they have us."

These observations are particularly appropriate for anyone entering the business world. In accounting, as in other areas of business, we frequently encounter ethical dilemmas. Some of these dilemmas are simple and easy to resolve. However, many are not, requiring difficult choices among allowable alternatives.

Companies that concentrate on "maximizing the bottom line," "facing the challenges of competition," and "stressing short-term results" place accountants in an environment of conflict and pressure. Basic questions such as, "Is this way of communicating financial information good or bad?" "Is it right or wrong?" "What should I do in the circumstance?" cannot always be answered by simply adhering to GAAP or following the rules of the profession. Technical competence is not enough when encountering ethical decisions.

Doing the right thing is not always easy or obvious. The pressures "to bend the rules," "to play the game," "to just ignore it" can be considerable. For example, "Will my decision affect my job performance negatively?", "Will my superiors be upset?", "Will my colleagues be unhappy with me?" are often questions business people face in making a tough ethical decision. The decision is more difficult because there is no comprehensive ethical system to provide guidelines.

Time, job, client, personal, and peer pressures can complicate the process of ethical sensitivity and selection among alternatives. Throughout this textbook, **we present ethical considerations to help sensitize you** to the type of situations you may encounter in the performance of your professional responsibility.

Conclusion

Bob Herz, FASB chairman, believes that there are three fundamental considerations the FASB must keep in mind in its standard-setting activities: (1) improvement in financial reporting, (2) simplification of the accounting literature and the standard-setting process, and (3) international convergence. These are notable objectives, and the Board is making good progress on all three dimensions. Issues such as off-balance-sheet financing, measurement of fair values, enhanced criteria for revenue recognition, and stock option accounting are examples of where the Board has exerted leadership. Improvements in financial reporting should follow.

Also, the Board is making it easier to understand what GAAP is. Presently GAAP is contained in a number of different documents. The lack of a single source makes it difficult to access and understand generally accepted principles. The Board is embarked on a long-term project ("the codification") that will compile GAAP in one document. This codification will organize existing GAAP by accounting topic regardless of its source (FASB Statements, APB Opinions, and so on). The codified standards will then be considered to be GAAP and to be authoritative, and all other literature will be considered non-authoritative.

Finally, international convergence is underway. Some projects already are completed and differences eliminated. Many more are on the drawing board. The crisis caused in the capital markets due to accounting irregularities of companies like **Enron, Krispy Kreme, Fannie Mae, Xerox,** and a host of others has caused the profession to reexamine its processes and standards. At present, we believe that the profession is reacting responsibly to remedy identified shortcomings.

OBJECTIVE 9
Understand issues related to ethics and financial accounting.

WHAT'S THE PRINCIPLE?
Financial information must be *representationally faithful*; that is, the numbers and descriptions match what really existed or happened.

Expanded Discussion of Ethical Issues in Financial Reporting

Expanded Discussion on International Accounting

You will want to read the CONVERGENCE CORNER on page 20 for discussion of the international convergence efforts and the reporting environment.

CONVERGENCE CORNER

International Financial Reporting

Most agree that there is a need for one set of international accounting standards. Here is why:

Multinational corporations. Today companies view the entire world as their market. For example, **Coca-Cola**, **Intel**, and **McDonald's** generate more than 50 percent of their sales outside the United States, and many foreign companies find their largest market to be the United States.

Mergers and acquisitions. The mergers that led to international giants **DaimlerChrysler** and **Vodafone/Mannesmann** suggest that we will see even more such mergers in the future.

Information technology. As communication barriers continue to topple through advances in technology, companies and individuals in different countries and markets are becoming comfortable buying and selling goods and services from one another.

Financial markets. Financial markets are some of the most significant international markets today. Whether it is currency, equity securities (stocks), bonds, or derivatives, there are active markets throughout the world trading these types of instruments.

RELEVANT FACTS

• iGAAP includes the standards, referred to as International Financial Reporting Standards (IFRS), developed by the IASB. The predecessor to the IASB issued International Accounting Standards (IAS). Both IFRS and IAS are considered iGAAP.

• The fact that there are differences between U.S. GAAP and iGAAP should not be surprising because standard setters have developed standards in response to different user needs. In some countries, the primary users of financial statements are private investors; in others, the primary users are tax authorities or central government planners. In the United States, investors and creditors have driven accounting-standard formulation.

• iGAAP tends to be simpler and less stringent in its accounting and disclosure requirements. U.S. GAAP is more detailed. This difference in approach has resulted in a debate about the merits of "principle-based" versus "rule-based" standards.

• Regulators have stated that by 2009 they want to eliminate the need for foreign companies that trade sharees in U.S. markets to reconcile their accounting with U.S. GAAP.

ABOUT THE NUMBERS

The IASB is a relatively new organization (formed in 2001). As a result, it has looked to the United States to determine the structure it should follow in establishing iGAAP. Thus, the standard-setting structure internationally is very similar to the standard-setting structure in the United States. Presented below is a chart of the international standard setting structure.

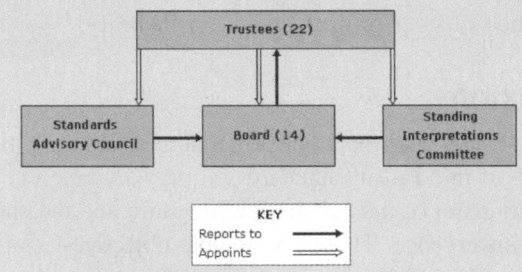

ON THE HORIZON

Both the IASB and the FASB are hard at work developing standards that will lead to the elimination of major differences in the way certain transactions are accounted for and reported. In fact, the IASB has stated that no new major standards will become effective until 2009. The major reason for this policy is to provide companies time to translate and implement iGAAP into practice.

The international standard-setting environment is changing rapidly. The task will not be easy, but conditions are conducive to convergence. As Mary Barth, a member of the IASB noted, "There is still a lot to do, but I would never have dreamed we would be working as closely with the FASB as we do today."

ACCOUNTING, ANALYSIS, PRINCIPLES

As the U.S. economy began to take shape in the decades after the Civil War, the era of Andrew Carnegie, John D. Rockefeller, and J.P. Morgan, regulation of companies was largely left to individual states. "The reality is that mandatory disclosure was not a particularly big deal at the state level" until well into the 20th century, says Joel Seligman, president of the University of Rochester and author of books on securities law.

In the absence of government regulation, any push for greater corporate openness largely fell to stock exchanges. In 1869, the New York Stock Exchange (NYSE) required that all shares of listed companies be registered at a bank or other appropriate agency. The move was aimed at stopping the practice of companies "watering" stock by issuing shares without telling anyone—thus secretly diluting the holdings of existing shareholders. The NYSE, according to its own official history, delisted the stock of a railroad for several months until the company agreed to comply with the new rule.

Accounting

Identify the two entities that are primarily responsible today for establishing generally accepted accounting principles. Explain the relationship of these two organizations to one another.

Analysis

Some of the early business reports in the middle 1930s were not heavy on verbiage. Many of the required reports were so bare-bones beyond the financial statements that an expert on financial accounting once commented that a person could read them "without being able to tell what business a company is in."

For example, the 1936 annual report of **American Express** ran nine pages, including a one-page auditor's opinion, two pages listing officers and directors, and two pages briefly describing some events of 1936. The financial tables did not include comparative numbers for 1935. In comparison, the following chart indicates the increase in the number of pages of American Express's annual report over an extended period of time.

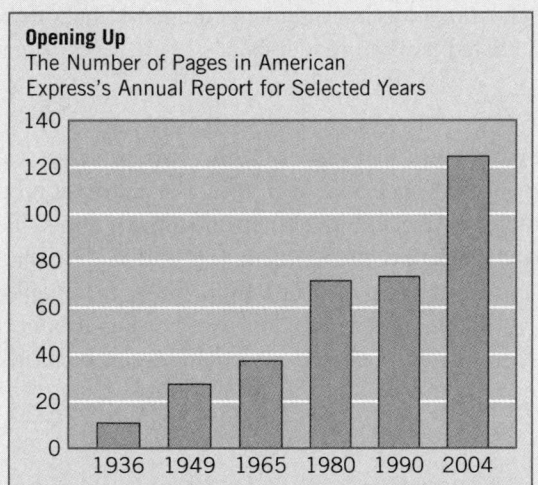

Opening Up
The Number of Pages in American Express's Annual Report for Selected Years

Source: Information in this problem, including the chart, is adapted from John R. Emshwiller, Corporate Governance (A Special Report), "Opening the Books: Corporate Disclosure Has Come a Long Way Over the Decades, But It Still Has a Ways to Go," *Wall Street Journal*, October 2005, p. R6.

Explain why American Express's annual report has increased so much in size over the last 70 years.

Principles

What are the accounting concepts or principles that companies use to justify the increase in financial information presented in annual reports?

Solution

Accounting

The two primary entities are the SEC and the FASB. The SEC is a federal agency. It administers the Securities Exchange Act of 1934 and several other acts. Most companies that issue securities to the public that are listed on a stock exchange are required to file audited financial statements with the SEC. In addition, the SEC has broad powers to prescribe, in whatever detail it desires, the accounting practices and standards to be employed by companies that fall within its jurisdiction.

The FASB is a private standard-setting body. Its mission is to establish and improve standards of financial accounting and reporting for the guidance and education of the public, which includes issuers, auditors, and users of financial information.

The SEC has affirmed its support for the FASB by indicating that the financial statements conforming to the standards set by the FASB are presumed to have substantial authoritative support. In short, the SEC requires registrants to adhere to GAAP. In addition, the SEC indicated in its reports to Congress that "it continues to believe that the initiative for establishing and improving accounting standards should remain in the private sector, subject to Commission oversight."

Analysis

There are many reasons why American Express's annual report, like those of most companies, has increased in size. Here are three:

1   *Complexity of the business environment.* The increasing complexity of business operations magnifies the difficulty of distilling economic events into summarized reports. Such areas as derivatives, leasing, business combinations, and pensions are complex, and extensive note disclosure is needed to understand the effects of these transactions.

2   *Necessity for timely information.* Users want information that is current and predictive, which leads to the presentation of more than just historical information.

3   *Accounting as a control and monitoring device.* The government has sought public disclosure of such phenomena as management compensation, off–balance-sheet financing arrangements, and related party transactions.

Principles

As will be discussed more fully in Chapter 2, the two primary qualities that accounting information must have are *relevance* and *reliability*. For information to be relevant today, it must be helpful in predicting the future, provide feedback about the past, and be timely. Given the complexity of the business environment, it is only natural that expansion of financial reporting will result. Furthermore, the information must be reliable, meaning it is representationally faithful, verifiable, and neutral. In many cases, it is necessary to describe the transactions in detail, because less-detailed information can be easily misinterpreted.

Key Terms

Summary of Learning Objectives

1 Identify the major financial statements and other means of financial reporting. Companies most frequently provide (1) the balance sheet, (2) the income statement, (3) the statement of cash flows, and (4) the statement of owners' or stockholders' equity. Financial reporting other than financial statements may take various forms. Examples include the president's letter and supplementary schedules in the corporate annual report, prospectuses, reports filed with government agencies, news releases, management's forecasts, and descriptions of a company's social or environmental impact.

2 Explain how accounting assists in the efficient use of scarce resources. Accounting provides reliable, relevant, and timely information to managers, investors, and creditors to allow resource allocation to the most efficient enterprises. Accounting also provides measurements of efficiency (profitability) and financial soundness.

3 Describe some of the challenges facing accounting. Financial reports fail to provide (1) some key performance measures widely used by management, (2) forward-looking information needed by investors and creditors, (3) sufficient information on a company's soft assets (intangibles), and (4) real-time financial information.

4 Identify the objectives of financial reporting. The objectives of financial reporting are to provide information that is (1) useful in investment and credit decisions, (2) useful in assessing cash flow prospects, and (3) about enterprise resources, claims to those resources, and changes in them.

5 Explain the need for accounting standards. The accounting profession has attempted to develop a set of standards that is generally accepted and universally practiced. Without this set of standards, each company would have to develop its own standards. Readers of financial statements would have to familiarize themselves with every company's peculiar accounting and reporting practices. As a result, it would be almost impossible to prepare statements that could be compared.

6 Identify the major policy-setting bodies and their role in the standard-setting process. The *Securities and Exchange Commission (SEC)* is a federal agency that has the broad powers to prescribe, in whatever detail it desires, the accounting standards to be employed by companies that fall within its jurisdiction. The *American Institute of Certified Public Accountants (AICPA)* issued standards through its Committee on Accounting Procedure and Accounting Principles Board. The *Financial Accounting Standards Board (FASB)* establishes and improves standards of financial accounting and reporting for the guidance and education of the public.

7 Explain the meaning of generally accepted accounting principles. Generally accepted accounting principles (GAAP) are those principles that have substantial authoritative support, such as FASB Standards, Interpretations, and Staff Positions, APB Opinions and Interpretations, AICPA Accounting Research Bulletins, and other authoritative pronouncements.

8 Describe the impact of user groups on the standard-setting process. User groups may want particular economic events accounted for or reported in a particular way, and they fight hard to get what they want. They especially target the FASB to influence changes in the existing standards and the development of new ones. Because of the accelerated rate of change and the increased complexity of our economy, these pressures have been multiplying. Accounting standards are as much a product of political action as they are of careful logic or empirical findings. The IASB is working with U.S. standard setters toward international convergence of standards.

9 Understand issues related to ethics and financial accounting. Financial accountants are called on for moral discernment and ethical decision making. Decisions sometimes are difficult because a public consensus has not emerged to formulate a comprehensive ethical system that provides guidelines in making ethical judgments.

Questions

1 Differentiate broadly between financial accounting and managerial accounting.

2 Differentiate between "financial statements" and "financial reporting."

3 How does accounting help the capital allocation process?

4 What are some of the major challenges facing the accounting profession?

5 What are the major objectives of financial reporting?

6 Of what value is a common set of standards in financial accounting and reporting?

7 What is the likely limitation of "general-purpose financial statements"?

8 In what way is the Securities and Exchange Commission concerned about and supportive of accounting principles and standards?

9 What was the Committee on Accounting Procedure, and what were its accomplishments and failings?

10 For what purposes did the AICPA in 1959 create the Accounting Principles Board?

11 Distinguish among Accounting Research Bulletins, Opinions of the Accounting Principles Board, and Statements of the Financial Accounting Standards Board.

12 If you had to explain or define "generally accepted accounting principles or standards," what essential characteristics would you include in your explanation?

13 In what ways was it felt that the statements issued by the Financial Accounting Standards Board would carry greater weight than the opinions issued by the Accounting Principles Board?

14 How are FASB discussion memoranda and FASB exposure drafts related to FASB "statements"?

15 Distinguish between FASB "statements of financial accounting standards" and FASB "statements of financial accounting concepts."

16 What is Rule 203 of the Code of Professional Conduct?

17 Rank from the most authoritative to the least authoritative, the following three items: FASB Technical Bulletins, AICPA Practice Bulletins, and FASB Standards.

18 The chairman of the FASB at one time noted that "the flow of standards can only be slowed if (1) producers focus less on quarterly earnings per share and tax benefits and more on quality products, and (2) accountants and lawyers rely less on rules and law and more on professional judgment and conduct." Explain his comment.

19 What is the purpose of FASB Staff Positions?

20 Explain the role of the Emerging Issues Task Force in establishing generally accepted accounting principles.

21 What is the purpose of the Governmental Accounting Standards Board?

22 What are some possible reasons why another organization, such as the Governmental Accounting Standards Board, should not issue financial reporting standards?

23 What are the sources of pressure that change and influence the development of accounting principles and standards?

24 Some individuals have indicated that the FASB must be cognizant of the economic consequences of its pronouncements. What is meant by "economic consequences"? What dangers exist if politics play too much of a role in the development of financial reporting standards?

25 If you were given complete authority in the matter, how would you propose that accounting principles or standards should be developed and enforced?

26 One writer recently noted that 99.4 percent of all companies prepare statements that are in accordance with GAAP. Why then is there such concern about fraudulent financial reporting?

27 What is the "expectations gap"? What is the profession doing to try to close this gap?

28 The Sarbanes-Oxley Act was enacted to combat fraud and curb poor reporting practices. What are some key provisions of this legislation?

29 A number of foreign countries have reporting standards that differ from those in the United States. What are some of the main reasons why reporting standards are often different among countries?

30 Why would it be advantageous for U.S. GAAP and International GAAP to be the same?

31 How are financial accountants challenged in their work to make ethical decisions? Is technical mastery of GAAP not sufficient to the practice of financial accounting?

ACCOUNTING IN ACTION

Financial Reporting and Analysis

■ Financial Statement Analysis

AIA1-1 Kate Jackson, a new staff accountant, is confused because of the complexities involving accounting standard setting. Specifically, she is confused by the number of bodies issuing financial reporting standards of one kind or another and the level of authoritative support that can be attached to these reporting standards. Kate decides that she must review the environment in which accounting standards are set, if she is to increase her understanding of the accounting profession.

Kate recalls that during her accounting education there was a chapter or two regarding the environment of financial accounting and the development of accounting standards. However, she remembers that her instructor placed little emphasis on these chapters.

Instructions

(a) Help Kate by identifying key organizations involved in accounting standard setting.

(b) Kate asks for guidance regarding authoritative support. Please assist her by explaining what is meant by authoritative support.

(c) Give Kate a historical overview of how standard setting has evolved so that she will not feel that she is the only one to be confused.

(d) What authority for compliance with GAAP has existed throughout the period of standard setting?

International Reporting Issues

AIA1-2 Michael Sharpe, former Deputy Chairman of the International Accounting Standards Board (IASB), made the following comments to the 63rd Annual Conference of the Financial Executives Institute (FEI).

There is an irreversible movement towards the harmonization of financial reporting throughout the world. The international capital markets require an end to:

1 The confusion caused by international companies announcing different results depending on the set of accounting standards applied. Recent announcements by **Daimler-Benz** [now **DaimlerChrysler**] highlight the confusion that this causes.

2 Companies in some countries obtaining unfair commercial advantages from the use of particular national accounting standards.

3 The complications in negotiating commercial arrangements for international joint ventures caused by different accounting requirements.

4 The inefficiency of international companies having to understand and use a myriad of different accounting standards depending on the countries in which they operate and the countries in which they raise capital and debt. Executive talent is wasted on keeping up to date with numerous sets of accounting standards and the never-ending changes to them.

5 The inefficiency of investment managers, bankers, and financial analysts as they seek to compare financial reporting drawn up in accordance with different sets of accounting standards.

6 Failure of many stock exchanges and regulators to require companies subject to their jurisdiction to provide comparable, comprehensive, and transparent financial reporting frameworks giving international comparability.

Instructions

(a) What is the International Accounting Standards Board?

(b) What stakeholders might benefit from the use of International Accounting Standards?

(c) What do you believe are some of the major obstacles to harmonization?

Concepts for Analysis

AIA1-3 **(Financial Accounting)** Alan Rodriquez has recently completed his first year of studying accounting. His instructor for next semester has indicated that the primary focus will be the area of financial accounting.

Instructions

(a) Differentiate between financial accounting and managerial accounting.

(b) One part of financial accounting involves the preparation of financial statements. What are the financial statements most frequently provided?

(c) What is the difference between financial statements and financial reporting?

AIA1-4 **(Objectives of Financial Reporting)** Celia Cruz, a recent graduate of the local state university, is presently employed by a large manufacturing company. She has been asked by Angeles Ochoa, controller, to prepare the company's response to a current Discussion Memorandum published by the Financial Accounting Standards Board (FASB). Cruz knows that the FASB has issued seven *Statements of Financial Accounting Concepts,* and she believes that these concept statements could be used to support the company's response to the Discussion Memorandum. She has prepared a rough draft of the response citing *Statement of Financial Accounting Concepts No. 1,* "Objectives of Financial Reporting by Business Enterprises."

Instructions

(a) Identify the three objectives of financial reporting as presented in *Statement of Financial Accounting Concepts No. 1 (SFAC No. 1)*.

(b) Describe the level of sophistication expected of the users of financial information by *SFAC No. 1*.

(CMA adapted)

AIA1-5 (Accounting Numbers and the Environment) Hardly a day goes by without an article appearing on the crises affecting many of our financial institutions in the United States. It is estimated that the savings and loan (S&L) debacle of the 1980s, for example, ended up costing $500 billion ($2,000 for every man, woman, and child in the United States). Some argue that if the S&Ls had been required to report their investments at market value instead of cost, large losses would have been reported earlier, which would have signaled regulators to close those S&Ls and, therefore, minimize the losses to U.S. taxpayers.

Instructions

Explain how reported accounting numbers might affect an individual's perceptions and actions. Cite two examples.

 AIA1-6 (Need for Accounting Standards) Some argue that having various organizations establish accounting principles is wasteful and inefficient. Rather than mandating accounting standards, each company could voluntarily disclose the type of information it considered important. In addition, if an investor wants additional information, the investor could contact the company and pay to receive the additional information desired.

Instructions

Comment on the appropriateness of this viewpoint.

AIA1-7 (AICPA's Role in Standard Setting) One of the major groups involved in the standard-setting process is the American Institute of Certified Public Accountants. Initially it was the primary organization that established accounting principles in the United States. Subsequently it relinquished most of its power to the FASB.

Instructions

(a) Identify the two committees of the AICPA that established accounting principles prior to the establishment of the FASB.

(b) Speculate as to why these two organizations failed. In your answer, identify steps the FASB has taken to avoid failure.

(c) What is the present role of the AICPA in the standard-setting environment?

AIA1-8 (FASB Role in Standard Setting) A press release announcing the appointment of the trustees of the new Financial Accounting Foundation stated that the Financial Accounting Standards Board (to be appointed by the trustees) ". . . will become the established authority for setting accounting principles under which corporations report to the shareholders and others."

Instructions

(a) Identify the sponsoring organization of the FASB and the process by which the FASB arrives at a decision and issues an accounting standard.

(b) Indicate the major types of pronouncements issued by the FASB and the purposes of each of these pronouncements.

AIA1-9 (Government Role in Standard Setting) Recently an article stated "the setting of accounting standards in the United States is now about 70 years old. It is a unique process in our society, one that has undergone numerous changes over the years. The standards are established by a private sector entity that has no dominant sponsor and is not part of any professional organization or trade association. The governmental entity that provides oversight, on the other hand, is far more a friend than a competitor or an antagonist."

Instructions

Identify the governmental entity that provides oversight and indicate its role in the standard-setting process.

 AIA1-10 (Politicization of Standard Setting) Some accountants have said that politicization in the development and acceptance of generally accepted accounting principles (i.e., standard setting) is taking place. Some use the term "politicization" in a narrow sense to mean the influence by governmental agencies, particularly the

Securities and Exchange Commission, on the development of generally accepted accounting principles. Others use it more broadly to mean the compromise that results when the bodies responsible for developing generally accepted accounting principles are pressured by interest groups (SEC, American Accounting Association, businesses through their various organizations, Institute of Management Accountants, financial analysts, bankers, lawyers, and so on).

Instructions

(a) The Committee on Accounting Procedure of the AICPA was established in the mid- to late 1930s and functioned until 1959, at which time the Accounting Principles Board came into existence. In 1973, the Financial Accounting Standards Board was formed and the APB went out of existence. Do the reasons these groups were formed, their methods of operation while in existence, and the reasons for the demise of the first two indicate an increasing politicization (as the term is used in the broad sense) of accounting standard setting? Explain your answer by indicating how the CAP, the APB, and the FASB operated or operate. Cite specific developments that tend to support your answer.

(b) What arguments can be raised to support the "politicization" of accounting standard setting?

(c) What arguments can be raised against the "politicization" of accounting standard setting?

(CMA adapted)

AIA1-11 (**Models for Setting Accounting Standards**) Presented below are three models for setting accounting standards.

1. The purely political approach, where national legislative action decrees accounting standards.
2. The private, professional approach, where financial accounting standards are set and enforced by private professional actions only.
3. The public/private mixed approach, where standards are basically set by private-sector bodies that behave as though they were public agencies and whose standards to a great extent are enforced through governmental agencies.

Instructions

(a) Which of these three models best describes standard setting in the United States? Comment on your answer.

(b) Why do companies, financial analysts, labor unions, industry trade associations, and others take such an active interest in standard setting?

(c) Cite an example of a group other than the FASB that attempts to establish accounting standards. Speculate as to why another group might wish to set its own standards.

AIA1-12 (**Standard-Setting Terminology**) Andrew Wyeth, an administrator at a major university, recently said, "I've got some CDs in my IRA, which I set up to beat the IRS." As elsewhere, in the world of accounting and finance, it often helps to be fluent in abbreviations and acronyms.

Instructions

Presented below is a list of common accounting acronyms. Identify the term for which each acronym stands, and provide a brief definition of each term.

(a)	AICPA	(e)	FAF	(i)	CPA	(m)	GASB
(b)	CAP	(f)	FASAC	(j)	FASB		
(c)	ARB	(g)	SOP	(k)	SEC		
(d)	APB	(h)	GAAP	(l)	IASB		

AIA1-13 (**Accounting Organizations and Documents Issued**) Presented below are a number of accounting organizations and types of documents they have issued.

Instructions

Match the appropriate document to the organization involved. Note that more than one document may be issued by the same organization. If no document is provided for an organization, write in "0."

Organization	Document
1. _____ Accounting Standards Executive Committee	(a) Opinions
2. _____ Accounting Principles Board	(b) Practice Bulletins
3. _____ Committee on Accounting Procedure	(c) Accounting Research Bulletins
4. _____ Financial Accounting Standards Board	(d) Financial Accounting Standards
	(e) Statements of Position

AIA1-14 (**Accounting Pronouncements**)   Standard setting bodies have issued a number of authoritative pronouncements. A list is provided on the left, below, with a description of these pronouncements on the right.

Instructions

Match the description to the pronouncements.

1. _____ Staff Positions
2. _____ Interpretations (of the Financial Accounting Standards Board)
3. _____ Statement of Financial Accounting Standards
4. _____ EITF Statements
5. _____ Opinions
6. _____ Statement of Financial Accounting Concepts

(a) Official pronouncements of the APB.

(b) Sets forth fundamental objectives and concepts that will be used in developing future standards.

(c) Primary document of the FASB that establishes GAAP.

(d) Provides additional guidance on implementing or applying FASB Standards or Interpretations.

(e) Provides guidance on how to account for new and unusual financial transactions that have the potential for creating diversity in financial reporting practices.

(f) Represent extensions or modifications of existing standards.

AIA1-15 (**Securities and Exchange Commission**)   The U.S. Securities and Exchange Commission (SEC) was created in 1934 and consists of five commissioners and a large professional staff. The SEC professional staff is organized into five divisions and several principal offices. The primary objective of the SEC is to support fair securities markets. The SEC also strives to foster enlightened stockholder participation in corporate decisions of publicly traded companies. The SEC has a significant presence in financial markets, the development of accounting practices, and corporation-shareholder relations, and has the power to exert influence on entities whose actions lie within the scope of its authority.

Instructions

(a) Explain from where the Securities and Exchange Commission receives its authority.

(b) Describe the official role of the Securities and Exchange Commission in the development of financial accounting theory and practices.

(c) Discuss the interrelationship between the Securities and Exchange Commission and the Financial Accounting Standards Board with respect to the development and establishment of financial accounting theory and practices.

(CMA adapted)

AIA1-16 (**Standard-Setting Process**)   In 1973, the responsibility for developing and issuing rules on accounting practices was given to the Financial Accounting Foundation and, in particular, to an arm of the foundation called the Financial Accounting Standards Board (FASB). The generally accepted accounting principles established by the FASB are enunciated through a publication series entitled *Statements of Financial Accounting Standards*. These statements are issued periodically, and over 150 have been issued. The statements have a significant influence on the way in which financial statements are prepared by U.S. corporations.

Instructions

(a) Describe the process by which a topic is selected or identified as appropriate for study by the Financial Accounting Standards Board (FASB).

(b) Once a topic is considered appropriate for consideration by the FASB, a series of steps is followed before a *Statement of Financial Accounting Standards* is issued. Describe the major steps in the process leading to the issuance of a standard.

(c) Identify at least three other organizations that influence the setting of generally accepted accounting principles (GAAP).

(CMA adapted)

AIA1-17 (**Economic Consequences**)   Presented on the next page are comments made in the financial press.

Instructions

Prepare responses to the requirements in each item.

(a) Rep. John Dingell, the ranking Democrat on the House Commerce Committee, threw his support behind the FASB's controversial derivatives accounting standard and encouraged the FASB to adopt the rule promptly. Indicate why a member of Congress might feel obligated to comment on this proposed FASB standard.

(b) In a strongly worded letter to Senator Lauch Faircloth (R-NC) and House Banking Committee Chairman Jim Leach (R-IA), the American Institute of Certified Public Accountants (AICPA) cautioned against government intervention in the accounting standard-setting process, warning that it had the potential of jeopardizing U.S. capital markets. Explain how government intervention could possibly affect capital markets adversely.

AIA1-18 **(Standard-Setting Process, Economic Consequences)** The following letter was sent to the SEC and the FASB by leaders of the business community.

Dear Sirs:

The FASB has been struggling with accounting for derivatives and hedging for many years. The FASB has now developed, over the last few weeks, a new approach that it proposes to adopt as a final standard. We understand that the Board intends to adopt this new approach as a final standard without exposing it for public comment and debate, despite the evident complexity of the new approach, the speed with which it has been developed and the significant changes to the exposure draft since it was released more than one year ago. Instead, the Board plans to allow only a brief review by selected parties, limited to issues of operationality and clarity, and would exclude questions as to the merits of the proposed approach.

As the FASB itself has said throughout this process, its mission does not permit it to consider matters that go beyond accounting and reporting considerations. Accordingly, the FASB may not have adequately considered the wide range of concerns that have been expressed about the derivatives and hedging proposal, including concerns related to the potential impact on the capital markets, the weakening of companies' ability to manage risk, and the adverse control implications of implementing costly and complex new rules imposed at the same time as other major initiatives, including the Year 2000 issues and a single European currency. We believe that these crucial issues must be considered, if not by the FASB, then by the Securities and Exchange Commission, other regulatory agencies, or Congress.

We believe it is essential that the FASB solicit all comments in order to identify and address all material issues that may exist before issuing a final standard. We understand the desire to bring this process to a prompt conclusion, but the underlying issues are so important to this nation's businesses, the customers they serve and the economy as a whole that expediency cannot be the dominant consideration. As a result, we urge the FASB to expose its new proposal for public comment, following the established due process procedures that are essential to acceptance of its standards, and providing sufficient time to affected parties to understand and assess the new approach.

We also urge the SEC to study the comments received in order to assess the impact that these proposed rules may have on the capital markets, on companies' risk management practices, and on management and financial controls. These vital public policy matters deserve consideration as part of the Commission's oversight responsibilities.

We believe that these steps are essential if the FASB is to produce the best possible accounting standard while minimizing adverse economic effects and maintaining the competitiveness of U.S. businesses in the international marketplace.

Very truly yours,

(This letter was signed by the chairs of 22 of the largest U.S. companies.)

Instructions

Answer the following questions.

(a) Explain the "due process" procedures followed by the FASB in developing a financial reporting standard.

(b) What is meant by the term "economic consequences" in accounting standard setting?

(c) What economic consequences arguments are used in this letter?

(d) What do you believe is the main point of the letter?

(e) Why do you believe a copy of this letter was sent by the business community to influential members of the United States Congress?

Professional Tools

Ethical Decision Making

AIA1-19 **(Issues Involving Standard Setting)** When the FASB issues new standards, the implementation date is usually 12 months from date of issuance, with early implementation encouraged. Paula Popovich, controller, discusses with her financial vice president the need for early implementation of a standard that would result in a fairer presentation of the company's financial condition and earnings. When the financial vice president determines that early implementation of the standard will adversely affect the reported net income for the year, he discourages Popovich from implementing the standard until it is required.

Instructions

Answer the following questions.

(a) What, if any, is the ethical issue involved in this case?
(b) Is the financial vice president acting improperly or immorally?
(c) What does Popovich have to gain by advocacy of early implementation?
(d) Which stakeholders might be affected by the decision against early implementation?

(CMA adapted)

AIA1-20 **(Financial Reporting Pressures)** Presented below is abbreviated testimony from Troy Normand in the **WorldCom** case. He was a manager in the corporate reporting department and is one of five individuals who pleaded guilty. He is testifying in hopes of receiving no prison time when he is ultimately sentenced.

Q. Mr. Normand, if you could just describe for the jury how the meeting started and what was said during the meeting?

A. I can't recall exactly who initiated the discussion, but right away Scott Sullivan acknowledged that he was aware we had problems with the entries, David Myers had informed him, and we were considering resigning.

He said that he respected our concerns but that we weren't being asked to do anything that he believed was wrong. He mentioned that he acknowledged that the company had lost focus quite a bit due to the preparations for the Sprint merger, and that he was putting plans in place and projects in place to try to determine where the problems were, why the costs were so high.

He did say he believed that the initial statements that we produced, that the line costs in those statements could not have been as high as they were, that he believes something was wrong and there was no way that the costs were that high.

I informed him that I didn't believe the entry we were being asked to do was right, that I was scared, and I didn't want to put myself in a position of going to jail for him or the company. He responded that he didn't believe anything was wrong, nobody was going to be going to jail, but that if it later was found to be wrong, that he would be the person going to jail, not me.

He asked that I stay, don't jump off the plane, let him land it softly, that's basically how he put it. And he mentioned that he had a discussion with Bernie Ebbers asking Bernie to reduce projections going forward and that Bernie had refused.

Q. Mr. Normand, you said that Mr. Sullivan said something about don't jump out of the plane. What did you understand him to mean when he said that?

A. Not to quit.

Q. During this meeting, did Mr. Sullivan say anything about whether you would be asked to make entries like this in the future?

A. Yes, he made a comment that from that point going forward we wouldn't be asked to record any entries, high-level late adjustments, that the numbers would be the numbers.

Q. What did you understand that to be mean, the numbers would be the numbers?

A. That after the preliminary statements were issued, with the exception of any normal transaction, valid transaction, we wouldn't be asked to be recording any more late entries.

Q. I believe you testified that Mr. Sullivan said something about the line cost numbers not being accurate. Did he ask you to conduct any analysis to determine whether the line cost numbers were accurate?

A. No, he did not.

Q. Did anyone ever ask you to do that?

A. No.

Q. Did you ever conduct any such analysis?

A. No, I didn't.

Q. During this meeting, did Mr. Sullivan ever provide any accounting justification for the entry you were asked to make?

A. No, he did not.

Q. Did anything else happen during the meeting?

A. I don't recall anything else.

Q. How did you feel after this meeting?

A. Not much better actually. I left his office not convinced in any way that what we were asked to do was right. However, I did question myself to some degree after talking with him wondering whether I was making something more out of what was really there.

Instructions

Answer the following questions.

(a) What appears to be the ethical issue involved in this case?
(b) Is Troy Normand acting improperly or immorally?
(c) What would you do if you were Troy Normand?
(d) Who are the major stakeholders in this case?

Financial Accounting Research (FARS)

AIA1-21 As a newly enrolled accounting major, you are anxious to better understand accounting institutions and sources of accounting literature. As a first step, you decide to explore the FASB's Statement of Financial Accounting Concepts No. 1 (CON 1).

Instructions

Using the **Financial Accounting Research System (FARS)** database, respond to the following items. (Provide text strings used in your search.)
(a) Find *Statement of Financial Accounting Concepts No. 1*. List three ways to access it on FARS.
(b) According to CON 1, "...financial reporting includes not only financial statements but also other means of communicating information." What other means are there of communicating information?
(c) According to CON 1, "...many people base economic decisions on their relationships to and knowledge about business enterprises and thus are potentially interested in the information provided by financial reporting." Indicate some of the users and the information they are most directly concerned with in economic decision making.

Professional Simulation

AIA1-22 Go to the book's companion website, at **www.wiley.com/college/warfield,** to find an interactive problem that simulates the computerized CPA exam. The professional simulation for this chapter asks you to address questions related to accounting principles.

What do the numbers mean?
Guideline Answers to Beyond the Numbers Questions

"It's Not the Economy Anymore, Stupid," p. 5

Q: Explain the difference between relevance and reliability. Why are these concepts important in reporting financial information?

A: Relevance and reliability are the two primary qualities that make accounting information useful for decision making. To be *relevant,* accounting information must be capable of making a difference in a decision. Information with no bearing on a decision is irrelevant. Accounting information is *reliable* to the extent that it is verifiable, is a faithful representation, and is reasonably free of error and bias.

Relevant information helps users predict the ultimate outcome of past, present, and future events. Reliability is a necessity, because most users have neither the time nor the expertise to evaluate the factual content of the information. These concepts will be discussed more fully in Chapter 2.

You Have to Step Back, p. 15

Q: Do you believe that standard-setters should issue principle-based standards or rule-based standards?

A: Those who advocate principle-based standards state that judgment is a necessary part of preparing financial statements. If standard-setters try to provide detailed guidance for every transaction, we get hundreds of pages of standards which are difficult to interpret and often lead to inconsistencies among standards. In fact, what happens is that more interpretations have to be issued to interpret the detailed rules. What are needed are objectives and principles stated for each standard, as well as guidance to help understand and apply the standard.

Those who favor a rule-based system note they do not want to apply judgment because such judgment can be second-guessed. They contend that due to our litigious environment, companies and auditors need the detailed rules to protect themselves from securities lawsuits and onerous legal liability.

The Economic Consequences of Goodwill, p. 17

Q: What is meant by the phrase *economic consequences of accounting standards?* Identify some accounting issue, other than the accounting for goodwill, that would have economic consequences.

A: *Economic consequences* means the impact of accounting reports on the wealth of issuers and users of financial information and the decision-making behavior resulting from that impact. It is hard to imagine any accounting standard that does not have economic consequences. The text discussed the example of accounting for goodwill. Other standards that have substantive economic consequences effects are accounting for pensions, leases, deferred income taxes, derivatives and financial instruments, and stock options.

Remember to check the book's companion website to find additional resources for this chapter.

CHAPTER 2

CONCEPTUAL FRAMEWORK UNDERLYING FINANCIAL ACCOUNTING

Show Me the Earnings!

The growth of new-economy business on the Internet has led to the development of new measures of performance. When **Priceline.com** splashed onto the dot-com scene, it touted steady growth in a measure called "unique offers by users" to explain its heady stock price. To draw investors to its stock, **Drugstore.com** focused on the number of "unique customers" at its website. After all, new businesses call for new performance measures, right?

Not necessarily. In fact, these indicators failed to show any consistent relationship between profits and website visits. Eventually, as the graphs below show, the profits never materialized, and stock prices fell. The lesson here: Although the new economy may require some new measures, investors need to be careful not to forget the reliable traditional ones.

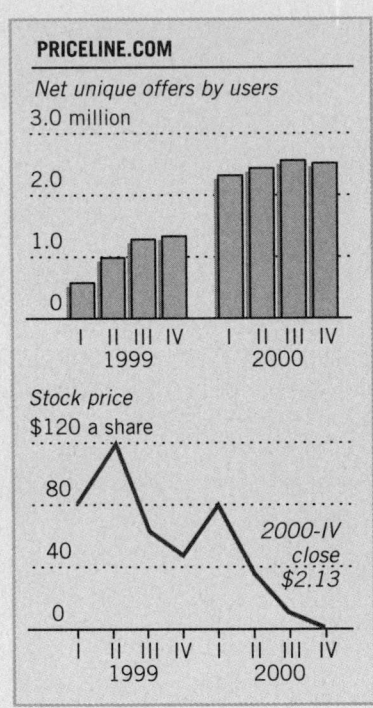

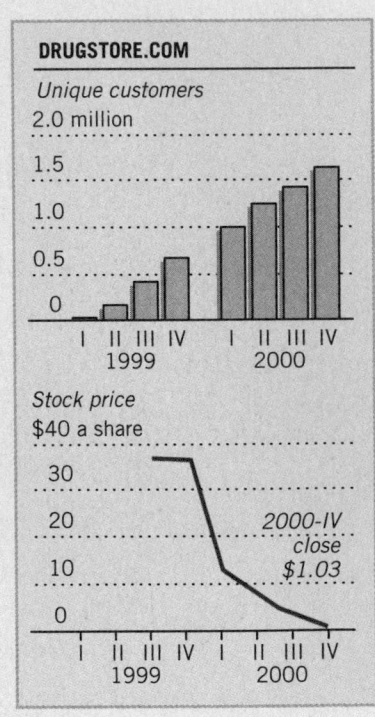

Source: Story and graphs adapted from Gretchen Morgenson, "How Did They Value Stocks? Count the Absurd Ways," *New York Times* (March 18, 2001), section 3, p. 1.

Preview of Chapter 2

As the opening story indicates, users of financial statements need relevant and reliable information. To help develop this type of financial information, financial accounting and reporting relies on a conceptual framework. *In this chapter, we discuss the basic concepts underlying the conceptual framework, as follows.*

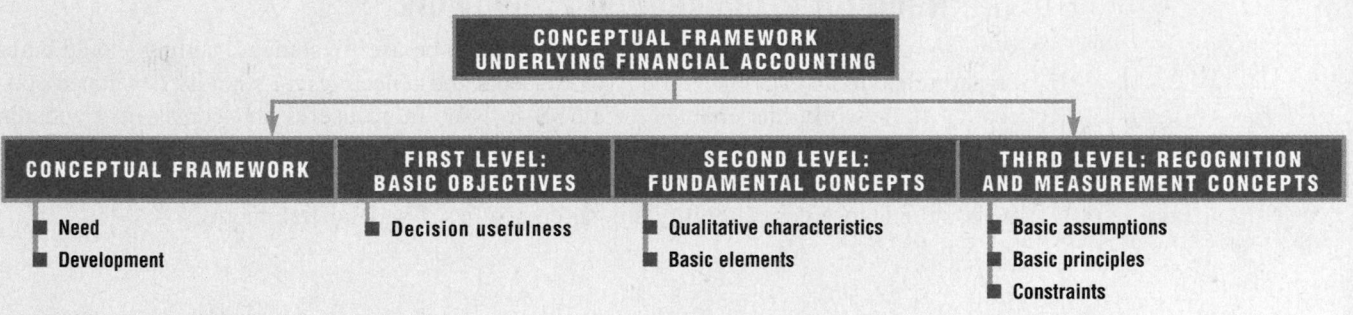

CONCEPTUAL FRAMEWORK UNDERLYING FINANCIAL ACCOUNTING

CONCEPTUAL FRAMEWORK	FIRST LEVEL: BASIC OBJECTIVES	SECOND LEVEL: FUNDAMENTAL CONCEPTS	THIRD LEVEL: RECOGNITION AND MEASUREMENT CONCEPTS
■ Need ■ Development	■ Decision usefulness	■ Qualitative characteristics ■ Basic elements	■ Basic assumptions ■ Basic principles ■ Constraints

Learning Objectives

After studying this chapter, you should be able to:

1. Describe the usefulness of a conceptual framework.
2. Describe the FASB's efforts to construct a conceptual framework.
3. Understand the objectives of financial reporting.
4. Identify the qualitative characteristics of accounting information.
5. Define the basic elements of financial statements.
6. Describe the basic assumptions of accounting.
7. Explain the application of the basic principles of accounting.
8. Describe the impact that constraints have on reporting accounting information.

Inside Chapter 2

- **What Do the Numbers Mean?**
  What's your principle? (p. 36)
  You may need a map (p. 42)
  Whose company is it? (p. 45)
  No take-backs (p. 49)
  Hollywood accounting (p. 50)
  Living in a material world (p. 55)
- **What's the Principle?** (pp. 37, 47)
- **Convergence Corner** (p. 57)
- **Accounting, Analysis, Principles** (p. 58)
  Prepare balance sheet.
  Analyze income measurement approaches.
  Consider expense recognition.

A **conceptual framework** is like a **constitution**: It is "a coherent system of interrelated objectives and fundamentals that can lead to consistent standards and that prescribes the nature, function, and limits of financial accounting and financial statements."[1] Many consider the FASB's real contribution to depend on the quality and utility of the conceptual framework.

The Need for a Conceptual Framework

OBJECTIVE 1

Describe the usefulness of a conceptual framework.

Why do we need a conceptual framework? First, to be useful, standard setting should build on and relate to an established body of concepts and objectives. A soundly developed conceptual framework thus enables the FASB to issue more useful and consistent standards over time. **A coherent set of standards and rules should result.** The framework should increase financial statement users' understanding of and confidence in financial reporting. It should enhance comparability among companies' financial statements.

What do the numbers mean?   What's Your Principle?

The need for a conceptual framework is highlighted by recent accounting scandals such as those at **Enron, Healthsouth**, and other companies. To restore public confidence in the financial reporting process, Congress passed the Sarbanes-Oxley Act of 2002 ("SOX"). One of the provisions of SOX is a requirement for the Securities and Exchange Commission (SEC) to evaluate the usefulness of "principles-based" accounting standards relative to the current set of accounting standards (which many argue are too "rules-based").

Some have suggested a move toward principles-based standards because they believe that companies exploited the detailed provisions in rules-based standards to manage accounting reports, rather than report the economic substance of transactions. For example, many of the off-balance-sheet arrangements of Enron avoided transparent reporting by barely achieving 3 percent outside equity ownership, a requirement in an obscure accounting standard interpretation. Enron's financial engineers were able to structure transactions to achieve a desired accounting treatment, even if that accounting treatment did not reflect the transaction's true nature.

In 2003 the SEC issued a report recommending that accounting standard setters move away from a rules-based approach toward a more principles-based approach ("Study Pursuant to Section 108(d) . . ."). If the profession adopts this approach, accounting standards will be more conceptual in nature, and the financial reporting objective of each standard will be more clearly stated. Top management's financial reporting responsibility will shift from demonstrating compliance with rules to demonstrating that a company has attained financial reporting objectives.

Source: "Study Pursuant to Section 108(d) of the Sarbanes-Oxley Act of 2002 on the Adoption by the United States Financial Reporting System of a Principles-Based Accounting System," *www.sec.gov/news/studies/ principlesbasedstand.htm.*

Beyond the Numbers

Some are concerned that principle-based rules will permit management too much discretion in applying accounting standards. What are the potential consequences for individual companies and markets as a whole of increased management judgment inherent in principle-based rules?

[1]"Conceptual Framework for Financial Accounting and Reporting: Elements of Financial Statements and Their Measurement," *FASB Discussion Memorandum* (Stamford, Conn.: FASB, 1976), page 1 of the "Scope and Implications of the Conceptual Framework Project" section. For an excellent discussion of the functions of the conceptual framework, see Reed K. Storey and Sylvia Storey, Special Report, "The Framework of Financial Accounting and Concepts" (Norwalk, Conn.: FASB, 1998), pp. 85–88.

Second, the profession should be able to more quickly solve new and emerging **practical problems by referring to an existing framework of basic theory**. For example, **Sunshine Mining** (a silver-mining company) sold two issues of bonds. It can redeem them either with $1,000 in cash or with 50 ounces of silver, whichever is worth more at maturity. Both bond issues have a stated interest rate of 8.5 percent. At what amounts should Sunshine or the buyers of the bonds record them? What is the amount of the premium or discount on the bonds? And how should Sunshine amortize this amount, if the bond redemption payments are to be made in silver (the future value of which is unknown at the date of issuance)? Sunshine cannot know, at the date of issuance, the value of future silver bond redemption payments.

It is difficult, if not impossible, for the FASB to prescribe the proper accounting treatment quickly for such situations. Practicing accountants, though, must resolve such problems on a daily basis. How? Through good judgment and with the help of a universally accepted conceptual framework, practitioners can quickly focus on an acceptable treatment.

Development of a Conceptual Framework

Over the years, numerous organizations developed and published their own conceptual frameworks, but no single framework was universally accepted and relied on in practice. In 1976 the FASB began to develop a conceptual framework that would be a basis for setting accounting standards and for resolving financial reporting controversies. The FASB has since issued six Statements of Financial Accounting Concepts that relate to financial reporting for business exterprises.[2] They are as follows.

OBJECTIVE 2
Describe the FASB's efforts to construct a conceptual framework.

1 **SFAC No. 1,** "Objectives of Financial Reporting by Business Enterprises," presents the goals and purposes of accounting.
2 **SFAC No. 2,** "Qualitative Characteristics of Accounting Information," examines the characteristics that make accounting information useful.
3 **SFAC No. 3,** "Elements of Financial Statements of Business Enterprises," provides definitions of financial statement items, e.g., assets, liabilities, revenues, and expenses.
4 **SFAC No. 5,** "Recognition and Measurement in Financial Statements of Business Enterprises," sets forth fundamental recognition and measurement criteria and guidance on what information to formally incorporate into financial statements and when.
5 **SFAC No. 6,** "Elements of Financial Statements," replaces *SFAC No. 3* and expands its scope to include not-for-profit organizations.
6 **SFAC No. 7,** "Using Cash Flow Information and Present Value in Accounting Measurements," provides a framework for using expected future cash flows and present values as a basis for measurement.

INTERNATIONAL INSIGHT

The IASB has also issued a conceptual framework. The FASB and the IASB have agreed on a joint project to develop a common conceptual framework—one that converges and improves upon the existing frameworks of the two boards.

Illustration 2-1 (page 38) provides an overview of the conceptual framework.[3] The first level lists the **objectives**—that is, the goals and purposes of accounting. Ideally, accounting standards developed according to a conceptual framework will result in more useful accounting reports. The second level provides the **qualitative characteristics** that make accounting information useful and the **elements** of financial statements (assets, liabilities, and so on). The third level identifies the **recognition and measurement concepts** used in establishing and applying accounting standards. These concepts include assumptions, principles, and constraints that describe the present reporting environment. We examine these three levels of the conceptual framework next.

WHAT'S THE PRINCIPLE?

The FASB uses the conceptual framework to guide it in developing accounting standards. Throughout the text, we use "What's the Principle?" boxes to highlight important concepts and principles as they relate to topics under discussion. As you study future chapters, do not hesitate to refer back to this chapter to review the important concepts and principles that are the foundation underlying financial accounting and reporting.

[2]The FASB also issued a Statement of Financial Accounting Concepts that relates to nonbusiness organizations: "Objectives of Financial Reporting by Nonbusiness Organizations," *Statement of Financial Accounting Concepts No. 4* (December 1980).
[3]Adapted from William C. Norby, *The Financial Analysts Journal* (March–April 1982), p. 22.

Illustration 2-1
Conceptual Framework
for Financial Reporting

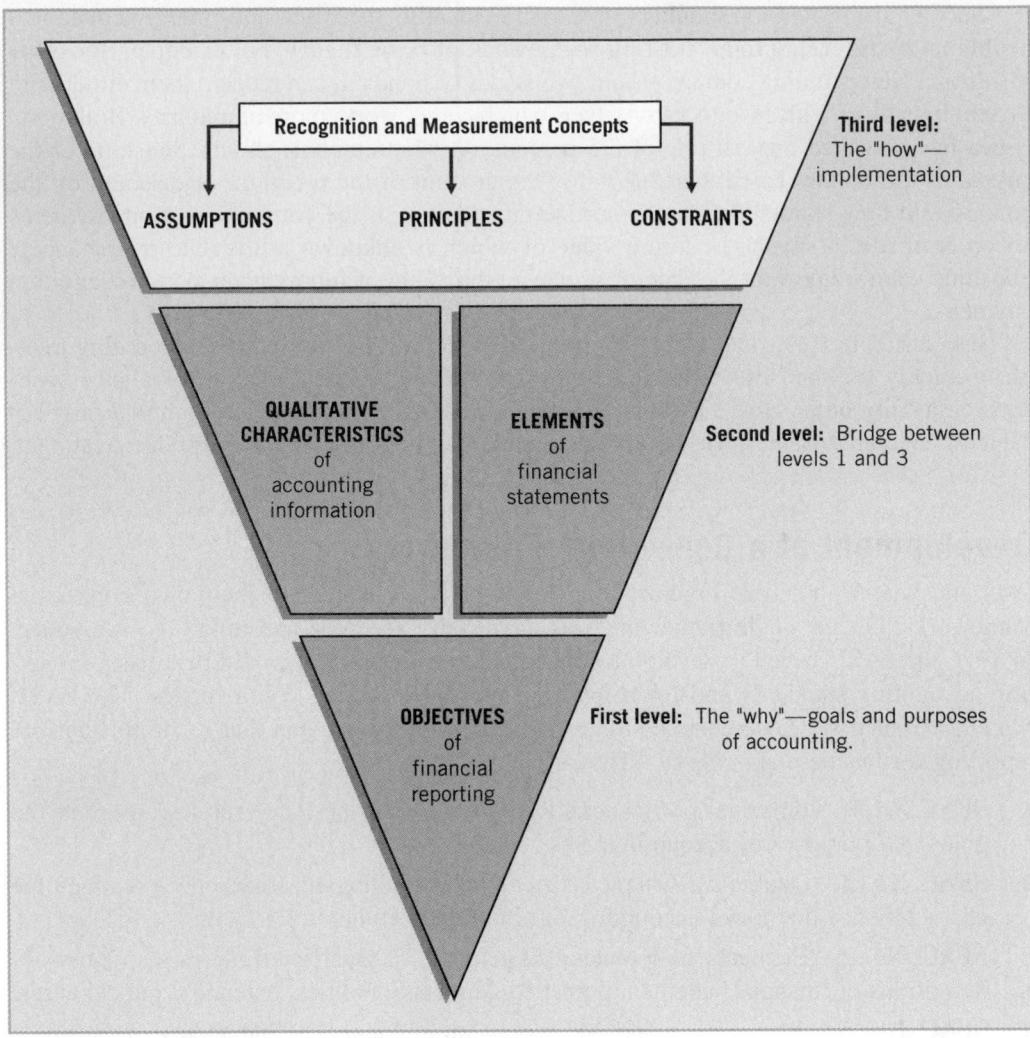

FIRST LEVEL: BASIC OBJECTIVES

OBJECTIVE 3

Understand the objectives of financial reporting.

As we discussed in Chapter 1, the **objectives of financial reporting** are to provide information that is: (1) useful to those making investment and credit decisions, who have a reasonable understanding of business and economic activities; (2) helpful to present and potential investors, creditors, and other users in assessing the amounts, timing, and uncertainty of future cash flows; and (3) about economic resources, the claims to those resources, and the changes in them.

The objectives, therefore, broadly concern information that is useful to investor and creditor decisions. That concern narrows to the investors' and creditors' interest in receiving cash from their investments in, or loans to, business enterprises. Finally, the objectives focus on the financial statements, which provide information useful in assessing future cash flows. This approach is referred to as **decision usefulness**.

To provide information to decision makers, companies prepare general-purpose financial statements. These statements provide the most useful information possible at the least cost. However, users do need reasonable knowledge of business and financial accounting matters to understand the information contained in financial statements. This point is important. It means that financial statement preparers assume a level of competence on the part of users. This assumption impacts the way and the extent to which companies report information.

SECOND LEVEL: FUNDAMENTAL CONCEPTS

The objectives (first level) focus on the goals and purposes of accounting. Later, we will discuss the ways these goals and purposes are implemented (third level). What, then, is the purpose of the second level? The second level provides conceptual building blocks that explain the qualitative characteristics of accounting information and define the elements of financial statements. That is, the second level forms a bridge between the **why** of accounting (the objectives) and the **how** of accounting (recognition and measurement).

Qualitative Characteristics of Accounting Information

Should companies like **Walt Disney** or **Kellogg's** provide information in their financial statements on how much it costs them to acquire their assets (historical cost basis) or how much the assets are currently worth (fair-value basis)? Should **PepsiCo** combine and show as one company the four main segments of its business, or should it report PepsiCo Beverages, Frito Lay, Quaker Foods, and PepsiCo International as four separate segments?

How does a company choose an acceptable accounting method, the amount and types of information to disclose, and the format in which to present it? The answer: By determining **which alternative provides the most useful information for decision-making purposes (decision usefulness)**. The FASB identified the **qualitative characteristics** of accounting information that distinguish better (more useful) information from inferior (less useful) information for decision-making purposes.[4] In addition, the FASB identified certain constraints (cost-benefit and materiality) as part of the conceptual framework (discussed later in the chapter). As Illustration 2-2 shows, the characteristics may be viewed as a hierarchy.

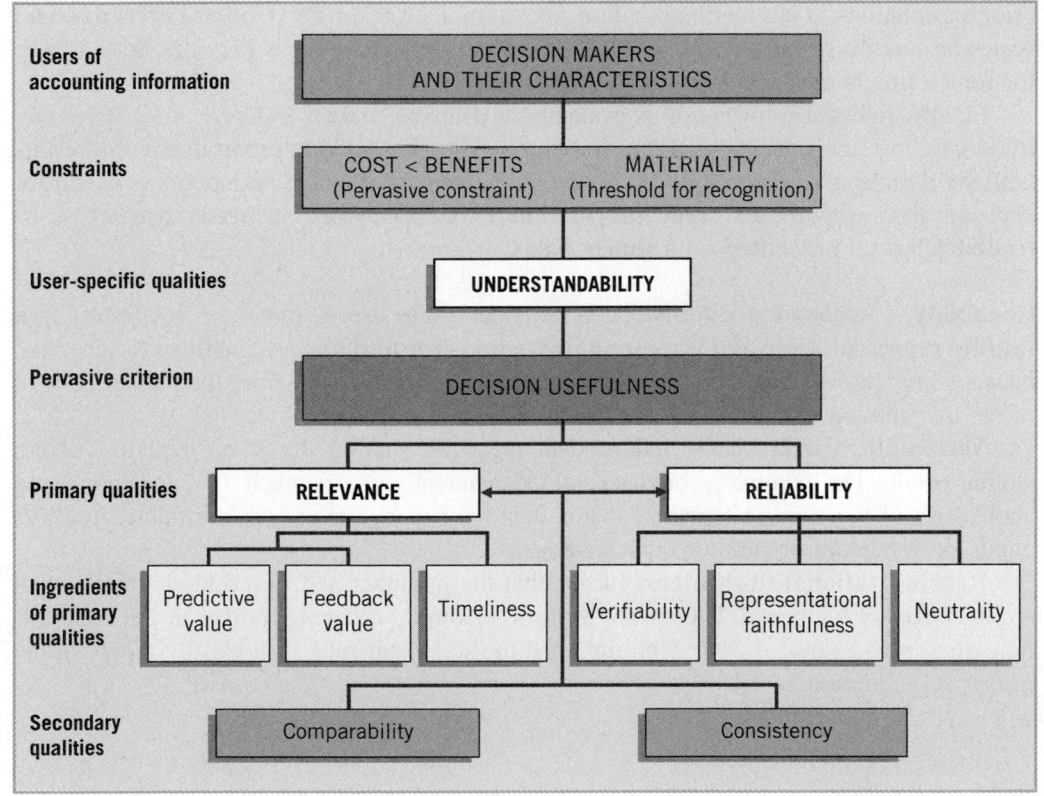

Illustration 2-2
Hierarchy of Accounting Qualities

[4]"Qualitative Characteristics of Accounting Information," *Statement of Financial Accounting Concepts No. 2* (Stamford, Conn.: FASB, May 1980).

Decision Makers (Users) and Understandability

Decision makers vary widely in the types of decisions they make, how they make decisions, the information they already possess or can obtain from other sources, and their ability to process the information. For information to be useful, there must be a connection (linkage) between these users and the decisions they make. This link, **understandability**, is the quality of information that lets reasonably informed users see its significance.

For example, assume that **IBM Corp.** issues a three-months' report that shows interim earnings way down. This interim report provides relevant and reliable information for decision-making purposes. Now say that some users, upon reading the report, decide to sell their stock. Other users, however, do not understand the report's content and significance. They are surprised when IBM declares a smaller year-end dividend and the value of the stock declines. Thus, although IBM presented highly relevant and reliable information, it was useless to those who did not understand it.

Primary Qualities: Relevance and Reliability

Relevance and reliability are the two primary qualities that make accounting information useful for decision making. As stated in FASB *Concepts Statement No. 2,* "the qualities that distinguish 'better' (more useful) information from 'inferior' (less useful) information are primarily the qualities of relevance and reliability, with some other characteristics that those qualities imply."[5]

Relevance. To be relevant, accounting information must be capable of making a difference in a decision.[6] Information with no bearing on a decision is irrelevant. Relevant information helps users predict the ultimate outcome of past, present, and future events. That is, it has **predictive value**. Relevant information also helps users confirm or correct prior expectations; it has **feedback value**. For example, when **UPS (United Parcel Service)** issues an interim report, the information in it is relevant because it provides both a basis for forecasting annual earnings and feedback on past performance.

Finally, relevant information is available to decision makers before it loses its capacity to influence their decisions. It has **timeliness**. If UPS waited to report its interim results until six months after the end of the period, the information would be much less useful for decision-making purposes. **For information to be relevant, it needs predictive or feedback value, presented on a timely basis.**

Reliability. Accounting information is reliable to the extent that **it is verifiable, is a faithful representation, and is reasonably free of error and bias.** Reliability is a necessity, because most users have neither the time nor the expertise to evaluate the factual content of the information.

Verifiability occurs when independent measurers, using the same methods, obtain similar results. For example, would several independent auditors reach the same conclusion about a set of financial statements? If not, then the statements are not verifiable. Auditors could not render an opinion on such statements.

Representational faithfulness means that the numbers and descriptions match what really existed or happened. If **General Motors'** income statement reports sales of $225 billion when it had sales of $193.5 billion, then the statement fails to faithfully represent the proper sales amount.

[5]Ibid., par. 15.
[6]Ibid., par. 47.

Neutrality means that a company cannot select information to favor one set of interested parties over another. Unbiased information must be the overriding consideration. For example, in the notes to financial statements, tobacco companies such as **R. J. Reynolds** should not suppress information about the numerous lawsuits that have been filed because of tobacco-related health concerns—even though such disclosure is damaging to the company.

Neutrality in standard setting has come under increasing attack. Some argue that the FASB should not issue standards that cause undesirable economic effects on an industry or company. We disagree. Standards must be free from bias, or we will no longer have credible financial statements. Without credible financial statements, individuals will no longer use this information. An analogy demonstrates the point: In the United States, many individuals bet on boxing matches because such contests are assumed not to be fixed. But nobody bets on wrestling matches. Why? Because the public assumes that wrestling matches are rigged. If financial information is biased (rigged), the public will lose confidence and no longer use it.

Secondary Qualities: Comparability and Consistency

Information about a company is more useful if decision makers can compare it with similar information about another company and with similar information about the same company at other points in time. The first of these qualities is **comparability**, and the second is **consistency**.

Comparability. Information that is measured and reported in a similar manner for different companies is considered comparable. Comparability enables users to identify the real similarities and differences in economic events between companies.

For example, the accounting for pensions in the United States differs from that in Japan. In the United States, companies record pension cost as incurred. In Japan, companies record little or no charge to income for these costs. As a result, it is difficult to compare and evaluate the financial results of **General Motors** or **Ford** to Japanese competitors. Also, resource allocation decisions involve evaluating alternatives. A valid evaluation can be made only if comparable information is available.

Consistency. When a company applies the same accounting treatment to similar events, from period to period, the company shows consistent use of accounting standards. The idea of consistency does not mean, however, that companies cannot switch from one accounting method to another. A company *can* change methods, but it must first demonstrate that the newly adopted method is preferable to the old. If approved, the company must then disclose the nature and effect of the accounting change, as well as the justification for it, in the financial statements for the period in which it made the change.[7] When a change in accounting principles occurs, the auditor refers to it in an explanatory paragraph of the audit report. This paragraph identifies the nature of the change and refers the reader to the note in the financial statements that discusses the change in detail.[8]

---

[7]Surveys indicate that users highly value consistency. They note that a change tends to destroy the comparability of data before and after the change. Some companies assist users to understand the pre- and post-change data. Generally, however, users say they lose the ability to analyze over time. It is hoped that the new standard on accounting changes will improve the comparability of the data before and after the change.

[8]"Reports on Audited Financial Statements," *Statement on Auditing Standards No. 58* (New York: AICPA, April 1988), par. 34.

Beyond touting nonfinancial measures to investors (see opening story), many companies increasingly promote the performance of their companies through the reporting of various "pro-forma" earnings measures. A recent survey of newswire reports found 36 instances of the reporting of pro-forma measures in just a three-day period.

Pro-forma measures are standard measures (such as earnings) that companies adjust, usually for one-time or nonrecurring items. For example, companies usually adjust earnings for the effects of an extraordinary item. Such adjustments make the numbers more comparable to numbers reported in periods without the unusual item.

However, rather than increasing comparability, it appears that some companies use pro-forma reporting to accentuate the positive in their results. Examples include **Yahoo! Inc.** and **Cisco**, which define pro-forma income after adding back payroll tax expense. **Level 8 Systems** transformed an operating loss into a pro-forma profit by adding back expenses for depreciation and amortization of intangible assets.

Lynn Turner, former Chief Accountant at the SEC, calls such earnings measures EBS— "Everything but Bad Stuff." To provide investors a more complete picture of company profitability, not the story preferred by management, the SEC issued Regulation G (REG G). REG G requires companies to reconcile non-GAAP financial measures to GAAP, thereby giving investors a roadmap to analyze adjustments companies make to their GAAP numbers to arrive at pro-forma results.

Sources: Adapted from Gretchen Morgenson, "How Did They Value Stocks? Count the Absurd Ways," *New York Times* (March 18, 2001), section 3, p. 1; and Gretchen Morgenson, "Expert Advice: Focus on Profit," *New York Times* (March 18, 2001), section 3, p. 14. See also SEC Regulation G, "Conditions for Use of Non-GAAP Financial Measures, "Release No. 33–8176 (March 28, 2003).

Beyond the Numbers

Can you think of possible motivations that companies might have to use pro-forma reporting to present their companies in a more favorable light?

Basic Elements

OBJECTIVE 5

Define the basic elements of financial statements.

An important aspect of developing any theoretical structure is the body of **basic elements** or definitions to be included in it. Accounting uses many terms with distinctive and specific meanings. These terms constitute the language of business or the jargon of accounting.

One such term is **asset**. Is it merely something we own? Or is an asset something we have the right to use, as in the case of leased equipment? Or is it anything of value used by a company to generate revenues—in which case, should we also consider the managers of a company as an asset?

As this example illustrates, it seems necessary, therefore, to develop basic definitions for the elements of financial statements. *Concepts Statement No. 6* defines the ten interrelated elements that most directly relate to measuring the performance and financial status of a business enterprise. We list them here for review and information purposes; you need not memorize these definitions at this point. We will explain and examine each of these elements in more detail in subsequent chapters.

ELEMENTS OF FINANCIAL STATEMENTS

ASSETS. Probable future economic benefits obtained or controlled by a particular entity as a result of past transactions or events.

LIABILITIES. Probable future sacrifices of economic benefits arising from present obligations of a particular entity to transfer assets or provide services to other entities in the future as a result of past transactions or events.

EQUITY. Residual interest in the assets of an entity that remains after deducting its liabilities. In a business enterprise, the equity is the ownership interest.

INVESTMENTS BY OWNERS. Increases in net assets of a particular enterprise resulting from transfers to it from other entities of something of value to obtain or increase ownership interests (or equity) in it. Assets are most commonly received as investments by owners, but that which is received may also include services or satisfaction or conversion of liabilities of the enterprise.

DISTRIBUTIONS TO OWNERS. Decreases in net assets of a particular enterprise resulting from transferring assets, rendering services, or incurring liabilities by the enterprise to owners. Distributions to owners decrease ownership interests (or equity) in an enterprise.

COMPREHENSIVE INCOME. Change in equity (net assets) of an entity during a period from transactions and other events and circumstances from nonowner sources. It includes all changes in equity during a period except those resulting from investments by owners and distributions to owners.

REVENUES. Inflows or other enhancements of assets of an entity or settlement of its liabilities (or a combination of both) during a period from delivering or producing goods, rendering services, or other activities that constitute the entity's ongoing major or central operations.

EXPENSES. Outflows or other using up of assets or incurrences of liabilities (or a combination of both) during a period from delivering or producing goods, rendering services, or carrying out other activities that constitute the entity's ongoing major or central operations.

GAINS. Increases in equity (net assets) from peripheral or incidental transactions of an entity and from all other transactions and other events and circumstances affecting the entity during a period except those that result from revenues or investments by owners.

LOSSES. Decreases in equity (net assets) from peripheral or incidental transactions of an entity and from all other transactions and other events and circumstances affecting the entity during a period except those that result from expenses or distributions to owners.[9]

The FASB classifies the elements into two distinct groups. The first group of three elements—assets, liabilities, and equity—describes amounts of resources and claims to resources at a **moment in time**. The other seven elements describe transactions, events, and circumstances that affect a company during a **period of time**. The first class, affected by elements of the second class, provides at any time the cumulative result of all changes. This interaction is referred to as "articulation." That is, key figures in one financial statement correspond to balances in another.

[9]"Elements of Financial Statements," *Statement of Financial Accounting Concepts No. 6* (Stamford, Conn.: FASB, December 1985), pp. ix and x.

Try it out!   A local broker has called you with a tip about an investment in bonds of a company that he feels is about to take off. The company, AROD, Inc. distributes sports memorabilia on the Internet. The bonds being issued by AROD mature in 10 years and promise a 10% yield. You tell the broker that before investing in this hot opportunity, you would like to see AROD's financial statements.

The broker sends you the statements, which are a year old and unaudited. AROD's owner, Roderick Andrews, prepared the statements. You review the statements, and they are quite impressive: AROD reported a profit of $3,500,000 and showed a low debt-equity ratio of .15 and a current ratio of 2.3. The statements provide no comparative amounts for prior years, and there are no note disclosures provided about AROD's accounting methods related to inventory, depreciation, liabilities, and so on.

Instructions

Answer the following questions.

a How can financial statements provide decision-useful information in this context?

b With a focus on relevance and reliability, why would it be unwise to base an investment decision on the financial statements provided by the broker?

Solution

a Before you invest in the bonds, you must decide whether to give your money to AROD in exchange for its promise to repay the bond principal and make interest payments on the bonds to provide the 10% yield on the investment. Financial statements containing information on earnings, cash flows, and financial position provide information that you (and other investors) can use to assess the likelihood that AROD will be able to repay the bond investors in the future. For example, the current ratio of 2.3 indicates that AROD has short term assets far in excess of its current obligations, which is a positive indicator that AROD will be able to make interest payments in the next year.

b The AROD statements are neither (1) relevant nor (2) reliable:

(1) With respect to relevance, this information must be *timely*. Because AROD's financial statements are a year old, they have lost their ability to influence an investor's decision; a lot could have changed in that one year. Another element of relevance is *predictive value*. AROD's accounting information is not relevant because it provides no reference to other years' profitability. Because developing trends are not reported, the information cannot help an investor predict future profitability. Closely related to predictive value is *feedback value*. These financial statements do not provide feedback on any strategies that the company may have used to increase profits.

(2) With respect to reliability, information must be *verifiable* by several independent parties. Because no independent auditor has verified these amounts, there is no way of knowing whether they are represented faithfully. For instance, an investor might like to believe that AROD earned $3,500,000 and that it had very favorable debt-to-equity and current ratios. However, unaudited financial statements do not give reasonable assurance about these claims. The fact that Mr. Andrews himself prepared these statements indicates a lack of *neutrality*. Because Andrews is not a disinterested third party, an investor cannot be sure that he did not prepare the financial statements to portray his business in the most favorable light.

THIRD LEVEL: RECOGNITION AND MEASUREMENT CONCEPTS

The third level of the framework consists of concepts that implement the basic objectives of level one. These concepts explain how companies should recognize, measure, and report financial elements and events. The FASB sets forth most of these in its *Statement of Financial Accounting Concepts No. 5,* "Recognition and Measurement in Financial Statements of Business Enterprises." According to *SFAC No. 5,* to be recognized, an item (event or transaction) must meet the definition of an "element of financial statements" as defined in *SFAC No. 6* and must be measurable. Most aspects of current practice follow these recognition and measurement concepts.

The accounting profession continues to use the concepts in *SFAC No. 5* as operational guidelines. Here, we identify the concepts as basic assumptions, principles, and constraints. Not everyone uses this classification system, so focus your attention more on **understanding the concepts** than on how we classify and organize them. These concepts serve as guidelines in responding to controversial financial reporting issues.

Basic Assumptions

Four basic **assumptions** underlie the financial accounting structure: (1) economic entity, (2) going-concern, (3) monetary unit, and (4) periodicity. We'll look at each in turn.

> **OBJECTIVE 6**
> Describe the basic assumptions of accounting.

Economic Entity Assumption

The **economic entity assumption means that economic activity can be identified with a particular unit of accountability**. In other words, a company keeps its activity separate and distinct from its owners and any other business unit. At the most basic level, the economic entity assumption dictates that **Panera Bread Company** record the company's financial activities separate from those of its owners and managers. Equally important, financial statement users need to be able to distinguish the activities and elements of different companies, such as **General Motors**, **Ford**, and **DaimlerChrysler**. If users could not distinguish the activities of different companies, how would they know which company financially outperformed the other?

The entity concept does not apply solely to the segregation of activities among competing companies, such as **Best Buy** and **Circuit City**. An individual, department, division, or an entire industry could be considered a separate entity if we choose to define it in this manner. Thus, **the entity concept does not necessarily refer to a legal entity**. A parent and its subsidiaries are separate **legal** entities, but merging their activities for accounting and reporting purposes does not violate the **economic entity** assumption.[10]

What do the numbers mean?   Whose Company Is It?

The importance of the entity assumption is illustrated by scandals involving **W. R. Grace** and **Adelphia**. In both cases, senior company employees entered into transactions that blurred the line between the employee's financial interests and those of the company. At Adelphia, among many other self-dealings, the company guaranteed over $2 billion of loans to the founding family. W. R. Grace used company funds to pay for an apartment and chef for the company chairman. As a result of these transactions, these insiders benefitted at the expense of shareholders. Additionally, the financial statements failed to disclose the transactions. Such disclosure would have allowed shareholders to sort out the impact of the employee transactions on company results.

Beyond the Numbers

(1) What element of reliability is negatively affected when companies violate the entity assumption, as in the cases of Adelphia and W.R. Grace? (2) How are shareholders affected when managers engage in illegal self-dealing that results in violation of the entity assumption?

---

[10]The concept of the entity is changing. For example, defining the "outer edges" of companies is now harder. Public companies often consist of multiple public subsidiaries, each with joint ventures, licensing arrangements, and other affiliations. Increasingly, companies form and dissolve joint ventures or customer-supplier relationships in a matter of months or weeks. These "virtual companies" raise accounting issues about how to account for the entity. See Steven H. Wallman, "The Future of Accounting and Disclosure in an Evolving World: The Need for Dramatic Change," *Accounting Horizons* (September 1995).

Going-Concern Assumption

Most accounting practices rely on the **going-concern assumption—the assumption that the company will have a long life**. Despite numerous business failures, most companies have a fairly high continuance rate. As a rule, we expect companies to last long enough to fulfill their objectives and commitments.

This assumption has significant implications. The historical cost principle would be of limited usefulness if we assume eventual liquidation. Under a liquidation approach, for example, a company would better state asset values at net realizable value (sales price less costs of disposal) than at acquisition cost. **Depreciation and amortization policies are justifiable and appropriate only if we assume some permanence to the company.** If a company adopts the liquidation approach, the current/noncurrent classification of assets and liabilities loses much of its significance. Labeling anything a fixed or long-term asset would be difficult to justify. Indeed, listing liabilities on the basis of priority in liquidation would be more reasonable.

The going-concern assumption applies in most business situations. **Only where liquidation appears imminent is the assumption inapplicable.** In these cases a total revaluation of assets and liabilities can provide information that closely approximates the company's net realizable value. You will learn more about accounting problems related to a company in liquidation in advanced accounting courses.

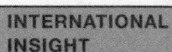

INTERNATIONAL INSIGHT

Due to their experiences with persistent inflation, several South American countries produce "constant-currency" financial reports. Typically, companies in these countries use a general price-level index to adjust for the effects of inflation.

Monetary Unit Assumption

The **monetary unit assumption** means that money is the common denominator of economic activity and provides an appropriate basis for accounting measurement and analysis. That is, the monetary unit is the most effective means of expressing to interested parties changes in capital and exchanges of goods and services. **The monetary unit is relevant, simple, universally available, understandable, and useful.** Application of this assumption depends on the even more basic assumption that quantitative data are useful in communicating economic information and in making rational economic decisions.

In the United States, accounting ignores price-level changes (inflation and deflation) and assumes that the unit of measure—the dollar—remains reasonably stable. We therefore use the monetary unit assumption to justify adding 1980 dollars to 2007 dollars without any adjustment. The FASB in *SFAC No. 5* indicated that it expects the dollar, unadjusted for inflation or deflation, to continue to be used to measure items recognized in financial statements. Only if circumstances change dramatically (such as if the United States experiences high inflation similar to that in many South American countries) will the FASB again consider "inflation accounting."

Accounting for Changing Prices

Periodicity Assumption

To measure the results of a company's activity accurately, we would need to wait until it liquidates. Decision makers, however, cannot wait that long for such information. Users need to know a company's performance and economic status on a timely basis so that they can evaluate and compare firms, and take appropriate actions. Therefore, companies must report information periodically.

The **periodicity** (or **time period**) **assumption** implies that a company can divide its economic activities into artificial time periods. These time periods vary, but the most common are monthly, quarterly, and yearly.

The shorter the time period, the more difficult it is to determine the proper net income for the period. A month's results usually prove less reliable than a quarter's results, and a quarter's results are likely to be less reliable than a year's results. Investors desire and demand that a company quickly process and disseminate information. Yet the quicker a company releases the information, the more likely the information will include errors. **This phenomenon provides an interesting example of the trade-off between relevance and reliability in preparing financial data.**

The problem of defining the time period becomes more serious as product cycles shorten and products become obsolete more quickly. Many believe that, given technology advances, companies need to provide more online, real-time financial information to ensure the availability of relevant information.

Basic Principles of Accounting

We generally use four basic **principles of accounting** to record transactions: (1) historical-cost, (2) revenue recognition, (3) matching, and (4) full disclosure. Again, we look at each in turn.

OBJECTIVE 7

Explain the application of the basic principles of accounting

Historical-Cost Principle

GAAP requires that companies account for and report most assets and liabilities on the basis of acquisition price. This is often referred to as the **historical-cost principle**. Cost has an important advantage over other valuations: **it is reliable**. To illustrate this advantage, consider the problems if companies select current selling price instead. Companies might have difficulty establishing a value for unsold items. Every member of the accounting department might value the assets differently. Further, how often would it be necessary to establish sales value? All companies close their accounts at least annually. Some compute their net income every month. These companies would have to place a sales value on every asset each time they wished to determine income. Critics raise similar objections against current cost (replacement cost, present value of future cash flows) and any other basis of valuation **except historical cost**.

WHAT'S THE PRINCIPLE?

Within the FASB's conceptual framework, a "principle," such as the historical cost principle, is a sub-element of recognition and measurement concepts.

What about liabilities? Do companies account for them on a cost basis? Yes, they do. Companies issue liabilities, such as bonds, notes, and accounts payable, in exchange for assets, or perhaps services, for an agreed-upon price. **This price, established by the exchange transaction, is the "cost" of the liability.** A company uses this amount to record the liability in the accounts and report it in financial statements.

In general, users prefer historical cost because it provides them with a reliable benchmark for measuring historical trends. However, **fair value information** may be more useful for certain types of assets and liabilities and in certain industries. For example, companies report many financial instruments, including derivatives, at fair value, and inventories at lower of cost or market. Certain industries, such as brokerage houses and mutual funds, prepare their basic financial statements on a fair value basis.

At initial acquisition, historical cost equals fair value. In subsequent periods, as market and economic conditions change, historical cost and fair value often diverge. As a result, fair value measures or estimates often provide more relevant information about the expected future cash flows related to the asset or liability. For example, when long-lived assets decline in value, a fair value measure determines any impairment loss.

The FASB now appears to support greater use of fair value measurements in the financial statements. The Board believes that fair value information is more relevant to users than historical cost. Fair value measurement, it is argued, provides better insight into the value of a company's asset and liabilities (its financial position) and provides a better basis for assessing future cash flow prospects.

The FASB has developed a standard on "Fair Value Measurements," which provides guidance on how to measure fair value. This standard applies to both financial and non-financial assets that are measured at fair value. As a result, we should now have increased consistency and comparability when fair value measurements are used in the financial statements and related notes. Such consistency and comparability is very much needed in light of controversies using fair values at companies like **Enron** (valuation of energy contracts) and **J. P. Morgan** (valuation of its bond portfolio). In addition, this new standard clarifies and incorporates the guidance in *Concepts Statement 7,* "Using Cash Flow

Information and Present Value in Accounting Measurements," for using present value techniques to estimate future cash flows, and it provides enhanced disclosure of fair value information.[11]

As we indicated above, we presently have a "mixed-attribute" system that permits the use of historical cost, fair value, and other valuation bases. Although the historical cost principle continues to be the primary basis for valuation, recording and reporting of fair value information is increasing.

Revenue Recognition Principle

A crucial question for many companies is when to recognize revenue. Revenue recognition generally occurs (1) when **realized** or **realizable** and (2) when **earned**. This approach has often been referred to as the **revenue recognition principle**.

A company **realizes** revenues when it exchanges products (goods or services), merchandise, or other assets for cash or claims to cash. Revenues are realizable when assets received or held are readily convertible into cash or claims to cash. Assets are readily convertible when they are salable or interchangeable in an active market at readily determinable prices without significant additional cost.

In addition to the first test (realized or realizable), a company delays recognition of revenues until earned. Revenues are considered **earned** when the company substantially accomplishes what it must do to be entitled to the benefits represented by the revenues.[12] Generally, an objective test, such as a sale, indicates the point at which a company recognizes revenue. The sale provides an objective and verifiable measure of revenue—the sales price. Any basis for revenue recognition short of actual sale opens the door to wide variations in practice. **Recognition at the time of sale provides a uniform and reasonable test.**

However, as Illustration 2-3 shows, exceptions to the rule exist. We discuss these exceptions in the following sections.

Illustration 2-3
Timing of Revenue
Recognition

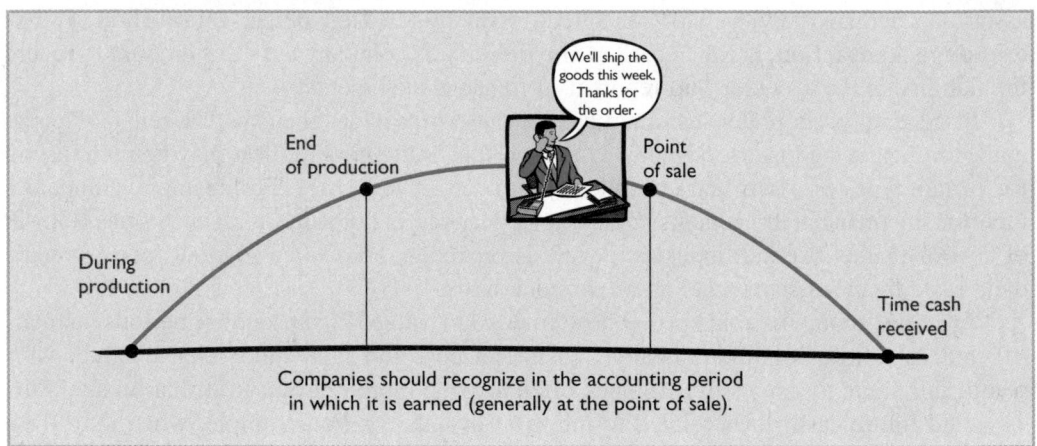

During Production.   A company can recognize revenue **before** it completes the job in certain long-term construction contracts. In this method, a company recognizes revenue periodically, based on the percentage of the job it has completed. Although technically a transfer of ownership has not occurred, the earning process is considered substantially completed at various stages of construction. If it is not possible to obtain dependable estimates of cost and progress, then a company delays revenue recognition until it completes the job.

---

[11]"Fair Value Measurement," *Statement of Financial Accounting Standards No. 157* (Norwalk, Conn.: FASB, September 2006).

[12]"Recognition and Measurement in Financial Statements of Business Enterprises," *Statement of Financial Accounting Concepts No. 5* (Stamford, Conn.: FASB, December 1984), par. 83(a) and (b).

At End of Production.   At times, a company may recognize revenue **after completion of the production cycle but before the sale takes place**. This occurs if products or other assets are salable in an active market at readily determinable prices without significant additional cost. An example is the mining of certain minerals. Once a company mines the mineral, a ready market at a quoted price exists. The same holds true for some agricultural products.

Upon Receipt of Cash.   **Receipt of cash is another basis for revenue recognition**. Companies use the cash-basis approach only when collection is uncertain at the time of sale.

One form of the cash basis is the **installment-sales method**. Here, a company requires payment in periodic installments over a long period of time. Its most common use is in retail, such as for farm and home equipment and furnishings. Companies frequently justify the installment-sales method based on the high risk of not collecting an account receivable. In some instances, this reasoning may be valid. Generally, though, if a sale has been completed, the company should recognize the sale; if bad debts are expected, the company should record them as separate estimates.

To summarize, a company records revenue in the period when realized or realizable and when earned. Normally, this is the date of sale. But circumstances may dictate application of the percentage-of-completion approach, the end-of-production approach, or the receipt-of-cash approach.

What do the numbers mean?   **No Take-Backs**

Investors in **Lucent Technologies** got an unpleasant surprise when the SEC forced the company to restate its financial results. What happened? Lucent violated one of the fundamental criteria for revenue recognition—the "no take-back" rule. This rule holds that a company should not book revenue on inventory that it shipped if the customer can return it at some point in the future. In this particular case, Lucent agreed to take back shipped inventory from its distributors if they could not sell the items to their customers.

Lucent recorded the sales on the shipped goods, which helped it report continued sales growth. However, Lucent's distributors did indeed return many of those shipped goods. The restatement erased $679 million in revenues, turning an operating profit into a loss. In response, Lucent's stock price declined $1.31 per share or 8.5 percent. Lucent has since changed its policy. It now records inventory as sold only when the final customer buys the equipment, not when Lucent ships the inventory to the distributor.

The lesson for investors: Review a company's revenue recognition policy for indications that revenues may be overstated due to generous return provisions for inventory. And remember, no take-backs!

Source: Adapted from S. Young, "Lucent Slashes First Quarter Outlook, Erases Revenue from Latest Quarter,"*Wall Street Journal Online Edition* (December 22, 2000).

Beyond the Numbers

(1) Lucent could have avoided its accounting problems simply by not allowing customers to return goods once they are sold. Would this be a good idea? Explain. (2) Lucent could facilitate sales by granting generous credit terms to its customers. If these customers do not pay, how does the accounting for these credit sales ensure that income is not overstated?

Matching Principle

In recognizing expenses, the approach is "Let the expense follow the revenues." Companies recognize expenses not when they pay wages or make a product, but when the work (service) or the product actually contributes to revenue. Thus, companies tie expense recognition to revenue recognition. This practice is referred to as the **matching principle**, because it dictates that **efforts (expenses) be matched with accomplishment (revenues) whenever it is reasonable and practicable to do so**.

Some costs, however, are difficult to associate with revenue. As a result, some other approach must be developed. Often, companies use a "rational and systematic" allocation policy that will approximate the matching principle. This type of expense recognition involves assumptions about the benefits that a company receives as well as the cost associated with those benefits. For example, a company like **Intel** or **Motorola** allocates the cost of a long-lived asset over all of the accounting periods during which it uses the asset because the asset contributes to the generation of revenue throughout its useful life.

Companies charge some costs to the current period as expenses (or losses) simply because they cannot determine a connection with revenue. Examples of these types of costs are officers' salaries and other administrative expenses.

What do the numbers mean? Hollywood Accounting

Hollywood accounting illustrates that the problem of expense recognition is as complex as that of revenue recognition. Following then-existing GAAP standards, major motion picture studios capitalized advertising and marketing costs, and then amortized these costs against revenues over the life of the film. As a result, many investors suggested that the studios overstated their profit numbers. Under a new GAAP standard, the studios must now amortize these costs over no more than three months. In many cases, the studios have to expense them immediately.

Similarly, the studios often allocated the costs related to abandoned projects to overhead, thus spreading them out over the lives of the successful projects. Not anymore. The studios must now expense these costs as incurred.

Here is a rough estimate of the amounts of capitalized advertising costs some major studios charged off in response to the change in GAAP.

Studio (Parent Company)	Capitalized Advertising (in millions)
Columbia Tri-Star (Sony)	$200
Paramount (Viacom)	200
20th Century Fox (News Corp)	150

The more conservative approach results from a stricter application of the definitions of assets and expenses. While many argue that advertising and marketing costs have future service potential, difficulty in reliably measuring these benefits suggests they are not assets. Therefore, a very short amortization period or immediate write-off is justified. Under these new guidelines, investors will have more reliable measures for assessing the performance of companies in this industry.

Beyond the Numbers

Some sports franchises attempt to portray franchise results more conservatively by recording as many expenses as possible. Such conservative accounting can give these businesses an advantage in negotiations with players or in securing concessions from local communities for stadiums and other services. Is conservative reporting by sports franchises a good thing or a bad thing with respect to accounting concepts? Explain.

Costs are generally classified into two groups: **product costs** and **period costs**. **Product costs**, such as material, labor, and overhead, attach to the product. Companies carry these costs into future periods if they recognize the revenue from the product in subsequent periods. **Period costs**, such as officers' salaries and other administrative expenses, attach to the period. Companies charge off such costs in the immediate period, even though benefits associated with these costs may occur in the future. Why? Because companies cannot determine a direct relationship between period costs and revenue. Illustration 2-4 summarizes these expense recognition procedures.

Type of Cost	Relationship	Recognition
Product costs: • Material • Labor • Overhead	Direct relationship between cost and revenue.	Recognize in period of revenue (matching).
Period costs: • Salaries • Administrative costs	No direct relationship between cost and revenue.	Expense as incurred.

Illustration 2-4
Expense Recognition

As indicated in the discussion of Hollywood accounting, there is some debate about the conceptual validity of the matching principle. A major concern is that matching permits companies to defer certain costs and treat them as assets on the balance sheet. In fact, these costs may not have future benefits. If abused, this principle permits the balance sheet to become a "dumping ground" for unmatched costs. In addition, there appears to be no objective definition of "systematic and rational."

Full Disclosure Principle

In deciding what information to report, companies follow the general practice of providing information that is of sufficient importance to influence the judgment and decisions of an informed user. Often referred to as the **full disclosure principle**, it recognizes that the nature and amount of information included in financial reports reflects a series of judgmental trade-offs. These trade-offs strive for (1) sufficient detail to disclose matters that **make a difference** to users, yet (2) sufficient condensation to make the **information understandable**, keeping in mind costs of preparing and using it.

Users find information about financial position, income, cash flows, and investments in one of three places: (1) within the main body of financial statements, (2) in the notes to those statements, or (3) as supplementary information.

As discussed in Chapter 1, the **financial statements** are the balance sheet, income statement, statement of cash flows, and statement of owners' equity. They are a structured means of communicating financial information. To be recognized in the main body of financial statements, **an item should meet the definition of a basic element, be measurable with sufficient certainty, and be relevant and reliable.**[13]

Disclosure is not a substitute for proper accounting. As a former chief accountant of the SEC noted, "Good disclosure does not cure bad accounting any more than an adjective or adverb can be used without, or in place of, a noun or verb." Thus, for example, cash-basis accounting for cost of goods sold is misleading, even if a company discloses accrual-basis amounts in the notes to the financial statements.

The **notes to financial statements** generally amplify or explain the items presented in the main body of the statements. If the main body of the financial statements gives an incomplete picture of the performance and position of the company, the notes should provide the additional information needed. Information in the notes does not have to be quantifiable, nor does it need to qualify as an element. Notes can be partially or totally narrative. Examples of notes include descriptions of the accounting policies and methods used in measuring the elements reported in the statements, explanations of uncertainties and contingencies, and statistics and details too voluminous for inclusion in the statements. The notes can be essential to understanding the company's performance and position.

Supplementary information may include details or amounts that present a different perspective from that adopted in the financial statements. It may be quantifiable information that is high in relevance but low in reliability. For example, oil and gas companies typically provide information on proven reserves as well as the related discounted cash flows.

[13]*SFAC No. 5*, par. 63.

Supplementary information may also include management's explanation of the financial information and its discussion of the significance of that information. For example, many business combinations have produced financing arrangements that demand new accounting and reporting practices and principles. In each of these situations, the same problem must be faced: making sure the company presents enough information to ensure that the **reasonably prudent investor** will not be misled.

We discuss the content, arrangement, and display of financial statements, along with other facets of full disclosure, in Chapters 4, 5, and 6.

Try it out! Orlando Bloom Company adheres to the following accounting procedures.

1 The company received an order for $22,000 from a customer for products the company has on hand. This order was shipped in January 2008. The company made the following entry in 2007.

Accounts Receivable	22,000	
Sales		22,000

2 During the year, the company purchased equipment through the issuance of common stock. The stock has a par value of $12,000 and a fair market value of $45,000. The fair market value of the equipment was not readily determinable. The company recorded the transaction as follows.

Equipment	12,000	
Common Stock		12,000

3 The company purchased materials on January 1, 2007, for $38,000 and recorded this amount in the inventory account. On December 31, 2007, the inventory is still on hand and could be purchased in the market for $45,000, so the company made the following entry.

Inventory	7,000	
Gain on Inventories		7,000

4 Depreciation expense on its buildings for the year is $30,000. Because the building was increasing in value during the year, the company recorded depreciation expense in retained earnings instead of income, through the following entry.

Retained Earnings	30,000	
Accumulated Depreciation—Buildings		30,000

Instructions

Comment on Orlando Bloom Company's application of the basic principles of accounting.

Solution

1 According to the *revenue recognition principle*, companies do not earn Sales Revenue until the goods change hands. In this case, Orlando Bloom should record the sale in 2008 instead of 2007. Regardless of whether the terms are f.o.b. shipping point or f.o.b. destination, the inventory changed hands in 2008.

2 According to the *historical cost principle*, companies should record assets at the fair market value of what is given up or the fair market value of what is received, whichever is more clearly evident. Note that it is not a violation of the historical-cost principle to use the fair market value of the stock—at acquisition, the historical cost and fair value are the same. Recording the asset at the par value of the stock has no conceptual validity, because par value is merely an arbitrary amount usually set at the date of incorporation.

3 This accounting violates the *historical-cost principle*. That is, Bloom should not recognize a gain until the inventory is sold. Rather it should record the inventory at historical cost; write-ups are not permitted. Note also that the *revenue recognition principle* states that companies should not recognize revenue until it is realized or realizable and is earned.

4 Depreciation is an allocation of cost, not an attempt to value assets. As a consequence, even if the value of the building is increasing, Bloom should match costs related to this building with revenues on the income statement, not as a charge against retained earnings.

Constraints

In providing information with the qualitative characteristics that make it useful, companies must consider two overriding factors that limit (constrain) the reporting. These **constraints** are: (1) the cost-benefit relationship and (2) materiality. We also review two other less-dominant yet important constraints that are part of the reporting environment: industry practices and conservatism.

Cost-Benefit Relationship

Too often, users assume that information is free. But preparers and providers of accounting information know that it is not. Therefore, companies must consider the **cost-benefit relationship**: They must weigh the costs of providing the information against the benefits that can be derived from using it. Standard-setting bodies and governmental agencies use cost-benefit analysis before making final their informational requirements. In order to justify requiring a particular measurement or disclosure, the benefits perceived to be derived from it must exceed the costs perceived to be associated with it.

A corporate executive made the following remark to the FASB about a proposed standard: "In all my years in the financial arena, I have never seen such an absolutely ridiculous proposal. . . . To dignify these 'actuarial' estimates by recording them as assets and liabilities would be virtually unthinkable except for the fact that the FASB has done equally stupid things in the past. . . . For God's sake, use common sense just this once."[14] Although extreme, this remark indicates the frustration expressed by members of the business community about standard setting, and whether the benefits of a given standard exceed the costs.

The difficulty in cost-benefit analysis is that the costs and especially the benefits are not always evident or measurable. The costs are of several kinds: costs of collecting and processing, of disseminating, of auditing, of potential litigation, of disclosure to competitors, and of analysis and interpretation. Benefits to preparers may include greater management control and access to capital at a lower cost. Users may receive better information for allocation of resources, tax assessment, and rate regulation. As noted earlier, benefits are generally more difficult to quantify than are costs.

The recent implementation of the provisions of the Sarbanes-Oxley Act of 2002 illustrates the challenges in assessing costs and benefits of standards. One study estimated the increased costs of complying with the new internal-control standards related to the financial reporting process to be an average of $7.8 million per company. However, the study concluded that ". . . quantifying the benefits of improved more reliable financial reporting is not fully possible."[15]

Despite the difficulty in assessing the costs and benefits of its standards, the FASB attempts to determine that each proposed standard will fill a significant need and that the costs

[14]"Decision-Usefulness: The Overriding Objective," *FASB Viewpoints* (October 19, 1983), p. 4.

[15]Charles Rivers and Associates, "Sarbanes-Oxley Section 404: Costs and Remediation of Deficiencies" letter from Deloitte and Touche, Ernst and Young, KPMG, and Pricewaterhouse-Coopers to the SEC (April 11, 2005).

imposed to meet the standard are justified in relation to overall benefits of the resulting information. In addition, the Board seeks input on costs and benefits as part of its due process.[16]

Materiality

The **materiality** constraint concerns an item's impact on a company's overall financial operations. An item is *material* if its inclusion or omission would influence or change the judgment of a reasonable person.[17] It is *immaterial,* and therefore irrelevant, if it would have no impact on a decision maker. In short, **it must make a difference** or a company need not disclose it.

The point involved here is of **relative size and importance**. If the amount involved is significant when compared with the other revenues and expenses, assets and liabilities, or net income of the company, sound and acceptable standards should be followed in reporting it. If the amount is so small that it is unimportant when compared with other items, applying a particular standard may be considered of less importance.

It is difficult to provide firm guidelines in judging when a given item is or is not material. Materiality varies both with relative amount and with relative importance. For example, the two sets of numbers presented below illustrate relative size.

Illustration 2-5
Materiality Comparison

	Company A	Company B
Sales	$10,000,000	$100,000
Costs and expenses	9,000,000	90,000
Income from operations	$ 1,000,000	$ 10,000
Unusual gain	$ 20,000	$ 5,000

During the period in question, the revenues and expenses, and therefore the net incomes of Company A and Company B, are proportional. Each reported an unusual gain. In looking at the abbreviated income figures for Company A, it appears insignificant whether the amount of the unusual gain is set out separately or merged with the regular operating income. The gain is only 2 percent of the net income. If merged, it would not seriously distort the net income figure. Company B has had an unusual gain of only $5,000. However, it is relatively much more significant than the larger gain realized by A. For Company B, an item of $5,000 amounts to 50 percent of its income from operations. Obviously, the inclusion of such an item in ordinary operating income would affect the amount of that income materially. Thus we see the importance of the **relative size** of an item in determining its materiality.

Companies and their auditors generally adopt the rule of thumb that anything under 5 percent of net income is considered immaterial. However, the SEC indicates that a company may use this percentage for an initial assessment of materiality, but it must also consider other factors.[18] For example, companies can no longer fail to record items in order to meet consensus analysts' earnings numbers, preserve a positive earnings trend, convert a loss to a profit or vice versa, increase management compensation, or hide an illegal transaction like a bribe. In other words, **companies must consider both quantitative and qualitative factors in determining whether an item is material**.

---

[16]For example, as part of its project on "Share-Based Payment," *SFAS No. 123R*, the Board conducted a field study and surveyed commercial software providers to collect information on the costs of measuring the fair values of share-based compensation arrangements.

[17]*SFAC No. 2*, par. 132, sets forth the essence of materiality: "The omission or misstatement of an item in a financial report is material if, in the light of surrounding circumstances, the magnitude of the item is such that it is probable that the judgment of a reasonable person relying upon the report would have been changed or influenced by the inclusion or correction of the item." The auditing profession also adopted this same concept of materiality. See "Audit Risk and Materiality in Conducting an Audit," *Statement on Auditing Standards No. 47* (New York: AICPA, 1983), par. 6.

[18]"Materiality," *SEC Staff Accounting Bulletin No. 99* (Washington, D.C.: SEC, 1999).

The SEC also indicated that in determining materiality, companies must consider each misstatement separately *and* the aggregate effect of all misstatements. At one time **General Dynamics** disclosed that its Resources Group improved its earnings by $5.8 million. At the same time, it disclosed that another subsidiary had taken write-offs of $6.7 million. Although both numbers exceeded the $2.5 million that General Dynamics as a whole earned for the year, the company disclosed neither as unusual because it considered the net effect on earnings as immaterial. **This practice is prohibited**; each item must be considered separately. Also, even though an individual item may be immaterial, it may be considered material when added to other immaterial items. Companies must disclose such items.

Materiality factors in a great many internal accounting decisions, too. Examples of such judgments that companies must make include: the amount of classification required in a subsidiary expense ledger, the degree of accuracy required in prorating expenses among the departments of a company, and the extent to which adjustments should be made for accrued and deferred items. Only by **the exercise of good judgment and professional expertise** can reasonable and appropriate answers be found, which is the materiality constraint sensibly applied.

What do the numbers mean?   Living in a Material World

The first line of defense for many companies caught "cooking the books" had been to argue that a questionable accounting item is immaterial. That defense has not been working so well lately, in the wake of the tougher rules on materiality issued by the SEC (*SAB 99*).

For example, the SEC alleged in a case against **Sunbeam** that the company racked up so many immaterial adjustments that they added up to a material misstatement that misled investors about the company's financial position. More recently, the SEC called for a number of companies, such as **Jack in the Box**, **McDonald's**, and **AIG**, to restate prior financial statements for the effects of incorrect accounting. In some cases, the restatements did not meet traditional materiality thresholds. Don Nicholaisen, then-SEC Chief Accountant, observed that whether the amount is material or not-material, some transactions appear to be "flat out intended to mislead investors." In essence, any wrong accounting for a transaction can represent important information to the users of financial statements.

Responding to new concerns about materiality, blue-chip companies such as **IBM** and **General Electric** are providing expanded disclosures of transactions that used to fall below the materiality radar. As a result, some good may yet come from the recent accounting failures.

Source: Adapted from K. Brown and J. Weil, "A Lot More Information Is 'Material' After Enron," *Wall Street Journal Online* (February 22, 2002); S. D. Jones and R. Gibson, "Restaurants Serve Up Restatements," *Wall Street Journal* (January 26, 2005), p. C3; and R. McTauge, "Nicholaisen Says Restatement Needed When Deal Lacks Business Purpose," *Securities Regulation & Law Reporter* (May 9, 2005).

Beyond the Numbers

Consider the following: Engone Company is preparing its year-end financial statements and is proposing a reduction in its bad debt allowance by an amount management believes is immaterial. By recording a smaller bad debt expense, the company will report EPS that just meets analysts' forecasts, and hence will avoid negative consequences for its stock price. What would you advise Engone management in order for its reporting to be in compliance with the materiality constraint?

Industry Practices

Another practical consideration is **industry practices**. **The peculiar nature of some industries and business concerns** sometimes requires departure from basic theory. For example, public-utility companies report noncurrent assets first on the balance sheet to highlight the industry's capital-intensive nature. Agricultural companies often report crops at market value because it is costly to develop accurate cost figures on individual crops.

Such variations from basic theory are infrequent, yet they do exist. Whenever we find what appears to be a violation of basic accounting theory, we should determine whether some peculiarity of the industry explains the violation before we criticize the procedures followed.

Conservatism

Few conventions in accounting are as misunderstood as the constraint of conservatism. **Conservatism** means **when in doubt, choose the solution that will be least likely to overstate assets and income.** Note that the conservatism convention does not urge that net assets or net income be *understated*. Unfortunately, some interpret conservatism to mean just that.

All that conservatism does, properly applied, is provide a reasonable guide in difficult situations: Refrain from overstatement of net income and net assets. Examples of conservatism in accounting are the use of the lower-of-cost-or-market approach in valuing inventories, and the rule that companies recognize accrued net losses on firm purchase commitments for goods for inventory. When in doubt, it is better to understate than overstate net income and net assets. Of course, if no doubt exists, there is no need to apply this constraint.

You will want to read the
CONVERGENCE CORNER
on the next page for
discussion of how international
convergence efforts relate to the
chapter topic.

Summary of the Structure

Illustration 2-6 presents the conceptual framework discussed in this chapter. It is similar to Illustration 2-1, except that it provides additional information for each level. We cannot overemphasize the usefulness of this conceptual framework in helping to understand many of the problem areas that we examine in later chapters.

Illustration 2-6
Conceptual Framework
for Financial Reporting

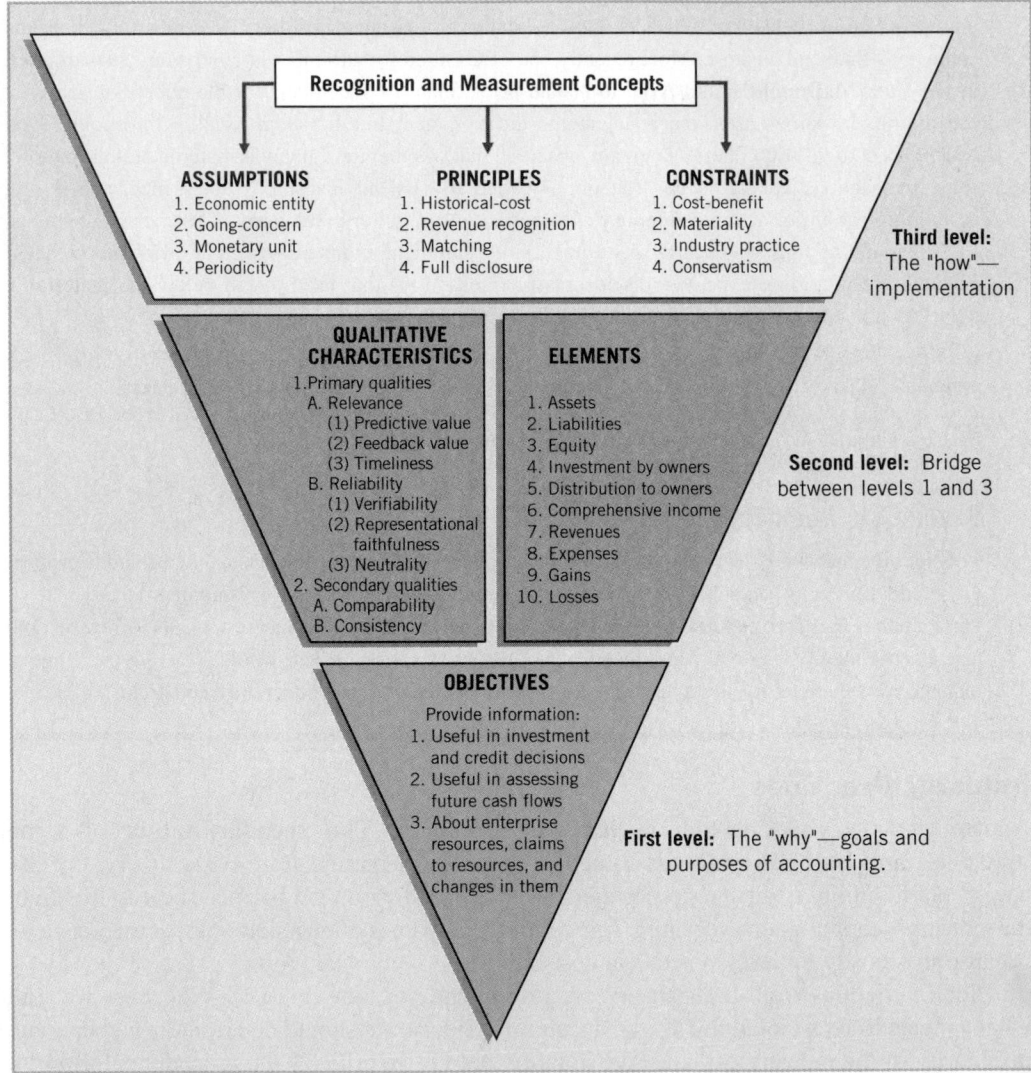

CONVERGENCE CORNER

The Conceptual Framework

In 2005, the IASB and the FASB agreed to work on a joint project to develop a common conceptual framework. This framework is based on the existing conceptual frameworks underlying U.S. GAAP and iGAAP. The objective of this joint project is to develop a conceptual framework that leads to developing standards that are principle-based and internally consistent and that leads to the most useful financial reporting.

RELEVANT FACTS

• The existing conceptual frameworks underlying U.S. GAAP and iGAAP are very similar. That is, they are organized in a similar manner (objectives, elements, qualitative characteristics, etc.). There is no real need to change many aspects of the existing frameworks, other than to converge different ways of discussing essentially the same concepts.

• The converged framework should be a single document, unlike the two conceptual frameworks that presently exist; it is unlikely that the basic structure related to the concepts will change.

• The IASB framework makes two assumptions. One assumption is that financial statements are prepared on an accrual basis; the other is that the reporting entity is a going concern. The FASB framework discusses accrual accounting extensively but does not identify it as an assumption, and it only briefly discusses the going concern concept.

ABOUT THE NUMBERS

The work on the conceptual framework is being done in phases. As indicated in the chart below, an exposure draft (ED) of phase A related to objectives and qualitative characteristics was issued in 2007. In addition, a discussion paper (DP) related to the reporting entity (phase D) was also issued in 2007.

Conceptual Framework Schedule	2007	2008	Timing not determined
Phase A: Objectives and qualitative characteristics	ED		
Phase B: Elements and recognition		DP	
Phase C: Measurement			DP
Phase D: Reporting entity	DP		
Phase E: Presentation and disclosure			DP
Phase F: Purpose and status			DP
Phase G: Application to not-for-profit entities			DP
Phase H: Remaining issues (Document type not yet determined)			

• There is some agreement that the role of financial reporting is to assist users in decision making. However, others note that another objective is to provide information on management's performance, often referred to as stewardship. It is likely that there will be much debate about the role of stewardship in the conceptual framework.

ON THE HORIZON

The IASB and the FASB face a difficult task in attempting to update, modify, and complete a converged conceptual framework. There are many difficult issues. For example: How do we trade off characteristics such as highly relevant information that is difficult to verify? How do we define control when we are developing a definition of an asset? Is a liability the future sacrifice itself or the obligation to make the sacrifice? Should a single measurement method, such as historical cost or fair value, be used, or does it depend on whether it is an asset or liability that is being measured? We are optimistic that the new document will be a significant improvement over its predecessors and will lead to principle-based standards that help users of the financial statements make better decisions.

ACCOUNTING, ANALYSIS, PRINCIPLES

William Murray achieved one of his life-long dreams by opening his own business, The Caddie Shack Diving Range, on May 1, 2008. He invested $20,000 of his own savings in the business. He paid $6,000 cash to have a small building constructed to house the operations and spent $800 on golf clubs, golf balls, and yardage signs. Murray leased 4 acres of land at a cost of $1,000 per month. (He paid the first month's rent in cash.) During the first month, advertising costs totaled $750, of which $150 was unpaid at the end of the month. Murray paid his three nephews $400 for retrieving golf balls. He deposited in the company's bank account all revenues from customers ($4,700). On May 15, Murray withdrew $800 in cash for personal use. On May 31, the company received a utility bill for $100, but did not immediately pay it. On May 31, the balance in the company bank account was $15,100.

Murray is feeling pretty good about results for the first month, but his estimate of profitability ranges from a loss of $4,900 to a profit of $1,650.

Accounting

a Prepare a balance sheet at May 31, 2008. (Murray appropriately records any depreciation expense on a quarterly basis.) How could Murray have determined that the business operated at a profit of $1,650?

b How could Murray conclude that the business operated at a loss of $4,900?

Analysis

c Assume Murray has asked you to become a partner in his business. Under the partnership agreement, after paying him $10,000, you would share equally in all future profits. Which of the two income measures above would be more useful in deciding whether to become a partner? Explain.

Principles

d What is income according to GAAP? What concepts do the differences in the three income measures for The Caddie Shack Driving Range illustrate?

Solution

Accounting

a A balance sheet for The Caddie Shack at May 31, 2008, would be:

Assets		Liabilities and Capital	
Cash	$15,100	Advertising payable	$ 150
Building	6,000	Utilities payable	100
Equipment	800	Original capital	20,000
		Change in capital	1,650
Total assets	$21,900		$21,900

Murray might conclude that income was $1,650 based on the change in capital from the beginning of the month to the end of the month.

b If Murray focused on the change in cash or the balance in the bank account, he would conclude that the company had a loss of $4,900 ($20,000 – $15,100). This is income measured *on a cash basis*.

Analysis

c The income measure of $1,650 is most relevant for assessing the future profitability and hence the payoffs to the owners. For example, charging the cost of the building and equipment to expense in the first month of operations understates income in the first month. These costs should be allocated to future periods of benefit through depreciation expense. Similarly, although not paid, the utilities were used to generate revenues so they should be recognized when incurred, not when paid.

Principles

d GAAP income is $1,650 plus the cash withdrawal of $800. Alternatively, the income statement for The Caddie Shack is:

Revenues	$4,700
Expenses	
Rent	1,000
Advertising	750
Wages	400
Utilities	100
Total expenses	2,250
Net income	$2,450

The key concept illustrated in the difference between the loss of $4,900 and profit of $1,650 is the *matching principle*, which calls for recognition of expenses when incurred, not when paid. Excluding the cash withdrawal from the measurement of income (the difference between income measures in parts **c** and **d**) is an application of the definition of basic elements. Cash withdrawals are distributions to owners, not an element of income (expenses or losses).

Key Terms

assumption, 45
comparability, 41
conceptual framework, 36
conservatism, 56
consistency, 41
constraints, 53
cost-benefit relationship, 53
decision usefulness, 38
earned (revenue), 48
economic entity assumption, 45
elements, basic, 42
feedback value, 40
full disclosure principle, 51
going-concern assumption, 46
historical-cost principle, 47
industry practices, 55
matching principle, 49
materiality, 54
monetary unit assumption, 46

neutrality, 41
notes to financial statements, 51
objectives of financial reporting, 38
period costs, 50
periodicity (time period) assumption, 46
predictive value, 40
principles of accounting, 47
product costs, 50
qualitative characteristics, 39
realizable (revenue), 48
realized (revenue), 48
relevance, 40
reliability, 40
representational faithfulness, 40
revenue recognition principle, 48
supplementary information, 51
timeliness, 40
understandability, 40
verifiability, 40

Summary of Learning Objectives

1 Describe the usefulness of a conceptual framework. The accounting profession needs a conceptual framework to: (1) build on and relate to an established body of concepts and objectives, (2) provide a framework for solving new and emerging practical problems, (3) increase financial statement users' understanding of and confidence in financial reporting, and (4) enhance comparability among companies' financial statements.

2 **Describe the FASB's efforts to construct a conceptual framework.** The FASB issued six Statements of Financial Accounting Concepts that relate to financial reporting for business enterprises. These concept statements provide the basis for the conceptual framework. They include objectives, qualitative characteristics, and elements. In addition, measurement and recognition concepts are developed.

3 **Understand the objectives of financial reporting.** Financial reporting should provide information that is: (1) useful to those making investment and credit decisions who have a reasonable understanding of business activities; (2) helpful to present and potential investors, creditors, and others in assessing future cash flows; and (3) about economic resources and the claims to and changes in them.

4 **Identify the qualitative characteristics of accounting information.** The overriding criterion by which accounting choices can be judged is decision usefulness—that is, providing information that is most useful for decision making. Relevance and reliability are the two primary qualities. Comparability and consistency are the secondary qualities, that make accounting information useful for decision making.

5 **Define the basic elements of financial statements.** The basic elements of financial statements are: (1) assets, (2) liabilities, (3) equity, (4) investments by owners, (5) distributions to owners, (6) comprehensive income, (7) revenues, (8) expenses, (9) gains, and (10) losses. We define these ten elements on page 37.

6 **Describe the basic assumptions of accounting.** Four basic assumptions underlying financial accounting are: (1) *Economic entity:* The activity of a company can be kept separate and distinct from its owners and any other business unit. (2) *Going-concern:* The company will have a long life. (3) *Monetary unit:* Money is the common denominator by which economic activity is conducted, and the monetary unit provides an appropriate basis for measurement and analysis. (4) *Periodicity:* The economic activities of a company can be divided into artificial time periods.

7 **Explain the application of the basic principles of accounting.** (1) *Historical-cost principle:* Existing GAAP requires that companies account for and report most assets and liabilities on the basis of acquisition price. (2) *Revenue recognition:* A company generally recognizes revenue when (a) realized or realizable and (b) earned. (3) *Matching principle:* A company recognizes expenses when the work (service) or the product actually makes its contribution to revenue. (4) *Full disclosure principle:* Companies generally provide information that is of sufficient importance to influence the judgment and decisions of an informed user.

8 **Describe the impact that constraints have on reporting accounting information.** The constraints and their impact are: (1) *Cost-benefit relationship:* The cost of providing the information must be weighed against the benefits that can be derived from using the information. (2) *Materiality:* Sound and acceptable standards should be followed if the amount involved is significant when compared with the other revenues and expenses, assets and liabilities, or net income of the company. (3) *Industry practices:* Follow the general practices in the company's industry, which sometimes requires departure from basic theory. (4) *Conservatism:* When in doubt, choose the solution that will be least likely to overstate net assets and net income.

REVIEW EXERCISE

Jeremy Roenick Corporation has hired you to review its accounting records prior to the closing of the revenue and expense accounts as of December 31, the end of the current fiscal year. The following information comes to your attention.

1   During the current year, Jeremy Roenick Corporation changed its policy in regard to expensing purchases of small tools. In the past, it had expensed these purchases because they amounted to less than 2% of net income. Now, the president has decided that the company should follow a policy of capitalization and subsequent depreciation. It is expected that purchases of small tools will not fluctuate greatly from year to year.

2   The company constructed a warehouse at a cost of $1,000,000. It had been depreciating the asset on a straight-line basis over 10 years. In the current year, the controller

doubled depreciation expense because the replacement cost of the warehouse had increased significantly.

3 When the balance sheet was prepared, the preparer omitted detailed information as to the amount of cash on deposit in each of several banks. Only the total amount of cash under a caption "Cash in banks" was presented.

4 On July 15 of the current year, Jeremy Roenick Corporation purchased an undeveloped tract of land at a cost of $320,000. The company spent $80,000 in subdividing the land and getting it ready for sale. An appraisal of the property at the end of the year indicated that the land was now worth $500,000. Although none of the lots were sold, the company recognized revenue of $180,000, less related expenses of $80,000, for a net income on the project of $100,000.

5 For a number of years the company used the FIFO method for inventory valuation purposes. During the current year, the president noted that all the other companies in the industry had switched to the LIFO method. The company decided not to switch to LIFO because net income would decrease $830,000.

Instructions

State whether or not you agree with the decisions made by Jeremy Roenick Corporation. Support your answers with reference, whenever possible, to the generally accepted principles, assumptions, and constraints applicable in the circumstances.

Solution

1 From the facts it is difficult to determine whether to agree or disagree. Consistency, of course, is violated in this situation, although its violation may not be material. Furthermore, the change of accounting policies regarding the treatment of small tools cannot be judged good or bad, but would depend on the circumstances. In this case, it seems that the result will be approximately the same whether the corporation capitalizes and expenses, or simply expenses each period, since the purchases are fairly uniform. Perhaps from a cost standpoint (expediency), it might be best to continue the present policy rather than become involved in detailed depreciation schedules, assuming that purchases remain fairly uniform. On the other hand, the president may believe there is a significant unrecorded asset that should be shown on the balance sheet. If such is the case, capitalization and subsequent depreciation would be more appropriate.

2 Disagree. At the present time, accountants do not recognize price level or current value adjustments in the accounts. Hence it is misleading to deviate from the cost principle, because conjecture or opinion can take place. Also, depreciation is not so much a matter of valuation as it is a means of cost allocation. Assets are not depreciated on the basis of a decline in their fair market value; rather, they are depreciated on the basis of a systematic charge of expired cost against revenues.

3 Agree. The full-disclosure principle recognizes that reasonable condensation and summarization of the details of a corporation's operations and financial position are essential to readability and comprehension. Thus, in determining what is full disclosure, the accountant must decide whether omission will mislead readers of the financial statements. Generally, companies present only the total amount of cash on a balance sheet, unless some special circumstance is involved (such as a possible restriction on the use of the cash). In most cases, however, the company's presentation would be considered appropriate and in accordance with the full disclosure principle.

4 Disagree. The historical-cost principle indicates that companies account for assets and liabilities on the basis of cost. If sales value were selected, for example, it would be extremely difficult to establish an appraisal value for the given item without selling it.

Note, too, that the revenue recognition principle provides guidance on when revenue should be recognized. Revenue should be recognized when (1) realized or realizable and (2) earned. In this case, the revenue was not earned because the critical event, "sale of the land," had not occurred.

5 From the facts it is difficult to determine whether to agree or disagree with the president. The president's approach is not a violation of any principle. Consistency requires that accounting entities give accountable events the same accounting treatment from period to period for a given business enterprise. It says nothing concerning consistency of accounting principles among business enterprises. From a comparability viewpoint, it might be useful to report the information on a LIFO basis, but as indicated above, there is no requirement to do so.

Questions

1 What is a conceptual framework? Why is a conceptual framework necessary in financial accounting?

2 What are the primary objectives of financial reporting as indicated in *Statement of Financial Accounting Concepts No. 1?*

3 What is meant by the term "qualitative characteristics of accounting information"?

4 Briefly describe the two primary qualities of useful accounting information.

5 According to the FASB conceptual framework, the objectives of financial reporting for business enterprises are based on the needs of the users of financial statements. Explain the level of sophistication that the Board assumes about the users of financial statements.

6 What is the distinction between comparability and consistency?

7 Why is it necessary to develop a definitional framework for the basic elements of accounting?

8 Expenses, losses, and distributions to owners are all decreases in net assets. What are the distinctions among them?

9 Revenues, gains, and investments by owners are all increases in net assets. What are the distinctions among them?

10 What are the four basic assumptions that underlie the financial accounting structure?

11 The life of a business is divided into specific time periods, usually a year, to measure results of operations for each such time period and to portray financial conditions at the end of each period.

(a) This practice is based on the accounting assumption that the life of the business consists of a series of time periods and that it is possible to measure accurately the results of operations for each period. Comment on the validity and necessity of this assumption.

(b) What has been the effect of this practice on accounting? What is its relation to the accrual system? What influence has it had on accounting entries and methodology?

12 What is the basic accounting problem created by the monetary unit assumption when there is significant inflation? What appears to be the FASB position on a stable monetary unit?

13 The chairman of the board of directors of the company for which you are chief accountant has told you that he has little use for accounting figures based on cost. He believes that replacement values are of far more significance to the board of directors than "out-of-date costs." Present some arguments to convince him that accounting data should still be based on cost.

14 When is revenue generally recognized? Why has the profession chosen that date as the point at which to recognize the revenue resulting from the entire producing and selling process?

15 Magnus Eatery operates a catering service specializing in business luncheons for large corporations. Magnus requires customers to place their orders 2 weeks in advance of the scheduled events. Magnus bills its customers on the tenth day of the month following the date of service and requires that payment be made within 30 days of the billing date. Conceptually, when should Magnus recognize revenue related to its catering service?

16 What is the difference between realized and realizable? Give an example of where the concept of realizable is used to recognize revenue.

17 What is the justification for the following deviations from recognizing revenue at the time of sale?

(a) Installment-sales method of recognizing revenue.

(b) Recognition of revenue at completion of production for certain agricultural products.

(c) The percentage-of-completion basis in long-term construction contracts.

18 Jane Hull Company paid $135,000 for a machine in 2008. The Accumulated Depreciation account has a balance of $46,500 at the present time. The company could sell the machine today for $150,000. The company president believes that the company has a "right to this gain." What does the president mean by this statement? Do you agree?

19 The text discussed three expense recognition methods (associating cause and effect, rational and systematic allocation, and immediate recognition) under the matching principle. Indicate the basic nature of each of these types of expenses and give two examples of each.

20 *Statement of Financial Accounting Concepts No. 5* identifies characteristics that an item must have before it is recognized in the financial statements. What are these characteristics?

21 Briefly describe the types of information concerning financial position, income, and cash flows that might be provided: (a) within the main body of the financial statements, (b) in the notes to the financial statements, or (c) as supplementary information.

22 In January 2008, Alan Jackson Inc. doubled the amount of its outstanding stock by selling on the market an additional 10,000 shares to finance an expansion of the business. You propose that this information be shown by a footnote on the balance sheet as of December 31, 2007. The president objects, claiming that this sale took place after December 31, 2007, and, therefore, should not be shown. Explain your position.

23 Describe the two major constraints inherent in the presentation of accounting information.

24 What are some of the costs of providing accounting information? What are some of the benefits of accounting information? Describe the cost-benefit factors that should be considered when new accounting standards are proposed.

25 How are materiality (and immateriality) related to the proper presentation of financial statements? What factors and measures should be considered in assessing the materiality of a misstatement in the presentation of a financial statement?

26 The treasurer of Joan Osborne Co. has heard that conservatism is a doctrine that is followed in accounting and, therefore, proposes that the company follow several policies that are conservative in nature. State your opinion with respect to each of the policies listed below.

(a) The company gives a 2-year warranty to its customers on all products sold. The company should enter as an expense this year the estimated warranty costs incurred from this year's sales instead of an expense in the period in the future when the warranty is made good.

(b) When sales are made on account, there is always uncertainty about whether the accounts are collectible. Therefore, the treasurer recommends recording the sale when the company receives the cash from the customers.

(c) A personal liability lawsuit is pending against the company. The treasurer believes there is an even chance that the company will lose the suit and have to pay damages of $200,000 to $300,000. The treasurer recommends that the company record a loss and create a liability in the amount of $300,000.

(d) The company should value the inventory at "cost or market, whichever is lower" because the losses from price declines should be recognized in the accounts in the period in which the price decline takes place.

Brief Exercises

BE2-1 Discuss whether the changes described in each of the cases below require recognition in the CPA's audit report as to consistency. (Assume that the amounts are material.)

(LO 4)

(a) The company changed its inventory method to FIFO from weighted-average, which had been used in prior years.

(b) The company disposed of one of the two subsidiaries that had been included in its consolidated statements for prior years.

(c) The estimated remaining useful life of plant property was reduced because of obsolescence.

(d) The company is using an inventory valuation method that is different from those used by all other companies in its industry.

BE2-2 Identify which qualitative characteristic of accounting information is best described in each item below. (Do not use relevance and reliability.)

(LO 4)

(a) Certified public accountants audit the annual reports of **Best Buy Co.**

(b) **Black & Decker** and **Cannondale Corporation** both use the FIFO cost flow assumption.

(c) **Starbucks Corporation** has used straight-line depreciation since it began operations.

(d) **Motorola** issues its quarterly reports immediately after each quarter ends.

(LO 5)   **BE2-3**   For each item below, indicate to which category of elements of financial statements it belongs.

(a) Retained earnings	(e) Depreciation	(h) Dividends
(b) Sales	(f) Loss on sale of equipment	(i) Gain on sale of investment
(c) Additional paid-in capital	(g) Interest payable	(j) Issuance of common stock
(d) Inventory		

(LO 6)   **BE2-4**   Identify which basic assumption of accounting is best described in each item below.

(a) The economic activities of **FedEx Corporation** are divided into 12-month periods for the purpose of issuing annual reports.

(b) **Solectron Corporation, Inc.** does not adjust amounts in its financial statements for the effects of inflation.

(c) **Walgreen Co.** reports current and noncurrent classifications in its balance sheet.

(d) The economic activities of **General Electric** and its subsidiaries are merged for accounting and reporting purposes.

(LO 7)   **BE2-5**   Identify which basic principle of accounting is best described in each item below.

(a) **Norfolk Southern Corporation** reports revenue in its income statement when it is earned instead of when the cash is collected.

(b) **Yahoo, Inc.** recognizes depreciation expense for a machine over the 2-year period during which that machine helps the company earn revenue.

(c) **Oracle Corporation** reports information about pending lawsuits in the notes to its financial statements.

(d) **Eastman Kodak Company** reports land on its balance sheet at the amount paid to acquire it, even though the estimated fair market value is greater.

(LO 8)   **BE2-6**   What accounting constraints are illustrated by the items below?

(a) Zip's Farms, Inc. reports agricultural crops on its balance sheet at market value.

(b) Crimson Tide Corporation does not accrue a contingent lawsuit gain of $650,000.

(c) Wildcat Company does not disclose any information in the notes to the financial statements unless the value of the information to financial statement users exceeds the expense of gathering it.

(d) Sun Devil Corporation expenses the cost of wastebaskets in the year they are acquired.

(LO 8)   **BE2-7**   Presented below are three different transactions related to materiality. Explain whether you would classify these transactions as material.

(a) Marcus Co. has reported a positive trend in earnings over the last 3 years. In the current year, it reduces its bad debt allowance to ensure another positive earnings year. The impact of this adjustment is equal to 3% of net income.

(b) Sosa Co. has an extraordinary gain of $3.1 million on the sale of plant assets and a $3.3 million loss on the sale of investments. It decides to net the gain and loss because the net effect is considered immaterial. Sosa Co.'s income for the current year was $10 million.

(c) Seliz Co. expenses all capital equipment under $25,000 on the basis that it is immaterial. The company has followed this practice for a number of years.

(LO 6)   **BE2-8**   If the going-concern assumption is not made in accounting, discuss the differences in the amounts shown in the financial statements for the following items.

(a) Land.

(b) Unamortized bond premium.

(c) Depreciation expense on equipment.

(d) Merchandise inventory.

(e) Prepaid insurance.

(LO 6, 7, 8)   **BE2-9**   What accounting assumption, principle, or modifying convention does **Target Corporation** use in each of the situations below?

(a) Target uses the lower-of-cost-or-market basis to value inventories.

(b) Target was involved in litigation over the last year. This litigation is disclosed in the financial statements.

(c) Target allocates the cost of its depreciable assets over the life it expects to receive revenue from these assets.

(d) Target records the purchase of a new **Dell** PC at its cash equivalent price.

(LO 5)   **BE2-10**   Explain how you would decide whether to record each of the following expenditures as an asset or an expense. Assume all items are material.

(a) Legal fees paid in connection with the purchase of land are $1,500.

(b) Benjamin Bratt, Inc. paves the driveway leading to the office building at a cost of $21,000.

(c) A meat market purchases a meat-grinding machine at a cost of $3,500.

(d) On June 30, Alan and Alda, medical doctors, pay 6 months' office rent to cover the month of July and the next 5 months.

(e) Tim Taylor's Hardware Company pays $9,000 in wages to laborers for construction on a building to be used in the business.

(f) Nancy Kwan's Florists pays wages of $2,100 for November to an employee who serves as driver of its delivery truck.

Exercises

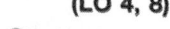

E2-1 **(Qualitative Characteristics)** *SFAC No. 2* identifies the qualitative characteristics that make accounting information useful. Presented below are a number of questions related to these qualitative characteristics and underlying constraints.

(LO 4, 8)

(a) What is the quality of information that enables users to confirm or correct prior expectations?

(b) Identify the two overall or pervasive constraints developed in *SFAC No. 2*.

(c) The chairman of the SEC at one time noted, "If it becomes accepted or expected that accounting principles are determined or modified in order to secure purposes other than economic measurement, we assume a grave risk that confidence in the credibility of our financial information system will be undermined." Which qualitative characteristic of accounting information should ensure that such a situation will not occur? (Do not use reliability.)

(d) Billy Owens Corp. switches from FIFO to average cost to FIFO over a 2-year period. Which qualitative characteristic of accounting information is *not* followed?

(e) Assume that the profession permits the savings and loan industry to defer losses on investments it sells, because immediate recognition of the loss may have adverse economic consequences on the industry. Which qualitative characteristic of accounting information is not followed? (Do not use relevance or reliability.)

(f) What are the two primary qualities that make accounting information useful for decision making?

(g) Rex Chapman, Inc. does not issue its first-quarter report until after the second quarter's results are reported. Which qualitative characteristic of accounting is not followed? (Do not use relevance.)

(h) Predictive value is an ingredient of which of the two primary qualities that make accounting information useful for decision-making purposes?

(i) Ronald Coles, Inc. is the only company in its industry to depreciate its plant assets on a straight-line basis. Which qualitative characteristic of accounting information may not be followed? (Do not use industry practices.)

(j) Jeff Malone Company has attempted to determine the replacement cost of its inventory. Three different appraisers arrive at substantially different amounts for this value. The president, nevertheless, decides to report the middle value for external reporting purposes. Which qualitative characteristic of information is lacking in these data? (Do not use reliability or representational faithfulness.)

E2-2 **(Qualitative Characteristics)** The qualitative characteristics that make accounting information useful for decision-making purposes are as follows.

(LO 4)

Relevance	Timeliness	Representational faithfulness
Reliability	Verifiability	Comparability
Predictive value	Neutrality	Consistency
Feedback value		

Instructions

Identify the appropriate qualitative characteristic(s) to be used given the information provided below.

(a) Qualitative characteristic being employed when companies in the same industry are using the same accounting principles.

(b) Quality of information that confirms users' earlier expectations.

(c) Imperative for providing comparisons of a company from period to period.

(d) Ignores the economic consequences of a standard or rule.

(e) Requires a high degree of consensus among individuals on a given measurement.

(f) Predictive value is an ingredient of this primary quality of information.

(g) Two qualitative characteristics that are related to both relevance and reliability.

(h) Neutrality is an ingredient of this primary quality of accounting information.
(i) Two primary qualities that make accounting information useful for decision-making purposes.
(j) Issuance of interim reports is an example of what primary ingredient of relevance?

(LO 4)

E2-3 (Qualitative Characteristics) Accounting information provides useful information about business transactions and events. Those who provide and use financial reports must often select and evaluate accounting alternatives. *FASB Statement of Financial Accounting Concepts No. 2*, "Qualitative Characteristics of Accounting Information," examines the characteristics of accounting information that make it useful for decision making. It also points out that various limitations inherent in the measurement and reporting process may necessitate trade-offs or sacrifices among the characteristics of useful information.

Instructions

(a) Describe briefly the following characteristics of useful accounting information.
    (1) Relevance   (4) Comparability
    (2) Reliability   (5) Consistency
    (3) Understandability

(b) For each of the following pairs of information characteristics, give an example of a situation in which one of the characteristics may be sacrificed in return for a gain in the other.
    (1) Relevance and reliability   (3) Comparability and consistency
    (2) Relevance and consistency   (4) Relevance and understandability

(c) What criterion should be used to evaluate trade-offs between information characteristics?

(LO 5)

E2-4 (Elements of Financial Statements) Ten interrelated elements that are most directly related to measuring the performance and financial status of an enterprise are listed below.

Assets	Distributions to owners	Expenses
Liabilities	Comprehensive income	Gains
Equity	Revenues	Losses
Investments by owners		

Instructions

Identify the element or elements from the list above that is/are associated with the 12 items below.

(a) Arises from peripheral or incidental transactions.
(b) Obligation to transfer resources arising from a past transaction.
(c) Increases ownership interest.
(d) Declares and pays cash dividends to owners.
(e) Increases in net assets in a period from nonowner sources.
(f) Items characterized by service potential or future economic benefit.
(g) Equals increase in assets less liabilities during the year, after adding distributions to owners and subtracting investments by owners.
(h) Arises from income statement activities that constitute the entity's ongoing major or central operations.
(i) Residual interest in the assets of the enterprise after deducting its liabilities.
(j) Increases assets during a period through sale of product.
(k) Decreases assets during the period by purchasing the company's own stock.
(l) Includes all changes in equity during the period, except those resulting from investments by owners and distributions to owners.

(LO 7)

E2-5 (Revenue Recognition and Matching Principle) On June 5, 2007, McCoy Corporation signed a contract with Sulu Associated under which Sulu agreed (1) to construct an office building on land owned by McCoy, (2) to accept responsibility for procuring financing for the project and finding tenants, and (3) to manage the property for 35 years. The annual net income from the project, after debt service, was to be divided equally between McCoy Corporation and Sulu Associates. Sulu was to accept its share of future net income as full payment for its services in construction, obtaining finances and tenants, and management of the project.

By May 31, 2008, the project was nearly completed and tenants had signed leases to occupy 90% of the available space at annual rentals totalling $4,000,000. The company estimated that, after operating expenses and debt service, the annual net income will amount to $1,500,000.

The management of Sulu Associates believed that (a) the economic benefit derived from the contract with McCoy should be reflected on its financial statements for the fiscal year ended May 31, 2008, and directed that revenue be accrued in an amount equal to the commercial value of the services Sulu had rendered during the year, (b) this amount be carried in contracts receivable, and (c) all related expenditures be charged against the revenue.

Instructions

(a) Explain the main difference between the economic concept of business income as reflected by Sulu's management and the measurement of income under generally accepted accounting principles.

(b) Discuss the factors to be considered in determining when revenue should be recognized for the purpose of accounting measurement of periodic income.

(c) Is the belief of Sulu's management in accordance with generally accepted accounting principles for the measurement of revenue and expense for the year ended May 31, 2008? Support your opinion by discussing the application to this case of the factors to be considered for asset measurement and revenue and expense recognition.

(AICPA adapted)

E2-6 **(Matching Principle)** Carlos Rodriguez sells and erects "shell houses," that is, frame structures that are completely finished on the outside but are unfinished on the inside except for flooring, partition studding, and ceiling joists. Shell houses are sold chiefly to customers who are handy with tools and who have time to do the interior wiring, plumbing, wall completion and finishing, and other work necessary to make the shell houses livable dwellings.

Rodriguez buys shell houses from a manufactorer in unassembled packages consisting of all lumber, roofing, doors, windows, and similar materials necessary to complete a shell house. When starting operations in a new area, Rodriguez buys or leases land as a site for its local warehouse, field office, and display houses. He erects sample display houses at a total cost of $20,000 to $29,000 including the cost of the unassembled packages. The chief element of cost of the display house is the unassembled packages; the assembly process is a short, low-cost operation. Every 3 to 7 years Rodriguez tears down old sample models or alters them into new models. Sample display houses have little salvage value because dismantling and moving costs amount to nearly as much as the cost of an unassembled package.

(LO 7)

Instructions

(a) Rodriguez must choose between (1) expensing the costs of sample display houses in the periods in which the expenditure is made and (2) spreading the costs over more than one period. Discuss the advantages of each method.

(b) Would it be preferable to amortize the cost of display houses on the basis of (1) the passage of time or (2) the number of shell houses sold? Explain.

(AICPA adapted)

E2-7 **(Assumptions, Principles, and Constraints)** Presented below are the assumptions, principles, and constraints used in this chapter.

(LO 6, 7, 8)

1. Economic entity assumption
2. Going-concern assumption
3. Monetary unit assumption
4. Periodicity assumption
5. Historical-cost principle
6. Matching principle
7. Full disclosure principle
8. Cost-benefit relationship
9. Materiality
10. Industry practices
11. Conservatism

Instructions

Identify by number the accounting assumption, principle, or constraint that describes each situation below. Do not use a number more than once.

(a) Recognizes expenses based on contribution to revenues in the proper period.

(b) Indicates that market value changes subsequent to purchase are not recorded in the accounts. (Do not use revenue recognition principle.)

(c) Ensures that all relevant financial information is reported.

(d) Rationale why plant assets are not reported at liquidation value. (Do not use historical cost principle.)

(e) Anticipates all losses, but reports no gains.

(f) Indicates that personal and business record keeping should be separately maintained.

(g) Separates financial information into time periods for reporting purposes.

(h) Permits the use of market value valuation in certain specific situations.

(i) Requires that information significant enough to affect the decision of reasonably informed users should be disclosed. (Do not use full disclosure principle.)

(j) Assumes that the dollar is the "measuring stick" used to report on financial performance.

(LO 6, 7, 8)

E2-8 **(Assumptions, Principles, and Constraints)** Presented below are a number of operational guidelines and practices that have developed over time.

Instructions

Select the assumption, principle, or constraint that most appropriately justifies these procedures and practices. (Do not use qualitative characteristics.)

(a) Market value changes are not recognized in the accounting records.
(b) Lower-of-cost-or-market is used to value inventories.
(c) Financial information is presented so that investors will not be misled.
(d) Intangible assets are capitalized and amortized over periods benefited.
(e) Repair tools are expensed when purchased.
(f) Agricultural companies use market value for purposes of valuing crops.
(g) Each enterprise is kept as a unit distinct from its owner or owners.
(h) All significant postbalance sheet events are reported.
(i) Revenue is recorded at point of sale.
(j) All important aspects of bond indentures are presented in financial statements.
(k) Rationale for accrual accounting.
(l) The use of consolidated statements is justified.
(m) Reporting must be done at defined time intervals.
(n) An allowance for doubtful accounts is established.
(o) All payments out of petty cash are charged to Miscellaneous Expense. (Do not use conservatism.)
(p) Goodwill is recorded only at time of purchase.
(q) No profits are anticipated and all possible losses are recognized.
(r) A company charges its sales commission costs to expense.

(LO 7)

E2-9 **(Full Disclosure Principle)** Presented below are a number of facts related to R. Kelly, Inc. Assume that the company did not mention these facts in the financial statements and the related notes.

Instructions

Assume that you are the auditor of R. Kelly, Inc. and that you have been asked to explain the appropriate accounting and related disclosure necessary for each of these items.

(a) The company decided that, for the sake of conciseness, it would report only net income on the income statement. Details as to revenues, cost of goods sold, and expenses were omitted.
(b) Equipment purchases of $170,000 were partly financed during the year through the issuance of a $110,000 note payable. The company offset the equipment against the note payable and reported plant assets at $60,000.
(c) R. Kelly has reported its ending inventory at $2,100,000 in the financial statements. No other information related to inventories is presented in the financial statements and related notes.

(LO 7)

E2-10 **(Accounting Principles—Comprehensive)** Presented below are a number of business transactions that occurred during the current year for Fresh Horses, Inc.

Instructions

In each of the situations, discuss the appropriateness of the journal entries in terms of generally accepted accounting principles.

(a) The president of Fresh Horses, Inc. used his expense account to purchase a new Suburban solely for personal use. The following journal entry was made.

Miscellaneous Expense	29,000	
Cash		29,000

(b) Merchandise inventory that cost $620,000 is reported on the balance sheet at $690,000, the expected selling price less estimated selling costs. The following entry was made to record this increase in value.

Merchandise Inventory	70,000	
Revenue		70,000

(c) The company is being sued for $500,000 by a customer who claims damages for personal injury apparently caused by a defective product. Company attorneys feel extremely confident that the company will have no liability for damages resulting from the situation. Nevertheless, the company decides to make the following entry.

Loss from Lawsuit	500,000	
Liability for Lawsuit		500,000

(d) Because the general level of prices increased during the current year, Fresh Horses, Inc. determined that there was a $16,000 understatement of depreciation expense on its equipment and decided to record it in its accounts. The following entry was made.

Depreciation Expense	16,000	
Accumulated Depreciation		16,000

(e) Fresh Horses, Inc. has been concerned about whether intangible assets could generate cash in case of liquidation. As a consequence, goodwill arising from a purchase transaction during the current year and recorded at $800,000 was written off as follows.

Retained Earnings	800,000	
Goodwill		800,000

(f) Because of a "fire sale," equipment obviously worth $200,000 was acquired at a cost of $155,000. The following entry was made.

Equipment	200,000	
Cash		155,000
Revenue		45,000

E2-11 (Accounting Principles—Comprehensive) Presented below is information related to Garth Brooks, Inc.　　　**(LO 7)**

Instructions

Comment on the appropriateness of the accounting procedures followed by Garth Brooks, Inc.

(a) Depreciation expense on the building for the year was $60,000. Because the building was increasing in value during the year, the controller decided to charge the depreciation expense to retained earnings instead of to net income. The following entry was recorded.

Retained Earnings	60,000	
Accumulated Depreciation – Buildings		60,000

(b) Materials were purchased on January 1, 2008, for $120,000 and this amount was entered in the Materials account. On December 31, 2008, the materials would have cost $141,000, so the following entry was made.

Inventory	21,000	
Gain on Inventories		21,000

(c) During the year, the company purchased equipment through the issuance of common stock. The stock had a par value of $135,000 and a fair market value of $450,000. The fair market value of the equipment was not easily determinable. The company recorded this transaction as follows.

Equipment	135,000	
Common Stock		135,000

(d) During the year, the company sold certain equipment for $285,000, recognizing a gain of $69,000. Because the controller believed that new equipment would be needed in the near future, she decided to defer the gain and amortize it over the life of any new equipment purchased.

(e) An order for $61,500 has been received from a customer for products on hand. This order was shipped on January 9, 2008. The company made the following entry in 2007.

Accounts Receivable	61,500	
Sales		61,500

See the book's companion website, at www.wiley.com/college/warfield, for Additional Exercises.

ACCOUNTING IN ACTION

P&G Financial Reporting and Analysis

■ Financial Reporting Issues: The Procter & Gamble Company

AIA2-1 The financial statements of **Procter & Gamble (P&G)** can be accessed at the book's website.

Instructions

Refer to P&G's financial statements and the accompanying notes to answer the following questions.

(a) Using the notes to the consolidated financial statements, determine P&G's revenue recognition policies. Discuss the impact of trade promotions on P&G's financial statements.

(b) Give two examples of where historical cost information is reported in P&G's financial statements and related notes. Give two examples of the use of fair value information reported in either the financial statements or related notes.

(c) How can we determine that the accounting principles used by P&G are prepared on a basis consistent with those of last year?

(d) What is P&G's accounting policy related to advertising? What accounting principle does P&G follow regarding accounting for advertising? Where are advertising expenses reported in the financial statements?

PEPSICO ■ Comparative Analysis: The Coca-Cola Company and PepsiCo, Inc.

AIA2-2 The financial statements of **The Coca-Cola Company** and **PepsiCo, Inc.** can be accessed at the book's website.

Instructions

Use information found at the book's website to answer the following questions.

(a) What are the primary lines of business of these two companies as shown in their notes to the financial statements?

(b) Which company has the dominant position in beverage sales?

(c) How are inventories for these two companies valued? What cost allocation method is used to report inventory? How does their accounting for inventories affect comparability between the two companies?

(d) Which company changed its accounting policies during 2006 which affected the consistency of the financial results from the previous year? What were these changes?

■ Financial Statement Analysis

AIA2-3 **Wal-Mart Stores** provided the following disclosure in a recent annual report.

> **Wal-Mart Stores**
>
> *New accounting pronouncement (partial)* . . . the Securities and Exchange Commission issued Staff Accounting Bulletin No. 101—"Revenue Recognition in Financial Statements" *(SAB 101)*. This SAB deals with various revenue recognition issues, several of which are common within the retail industry. As a result of the issuance of this SAB . . . the Company is currently evaluating the effects of the SAB on its method of recognizing revenues related to layaway sales and will make any accounting method changes necessary during the first quarter of [next year].

In response to *SAB 101*, Wal-Mart changed its revenue recognition policy for layaway transactions, in which Wal-Mart sets aside merchandise for customers who make partial payment. Before the change, Wal-Mart recognized all revenue on the sale at the time of the layaway. After the change, Wal-Mart does not recognize revenue until customers satisfy all payment obligations and take possession of the merchandise.

Instructions

(a) Discuss the expected effect on income (1) in the year that Wal-Mart makes the changes in its revenue recognition policy, and (2) in the years following the change.

(b) Evaluate the extent to which Wal-Mart's previous revenue policy was consistent with the revenue recognition principle.

(c) If all retailers had used a revenue recognition policy similar to Wal-Mart's before the change, are there any concerns with respect to the qualitative characteristic of comparability? Explain.

AIA2-4 Presented below is a statement that appeared about **Weyerhaeuser Company** in a financial magazine.

> The land and timber holdings are now carried on the company's books at a mere $422 million. The value of the timber alone is variously estimated at $3 billion to $7 billion and is rising all the time. "The understatement of the company is pretty severe," conceded Charles W. Bingham, a senior vice-president. Adds Robert L. Schuyler, another senior vice-president: "We have a whole stream of profit nobody sees and there is no way to show it on our books."

Instructions

(a) What does Schuyler mean when he says, "We have a whole stream of profit nobody sees but there is no way to show it on our books."

(b) If the understatement of the company's assets is severe, why does accounting not report this information?

■ International Reporting Issues

AIA2-5 As discussed in Chapter 1, the **International Accounting Standards Board (IASB)** develops accounting standards for many international companies. The IASB also has developed a conceptual framework to help guide the setting of accounting standards. Following is an overview of the IASB framework.

Objective of Financial Statements
>   To provide information about the financial position, performance, and changes in financial position of an enterprise that is useful to a wide range of users in making economic decisions.

Underlying Assumptions
>   Accrual basis   Going concern

Qualitative Characteristics of Financial Statements

Understandability	Reliability	Reliability (continued)
Relevance	Faithful representation	Prudence
Materiality	Substance over form	Completeness
	Neutrality	Comparability

Constraints on Relevant and Reliable Information
>   Timeliness
>   Balance between benefit and cost
>   Balance between qualitative characteristics

True and Fair Presentation

Elements of Financial Statements

Asset: A resource controlled by the enterprise as a result of past events and from which future economic benefits are expected to flow to the enterprise.

Liability: A present obligation of the enterprise arising from past events, the settlement of which is expected to result in an outflow from the enterprise of resources embodying economic benefits.

Equity: The residual interest in the assets of the enterprise after deducting all its liabilities.

Income: Increases in economic benefits during the accounting period in the form of inflows or enhancements of assets or decreases of liabilities that result in increases in equity, other than those relating to contributions from equity participants.

Expenses: Decreases in economic benefits during the accounting period in the form of outflows or depletions of assets or incurrences of liabilities that result in decreases in equity, other than those relating to distributions to equity participants.

Instructions

Identify at least three similarities and at least three differences between the FASB and IASB conceptual frameworks as revealed in the above overview.

Concepts for Analysis

AIA2-6 **(Conceptual Framework—General)** Roger Morgan has some questions regarding the theoretical framework in which standards are set. He knows that the FASB and other predecessor organizations have attempted to develop a conceptual framework for accounting theory formulation. Yet, Roger's supervisors have indicated that these theoretical frameworks have little value in the practical sense (i.e., in the real world). Roger did notice that accounting standards seem to be established after the fact rather than before. He thought this indicated a lack of theory structure but never really questioned the process at school because he was too busy doing the homework.

Roger feels that some of his anxiety about accounting theory and accounting semantics could be alleviated by identifying the basic concepts and definitions accepted by the profession and considering them in light of his current work. By doing this, he hopes to develop an appropriate connection between theory and practice.

Instructions

(a) Help Roger recognize the purpose of and benefit of a conceptual framework.

(b) Identify any *Statements of Financial Accounting Concepts* issued by FASB that may be helpful to Roger in developing his theoretical background.

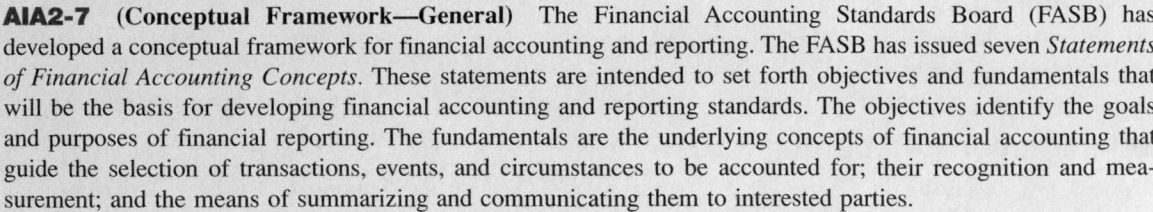

AIA2-7 (Conceptual Framework—General) The Financial Accounting Standards Board (FASB) has developed a conceptual framework for financial accounting and reporting. The FASB has issued seven *Statements of Financial Accounting Concepts*. These statements are intended to set forth objectives and fundamentals that will be the basis for developing financial accounting and reporting standards. The objectives identify the goals and purposes of financial reporting. The fundamentals are the underlying concepts of financial accounting that guide the selection of transactions, events, and circumstances to be accounted for; their recognition and measurement; and the means of summarizing and communicating them to interested parties.

The purpose of *Statement of Financial Accounting Concepts No. 2*, "Qualitative Characteristics of Accounting Information," is to examine the characteristics that make accounting information useful. The characteristics or qualities of information discussed in SFAC No. 2 are the ingredients that make information useful and the qualities to be sought when accounting choices are made.

Instructions

(a) Identify and discuss the benefits that can be expected to be derived from the FASB's conceptual framework study.

(b) What is the most important quality for accounting information as identified in *Statement of Financial Accounting Concepts No. 2*? Explain why it is the most important.

(c) *Statement of Financial Accounting Concepts No. 2* describes key characteristics or qualities for accounting information. Briefly discuss the importance of any three of these qualities for financial reporting purposes.

(CMA adapted)

AIA2-8 (Objectives of Financial Reporting) Regis Gordon and Kathy Medford are discussing various aspects of the FASB's pronouncement *Statement of Financial Accounting Concepts No. 1*, "Objectives of Financial Reporting by Business Enterprises." Regis indicates that this pronouncement provides little, if any, guidance to the practicing professional in resolving accounting controversies. He believes that the statement provides such broad guidelines that it would be impossible to apply the objectives to present-day reporting problems. Kathy concedes this point but indicates that objectives are still needed to provide a starting point for the FASB in helping to improve financial reporting.

Instructions

(a) Indicate the basic objectives established in *Statement of Financial Accounting Concepts No. 1*.

(b) What do you think is the meaning of Kathy's statement that the FASB needs a starting point to resolve accounting controversies?

AIA2-9 (Revenue Recognition and Matching Principle) After the presentation of your report on the examination of the financial statements to the board of directors of Bones Publishing Company, one of the new directors expresses surprise that the income statement assumes that an equal proportion of the revenue is earned with the publication of every issue of the company's magazine. She feels that the "crucial event" in the process of earning revenue in the magazine business is the cash sale of the subscription. She says that she does not understand why most of the revenue cannot be "recognized" in the period of the sale.

Instructions

(a) List the various accepted times for recognizing revenue and explain when the methods are appropriate.

(b) Discuss the propriety of timing the recognition of revenue in Bones Publishing Company's accounts with:

(1) The cash sale of the magazine subscription.

(2) The publication of the magazine every month.

(3) Both events, by recognizing a portion of the revenue with the cash sale of the magazine subscription and a portion of the revenue with the publication of the magazine every month.

AIA2-10 (Matching Principle) An accountant must be familiar with the concepts involved in determining earnings of a business entity. The amount of earnings reported for a business entity is dependent on the proper recognition, in general, of revenue and expense for a given time period. In some situations, costs are recognized as expenses at the time of product sale. In other situations, guidelines have been developed for recognizing costs as expenses or losses by other criteria.

Instructions

(a) Explain the rationale for recognizing costs as expenses at the time of product sale.

(b) What is the rationale underlying the appropriateness of treating costs as expenses of a period instead of assigning the costs to an asset? Explain.

(c) In what general circumstances would it be appropriate to treat a cost as an asset instead of as an expense? Explain.

(d) Some expenses are assigned to specific accounting periods on the basis of systematic and rational allocation of asset cost. Explain the underlying rationale for recognizing expenses on the basis of systematic and rational allocation of asset cost.

(e) Identify the conditions under which it would be appropriate to treat a cost as a loss.

(AICPA adapted)

AIA2-11 **(Matching Principle)** Accountants try to prepare income statements that are as accurate as possible. A basic requirement in preparing accurate income statements is to match costs against revenues properly. Proper matching of costs against revenues requires that costs resulting from typical business operations be recognized in the period in which they expired.

Instructions

(a) List three criteria that can be used to determine whether such costs should appear as charges in the income statement for the current period.

(b) As generally presented in financial statements, the following items or procedures have been criticized as improperly matching costs with revenues. Briefly discuss each item from the viewpoint of matching costs with revenues and suggest corrective or alternative means of presenting the financial information.

    (1) Receiving and handling costs.

    (2) Valuation of inventories at the lower of cost or market.

    (3) Cash discounts on purchases.

AIA2-12 **(Qualitative Characteristics)** Recently, your Uncle Waldo Ralph, who knows that you always have your eye out for a profitable investment, has discussed the possibility of your purchasing some corporate bonds. He suggests that you may wish to get in on the "ground floor" of this deal. The bonds being issued by Cricket Corp. are 10-year debentures which promise a 40% rate of return. Cricket manufactures novelty/party items.

    You have told Waldo that, unless you can take a look at Cricket's financial statements, you would not feel comfortable about such an investment. Believing that this is the chance of a lifetime, Uncle Waldo has procured a copy of Cricket's most recent, unaudited financial statements which are a year old. These statements were prepared by Mrs. John Cricket. You peruse these statements, and they are quite impressive. The balance sheet showed a debt-to-equity ratio of 0.10 and, for the year shown, the company reported net income of $2,424,240.

    The financial statements are not shown in comparison with amounts from other years. In addition, no significant note disclosures about inventory valuation, depreciation methods, loan agreements, etc. are available.

Instructions

Write a letter to Uncle Waldo explaining why it would be unwise to base an investment decision on the financial statements that he has provided. Explain why these financial statements are neither relevant nor reliable.

Professional Tools

■ Ethical Decision Making

AIA2-13 **(Matching)** Hinckley Nuclear Power Plant will be "mothballed" at the end of its useful life (approximately 20 years) at great expense. The matching principle requires that expenses be matched to revenue. Accountants Jana Kingston and Pete Henning argue whether it is better to allocate the expense of mothballing over the next 20 years or ignore it until mothballing occurs.

Instructions

Answer the following questions.

(a) What stakeholders should be considered?

(b) What ethical issue, if any, underlies the dispute?

(c) What alternatives should be considered?

(d) Assess the consequences of the alternatives.

(e) What decision would you recommend?

■ Financial Accounting and Research (FARS)

AIA2-14 Your aunt recently received the annual report for a company in which she has invested. The report notes that the statements have been prepared in accordance with "generally accepted accounting principles." She has also heard that certain terms have special meanings in accounting relative to everyday use. She would like you to explain the meaning of terms she has come across related to accounting.

Instructions

Using the **Financial Accounting Research System (FARS)** database, respond to the following items. (Provide text strings used in your search.)

(a) How is "materiality" defined in the conceptual framework?

(b) The concepts statements provide several examples in which specific quantitative materiality guidelines are provided to firms. Identity at least two of these examples. Do you think the materiality guidelines should be quantified? Why or why not?

(c) The concepts statements discuss the concept of "articulation" between financial statement elements. Briefly summarize the meaning of this term and how it relates to an entity's financial statements.

■ Professional Simulation

AIA2-15 Go to the book's website, at **www.wiley.com/college/warfield**, to find an interactive problem that simulates the computerized CPA exam. The professional simulation for this chapter asks you to address questions related to the conceptual framework.

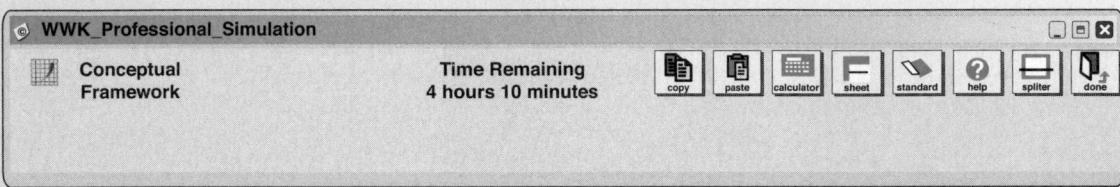

WWK_Professional_Simulation		
Conceptual Framework	Time Remaining 4 hours 10 minutes	copy paste calculator sheet standard help spliter done

---

What do the numbers mean?

Guideline Answers to Beyond the Numbers Questions

What's Your Principle?, p. 36

Q: Some are concerned that principle-based rules will permit management too much discretion in applying accounting standards. What are the potential consequences for individual companies and markets as a whole of increased management judgment inherent in principle-based rules?

A: If managers use the additional discretion in principle-based rules in order to report company performance in a more favorable light, such reporting will not meet the objectives of financial reporting. Such reporting will be biased or will lack neutrality. If investors and creditors suspect biased reporting, they will discount the prices of companies whose managers exploit the discretion in principle-based rules. This could affect the overall market and even companies with managers who do not abuse the discretion, if the market is unable to distinguish between good and bad discretion.

You May Need a Map, p. 42

Q: Can you think of possible motivations that companies might have to use pro-forma reporting to present their companies in a more favorable light?

A: Because reported earnings can affect stock prices, by reporting more favorable earnings, companies can keep their stock price up. If they hold stock options or have other forms of compensation based on stock price, managers might benefit from higher stock prices. In addition, to the extent that the markets view companies with high stock prices more favorably, companies will be able to raise capital at lower cost—at least in the short term, until the market finds out that the reported earnings were inflated through pro-forma reporting.

Guideline Answers, continued

Whose Company Is It?, p. 45

Q: What element of reliability is negatively affected when companies violate the entity assumption, as in the cases of Adelphia and W.R. Grace?

A: When non-entity transactions (e.g., paying for the chairman's chef, loans to management) are reflected in the company's financial statements, then the financial statements are not *representationally faithful*. That is, the financial statements of Adelphia should reflect only transactions affecting the company and not those affecting management personally.

Q: How are shareholders affected when managers engage in illegal self-dealing that results in violation of the entity assumption?

A: Because the illegal actions at Adelphia and W.R. Grace negatively impact the reliability of these companies' financial reports, the market will question the credibility of the reports. Consequently, these companies' share prices will bear an information-risk discount, which will reduce the amount shareholders receive when they sell their shares.

No Take-Backs!, p. 49

Q: Lucent could have avoided its accounting problems simply by not allowing customers to return goods once they are sold. Would this be a good idea? Explain.

A: Granting return privileges to customers is likely an expected custom in this industry. It would not be a good idea for Lucent to drop its returns policy, lest it lose customers' business altogether. Note that the accounting rules do not say you cannot allow returns—only that the accounting for the returns contribute to a faithful reporting of the actual sales results.

Q: Lucent could facilitate sales by granting generous credit terms to its customers. If these customers do not pay, how

does the accounting for these credit sales ensure that income is not overstated?

A: Selling goods on credit raises concerns about the realizability revenue-recognition criterion. That is, will Lucent get paid and have an inflow or other enhancement of assets as a result of the sale? Similar to the accounting for returns, if companies can reliably estimate bad debts related to credit sales (and record bad debt expense in the period of the sale), it is acceptable to record revenue from credit sales.

Hollywood Accounting, p. 50

Q: Some sports franchises attempt to portray franchise results more conservatively by recording as many expenses as possible. Such conservative accounting can give these businesses an advantage in negotiations with players or in securing concessions from local communities for stadiums and other services. Is conservative reporting by sports franchises a good thing or a bad thing with respect to accounting concepts? Explain.

A: Such reporting violates the neutrality element of reliability. By recording as many expenses as possible, the franchise owners can report lower (conservative) earnings. However, such reporting is biased (in this case, downward or conservatively) in favor of one party (the owners) relative to others (the players and/or local communities.)

Living in a Material World, p. 55

Q: What would you advise Engone management in order for its reporting to be in compliance with GAAP materiality concepts?

A: Advise Engone Management against such "meeting and beating" reporting, even if the extent of the earnings management is a small amount. As indicated in the chapter, companies must consider other factors besides the magnitude of the accounting adjustment when assessing materiality. Although the amount of the change in the bad debt adjustment is small, it permits Engone to meet

analysts' consensus earnings numbers. This is considered material because the company would bear significant negative consequences in the absence of the earnings management. That is, advise management to consider both quantitative and qualitative factors in determining whether an item is material. If management believes that there are valid reasons to reduce the bad debt provision, they will want to consider expanded disclosure to explain this accounting judgment, like that provided by General Electric and IBM.

Remember to check the book's companion website to find additional resources for this chapter.

CHAPTER 3

THE ACCOUNTING INFORMATION SYSTEM

Needed: A Reliable Information System

Maintaining a set of accounting records is not optional. The **Internal Revenue Service (IRS)** requires that businesses prepare and retain a set of records and documents that can be audited. The Foreign Corrupt Practices Act (federal legislation) requires public companies to ". . . make and keep books, records, and accounts, which, in reasonable detail, accurately and fairly reflect the transactions and dispositions of the assets. . . ." But beyond these two reasons, a company that fails to keep an accurate record of its business transactions may lose revenue and is more likely to operate inefficiently.

Consider, for example, the **Long Island Railroad (LIRR)**, once one of the nation's busiest commuter lines. The LIRR lost money because of poor recordkeeping. It forgot to bill some customers, mistakenly paid some payables twice, and neglected to record redemptions of bonds. **FFP Marketing**, which operates convenience stores in 11 states, provides another example. The SEC forced it to restate earnings when an audit uncovered faulty bookkeeping for its credit card accounts and fuel payables.

Inefficient accounting also cost the **City of Cleveland**, Ohio. An audit discovered over 313 examples of dysfunctional accounting, costing taxpayers over $1.3 million. Its poor accounting system resulted in the Cleveland treasurer's ignorance of available cash, which led to missed investment opportunities. Further, delayed recording of pension payments created the false impression of $13 million in the city coffers.

Even the use of computers is no assurance of accuracy and efficiency. "The conversion to a new system called MasterNet fouled up data processing records to the extent that **Bank of America** was frequently unable to produce or deliver customer statements on a timely basis," said an executive at one of the country's largest banks.

Although these situations may occur only rarely in large organizations, they illustrate the point: Companies must properly maintain accounts and detailed records or face unnecessary costs. The SEC suspended trading in FFP Marketing's stock until it corrected the errors and re-issued financial statements. The City of Cleveland's municipal bond rating took a hit because of its poor accounting practices.

Preview of Chapter 3

As the opening story indicates, a reliable information system is a necessity for all companies. The purpose of this chapter is to explain and illustrate the features of an accounting information system. *The content and organization of this chapter are as follows.*

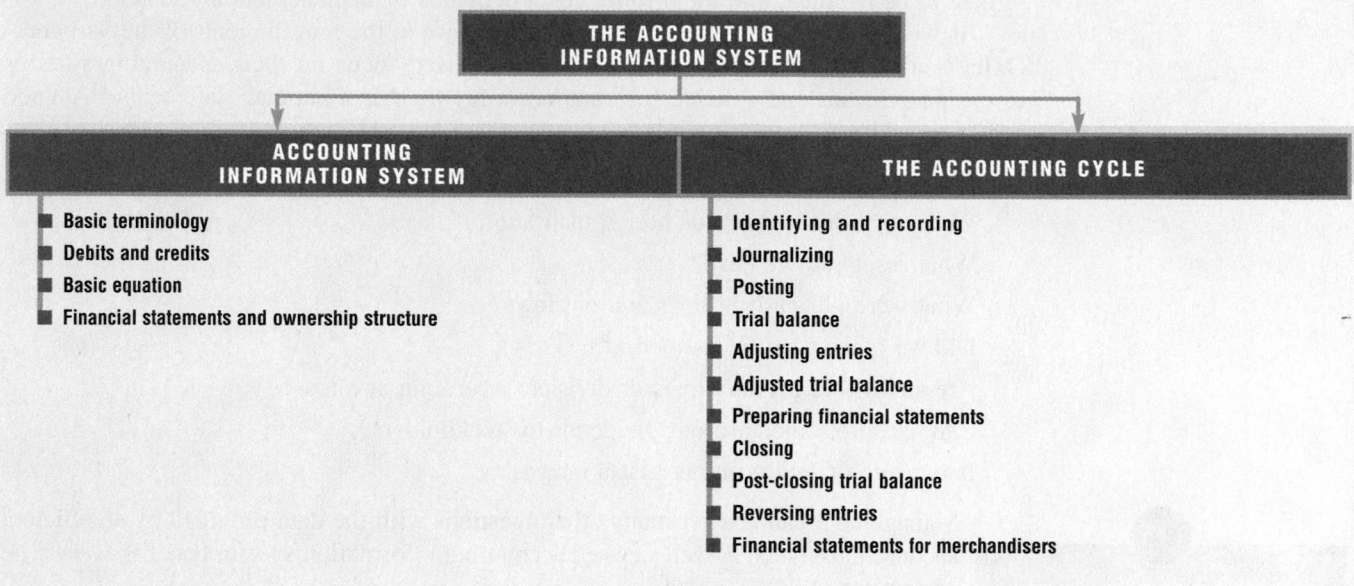

THE ACCOUNTING INFORMATION SYSTEM

ACCOUNTING INFORMATION SYSTEM
- Basic terminology
- Debits and credits
- Basic equation
- Financial statements and ownership structure

THE ACCOUNTING CYCLE
- Identifying and recording
- Journalizing
- Posting
- Trial balance
- Adjusting entries
- Adjusted trial balance
- Preparing financial statements
- Closing
- Post-closing trial balance
- Reversing entries
- Financial statements for merchandisers

Learning Objectives

After studying this chapter, you should be able to:

1. Understand basic accounting terminology.
2. Explain double-entry rules.
3. Identify steps in the accounting cycle.
4. Record transactions in journals, post to ledger accounts, and prepare a trial balance.
5. Explain the reasons for preparing adjusting entries.
6. Prepare financial statements from the adjusted trial balance.
7. Prepare closing entries.
8. Explain how to adjust inventory accounts at year-end.

Inside Chapter 3

- **What Do the Numbers Mean?**
  Am I covered? (p. 100)
  24/7 accounting (p. 104)
  Statements, please (p. 107)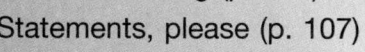
- **What's the Principle?** (pp. 78, 84, 84, 91)
- **Accounting, Analysis, Principles** (p. 111)
  Prepare adjusting entries.
  Compare usefulness of income before and after adjusting entries.
  Assess impact of timeliness on reliability.
- **Convergence Corner** (p. 113)

ACCOUNTING INFORMATION SYSTEM

An **accounting information system** collects and processes transaction data and then disseminates the financial information to interested parties. Accounting information systems vary widely from one business to another. Various factors shape these systems: the nature of the business and the transactions in which it engages, the size of the firm, the volume of data to be handled, and the informational demands of management and others.

As we discussed in Chapters 1 and 2, in response to the requirements of the Sarbanes-Oxley Act of 2002, companies are placing a renewed focus on their accounting systems to ensure relevant and reliable information is reported in financial statements.[1] A good accounting information system helps management answer such questions as:

How much and what kind of debt is outstanding?

Were our sales higher this period than last?

What assets do we have?

What were our cash inflows and outflows?

Did we make a profit last period?

Are any of our product lines or divisions operating at a loss?

Can we safely increase our dividends to stockholders?

Is our rate of return on net assets increasing?

Management can answer many other questions with the data provided by an efficient accounting system. A well-devised accounting information system benefits every type of company.

WHAT'S THE PRINCIPLE?

A good information system provides information that is useful both to internal decision-makers (managers) and to external decision-makers (investors and creditors).

Basic Terminology

Financial accounting rests on a set of concepts (discussed in Chapters 1 and 2) for identifying, recording, classifying, and interpreting transactions and other events relating to enterprises. You therefore need to understand the **basic terminology employed in collecting accounting data**.

OBJECTIVE 1
Understand basic accounting terminology.

BASIC TERMINOLOGY

EVENT. A happening of consequence. An event generally is the source or cause of changes in assets, liabilities, and equity. Events may be external or internal.

TRANSACTION. An **external event** involving a transfer or exchange between two or more entities.

ACCOUNT. A systematic arrangement that shows the effect of transactions and other events on a specific element (asset, liability, and so on). Companies keep a separate account for each asset, liability, revenue, and expense, and for capital (owners' equity).

REAL AND NOMINAL ACCOUNTS. **Real** (permanent) **accounts** are asset, liability, and equity accounts; they appear on the balance sheet. **Nominal** (temporary) **accounts** are revenue, expense, and dividend accounts; except for dividends, they appear on the income statement. Companies periodically close nominal accounts; they do not close real accounts.

[1]One study of first compliance with the internal-control testing provisions of the Sarbanes-Oxley Act documented material weaknesses for about 13 percent of companies reporting in 2004 and 2005. L. Townsend, "Internal Control Deficiency Disclosures–Interim Alert," *Yellow Card–Interim Trend Alert* (April 12, 2005) Glass, Lewis & Co., LLC.

LEDGER. The book (or computer printouts) containing the accounts. A **general ledger** is a collection of all the asset, liability, owners' equity, revenue, and expense accounts. A **subsidiary ledger** contains the details related to a given general ledger account.

JOURNAL. The "book of original entry" where the company initially records transactions and selected other events. Various amounts are transferred from the book of original entry, the journal, to the ledger.

POSTING. The process of transferring the essential facts and figures from the book of original entry to the ledger accounts.

TRIAL BALANCE. The list of all open accounts in the ledger and their balances. The trial balance taken immediately after all adjustments have been posted is called an **adjusted trial balance**. A trial balance taken immediately after closing entries have been posted is called a **post-closing or after-closing trial balance**. Companies may prepare a trial balance at any time.

ADJUSTING ENTRIES. Entries made at the end of an accounting period to bring all accounts up to date on an accrual basis, so that the company can prepare correct financial statements.

FINANCIAL STATEMENTS. Statements that reflect the collection, tabulation, and final summarization of the accounting data. Four statements are involved: (1) The **balance sheet** shows the financial condition of the enterprise at the end of a period. (2) The **income statement** measures the results of operations during the period. (3) The **statement of cash flows** reports the cash provided and used by operating, investing, and financing activities during the period. (4) The **statement of retained earnings** reconciles the balance of the retained earnings account from the beginning to the end of the period.

CLOSING ENTRIES. The formal process by which the enterprise reduces all nominal accounts to zero and determines and transfers the net income or net loss to an owners' equity account. Also known as "closing the ledger," "closing the books," or merely "closing."

Debits and Credits

The terms **debit** (Dr.) and **credit** (Cr.) mean left and right, respectively. These terms do not mean increase or decrease, but instead describe *where* a company makes entries in the recording process. That is, when a company enters an amount on the left side of an account, it **debits** the account. When it makes an entry on the right side, it **credits** the account. When comparing the totals of the two sides, an account shows a **debit balance** if the total of the debit amounts exceeds the credits. An account shows a **credit balance** if the credit amounts exceed the debits.

The positioning of debits on the left and credits on the right is simply an accounting custom. We could function just as well if we reversed the sides. However, the United States adopted the custom, now the rule, of having debits on the left side of an account and credits on the right side, similar to the custom of driving on the right-hand side of the road. This rule applies to all accounts.

The equality of debits and credits provides the basis for the double-entry system of recording transactions (sometimes referred to as double-entry bookkeeping). Under the universally used **double-entry accounting** system, a company records the dual (two-sided) effect of each transaction in appropriate accounts. This system provides a logical method for recording transactions. It also offers a means of proving the accuracy of the recorded amounts. If a company records every transaction with equal debits and credits, then the sum of all the debits to the accounts must equal the sum of all the credits.

OBJECTIVE 2
Explain double-entry rules.

Illustration 3-1 presents the basic guidelines for an accounting system. Increases to all asset and expense accounts occur on the left (or debit side) and decreases on the right (or credit side). Conversely, increases to all liability and revenue accounts occur on the right (or credit side) and decreases on the left (or debit side). A company increases stockholders' (owners') equity accounts, such as Common Stock and Retained Earnings, on the credit side, but increases Dividends on the debit side.

Illustration 3-1
Double-entry (Debit and Credit) Accounting System

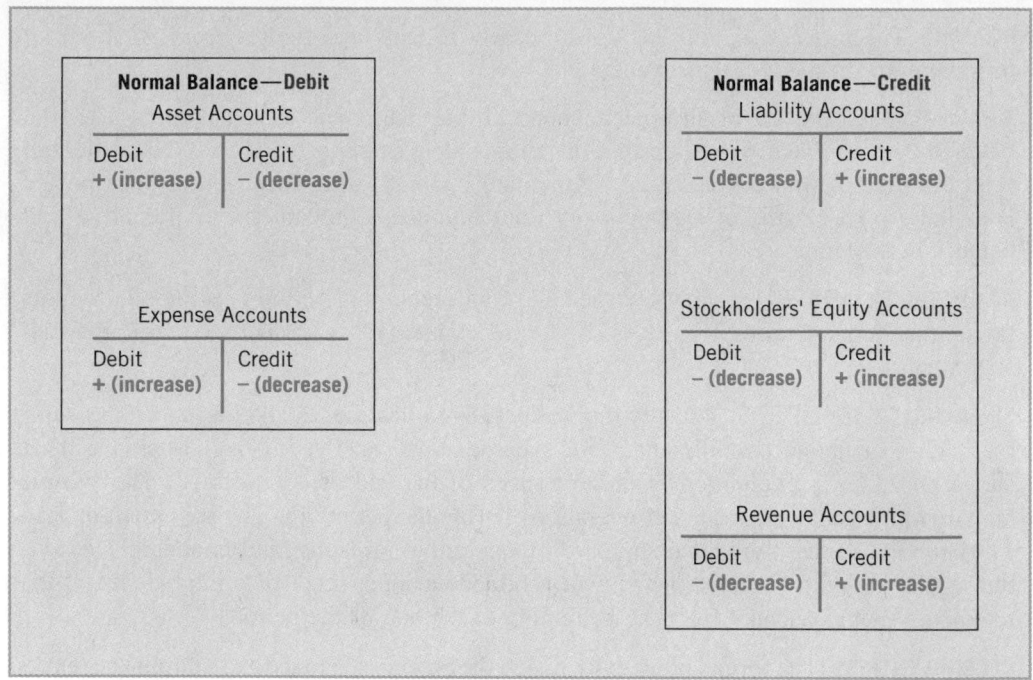

Basic Equation

In a double-entry system, for every debit there must be a credit, and vice versa. This leads us, then, to the basic equation in accounting (Illustration 3-2).

Illustration 3-2
The Basic Accounting Equation

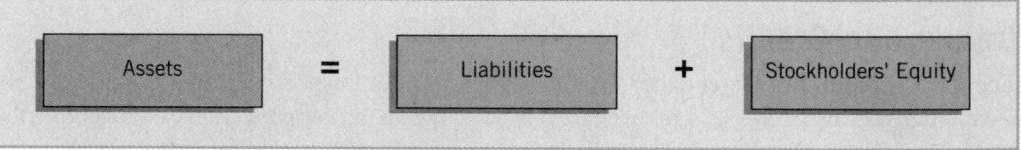

Illustration 3-3 expands this equation to show the accounts that make up stockholders' equity. The figure also shows the debit/credit rules and effects on each type of account. Study this diagram carefully. It will help you understand the fundamentals of the double-entry system. Like the basic equation, the expanded basic equation must also balance (total debits equal total credits).

Illustration 3-3
Expanded Basic Equation and Debit/Credit Rules and Effects

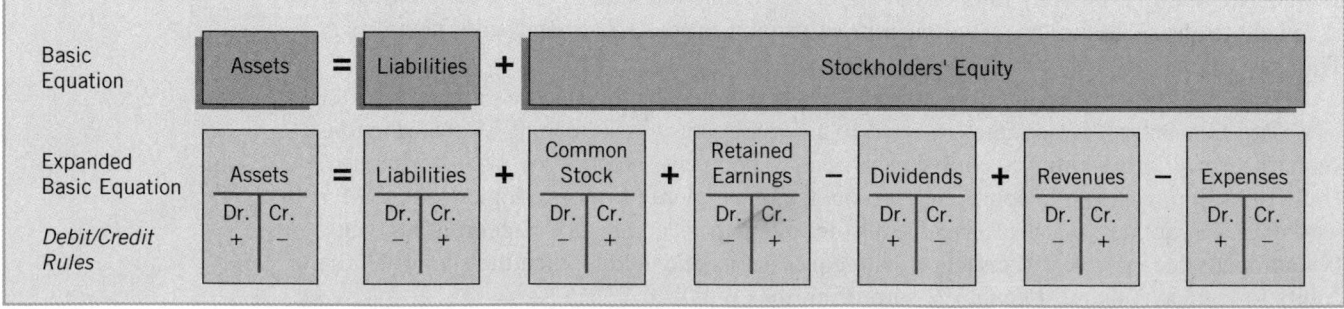

Every time a transaction occurs, the elements of the equation change. However, the basic equality remains. To illustrate, consider the following eight different transactions for Perez Inc.

1 Owners invest $40,000 in exchange for common stock.

Assets + 40,000	=	Liabilities	+	Stockholders' Equity + 40,000

2 Disburse $600 cash for secretarial wages.

Assets − 600	=	Liabilities	+	Stockholders' Equity − 600 (expense)

3 Purchase office equipment priced at $5,200, giving a 10 percent promissory note in exchange.

Assets + 5,200	=	Liabilities +5,200	+	Stockholders' Equity

4 Receive $4,000 cash for services rendered.

Assets + 4,000	=	Liabilities	+	Stockholders' Equity + 4,000 (revenue)

5 Pay off a short-term liability of $7,000.

Assets − 7,000	=	Liabilities − 7,000	+	Stockholders' Equity

6 Declare a cash dividend of $5,000.

Assets	=	Liabilities + 5,000	+	Stockholders' Equity − 5,000

7 Convert a long-term liability of $80,000 into common stock.

Assets	=	Liabilities − 80,000	+	Stockholders' Equity + 80,000

8 Pay cash of $16,000 for a delivery van.

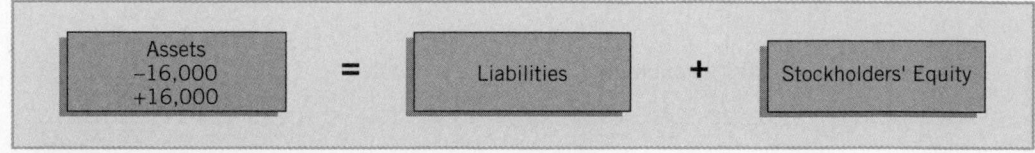

Financial Statements and Ownership Structure

The stockholders' equity section of the balance sheet reports common stock and retained earnings. The income statement reports revenues and expenses. The statement of retained earnings (often referred to as the retained earnings statement) reports dividends. Because a company transfers dividends, revenues, and expenses to retained earnings at the end of the period, a change in any one of these three items affects stockholders' equity. Illustration 3-4 shows the stockholders' equity relationships.

Illustration 3-4
Financial Statements and
Ownership Structure

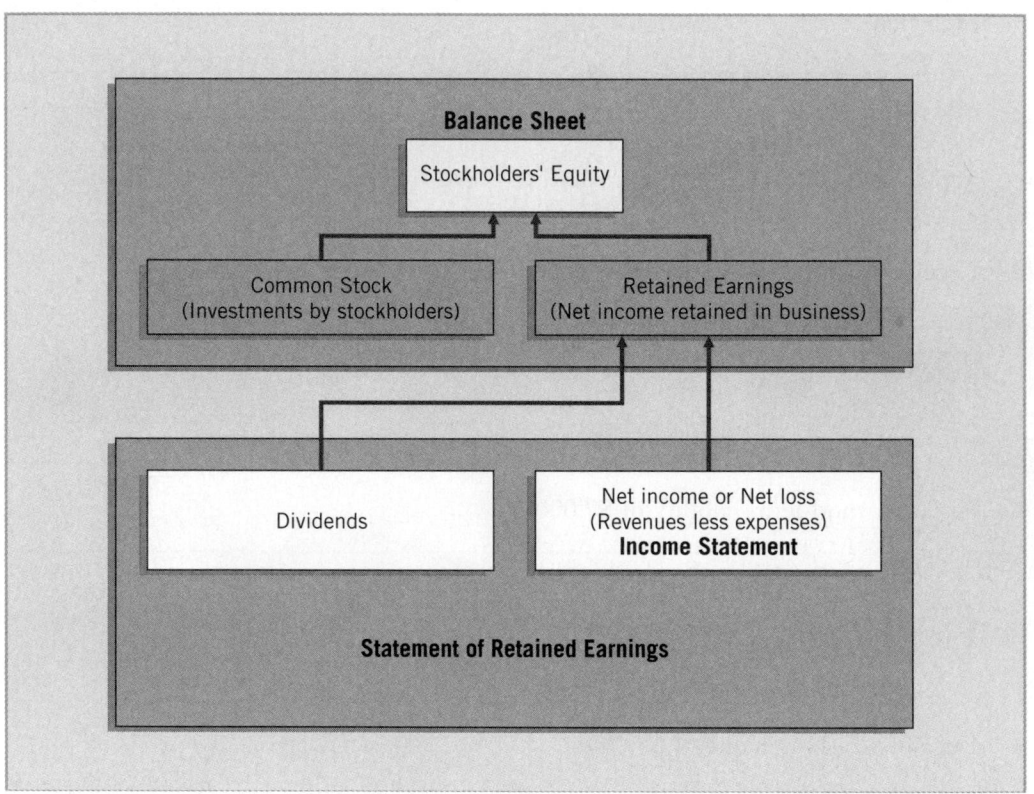

The enterprise's ownership structure dictates the types of accounts that are part of or affect the equity section. A corporation commonly uses Common Stock, Additional Paid-in Capital, Dividends, and Retained Earnings accounts. A proprietorship or a partnership uses a Capital account and a Drawing account: A Capital account indicates the owner's or owners' investment in the company. A Drawing account tracks withdrawals by the owner(s).

Illustration 3-5 summarizes and relates the transactions affecting owners' equity to the nominal (temporary) and real (permanent) classifications and to the types of business ownership.

Illustration 3-5
Effects of Transactions on
Owners' Equity Accounts

Transactions Affecting Owners' Equity	Impact on Owners' Equity	Ownership Structure			
		Proprietorships and Partnerships		Corporations	
		Nominal (Temporary) Accounts	Real (Permanent) Accounts	Nominal (Temporary) Accounts	Real (Permanent) Accounts
Investment by owner(s)	Increase		Capital		Common Stock and related accounts
Revenues earned	Increase	Revenue ⎫		Revenue ⎫	
Expenses incurred	Decrease	Expense ⎬ Capital		Expense ⎬ Retained	
Withdrawal by owner(s)	Decrease	Drawing ⎭		Dividends ⎭ Earnings	

THE ACCOUNTING CYCLE

Illustration 3-6 shows the steps in the **accounting cycle**. An enterprise normally uses these accounting procedures to record transactions and prepare financial statements.

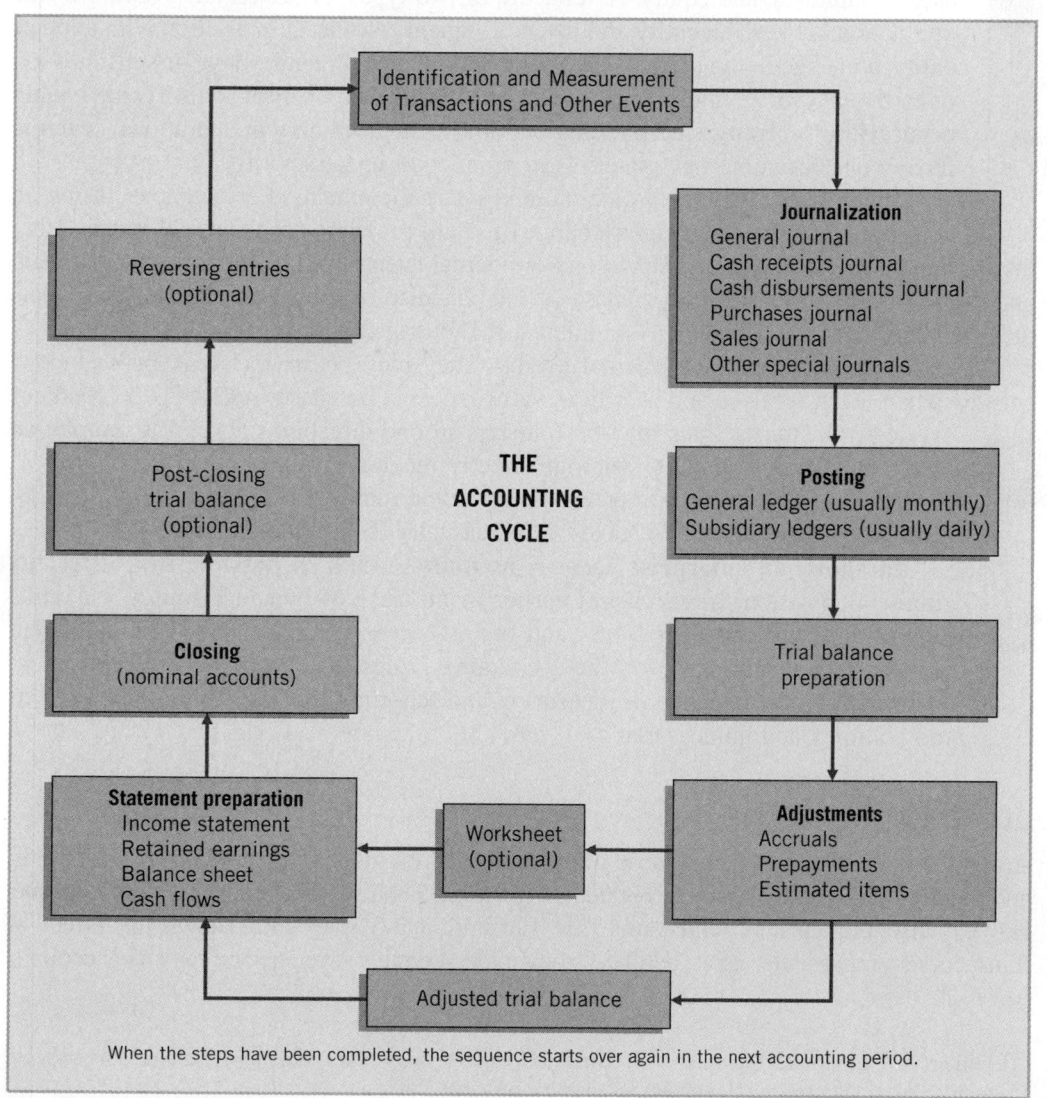

Illustration 3-6
The Accounting Cycle

OBJECTIVE 3
Identify steps in the accounting cycle.

Accounting Cycle Tutorial

Identifying and Recording Transactions and Other Events

The first step in the accounting cycle is analysis of transactions and selected other events. The first problem is to determine what to record. Although GAAP provides guidelines, no simple rules exist that state which events a company should record. Although changes in a company's personnel or managerial policies may be important, the company should not record these items in the accounts. On the other hand, a company should record all cash sales or purchases—no matter how small.

The concepts we presented in Chapter 2 determine what to recognize in the accounts. An item should be recognized in the financial statements if it is an element, is measurable, and is relevant and reliable. Consider human resources. **R. G. Barry & Co.** at one time reported as supplemental data total assets of $14,055,926, including $986,094 for "Net investments in human resources." **AT&T** and **ExxonMobil Company** also experimented with human resource accounting. Should we value employees for balance sheet and income statement purposes? Certainly skilled employees are an important asset (highly relevant), but the problems of determining their value and measuring it reliably have not yet been solved. Consequently, human resources are not recorded. Perhaps when measurement techniques become more sophisticated and accepted, such information will be presented, if only in supplemental form.

WHAT'S THE PRINCIPLE?

Assets are probable economic benefits controlled by a particular entity as a result of a past transaction or event. Do human resources of a company meet this definition?

The FASB uses the phrase "transactions and other events and circumstances that affect a business enterprise" to describe the sources or causes of changes in an entity's assets, liabilities, and equity.[2] Events are of two types: (1) **External events** involve interaction between an entity and its environment, such as a transaction with another entity, a change in the price of a good or service that an entity buys or sells, a flood or earthquake, or an improvement in technology by a competitor. (2) **Internal events** occur within an entity, such as using buildings and machinery in operations, or transferring or consuming raw materials in production processes.

Many events have both external and internal elements. For example, hiring an employee, which involves an exchange of salary for labor, is an external event. Using the services of labor is part of production, an internal event. Further, an entity may initiate and control events, such as the purchase of merchandise or use of a machine. Or, events may be beyond its control, such as an interest rate change, theft, or a tax hike.

WHAT'S THE PRINCIPLE?

In many cases, the decision on whether to recognize an item in the financial statements comes down to a trade-off between the qualitative characteristics of relevance and reliability.

Transactions are types of external events. They may be an exchange between two entities where each receives and sacrifices value, such as purchases and sales of goods or services. Or, transactions may be transfers in one direction only. For example, an entity may incur a liability without directly receiving value in exchange, such as charitable contributions. Other examples include investments by owners, distributions to owners, payment of taxes, gifts, casualty losses, and thefts.

In short, an enterprise records as many events as possible that affect its financial position. As discussed earlier in the case of human resources, it omits some events because of tradition and others because of complicated measurement problems. Recently, however, the accounting profession shows more receptiveness to accepting the challenge of measuring and reporting events previously viewed as too complex and immeasurable.

Journalizing

OBJECTIVE 4
Record transactions in journals, post to ledger accounts, and prepare a trial balance.

A company records in **accounts** those transactions and events that affect its assets, liabilities, and equities. The **general ledger** contains all the asset, liability, stockholders' equity, revenue, and expense accounts. A **T-account** (see Illustration 3-3, page 80) shows the effect of transactions on particular asset, liability, stockholders' equity, revenue, and expense accounts.

[2]"Elements of Financial Statements of Business Enterprises," *Statement of Financial Accounting Concepts No. 6* (Stamford, Conn.: FASB, 1985), pp. 259–260.

In practice, companies do not record transactions and selected other events originally in the ledger. A transaction affects two or more accounts, each of which is on a different page in the ledger. Therefore, in order to have a complete record of each transaction or other event in one place, a company uses a **journal** (also called "the book of original entry"). In its simplest form, a **general journal** chronologically lists transactions and other events, expressed in terms of debits and credits to accounts.

Illustration 3-7 depicts the technique of journalizing, using the first two transactions for Softbyte Inc. These transactions were:

September 1   Stockholders invested $15,000 cash in the corporation in exchange for shares of stock.

Purchased computer equipment for $7,000 cash.

The J1 indicates these two entries are on the first page of the general journal.

General Journal				J1
Date	Account Titles and Explanation	Ref.	Debit	Credit
2008				
Sept. 1	Cash		15,000	
	Common Stock			15,000
	(Issued shares of stock for cash)			
1	Computer Equipment		7,000	
	Cash			7,000
	(Purchased equipment for cash)			

Illustration 3-7
Technique of Journalizing

Each **general journal entry** consists of four parts: (1) the accounts and amounts to be debited (Dr.), (2) the accounts and amounts to be credited (Cr.), (3) a date, and (4) an explanation. A company enters debits first, followed by the credits (slightly indented). The explanation begins below the name of the last account to be credited and may take one or more lines. A company completes the "Ref." column at the time it posts the accounts.

In some cases, a company uses **special journals** in addition to the general journal. Special journals summarize transactions possessing a common characteristic (e.g., cash receipts, sales, purchases, cash payments). As a result, using them reduces bookkeeping time.

Expanded Discussion of Special Journals

Posting

The procedure of transferring journal entries to the ledger accounts is called **posting**. Posting involves the following steps.

1 In the ledger, enter in the appropriate columns of the debited account(s) the date, journal page, and debit amount shown in the journal.

2 In the reference column of the journal, write the account number to which the debit amount was posted.

3 In the ledger, enter in the appropriate columns of the credited account(s) the date, journal page, and credit amount shown in the journal.

4 In the reference column of the journal, write the account number to which the credit amount was posted.

Illustration 3-8 (page 86) diagrams these four steps, using the first journal entry of Softbyte Inc. The illustration shows the general ledger accounts in **standard account form**. Some companies call this form the **three-column form of account** because it has three money columns—debit, credit, and balance. The balance in the account is determined after each transaction. The explanation space and reference columns provide special information about the transaction. The boxed numbers indicate the sequence of the steps.

Illustration 3-8
Posting a Journal Entry

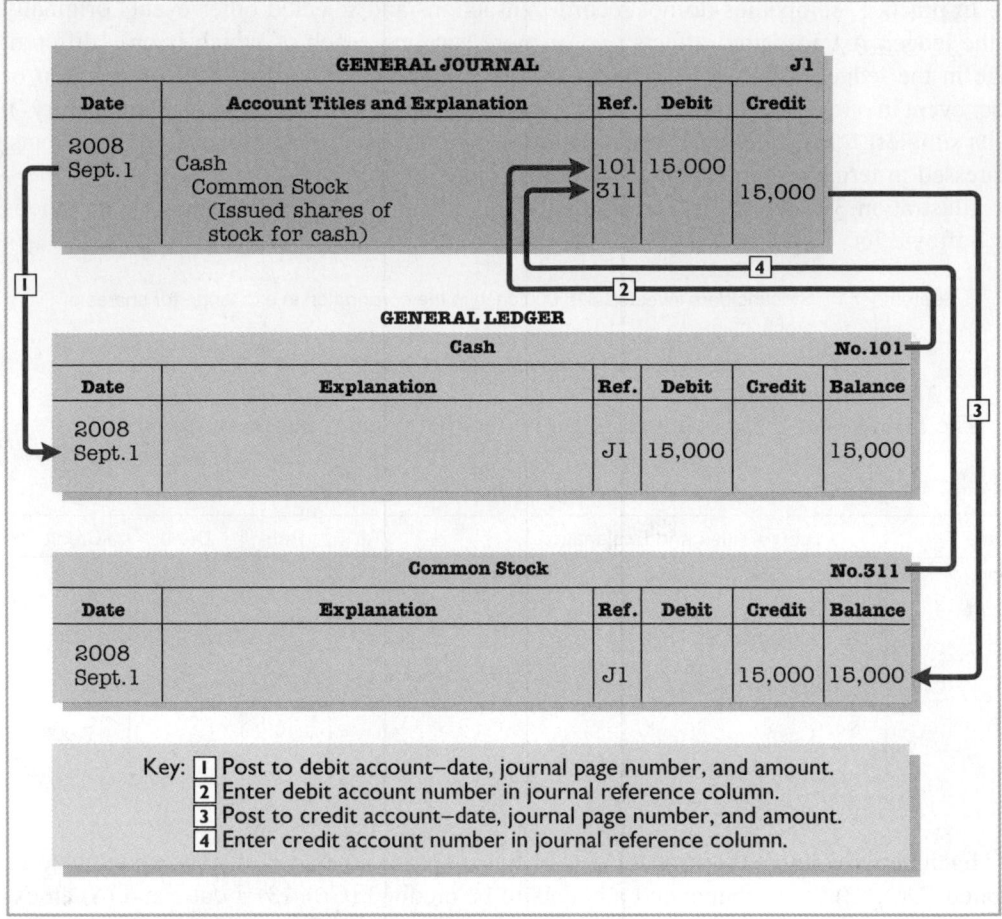

Key: ☐1 Post to debit account—date, journal page number, and amount.
☐2 Enter debit account number in journal reference column.
☐3 Post to credit account—date, journal page number, and amount.
☐4 Enter credit account number in journal reference column.

The numbers in the "Ref." column of the general journal refer to the ledger accounts to which a company posts the respective items. For example, the "101" placed in the column to the right of "Cash" indicates that the company posted this $15,000 item to Account No. 101 in the ledger.

The posting of the general journal is completed when a company records all of the posting reference numbers opposite the account titles in the journal. Thus the number in the posting reference column serves two purposes: (1) It indicates the ledger account number of the account involved. (2) It indicates the completion of posting for the particular item. Each company selects its own numbering system for its ledger accounts. Many begin numbering with asset accounts and then follow with liabilities, stockholders' equity, revenue, and expense accounts, in that order.

The ledger accounts in Illustration 3-8 show the accounts after completion of the posting process. The reference J1 (General Journal, page 1) indicates the source of the data transferred to the ledger account.

Expanded Example. To show an expanded example of the basic steps in the recording process, we use the October transactions of Pioneer Advertising Agency Inc. Pioneer's accounting period is a month. Illustrations 3-9 through 3-18 show the journal entry and posting of each transaction. For simplicity, we use a T-account form instead of the standard account form. Study the transaction analyses carefully.

The purpose of transaction analysis is (1) to identify the type of account involved, and (2) to determine whether a debit or a credit is required. You should always perform this type of analysis before preparing a journal entry. Doing so will help you understand the journal entries discussed in this chapter as well as more complex journal entries in later chapters. Keep in mind that every journal entry affects one or more of the following items: assets, liabilities, stockholders' equity, revenues, or expenses.

1 October 1: Stockholders invest $100,000 cash in an advertising venture to be known as Pioneer Advertising Agency Inc.

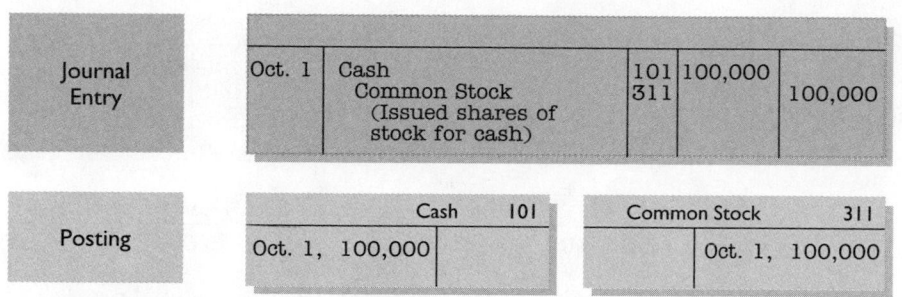

Illustration 3-9
Investment of Cash by Stockholders

2 October 1: Pioneer Advertising purchases office equipment costing $50,000 by signing a 3-month, 12%, $50,000 note payable.

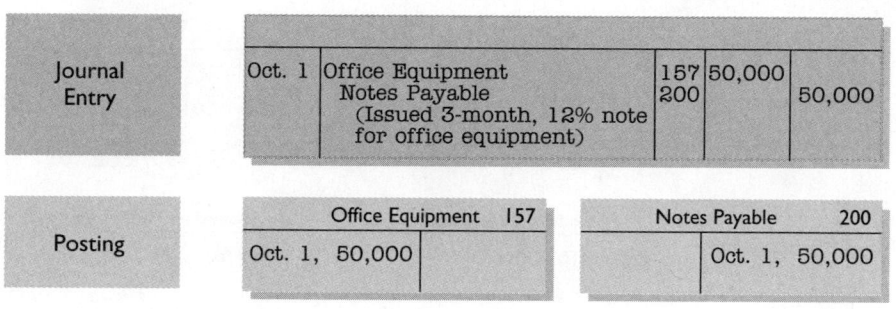

Illustration 3-10
Purchase of Office Equipment

3 October 2: Pioneer Advertising receives a $12,000 cash advance from R. Knox, a client, for advertising services that are expected to be completed by December 31.

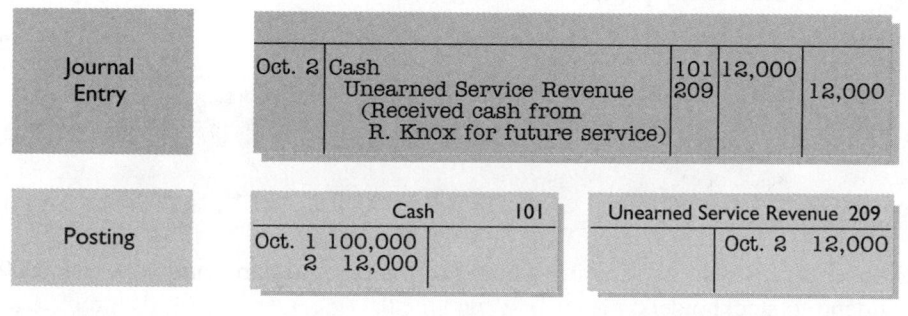

Illustration 3-11
Receipt of Cash for Future Service

4 October 3: Pioneer Advertising pays $9,000 office rent, in cash, for October.

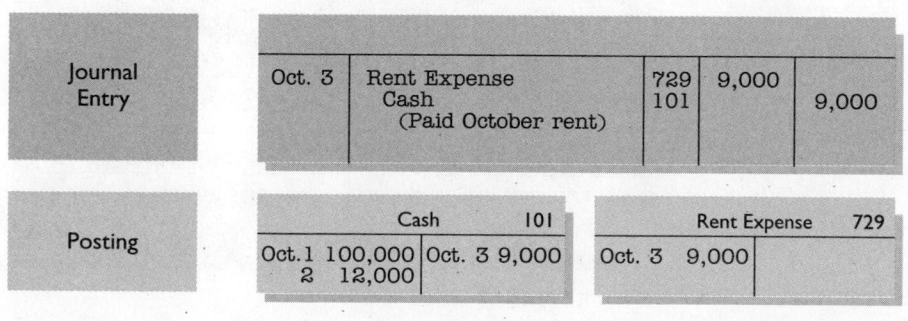

Illustration 3-12
Payment of Monthly Rent

5 October 4: Pioneer Advertising pays $6,000 for a one-year insurance policy that will expire next year on September 30.

Illustration 3-13
Payment for Insurance

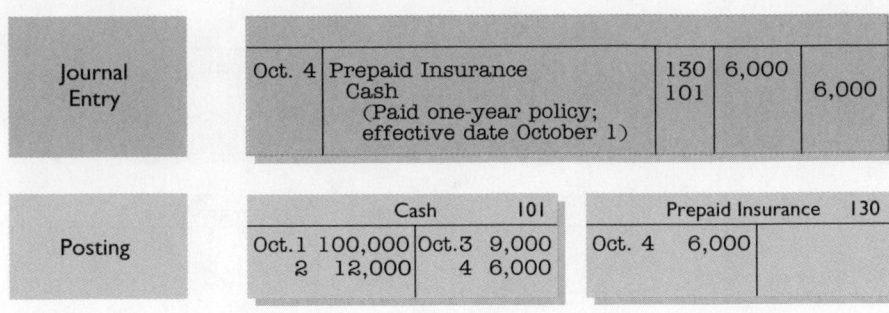

6 October 5: Pioneer Advertising purchases, for $25,000 on account, an estimated 3-month supply of advertising materials from Aero Supply.

Illustration 3-14
Purchase of Supplies on Account

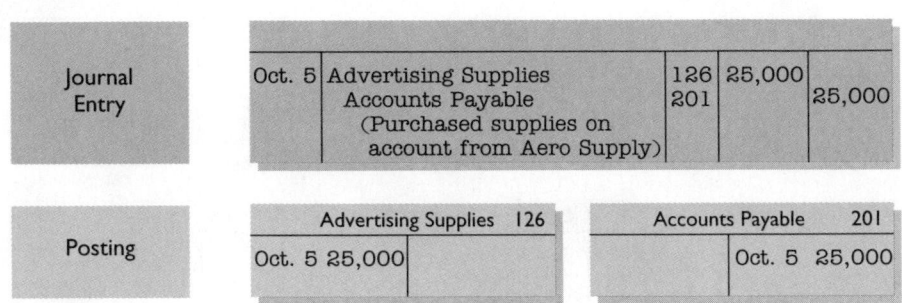

7 October 9: Pioneer Advertising signs a contract with a local newspaper for advertising inserts (flyers) to be distributed starting the last Sunday in November. Pioneer will start work on the content of the flyers in November. Payment of $7,000 is due following delivery of the Sunday papers containing the flyers.

Illustration 3-15
Signing a Contract

A business transaction has not occurred. There is only an agreement between Pioneer Advertising and the newspaper for the services to be provided in November. Therefore, no journal entry is necessary in October.

8 October 20: Pioneer Advertising's board of directors declares and pays a $5,000 cash dividend to stockholders.

Illustration 3-16
Declaration and Payment of Dividend by Corporation

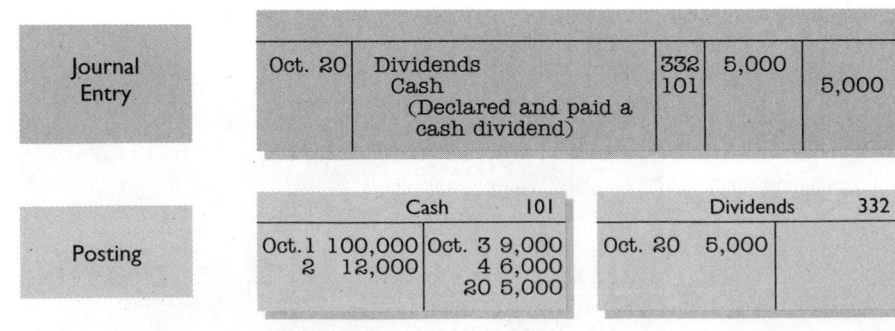

9 October 26: Pioneer Advertising pays employee salaries in cash. Employees are paid once a month, every four weeks. The total payroll is $10,000 per week, or $2,000 per day. In October, the pay period began on Monday, October 1. As a result, the pay period ended on Friday, October 26, with salaries of $40,000 being paid.

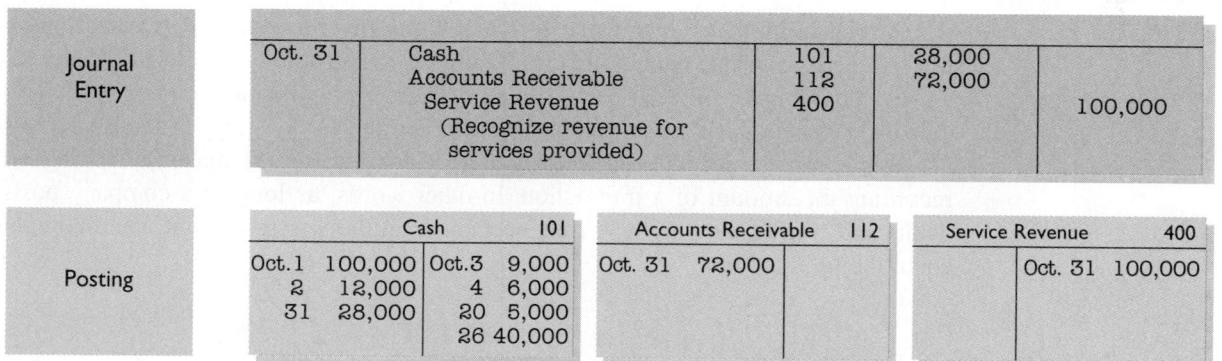

Illustration 3-17
Payment of Salaries

10 October 31: Pioneer Advertising receives $28,000 in cash and bills Copa Company $72,000 for advertising services of $100,000 provided in October.

Illustration 3-18
Recognize Revenue for
Services Provided

Journal Entry	Oct. 31	Cash	101	28,000	
		Accounts Receivable	112	72,000	
		Service Revenue	400		100,000
		(Recognize revenue for services provided)			

	Cash	101		Accounts Receivable	112		Service Revenue	400
Posting	Oct.1 100,000	Oct.3 9,000		Oct. 31 72,000				Oct. 31 100,000
	2 12,000	4 6,000						
	31 28,000	20 5,000						
		26 40,000						

Trial Balance

A **trial balance** lists accounts and their balances at a given time. A company usually prepares a trial balance at the end of an accounting period. The trial balance lists the accounts in the order in which they appear in the ledger, with debit balances listed in the left column and credit balances in the right column. The totals of the two columns must agree.

The trial balance proves the mathematical equality of debits and credits after posting. Under the double-entry system this equality occurs when the sum of the debit account balances equals the sum of the credit account balances. A trial balance also uncovers errors in journalizing and posting. In addition, it is useful in the preparation of financial statements. The procedures for preparing a trial balance consist of:

1 Listing the account titles and their balances.

2 Totaling the debit and credit columns.

3 Proving the equality of the two columns.

For example, Illustration 3-19 presents the trial balance prepared from the ledger of Pioneer Advertising Agency Inc. Note that the total debits ($287,000) equal the total credits ($287,000). A trial balance also often shows account numbers to the left of the account titles.

Illustration 3-19
Trial Balance (Unadjusted)

Pioneer Advertising Agency Inc.
Trial Balance
October 31, 2008

	Debit	Credit
Cash	$ 80,000	
Accounts Receivable	72,000	
Advertising Supplies	25,000	
Prepaid Insurance	6,000	
Office Equipment	50,000	
Notes Payable		$ 50,000
Accounts Payable		25,000
Unearned Service Revenue		12,000
Common Stock		100,000
Dividends	5,000	
Service Revenue		100,000
Salaries Expense	40,000	
Rent Expense	9,000	
	$287,000	$287,000

A trial balance does not prove that a company recorded all transactions or that the ledger is correct. Numerous errors may exist even though the trial balance columns agree. For example, the trial balance may balance even when a company (1) fails to journalize a transaction, (2) omits posting a correct journal entry, (3) posts a journal entry twice, (4) uses incorrect accounts in journalizing or posting, or (5) makes offsetting errors in recording the amount of a transaction. In other words, as long as a company posts equal debits and credits, even to the wrong account or in the wrong amount, the total debits will equal the total credits.

Try it out! After learning the basics of the delivery business working at **FedEx**, on April 1, 2008, Brett George decided to open his own delivery business to serve the downtown area. The following events and transactions occurred to get the business, Brett's Midtown Delivery, up and running.

April 1	Brett invested $10,000 of his savings to start the business and opened a checking account.
1	Brett rented office space on the city square by paying the first 3 months' rent in advance, $450.
5	Purchased office supplies, $200.
25	Collected $600 for delivery services provided.
30	Paid $90 for telephone and Internet services for the first month.

Instructions

a Prepare journal entries for the above transactions. (Omit explanations.)

b Prepare a trial balance for Brett's Midtown Delivery at April 30, 2008.

Solution

a General journal

				Debit	Credit
April	1	Cash		10,000	
			Brett George, Capital		10,000
	1	Prepaid Rent		450	
			Cash		450
	5	Supplies		200	
			Cash		200
	25	Cash		600	
			Delivery Revenue		600
	30	Telephone/ Internet Expense		90	
			Cash		90

b

Brett's Midtown Delivery
Trial Balance
April 30, 2008

	Debit	Credit
Cash ($10,000 − $450 − $200 + $600 − $90)	$ 9,860	_____
Supplies	200	
Prepaid Rent	450	
Brett George, Capital		$10,000
Delivery Revenue		600
Telephone/Internet Expense	90	_____
	$10,600	$10,600

Adjusting Entries

In order for a company, like **McDonald's**, to record revenues in the period in which it earns them, and to recognize expenses in the period in which it incurs them, McDonald's makes **adjusting entries** at the end of the accounting period. In short, adjustments ensure that McDonald's follows the revenue recognition and matching principles.

OBJECTIVE 5
Explain the reasons for preparing adjusting entries.

The use of adjusting entries makes it possible to report on the balance sheet the appropriate assets, liabilities, and owners' equity at the statement date. Adjusting entries also make it possible to report on the income statement the proper revenues and expenses for the period. However, the trial balance—the first pulling together of the transaction data—may not contain up-to-date and complete data. This occurs for the following reasons.

1 Some events are not journalized daily because it is not expedient. Examples are the consumption of supplies and the earning of wages by employees.

2 Some costs are not journalized during the accounting period because these costs expire with the passage of time rather than as a result of recurring daily transactions. Examples of such costs are building and equipment deterioration and rent and insurance.

3 Some items may be unrecorded. An example is a utility service bill that will not be received until the next accounting period.

WHAT'S THE PRINCIPLE?

Adjusting entries are needed to ensure accurate reporting of the amounts reported in both the balance sheet and income statement.

Adjusting entries are required every time a company, such as **The Coca-Cola Company**, prepares financial statements. At that time, Coca-Cola must analyze each account in the trial balance to determine whether it is complete and up-to-date for financial statement purposes. The analysis requires a thorough understanding of

Coca-Cola's operations and the interrelationship of accounts. Because of this involved process, usually a skilled accountant prepares the adjusting entries. In gathering the adjustment data, Coca-Cola may need to make inventory counts of supplies and repair parts. Further, it may prepare supporting schedules of insurance policies, rental agreements, and other contractual commitments. Companies often prepare adjustments after the balance sheet date. However, they date the entries as of the balance sheet date.

Types of Adjusting Entries

Adjusting entries are classified as either prepayments or accruals. Each of these classes has two subcategories, as Illustration 3-20 shows.

Illustration 3-20
Classes of Adjusting
Entries

Prepayments	Accruals
1. **Prepaid Expenses.** Expenses paid in cash and recorded as assets before they are used or consumed.	3. **Accrued Revenues.** Revenues earned but not yet received in cash or recorded.
2. **Unearned Revenues.** Revenues received in cash and recorded as liabilities before they are earned.	4. **Accrued Expenses.** Expenses incurred but not yet paid in cash or recorded.

We review specific examples and explanations of each type of adjustment in subsequent sections. We base each example on the October 31 trial balance of Pioneer Advertising Agency Inc. (Illustration 3-19). We assume that Pioneer uses an accounting period of one month. Thus, Pioneer will make monthly adjusting entries, dated October 31.

Adjusting Entries for Prepayments

As we indicated earlier, prepayments are either prepaid expenses or unearned revenues. Adjusting entries for prepayments, required at the statement date, record the portion of the prepayment that represents the **expense incurred or the revenue earned** in the current accounting period.

If a company does not make an adjustment for these prepayments, the asset and liability are overstated, and the related expense and revenue are understated. For example, in Pioneer's trial balance (Illustration 3-19), the balance in the asset Advertising Supplies shows only supplies purchased. This balance is overstated; the related expense account, Supplies Expense, is understated because the cost of supplies used has not been recognized. Thus the adjusting entry for prepayments will decrease a balance sheet account and increase an income statement account. Illustration 3-21 (next page) shows the effects of adjusting entries for prepayments.

Prepaid Expenses.   Assets paid for and recorded before a company uses them are called **prepaid expenses**. When a company incurs a cost, it debits an asset account to show the service or benefit it will receive in the future. Prepayments often occur in regard to insurance, supplies, advertising, and rent. In addition, companies make prepayments when purchasing buildings and equipment.

Prepaid expenses expire either with the passage of time (e.g., rent and insurance) or **through use and consumption** (e.g., supplies). The expiration of these costs does not require daily recurring entries, an unnecessary and impractical task. Accordingly, a company, like **Walgreens**, usually postpones the recognition of such cost expirations until it prepares financial statements. At each statement date, Walgreens makes adjusting entries to record the expenses that apply to the current accounting period and to show the unexpired costs in the asset accounts.

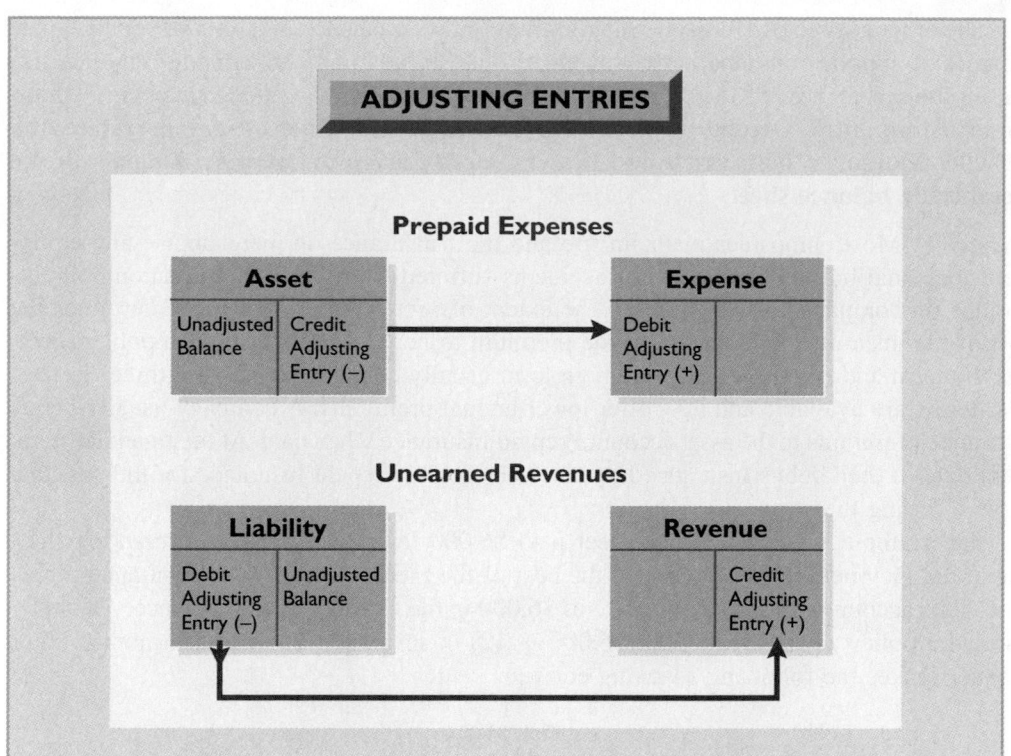

Illustration 3-21
Adjusting Entries for
Prepayments

As was shown above, prior to adjustment, assets are overstated and expenses are understated. Thus, the prepaid expense adjusting entry results in a debit to an expense account and a credit to an asset account.

Supplies. A business enterprise may use several different types of supplies. For example, a CPA firm will use office supplies such as stationery, envelopes, and accounting paper. An advertising firm will stock advertising supplies such as graph paper, video film, and poster paper. Supplies are generally debited to an asset account when they are acquired. Recognition of supplies used is generally deferred until the adjustment process. At that time, a physical inventory (count) of supplies is taken. The difference between the balance in the Supplies (asset) account and the cost of supplies on hand represents the supplies used (expense) for the period.

For example, Pioneer (see Illustration 3-19) purchased advertising supplies costing $25,000 on October 5. Pioneer therefore debited the asset Advertising Supplies. This account shows a balance of $25,000 in the October 31 trial balance. An inventory count at the close of business on October 31 reveals that $10,000 of supplies are still on hand. Thus, the cost of supplies used is $15,000 ($25,000 − $10,000). Pioneer makes the following adjusting entry.

Supplies

Oct. 5

Supplies purchased;
record asset

Oct. 31

Supplies used;
record supplies expense

		A	=	L	+	SE
						−15,000
−15,000						

Cash Flows
no effect

Oct. 31

Advertising Supplies Expense	15,000	
Advertising Supplies		15,000
(To record supplies used)		

After Pioneer posts the adjusting entry, the two supplies accounts in T-account form show the following.

Illustration 3-22
Supplies Accounts after
Adjustment

Advertising Supplies				Advertising Supplies Expense		
10/ 5	25,000	10/31	Adj. 15,000	10/31	Adj. 15,000	
10/31	Bal. 10,000					

Insurance

Oct. 4

Insurance purchased;
record asset

Insurance Policy			
Oct	Nov	Dec	Jan
$500	$500	$500	$500
Feb	March	April	May
$500	$500	$500	$500
June	July	Aug	Sept
$500	$500	$500	$500
I YEAR $6,000			

Oct. 31
Insurance expired;
record insurance expense

A	=	L	+	SE
				−500
−500				

Cash Flows
no effect

The asset account Advertising Supplies now shows a balance of $10,000, which equals the cost of supplies on hand at the statement date. In addition, Advertising Supplies Expense shows a balance of $15,000, which equals the cost of supplies used in October. **Without an adjusting entry, October expenses are understated and net income overstated by $15,000. Moreover, both assets and owners' equity are overstated by $15,000 on the October 31 balance sheet.**

Insurance. Most companies maintain fire and theft insurance on merchandise and equipment, personal liability insurance for accidents suffered by customers, and automobile insurance on company cars and trucks. The extent of protection against loss determines the cost of the insurance (the amount of the premium to be paid.) The insurance policy specifies the term and coverage. The minimum term usually covers one year, but three- to five-year terms are available and may offer lower annual premiums. A company usually debits insurance premiums to the asset account Prepaid Insurance when paid. At the financial statement date, it then debits Insurance Expense and credits Prepaid Insurance for the cost that expired during the period.

For example, on October 4, Pioneer paid $6,000 for a one-year fire insurance policy, beginning October 1. Pioneer debited the cost of the premium to Prepaid Insurance at that time. This account still shows a balance of $6,000 in the October 31 trial balance. An analysis of the policy reveals that $500 ($6,000 ÷ 12) of insurance expires each month. Thus, Pioneer makes the following adjusting entry.

Oct. 31

Insurance Expense	500	
Prepaid Insurance		500
(To record insurance expired)		

After Pioneer posts the adjusting entry, the insurance-related accounts show:

Illustration 3-23
Insurance Accounts after
Adjustment

Prepaid Insurance					Insurance Expense		
10/ 4	6,000	10/31	Adj. 500	10/31	Adj. 500		
10/31	Bal. 5,500						

Depreciation

Oct. I

Office equipment purchased;
record asset ($50,000)

Office Equipment			
Oct	Nov	Dec	Jan
$400	$400	$400	$400
Feb	March	April	May
$400	$400	$400	$400
June	July	Aug	Sept
$400	$400	$400	$400
Depreciation = $4,800/year			

Oct. 31
Depreciation recognized;
record depreciation expense

The asset Prepaid Insurance shows a balance of $5,500, which represents the unexpired cost for the remaining 11 months of coverage. At the same time, the balance in Insurance Expense equals the insurance cost that expired in October. **Without an adjusting entry, October expenses are understated by $500 and net income overstated by $500. Moreover, both assets and owners' equity also are overstated by $500 on the October 31 balance sheet.**

Depreciation. Companies, like **Caterpillar** or **Boeing**, typically own various productive facilities, such as buildings, equipment, and motor vehicles. These assets provide a service for a number of years. The term of service is commonly referred to as the **useful life** of the asset. Because Caterpillar, for example, expects an asset such as a building to provide service for many years, Caterpillar records the building as an asset, rather than an expense, in the year the building is acquired. Caterpillar records such assets at cost, as required by the historical cost principle.

According to the matching principle, Caterpillar should report a portion of the cost of a long-lived asset as an expense during each period of the asset's useful life. The process of **depreciation** allocates the cost of an asset to expense over its useful life in a rational and systematic manner.

Need for depreciation adjustment. Generally accepted accounting principles (GAAP) view the acquisition of productive facilities as a long-term prepayment for services. The need for making periodic adjusting entries for depreciation is, therefore, the same as we described for other prepaid expenses. That is, a company recognizes the expired cost (expense) during the period and reports the unexpired cost (asset) at the end of the period. The primary causes of depreciation of a productive facility are actual use, deterioration due to the elements, and obsolescence. For example, at the time Caterpillar acquires an asset, the effects of these factors cannot be known with certainty. Therefore, Caterpillar must estimate them. **Thus, depreciation is an estimate rather than a factual measurement of the expired cost.**

To estimate depreciation expense, Caterpillar often divides the cost of the asset by its useful life. For example, if Caterpillar purchases equipment for $10,000 and expects its useful life to be 10 years, Caterpillar records annual depreciation of $1,000.

In the case of Pioneer Advertising, it estimates depreciation on its office equipment to be $4,800 a year (cost $50,000 less salvage value $2,000 divided by useful life of 10 years), or $400 per month. Accordingly, Pioneer recognizes depreciation for October by the following adjusting entry.

	Oct. 31		
Depreciation Expense		400	
Accumulated Depreciation—Office Equipment			400
(To record monthly depreciation)			

A	=	L	+	SE
				−400
−400				

Cash Flows
no effect

After Pioneer posts the adjusting entry, the accounts show the following.

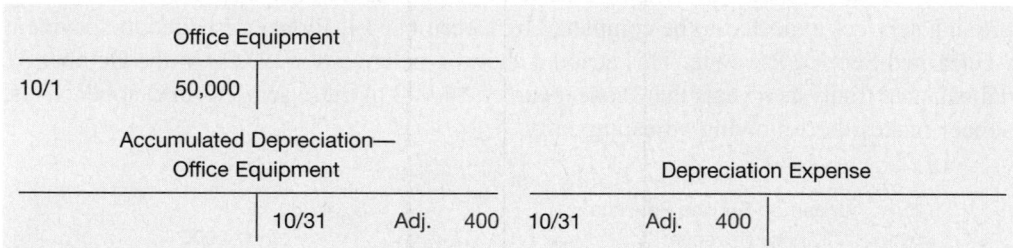

Illustration 3-24
Accounts after Adjustment for Depreciation

The balance in the accumulated depreciation account will increase $400 each month. Therefore, after journalizing and posting the adjusting entry at November 30, the balance will be $800.

Statement presentation. Accumulated Depreciation—Office Equipment is a contra asset account. A **contra asset account** offsets an asset account on the balance sheet. This means that the accumulated depreciation account offsets the Office Equipment account on the balance sheet. Its normal balance is a credit. Pioneer uses this account instead of crediting Office Equipment in order to disclose both the original cost of the equipment and the total expired cost to date. In the balance sheet, Pioneer deducts Accumulated Depreciation—Office Equipment from the related asset account as follows.

Office equipment	$50,000	
Less: Accumulated depreciation—office equipment	400	$49,600

Illustration 3-25
Balance Sheet Presentation of Accumulated Depreciation

The **book value** of any depreciable asset is the difference between its cost and its related accumulated depreciation. In Illustration 3-25, the book value of the equipment at the balance sheet date is $49,600. Note that the asset's book value generally differs from its market value because depreciation is not a matter of valuation but rather a means of cost allocation.

Note also that depreciation expense identifies that portion of the asset's cost that expired in October. As in the case of other prepaid adjustments, without this adjusting entry, total assets, total owners' equity, and net income are overstated, and depreciation expense is understated.

A company records depreciation expense for each piece of equipment, such as delivery or store equipment, and for all buildings. A company also establishes related accumulated depreciation accounts for the above, such as Accumulated Depreciation—Delivery Equipment; Accumulated Depreciation—Store Equipment; and Accumulated Depreciation—Buildings.

Unearned Revenues. Revenues received in cash and recorded as liabilities before a company earns them are called **unearned revenues**. Such items as rent, magazine subscriptions, and customer deposits for future service may result in unearned revenues. Airlines, such as **Northwest, American,** and **Southwest,** treat receipts from the sale of tickets as unearned revenue until they provide the flight service. Tuition received prior to the start of a semester is another example of unearned revenue. Unearned revenues are the opposite of prepaid expenses. Indeed, unearned revenue on the books of one company is likely to be a prepayment on the books of the company that made the advance payment. For example, if we assume identical accounting periods, a landlord will have unearned rent revenue when a tenant has prepaid rent.

When a company, such as **Intel**, receives payment for services to be provided in a future accounting period, it credits an unearned revenue (a liability) account to recognize the obligation that exists. It subsequently earns the revenues through rendering service to a customer. However, making daily recurring entries to record this revenue is impractical. Therefore, Intel delays recognition of earned revenue until the adjustment process. Then Intel makes an adjusting entry to record the revenue that it earned and to show the liability that remains. In the typical case, liabilities are overstated and revenues are understated prior to adjustment. **Thus, the adjusting entry for unearned revenues results in a debit (decrease) to a liability account and a credit (increase) to a revenue account.**

For example, Pioneer Advertising received $12,000 on October 2 from R. Knox for advertising services expected to be completed by December 31. Pioneer credited the payment to Unearned Service Revenue. This account shows a balance of $12,000 in the October 31 trial balance. Analysis reveals that Pioneer earned $4,000 of these services in October. Thus, Pioneer makes the following adjusting entry.

Unearned Revenues

Oct. 2

Cash is received in advance; liability is recorded

Oct. 31

Service is provided; revenue is recorded

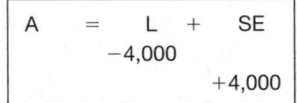

A	=	L	+	SE
		−4,000		
				+4,000

Cash Flows
no effect

Illustration 3-26
Service Revenue
Accounts after
Prepayments Adjustment

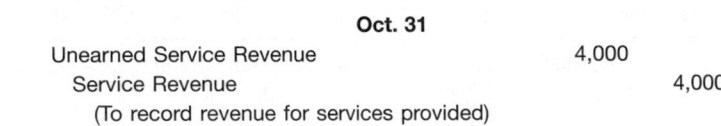

Oct. 31		
Unearned Service Revenue	4,000	
Service Revenue		4,000
(To record revenue for services provided)		

After Pioneer posts the adjusting entry, the accounts show the following.

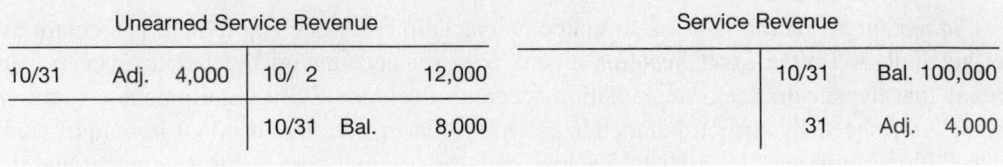

Unearned Service Revenue						Service Revenue			
10/31	Adj.	4,000	10/ 2		12,000		10/31	Bal.	100,000
			10/31	Bal.	8,000		31	Adj.	4,000

The liability Unearned Service Revenue now shows a balance of $8,000, which represents the remaining advertising services expected to be performed in the future. At the same time, Service Revenue shows total revenue earned in October of $104,000. **Without this adjustment, revenues and net income are understated by $4,000 in the income statement. Moreover, liabilities are overstated and owners' equity are understated by $4,000 on the October 31 balance sheet.**

Adjusting Entries for Accruals

The second category of adjusting entries is accruals. Companies make adjusting entries for accruals to record unrecognized revenues earned and expenses incurred in the current accounting period. Without an accrual adjustment, the revenue account (and the related asset account) or the expense account (and the related liability account) are understated. Thus, the adjusting entry for accruals **will increase both a balance sheet and an income statement account**. Illustration 3-27 shows adjusting entries for accruals.

Illustration 3-27
Adjusting Entries for
Accruals

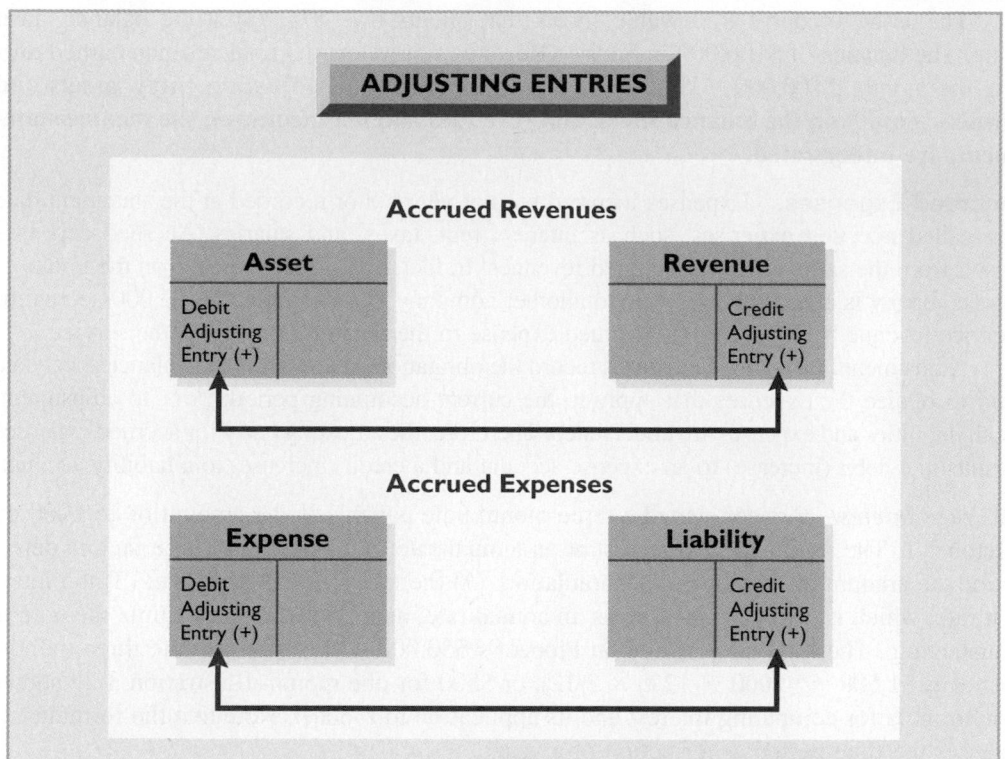

Accrued Revenues

Oct. 31

Service is provided;
revenue and receivable
are recorded

Nov.
Cash is received;
receivable is reduced

Accrued Revenues. Revenues earned but not yet received in cash or recorded at the statement date are **accrued revenues**. A company accrues revenues with the passing of time, as in the case of interest revenue and rent revenue. Because interest and rent do not involve daily transactions, these items are often unrecorded at the statement date. Or accrued revenues may result from unbilled or uncollected services that a company performed, as in the case of commissions and fees. A company does not record commissions or fees daily, because only a portion of the total service has been provided.

An adjusting entry shows the receivable that exists at the balance sheet date and records the revenue that a company earned during the period. Prior to adjustment both assets and revenues are understated. Accordingly, **an adjusting entry** for accrued revenues results in a debit (increase) to an asset account and a credit (increase) to a revenue account.

In October Pioneer earned $2,000 for advertising services that it did not bill to clients before October 31. Pioneer therefore did not yet record these services. Thus, Pioneer makes the following adjusting entry.

	Oct. 31		
Accounts Receivable		2,000	
Service Revenue			2,000
(To record revenue for services provided)			

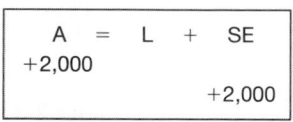

A	=	L	+	SE
+2,000				
				+2,000

Cash Flows
no effect

After Pioneer posts the adjusting entry, the accounts show the following.

Accounts Receivable					Service Revenue		
10/31	72,000			10/31			100,000
31	Adj. 2,000			31			4,000
				31		Adj.	2,000
10/31	Bal. 74,000			10/31			Bal. 106,000

Illustration 3-28
Receivable and Revenue
Accounts after Accrual
Adjustment

The asset Accounts Receivable shows that clients owe $74,000 at the balance sheet date. The balance of $106,000 in Service Revenue represents the total revenue earned during the month ($100,000 + $4,000 + $2,000). **Without an adjusting entry, assets and owners' equity on the balance sheet, and revenues and net income on the income statement, are understated.**

Accrued Expenses.   Expenses incurred but not yet paid or recorded at the statement date are called **accrued expenses**, such as interest, rent, taxes, and salaries. Accrued expenses result from the same causes as accrued revenues. In fact, an accrued expense on the books of one company is an accrued revenue to another company. For example, the $2,000 accrual of service revenue by Pioneer is an accrued expense to the client that received the service.

Adjustments for accrued expenses record the obligations that exist at the balance sheet date and recognize the expenses that apply to the current accounting period. Prior to adjustment, both liabilities and expenses are understated. Therefore, the adjusting entry for accrued expenses results in a debit (increase) to an expense account and a credit (increase) to a liability account.

Accrued Interest.   Pioneer signed a three-month note payable in the amount of $50,000 on October 1. The note requires interest at an annual rate of 12 percent. Three factors determine the amount of the interest accumulation: (1) the face value of the note; (2) the interest rate, which is always expressed as an annual rate; and (3) the length of time the note is outstanding. The total interest due on Pioneer's $50,000 note at its due date three months hence is $1,500 ($50,000 × 12% × 3/12), or $500 for one month. Illustration 3-29 shows the formula for computing interest and its application to Pioneer. Note that the formula expresses the time period as a fraction of a year.

Illustration 3-29
Formula for Computing
Interest

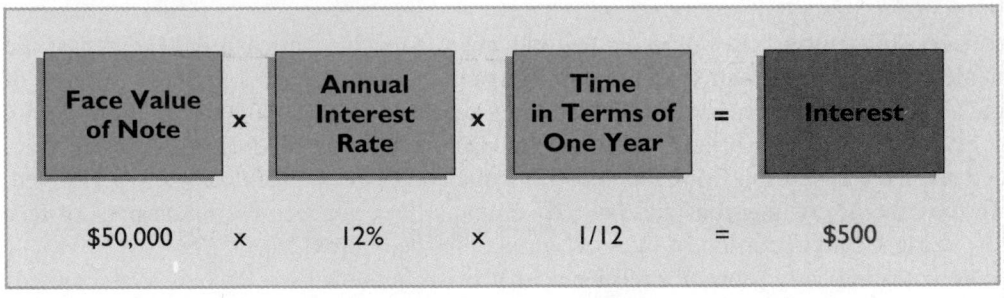

Pioneer makes the accrued expense adjusting entry at October 31 as follows.

A	=	L	+	SE
				−500
		+500		

Cash Flows
no effect

Oct. 31

Interest Expense	500	
Interest Payable		500
(To record interest on notes payable)		

After Pioneer posts this adjusting entry, the accounts show the following.

Illustration 3-30
Interest Accounts after
Adjustment

Interest Expense			Interest Payable		
10/31	500			10/31	500

Interest Expense shows the interest charges applicable to the month of October. Interest Payable shows the amount of interest owed at the statement date. Pioneer will not pay this amount until the note comes due at the end of three months. Why does Pioneer use the Interest Payable account instead of crediting Notes Payable? By recording interest payable separately, Pioneer discloses the two types of obligations (interest and principal) in the accounts and statements. **Without this adjusting entry, both liabilities and interest expense are understated, and both net income and owners' equity are overstated.**

Accrued Salaries. Companies pay for some types of expenses, such as employee salaries and commissions, after the services have been performed. For example, Pioneer last paid salaries on October 26. It will not pay salaries again until November 23. However, as shown in the calendar below, three working days remain in October (October 29–31).

At October 31, the salaries for these days represent an accrued expense and a related liability to Pioneer. The employees receive total salaries of $10,000 for a five-day work week, or $2,000 per day. Thus, accrued salaries at October 31 are $6,000 ($2,000 × 3). Pioneer makes the adjusting entry as follows.

Oct. 31

Salaries Expense	6,000	
Salaries Payable		6,000
(To record accrued salaries)		

A	=	L	+	SE
				−6,000
		+6,000		

Cash Flows
no effect

After Pioneer posts this adjusting entry, the accounts show the following.

Salaries Expense			Salaries Payable	
10/26 40,000				10/31 Adj. 6,000
31 Adj. 6,000				
10/31 Bal. 46,000				

Illustration 3-31
Salary Accounts after Adjustment

After this adjustment, the balance in Salaries Expense of $46,000 (23 days × $2,000) is the actual salary expense for October. The balance in Salaries Payable of $6,000 is the amount of the liability for salaries owed as of October 31. **Without the $6,000 adjustment for salaries, both Pioneer's expenses and liabilities are understated by $6,000.**

Pioneer pays salaries every four weeks. Consequently, the next payday is November 23, when it will again pay total salaries of $40,000. The payment consists of $6,000 of salaries payable at October 31 plus $34,000 of salaries expense for November (17 working days as shown in the November calendar × $2,000). Therefore, Pioneer makes the following entry on November 23.

Nov. 23

Salaries Payable	6,000	
Salaries Expense	34,000	
Cash		40,000
(To record November 23 payroll)		

A	=	L	+	SE
		−6,000		
				−34,000
−40,000				

Cash Flows
−40,000

This entry eliminates the liability for Salaries Payable that Pioneer recorded in the October 31 adjusting entry. This entry also records the proper amount of Salaries Expense for the period between November 1 and November 23.

What do the numbers mean?

Rather than purchasing insurance to cover casualty losses and other obligations, some companies "self-insure." That is, a company decides to pay for any possible claims, as they arise, out of its own resources. The company also purchases an insurance policy to cover losses that exceed certain amounts.

For example, **Almost Family, Inc.**, a healthcare services company, has a self-insured employee health-benefit program. However, Almost Family ran into accounting problems when it failed to record an accrual of the liability for benefits not covered by its back-up insurance policy. This led to restatement of Almost Family's fiscal results for the accrual of the benefit expense.

Beyond the Numbers

Companies must be careful when accounting for self-insurance so that the assets, liabilities, and expenses are recorded according to good accounting principles. Assume that Almost Family, Inc. made the following entry in establishing a reserve for future insurance losses.

Insurance Expense	10,000	
Insurance Liability		10,000

Discuss the propriety of this accounting for potential insurance losses. Focus on the conceptual definition of liabilities.

Bad Debts

Oct. 31
Uncollectible accounts;
record bad debt expense

A	=	L	+	SE
				−1,600
−1,600				

Bad Debts. Proper matching of revenues and expenses dictates recording bad debts as an expense of the period in which a company earned revenue instead of the period in which the company writes off the accounts or notes. The proper valuation of the receivable balance also requires recognition of uncollectible receivables. Proper matching and valuation require an adjusting entry.

At the end of each period, a company, such as **General Mills**, estimates the amount of receivables that will later prove to be uncollectible. General Mills bases the estimate on various factors: the amount of bad debts it experienced in past years, general economic conditions, how long the receivables are past due, and other factors that indicate the extent of uncollectibility. To illustrate, assume that, based on past experience, Pioneer reasonably estimates a bad debt expense for the month of $1,600. It makes the adjusting entry for bad debts as follows.

Oct. 31

Bad Debt Expense	1,600	
Allowance for Doubtful Accounts		1,600
(To record monthly bad debt expense)		

After Pioneer posts the adjusting entry, the accounts show the following.

Illustration 3-32
Accounts after Adjustment for Bad Debt Expense

Accounts Receivable

| 10/ 1 | 72,000 | |
| 31 | Adj. 2,000 | |

Allowance for Doubtful Accounts		Bad Debt Expense	
	10/31 Adj. 1,600	10/31 Adj. 1,600	

A company often expresses bad debts as a percentage of the revenue on account for the period. Or a company may compute bad debts by adjusting the Allowance for Doubtful Accounts to a certain percentage of the trade accounts receivable and trade notes receivable at the end of the period.

Adjusted Trial Balance

After journalizing and posting all adjusting entries, Pioneer prepares another trial balance from its ledger accounts. This trial balance is called an **adjusted trial balance**. It shows the balance of all accounts, including those adjusted, at the end of the accounting period. The adjusted trial balance thus shows the effects of all financial events that occurred during the accounting period.

Pioneer Advertising Agency Inc.
Adjusted Trial Balance
October 31, 2008

	Debit	Credit
Cash	$ 80,000	
Accounts Receivable	74,000	
Allowance for Doubtful Accounts		$ 1,600
Advertising Supplies	10,000	
Prepaid Insurance	5,500	
Office Equipment	50,000	
Accumulated Depreciation—		
Office Equipment		400
Notes Payable		50,000
Accounts Payable		25,000
Interest Payable		500
Unearned Service Revenue		8,000
Salaries Payable		6,000
Common Stock		100,000
Dividends	5,000	
Service Revenue		106,000
Salaries Expense	46,000	
Advertising Supplies Expense	15,000	
Rent Expense	9,000	
Insurance Expense	500	
Interest Expense	500	
Depreciation Expense	400	
Bad Debt Expense	1,600	
	$297,500	$297,500

Illustration 3-33
Adjusted Trial Balance

Try it out! Brett's Midtown Delivery has completed the first month of operations, and Brett has contacted you to help him assess the financial performance of his business. He provides the following unadjusted trial balance.

Brett's Midtown Delivery
Unadjusted Trial Balance
April 30, 2008

	Debit	Credit
Cash	$ 9,860*	
Supplies	200	
Prepaid Rent	450	
Brett George, Capital		$10,000
Delivery Revenue		600
Telephone/Internet Expense	90	
	$10,600	$10,600

* $10,000 − $450 − $200 + $600 − $90

Brett provides the following additional information.

1 Supplies on hand at April 30, $100.

2 Prepaid rent covers occupancy for April, May, and June.

3 Brett hired a receptionist and a part-time courier toward the end of the month. Their wages of $350 for the last week of the month will not be paid until May 5, 2008.

4 Brett entered into an agreement on April 15 with a local law office to provide delivery services on a monthly basis. Brett will be paid $360 on the 15th of each month, beginning May 15, 2008. Brett provided delivery services on the contract in the last half of April.

Instructions

a Prepare the adjusting entries for these transactions.

b Prepare an adjusted trial balance for Brett's Midtown Delivery at April 30, 2008.

c What is Brett's income for the month?

Solution

a Adjusting entries:

1	Supplies Expense	100	
	Supplies		100
2	Rent Expense	150	
	Prepaid Rent		150
3	Wages Expense	350	
	Wages Payable		350
4	Accounts Receivable	180	
	Delivery Revenue		180

b

Brett's Midtown Delivery
Adjusted Trial Balance
April 30, 2008

	Trial Balance Dr.	Trial Balance Cr.	Adjustments Dr.	Adjustments Cr.	Adjusted Trial Balance Dr.	Adjusted Trial Balance Cr.
Cash	$ 9,860*				$ 9,860	
Accounts Receivable			$180		180	
Supplies	200			$100	100	
Prepaid Rent	450			150	300	
Wages Payable				350		$ 350
Brett George, Capital		10,000				10,000
Delivery Revenue		600		180		780
Telephone/Internet Expense	90				90	
Rent Expense			150		150	
Supplies Expense			100		100	
Wages Expense			350		350	
	$10,600	$10,600	$780	$780	$11,130	$11,130

*$10,000 − $450 − $200 + $600 − $90

c Income for the month = $90 ($780 − $90 − $150 − $100 − $350)

Preparing Financial Statements

Pioneer can prepare financial statements directly from the adjusted trial balance. Illustrations 3-34 and 3-35 show the interrelationships of data in the adjusted trial balance and the financial statements.

OBJECTIVE 6

Prepare financial statements from the adjusted trial balance.

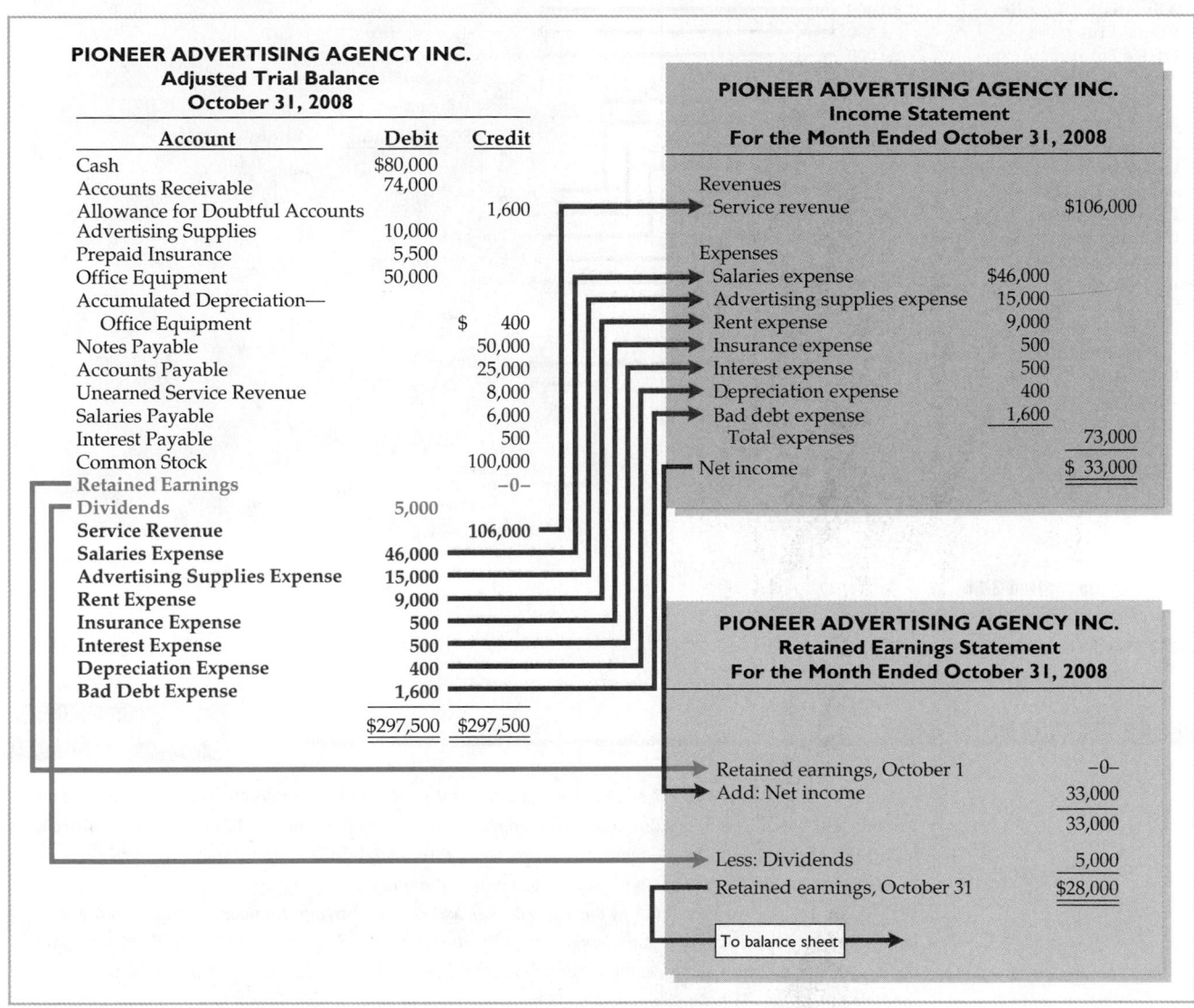

Illustration 3-34
Preparation of the Income Statement and Retained Earnings Statement from the Adjusted Trial Balance

As Illustration 3-34 shows, Pioneer begins preparation of the income statement from the revenue and expense accounts. It derives the retained earnings statement from the retained earnings and dividends accounts and the net income (or net loss) shown in the income statement. As Illustration 3-35 (page 104) shows, Pioneer then prepares the balance sheet from the asset and liability accounts, the common stock account, and the ending retained earnings balance as reported in the retained earnings statement.

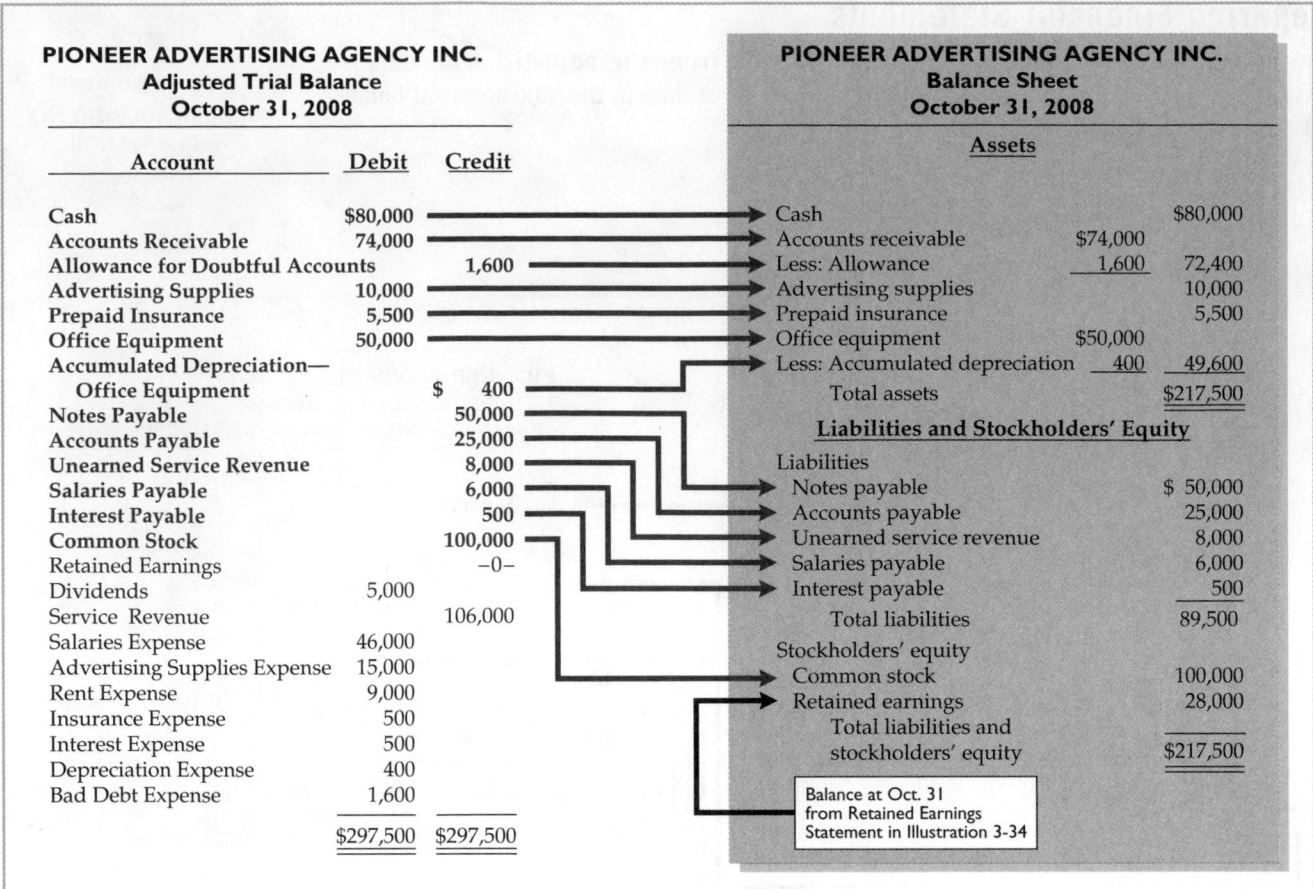

Illustration 3-35
Preparation of the
Balance Sheet from the
Adjusted Trial Balance

What do the numbers mean?   24/7 Accounting

To achieve the vision of "24/7 accounting," a company must be able to update revenue, income, and balance sheet numbers every day within the quarter and publish them on the Internet. Such real-time reporting responds to the demand for more timely financial information made available to all investors—not just to analysts with access to company management.

Two obstacles typically stand in the way of 24/7 accounting: having the necessary accounting systems to close the books on a daily basis, and reliability concerns associated with unaudited real-time data. Only a few companies have the necessary accounting capabilities. **Cisco Systems**, which pioneered the concept of the 24-hour close, is one such company.

Beyond the Numbers

What users might benefit from receiving daily financial statements? Discuss the decisions to be made with the financial statements and how more timely statements can improve those decisions.

Closing

OBJECTIVE 7

Prepare closing entries.

Basic Process

The **closing process** reduces the balance of nominal (temporary) accounts to zero in order to prepare the accounts for the next period's transactions. In the closing process Pioneer transfers all of the revenue and expense account balances (income statement items) to a clearing or suspense account called Income Summary. The Income Summary account matches revenues and expenses.

Pioneer uses this clearing account only at the end of each accounting period. The account represents the net income or net loss for the period. It then transfers the net result of this matching (the net income or net loss) to an owners' equity account. (For a corporation, the owners' equity account is retained earnings; for proprietorships and partnerships, it is a capital account.) Companies post all such **closing entries** to the appropriate general ledger accounts.

Closing Entries

In practice, companies generally prepare closing entries only at the end of a company's annual accounting period. However, to illustrate the journalizing and posting of closing entries, we will assume that Pioneer Advertising Agency Inc. closes its books monthly. Illustration 3-36 shows the closing entries at October 31.

Illustration 3-36
Closing Entries Journalized

General Journal			J3
Date	Account Titles and Explanation	Debit	Credit
	Closing Entries		
	(1)		
Oct. 31	Service Revenue	106,000	
	Income Summary		106,000
	(To close revenue account)		
	(2)		
31	Income Summary	73,000	
	Advertising Supplies Expense		15,000
	Depreciation Expense		400
	Insurance Expense		500
	Salaries Expense		46,000
	Rent Expense		9,000
	Interest Expense		500
	Bad Debt Expense		1,600
	(To close expense accounts)		
	(3)		
31	Income Summary	33,000	
	Retained Earnings		33,000
	(To close net income to retained earnings)		
	(4)		
31	Retained Earnings	5,000	
	Dividends		5,000
	(To close dividends to retained earnings)		

A couple of cautions about preparing closing entries: (1) Avoid unintentionally doubling the revenue and expense balances rather than zeroing them. (2) Do not close Dividends through the Income Summary account. **Dividends are not expenses, and they are not a factor in determining net income.**

Posting Closing Entries

Illustration 3-37 (page 106) shows the posting of closing entries and the ruling of accounts. All temporary accounts have zero balances after posting the closing entries. In addition, note that the balance in Retained Earnings represents the accumulated undistributed earnings of Pioneer at the end of the accounting period. Pioneer reports this amount in the balance sheet as the ending amount reported on the retained earnings statement. As noted above, **Pioneer uses the Income Summary account only in closing**. It does not journalize and post entries to this account during the year.

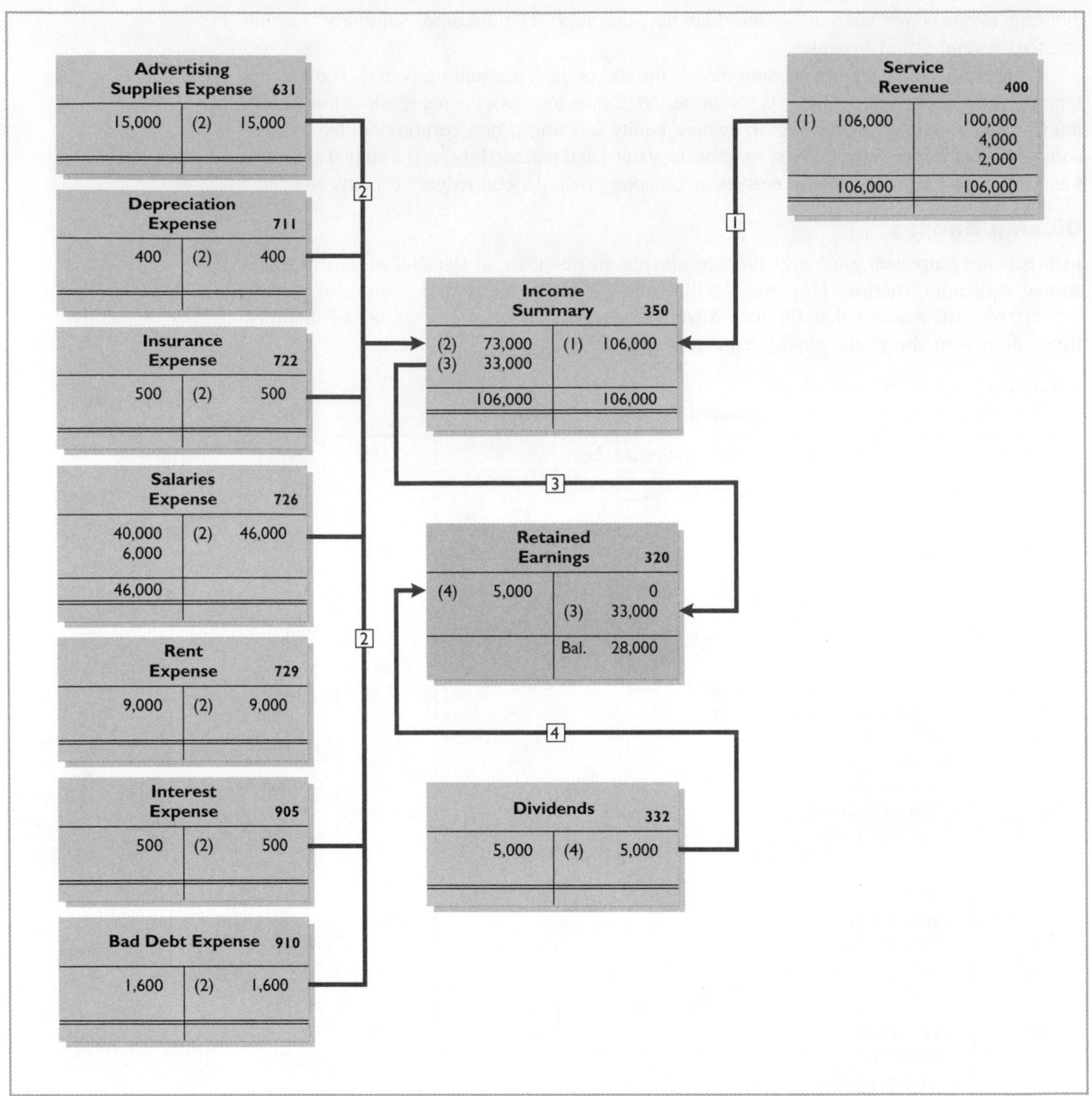

Illustration 3-37
Posting of Closing Entries

As part of the closing process, Pioneer totals, balances, and double-rules the **temporary accounts**—revenues, expenses, and dividends—as shown in T-account form in Illustration 3-37. It does not close the **permanent accounts**—assets, liabilities, and stockholders' equity (Common Stock and Retained Earnings). Instead, the preparer draws a single rule beneath the current-period entries, and enters beneath the single rules the account balance to be carried forward to the next period. (For example, see Retained Earnings.)

After the closing process, each income statement account and the Dividends account are balanced out to zero and are ready for use in the next accounting period.

Post-Closing Trial Balance

Recall that a trial balance is prepared after entering the regular transactions of the period, and that a second trial balance (the adjusted trial balance) occurs after posting the adjusting entries. A company may take a third trial balance after posting the closing entries. The trial balance after closing, called the **post-closing trial balance**, consists only of asset, liability, and owners' equity accounts—the real accounts.

Reversing Entries

After preparing the financial statements and closing the books, a company may reverse some of the adjusting entries before recording the regular transactions of the next period. Such entries are called **reversing entries**. A company makes a reversing entry at the beginning of the next accounting period; this entry is the exact opposite of the related adjusting entry made in the previous period. Making reversing entries is an optional step in the accounting cycle that a company may perform at the beginning of the next accounting period. Appendix 3A discusses reversing entries in more detail.

The Accounting Cycle Summarized

A summary of the steps in the accounting cycle shows a logical sequence of the accounting procedures used during a fiscal period:

1 Enter the transactions of the period in appropriate journals.

2 Post from the journals to the ledger (or ledgers).

3 Take an unadjusted trial balance (trial balance).

4 Prepare adjusting journal entries and post to the ledger(s).

5 Take a trial balance after adjusting (adjusted trial balance).

6 Prepare the financial statements from the second trial balance.

7 Prepare closing journal entries and post to the ledger(s).

8 Take a trial balance after closing (post-closing trial balance).

9 Prepare reversing entries (optional) and post to the ledger(s).

A company normally completes all of these steps in every fiscal period.

What do the numbers mean?	Statements, Please

The use of a worksheet at the end of each month or quarter enables a company to prepare interim financial statements even though it closes the books only at the end of each year. For example, assume that **Google** closes its books on December 31, but it wants monthly financial statements. To do this, at the end of January, Google prepares an adjusted trial balance (using a worksheet as illustrated in Appendix 3B) to supply the information needed for statements for January.

At the end of February, it uses a worksheet again. Note that because Google did not close the accounts at the end of January, the income statement taken from the adjusted trial balance on February 28 will present the net income for two months. If Google wants an income statement for only the month of February, the company obtains it by subtracting the items in the January income statement from the corresponding items in the income statement for the two months of January and February.

If Google executes such a process daily, it can realize "24/7 accounting" (see box on page 104).

Beyond the Numbers

Most agree that users benefit from receiving more timely information. However, companies must also consider the costs of such reporting. Choose a financial statement item that requires adjustment when the books are closed (and financial statements prepared) and discuss the costs of preparing this adjustment on a daily basis.

Financial Statements for a Merchandising Company

Pioneer Advertising Agency Inc. is a service company. We now will show a detailed set of financial statements for a merchandising company, Uptown Cabinet Corp. The financial statements on pages 108 and 109 are prepared from the adjusted trial balance.

Income Statement

The income statement for Uptown is self-explanatory. The income statement classifies amounts into such categories as gross profit on sales, income from operations, income before taxes, and net income. Although earnings per share information is required to be shown on the face of the income statement for a corporation, we omit this item here; it will be discussed more fully later in the text. *(For homework problems, do not present earnings per share information unless required to do so).*

Illustration 3-38
An Income Statement

Uptown Cabinet Corp. Income Statement For the Year Ended December 31, 2008			
Net sales			$400,000
Cost of goods sold			316,000
Gross profit on sales			84,000
Selling expenses			
Sales salaries expense		$20,000	
Traveling expense		8,000	
Advertising expense		2,200	
Total selling expenses		30,200	
Administrative expenses			
Salaries, office and general	$19,000		
Depreciation expense—furniture and equipment	6,700		
Property tax expense	5,300		
Rent expense	4,300		
Bad debt expense	1,000		
Telephone and Internet expense	600		
Insurance expense	360		
Total administrative expenses		37,260	
Total selling and administrative expenses			67,460
Income from operations			16,540
Other revenues and gains			
Interest revenue			800
			17,340
Other expenses and losses			
Interest expense			1,700
Income before income taxes			15,640
Income taxes			3,440
Net income			$ 12,200

Statement of Retained Earnings

A corporation may retain the net income earned in the business, or it may distribute it to stockholders by payment of dividends. In the illustration, Uptown added the net income earned during the year to the balance of retained earnings on January 1, thereby increasing the balance of retained earnings. Deducting dividends of $2,000 results in the ending retained earnings balance of $26,400 on December 31.

Illustration 3-39
A Statement of
Retained Earnings

Uptown Cabinet Corp. Statement of Retained Earnings For the Year Ended December 31, 2008	
Retained earnings, January 1	$16,200
Add: Net income	12,200
	28,400
Less: Dividends	2,000
Retained earnings, December 31	$26,400

Balance Sheet

The balance sheet for Uptown is a classified balance sheet. Interest receivable, prepaid insurance, and prepaid rent expense are included as current assets. Uptown considers these assets current because they will be converted into cash or used by the business within a relatively short period of time. Uptown deducts the amount of Allowance for Doubtful Accounts from the total of accounts, notes, and interest receivable because it estimates that only $54,800 of $57,800 will be collected in cash.

In the property, plant, and equipment section, Uptown deducts the accumulated depreciation from the cost of the furniture and equipment. The difference represents the book or carrying value of the furniture and equipment.

The balance sheet shows property tax payable as a current liability because it is an obligation that is payable within a year. The balance sheet also shows other short-term liabilities such as accounts payable.

The bonds payable, due in 2016, are long-term liabilities. As a result, the balance sheet shows the account in a separate section. (The company paid interest on the bonds on December 31.)

Because Uptown is a corporation, the capital section of the balance sheet, called the stockholders' equity section in the illustration, differs somewhat from the capital section for a proprietorship. Total stockholders' equity consists of the common stock, which is the original investment by stockholders, and the earnings retained in the business. *For homework purposes, unless instructed otherwise, prepare an unclassified balance sheet.*

Illustration 3-40
A Balance Sheet

Uptown Cabinet Corp.
Balance Sheet
As of December 31, 2008

Assets

Current assets			
Cash			$ 1,200
Notes receivable	$16,000		
Accounts receivable	41,000		
Interest receivable	800	$57,800	
Less: Allowance for doubtful accounts		3,000	54,800
Merchandise inventory			40,000
Prepaid insurance			540
Prepaid rent expense			500
Total current assets			97,040
Property, plant, and equipment			
Furniture and equipment		67,000	
Less: Accumulated depreciation		18,700	
Total property, plant, and equipment			48,300
Total assets			$145,340

Liabilities and Stockholders' Equity

Current liabilities			
Notes payable			$ 20,000
Accounts payable			13,500
Property tax payable			2,000
Income tax payable			3,440
Total current liabilities			38,940
Long-term liabilities			
Bonds payable, due June 30, 2016			30,000
Total liabilities			68,940
Stockholders' equity			
Common stock, $5.00 par value, issued and outstanding, 10,000 shares		$50,000	
Retained earnings		26,400	
Total stockholders' equity			76,400
Total liabilities and stockholders' equity			$145,340

Closing Entries

Uptown makes closing entries as follows on December 31, 2008.

General Journal		
December 31, 2008		
Interest Revenue	800	
Sales	400,000	
Income Summary		400,800
(To close revenues to Income Summary)		
Income Summary	388,600	
Cost of Goods Sold		316,000
Sales Salaries Expense		20,000
Traveling Expense		8,000
Advertising Expense		2,200
Salaries, Office and General		19,000
Depreciation Expense—Furniture and Equipment		6,700
Rent Expense		4,300
Property Tax Expense		5,300
Bad Debt Expense		1,000
Telephone and Internet Expense		600
Insurance Expense		360
Interest Expense		1,700
Income Tax Expense		3,440
(To close expenses to Income Summary)		
Income Summary	12,200	
Retained Earnings		12,200
(To close Income Summary to Retained Earnings)		
Retained Earnings	2,000	
Dividends		2,000
(To close Dividends to Retained Earnings)		

Inventory and Cost of Goods Sold

OBJECTIVE 8

Explain how to adjust inventory accounts at year-end.

Because Uptown is a merchandising company, it has inventory. Companies with inventory generally use a **perpetual inventory system**. With such a system, a company records the cost of the inventory purchased and sold directly in the Inventory account as the purchases and sales occur. Therefore, the balance in the Inventory account should represent the ending inventory amount, and no adjusting entries are needed. To ensure this accuracy, a physical count of the items in inventory is performed on an annual basis.

With the perpetual inventory system, because the company debits purchases directly to the Inventory account, it does not use a Purchases account. However, the company does use a Cost of Goods Sold account to accumulate the issuances from inventory. That is, when inventory is sold, the company credits the cost of the sold goods to Inventory and debits Cost of Goods Sold. In closing the accounts, the company credits Cost of Goods Sold and debits Income Summary.

With a **periodic inventory system**, a company uses a Purchases account to record purchases of inventory during the period. Here, the Inventory account remains **unchanged** during the period. The Inventory account represents the beginning inventory amount throughout the period. Then, at the end of the accounting period the company must adjust the inventory account by **closing out the beginning inventory amount** and **recording the ending inventory amount**. A company determines the ending inventory by physically counting the items on hand and valuing them at cost or at the lower-of-cost-or-market. Under the periodic inventory system, a company therefore determines the cost of goods sold by adding the beginning inventory together with net purchases and deducting the ending inventory.

To illustrate how to compute cost of goods sold with a periodic inventory system, assume that Collegiate Apparel Shop begins with an inventory of $30,000. It records purchases of $200,000, transportation-in of $6,000, purchase returns and allowances of

CONVERGENCE CORNER

Accounting Information Systems

As indicated in Chapter 3, companies must have an effective accounting system. In the wake of accounting scandals at companies like **Sunbeam**, **Rite-Aid**, **Xerox**, and **WorldCom**, U.S. lawmakers demanded higher assurance on the quality of accounting reports. Since the passage of the Sarbanes-Oxley Act of 2002 (SOX), companies that trade on U.S. exchanges are required to place renewed focus on their accounting systems to ensure accurate reporting.

RELEVANT FACTS

- Internal controls are a system of checks and balances designed to prevent and detect fraud and errors. While most companies have these systems in place, many have never completely documented them nor had an independent auditor attest to their effectiveness. Both of these actions are required under SOX.

- Companies find that internal control review is a costly process but badly needed. One study estimates the cost of compliance for U.S. companies at over $35 billion, with audit fees doubling in the first year of compliance. At the same time, examination of internal controls indicates lingering problems in the way companies operate. One study of first compliance with the internal-control testing provisions documented material weaknesses for about 13 percent of companies reporting in 2004 and 2005.

- The enhanced internal control standards apply only to large public companies listed on U.S. exchanges. There is continuing debate over whether foreign issuers should have to comply with this extra layer of regulation.[1]

ABOUT THE NUMBERS

Debate about requiring foreign companies to comply with SOX centers on whether the higher costs of a good information system are making the U.S. securities markets less competitive. Presented below are statistics for initial public offerings (IPOs) in the years since the passage of SOX.

Share of IPO proceeds: U.S., Europe, and China
(U.S. $, billions)

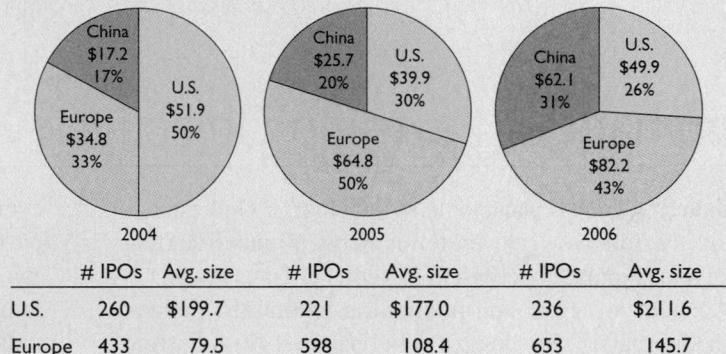

	# IPOs	Avg. size	# IPOs	Avg. size	# IPOs	Avg. size
U.S.	260	$199.7	221	$177.0	236	$211.6
Europe	433	79.5	598	108.4	653	145.7
China	208	82.5	98	260.9	140	444.0

Source: PricewaterhouseCoopers, U.S. IPO Watch: 2006 Analysis and Trends.

Note the U.S. share of IPOs has steadily declined, and some critics of the SOX provisions attribute the decline to the increased cost of complying with the internal control rules.

Others, looking at these same trends, are not so sure about SOX being the cause of the relative decline of U.S. IPOs. These commentators argue that growth in non-U.S. markets is a natural consequence of general globalization of capital flows.

[1]Greg Ip, Kara Scannel, and Deborah Solomon, "Trade Winds in Call to Deregulate Business, A Global Twist," *Wall Street Journal,* January 25, 2007, p. A1.

 ## ON THE HORIZON

High-quality international accounting requires both high-quality accounting standards and high-quality auditing. Similar to the convergence of U.S. GAAP and iGAAP, there is a movement to improve international auditing standards. The International Auditing and Assurance Standards Board (IAASB) functions as an independent standard-setting body. It works to establish high-quality auditing and assurance and quality-control standards throughout the world. Whether the IAASB adopts internal control provisions similar to those in SOX remains to be seen. You can follow developments in the international audit arena at *http://www.ifac.org/iaasb/.*

Key Terms

account, 78
accounting cycle, 83
accounting information system, 78
accrued expenses, 98
accrued revenues, 97
adjusted trial balance, 101
adjusting entry, 78, 91
balance sheet, 79
book value, 95
closing entries, 79, 105
closing process, 104
contra asset account, 95
credit, 79
debit, 79
depreciation, 94
double-entry accounting, 79
event, 78
financial statements, 79
general journal, 85
general ledger, 84

income statement, 79
journal, 79
ledger, 79
nominal accounts, 78
periodic inventory system, 110
perpetual inventory system, 110
post-closing trial balance, 107
posting, 79, 85
prepaid expenses, 92
real accounts, 78
reversing entries, 107
special journals, 85
statement of cash flows, 79
statement of retained earnings, 79
T-account, 84
transaction, 78
trial balance, 79, 89
unearned revenues, 96
useful life, 94

Summary of Learning Objectives

1 Understand basic accounting terminology. Understanding the following eleven terms helps in understanding key accounting concepts: (1) Event. (2) Transaction. (3) Account. (4) Real and nominal accounts. (5) Ledger. (6) Journal. (7) Posting. (8) Trial balance. (9) Adjusting entries. (10) Financial statements. (11) Closing entries.

2 Explain double-entry rules. The left side of any account is the debit side; the right side is the credit side. All asset and expense accounts are increased on the left or debit side and decreased on the right or credit side. Conversely, all liability and revenue accounts are increased on the right or credit side and decreased on the left or debit side. Stockholders' equity accounts, Common Stock and Retained Earnings, are increased on the credit side. Dividends is increased on the debit side.

3. Identify steps in the accounting cycle. The basic steps in the accounting cycle are (1) identifying and measuring transactions and other events; (2) journalizing; (3) posting; (4) preparing an unadjusted trial balance; (5) making adjusting entries; (6) preparing an adjusted trial balance; (7) preparing financial statements; and (8) closing.

4 Record transactions in journals, post to ledger accounts, and prepare a trial balance. The simplest journal form chronologically lists transactions and events expressed in terms of debits and credits to particular accounts. The items entered in a general journal must be transferred (posted) to the general ledger. Companies should prepare an unadjusted trial balance at the end of a given period after they have recorded the entries in the journal and posted them to the ledger.

5 Explain the reasons for preparing adjusting entries. Adjustments achieve a proper matching of revenues and expenses, so as to determine net income for the current period and to achieve an accurate statement of end-of-the-period balances in assets, liabilities, and owners' equity accounts.

6 Prepare financial statements from the adjusted trial balance. Companies can prepare financial statements directly from the adjusted trial balance. The income statement is prepared from the revenue and expense accounts. The statement of retained earnings is prepared from the retained earnings account, dividends, and net income (or net loss). The balance sheet is prepared from the asset, liability, and equity accounts.

7 Prepare closing entries. In the closing process, the company transfers all of the revenue and expense account balances (income statement items) to a clearing account called Income Summary, which is used only at the end of the fiscal year. Revenues and expenses are matched in the Income Summary account. The net result of this matching represents the net income or net loss for the period. That amount is then transferred to an owners' equity account (Retained Earnings for a corporation and capital accounts for proprietorships and partnerships).

8 Explain how to adjust inventory accounts at year-end.
Under a perpetual inventory system the balance in the Inventory account represents the ending inventory amount. When companies maintain the inventory records in a periodic inventory system, they use a Purchases account; the Inventory account is unchanged during the period. The Inventory account represents the beginning inventory amount throughout the period. At the end of the accounting period the company must adjust the Inventory account by closing out the beginning inventory amount and recording the ending inventory amount.

BEHIND THE NUMBERS
APPENDIX 3A
USING REVERSING ENTRIES

Use of reversing entries simplifies the recording of transactions in the next accounting period. The use of reversing entries, however, does not change the amounts reported in the financial statements for the previous period.

Example of Reversing Entries—Accruals

A company most often uses reversing entries to reverse two types of adjusting entries: accrued revenues and accrued expenses. To illustrate the optional use of reversing entries for accrued expenses, we use the following transaction and adjustment data.

> **OBJECTIVE 9**
> **Identify adjusting entries that may be reversed.**

1 October 24 (initial salary entry): Paid $4,000 of salaries incurred between October 10 and October 24.

2 October 31 (adjusting entry): Incurred salaries between October 25 and October 31 of $1,200, to be paid in the November 8 payroll.

3 November 8 (subsequent salary entry): Paid salaries of $2,500. Of this amount, $1,200 applied to accrued wages payable at October 31 and $1,300 to wages payable for November 1 through November 8.

Illustration 3A-1 (page 116) shows the comparative entries.

The comparative entries show that the first three entries are the same whether or not the company uses reversing entries. The last two entries differ. The November 1 reversing entry eliminates the $1,200 balance in Salaries Payable, created by the October 31 adjusting entry. The reversing entry also creates a $1,200 credit balance in the Salaries Expense account. As you know, it is unusual for an expense account to have a credit balance. However, the balance is correct in this instance. Why? Because the company will debit the entire amount of the first salary payment in the new accounting period to Salaries Expense. This debit eliminates the credit balance. The resulting debit balance in the expense account will equal the salaries expense incurred in the new accounting period ($1,300 in this example).

When a company makes reversing entries, it debits all cash payments of expenses to the related expense account. This means that on November 8 (and every payday) the company debits Salaries Expense for the amount paid without regard to the existence of any accrued salaries payable. Repeating the same entry simplifies the recording process in an accounting system.

Reversing Entries Not Used			Reversing Entries Used		
Initial Salary Entry					
Oct. 24	Salaries Expense	4,000	Oct. 24	Salaries Expense	4,000
	Cash	4,000		Cash	4,000
Adjusting Entry					
Oct. 31	Salaries Expense	1,200	Oct. 31	Salaries Expense	1,200
	Salaries Payable	1,200		Salaries Payable	1,200
Closing Entry					
Oct. 31	Income Summary	5,200	Oct. 31	Income Summary	5,200
	Salaries Expense	5,200		Salaries Expense	5,200
Reversing Entry					
Nov. 1	No entry is made.		Nov. 1	Salaries Payable	1,200
				Salaries Expense	1,200
Subsequent Salary Entry					
Nov. 8	Salaries Payable	1,200	Nov. 8	Salaries Expense	2,500
	Salaries Expense	1,300		Cash	2,500
	Cash	2,500			

Illustration 3A-1
Comparison of Entries for Accruals, with and without Reversing Entries

Example of Reversing Entries—Prepayments

Up to this point, we assumed the recording of all prepayments as prepaid expense or unearned revenue. In some cases, though, a company records prepayments directly in expense or revenue accounts. When this occurs, a company may also reverse prepayments.

To illustrate the use of reversing entries for prepaid expenses, we use the following transaction and adjustment data.

1 December 10 (initial entry): Purchased $20,000 of office supplies with cash.

2 December 31 (adjusting entry): Determined that $5,000 of office supplies are on hand.

Illustration 3A-2 shows the comparative entries.

Illustration 3A-2
Comparison of Entries for Prepayments, with and without Reversing Entries

Reversing Entries Not Used			Reversing Entries Used		
Initial Purchase of Supplies Entry					
Dec. 10	Office Supplies	20,000	Dec. 10	Office Supplies Expense	20,000
	Cash	20,000		Cash	20,000
Adjusting Entry					
Dec. 31	Office Supplies Expense	15,000	Dec. 31	Office Supplies	5,000
	Office Supplies	15,000		Office Supplies Expense	5,000
Closing Entry					
Dec. 31	Income Summary	15,000	Dec. 31	Income Summary	15,000
	Office Supplies Expense	15,000		Office Supplies Expense	15,000
Reversing Entry					
Jan. 1	No entry		Jan. 1	Office Supplies Expense	5,000
				Office Supplies	5,000

After the adjusting entry on December 31 (regardless of whether using reversing entries), the asset account Office Supplies shows a balance of $5,000, and Office Supplies Expense shows a balance of $15,000. If the company initially debits Office Supplies Expense when it purchases the supplies, it then makes a reversing entry to return to the expense account the cost of unconsumed supplies. The company then continues to debit Office Supplies Expense for additional purchases of office supplies during the next period.

Prepaid items are generally entered in real accounts (assets and liabilities), thus making reversing entries unnecessary. This approach is used because it is advantageous for items that a company needs to apportion over several periods (e.g., supplies and parts inventories). However, for other items that do not follow this regular pattern and that may or may not involve two or more periods, a company ordinarily enters them initially in revenue or expense accounts. The revenue and expense accounts may not require adjusting, and the company thus systematically closes them to Income Summary.

Using the nominal accounts adds consistency to the accounting system. It also makes the recording more efficient, particularly when a large number of such transactions occur during the year. For example, the bookkeeper knows to expense invoice items (except for capital asset acquisitions). He or she need not worry whether an item will result in a prepaid expense at the end of the period, because the company will make adjustments at the end of the period.

Expanded Discussion of Cash Basis versus Accrual Basis Accounting

Summary of Reversing Entries

We summarize guidelines for reversing entries as follows.

1 All accrued items should be reversed.

2 All prepaid items for which a company debited or credited the original cash transaction to an expense or revenue account should be reversed.

3 Adjusting entries for depreciation and bad debts are not reversed.

Recognize that reversing entries do not have to be used. Therefore, some accountants avoid them entirely.

Summary of Learning Objective for Appendix 3A

9 Identify adjusting entries that may be reversed. Reversing entries are most often used to reverse two types of adjusting entries: accrued revenues and accrued expenses. Prepayments may also be reversed if the initial entry to record the transaction is made to an expense or revenue account.

BEHIND THE NUMBERS APPENDIX 3B	USING A WORKSHEET: THE ACCOUNTING CYCLE REVISITED

In this appendix we provide an additional example of the end-of-period steps in the accounting cycle and illustrate the use of a worksheet in this process. Using a **worksheet** often facilitates the end-of-period (monthly, quarterly, or annually) accounting and reporting process. Use of a worksheet helps a company prepare the financial statements on a more timely basis. How? With a worksheet, a company need not wait until it journalizes and posts the adjusting and closing entries.

A company prepares a worksheet either on columnar paper or within an electronic spreadsheet. In either form, a company uses the worksheet to adjust account balances and to prepare financial statements.

The worksheet does not replace the financial statements. Instead, it is an informal device for accumulating and sorting information needed for the financial statements.

OBJECTIVE 10

Prepare a 10-column worksheet.

Completing the worksheet provides considerable assurance that a company properly handled all of the details related to the end-of-period accounting and statement preparation. The 10-column worksheet in Illustration 3B-1 (page 119) provides columns for the first trial balance, adjustments, adjusted trial balance, income statement, and balance sheet.

Worksheet Columns

Trial Balance Columns

Uptown Cabinet Corp., shown in Illustration 3B-1, obtains data for the trial balance from its ledger balances at December 31. The amount for Merchandise Inventory, $40,000, is the year-end inventory amount, which results from the application of a perpetual inventory system.

Adjustments Columns

After Uptown enters all adjustment data on the worksheet, it establishes the equality of the adjustment columns. It then extends the balances in all accounts to the adjusted trial balance columns.

Adjustments Entered on the Worksheet

Items (a) through (g) below serve as the basis for the adjusting entries made in the worksheet for Uptown shown in Illustration 3B-1.

(a) Depreciation of furniture and equipment at the rate of 10% per year based on original cost of $67,000.

(b) Estimated bad debts of one-quarter of 1 percent of sales ($400,000).

(c) Insurance expired during the year, $360.

(d) Interest accrued on notes receivable as of December 31, $800.

(e) The Rent Expense account contains $500 rent paid in advance, which is applicable to next year.

(f) Property taxes accrued December 31, $2,000.

(g) Income tax payable estimated $3,440.

The adjusting entries shown on the December 31, 2008, worksheet are as follows.

	(a)		
Depreciation Expense—Furniture and Equipment		6,700	
Accumulated Depreciation—Furniture and Equipment			6,700
	(b)		
Bad Debt Expense		1,000	
Allowance for Doubtful Accounts			1,000
	(c)		
Insurance Expense		360	
Prepaid Insurance			360
	(d)		
Interest Receivable		800	
Interest Revenue			800
	(e)		
Prepaid Rent Expense		500	
Rent Expense			500
	(f)		
Property Tax Expense		2,000	
Property Tax Payable			2,000
	(g)		
Income Tax Expense		3,440	
Income Tax Payable			3,440

Uptown Cabinet transfers the adjusting entries to the Adjustments columns of the worksheet, often designating each by letter. The trial balance lists any new accounts resulting from the adjusting entries, as illustrated on the worksheet. (For example, see the accounts listed in rows 27 through 35 in Illustration 3B-1.) Uptown then totals and balances the Adjustments columns.

Adjusted Trial Balance

The adjusted trial balance shows the balance of all accounts after adjustment at the end of the accounting period. For example, Uptown adds the $2,000 shown opposite the Allowance for Doubtful Accounts in the Trial Balance Cr. column to the $1,000 in the Adjustments Cr. column. The company then extends the $3,000 total to the Adjusted Trial Balance Cr. column. Similarly, Uptown reduces the $900 debit opposite Prepaid Insurance by the $360 credit in the Adjustments column. The result, $540, is shown in the Adjusted Trial Balance Dr. column.

Income Statement and Balance Sheet Columns

Uptown extends all the debit items in the Adjusted Trial Balance columns into the Income Statement or Balance Sheet columns to the right. It similarly extends all the credit items.

The next step is to total the Income Statement columns. Uptown needs the amount of net income or loss for the period to balance the debit and credit columns. The net income of $12,200 is shown in the Income Statement Dr. column because revenues exceeded expenses by that amount.

Illustration 3B-1

Use of a Worksheet

UPTOWN CABINET CORP.
Ten–Column Worksheet for The Year Ended December 31, 2008

	A	B	C	D	E	F	G	H	I	J	K
	Accounts	**Trial Balance**		**Adjustments**		**Adjusted Trial Balance**		**Income Statement**		**Balance Sheet**	
1		Dr.	Cr.	Dr.	Cr.	Dr.	Cr.	Dr.	Cr.	Dr.	Cr.
2	Cash	1,200				1,200				1,200	
3	Notes Receivable	16,000				16,000				16,000	
4	Accounts Receivable	41,000				41,000				41,000	
5	Allowance for Doubtful Accounts		2,000		(b) 1,000		3,000				3,000
6	Merchandise Inventory	40,000				40,000				40,000	
7	Prepaid Insurance	900			(c) 360	540				540	
8	Furniture and Equipment	67,000				67,000				67,000	
9	Accumulated Depreciation- Furniture and Equipment		12,000		(a) 6,700		18,700				18,700
10	Notes Payable		20,000				20,000				20,000
11	Accounts Payable		13,500				13,500				13,500
12	Bonds Payable		30,000				30,000				30,000
13	Common Stock		50,000				50,000				50,000
14	Retained Earnings, Jan. 1, 2008		16,200				16,200				16,200
15	Dividends	2,000				2,000				2,000	
16	Sales		400,000				400,000		400,000		
17	Cost of Goods Sold	316,000				316,000		316,000			
18	Sales Salaries Expense	20,000				20,000		20,000			
19	Advertising Expense	2,200				2,200		2,200			
20	Traveling Expense	8,000				8,000		8,000			
21	Salaries, Office and General	19,000				19,000		19,000			
22	Telephone and Internet Expense	600				600		600			
23	Rent Expense	4,800			(e) 500	4,300		4,300			
24	Property Tax Expense	3,300		(f) 2,000		5,300		5,300			
25	Interest Expense	1,700				1,700		1,700			
26	Totals	543,700	543,700								
27	Depreciation Expense- Furniture and Equipment			(a) 6,700		6,700		6,700			
28	Bad Debt Expense			(b) 1,000		1,000		1,000			
29	Insurance Expense			(c) 360		360		360			
30	Interest Receivable			(d) 800		800				800	
31	Interest Revenue				(d) 800		800		800		
32	Prepaid Rent Expense			(e) 500		500				500	
33	Property Tax Payable				(f) 2,000		2,000				2,000
34	Income Tax Expense			(g) 3,440				3,440			
35	Income Tax Payable				(g) 3,440						3,440
36	Totals			14,800	14,800	554,200	554,200	388,600	400,800		
37	Net Income							12,200			12,200
38	Totals							400,800	400,800	169,040	169,040
39											
40											
41											
42											
43											

Sheet1 / Sheet2 / Sheet3

Uptown then balances the Income Statement columns. The company also enters the net income of $12,200 in the Balance Sheet Cr. column as an increase in retained earnings.

Preparing Financial Statements from a Worksheet

The worksheet provides the information needed for preparation of the financial statements without reference to the ledger or other records. In addition, the worksheet sorts the data into appropriate columns, which facilitates the preparation of the statements. The financial statements for Uptown Cabinet are shown in Chapter 3, pages 108 and 109.

Key Term for Appendix 3B

worksheet, 117

Summary of Learning Objective for Appendix 3B

10 Prepare a 10-column worksheet. The 10-column worksheet provides columns for the first trial balance, adjustments, adjusted trial balance, income statement, and balance sheet. The worksheet does not replace the financial statements. Instead, it is an informal device for accumulating and sorting information needed for the financial statements.

REVIEW EXERCISE

Nalezny Advertising Agency was founded by Casey Hayward in January 2005. Presented below are both the adjusted and unadjusted trial balances as of December 31, 2008.

Nalezny Advertising Agency
Trial Balance
December 31, 2008

	Unadjusted		Adjusted	
	Dr.	Cr.	Dr.	Cr.
Cash	$ 11,000		$ 11,000	
Accounts Receivable	20,000		21,500	
Art Supplies	8,400		5,000	
Printing Equipment	60,000		60,000	
Accumulated Depreciation		$ 28,000		$ 35,000
Accounts Payable		5,000		5,000
Unearned Advertising Revenue		7,000		5,600
Salaries Payable		–0–		1,300
Common Stock		10,000		10,000
Retained Earnings		4,800		4,800
Advertising Revenue		58,600		61,500
Salaries Expense	10,000		11,300	
Depreciation Expense			7,000	
Art Supplies Expense			3,400	
Rent Expense	4,000		4,000	
	$113,400	$113,400	$123,200	$123,200

Instructions

a Journalize the annual adjusting entries that were made.

b Prepare an income statement for the year ending December 31, 2008, and a balance sheet at December 31.

c Describe the remaining steps in the accounting cycle to be completed by Nalezny for 2008.

Solution

a

Dec. 31	Accounts Receivable	1,500	
	Advertising Revenue		1,500
31	Unearned Advertising Revenue	1,400	
	Advertising Revenue		1,400
31	Art Supplies Expense	3,400	
	Art Supplies		3,400
31	Depreciation Expense	7,000	
	Accumulated Depreciation		7,000
31	Salaries Expense	1,300	
	Salaries Payable		1,300

b

Nalezny Advertising Agency
Income Statement
For the Year Ended December 31, 2008

Revenues		
Advertising revenue		$61,500
Expenses		
Salaries expense	$11,300	
Depreciation expense	7,000	
Rent expense	4,000	
Art supplies expense	3,400	
Total expenses		25,700
Net income		$35,800

Nalezny Advertising Agency
Balance Sheet
December 31, 2008

Assets

Cash		$11,000
Accounts receivable		21,500
Art supplies		5,000
Printing equipment	$60,000	
Less: Accumulated depreciation—Printing equipment	35,000	25,000
Total assets		$62,500

Liabilities and Stockholders' Equity

Liabilities		
Accounts payable		$5,000
Unearned advertising revenue		5,600
Salaries payable		1,300
Total liabilities		11,900

Stockholders' equity			
Common stock		$10,000	
Retained earnings		40,600*	50,600
Total liabilities and stockholders' equity			$62,500

*Retained earnings, Jan. 1, 2008	$ 4,800	
Add: Net income	35,800	
Retained earnings, Dec. 31, 2008	$40,600	

c Following preparation of financial statements (see Illustration 3-34, 3-35), Nalezny would prepare closing entries to reduce the temporary accounts to zero. Some companies prepare a post-closing trial balance and reversing entries.

Questions

Note: All **asterisked** assignment materials relate to material contained in the appendices to the chapter.

1 Give an example of a transaction that results in:

(a) A decrease in an asset and a decrease in a liability.

(b) A decrease in one asset and an increase in another asset.

(c) A decrease in one liability and an increase in another liability.

2 Do the following events represent business transactions? Explain your answer in each case.

(a) A computer is purchased on account.

(b) A customer returns merchandise and is given credit on account.

(c) A prospective employee is interviewed.

(d) The owner of the business withdraws cash from the business for personal use.

(e) Merchandise is ordered for delivery next month.

3 Name the accounts debited and credited for each of the following transactions.

(a) Billing a customer for work done.

(b) Receipt of cash from customer on account.

(c) Purchase of office supplies on account.

(d) Purchase of 15 gallons of gasoline for the delivery truck.

4 Why are revenue and expense accounts called temporary or nominal accounts?

5 Omar Morena, a fellow student, contends that the double-entry system means that each transaction must be recorded twice. Is Omar correct? Explain.

6 Is it necessary that a trial balance be prepared periodically? What purpose does it serve?

7 Indicate whether each of the items below is a real or nominal account and whether it appears in the balance sheet or the income statement.

(a) Prepaid Rent.

(b) Salaries and Wages Payable.

(c) Merchandise Inventory.

(d) Accumulated Depreciation.

(e) Office Equipment.

(f) Service Revenue.

(g) Office Salaries Expense.

(h) Supplies on Hand.

8 Employees are paid every Saturday for the preceding work week. If a balance sheet is prepared on Wednesday, December 31, what does the amount of wages earned during the first three days of the week (12/29, 12/30, 12/31) represent? Explain.

9 (a) How do the components of revenues and expenses differ between a merchandising company and a service enterprise? (b) Explain the income measurement process of a merchandising company.

10 What is the purpose of the Cost of Goods Sold account? (Assume a periodic inventory system.)

11 Under a perpetual system, what is the purpose of the Cost of Goods Sold account?

12 If the $3,900 cost of a new microcomputer and printer purchased for office use were recorded as a debit to Purchases, what would be the effect of the error on the balance sheet and income statement in the period in which the error was made?

13 What differences are there between the trial balance before closing and the trial balance after closing with respect to the following accounts?

(a) Accounts Payable.

(b) Expense accounts.

(c) Revenue accounts.

(d) Retained Earnings account.

(e) Cash.

14 What are adjusting entries and why are they necessary?

15 What are closing entries and why are they necessary?

16 John Damon, maintenance supervisor for Red Sox Insurance Co., has purchased a riding lawnmower and accessories to be used in maintaining the grounds around corporate head-quarters. He has sent the following information to the accounting department.

Cost of mower and		Date purchased	7/1/08
accessories	$3,000	Monthly salary of	
Estimated useful life	5 yrs	groundskeeper	$1,100
		Estimated annual	
		fuel cost	$150

Compute the amount of depreciation expense (related to the mower and accessories) that should be reported on Red Sox's December 31, 2008, income statement. Assume straight-line depreciation.

17 Selanne Enterprises made the following entry on December 31, 2008.

Interest Expense	10,000	
Interest Payable		10,000
(To record interest expense due on loan		
from Anaheim National Bank.)		

What entry would Anaheim National Bank make regarding its outstanding loan to Selanne Enterprises? Explain why this must be the case.

*18 What are reversing entries, and why are they used?

*19 "A worksheet is a permanent accounting record, and its use is required in the accounting cycle." Do you agree? Explain.

Brief Exercises

BE3-1 Transactions for Argot Company for the month of May are presented below. Prepare journal entries for each of these transactions. (You may omit explanations.)   **(LO 4)**

May	1	B.D. Argot invests $3,000 cash in exchange for common stock in a small welding corporation.
	3	Buys equipment on account for $1,100.
	13	Pays $400 to landlord for May rent.
	21	Bills Noble Corp. $500 for welding work done.

BE3-2 Brett Favre Repair Shop (a sole proprietorship) had the following transactions during the first month of business. Journalize the transactions. (Omit explanations.)   **(LO 4, 5)**

Aug.	2	Invested $12,000 cash and $2,500 of equipment in the business.
	7	Purchased supplies on account for $400. (Debit asset account.)
	12	Performed services for clients, for which $1,300 was collected in cash and $670 was billed to the clients.
	15	Paid August rent $600.
	19	Counted supplies and determined that only $270 of the supplies purchased on August 7 are still on hand.

BE3-3 On July 1, 2008, Blair Co. pays $18,000 to Hindi Insurance Company for a 3-year insurance contract. Both companies have fiscal years ending December 31. For Blair Co. journalize the entry on July 1 and the adjusting entry on December 31.   **(LO 4, 5)**

BE3-4 Using the data in BE3-3, journalize the entry on July 1 and the adjusting entry on December 31 for Hindi Insurance Company. Hindi uses the accounts Unearned Insurance Revenue and Insurance Revenue.   **(LO 4, 5)**

BE3-5 Assume that on February 1, **Procter & Gamble (P&G)** paid $840,000 in advance for 2 years' insur-ance coverage. Prepare P&G's February 1 journal entry and the annual adjusting entry on June 30.   **(LO 4, 5)**

BE3-6 Mogilny Corporation owns a warehouse. On November 1, it rented storage space to a lessee (tenant) for 3 months for a total cash payment of $2,700 received in advance. Prepare Mogilny's November 1 journal en-try and the December 31 annual adjusting entry.   **(LO 4, 5)**

(LO 4, 5)   **BE3-7** Catherine Janeway Company's weekly payroll, paid on Fridays, totals $6,000. Employees work a 5-day week. Prepare Janeway's adjusting entry on Wednesday, December 31, and the journal entry to record the $6,000 cash payment on Friday, January 2.

(LO 5)   **BE3-8** Included in Martinez Company's December 31 trial balance is a note receivable of $10,000. The note is a 4-month, 12% note dated October 1. Prepare Martinez's December 31 adjusting entry to record $300 of accrued interest, and the February 1 journal entry to record receipt of $10,400 from the borrower.

(LO 5)   **BE3-9** Prepare the following adjusting entries at August 31 for **Walgreens**.

(a) Interest on notes payable of $400 is accrued.
(b) Fees earned but unbilled total $1,400.
(c) Salaries earned by employees of $700 have not been recorded.
(d) Bad debt expense for year is $900.

Use the following account titles: Service Revenue, Accounts Receivable, Interest Expense, Interest Payable, Salaries Expense, Salaries Payable, Allowance for Doubtful Accounts, and Bad Debt Expense.

(LO 5)   **BE3-10** At the end of its first year of operations, the trial balance of Rafael Company shows Equipment $30,000 and zero balances in Accumulated Depreciation—Equipment and Depreciation Expense. Depreciation for the year is estimated to be $3,000. Prepare the adjusting entry for depreciation at December 31, and indicate the balance sheet presentation for the equipment at December 31.

(LO 8)   **BE3-11** Willis Corporation has beginning inventory $81,000; Purchases $540,000; Freight-in $16,200; Purchase Returns $5,800; Purchase Discounts $5,000; and ending inventory $70,200. Compute cost of goods sold.

(LO 7)   **BE3-12** Karen Sepaniak has year-end account balances of Sales $828,900; Interest Revenue $13,500; Cost of Goods Sold $556,200; Operating Expenses $189,000; Income Tax Expense $35,100; and Dividends $18,900. Prepare the year-end closing entries.

(LO 9)   ***BE3-13** Assume that **Best Buy** made a December 31 adjusting entry to debit Salaries Expense and credit Salaries Payable for $3,600 for one of its departments. On January 2, Best Buy paid the weekly payroll of $6,000. Prepare Best Buy's (a) January 1 reversing entry; (b) January 2 entry (assuming the reversing entry was prepared); and (c) January 2 entry (assuming the reversing entry was not prepared).

Exercises

(LO 4)   **E3-1** (Transaction Analysis—Service Company)   Beverly Crusher is a licensed CPA. During the first month of operations of her business (a sole proprietorship), the following events and transactions occurred.

April	2	Invested $32,000 cash and equipment valued at $14,000 in the business.
	2	Hired a secretary-receptionist at a salary of $290 per week payable monthly.
	3	Purchased supplies on account $700. (Debit an asset account.)
	7	Paid office rent of $600 for the month.
	11	Completed a tax assignment and billed client $1,100 for services rendered. (Use Service Revenue account.)
	12	Received $3,200 advance on a management consulting engagement.
	17	Received cash of $2,300 for services completed for Ferengi Co.
	21	Paid insurance expense $110.
	30	Paid secretary-receptionist $1,160 for the month.
	30	A count of supplies indicated that $120 of supplies had been used.
	30	Purchased a new computer for $6,100 with personal funds. (The computer will be used exclusively for business purposes.)

Instructions

Journalize the transactions in the general journal. (Omit explanations.)

(LO 4)   **E3-2** (Corrected Trial Balance)   The trial balance of Wanda Landowska Company (shown on the next page) does not balance. Your review of the ledger reveals the following: (a) Each account had a normal balance. (b) The debit footings in Prepaid Insurance, Accounts Payable, and Property Tax Expense were each understated $100. (c) A transposition error was made in Accounts Receivable and Service Revenue; the correct balances for Accounts Receivable and Service Revenue are $2,750 and $6,690, respectively. (d) A debit posting to Advertising Expense of $300 was omitted. (e) A $1,500 cash drawing by the owner was debited to Wanda Landowska, Capital, and credited to Cash.

Wanda Landowska Company
Trial Balance
April 30, 2008

	Debit	Credit
Cash	$ 4,800	
Accounts Receivable	2,570	
Prepaid Insurance	700	
Equipment		$ 8,000
Accounts Payable		4,500
Property Tax Payable	560	
Wanda Landowska, Capital		11,200
Service Revenue	6,960	
Salaries Expense	4,200	
Advertising Expense	1,100	
Property Tax Expense		800
	$20,890	$24,500

Instructions

Prepare a correct trial balance.

E3-3 (Corrected Trial Balance) The trial balance of Blues Traveler Corporation does not balance. (LO 4)

Blues Traveler Corporation
Trial Balance
April 30, 2008

	Debit	Credit
Cash	$ 5,912	
Accounts Receivable	5,240	
Supplies on Hand	2,967	
Furniture and Equipment	6,100	
Accounts Payable		$ 7,044
Common Stock		8,000
Retained Earnings		2,000
Service Revenue		5,200
Office Expense	4,320	
	$24,539	$22,244

An examination of the ledger shows these errors.

1. Cash received from a customer on account was recorded (both debit and credit) as $1,380 instead of $1,830.
2. The purchase on account of a computer costing $3,200 was recorded as a debit to Office Expense and a credit to Accounts Payable.
3. Services were performed on account for a client, $2,250, for which Accounts Receivable was debited $2,250 and Service Revenue was credited $225.
4. A payment of $95 for telephone charges was entered as a debit to Office Expenses and a debit to Cash.
5. The Service Revenue account was totaled at $5,200 instead of $5,280.

Instructions

From this information prepare a corrected trial balance.

E3-4 (Corrected Trial Balance) The trial balance of Watteau Co. (shown on the next page) does not balance. (LO 4)

Watteau Co.
Trial Balance
June 30, 2008

	Debit	Credit
Cash		$ 2,870
Accounts Receivable	$ 3,231	
Supplies	800	
Equipment	3,800	
Accounts Payable		2,666
Unearned Service Revenue	1,200	
Common Stock		6,000
Retained Earnings		3,000
Service Revenue		2,380
Wages Expense	3,400	
Office Expense	940	
	$13,371	$16,916

Each of the listed accounts should have a normal balance per the general ledger. An examination of the ledger and journal reveals the following errors.

1. Cash received from a customer on account was debited for $570, and Accounts Receivable was credited for the same amount. The actual collection was for $750.
2. The purchase of a computer printer on account for $500 was recorded as a debit to Supplies for $500 and a credit to Accounts Payable for $500.
3. Services were performed on account for a client for $890. Accounts Receivable was debited for $890 and Service Revenue was credited for $89.
4. A payment of $65 for telephone charges was recorded as a debit to Office Expense for $65 and a debit to Cash for $65.
5. When the Unearned Service Revenue account was reviewed, it was found that $325 of the balance was earned prior to June 30.
6. A debit posting to Wages Expense of $670 was omitted.
7. A payment on account for $206 was credited to Cash for $206 and credited to Accounts Payable for $260.
8. A dividend of $575 was debited to Wages Expense for $575 and credited to Cash for $575.

Instructions

Prepare a correct trial balance. (*Note:* It may be necessary to add one or more accounts to the trial balance.)

(LO 5)

E3-5 **(Adjusting Entries)** The ledger of Duggan Rental Agency on March 31 of the current year includes the following selected accounts before adjusting entries have been prepared.

	Debit	Credit
Prepaid Insurance	$ 3,600	
Supplies	2,800	
Equipment	25,000	
Accumulated Depreciation—Equipment		$ 8,400
Notes Payable		20,000
Unearned Rent Revenue		9,300
Rent Revenue		60,000
Interest Expense	–0–	
Wage Expense	14,000	

An analysis of the accounts shows the following.

1. The equipment depreciates $250 per month.
2. One-third of the unearned rent was earned during the quarter.
3. Interest of $500 is accrued on the notes payable.
4. Supplies on hand total $850.
5. Insurance expires at the rate of $300 per month.

Instructions

Prepare the adjusting entries at March 31, assuming that adjusting entries are made quarterly. Additional accounts are: Depreciation Expense; Insurance Expense; Interest Payable; and Supplies Expense. (Omit explanations.)

E3-6 (Adjusting Entries) Karen Weller, D.D.S., opened a dental practice on January 1, 2008. During the first month of operations the following transactions occurred.

(LO 5)

1. Performed services for patients who had dental plan insurance. At January 31, $750 of such services was earned but not yet billed to the insurance companies.
2. Utility expenses incurred but not paid prior to January 31 totaled $520.
3. Purchased dental equipment on January 1 for $80,000, paying $20,000 in cash and signing a $60,000, 3-year note payable. The equipment depreciates $400 per month. Interest is $500 per month.
4. Purchased a one-year malpractice insurance policy on January 1 for $12,000.
5. Purchased $1,600 of dental supplies. On January 31, determined that $500 of supplies were on hand.

Instructions

Prepare the adjusting entries on January 31. (Omit explanations.) Account titles are: Accumulated Depreciation—Dental Equipment; Depreciation Expense; Service Revenue; Accounts Receivable; Insurance Expense; Interest Expense; Interest Payable; Prepaid Insurance; Supplies; Supplies Expense; Utilities Expense; and Utilities Payable.

E3-7 (Analyze Adjusted Data) A partial adjusted trial balance of Piper Company at January 31, 2008, shows the following.

(LO 5)

Piper Company Adjusted Trial Balance January 31, 2008		
	Debit	Credit
Supplies	$ 700	
Prepaid Insurance	2,400	
Salaries Payable		$ 800
Unearned Revenue		750
Supplies Expense	950	
Insurance Expense	400	
Salaries Expense	1,800	
Service Revenue		2,000

Instructions

Answer the following questions, assuming the year begins January 1.

(a) If the amount in Supplies Expense is the January 31 adjusting entry, and $850 of supplies was purchased in January, what was the balance in Supplies on January 1?
(b) If the amount in Insurance Expense is the January 31 adjusting entry, and the original insurance premium was for one year, what was the total premium and when was the policy purchased?
(c) If $2,500 of salaries was paid in January, what was the balance in Salaries Payable at December 31, 2007?
(d) If $1,600 was received in January for services performed in January, what was the balance in Unearned Revenue at December 31, 2007?

E3-8 (Adjusting Entries) Andy Roddick is the new owner of Ace Computer Services. At the end of August 2008, his first month of ownership, Roddick is trying to prepare monthly financial statements. Below is some information related to unrecorded expenses that the business incurred during August.

(LO 5)

1. At August 31, Roddick owed his employees $1,900 in wages that will be paid on September 1.
2. At the end of the month he had not yet received the month's utility bill. Based on past experience, he estimated the bill would be approximately $600.
3. On August 1, Roddick borrowed $30,000 from a local bank on a 15-year mortgage. The annual interest rate is 8%.
4. A telephone bill in the amount of $117 covering August charges is unpaid at August 31.

Instructions

Prepare the adjusting journal entries as of August 31, 2008, suggested by the information above.

(LO 5)

E3-9 (**Adjusting Entries**) Selected accounts of Urdu Company are shown below.

Supplies				Accounts Receivable			
Beg. Bal.	800	10/31	470	10/17	2,400		
				10/31	1,650		

Salaries Expense				Salaries Payable			
10/15	800					10/31	600
10/31	600						

Unearned Service Revenue				Supplies Expense			
10/31	400	10/20	650	10/31	470		

Service Revenue			
		10/17	2,400
		10/31	1,650
		10/31	400

Instructions

From an analysis of the T-accounts, reconstruct (a) the October transaction entries, and (b) the adjusting journal entries that were made on October 31, 2008. Prepare explanations for each journal entry.

(LO 5)

E3-10 (**Adjusting Entries**) Greco Resort opened for business on June 1 with eight air-conditioned units. Its trial balance on August 31 is as follows.

Greco Resort
Trial Balance
August 31, 2008

	Debit	Credit
Cash	$ 19,600	
Prepaid Insurance	4,500	
Supplies	2,600	
Land	20,000	
Cottages	120,000	
Furniture	16,000	
Accounts Payable		$ 4,500
Unearned Rent Revenue		4,600
Mortgage Payable		60,000
Common Stock		91,000
Retained Earnings		9,000
Dividends	5,000	
Rent Revenue		76,200
Salaries Expense	44,800	
Utilities Expense	9,200	
Repair Expense	3,600	
	$245,300	$245,300

Other data:

1. The balance in prepaid insurance is a one-year premium paid on June 1, 2008.
2. An inventory count on August 31 shows $450 of supplies on hand.
3. Annual depreciation rates are cottages (4%) and furniture (10%). Salvage value is estimated to be 10% of cost.
4. Unearned Rent Revenue of $3,800 was earned prior to August 31.
5. Salaries of $375 were unpaid at August 31.
6. Rentals of $800 were due from tenants at August 31.
7. The mortgage (dated June 1, 2008) has an interest rate of 8% per year.

Instructions

(a) Journalize the adjusting entries on August 31 for the 3-month period June 1–August 31. (Omit explanations.)

(b) Prepare an adjusted trial balance on August 31.

E3-11 (Prepare Financial Statements) The adjusted trial balance of Anderson Cooper Co. as of December 31, 2008, contains the following.

Anderson Cooper Co.
Adjusted Trial Balance
December 31, 2008

Account Titles	Dr.	Cr.
Cash	$19,472	
Accounts Receivable	6,920	
Prepaid Rent	2,280	
Equipment	18,050	
Accumulated Depreciation		$ 4,895
Notes Payable		5,700
Accounts Payable		5,472
Common Stock		20,000
Retained Earnings		11,310
Dividends	3,000	
Service Revenue		11,590
Salaries Expense	6,840	
Rent Expense	2,260	
Depreciation Expense	145	
Interest Expense	83	
Interest Payable		83
	$59,050	$59,050

Instructions

(a) Prepare an income statement.

(b) Prepare a statement of retained earnings.

(c) Prepare a classified balance sheet.

E3-12 (Prepare Financial Statements) Santo Design Agency was founded by Thomas Grant in January 2004. Presented below is the adjusted trial balance as of December 31, 2008.

Santo Design Agency
Adjusted Trial Balance
December 31, 2008

	Dr.	Cr.
Cash	$ 11,000	
Accounts Receivable	21,500	
Art Supplies	5,000	
Prepaid Insurance	2,500	
Printing Equipment	60,000	
Accumulated Depreciation		$ 35,000
Accounts Payable		5,000
Interest Payable		150
Notes Payable		5,000
Unearned Advertising Revenue		5,600
Salaries Payable		1,300
Common Stock		10,000
Retained Earnings		3,500
Advertising Revenue		61,500
Salaries Expense	11,300	
Insurance Expense	850	
Interest Expense	500	
Depreciation Expense	7,000	
Art Supplies Expense	3,400	
Rent Expense	4,000	
	$127,050	$127,050

Instructions

(a) Prepare an income statement and a statement of retained earnings for the year ending December 31, 2008, and an unclassified balance sheet at December 31.

(b) Answer the following questions.
  (1) If the note has been outstanding 6 months, what is the annual interest rate on that note?
  (2) If the company paid $17,500 in salaries in 2008, what was the balance in Salaries Payable on December 31, 2007?

(LO 7)   **E3-13** (Closing Entries)   The adjusted trial balance of Lopez Company shows the following data pertaining to sales at the end of its fiscal year, October 31, 2007: Sales $800,000, Freight-out $12,000, Sales Returns and Allowances $24,000, and Sales Discounts $15,000.

Instructions

(a) Prepare the sales revenue section of the income statement.

(b) Prepare separate closing entries for (1) sales and (2) the contra accounts to sales.

(LO 7)   **E3-14** (Closing Entries)   Presented below is information related to Gonzales Corporation for the month of January 2008.

Cost of goods sold	$208,000	Salary expense	$ 61,000
Freight-out	7,000	Sales discounts	8,000
Insurance expense	12,000	Sales returns and allowances	13,000
Rent expense	20,000	Sales	350,000

Instructions

Prepare the necessary closing entries.

(LO 8)   **E3-15** (Missing Amounts)   Presented below is financial information for two different companies.

	Alatorre Company	Eduardo Company
Sales	$90,000	(d)
Sales returns	(a)	$ 5,000
Net sales	81,000	95,000
Cost of goods sold	56,000	(e)
Gross profit	(b)	38,000
Operating expenses	15,000	23,000
Net income	(c)	15,000

Instructions

Compute the missing amounts.

(LO 8)   **E3-16** (Find Missing Amounts—Periodic Inventory)   Financial information is presented below for four different companies.

	Pamela's Cosmetics	Dean's Grocery	Anderson Wholesalers	Baywatch Supply Co.
Sales	$78,000	(c)	$144,000	$100,000
Sales returns	(a)	$ 5,000	12,000	9,000
Net sales	74,000	94,000	132,000	(g)
Beginning inventory	16,000	(d)	44,000	24,000
Purchases	88,000	100,000	(e)	85,000
Purchase returns	6,000	10,000	8,000	(h)
Ending inventory	(b)	48,000	30,000	28,000
Cost of goods sold	64,000	72,000	(f)	72,000
Gross profit	10,000	22,000	18,000	(i)

Instructions

Determine the missing amounts (a–i). Show all computations.

(LO 8)   **E3-17** (Cost of Goods Sold Section—Periodic Inventory)   The trial balance of the Neville Mariner Company at the end of its fiscal year, August 31, 2008, includes the following accounts: Merchandise Inventory $17,500; Purchases $149,400; Sales $200,000; Freight-in $4,000; Sales Returns and Allowances $4,000; Freight-out $1,000; and Purchase Returns and Allowances $2,000. The ending merchandise inventory is $25,000.

Instructions

Prepare a cost of goods sold section for the year ending August 31.

E3-18 (Closing Entries for a Corporation) Presented below are selected account balances for Homer Winslow Co. as of December 31, 2008.   (LO 7)

Merchandise Inventory 12/31/08	$ 60,000	Cost of Goods Sold	$225,700
Common Stock	75,000	Selling Expenses	16,000
Retained Earnings	45,000	Administrative Expenses	38,000
Dividends	18,000	Income Tax Expense	30,000
Sales Returns and Allowances	12,000		
Sales Discounts	15,000		
Sales	410,000		

Instructions

Prepare closing entries for Homer Winslow Co. on December 31, 2008. (Omit explanations.)

E3-19 (Transactions of a Corporation, Including Investment and Dividend) Scratch Miniature Golf and Driving Range Inc. was opened on March 1 by Scott Verplank. The following selected events and transactions occurred during March.   (LO 4)

Mar.	1	Invested $50,000 cash in the business in exchange for common stock.
	3	Purchased Michelle Wie's Golf Land for $38,000 cash. The price consists of land $10,000; building $22,000; and equipment $6,000. (Make one compound entry.)
	5	Advertised the opening of the driving range and miniature golf course, paying advertising expenses of $1,600.
	6	Paid cash $1,480 for a one-year insurance policy.
	10	Purchased golf equipment for $2,500 from Singh Company, payable in 30 days.
	18	Received golf fees of $1,200 in cash.
	25	Declared and paid a $500 cash dividend.
	30	Paid wages of $900.
	30	Paid Singh Company in full.
	31	Received $750 of fees in cash.

Scratch uses the following accounts: Cash; Prepaid Insurance; Land; Buildings; Equipment; Accounts Payable; Common Stock; Dividends; Service Revenue; Advertising Expense; and Wages Expense.

Instructions

Journalize the March transactions. (Provide explanations for the journal entries.)

*E3-20 (Adjusting and Reversing Entries) When the accounts of Daniel Barenboim Inc. are examined, the adjusting data listed below are uncovered on December 31, the end of an annual fiscal period.   (LO 5, 9)

1. The prepaid insurance account shows a debit of $5,280, representing the cost of a 2-year fire insurance policy dated August 1 of the current year.
2. On November 1, Rental Revenue was credited for $1,800, representing revenue from a subrental for a 3-month period beginning on that date.
3. Purchase of advertising materials for $800 during the year was recorded in the Advertising Expense account. On December 31, advertising materials of $290 are on hand.
4. Interest of $770 has accrued on notes payable.

Instructions

Prepare the following in general journal form.

(a) The adjusting entry for each item.
(b) The reversing entry for each item where appropriate.

*E3-21 (Worksheet) Presented on the next page are selected accounts for Alvarez Company as reported in the worksheet at the end of May 2008.   (LO 10)

Accounts	Adjusted Trial Balance Dr.	Cr.	Income Statement Dr.	Cr.	Balance Sheet Dr.	Cr.
Cash	9,000					
Merchandise Inventory	80,000					
Sales		450,000				
Sales Returns and Allowances	10,000					
Sales Discounts	5,000					
Cost of Goods Sold	250,000					

Instructions

Complete the worksheet by extending amounts reported in the adjusted trial balance to the appropriate columns in the worksheet. Do not total individual columns.

(LO 6, 10)   *E3-22 (**Worksheet and Balance Sheet Presentation**)   The adjusted trial balance for Ed Bradley Co. is presented in the following worksheet for the month ended April 30, 2008.

Ed Bradley Co.
Worksheet (partial)
For the Month Ended April 30, 2008

Account Titles	Adjusted Trial Balance Dr.	Cr.	Income Statement Dr.	Cr.	Balance Sheet Dr.	Cr.
Cash	$19,472					
Accounts Receivable	6,920					
Prepaid Rent	2,280					
Equipment	18,050					
Accumulated Depreciation		$ 4,895				
Notes Payable		5,700				
Accounts Payable		5,472				
Bradley, Capital		34,960				
Bradley, Drawing	6,650					
Service Revenue		11,590				
Salaries Expense	6,840					
Rent Expense	2,260					
Depreciation Expense	145					
Interest Expense	83					
Interest Payable		83				

Instructions

Complete the worksheet and prepare a classified balance sheet.

(LO 10)   *E3-23 (**Partial Worksheet Preparation**)   Jurassic Park Co. prepares monthly financial statements from a worksheet. Selected portions of the January worksheet showed the following data.

Jurassic Park Co.
Worksheet (partial)
For the Month Ended January 31, 2008

Account Title	Trial Balance Dr.	Cr.	Adjustments Dr.	Cr.	Adjusted Trial Balance Dr.	Cr.
Supplies	3,256			(a) 1,500	1,756	
Accumulated Depreciation		6,682		(b) 257		6,939
Interest Payable		100		(c) 50		150
Supplies Expense			(a) 1,500		1,500	
Depreciation Expense			(b) 257		257	
Interest Expense			(c) 50		50	

During February no events occurred that affected these accounts, but at the end of February the following information was available.

(a) Supplies on hand	$715
(b) Monthly depreciation	$257
(c) Accrued interest	$ 50

Instructions

Reproduce the data that would appear in the February worksheet, and indicate the amounts that would be shown in the February income statement.

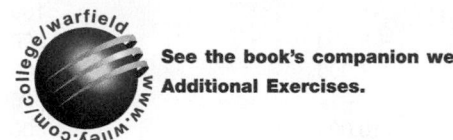

See the book's companion website, www.wiley.com/college/warfield, for Additional Exercises.

Problems

P3-1 **(Transactions, Financial Statements—Service Company)**   Listed below are the transactions of Shigeki Muruyama, D.D.S., for the month of September. **(LO 4, 6, 7)**

Sept.	1	Muruyama begins practice as a dentist and invests $20,000 cash.
	2	Purchases furniture and dental equipment on account from Green Jacket Co. for $17,280.
	4	Pays rent for office space, $680 for the month.
	4	Employs a receptionist, Michael Bradley.
	5	Purchases dental supplies for cash, $942.
	8	Receives cash of $1,690 from patients for services performed.
	10	Pays miscellaneous office expenses, $430.
	14	Bills patients $5,120 for services performed.
	18	Pays Green Jacket Co. on account, $3,600.
	19	Withdraws $3,000 cash from the business for personal use.
	20	Receives $980 from patients on account.
	25	Bills patients $2,110 for services performed.
	30	Pays the following expenses in cash: office salaries $1,400; miscellaneous office expenses $85.
	30	Dental supplies used during September, $330.

Instructions

(a) Enter the transactions shown above in appropriate general ledger accounts (use T-accounts). Use the following ledger accounts: Cash; Accounts Receivable; Supplies on Hand; Furniture and Equipment; Accumulated Depreciation; Accounts Payable; Shigeki Muruyama, Capital; Service Revenue; Rent Expense; Miscellaneous Office Expense; Office Salaries Expense; Supplies Expense; Depreciation Expense; and Income Summary. Allow 10 lines for the Cash and Income Summary accounts, and 5 lines for each of the other accounts needed. Record depreciation using a 5-year life on the furniture and equipment, the straight-line method, and no salvage value. Do not use a drawing account.
(b) Prepare an adjusted trial balance.
(c) Prepare an income statement, an unclassified balance sheet, and a statement of owner's equity.
(d) Close the ledger.
(e) Prepare a post-closing trial balance.

P3-2 **(Adjusting Entries and Financial Statements)**   Yount Advertising Agency was founded in January 2004. Presented below are adjusted and unadjusted trial balances as of December 31, 2008. **(LO 5, 6)**

Yount Advertising Agency
Trial Balance
December 31, 2008

	Unadjusted		Adjusted	
	Dr.	Cr.	Dr.	Cr.
Cash	$ 11,000		$ 11,000	
Accounts Receivable	20,000		21,500	
Art Supplies	8,400		5,000	
Prepaid Insurance	3,350		2,500	
Printing Equipment	60,000		60,000	
Accumulated Depreciation		$ 28,000		$ 35,000
Accounts Payable		5,000		5,000
Interest Payable		–0–		150
Notes Payable		5,000		5,000
Unearned Advertising Revenue		7,000		5,600
Salaries Payable		–0–		1,300
Common Stock		10,000		10,000
Retained Earnings		3,500		3,500
Advertising Revenue		58,600		61,500
Salaries Expense	10,000		11,300	
Insurance Expense			850	
Interest Expense	350		500	
Depreciation Expense			7,000	
Art Supplies Expense			3,400	
Rent Expense	4,000		4,000	
	$117,100	$117,100	$127,050	$127,050

Instructions

(a) Journalize the annual adjusting entries that were made. (Omit explanations.)

(b) Prepare an income statement and a statement of retained earnings for the year ending December 31, 2008, and an unclassified balance sheet at December 31.

(c) Answer the following questions.

   (1) If the note has been outstanding 3 months, what is the annual interest rate on that note?

   (2) If the company paid $13,500 in salaries in 2008, what was the balance in Salaries Payable on December 31, 2007?

(LO 5)   **P3-3** (**Adjusting Entries**)   A review of the ledger of Oklahoma Company at December 31, 2008, produces the following data pertaining to the preparation of annual adjusting entries.

1. Salaries Payable $0. There are eight salaried employees. Salaries are paid every Friday for the current week. Five employees receive a salary of $700 each per week, and three employees earn $500 each per week. December 31 is a Tuesday. Employees do not work weekends. All employees worked the last 2 days of December.

2. Unearned Rent Revenue $369,000. The company began subleasing office space in its new building on November 1. Each tenant is required to make a $5,000 security deposit that is not refundable until occupancy is terminated. At December 31, the company had the following rental contracts that are paid in full for the entire term of the lease.

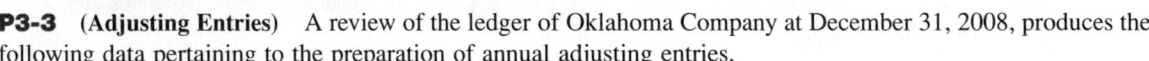

Date	Term (in months)	Monthly Rent	Number of Leases
Nov. 1	6	$4,000	5
Dec. 1	6	$8,500	4

3. Prepaid Advertising $13,200. This balance consists of payments on two advertising contracts. The contracts provide for monthly advertising in two trade magazines. The terms of the contracts are as shown at the top of page 135.

Contract	Date	Amount	Number of Magazine Issues
A650	May 1	$6,000	12
B974	Oct. 1	7,200	24

The first advertisement runs in the month in which the contract is signed.

4. Notes Payable $80,000. This balance consists of a note for one year at an annual interest rate of 12%, dated June 1.

Instructions

Prepare the adjusting entries at December 31, 2008. (Show all computations).

P3-4 (**Financial Statements, Adjusting and Closing Entries**) The trial balance of Daphne Main Fashion Center contained the following accounts at November 30, the end of the company's fiscal year.

(LO 4, 5, 6, 7)

Daphne Main Fashion Center
Trial Balance
November 30, 2008

	Debit	Credit
Cash	$ 26,700	
Accounts Receivable	33,700	
Merchandise Inventory	45,000	
Store Supplies	5,500	
Store Equipment	85,000	
Accumulated Depreciation—Store Equipment		$ 18,000
Delivery Equipment	48,000	
Accumulated Depreciation—Delivery Equipment		6,000
Notes Payable		51,000
Accounts Payable		48,500
Common Stock		90,000
Retained Earnings		8,000
Sales		757,200
Sales Returns and Allowances	4,200	
Cost of Goods Sold	497,400	
Salaries Expense	140,000	
Advertising Expense	26,400	
Utilities Expense	14,000	
Repair Expense	12,100	
Delivery Expense	16,700	
Rent Expense	24,000	
	$978,700	$978,700

Adjustment data:

1. Store supplies on hand totaled $3,500.
2. Depreciation is $9,000 on the store equipment and $7,000 on the delivery equipment.
3. Interest of $11,000 is accrued on notes payable at November 30.

Other data:

1. Salaries expense is 70% selling and 30% administrative.
2. Rent expense and utilities expense are 80% selling and 20% administrative.
3. $30,000 of notes payable are due for payment next year.
4. Repair expense is 100% administrative.

Instructions

(a) Journalize the adjusting entries.
(b) Prepare an adjusted trial balance.
(c) Prepare a multiple-step income statement and retained earnings statement for the year and a classified balance sheet as of November 30, 2008.
(d) Journalize the closing entries.
(e) Prepare a post-closing trial balance.

P3-5 (**Adjusting Entries**) The accounts listed on the next page appeared in the December 31 trial balance of the Jane Alexander Theater.

(LO 5)

	Debit	Credit
Equipment	$192,000	
Accumulated Depreciation—Equipment		$ 60,000
Notes Payable		90,000
Admissions Revenue		380,000
Advertising Expense	13,680	
Salaries Expense	57,600	
Interest Expense	1,400	

Instructions

(a) From the account balances listed above and the information given below, prepare the annual adjusting entries necessary on December 31. (Omit explanations.)

    (1) The equipment has an estimated life of 16 years and a salvage value of $40,000 at the end of that time. (Use straight-line method.)

    (2) The note payable is a 90-day note given to the bank October 20 and bearing interest at 10%. (Use 360 days for denominator.)

    (3) In December 2,000 coupon admission books were sold at $25 each. They could be used for admission any time after January 1.

    (4) Advertising expense paid in advance and included in Advertising Expense $1,100.

    (5) Salaries accrued but unpaid $4,700.

(b) What amounts should be shown for each of the following on the income statement for the year?

    (1) Interest expense.   (3) Advertising expense.

    (2) Admissions revenue.   (4) Salaries expense.

(LO 5, 6)   **P3-6** **(Adjusting Entries and Financial Statements)** Presented below are the trial balance and the other information related to Carlos Beltran, a consulting engineer.

<table>
<tr><td colspan="3" align="center">**Carlos Beltran, Consulting Engineer**
Trial Balance
December 31, 2008</td></tr>
<tr><td></td><td align="center">Debit</td><td align="center">Credit</td></tr>
<tr><td>Cash</td><td>$ 31,500</td><td></td></tr>
<tr><td>Accounts Receivable</td><td>49,600</td><td></td></tr>
<tr><td>Allowance for Doubtful Accounts</td><td></td><td>$ 750</td></tr>
<tr><td>Engineering Supplies Inventory</td><td>1,960</td><td></td></tr>
<tr><td>Unexpired Insurance</td><td>1,100</td><td></td></tr>
<tr><td>Furniture and Equipment</td><td>25,000</td><td></td></tr>
<tr><td>Accumulated Depreciation—Furniture and Equipment</td><td></td><td>6,250</td></tr>
<tr><td>Notes Payable</td><td></td><td>7,200</td></tr>
<tr><td>Carlos Beltran, Capital</td><td></td><td>35,010</td></tr>
<tr><td>Service Revenue</td><td></td><td>100,000</td></tr>
<tr><td>Rent Expense</td><td>9,750</td><td></td></tr>
<tr><td>Office Salaries Expense</td><td>28,500</td><td></td></tr>
<tr><td>Heat, Light, and Water Expense</td><td>1,080</td><td></td></tr>
<tr><td>Miscellaneous Office Expense</td><td>720</td><td></td></tr>
<tr><td></td><td>$149,210</td><td>$149,210</td></tr>
</table>

1. Fees received in advance from clients $6,900.
2. Services performed for clients that were not recorded by December 31, $4,900.
3. Bad debt expense for the year is $1,430.
4. Insurance expired during the year $480.
5. Furniture and equipment is being depreciated at $12\frac{1}{2}\%$ per year.
6. Carlos Beltran gave the bank a 90-day, 10% note for $7,200 on December 1, 2008.
7. Rent of the building is $750 per month. The rent for 2008 has been paid, as has that for January 2009.
8. Office salaries earned but unpaid December 31, 2008, $2,510.

Instructions

(a) From the trial balance and other information given, prepare annual adjusting entries as of December 31, 2008. (Omit explanations.)

(b) Prepare an income statement for 2008, a classified balance sheet, and a statement of owner's equity. Carlos Beltran withdrew $17,000 cash for personal use during the year.

P3-7 (**Adjusting Entries and Financial Statements**) Ana Alicia Advertising Corp. was founded in January **(LO 5, 6)**
2004. Presented below are the adjusted and unadjusted trial balances as of December 31, 2008.

Ana Alicia Advertising Corp.
Trial Balance
December 31, 2008

	Unadjusted Dr.	Unadjusted Cr.	Adjusted Dr.	Adjusted Cr.
Cash	$ 7,000		$ 7,000	
Accounts Receivable	19,000		22,000	
Art Supplies	8,500		5,500	
Prepaid Insurance	3,250		2,500	
Printing Equipment	60,000		60,000	
Accumulated Depreciation		$ 27,000		$ 33,750
Accounts Payable		5,000		5,000
Interest Payable				150
Notes Payable		5,000		5,000
Unearned Service Revenue		7,000		5,600
Salaries Payable				1,500
Common Stock		10,000		10,000
Retained Earnings		4,500		4,500
Service Revenue		58,600		63,000
Salaries Expense	10,000		11,500	
Insurance Expense			750	
Interest Expense	350		500	
Depreciation Expense			6,750	
Art Supplies Expense	5,000		8,000	
Rent Expense	4,000		4,000	
	$117,100	$117,100	$128,500	$128,500

Instructions

(a) Journalize the annual adjusting entries that were made. (Omit explanations.)
(b) Prepare an income statement and a statement of retained earnings for the year ending December 31, 2008, and an unclassified balance sheet at December 31, 2008.
(c) Answer the following questions.
   (1) If the useful life of equipment is 8 years, what is the expected salvage value?
   (2) If the note has been outstanding 3 months, what is the annual interest rate on that note?
   (3) If the company paid $12,500 in salaries in 2008, what was the balance in Salaries Payable on December 31, 2007?

P3-8 (**Adjusting and Closing**) Following is the trial balance of the Platteville Golf Club, Inc. as of December **(LO 4, 5,**
31. The books are closed annually on December 31. **6, 7)**

Platteville Golf Club, Inc.
Trial Balance
December 31

	Debit	Credit
Cash	$ 15,000	
Accounts Receivable	13,000	
Allowance for Doubtful Accounts		$ 1,100
Prepaid Insurance	9,000	
Land	350,000	
Buildings	120,000	
Accumulated Depreciation—Buildings		38,400
Equipment	150,000	
Accumulated Depreciation—Equipment		70,000
Common Stock		400,000
Retained Earnings		82,000
Dues Revenue		200,000
Greens Fee Revenue		8,100
Rental Revenue		15,400
Utilities Expense	54,000	
Salaries Expense	80,000	
Maintenance Expense	24,000	
	$815,000	$815,000

Instructions

(a) Enter the balances in ledger accounts. Allow five lines for each account.

(b) From the trial balance and the information given, prepare annual adjusting entries and post to the ledger accounts. (Omit explanations.)

    (1) The buildings have an estimated life of 25 years with no salvage value (straight-line method).

    (2) The equipment is depreciated at 10% per year.

    (3) Insurance expired during the year $3,500.

    (4) The rental revenue represents the amount received for 11 months for dining facilities. The December rent has not yet been received.

    (5) It is estimated that 15% of the accounts receivable will be uncollectible.

    (6) Salaries earned but not paid by December 31, $3,600.

    (7) Dues paid in advance by members $8,900.

(c) Prepare an adjusted trial balance.

(d) Prepare closing entries and post.

(LO 4, 5, 6, 7)   **P3-9** **(Adjusting and Closing)**   Presented below is the December 31 trial balance of Nancy Drew Boutique.

Nancy Drew Boutique
Trial Balance
December 31

	Debit	Credit
Cash	$ 18,500	
Accounts Receivable	42,000	
Allowance for Doubtful Accounts		$ 700
Inventory, December 31	80,000	
Prepaid Insurance	5,100	
Furniture and Equipment	84,000	
Accumulated Depreciation—Furniture and Equipment		35,000
Notes Payable		28,000
Common Stock		80,600
Retained Earnings		10,000
Sales		600,000
Cost of Goods Sold	398,000	
Sales Salaries Expense	50,000	
Advertising Expense	6,700	
Administrative Salaries Expense	65,000	
Office Expense	5,000	
	$754,300	$754,300

Instructions

(a) Construct T-accounts and enter the balances shown.

(b) Prepare adjusting journal entries for the following and post to the T-accounts. (Omit explanations.) Open additional T-accounts as necessary. (The books are closed yearly on December 31.)

    (1) Bad debts are estimated to be $1,400.

    (2) Furniture and equipment is depreciated based on a 6-year life (no salvage value).

    (3) Insurance expired during the year $2,550.

    (4) Interest accrued on notes payable $3,360.

    (5) Sales salaries earned but not paid $2,400.

    (6) Advertising paid in advance $700.

    (7) Office supplies on hand $1,500, charged to Office Expense when purchased.

(c) Prepare closing entries and post to the accounts.

(LO 5, 6, 7, 10)   ***P3-10** **(Worksheet, Balance Sheet, Adjusting and Closing Entries)**   Noah's Ark has a fiscal year ending on September 30. Selected data from the September 30 work sheet are presented on the next page.

Noah's Ark
Worksheet
For the Year Ended September 30, 2008

	Trial Balance Dr.	Trial Balance Cr.	Adjusted Trial Balance Dr.	Adjusted Trial Balance Cr.
Cash	37,400		37,400	
Supplies	18,600		1,200	
Prepaid Insurance	31,900		3,900	
Land	80,000		80,000	
Equipment	120,000		120,000	
Accumulated Depreciation		36,200		43,000
Accounts Payable		14,600		14,600
Unearned Admissions Revenue		2,700		1,700
Mortgage Payable		50,000		50,000
N. Y. Berge, Capital		109,700		109,700
N. Y. Berge, Drawing	14,000		14,000	
Admissions Revenue		278,500		279,500
Salaries Expense	109,000		109,000	
Repair Expense	30,500		30,500	
Advertising Expense	9,400		9,400	
Utilities Expense	16,900		16,900	
Property Taxes Expense	18,000		21,000	
Interest Expense	6,000		12,000	
Totals	491,700	491,700		
Insurance Expense			28,000	
Supplies Expense			17,400	
Interest Payable				6,000
Depreciation Expense			6,800	
Property Taxes Payable				3,000
Totals			507,500	507,500

Instructions

(a) Prepare a complete worksheet.
(b) Prepare a classified balance sheet. (*Note:* $10,000 of the mortgage payable is due for payment in the next fiscal year.)
(c) Journalize the adjusting entries using the worksheet as a basis.
(d) Journalize the closing entries using the worksheet as a basis.
(e) Prepare a post-closing trial balance.

ACCOUNTING IN ACTION

Financial Reporting and Analysis

P&G

■ Financial Reporting Issues: The Procter & Gamble Company

AIA3-1 The financial statements of **Procter & Gamble (P&G)** can be accessed at the book's website.

Instructions

Refer to P&G's financial statements and the accompanying notes to answer the following questions.

(a) What were P&G's total assets at June 30, 2006? At June 30, 2005?
(b) How much cash (and cash equivalents) did P&G have on June 30, 2006?
(c) What were P&G's research and development costs in 2004? In 2006?
(d) What were P&G's revenues in 2004? In 2006?

(e) Using P&G's financial statements and related notes, identify items that may result in adjusting entries for prepayments and accruals.

(f) What were the amounts of P&G's depreciation and amortization expense in 2004, 2005, and 2006?

PEPSICO ■ Comparative Analysis: The Coca-Cola Company and PepsiCo, Inc.

AIA3-2   The financial statements of **The Coca-Cola Company** and **PepsiCo, Inc.** can be accessed at the book's website.

Instructions

Use information found at the book's website to answer the following questions.

(a) Which company had the greater percentage increase in total assets from 2005 to 2006?

(b) Using the Selected Financial Data section of these two companies, determine their 5-year growth rates related to net sales and income from continuing operations.

(c) Which company had more depreciation and amortization expense for 2006? Provide a rationale as to why there is a difference in these amounts between the two companies.

■ Financial Statement Analysis

AIA3-3   **Kellogg Company** has its headquarters in Battle Creek, Michigan. The company manufactures and sells ready-to-eat breakfast cereals and convenience foods including cookies, toaster pastries, and cereal bars. Selected data from Kellogg Company's 2005 annual report follows (dollar amounts in millions).

Kellogg Company	2005	2004	2003
Sales	$10,177.20	$9,613.90	$8,811.50
Gross profit %	44.90%	44.90%	44.40%
Operating profit	$1,750.30	$1,681.10	$1,544.10
Net cash flow less capital expenditures	$769.10	$950.40	$923.80
Net earnings	$980.40	$890.60	$787.10

In its 2005 annual report, Kellogg Company disclosed that

> . . . "We met or exceeded our goals while investing in our brands, our people, and our future. We have a proven, focused strategy and pragmatic operating principles in Volume to Value and Manage for Cash that keep us focused on the right metrics. All of this, in combination with our realistic growth targets, drives sustainable and dependable performance."

Instructions

(a) Compute the percentage change in sales, operating profit, net cash flow, and net earnings from year to year for the years presented.

(b) Evaluate Kellogg's performance. Which trend seems most favorable? Which trend seems least favorable? What are the implications of these trends for Kellogg's sustainable performance objectives? Explain.

AIA3-4   **Laser Recording Systems**, founded in 1981, produces disks for use in the home market. The following is an excerpt from Laser Recording Systems' financial statements (all dollars in thousands).

Laser Recording Systems
Management Discussion

Accrued liabilities increased to $1,642 at January 31, from $138 at the end of the previous fiscal year. Compensation and related accruals increased $195 due primarily to increases in accruals for severance, vacation, commissions, and relocation expenses. Accrued professional services increased by $137 primarily as a result of legal expenses related to several outstanding contractual disputes. Other expenses increased $35, of which $18 was for interest payable.

Instructions

(a) Can you tell from the discussion whether Laser Recording Systems has prepaid its legal expenses and is now making an adjustment to the asset account Prepaid Legal Expenses, or whether the company is handling the legal expense via an accrued expense adjustment?

(b) Identify each of the adjustments Laser Recording Systems is discussing as one of the four types of possible adjustments discussed in the chapter. How is net income ultimately affected by each of the adjustments?

(c) What journal entry did Laser Recording make to record the accrued interest?

AIA3-5 **Chieftain International, Inc.,** is an oil and natural gas exploration and production company. A recent balance sheet reported $208 million in assets with only $4.6 million in liabilities, all of which were short-term accounts payable.

During the year, Chieftain expanded its holdings of oil and gas rights, drilled 37 new wells, and invested in expensive 3-D seismic technology. The company generated $19 million cash from operating activities and paid no dividends. It had a cash balance of $102 million at the end of the year.

Instructions

(a) Name at least two advantages to Chieftain from having no long-term debt. Can you think of disadvantages?

(b) What are some of the advantages to Chieftain from having this large a cash balance? What is a disadvantage?

(c) Why do you suppose Chieftain has the $4.6 million balance in accounts payable, since it appears that it could have made all its purchases for cash?

Professional Tools

■ Financial Accounting Research (FARS)

AIA3-6 Recording transactions in the accounting system requires knowledge of the important characteristics of the elements of financial statements, such as assets and liabilities. In addition, accountants must understand the inherent uncertainty in accounting measures and distinctions between related accounting concepts that are important in evaluating the effects of transactions on the financial statements.

Instructions

Using the **Financial Accounting Research System (FARS)** database, provide explanations for the following items. (Provide text strings used in your search.)

(a) The three essential characteristics of assets.

(b) The three essential characteristics of liabilities.

(c) Uncertainty and its effect on financial statements.

(d) The difference between realization and recognition.

■ Professional Simulation

AIA3-7 Go to the book's website, at www.wiley.com/college/kieso, to find an interactive problem that simulates the computerized CPA exam. The professional simulation for this chapter asks you to address questions related to an income statement and balance sheet.

<u>**What do the numbers mean?**</u>   **Guideline Answers to Beyond the Numbers Questions**

Am I Covered?, p. 100

Q: Assume that Almost Family, Inc. made the following entry in establishing a reserve for future insurance losses.

Insurance Expense   10,000
    Insurance Liability   10,000

Discuss the propriety of this accounting for potential insurance losses. Focus on the conceptual definition of liabilities.

A: Because the event which results in the obligation has not yet occurred, recording an expense and liability is not appropriate. According to *Concepts Statement No. 6*, "Liabilities are probable future sacrifices of economic benefits arising from present obligations of a particular entity to transfer assets or provide services to other entities in the future *as a result of past transactions or events*." Since the casualty loss has not yet occurred, there is no liability.

24/7 Accounting, p. 104

Q: What users might benefit from receiving daily financial statements? Discuss the decisions to be made with the financial statements and how more timely statements can improve those decisions.

A: For example, a loan officer might need to decide whether to renew a loan that matures partway through the month. If the company's financial condition has changed since the last financial statement date, up-to-date information on the company's operating results (income), liquidity, and financial flexibility would be useful in evaluating whether the company can repay the loan if renewed. Or consider an investor deciding whether to add or drop the company's stock to/from his or her portfolio prior to the end of the year. Timely information on cash flows and earnings is needed now to make an informed investment decision.

Statements, Please, p. 107

Q: Choose a financial statement item that requires adjustment when the books are closed (and financial statements prepared) and discuss the costs of preparing this adjustment on a daily basis.

A: To record bad debt expense, the company needs to prepare an analysis of uncollectible accounts, either as a percentage of sales or accounts receivable. This will require staff time and computer resources. If performed on a daily basis, the costs would add up quickly. A similar set of costs would be incurred in performing accurate inventory and sales cutoffs to determine cost of goods sold and inventory amounts on a daily basis.

Remember to check the book's companion website to find additional resources for this chapter.

CHAPTER 4
BALANCE SHEET

"There Ought to Be a Law"

As one manager noted, "There ought to be a law in this country that before you are allowed to buy a stock, you have to be able to read a balance sheet." We agree and the same can be said for a statement of cash flows.

Krispy Kreme Doughnuts provides a good example of how stunning earnings growth can hide real problems. Not long ago the doughnut maker was a glamour stock, with a 60 percent earnings per share growth rate and a price-earnings ratio around 70. Seven months later its stock price had dropped 72 percent. Krispy Kreme, alleged some of its stockholders, may have been stuffing its channels with too many doughnuts (inflating its revenues) and not taking enough bad debt expense (which inflated both assets and income). Krispy Kreme also had weak cash flow from operating activities. Most financially sound companies throw off positive cash flow, but Krispy Kreme's cash flow was negative. Thus, the company's quality of earnings was suspect.

For comparison, here are examples of how one rating agency rated some other companies' earnings quality, using some key balance sheet and cash flow measures.

Company	Earnings-Quality Indicators
Earnings-Quality Winners	
Avon Products	Strong cash flow
Capital One Financial	Conservatively capitalized
Ecolab	Good management of working capital
Timberland	Minimal off–balance sheet commitments
Earnings-Quality Losers	
Ford Motor	High debt and underfunded pension plan
Kroger	High goodwill and debt
Ryder System	Negative free cash flows
Teco Energy	Selling assets to meet liquidity needs

These examples illustrate that earnings declines (and falling stock prices) can often be predicted by using the balance sheet and related cash flow information. And just as deteriorating balance sheets warn of trouble, improving balance sheet and cash flow information is a leading indicator of improved earnings.

Sources: Adapted from Gretchen Morgenson, "How Did They Value Stocks? Count the Absurd Ways," *New York Times on the Web* (March 18, 2001); and K. Badanhausen, J. Gage, C. Hall, and M. Ozanian, "Beyond Balance Sheet Earnings Quality," *Forbes* (January 29, 2005).

Preview of Chapter 4

Readers of the financial statements sometimes ignore important information in the balance sheet and related cash flow information. As our opening story shows, analyzing the balance sheet helps investors avoid surprises in earnings. In this chapter we examine the many different types of assets, liabilities, and stockholders' equity items that affect the balance sheet, *as follows.*

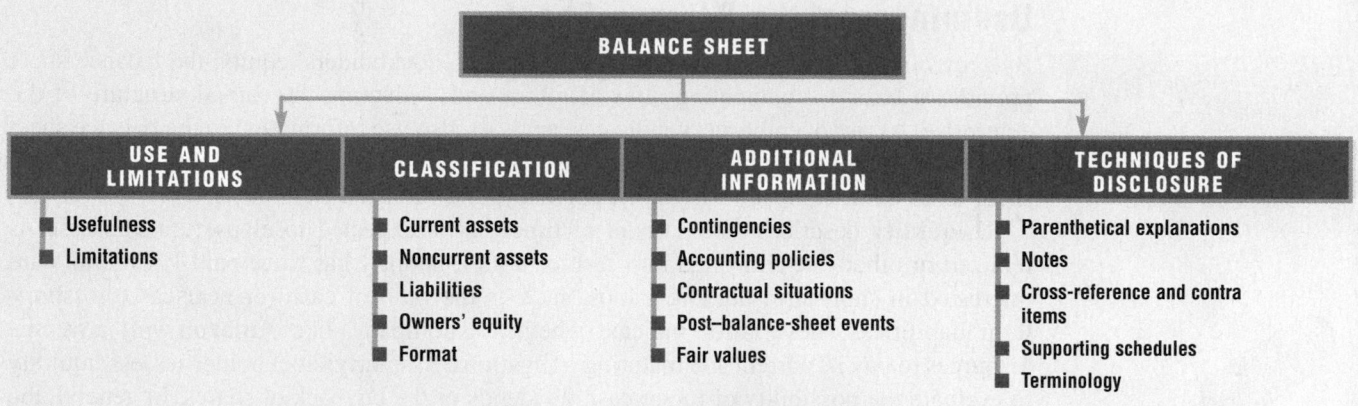

BALANCE SHEET			
USE AND LIMITATIONS	**CLASSIFICATION**	**ADDITIONAL INFORMATION**	**TECHNIQUES OF DISCLOSURE**
■ Usefulness ■ Limitations	■ Current assets ■ Noncurrent assets ■ Liabilities ■ Owners' equity ■ Format	■ Contingencies ■ Accounting policies ■ Contractual situations ■ Post–balance-sheet events ■ Fair values	■ Parenthetical explanations ■ Notes ■ Cross-reference and contra items ■ Supporting schedules ■ Terminology

Learning Objectives

After studying this chapter, you should be able to:

1. Explain the uses and limitations of a balance sheet.

2. Identify the major classifications of the balance sheet.

3. Prepare a classified balance sheet using the report and account formats.

4. Determine which balance sheet information requires supplemental disclosure.

5. Describe the major disclosure techniques for the balance sheet.

Inside Chapter 4

■ **What Do the Numbers Mean?**
Grounded (p. 146)
"Show me the assets!" (p. 157)
Warning signals (p. 162)
What about your commitments? (p. 164)

■ **What's the Principle?** (pp. 151, 161, 163, 165, 168)

■ **Convergence Corner** (p. 171)

■ **Accounting, Analysis, Principles** (p. 172)
Prepare a classified balance sheet.
Analyze creditworthiness.
Assess usefulness of balance sheet information.

USE AND LIMITATIONS

The **balance sheet**, sometimes referred to as the **statement of financial position,** reports the assets, liabilities, and stockholders' equity of a business enterprise at a specific date.[1] This financial statement provides information about the nature and amounts of investments in enterprise resources, obligations to creditors, and the owners' equity in net resources. It therefore helps in predicting the amounts, timing, and uncertainty of future cash flows.

Usefulness of the Balance Sheet

OBJECTIVE 1

Explain the uses and limitations of a balance sheet.

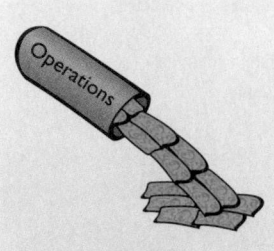

How quickly will my assets convert to cash?

Obligation Ocean

We are drowning in a sea of debt!

By providing information on assets, liabilities, and stockholders' equity, the balance sheet provides a basis for computing rates of return and evaluating the capital structure of the enterprise. As our opening story indicates, analysts also use information in the balance sheet to assess a company's risk[2] and future cash flows. In this regard, analysts use the balance sheet to assess a company's liquidity, solvency, and financial flexibility.

Liquidity describes "the amount of time that is expected to elapse until an asset is realized or otherwise converted into cash or until a liability has to be paid."[3] Creditors are interested in short-term liquidity ratios, such as the ratio of cash (or near cash) to short-term liabilities. These ratios indicate whether a company, like **Amazon** will have the resources to pay its current and maturing obligations. Similarly, stockholders assess liquidity to evaluate the possibility of future cash dividends or the buyback of shares. In general, the greater Amazon's liquidity, the lower its risk of failure.

Solvency refers to the ability of a company to pay its debts as they mature. For example, when a company carries a high level of long-term debt relative to assets, it has lower solvency than a similar company with a low level of long-term debt. Companies with higher debt are relatively more risky. Why? Because they will need more of their assets to meet these fixed obligations (interest and principal payments).

Liquidity and solvency affect a company's **financial flexibility,** which measures the "ability of an enterprise to take effective actions to alter the amounts and timing of cash flows so it can respond to unexpected needs and opportunities."[4] For example, a company may become

---

[1]*Accounting Trends and Techniques—2006* indicates that approximately 96 percent of the companies surveyed used the term "balance sheet." The term "statement of financial position" is used infrequently, although it is conceptually appealing.

[2]Risk conveys the unpredictability of future events, transactions, circumstances, and results of the company.

[3]"Reporting Income, Cash Flows, and Financial Position of Business Enterprises," *Proposed Statement of Financial Accounting Concepts* (Stamford, Conn.: FASB, 1981), par. 29.

[4]"Reporting Income, Cash Flows, and Financial Position of Business Enterprises," *Proposed Statement of Financial Accounting Concepts* (Stamford, Conn.: FASB, 1981), par. 25.

What do the numbers mean?   Grounded

The terrorist attacks of September 11, 2001, showed how vulnerable the major airlines are to falling demand for their services. Since this infamous date, major airlines have reduced capacity and slashed jobs to avoid bankruptcy. Also, **United Airlines,** the second-largest U.S. air carrier, **US Airways,** the seventh-largest U.S. carrier, **ATA,** the tenth-largest carrier, and several smaller competitors have filed for bankruptcy. In a recent annual report, **Delta Airlines** made the following statements, and its auditors noted that there is substantial doubt about the company's ability to continue as a going concern.

"If we are unsuccessful in further reducing our operating costs. . . we will need to restructure our costs under Chapter 11 of the U.S. Bankruptcy Code. . . "We have substantial liquidity needs and there is no assurance that we will be able to obtain the necessary financing to meet those needs on acceptable terms, if at all."

The financial distress related to the airline industry was not an insider's secret. The airlines' balance sheets clearly revealed their financial inflexibility and low liquidity even before September 11. For example, major airlines such as **Braniff**, **Continental**, **Eastern**, **Midway**, and **America West** declared bankruptcy before September 11. Conversely some airlines have done well. In 2006, **Southwest Airlines** recorded its thirty-fourth consecutive year of profitability.

Beyond the Numbers

In assessing a company's financial flexibility, a high proportion of debt relative to stockholders' equity is considered a signal that the company may be financially inflexible. Explain why that statement is true.

---

so loaded with debt—so financially inflexible—that it has limited or nonexistent sources of cash to finance expansion or to pay off maturing debt. A company with a high degree of financial flexibility is better able to survive bad times, to recover from unexpected setbacks, and to take advantage of profitable and unexpected investment opportunities. Generally, the greater an enterprise's financial flexibility, the lower its risk of failure.

Limitations of the Balance Sheet

Some of the major limitations of the balance sheet are:

Hmm... I wonder if they will pay me back?

1 Companies state most assets and liabilities at **historical cost**. As a result, the information reported in the balance sheet has high reliability. But it is often criticized for not reporting a more relevant fair value. For example, **Georgia Pacific** owns timber and other assets that may appreciate in value after purchase. Yet, Georgia Pacific reports any increase only if and when it sells the assets.

2 Companies use **judgments and estimates** to determine many of the items reported in the balance sheet. For example, in its balance sheet, **Dell** estimates the amount of receivables that it will collect, the useful life of its warehouses, and the number of computers that will be returned under warranty.

3 The balance sheet necessarily **omits many items that are of financial value** but that a company cannot record objectively. For example, the knowledge and skill of **Intel** employees in developing new computer chips are arguably the company's most significant asset. However, because Intel cannot reliably measure the value of its employees and other intangible assets (customer base, research superiority, and reputation), it cannot recognize these items in the balance sheet. Similarly, companies report many other liabilities in an "off–balance-sheet" manner, if at all.

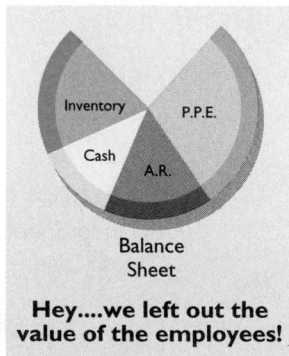

Balance Sheet

Hey....we left out the value of the employees!

The bankruptcy of **Enron**, the seventh-largest U.S. company, highlights the omission of important items in the balance sheet. In Enron's case, it failed to disclose certain off–balance-sheet financing obligations in its main financial statements.[5]

---

[5]We discuss several of these omitted items (such as leases and other off–balance-sheet arrangements) in later chapters. See Wayne Upton, Jr., Special Report: *Business and Financial Reporting, Challenges from the New Economy* (Norwalk, Conn.: FASB, 2001).

CLASSIFICATION IN THE BALANCE SHEET

BJECTIVE **2**

Identify the major classifications of the balance sheet.

Balance sheet accounts are **classified** so that companies can group together similar items to arrive at significant subtotals. Furthermore, classification reveals important relationships.

The FASB has often noted that the parts and subsections of financial statements can be more informative than the whole. Therefore, the FASB discourages the reporting of summary accounts alone (total assets, net assets, total liabilities, etc.). Instead, companies should report and classify individual items in sufficient detail to permit users to assess the amounts, timing, and uncertainty of future cash flows, as well as the evaluation of liquidity and financial flexibility, profitability, and risk.

To classify items in financial statements, companies group those items with similar characteristics and separate items with different characteristics.[6] For example, companies should report the following items separately:

1 Assets that differ in their **type or expected function** in the company's central operations or other activities. For example, **IBM** reports merchandise inventories separately from property, plant, and equipment.

2 Assets and liabilities with **different implications for the company's financial flexibility.** For example, a company like **Walgreens**, which uses assets in its operations, should report them separately from assets held for investment and assets subject to restrictions, such as leased equipment.

3 Assets and liabilities with **different general liquidity characteristics**. For example, **Boeing Company** reports cash separately from inventories.

The three general classes of items included in the balance sheet are assets, liabilities, and equity. We defined them in Chapter 2 as follows.

ELEMENTS OF THE BALANCE SHEET

1 ASSETS. Probable future economic benefits obtained or controlled by a particular entity as a result of past transactions or events.

2 LIABILITIES. Probable future sacrifices of economic benefits arising from present obligations of a particular entity to transfer assets or provide services to other entities in the future as a result of past transactions or events.

3 EQUITY. Residual interest in the assets of an entity that remains after deducting its liabilities. In a business enterprise, the equity is the ownership interest.[7]

These items are then divided into several subclassifications. Illustration 4-1 indicates the general format of balance sheet presentation.

Illustration 4-1
Balance Sheet Classifications

Assets	Liabilities and Owners' (Stockholders') Equity
Current assets	Current liabilities
Long-term investments	Long-term liabilities
Property, plant, and equipment	Owners' (Stockholders') equity
Intangible assets	Capital stock
Other assets	Additional paid-in capital
	Retained earnings

[6]"Reporting Income, Cash Flows, and Financial Positions of Business Enterprises," *Proposed Statement of Financial Accounting Concepts* (Stamford, Conn.: FASB, 1981), par. 51.

[7]"Elements of Financial Statements of Business Enterprises," *Statement of Financial Accounting Concepts No. 6* (Stamford, Conn.: FASB, 1985), pars. 25, 35 and 49.

A company may classify the balance sheet in some other manner, but you usually see little departure from these major subdivisions in practice. A proprietorship or partnership does present the classifications within the owners' equity section a little differently, as we will show later in the chapter.

Current Assets

Current assets are cash and other assets a company expects to convert into cash, sell, or consume either in one year or in the operating cycle, whichever is longer. The operating cycle is the average time between when a company acquires materials and supplies and when it receives cash for sales of the product (for which it acquired the materials and supplies). The cycle operates from cash through inventory, production, receivables, and back to cash. When several operating cycles occur within one year, a company uses the one-year period. If the operating cycle is more than one year, the longer period is used. **Companies present current assets in the balance sheet in order of liquidity.**

The five major items found in the current assets section and their bases of valuation are shown in Illustration 4-2.

Item	Basis of Valuation
Cash and cash equivalents	Fair value
Short-term investments	Generally, fair value
Receivables	Estimated amount collectible
Inventories	Lower of cost or market
Prepaid expenses	Cost

Illustration 4-2
Current Assets and Basis of Valuation

A company does not report these five items as current assets if it does not expect to realize them in one year or in the operating cycle, whichever is longer. For example, a company excludes cash restricted for purposes other than payment of current obligations or for use in current operations from the current assets section. **Generally, if a company expects to convert an asset into cash or to use it to pay a current liability within a year or the operating cycle, whichever is longer, it classifies the asset as current.** This rule, however, is subject to interpretation. A company classifies an investment in common stock as either a current asset or a noncurrent asset depending on management's intent. When it has small holdings of common stocks or bonds that it will hold long-term, it should not classify them as current.

Although a current asset is well defined, certain theoretical problems develop. For example, how is including prepaid expense in the current assets section justified? The rationale is that if a company did not pay these items in advance, it would instead need to use other current assets during the operating cycle. If we follow this logic to its ultimate conclusion, however, any asset previously purchased saves the use of current assets during the operating cycle and would be considered current.

Another problem occurs in the current asset definition when a company consumes fixed assets during the operating cycle. The accounting profession's position on this matter would indicate that a company should place an amount equal to the current depreciation and amortization charges on the noncurrent assets in the current assets section at the beginning of the year, because it will consume them in the next operating cycle. However, most ignore this conceptual problem. This illustrates that the formal distinction made between current and noncurrent assets is somewhat arbitrary.

Cash

Cash is generally considered to be currency and demand deposits (monies available on demand at a financial institution.) **Cash equivalents** are short-term highly liquid investments that will mature within three months or less. Most companies use the caption "Cash and cash equivalents" and indicate that this amount approximates fair value. A company must disclose any restrictions or commitments on its availability of cash. As an example, see the excerpt from the annual report of **Alterra Healthcare Corp.** in Illustration 4-3.

Illustration 4-3
Balance Sheet
Presentation of
Restricted Cash

Alterra Healthcare Corp.

Current assets	
Cash	$18,728,000
Restricted cash and investments (Note 7)	7,191,000

Note 7: Restricted Cash and Investments. Restricted cash and investments consist of certificates of deposit restricted as collateral for lease arrangements and debt service with interest rates ranging from 4.0% to 5.5%.

Alterra Healthcare restricted cash to meet an obligation due currently. Therefore, Alterra included this restricted cash under current assets. If a company restricts cash for purposes other than current obligations, it excludes the cash from current assets. Illustration 4-4 shows an example of this, excerpted from the annual report of **Owens Corning, Inc.**

Illustration 4-4
Balance Sheet
Presentation of Current
and Noncurrent
Restricted Cash

Owens Corning, Inc.
(in millions)

Current assets	
Cash and cash equivalents	$ 70
Restricted securities—Fibreboard—current portion (Note 23)	900
Other assets	
Restricted securities—Fibreboard (Note 23)	938

Note 23 (in part). The Insurance Settlement funds are held in and invested by the Fibreboard Settlement Trust (the "Trust") and are available to satisfy Fibreboard's pending and future asbestos related liabilities. . . . The assets of the Trust are comprised of cash and marketable securities (collectively, the "Trust Assets") and are reflected on Owens Corning's consolidated balance sheet as restricted assets. These assets are reflected as current assets or other assets, with each category denoted "Restricted securities—Fibreboard."

Short-Term Investments

Companies group investments in debt and equity securities into three separate portfolios for valuation and reporting purposes:

Held-to-maturity: Debt securities that a company has the positive intent and ability to hold to maturity.

Trading: Debt and equity securities bought and held primarily for sale in the near term to generate income on short-term price differences.

Available-for-sale: Debt and equity securities not classified as held-to-maturity or trading securities.

A company reports trading securities (whether debt or equity) as current assets. It classifies individual held-to-maturity and available-for-sale securities as current or noncurrent depending on the circumstances. It should report held-to-maturity securities at amortized cost. All trading and available-for-sale securities are reported at fair value.[8] For example, see the excerpt in Illustration 4-5 from the annual report of **Intuit Inc.** with respect to its available-for-sale investments.

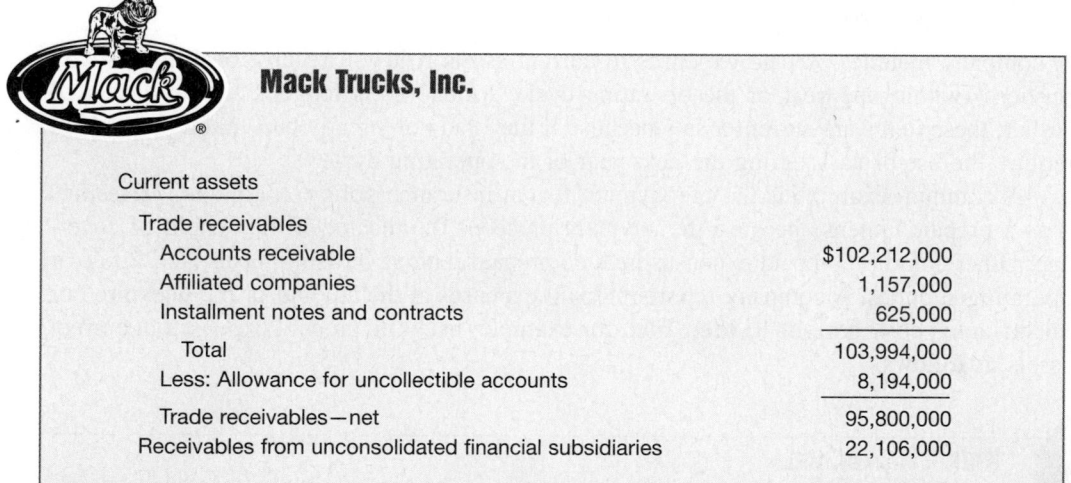

Intuit Inc.
(in thousands)

Assets

Cash and cash equivalents	$ 170,043
Short-term investments **(Note 2)**	1,036,785

Note 2: (In Part). The following schedule summarizes the estimated fair value of our short-term investments (all available-for-sale):

Corporate notes	$ 50,471
Municipal bonds	931,374
U.S. government securities	54,913

Illustration 4-5
Balance Sheet
Presentation of
Investments in Securities

Receivables

A company should clearly identify any anticipated loss due to uncollectible accounts, the amount and nature of any nontrade receivables, and any receivables used as collateral. Major categories of receivables should be shown in the balance sheet or the related notes. For receivables arising from unusual transactions (such as sale of property, or a loan to affiliates or employees), companies should separately classify these as long-term, unless collection is expected within one year. **Mack Trucks, Inc.** reported its receivables as follows.

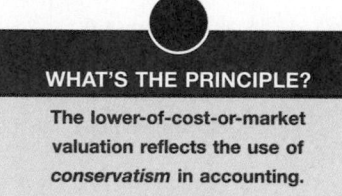

Mack Trucks, Inc.

Current assets

Trade receivables

Accounts receivable	$102,212,000
Affiliated companies	1,157,000
Installment notes and contracts	625,000
Total	103,994,000
Less: Allowance for uncollectible accounts	8,194,000
Trade receivables—net	95,800,000
Receivables from unconsolidated financial subsidiaries	22,106,000

Illustration 4-6
Balance Sheet
Presentation of
Receivables

Inventories

To present inventories properly, a company discloses the basis of valuation (e.g., lower-of-cost-or-market) and the method of pricing (e.g., FIFO or LIFO). A manufacturing concern, like **Abbott Laboratories** shown in Illustration 4-7 (page 152), also indicates the stage of completion of the inventories.

WHAT'S THE PRINCIPLE?
The lower-of-cost-or-market valuation reflects the use of *conservatism* in accounting.

[8]"Accounting for Certain Investments in Debt and Equity Securities," *Statement of Financial Accounting Standards No. 115* (Norwalk, Conn.: FASB, 1993).

Illustration 4-7
Balance Sheet
Presentation of
Inventories, Showing
Stage of Completion

Abbott Laboratories
(in thousands)

Current assets

Inventories	
Finished products	$ 772,478
Work in process	338,818
Materials	384,148
Total inventories	1,495,444

Note 1 (in part): Inventories.   Inventories are stated at the lower of cost (first-in, first-out basis) or market.

Weyerhaeuser Company, a forestry company and lumber manufacturer with several finished-goods product lines, reported its inventory as follows.

Illustration 4-8
Balance Sheet
Presentation of
Inventories, Showing
Product Lines

Weyerhaeuser Company

Current assets

Inventories—at FIFO lower of cost or market	
Logs and chips	$ 68,471,000
Lumber, plywood and panels	86,741,000
Pulp, newsprint and paper	47,377,000
Containerboard, paperboard, containers and cartons	59,682,000
Other products	161,717,000
Total product inventories	423,988,000
Materials and supplies	175,540,000

Prepaid Expenses

A company includes prepaid expenses in current assets if it will receive benefits (usually services) within one year or the operating cycle, whichever is longer.[9] As we discussed earlier, these items are current assets because if they had not already been paid, they would require the use of cash during the next year or the operating cycle.

A common example is the prepayment for an insurance policy. A company classifies it as a prepaid expense because the payment precedes the receipt of the benefit of coverage. Other common prepaid expenses include prepaid rent, advertising, taxes, and office or operating supplies. A company reports prepaid expenses at the amount of the unexpired or unconsumed cost. **Knight Ridder, Inc.**, for example, listed its prepaid expenses in current assets as follows.

Illustration 4-9
Balance Sheet
Presentation of
Prepaid Expenses

Knight Ridder, Inc.
(in thousands)

Current assets

Cash, including short-term cash investments of $7,001	$ 41,661
Accounts receivable, net of allowances of $20,238	416,498
Inventories	52,786
Prepaids	30,767
Other current assets	34,382

[9]*Accounting Trends and Techniques—2006* in its survey of 600 annual reports identified 378 companies that reported prepaid expenses.

Companies often include insurance and other prepayments for two or three years in current assets even though part of the advance payment applies to periods beyond one year or the current operating cycle.

Noncurrent Assets

Noncurrent assets are those that do not meet the definition of current assets. They include a variety of items, as we discuss in the following sections.

Long-Term Investments

Long-term investments, often referred to simply as **investments,** normally consist of one of four types:

1 Investments in securities, such as bonds, common stock, or long-term notes.

2 Investments in tangible fixed assets not currently used in operations, such as land held for speculation.

3 Investments set aside in special funds such as a sinking fund, pension fund, or plant expansion fund. This includes the cash surrender value of life insurance.

4 Investments in nonconsolidated subsidiaries or affiliated companies.

Companies expect to hold long-term investments for many years. They usually present them on the balance sheet just below "Current assets," in a separate section called Investments. Realize that many securities classified as long-term investments are, in fact, readily marketable. But a company does not include them as current assets unless it *intends* to convert them to cash in the short-term—within a year or in the operating cycle, whichever is longer. As indicated earlier, securities classified as available-for-sale are reported at fair value, and held-to-maturity securities are reported at amortized cost.

Motorola, Inc. reported its investments section between "Property, plant, and equipment" and "Other assets" in the following manner.

Motorola, Inc.
(in millions)

Investments	
Equity investments	$ 872
Other investments	2,567
Fair value adjustment to available-for-sale securities	2,487
Total	$5,926

Illustration 4-10
Balance Sheet Presentation of Long-Term Investments

Property, Plant, and Equipment

Property, plant, and equipment are assets of a durable nature used in the regular operations of the business. These assets consist of physical property such as land, buildings, machinery, furniture, tools, and wasting resources (timberland, minerals). With the exception of land, a company either depreciates (e.g., buildings) or depletes (e.g., timberlands or oil reserves) these assets.

Mattel, Inc., a manufacturer of toys and games, presented its property, plant, and equipment in its balance sheet as shown in Illustration 4-11 (page 154).

Mattel, Inc.

Property, plant, and equipment

Land	$ 32,793,000
Buildings	257,430,000
Machinery and equipment	564,244,000
Capitalized leases	23,271,000
Leasehold improvements	74,988,000
	952,726,000
Less: Accumulated depreciation	472,986,000
	479,740,000
Tools, dies and molds, net	168,092,000
Property, plant, and equipment, net	647,832,000

Illustration 4-11
Balance Sheet
Presentation of Property,
Plant, and Equipment

A company usually discloses in notes to the statements the basis of valuing property, plant, and equipment, any liens against the properties, and accumulated depreciation.

Intangible Assets

Intangible assets lack physical substance and are not financial instruments. They include patents, copyrights, franchises, goodwill, trademarks, trade names, and customer lists. A company writes off (amortizes) limited-life intangible assets over their useful lives. It periodically assesses indefinite-life intangibles (such as goodwill) for impairment. Intangibles can represent significant economic resources, yet financial analysts often ignore them.

PepsiCo, Inc. reported intangible assets in its balance sheet as follows.

Illustration 4-12
Balance Sheet
Presentation of Intangible
Assets

PEPSICO
PepsiCo, Inc.
(in millions)

Intangible assets

Goodwill	$3,374
Trademarks	1,320
Other identifiable intangibles	147
Total intangibles	$4,841

Other Assets

The items included in the section "Other assets" vary widely in practice. Some include items such as long-term prepaid expenses, pension assets, noncurrent receivables, assets in special funds, deferred income taxes, property held for sale, and restricted cash or securities. A company should restrict this section to include only unusual items sufficiently different from assets included in specific categories.

Try it out! Williams Co. reported the following assets in its balance sheet at October 31, 2008.

Cash	$ 79,000
Accounts receivable (net)	50,500
Inventories	50,000
Equipment (net)	84,000
Patents	11,000
	$274,500

The company provides the following additional information.

1 Cash included $800 petty cash and $17,000 in a plant expansion fund.

2 The net accounts receivable is comprised of (a) accounts receivable $62,000 and (b) allowance for doubtful accounts $11,500.

3 Merchandise inventory costing $5,500 was shipped on consignment on October 31, 2008. The bookkeeper recorded the shipment as a debit to Accounts Receivable and a credit to Inventory.

4 Equipment had a cost of $96,000 and accumulated depreciation of $12,000.

Instructions

Prepare a corrected assets section of the balance sheet for Williams Co. at October 31, 2008, from the available information.

Solution

Williams Co.
Balance Sheet
October 31, 2008

Assets

Current assets			
Cash		$62,000*	
Accounts receivable	$56,500**		
Less: Allowance for doubtful accounts	11,500	45,000	
Inventories		55,500***	
Total current assets			$162,500
Long-term investments			
Plant expansion fund			17,000
Property, plant, and equipment			
Equipment		96,000	
Less: Accumulated depreciation— equipment		12,000	84,000
Intangible assets			
Patents			11,000
Total assets			$274,500

* ($79,000 − $17,000)
** ($62,000 − $5,500)
*** ($50,000 + $5,500)

Liabilities

Similar to assets, companies classify liabilities as current or long-term.

Current Liabilities

Current liabilities are the obligations that a company reasonably expects to liquidate either through the use of current assets or the creation of other current liabilities. This concept includes:

1 Payables resulting from the acquisition of goods and services: accounts payable, wages payable, taxes payable, and so on.

2 Collections received in advance for the delivery of goods or performance of services such as unearned rent revenue or unearned subscriptions revenue.

3 Other liabilities whose liquidation will take place within the operating cycle such as the portion of long-term bonds to be paid in the current period, or short-term obligations arising from purchase of equipment.

At times, a liability payable next year is not included in the current liabilities section. This occurs either when the company expects to refinance the debt through another long-term issue[10] or to retire the debt out of noncurrent assets. This approach is used because liquidation does not result from the use of current assets or the creation of other current liabilities.

Companies do not report current liabilities in any consistent order. In general though, companies most commonly list first notes payable, accounts payable, or short-term debt. Companies usually list last income taxes payable, current maturities of long-term debt, or other current liabilities. For example, see **Halliburton Company**'s current liabilities section in Illustration 4-13.

Illustration 4-13
Balance Sheet
Presentation of
Current Liabilities

Halliburton Company
(in millions)

Current liabilities	
Short-term notes payable	$1,570
Accounts payable	782
Accrued employee compensation and benefits	267
Unearned revenues	386
Income taxes payable	113
Accrued special charges	6
Current maturities of long-term debt	8
Other current liabilities	694
Total current liabilities	3,826

Current liabilities include such items as trade and nontrade notes and accounts payable, advances received from customers, and current maturities of long-term debt. If material, companies classify income taxes and other accrued items separately. A company should fully describe in the notes any information about a secured liability—for example, stock held as collateral on notes payable—to identify the assets providing the security.

The excess of total current assets over total current liabilities is referred to as **working capital** (sometimes called **net working capital**). Working capital represents the net amount of a company's relatively liquid resources. That is, it is the liquid buffer available

[10]"Classification of Short-term Obligations Expected to Be Refinanced," *Statement of Financial Accounting Standards No. 6* (Stamford, Conn.: FASB, 1975).

to meet the financial demands of the operating cycle. Companies seldom disclose an amount for working capital on the balance sheet. But bankers and other creditors compute it as an indicator of the short-run liquidity of a company. To determine the actual liquidity and availability of working capital to meet current obligations, however, requires analyis of the composition of the current assets and their nearness to cash.

What do the numbers mean? "Show Me the Assets!"

Recently, concerned about the liquidity and solvency of many dot-com companies, creditors have demanded more assurance that these companies can pay their bills when due. A key indicator for creditors is the amount of working capital. For example, when a report published early in 2001 predicted that **Amazon.com**'s working capital would turn negative, the company's vendors began to explore steps that would ensure that Amazon would pay them.

Some vendors demanded that their Internet customers sign notes stating that the goods shipped to them serve as collateral for the transaction. Other vendors began shipping goods on *consignment*— an arrangement whereby the vendor retains ownership of the goods until a third party buys and pays for them. Such creditor-protection measures for dot-coms arise from creditors' concerns about Internet companies' lack of tangible assets that they can convert to cash to meet short-term obligations. For example, the primary asset for many Internet companies is its customer list. However, these lists have little resale value because privacy agreements prohibit sharing the customer information. Thus, with fewer hard assets that they can convert to cash, dot-coms can experience a more severe credit squeeze as vendors curtail shipments or take other measures to limit their financial risk. Such actions can further erode a company's liquidity and financial flexibility.

Beyond the Numbers

What is working capital? Why is it important that analysts look beyond the working capital number and examine the items that comprise working capital?

Long-Term Liabilities

Long-term liabilities, often referred to as **long-term debt**, are obligations that a company does not reasonably expect to liquidate within the normal operating cycle. Instead, it expects to pay them at some date beyond that time. Bonds payable, notes payable, some deferred income tax amounts, lease obligations, and pension obligations are the most common examples. It is desirable to report any premium or discount separately as an addition to or a subtraction from the bonds payable. Companies provide a great deal of supplementary disclosure for this section, because most long-term debt is subject to various covenants and restrictions for the protection of lenders.[11] Companies classify long-term liabilities that mature within the current operating cycle as *current* liabilities if payment of the obligation requires the use of current assets.

Generally, long-term liabilities are of three types:

1 Obligations arising from specific financing situations, such as the issuance of bonds, long-term lease obligations, and long-term notes payable.

2 Obligations arising from the ordinary operations of the company, such as pension obligations and deferred income tax liabilities.

---

[11]Companies usually explain the pertinent rights and privileges of the various securities (both debt and equity) outstanding in the notes to the financial statements. Examples of information that companies should disclose are dividend and liquidation preferences, participation rights, call prices and dates, conversion or exercise prices or rates and pertinent dates, sinking fund requirements, unusual voting rights, and significant terms of contracts to issue additional shares. "Disclosure of Information about Capital Structure," *Statement of Financial Accounting Standards No. 129* (Norwalk: FASB, 1997), par. 4.

3 Obligations that depend on the occurrence or nonoccurrence of one or more future events to confirm the amount payable, or the payee, or the date payable, such as service or product warranties and other contingencies.

Companies frequently describe in notes to the financial statements the terms of all long-term liability agreements (including maturity date or dates, rates of interest, nature of obligation, and any security pledged to support the debt). Illustration 4-14 provides an example of this, taken from an excerpt from **The Great Atlantic & Pacific Tea Company**'s financials.

Illustration 4-14
Balance Sheet
Presentation of Long-
Term Debt

The Great Atlantic & Pacific Tea Company, Inc.

Total current liabilities	$978,109,000
Long-term debt (See note)	254,312,000
Obligations under capital leases	252,618,000
Deferred income taxes	57,167,000
Other non-current liabilities	127,321,000

Note: Indebtedness. Debt consists of:

9.5% Senior notes, due in annual installments of $10,000,000	$ 40,000,000
Mortgages and other notes due through 2013 (average interest rate of 9.9%)	107,604,000
Bank borrowings at 9.7%	67,225,000
Commercial paper at 9.4%	100,102,000
	314,931,000
Less: Current portion	(60,619,000)
Total long-term debt	$254,312,000

Owners' (Stockholders') Equity

The **owners' equity** (**stockholders' equity**) section is one of the most difficult sections to prepare and understand. This is due to the complexity of capital stock agreements and the various restrictions on stockholders' equity imposed by state corporation laws, liability agreements, and boards of directors. Companies usually divide the section into three parts:

STOCKHOLDERS' EQUITY SECTION

1 CAPITAL STOCK. The par or stated value of the shares issued.

2 ADDITIONAL PAID-IN CAPITAL. The excess of amounts paid in over the par or stated value.

3 RETAINED EARNINGS. The corporation's undistributed earnings.

For capital stock, companies must disclose the authorized, issued, and outstanding par value amounts. A company usually presents the additional paid-in capital in one amount, although subtotals are informative if the sources of additional capital are varied and material. The retained earnings amount may be divided between *unappropriated* (the amount that is usually available for dividend distribution) and *restricted* (e.g., by bond indentures or other loan agreements) amounts. In addition, companies show any capital stock reacquired (treasury stock) as a reduction of stockholders' equity.

The ownership accounts (stockholders' equity) in a corporation differ considerably from ownership accounts in a partnership or proprietorship. Partners show separately their permanent capital accounts and the balance in their temporary accounts (drawing accounts). Proprietors ordinarily use a single capital account that handles all of the owner's equity transactions.

Illustration 4-15 presents an example of the stockholders' equity section from **Quanex Corporation**.

Quanex Corporation (in thousands)	
Stockholders' equity	
Preferred stock, no par value, 1,000,000 shares authorized;	
345,000 issued and outstanding	$ 86,250
Common stock, $0.50 par value, 25,000,000 shares authorized;	
13,638,005 shares issued and outstanding	6,819
Additional paid-in capital	87,260
Retained earnings	57,263
	$237,592

Illustration 4-15
Balance Sheet
Presentation of
Stockholders' Equity

Try it out! The trial balance at December 31, 2008, for Modest Mouse Co. showed the following credit balances.

Accounts Payable	$ 148,000
Allowance for Doubtful Accounts	8,700
Accumulated Depreciation—Equipment	140,000
Accrued Expenses	49,200
Notes Payable	94,000
Bonds Payable	400,000
Common Stock ($1 par)	500,000
Additional Paid-in Capital	45,000
Retained Earnings	138,000
	$1,522,900

The company provides the following additional information.

1   The notes payable represent bank loans that are secured by long-term investments carried at $120,000. These bank loans are due in 2009.

2   The bonds payable bear interest at 11% payable every December 31 and are due January 1, 2019.

3   On December 1, 2008, Modest Mouse received $10,000 cash payment for services to be provided in 2009. The bookkeeper debited Cash and credited Revenue.

4   On December 30, 2008, Modest Mouse declared dividends of $20,000 to be paid January 10, 2009. The company plans to record the dividends when paid.

Instructions

Prepare the corrected liability and stockholders' equity sections of the balance sheet for Modest Mouse Co. at December 31, 2008, from the available information.

Solution

Modest Mouse Co.
Balance Sheet (partial)
December 31, 2008

Liabilities and Stockholders' Equity

Current liabilities

Notes payable (secured by			
investments which cost $120,000)	$ 94,000		
Accounts payable	148,000		
Dividends payable	20,000		
Unearned revenue	10,000		
Accrued expenses	49,200		
Total current liabilities			$ 321,200

Long-term liabilities

11% bonds payable, due January 1, 2019			400,000
Total liabilities			721,200

Stockholders' equity

Common stock			
Shares at $1 par value;			
500,000 issued and			
outstanding	$500,000		
Additional paid-in capital	45,000	545,000	
Retained earnings		108,000*	
Total stockholders' equity			653,000
Total liabilities and stockholders' equity			$1,374,200

* ($138,000 − $10,000 − $20,000)

OBJECTIVE 3

Prepare a classified balance sheet using the report and account formats.

Balance Sheet Format

One common arrangement that companies follow in the presentation of a classified balance sheet is the **account form**. It lists assets by sections on the left side and liabilities and stockholders' equity by sections on the right side. The main disadvantage is the need for two facing pages.

To avoid this disadvantage, some companies use the **report form**, shown in Illustration 4-16 (page 161). It lists liabilities and stockholders' equity directly below assets on the same page.[12]

Companies infrequently use other balance sheet formats. For example, some companies deduct current liabilities from current assets to arrive at working capital. Alternatively, some deduct all liabilities from all assets.

---

[12]*Accounting Trends and Techniques—2006* indicates that all of the 600 companies surveyed use either the "report form" (506) or the "account form" (94), sometimes collectively referred to as the "customary form."

Illustration 4-16
Classified Report Form
Balance Sheet

Scientific Products, Inc.
Balance Sheet
December 31, 2008

Assets

Current assets

Cash		$ 42,485
Available-for-sale securities—at fair value		28,250
Accounts receivable	$165,824	
Less: Allowance for doubtful accounts	1,850	163,974
Notes receivable		23,000
Inventories—at average cost		489,713
Supplies on hand		9,780
Prepaid expenses		16,252
Total current assets		$ 773,454

Long-term investments

Investments in Warren Co.		87,500

Property, plant, and equipment

Land—at cost		125,000
Buildings—at cost	975,800	
Less: Accumulated depreciation	341,200	634,600
Total property, plant, and equipment		759,600

Intangible assets

Goodwill		100,000
Total assets		$1,720,554

Liabilities and Stockholders' Equity

Current liabilities

Notes payable to banks	$ 50,000	
Accounts payable	197,532	
Accrued interest on notes payable	500	
Income taxes payable	62,520	
Accrued salaries, wages, and other liabilities	9,500	
Deposits received from customers	420	
Total current liabilities		$ 320,472

Long-term liabilities

Twenty-year 12% debentures, due January 1, 2018		500,000
Total liabilities		820,472

Stockholders' equity

Paid in on capital stock		
Preferred, 7% cumulative		
Authorized, issued, and outstanding, 30,000 shares of $10 par value	$300,000	
Common		
Authorized, 500,000 shares of $1 par value; issued and outstanding, 400,000 shares	400,000	
Additional paid-in capital	37,500	737,500
Retained earnings		162,582
Total stockholders' equity		900,082
Total liabilities and stockholders' equity		$1,720,554

Presentation of Balance Sheet Formats for Various Real Companies

college/warfield
www.wiley.com

Analysts use balance sheet information in models designed to predict financial distress. A bankruptcy-prediction model pioneered by E. I. Altman combines balance sheet and income measures in the following equation to derive a "Z-score."

$$Z = \frac{\text{Working capital}}{\text{Total assets}} \times 1.2 + \frac{\text{Retained earnings}}{\text{Total assets}} \times 1.4 + \frac{\text{EBIT}}{\text{Total assets}} \times 3.3$$

$$+ \frac{\text{Sales}}{\text{Total assets}} \times 0.99 + \frac{\text{MV equity}}{\text{Total liabilities}} \times 0.6$$

Following extensive testing, Altman found that companies with Z-scores above 3.0 are unlikely to fail. Those with Z-scores below 1.81 are very likely to fail. Although Altman developed the original model for publicly held manufacturing companies, the model has been modified to apply to companies in various industries, to emerging companies, and to companies not traded in public markets.

At one time, the use of Z-scores was virtually unheard of among practicing accountants. Today, auditors, management consultants, and courts of law use this measure. In addition, banks use Z-scores for loan evaluation. While a low score does not guarantee bankruptcy, the model has been proven accurate in many situations.

Source: Adapted from E. I. Altman and E. Hotchkiss, *Corporate Financial Distress and Bankruptcy*, 3rd edition (New York: John Wiley and Sons, 2005).

Beyond the Numbers

Explain why the ratios that are part of Altman's bankruptcy prediction model are significant in forecasting financial distress.

ADDITIONAL INFORMATION REPORTED

The balance sheet is not complete if a company simply lists the assets, liabilities, and owners' equity accounts. It still needs to provide important supplemental information. This may be information not presented elsewhere in the statement, or it may elaborate on items in the balance sheet.

Five types of information normally are supplemental to the account titles and amounts presented in the balance sheet.

OBJECTIVE 4
Determine which balance sheet information requires supplemental disclosure.

SUPPLEMENTAL BALANCE SHEET INFORMATION

1 **CONTINGENCIES.** Material events that have an uncertain outcome.

2 **ACCOUNTING POLICIES.** Explanations of the valuation methods used or the basic assumptions made concerning inventory valuations, depreciation methods, investments in subsidiaries, etc.

3 **CONTRACTUAL SITUATIONS.** Explanations of certain restrictions or covenants attached to specific assets or, more likely, to liabilities.

4 **POST–BALANCE-SHEET DISCLOSURES.** Disclosures of certain events that have occurred after the balance sheet date but before the financial statements have been issued.

5 **FAIR VALUES.** Disclosures of fair values, particularly for financial instruments.

We discuss these five types of additional information in the following sections.

Contingencies

A **contingency** is an existing situation involving uncertainty as to possible gain (*gain contingency*) or loss (*loss contingency*) that will ultimately be resolved when one or more future events occur or fail to occur. In short, contingencies are material events with an uncertain future. Examples of gain contingencies are tax operating loss carryforwards or company litigation against another party. Typical loss contingencies relate to litigation, environmental issues, possible tax assessments, or government investigation. We examine the accounting and reporting requirements involving contingencies more fully in Chapter 12.

> **WHAT'S THE PRINCIPLE?**
>
> The basis for including additional information should meet the *full disclosure principle*. That is, the information should be of sufficient importance to influence the judgment of an informed user.

Accounting Policies

APB Opinion No. 22 recommends disclosure for all significant accounting principles and methods that involve selection from among alternatives or those that are peculiar to a given industry.[13] For instance, companies can compute inventories under several cost flow assumptions (e.g., LIFO and FIFO), depreciate plant and equipment under several accepted methods (e.g., double-declining balance and straight-line), and carry investments at different valuations (e.g., cost, equity, and fair value). Sophisticated users of financial statements know of these possibilities and examine the statements closely to determine the methods used.

Companies must also disclose information about the nature of their operations, the use of estimates in preparing financial statements, certain significant estimates, and vulnerabilities due to certain concentrations.[14] Illustration 4-17 shows an example of such a disclosure.

Illustration 4-17
Balance Sheet Disclosure of Significant Risks and Uncertainties

Chesapeake Corporation

Risks and Uncertainties. Chesapeake operates in three business segments which offer a diversity of products over a broad geographic base. The Company is not dependent on any single customer, group of customers, market, geographic area or supplier of materials, labor or services. Financial statements include, where necessary, amounts based on the judgments and estimates of management. These estimates include allowances for bad debts, accruals for landfill closing costs, environmental remediation costs, loss contingencies for litigation, self-insured medical and workers' compensation insurance and income taxes and determinations of discount and other rate assumptions for pensions and postretirement benefit expenses.

Disclosure of significant accounting principles and methods and of risks and uncertainties is particularly useful if placed in a separate **Summary of Significant Accounting Policies** preceding the notes to the financial statements or as the initial note.

Contractual Situations

If significant, companies should disclose contractual situations in the notes to the financial statements. For example, they must clearly state the essential provisions of lease contracts, pension obligations, and stock option plans in the notes. Analysts want to know not only the amount of the liabilities, but also how the different contractual provisions affect the company at present and in the future.

Companies must disclose contractual situations if they are material. Examples would be commitments related to obligations to maintain working capital, to limit the payment of dividends, to restrict the use of assets, and to require the maintenance of certain financial ratios. Management must exercise considerable judgment to determine whether omission

[13]"Disclosure of Accounting Policies," Opinions of the Accounting Principles Board No. 22 (New York: AICPA, 1972).

[14]"Disclosure of Certain Significant Risks and Uncertainties," *Statement of Position 94-6* (New York: AICPA, 1994).

of such information is misleading. The rule in this situation is, "When in doubt, disclose." It is better to disclose a little too much information than not enough.

<u>**What do the numbers mean?**</u>   **What About Your Commitments?**

Many of the accounting scandals of recent years related to the nondisclosures of significant contractual obligations. The SEC has now mandated that companies disclose contractual obligations in a tabular summary in the management discussion and analysis section of the company's annual report. Presented below is an example of **Procter & Gamble**'s disclosure.

Contractual Commitments as of June 30, 2006

(in millions of dollars)	Total	Less Than 1 Year	1–3 Years	3–5 Years	After 5 Years
Recorded Liabilities					
Total debt	$37,501	$2,059	$22,699	$3,752	$ 8,991
Capital leases	632	90	278	92	172
Wella Domination and Profit Transfer Agreement	207	207	—	—	—
Other					
Interest payments relating to long-term debt	11,923	1,850	2,485	1,087	6,501
Operating leases	1,399	269	394	308	428
Minimum pension funding [1]	1,136	398	738	—	—
Purchase obligations [2]	5,700	1,940	1,593	1,002	1,165
Total Contractual Commitments	58,498	6,813	28,187	6,241	17,257

(1) Represents future pension payments to comply with local funding requirements. The projected payments beyond fiscal year 2009 are not currently determinable.

(2) Primarily reflects future contractual payments under various take-or-pay arrangements entered into as part of the normal course of business.

Beyond the Numbers

How will tabular displays of contractual obligations help investors?

Post–Balance-Sheet Events (Subsequent Events)

Notes to the financial statements should explain any significant financial events that took place after the formal balance sheet date but before a company finally issued it. These events are referred to as **post–balance-sheet events, events subsequent to the balance sheet date**, or just plain **subsequent events**.

A period of several weeks, and sometimes months, may elapse after the end of the fiscal year before a company issues the financial statements. The activities involved in issuing the statements—taking and pricing the inventory, reconciling subsidiary ledgers with controlling accounts, preparing necessary adjusting entries, ensuring the entry for all transactions for the period, obtaining an audit of the financial statements by independent certified public accountants, and printing the annual report—all take time. During the period between the balance sheet date and its distribution to stockholders and creditors, important transactions or other events may occur that materially affect the company's financial position or operating situation. Illustration 4-18 shows how the subsequent events period is time-diagrammed.

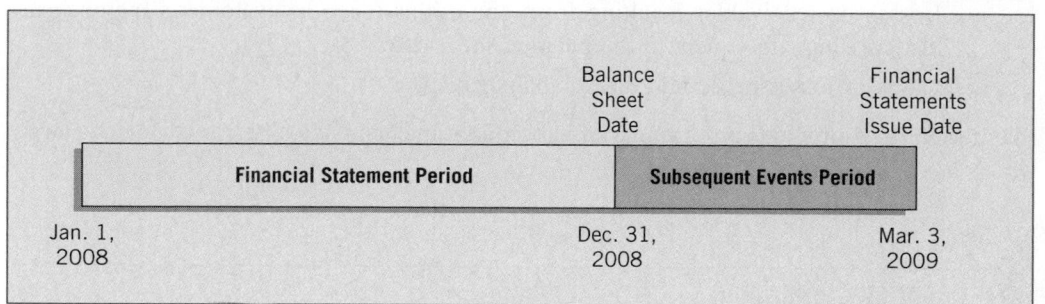

Illustration 4-18
Time Periods for
Subsequent Events

Many who read a recent balance sheet believe the balance sheet condition is constant and tend to project that condition into the future. However, readers must be told if the company has sold one of its plants, acquired a subsidiary, suffered extraordinary losses, settled significant litigation, or experienced any other important event in the post–balance-sheet period. Without an explanation in a note, the reader might be misled and draw inappropriate conclusions.

Two types of events or transactions occurring after the balance sheet date may have a material effect on the financial statements or may need to be considered to interpret these statements accurately:

1 Events that provide additional evidence about conditions that existed at the balance sheet date, affect the estimates used in preparing financial statements, and, therefore, result in needed adjustments. Companies must use all information available prior to the issuance of the financial statements to evaluate estimates previously made. To ignore these subsequent events is to pass up an opportunity to improve the accuracy of the financial statements. This first type encompasses information that a company would record in the accounts had it been known at the balance sheet date.

> **WHAT'S THE PRINCIPLE?**
>
> The *periodicity* or *time period assumption* implies that economic activities of a company can be divided into artificial time periods for purpose of analysis.

For example, if a loss on an account receivable results from a customer's bankruptcy subsequent to the balance sheet date, the company adjusts the financial statements before their issuance. The bankruptcy stems from the customer's poor financial health existing at the balance sheet date.

The same criterion applies to settlements of litigation. A company must adjust the financial statements if the events that gave rise to the litigation, such as personal injury or patent infringement, took place prior to the balance sheet date. If the event took place subsequent to the balance sheet date, no adjustment is necessary but disclosure is. To illustrate, a loss resulting from a customer's fire or flood after the balance sheet date is not indicative of conditions existing at that date. Thus, adjustment of the financial statements is not necessary.

2 Events that provide evidence about conditions that did not exist at the balance sheet date but arise subsequent to that date and do not require adjustment of the financial statements. A company may need to disclose some of these events to keep the financial statements from being misleading. These disclosures take the form of notes, supplemental schedules, or even pro forma, "as if" financial data prepared as if the event had occurred on the balance sheet date. Examples of such events that require disclosure (but do not result in adjustment) include:

a Sale of bonds or capital stock; stock splits or stock dividends.

b Business combination pending or effected.

c Settlement of litigation when the event giving rise to the claim took place subsequent to the balance sheet date.

d Loss of plant or inventories from fire or flood.

    e   Losses on receivables resulting from conditions (such as customer's major casu-
alty) arising subsequent to the balance sheet date.

    f   Gains or losses on certain marketable securities.[15]

Illustration 4-19 provides an example of subsequent events disclosure for **Goodrich Corp.**,
which has a December 31 year-end.

Illustration 4-19
Disclosure of
Subsequent Events

Goodrich Corporation

Note W. Subsequent Event   On February 16, 2004 the Company was notified by Pratt & Whitney, a
United Technologies Company, that it will not meet the requirements for original equipment PW4000
engine components after the Company completes delivery of 45 shipsets (2 units per shipset) through
early 2005. The Company had originally forecasted 90 shipsets to be delivered through 2009. As a
result of this action, the total estimated revenue associated with this contract has been significantly
reduced and anticipated cost reductions related to future deliveries under this contract will not occur.

    The notice of termination is considered a Type 1 subsequent event under generally accepted
accounting principles, the effects of which must be reflected in the Company's 2003 financial statements. As a result, the Company recorded a pre-tax charge of $15.1 million, as of December 31, 2003
related to this contract. The charge includes impairment of excess over average inventory of $7.0 million
and $8.1 million for forward losses relating to the reduction in forecasted contract revenue and the
increase in costs.

**Many subsequent events or developments are not likely to require either adjust-
ment of or disclosure in the financial statements.** Typically, companies communicate
these non-accounting events or conditions by other means. These events include legislation, product changes, management changes, strikes, unionization, marketing agreements,
and loss of important customers.

Fair Values

As we discussed in Chapter 2, companies use historical cost as the primary valuation basis
in financial statements. However, fair value information may be more useful than historical
cost for certain types of assets and liabilities. This is particularly so in the case of financial
instruments.[16] **Financial instruments** are defined as cash, an ownership interest, or a contractual right to receive or obligation to deliver cash or another financial instrument. Contractual rights to receive cash or other financial instruments are assets. Contractual obligations
to pay are liabilities. Cash, investments, accounts receivable, and payables are examples of
financial instruments. Financial instruments are increasing both in use and variety.

    Companies must disclose both the carrying value and the estimated fair values of their
financial instruments. For example, **YUM! Inc.** provides extensive disclosures of the fair

---

[15]"Subsequent Events," *Statement on Auditing Standards No. 1* (New York: AICPA, 1973),
pp. 123–124. *Accounting Trends and Techniques—2006* listed the following types of subsequent
events and their frequency of occurrence among the 600 companies surveyed: business combinations
pending or effected, 99; debt incurred, reduced, or refinanced, 62; capital stock issued or repurchased,
39; discontinued operations, 38; litigation, 33; restructuring/bankruptcy, 26; stock splits or dividends,
stock rights, 20; employee benefit plans, 14.

[16]The FASB has issued two recent standards related to fair value measurement, In *Statement of
Financial Accounting Standard No. 157*, "Fair Value Measurements" (FASB: September 2006), the
Board has developed a single definition of fair value when fair value is a required measurement in
GAAP. *Statement of Financial Accounting Standard No. 159*, "The Fair Value Option for Financial
Assets and Financial Liabilities—Including an amendment of FASB Statement No. 115" (FASB:
February 2007) gives companies the option to use fair value for recording financial assets and
liabilities. This latter standard likely will result in more use of fair values in financial statements.

value of its financial instrument assets and liabilities, as shown in Illustration 4-20. We provide more extensive discussion of financial instrument accounting and reporting in Chapters 8, 12, 13, and 14.

YUM! Brands Inc.

The carrying amounts and fair values of our other financial instruments subject to fair value disclosures are as follows:

	Carrying Amount	Fair Value
Debt		
Short-term borrowings and long-term debt, excluding capital leases and the derivative instrument adjustments	$ 1,925	$ 2,181
Debt-related derivative instruments		
Open contracts in a net asset position	31	31
Lease guarantees	8	37
Guarantees of supporting financial arrangements of certain franchisees, unconsolidated affiliates and other third parties	8	10
Letters of credit	–	3

We estimated the fair value of debt, debt-related derivative instruments, foreign currency-related derivative instruments, guarantees and letters of credit using market quotes and calculations based on market rates.

Illustration 4-20
Disclosure of Financial Instrument Fair Values

TECHNIQUES OF DISCLOSURE

Companies should disclose as completely as possible the effect of various contingencies on financial condition, the methods of valuing assets, and the company's contracts and agreements. To disclose this pertinent information, companies may use parenthetical explanations, notes, cross-reference and contra items, and supporting schedules.

OBJECTIVE 5
Describe the major disclosure techniques for the balance sheet.

Parenthetical Explanations

Companies often provide additional information by parenthetical explanations following the item. Illustration 4-21 shows parenthetical disclosure of shares of common stock issued by **Ford Motor Company**.

Ford Motor Company

Stockholders' equity (in millions)

Common stock, par value $0.01 per share (1,837 million shares issued) $18

Illustration 4-21
Parenthetical Explanation

This additional pertinent balance sheet information adds clarity and completeness. It has an advantage over a note because it brings the additional information into the body of the statement where readers will less likely overlook it. Companies, however, should avoid lengthy parenthetical explanations, which might be distracting.

Notes

Companies use notes if they cannot conveniently show additional explanations as parenthetical explanations. Illustration 4-22 shows how **International Paper Company** reported its inventory costing methods in accompanying notes.

Illustration 4-22
Note Disclosure

International Paper Company

Note 11

Inventories by major category were (millions):

Raw materials	$ 371
Finished pulp, paper and packaging products	1,796
Finished lumber and panel products	184
Operating supplies	351
Other	16
Total inventories	$2,718

The last-in, first-out inventory method is used to value most of International Paper's U.S. inventories. Approximately 70% of total raw materials and finished products inventories were valued using this method. If the first-in, first-out method had been used, it would have increased total inventories balances by approximately $170 million.

Companies commonly use notes to disclose the following: the existence and amount of any preferred stock dividends in arrears, the terms of or obligations imposed by purchase commitments, special financial arrangements and instruments, depreciation policies, any changes in the application of accounting principles, and the existence of contingencies.

WHAT'S THE PRINCIPLE?

The user-specific quality of *understandability* requires accountants to be careful in describing transactions and events.

Notes therefore must present all essential facts as completely and succinctly as possible. Careless wording may mislead rather than aid readers. Notes should *add* to the total information made available in the financial statements, not raise unanswered questions or contradict other portions of the statements. The following three notes illustrate a common method of presenting such information.

Illustration 4-23
More Note Disclosures

Consolidated Papers, Inc.

Note 7: Commitments. The company had capital expenditure purchase commitments outstanding of approximately $17 million.

Alberto-Culver Company

Note 3: Long-Term Debt. Various borrowing arrangements impose restrictions on such items as total debt, working capital, dividend payments, treasury stock purchases and interest expense. The company was in compliance with these arrangements and $68 million of consolidated retained earnings was not restricted as to the payment of dividends and purchases of treasury stock.

Willamette Industries, Inc.

Note 4: Property, Plant, and Equipment (partial). The company changed its accounting esti-mates relating to depreciation. The estimated service lives for most machinery and equipment were extended five years. The change was based upon a study performed by the company's engineering department, comparisons to typical industry practices, and the effect of the company's extensive capital investments which have resulted in a mix of assets with longer productive lives due to technological advances. As a result of the change, net income was increased $51,900, or $0.46 per diluted share.

Illustration 4-23
More Note Disclosures
(continued)

Cross-Reference and Contra Items

Companies often "cross-reference" a direct relationship between an asset and a liability on the balance sheet. For example, Illustration 4-24 shows how a company, on December 31, 2008, might cross-reference bonds payable in the current assets section and the amount of bonds payable to be redeemed within one year among the current liabilities.

Current assets (in part)	
Cash on deposit with sinking fund trustee for redemption of bonds payable—see Current liabilities	$800,000

Current liabilities (in part)	
Bonds payable to be redeemed in 2009—see Current assets	$2,300,000

Illustration 4-24
Cross-Referencing and
Contra Items

This cross-reference points out that the company will redeem $2,300,000 of bonds payable currently (in 2009), for which it has set aside only $800,000. Therefore, it needs additional cash—from unrestricted cash, from sales of investments, from profits, or from some other source. Alternatively, the company could instead show the same information parenthetically.

Another common disclosure procedure is to establish contra or adjunct accounts. A **contra account** on a balance sheet reduces either an asset, liability, or owners' equity ac-count. Examples include Accumulated Depreciation and Discount on Bonds Payable. Con-tra accounts provide some flexibility in presenting the financial information. With the use of the Accumulated Depreciation account, for example, a reader of the statement can see the original cost of the asset as well as the depreciation to date.

An **adjunct account**, on the other hand, increases either an asset, liability, or owners' equity account. An example is Premium on Bonds Payable, which, when added to the Bonds Payable account, describes the total bond liability of the company.

Supporting Schedules

Often a company needs a separate schedule to present more detailed information about certain assets or liabilities. The two parts of Illustration 4-25 (below and on page 170) demonstrate disclosure by supporting schedules.

Property, plant, and equipment	
Land, buildings, equipment, and other fixed assets—net (see Schedule 3)	$643,300

Illustration 4-25
Disclosure through Use of
Supporting Schedules

Illustration 4-25
Disclosure through Use of
Supporting Schedules
(continued)

Schedule 3
Land, Buildings, Equipment, and Other Fixed Assets

	Total	Land	Buildings	Equip.	Other Fixed Assets
Balance January 1, 2008	$740,000	$46,000	$358,000	$260,000	$76,000
Additions in 2008	161,200		120,000	38,000	3,200
	901,200	46,000	478,000	298,000	79,200
Assets retired or sold in 2008	31,700			27,000	4,700
Balance December 31, 2008	869,500	46,000	478,000	271,000	74,500
Depreciation taken to January 1, 2008	196,000		102,000	78,000	16,000
Depreciation taken in 2008	56,000		28,000	24,000	4,000
	252,000		130,000	102,000	20,000
Depreciation on assets retired in 2008	25,800			22,000	3,800
Depreciation accumulated December 31, 2008	226,200		130,000	80,000	16,200
Book value of assets	$643,300	$46,000	$348,000	$191,000	$58,300

Terminology

The account titles in the general ledger do not necessarily represent the best terminology for balance sheet purposes. Companies often use brief account titles and include technical terms understood only by accountants. Yet, many persons unacquainted with accounting terminology examine balance sheets. Thus balance sheets should contain descriptions that readers will generally understand and clearly interpret.

For example, in the past companies used the term *reserve* in several ways: to describe amounts deducted from assets (contra accounts such as accumulated depreciation and allowance for doubtful accounts) and as a part of the title of contingent or estimated liabilities. Because of the different meanings attached to this term, misinterpretation often resulted from its use. The profession now recommends that companies use the word **reserve** only to describe an appropriation of retained earnings. This more selective use of "reserve" has resulted in a better understanding of its significance when it appears in a balance sheet. Despite this more selective use, however, the term "appropriated" appears more logical, and its use should be encouraged.

For years the profession has recommended that companies discontinue the use of the word *surplus* in balance sheet presentations of owners' equity. The use of the terms *capital surplus, paid-in surplus*, and *earned surplus* is confusing. Although condemned by the profession, these terms appear all too frequently in current financial statements.

You will want to read the CONVERGENCE CORNER
on the next page for
discussion of how international convergence efforts relate to the balance sheet.

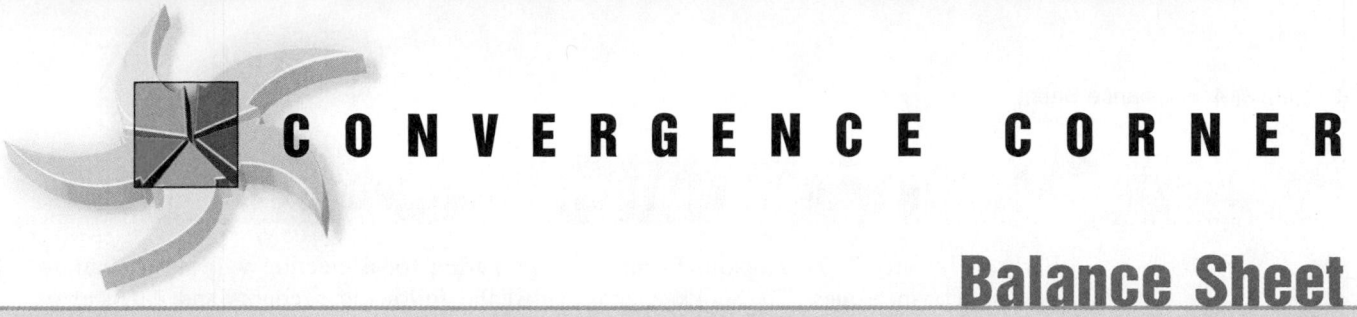

Balance Sheet

As in U.S. GAAP, the balance sheet is a required statement for iGAAP. In addition, the content and presentation of an iGAAP balance sheet are similar to that used for U.S. GAAP. The disclosure requirements related to the balance sheet are much more extensive and detailed in the United States. *IAS 1*, "Presentation of Financial Statements," provides the overall iGAAP requirements for balance sheet information.

 RELEVANT FACTS

• iGAAP has a standard on financial statement presentation *IAS 1*, which requires that companies report specific items on the balance sheet. No such general standard exists in U.S. GAAP. However under U.S. GAAP, public companies must follow SEC regulations, which require specific line items. In addition, specific U.S. GAAP standards mandate certain forms of reporting balance sheet information.

• There are many similarities between U.S. and iGAAP related to presentation of comparative prior-period information, and current/noncurrent classification for assets and liabilities.

• Interestingly, iGAAP statements may report property, plant, and equipment first in the balance sheet. Some companies report the subtotal "net assets," which equals total assets minus total liabilities.

• While the use of the term "reserve" is discouraged in U.S. GAAP, there is no such prohibition in iGAAP.

ABOUT THE NUMBERS

U.S. GAAP and iGAAP differ in the iGAAP provision for revaluations of property, plant, and equipment. To illustrate, Richardson Company uses iGAAP and has property and equipment on an historical cost basis of 2,000,000 euros. At the end of the year, Richardson performs an appraisal and determines that its property and equipment had a revaluation increase of 243,000 euros. Richardson makes the following entry to record this revaluation.

Property and Equipment	243,000	
Revaluation Equity		243,000

As indicated, property and equipment are increased as well as stockholders' equity. Each reporting period, the company revalues property and equipment to approximate fair value. Under iGAAP, Richardson provides the following note to explain the change in the revaluation equity account from one period to the next.

Note 30 Reserves (in part)	2008 (euros 000)
Properties revaluation reserve	
Balance at beginning of year	11,345
Increase/(decrease) on revaluation of plant and equipment	243
Impairment losses	–
Reversals of impairment losses	–
Balance at end of year	11,588

 ON THE HORIZON

The IASB and the FASB are working on a project to converge their standards related to financial statement presentation. A key feature of the proposed framework for financial statement presentation is that each of the statements will be organized in the same format to separate an entity's financing activities from its operating and other (investing) activities and to further separate financing activities into transactions with owners and creditors. Thus, the same classifications used in the balance sheet would also be used in the income statement and the statement of cash flows. You can follow the joint financial presentation project at the following link: *http://www.fasb.org/project/financial statement presentation.shtml*.

The FASB also has a project to consider whether certain differences between U.S. GAAP and the corresponding iGAAP (*IAS 10*, "Events after the Balance Sheet Date") could be converged. These differences relate to the dates through which subsequent events are considered and provisions related to the re-issuance of financial statements in the presence of subsequent events.

ACCOUNTING, ANALYSIS, PRINCIPLES

Early in January 2009, Hopkins Company is preparing for a meeting with its bankers to discuss a loan request. Its bookkeeper provided the following accounts and balances at December 31, 2008.

	Debit	Credit
Cash	$ 75,000	
Accounts Receivable (net)	38,500	
Inventories	65,300	
Equipment (net)	84,000	
Patents	15,000	
Notes and Accounts Payable		$ 52,000
Notes Payable (due 2010)		75,000
Common Stock		100,000
Retained Earnings		50,800
	$277,800	$277,800

Except for the following items, Hopkins has recorded all adjustments in the accounts.

1 Cash includes $500 petty cash and $15,000 in a bond sinking fund.

2 The net accounts receivable is comprised of (a) accounts receivable $52,000 and (b) allowance for doubtful accounts $13,500.

3 Equipment had a cost of $112,000 and accumulated depreciation of $28,000.

4 On January 8, 2009, one of Hopkins' customers declared bankruptcy. At December 31, 2008, this company owed Hopkins $9,000.

Accounting

Prepare a corrected classified balance sheet for Hopkins Company at December 31, 2008.

Analysis

Hopkins' bank is considering granting an additional loan in the amount of $45,000, which will be due December 31, 2009. How can the information in the balance sheet provide useful information to the bank about Hopkins' ability to repay the loan, if renewed?

Principles

In the upcoming meeting with the bank, Hopkins plans to provide additional information about the fair value of its equipment and some internally generated intangible assets related to its customer lists. This information indicates that Hopkins has significant unrealized gains on these assets, which are not reflected on the balance sheet. What objections is the bank likely to raise about the usefulness of this information in evaluating Hopkins for the loan renewal?

Solution

Accounting

Hopkins Company
Balance Sheet
December 31, 2008

Assets

Current assets		
Cash ($75,000 − $15,000)		$ 60,000
Accounts receivable ($52,000 − $9,000)	$ 43,000	
Less: Allowance for doubtful		
accounts ($13,500 − $9,000)	4,500	38,500
Inventories		65,300
Total current assets		163,800
Long-term investments		
Bond sinking fund		15,000
Property, plant, and equipment		
Equipment	112,000	
Less: Accumulated depreciation—equipment	28,000	84,000
Intangible assets		
Patents		15,000
Total assets		$277,800

Liabilities and Stockholders' Equity

Current liabilities		
Notes and accounts payable	$ 52,000	
Long-term liabilities		
Notes payable (due 2010)	75,000	
Total liabilities		$127,000
Stockholders' equity		
Common stock	100,000	
Retained earnings	50,800	
Total stockholders' equity		150,800
Total liabilities and stockholders' equity		$277,800

Analysis

The classified balance sheet provides subtotals for current assets and current liabilities, which are assets expected to be converted to cash (or liabilities expected to be paid from cash) in the next year or operating cycle. Thus, an analysis of current assets relative to current liabilities provides information relevant to assessing Hopkins' ability to repay a loan within the next year. Specifically, current assets in excess of current liabilities (working capital) is $111,800 ($163,800 − $52,000.) This seems to be a safe liquidity cushion relative to an additional loan of $45,000. Of course, the loan officer also would evaluate Hopkins' earnings and cash flows in the analysis.

Principles

The primary objection that the bank is likely to raise about this supplemental information is the reliability of the estimates of fair values for the long-lived assets and the internally generated intangibles. In addition, the loan officer might not consider information about these long-term assets to be that relevant to the loan decision, because the loan is short-term.

Key Terms

Summary of Learning Objectives

1 Explain the uses and limitations of a balance sheet. The balance sheet provides information about the nature and amounts of investments in enterprise resources, obligations to creditors, and the owners' equity in net resources. The balance sheet contributes to financial reporting by providing a basis for (1) computing rates of return, (2) evaluating the capital structure of the enterprise, and (3) assessing the liquidity, solvency, and financial flexibility of the enterprise.

The limitations of a balance sheet are as follows: (1) The balance sheet does not reflect fair value because accountants use a historical cost basis in valuing and reporting assets and liabilities. (2) Companies must use judgment and estimates to determine amounts such as the collectibility of receivables, the salability of inventory, and the useful life of long-term tangible and intangible assets. (3) The balance sheet omits many items that are of financial value to the business but cannot be recorded objectively, such as human resources, customer base, and reputation.

2 Identify the major classifications of the balance sheet. The general elements of the balance sheet are assets, liabilities, and equity. The major classifications of assets are current assets; long-term investments; property, plant, and equipment; intangible assets; and other assets. The major classifications of liabilities are current and long-term liabilities. The balance sheet of a corporation generally classifies owners' equity as capital stock, additional paid-in capital, and retained earnings.

3 Prepare a classified balance sheet using the report and account formats. The report form lists liabilities and stockholders' equity directly below assets on the same page. The account form lists assets by sections on the left side, and liabilities and stockholders' equity by sections on the right side.

4 Determine which balance sheet information requires supplemental disclosure. Five types of information normally are supplemental to account titles and amounts presented in the balance sheet: (1) *Contingencies:* Material events that have an uncertain outcome. (2) *Accounting policies:* Explanations of the valuation methods used or the basic assumptions made concerning inventory valuation, depreciation methods, investments in subsidiaries, etc. (3) *Contractual situations:* Explanations of certain restrictions or covenants attached to specific assets or, more likely, to liabilities. (4) *Post–balance-sheet events:* Events occurring after the balance date but before issuance of statements. (5) *Fair values:* Disclosures related to fair values, particularly related to financial instruments.

5 Describe the major disclosure techniques for the balance sheet. Companies use four methods to disclose pertinent information in the balance sheet: (1) *Parenthetical explanations:* Parenthetical information provides additional information or description following the item. (2) *Notes:* A company uses notes if it cannot conveniently show additional explanations or descriptions as parenthetical explanations. (3) *Cross-reference and contra items:* Companies "cross-reference" a direct relationship between an asset and a liability on the balance sheet. (4) *Supporting schedules:* Often a company needs a separate schedule to present more detailed information about certain assets or liabilities, because the balance sheet provides just a single summary item.

REVIEW EXERCISE

Presented below is a condensed balance sheet of James Henry Corporation.

James Henry Corporation
Balance Sheet
December 31, 2008

Current assets	$ 82,000	Current liabilities	$ 82,000
Long-term investments	124,000	Long-term liabilities	265,000
Property, plant, and equipment	301,000	Stockholders' equity	235,000
Intangibles	75,000		$582,000
	$582,000		

Additional information:

1 The current assets include: cash $50,000; accounts receivable $45,000, less $5,000 allowance for doubtful accounts; advances from customers $9,000; and prepaid insurance $1,000.

2 Investments include: investment in subsidiary $82,000; premium on bonds payable $4,000; patents $16,000; treasury stock at cost of $20,000; and held-to-maturity securities, at amortized cost $10,000.

3 Property, plant, and equipment consists of: buildings $180,000 less accumulated depreciation of $30,000; land held for speculation $75,000; equipment of $95,000 less accumulated depreciation of $25,000; and a refundable deposit on rental equipment of $6,000 on a lease that ends in 2 months.

4 Intangible assets include goodwill of $75,000.

5 Current liabilities include: accounts payable $47,000; and a note payable (due in 90 days) $35,000.

6 Long-term liabilities consist of: bonds payable $150,000; preferred stock, $100 par, $100,000; and cash dividends payable $15,000.

7 Stockholders' equity consists of: common stock, $1 par, $80,000; additional paid-in capital $40,000; and retained earnings $115,000.

Instructions

From the information provided, prepare a classified balance sheet at December 31, 2008, showing the details of each classification.

Solution

James Henry Corporation
Balance Sheet
December 31, 2008

Assets

Current assets

Cash		$50,000	
Accounts receivable	$ 45,000		
Less: Allowance for doubtful accounts	5,000	40,000	
Prepaid insurance		1,000	
Deposits		6,000	$ 97,000

Long-term investments			
Held-to-maturity securities, at amortized cost		10,000	
Land held for speculation		75,000	
Investment in subsidiary		82,000	167,000
Property, plant, and equipment			
Building	180,000		
Less: Accumulated depreciation	30,000	150,000	
Equipment	95,000		
Less: Accumulated depreciation	25,000	70,000	220,000
Intangible assets			
Goodwill		75,000	
Patents		16,000	91,000
Total assets			$575,000

Liabilities and Stockholders' Equity

Current liabilities		
Notes payable	$ 35,000	
Accounts payable	47,000	
Advances from customers	9,000	
Dividends payable	15,000	
Total current liabilities		$106,000
Long-term liabilities		
Bonds payable	150,000	
Plus: Premium on bonds	4,000	154,000
Total liabilities		260,000
Stockholders' equity		
Preferred stock, $100 par, 1,000 shares issued	100,000	
Common stock, $1 par, 80,000 shares issued	80,000	
Additional paid-in capital	40,000	220,000
Retained earnings		115,000
Less: Treasury stock, at cost		(20,000)
Total stockholders' equity		315,000
Total liabilities and stockholders' equity		$575,000

Questions

1 How does information from the balance sheet help users of the financial statements?

2 What is meant by solvency? What information in the balance sheet can be used to assess a company's solvency?

3 A recent financial magazine indicated that a drug company had good financial flexibility. What is meant by financial flexibility, and why is it important?

4 Discuss at least two situations in which estimates could affect the usefulness of information in the balance sheet.

5 Jones Company reported an increase in inventories in the past year. Discuss the effect of this change on the current ratio (current assets ÷ current liabilities). What does this tell a statement user about Jones Company's liquidity?

6 What is meant by liquidity? Rank the following assets from one to five in order of liquidity.

(a) Goodwill.

(b) Inventories.

(c) Buildings.

(d) Short-term investments.

(e) Accounts receivable.

7 What are the major limitations of the balance sheet as a source of information?

8 Discuss at least two items that are important to the value of companies like **Intel** or **IBM** but that are not recorded in their balance sheets. What are some reasons why these items are not recorded in the balance sheet?

9 How does separating current assets from property, plant, and equipment in the balance sheet help analysts?

10 In its December 31, 2008, balance sheet Oakley Corporation reported as an asset, "Net notes and accounts receivable, $7,100,000." What other disclosures are necessary?

11 Should available-for-sale securities always be reported as a current asset? Explain.

12 What is the relationship between current assets and current liabilities?

13 The New York Knicks, Inc. sold 10,000 season tickets at $1,000 each. By December 31, 2008, 18 of the 40 home games had been played. What amount should be reported as a current liability at December 31, 2008?

14 What is working capital? How does working capital relate to the operating cycle?

15 In what section of the balance sheet should the following items appear, and what balance sheet terminology would you use?

(a) Treasury stock (recorded at cost).

(b) Checking account at bank.

(c) Land (held as an investment).

(d) Appropriation for sinking fund.

(e) Unamortized premium on bonds payable.

(f) Copyrights.

(g) Pension fund assets.

(h) Premium on capital stock.

(i) Long-term investments (pledged against bank loans payable).

16 Where should the following items be shown on the balance sheet, if shown at all?

(a) Allowance for doubtful accounts.

(b) Merchandise held on consignment.

(c) Advances received on sales contract.

(d) Cash surrender value of life insurance.

(e) Land.

(f) Merchandise out on consignment.

(g) Pension fund on deposit with a trustee (under a trust revocable at depositor's option).

(h) Franchises.

(i) Accumulated depreciation of plant and equipment.

(j) Materials in transit—purchased f.o.b. destination.

17 State the generally accepted accounting principle (standard) applicable to the balance sheet valuation of each of the following assets.

(a) Trade accounts receivable.

(b) Land.

(c) Inventories.

(d) Trading securities (common stock of other companies).

(e) Prepaid expenses.

18 Refer to the definition of assets on page 148. Discuss how a leased building might qualify as an asset of the lessee under this definition.

19 Christine Agazzi says, "Retained earnings should be reported as an asset, since it is earnings which are reinvested in the business." How would you respond to Agazzi?

20 The creditors of Nick Anderson Company agree to accept promissory notes for the amount of its indebtedness with a proviso that two-thirds of the annual profits must be applied to their liquidation. How should these notes be reported on the balance sheet of the issuing company? Give a reason for your answer.

21 What is the Altman Z-score? What balance sheet information is used in computing a Z-score?

22 What are the major types of subsequent events? Indicate how each of the following subsequent events would be reported.

(a) Collection of a note written off in a prior period.

(b) Issuance of a large preferred stock offering.

(c) Acquisition of a company in a different industry.

(d) Destruction of a major plant in a flood.

(e) Death of the company's chief executive officer (CEO).

(f) Settlement of a four-week strike at additional wage costs.

(g) Settlement of a federal income tax case at considerably more tax than anticipated at year-end.

(h) Change in the product mix from consumer goods to industrial goods.

23 What are some of the techniques of disclosure for the balance sheet?

24 What is a "Summary of Significant Accounting Policies"?

25 What types of contractual obligations must be disclosed in great detail in the notes to the balance sheet? Why do you think these detailed provisions should be disclosed?

26 What is the profession's recommendation in regard to the use of the term "surplus"? Explain.

Brief Exercises

(LO 3) **BE4-1** La Bouche Corporation has the following accounts included in its December 31, 2008, trial balance: Accounts Receivable $110,000; Inventories $290,000; Allowance for Doubtful Accounts $8,000; Patents $72,000; Prepaid Insurance $9,500; Accounts Payable $77,000; Cash $27,000. Prepare the current assets section of the balance sheet listing the accounts in proper sequence.

(LO 3) **BE4-2** Jodi Corporation's adjusted trial balance contained the following asset accounts at December 31, 2008: Cash $7,000; Land $40,000; Patents $12,500; Accounts Receivable $90,000; Prepaid Insurance $5,200; Inventory $34,000; Allowance for Doubtful Accounts $4,000; Trading Securities $11,000. Prepare the current assets section of the balance sheet, listing the accounts in proper sequence.

(LO 3) **BE4-3** Included in Goo Goo Dolls Company's December 31, 2008, trial balance are the following accounts: Prepaid Rent $5,200; Held-to-Maturity Securities $61,000; Unearned Fees $17,000; Land Held for Investment $39,000; Long-term Receivables $42,000. Prepare the long-term investments section of the balance sheet.

(LO 3) **BE4-4** Adam Ant Company's December 31, 2008, trial balance includes the following accounts: Inventories $120,000; Buildings $207,000; Accumulated Depreciation–Equipment $19,000; Equipment $190,000; Land Held for Investment $46,000; Accumulated Depreciation–Buildings $45,000; Land $61,000; Timberland $70,000. Prepare the property, plant, and equipment section of the balance sheet.

(LO 3) **BE4-5** Mason Corporation has the following accounts included in its December 31, 2008, trial balance: Trading Securities $21,000; Goodwill $150,000; Prepaid Insurance $12,000; Patents $220,000; Franchises $110,000. Prepare the intangible assets section of the balance sheet.

(LO 3) **BE4-6** Mickey Snyder Corporation's adjusted trial balance contained the following asset accounts at December 31, 2008: Prepaid Rent $12,000; Goodwill $40,000; Franchise Fees Receivable $2,000; Franchises $47,000; Patents $33,000; Trademarks $10,000. Prepare the intangible assets section of the balance sheet.

(LO 3) **BE4-7** John Hawk Corporation's adjusted trial balance contained the following liability accounts at December 31, 2008: Bonds Payable (due in 3 years) $100,000; Accounts Payable $72,000; Notes Payable (due in 90 days) $12,500; Accrued Salaries $4,000; Income Taxes Payable $7,000. Prepare the current liabilities section of the balance sheet.

(LO 3) **BE4-8** Included in Ewing Company's December 31, 2008, trial balance are the following accounts: Accounts Payable $240,000; Pension Liability $375,000; Discount on Bonds Payable $24,000; Advances from Customers $41,000; Bonds Payable $400,000; Wages Payable $27,000; Interest Payable $12,000; Income Taxes Payable $29,000. Prepare the current liabilities section of the balance sheet.

(LO 3) **BE4-9** Use the information presented in BE4-8 for Ewing Company to prepare the long-term liabilities section of the balance sheet.

(LO 3) **BE4-10** Kevin Flynn Corporation's adjusted trial balance contained the following accounts at December 31, 2008: Retained Earnings $120,000; Common Stock $700,000; Bonds Payable $100,000; Additional Paid-in Capital $200,000; Goodwill $55,000; Treasury Stock $150,000. Prepare the stockholders' equity section of the balance sheet.

(LO 3) **BE4-11** Young Company's December 31, 2008, trial balance includes the following accounts: Investment in Common Stock $70,000; Retained Earnings $114,000; Trademarks $31,000; Preferred Stock $172,000; Common Stock $55,000; Deferred Income Taxes $88,000; Additional Paid-in Capital $174,000. Prepare the stockholders' equity section of the balance sheet.

Exercises

(LO 2, 3) **E4-1** (**Balance Sheet Classifications**) Presented below are a number of balance sheet accounts of Deep Blue Something, Inc.

(a) Investment in Preferred Stock.
(b) Treasury Stock.
(c) Common Stock.
(d) Cash Dividends Payable.

(e) Accumulated Depreciation.
(f) Warehouse in Process of Construction.
(g) Petty Cash.
(h) Accrued Interest on Notes Payable.

(i) Deficit.
(j) Trading Securities.
(k) Income Taxes Payable.

(l) Unearned Subscription Revenue.
(m) Work in Process.
(n) Accrued Vacation Pay.

Instructions

For each of the accounts above, indicate the proper balance sheet classification. In the case of borderline items, indicate the additional information that would be required to determine the proper classification.

E4-2 **(Classification of Balance Sheet Accounts)** Presented below are the captions of Faulk Company's balance sheet. **(LO 2, 3)**

(a) Current assets
(b) Investments
(c) Property, plant, and equipment
(d) Intangible assets
(e) Other assets

(f) Current liabilities
(g) Long-term liabilities
(h) Capital stock
(i) Additional paid-in capital
(j) Retained earnings

Instructions

Indicate by letter where each of the following items would be classified.

1. Preferred stock.
2. Goodwill.
3. Wages payable.
4. Trade accounts payable.
5. Buildings.
6. Trading securities.
7. Current portion of long-term debt.
8. Premium on bonds payable.
9. Allowance for doubtful accounts.
10. Accounts receivable.
11. Cash surrender value of life insurance.
12. Notes payable (due next year).
13. Office supplies.
14. Common stock.
15. Land.
16. Bond sinking fund.
17. Merchandise inventory.
18. Prepaid insurance.
19. Bonds payable.
20. Taxes payable.

E4-3 **(Classification of Balance Sheet Accounts)** Assume that Fielder Enterprises uses the following headings on its balance sheet. **(LO 2, 3)**

(a) Current assets
(b) Investments
(c) Property, plant, and equipment
(d) Intangible assets
(e) Other assets

(f) Current liabilities
(g) Long-term liabilities
(h) Capital stock
(i) Paid-in Capital in excess of par
(j) Retained earnings

Instructions

Indicate by letter how each of the following usually should be classified. If an item should appear in a note to the financial statements, use the letter "N" to indicate this fact. If an item need not be reported at all on the balance sheet, use the letter "X."

1. Unexpired insurance.
2. Stock owned in affiliated companies.
3. Unearned subscriptions revenue.
4. Advances to suppliers.
5. Unearned rent revenue.
6. Preferred stock.
7. Premium on preferred stock.
8. Copyrights.
9. Petty cash fund.
10. Sales tax payable.
11. Accrued interest on notes receivable.
12. Twenty-year issue of bonds payable that will mature within the next year. (No sinking fund exists, and refunding is not planned.)
13. Machinery retired from use and held for sale.
14. Fully depreciated machine still in use.
15. Accrued interest on bonds payable.
16. Salaries that company budget shows will be paid to employees within the next year.
17. Discount on bonds payable. (Assume related to bonds payable in No. 12.)
18. Accumulated depreciation.

(LO 2, 3)   **E4-4   (Preparation of a Classified Balance Sheet)**   Assume that Denis Savard Inc. has the following accounts at the end of the current year.

1. Common Stock.
2. Discount on Bonds Payable.
3. Treasury Stock (at cost).
4. Notes Payable, short-term.
5. Raw Materials.
6. Preferred Stock Investments— Long-term.
7. Unearned Rent Revenue.
8. Work in Process.
9. Copyrights.
10. Buildings.
11. Notes Receivable (short-term).
12. Cash.
13. Accrued Salaries Payable.
14. Accumulated Depreciation—Buildings.
15. Cash Restricted for Plant Expansion.
16. Land Held for Future Plant Site.
17. Allowance for Doubtful Accounts— Accounts Receivable.
18. Retained Earnings.
19. Premium on Common Stock.
20. Unearned Subscriptions Revenue.
21. Receivables—Officers (due in one year).
22. Finished Goods.
23. Accounts Receivable.
24. Bonds Payable (due in 4 years).

Instructions

Prepare a classified balance sheet in good form (no monetary amounts are necessary).

(LO 3)   **E4-5   (Preparation of a Corrected Balance Sheet)**   Uhura Company has decided to expand its operations. The bookkeeper recently completed the balance sheet presented below in order to obtain additional funds for expansion.

Uhura Company
Balance Sheet
For the Year Ended 2008

Current assets	
Cash	$230,000
Accounts receivable (net) Allowance 17000	340,000
Inventories at lower of average cost or market	401,000
Trading securities—at cost (fair value $120,000)	140,000 120 000
Property, plant, and equipment	
Building (net) acc dep 160 000	570,000
Office equipment (net) acc dep 105 000	160,000
Land held for future use	175,000
Intangible assets	
Goodwill	80,000
Cash surrender value of life insurance	90,000
Prepaid expenses	12,000
Current liabilities	
Accounts payable	135,000
Notes payable (due next year)	125,000
Pension obligation	82,000
Rent payable	49,000
Premium on bonds payable	53,000
Long-term liabilities	
Bonds payable	500,000
Stockholders' equity	
Common stock, $1 par, authorized	
400,000 shares, issued 290,000	290,000
Additional paid-in capital	160,000
Retained earnings	? 784

LT Investment

Instructions

Prepare a revised balance sheet given the available information. Assume that the accumulated depreciation balance for the buildings is $160,000 and for the office equipment, $105,000. The allowance for doubtful accounts has a balance of $17,000. The pension obligation is considered a long-term liability.

E4-6 **(Corrections of a Balance Sheet)** The bookkeeper for Geronimo Company has prepared the following balance sheet as of July 31, 2008.

(LO 2, 3)

Geronimo Company			
Balance Sheet			
July 31, 2008			
Cash	$ 69,000	Notes and accounts payable	$ 44,000
Accounts receivable (net)	40,500	Long-term liabilities	75,000
Inventories	60,000	Stockholders' equity	155,500
Equipment (net)	84,000		$274,500
Patents	21,000		
	$274,500		

The following additional information is provided.

1. Cash includes $1,200 in a petty cash fund and $15,000 in a bond sinking fund.

2. The net accounts receivable balance is comprised of the following three items: (a) accounts receivable—debit balances $52,000; (b) accounts receivable—credit balances $8,000; (c) allowance for doubtful accounts $3,500.

3. Merchandise inventory costing $5,300 was shipped out on consignment on July 31, 2008. The ending inventory balance does not include the consigned goods. Receivables in the amount of $5,300 were recognized on these consigned goods.

4. Equipment had a cost of $112,000 and an accumulated depreciation balance of $28,000.

5. Taxes payable of $6,000 were accrued on July 31. Geronimo Company, however, had set up a cash fund to meet this obligation. This cash fund was not included in the cash balance, but was offset against the taxes payable amount.

Instructions

Prepare a corrected classified balance sheet as of July 31, 2008, from the available information, adjusting the account balances using the additional information.

E4-7 **(Current Assets Section of the Balance Sheet)** Presented below are selected accounts of Yasunari Kawabata Company at December 31, 2008.

(LO 3, 4)

Finished Goods	$ 52,000	Cost of Goods Sold	$2,100,000
Revenue Received in Advance	90,000	Notes Receivable	40,000
Equipment	253,000	Accounts Receivable	161,000
Work-in-Process	34,000	Raw Materials	207,000
Cash	37,000	Supplies Expense	60,000
Short-term Investments in Stock	31,000	Allowance for Doubtful Accounts	12,000
Customer Advances	36,000	Licenses	18,000
Cash Restricted for Plant Expansion	50,000	Additional Paid-in Capital	88,000
		Treasury Stock	22,000

The following additional information is available.

1. Inventories are valued at lower of cost or market using LIFO.

2. Equipment is recorded at cost. Accumulated depreciation, computed on a straight-line basis, is $50,600.

3. The short-term investments have a fair value of $29,000. (Assume they are trading securities.)

4. The notes receivable are due April 30, 2010, with interest receivable every April 30. The notes bear interest at 12%. (Hint: Accrue interest due on December 31, 2008.)

5. The allowance for doubtful accounts applies to the accounts receivable. Accounts receivable of $50,000 are pledged as collateral on a bank loan.

6. Licenses are recorded net of accumulated amortization of $14,000.

7. Treasury stock is recorded at cost.

Instructions

Prepare the current assets section of Yasunari Kawabata Company's December 31, 2008, balance sheet, with appropriate disclosures.

(LO 2)   **E4-8   (Current vs. Long-term Liabilities)**   Frederic Chopin Corporation is preparing its December 31, 2008, balance sheet. The following items may be reported as either a current or long-term liability.

1. On December 15, 2008, Chopin declared a cash dividend of $2.50 per share to stockholders of record on December 31. The dividend is payable on January 15, 2009. Chopin has issued 1,000,000 shares of common stock, of which 50,000 shares are held in treasury.

2. At December 31, bonds payable of $100,000,000 are outstanding. The bonds pay 12% interest every September 30 and mature in installments of $25,000,000 every September 30, beginning September 30, 2009.

3. At December 31, 2007, customer advances were $12,000,000. During 2008, Chopin collected $30,000,000 of customer advances, and advances of $25,000,000 were earned.

Instructions

For each item above indicate the dollar amounts to be reported as a current liability and as a long-term liability, if any.

(LO 2, 3)   **E4-9   (Current Assets and Current Liabilities)**   The current assets and liabilities sections of the balance sheet of Allessandro Scarlatti Company appear as follows.

Allessandro Scarlatti Company
Balance Sheet (partial)
December 31, 2008

Cash		$ 40,000	Accounts payable	$ 61,000
Accounts receivable	$89,000		Notes payable	67,000
Less: Allowance for				$128,000
doubtful accounts	7,000	82,000		
Inventories		171,000		
Prepaid expenses		9,000		
		$302,000		

The following errors in the corporation's accounting have been discovered:

1. January 2009 cash disbursements entered as of December 2008 included payments of accounts payable in the amount of $39,000, on which a cash discount of 2% was taken.

2. The inventory included $27,000 of merchandise that had been received at December 31 but for which no purchase invoices had been received or entered. Of this amount, $12,000 had been received on consignment; the remainder was purchased f.o.b. destination, terms 2/10, n/30.

3. Sales for the first four days in January 2009 in the amount of $30,000 were entered in the sales book as of December 31, 2008. Of these, $21,500 were sales on account and the remainder were cash sales.

4. Cash, not including cash sales, collected in January 2009 and entered as of December 31, 2008, totaled $35,324. Of this amount, $23,324 was received on account after cash discounts of 2% had been deducted; the remainder represented the proceeds of a bank loan.

Instructions

(a) Restate the current assets and liabilities sections of the balance sheet in accordance with good accounting practice. (Assume that both accounts receivable and accounts payable are recorded gross.)

(b) Determine the net effect of your adjustments on Allesandro Scarlatti Company's retained earnings balance.

E4-10 (Current Liabilities) Norma Smith is the controller of Baylor Corporation and is responsible for the preparation of the year-end financial statements. The following transactions occurred during the year. **(LO 3)**

(a) On December 20, 2008, an employee filed a legal action against Baylor for $100,000 for wrongful dismissal. Management believes the action to be frivolous and without merit. The likelihood of payment to the employee is remote.

(b) Bonuses to key employees based on net income for 2008 are estimated to be $150,000.

(c) On December 1, 2008, the company borrowed $600,000 at 8% per year. Interest is paid quarterly.

(d) Credit sales for the year amounted to $10,000,000. Baylor's expense provision for doubtful accounts is estimated to be 3% of credit sales.

(e) On December 15, 2008, the company declared a $2.00 per share dividend on the 40,000 shares of common stock outstanding, to be paid on January 5, 2009.

(f) During the year, customer advances of $160,000 were received; $50,000 of this amount was earned by December 31, 2008.

Instructions

For each item above, indicate the dollar amount to be reported as a current liability. If a liability is not reported, explain why.

E4-11 (Balance Sheet Preparation) Presented below is the adjusted trial balance of Kelly Corporation at December 31, 2008. **(LO 3)**

	Debits	Credits
Cash	$?	
Office Supplies	1,200	
Prepaid Insurance	1,000	
Equipment	48,000	
Accumulated Depreciation—Equipment		$ 4,000
Trademarks	950	
Accounts Payable		10,000
Wages Payable		500
Unearned Service Revenue		2,000
Bonds Payable, due 2015		9,000
Common Stock		10,000
Retained Earnings		25,000
Service Revenue		10,000
Wages Expense	9,000	
Insurance Expense	1,400	
Rent Expense	1,200	
Interest Expense	900	
Total	$?	$?

Additional information:

1. Net loss for the year was $2,500.
2. No dividends were declared during 2008.

Instructions

Prepare a classified balance sheet as of December 31, 2008.

(LO 3)

E4-12 (Preparation of a Balance Sheet) Presented below is the trial balance of John Nalezny Corporation at December 31, 2008.

	Debits	Credits
Cash	$ 197,000	
Sales		$ 8,100,000
Trading Securities (at cost, $145,000)	153,000	
Cost of Goods Sold	4,800,000	
Long-term Investments in Bonds	299,000	
Long-term Investments in Stocks	277,000	
Short-term Notes Payable		90,000
Accounts Payable		455,000
Selling Expenses	2,000,000	
Investment Revenue		63,000
Land	260,000	
Buildings	1,040,000	
Dividends Payable		136,000
Accrued Liabilities		96,000
Accounts Receivable	435,000	
Accumulated Depreciation—Buildings		152,000
Allowance for Doubtful Accounts		25,000
Administrative Expenses	900,000	
Interest Expense	211,000	
Inventories	597,000	
Extraordinary Gain		80,000
Long-term Notes Payable		900,000
Equipment	600,000	
Bonds Payable		1,000,000
Accumulated Depreciation—Equipment		60,000
Franchise (net of $80,000 amortization)	160,000	
Common Stock ($5 par)		1,000,000
Treasury Stock	191,000	
Patent (net of $30,000 amortization)	195,000	
Retained Earnings		78,000
Additional Paid-in Capital		80,000
Totals	$12,315,000	$12,315,000

Instructions

Prepare a balance sheet at December 31, 2008, for John Nalezny Corporation. Ignore income taxes.

(LO 4)

E4-13 (Post–Balance-Sheet Events) Madrasah Corporation issued its financial statements for the year ended December 31, 2008, on March 10, 2009. The following events took place early in 2009.

(a) On January 10, 10,000 shares of $5 par value common stock were issued at $66 per share.

(b) On March 1, Madrasah determined after negotiations with the Internal Revenue Service that income taxes payable for 2008 should be $1,270,000. At December 31, 2008, income taxes payable were recorded at $1,100,000.

Instructions

Discuss how the preceding post–balance-sheet events should be reflected in the 2008 financial statements.

(LO 4)

E4-14 (Post–Balance-Sheet Events) For each of the following subsequent (post–balance-sheet) events, indicate whether a company should (a) adjust the financial statements, (b) disclose in notes to the financial statements, or (c) neither adjust nor disclose.

_____ 1. Settlement of federal tax case at a cost considerably in excess of the amount expected at year-end.

_____ 2. Introduction of a new product line.

_____ **3.** Loss of assembly plant due to fire.

_____ **4.** Sale of a significant portion of the company's assets.

_____ **5.** Retirement of the company president.

_____ **6.** Prolonged employee strike.

_____ **7.** Loss of a significant customer.

_____ **8.** Issuance of a significant number of shares of common stock.

_____ **9.** Material loss on a year-end receivable because of a customer's bankruptcy.

_____**10.** Hiring of a new president.

_____**11.** Settlement of prior year's litigation against the company.

_____**12.** Merger with another company of comparable size.

 **See the book's companion website, at www.wiley.com/college/warfield, for Additional Exercises.**

Problems

P4-1 **(Preparation of a Classified Balance Sheet, Periodic Inventory)** Presented below is a list of accounts **(LO 2, 3)** in alphabetical order.

Accounts Receivable

Accrued Wages

Accumulated Depreciation—Buildings

Accumulated Depreciation—Equipment

Advances to Employees

Advertising Expense

Allowance for Doubtful Accounts

Bond Sinking Fund

Bonds Payable

Building

Cash in Bank

Cash on Hand

Cash Surrender Value of Life Insurance

Commission Expense

Common Stock

Copyright

Dividends Payable

Equipment

Gain on Sale of Equipment

Interest Receivable

Inventory—Beginning

Inventory—Ending

Land

Land for Future Plant Site

Loss from Flood

Notes Payable

Patent

Payroll Taxes Payable

Pension Obligations

Petty Cash

Preferred Stock

Premium on Bonds Payable

Premium on Preferred Stock

Prepaid Rent

Purchases

Purchase Returns and Allowances

Retained Earnings

Sales

Sales Discounts

Sales Salaries

Trading Securities

Transportation-in

Treasury Stock (at cost)

Unearned Subscriptions Revenue

Instructions

Prepare a classified balance sheet in good form. (No monetary amounts are to be shown.)

(LO 2, 3)

P4-2 **(Balance Sheet Preparation)** Presented below are a number of balance sheet items for Letterman, Inc., for the current year, 2008.

Goodwill	$ 125,000	Accumulated depreciation—equipment	$ 292,000
Payroll taxes payable	177,591	Inventories	239,800
Bonds payable	300,000	Rent payable—short-term	45,000
Discount on bonds payable	15,000	Taxes payable	98,362
Cash	360,000	Long-term rental obligations	480,000
Land	480,000	Common stock, $1 par value	200,000
Notes receivable	545,700	Preferred stock, $10 par value	150,000
Notes payable to banks	265,000	Prepaid expenses	87,920
Accounts payable	590,000	Equipment	1,470,000
Retained earnings	?	Trading securities	121,000
Income taxes receivable	97,630	Accumulated depreciation—building	170,200
Unsecured notes payable (long-term)	1,600,000	Building	1,640,000

Instructions

Prepare a classified balance sheet in good form. Common stock authorized was 400,000 shares, and preferred stock authorized was 20,000 shares. Assume that notes receivable and notes payable are short-term, unless stated otherwise. Cost and fair value of trading securities are the same.

(LO 3, 4)

P4-3 **(Balance Sheet Adjustment and Preparation)** The adjusted trial balance of Side Kicks Company and other related information for the year 2008 is presented below.

<table>
<tr><td colspan="3" align="center">**Side Kicks Company**
Adjusted Trial Balance
December 31, 2008</td></tr>
<tr><td></td><td align="center">Debits</td><td align="center">Credits</td></tr>
<tr><td>Cash</td><td>$ 41,000</td><td></td></tr>
<tr><td>Accounts Receivable</td><td>163,500</td><td></td></tr>
<tr><td>Allowance for Doubtful Accounts</td><td></td><td>$ 8,700</td></tr>
<tr><td>Prepaid Insurance</td><td>5,900</td><td></td></tr>
<tr><td>Inventory</td><td>308,500</td><td></td></tr>
<tr><td>Long-term Investments</td><td>339,000</td><td></td></tr>
<tr><td>Land</td><td>85,000</td><td></td></tr>
<tr><td>Construction Work in Progress</td><td>124,000</td><td></td></tr>
<tr><td>Patents</td><td>36,000</td><td></td></tr>
<tr><td>Equipment</td><td>400,000</td><td></td></tr>
<tr><td>Accumulated Depreciation of Equipment</td><td></td><td>140,000</td></tr>
<tr><td>Unamortized Discount on Bonds Payable</td><td>20,000</td><td></td></tr>
<tr><td>Accounts Payable</td><td></td><td>148,000</td></tr>
<tr><td>Accrued Expenses</td><td></td><td>49,200</td></tr>
<tr><td>Notes Payable</td><td></td><td>94,000</td></tr>
<tr><td>Bonds Payable</td><td></td><td>400,000</td></tr>
<tr><td>Capital Stock</td><td></td><td>500,000</td></tr>
<tr><td>Premium on Capital Stock</td><td></td><td>45,000</td></tr>
<tr><td>Retained Earnings</td><td></td><td>138,000</td></tr>
<tr><td></td><td>$1,522,900</td><td>$1,522,900</td></tr>
</table>

Additional information:

1. The LIFO method of inventory value is used.

2. The cost and fair value of the long-term investments that consist of stocks and bonds is the same.

3. The amount of the Construction Work in Progress account represents the costs expended to date on a building in the process of construction. (The company rents factory space at the present time.) The land on which the building is being constructed cost $85,000, as shown in the trial balance.

4. The patents were purchased by the company at a cost of $40,000 and are being amortized on a straight-line basis.

5. Of the unamortized discount on bonds payable, $2,000 will be amortized in 2009.

6. The notes payable represent bank loans that are secured by long-term investments carried at $120,000. These bank loans are due in 2009.

7. The bonds payable bear interest at 11% payable every December 31, and are due January 1, 2019.

8. Six hundred thousand shares of common stock of a par value of $1 were authorized, of which 500,000 shares were issued and outstanding.

Instructions

Prepare a balance sheet as of December 31, 2008, so that all important information is fully disclosed.

P4-4 **(Preparation of a Corrected Balance Sheet)** Presented below is the balance sheet of Russell Crowe Corporation as of December 31, 2008.

(LO 3)

Russell Crowe Corporation
Balance Sheet
December 31, 2008

Assets

Goodwill (Note 2)	$ 120,000
Buildings (Note 1)	1,640,000
Inventories	312,100
Land	750,000
Accounts receivable	170,000
Treasury stock (50,000 shares, no par)	87,000
Cash on hand	175,900
Assets allocated to trustee for plant expansion	
Cash in bank	70,000
U.S. Treasury notes, at cost and fair value	138,000
	$3,463,000

Equities

Notes payable (Note 3)	$ 600,000
Common stock, authorized and issued, 1,000,000 shares, no par	1,150,000
Retained earnings	658,000
Appreciation capital (Note 1)	570,000
Federal income taxes payable	75,000
Reserve for depreciation of building	410,000
	$3,463,000

Note 1: Buildings are stated at cost, except for one building that was recorded at appraised value. The excess of appraisal value over cost was $570,000. Depreciation has been recorded based on cost.

Note 2: Goodwill in the amount of $120,000 was recognized because the company believed that book value was not an accurate representation of the fair market value of the company. The gain of $120,000 was credited to Retained Earnings.

Note 3: Notes payable are long-term except for the current installment due of $100,000.

Instructions

Prepare a corrected classified balance sheet in good form. The notes above are for information only.

(LO 3)

P4-5 **(Balance Sheet Adjustment and Preparation)** Presented below is the balance sheet of Stephen King Corporation for the current year, 2008.

	Stephen King Corporation **Balance Sheet** **December 31, 2008**		
Current assets	$ 435,000	Current liabilities	$ 330,000
Investments	640,000	Long-term liabilities	1,000,000
Property, plant, and equipment	1,720,000	Stockholders' equity	1,770,000
Intangible assets	305,000		$3,100,000
	$3,100,000		

The following information is presented.

1. The current assets section includes: cash $114,000, accounts receivable $170,000 less $10,000 for allowance for doubtful accounts, inventories $180,000, and unearned revenue $5,000. Inventories are stated on the lower of FIFO cost or market.

2. The investments section includes: the cash surrender value of a life insurance contract $40,000; investments in common stock, short-term (trading) $80,000 and long-term (available-for-sale) $270,000; and bond sinking fund $250,000. The cost and fair value of investments in common stock are the same.

3. Property, plant, and equipment includes: buildings $1,040,000 less accumulated depreciation $360,000; equipment $450,000 less accumulated depreciation $180,000; land $500,000; and land held for future use $270,000.

4. Intangible assets include: a franchise $165,000; goodwill $100,000; and discount on bonds payable $40,000.

5. Current liabilities include: accounts payable $90,000; notes payable—short-term $80,000 and long-term $120,000; and taxes payable $40,000.

6. Long-term liabilities are composed solely of 10% bonds payable due 2016.

7. Stockholders' equity has: preferred stock, no par value, authorized 200,000 shares, issued 70,000 shares for $450,000; and common stock, $1 par value, authorized 400,000 shares, issued 100,000 shares at an average price of $10. In addition, the corporation has retained earnings of $320,000.

Instructions

Prepare a balance sheet in good form, adjusting the amounts in each balance sheet classification as affected by the information given above.

(LO 3, 4)

P4-6 **(Corrected Balance Sheet—Subsequent Events)** Your firm has been engaged to examine the financial statements of Will Smith Corporation for the year 2008. The bookkeeper who maintains the financial records has prepared all the unaudited financial statements for the corporation since its organization on January 2, 2004. The client provides you with the information below.

	Will Smith Corporation **Balance Sheet** **December 31, 2008**		
Assets		**Liabilities**	
Current assets	$1,881,100	Current liabilities	$ 962,400
Other assets	5,171,400	Long-term liabilities	1,439,500
		Capital	4,650,600
	$7,052,500		$7,052,500

An analysis of current assets discloses the following:

Cash (restricted in the amount of $400,000 for plant expansion)	$ 571,000
Investments in land	185,000
Accounts receivable less allowance of $30,000	480,000
Inventories (LIFO flow assumption)	645,100
	$1,881,100

Other assets include:

Prepaid expenses	$ 47,400
Plant and equipment less accumulated depreciation of $1,430,000	4,130,000
Cash surrender value of life insurance	84,000
Unamortized bond discount	49,500
Notes receivable (short-term)	162,300
Goodwill	252,000
Land	446,200
	$5,171,400

Current liabilities include:

Accounts payable	$ 510,000
Notes payable (due 2010)	157,400
Estimated income taxes payable	145,000
Premium on common stock	150,000
	$ 962,400

Long-term liabilities include:

Unearned revenue	$ 489,500
Dividends payable (cash)	200,000
8% bonds payable (due May 1, 2013)	750,000
	$1,439,500

Capital includes:

Retained earnings	$2,810,600
Capital stock, par value $10; authorized 200,000 shares, 184,000 shares issued	1,840,000
	$4,650,600

The supplementary information below is also provided.

1. On May 1, 2008, the corporation issued at 93.4, $750,000 of bonds to finance plant expansion. The long-term bond agreement provided for the annual payment of interest every May 1. The existing plant was pledged as security for the loan. Use the straight-line method for discount amortization.

2. The bookkeeper made the following mistakes.
    (a) In 2006, the ending inventory was overstated by $183,000. The ending inventories for 2007 and 2008 were correctly computed.
    (b) In 2008, accrued wages in the amount of $275,000 were omitted from the balance sheet and these expenses were not charged on the income statement.
    (c) In 2008, a gain of $175,000 (net of tax) on the sale of certain plant assets was credited directly to retained earnings.

3. A major competitor has introduced a line of products that will compete directly with Smith's primary line, now being produced in a specially designed new plant. Because of manufacturing innovations, the competitor's line will be of comparable quality but priced 50% below Smith's line. The competitor announced its new line on January 14, 2009. Smith indicates that the company will meet the lower prices that are high enough to cover variable manufacturing and selling expenses, but permit recovery of only a portion of fixed costs.

4. You learned on January 28, 2009, prior to completion of the audit, of heavy damage because of a recent fire to one of Smith's two plants; the loss will not be reimbursed by insurance. The newspapers described the event in detail.

Instructions

Analyze the above information to prepare a corrected balance sheet for Smith in accordance with proper accounting and reporting principles. Prepare a description of any notes that might need to be prepared. The books are closed and adjustments to income are to be made through retained earnings.

(LO 4)   **P4-7   (Post–Balance-Sheet Events)**   At December 31, 2007, Joni Brandt Corp. has assets of $10,000,000, liabilities of $6,000,000, common stock of $2,000,000 (representing 2,000,000 shares of $1.00 par common stock), and retained earnings of $2,000,000. Net sales for the year 2007 were $18,000,000, and net income was $800,000. As auditors of this company, you are making a review of subsequent events on February 13, 2008, and you find the following.

1. On February 3, 2008, one of Brandt's customers declared bankruptcy. At December 31, 2007, this company owed Brandt $300,000, of which $40,000 was paid in January, 2008.

2. On January 18, 2008, one of the three major plants of the client burned.

3. On January 23, 2008, a strike was called at one of Brandt's largest plants, which halted 30% of its production. As of today (February 13) the strike has not been settled.

4. A major electronics enterprise has introduced a line of products that would compete directly with Brandt's primary line, now being produced in a specially designed new plant. Because of manufacturing innovations, the competitor has been able to achieve quality similar to that of Brandt's products, but at a price 50% lower. Brandt officials say they will meet the lower prices, which are high enough to cover variable manufacturing and selling costs but which permit recovery of only a portion of fixed costs.

5. Merchandise traded in the open market is recorded in the company's records at $1.40 per unit on December 31, 2007. This price had prevailed for 2 weeks, after release of an official market report that predicted vastly enlarged supplies; however, no purchases were made at $1.40. The price throughout the preceding year had been about $2.00, which was the level experienced over several years. On January 18, 2008, the price returned to $2.00, after public disclosure of an error in the official calculations of the prior December, correction of which destroyed the expectations of excessive supplies. Inventory at December 31, 2007, was on a lower of cost or market basis.

6. On February 1, 2008, the board of directors adopted a resolution accepting the offer of an investment banker to guarantee the marketing of $1,200,000 of preferred stock.

Instructions

State in each case how the 2007 financial statements would be affected, if at all.

ACCOUNTING IN ACTION

Financial Reporting and Analysis

■ Financial Reporting Issues: The Procter & Gamble Company

AIA4-1   The financial statements of **Procter & Gamble (P&G)** can be accessed at the book's website.

Instructions

Refer to P&G's financial statements and the accompanying notes to answer the following questions.

(a) What alternative formats could P&G have adopted for its balance sheet? Which format did it adopt?

(b) Identify the various techniques of disclosure P&G might have used to disclose additional pertinent financial information. Which technique does it use in its financials?

(c) In what classifications are P&G's investments reported? What valuation basis does P&G use to report its investments? How much working capital did P&G have on June 30, 2006? On June 30, 2005?

(d) Does P&G report any subsequent events? If so, what is the nature of the event(s) reported?

PEPSICO ■ Comparative Analysis: The Coca-Cola Company and PepsiCo, Inc.

AIA4-2   The financial statements of **The Coca-Cola Company** and **PepsiCo, Inc.** can be accessed at the book's website.

Instructions

Use information found at the book's website to answer the following questions.

(a) What format(s) did these companies use to present their balance sheets? *report form*

(b) How much working capital did each of these companies have at the end of 2006? Speculate as to their rationale for the amount of working capital they maintain.

(c) What is the most significant difference in the asset structure of the two companies? What causes this difference?

(d) What are the companies' annual and 4-year (2002–2006) growth rates in total assets and long-term debt?

■ Financial Statement Analysis

AIA4-3 **Uniroyal Technology Corporation (UTC)**, with corporate offices in Sarasota, Florida, is organized into three operating segments. The high-performance plastics segment is responsible for research, development, and manufacture of a wide variety of products, including orthopedic braces, graffiti-resistant seats for buses and airplanes, and a static-resistant plastic used in the central processing units of microcomputers. The coated fabrics segment manufactures products such as automobile seating, door and instrument panels, and specialty items such as waterproof seats for personal watercraft and stain-resistant, easy-cleaning upholstery fabrics. The foams and adhesives segment develops and manufactures products used in commercial roofing applications.

The following items relate to operations in a recent year.

1. Serious pressure was placed on profitability by sharply increasing raw material prices. Some raw materials increased in price 50% during the past year. Cost containment programs were instituted and product prices were increased whenever possible, which resulted in profit margins actually improving over the course of the year.

2. The company entered into a revolving credit agreement, under which UTC may borrow the lesser of $15,000,000 or 80% of eligible accounts receivable. At the end of the year, approximately $1,000,000 was outstanding under this agreement. The company plans to use this line of credit in the upcoming year to finance operations and expansion.

Instructions

(a) Should investors be informed of raw materials price increases, such as described in item 1? Does the fact that the company successfully met the challenge of higher prices affect the answer? Explain.

(b) How should the information in item 2 be presented in the financial statements of UTC?

AIA4-4 **Sherwin-Williams**, based in Cleveland, Ohio, manufactures a wide variety of paint and other coatings, which are marketed through its specialty stores and in other retail outlets. The company also manufactures paint for automobiles. The Automotive Division has had financial difficulty. During a recent year, five branch locations of the Automotive Division were closed, and new management was put in place for the branches remaining.

The following titles were shown on Sherwin-Williams's balance sheet for that year.

Accounts payable	Machinery and equipment
Accounts receivable, less allowance	Other accruals
Accrued taxes	Other capital
Buildings	Other current assets
Cash and cash equivalents	Other long-term liabilities
Common stock	Postretirement obligations other than pensions
Employee compensation payable	Retained earnings
Finished goods inventories	Short-term investments
Intangibles and other assets	Taxes payable
Land	Work in process and raw materials inventories
Long-term debt	

Instructions

(a) Organize the accounts in the general order in which they would have been presented in a classified balance sheet.

(b) When several of the branch locations of the Automotive Division were closed, what balance sheet accounts were most likely affected? Did the balance in those accounts decrease or increase?

AIA4-5 Shown on page 192 is the SEC-mandated disclosure of contractual obligations provided by **Deere & Company** in a recent annual report. Deere & Company reported current assets of $17,855 and total current liabilities of $7,888. All dollars are in millions.

Deere & Company

Aggregate Contractual Obligations

Most of the company's contractual obligations to make payments to third parties are debt obligations. In addition, the company has off-balance sheet obligations for the purchases of raw materials and services along with agreements for future lease payments. The payment schedule for these contractual obligations in millions of dollars is as follows:

	Total	Less than 1 year	1–3 years	3–5 years	More than 5 years
Total debt					
Equipment Operations	$ 2,958	$ 312	$ 281	$ 8	$2,357
Financial Services	11,265	3,146	4,393	1,541	2,185
Total	14,223	3,458	4,674	1,549	4,542
Purchase obligations	2,306	2,274	32		
Operating leases	367	75	130	59	103
Capital leases	12	2	3	2	5
Contractual obligations	$16,908	$5,809	$4,839	$1,610	$4,650

Instructions

(a) Compute Deere & Company's working capital and current ratio (current assets ÷ current liabilities) with and without the contractual obligations reported in the schedule.

(b) Briefly discuss how the information provided in the contractual obligation disclosure would be useful in evaluating Deere & Company for loans: (1) due in one year, (2) due in five years.

■ International Reporting Issues

AIA4-6 Presented below is the balance sheet for **Tomkins PLC**, a British company, which prepares its statements using international reporting standards.

Instructions

(a) Identify at least three differences in balance sheet reporting between British and U.S. firms, as shown in Tomkins's balance sheet.

(b) Review Tomkins's balance sheet and identify how the format of this financial statement provides useful information, as illustrated in the chapter.

♦TOMKINS

Tomkins PLC

**Consolidated Balance Sheet
at December 31, 2005**

Non-current assets	£ million
Goodwill	319.5
Other intangible assets	22.0
Property, plant and equipment	831.7
Investments in associates	4.4
Other	121.7
	1,299.3
Current assets	
Inventories	444.7
Trade and other receivables	583.7
Income tax recoverable	4.1
Available-for-sale investments	2.2
Cash and cash equivalents	230.9
	1,265.6
Assets held for sale	13.4
Total assets	2,578.3

Current liabilities	
Bank overdrafts, leases	(43.9)
Trade and other payables	(442.3)
Income tax liabilities	(17.6)
Provisions	(41.3)
	(545.1)
Non-current liabilities	
Bank and other loans	(531.0)
Obligations under finance leases	(9.9)
Trade and other payables	(15.3)
Post-employment benefit obligations	(296.3)
Deferred tax liabilities	(50.0)
Income tax liabilities	(94.9)
Provisions	(18.2)
	(1,015.6)
Convertible cumulative preference shares	(304.7)
	(1,320.3)
Total liabilities	(1,865.4)
Net assets	712.9
Capital and reserves	
Ordinary share capital	38.7
Share premium account	95.8
Own shares	461.9
Capital redemption reserve	(8.7)
Currency translation reserve	32.5
Retained profit/(losses)	44.3
Shareholders' equity	664.5
Minority interests	48.4
Total equity	712.9
	712.9

Concepts for Analysis

AIA4-7 (**Reporting the Financial Effects of Varied Transactions**) In an examination of Juan Acevedo Corporation as of December 31, 2008, you have learned that the following situations exist. No entries have been made in the accounting records for these items.

1. The corporation erected its present factory building in 1993. Depreciation was calculated by the straight-line method, using an estimated useful life of 35 years. Early in 2008, the board of directors conducted a careful survey and estimated that the factory building had a remaining useful life of 25 years as of January 1, 2008.

2. When calculating the accrual for officers' salaries at December 31, 2008, it was discovered that the accrual for officers' salaries for December 31, 2007, had been overstated.

3. On December 15, 2008, Acevedo Corporation declared a 1% common stock dividend on its common stock outstanding, payable February 1, 2009, to the common stockholders of record December 31, 2008.

Instructions

Describe fully how each of the items above should be reported in the financial statements of Acevedo Corporation for the year 2008.

AIA4-8 (**Current Asset and Liability Classification**) Below and on page 194 are the titles of a number of debit and credit accounts as they might appear on the balance sheet of Ethan Allen Corporation as of October 31, 2008.

Debits	Credits
Interest Accrued on U.S. Government	Capital Stock—Preferred
Securities	11% First Mortgage Bonds, due in 2015
Notes Receivable	Preferred Cash Dividend, payable Nov. 1, 2008
Petty Cash Fund	Allowance for Doubtful Accounts Receivable
U.S. Government Securities	Federal Income Taxes Payable

Debits	Credits
Treasury Stock	Customers' Advances (on contracts to be completed next year)
Unamortized Bond Discount	Premium on Bonds Redeemable in 2008
Cash in Bank	Officers' 2008 Bonus Accrued
Land	Accrued Payroll
Inventory of Operating Parts and Supplies	Notes Payable
Inventory of Raw Materials	Accrued Interest on Bonds
Patents	Accumulated Depreciation
Cash and U.S. Government Bonds Set Aside for Property Additions	Accounts Payable
Investment in Subsidiary	Capital in Excess of Par
Accounts Receivable	Accrued Interest on Notes Payable
U.S. Government Contracts	8% First Mortgage Bonds, to be redeemed in 2008 out of current assets
Regular	
Installments—Due Next Year	
Installments—Due After Next year	
Goodwill	
Inventory of Finished Goods	
Inventory of Work in Process	
Deficit	

Instructions

Select the current asset and current liability items from among these debits and credits. If there appear to be certain borderline cases that you are unable to classify without further information, mention them and explain your difficulty, or give your reasons for making questionable classifications, if any.

(AICPA adapted)

 AIA4-9 **(Critique of Balance Sheet Format and Content)** Presented below is the balance sheet of Bellemy Brothers Corporation (000s omitted).

Bellemy Brothers Corporation
Balance Sheet
December 31, 2008

Assets

Current assets		
Cash	$26,000	
Short-term investments	18,000	
Accounts receivable	25,000	
Merchandise inventory	20,000	
Supplies inventory	4,000	
Stock investment in Subsidiary Company	20,000	$113,000
Investments		
Treasury stock		25,000
Property, plant, and equipment		
Buildings and land	91,000	
Less: Reserve for depreciation	31,000	60,000
Other assets		
Cash surrender value of life insurance		19,000
		$217,000

Liabilities and Capital

Current liabilities		
Accounts payable	$22,000	
Reserve for income taxes	15,000	
Customers' accounts with credit balances	1	$ 37,001

Deferred credits		
Unamortized premium on bonds payable		2,000
Long-term liabilities		
Bonds payable		60,000
Total liabilities		99,001
Capital stock		
Common stock, par $5	85,000	
Earned surplus	24,999	
Cash dividends declared	8,000	117,999
		$217,000

Instructions

Evaluate the balance sheet presented. State briefly the proper treatment of any item criticized.

AIA4-10 (**Identifying Balance Sheet Deficiencies**) The financial statement below was prepared by employees of your client, Walt Whitman Co. The statement is unaccompanied by notes.

Walt Whitman Co.
Balance Sheet
November 30, 2008

Current assets			
Cash		$ 100,000	
Accounts receivable (less allowance of $30,000 for doubtful accounts)		419,900	
Inventories		1,954,000	$2,473,900
Less: Current liabilities			
Accounts payable		306,400	
Accrued payroll		28,260	
Accrued interest on mortgage note		12,000	
Estimated taxes payable		66,000	412,660
Net working capital			2,061,240
Property, plant, and equipment (at cost)			

	Cost	Depreciation	Value	
Land and buildings	$ 983,300	$410,000	$ 573,300	
Machinery and equipment	1,135,700	568,699	567,001	
	$2,119,000	$978,699		1,140,301

Deferred charges			
Prepaid taxes and other expenses		23,700	
Unamortized discount on mortgage note		10,800	34,500
Total net working capital and noncurrent assets			3,236,041
Less: Deferred liabilities			
Mortgage note payable		300,000	
Unearned revenue		1,808,000	2,108,000
Total net assets			$1,128,041
Stockholders' equity			
10% Preferred stock at par value			$ 300,000
Common stock at par value			397,000
Paid-in surplus			210,000
Retained earnings			265,641
Treasury stock at cost (400 shares)			(44,600)
Total stockholders' equity			$1,128,041

Instructions

Indicate the deficiencies, if any, in the previous balance sheet in regard to form, terminology, descriptions, content, and the like.

Professional Tools

■ Ethical Decision Making

AIA4-11 **(Presentation of Property, Plant, and Equipment)** Andrea Pafko, corporate comptroller for Nicholson Industries, is trying to decide how to present "Property, plant, and equipment" in the balance sheet. She realizes that the statement of cash flows will show that the company made a significant investment in purchasing new equipment this year, but overall she knows the company's plant assets are rather old. She feels that she can disclose one figure titled "Property, plant, and equipment, net of depreciation," and the result will be a low figure. However, it will not disclose the age of the assets. If she chooses to show the cost less accumulated depreciation, the age of the assets will be apparent. She proposes the following.

Property, plant, and equipment, net of depreciation	$10,000,000
rather than	
Property, plant, and equipment	$50,000,000
Less: Accumulated depreciation	(40,000,000)
Net book value	$10,000,000

Instructions

Answer the following questions.

(a) What are the ethical issues involved?
(b) What should Pafko do?

■ Financial Accounting Research (FARS)

AIA4-12 In light of the disclosure principle, investors and creditors need to know the balances for assets, liabilities, and equity as well as the accounting policies adopted by management to measure the items reported in the balance sheet.

Instructions

Using the **Financial Accounting Research System (FARS)** database, respond to the following items. (Provide text strings used in your search.)

(a) Identify the statement that addresses the disclosure of accounting policies.
(b) How are "Accounting Policies" defined in the standard?
(c) What are the three scenarios that would result in detailed disclosure of the accounting methods used?
(d) What are some examples of common disclosures that are required under this statement?

■ Professional Simulation

AIA4-13 Go to the book's companion website, at **www.wiley.com/college/warfield**, to find an interactive problem that simulates the computerized CPA exam. The professional simulation for this chapter asks you to address questions related to the balance sheet.

What do the numbers mean?

Grounded, p. 146

Q: In assessing a company's financial flexibility, a high proportion of debt relative to stockholders' equity is considered a signal that the company may be financially inflexible. Explain why that statement is true.

A: A company that has a large amount of debt relative to stockholders' equity is generally considered to be financially inflexible. If interest rates increase, its cost of funding projects will increase. In good economic times, the company may be able to pay for the increased interest payments. However, in this situation, a company may be prevented from taking advantage of additional opportunities. In poor economic conditions, the company's cash flows from operations may not cover the principal and interest payments required. As a result its may be forced to sell off assets or issue stock at distressed prices to generate additional funds.

High debt levels are not always bad, though. Public utilities, for example, have high debt levels because their cash flows are generally fairly constant in good and bad times. Consequently, the debt has a lower cost relative to equity financing for this industry.

"Show Me the Assets!," p. 157

Q: What is working capital? Why is it important that analysts look beyond the working capital number and examine the items that comprise working capital?

A: The excess of total current assets over total current liabilities is referred to as working capital. Working capital consists of assets such as cash, receivables, inventory, and prepaid expenses and of liabilities such as accounts payable and notes payable. The working capital number provides a quick way of evaluating a company's liquidity.

However, analysts have to be careful in assessing working capital because if receivables and inventory are increasing but sales are not, the company's liquidity and financial flexibility may be decreasing. Cash is quite liquid, but many of the other items in current assets may be illiquid if the company is experiencing economic hardship.

Warning Signs, p. 162

Q: Explain why the ratios that are part of Altman's bankruptcy prediction model are significant in forecasting financial distress.

A: The first ratio is working capital to total assets. A low working capital indicates lack of liquidity and therefore possible financial distress.

The second ratio is retained earnings to total assets. A low retained earnings indicates that earnings are not significant and that the company may have a capital structure that has too much debt.

Third, the ratio of EBIT (earnings before interest and taxes) to total assets is a measure of profitability. A low EBIT indicates that earnings may not be significant, which is an indicator of financial distress.

The ratio of sales to total assets provides an indication of how efficiently the company uses it assets in generating sales. The lower the sales to total assets, the less efficiently the assets are being used.

Finally, the market value of equity to total liabilities provides a better understanding of the capital structure of the company. A low ratio of market value of equity to debt signals that the company has low financial flexibility.

By using this set of ratios, Altman has combined income and balance sheet information to arrive at a model which has become quite successful in predicting financial distress.

What About Your Commitments?, p. 164

Q: How will tabular displays of contractual obligations help investors?

A: According to the SEC, the table of contractual obligations will help investors to assess a company's short-term and long-term liquidity and capital resource needs and demands. It will provide a brief summary of future obligations, including those not currently reported as liabilities on a company's balance sheet (such as purchase obligations, payments for operating leases, and contracted expenditures). Furthermore, the SEC believes that the table will improve an investor's ability to compare companies.

This table should help investors because it collects information about future contractual cash flows in one place. Before, the investor had to search through the notes to the financial statements, and in some cases the information was not reported.

Remember to check the book's companion website to find additional resources for this chapter.

CHAPTER 5

INCOME STATEMENT AND RELATED INFORMATION

Which Income Number?

Recently, 40 percent of the companies in the Standards and Poor's 500 provided investors a choice in reported income numbers. In addition to income measured according to generally accepted accounting principles (GAAP), companies also reported an income measure that they adjusted for certain items. Companies make these adjustments because they believe the items are not representative of operating results. In some cases these adjustments are quite large. As we show in the following table, in a recent quarter the reporting of such "pro forma" income measures put a very different spin on operating results. In some cases (**JDS-Uniphase**, **Checkfree**, **PMC-Sierra**, and **Yahoo!**), a loss under GAAP measurement rules became an operating profit after proforma adjustments.

Company	Earnings Per Share	
	Pro Forma	GAAP
JDS-Uniphase	$0.14	−$1.13
Checkfree	0.04	−1.17
Amazon.com	−0.22	−0.66

Company	Earnings Per Share	
	Pro Forma	GAAP
PMC-Sierra	0.02	−0.38
Qualcomm	0.29	0.18
Yahoo	0.01	−0.02

Characteristic of pro forma reporting practices is Amazon.com. It adjusted for items such as stock-based compensation, amortization of goodwill and intangibles, impairment charges, and equity in losses of investees. All of these adjustments make pro forma earnings higher than GAAP income. In its earnings announcement, Amazon defended its pro forma reporting, saying that it gives better insight into the fundamental operations of the business.

So what's wrong with focusing investors on the fundamentals of the business? According to Ed Jenkins, former chair of the FASB, one problem is that there are no standards for the reporting of pro forma numbers. As a result, investors will have a hard time comparing Amazon's pro forma measure with that reported by another company, which has a different idea of what is fundamental to its business. Also, there is concern that companies may use pro forma reporting to deflect investor attention from bad news. In response, the SEC issued Regulation G, which requires companies to reconcile non-GAAP financial measures to GAAP. This regulation provides investors with a roadmap to analyze adjustments companies make to their GAAP numbers to arrive at pro forma results.

Sources: Story adapted from David Henry, "The Numbers Game," *Business Week* (May 14, 2001), pp. 100–110. See also SEC Regulation G, "Conditions for Use of Non-GAAP Financial Measures," *Release No. 33-8176* (March 28, 2003).

Preview of Chapter 5

As we indicate in the opening story, investors need complete and comparable information on income and its components to assess company profitability correctly. In this chapter we examine the many different types of revenues, expenses, gains, and losses that affect the income statement and related information, *as follows.*

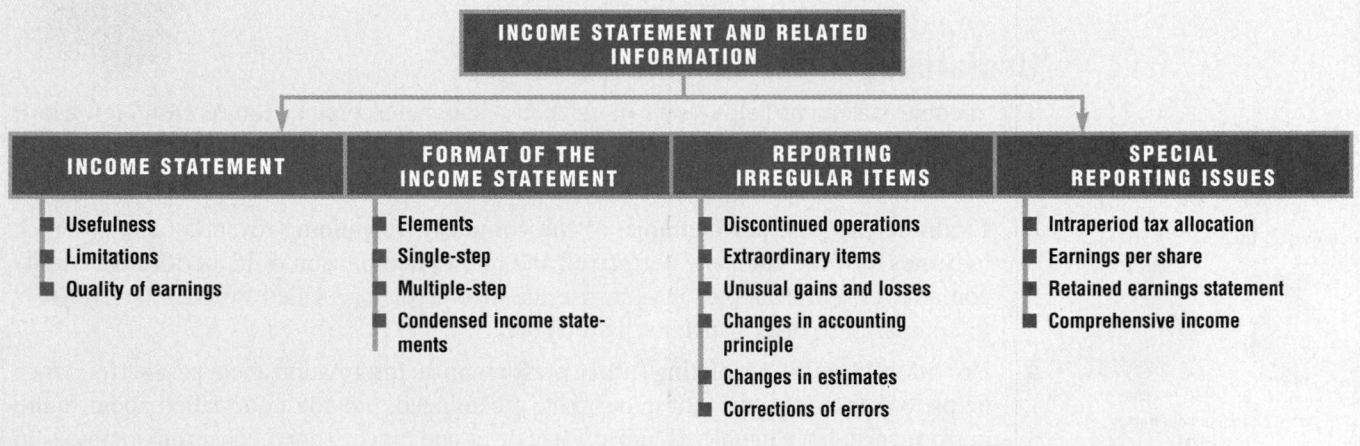

INCOME STATEMENT AND RELATED INFORMATION			
INCOME STATEMENT	**FORMAT OF THE INCOME STATEMENT**	**REPORTING IRREGULAR ITEMS**	**SPECIAL REPORTING ISSUES**
■ Usefulness ■ Limitations ■ Quality of earnings	■ Elements ■ Single-step ■ Multiple-step ■ Condensed income statements	■ Discontinued operations ■ Extraordinary items ■ Unusual gains and losses ■ Changes in accounting principle ■ Changes in estimates ■ Corrections of errors	■ Intraperiod tax allocation ■ Earnings per share ■ Retained earnings statement ■ Comprehensive income

Learning Objectives

After studying this chapter, you should be able to:

1. Understand the uses and limitations of an income statement.
2. Prepare a single-step income statement.
3. Prepare a multiple-step income statement.
4. Explain how to report irregular items.
5. Explain intraperiod tax allocation.
6. Identify where to report earnings per share information.
7. Prepare a retained earnings statement.
8. Explain how to report other comprehensive income.

Inside Chapter 5

■ **What Do the Numbers Mean?**
Manage up, manage down (p. 202)
Are one-time charges bugging you? (p. 210)
Extraordinary times (p. 212)

■ **What's the Principle?** (pp. 201, 207, 215, 217)

■ **Convergence Corner** (p. 225)

■ **Accounting, Analysis, Principles** (p. 226)
Prepare income statements and statement of retained earnings.
Explain the usefulness of a multiple-step income statement.
Discuss conceptual merits of irregular-item reporting.

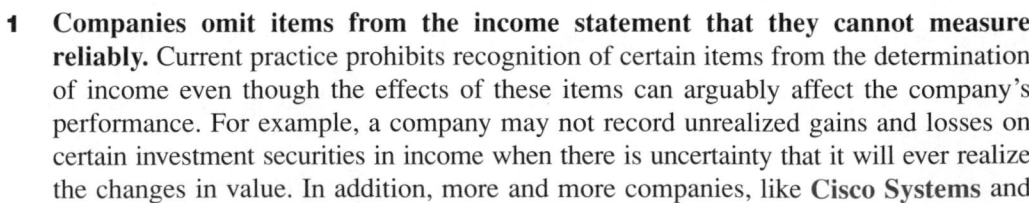

INCOME STATEMENT

OBJECTIVE 1
Understand the uses and limitations of an income statement.

The **income statement** is the report that measures the success of company operations for a given period of time. (It is also often called the statement of income or statement of earnings.[1]) The business and investment community uses the income statement to determine profitability, investment value, and creditworthiness. It provides investors and creditors with information that helps them predict the **amounts, timing, and uncertainty of future cash flows**.

Usefulness of the Income Statement

The income statement helps users of financial statements predict future cash flows in a number of ways. For example, investors and creditors use the income statement information to:

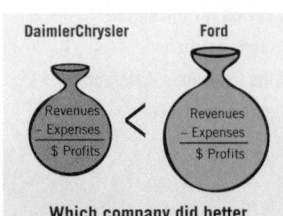

DaimlerChrysler / **Ford**
Which company did better last year?

1 **Evaluate the past performance of the company.** Examining revenues and expenses indicates how the company performed and allows comparison of its performance to its competitors. For example, analysts use the income data provided by **DaimlerChrysler** to compare its performance to that of **Ford**.

2 **Provide a basis for predicting future performance.** Information about past performance helps to determine important trends that, if continued, provide information about future performance. For example, **General Electric** at one time reported consistent increases in revenues. Obviously past success does not necessarily translate into future success. However, analysts can better predict future revenues, and hence earnings and cash flows, if a reasonable correlation exists between past and future performance.

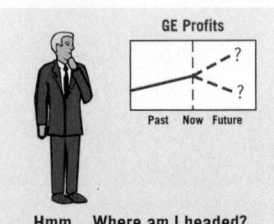

GE Profits
Past Now Future
Hmm....Where am I headed?

3 **Help assess the risk or uncertainty of achieving future cash flows.** Information on the various components of income—revenues, expenses, gains, and losses—highlights the relationships among them. It also helps to assess the risk of not achieving a particular level of cash flows in the future. For example, investors and creditors often segregate **IBM**'s operating performance from other nonrecurring sources of income because IBM primarily generates revenues and cash through its operations. Thus, results from continuing operations usually have greater significance for predicting future performance than do results from nonrecurring activities and events.

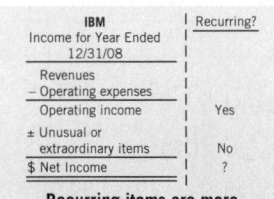

IBM Income for Year Ended 12/31/08	Recurring?
Revenues	
− Operating expenses	
Operating income	Yes
± Unusual or extraordinary items	No
$ Net Income	?

Recurring items are more certain in the future.

In summary, information in the income statement—revenues, expenses, gains, and losses—helps users evaluate past performance. It also provides insights into the likelihood of achieving a particular level of cash flows in the future.

Limitations of the Income Statement

Because net income is an estimate and reflects a number of assumptions, income statement users need to be aware of certain limitations associated with its information. Some of these limitations include:

Exp Exp
Rev Rev Rev
Profits
Unrealized Earnings
Brand value
You left something out!

1 **Companies omit items from the income statement that they cannot measure reliably.** Current practice prohibits recognition of certain items from the determination of income even though the effects of these items can arguably affect the company's performance. For example, a company may not record unrealized gains and losses on certain investment securities in income when there is uncertainty that it will ever realize the changes in value. In addition, more and more companies, like **Cisco Systems** and

---

[1]*Accounting Trends and Techniques—2006* (New York: AICPA) indicates that out of 600 companies surveyed, 255 used the term *income* in the title of income statements, 254 used *operations* (many companies had net losses), and 86 used *earnings*.

Microsoft, experience increases in value due to brand recognition, customer service, and product quality. A common framework for identifying and reporting these types of values is still lacking.

2 **Income numbers are affected by the accounting methods employed.** One company may depreciate its plant assets on an accelerated basis; another chooses straight-line depreciation. Assuming all other factors are equal, the first company will report lower income. In effect, we are comparing apples to oranges.

3 **Income measurement involves judgment.** For example, one company in good faith may estimate the useful life of an asset to be 20 years while another company uses a 15-year estimate for the same type of asset. Similarly, some companies may make optimistic estimates of future warranty returns and bad debt write-offs, which results in lower expense and higher income.

In summary, several limitations of the income statement reduce the usefulness of its information for predicting the amounts, timing, and uncertainty of future cash flows.

Quality of Earnings

So far, our discussion has highlighted the importance of information in the income statement for investment and credit decisions, including the evaluation of the company and its managers.[2] Companies try to meet or beat Wall Street expectations so that the market price of their stock and the value of management's stock options increase. As a result, companies have incentives to manage income to meet earnings targets or to make earnings look less risky.

Recently, the SEC has expressed concern that the motivations to meet earnings targets may override good business practices. This erodes the quality of earnings and the quality of financial reporting. As indicated by one SEC chairman, "Managing may be giving way to manipulation; integrity may be losing out to illusion."[3] As a result, the SEC has started to take decisive action to prevent the practice of earnings management.

What is **earnings management**? It is often defined as the planned timing of revenues, expenses, gains, and losses to smooth out bumps in earnings. In most cases, companies use earnings management to increase income in the current year at the expense of income in future years. For example, they prematurely recognize sales (i.e., before earned) in order to boost earnings. As one commentator noted, ". . . it's like popping a cork in [opening] a bottle of wine before it is ready."

Companies also use earnings management to decrease current earnings in order to increase income in the future. The classic case is the use of "cookie jar" reserves. Companies establish these reserves by using unrealistic assumptions to estimate liabilities for such items as loan losses, restructuring charges, and warranty returns. The companies then reduce these reserves in the future to increase reported income in the future.

Such earnings management negatively affects the **quality of earnings** if it distorts the information in a way that is less useful for predicting future earnings and cash flows. Markets rely on trust. The bond between shareholders and the company must remain strong. Investors or others losing faith in the numbers reported in the financial statements will damage U.S. capital markets. As we mentioned in the opening story, we need heightened scrutiny of income measurement and reporting to ensure the quality of earnings and investors' confidence in the income statement.

---

[2]In support of the usefulness of income information, accounting researchers have documented an association between the market prices of companies and reported income. See W. H. Beaver, "Perspectives on Recent Capital Markets Research," *The Accounting Review* (April 2002), pp. 453–474.

[3]A. Levitt, "The Numbers Game." Remarks to NYU Center for Law and Business, September 28, 1998 (Securities and Exchange Commission, 1998).

Managing earnings up or down adversely affects the quality of earnings. For example, **W. R. Grace** managed earnings down by taking excess "cookie jar" reserves in good earnings years. During the early 1990s, Grace was growing fast, with profits increasing 30 percent annually. Analysts' targets had Grace growing 24 percent each year. Worried about meeting these growth expectations, Grace began stashing away excess profits in an all-purpose reserve (a "cookie jar"). In 1995, when profits fell below expectations, Grace wanted to reduce this reserve and so increase income. The SEC objected, noting this violated generally accepted accounting principles.

More recently, **MicroStrategy** managed earnings up by booking revenue for future software upgrades, even though it had not yet delivered them. And **Rent-Way, Inc.** managed its earnings up by understating some $65 million in expenses relating to such items as automobile maintenance and insurance payments.

Does the market value accounting quality? Apparently so: The stock of each of these companies took a beating in the marketplace when the earnings management practices came to light. For example, Rent-Way's stock price plummeted from above $25 per share to below $10 per share when it announced restatements for its improper expense accounting. So, whether managing earnings up or down, companies had better be prepared to pay the price for poor accounting quality.

Beyond the Numbers

If companies "pay a price" when the market discovers the use of cookie jar reserves in prior years, what are some of the incentives to manage earnings down today in order to report better results in the future?

FORMAT OF THE INCOME STATEMENT

Elements of the Income Statement

Net income results from revenue, expense, gain, and loss transactions. The income statement summarizes these transactions. This method of income measurement, the **transaction approach**, focuses on the income-related activities that have occurred during the period.[4] The statement can further classify income by customer, product line, or function or by operating and nonoperating, continuing and discontinued, and regular and irregular categories.[5] The following lists more formal definitions of income-related items, referred to as the major elements of the income statement.

ELEMENTS OF FINANCIAL STATEMENTS

REVENUES. Inflows or other enhancements of assets of an entity or settlements of its liabilities during a period from delivering or producing goods, rendering services, or other activities that constitute the entity's ongoing major or central operations.

EXPENSES. Outflows or other using-up of assets or incurrences of liabilities during a period from delivering or producing goods, rendering services, or carrying out other activities that constitute the entity's ongoing major or central operations.

[4]The most common alternative to the transaction approach is the **capital maintenance approach** to income measurement. Under this approach, a company determines income for the period based on the change in equity, after adjusting for capital contributions (e.g., investments by owners) or distributions (e.g., dividends). The main drawback associated with the capital maintenance approach is that the components of income are not evident in its measurement. The Internal Revenue Service uses the capital maintenance approach to identify unreported income and refers to this approach as the "net worth check."

[5]The term "irregular" encompasses transactions and other events that are derived from developments outside the normal operations of the business.

GAINS. Increases in equity (net assets) from peripheral or incidental transactions of an entity except those that result from revenues or investments by owners.

LOSSES. Decreases in equity (net assets) from peripheral or incidental transactions of an entity except those that result from expenses or distributions to owners.[6]

Revenues take many forms, such as sales, fees, interest, dividends, and rents. Expenses also take many forms, such as cost of goods sold, depreciation, interest, rent, salaries and wages, and taxes. Gains and losses also are of many types, resulting from the sale of investments or plant assets, settlement of liabilities, write-offs of assets due to impairments or casualty.

The distinction between revenues and gains, and between expenses and losses, depend to a great extent on the typical activities of the company. For example, when **McDonald's** sells a hamburger, it records the selling price as revenue. However, when McDonald's sells land, it records any excess of the selling price over the book value as a gain. This difference in treatment results because the sale of the hamburger is part of McDonald's regular operations. The sale of land is not.

We cannot overemphasize the importance of reporting these elements. Most decision makers find the *parts* of a financial statement to be more useful than the whole. As we indicated earlier, investors and creditors are interested in predicting the amounts, timing, and uncertainty of future income and cash flows. Having income statement elements shown in some detail and in comparison with prior years' data allows decision makers to better assess future income and cash flows.

> **INTERNATIONAL INSIGHT**
>
> Companies in some countries (e.g., Germany) prepare financial reporting on the same basis as tax returns. In such cases, companies have incentives to *minimize* reported income.

Single-Step Income Statements

In reporting revenues, gains, expenses, and losses, companies often use a format known as the **single-step income statement**. The single-step statement consists of just two groupings: revenues and expenses. Expenses are deducted from revenues to arrive at net income or loss, hence the expression "single-step." Frequently companies report income tax separately as the last item before net income to indicate its relationship to income before income tax. Illustration 5-1 shows the single-step income statement of Dan Deines Company.

> **OBJECTIVE 2**
>
> **Prepare a single-step income statement.**

Dan Deines Company
Income Statement
For The Year Ended December 31, 2008

Revenues	
Net sales	$2,972,413
Dividend revenue	98,500
Rental revenue	72,910
Total revenues	3,143,823
Expenses	
Cost of goods sold	1,982,541
Selling expenses	453,028
Administrative expenses	350,771
Interest expense	126,060
Income tax expense	66,934
Total expenses	2,979,334
Net income	$ 164,489
Earnings per common share	$1.74

Illustration 5-1
Single-Step Income Statement

---

[6]"Elements of Financial Statements," *Statement of Financial Accounting Concepts No. 6* (Stamford, Conn.: FASB, 1985), pars. 78–89.

Companies that use the single-step income statement in financial reporting typically do so because of its simplicity. In recent years, though, the multiple-step form has gained popularity.[7]

The primary advantage of the single-step format lies in its simple presentation and the absence of any implication that one type of revenue or expense item has priority over another. This format thus eliminates potential classification problems.

Multiple-Step Income Statements

OBJECTIVE 3
Prepare a multiple-step income statement.

Some contend that including other important revenue and expense classifications makes the income statement more useful. These further classifications include:

1 A separation of operating and nonoperating activities of the company. For example, companies often present income from operations followed by sections entitled "Other revenues and gains" and "Other expenses and losses." These other categories include such transactions as interest revenue and expense, gains or losses from sales of long-term assets, and dividends received.

2 A classification of expenses by functions, such as merchandising (cost of goods sold), selling, and administration. This permits immediate comparison with costs of previous years and with other departments in the same year.

Companies use a **multiple-step income statement** to recognize these additional relationships. This statement separates operating transactions from nonoperating transactions, and matches costs and expenses with related revenues. It highlights certain intermediate components of income that analysts use to compute ratios for assessing the performance of the company.

Intermediate Components of the Income Statement

When a company uses a multiple-step income statement, it may prepare some or all of the following sections or subsections.

INCOME STATEMENT SECTIONS

1 **OPERATING SECTION.** A report of the revenues and expenses of the company's principal operations.
   (a) **Sales or Revenue Section**. A subsection presenting sales, discounts, allowances, returns, and other related information. Its purpose is to arrive at the net amount of sales revenue.
   (b) **Cost of Goods Sold Section**. A subsection that shows the cost of goods that were sold to produce the sales.
   (c) **Selling Expenses**. A subsection that lists expenses resulting from the company's efforts to make sales.
   (d) **Administrative or General Expenses**. A subsection reporting expenses of general administration.

2 **NONOPERATING SECTION.** A report of revenues and expenses resulting from secondary or auxiliary activities of the company. In addition, special gains and losses that are

[7]*Accounting Trends and Techniques—2006* (New York: AICPA). Of the 600 companies surveyed by the AICPA, 495 employed the multiple-step form, and 105 employed the single-step income statement format. This is a reversal from 1983, when 314 used the single-step form and 286 used the multiple-step form.

infrequent or unusual, but not both, are normally reported in this section. Generally these items break down into two main subsections:

(a) Other Revenues and Gains. A list of the revenues earned or gains incurred, generally net of related expenses, from nonoperating transactions.

(b) Other Expenses and Losses. A list of the expenses or losses incurred, generally net of any related incomes, from nonoperating transactions.

3 INCOME TAX. A short section reporting federal and state taxes levied on income from continuing operations.

4 DISCONTINUED OPERATIONS. Material gains or losses resulting from the disposition of a segment of the business.

5 EXTRAORDINARY ITEMS. Unusual and infrequent material gains and losses.

6 EARNINGS PER SHARE.

Although the content of the operating section is always the same, the organization of the material can differ. The breakdown above uses a **natural expense classification**. Manufacturing concerns and merchandising companies in the wholesale trade commonly use this. Another classification of operating expenses, recommended for retail stores, uses a **functional expense classification** of administrative, occupancy, publicity, buying, and selling expenses.

Usually, financial statements provided to external users have less detail than internal management reports. Internal reports include more expense categories—usually grouped along lines of responsibility. This detail allows top management to judge staff performance. Irregular transactions such as discontinued operations and extraordinary items are reported separately, following income from continuing operations.

Dan Deines Company's statement of income illustrates the multiple-step income statement. This statement, shown in Illustration 5-2, includes items 1, 2, 3, and 6 from the list starting on page 204.[8] Note that in arriving at net income, the statement presents three subtotals of note:

1 Net sales revenue.

2 Gross profit on sales.

3 Income from operations.

The disclosure of net sales revenue is useful because Deines reports regular revenues as a separate item. It discloses irregular or incidental revenues elsewhere in the income statement. As a result, analysts can more easily understand and assess trends in revenue from continuing operations.

Similarly, the reporting of gross profit provides a useful number for evaluating performance and predicting future earnings. Statement readers may study the trend in gross profits to determine how successfully a company uses its resources. They also may use that information to understand how competitive pressure affected profit margins.

Finally, disclosing income from operations highlights the difference between regular and irregular or incidental activities. This disclosure helps users recognize that incidental or irregular activities are unlikely to continue at the same level. Furthermore, disclosure of operating earnings may assist in comparing different companies and assessing operating efficiencies.

---

[8]Companies must include *earnings per share* or *net loss per share* on the face of the income statement.

Illustration 5-2
Multiple-Step Income
Statement

**Income Statements for
Real Companies**

Dan Deines Company
Income Statement
For the Year Ended December 31, 2008

Sales Revenue			
Sales			$3,053,081
Less: Sales discounts		$ 24,241	
Sales returns and allowances		56,427	80,668
Net sales revenue			2,972,413
Cost of Goods Sold			
Merchandise inventory, Jan. 1, 2008		461,219	
Purchases	$1,989,693		
Less: Purchase discounts	19,270		
Net purchases	1,970,423		
Freight and transportation-in	40,612	2,011,035	
Total merchandise available for sale		2,472,254	
Less: Merchandise inventory, Dec. 31, 2008		489,713	
Cost of goods sold			1,982,541
Gross profit on sales			989,872
Operating Expenses			
Selling expenses			
Sales salaries and commissions	202,644		
Sales office salaries	59,200		
Travel and entertainment	48,940		
Advertising expense	38,315		
Freight and transportation-out	41,209		
Shipping supplies and expense	24,712		
Postage and stationery	16,788		
Depreciation of sales equipment	9,005		
Telephone and Internet expense	12,215	453,028	
Administrative expenses			
Officers' salaries	186,000		
Office salaries	61,200		
Legal and professional services	23,721		
Utilities expense	23,275		
Insurance expense	17,029		
Depreciation of building	18,059		
Depreciation of office equipment	16,000		
Stationery, supplies, and postage	2,875		
Miscellaneous office expenses	2,612	350,771	803,799
Income from operations			186,073
Other Revenues and Gains			
Dividend revenue		98,500	
Rental revenue		72,910	171,410
			357,483
Other Expenses and Losses			
Interest on bonds and notes			126,060
Income before income tax			231,423
Income tax			66,934
Net income			$ 164,489
Earnings per common share			$1.74

Condensed Income Statements

In some cases a single income statement cannot possibly present all the desired expense detail. To solve this problem, a company includes only the totals of expense groups in the statement of income. It then also prepares supplementary schedules to support the totals. This format may thus reduce the income statement itself to a few lines on a single sheet. For this reason, readers who wish to study all the reported data on operations must give their attention to the supporting schedules. For example, consider the income statement shown in Illustration 5-3 for Dan Deines Company. This statement is a condensed version of the more detailed multiple-step statement presented earlier. It is more representative of the type found in practice.

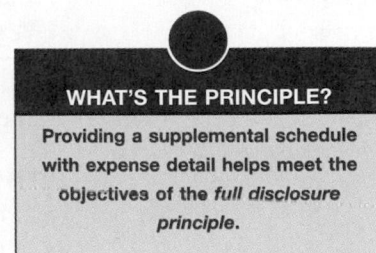

WHAT'S THE PRINCIPLE?

Providing a supplemental schedule with expense detail helps meet the objectives of the *full disclosure principle.*

Illustration 5-3
Condensed Income Statement

Dan Deines Company		
Income Statement		
For the Year Ended December 31, 2008		
Net sales		$2,972,413
Cost of goods sold		1,982,541
Gross profit		989,872
Selling expenses (see Note D)	$453,028	
Administrative expenses	350,771	803,799
Income from operations		186,073
Other revenues and gains		171,410
		357,483
Other expenses and losses		126,060
Income before income tax		231,423
Income tax		66,934
Net income		$ 164,489
Earnings per share		$1.74

Illustration 5-4 shows an example of a supporting schedule, cross-referenced as Note D and detailing the selling expenses.

Illustration 5-4
Sample Supporting Schedule

Note D: Selling expenses	
Sales salaries and commissions	$202,644
Sales office salaries	59,200
Travel and entertainment	48,940
Advertising expense	38,315
Freight and transportation-out	41,209
Shipping supplies and expense	24,712
Postage and stationery	16,788
Depreciation of sales equipment	9,005
Telephone and Internet expense	12,215
Total selling expenses	$453,028

How much detail should a company include in the income statement? On the one hand, a company wants to present a simple, summarized statement so that readers can readily discover important factors. On the other hand, it wants to disclose the results of all activities and to provide more than just a skeleton report. As we showed above, the income statement always includes certain basic elements, but companies can present them in various formats.

Try it out! Selected financial information for Jones Company at December 31, 2008, is as follows: Sales $2,300,000; cost of goods sold $1,300,000; selling expenses $200,000; administrative expenses $450,000; interest revenue $12,000; interest expense $54,000. Jones has 100,000 shares outstanding and its tax rate is 35%.

Instructions

a   Prepare a multiple-step income statement.

b   In 2007, Jones had a gross profit margin (Gross profit ÷ Sales) of 46%. Compute the gross profit margin for 2008, and discuss its relevance to Jones's operating performance in 2008.

Solution

a

Jones Company
Income Statement
For the Year Ended December 31, 2008

Sales		$2,300,000
Cost of goods sold		1,300,000
Gross profit		1,000,000
Selling expenses	$200,000	
Administrative expenses	450,000	650,000
Income from operations		350,000
Other revenue and gains		
Interest revenue		12,000
		362,000
Other expenses and losses		
Interest expense		54,000
Income before income tax		308,000
Income tax		107,800
Net income		$ 200,200
Earnings per share ($200,200 ÷ 100,000 shares)		$2.00

b   The gross profit margin for 2008 is 43.5% ($1,000,000 ÷ $2,300,000). The decline indicates that the cost of products relative to sales has declined, possibly due to competitive price pressure or increasing costs. Note that reporting income in a multiple-step format permits analysis based on income subtotals.

REPORTING IRREGULAR ITEMS

As the use of a multiple-step or condensed income statement illustrates, GAAP allows flexibility in the presentation of the components of income. However, the FASB developed specific guidelines in two important areas: what to include in income and how to report certain unusual or irregular items.

What should be included in net income has been a controversy for many years. For example, should companies report irregular gains and losses, and corrections of revenues and expenses of prior years, as part of retained earnings? Or should companies first present them in the income statement and then carry them to retained earnings?

This issue is extremely important because the number and magnitude of irregular items are substantial. For example, Illustration 5-5 identifies the most common types and number of irregular items reported in a survey of 600 large companies. Notice that more than 40 percent of the surveyed firms reported restructuring charges, which often contain write-offs and other one-time items. About 17 percent of the surveyed firms reported either an extraordinary item or a discontinued operation charge.[9]

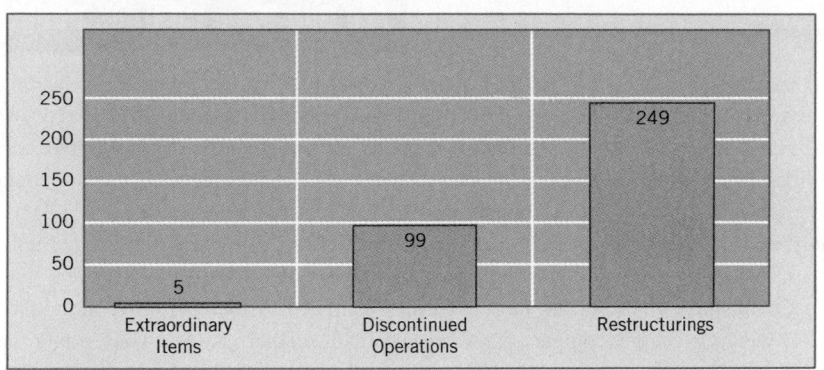

Illustration 5-5
Number of Irregular Items
Reported in a Recent Year
by 600 Large Companies

As our opening story discusses, we need consistent and comparable income reporting practices to avoid "promotional" information reported by companies. Developing a framework for reporting irregular items is important to ensure reliable income information.[10]

Some users advocate a **current operating performance approach** to income reporting. These analysts argue that the most useful income measure reflects only regular and recurring revenue and expense elements. Irregular items do not reflect a company's future earning power.

In contrast, others warn that a focus on operating income potentially misses important information about a company's performance. Any gain or loss experienced by the company, whether directly or indirectly related to operations, contributes to its long-run profitability. As one analyst notes, "write-offs matter. . . . They speak to the volatility of (past) earnings."[11] As a result, analysts can use some nonoperating items to assess the riskiness of future earnings. Furthermore, determining which items are operating and which are irregular requires judgment. This might lead to differences in the treatment of irregular items and to possible manipulation of income measures.

So, what to do? The accounting profession has adopted a **modified all-inclusive concept** and requires application of this approach in practice. This approach indicates that companies record just about all items, including irregular ones, as part of net income.[12] In addition, companies are required to highlight irregular items in the financial statements so that users can better determine the long-run earning power of the company.

Irregular items fall into six general categories, which we discuss in the following sections:

1 Discontinued operations.

2 Extraordinary items.

INTERNATIONAL INSIGHT

In many countries the "modified all-inclusive" income statement approach does not parallel that of the U.S. For example, companies in these countries take some gains and losses directly to owners' equity accounts instead of reporting them on the income statement.

---

[9]*Accounting Trends and Techniques—2006* (New York: AICPA).

[10]The FASB and other international accounting standard setters continue to study the best way to report income. See *www.fasb.org/project/financial_statement_presentation.shtml*.

[11]D. McDermott, "Latest Profit Data Stir Old Debate Between Net and Operating Income," *Wall Street Journal* (May 3, 1999).

[12]The FASB issued a statement of concepts that offers some guidance on this topic—"Recognition and Measurement in Financial Statements of Business Enterprises," *Statement of Financial Accounting Concepts No. 5* (Stamford, Conn.: FASB, 1984).

    3   Unusual gains and losses.

    4   Changes in accounting principle.

    5   Changes in estimates.

    6   Corrections of errors.

What do the numbers mean?   Are One-Time Charges Bugging You?

Which number—net income or income from operations—should an analyst use in evaluating companies that have unusual items? Some argue that operating income better represents what will happen in the future. Others note that special items are often no longer special. For example, one study noted that in one year, companies in the Standard & Poor's 500 index wrote off items totaling $165 billion—more than in the prior five years combined.

A study by Multex.com and the *Wall Street Journal* indicated that analysts should not ignore these charges. Based on data for companies taking unusual charges from 1996–2001, the study documented that companies reporting the largest unusual charges had more negative stock price performance following the charge, compared to companies with smaller charges. Thus, rather than signaling the end of bad times, these unusual charges indicated poorer future earnings.

In fact, some analysts use these charges to weed out stocks that may be headed for a fall. Following the "cockroach theory," any charge indicating a problem raises the probability of more problems. Thus, investors should be wary of the increasing use of restructuring and other one-time charges, which may bury expenses that signal future performance declines.

Source: Adapted from J. Weil and S. Liesman, "Stock Gurus Disregard Most Big Write-offs, But They Often Hold Vital Clues to Outlook," *Wall Street Journal Online* (December 31, 2001).

Beyond the Numbers

Can so-called one-time charges be used to manage earnings similar to cookie jar reserves? Explain.

Discontinued Operations

As Illustration 5-5 (page 209) shows, one of **the most common types of irregular items is discontinued operations. A discontinued operation** occurs when two things happen: (a) a company eliminates the results of operations and cash flows of a *component* from its ongoing operations, and (b) there is no significant continuing involvement in that component after the disposal transaction.

To illustrate a **component**, **S. C. Johnson** manufactures and sells consumer products. It has several product groups, each with different product lines and brands. For S. C. Johnson, a product group is the lowest level at which it can clearly distinguish the operations and cash flows from the rest of the company's operations. Therefore each product group is a component of the company. If a component were disposed of, S. C. Johnson would classify it as a discontinued operation.

Here is another example. Assume that Softso Inc. has experienced losses with certain brands in its beauty-care products group. As a result, Softso decides to sell that part of its business. It will discontinue any continuing involvement in the product group after the sale. In this case, Softso eliminates the operations and the cash flows of the product group from its ongoing operations, and reports it as a discontinued operation.

On the other hand, assume Softso decides to remain in the beauty-care business but will discontinue the brands that experienced losses. Because Softso cannot differentiate the cash flows from the brands from the cash flows of the product group as a whole, it cannot consider the brands a component. Softso does not classify any gain or loss on the sale of the brands as a discontinued operation.

Companies report as discontinued operations (in a separate income statement category) the gain or loss from **disposal of a component of a business**. In addition, companies report the **results of operations of a component that has been or will be disposed of** separately from continuing operations. Companies show the effects of discontinued operations net of tax as a separate category, after continuing operations but before extraordinary items.[13]

To illustrate, Multiplex Products, Inc., a highly diversified company, decides to discontinue its electronics division. During the current year, the electronics division lost $300,000 (net of tax). Multiplex sold the division at the end of the year at a loss of $500,000 (net of tax). Multiplex shows the information on the current year's income statement as follows.

Income from continuing operations		$20,000,000
Discontinued operations		
Loss from operation of discontinued electronics division (net of tax)	$300,000	
Loss from disposal of electronics division (net of tax)	500,000	800,000
Net income		$19,200,000

Illustration 5-6
Income Statement
Presentation of
Discontinued Operations

Companies use the subtotal "**Income from continuing operations**" only when gains or losses on discontinued operations occur.

Extraordinary Items

Extraordinary items are nonrecurring **material** items that differ significantly from a company's typical business activities. The criteria for extraordinary items are as follows.

Extraordinary items are events and transactions that are distinguished by their unusual nature and by the infrequency of their occurrence. Classifying an event or transaction as an extraordinary item requires meeting **both** of the following criteria:

a   **Unusual Nature.** The underlying event or transaction should possess a high degree of abnormality and be of a type clearly unrelated to, or only incidentally related to, the ordinary and typical activities of the company, taking into account the environment in which it operates.

b   **Infrequency of Occurrence.** The underlying event or transaction should be of a type that the company does not reasonably expect to recur in the foreseeable future, taking into account the environment in which the company operates.[14]

For further clarification, the following gains and losses are **not extraordinary items**.

a   Write-down or write-off of receivables, inventories, equipment leased to others, deferred research and development costs, or other intangible assets.

b   Gains or losses from exchange or translation of foreign currencies, including those relating to major devaluations and revaluations.

c   Gains or losses on disposal of a component of an entity (reported as a discontinued operation).

d   Other gains or losses from sale or abandonment of property, plant, or equipment used in the business.

e   Effects of a strike, including those against competitors and major suppliers.

f   Adjustment of accruals on long-term contracts.[15]

The above items are not considered extraordinary "because they are usual in nature and may be expected to recur as a consequence of customary and continuing business activities."

---

[13]"Accounting for the Impairment or Disposal of Long-Lived Assets," *Statement of Financial Accounting Standards No. 144* (Norwalk, Conn.: FASB, 2001), par. 4. This standard requires discontinued-operation reporting, even though the assets disposed of (i.e., component of the business) do not meet the definition of a business segment.

[14]"Reporting the Results of Operations," *Opinions of the Accounting Principles Board No. 30* (New York: AICPA, 1973), par. 20.

[15]Ibid., par. 23, as amended by "Accounting for the Impairment or Disposal of Long-lived Assets," *Statement of Financial Accounting Standards No. 144* (Norwalk, Conn.: FASB, 2001).

Only rarely does an event or transaction clearly meet the criteria for an extraordinary item.[16] For example, a company classifies gains or losses such as (a) and (d) above as extraordinary if they **resulted directly from a major casualty** (such as an earthquake), **an expropriation**, or a **prohibition under a newly enacted law or regulation**. Such circumstances clearly meet the criteria of unusual and infrequent. For example, **Weyerhaeuser Company** (forest and lumber) incurred an extraordinary item (an approximate $36 million loss) as a result of volcanic activity at Mount St. Helens. The eruption destroyed standing timber, logs, buildings, equipment, and transportation systems covering 68,000 acres.

In determining whether an item is extraordinary, **a company must consider the environment in which it operates**. The environment includes such factors as industry characteristics, geographic location, and the nature and extent of governmental regulations. Thus, the FASB accords extraordinary item treatment to the loss from hail damages to a tobacco grower's crops if hailstorm damage in its locality is rare. On the other hand, frost damage to a citrus grower's crop in Florida does not qualify as extraordinary because frost damage normally occurs there every three or four years.

Similarly, when a company sells the only significant security investment it has ever owned, the gain or loss meets the criteria of an extraordinary item. Another company, however, that has a portfolio of securities acquired for investment purposes would not report such a sales as an extraordinary item. Sale of such securities is part of its ordinary and typical activities.[17]

What do the numbers mean?   Extraordinary Times

No recent event better illustrates the difficulties of determining whether a transaction meets the definition of extraordinary than the financial impacts of the terrorist attack on the World Trade Center on September 11, 2001.

To many, this event, which resulted in the tragic loss of lives, jobs, and in some cases, entire businesses, clearly meets the criteria for unusual and infrequent. For example, in the wake of the terrorist attack that destroyed the World Trade Center and turned much of lower Manhattan including Wall Street into a war zone, airlines, insurance companies, and other businesses recorded major losses due to property damage, business disruption, and suspension of airline travel and of securities trading.

But, to the surprise of many, the FASB did not permit extraordinary item reporting for losses arising from the terrorist attacks. The reason? After much deliberation, the Emerging Issues Task Force (EITF) of the FASB decided that measurement of the possible loss was too difficult. Take the airline industry as an example: What portion of the airlines' losses after September 11 was related to the terrorist attack, and what portion was due to the ongoing recession? Also, the FASB did not want companies to use the attack as a reason for reporting as extraordinary some losses that had little direct relationship to the attack. Indeed, energy company AES and shoe retailer Footstar, who both were experiencing profit pressure before 9/11, put some of the blame for their poor performance on the attack.

Source: Julie Creswell, "Bad News Bearers Shift the Blame," *Fortune* (October 15, 2001), p. 44.

Beyond the Numbers

Explain how the accounting for the financial impacts of 9/11 illustrates a tradeoff between the two primary qualities of accounting information, as discussed in the FASB's conceptual framework.

---

[16]*Accounting Trends and Techniques—2006* (New York: AICPA) indicates that just 5 of the 600 companies surveyed reported an extraordinary item.

[17]Debt extinguishments had been the most common reason for companies reporting extraordinary items. The FASB has now eliminated extraordinary item treatment for these gains and losses, unless they are both unusual and infrequent in nature ("Rescission of FASB Statements No. 4, 44, and 64 and Technical Corrections," *Statement of Financial Accounting Standards No. 145* (Norwalk, Conn.: FASB, 2002). Thus, reporting an extraordinary item has to become a rare event.

In addition, considerable judgment must be exercised in determining whether to report an item as extraordinary. For example, the government condemned the forestlands of some paper companies to preserve state or national parks or forests. Is such an event extraordinary, or is it part of a paper company's normal operations? Such determination is not easy. Much depends on the frequency of previous condemnations, the expectation of future condemnations, materiality, and the like.[18]

Companies must show extraordinary items net of taxes in a separate section in the income statement, usually just before net income. After listing the usual revenues, expenses, and income taxes, the remainder of the statement shows the following.

Income before extraordinary items
Extraordinary items (less applicable income tax of $_____)
Net income

Illustration 5-7
Income Statement Placement of Extraordinary Items

For example, Illustration 5-8 shows how **Keystone Consolidated Industries** reported an extraordinary loss.

Keystone Consolidated Industries, Inc.

Income before extraordinary item	$11,638,000
Extraordinary item—flood loss (Note E)	1,216,000
Net income	$10,422,000

Note E: Extraordinary Item. The Keystone Steel and Wire Division's Steel Works experienced a flash flood on June 22. The extraordinary item represents the estimated cost, net of related income taxes of $1,279,000, to restore the steel works to full operation.

Illustration 5-8
Income Statement Presentation of Extraordinary Items

Unusual Gains and Losses

Because of the restrictive criteria for extraordinary items, financial statement users must carefully examine the financial statements for items that are **unusual or infrequent but not both**. Recall that companies cannot consider items such as write-downs of inventories and transaction gains and losses from fluctuation of foreign exchange as extraordinary items. Thus, companies sometimes show these items with their normal recurring revenues and expenses. If not material in amount, companies combine these with other items in the income statement. If material, companies must disclose them separately, and report them **above** "Income (loss) before extraordinary items."

For example, **PepsiCo, Inc.** presented an unusual charge in its income statement, as Illustration 5-9 (page 214) shows.

Restructuring charges, like the one PepsiCo reported, have been common in recent years (see also Illustration 5-5). A **restructuring charge** relates to a major reorganization of company affairs, such as costs associated with employee layoffs, plant closing

---

[18]Because assessing the materiality of individual items requires judgment, determining what is extraordinary is difficult. However, in making materiality judgments, companies should consider extraordinary items individually, and not in the aggregate. "Reporting the Results of Operations," op. cit., par. 24.

Illustration 5-9
Income Statement
Presentation of
Unusual Charges

PEPSICO
PepsiCo, Inc.
(in millions)

Net sales	$20,917
Costs and expenses, net	
Cost of sales	8,525
Selling, general, and administrative expenses	9,241
Amortization of intangible assets	199
Unusual items (Note 2)	290
Operating income	$ 2,662

Note 2 (Restructuring Charge)

Dispose and write down assets	$183
Improve productivity	94
Strengthen the international bottler structure	13
Net loss	$290

The net charge to strengthen the international bottler structure includes proceeds of $87 million associated with a settlement related to a previous Venezuelan bottler agreement, which were partially offset by related costs.

costs, write-offs of assets, and so on. A company should not report a restructuring charge as an extraordinary item, because these write-offs are part of a company's ordinary and typical activities.

Companies tend to **report unusual items in a separate section just above** "**Income from operations before income taxes**" **and** "**Extraordinary items**," especially when there are multiple unusual items. For example, when **General Electric Company** experienced multiple unusual items in one year, it reported them in a separate "Unusual items" section of the income statement below "Income before unusual items and income taxes." When preparing a multiple-step income statement for homework purposes, you should report unusual gains and losses in the "Other revenues and gains" or "Other expenses and losses" section unless you are instructed to prepare a separate unusual items section.[19]

In dealing with events that are either unusual or nonrecurring but not both, the profession attempted to prevent a practice that many believed was misleading. Companies often reported such transactions on a net-of-tax basis and prominently displayed the earnings per share effect of these items. Although not captioned "Extraordinary items," companies presented them in the same manner. Some had referred to these as "first cousins" to extraordinary items.

As a consequence, the Board specifically **prohibited a net-of-tax treatment for such items**, to ensure that users of financial statements can easily differentiate extraordinary items—reported net of tax—from material items that are unusual or infrequent, but not both.

---

[19]Many companies report "one-time items." However, some companies take restructuring charges practically every year. **Citicorp** (now **Citigroup**) took restructuring charges six years in a row, between 1988 and 1993; **Eastman Kodak Co.** did so five out of six years in 1989 to 1994. Research indicates that the market discounts the earnings of companies that report a series of "nonrecurring" items. Such evidence supports the contention that these elements reduce the quality of earnings. J. Elliott and D. Hanna, "Repeated Accounting Write-offs and the Information Content of Earnings," *Journal of Accounting Research* (Supplement, 1996).

Changes in Accounting Principle

Changes in accounting occur frequently in practice, because important events or conditions may be in dispute or uncertain at the statement date. One type of accounting change results when a company adopts a different accounting principle. Changes in accounting principle include a change in the method of inventory pricing from FIFO to average cost, or a change in accounting for construction contracts from the percentage-of-completion to the completed-contract method.[20]

A company recognizes a change in accounting principle by making a **retrospective adjustment** to the financial statements. Such an adjustment recasts the prior years' statements on a basis consistent with the newly adopted principle. The company records the cumulative effect of the change for prior periods as an adjustment to beginning retained earnings of the earliest year presented.

To illustrate, Gaubert Inc. decided in March 2008 to change from FIFO to weighted-average inventory pricing. Gaubert's income before taxes, using the new weighted-average method in 2008, is $30,000. Illustration 5-10 presents the pretax income data for 2006 and 2007 for this example.

Year	FIFO	Weighted-Average Method	Excess of FIFO over Weighted-Average Method
2006	$40,000	$35,000	$5,000
2007	30,000	27,000	3,000
Total			$8,000

Illustration 5-10
Calculation of a Change in Accounting Principle

Illustration 5-11 shows the information Gaubert presented in its comparative income statements, based on a 30 percent tax rate.

	2008	2007	2006
Income before income tax	$30,000	$27,000	$35,000
Income tax	9,000	8,100	10,500
Net income	$21,000	$18,900	$24,500

Illustration 5-11
Income Statement Presentation of a Change in Accounting Principle

Thus, under the retrospective approach, the company recasts the prior years' income numbers under the newly adopted method. This approach thus preserves comparability across years.

Changes in Estimates

Estimates are inherent in the accounting process. For example, companies estimate useful lives and salvage values of depreciable assets, uncollectible receivables, inventory obsolescence, and the number of periods expected to benefit from a particular expenditure.

---

[20]"Accounting Changes and Error Corrections," *Statement of Financial Accounting Standards No. 154* (Norwalk, Conn.: FASB, 2005). In Chapter 18, we examine in greater detail the problems related to accounting changes.

WHAT'S THE PRINCIPLE?

Companies can change principles, but they must demonstrate that the newly adopted principle is preferable to the old one. Such changes result in lost consistency from period to period.

Not infrequently, due to time, circumstances, or new information, even estimates originally made in good faith must be changed. A company accounts for such **changes in estimates** in the period of change if they affect only that period, or in the period of change and future periods if the change affects both.

To illustrate a change in estimate that affects only the period of change, assume that DuPage Materials Corp. consistently estimated its bad debt expense at 1 percent of credit sales. In 2008 however, DuPage determines that it must revise upward the estimate of bad debts for the current year's credit sales to 2 percent, or double the prior years' percentage. The 2 percent rate is necessary to reduce accounts receivable to net realizable value. Using 2 percent results in a bad debt charge of $240,000, or double the amount using the 1 percent estimate for prior years, DuPage records the provision at December 31, 2008, as follows.

Bad Debt Expense	240,000	
Allowance for Doubtful Accounts		240,000

DuPage includes the entire change in estimate in 2008 income because the change does not affect future periods. **Companies do not handle changes in estimate retrospectively.** That is, such changes are not carried back to adjust prior years. (We examine changes in estimate that affect both the current and future periods in greater detail in Chapter 18.) **Changes in estimate are not considered errors or extraordinary items.**

Corrections of Errors

Errors occur as a result of mathematical mistakes, mistakes in the application of accounting principles, or oversight or misuse of facts that existed at the time financial statements were prepared. In recent years, many companies have corrected for errors in their financial statements. For example, one consulting group noted that error-driven restatements were up 17 percent (to 1,876 restatements) in 2006 for publicly traded U.S. and foreign companies.[21] The most common errors involved improper reporting of debt and equity instruments, accounting for stock options, cash flow reporting, and taxes.

Companies must correct errors by making proper entries in the accounts and reporting the corrections in the financial statements. Corrections of errors are treated as **prior period adjustments**, similar to changes in accounting principles. Companies record a correction of an error in the year in which it is discovered. They report the error in the financial statements as an adjustment to the beginning balance of retained earnings. If a company prepares comparative financial statements, it should restate the prior statements for the effects of the error.

To illustrate, in 2008, Hillsboro Co. determined that it incorrectly overstated its accounts receivable and sales revenue by $100,000 in 2007. In 2008, Hillboro makes the following entry to correct for this error (ignore income taxes).

Retained Earnings	100,000	
Accounts Receivable		100,000

Retained Earnings is debited because sales revenue, and therefore net income, was overstated in a prior period. Accounts Receivable is credited to reduce this overstated balance to the correct amount.

Summary of Irregular Items

The public accounting profession now tends to accept a modified all-inclusive income concept instead of the current operating performance concept. Except for changes in accounting principle and error corrections, which are charged or credited directly to retained

---

[21]David Reilly, "Restatements Still Bedevil Firms," *Wall Street Journal* (February 12, 2007), p. C7.

earnings, companies close all other irregular gains or losses or nonrecurring items to Income Summary and include them in the income statement.

Of these irregular items, companies classify **discontinued operations of a component** of a business as a separate item in the income statement, after "Income from continuing operations." Companies show the **unusual, material, nonrecurring items** that significantly differ from the typical or customary business activities in a separate "Extraordinary items" section below "Discontinued operations." They separately disclose other items of a material amount that are of an **unusual or nonrecurring** nature and are **not considered extraordinary**.

Because of the numerous intermediate income figures created by the reporting of these irregular items, readers must carefully evaluate earnings information reported by the financial press. Illustration 5-12 summarizes the basic concepts that we previously discussed. Although simplified, the chart provides a useful framework for determining the treatment of special items affecting the income statement.

WHAT'S THE PRINCIPLE?

The AICPA Special Committee on Financial Reporting indicates a company's core activities—usual and recurring events—provide the best historical data from which users determine trends and relationships and make their predictions about the future. Therefore, companies should separately display the effects of core and noncore activities.

Illustration 5-12
Summary of Irregular Items in the Income Statement

Type of Situation[a]	Criteria	Examples	Placement on Income Statement
Discontinued operations	Disposal of a component of a business for which the company can clearly distinguish operations and cash flows from the rest of the company's operations.	Sale by diversified company of major division that represents only activities in electronics industry. Food distributor that sells wholesale to supermarket chains and through fast-food restaurants decides to discontinue the division that sells to one of two classes of customers.	Show in separate section after continuing operations but before extraordinary items. (Shown net of tax.)
Extraordinary items	Material, and both unusual and infrequent (nonrecurring).	Gains or losses resulting from casualties, an expropriation, or a prohibition under a new law.	Show in separate section entitled "Extraordinary items." (Shown net of tax.)
Unusual gains or losses, not considered extraordinary	Material; character typical of the customary business activities; unusual or infrequent but not both.	Write-downs of receivables, inventories; adjustments of accrued contract prices; gains or losses from fluctuations of foreign exchange; gains or losses from sales of assets used in business.	Show in separate section above income before extraordinary items. Often reported in "Other revenues and gains" or "Other expenses and losses" section. (Not shown net of tax.)
Changes in principle	Change from one generally accepted principle to another.	Change in the basis of inventory pricing from FIFO to average cost.	Recast prior years' income statements on the same basis as the newly adopted principle.
Changes in estimates	Normal, recurring corrections and adjustments.	Changes in the realizability of receivables and inventories; changes in estimated lives of equipment, intangible assets; changes in estimated liability for warranty costs, income taxes, and salary payments.	Show change only in the affected accounts. (Not shown net of tax.)
Corrections of errors	Mistake, misuse of facts.	Error in reporting revenue.	~~statement of net earnings~~ Restate prior years' income statements to correct for error.

[a]This summary provides only the general rules to be followed in accounting for the various situations described above. Exceptions do exist in some of these situations.

Try it out! Sloan Corporation reported the following income-related information for the year ended December 31, 2008: Income from continuing operations $240,000. The following irregular items have not yet been considered by Sloan: Extraordinary loss (net of tax) $20,000; gain on disposal of a component of the business (net of tax) $35,000; restructuring charge $45,000.

Instructions

Determine the amounts for: (a) income from continuing operations and (b) net income. Sloan's tax rate is 30%.

Solution

a Income from continuing operations

= $240,000 less restructuring, adjusted for taxes
= $240,000 − [$45,000 × (1 − .30)] = $208,500

b
Income from continuing operations	$208,500
Discontinued operations	35,000
Extraordinary loss	(20,000)
Net income	$223,500

SPECIAL REPORTING ISSUES

Intraperiod Tax Allocation

OBJECTIVE 5

Explain intraperiod tax allocation.

Companies report irregular items (except for unusual gains and losses) on the income statement or statement of retained earnings net of tax. This procedure is called **intraperiod tax allocation**, that is, allocation within a period. It relates the income tax expense (sometimes referred to as the income tax provision) of the fiscal period to the **specific items** that give rise to the amount of the tax provision.

Intraperiod tax allocation helps financial statement users better understand the impact of income taxes on the various components of net income. For example, readers of financial statements will understand how much income tax expense relates to "income from continuing operations" and how much relates to certain irregular transactions and events. This approach should help users to better predict the amount, timing, and uncertainty of future cash flows. In addition, intraperiod tax allocation discourages statement readers from using pretax measures of performance when evaluating financial results, and thereby recognizes that income tax expense is a real cost.

Companies use intraperiod tax allocation on the income statement for the following items: (1) income from continuing operations, (2) discontinued operations, and (3) extraordinary items. The general concept is "**let the tax follow the income**."

To compute the income tax expense attributable to "Income from continuing operations," a company would find the income tax expense related to both the revenue and expense transactions used in determining this income. (In this computation, the company does not consider the tax consequences of items excluded from the determination of "Income from continuing operations.") Companies then associate a separate tax effect with each irregular item (e.g., discontinued operations and extraordinary items). Here we look in more detail at calculation of intraperiod tax allocation for extraordinary gains and losses.

Extraordinary Gains

In applying the concept of intraperiod tax allocation, assume that Schindler Co. has income before income tax and extraordinary item of $250,000. It has an extraordinary gain of $100,000 from a condemnation settlement received on one its properties. Assuming a 30 percent income tax rate, Schindler presents the following information on the income statement.

Income before income tax and extraordinary item		$250,000
Income tax		75,000
Income before extraordinary item		175,000
Extraordinary gain—condemnation settlement	$100,000	
Less: Applicable income tax	30,000	70,000
Net income		$245,000

Illustration 5-13
Intraperiod Tax Allocation, Extraordinary Gain

Schindler determines the income tax of $75,000 ($250,000 × 30%) attributable to "Income before income tax and extraordinary item" from revenue and expense transactions related to this income. Schindler omits the tax consequences of items excluded from the determination of "Income before income tax and extraordinary item." The company shows a separate tax effect of $30,000 as "Extraordinary gain—condemnation settlement."

Extraordinary Losses

To illustrate the reporting of an extraordinary loss, assume that Schindler Co. has income before income tax and extraordinary item of $250,000. It suffers an extraordinary loss from a major casualty of $100,000. Assuming a 30 percent tax rate, Schindler presents the income tax on the income statement as shown in Illustration 5-14. In this case, the loss provides a positive tax benefit of $30,000. Schindler, therefore, subtracts it from the $100,000 loss.

Income before income tax and extraordinary item		$250,000
Income tax		75,000
Income before extraordinary item		175,000
Extraordinary item—loss from casualty	$100,000	
Less: Applicable income tax reduction	30,000	70,000
Net income		$105,000

Illustration 5-14
Intraperiod Tax Allocation, Extraordinary Loss

Companies may also report the tax effect of an extraordinary item by means of a note disclosure, as illustrated below.

Income before income tax and extraordinary item	$250,000	
Income tax	75,000	
Income before extraordinary item	175,000	
Extraordinary item, less applicable income tax reduction (Note 1)	70,000	
Net income	$105,000	

Illustration 5-15
Note Disclosure of Intraperiod Tax Allocation

Note 1: During the year the Company suffered a major casualty loss of $70,000, net of applicable income tax reduction of $30,000.

<table>
<tr><td>

OBJECTIVE 6

Identify where to report earnings per share information.

</td></tr>
</table>

Earnings per Share

A company customarily sums up the results of its operations in one important figure: net income. However, the financial world has widely accepted an even more distilled and compact figure as the most significant business indicator—**earnings per share** (EPS).

The computation of earnings per share is usually straightforward. **Earnings per share is net income minus preferred dividends (income available to common stockholders), divided by the weighted average of common shares outstanding.**[22]

To illustrate, assume that Lancer, Inc. reports net income of $350,000. It declares and pays preferred dividends of $50,000 for the year. The weighted average number of common shares outstanding during the year is 100,000 shares. Lancer computes earnings per share of $3, as shown in Illustration 5-16.

Illustration 5-16
Equation Illustrating
Computation of Earnings
per Share

$$\frac{\text{Net Income} - \text{Preferred Dividends}}{\text{Weighted Average of Common Shares Outstanding}} = \text{Earnings per Share}$$

$$\frac{\$350,000 - \$50,000}{100,000} = \$3$$

Note that EPS measures the number of dollars earned by each share of common stock. It does not represent the dollar amount paid to stockholders in the form of dividends.

Prospectuses, proxy material, and annual reports to stockholders commonly use the "net income per share" or "earnings per share" ratio. The financial press, statistical services like Standard & Poor's, and Wall Street securities analysts also highlight EPS. Because of its importance, **companies must disclose earnings per share on the face of the income statement**. A company that reports a discontinued operation or an extraordinary item must report per share amounts for these line items either on the face of the income statement or in the notes to the financial statements.[23]

To illustrate, consider the income statement for Poquito Industries Inc. shown in Illustration 5-17 (page 221). Notice the order in which Poquito shows the data, with per share information at the bottom. Assume that the company had 100,000 shares outstanding for the entire year. The Poquito income statement, as Illustration 5-17 shows, is highly condensed. Poquito would need to describe items such as "Unusual charge," "Discontinued operations," and "Extraordinary item" fully and appropriately in the statement or related notes.

Many corporations have simple capital structures that include only common stock. For these companies, a presentation such as "Earnings per common share" is appropriate on the income statement. In many instances, however, companies' earnings per share are subject to dilution (reduction) in the future because existing contingencies permit the issuance of additional common shares.[24]

In summary, the simplicity and availability of EPS figures lead to their widespread use. Because of the importance that the public, even the well-informed public, attaches to earnings per share, companies must make the EPS figure as meaningful as possible.

---

[22]In calculating earnings per share, companies deduct preferred dividends from net income if the dividends are declared or if they are cumulative though not declared.

[23]"Earnings Per Share," *Statement of Financial Accounting Standards No. 128* (Norwalk, Conn.: FASB, 1996).

[24]Ibid. We discuss the computational problems involved in accounting for these dilutive securities in earnings per share computations in Chapter 18.

Illustration 5-17
Income Statement

Poquito Industries Inc.
Income Statement
For the Year Ended December 31, 2008

Sales revenue		$1,420,000
Cost of goods sold		600,000
Gross profit		820,000
Selling and administrative expenses		320,000
Income from operations		500,000
Other revenues and gains		
Interest revenue		10,000
Other expenses and losses		
Loss on disposal of part of Textile Division	$ (5,000)	
Unusual charge—loss on sale of investments	(45,000)	(50,000)
Income from continuing operations before income tax		460,000
Income tax		184,000
Income from continuing operations		276,000
Discontinued operations		
Income from operations of Pizza Division, less		
applicable income tax of $24,800	54,000	
Loss on disposal of Pizza Division, less		
applicable income tax of $41,000	(90,000)	(36,000)
Income before extraordinary item		240,000
Extraordinary item—loss from earthquake, less		
applicable income tax of $23,000		(45,000)
Net income		$ 195,000
Per share of common stock		
Income from continuing operations		$2.76
Income from operations of discontinued division, net of tax		0.54
Loss on disposal of discontinued operation, net of tax		(0.90)
Income before extraordinary item		2.40
Extraordinary loss, net of tax		(0.45)
Net income		$1.95

Retained Earnings Statement

Net income increases retained earnings. A net loss decreases retained earnings. Both cash and stock dividends decrease retained earnings. Changes in accounting principles (generally) and prior period adjustments may increase or decrease retained earnings. Companies charge or credit these adjustments (net of tax) to the opening balance of retained earnings. This excludes the adjustments from the determination of net income for the current period.

Companies may show retained earnings information in different ways. For example, some companies prepare a separate retained earnings statement, as Illustration 5-18 shows.

The reconciliation of the beginning to the ending balance in retained earnings provides information about why net assets increased or decreased during the year. The association of dividend distributions with net income for the period indicates what management is doing with earnings: It may be "plowing back" into the business part or all of the earnings, distributing all current income, or distributing current income plus the accumulated earnings of prior years.[25]

> **OBJECTIVE 7**
> **Prepare a retained earnings statement.**

[25]*Accounting Trends and Techniques—2006* (New York: AICPA) indicates that most companies (590 of 600 surveyed) present changes in retained earnings either within the statement of stockholders' equity (586 firms) or in a separate statement of retained earnings. Only 3 of the 600 companies prepare a combined statement of income and retained earnings.

Illustration 5-18
Retained Earnings
Statement

Tiger Woods Inc.
Retained Earnings Statement
For the Year Ended December 31, 2008

Retained earnings, January 1, as reported		$1,050,000
Correction for understatement of net income in prior period		
(inventory error)		50,000
Retained earnings, January 1, as adjusted		1,100,000
Add: Net income		360,000
		1,460,000
Less: Cash dividends	$100,000	
Stock dividends	200,000	300,000
Retained earnings, December 31		$1,160,000

Restrictions of Retained Earnings

Companies often restrict retained earnings to comply with contractual requirements, board of directors' policy, or current necessity. Generally, companies disclose in the notes to the financial statements the amounts of restricted retained earnings. In some cases, companies transfer the amount of retained earnings restricted to an account titled **Appropriated Retained Earnings**. The retained earnings section may therefore report two separate amounts—(1) retained earnings free (unrestricted) and (2) retained earnings appropriated (restricted). The total of these two amounts equals the total retained earnings.

Comprehensive Income

Companies generally include in income all revenues, expenses, and gains and losses recognized during the period. These items are classified within the income statement so that financial statement readers can better understand the significance of various components of net income. Changes in accounting principles and corrections of errors are excluded from the calculation of net income because their effects relate to prior periods.

In recent years, there is increased use of fair values for measuring assets and liabilities. Furthermore, possible reporting of gains and losses related to changes in fair value have placed a strain on income reporting. Because fair values are continually changing, some argue that recognizing these gains and losses in net income is misleading. The FASB agrees and has identified a limited number of transactions that should be recorded directly to stockholders equity. One example is unrealized gains and losses on available-for-sale securities.[26] These gains and losses are excluded from net income, thereby reducing volatility in net income due to fluctuations in fair value.

Companies include these items that bypass the income statement in a measure called comprehensive income. **Comprehensive income** includes all changes in equity during a period *except* those resulting from investments by owners and distributions to owners. Comprehensive income, therefore, includes the following: all revenues and gains, expenses and losses reported in net income, and all gains and losses that bypass net income but affect stockholders' equity. These items—non-owner changes in equity that bypass the income statement—are referred to as **other comprehensive income**.

The FASB decided that companies must display the components of other comprehensive income in one of three ways: **(1) a second income statement; (2) a combined statement**

OBJECTIVE 8

Explain how to report other comprehensive income.

---

[26]We further discuss available-for-sale securities in Chapter 14. Additional examples of other comprehensive items are translation gains and losses on foreign currency, some pension gains and losses, and unrealized gains and losses on certain hedging transactions.

of comprehensive income; or (3) as a part of the statement of stockholders' equity. [27]
Regardless of the format used, companies must add net income to other comprehensive income
to arrive at comprehensive income. Companies are not required to report earnings per share
information related to comprehensive income.[28]

To illustrate, assume that V. Gill Inc. reports the following information for 2008: sales
revenue $800,000; cost of goods sold $600,000; operating expenses $90,000; and an unre-
alized holding gain on available-for-sale securities of $30,000, net of tax.

Second Income Statement

Illustration 5-19 shows the two-income statement format, using information for V. Gill.
Reporting comprehensive income in a separate statement indicates that the gains and
losses identified as other comprehensive income have the same status as traditional gains
and losses. Placing net income as the starting point in the comprehensive income statement highlights the relationship of the statement to the traditional income statement.

Illustration 5-19
Two-Statement Format:
Comprehensive Income

V. Gill Inc.
Income Statement
For the Year Ended December 31, 2008

Sales revenue	$800,000
Cost of goods sold	600,000
Gross profit	200,000
Operating expenses	90,000
Net income	$110,000

V. Gill Inc.
Comprehensive Income Statement
For the Year Ended December 31, 2008

Net income	$110,000
Other comprehensive income	
Unrealized holding gain, net of tax	30,000
Comprehensive income	$140,000

Combined Statement of Comprehensive Income

The second approach to reporting other comprehensive income provides a **combined
statement** of comprehensive income. In this approach, the traditional net income is a subtotal, with total comprehensive income shown as a final total. The combined statement has
the advantage of not requiring the creation of a new financial statement. However, burying
net income as a subtotal on the statement is a disadvantage.

Statement of Stockholders' Equity

A third approach reports other comprehensive income items in a **statement of stockholders' equity**. This statement reports the changes in each stockholder's equity account
and in total stockholders' equity during the year. Companies often prepare **in columnar**

[27]"Reporting Comprehensive Income," *Statement of Financial Accounting Standards No. 130* (Norwalk, Conn.: FASB, June 1997). *Accounting Trends and Techniques—2006* (New York: AICPA)
indicates that for the 600 companies surveyed, 579 report comprehensive income. Most companies (478 of 580) include comprehensive income as part of the statement of stockholders' equity.

[28]A company must display the components of other comprehensive income either (1) net of related
tax effects, or (2) before related tax effects, with one amount shown for the aggregate amount of tax
related to the total amount of other comprehensive income.

form the statement of stockholders' equity. In this format, they use columns for each account and for total stockholders' equity.

To illustrate, assume the same information for V. Gill. The company had the following stockholder equity account balances at the beginning of 2008: Common Stock $300,000; Retained Earnings $50,000; and Accumulated Other Comprehensive Income $60,000. No changes in the Common Stock account occurred during the year. Illustration 5-20 shows a statement of stockholders' equity for V. Gill.

Illustration 5-20
Presentation of Comprehensive Income Items in Stockholders' Equity Statement

V. Gill Inc.
Statement of Stockholders' Equity
For the Year Ended December 31, 2008

	Total	Comprehensive Income	Retained Earnings	Accumulated Other Comprehensive Income	Common Stock
Beginning balance	$410,000		$ 50,000	$60,000	$300,000
Comprehensive income					
Net income	110,000	$110,000	110,000		
Other comprehensive income					
Unrealized holding gain, net of tax	30,000	30,000		30,000	
Comprehensive income		$140,000			
Ending balance	$550,000		$160,000	$90,000	$300,000

Examples of Comprehensive Income Reporting

Because many companies already provide a statement of stockholders' equity, adding additional columns to display information related to comprehensive income is not costly.

Balance Sheet Presentation

Regardless of the display format used, V. Gill reports the **accumulated other comprehensive income** of $90,000 in the stockholders' equity section of the balance sheet as follows.

Illustration 5-21
Presentation of Accumulated Other Comprehensive Income in the Balance Sheet

V. Gill Inc.
Balance Sheet
December 31, 2008
(Stockholders' Equity Section)

Stockholders' equity	
Common stock	$300,000
Retained earnings	160,000
Accumulated other comprehensive income	90,000
Total stockholders' equity	$550,000

You will want to read the CONVERGENCE CORNER on the next page for discussion of how international convergence efforts relate to the income statement.

By providing information on the components of comprehensive income, as well as accumulated other comprehensive income, the company communicates information about all changes in net assets.[29] With this information, users will better understand the quality of the company's earnings.

[29]Corrections of errors and changes in accounting principles are not considered other comprehensive income items.

CONVERGENCE CORNER

Income Statement

As in U.S. GAAP, the statement of income is a required statement for iGAAP. In addition, the content and presentation of an iGAAP income statement is similar to the one used for U.S. GAAP. *IAS 1*, "Presentation of Financial Statements," provides general guidelines for the reporting of income statement information. Subsequently, a number of international standards have been issued that provide additional guidance to issues related to income statement presentation.

 RELEVANT FACTS

• Under iGAAP, companies must classify expenses by either nature or function. Classification by *nature* leads to descriptions such as the following: salaries, depreciation expense, utilities expense, and so on. Classification *by function* leads to descriptions like administration, distribution, and manufacturing. If a company uses the functional expense method on the income statement, disclosure by nature is required in the notes to the financial statements.

• Presentation of the income statement under U.S. GAAP follows either a single-step or multiple-step format. iGAAP does not mention a single-step or multiple-step approach. In addition, under U.S. GAAP, companies must report an item as extraordinary if it is unusual in nature and infrequent in occurrence. Extraordinary items are prohibited under iGAAP.

• Under iGAAP, companies are required to prepare as a primary financial statement either a statement of stockholder' equity similar to the one prepared under U.S. GAAP or a statement of recognized income and expense (called a *SoRIE*).

• Both iGAAP and U.S. GAAP have items that are recognized in equity as part of comprehensive income but do not affect net income. U.S. GAAP provides three possible formats for presenting this information: single income statement, combined income statement of comprehensive income, in the statement of stockholder' equity. iGAAP allows either the statement of stockholders' equity approach or the SoRIE format.

• Under iGAAP revaluation of land, buildings, and intangible assets is permitted. The effect of this difference is that application of iGAAP results in more transactions affecting equity but not net income.

 ABOUT THE NUMBERS

As indicated, under iGAAP companies can prepare a statement of recognized income and expense (SoRIE). A SoRIE reports the net income or loss for the period and all the income and expense items that are included in comprehensive income but not net income until realized. Here is a SoRIE for Hulce Inc.

Hulce Inc. Statement of Recognized Income and Expense For the Year Ended 2008 (in million of U.S. dollars)	
Unrealized gain related to revaluation of land	$100
Unrealized loss related to available for sale securities	(60)
Unrealized gain related to revaluation of intangibles	80
Items not recognized on the income statement	120
Net income	400
Total recognized income and expense	$520
Cumulative effect of a change in accounting principle	$118

(Supplementary information in the notes to the financial statements is required to show other changes in capital accounts resulting from transactions with owners as well as changes in retained earnings.)

If a company presents information by means of a SoRIE, it would not prepare a traditional statement of stockholders' equity.

 ON THE HORIZON

The IASB and FASB are working on a project that would rework the structure of financial statements. In phase 1 of this project, a major focus is on the reporting of revenues and expenses. What appears likely is an amendment to *IAS 1* that would bring it largely into line with the equivalent U.S. standard, *SFAS No. 130*, "Reporting of Comprehensive Income," discussed in this chapter. A proposed amendment to *IAS 1* would present all income and expenses separately from changes in equity that arise from transactions with its owners. Companies would have a choice of presenting income and expenses in a single statement or in two statements (the two approaches discussed in this chapter). The option to report this information solely in the statement of stockholders' equity or by use of the SoRIE approach would not be permitted.

The second stage of this project will address the issue of how to classify various items in the income statement. A main goal of this new approach is to provide information that better represents how businesses are run. In addition, this approach draws attention away from just one number—net income.

ACCOUNTING, ANALYSIS, PRINCIPLES

Counting Crows Inc. provided the following information for the year 2008: Income tax applicable to income from continuing operations $187,000; income tax applicable to loss on discontinued operations $25,500; income tax applicable to extraordinary gain $32,300; and unrealized holding gain on available for sale securities $17,000, less applicable tax of $2,000.

Extraordinary gain	$95,000	Retained earnings, January 1,	
Loss on discontinued		2008	$600,000
operations	75,000	Cost of goods sold	850,000
Administrative expenses	240,000	Selling expenses	300,000
Rent revenue	40,000	Sales	1,900,000
Cash dividends declared	80,000		

Shares outstanding during 2008 were100,000.

Accounting

a   Prepare a single step income statement for 2008.

b   Prepare a statement of retained earnings for 2008.

c   Prepare a statement of comprehensive income using the second income statement format.

Analysis

Explain how a multiple-step income statement format can provide useful information to a financial statement user.

Principles

In a recent meeting with its auditor, Counting Crows's management argued that the company should be able to prepare a pro forma income statement with some one-time administrative expenses reported similar to extraordinary items and discontinued operations. Is such reporting consistent with the qualitative characteristics of accounting information as discussed in the conceptual framework? Explain.

Solution

Accounting

a

Counting Crows Inc.
Income Statement
For the Year Ended December 31, 2008

Revenues	
Sales	$1,900,000
Rent revenue	40,000
Total revenues	1,940,000
Expenses	
Cost of goods sold	850,000
Selling expenses	300,000
Administrative expenses	240,000
Total expenses	1,390,000

Income from continuing operations before income tax		550,000
Income tax		187,000
Income from continuing operations		363,000
Discontinued operations		
Loss on discontinued operations	$75,000	
Less: Applicable income tax reduction	25,500	49,500
Income before extraordinary items		313,500
Extraordinary items		
Extraordinary gain	95,000	
Less: Applicable income tax	32,300	62,700
Net income		$ 376,200
Per share of common stock		
Income from continuing operations ($363,000 ÷ 100,000)		$3.63
Loss on discontinued operations, net of tax		(0.50)
Income before extraordinary items ($313,500 ÷ 100,000)		3.13
Extraordinary gain, net of tax		0.63
Net income ($376,200 ÷ 100,000)		$3.76

b

Counting Crows Inc.
Retained Earnings Statement
For the Year Ended December 31, 2008

Retained earnings, January 1	$600,000
Net income	376,200
	$976,200
Dividends declared	(80,000)
Retained earnings, December 31	$896,200

c

Counting Crows Inc.
Statement of Comprehensive Income
For the Year Ended December 31, 2008

Net income	$376,200
Other comprehensive income	
Unrealized holding gain, net of tax	15,000
Comprehensive income	$391,200

Analysis

The multiple-step income statement recognizes important relationships between income statement elements. For example, by separating operating transactions from nonoperating transactions, the statement user can distinguish between elements with differing implications for future operating results. In addition, the multiple-step format generally matches costs and expenses with related revenues (e.g., cost of goods sold with sales to yield a gross profit measure). Finally, the multiple-step format highlights certain intermediate components of income that analysts use to compute ratios for assessing the performance of the company.

Principles

Pro forma reporting is inconsistent with the conceptual framework's qualitative characteristic of comparability. For example, similar to the discussion in the opening story, if Counting Crows Inc. classifies some items in a pro forma manner but other companies do not, investors and creditors will not be able to compare the reported incomes. This is the reason the SEC issued Regulation G, which requires companies that issue pro forma income reports to provide reconciliation to income measured under GAAP, which interested parties can then compare across companies.

Key Terms

accumulated other comprehensive income, 224
appropriated retained earnings, 222
capital maintenance approach, 202 (ftn)
changes in estimates, 216
comprehensive income, 222
current operating performance approach, 209
discontinued operation, 210
earnings management, 201
earnings per share, 220
extraordinary items, 211
income statement, 200

intraperiod tax allocation, 218
irregular items, 209
modified all-inclusive concept, 209
multiple-step income statement, 204
other comprehensive income, 222
prior period adjustments, 216
quality of earnings, 201
single-step income statement, 203
statement of stockholders' equity, 224
transaction approach, 202

Summary of Learning Objectives

1 Understand the uses and limitations of an income statement. The income statement provides investors and creditors with information that helps them predict the amounts, timing, and uncertainty of future cash flows. Also, the income statement helps users determine the risk (level of uncertainty) of not achieving particular cash flows. The limitations of an income statement are: (1) The statement does not include many items that contribute to general growth and well-being of a company. (2) Income numbers are often affected by the accounting methods used. (3) Income measures are subject to estimates.

The *transaction approach* focuses on the activities that occurred during a given period. Instead of presenting only a net change in net assets, it discloses the components of the change. The transaction approach to income measurement requires the use of revenue, expense, loss, and gain accounts.

2 Prepare a single-step income statement. In a single-step income statement, just two groupings exist: revenues and expenses. Expenses are deducted from revenues to arrive at net income or loss—a single subtraction. Frequently, companies report income tax separately as the last item before net income.

3 Prepare a multiple-step income statement. A multiple-step income statement shows two further classifications: (1) a separation of operating results from those obtained through the subordinate or nonoperating activities of the company; and (2) a classification of expenses by functions, such as merchandising or manufacturing, selling, and administration.

4 Explain how to report irregular items. Companies generally close irregular gains or losses or nonrecurring items to Income Summary and include them in the income statement as follows: (1) Discontinued operations of a component of a business are classified as a separate item, after continuing operations. (2) The unusual, material, nonrecurring items that are significantly different from the customary business activities are shown in a separate section for extraordinary items, below discontinued operations. (3) Other items of a material amount that are of an unusual or nonrecurring nature and are not considered extraordinary are separately disclosed as a component of continuing operations. Changes in accounting principle and corrections of errors are adjusted through retained earnings.

5 Explain intraperiod tax allocation. Companies should relate the tax expense for the year to specific items on the income statement to provide a more informative disclosure to statement users. This procedure, intraperiod tax allocation, relates the income tax expense for the fiscal period to the following items that affect the amount of the tax provisions: (1) income from continuing operations, (2) discontinued operations, and (3) extraordinary items.

6 Identify where to report earnings per share information. Because of the inherent dangers of focusing attention solely on earnings per share, the profession concluded that companies must disclose earnings per share on the face of the income statement. A company that reports a discontinued operation or an extraordinary item must report per share amounts for these line items either on the face of the income statement or in the notes to the financial statements.

7 Prepare a retained earnings statement. The retained earnings statement should disclose net income (loss), dividends, adjustments due to changes in accounting principles, error corrections, and restrictions of retained earnings.

8 Explain how to report other comprehensive income. Companies report the components of other comprehensive income in a second statement, a combined statement of comprehensive income, or in a statement of stockholders' equity.

REVIEW EXERCISE

Presented below are ten income statements items from Ritter Corporation for the year ended December 31, 2008.

Sales	$3,200,000
Cost of goods sold	1,650,000
Interest revenue	10,000
Loss from abandonment of plant assets	60,000
Gain from extinguishment of debt	100,000
Selling expenses	340,000
Administrative expenses	280,000
Effect of change in estimated useful lives of fixed assets	50,000
Loss from earthquake (unusual and infrequent)	40,000
Gain on disposal of a component of Ritter's business	90,000

Instructions

Using the information above, prepare a condensed multiple-step income statement. Assume a tax rate of 30% and 100,000 shares of common stock outstanding during 2008.

Solution

Ritter Corporation
Income Statement
For the Year Ended December 31, 2008

Sales		$3,200,000
Cost of goods sold		1,650,000
Gross profit		1,550,000
Selling expenses	$340,000	
Administrative expenses	280,000	620,000
Income from operations		930,000
Other revenues and gains		
Interest revenue	10,000	
Gain on debt extinguishment	100,000	110,000
Other expenses and losses		
Loss from plant abandonment		(60,000)
Income before income taxes		980,000
Income taxes (30%)		294,000
Income from continuing operations		686,000
Discontinued operations		
Gain from disposal of component of business	90,000	
Less: Applicable income tax	27,000	63,000
Income before extraordinary items		749,000
Extraordinary items		
Loss from earthquake	40,000	
Less: Applicable income tax	12,000	(28,000)
Net income		$721,000

(continued)

Per share of common stock	
Income from continuing operations	$6.86
Discontinued operations	0.63
Income before extraordinary items	7.49
Extraordinary item, loss from earthquake, net of tax	(0.28)
Net income	$7.21

Questions

1 What kinds of questions about future cash flows do investors and creditors attempt to answer with information in the income statement?

2 How can information based on past transactions be used to predict future cash flows?

3 Identify at least two situations in which important changes in value are not reported in the income statement.

4 Identify at least two situations in which application of different accounting methods or accounting estimates results in difficulties in comparing companies.

5 Explain the transaction approach to measuring income. Why is the transaction approach to income measurement preferable to other ways of measuring income?

6 What is earnings management?

7 How can earnings management affect the quality of earnings?

8 Why should caution be exercised in the use of the income figure derived in an income statement? What are the objectives of generally accepted accounting principles in their application to the income statement?

9 A *Wall Street Journal* article noted that **MicroStrategy** reported higher income than its competitors by using a more aggressive policy for recognizing revenue on future upgrades to its products. Some contend that MicroStrategy's quality of earnings is low. What does the term "quality of earnings" mean?

10 What is the major distinction (a) between revenues and gains and (b) between expenses and losses?

11 What are the advantages and disadvantages of the single-step income statement?

12 What is the basis for distinguishing between operating and nonoperating items?

13 Distinguish between the modified all-inclusive income statement and the current operating performance income statement. According to present generally accepted accounting principles, which is recommended? Explain.

14 How should correction of errors be reported in the financial statements?

15 Discuss the appropriate treatment in the financial statements of each of the following.

(a) An amount of $113,000 realized in excess of the cash surrender value of an insurance policy on the life of one of the founders of the company who died during the year.

(b) A profit-sharing bonus to employees computed as a percentage of net income.

(c) Additional depreciation on factory machinery because of an error in computing depreciation for the previous year.

(d) Rent received from subletting a portion of the office space.

(e) A patent infringement suit, brought 2 years ago against the company by another company, was settled this year by a cash payment of $725,000.

(f) A reduction in the Allowance for Doubtful Accounts balance, because the account appears to be considerably in excess of the probable loss from uncollectible receivables.

16 Indicate where the following items would ordinarily appear on the financial statements of Allepo, Inc. for the year 2008.

(a) The service life of certain equipment was changed from 8 to 5 years. If a 5-year life had been used previously, additional depreciation of $425,000 would have been charged.

(b) In 2008 a flood destroyed a warehouse that had a book value of $1,600,000. Floods are rare in this locality.

(c) In 2008 the company wrote off $1,000,000 of inventory that was considered obsolete.

(d) An income tax refund related to the 2005 tax year was received.

(e) In 2005, a supply warehouse with an expected useful life of 7 years was erroneously expensed.

(f) Allepo, Inc. changed from weighted-average to FIFO inventory pricing.

17 Give the section of a multiple-step income statement in which each of the following is shown.

(a) Loss on inventory write-down.

(b) Loss from strike.

(c) Bad debt expense.

(d) Loss on disposal of a component of the business.

(e) Gain on sale of machinery.

(f) Interest revenue.

(g) Depreciation expense.

(h) Material write-offs of notes receivable.

18 Barry Zito Land Development, Inc. purchased land for $70,000 and spent $30,000 developing it. It then sold the land for $160,000. Tom Glavine Manufacturing purchased land for a future plant site for $100,000. Due to a change in plans, Glavine later sold the land for $160,000. Should these two companies report the land sales, both at gains of $60,000, in a similar manner?

19 You run into Rex Grossman at a party and begin discussing financial statements. Rex says, "I prefer the single-step income statement because the multiple-step format generally overstates income." How should you respond to Rex?

20 Federer Corporation has eight expense accounts in its general ledger which could be classified as selling expenses. Should Federer report these eight expenses separately in its income statement or simply report one total amount for selling expenses?

21 El Duque Investments reported an unusual gain from the sale of certain assets in its 2008 income statement. How does intraperiod tax allocation affect the reporting of this unusual gain?

22 What effect does intraperiod tax allocation have on reported net income?

23 Letterman Company computed earnings per share as follows.

$$\frac{\text{Net income}}{\text{Common shares outstanding at year-end}}$$

Letterman has a simple capital structure. What possible errors might the company have made in the computation? Explain.

24 Governator Corporation reported 2008 earnings per share of $7.21. In 2009, Governator reported earnings per share as follows.

On income before extraordinary item	$6.40
On extraordinary item	1.88
On net income	$8.28

Is the increase in earnings per share from $7.21 to $8.28 a favorable trend?

25 What is meant by "tax allocation within a period"? What is the justification for such practice?

26 When does tax allocation within a period become necessary? How should this allocation be handled?

27 During 2008, Natsume Sozeki Company earned income of $1,000,000 before income taxes and realized a gain of $450,000 on a government-forced condemnation sale of a division plant facility. The income is subject to income taxation at the rate of 34%. The gain on the sale of the plant is taxed at 30%. Proper accounting suggests that the unusual gain be reported as an extraordinary item. Illustrate an appropriate presentation of these items in the income statement.

28 On January 30, 2007, a suit was filed against Pierogi Corporation under the Environmental Protection Act. On August 6, 2008, Pierogi Corporation agreed to settle the action and pay $920,000 in damages to certain current and former employees. How should this settlement be reported in the 2008 financial statements? Discuss.

29 Tiger Paper Company decided to close two small pulp mills in Conway, New Hampshire, and Corvallis, Oregon. Would these closings be reported in a separate section entitled "Discontinued operations after income from continuing operations"? Discuss.

30 What major types of items are reported in the retained earnings statement?

31. Generally accepted accounting principles usually require the use of accrual accounting to "fairly present" income. If the cash receipts and disbursements method of accounting will "clearly reflect" taxable income, why does this method not usually also "fairly present" income?

32 State some of the more serious problems encountered in seeking to achieve the ideal measurement of periodic net income. Explain what accountants do as a practical alternative.

33 What is meant by the terms *elements* and *items* as they relate to the income statement? Why might items have to be disclosed in the income statement?

34 What are the three ways that other comprehensive income may be displayed (reported)?

35 How should the disposal of a component of a business be disclosed in the income statement?

Brief Exercises

(LO 2)   **BE5-1**   Tim Allen Co. had sales revenue of $540,000 in 2008. Other items recorded during the year were:

Cost of goods sold	$320,000
Wage expense	120,000
Income tax expense	25,000
Increase in value of company reputation	15,000
Other operating expenses	10,000
Unrealized gain on value of patents	20,000

Prepare a single-step income statement for Allen for 2008. Allen has 100,000 shares of stock outstanding.

(LO 2)   **BE5-2**   Turner Corporation had net sales of $2,400,000 and interest revenue of $31,000 during 2008. Expenses for 2008 were: cost of goods sold $1,250,000; administrative expenses $212,000; selling expenses $280,000; interest expense $45,000. Turner's tax rate is 30%. The corporation had 100,000 shares of common stock authorized and 70,000 shares issued and outstanding during 2008. Prepare a single-step income statement for the year ended December 31, 2008.

(LO 3)   **BE5-3**   Using the information provided in BE5-2, prepare a condensed multiple-step income statement for Turner Corporation.

(LO 3, 4)   **BE5-4**   Green Day Corporation had income from continuing operations of $12,600,000 in 2008. During 2008, it disposed of its restaurant division at an after-tax loss of $189,000. Prior to disposal, the division operated at a loss of $315,000 (net of tax) in 2008. Green Day had 10,000,000 shares of common stock outstanding during 2008. Prepare a partial income statement for Green Day beginning with income from continuing operations.

(LO 4, 5)   **BE5-5**   J. Depp Corporation had income before income taxes for 2008 of $7,300,000. In addition, it suffered an unusual and infrequent pretax loss of $770,000 from a volcano eruption. The corporation's tax rate is 30%. Prepare a partial income statement for J. Depp beginning with income before income taxes. The corporation had 5,000,000 shares of common stock outstanding during 2008.

(LO 4)   **BE5-6**   During 2008 Lebron James Company changed from FIFO to weighted-average inventory pricing. Pretax income in 2007 and 2006 (James's first year of operations) under FIFO was $160,000 and $180,000, respectively. Pretax income using weighted-average pricing in the prior years would have been $145,000 in 2007 and $170,000 in 2006. In 2008, Lebron James Company reported pretax income (using weighted-average pricing) of $190,000. Show comparative income statements for Lebron James Company, beginning with "Income before income tax," as presented on the 2008 income statement. (The tax rate in all years is 30%.)

(LO 4)   **BE5-7**   Jana Kingston Company has recorded bad debt expense in the past at a rate of $1\frac{1}{2}\%$ of net sales. In 2008, Kingston decides to increase its estimate to 2%. If the new rate had been used in prior years, cumulative bad debt expense would have been $380,000 instead of $285,000. In 2008, bad debt expense will be $120,000 instead of $90,000. If Kingston's tax rate is 30%, what amount should it report as the cumulative effect of changing the estimated bad debt rate?

(LO 6)   **BE5-8**   In 2008, Stills Corporation reported net income of $1,200,000. It declared and paid preferred stock dividends of $250,000. During 2008, Stills had a weighted average of 190,000 common shares outstanding. Compute Stllls's 2008 earnings per share.

(LO 7)   **BE5-9**   Lincoln Corporation has retained earnings of $675,000 at January 1, 2008. Net income during 2008 was $2,400,000, and cash dividends declared and paid during 2008 totaled $75,000. Prepare a retained earnings statement for the year ended December 31, 2008.

(LO 4, 7)   **BE5-10**   Using the information from BE5-9, prepare a retained earnings statement for the year ended December 31, 2008. Assume an error was discovered: land costing $80,000 (net of tax) was charged to repairs expense in 2005.

(LO 8)   **BE5-11**   On January 1, 2008, Creative Works Inc. had cash and common stock of $60,000. At that date the company had no other asset, liability or equity balances. On January 2, 2008, it purchased for cash $20,000 of equity securities that it classified as available-for-sale. It received cash dividends of $3,000 during the year on these securities. In addition, it has an unrealized holding gain on these securities of $5,000 net of tax. Determine the following amounts for 2008: (a) net income; (b) comprehensive income; (c) other comprehensive income; and (d) accumulated other comprehensive income (end of 2008).

Exercises

E5-1 **(Computation of Net Income)**   Presented below are changes in all the account balances of Fritz Reiner Furniture Co. during the current year, except for retained earnings.

(LO 2)

	Increase (Decrease)		Increase (Decrease)
Cash	$ 79,000	Accounts Payable	$(51,000)
Accounts Receivable (net)	45,000	Bonds Payable	82,000
Inventory	127,000	Common Stock	125,000
Investments	(47,000)	Additional Paid-in Capital	13,000

Instructions

Compute the net income for the current year, assuming that there were no entries in the Retained Earnings account except for net income and a dividend declaration of $19,000 which was paid in the current year.

E5-2 **(Income Statement Items)**   Presented below are certain account balances of Paczki Products Co.

(LO 2)

Rental revenue	$ 6,500	Sales discounts	$ 7,800
Interest expense	12,700	Selling expenses	99,400
Beginning retained earnings	114,400	Sales	390,000
Ending retained earnings	134,000	Income tax	31,000
Dividend revenue	71,000	Cost of goods sold	184,400
Sales returns	12,400	Administrative expenses	82,500

Instructions

From the foregoing, compute the following: (a) total net revenue, (b) net income, (c) dividends declared during the current year.

E5-3 **(Single-Step Income Statement)**   The financial records of LeRoi Jones Inc. were destroyed by fire at the end of 2008. Fortunately the controller had kept certain statistical data related to the income statement as presented below.

(LO 2)

1. The beginning merchandise inventory was $92,000 and decreased 20% during the current year.
2. Sales discounts amount to $17,000.
3. 20,000 shares of common stock were outstanding for the entire year.
4. Interest expense was $20,000.
5. The income tax rate is 30%.
6. Cost of goods sold amounts to $500,000.
7. Administrative expenses are 20% of cost of goods sold but only 8% of gross sales.
8. Four-fifths of the operating expenses relate to sales activities.

Instructions

From the foregoing information prepare an income statement for the year 2008 in single-step form.

E5-4 **(Multiple-Step and Single-Step)**   Two accountants for the firm of Elwes and Wright are arguing about the merits of presenting an income statement in a multiple-step versus a single-step format. The discussion involves the following 2008 information related to P. Bride Company ($000 omitted).

(LO 2, 3)

Administrative expense	
Officers' salaries	$ 4,900
Depreciation of office furniture and equipment	3,960
Cost of goods sold	60,570
Rental revenue	17,230
Selling expense	
Transportation-out	2,690
Sales commissions	7,980
Depreciation of sales equipment	6,480
Sales	96,500
Income tax	9,070
Interest expense	1,860

Instructions

(a) Prepare an income statement for the year 2008 using the multiple-step form. Common shares outstanding for 2008 total 40,550 (000 omitted).

(b) Prepare an income statement for the year 2008 using the single-step form.

(c) Which one do you prefer? Discuss.

(LO 3, 4)

E5-5 **(Multiple-Step and Extraordinary Items)** The following balances were taken from the books of Alonzo Corp. on December 31, 2008.

Interest revenue	$ 86,000	Accumulated depreciation—equipment	$ 40,000
Cash	51,000	Accumulated depreciation—building	28,000
Sales	1,380,000	Notes receivable	155,000
Accounts receivable	150,000	Selling expenses	194,000
Prepaid insurance	20,000	Accounts payable	170,000
Sales returns and allowances	150,000	Bonds payable	100,000
Allowance for doubtful		Administrative and general	
accounts	7,000	expenses	97,000
Sales discounts	45,000	Accrued liabilities	32,000
Land	100,000	Interest expense	60,000
Equipment	200,000	Notes payable	100,000
Building	140,000	Loss from earthquake damage	
Cost of goods sold	621,000	(extraordinary item)	150,000
		Common stock	500,000
		Retained earnings	21,000

Assume the total effective tax rate on all items is 34%.

Instructions

Prepare a multiple-step income statement; 100,000 shares of common stock were outstanding during the year.

(LO 2, 3)

E5-6 **(Multiple-Step and Single-Step)** The accountant of Kooks Shoe Co. has compiled the following information from the company's records as a basis for an income statement for the year ended December 31, 2008.

Rental revenue	$ 29,000
Interest on notes payable	18,000
Market appreciation on land above cost	31,000
Wages and salaries—sales	114,800
Materials and supplies—sales	17,600
Income tax	37,400
Wages and salaries—administrative	135,900
Other administrative expenses	51,700
Cost of goods sold	496,000
Net sales	980,000
Depreciation on plant assets (70% selling, 30% administrative)	65,000
Cash dividends declared	16,000

There were 20,000 shares of common stock outstanding during the year.

Instructions

(a) Prepare a multiple-step income statement.

(b) Prepare a single-step income statement.

(c) Which format do you prefer? Discuss.

(LO 2, 4, 6)

E5-7 **(Income Statement, EPS)** Presented below are selected ledger accounts of Tucker Corporation as of December 31, 2008.

Cash	$ 50,000
Administrative expenses	100,000
Selling expenses	80,000
Net sales	540,000
Cost of goods sold	210,000
Cash dividends declared (2008)	20,000
Cash dividends paid (2008)	15,000
Discontinued operations (loss before income taxes)	40,000

Depreciation expense, not recorded in 2007	30,000
Retained earnings, December 31, 2007	90,000
Effective tax rate 30%	

Instructions

(a) Compute net income for 2008.

(b) Prepare a partial income statement beginning with income from continuing operations before income tax, and including appropriate earnings per share information. Assume 10,000 shares of common stock were outstanding during 2008.

E5-8 **(Multiple-Step Income Statement with Retained Earnings)** Presented below is information related to Ivan Calderon Corp. for the year 2008.

(LO 3, 4, 5, 6, 7)

Net sales	$1,300,000	Write-off of inventory due to obsolescence	$ 80,000
Cost of goods sold	780,000	Depreciation expense omitted by accident in 2007	55,000
Selling expenses	65,000	Casualty loss (extraordinary item) before taxes	50,000
Administrative expenses	48,000	Cash dividends declared	45,000
Dividend revenue	20,000	Retained earnings at December 31, 2007	980,000
Interest revenue	7,000	Effective tax rate of 34% on all items	

Instructions

(a) Prepare a multiple-step income statement for 2008. Assume that 60,000 shares of common stock are outstanding.

(b) Prepare a separate retained earnings statement for 2008.

E5-9 **(Extraordinary Items)** Jeff Foxworthy, vice-president of finance for Gorillaz Company, has recently been asked to discuss with the company's division controllers the proper accounting for extraordinary items. Jeff Foxworthy prepared the factual situations presented below as a basis for discussion.

(LO 3, 4)

1. An earthquake destroys one of the oil refineries owned by a large multinational oil company. Earthquakes are rare in this geographical location.

2. A publicly held company has incurred a substantial loss in the unsuccessful registration of a bond issue.

3. A large portion of a cigarette manufacturer's tobacco crops are destroyed by a hailstorm. Severe damage from hailstorms is rare in this locality.

4. A large diversified company sells a block of shares from its portfolio of securities acquired for investment purposes.

5. A company that operates a chain of warehouses sells the excess land surrounding one of its warehouses. When the company buys property to establish a new warehouse, it usually buys more land than it expects to use for the warehouse with the expectation that the land will appreciate in value. Twice during the past 5 years the company sold excess land.

6. A company experiences a material loss in the repurchase of a large bond issue that has been outstanding for 3 years. The company regularly repurchases bonds of this nature.

7. A railroad experiences an unusual flood loss to part of its track system. Flood losses normally occur every 3 or 4 years.

8. A machine tool company sells the only land it owns. The land was acquired 10 years ago for future expansion, but shortly thereafter the company abandoned all plans for expansion but decided to hold the land for appreciation.

Instructions

Determine whether the foregoing items should be classified as extraordinary items. Present a rationale for your position.

E5-10 **(Classification of Income Statement Items)** As audit partner for Noriyuki and Morita, you are in charge of reviewing the classification of unusual items that have occurred during the current year. The following material items have come to your attention.

(LO 3, 4)

1. A merchandising company incorrectly overstated its ending inventory 2 years ago by a material amount. Inventory for all other periods is correctly computed.

2. An automobile dealer sells for $137,000 an extremely rare 1930 S type Invicta which it purchased for $21,000 10 years ago. The Invicta is the only such display item the dealer owns.

3. A drilling company during the current year extended the estimated useful life of certain drilling equipment from 9 to 15 years. As a result, depreciation for the current year was materially lowered.

4. A retail outlet changed its computation for bad debt expense from 1% to ½ of 1% of sales because of changes in its customer clientele.

5. A mining concern sells a foreign subsidiary engaged in uranium mining, although it (the seller) continues to engage in uranium mining in other countries.

6. A company changes from the average cost method to the FIFO method for inventory costing.

7. A construction company, at great expense, prepared a major proposal for a government loan. The loan is not approved.

8. A water pump manufacturer has had large losses resulting from a strike by its employees early in the year.

9. Depreciation for a prior period was incorrectly understated by $950,000. The error was discovered in the current year.

10. A large sheep rancher suffered a major loss because the state required that all sheep in the state be killed to halt the spread of a rare disease. Such a situation has not occurred in the state for 20 years.

11. A food distributor that sells wholesale to supermarket chains and to fast-food restaurants (two distinguishable classes of customers) decides to discontinue the division that sells to one of the two classes of customers.

Instructions

From the foregoing information, indicate in what section of the income statement or retained earnings statement these items should be classified. Provide a brief rationale for your position.

(LO 6) **E5-11** **(Earnings per Share)** The stockholders' equity section of Tkachuk Corporation appears below as of December 31, 2008.

8% preferred stock, $50 par value, authorized		
100,000 shares, outstanding 90,000 shares		$ 4,500,000
Common stock, $1.00 par, authorized and issued 10 million shares		10,000,000
Additional paid-in capital		20,500,000
Retained earnings	$134,000,000	
Net income	33,000,000	167,000,000
		$202,000,000

Net income for 2008 reflects a total effective tax rate of 34%. Included in the net income figure is a loss of $18,000,000 (before tax) as a result of a major casualty, which should be classified as an extraordinary item. Preferred stock dividends of $360,000 were declared and paid in 2008. Dividends of $1,000,000 were declared and paid to common stockholders in 2008.

Instructions

Compute earnings per share data as it should appear on the income statement of Tkachuk Corporation.

(LO 3, 4, 5, 6) **E5-12** **(Condensed Income Statement—Periodic Inventory Method)** Presented below are selected ledger accounts of Spock Corporation at December 31, 2008.

Cash	$ 185,000	Sales salaries	$284,000
Merchandise inventory	535,000	Office salaries	346,000
Sales	4,275,000	Purchase returns	15,000
Advances from customers	117,000	Sales returns	79,000
Purchases	2,786,000	Transportation-in	72,000
Sales discounts	34,000	Accounts receivable	142,500
Purchase discounts	27,000	Sales commissions	83,000
Travel and entertainment—sales	69,000	Telephone—sales	17,000
Accounting and legal services	33,000	Utilities—office	32,000
Insurance expense—office	24,000	Miscellaneous office expenses	8,000
Advertising	54,000	Rental revenue	240,000
Transportation-out	93,000	Extraordinary loss (before tax)	70,000
Depreciation of office equipment	48,000	Interest expense	176,000
Depreciation of sales equipment	36,000	Common stock ($10 par)	900,000

Spock's effective tax rate on all items is 34%. A physical inventory indicates that the ending inventory is $686,000.

Instructions

Prepare a condensed 2008 income statement for Spock Corporation.

E5-13 (Retained Earnings Statement) Carlos Zambrano Corporation began operations on January 1, 2005. **(LO 7)**
During its first 3 years of operations, Zambrano reported net income and declared dividends as follows.

	Net income	Dividends declared
2005	$ 40,000	$ –0–
2006	125,000	50,000
2007	160,000	50,000

The following information relates to 2008.

Income before income tax	$240,000
Prior period adjustment: understatement of 2006 depreciation expense (before taxes)	$ 25,000
Cumulative decrease in income from change in inventory methods (before taxes)	$ 35,000
Dividends declared (of this amount, $25,000 will be paid on Jan. 15, 2009)	$100,000
Effective tax rate	40%

Instructions

(a) Prepare a 2008 retained earnings statement for Carlos Zambrano Corporation.
(b) Assume Carlos Zambrano Corp. restricted retained earnings in the amount of $70,000 on December 31, 2008. After this action, what would Zambrano report as total retained earnings in its December 31, 2008, balance sheet?

E5-14 (Earnings per Share) At December 31, 2007, Shiga Naoya Corporation had the following stock **(LO 4,**
outstanding. **5, 6)**

10% cumulative preferred stock, $100 par, 107,500 shares	$10,750,000
Common stock, $5 par, 4,000,000 shares	20,000,000

During 2008, Shiga Naoya did not issue any additional common stock. The following also occurred during 2008.

Income from continuing operations before taxes	$23,650,000
Discontinued operations (loss before taxes)	$ 3,225,000
Preferred dividends declared	$ 1,075,000
Common dividends declared	$ 2,200,000
Effective tax rate	35%

Instructions

Compute earnings per share data as it should appear in the 2008 income statement of Shiga Naoya Corporation. (Round to two decimal places.)

E5-15 (Change in Accounting Principle) Tim Mattke Company began operations in 2006 and for simplicity **(LO 4,**
reasons, adopted weighted-average pricing for inventory. In 2008, in accordance with other companies in its indus- **5, 6)**
try, Mattke changed its inventory pricing to FIFO. The pretax income data is reported below.

Year	Weighted-Average	FIFO
2006	$370,000	$395,000
2007	390,000	430,000
2008	410,000	450,000

Instructions

(a) What is Mattke's net income in 2008? Assume a 35% tax rate in all years.
(b) Compute the cumulative effect of the change in accounting principle from weighted-average to FIFO inventory pricing.
(c) Show comparative income statements for Tim Mattke Company, beginning with income before income tax, as presented on the 2008 income statement.

E5-16 (Comprehensive Income) Roxanne Carter Corporation reported the following for 2008: net sales **(LO 3,**
$1,200,000; cost of goods sold $750,000; selling and administrative expenses $320,000; and an unrealized hold- **8)**
ing gain on available-for-sale securities $18,000.

Instructions

Prepare a statement of comprehensive income, using the two-income statement format. Ignore income taxes and earnings per share.

(LO 7, 8)

E5-17 **(Comprehensive Income)** C. Reither Co. reports the following information for 2008: sales revenue $700,000; cost of goods sold $500,000; operating expenses $80,000; and an unrealized holding loss on available-for-sale securities for 2008 of $60,000. It declared and paid a cash dividend of $10,000 in 2008.

C. Reither Co. has January 1, 2008, balances in common stock $350,000; accumulated other comprehensive income $80,000; and retained earnings $90,000. It issued no stock during 2008.

Instructions

Prepare a statement of stockholders' equity.

(LO 2, 4, 5, 6, 7, 8)

E5-18 **(Various Reporting Formats)** The following information was taken from the records of Roland Carlson Inc. for the year 2008. Income tax applicable to income from continuing operations $187,000; income tax applicable to loss on discontinued operations $25,500; income tax applicable to extraordinary gain $32,300; income tax applicable to extraordinary loss $20,400; and unrealized holding gain on available-for-sale securities $15,000.

Extraordinary gain	$ 95,000	Cash dividends declared	$ 150,000
Loss on discontinued operations	75,000	Retained earnings January 1, 2008	600,000
Administrative expenses	240,000	Cost of goods sold	850,000
Rent revenue	40,000	Selling expenses	300,000
Extraordinary loss	60,000	Sales	1,900,000

Shares outstanding during 2008 were 100,000.

Instructions

(a) Prepare a single-step income statement for 2008.
(b) Prepare a retained earnings statement for 2008.
(c) Show how comprehensive income is reported using the second income statement format.

 **See the book's companion website, at www.wiley.com/college/warfield, for Additional Exercises**

Problems

(LO 3, 4, 5, 6, 7)

P5-1 **(Multiple-Step Income, Retained Earnings)** Presented below is information related to P. J. Harvey Company for 2008.

Retained earnings balance, January 1, 2008	$ 980,000
Sales for the year	25,000,000
Cost of goods sold	17,000,000
Interest revenue	70,000
Selling and administrative expenses	4,700,000
Write-off of goodwill (not tax deductible)	820,000
Income taxes for 2008	905,000
Gain on the sale of investments (normal recurring)	110,000
Loss due to flood damage—extraordinary item (net of tax)	390,000
Loss on the disposition of the wholesale division (net of tax)	440,000
Loss on operations of the wholesale division (net of tax)	90,000
Dividends declared on common stock	250,000
Dividends declared on preferred stock	70,000

Instructions

Prepare a multiple-step income statement and a retained earnings statement. P. J. Harvey Company decided to discontinue its entire wholesale operations and to retain its manufacturing operations. On September 15, P. J. Harvey sold the wholesale operations to Rogers Company. During 2008, there were 300,000 shares of common stock outstanding all year.

(LO 2, 6, 7)

P5-2 **(Single-Step Income, Retained Earnings, Periodic Inventory)** Presented on page 239 is the trial balance of Mary J. Blige Corporation at December 31, 2008.

Mary J. Blige Corporation
Trial Balance
Year Ended December 31, 2008

	Debits	Credits
Purchase Discounts		$ 10,000
Cash	$ 205,100	
Accounts Receivable	105,000	
Rent Revenue		18,000
Retained Earnings		260,000
Salaries Payable		18,000
Sales		1,000,000
Notes Receivable	110,000	
Accounts Payable		49,000
Accumulated Depreciation—Equipment		28,000
Sales Discounts	14,500	
Sales Returns	17,500	
Notes Payable		70,000
Selling Expenses	232,000	
Administrative Expenses	99,000	
Common Stock		300,000
Income Tax Expense	38,500	
Cash Dividends	45,000	
Allowance for Doubtful Accounts		5,000
Supplies	14,000	
Freight-in	20,000	
Land	70,000	
Equipment	140,000	
Bonds Payable		100,000
Gain on Sale of Land		30,000
Accumulated Depreciation—Building		19,600
Merchandise Inventory	89,000	
Building	98,000	
Purchases	610,000	
Totals	$1,907,600	$1,907,600

A physical count of inventory on December 31 resulted in an inventory amount of $124,000.

Instructions

Prepare a single-step income statement and a retained earnings statement. Assume that the only changes in retained earnings during the current year were from net income and dividends. Thirty thousand shares of common stock were outstanding the entire year.

P5-3 (Irregular Items) Tony Rich Inc. reported income from continuing operations before taxes during 2008 of $790,000. Additional transactions occurring in 2008 but not considered in the $790,000 are as follows.

(LO 4, 5, 6)

1. The corporation experienced an uninsured flood loss (extraordinary) in the amount of $80,000 during the year. The tax rate on this item is 46%.

2. At the beginning of 2006, the corporation purchased a machine for $54,000 (salvage value of $9,000) that had a useful life of 6 years. The bookkeeper used straight-line depreciation for 2006, 2007, and 2008 but failed to deduct the salvage value in computing the depreciation base.

3. Sale of securities held as a part of its portfolio resulted in a loss of $57,000 (pretax).

4. When its president died, the corporation realized $110,000 from an insurance policy. The cash surrender value of this policy had been carried on the books as an investment in the amount of $46,000 (the gain is nontaxable).

5. The corporation disposed of its recreational division at a loss of $115,000 before taxes. Assume that this transaction meets the criteria for discontinued operations.

6. The corporation decided to change its method of inventory pricing from average cost to the FIFO method. The effect of this change on prior years is to increase 2006 income by $60,000 and decrease 2007 income by $20,000 before taxes. The FIFO method has been used for 2008. The tax rate on these items is 40%.

Instructions

Prepare an income statement for the year 2008 starting with income from continuing operations before taxes. Compute earnings per share as it should be shown on the face of the income statement. Common shares outstanding for the year are 80,000 shares. (Assume a tax rate of 30% on all items, unless indicated otherwise.)

(LO 3, 4, 5, 7)

P5-4 **(Multiple- and Single-Step Income, Retained Earnings)** The following account balances were included in the trial balance of J.R. Reid Corporation at June 30, 2008.

Sales	$1,678,500	Depreciation of office furniture	
Sales discounts	31,150	and equipment	$ 7,250
Cost of goods sold	896,770	Real estate and other local taxes	7,320
Sales salaries	56,260	Bad debt expense—selling	4,850
Sales commissions	97,600	Building expense—prorated	
Travel expense—salespersons	28,930	to administration	9,130
Freight-out	21,400	Miscellaneous office expenses	6,000
Entertainment expense	14,820	Sales returns	62,300
Telephone and Internet expense—sales	9,030	Dividends received	38,000
Depreciation of sales equipment	4,980	Bond interest expense	18,000
Building expense—prorated to sales	6,200	Income taxes	133,000
Miscellaneous selling expenses	4,715	Depreciation understatement due	
Office supplies used	3,450	to error—2005 (net of tax)	17,700
Telephone and Internet expense—		Dividends declared on	
administration	2,820	preferred stock	9,000
		Dividends declared on common	
		stock	32,000

The Retained Earnings account had a balance of $337,000 at July 1, 2007. There are 80,000 shares of common stock outstanding.

Instructions

(a) Using the multiple-step form, prepare an income statement and a retained earnings statement for the year ended June 30, 2008.

(b) Using the single-step form, prepare an income statement and a retained earnings statement for the year ended June 30, 2008.

(LO 4, 5, 6, 7)

P5-5 **(Irregular Items)** Presented below is a combined single-step income and retained earnings statement for Sandy Freewalt Company for 2008.

		(000 omitted)
Net sales		$640,000
Costs and expenses		
Cost of goods sold		500,000
Selling, general, and administrative expenses		66,000
Other, net		17,000
		583,000
Income before income tax		57,000
Income tax		19,400
Net income		37,600
Retained earnings at beginning of period, as previously reported	$141,000	
Adjustment required for correction of error	(7,000)	
Retained earnings at beginning of period, as restated		134,000
Dividends on common stock		(12,200)
Retained earnings at end of period		$159,400

Additional facts are as follows.

1. "Selling, general, and administrative expenses" for 2008 included a usual but infrequently occurring charge of $10,500,000.

2. "Other, net" for 2008 included an extraordinary item (charge) of $9,000,000. If the extraordinary item (charge) had not occurred, income taxes for 2008 would have been $22,400,000 instead of $19,400,000.

3. "Adjustment required for correction of an error" was a result of a change in estimate (useful life of certain assets reduced to 8 years and a catch-up adjustment made).

4. Sandy Freewalt Company disclosed earnings per common share for net income in the notes to the financial statements.

Instructions

Determine from these additional facts whether the presentation of the facts in the Sandy Freewalt Company income and retained earnings statement is appropriate. If the presentation is not appropriate, describe the appropriate presentation and discuss its theoretical rationale. (Do not prepare a revised statement.)

P5-6 **(Retained Earnings Statement, Prior Period Adjustment)**   Below is the retained earnings account for the year 2008 for LeClair Corp.

(LO 4, 5, 7)

Retained earnings, January 1, 2008		$257,600
Add:		
Gain on sale of investments (net of tax)	$41,200	
Net income	84,500	
Refund on litigation with government, related to the year 2005 (net of tax)	21,600	
Recognition of income earned in 2007, but omitted from income statement in that year (net of tax)	25,400	172,700
		430,300
Deduct:		
Loss on discontinued operations (net of tax)	25,000	
Write-off of goodwill (net of tax)	60,000	
Cumulative effect on income of prior years in changing from LIFO to FIFO inventory valuation in 2008 (net of tax)	18,200	
Cash dividends declared	32,000	135,200
Retained earnings, December 31, 2008		$295,100

Instructions

(a) Prepare a corrected retained earnings statement. LeClair Corp. normally sells investments of the type mentioned above. FIFO inventory was used in 2008 to compute net income.

(b) State where the items that do not appear in the corrected retained earnings statement should be shown.

P5-7 **(Income Statement, Irregular Items)**   Rap Corp. has 100,000 shares of common stock outstanding. In 2008, the company reports income from continuing operations before income tax of $1,210,000. Additional transactions not considered in the $1,210,000 are as follows.

(LO 4, 5, 6)

1. In 2008, Rap Corp. sold equipment for $40,000. The machine had originally cost $80,000 and had accumulated depreciation of $36,000. The gain or loss is considered ordinary.

2. The company discontinued operations of one of its subsidiaries during the current year at a loss of $190,000 before taxes. Assume that this transaction meets the criteria for discontinued operations. The loss on operations of the discontinued subsidiary was $90,000 before taxes; the loss from disposal of the subsidiary was $100,000 before taxes.

3. An internal audit discovered that amortization of intangible assets was understated by $35,000 (net of tax) in a prior period. The amount was charged against retained earnings.

4. The company had a gain of $145,000 on the condemnation of much of its property. The gain is taxed at a total effective rate of 40%. Assume that the transaction meets the requirements of an extraordinary item.

Instructions

Analyze the above information and prepare an income statement for the year 2008, starting with income from continuing operations before income tax. Compute earnings per share as it should be shown on the face of the income statement. (Assume a total effective tax rate of 38% on all items, unless otherwise indicated.)

ACCOUNTING IN ACTION

Financial Reporting and Analysis

■ Financial Reporting Issues: The Procter & Gamble Company

AIA5-1   The financial statements of **Procter & Gamble (P&G)** can be accessed at the book's website.

Instructions

Refer to P&G's financial statements and the accompanying notes to answer the following questions.

(a) What type of income statement format does P&G use? Indicate why this format might be used to present income statement information.

(b) What are P&G's primary revenue sources?

(c) Compute P&G's gross profit for each of the years 2004–2006. Explain why gross profit increased in 2006.

(d) Why does P&G make a distinction between operating and nonoperating revenue?

(e) What financial ratios did P&G choose to report in its "Financial Summary" section covering the years 1996–2006?

PEPSICO ■ Comparative Analysis: The Coca-Cola Company and PepsiCo, Inc.

AIA5-2   The financial statements of **The Coca-Cola Company** and **PepsiCo, Inc.** can be accessed at the book's website.

Instructions

Use information found at the book's website to answer the following questions.

(a) What type of income format(s) is used by these two companies? Identify any differences in income statement format between these two companies.

(b) What are the gross profits, operating profits, and net incomes for these two companies over the 3-year period 2004–2006? Which company has had better financial results over this period of time?

(c) Identify the irregular items reported by these two companies in their income statements over the 3-year period 2004–2006. Do these irregular items appear to be significant?

(d) Refer to Coca-Cola's Management Analysis section under "Operations Review." Explain how discussion of "Selling, General and Administrative Expenses" illustrates the income reporting in a condensed income statement.

■ Financial Statement Analysis

AIA5-3   **(Bankruptcy Prediction)**   The Z-score bankruptcy prediction model uses balance sheet and income information to arrive at a Z-score, which analysts can use to predict financial distress:

$$Z = \frac{\text{Working capital}}{\text{Total assets}} \times 1.2 + \frac{\text{Retained earnings}}{\text{Total assets}} \times 1.4 + \frac{\text{EBIT}}{\text{Total assets}} \times 3.3 + \frac{\text{Sales}}{\text{Total assets}} \times .99$$

$$+ \frac{\text{MV equity}}{\text{Total liabilities}} \times 0.6$$

EBIT is earnings before interest and taxes. MV Equity is the market value of common equity, which can be determined by multiplying stock price by shares outstanding.

Following extensive testing, it has been shown that companies with Z-scores above 3.0 are unlikely to fail; those with Z-scores below 1.81 are very likely to fail. While the original model was developed for publicly held manufacturing companies, the model has been modified to apply to companies in various industries, emerging companies, and companies not traded in public markets.

Instructions

(a) Use information in the financial statements of a company like **Walgreens** or **Deere & Co.** to compute the Z-score for the past 2 years.

(b) Interpret your result. Where does the company fall in the financial distress range?

(c) The Z-score uses EBIT as one of its elements. Why do you think this income measure is used?

AIA5-4 **Dresser Industries** provides products and services to oil and natural gas exploration, production, transmission and processing companies. A recent income statement is reproduced below. Dollar amounts are in millions.

Dresser Industries

Income Statement

Sales	$2,697.0
Service revenues	1,933.9
Share of earnings of unconsolidated affiliates	92.4
Total revenues	4,723.3
Cost of sales	1,722.7
Cost of services	1,799.9
Total costs of sales and services	3,522.6
Gross earnings	1,200.7
Selling, engineering, administrative and general expenses	(919.8)
Special charges	(70.0)
Other income (deductions)	
Interest expense	(47.4)
Interest earned	19.1
Other, net	4.8
Earnings before income taxes and other items below	187.4
Income taxes	(79.4)
Minority interest	(10.3)
Earnings from continuing operations	97.7
Discontinued operations	(35.3)
Earnings before extraordinary items	62.4
Extraordinary items	(6.3)
Net earnings	$56.1

Instructions

Assume that 177,636,000 shares of stock were issued and outstanding. Prepare the per-share portion of the income statement. Remember to begin with "Income from continuing operations."

AIA5-5 One of the more closely watched ratios by investors is the price/earnings or P/E ratio. By dividing price per share by earnings per share, analysts get insight into the value the market attaches to a company's earnings. More specifically, a high P/E ratio (in comparison to companies in the same industry) may suggest the stock is overpriced. Also, there is some evidence that companies with low P/E ratios are underpriced and tend to outperform the market. However, the ratio can be misleading.

P/E ratios are sometime misleading because the E (earnings) is subject to a number of assumptions and estimates that could result in overstated earnings and a lower P/E. Some analysts conduct "revenue analysis" to evaluate the quality of an earnings number. Revenues are less subject to management estimates and all earnings must begin with revenues. These analysts also compute the price-to-sales ratio (PSR = price per share ÷ sales per share) to assess whether a company is performing well compared to similar companies. If a company has a price-to-sales ratio significantly higher than its competitors, investors may be betting on a stock that has yet to prove itself. [*Source*: Janice Revell, "Beyond P/E," *Fortune* (May 28, 2001), p. 174.]

Instructions

(a) Identify some of the estimates or assumptions that could result in overstated earnings.

(b) Compute the P/E ratio and the PSR for **Tootsie Roll** and **Hershey's** for 2005.

(c) Use these data to compare the quality of each company's earnings.

■ International Reporting Issues

AIA5-6   Presented below is the income statement for a British company **Avon Rubber PLC**.

Avon Rubber PLC

**Consolidated Profit and Loss Account
for the year ended 30 September**

	Before exceptional items £'000	Exceptional items £'000	Total £'000
Turnover	250,509	–	250,509
Cost of sales	(209,739)	–	(209,739)
Gross profit	40,770	–	40,770
Net operating expenses (including £681,000 (2002; £626,000) goodwill amortisation)	(30,349)	(6,701)	(37,050)
Operating profit	10,421	(6,701)	3,720
Share of profits of joint venture and associate	21	–	21
Total operating profit including joint venture and associate	10,442	(6,701)	3,741
Loss on disposal of fixed assets	—	(1,205)	(1,205)
Loss on disposal of operations	—	(568)	(568)
Profit on ordinary activities before interest	10,442	(8,474)	1,968
Interest receivable	609	–	609
Interest payable	(4,032)	–	(4,032)
Profit /(loss) on ordinary activities before taxation	7,019	(8,474)	(1,455)
Taxation	(2,810)	2,500	(310)
Profit /(loss) on ordinary activities after taxation	4,209	(5,974)	(1,765)
Minority interests	194	–	194
Profit/(loss) for the financial year	4,403	(5,974)	(1,571)
Dividends	(2,031)	–	(2,031)
Retained profit/(loss) for the financial year	2,372	(5,974)	(3,602)
Earnings/(loss) per ordinary share Basic			(5.7)p

Instructions

(a) Review the Avon Rubber income statement and identify at least three differences between the British income statement and an income statement of a U.S. company as presented in the chapter.

(b) Identify any irregular items reported by Avon Rubber. Is the reporting of these irregular items in Avon's income statement similar to reporting of these items in U.S. companies' income statements? Explain.

Concepts for Analysis

AIA5-7 **(Identification of Income Statement Deficiencies)** John Amos Corporation was incorporated and began business on January 1, 2008. It has been successful and now requires a bank loan for additional working capital to finance expansion. The bank has requested an audited income statement for the year 2008. The accountant for John Amos Corporation provides you with the following income statement which John Amos plans to submit to the bank.

John Amos Corporation
Income Statement

Sales		$850,000
Dividends		32,300
Gain on recovery of insurance proceeds from		
earthquake loss (extraordinary)		38,500
		920,800
Less:		
Selling expenses	$101,100	
Cost of goods sold	510,000	
Advertising expense	13,700	
Loss on obsolescence of inventories	34,000	
Loss on discontinued operations	48,600	
Administrative expense	73,400	780,800
Income before income tax		140,000
Income tax		56,000
Net income		$ 84,000

Instructions

Indicate the deficiencies in the income statement presented above. Assume that the corporation desires a single-step income statement.

AIA5-8 **(Income Reporting Deficiencies)** The following represents a recent income statement for **Boeing**  **Company**.

	($ in millions)
Sales	$21,924
Costs and expenses	20,773
Income from operations	1,151
Other income	122
Interest and debt expense	(130)
Earnings before income taxes	1,143
Income taxes	(287)
Net income	$ 856

Instructions

(a) Indicate the deficiencies in the income statement.
(b) What recommendations would you make to Boeing to improve the usefulness of its income statement?

AIA5-9 **(Earnings Management)** Grace Inc. has recently reported steadily increasing income. The company reported income of $20,000 in 2005, $25,000 in 2006, and $30,000 in 2007. A number of market analysts have recommended that investors buy the stock because they expect the steady growth in income to continue. Grace is approaching the end of its fiscal year in 2008, and it again appears to be a good year. However, it has not yet recorded warranty expense.

Based on prior experience, this year's warranty expense should be around $5,000, but some managers have approached the controller to suggest a larger, more conservative warranty expense should be recorded this year.

Income before warranty expense is $43,000. Specifically, by recording an $8,000 warranty accrual this year, Grace could report an increase in income for this year and still be in a position to cover its warranty costs in future years.

Instructions

(a) What is earnings management?

(b) Assume income before warranty expense is $43,000 for both 2008 and 2009 and that total warranty expense over the 2-year period is $10,000. What is the effect of the proposed accounting in 2008? In 2009?

(c) What is the appropriate accounting in this situation?

AIA5-10 **(Income Reporting Items)** Woody Allen Corp. is an entertainment firm that derives approximately 30% of its income from the Casino Royale Division, which manages gambling facilities. As auditor for Woody Allen Corp., you have recently overheard the following discussion between the controller and financial vice-president.

VICE-PRESIDENT: If we sell the Casino Royale Division, it seems ridiculous to segregate the results of the sale in the income statement. Separate categories tend to be absurd and confusing to the stockholders. I believe that we should simply report the gain on the sale as other income or expense without detail.

CONTROLLER: Professional pronouncements would require that we disclose this information separately in the income statement. If a sale of this type is considered unusual and infrequent, it must be reported as an extraordinary item.

VICE-PRESIDENT: What about the walkout we had last month when employees were upset about their commission income? Would this situation not also be an extraordinary item?

CONTROLLER: I am not sure whether this item would be reported as extraordinary or not.

VICE-PRESIDENT: Oh well, it doesn't make any difference because the net effect of all these items is immaterial, so no disclosure is necessary.

Instructions

(a) On the basis of the foregoing discussion, answer the following questions: Who is correct about handling the sale? What would be the correct income statement presentation for the sale of the Casino Royale Division?

(b) How should the walkout by the employees be reported?

(c) What do you think about the vice-president's observation on materiality?

(d) What are the earnings per share implications of these topics?

AIA5-11 **(Identification of Income Statement Weaknesses)** The following financial statement was prepared by employees of Cynthia Taylor Corporation.

Cynthia Taylor Corporation
Income Statement
Year Ended December 31, 2008

Revenues	
Gross sales, including sales taxes	$1,044,300
Less: Returns, allowances, and cash discounts	56,200
Net sales	988,100
Dividends, interest, and purchase discounts	30,250
Recoveries of accounts written off in prior years	13,850
Total revenues	1,032,200
Costs and expenses	
Cost of goods sold, including sales taxes	465,900
Salaries and related payroll expenses	60,500
Rent	19,100
Freight-in and freight-out	3,400
Bad debt expense	27,800
Total costs and expenses	576,700

Income before extraordinary items	455,500
Extraordinary items	
Loss on discontinued styles (Note 1)	71,500
Loss on sale of marketable securities (Note 2)	39,050
Loss on sale of warehouse (Note 3)	86,350
Total extraordinary items	196,900
Net income	$ 258,600
Net income per share of common stock	$2.30

Note 1: New styles and rapidly changing consumer preferences resulted in a $71,500 loss on the disposal of discontinued styles and related accessories.

Note 2: The corporation sold an investment in marketable securities at a loss of $39,050. The corporation normally sells securities of this nature.

Note 3: The corporation sold one of its warehouses at an $86,350 loss.

Instructions

Identify and discuss the weaknesses in classification and disclosure in the single-step income statement above. You should explain why these treatments are weaknesses and what the proper presentation of the items would be in accordance with GAAP.

AIA5-12 **(Comprehensive Income)** Ferguson Arthur, Jr., controller for Jenkins Corporation, is preparing the company's financial statements at year-end. Currently, he is focusing on the income statement and determining the format for reporting comprehensive income. During the year, the company earned net income of $400,000 and had unrealized gains on available-for-sale securities of $20,000. In the previous year net income was $410,000, and the company had no unrealized gains or losses.

Instructions

(a) Show how income and comprehensive income will be reported on a comparative basis for the current and prior years, using the separate income statement format.

(b) Show how income and comprehensive income will be reported on a comparative basis for the current and prior years, using the combined income statement format.

(c) Which format should Arthur recommend?

Professional Tools

■ Ethical Decision Making

AIA5-13 **(Earnings Management)** Arthur Miller, controller for the Salem Corporation, is preparing the company's income statement at year-end. He notes that the company lost a considerable sum on the sale of some equipment it had decided to replace. Since the company has sold equipment routinely in the past, Miller knows the losses cannot be reported as extraordinary. He also does not want to highlight it as a material loss since he feels that will reflect poorly on him and the company. He reasons that if the company had recorded more depreciation during the assets' lives, the losses would not be so great. Since depreciation is included among the company's operating expenses, he wants to report the losses along with the company's expenses, where he hopes it will not be noticed.

Instructions

(a) What are the ethical issues involved?

(b) What should Miller do?

■ Financial Accounting Research (FARS)

AIA5-14 Your client took accounting a number of years ago and was unaware of comprehensive income reporting. He is not convinced that any accounting standards exist for comprehensive income.

Instructions

Using the **Financial Accounting Research System (FARS)** database, respond to the following items. (Provide text strings used in your search.)

(a) What statement addresses comprehensive income directly? When was it issued?

(b) Provide the definition of comprehensive income.

(c) Define classifications within net income; give examples.

(d) Define classifications within other comprehensive income; give examples.

(e) What are reclassification adjustments?

■ Professional Simulation

AIA5-15 Go to the book's website, at **www.wiley.com/college/warfield**, to find an interactive problem that simulates the computerized CPA exam. The professional simulation for this chapter asks you to compute various income amounts.

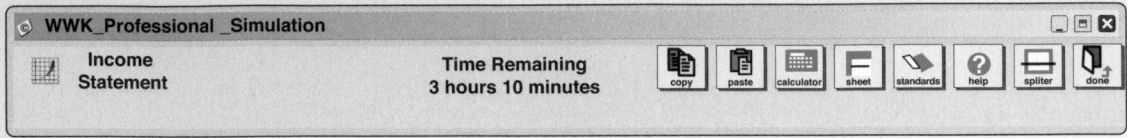

WWK_Professional _Simulation		
Income Statement	Time Remaining 3 hours 10 minutes	copy paste calculator sheet standards help splitter done

What do the numbers mean?

Guideline Answers to Beyond the Numbers Questions

Manage Up, Manage Down, p. 202

Q: If companies "pay a price" when the market discovers the use of cookie jar reserves in prior years, what are some of the incentives to manage earnings down today in order to report better results in the future?

A: As mentioned in the story, companies might wish to impress the market with a steadily increasing income stream in future years. In addition, by reporting higher earnings in future periods, earnings-based management bonuses may be higher and some debt covenants based on earnings (and therefore retained earnings) might be relaxed if higher income is reported in future periods.

Are One-Time Charges Bugging You?, p. 210

Q: Can so-called one-time charges be used to manage earnings similar to cookie jar reserves? Explain.

A: Yes. Take the example of an impairment charge. Consider a company that is already having a bad year and management thinks it might have to record an impairment charge on an asset sometime in the next few years. By taking the impairment charge in the current period ("taking a bath"), the company's reported income in the future will be higher.

Extraordinary Times, p. 212

Q: Explain how the accounting for the financial impacts of 9/11 illustrates a tradeoff between the two primary qualities of accounting information, as discussed in the FASB's conceptual framework.

A: The primary qualities of accounting information are relevance and reliability. In the case of the 9/11 charges, given the unusual and infrequent nature of the terrorist attacks, more relevant information would be provided if the amounts arising from the terrorist attacks were reported as an extraordinary item. For example, given their nonrecurring nature, the 9/11 charges have little predictive value. However, as indicated in the story, relevance must be evaluated against how reliably companies can measure the income effects arising from the terrorist attacks versus other economic forces (slowing economy, etc.). In the end, the FASB came down on the side of reliability.

Remember to check the book's companion website to find additional resources for this chapter.

CHAPTER 6
STATEMENT OF CASH FLOWS

Don't Take Cash Flow for Granted

Investors usually look to net income as a key indicator of a company's financial health and future prospects. The following graph shows the net income of one company over a 7-year period.

The company showed a pattern of consistent profitability and even some periods of income growth. Between years 1 and 4, net income for this company grew by 32 percent, from $31 million to $41 million. Does this company look like a good investment? Would you expect its profitability to continue? The company had consistently paid dividends and interest. Would you expect it to continue to do so? Investors answered "yes" to all three of these questions, by buying the company's stock.

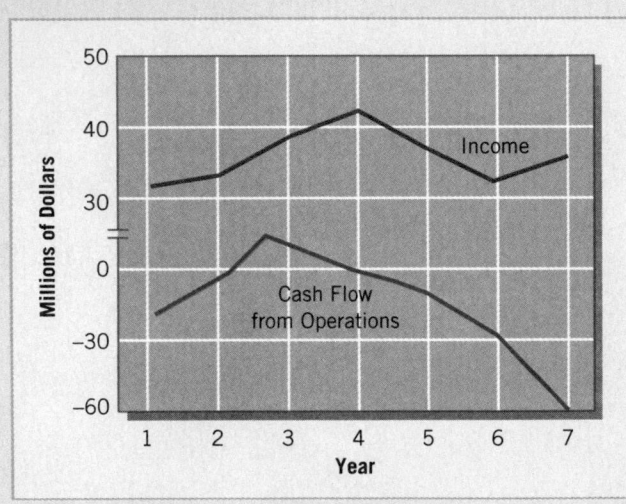

Eighteen months later, this company—**W. T. Grant**—filed for bankruptcy, in what was then the largest bankruptcy filing in the United States. As indicated by the second line in the graph, the company had experienced several years of negative cash flow from its operations, even though it reported profits. How could this happen? It was partly because the sales that W. T. Grant reported on the income statement were made on credit, and the company was having trouble collecting the receivables from the sales, causing cash flow to be less than the net income. Analysis of the cash flows would have provided an early warning signal of W. T. Grant's operating problems.

Source: Adapted from James A. Largay III and Clyde P. Stickney, "Cash Flows, Ratio Analysis, and the W. T. Grant Company Bankruptcy," *Financial Analysts Journal* (July–August 1980), p. 51.

Preview of Chapter 6

As the story about W. T. Grant indicates, the balance sheet, income statement, and retained earnings statement do not always show the whole picture of the financial condition of a company or institution. In fact, looking at the financial statements of some well-known companies, a thoughtful investor might ask questions like these: How did **Eastman Kodak** finance cash dividends of $649 million in a year in which it earned only $17 million? How could **United Airlines** purchase new planes that cost $1.9 billion in a year in which it reported a net loss of over $2 billion? How did the companies that spent a combined fantastic $3.4 trillion on mergers and acquisitions in a recent year finance those deals? Answers to these and similar questions can be found in this chapter, which illustrates the statement of cash flows.

The content and organization of this chapter are as follows.

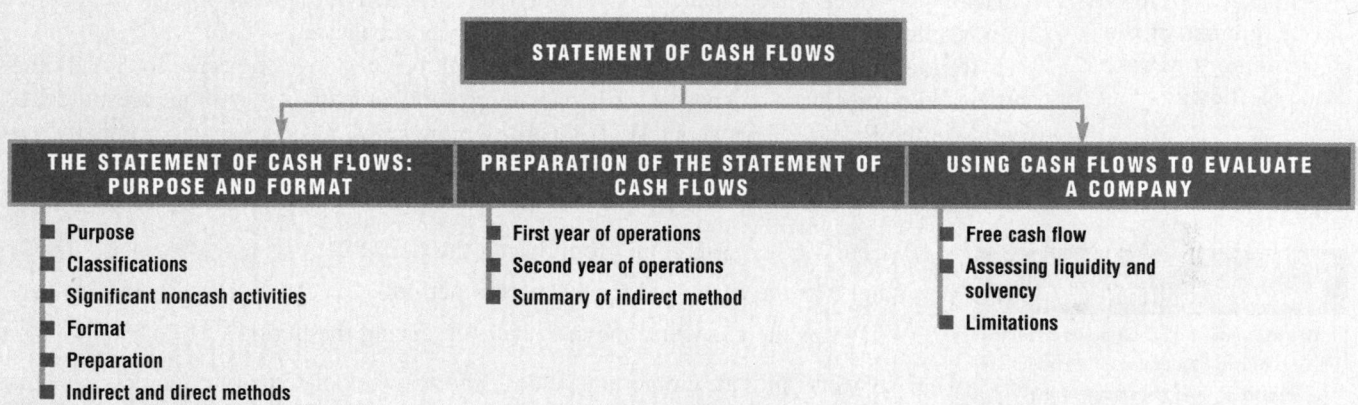

STATEMENT OF CASH FLOWS		
THE STATEMENT OF CASH FLOWS: PURPOSE AND FORMAT	**PREPARATION OF THE STATEMENT OF CASH FLOWS**	**USING CASH FLOWS TO EVALUATE A COMPANY**
■ Purpose ■ Classifications ■ Significant noncash activities ■ Format ■ Preparation ■ Indirect and direct methods	■ First year of operations ■ Second year of operations ■ Summary of indirect method	■ Free cash flow ■ Assessing liquidity and solvency ■ Limitations

Learning Objectives

After studying this chapter, you should be able to:

1. Indicate the primary purpose of the statement of cash flows.
2. Distinguish among operating, investing, and financing activities.
3. Identify sources of information for preparing the statement of cash flows.
4. Differentiate between net income and net cash provided by operating activities.
5. Determine net cash from investing and financing activities.
6. Prepare a statement of cash flows.
7. Analyze the statement of cash flows.

Inside Chapter 6

- **What Do the Numbers Mean?**
  Don't be misled by net income (p. 254)
  Losing the faith (p. 257)
  Pumping up cash (p. 260)
  "How's my cash flow?" (p. 271)
- **What's the Principle?** (pp. 252, 254, 259, 266)
- **Convergence Corner** (p. 273)
- **Accounting, Analysis, Principles** (p. 274)
  Prepare a statement of cash flows.
  Compute free cash flow.
  Understand objectives of financial reporting.

THE STATEMENT OF CASH FLOWS: PURPOSE AND FORMAT

The basic financial statements we have presented so far provide only limited information about a company's cash flows (cash receipts and cash payments). For example, comparative balance sheets show the increase in property, plant, and equipment during the year. But they do not show how the additions were financed or paid for. The income statement shows net income. But it does not indicate the amount of cash generated by operating activities. The retained earnings statement shows cash dividends declared but not the cash dividends paid during the year. None of these statements presents a detailed summary of the **net change in cash** as a result of operating, investing, and financing activities during the period. To fill this need, the FASB requires the statement of cash flows (also called the cash flow statement.)[1]

Purpose of the Statement of Cash Flows

OBJECTIVE 1

Indicate the usefulness of the statement of cash flows.

The primary purpose of the **statement of cash flows** is to provide information about cash receipts, cash payments, and the net change in cash resulting from the operating, investing, and financing activities of a company during the period. These activities involving cash are reported in a format that reconciles the beginning and ending cash balances.

Reporting the causes of changes in cash is useful because investors, creditors, and other interested parties want to know what is happening to a company's most liquid resource, its cash. As the Feature Story about **W. T. Grant** demonstrates, to understand a company's financial position it is essential to understand its cash flows. The statement of cash flows provides answers to the following simple, but important, questions about an enterprise.

WHAT'S THE PRINCIPLE?

The statement of cash flows meets one of the objectives of financial reporting—to help assess the amounts, timing, and uncertainty of future cash flows.

- Where did the cash come from during the period?
- What was the cash used for during the period?
- What was the change in the cash balance during the period?

The answers provide important clues about whether dynamic companies like **Microsoft** and **Oracle** will be able to continue to thrive and invest in new opportunities. The statement of cash flows also provides clues about whether a struggling company will survive or perish.

Classification of Cash Flows

OBJECTIVE 2

Distinguish among operating, investing, and financing activities.

The statement of cash flows classifies cash receipts and cash payments into operating, investing, and financing activities.[2] Transactions within each activity are as follows.

1 **Operating activities** include the cash effects of transactions that create revenues and expenses. They thus enter into the determination of net income.

2 **Investing activities** include (a) purchasing and disposing of investments and productive long-lived assets using cash, and (b) lending money and collecting the loans.

3 **Financing activities** include (a) obtaining cash from issuing debt and repaying the amounts borrowed, and (b) obtaining cash from stockholders and paying them dividends.

---

[1]"Statement of Cash Flows," *Statement of Financial Accounting Standards No. 95* (Stamford, Conn.: FASB, 1987).

[2]The basis recommended by the FASB for the statement of cash flows is actually "cash and cash equivalents." **Cash equivalents** are short-term, highly liquid investments that are both: (a) readily convertible to known amounts of cash, and (b) so near their maturity that they present insignificant risk of changes in interest rates. Generally, only investments with original maturities of three months or less qualify under this definition. Examples of cash equivalents are Treasury bills, commercial paper, and money market funds purchased with cash that is in excess of immediate needs.

We use the term "cash" throughout our discussion and illustrations in this chapter. By that term, we mean cash and cash equivalents when reporting the cash flows and the net increase or decrease in cash.

The operating activities category is the most important because it shows the cash provided or used by company operations. Ultimately a company must generate cash from its operating activities in order to continue as a going concern and to expand.

Illustration 6-1 lists typical cash receipts and cash payments within each of the three activities. **Study the list carefully.** It will prove very useful in solving homework exercises and problems.

Types of Cash Inflows and Outflows

Operating
 Cash inflows
  From sales of goods or services.
  From returns on loans (interest) and on equity
   securities (dividends).
 Cash outflows   } Income
  To suppliers for inventory.   Statement
  To employees for services.   Items
  To government for taxes.
  To lenders for interest.
  To others for expenses.

Investing
 Cash inflows
  From sale of property, plant, and equipment.
  From sale of debt or equity securities of other entities.   Generally,
  From collection of principal on loans to other entities.   Long-Term
 Cash outflows   Asset Items
  To purchase property, plant, and equipment.
  To purchase debt or equity securities of other entities.
  To make loans to other entities.

Financing
 Cash inflows   Generally,
  From sale of equity securities.   Long-Term
  From issuance of debt (bonds and notes).   Liability
 Cash outflows   and Equity
  To stockholders as dividends.   Items
  To redeem long-term debt or reacquire capital stock.

Illustration 6-1
Typical Classification of Cash Flows Shown in the Statement of Cash Flows

Note the following general guidelines:

1 **Operating activities** involve income statement items.

2 **Investing activities** involve cash flows resulting from changes in investments and long-term asset items.

3 **Financing activities** involve cash flows resulting from changes in long-term liability and stockholders' equity items.

As you can see, some cash flows relating to investing or financing activities are classified as operating activities. Examples include receipts of investment revenue (interest and dividends), and payments of interest to lenders. Why are these considered operating activities? **Because these items are reported in the income statement**, where results of operations are shown.[3]

[3]For exceptions to the treatment of purchases and sales of loans and securities by banks and brokers, see *Statement of Financial Accounting Standards No. 102* (February 1989) and James Don Edwards and Cynthia D. Heagy, "Relevance Gained: FASB Modifies Cash Flow Statement Requirements for Banks," *Journal of Accountancy* (June 1991). Banks and brokers are required to classify cash flows from purchases and sales of loans and securities specifically for resale and carried at market value **as operating activities.** This requirement recognizes that for these firms, these assets are similar to inventory in other businesses.

Significant Noncash Activities

Not all of a company's significant activities involve cash. Examples of significant non-cash activities are:

1 Issuance of common stock to purchase assets.

2 Conversion of bonds into common stock.

3 Issuance of debt to purchase assets.

4 Exchanges of plant assets.

Companies do not report in the body of the statement of cash flows significant financing and investing activities that do not affect cash. They report these activities in either a **separate schedule** at the bottom of the statement of cash flows or in a **separate note or supplementary schedule** to the financial statements.

The reporting of these noncash activities in a separate schedule satisfies the **full disclosure principle.** In solving homework assignments you should present significant noncash investing and financing activities in a separate schedule at the bottom of the statement of cash flows. (See lower section of Illustration 6-2, on the next page, for an example.)

What do the numbers mean?   Don't Be Misled by Net Income

Net income is not the same as net cash provided by operations. The following results from annual reports for 2006 ($ in millions) illustrate the differences. Note the wide disparity among these companies, all of which engaged in similar types of retail merchandising.

Company	Net Income	Net Cash Provided by Operations
Nordstrom	$ 551	$ 776
Wal-Mart Stores, Inc.	11,231	17,633
J. C. Penney Company, Inc.	1,088	1,419
Sears Holdings	858	2,298
Target Corporation	2,408	4,451

Beyond the Numbers

For all of the companies listed above, the cash-basis amount "Net cash provided by operations," from the statement of cash flows, is much greater than the accrual-basis amount "Net income," from the income statement. What explanation can you give for this difference?

Format of the Statement of Cash Flows

The general format of the statement of cash flows presents the results of the three activities discussed previously—operating, investing, and financing—plus the significant noncash investing and financing activities. Illustration 6-2 (page 255) shows a widely used form of the statement of cash flows.

The cash flows from operating activities section always appears first, followed by the investing activities and the financing activities sections. Note also that, **the individual inflows and outflows from investing and financing activities are reported separately**. Thus, the cash outflow for the purchase of property, plant, and equipment is reported separately from the cash inflow from the sale of property, plant, and equipment. Similarly, the cash inflow from the issuance of debt securities is reported separately from the cash outflow

The Statement of Cash Flows: Purpose and Format **255**

Illustration 6-2
Format of Statement of
Cash Flows

Company Name Statement of Cash Flows Period Covered		
Cash flows from operating activities		
(List of individual items)	XX	
Net cash provided (used) by operating activities		XXX
Cash flows from investing activities		
(List of individual inflows and outflows)	XX	
Net cash provided (used) by investing activities		XXX
Cash flows from financing activities		
(List of individual inflows and outflows)	XX	
Net cash provided (used) by financing activities		XXX
Net increase (decrease) in cash		XXX
Cash at beginning of period		XXX
Cash at end of period		XXX
Noncash investing and financing activities		
(List of individual noncash transactions)		XXX

INTERNATIONAL INSIGHT

International Accounting Standard 7 requires a statement of cash flows. Both international standards and U.S. GAAP specify that companies must classify the cash flows as operating, investing, or financing.

for the retirement of debt. If a company did not report the inflows and outflows separately, it would obscure the investing and financing activities of the enterprise. This would make it more difficult for the user to assess future cash flows.

The reported operating, investing, and financing activities result in net cash either **provided or used** by each activity. The amounts of net cash provided or used by each activity then are totaled. The result is the net increase (decrease) in cash for the period. This amount is then added to or subtracted from the beginning-of-period cash balance to obtain the end-of-period cash balance. Finally, any significant noncash investing and financing activities are reported in a separate schedule at the bottom of the statement.

Try it out! During its first week, Duffy & Stevenson Company had these transactions.

1 Issued 100,000 shares of $5 par value common stock for $800,000 cash.
2 Borrowed $200,000 from Castle Bank, signing a 5-year note bearing 8% interest.
3 Purchased two semi-trailer trucks for $170,000 cash.
4 Paid employees $12,000 for salaries and wages.
5 Collected $20,000 cash for services rendered.

Instructions

Classify each of these transactions by type of cash flow activity.

Solution

1 Financing activity
2 Financing activity
3 Investing activity
4 Operating activity
5 Operating activity

Preparing the Statement of Cash Flows

Companies prepare the statement of cash flows differently from the three other basic financial statements. First, they do not prepare it from an adjusted trial balance. The statement requires detailed information concerning the changes in account balances that occurred between two points in time. An adjusted trial balance will not provide the necessary data. Second, the statement of cash flows deals with cash receipts and payments. As a result, a company must adjust the effects of the use of accrual accounting **to determine cash flows**.

The information to prepare this statement usually comes from three sources:

OBJECTIVE 3

Identify sources of information for preparing the statement of cash flows.

- **Comparative balance sheets.** Information in the comparative balance sheets indicates the amount of the changes in assets, liabilities, and stockholders' equities from the beginning to the end of the period.

- **Current income statement.** Information in this statement helps determine the amount of cash provided or used by operations during the period.

- **Additional information.** Such information includes transaction data that are needed to determine how cash was provided or used during the period.

Preparing the statement of cash flows from these data sources involves three major steps, explained in Illustration 6-3.

Illustration 6-3
Three Major Steps in Preparing the Statement of Cash Flows

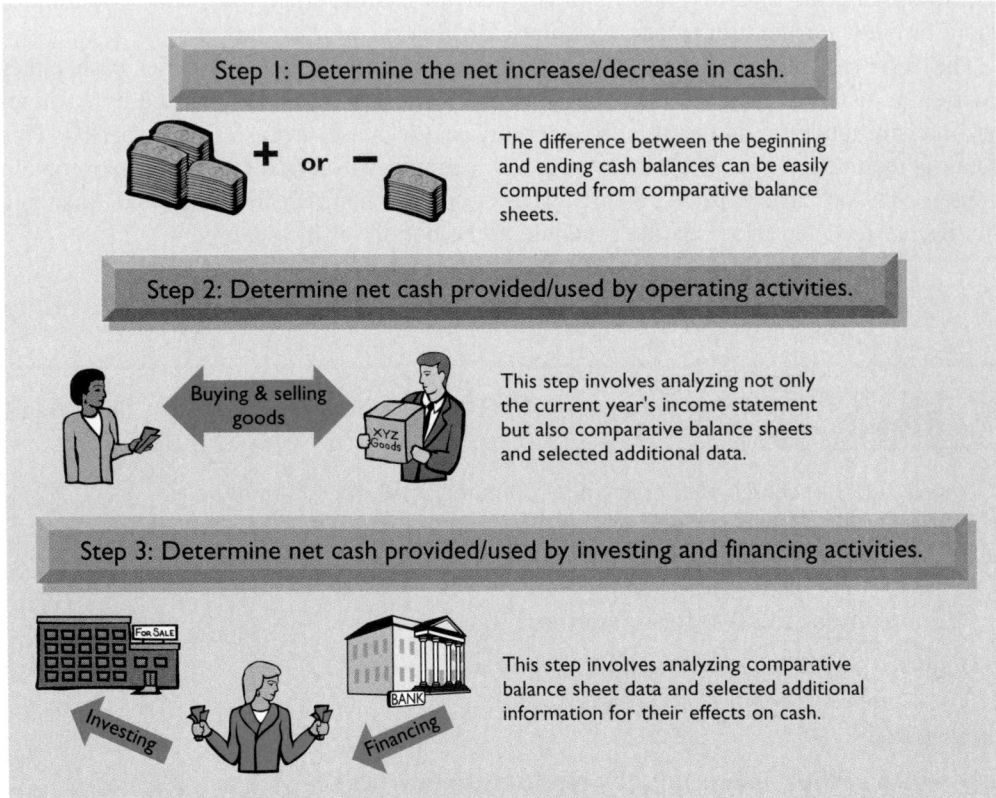

Start by identifying the change in cash during the period. Has cash increased or decreased during the year? Second, determine the net cash provided/used by operating activities. Third, determine the net cash provided/used by investing and financing activities.

Indirect and Direct Methods

In order to determine the cash provided/used by operating activities, the company **must convert net income from an accrual basis to a cash basis**. They can make this conversion by either of two methods: indirect or direct. **Both methods arrive at the same total amount** for "Net cash provided by operating activities." They differ in disclosing the items that make up the total amount. Note that the two different methods affect **only the operating activities section**. The investing activities and financing activities sections **are not affected by the choice of method**.

The indirect method is used extensively in practice—by about 99% of companies in a recent survey.[4] Companies favor the indirect method for three reasons: (1) It is easier to prepare, (2) it focuses on the differences between net income and net cash flow from operating activities, and (3) it tends to reveal less company information to competitors.

Others, however, favor the direct method. This method is more consistent with the objective of a statement of cash flows because it shows operating cash receipts and payments. The FASB has expressed a preference for the direct method but allows the use of either method. When the direct method is used, the net cash flow from operating activities as computed using the indirect method must also be reported in a separate schedule.[5]

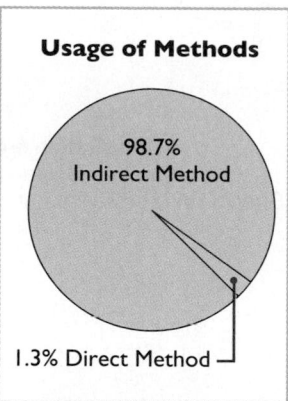

Usage of Methods

98.7% Indirect Method

1.3% Direct Method

What do the numbers mean?

Losing the Faith

During the 1990s, analysts increasingly used cash-flow-based measures of income, such as cash flow provided by operations, instead of or in addition to net income. The reason for the change was that they were losing faith in accrual-accounting-based net income numbers. Sadly, these days even cash flow from operations isn't always what it seems to be.

For example, in 2002 **WorldCom, Inc.** disclosed that it had improperly capitalized expenses: It moved $3.8 billion of cash outflows from the "Cash from operating activities" section of the cash flow statement to the "Investing activities" section, thereby greatly enhancing cash provided by operating activities. Similarly, in 2002 **Dynegy, Inc.** restated its cash flow statement so that $300 million tied to its complex natural gas trading operation was removed from cash flow from operations and put into the financing section—a drop of 37% in cash flow from operations.

Source: Henny Sender, "Sadly, These Days Even Cash Flow Isn't Always What It Seems To Be," *Wall Street Journal Online* (May 8, 2002).

Beyond the Numbers

Since these and numerous other financial accounting corrections and misstatements were reported in 2000, 2001, and 2002, what actions have been taken to curb such misdeeds?

PREPARATION OF THE STATEMENT OF CASH FLOWS

To explain and illustrate the indirect method, we will use the transactions of Computer Services Company for two years, 2008 and 2009, to prepare annual statements of cash flows. We will show basic transactions in the first year, with additional transactions added in the second year.

First Year of Operations—2008

Computer Services Company started on January 1, 2008, when it issued 50,000 shares of $1 par value common stock for $50,000 cash. The company rented its office space and furniture and performed consulting services throughout the first year. The comparative balance sheets for the beginning and end of 2008, showing increases or decreases, appear

---

[4]*Accounting Trends and Techniques—2006* (New York: American Institute of Certified Public Accountants, 2006).

[5]We illustrate the indirect method because of its extensive use in practice. Appendix B (at the end of the book) presents an expanded discussion of preparation of the statement of cash flows, including the direct method.

in Illustration 6-4. The income statement and additional information for Computer Services Company are shown in Illustration 6-5.

Illustration 6-4
Comparative Balance Sheets with Increases and Decreases

Computer Services Company
Comparative Balance Sheets

Assets	Dec. 31, 2008	Jan. 1, 2008	Change Increase/Decrease
Cash	$34,000	$0	$34,000 increase
Accounts receivable	30,000	0	30,000 increase
Equipment	10,000	0	10,000 increase
Total	$74,000	$0	
Liabilities and Stockholders' Equity			
Accounts payable	$ 4,000	$0	$ 4,000 increase
Common stock	50,000	0	50,000 increase
Retained earnings	20,000	0	20,000 increase
Total	$74,000	$0	

Illustration 6-5
Income Statement and Additional Information, 2008

Computer Services Company
Income Statement
For the Year Ended December 31, 2008

Revenues	$85,000
Operating expenses	40,000
Income before income tax	45,000
Income tax	10,000
Net income	$35,000

Additional information:

(a) Examination of selected data indicates that a dividend of $15,000 was declared and paid during the year.

(b) The equipment was purchased at the end of 2008. No depreciation was taken in 2008.

Determining the Net Increase/Decrease In Cash (Step 1)

To prepare a statement of cash flows, the first step is to **determine the net increase or decrease in cash**. This is a simple computation. For example, Computer Services Company had no cash on hand at the beginning of 2008. It had $34,000 on hand at the end of the year. Thus, the change in cash for 2008 was an increase of $34,000.

Determining Net Cash Provided/Used by Operating Activities (Step 2)

OBJECTIVE 4

Differentiate between net income and net cash provided by operating activities.

To determine net cash provided by operating activities under the indirect method, **net income is adjusted for items that did not affect cash**. A useful starting point in determining net cash provided by operating activities is to understand **why** net income must be converted. Under generally accepted accounting principles, most companies use the accrual basis of accounting. The accrual basis requires that revenue be recorded when earned and that expenses be recorded when incurred. Earned revenues may include credit sales that have not been collected in cash. Expenses incurred may include costs that have not been paid in cash. Under the accrual basis of accounting, net income does not indicate the net cash provided by operating activities. Therefore, under the indirect method, net income must be adjusted to convert certain items to the cash basis.

The **indirect method** (or **reconciliation method**) starts with net income and converts it to net cash provided by operating activities. In other words, **the indirect method adjusts net income for items that affected reported net income but did not affect cash**. Illustration 6-6 shows this adjustment. That is, noncash charges in the income statement are added back to net income. Likewise, noncash credits are deducted. The result is net cash provided by operating activities.

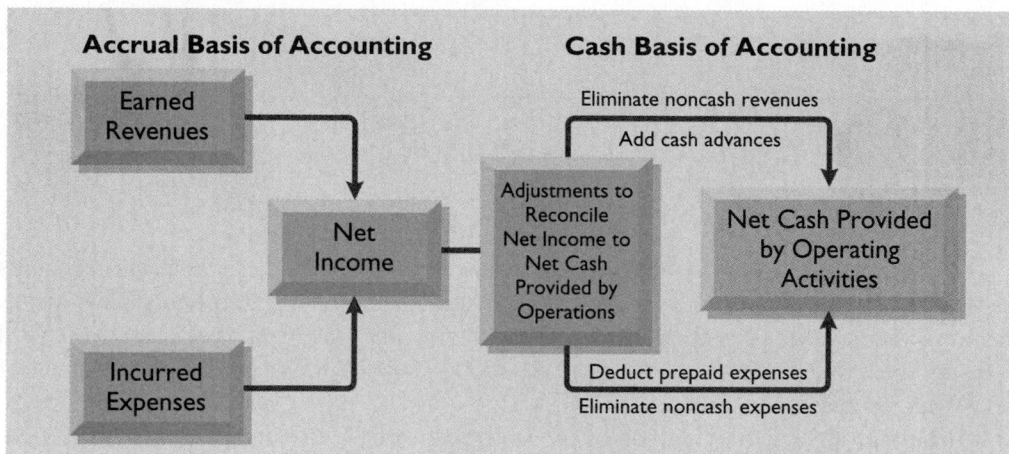

Illustration 6-6
Net Income Versus Net Cash Provided by Operating Activities

A useful starting point in identifying the adjustments to net income is the current asset and current liability accounts other than cash. Those accounts—receivables, payables, prepayments, and inventories—should be analyzed for their effects on cash. We do that next for various accounts.

WHAT'S THE PRINCIPLE?

Income from operations and cash flow from operating activities are different. Income from operations is based on accrual accounting; cash flow from operating activities is prepared on a cash basis.

Increase in Accounts Receivable.   When accounts receivable increase during the year, revenues on an accrual basis are higher than revenues on a cash basis. In other words, operations of the period led to revenues, **but not all of these revenues resulted in an increase in cash**. Some of the revenues resulted in an increase in accounts receivable.

For example, Computer Services Company, in its first year of operations, had revenues of $85,000, but it collected only $55,000 in cash. Thus, on an accrual basis revenue was $85,000, but on a cash basis we would record only the $55,000 received during the period. Illustration 6-7 shows that, to convert net income to net cash provided by operating activities, the increase of $30,000 in accounts receivable must be deducted from net income.

	Accounts Receivable		
Jan. 1 Balance	0	Receipts from customers	55,000
Revenues	85,000		
Dec. 31 Balance	30,000		

Illustration 6-7
Analysis of Accounts Receivable

Increase in Accounts Payable.   In the first year, operating expenses incurred on account were credited to Accounts Payable. When accounts payable increase during the year, operating expenses on an accrual basis are higher than they are on a cash basis. For Computer

Services Company, operating expenses reported in the income statement were $40,000. However, since Accounts Payable increased $4,000, only $36,000 ($40,000 − $4,000) of the expenses were paid in cash. To convert net income to net cash provided by operating activities, the increase of $4,000 in accounts payable must be added to net income.

The T account analysis in Illustration 6-8 indicates that payments to creditors are less than operating expenses.

Illustration 6-8

Analysis of Accounts Payable

		Accounts Payable		
Payments to creditors	36,000	Jan. 1	Balances	0
			Operating expenses	40,000
		Dec. 31	Balance	4,000

For Computer Services Company, the changes in accounts receivable and accounts payable were the only changes in current asset and current liability accounts. This means that any other revenues or expenses reported in the income statement were received or paid in cash. Thus, the income tax expense of $10,000 was paid in cash, and no adjustment of net income is necessary.

The operating activities section of the statement of cash flows for Computer Services Company is shown in Illustration 6-9.

Illustration 6-9

Operating Activities Section, 2008—Indirect Method

Computer Services Company
Statement of Cash Flows (partial)—Indirect Method
For the Year Ended December 31, 2008

Cash flows from operating activities		
Net income		$35,000
Adjustments to reconcile net income to net cash		
provided by operating activities:		
Increase in accounts receivable	$(30,000)	
Increase in accounts payable	4,000	(26,000)
Net cash provided by operating activities		$ 9,000

What do the numbers mean?   Pumping Up Cash

Due to recent concerns about a decline in the quality of earnings, some investors have been focusing on cash flow. Management has an incentive to make operating cash flow look good, because Wall Street has paid a premium for companies that generate a lot of cash from operations, rather than through borrowings. However, similar to earnings, companies have ways to pump up cash flow from operations.

One way that companies can boost their operating cash flow is by "securitizing" receivables. That is, companies can speed up cash collections by selling their receivables. For example, **Federated Department Stores** reported a $2.2 billion increase in cash flow from operations. This seems impressive until you read the fine print, which indicates that a big part of the increase was due to the sale of receivables. As discussed in this section, decreases in accounts receivable increase cash flow from operations. So while it appeared that Federated's core operations had improved, the company really did little more than accelerate collections of its receivables. In fact, the cash flow from the securitizations represented more than half of Federated's operating cash flow. Thus, just like earnings, cash flow can be of high or low quality.

Source: Adapted from Ann Tergesen, "Cash Flow Hocus Pocus," *Business Week* (July 16, 2002), pp. 130–131. *See also* Bear Stearns Equity Research, *Accounting Issues: Cash Flow Metrics* (June 2006).

Beyond the Numbers

Why would financial statement readers focus on the information in the statement of cash flows when earnings quality is low?

Determining Net Cash Provided/Used by Investing and Financing Activities (Step 3)

The third and final step in preparing the statement of cash flows begins with a study of the balance sheet. We look at it to determine changes in noncurrent accounts. The change in each noncurrent account is then analyzed to determine the effect, if any, the changes had on cash.

For Computer Services Company, the three noncurrent accounts are Equipment, Common Stock, and Retained Earnings. All three have increased during the year. What caused these increases? No transaction data are given for the increases in Equipment of $10,000 and Common Stock of $50,000. When other explanations are lacking, we assume that any differences involve cash. Thus, the increase in Equipment is assumed to be a purchase of equipment for $10,000 cash. This purchase is reported as a cash outflow in the investing activities section. The increase in Common Stock is assumed to result from the issuance of common stock for $50,000 cash. The issuance of common stock is reported as an inflow of cash in the financing activities section of the statement of cash flows. In doing your homework, assume that **any unexplained differences in noncurrent accounts involve cash**.

The reasons for the net increase of $20,000 in the Retained Earnings account are determined by analysis. First, net income increased retained earnings by $35,000. Second, the additional information provided below the income statement in Illustration 6-5 indicates that a cash dividend of $15,000 was declared and paid. The $35,000 increase due to net income is reported in the operating activities section. The cash dividend paid is reported in the financing activities section.

This analysis can also be made directly from the Retained Earnings account in the ledger of Computer Services Company as shown in Illustration 6-10.

> OBJECTIVE **5**
> Determine net cash from investing and financing activities.

Retained Earnings

Dec. 31 Cash dividend	15,000	Jan. 1 Balance	0
		Dec. 31 Net income	35,000
		Dec. 31 Balance	20,000

Illustration 6-10
Analysis of Retained Earnings

The $20,000 increase in Retained Earnings in 2008 is a net change. When a net change in a noncurrent balance sheet account has occurred during the year, it generally is necessary to report the causes of the net change separately in the statement of cash flows.

Statement of Cash Flows—2008

Having completed the three steps above, we can prepare the statement of cash flows. The statement starts with the operating activities section, followed by the investing activities

> OBJECTIVE **6**
> Prepare a statement of cash flows.

section, and then the financing activities section. The 2008 statement of cash flows for Computer Services is shown in Illustration 6-11.

Illustration 6-11
Statement of Cash Flows,
2008—Indirect Method

Computer Services Company
Statement of Cash Flows
For the Year Ended December 31, 2008

Cash flows from operating activities		
Net income		$35,000
Adjustments to reconcile net income to net cash		
provided by operating activities:		
Increase in accounts receivable	$(30,000)	
Increase in accounts payable	4,000	(26,000)
Net cash provided by operating activities		9,000
Cash flows from investing activities		
Purchase of equipment	(10,000)	
Net cash used by investing activities		(10,000)
Cash flows from financing activities		
Issuance of common stock	50,000	
Payment of cash dividends	(15,000)	
Net cash provided by financing activities		35,000
Net increase in cash		34,000
Cash at beginning of period		0
Cash at end of period		$34,000

Computer Services Company's statement of cash flows for 2008 shows that operating activities **provided** $9,000 cash. Investing activities **used** $10,000 cash. Financing activities **provided** $35,000 cash. The increase in cash of $34,000 reported in the statement of cash flows agrees with the increase of $34,000 shown as the change in the Cash account in the comparative balance sheets.

Second Year of Operations—2009

Illustrations 6-12 and 6-13 present information related to the second year of operations for Computer Services Company.

Illustration 6-12
Comparative Balance
Sheets with Increases and
Decreases

Computer Services Company
Comparative Balance Sheets
December 31

Assets	2009	2008	Change Increase/Decrease	
Cash	$ 56,000	$34,000	$ 22,000	increase
Accounts receivable	20,000	30,000	10,000	decrease
Prepaid expenses	4,000	0	4,000	increase
Land	130,000	0	130,000	increase
Building	160,000	0	160,000	increase
Accumulated depreciation—building	(11,000)	0	11,000	increase
Equipment	27,000	10,000	17,000	increase
Accumulated depreciation—equipment	(3,000)	0	3,000	increase
Total	$383,000	$74,000		

Liabilities and Stockholders' Equity

Accounts payable	$ 59,000	$ 4,000	$ 55,000	increase
Bonds payable	130,000	0	130,000	increase
Common stock	50,000	50,000	0	
Retained earnings	144,000	20,000	124,000	increase
Total	$383,000	$74,000		

Illustration 6-13
Income Statement and
Additional Information,
2009

Computer Services Company
Income Statement
For the Year Ended December 31, 2009

Revenues		$507,000
Operating expenses (excluding depreciation)	$261,000	
Depreciation expense	15,000	
Loss on sale of equipment	3,000	279,000
Income before income tax		228,000
Income tax		89,000
Net income		$139,000

Additional information:
(a) In 2009 the company declared and paid a $15,000 cash dividend.
(b) The company obtained land through the issuance of $130,000 of long-term bonds.
(c) An office building costing $160,000 was purchased for cash. Equipment costing $25,000 was also purchased for cash.
(d) During 2009 the company sold equipment with a book value of $7,000 (cost $8,000 less accumulated depreciation $1,000) for $4,000 cash.

Determining the Net Increase/Decrease in Cash (Step 1)

To prepare a statement of cash flows from this information, the first step is to **determine the net increase or decrease in cash**. As indicated from the information presented, cash increased $22,000 ($56,000 − $34,000).

Determining Net Cash Provided/Used by Operating Activities (Step 2)

As in step 2 in 2008, net income on an accrual basis must be adjusted to arrive at net cash provided/used by operating activities. Explanations for the adjustments to net income for Computer Services Company in 2009 are as follows.

Decrease in Accounts Receivable. Accounts receivable decreases during the period because cash receipts are higher than revenues reported on an accrual basis. To adjust net income to net cash provided by operating activities, the decrease of $10,000 in accounts receivable must be added to net income.

Increase in Prepaid Expenses. Prepaid expenses increase during a period because cash paid for expenses is greater than expenses reported on an accrual basis. Cash payments have been made in the current period, but expenses (as charges to the income statement) have been deferred to future periods. To convert net income to net cash provided by operating activities, the $4,000 increase in prepaid expenses must be deducted from net income. An increase in prepaid expenses results in a decrease in cash during the period.

Increase in Accounts Payable. Like the increase in 2008, the 2009 increase of $55,000 in accounts payable must be added to net income in order to convert to net cash provided by operating activities.

Depreciation Expense. During 2009 Computer Services Company reported depreciation expense of $15,000. Of this amount, $11,000 related to the building and $4,000 to the equipment. These two amounts were determined by analyzing the accumulated depreciation accounts in the balance sheets, as follows.

Increase in Accumulated Depreciation—Building. As shown in Illustration 6-12, the Accumulated Depreciation—Building account increased $11,000. This change represents the depreciation expense on the building for the year. **Depreciation expense is a noncash charge; thus it is added back to net income** in order to arrive at net cash provided by operating activities.

Increase in Accumulated Depreciation—Equipment. The Accumulated Depreciation—Equipment account increased $3,000. But this change does not represent the total depreciation expense for the year. The additional information indicates why not: This account was decreased (debited $1,000) as a result of the sale of some equipment. Thus, depreciation expense for 2009 was $4,000 ($3,000 + $1,000). This amount is **added to net income** to determine net cash provided by operating activities. The T account in Illustration 6-14 provides information about the changes that occurred in this account in 2009.

Illustration 6-14
Analysis of Accumulated Depreciation—Equipment

Accumulated Depreciation—Equipment				
Accumulated depreciation on equipment sold	1,000	Jan. 1	Balance	0
			Depreciation expense	4,000
		Dec. 31	Balance	3,000

Depreciation expense of $11,000 on the building plus depreciation expense of $4,000 on the equipment equals the depreciation expense of $15,000 reported on the income statement.

Other charges to expense **that do not require the use of cash**, such as the amortization of intangible assets, are treated in the same manner as depreciation. Depreciation and similar noncash charges are frequently listed in the statement of cash flows as the first adjustments to net income.

Loss on Sale of Equipment. On the income statement, Computer Services Company reported a $3,000 loss on the sale of equipment (book value $7,000 less cash proceeds $4,000). The loss reduced net income **but did not reduce cash**. Thus, the loss is **added to net income** in determining net cash provided by operating activities.[6]

As a result of the previous adjustments, net cash provided by operating activities is $218,000, as computed in Illustration 6-15 (page 265).

Determining Net Cash Provided/Used by Investing and Financing Activities (Step 3)

The final step involves analyzing the remaining changes in balance sheet accounts to determine net cash provided/used by investing and financing activities.

---

[6]If a gain on sale occurs, the treatment is the opposite: To allow a gain to flow through to net cash provided by operating activities would be double-counting the gain—once in net income and again in the investing activities section as part of the cash proceeds from sale. As a result, a gain is deducted from net income in reporting net cash provided by operating activities.

Illustration 6-15
Operating Activities
Section, 2009—Indirect
Method

Computer Services Company
Statement of Cash Flows (partial)
For the Year Ended December 31, 2009

Cash flows from operating activities		
Net income		$ 139,000
Adjustments to reconcile net income to net cash provided by operating activities:		
Depreciation expense	$15,000	
Loss on sale of equipment	3,000	
Decrease in accounts receivable	10,000	
Increase in prepaid expenses	(4,000)	
Increase in accounts payable	55,000	79,000
Net cash provided by operating activities		$218,000

Increase in Land. As indicated from the change in the Land account and the additional information, land of $130,000 was purchased through the issuance of long-term bonds. The issuance of bonds payable for land has no effect on cash. But it is a significant noncash investing and financing activity that merits disclosure in a separate schedule at the bottom of the statement of cash flows.

Increase in Building. As the additional information indicates, an office building was acquired using cash of $160,000. This transaction is a cash outflow reported in the investing activities section.

Increase in Equipment. The Equipment account increased $17,000. The additional information explains that this was a net increase that resulted from two transactions: (1) a purchase of equipment for $25,000 and (2) the sale for $4,000 of equipment costing $8,000. These transactions are classified as investing activities. Each transaction should be reported separately. Thus, the purchase of equipment should be reported as an outflow of cash for $25,000. The sale of equipment should be reported as an inflow of cash for $4,000. Illustration 6-16 shows the reasons for the change in this account during the year.

Illustration 6-16
Analysis of Equipment

	Equipment			
Jan. 1	Balance	10,000	Cost of equipment sold	8,000
	Purchase of equipment	25,000		
Dec. 31	Balance	27,000		

Increase in Bonds Payable. The Bonds Payable account increased $130,000. As shown in the additional information, land was acquired through the issuance of these bonds. As indicated earlier, this noncash transaction is reported in a separate schedule at the bottom of the statement.

Increase in Retained Earnings. Retained Earnings increased $124,000 during the year. This increase can be explained by two factors: (1) Net income of $139,000 increased Retained Earnings. (2) Dividends of $15,000 decreased Retained Earnings. Net income is converted to net cash provided by operating activities in the operating activities section. Payment of the dividends is a **cash outflow that is reported as a financing activity**.

Statement of Cash Flows—2009

Combining the previous items, we obtain a statement of cash flows for 2009 for Computer Services Company as presented in Illustration 6-17 on the next page.

Illustration 6-17
Statement of Cash Flows,
2009—Indirect Method

Computer Services Company
Statement of Cash Flows
For the Year Ended December 31, 2009

Cash flows from operating activities		
Net income		$139,000
Adjustments to reconcile net income to net cash		
provided by operating activities:		
Depreciation expense	$ 15,000	
Loss on sale of equipment	3,000	
Decrease in accounts receivable	10,000	
Increase in prepaid expenses	(4,000)	
Increase in accounts payable	55,000	79,000
Net cash provided by operating activities		218,000
Cash flows from investing activities		
Purchase of building	(160,000)	
Purchase of equipment	(25,000)	
Sale of equipment	4,000	
Net cash used by investing activities		(181,000)
Cash flows from financing activities		
Payment of cash dividends	(15,000)	
Net cash used by financing activities		(15,000)
Net increase in cash		22,000
Cash at beginning of period		34,000
Cash at end of period		$ 56,000
Noncash investing and financing activities		
Issuance of bonds payable to purchase land		$130,000

WHAT'S THE PRINCIPLE?

Reporting noncash
activities on the face of the
statement or in a separate schedule
satisfies the full disclosure principle.

Summary of Conversion to Net Cash Provided by Operating Activities—Indirect Method

As shown in the previous illustrations, the statement of cash flows prepared by the indirect method starts with net income. It then adds or deducts items not affecting cash, to arrive at net cash provided by operating activities. The additions and deductions consist of (1) changes in specific current assets and current liabilities and (2) noncash charges reported in the income statement. A summary of the adjustments for current assets and current liabilities is provided in Illustration 6-18.

Illustration 6-18
Adjustments for Current
Assets and Current
Liabilities

	Adjustments to Convert Net Income to Net Cash Provided by Operating Activities	
Current Assets and Current Liabilities	**Add to Net Income**	**Deduct from Net Income**
Accounts receivable	Decrease	Increase
Inventory	Decrease	Increase
Prepaid expenses	Decrease	Increase
Accounts payable	Increase	Decrease
Accrued expenses payable	Increase	Decrease

Adjustments for the noncash charges reported in the income statement are made as shown in Illustration 6-19.

Noncash Charges	Adjustments to Convert Net Income to Net Cash Provided by Operating Activities
Depreciation expense	Add
Patent amortization expense	Add
Loss on sale of asset	Add

Illustration 6-19
Adjustments for Noncash Charges

Try it out! Presented below is information related to Callahan Company.

Instructions

Use the following information to prepare a statement of cash flows using the **indirect method**.

Callahan Company
Comparative Balance Sheets
December 31

Assets	2008	2007	Change Increase/Decrease
Cash	$ 54,000	$ 37,000	$ 17,000 Increase
Accounts receivable	68,000	26,000	42,000 Increase
Inventories	54,000	–0–	54,000 Increase
Prepaid expenses	4,000	6,000	2,000 Decrease
Land	45,000	70,000	25,000 Decrease
Buildings	200,000	200,000	–0–
Accumulated depreciation—buildings	(21,000)	(11,000)	10,000 Increase
Equipment	193,000	68,000	125,000 Increase
Accumulated depreciation—equipment	(28,000)	(10,000)	18,000 Increase
Totals	$569,000	$386,000	

Liabilities and Stockholders' Equity			
Accounts payable	$ 23,000	$ 40,000	$ 17,000 Decrease
Accrued expenses payable	10,000	–0–	10,000 Increase
Bonds payable	110,000	150,000	40,000 Decrease
Common stock ($1 par)	220,000	60,000	160,000 Increase
Retained earnings	206,000	136,000	70,000 Increase
Totals	$569,000	$386,000	

Callahan Company
Income Statement
For the Year Ended December 31, 2008

Revenues		$890,000
Cost of goods sold	$465,000	
Operating expenses	221,000	
Interest expense	12,000	
Loss on sale of equipment	2,000	700,000
Income before income tax		190,000
Income tax		65,000
Net income		$125,000

Additional Information

1   Operating expenses include depreciation expense of $33,000 and charges from pre-paid expenses of $2,000.

2   The company sold land at its book value for cash.

3   The company declared and paid cash dividends of $55,000 in 2008.

4   The company paid interest expense of $12,000 in cash.

5   The company purchased with cash equipment with a cost of $166,000. It sold for $34,000 cash equipment with a cost of $41,000 and a book value of $36,000.

6   The company redeemed for cash bonds of $10,000 at their book value. It converted bonds of $30,000 into common stock.

7   The company issued for cash common stock ($1 par) of $130,000.

Solution

Callahan Company
Statement of Cash Flows—Indirect Method
For the Year Ended December 31, 2008

Cash flows from operating activities		
Net income		$125,000
Adjustments to reconcile net income to net cash		
provided by operating activities:		
Depreciation expense	$ 33,000	
Loss on sale of equipment	2,000	
Increase in accounts receivable	(42,000)	
Increase in inventories	(54,000)	
Decrease in prepaid expenses	2,000	
Decrease in accounts payable	(17,000)	
Increase in accrued expenses payable	10,000	(66,000)
Net cash provided by operating activities		59,000
Cash flows from investing activities		
Sale of land	25,000	
Sale of equipment	34,000	
Purchase of equipment	(166,000)	
Net cash used by investing activities		(107,000)
Cash flows from financing activities		
Redemption of bonds	(10,000)	
Sale of common stock	130,000	
Payment of dividends	(55,000)	
Net cash provided by financing activities		65,000
Net increase in cash		17,000
Cash at beginning of period		37,000
Cash at end of period		$ 54,000
Noncash investing and financing activities		
Conversion of bonds into common stock		$ 30,000

USING CASH FLOWS TO EVALUATE A COMPANY

Traditionally, investors and creditors have most commonly used ratios based on accrual accounting. In this section we introduce **cash-flow measures** of analysis.

Free Cash Flow

In the statement of cash flows, cash provided by operating activities is intended to indicate the cash-generating capability of the company. Analysts have noted, however, that **cash provided by operating activities fails to take into account that a company must invest in new fixed assets** just to maintain its current level of operations. Companies also must at least **maintain dividends at current levels** to satisfy investors. A measurement that takes these necessary outflows into account while providing insight regarding a company's cash-generating ability is free cash flow. **Free cash flow** describes the cash remaining from operations after adjusting for capital expenditures and dividends. Illustration 6-20 shows the formula for computing free cash flow. (Alternative definitions also exist.)

Free Cash Flow	=	Cash Provided by Operations	−	Capital Expenditures	−	Cash Dividends

OBJECTIVE 7
Analyze the statement of cash flows.

Illustration 6-20
Free Cash Flow Formula

Consider the following example: Suppose that MPC produced and sold 10,000 personal computers this year. It reported $100,000 cash provided by operating activities. In order to maintain production at 10,000 computers, MPC invested $15,000 in equipment. It chose to pay $5,000 in dividends. Its free cash flow was $80,000 ($100,000 − $15,000 − $5,000). The company could use this $80,000 either to purchase new assets to expand the business or to pay an $80,000 dividend and continue to produce 10,000 computers.

Illustration 6-21 provides basic information excerpted from the 2006 statement of cash flows of **Microsoft Corporation**.

Microsoft Corporation

Statement of Cash Flows (partial)
2006 (in millions)

Cash provided by operations		$14,404
Cash flows from investing activities		
Additions to property, plant, and equipment	$ (1,578)	
Acquisitions	(649)	
Purchases of investments	(51,117)	
Sales of investments, security lending	61,347	
Cash provided by investing activities		8,003
Cash paid for dividends on common stock		(3,545)

Illustration 6-21
Microsoft Cash Flow Information ($ in millions)

Illustration 6-22 calculates Microsoft's free cash flow.

Cash provided by operating activities	$14,404
Less: Expenditures on property, plant, and equipment	1,578
Dividends paid	3,545
Free cash flow	**$ 9,281**

Illustration 6-22
Calculation of Microsoft's Free Cash Flow ($ in millions)

This free cash flow of $9.281 billion is a tremendous amount of cash generated in a single year. Microsoft can use it to acquire new assets, retire stock or debt, or pay dividends. While this amount is less than Microsoft's 2006 net income of $12,599 million, the nearly $10 billion of cash remaining after making capital expenditures and dividends lends additional credibility to Microsoft's income number as an indicator of potential future performance.

Oracle Corporation is the world's largest seller of database software and information management services. Like Microsoft, its success depends on continuing to improve its existing products while developing new products to keep pace with rapid changes in technology. Oracle's free cash flow for 2006 was $4.305 billion. This measure is impressive, but significantly less than Microsoft's amazing ability to generate cash.

Assessing Liquidity and Solvency Using Cash Flows

Ratios commonly used to analyze a company's liquidity and solvency employ accrual-based numbers from the income statement and balance sheet. In this section we focus on ratios that are cash-based rather than accrual-based. That is, instead of using numbers from the income statement, these ratios use numbers from the statement of cash flows.

Many analysts are critical of accrual-based numbers because they feel that the adjustment process allows too much management discretion. These analysts like to supplement accrual-based analysis with measures that use the cash flow statement. One disadvantage of these cash-based measures is that, unlike the more commonly employed accrual-based measures, there are no readily available industry averages for comparison. In the following discussion we use cash flow–based ratios to analyze Microsoft. In addition to the cash flow information provided in Illustration 6-22, we need the following information related to Microsoft.

($ in millions)	2006	2005
Current liabilities	$22,442	$16,877
Total liabilities	29,493	22,700
Current assets	49,010	48,737
Total assets	69,597	70,815

Liquidity

Liquidity is the ability of a business to meet its immediate obligations. One measure of liquidity is the *current ratio*: current assets divided by current liabilities. A disadvantage of the current ratio is that it uses year-end balances of current asset and current liability accounts. These year-end balances may not be representative of the company's position during most of the year.

A ratio that partially corrects this problem is the **current cash debt coverage ratio**. It is computed as cash provided by operating activities divided by average current liabilities. Because cash provided by operating activities involves the entire year rather than a balance at one point in time, it is often considered a better representation of liquidity on the average day. The ratio for **Microsoft Corporation** is calculated as shown in Illustration 6-23, with comparative numbers given for **Oracle**. For comparative purposes, we have also provided each company's current ratio.

Illustration 6-23
Current Cash Debt Coverage Ratio

$$\text{Current Cash Debt Coverage Ratio} = \frac{\text{Cash Provided by Operations}}{\text{Average Current Liabilities}}$$

($ in millions)	Current cash debt coverage ratio	Current ratio
Microsoft	$\dfrac{\$14,404}{(\$22,442 + \$16,877)/2} = .73$ times	2.18 times
Oracle	.61 times	1.42 times

Microsoft's net cash provided by operating activities is approximately .73 times its average current liabilities. Oracle's ratio of .61 times, though not a cause for concern, is substantially lower than that of Microsoft. Keep in mind that Microsoft's cash position is extraordinary. For example, many large companies now have current ratios in the range of

1.0. By this standard, Oracle's current ratio of 1.42 : 1 is respectable; Microsoft's current ratio of 2.18 : 1 is very strong.

Solvency

Solvency is the ability of a company to survive over the long term. A measure of solvency that uses cash figures is the **cash debt coverage ratio**. It is computed as the ratio of cash provided by operating activities to total debt, as represented by average total liabilities. This ratio indicates a company's ability to repay its liabilities from cash generated from operations—that is, without having to liquidate productive assets such as property, plant, and equipment. The cash debt coverage ratios for **Microsoft** and **Oracle** for 2006 are given in Illustration 6-24 For comparative purposes, the debt to total assets ratios for each company are also provided.

	Cash Debt Coverage Ratio $=$ Cash Provided by Operations / Average Total Liabilities	
($ in millions)	**Cash debt coverage ratio**	**Debt to total assets ratio**
Microsoft	$\dfrac{\$14{,}404}{(\$29{,}493 + \$22{,}700)/2} = .55$ times	.42 times
Oracle	.38 times	.48 times

Illustration 6-24
Cash Debt Coverage Ratio

Microsoft has relatively fewer long-term obligations. Thus, its cash debt coverage ratio is similar to its current cash debt coverage ratio. Obviously, Microsoft is very solvent. Oracle has some long-term debt with a debt to total assets ratio of 48.3% Its cash debt coverage ratio of .38 times is 69% of Microsoft's. Neither the cash nor accrual measures suggest any cause for concern for either company.

What do the numbers mean?   "How's My Cash Flow?"

To evaluate overall cash flow, it is useful to understand where in the product life cycle a company is. Generally, companies move through several stages of development, which have implications for cash flow. As the graph below shows, the pattern of cash flows from operating, financing, and investing activities varies depending on the stage of the product life cycle.

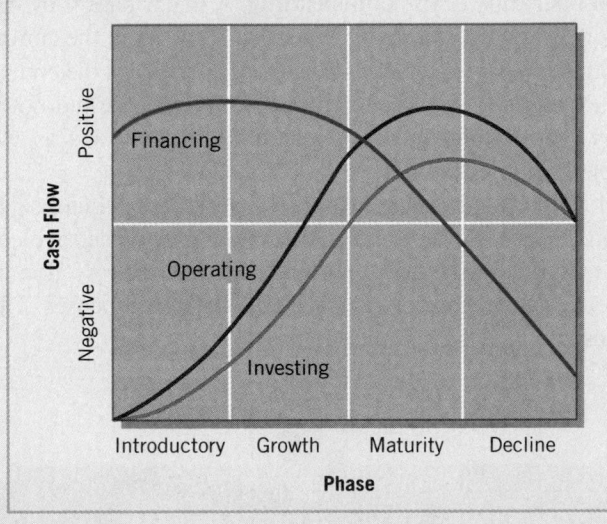

(continued)

In the *introductory phase*, the product is likely not generating much revenue. (That is, operating cash flow is negative.) Because the company is making heavy investments to get a product off the ground, cash flow from investment is negative, and financing cash flows are positive.

As the product moves to the *growth* and *maturity phases*, these cash flow relationships reverse. The product generates more cash flow from operations, which the company can use to cover investments needed to support the product, and less cash is needed from financing. So, is a negative operating cash flow bad? Not always. It depends on the product life cycle.

Source: Adapted from Paul D. Kimmel, Jerry J. Weygandt, and Donald E. Kieso, *Financial Accounting: Tools for Business Decision Making,* 4th ed. (New York: John Wiley & Sons, 2007), p. 591.

Beyond the Numbers

Until recently, **Microsoft** had never paid a cash dividend; beginning in 2003, Microsoft has paid a dividend every year. What part of the product life cycle do you think Microsoft is in? Explain.

Limitations of the Statement of Cash Flows

As indicated throughout this chapter, the statement of cash flows can be very valuable in examining the liquidity, solvency, and to a certain extent the financial performance of a company. However, you should recognize that this statement has two major limitations.

1 **Cash flow from operations is not accrual net income.** Some believe that the cash income (cash flows from operations) is more reliable than net income and hence a better measure to predict future cash flows. In other words, in this view, cash is the real bottom line and should be used to evaluate financial performance. However, the accrual basis, not the cash basis, recognizes all aspects of financial performance. Accrual-basis accounting provides more timely information about a company's cash flows by reporting these cash inflows and outflows associated with earnings activities as soon as these cash flows can be estimated with a reasonable degree of certainty. Receivables and payables are forecasters of future cash inflows and outflows. In other words, accrual-basis accounting aids in predicting future cash flows by reporting transactions with cash consequences at the time the transactions occur, rather when the cash is received or paid. Sole reliance on the statement of cash flows would ignore these consequences.

2 **Cash flow from operations can be misleading.** A major part of the fraud at **Worldcom** involved the capitalization of operating expenses. As a result, the company overstated net income. The same was true for the cash flow from operations; the company reported these cash operating expenses as investing activities and therefore did not reduce cash flows from operations. Thus, companies can manipulate cash flows as well as net income through the capitalization technique.

You should also recognize that, all other factors being equal, capital-intensive companies have a higher cash flow from operations than labor-intensive companies. The reason: Purchases of capital assets are reported in the investing section of the statement of cash flows, whereas labor costs are reported as operating expenses. Thus cash flow from operations is biased upwards for capital-intensive companies.

You will want to read the CONVERGENCE CORNER on the next page for discussion of how international convergence efforts relate to the statement of cash flows.

CONVERGENCE CORNER

Statement of Cash Flows

As in U.S. GAAP, the statement of cash flows is a required statement for iGAAP. In addition, the content and presentation of an iGAAP balance sheet is similar to one used for U.S. GAAP. However, the disclosure requirements related to the statement of cash flows are more extensive under U.S. GAAP. *IAS 7*, "Cash Flow Statements," provides the overall iGAAP requirements for cash flow information.

 RELEVANT FACTS

• Companies preparing financial statements under iGAAP must prepare a statement of cash flows as an integral part of the financial statements.

• Both iGAAP and U.S. GAAP require that the statement of cash flows should have three major sections—operating, investing and financing—along with changes in cash and cash equivalents.

• Similar to U.S. GAAP, the cash flow statement can be prepared using either the indirect or direct method under iGAAP. In both U.S. and international settings, companies choose for the most part to use the indirect method for reporting net cash flows from operating activities.

• iGAAP encourages companies to disclose the aggregate amount of cash flows that are attributable to the increase in operating capacity separately from those cash flows that are required to maintain operating capacity.

• The definition of cash equivalents used in iGAAP is similar to that used in U.S. GAAP. A major difference is that in certain situations bank overdrafts are considered part of cash and cash equivalents under iGAAP (which is not the case in U.S. GAAP). Under U.S. GAAP, bank overdrafts are classified as financing activities.

• iGAAP requires that noncash investing and financing activities be excluded from the statement of cash flows. Instead, these noncash activities should be reported elsewhere. This requirement is interpreted to mean that noncash investing and financing activities should be disclosed in the notes to the financial statements instead of in the financial statements. Under U.S. GAAP, companies may present this information in the cash flow statement.

 ABOUT THE NUMBERS

One area where there can be substantive differences between iGAAP and U.S. GAAP relates to the classification of interest, dividends, and taxes. The following table indicates the differences between the two approaches.

Item	iGAAP	U.S. GAAP
Interest paid	Operating or financing	Operating
Interest received	Operating or investing	Operating
Dividends paid	Operating or financing	Financing
Dividends received	Operating or investing	Operating
Taxes paid	Operating—unless specific identification with financing or investing	Operating[1,2]

[1] U.S. GAAP has additional disclosure rules
[2] U.S. GAAP has specific rules regarding the classification of the benefit associated with share-based compensation arrangements and the classification of derivatives that contain a financing element

Source: PricewaterhouseCoopers, *Similarities and Difference—A Comparison of IFRS and U.S. GAAP* (October 2006).

As indicated, the major difference is that iGAAP provides more alternatives for disclosing certain items.

 ON THE HORIZON

Presently, the FASB and the IASB are involved in a joint project on the presentation and organization of information in the financial statements. With respect to the cash flow statement specifically, the notion of *cash equivalents* will probably not be retained. The definition of cash in the existing literature would be retained, and the statement of cash flows would present information on changes in cash only. In addition, the FASB favors presentation of operating cash flows using the direct method only. However, the majority of IASB members express a preference for not requiring use of the direct method of reporting operating cash flows. So the two Boards will have to resolve their differences in this area in order to issue a converged standard for the statement of cash flows.

ACCOUNTING, ANALYSIS, PRINCIPLES

The income statement for the year ended December 31, 2008, for Laskowski Manufacturing Company contains the following condensed information.

Laskowski Company
Income Statement

Revenues		$6,583,000
Operating expenses (excluding depreciation)	$4,920,000	
Depreciation expense	880,000	5,800,000
Income before income tax		783,000
Income tax		353,000
Net income		$ 430,000

Included in operating expenses is a $24,000 loss resulting from the sale of machinery for $270,000 cash. The company purchased machinery at a cost of $750,000.

Laskowski reports the following balances on its comparative balance sheets at December 31.

Laskowski Manufacturing Company
Comparative Balance Sheets (partial)

	2008	2007
Cash	$672,000	$130,000
Accounts receivable	775,000	610,000
Inventories	834,000	867,000
Accounts payable	521,000	501,000

Income tax expense of $353,000 represents the amount paid in 2008. Dividends declared and paid in 2008 totaled $200,000.

Accounting

Prepare the statement of cash flows using the indirect method.

Analysis

Laskowski has an aggressive growth plan, which will require significant investments in plant and equipment over the next several years. Preliminary plans call for an investment of over $500,000 in the next year. Compute Laskowski's free cash flow and use it to evaluate the investment plans with the use of only internally generated funds.

 **Principles**

How does the statement of cash flows contribute to achieving the objectives of financial reporting?

Solution

Accounting

Laskowski Company
Statement of Cash Flows—Indirect Method
For the Year Ended December 31, 2008

Cash flows from operating activities	
Net income	$ 430,000
Adjustments to reconcile net income to net cash	

provided by operating activities:

Depreciation expense	$ 880,000	
Loss on sale of machinery	24,000	
Increase in accounts receivable	(165,000)	
Decrease in inventories	33,000	
Increase in accounts payable	20,000	792,000
Net cash provided by operating activities		1,222,000
Cash flows from investing activities		
Sale of machinery	270,000	
Purchase of machinery	(750,000)	
Net cash used by investing activities		(480,000)
Cash flows from financing activities		
Payment of cash dividends		(200,000)
Net increase in cash		542,000
Cash at beginning of period		130,000
Cash at end of period		$ 672,000

Analysis

Laskowski's free cash flow is:

Net cash provided by operating activities	$1,222,000
Less: Purchase of machinery	750,000
Dividends	200,000
Free cash flow	$ 272,000

Laskowski's free cash flow for the current year ($272,000) is less than the amount needed for expansion next year ($500,000). Thus, assuming operations at roughly the same level in future periods, Laskowski's free cash flow will not be sufficient to fund the expansion plan. The company might explore reducing the dividend or securing additional funds for the expansion through a borrowing.

Principles

According to *Statement of Financial Accounting Concepts No. 1,*

> Financial reporting should provide information that is useful to present and potential investors and creditors and other users in making rational investment, credit, and similar decisions. (Introduction)

More specifically,

> Financial reporting should provide information about the economic resources of an enterprise, the claims to those resources (obligations of the enterprise to transfer resources to other entities and owners' equity), and the effects of transactions, events, and circumstances that change resources and claims to those resources. (par. 40).

By reporting on cash provided by operations, and the sources and uses of cash from investing and financing decisions, the statement of cash flows provides information on the most liquid of company resources.

Key Terms

Cash debt coverage ratio, 271
Cash equivalents, 252
Current cash debt coverage ratio, 270
Financing activities, 252
Free cash flow, 269

Indirect method, 259
Investing activities, 252
Operating activities, 252
Statement of cash flows, 252

Summary of Learning Objectives

1 Indicate the primary purpose of the statement of cash flows. The statement of cash flows provides information about the cash receipts, cash payments, and net change in cash resulting from the operating, investing, and financing activities of a company during the period.

2 Distinguish among operating, investing, and financing activities. Operating activities include the cash effects of transactions that enter into the determination of net income. Investing activities involve cash flows resulting from changes in investments and long-term asset items. Financing activities involve cash flows resulting from changes in long-term liability and stockholders' equity items.

3 Identity sources of information for a statement of cash flows. The information to prepare the statement usually comes from three sources: (1) *Comparative balance sheets.* Information in these statements indicates the amount of the changes in assets, liabilities, and equities during the period. (2) *Current income statement.* Information in this statement is used in determining the cash provided by operations during the period. (3) *Selected transaction data.* These data from the general ledger provide additional detailed information needed to determine how cash was provided or used during the period.

4 Differentiate between net income and net cash provided by operating activities. Companies must adjust net income on an accural basis to determine net cash flow from operating activities because some expenses and losses do not cause cash outflows, and some revenues and gains do not provide cash inflows.

5 Determine net cash flows from investing and financing activities. Once a company has computed the net cash flow from operating activities, the next step is to determine whether any other changes in balance sheet accounts caused an increase or decrease in cash. Net cash flows from investing and financing activities can be determined by examining the changes in noncurrent balance sheet accounts.

6 Prepare a statement of cash flows. Preparing the statement involves three major steps: (1) *Determine the change in cash.* This is difference betwen the beginning and the ending cash balance shown on the comparative balance sheets. (2) *Determine the net cash flow from operating activities.* This procedure is complex; it involves analyzing not only the current year's income statement but also the comparative balance sheets and the selected transaction data. (3) *Determine cash flows from investing and financing activities.* Analyze all other changes in the balance sheet accounts to determine the effects on cash.

7 Use the statement of cash flows to evaluate a company. A number of measures can be derived by using information from the statement of cash flows as well as the other required financial statements. Free cash flow indicates the amount of cash a company generated during the current year that is available for the payment of dividends or for expansion. Liquidity can be measured with the current cash debt coverage ratio (cash provided by operating activities divided by average current liabilities). Solvency can be measured by the cash debt coverage ratio (cash provided by operating activities divided by average total liabilities).

APPENDIX 6A | RATIO ANALYSIS—A REFERENCE

OBJECTIVE 8

Identify the major types of financial ratios and what they measure.

Using Ratios to Analyze Financial Performance

Analysts and other interested parties can gather qualitative information from financial statements by examining relationships between items on the statements and identifying trends in these relationships. A useful starting point in developing this information is the application of ratio analysis.

A **ratio** expresses the mathematical relationship between one quantity and another. **Ratio analysis** expresses the relationship among selected financial statement data. The relationship is expressed in terms of either a percentage, a rate, or a simple proportion.

To illustrate, recently **IBM Corporation** had current assets of $41,338 million and current liabilities of $29,226 million. The relationship is determined by dividing current assets by current liabilities. The alternative means of expression are:

> **Percentage:** Current assets are 141% of current liabilities.
> **Rate:** Current assets are 1.41 times as great as current liabilities.
> **Proportion:** The relationship of current assets to liabilities is 1.41 : 1.

For analysis of financial statements, we classify ratios into four types, as follows.

MAJOR TYPES OF RATIOS

LIQUIDITY RATIOS. Measures of the enterprise's short-run ability to pay its maturing obligations.

ACTIVITY RATIOS. Measures of how effectively the enterprise is using the assets employed.

PROFITABILITY RATIOS. Measures of the degree of success or failure of a given enterprise or division for a given period of time.

COVERAGE RATIOS. Measures of the degree of protection for long-term creditors and investors.

Expanded Discussion of Financial Statement Analysis

Throughout the remainder of the textbook, we provide ratios to help you understand and interpret the information presented. Illustration 6A-1 below and on the next page presents the ratios that we will use throughout the text. You should find this chart helpful as you examine these ratios in more detail in the following chapters.

Illustration 6A-1
A Summary of Financial Ratios

Ratio	Formula	Purpose or Use
I. Liquidity ratios		
1. Current ratio	$\dfrac{\text{Current assets}}{\text{Current liabilities}}$	Measures short-term debt-paying ability.
2. Quick or acid-test ratio	$\dfrac{\text{Cash, marketable securities, and receivables (net)}}{\text{Current liabilities}}$	Measures immediate short-term liquidity.
3. Current cash debt coverage ratio	$\dfrac{\text{Net cash provided by operating activities}}{\text{Average current liabilities}}$	Measures a company's ability to pay off its current liabilities in a given year from its operations.
II. Activity ratios		
4. Receivables turnover	$\dfrac{\text{Net sales}}{\text{Average trade receivables (net)}}$	Measures liquidity of receivables.
5. Inventory turnover	$\dfrac{\text{Cost of goods sold}}{\text{Average inventory}}$	Measures liquidity of inventory.
6. Asset turnover	$\dfrac{\text{Net sales}}{\text{Average total assets}}$	Measures how efficiently assets are used to generate sales.

Illustration 6A-1
(Continued)

Ratio	Formula	Purpose or Use
III. Profitability ratios		
7. Profit margin on sales	$\dfrac{\text{Net income}}{\text{Net sales}}$	Measures net income generated by each dollar of sales.
8. Rate of return on assets	$\dfrac{\text{Net income}}{\text{Average total assets}}$	Measures overall profitability on assets.
9. Rate of return on common stock equity	$\dfrac{\text{Net income minus preferred dividends}}{\text{Average common stockholders' equity}}$	Measures return on common stockholders' investment.
10. Earnings per share	$\dfrac{\text{Net income minus preferred dividends}}{\text{Weighted shares outstanding}}$	Measures net income earned on each share of common stock.
11. Price-earnings ratio	$\dfrac{\text{Market price of stock}}{\text{Earnings per share}}$	Measures the ratio of the market price per share to earnings per share.
12. Payout ratio	$\dfrac{\text{Cash dividends}}{\text{Net income}}$	Measures percentage of earnings distributed in the form of cash dividends.
IV. Coverage ratios		
13. Debt to total assets	$\dfrac{\text{Total debt}}{\text{Total assets}}$	Measures the percentage of total assets provided by creditors.
14. Times interest earned	$\dfrac{\text{Income before interest charges and taxes}}{\text{Interest charges}}$	Measures ability to meet interest payments as they come due.
15. Cash debt coverage ratio	$\dfrac{\text{Net cash provided by operating activities}}{\text{Average total liabilities}}$	Measures a company's ability to repay its total liabilities in a given year from its operations.
16. Book value per share	$\dfrac{\text{Common stockholders' equity}}{\text{Outstanding shares}}$	Measures the amount each share would receive if the company were liquidated at the amounts reported on the balance sheet.

Key Terms for Appendix 6A

Summary of Learning Objective for Appendix 6A

8 **Identify the major types of financial ratios and what they measure.** Ratios express the mathematical relationship between one quantity and another, in terms of either a percentage, a rate, or a proportion. *Liquidity ratios* measure the short-run ability to pay maturing obligations. *Activity ratios* measure the effectiveness of asset usage. *Profitability* ratios measure the success or failure of an enterprise. *Coverage ratios* measure the degree of protection for long-term creditors and investors.

Review Exercise **279**

REVIEW EXERCISE

Data presented below are from the records of Antonio Brasileiro Company.

	December 31, 2008	December 31, 2007
Cash	$ 15,000	$ 8,000
Current assets other than cash	85,000	60,000
Long-term investments	10,000	53,000
Plant assets	335,000	215,000
	$445,000	$336,000
Accumulated depreciation	$ 20,000	$ 40,000
Current liabilities	40,000	22,000
Bonds payable	75,000	–0–
Common stock	254,000	254,000
Retained earnings	56,000	20,000
	$445,000	$336,000

Additional information:

1 In 2008 the company sold for $34,000 held-to-maturity securities carried at a cost of $43,000 on December 31, 2007. The loss (not extraordinary) was incorrectly charged directly to Retained Earnings.

2 In 2008 the company sold for $8,000 plant assets that cost $50,000 and were 80% depreciated. The loss (not extraordinary) was incorrectly charged directly to Retained Earnings.

3 Net income as reported on the income statement for the year was $57,000.

4 The company paid dividends totaling $10,000.

5 Depreciation charged for the year was $20,000.

Instructions

Prepare a statement of cash flows for the year 2008 using the indirect method.

Solution

Antonio Brasileiro Company
Statement of Cash Flows
for the Year Ended December 31, 2008
Indirect Method

Cash flows from operating activities		
Net income ($57,000 − $9,000 − $2,000)		$ 46,000
Adjustments to reconcile net income to net cash		
provided by operating activities:		
Depreciation expense	$ 20,000	
Loss on sale of investments	9,000	
Loss on sale of plant assets	2,000	

Increase in current assets other than cash	(25,000)	
Increase in current liabilities	18,000	24,000
Net cash provided by operating activities		70,000
Cash flows from investing activities		
Sale of plant assets	8,000	
Sale of held-to-maturity investments	34,000	
Purchase of plant assets*	(170,000)	
Net cash used by investing activities		(128,000)
Cash flows from financing activities		
Issuance of bonds payable	75,000	
Payment of dividends	(10,000)	
Net cash provided by financing activities		65,000
Net increase in cash		7,000
Cash balance, January 1, 2008		8,000
Cash balance, December 31, 2008		$ 15,000

*Supporting computation (purchase of plant assets):

Plant assets, December 31, 2007	$215,000	
Less: Plant assets sold	(50,000)	
	165,000	
Plant assets, December 31, 2008	335,000	
Plant assets purchased during 2008	$170,000	

Questions

Note: All **asterisked** assignment materials relate to material contained in appendix to the chapter.

1 What is a statement of cash flows?

2 John Stiller maintains that the statement of cash flows is an optional financial statement. Do you agree? Explain.

3 What questions about cash are answered by the statement of cash flows?

4 Distinguish among the three activities reported in the statement of cash flows.

5 (a) What are the major sources (inflows) of cash in a statement of cash flows?

(b) What are the major uses (outflows) of cash?

6 Why is it important to disclose certain noncash transactions? How should they be disclosed?

7 Wilma Flintstone and Barny Rublestone were discussing the format of the statement of cash flows of Rock Candy Co. At the bottom of Rock Candy's statement of cash flows was a separate section entitled "Noncash investing and financing activities." Give three examples of significant noncash transactions that would be reported in this section.

8 Why is it necessary to use comparative balance sheets, a current income statement, and certain transaction data in preparing a statement of cash flows?

9 Contrast the advantages and disadvantages of the direct and indirect methods of preparing the statement of cash flows. Are both methods acceptable? Which method is preferred by the FASB? Which method is more popular?

10 When the total cash inflows exceed the total cash outflows in the statement of cash flows, how and where is this excess identified?

11 Describe the indirect method for determining net cash provided (used) by operating activities.

12 Why is it necessary to convert accrual-based net income to cash-basis income when preparing a statement of cash flows?

13 The president of Frogger Company is puzzled. During the last year, the company experienced a net loss of $800,000, yet its cash increased $300,000 during the same period of time. Explain to the president how this could occur.

14 Identify five items that are adjustments to convert net income to net cash provided by operating activities under the indirect method.

15 Why and how is depreciation expense reported in a statement prepared using the indirect method?

16 Identify two noncash charges other than depreciation expense that are treated like depreciation expense in the statement of cash flows.

17 During 2008 Steinbrenner Company converted $1,700,000 of its total $2,000,000 of bonds payable into common stock.

Indicate how the transaction would be reported on a statement of cash flows, if at all.

18 What does free cash flow indicate, and how is it calculated?

19 Give examples of accrual-based and cash-based ratios to measure each of these characteristics of a company:

(a) Liquidity.

(b) Solvency.

20 What are the limitations of the statement of cash flows?

Brief Exercises

BE6-1 Each of these items must be considered in preparing a statement of cash flows for Jerry Co. for the year ended December 31, 2008. For each item, indicate its classification in the statement of cash flows for 2008.

(a) Issued bonds for $200,000 cash.
(b) Purchased equipment for $150,000 cash.
(c) Sold land costing $20,000 for $20,000 cash.
(d) Declared and paid a $50,000 cash dividend.

(LO 2)

BE6-2 Classify each item as an operating, investing, or financing activity. Assume all items involve cash unless there is information to the contrary.

(a) Purchase of equipment. (d) Depreciation.
(b) Sale of building.   (e) Payment of dividends.
(c) Redemption of bonds.   (f) Issuance of common stock.

(LO 2)

BE6-3 The following T account is a summary of the cash account of Elkhart Company.

(LO 2)

Cash (Summary Form)			
Balance, Jan. 1	8,000		
Receipts from customers	364,000	Payments for goods	200,000
Dividends on stock investments	6,000	Payments for operating expenses	140,000
Proceeds from sale of equipment	36,000	Interest paid	10,000
Proceeds from issuance of		Taxes paid	8,000
bonds payable	200,000	Dividends paid	50,000
Balance, Dec. 31	206,000		

What amount of net cash provided (used) by financing activities should be reported in the statement of cash flows?

BE6-4

(LO 4)

(a) Why is cash from operations likely to be lower than reported net income during the growth phase?
(b) Why is cash from investing often positive during the late maturity phase and during the decline phase?

BE6-5 Salvador, Inc. reported net income of $2.5 million in 2008. Depreciation for the year was $260,000, accounts receivable decreased $350,000, and accounts payable decreased $280,000. Compute net cash provided by operating activities using the indirect approach.

(LO 4)

BE6-6 The net income for Castle Co. for 2008 was $280,000. For 2008 depreciation on plant assets was $60,000, and the company incurred a loss on sale of plant assets of $12,000. Compute net cash provided by operating activities under the indirect method.

(LO 4)

(LO 4)

BE6-7 The comparative balance sheets for Holders Company show these changes in noncash current asset accounts: accounts receivable decrease $80,000, prepaid expenses increase $18,000, and inventories increase $30,000. Compute net cash provided by operating activities using the indirect method assuming that net income is $200,000.

(LO 5)

BE6-8 The T accounts for Equipment and the related Accumulated Depreciation for Triangle Art Company at the end of 2008 are shown here.

Equipment				Accumulated Depreciation			
Beg. bal.	80,000	Disposals	22,000	Disposals	5,500	Beg. bal.	44,500
Acquisitions	41,600					Depr. exp.	12,000
End. bal.	99,600					End. bal.	51,000

In addition, Triangle Art Company's income statement reported a loss on the sale of equipment of $7,500. What amount was reported on the statement of cash flows as "cash flow from sale of equipment"?

(LO 7)

BE6-9 **Cypress Semiconductor Corporation** in one year reported cash provided by operations of $95,100,000, cash used in investing of $322,500,000, and cash used in financing of $213,700,000. In addition, cash spent for fixed assets during the period was $176,800,000. Average current liabilities were $276,950,000, and average total liabilities were $1,026,050,000. No dividends were paid. Calculate the following:

(a) Free cash flow.
(b) Current cash debt coverage ratio.

(LO 7)

BE6-10 Jain Corporation reported cash provided by operating activities of $300,000, cash used by investing activities of $250,000, and cash provided by financing activities of $70,000. In addition, cash spent for capital assets during the period was $200,000. Average current liabilities were $150,000, and average total liabilities were $225,000. No dividends were paid. Calculate these values:

(a) Free cash flow.
(b) Current cash debt coverage ratio.

(LO 7)

BE6-11 **Alliance Atlantis Communication Inc.** reported a 30% increase in cash flow in the same quarter that it released its very successful movie *Austin Powers: They Spy Who Shagged Me*. The film earned more than $20 million in box office sales. Alliance reported cash provided by operating activities of $234,983,000 and revenues of $163,309,000. An amount of $258,000 was paid for preferred dividends. Cash spent on plant asset additions during the quarter was $4,318,000. Calculate free cash flow.

Exercises

(LO 2)

E6-1 **(Statement of Cash Flows—Classifications)** Big Salad Corporation had these transactions during 2008.
(a) Issued $50,000 par value common stock for cash.
(b) Purchased a machine for $30,000, giving a long-term note in exchange.
(c) Issued $200,000 par value common stock upon conversion of bonds having a face value of $200,000.
(d) Declared and paid a cash dividend of $18,000.
(e) Sold a long-term investment with a cost of $15,000 for $15,000 cash.
(f) Collected $16,000 of accounts receivable.
(g) Paid $18,000 on accounts payable.

Instructions

Analyze the transactions and indicate whether each transaction resulted in a cash flow from operating activities, investing activities, financing activities, or noncash investing and financing activities.

(LO 2)

E6-2 **(Statement of Cash Flows—Classifications)** An analysis of comparative balance sheets, the current year's income statement, and the general ledger accounts of Coffee Table Corp. uncovered the following items. Assume all items involve cash unless there is information to the contrary.
(a) Payment of interest on notes payable.
(b) Exchange of land for patent.
(c) Sale of building at book value.
(d) Payment of dividends.

(e) Depreciation.
(f) Receipt of dividends on investment in stock.
(g) Receipt of interest on notes receivable.
(h) Issuance of capital stock.
(i) Amortization of patent.

(j) Issuance of bonds for land.
(k) Purchase of land.
(l) Conversion of bonds into common stock.
(m) Loss on sale of land.
(n) Retirement of bonds.

Instructions

Indicate how each item should be classified in the statement of cash flows using these four major classifications: operating activity (indirect method), investing activity, financing activity, and significant noncash investing and financing activity.

E6-3 (Statement of Cash Flows—Classifications) The major classifications of activities reported in the statement of cash flows are operating, investing, and financing.

(LO 2)

Below is a list of common transactions.

(a) Issuance of capital stock.
(b) Purchase of land and building.
(c) Redemption of bonds.
(d) Sale of equipment.
(e) Depreciation of machinery.
(f) Amortization of patent.
(g) Issuance of bonds for plant assets.

(h) Payment of cash dividends.
(i) Exchange of furniture for office equipment.
(j) Purchase of treasury stock.
(k) Loss on sale of equipment.
(l) Increase in accounts receivable during the year.
(m) Decrease in accounts payable during the year.

Instructions

Classify each of the transactions above as:

1. Operating activity—add to net income.
2. Operating activity—deduct from net income.
3. Investing activity.
4. Financing activity.
5. Not reported as a cash flow.

E6-4 (Preparation of Operating Activities Section) Poppy Company reported net income of $195,000 for 2008. Poppy also reported depreciation expense of $45,000 and a loss of $5,000 on the sale of equipment. The comparative balance sheet shows a decrease in accounts receivable of $15,000 for the year, a $12,000 increase in accounts payable, and a $4,000 decrease in prepaid expenses.

(LO 4)

Instructions

Prepare the operating activities section of the statement of cash flows for 2008, using the indirect method.

E6-5 (Preparation of Operating Activities Section) The current sections of DoubleDip Inc.'s balance sheets at December 31, 2007 and 2008, are presented here.

(LO 4)

	2008	2007
Current assets		
Cash	$105,000	$ 99,000
Accounts receivable	120,000	89,000
Inventory	148,000	172,000
Prepaid expenses	27,000	22,000
Total current assets	$400,000	$382,000
Current liabilities		
Accrued expenses payable	$ 15,000	$ 5,000
Accounts payable	85,000	92,000
Total current liabilities	$100,000	$ 97,000

DoubleDip's net income for 2008 was $153,000. Depreciation expense was $19,000.

Instructions

Prepare the net cash provided by operating activities section of the company's statement of cash flows for the year ended December 31, 2008, using the indirect method.

(LO 4, 5) **E6-6** (Partial Statement of Cash Flows) These three accounts appear in the general ledger of Bosco Corp. during 2008.

Equipment

Date		Debit	Credit	Balance
Jan. 1	Balance			160,000
July 31	Purchase of equipment	70,000		230,000
Sept. 2	Cost of equipment constructed	53,000		283,000
Nov. 10	Cost of equipment sold		39,000	244,000

Accumulated Depreciation—Equipment

Date		Debit	Credit	Balance
Jan. 1	Balance			71,000
Nov. 10	Accumulated depreciation on equipment sold	30,000		41,000
Dec. 31	Depreciation for year		28,000	69,000

Retained Earnings

Date		Debit	Credit	Balance
Jan. 1	Balance			105,000
Aug. 23	Dividends (cash)	14,000		91,000
Dec. 31	Net income		67,000	158,000

Instructions

From the postings in the accounts, indicate how the information is reported on a statement of cash flows using the indirect method. The loss on sale of equipment was $3,000. (*Hint:* Purchase of equipment is reported in the investing activities section as a decrease in cash of $70,000.)

(LO 6, 7) **E6-7** (Statement of Cash Flows, Analysis) Here is a comparative balance sheet for Puffed Up Company:

Puffed Up Company Comparative Balance Sheet December 31		
Assets	2008	2007
Cash	$ 63,000	$ 22,000
Accounts receivable	85,000	76,000
Inventories	170,000	189,000
Land	75,000	100,000
Equipment	270,000	200,000
Accumulated depreciation	(66,000)	(32,000)
Total	$597,000	$555,000
Liabilities and Stockholders' Equity		
Accounts payable	$ 39,000	$ 47,000
Bonds payable	150,000	200,000
Common stock ($1 par)	216,000	174,000
Retained earnings	192,000	134,000
Total	$597,000	$555,000

Additional information:

1. Net income for 2008 was $98,000. Land was sold at cost. ✓
2. Cash dividends of $40,000 were declared and paid. ✓
3. Bonds payable amounting to $50,000 were redeemed for cash $50,000. ✓
4. Common stock was issued for $42,000 cash. ✓
5. Sales for 2008 were $978,000.

Instructions

(a) Prepare a statement of cash flows for 2008 using the indirect method.
(b) Compute these cash-basis ratios:

  (1) Current cash debt coverage.
  (2) Cash debt coverage.

E6-8 **(Preparation of Statement of Cash Flows)** The comparative balance sheets of Constantine Cavamanlis **(LO 6)**
Inc. at the beginning and the end of the year 2008 appear below.

Constantine Cavamanlis Inc. Balance Sheets			
Assets	Dec. 31, 2008	Jan. 1, 2008	Inc./Dec.
Cash	$ 45,000	$ 13,000	$32,000 Inc.
Accounts receivable	91,000	88,000	3,000 Inc.
Equipment	39,000	22,000	17,000 Inc.
Less: Accumulated depreciation	(17,000)	(11,000)	6,000 Inc.
Total	$158,000	$112,000	
Liabilities and Stockholders' Equity			
Accounts payable	$ 20,000	$ 15,000	5,000 Inc.
Common stock	100,000	80,000	20,000 Inc.
Retained earnings	38,000	17,000	21,000 Inc.
Total	$158,000	$112,000	

  Net income of $44,000 was reported and dividends of $23,000 were paid in 2008. New equipment was purchased and none was sold.

Instructions

Prepare a statement of cash flows for the year 2008.

E6-9 **(Preparation of Statement of Cash Flows)** Presented below is a condensed version of the compara- **(LO 6, 7)**
tive balance sheets for Zubin Mehta Corporation for the last two years at December 31.

	2008	2007
Cash	$ 177,000	$ 78,000
Accounts receivable	180,000	185,000
Investments	52,000	74,000
Equipment	298,000	240,000
Less: Accumulated depreciation	(106,000)	(89,000)
Current liabilities	134,000	151,000
Capital stock	160,000	160,000
Retained earnings	307,000	177,000

Additional information:
Investments were sold at a loss (not extraordinary) of $10,000; no equipment was sold; cash dividends paid were $30,000; and net income was $160,000.

Instructions

(a) Prepare a statement of cash flows for 2008 for Zubin Mehta Corporation.
(b) Determine Zubin Mehta Corporation's free cash flow.

(LO 7)   **E6-10** **(Analysis of Cash Flows)**   Presented here is 2006 information for **PepsiCo, Inc.** and **The Coca-Cola Company**.

($ in millions)	PepsiCo	Coca-Cola
Cash provided by operations	$ 6,084	$ 5,957
Average current liabilities	8,133	9,363
Average total liabilities	16,019	13,058
Net income	5,642	5,080
Sales	35,139	24,088

Instructions

Using the cash-based ratios presented in this chapter, compute and comment on the **(a)** liquidity and **(b)** solvency of the two companies.

(LO 7)   **E6-11** **(Analysis of Cash Flows)**   Information for two companies in the same industry, Rita Corporation and Les Corporation, is presented here.

	Rita Corporation	Les Corporation
Cash provided by operating activities	$200,000	$200,000
Average current liabilities	50,000	100,000
Average total liabilities	200,000	250,000
Net earnings	200,000	200,000
Sales	400,000	800,000

Instructions

Using the cash-based ratios presented in this chapter, compute and comment on the (a) liquidity and (b) solvency of the two companies.

See the book's companion website, at www.wiley.com/college/warfield, for Additional Exercises

Problems

(LO 2)   **P6-1** **(Statement of Cash Flows—Classification)**   The following transactions took place during a recent fiscal year.

Transaction	Where Reported on Statement	Cash Inflow, Outflow, or No Effect?
(a) Recorded depreciation expense on the plant assets.		
(b) Incurred a loss on disposal of plant assets.		
(c) Acquired a building by paying cash.		
(d) Made principal repayments on a mortgage.		
(e) Issued common stock.		
(f) Purchased shares of another company to be held as a long-term equity investment.		
(g) Paid dividends to common stockholders.		
(h) Sold inventory on credit. The company uses a perpetual inventory system.		
(i) Purchased inventory on credit.		
(j) Paid wages to employees.		

Instructions

Complete the table indicating whether each item (1) should be reported as an operating (O) activity, investing (I) activity, financing (F) activity, or as a noncash (NC) transaction reported in a separate schedule, and (2) represents a cash inflow or cash outflow or has no cash flow effect. Assume use of the indirect approach.

P6-2 **(Statement of Cash Flows—Classifications)** The following selected account balances relate to the plant asset accounts of Trudeau Inc. at year-end.   **(LO 2, 5)**

	2008	2007
Accumulated depreciation—buildings	$337,500	$300,000
Accumulated depreciation—equipment	144,000	96,000
Buildings	750,000	750,000
Depreciation expense	101,500	85,500
Equipment	300,000	240,000
Land	100,000	70,000
Loss on sale of equipment	1,000	–0–

Additional information:

1. Trudeau purchased $80,000 of equipment and $30,000 of land for cash in 2008.
2. Trudeau also sold equipment in 2008.

Instructions

(a) Determine the amounts of any cash inflows or outflows related to the plant asset accounts in 2008.
(b) Indicate where each of the cash inflows or outflows identified in (a) would be classified on the statement of cash flows.

P6-3 **(Cash Flow from Operations)** The income statement of Kroncke Company is presented here.   **(LO 4)**

<table>
<tr><td colspan="3" align="center">**Kroncke Company**
Income Statement
For the Year Ended December 31, 2008</td></tr>
<tr><td>Sales</td><td></td><td>$5,400,000</td></tr>
<tr><td>Cost of goods sold</td><td></td><td></td></tr>
<tr><td> Beginning inventory</td><td>$1,780,000</td><td></td></tr>
<tr><td> Purchases</td><td>3,430,000</td><td></td></tr>
<tr><td> Goods available for sale</td><td>5,210,000</td><td></td></tr>
<tr><td> Ending inventory</td><td>1,920,000</td><td></td></tr>
<tr><td> Total cost of goods sold</td><td></td><td>3,290,000</td></tr>
<tr><td>Gross profit</td><td></td><td>2,110,000</td></tr>
<tr><td>Operating expenses</td><td></td><td></td></tr>
<tr><td> Selling expenses</td><td>400,000</td><td></td></tr>
<tr><td> Administrative expense</td><td>525,000</td><td></td></tr>
<tr><td> Depreciation expense</td><td>125,000</td><td></td></tr>
<tr><td> Amortization expense</td><td>20,000</td><td>1,070,000</td></tr>
<tr><td>Net income</td><td></td><td>$1,040,000</td></tr>
</table>

Additional information:

1. Accounts receivable decreased $510,000 during the year.
2. Prepaid expenses increased $170,000 during the year.
3. Accounts payable to merchandise suppliers increased $50,000 during the year.
4. Accrued expenses payable increased $165,000 during the year.

Instructions

Prepare the operating activities section of the statement of cash flows for the year ended December 31, 2008, for Kroncke Company, using the indirect method.

P6-4 **(Cash Flow from Operations)** The income statement of Kraemer Inc. reported the following condensed information.

(LO 4)

Kraemer Inc.
Income Statement
For the Year Ended December 31, 2008

Revenues	$545,000
Operating expenses	400,000
Income from operations	145,000
Income tax expense	47,000
Net income	$ 98,000

Kraemer's balance sheet contained these comparative data at December 31.

	2008	2007
Accounts receivable	$50,000	$70,000
Accounts payable	30,000	41,000
Income taxes payable	10,000	4,000

Kraemer has no depreciable assets. Accounts payable pertain to operating expenses.

Instructions

Prepare the operating activities section of the statement of cash flows using the indirect method.

(LO 6, 7) **P6-5** (**Preparation and Analysis of Statement of Cash Flows**) Here are the financial statements of YoYo Company.

YoYo Company
Comparative Balance Sheets
December 31

Assets		2008		2007
Cash		$ 26,000		$ 33,000
Accounts receivable		28,000		14,000
Merchandise inventory		38,000		25,000
Property, plant, and equipment	$70,000		$78,000	
Less: Accumulated depreciation	(27,000)	43,000	(24,000)	54,000
Total		$135,000		$126,000
Liabilities and Stockholders' Equity				
Accounts payable		$ 31,000		$ 43,000
Income taxes payable		26,000		20,000
Bonds payable		20,000		10,000
Common stock		25,000		25,000
Retained earnings		33,000		28,000
Total		$135,000		$126,000

YoYo Company
Income Statement
For the Year Ended December 31, 2008

Sales		$286,000
Cost of goods sold		194,000
Gross profit		92,000
Selling expenses	$28,000	
Administrative expenses	9,000	37,000
Income from operations		55,000
Interest expense		7,000
Income before income taxes		48,000
Income tax expense		7,000
Net income		$ 41,000

Additional data:

1. Dividends of $36,000 were declared and paid.

2. During the year equipment was sold for $10,000 cash. This equipment cost $15,000 originally and had a book value of $10,000 at the time of sale.

3. All depreciation expense, $8,000, is in the selling expense category.

4. All sales and purchases are on account.

5. Additional equipment was purchased for $7,000 cash.

Instructions

(a) Prepare a statement of cash flows using the indirect method.

(b) Compute these cash-basis measures:

(1) Current cash debt coverage ratio.
(2) Cash debt coverage ratio.
(3) Free cash flow.

P6-6 **(Preparation of Statement of Cash Flows)** Condensed financial data of George Company follow. **(LO 6)**

George Company Comparative Balance Sheets December 31		
Assets	2008	2007
Cash	$ 92,700	$ 33,400
Accounts receivable	80,800	37,000
Inventories	121,900	102,650
Investments	84,500	107,000
Plant assets	310,000	205,000
Accumulated depreciation	(49,500)	(40,000)
Total	$640,400	$445,050
Liabilities and Stockholders' Equity		
Accounts payable	$ 62,700	$ 48,280
Accrued expenses payable	12,100	18,830
Bonds payable	140,000	70,000
Common stock	250,000	200,000
Retained earnings	175,600	107,940
Total	$640,400	$445,050

George Company Income Statement Data For the Year Ended December 31, 2008		
Sales		$297,500
Gain on sale of plant assets		5,000
		302,500
Less:		
Cost of goods sold	$99,460	
Operating expenses, excluding depreciation expense	14,670	
Depreciation expense	35,500	
Income taxes	7,270	
Interest expense	2,940	159,840
Net income		$142,660

Additional information:

1. New plant assets costing $141,000 were purchased for cash during the year.

2. Investments were sold at cost.

3. Plant assets costing $36,000 were sold for $15,000, resulting in a gain of $5,000.

4. A cash dividend of $75,000 was declared and paid during the year.

Instructions

Prepare a statement of cash flows using the indirect method.

(LO 6)   **P6-7   (Preparation of Statement of Cash Flows)**   Presented here is the comparative balance sheet for Perry Company at December 31.

Perry Company Comparative Balance Sheets December 31		
Assets	2008	2007
Cash	$ 26,000	$ 57,000
Accounts receivable	77,000	64,000
Inventory	192,000	140,000
Prepaid expenses	12,140	16,540
Land	105,000	150,000
Equipment	215,000	175,000
Accumulated depreciation—equipment	(70,000)	(42,000)
Building	250,000	250,000
Accumulated depreciation—building	(70,000)	(50,000)
Total	$737,140	$760,540
Liabilities and Stockholders' Equity		
Accounts payable	$ 63,000	$ 45,000
Bonds payable	235,000	265,000
Common stock, $1 par	280,000	250,000
Retained earnings	159,140	200,540
Total	$737,140	$760,540

Additional information:

1. Operating expenses include depreciation expense $65,000 and charges from prepaid expenses of $4,400.

2. Land was sold for cash at cost.

3. Cash dividends of $74,290 were paid.

4. Net income for 2008 was $32,890.

5. Equipment was purchased for $80,000 cash. In addition, equipment costing $40,000 with a book value of $23,000 was sold for $25,000 cash.

6. Bonds were converted at face value by issuing 30,000 shares of $1 par value common stock.

Instructions

Prepare a statement of cash flows for 2008 using the indirect method.

(LO 7)   **P6-8   (Analysis of Cash Flow Information)**   The following transactions took place during the year.

Transactions	Free Cash Flow ($125,000)	Current Cash Debt Coverage Ratio (0.5x)	Cash Debt Coverage Ratio (0.3x)
(a) Recorded cash sales $8,000.			
(b) Purchased inventory for $1,500 cash.			
(c) Purchased new equipment $10,000; signed a short-term note payable for the cost of the equipment.			
(d) Paid a $20,000 cash dividend to common stockholders.			
(e) Acquired a building for $750,000, by signing a mortgage payable for $450,000 and issuing common stock for the balance.			
(f) Made a principal payment on the mortgage currently due, $45,000.			

Instructions

For each transaction listed on page 290, indicate whether it will increase (I), decrease (D), or have no effect (NE) on the ratios.

P6-9 **(Preparation and Analysis of Statement of Cash Flows)** Presented below are the financial state-ments of Newman Company.

(LO 6, 7)

Newman Company
Comparative Balance Sheets
December 31

Assets	2008	2007
Cash	$ 31,000	$ 20,000
Accounts receivable	38,000	14,000
Merchandise inventory	27,000	20,000
Property, plant, and equipment	60,000	78,000
Accumulated depreciation	(30,000)	(24,000)
Total	$126,000	$108,000
Liabilities and Stockholders' Equity		
Accounts payable	$ 29,000	$ 15,000
Income taxes payable	7,000	8,000
Bonds payable	27,000	33,000
Common stock	18,000	14,000
Retained earnings	45,000	38,000
Total	$126,000	$108,000

Newman Company
Income Statement
For the Year Ended December 31, 2008

Sales		$242,000
Cost of goods sold		175,000
Gross profit		67,000
Selling expenses	$18,000	
Administrative expenses	6,000	24,000
Income from operations		43,000
Interest expense		3,000
Income before income taxes		40,000
Income tax expense		6,000
Net income		$ 34,000

Additional data:

1. Dividends declared and paid were $27,000.

2. During the year equipment was sold for $8,500 cash. This equipment cost $18,000 originally and had a book value of $8,500 at the time of sale.

3. All depreciation expense is in the selling expense category.

4. All sales and purchases are on account.

Instructions

(a) Prepare a statement of cash flows using the indirect method.
(b) Compute these cash-basis measures:
  (1) Current cash debt coverage ratio.
  (2) Cash debt coverage ratio.
  (3) Free cash flow.

(LO 6)   **P6-10** **(Preparation of Statement of Cash Flows)** Condensed financial data of Elly Inc. follow.

Elly Inc.
Comparative Balance Sheets
December 31

Assets	2008	2007
Cash	$ 97,800	$ 48,400
Accounts receivable	95,800	33,000
Inventories	112,500	102,850
Prepaid expenses	28,400	26,000
Investments	128,000	114,000
Plant assets	270,000	242,500
Accumulated depreciation	(50,000)	(52,000)
Total	$682,500	$514,750

Liabilities and Stockholders' Equity		
Accounts payable	$102,000	$ 67,300
Accrued expenses payable	16,500	17,000
Bonds payable	110,000	150,000
Common stock	220,000	175,000
Retained earnings	234,000	105,450
Total	$682,500	$514,750

Elly Inc.
Income Statement Data
For the Year Ended December 31, 2008

Sales		$392,780
Less:		
Cost of goods sold	$135,460	
Operating expenses, excluding depreciation	12,410	
Depreciation expense	46,500	
Income taxes	7,280	
Interest expense	4,730	
Loss on sale of plant assets	7,500	213,880
Net income		$178,900

Additional information:

1. New plant assets costing $85,000 were purchased for cash during the year.

2. Old plant assets having an original cost of $57,500 were sold for $1,500 cash.

3. Bonds matured and were paid off at face value for cash.

4. A cash dividend of $50,350 was declared and paid during the year.

Instructions

Prepare a statement of cash flows using the indirect method.

ACCOUNTING IN ACTION

Financial Reporting and Analysis

■ Financial Reporting Issues: The Procter & Gamble Company

AIA6-1   The financial statements of **Procter & Gamble (P&G)** can be accessed at the book's website.

Instructions

Refer to P&G's financial statements and the accompanying notes to answer the following questions.

(a) Which method of computing net cash provided by operating activities does P&G use? What were the amounts of cash provided by operations for the years 2004, 2005, and 2006? Which two items were most responsible for the increase in cash provided by operating activities in 2006?

(b) What was the most significant item in the cash flows used for the investing activities section in 2006? What was the most significant item in the cash flows used for the financing activities section in 2006?

(c) Where is depreciation reported in P&G's statement of cash flows? Why is depreciation added to net income in the statement of cash flows?

■ Comparative Analysis: The Coca-Cola Company and PepsiCo, Inc.   **PEPSICO**

AIA6-2   The financial statements of **The Coca-Cola Company** and **PepsiCo, Inc.** can be accessed at the book's website.

Instructions

Use information found at the book's website to answer the following questions.

(a) What method of computing net cash provided by operating activities does Coca-Cola use? What method does PepsiCo use? What were the amounts of cash provided by operating activities reported by Coca-Cola and PepsiCo in 2006?

(b) What was the most significant item reported by Coca-Cola and PepsiCo in 2006 in their investing activities sections? What is the most significant item reported by Coca-Cola and PepsiCo in 2006 in their financing activities sections?

(c) What were these two companies' trends in net cash provided by operating activities over the period 2004 to 2006?

(d) Where is "depreciation and amortization" reported by Coca-Cola and PepsiCo in their statements of cash flows? What is the amount and why does it appear in that section of the statement of cash flows?

(e) Based on the information contained in Coca-Cola's and PepsiCo's financial statements, compute free cash flow. What conclusions concerning the management of cash can be drawn from the free cash flow analysis?

■ Financial Statement Analysis

AIA6-3   **Vermont Teddy Bear Co.** was founded in the early 1980s. The company designs and manufactures American-made teddy bears and markets them primarily as gifts called Bear-Grams or Teddy Bear-Grams. Bear-Grams are personalized teddy bears delivered directly to the recipient for special occasions such as birthdays and anniversaries. The Shelburne, Vermont, company's primary markets are New York, Boston, and Chicago. Sales have jumped dramatically in recent years. Such dramatic growth has significant implications for cash flows. Provided below are the cash flow statements for two recent years for the company.

Vermont Teddy Bear Co.

Cash Flow Statements

	Current Year	Prior Year
Cash flows from operating activities:		
Net income	$ 17,523	$ 838,955
Adjustments to reconcile net income to net		
cash provided by operating activities		
Deferred income taxes	(69,524)	(146,590)
Depreciation and amortization	316,416	181,348

	Current Year	Prior Year
Changes in assets and liabilities:		
Accounts receivable, trade	(38,267)	(25,947)
Inventories	(1,599,014)	(1,289,293)
Prepaid and other current assets	(444,794)	(113,205)
Deposits and other assets	(24,240)	(83,044)
Accounts payable	2,017,059	(284,567)
Accrued expenses	61,321	170,755
Accrued interest payable, debentures	—	(58,219)
Other	—	(8,960)
Income taxes payable	—	117,810
Net cash provided by (used for) operating activities	236,480	(700,957)
Net cash used for investing activities	(2,102,892)	(4,422,953)
Net cash (used for) provided by financing activities	(315,353)	9,685,435
Net change in cash and cash equivalents	(2,181,765)	4,561,525

Other information:

Current liabilities	$ 4,055,465	$ 1,995,600
Total liabilities	4,620,085	2,184,386
Net sales	20,560,566	17,025,856

Instructions

(a) Note that net income in the current year was only $17,523 compared to prior-year income of $838,955, but cash flow from operations was $236,480 in the current year and a negative $700,957 in the prior year. Explain the causes of this apparent paradox.

(b) Evaluate Vermont Teddy Bear's liquidity and solvency for the current year using cash flow-based ratios.

AIA6-4 The incredible growth of **Amazon.com** has put fear into the hearts of traditional retailers. Amazon.com's stock price has soared to amazing levels. However, it is often pointed out in the financial press that the company did not report a profit until 2003 (several years after it went public). The following financial information is taken from the 2003 financial statements of Amazon.com.

($ in millions)	2003	2002
Current assets	$1,821	$1,616
Total assets	2,162	1,990
Current liabilities	1,253	1,066
Total liabilities	3,198	3,343
Cash provided by operations	392	174
Capital expenditures	46	39
Dividends paid	–0–	–0–
Net income (loss)	35	(149)
Sales	5,264	3,933

Instructions

(a) Calculate free cash flow for Amazon.com for 2003 and 2002, and discuss the company's ability to finance expansion from internally generated cash. Thus far, Amazon.com has avoided purchasing large warehouses. Instead, it has used those of others. It is possible, however, that in order to increase customer satisfaction the company may have to build its own warehouses. If this happens, how might your impression of its ability to finance expansion change?

(b) Discuss any potential implications of the change in Amazon.com's cash provided by operations from 2002 to 2003.

(c) Based on your findings in parts (a) and (b), can you conclude whether Amazon.com's amazing stock price is justified?

■ International Reporting Issues

AIA6-5 The statement of cash flows has become a commonly provided financial statement by companies throughout the world. It is interesting to note, however, that its format does vary across countries. The statement of cash flows below is from the financial statements of Irish pharmaceutical company **Élan Corporation**.

Élan Corporation

Consolidated Statement of Cash Flows

	Year Ended 31 December $m
Cash Flow from Operating Activities	(322.3)
Returns on Investments and Servicing of Finance	
Interest received	24.2
Interest paid	(281.9)
Cash outflow from returns on investments and servicing of finance	(257.7)
Taxation	(8.9)
Capital Expenditure and Financial Investment	
Additions to property, plant and equipment	(33.7)
Receipts from disposal of property, plant and equipment	27.9
Payments to acquire intangible assets	(144.8)
Receipts from disposal of intangible assets	0.5
Payments to acquire Pharma Marketing/Autoimmune product royalty rights	(297.6)
Payments to acquire financial fixed assets	(13.9)
Receipts from disposal of financial fixed assets	329.3
Cash outflow from capital expenditure and financial investment	(132.3)
Acquisitions and Disposals	
Cash received on disposal of businesses	546.9
Cash received on disposal of subsidiaries	46.1
Cash inflow from acquisitions and disposals	593.0
Cash outflow before use of liquid resources and financing	(128.2)
Management of Liquid Resources	14.5
Financing	
Proceeds from issue of share capital	167.9
Issue of loan notes	460.0
Repurchase of LYONs	(687.5)
Repayment of loans	(83.2)
Cash (outflow)/inflow from financing	(142.8)
Net (decrease)/increase in cash	(256.5)
The accompanying notes are an integral part of these financial statements.	
Reconciliation of Net Cash Flow to Movement in Net Debt	
(Decrease)/increase in cash for the period	(256.5)
Cash inflow from movement in liquid resources	(14.5)
	(271.0)
Repayment of loans	83.2
Repurchase of LYONs	803.4
Issue of loan notes	(460.0)
Change in net debt resulting from cash flows	155.6
Non-cash movement—translation differences	12.5
Non-cash movement—notes	(18.0)
Non-cash movement—other	(1.2)
Decrease/(increase) in net debt	148.9

Instructions

(a) What similarities to U.S. cash flow statements do you notice in terms of general format, as well as terminology?

(b) What differences do you notice in terms of general format, as well as terminology?

Concepts for Analysis

AIA6-6 **(SCF Theory and Analysis of Transactions)** John Lee Hooker Company is a young and growing producer of electronic measuring instruments and technical equipment. You have been retained by Hooker to advise it in the preparation of a statement of cash flows using the indirect method. For the fiscal year ended October 31, 2008, you have obtained the following information concerning certain events and transactions of Hooker.

1. The amount of reported earnings for the fiscal year was $800,000, which included a deduction for a loss of $110,000 on the sale of land. Cash proceeds were $30,000.
2. Depreciation expense of $315,000 was included in the income statement.
3. Uncollectible accounts receivable of $40,000 were written off against the allowance for doubtful accounts. Also, $51,000 of bad debt expense was included in determining income for the fiscal year, and the same amount was added to the allowance for doubtful accounts.
4. A gain of $9,000 was realized on the sale of a machine. It originally cost $75,000, of which $30,000 was undepreciated on the date of sale.
5. On July 3, 2008, building and land were purchased for $700,000. Hooker gave in payment $75,000 cash, $200,000 market value of its unissued common stock, and signed a $425,000 mortgage note payable.
6. On August 3, 2008, $800,000 face value of Hooker's 10% convertible debentures were converted into $150,000 par value of its common stock. The bonds were originally issued at face value.

Instructions

Explain whether each of the six numbered items above is a source or use of cash, and explain how it should be disclosed in John Lee Hooker's statement of cash flows for the fiscal year ended October 31, 2008. If any item is neither a source nor a use of cash, explain why it is not, and indicate the disclosure, if any, that should be made of the item in John Lee Hooker's statement of cash flows for the fiscal year ended October 31, 2008.

AIA6-7 **(Analysis of Transactions' Effect on SCF)** Each of the following items must be considered in preparing a statement of cash flows for Buddy Guy Fashions Inc. for the year ended December 31, 2008.

1. Fixed assets that had cost $20,000 6½ years before and were being depreciated on a 10-year basis, with no estimated scrap value, were sold for $5,250.
2. During the year, goodwill of $15,000 was considered impaired and was completely written off to expense.
3. During the year, 500 shares of common stock with a stated value of $25 a share were issued for $34 a share.
4. The company sustained a net loss for the year of $2,100. Depreciation amounted to $2,000 and patent amortization was $400.
5. Uncollectible accounts receivable in the amount of $2,000 were written off against the Allowance for Doubtful Accounts.
6. Investments (available-for-sale) that cost $12,000 when purchased 4 years earlier were sold for $10,600. The loss was considered ordinary.
7. Bonds payable with a par value of $24,000 on which there was an unamortized bond premium of $2,000 were redeemed at 103. The gain was credited to ordinary income.

Instructions

For each item, state where it is to be shown in the statement and then how you would present the necessary information, including the amount. Consider each item to be independent of the others. Assume that correct entries were made for all transactions as they took place.

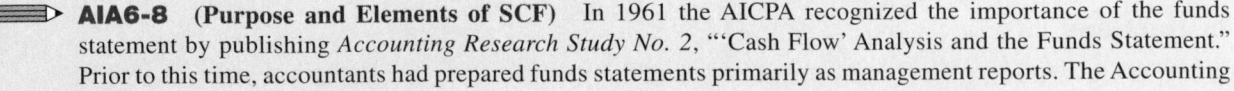 **AIA6-8** **(Purpose and Elements of SCF)** In 1961 the AICPA recognized the importance of the funds statement by publishing *Accounting Research Study No. 2*, "'Cash Flow' Analysis and the Funds Statement." Prior to this time, accountants had prepared funds statements primarily as management reports. The Accounting

Principles Board responded by issuing *APB Opinion No. 3*, "The Statement of Source and Application of Funds," which recommended that a statement of source and application of funds be presented on a supplementary basis. Because of the favorable response of the business community to this pronouncement, the APB issued *Opinion No. 19*, "Reporting Changes in Financial Position" in 1971. This opinion required that a statement of changes in financial position be presented as a basic financial statement and be covered by the auditor's report.

In 1981 the Financial Accounting Standards Board reconsidered funds flow issues as part of the conceptual framework project. At this time, the FASB decided that cash flow reporting issues should be considered at the standards level. Subsequent deliberations resulted in *Statement of Financial Accounting Standards (SFAS) No. 95*, "Statement of Cash Flows."

Instructions

(a) Explain the purposes of the statement of cash flows.
(b) List and describe the three categories of activities that must be reported in the statement of cash flows.
(c) Identify and describe the two methods that are allowed for reporting cash flows from operations.
(d) Describe the financial statement presentation of noncash investing and financing transactions. Include in your description an example of a noncash investing and financing transaction.

AIA6-9 **(Cash Flow Analysis)** The partner in charge of the James Spencer Corporation audit comes by your desk and leaves a letter he has started to the CEO and a copy of the cash flow statement for the year ended December 31, 2008. Because he must leave on an emergency, he asks you to finish the letter by explaining: (1) the disparity between net income and cash flow; (2) the importance of operating cash flow; (3) the renewable source(s) of cash flow; and (4) possible suggestions to improve the cash position.

James Spencer Corporation
Statement of Cash Flows
For the Year Ended December 31, 2008

Cash flows from operating activities		
Net income		$100,000
Adjustments to reconcile net income to net cash provided by operating activities:		
Depreciation expense	$ 10,000	
Amortization expense	1,000	
Loss on sale of fixed assets	5,000	
Increase in accounts receivable (net)	(40,000)	
Increase in inventory	(35,000)	
Decrease in accounts payable	(41,000)	(100,000)
Net cash provided by operating activities		– 0 –
Cash flows from investing activities		
Sale of plant assets	$ 25,000	
Purchase of equipment	(100,000)	
Purchase of land	(200,000)	
Net cash used by investing activities		(275,000)
Cash flows from financing activities		
Payment of dividends	$ (10,000)	
Redemption of bonds	(100,000)	
Net cash used by financing activities		(110,000)
Net decrease in cash		(385,000)
Cash balance, January 1, 2008		400,000
Cash balance, December 31, 2008		$ 15,000

Date

James Spencer, III, CEO
James Spencer Corporation
125 Wall Street
Middleton, Kansas 67458

Dear Mr. Spencer:

I have good news and bad news about the financial statements for the year ended December 31, 2008. The good news is that net income of $100,000 is close to what we predicted in the strategic plan last year, indicating strong performance this year. The bad news is that the cash balance is seriously low. Enclosed is the Statement of Cash Flows, which best illustrates how both of these situations occurred simultaneously. . . .

Instructions

Complete the letter to the CEO, including the four components requested by your boss.

Professional Tools

■ Ethical Decision Making

AIA6-10 Durocher Guitar Company is in the business of manufacturing top-quality, steel-string folk guitars. In recent years the company has experienced working capital problems resulting from the procurement of factory equipment, the unanticipated buildup of receivables and inventories, and the payoff of a balloon mortgage on a new manufacturing facility. The founder and president of the company, Laraine Durocher, has attempted to raise cash from various financial institutions, but to no avail because of the company's poor performance in recent years. In particular, the company's lead bank, First Financial, is especially concerned about Durocher's inability to maintain a positive cash position. The commercial loan officer from First Financial told Laraine, "I can't even consider your request for capital financing unless I see that your company is able to generate positive cash flows from operations."

Thinking about the banker's comment, Laraine came up with what she believes is a good plan: With a more attractive statement of cash flows, the bank might be willing to provide long-term financing. To "window dress" cash flows, the company can sell its accounts receivables to factors and liquidate its raw material inventories. These rather costly transactions would generate lots of cash. As the chief accountant for Durocher Guitar, it is your job to tell Laraine what you think of her plan.

Instructions

Answer the following questions.
(a) What are the ethical issues related to Laraine Durocher's idea?
(b) What would you tell Laraine Durocher?

AIA6-11 Tappit Corporation is a medium-sized wholesaler of automotive parts. It has ten stockholders, who have been paid a total of $1 million in cash dividends for eight consecutive years. The policy of the Board of Directors requires that in order for this dividend to be declared, net cash provided by operating activities as reported in Tappit's current year's statement of cash flows must be in excess of $1 million. President and CEO Ray Thomas's job is secure so long as he produces annual operating cash flows to support the usual dividend.

At the end of the current year, controller Jon Lawler presents president Thomas with some disappointing news: The net cash provided by operating activities is calculated, by the indirect method, to be only $970,000. The president says to Jon, "We must get that amount above $1 million. Isn't there some way to increase operating cash flow by another $30,000?" Jon answers, "These figures were prepared by my assistant. I'll go back to my office and see what I can do." The president replies, "I know you won't let me down, Jon."

Upon close scrutiny of the statement of cash flows, Jon concludes that he can get the operating cash flows above $1 million by reclassifying a $60,000, 2-year note payable listed in the financing activities section as "Proceeds from bank loan—$60,000." He will report the note instead as "Increase in payables—$60,000" and treat it as an adjustment of net income in the operating activities section. He returns to the president saying, "You can tell the Board to declare their usual dividend. Our net cash flow provided by operating activities is $1,030,000." "Good man, Jon! I knew I could count on you," exults the president.

Instructions

(a) Who are the stakeholders in this situation?
(b) Was there anything unethical about the president's actions? Was there anything unethical about the controller's actions?
(c) Are the Board members or anyone else likely to discover the misclassification?

■ Financial Accounting Research (FARS)

AIA6-12 As part of the year-end accounting process for your company, you are preparing the statement of cash flows according to GAAP. One of your team, a finance major, believes the statement should be prepared to report the change in working capital, because analysts often use working capital in ratio analysis. Your supervisor would like research conducted to verify the basis for preparing the statement of cash flows.

Instructions

Using the **Financial Accounting Research System (FARS)** database (provide text strings used in the search), provide responses to the following items.

(a) Has GAAP ever allowed the statement of cash flows to be prepared on the basis of working capital?

(b) What are the problems with using working capital as a concept of funds? Why is cash a more useful concept of funds?

(c) What information is provided in a statement of cash flows?

(d) List some of the typical cash inflows and outflows from operations.

■ Professional Simulation

AIA6-13 Go to the book's companion website, at **www.wiley.com/college/warfield**, to find an interactive problem that simulates the computerized CPA exam. The professional simulation for this chapter asks you to address questions related to the statement of cash flows.

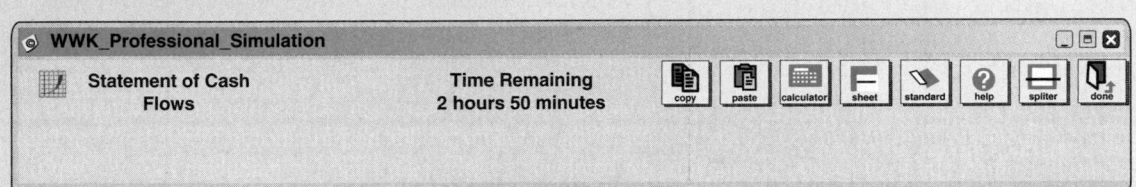

What do the numbers mean?	Guideline Answers to Beyond the Numbers Questions

Don't Be Misled by Net Income, p. 254

Q: For all of the companies listed in the box, the cash-basis amount "Net cash provided by operations," from the statement of cash flows, is much greater than the accrual-basis amount "Net income," from the income statement. What explanation can you give for this difference?

A: The differences can be explained by the reported amounts of revenues and expenses. The accrual-basis income statements for these companies evidently report lower revenues or greater expenses, or both, than a cash-basis statement of cash flows. A cash-basis statement would not report revenue that has been earned but for which the cash has not been received, nor would it match expenses with earned revenues. Because of these violations of, respectively, the revenue recognition and the matching principles, cash-basis income **statements** *are prohibited under GAAP.*

Losing the Faith, p. 257

Q: Since these and numerous other financial accounting corrections and misstatements were reported in 2000, 2001, and 2002, what actions have been taken to curb such misdeeds?

A: The federal government has passed legislation—the Sarbanes-Oxley Act—that (1) requires corporate boards to assume more responsibility for accurate and transparent financial reporting, and (2) levies stronger sanctions (jail terms) on abusers. The accounting profession has issued *Statements on Auditing Standard No. 99,* which requires independent auditors to include fraud detection procedures in their audits.

(continued)

Guideline Answers, continued

Pumping Up Cash, p. 260

Q: Why would financial statement readers focus on the information in the statement of cash flows when earnings quality is low?

A: As discussed in Chapter 5, earnings quality is low if the reported earnings do not reflect the underlying economics of the company's operations, which makes them less useful for predicting future cash flows. Because of the many estimates inherent in accrual-accounting measurement, earnings may be less reflective of the underlying economics, and in fact may be misleading if the company has managed the earnings. Because the measurement of cash flows is less subject to estimation, cash flow may provide a more reliable measure of company performance. In addition, the reconciliation from net income to cash flow from operations allows statement readers to see the sources of differences between cash flow and income, and thereby assess the reliability of net income.

"How's My Cash Flow?," p. 271

Q: Until recently, Microsoft had never paid a cash dividend; beginning in 2003, Microsoft has paid a dividend every year. What part of the product life cycle do you think Microsoft is in? Explain.

A: Microsoft has likely entered, or is transitioning to, the maturity stage. The payment of cash dividends has a negative effect on cash provided by financing activities. According to the graph in the box, we expect financing cash to begin trending down for companies entering the maturity stage. Thus, as Microsoft has reaped the rewards of R&D and other investments in its products, sales from these products increase operating cash flows, which the company can distribute to owners in the form of dividends. Indeed, Microsoft had accumulated so much cash that in 2005 it paid a $36 billion dividend to its shareholders.

Remember to check the book's companion website to find additional resources for this chapter.

CHAPTER 7

REVENUE RECOGNITION

It's Back

Several years after passage, the accounting world continues to be preoccupied with the Sarbanes-Oxley Act of 2002 (Sarbox, or SOX). Unfortunately, Sarbox did not solve one of the classic accounting issues—how to properly account for revenue. In fact, revenue recognition practices are the most prevalent reasons why accounting restatements have increased dramatically since passage of Sarbox. A number of the revenue recognition issues relate to possible fraudulent behavior by company executives and employees. Consider some recent SEC actions:

- The SEC charged the former co-chairman and CEO of **Qwest Communications International Inc.** and eight other former Qwest officers and employees with fraud and other violations of the federal securities laws. Three of these people fraudulently characterized nonrecurring revenue from one-time sales as revenue from recurring data and Internet services. The SEC press release notes that internal correspondence indicated that Qwest was dependent on these transactions to fill the gap between actual and projected revenue.

- The SEC filed a complaint against three former senior officers of **iGo Corp.** alleging that the defendants collectively caused iGo to improperly recognize revenue on consignment sales and products that were not shipped or that were shipped after the end of a fiscal quarter.

- The SEC filed a complaint against the former CEO and chairman of **Homestore Inc.** and its former executive vice president of business development, alleging that they engaged in a fraudulent scheme to overstate advertising and subscription revenues. The scheme involved a complex structure of "round-trip" transactions using various third-party companies that, in essence, allowed Homestore to recognize its own cash as revenue.

Though the cases cited involved fraud and irregularity, not all revenue recognition errors are intentional. For example, in April 2005 **American Home Mortgage Investment Corp.** announced that it would reverse revenue recognized from its fourth-quarter 2004 loan securitization and would recognize it in the first quarter of 2005 instead. As a result, American Home restated its financial results for 2004.

So, how does a company ensure that revenue transactions are recorded properly? Some answers will become apparent after you study this chapter.

Source: Adapted from Cheryl de Mesa Graziano, "Revenue Recognition: A Perennial Problem ," *Financial Executive* (July 14, 2005), *www.fei.org/mag/articles/7-2005_revenue.cfm.*

Preview of Chapter 7

As indicated in the opening story, "When should revenue be recognized?" is a complex question. The many methods of marketing products and services make it difficult to develop guidelines that will apply to all situations. The purpose of this chapter is to provide you with general guidelines used in most business transactions. *The content and organization of the chapter are as follows.*

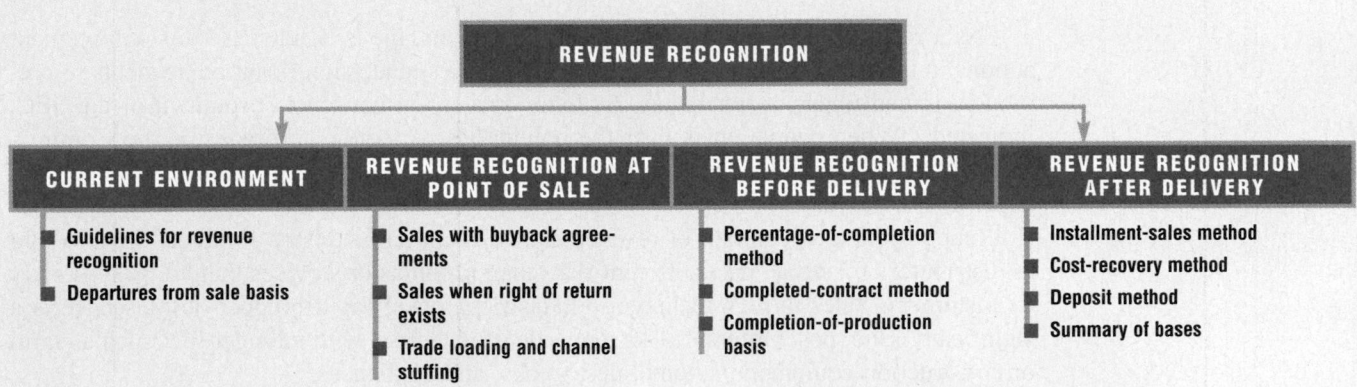

REVENUE RECOGNITION			
CURRENT ENVIRONMENT	**REVENUE RECOGNITION AT POINT OF SALE**	**REVENUE RECOGNITION BEFORE DELIVERY**	**REVENUE RECOGNITION AFTER DELIVERY**
■ Guidelines for revenue recognition ■ Departures from sale basis	■ Sales with buyback agreements ■ Sales when right of return exists ■ Trade loading and channel stuffing	■ Percentage-of-completion method ■ Completed-contract method ■ Completion-of-production basis	■ Installment-sales method ■ Cost-recovery method ■ Deposit method ■ Summary of bases

Learning Objectives

After studying this chapter, you should be able to:

1. Apply the revenue recognition principle.
2. Describe accounting issues involved with revenue recognition at point of sale.
3. Apply the percentage-of-completion method for long-term contracts.
4. Apply the completed-contract method for long-term contracts.
5. Describe the installment-sales and cost-recovery methods of accounting.

Inside Chapter 7

- ■ **What Do the Numbers Mean?**
  Grossed out (p. 308)
  No take-backs, revisited (p. 311)
  Less conservative (p. 317)
  The check is in the mail (p. 319)
  Liability or revenue? (p. 324)

- ■ **What's the Principle?** (p. 307, 309, 313, 316, 317, 319)

- ■ **Convergence Corner** (p. 325)

- ■ **Accounting, Analysis, Principles** (p. 326)
  Account for long-term contracts, installment sale.
  Compute free cash flow.
  Discuss tradeoff between relevance and reliability.

THE CURRENT ENVIRONMENT

According to one study, revenue recognition has been the largest single source of public-company restatements over the past decade. The study noted the following:

1 Restatements for improper revenue recognition result in larger drops in market capitalization than any other type of restatement.

2 Revenue problems caused eight of the top ten market value losses in a recent year.

3 Of the ten companies, the leading three lost $20 billion in market value in just three days following disclosure of revenue recognition problems.[1]

As a result of such revenue recognition problems, the SEC increased its enforcement actions in this area. In some of these cases companies made significant adjustments to previously issued financial statements. As Lynn Turner, former chief accountant of the SEC, indicated, "When people cross over the boundaries of legitimate reporting, the Commission will take appropriate action to ensure the fairness and integrity that investors need and depend on every day."[2]

Inappropriate recognition of revenue can occur in any industry. Products that are sold to distributors for resale pose different risks than products or services that are sold directly to customers. Sales in high-technology industries, where rapid product obsolescence is a significant issue, pose different risks than sale of inventory with a longer life, such as farm or construction equipment, automobiles, trucks, and appliances.[3]

The SEC has expressed concern that Internet companies (dot-coms) are increasing their revenue by including product sales in their revenue even though they are acting only as the distributor (intermediary) on behalf of other companies. Instead, these companies should be reporting only a distribution (brokerage) fee for selling another company's products.[4]

Guidelines for Revenue Recognition

OBJECTIVE 1

Apply the revenue recognition principle.

In general, the guidelines for revenue recognition are quite broad. Certain industries have very specific additional guidelines that provide further insight into when revenue should be recognized. The **revenue recognition principle** provides that companies should recognize[5] revenue (1) when it is realized or realizable and (2) when it is earned.[6] Revenues are **realized** when a company exchanges goods and services for cash or claims to cash (receivables).

[1]PricewaterhouseCoopers, "Current Developments for Audit Committees 2002" (Florham Park, N.J.: PricewaterhouseCoopers, 2002), p. 65.

[2]The Sarbanes-Oxley Act of 2002 also makes it clear that Congress will not tolerate abuses of the financial reporting process and that those who fail to adhere to "certain standards" will be prosecuted.

[3]Adapted from American Institute of Certified Public Accountants, Inc., *Audit Issues in Revenue Recognition* (New York: AICPA, 1999).

[4]The SEC noted that if a company performs as an agent or broker without assuming the risks and rewards of ownership of the goods, it should report sales on a net (fee) basis. See "Revenue Recognition in Financial Statements," *SEC Staff Accounting Bulletin No. 101* (December 3, 1999).

[5]Recognition is "the process of formally recording or incorporating an item in the accounts and financial statements of an entity" (*SFAC No. 3*, par. 83). "Recognition includes depiction of an item in both words and numbers, with the amount included in the totals of the financial statements" (*SFAC No. 5*, par. 6). For an asset or liability, recognition involves recording acquisition or incurrence of the item and also later changes in it, including removal from the financial statements previously recognized.

Recognition is not the same as realization, although you may find the two sometimes used interchangeably in accounting literature and practice. *Realization* is "the process of converting non-cash resources and rights into money and is most precisely used in accounting and financial reporting to refer to sales of assets for cash or claims to cash" (*SFAC No. 3*, par. 83).

[6]"Recognition and Measurement in Financial Statements of Business Enterprises," *Statement of Financial Accounting Concepts No. 5* (Stamford, Conn.: FASB, 1984), par. 83.

Revenues are **realizable** when assets received in exchange are readily convertible to known amounts of cash or claims to cash. Revenues are **earned** when a company has substantially accomplished what it must do to be entitled to the benefits represented by the revenues—that is, when the earnings process is complete or virtually complete.[7]

Four revenue transactions are recognized in accordance with this principle:

1 Companies recognize revenue from selling products at the date of sale. This date is usually interpreted to mean the date of delivery to customers.

2 Companies recognize revenue from services rendered when services have been performed and are billable.

3 Companies recognize revenue from permitting others to use enterprise assets, such as interest, rent, and royalties, as time passes or as the assets are used.

4 Companies recognize revenue from disposing of assets other than products at the date of sale.

WHAT'S THE PRINCIPLE?

Revenues are inflows of assets and/or settlements of liabilities from delivering or producing goods, rendering services, or other earning activities that constitute an enterprise's ongoing major or central operations during a period.

These revenue transactions are diagrammed in Illustration 7-1.

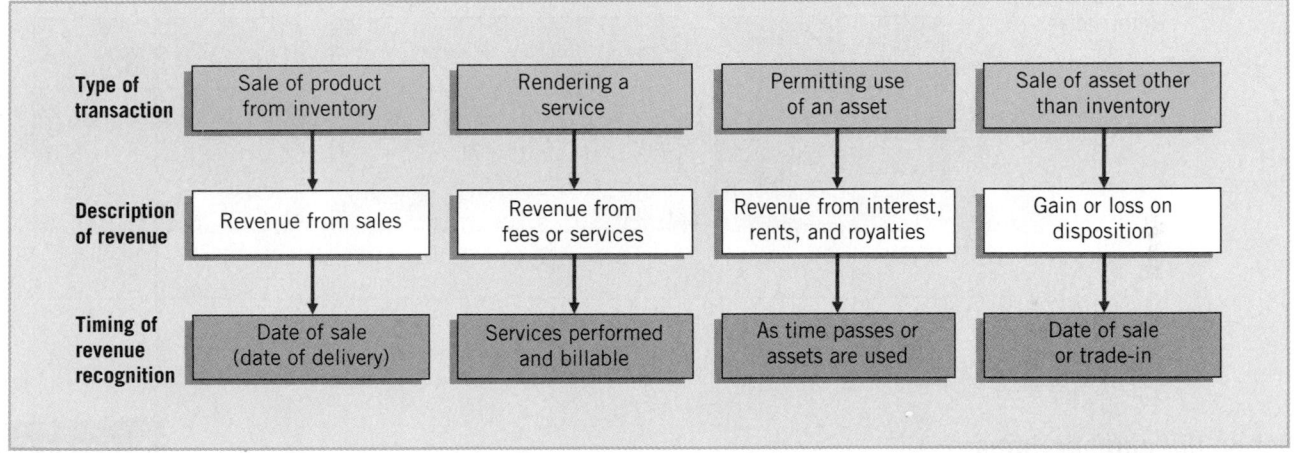

Illustration 7-1
Revenue Recognition Classified by Nature of Transaction

Departures from the Sale Basis

The statements in the preceding list are the basis of accounting for revenue transactions. In practice there are departures from the revenue recognition principle (e.g., the full accrual method). Companies sometimes recognize revenue at other points in the earning process, owing in great measure to the considerable variety of revenue transactions.[8]

An FASB study found some common **reasons for departures from the sale basis**.[9] One reason is a desire to **recognize earlier** than the time of sale the effect of earning activities. Earlier recognition is appropriate if there is a high degree of certainty about the amount of revenue earned. A second reason is a desire to **delay recognition** of revenue beyond the time of sale. Delayed recognition is appropriate if the degree of uncertainty concerning the amount of either revenue or costs is sufficiently high or if the sale does not represent substantial completion of the earnings process.

---

[7]Gains (as contrasted to revenues) commonly result from transactions and other events that do not involve an "earning process." For gain recognition, being earned is generally less significant than being realized or realizable. Companies commonly recognize gains at the time of sale of an asset, disposition of a liability, or when prices of certain assets change.

[8]The FASB and IASB are now involved in a joint project on revenue recognition. This is discussed more fully in the Convergence Corner on page 325.

[9]Henry R. Jaenicke, *Survey of Present Practices in Recognizing Revenues, Expenses, Gains, and Losses,* A Research Report (Stamford, Conn.: FASB, 1981), p. 11.

This chapter focuses on two of the four general types of revenue transactions described earlier: (1) selling products and (2) rendering services. Both of these are **sales transactions**. In several other sections of the textbook we discuss the other two types of revenue transactions—revenue from permitting others to use enterprise assets, and revenue from disposing of assets other than products.

Our discussion of product sales transactions in this chapter is organized around the following topics:

1 Revenue recognition at point of sale (delivery).

2 Revenue recognition before delivery.

3 Revenue recognition after delivery.

4 Revenue recognition for special sales transactions—franchises and consignments.

Illustration 7-2 depicts this organization of revenue recognition topics.

Examples of Revenue Recognition Policies

Illustration 7-2
Revenue Recognition Alternatives

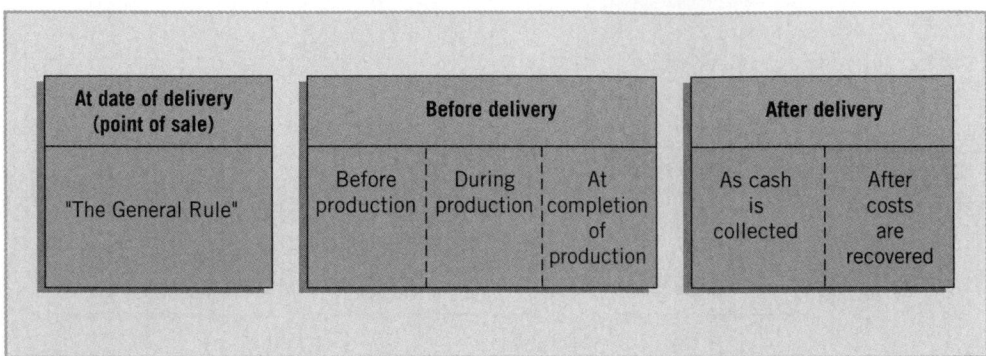

At date of delivery (point of sale)	Before delivery			After delivery	
"The General Rule"	Before production	During production	At completion of production	As cash is collected	After costs are recovered

What do the numbers mean? Grossed Out

Consider **Priceline.com**, the company made famous by William Shatner's ads about "naming your own price" for airline tickets and hotel rooms. In one of its quarterly SEC filings, Priceline reported that it earned $152 million in revenues. But that included the full amount customers paid for tickets, hotel rooms, and rental cars. Traditional travel agencies call that amount "gross bookings," not revenues. And much like regular travel agencies, Priceline keeps only a small portion of gross bookings—namely, the spread between the customers' accepted bids and the price it paid for the merchandise. The rest, which Priceline calls "product costs," it pays to the airlines and hotels that supply the tickets and rooms.

However, Priceline's product costs came to $134 million, leaving Priceline just $18 million of what it calls "gross profit" and what most other companies would call revenues. And that's before all of Priceline's other costs—like advertising and salaries—which netted out to a loss of $102 million. The difference isn't academic. Priceline stock traded at about 23 times its reported revenues but at a mind-boggling 214 times its "gross profit." This and other aggressive recognition practices led the SEC to issue stricter revenue recognition guidance indicating that if a company performs as an agent or broker without assuming the risks and rewards of ownership of the goods, the company should report sales on a net (fee) basis.

Source: "Revenue Recognition in Financial Statements," *SEC Staff Accounting Bulletin No. 101* (December 3, 1999) and "Revenue Recognition," *SEC Staff Accounting Bulletin No. 104* (December 17, 2003). See also Jeremy Kahn, "Presto Chango! Sales Are Huge," *Fortune* (March 20, 2000), p. 44.

Beyond the Numbers

What qualitative characteristic of accounting information is affected when Priceline reports its gross bookings in a unique fashion? Explain.

REVENUE RECOGNITION AT POINT OF SALE (DELIVERY)

According to the FASB in *Concepts Statement No. 5*, companies usually meet the two conditions for recognizing revenue (being realized or realizable and being earned) by the time that they deliver product or merchandise or render services to customers.[10] Therefore, companies commonly recognize revenues from manufacturing and selling activities at **point of sale** (usually meaning delivery).[11] Problems of implementation, however, can arise. Three such situations are discussed below: (1) sales with buyback agreements, (2) sales when right of return exists, and (3) trade loading and channel stuffing.

> **OBJECTIVE 2**
> **Describe accounting issues involved with revenue recognition at point of sale.**

Sales with Buyback Agreements

If a company sells a product in one period and agrees to buy it back in the next accounting period, has the company sold the product? Legal title has transferred in this situation, but the economic substance of the transaction is that the seller retains the risks of ownership. Therefore the profession has curtailed recognition of revenue using this practice. When a repurchase agreement exists at a set price and this price covers all costs of the inventory plus related holding costs, the inventory and related liability remain on the seller's books.[12] In other words, no sale.

Sales When Right of Return Exists

Whether cash or credit sales are involved, a special problem arises with claims for returns and allowances. In Chapter 9 we present the accounting treatment for normal returns and allowances. However, certain companies experience such a **high rate of returns**—a high ratio of returned merchandise to sales—that they find it necessary to postpone reporting sales until the return privilege has substantially expired.

For example, in the publishing industry the rate of return approaches 25 percent for hardcover books and 65 percent for some magazines. Other types of companies that experience high return rates are perishable-food dealers, distributors who sell to retail outlets, record and tape companies, and some toy and sporting goods manufacturers. Returns in these industries are frequently made either through a right of contract or as a matter of practice involving "guaranteed sales" agreements or consignments.

> **WHAT'S THE PRINCIPLE?**
> This is an example of *realized* but *unearned revenue*. When high rates of return exist and cannot be reasonably estimated, a question arises as to whether the company has substantially completed the earnings process.

Three alternative revenue recognition methods are available when the right of return exposes the seller to continued risks of ownership. These are: (1) not recording a sale until all return privileges have expired; (2) recording the sale, but reducing sales by an estimate of future returns; and (3) recording the sale and accounting for the returns as they occur. The FASB concluded that if a company sells its product but gives the buyer the right to return it, then the company should recognize revenue

---

[10]The SEC believes that revenue is realized or realizable and earned when all of the following four criteria are met: (1) Persuasive evidence of an arrangement exists. (2) Delivery has occurred or services have been rendered. (3) The seller's price to the buyer is fixed or determinable. (4) Collectibility is reasonably assured. See "Revenue Recognition in Financial Statements," *SEC Staff Accounting Bulletin No. 101* (December 3, 1999) and "Revenue Recognition," *SEC Staff Accounting Bulletin No. 104* (December 17, 2003). The SEC provided more specific guidance because the general criteria were difficult to interpret.

[11]*Statement of Financial Accounting Concepts No. 5,* op. cit., par. 84.

[12]"Accounting for Product Financing Arrangements," *Statement of Financial Accounting Standards No. 49* (Stamford, Conn.: FASB, 1981).

from the sales transaction at the time of sale *only if all of the following* six conditions have been met.[13]

1 The seller's price to the buyer is substantially fixed or determinable at the date of sale.

2 The buyer has paid the seller, or the buyer is obligated to pay the seller, and the obligation is not contingent on resale of the product.

3 The buyer's obligation to the seller would not be changed in the event of theft or physical destruction or damage of the product.

4 The buyer acquiring the product for resale has economic substance apart from that provided by the seller.

5 The seller does not have significant obligations for future performance to directly bring about resale of the product by the buyer.

6 The seller can reasonably estimate the amount of future returns.

What if the six conditions are not met? In that case, the company must recognize sales revenue and cost of sales either when the return privilege has substantially expired or when those six conditions subsequently are met, **whichever occurs first**. In the income statement, the company must reduce sales revenue and cost of sales by the amount of the estimated returns.

Trade Loading and Channel Stuffing

INTERNATIONAL INSIGHT

International standards provide general revenue recognition principles that are consistent with U.S. GAAP but that contain limited detailed or industry-specific guidance.

Some companies record revenues at date of delivery with neither buyback nor unlimited return provisions. Although they appear to be following acceptable point-of-sale revenue recognition practices, they are recognizing revenues and earnings prematurely.

For example, the domestic cigarette industry at one time engaged in a distribution practice known as **trade loading**. Said one commentator about this practice, "Trade loading is a crazy, uneconomic, insidious practice through which manufacturers—trying to show sales, profits, and market share they don't actually have—induce their wholesale customers, known as the trade, to buy more product than they can promptly resell."[14] In total, the cigarette industry appears to have exaggerated a couple years' operating profits by as much as $600 million by taking the profits from future years.

In the computer software industry a similar practice is referred to as **channel stuffing**. When a software maker needed to make its financial results look good, it offered deep discounts to its distributors to overbuy, and then recorded revenue when the software left the loading dock.[15] Of course, the distributors' inventories became bloated and the marketing channel got filled with product, but the software maker's current-period financials were improved. However, financial results in future periods suffered, unless the company repeated the process.

Trade loading and channel stuffing hype sales, distort operating results, and "window dress" financial statements. If used without an appropriate allowance for sales returns, channel stuffing is a classic example of booking tomorrow's revenue today. **The profession needs to discourage the practices of trade loading and channel stuffing.** Business managers need to be aware of the ethical dangers of misleading the financial community by engaging in such practices to improve their financial statements.

---

[13]"Revenue Recognition When Right of Return Exists," *Statement of Financial Accounting Standards No. 48* (Stamford, Conn.: FASB, 1981), par. 6.

[14]"The $600 Million Cigarette Scam," *Fortune* (December 4, 1989), p. 89.

[15]"Software's Dirty Little Secret," *Forbes* (May 15, 1989), p. 128.

What do the numbers mean?

You may recall from an earlier discussion in Chapter 2 (page 49) that investors in **Lucent Technologies** were negatively affected when Lucent violated the "no take-back" rule. This fundamental criterion for revenue recognition holds that revenue should not be booked on inventory that is shipped if the customer can return it at some point in the future. In this particular case, Lucent agreed to take back shipped inventory from its distributors, if the distributors were unable to sell the items to their customers.

In essence, Lucent was "stuffing the channel." By booking sales when goods were shipped, even though it most likely would get them back, Lucent was able to report continued sales growth. However, Lucent investors got a nasty surprise when distributors returned the goods and Lucent had to restate its financial results. The restatement erased $679 million in revenues, turning an operating profit into a loss. In response to this bad news, Lucent's stock price declined $1.31 per share, or 8.5 percent.

Lucent is not alone in this practice. In a recent variation, **Diebold** recorded sales on voting machines that were shipped without memory cards. Such machines were not functional, so genuine delivery did not occur. As a result, Diebold issued a restatement to recognize the revenue in a later quarter.

Additional Disclosures of Revenue Recognition Policies

Investors can be tipped off to potential channel stuffing by carefully reviewing a company's revenue recognition policy for generous return policies and by watching inventory and receivable levels. An increase in both sales and receivables is one sign that customers are not paying for goods shipped on credit. Also, growing inventory levels may indicate that customers have all the goods they need. Both scenarios suggest a higher likelihood of goods being returned and of revenues and income being restated. So remember, no take-backs!.

Sources: S. Young, "Lucent Slashes First Quarter Outlook, Erases Revenue from Latest Quarter," *Wall Street Journal Online* (December 22, 2000); Tracey Byrnes, "Too Many Thin Mints: Spotting the Practice of Channel Stuffing," *Wall Street Journal Online* (February 7, 2002); and J. Ciesielski, "Diebold's SEC Inquiry," The Accounting Observer's Weblog, *www.accountingobserver.com/blog/*(accessed May 12, 2006).

Beyond the Numbers

Explain how the Lucent and Diebold cases illustrate violation of revenue recognition criteria.

Try it out! Madison Company manufactures miniature circuit boards that it sells to cell phone manufacturers. In 2008 Madison shipped circuit boards with a sales value of $1,000,000. Presented below are four independent situations related to Madison.

a All sales are for cash. Based on historical experience, Madison estimates that 2% of shipped boards will be returned under its product guarantee provisions.

b One-half of the sales are under the same terms as described in (a). The other half of the sales are for a new product. Madison has little reliable historical data on possible returns on the new products.

c One-half of the sales are under the same terms as in (a). The remaining sales are to customers who have very uncertain credit-paying ability. Madison is unable to develop reliable estimates of collections on sales to these customers.

d All of the sales are for a product of which customers are not ready to receive shipment. Madison ships the product anyway and gives the customers the right to return it next year, if they do not use it.

Instructions

For each of the independent situations, address the following two issues.

1 How much net revenue (sales less allowances) should Madison recognize in 2008?

2 Identify the revenue recognition criteria illustrated and how the criteria are applied in that situation.

Solution

a Net revenue to recognize: $980,000 = $1,000,000 − (2% × $1,000,000). Revenue is recognized after an allowance for returns.

b Net revenue to recognize: $490,000 = [$1,000,000 − $500,000 − ($500,000 × 2%).] Half of the sales will not be recognized as revenue until the return period expires. Similar to (a), the other half can be recognized after a 2% allowance for returns.

c Net revenue to recognize: $490,000 = [$1,000,000 − $500,000 − ($500,000 × 2%).] One-half of the sales are not realizable, given the uncertainty of getting paid. The other half can be recognized as revenue, after an allowance for returns.

d Net revenue to recognize: $0. The revenue is neither realized or realizable (customers have not paid) nor earned (customers can return the product at their option). This is an example of channel stuffing.

REVENUE RECOGNITION BEFORE DELIVERY

For the most part, companies use recognition at the point of sale (delivery) because at point of sale, most of the uncertainties concerning the earning process are removed and the exchange price is known. Under certain circumstances, however, companies recognize revenue **prior to** completion and delivery. The most notable example is long-term construction contract accounting where the *percentage-of-completion* method applies.

Long-term contracts frequently provide that the seller (builder) may bill the purchaser at intervals, as they reach various points in the project. Examples of such long-term contracts are construction-type contracts, development of military and commercial aircraft, weapons-delivery systems, and space-exploration hardware. When the project consists of separable units such as a group of buildings or miles of roadway, companies may transfer title and may bill at stated stages of completion, such as the completion of each building unit or every 10 miles of road. Such contract provisions provide for delivery in installments. The accounting records should report this by recording sales when installments are "delivered."[16]

The profession recognizes two distinctly different methods of accounting for long-term construction contracts.[17] They are:

1 **Percentage-of-completion method:** Companies recognize revenues and gross profit each period based upon the progress of the construction—that is, the percentage of completion.

2 **Completed-contract method:** Companies recognize revenues and gross profit only when the contract is completed.

---

[16]*Statement of Financial Accounting Concepts No. 5,* par. 84, item c.

[17]*Accounting Trends and Techniques—2006* (New York: AICPA) reports that, of the 131 of its 600 sample companies that referred to long-term construction contracts, 125 used the percentage-of-completion method and 6 used the completed-contract method.

The rationale for using percentage-of-completion accounting is that under most of these contracts the buyer and seller have enforceable rights. The buyer has the legal right to require specific performance on the contract. The seller has the right to require progress payments that provide evidence of the buyer's ownership interest. As a result, a continuous sale occurs as the work progresses. Companies should recognize revenue according to that progression.

Companies must use the percentage-of-completion method when estimates of progress toward completion, revenues, and costs are reasonably dependable and **all of the following conditions** exist.[18]

WHAT'S THE PRINCIPLE?

Departure from the general revenue recognition criteria by recognizing revenue before delivery is designed to provide more useful (timely) information about the profitability of long-term contracts.

1 The contract clearly specifies the enforceable rights regarding goods or services to be provided and received by the parties, the consideration to be exchanged, and the manner and terms of settlement.

2 The buyer can be expected to satisfy all obligations under the contract.

3 The contractor can be expected to perform the contractual obligations.

Companies should use the completed-contract method only under the following conditions: (1) when a company has primarily short-term contracts, (2) when the company cannot meet the conditions for using the percentage-of-completion method, or (3) when there are inherent hazards in the contract beyond the normal, recurring business risks. The presumption is that **percentage-of-completion is the better method**. Therefore, companies should use **the completed-contract method only when the percentage-of-completion method is inappropriate**.

We discuss the two methods of accounting for long-term construction contracts in the sections that follow.

Percentage-of-Completion Method

The **percentage-of-completion method** recognizes revenues, costs, and gross profit as progress is made toward completion on a long-term contract. To defer recognition of these items until completion of the entire contract is to misrepresent the efforts (costs) and accomplishments (revenues) of the interim accounting periods. In order to apply the percentage-of-completion method, companies must have some basis or standard for measuring the progress toward completion at particular interim dates.

One of the common techniques that companies use to determine the progress toward completion is the **cost-to-cost basis**. Under the cost-to-cost basis, companies measure the percentage of completion by comparing costs incurred to date with the most recent estimate of the total costs to complete the contract. Illustration 7-3 shows the formula for the percentage of completion.

OBJECTIVE 3

Apply the percentage-of-completion method for long-term contracts.

| Costs Incurred to Date | ÷ | Most Recent Estimate of Total Costs | = | Percent Complete |

Illustration 7-3
Formula for Percentage of Completion, Cost-to-Cost Basis

Once a company knows the percentage that costs incurred bear to total estimated costs, it applies that percentage to the total revenue or the estimated total gross profit on the

[18]"Accounting for Performance of Construction-Type and Certain Production-Type Contracts," *Statement of Position 81-1* (New York: AICPA, 1981), par. 23.

contract. The resulting amount is the revenue or the gross profit to be recognized to date. Illustration 7-4 shows this computation.

Illustration 7-4
Formula for Total Revenue
to Be Recognized to Date

Percent Complete	×	Estimated Total Revenue (or Gross Profit)	=	Revenue (or Gross Profit) to Be Recognized to Date

To find the amounts of revenue and gross profit recognized each period, the company would subtract total revenue or gross profit recognized in prior periods, as shown in Illustration 7-5.

Revenue (or Gross Profit) to Be Recognized to Date	−	Revenue (or Gross Profit) Recognized in Prior Periods	=	Current Period Revenue (or Gross Profit)

The profession specifically recommends the cost-to-cost method (without excluding other bases for measuring progress toward completion). Therefore we have adopted it for use in our illustrations.[19]

Example of Percentage-of-Completion Method— Cost-to-Cost Basis

To illustrate the percentage-of-completion method, assume that Hardhat Construction Company has a contract to build a $4,500,000 bridge, at an estimated cost of $4,000,000. The contract is to start in July 2007, and the bridge is expected to be completed in October 2009. The following data pertain to the construction period. (Note that by the end of 2008 Hardhat has revised the estimated total cost from $4,000,000 to $4,050,000.)

	2007	2008	2009
Costs to date	$1,000,000	$2,916,000	$4,050,000
Estimated costs to complete	3,000,000	1,134,000	—

The percentage complete would be computed as shown in Illustration 7-6. In this illustration, the costs incurred to date as a proportion of the estimated total costs are a measure of the extent of progress toward completion.

[19]Committee on Accounting Procedure, "Long-Term Construction-Type Contracts," *Accounting Research Bulletin No. 45* (New York: AICPA, 1955), p. 7.

	2007	2008	2009
Contract price	$4,500,000	$4,500,000	$4,500,000
Less: Estimated costs			
Costs to date	1,000,000	2,916,000	4,050,000
Estimated costs to complete	3,000,000	1,134,000	–
Estimated total costs	4,000,000	4,050,000	4,050,000
Estimated total gross profit	$ 500,000	$ 450,000	$ 450,000
Percent complete	25%	72%	100%
	$\left(\dfrac{\$1,000,000}{\$4,000,000}\right)$	$\left(\dfrac{\$2,916,000}{\$4,050,000}\right)$	$\left(\dfrac{\$4,050,000}{\$4,050,000}\right)$

Illustration 7-7 shows calculation of the estimated revenue and gross profit to be recognized for each year.

	2007	2008	2009
Revenue recognized in:			
2007 $4,500,000 × 25%	$1,125,000		
2008 $4,500,000 × 72%		$3,240,000	
Less: Revenue recognized in 2007		1,125,000	
Revenue in 2008		$2,115,000	
2009 $4,500,000 × 100%			$4,500,000
Less: Revenue recognized in			
2007 and 2008			3,240,000
Revenue in 2009			$1,260,000
Gross profit recognized in:			
2007 $500,000 × 25%	$ 125,000		
2008 $450,000 × 72%		$ 324,000	
Less: Gross profit recognized in 2007		125,000	
Gross profit in 2008		$ 199,000	
2009 $450,000 × 100%			$ 450,000
Less: Gross profit recognized in			
2007 and 2008			324,000
Gross profit in 2009			$ 126,000

Thus, in each year of the contract, to determine the percentage completed, Hardhat combines realized costs with new estimates of expected costs to complete the project.

This example contained a **change in estimate** in the second year, 2008. At that time, the estimated total costs increased from $4,000,000 to $4,050,000. The company accounts for the change in estimate in a **cumulative catch-up manner**. To do so, it first adjusts the percent completed to the new estimate of total costs. It then deducts the amount of revenues and gross profit recognized in prior periods from revenues and gross profit computed for progress to date. That is, Hardhat accounts for the change in estimate **in the period of change**. The effect of this treatment is that the balance sheet at the end of the period of change and the accounting in subsequent periods are as they would have been if the revised estimate had been the original estimate. Appendix 7A shows the journal entries that Hardhat would record in each year of the contract.

Completed-Contract Method

Under the **completed-contract method**, companies recognize revenue and gross profit only at point of sale—that is, when the contract is completed. Under this method, companies accumulate costs of long-term contracts in process, but they **do not record interim charges or credits to income statement accounts for revenues, costs, and gross profit**.

The completed-contract method has a key advantage: Reported revenue is based on final results rather than on estimates of unperformed work. Its major disadvantage is that when a contract extends into more than one accounting period, the method does not reflect current performance. Although operations may be fairly uniform during the period of the contract, companies do not report revenue until the year of completion, creating a distortion of earnings.

Comparing the two methods in relation to the same bridge project, Hardhat Construction Company would have recognized gross profit as follows.

Illustration 7-8
Comparison of Gross Profit Recognized under Different Methods

	Percentage-of-Completion	Completed-Contract
2007	$125,000	$ 0
2008	199,000	0
2009	126,000	450,000

Long-Term Contract Losses

Cost estimates at the end of the current period may indicate that a loss will result upon completion of the entire contract. Under both the percentage-of-completion and the completed-contract methods, companies **must recognize the entire expected contract loss in the current period**. This treatment for unprofitable contracts is consistent with the accounting custom of anticipating foreseeable losses to avoid overstatement of current and future income (conservatism).

Example of Long-Term Contract Losses

To illustrate the accounting for an overall loss on a long-term contract, assume that at December 31, 2008, Hardhat Construction Company estimates the costs to complete the bridge contract at $1,640,250 instead of $1,134,000. Revised estimates relative to the bridge contract appear in Illustration 7-9.

Illustration 7-9
Computation of Loss on Contract

	2007 Original Estimates	2008 Revised Estimates
Contract price	$4,500,000	$4,500,000
Estimated total cost	4,000,000	4,556,250*
Estimated gross profit	$ 500,000	
Estimated loss		$ (56,250)

*($2,916,000 + $1,640,250)

Under the percentage-of-completion method, Hardhat had recognized $125,000 of gross profit in 2007 (see Illustration 7-7). This $125,000 must be offset in 2008 because Hardhat no longer expects to realize that profit. In addition, Hardhat must recognize the total estimated loss of $56,250 in 2008 since companies must recognize losses as soon as they are estimable. Therefore, in 2008 Hardhat must recognize a total loss of $181,250 ($125,000 + $56,250).

Under the **completed-contract method**, Hardhat also would recognize the contract loss of $56,250 in the year in which it became evident. Because the company recognized no previous income, its total loss reported in 2008 is $56,250.

What do the numbers mean?

Halliburton provides engineering- and construction-related services around the world. Much of the company's work is completed under contract over long periods of time. The company uses percentage-of-completion accounting. Recently the SEC started enforcement proceedings against the company related to its accounting for contract claims and disagreements with customers, including those arising from change orders and disputes about billable amounts and costs associated with a construction delay.

Prior to 1998 Halliburton took a very conservative approach to its accounting for disputed claims. As stated in the company's 1997 annual report, "Claims for additional compensation are recognized during the period such claims are resolved." That is, the company waited until all disputes were resolved before recognizing associated revenues. In contrast, in 1998 the company recognized revenue for disputed claims before their resolution, using estimates of amounts expected to be recovered. Such revenue and its related profit are more tentative and are subject to possible later adjustment than revenue and profit recognized when all claims have been resolved. As a case in point, the company noted that it incurred losses of $99 million in 1998 related to customer claims.

The accounting method put in place in 1998 is more aggressive than the company's former policy, but it is still within the boundaries of generally accepted accounting principles. However, the SEC noted that over six quarters, Halliburton failed to disclose its change in accounting practice. In the absence of any disclosure the SEC believed the investing public was misled about the precise nature of Halliburton's income in comparison to prior periods. The Halliburton situation illustrates the difficulty of using estimates in percentage-of-completion accounting and the impact of those estimates on the financial statements.

Sources: "Failure to Disclose a 1998 Change in Accounting Practice," SEC (August 3, 2004), *www.sec.gov/news/press/2004-104.htm*; "Accounting Ace Charles Mulford Answers Accounting Questions," *Wall Street Journal Online* (June 7, 2002).

Beyond the Numbers

How does the Halliburton case illustrate the qualitative characteristic of consistency? Explain the importance of the full disclosure principle in this case

Completion-of-Production Basis

In certain cases companies recognize revenue at the completion of production even though no sale has been made. Examples of such situations involve precious metals or agricultural products with assured prices. Under the **completion-of-production basis**, companies recognize revenue when they mine these metals or harvest agricultural crops. Several conditions apply to sales of these products: The sales price is reasonably assured, the units are interchangeable, and no significant costs are involved in distributing the product. When sale or cash receipt precedes production and delivery, as in the case of magazine subscriptions, companies may recognize revenues as earned by production and delivery.[20]

WHAT'S THE PRINCIPLE?

This is not an exception to the revenue recognition principle. At the completion of production, realization is virtually assured and the company has substantially completed the earning process.

---

[20]Such revenue satisfies the criteria of *Concepts Statement No. 5* since the assets are readily realizable and the earning process is virtually complete (see par. 84, items b and c).

Try it out! Lostdorf Construction Company uses percentage-of-completion accounting for its long-term contracts. The following data are available at the end of 2007 for two construction projects which were started in 2007.

Project	Total Price	Costs Incurred to Date 12/31/2007	Additional Costs to Complete
1	$1,200	$700	$300
2	580	400	100

Instructions

a How much gross profit should Lostdorf recognize on these two contracts in 2007?

b At the end of 2008, assume that Lostdorf completes project 1 (total costs = $1,050). Project 2 is not completed. Total costs incurred to date on project 2 are $500, and estimated additional costs to complete the project are $110. Given this new information, determine the gross profit that Lostdorf should recognize on projects 1 and 2 in 2008.

c Now assume Lostdorf uses the completed-contract method. Assuming the facts in (a) and (b), how much gross profit should the company recognize on project 1 in 2008?

Solution

		Cost-to-Cost Ratio	% Complete	Total Gross Profit	Gross Profit Recognized
a	**2007**				
	Project 1	$\dfrac{\$700}{(\$700 + \$300)}$	70%	$1,200 − $1,000 = $200	$140 (70% × $200)
	Project 2	$\dfrac{\$400}{(\$400 + \$100)}$	80%	$580 − $500 = $80	$64 (80% × $80)
b	**2008**				
	Project 1	$\dfrac{\$1,050}{\$1050}$	100%	$1,200 − $1,050 = $150	$150 − $140 = $10
	Project 2	NA—loss	NA—loss	$580 − ($500 + $110) = $30 loss	$30 loss − $64 (2007 GP) = $94 loss in 2008
c	**2008** Project 1— Completed-Contract	NA	100%	$1,200 − $1,050 = $150	$150 recognized in year completed

REVENUE RECOGNITION AFTER DELIVERY

In some cases, the collection of the sales price is not reasonably assured and so companies defer revenue recognition. In such instances, they generally employ one of two methods to defer revenue recognition until the cash is received: **the installment-sales method** or **the**

cost-recovery method. Companies sometimes use a third method, **the deposit method**, when they receive cash prior to delivery or transfer of the property. Because the sale transaction is incomplete, they record the cash payment as a deposit.

Installment-Sales Method

The installment-sales method emphasizes collection rather than sale. It recognizes income in the periods of collection rather than in the period of sale. This method is justified on the basis that when there is no reasonable approach for estimating the degree of collectibility, companies should not recognize revenue until cash is collected.

The expression "installment sales" generally describes any type of sale for which payment is required in periodic installments over an extended period of time. All types of home and farm equipment and furnishings are sold on an installment basis. The term is also sometimes used in the heavy equipment industry in which buyers of machine installations pay over a long period. Another application of the method is in land development sales.

Some justify use of the installment-sales method on the grounds that the risk of not collecting an account receivable may be so great that the sale itself is not sufficient evidence that recognition should occur. In some cases this reasoning may be valid, but not in a majority of cases. The general approach is that if a company has completed a sale, it should recognize the sale. If the seller expects bad debts, it should record them as separate estimates of uncollectibles. Although collection expenses, repossession expenses, and bad debts are an unavoidable part of installment sales, companies should be able to reasonably predict these costs and the collectibility of the receivables.

We study this topic because the method is acceptable in cases where a company cannot determine a reasonable basis of estimating the degree of collectibility. In addition, weaknesses in the sales method of revenue recognition sometimes apply to franchise operations and to land development ventures. Application of the installment-sales method to **franchise and license operations** resulted in an abuse described as "front-end loading." Front-end loading recognized revenue prematurely, such as the point at which the franchisor granted the franchise rather than as the franchisee earned revenue or received cash. Many **land development** ventures were susceptible to the same abuses. As a result, the FASB prescribes application of the installment-sales method of accounting for sales of real estate under certain circumstances.[21]

> **OBJECTIVE 5**
> **Describe the installment-sales and cost-recovery methods of accounting.**

> **WHAT'S THE PRINCIPLE?**
> The installment-sales method represents a departure from accrual accounting. Cash-basis is used due to uncertainty in realization of installment-sales payments.

Expanded Discussion of the Accounting for Franchises

What do the numbers mean? | The Check Is in the Mail

Datapoint Corp. encouraged its customers to load up with large shipments at the end of the year, allowing Datapoint to report these shipments as revenues, even though payment hadn't been collected. Unfortunately, some of the customers either went broke or quit paying for the equipment received. As a result, the company had to record substantial bad debts or in some cases reverse previously recorded sales. If Datapoint had used a less aggressive revenue recognition method, such as the installment-sales method, it would not have reported this revenue.

As a result, revenue recognition practices that are cash-basis oriented, such as the installment-sales method, are becoming more acceptable as it becomes difficult to tell when a sale is a sale.

Beyond the Numbers

To get better control of its revenue recognition policies, a company like Datapoint Corp. could tighten up its policies on credit sales to require customers to pay more cash before the company ships its product. Discuss some of the pros and cons of such a strategy.

---

[21]"Accounting for Sales of Real Estate," *Statement of Financial Accounting Standards No. 66* (Norwalk, Conn.: FASB, 1982), pars. 45–47.

Example of the Installment-Sales Method

Under the installment-sales method, each cash collection from a customer consists of (1) a partial recovery of the cost of the goods sold, and (2) partial gross profit from the sale. For example, if the gross profit rate at the date of sale is 40 percent, each subsequent receipt consists of 60 percent recovery of cost of goods sold and 40 percent gross profit. Illustration 7-10 shows the formula to recognize gross profit under this method.

Illustration 7-10
Gross Profit Formula—
Installment-Sales Method

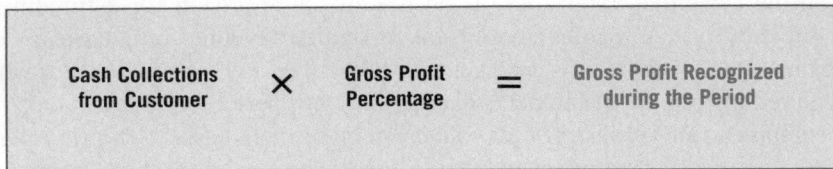

To illustrate, assume that an Iowa farm machinery dealer in the first year of operations had installment sales of $600,000 and a cost of goods sold on installment of $420,000. Total gross profit is, therefore, $180,000 ($600,000 − $420,000), and the gross profit percentage is 30 percent ($180,000 ÷ $600,000). The collections on the installment sales were as follows: first year $280,000 (down payment plus monthly payments); second year $200,000; and third year $120,000. Illustration 7-11 summarizes the collections of cash and recognition of the gross profit. (This illustration ignores interest charges.)

Illustration 7-11
Gross Profit Recognized—
Installment-Sales Method

Year	Cash Collected	×	Gross Profit Percentage	=	Gross Profit Recognized
2006	$280,000		30%		$ 84,000
2007	200,000		30%		60,000
2008	120,000		30%		36,000
Total	$600,000				$180,000

Under the installment-sales method, companies therefore recognize gross profit **in the period in which they collect the cash**.

As indicated earlier, some justify use of the installment-sales method when the risk of not collecting an account receivable may be such that the sale is not sufficient evidence for revenue to be recognized.

To illustrate the installment-sales method for the sale of merchandise in a more complex situation, assume the following data.

Illustration 7-12
Installment-Sales Data

	2007	2008	2009
Installment sales	$200,000	$250,000	$240,000
Cost of installment sales	150,000	190,000	168,000
Gross profit	$ 50,000	$ 60,000	$ 72,000
Rate of gross profit on sales	25%[a]	24%[b]	30%[c]
Cash receipts			
2007 sales	$60,000	$100,000	$ 40,000
2008 sales		100,000	125,000
2009 sales			80,000

[a] $\dfrac{\$50,000}{\$200,000}$ [b] $\dfrac{\$60,000}{\$250,000}$ [c] $\dfrac{\$72,000}{\$240,000}$

The company computes realized gross profit for the year 2007 as follows.

2007	
Rate of gross profit current year	25%
Cash collected on current year's sales	$60,000
Realized gross profit (25% of $60,000)	15,000

Illustration 7-13
Computation of Realized and Deferred Gross Profit, Year 1

Illustration 7-14 shows the realized gross profit for the year 2008.

2008	
Current year's sales	
Rate of gross profit	24%
Cash collected on current year's sales	$100,000
Realized gross profit (24% of $100,000)	24,000
Prior year's sales	
Rate of gross profit—2007	25%
Cash collected on 2007 sales	$100,000
Gross profit realized in 2008 on 2007 sales (25% of $100,000)	25,000
Total gross profit realized in 2008	
Realized on collections of 2007 sales	$ 25,000
Realized on collections of 2008 sales	24,000
Total	$ 49,000

Illustration 7-14
Computation of Realized and Deferred Gross Profit, Year 2

Note that to arrive at the realized gross profit, the company must apply the gross profit rate of each year's sales to cash collections of accounts receivable from that year's sales.

In 2009, the total gross profit realized would be $64,000, as shown by the computations in Illustration 7-15.

2009	
Current year's sales	
Rate of gross profit	30%
Cash collected on current year's sales	$ 80,000
Gross profit realized on 2009 sales (30% of $80,000)	24,000
Prior years' sales	
2007 sales	
Rate of gross profit	25%
Cash collected	$ 40,000
Gross profit realized in 2009 on 2007 sales (25% of $40,000)	10,000
2008 sales	
Rate of gross profit	24%
Cash collected	$125,000
Gross profit realized in 2009 on 2008 sales (24% of $125,000)	30,000
Total gross profit realized in 2009	
Realized on collections of 2007 sales	$ 10,000
Realized on collections of 2008 sales	30,000
Realized on collections of 2009 sales	24,000
Total	$ 64,000

Illustration 7-15
Computation of Realized and Deferred Gross Profit, Year 3

Appendix 7A presents expanded discussion of installment-sales accounting, including journal entries.

Cost-Recovery Method

Under the **cost-recovery method**, companies **do not recognize profit until the buyer's cash payments exceed the seller's cost of the merchandise sold**. After the seller has recovered all costs, it records as income any additional cash collections. *APB Opinion No. 10* allows a seller to use the cost-recovery method to account for sales in which "there is no reasonable basis for estimating collectibility." This method is required under *FASB Statements No. 45* (franchises) and *No. 66* (real estate) where a high degree of uncertainty exists related to the collection of receivables.[22]

To illustrate the cost-recovery method, assume that early in 2007 Fesmire Manufacturing sells inventory to Higley Company. The cost of the inventory is $25,000, and the sale price is $36,000, with payments receivable of $18,000 in 2007, $12,000 in 2008, and $6,000 in 2009. Assuming Fesmire collects the cash on schedule, the amount of gross profit recognized annually under the cost-recovery method is as shown in Illustration 7-16.

Illustration 7-16
Computation of Gross Profit—Cost-Recovery Method

Year	Cash Received	Original Cost Recovered	Balance of Unrecovered Cost	Gross Profit Realized
Beginning balance	—	—	$25,000	—
12/31/07	$18,000	$18,000	7,000	$ –0–
12/31/08	12,000	7,000	–0–	5,000
12/31/09	6,000	–0–	–0–	6,000

As shown, unlike the installment-sales method which recognizes income as cash is collected, the cost-recovery method recognizes profit only when cash collections exceed the total cost of the goods sold.

Deposit Method

In some cases, companies receive cash from the buyer before transfer of the goods or property. Because there is not sufficient transfer of the risks and rewards of ownership, the company does not (yet) record a sale. In such cases the seller has not performed under the contract and has no claim against the purchaser. The method of accounting for these incomplete transactions is the **deposit method**.

Under the deposit method the seller reports the cash received from the buyer as a deposit on the contract and classifies it on the balance sheet as a liability (refundable deposit or unearned revenue). The seller continues to report the property as an asset on its balance sheet, along with any related existing debt. Also, the seller continues to charge depreciation expense as a period cost for the property. The seller **does not recognize revenue or income until the sale is complete**.[23] At that time, the seller closes the deposit account and applies to the sale one of the revenue recognition methods discussed in this chapter.

---

[22]"Omnibus Opinion—1966," *Opinions of the Accounting Principles Board No. 10* (New York: AICPA, 1969), footnote 8, page 149; "Accounting for Franchise Fee Revenue," *Statement of Financial Accounting Standards No. 45* (Stamford, Conn.: FASB, 1981), par. 6; "Accounting for Sales of Real Estate," *Statement of Financial Accounting Standards No. 66,* pars. 62 and 63.

[23]*Statement of Financial Accounting Standards No. 66,* par. 65.

The **major difference between the installment-sales or cost-recovery methods and the deposit method** is this: The installment-sales and cost-recovery methods assume that the seller has performed on the contract, but cash collection is highly uncertain. In the deposit method, the seller has not performed and no legitimate claim exists. The deposit method postpones recognizing a sale until the seller can determine whether a sale has occurred for accounting purposes. Revenue recognition is delayed until a future event occurs. If there has not been sufficient transfer of risks and rewards of ownership, even if a deposit has been received, the seller postpones recognition of the sale until sufficient transfer has occurred. In that sense, the deposit method is not a revenue recognition method, whereas the installment-sales and cost-recovery methods are.

SUMMARY OF REVENUE RECOGNITION BASES

Illustration 7-17 summarizes the revenue recognition bases or methods, the criteria for their use, and the reasons for departing from the sale basis.

Illustration 7-17
Revenue Recognition
Bases Other Than the
Sale Basis for Products[24]

Recognition Basis (or Method of Applying a Basis)	Criteria for Use	Reason(s) for Departing from Sale Basis
Percentage-of-completion method	Long-term construction of property; dependable estimates of extent of progress and cost to complete; reasonable assurance of collectibility of contract price; expectation that both contractor and buyer can meet obligations; and absence of inherent hazards that make estimates doubtful.	Availability of evidence of ultimate proceeds; better measure of periodic income; avoidance of fluctuations in revenues, expenses, and income; performance is a "continuous sale" and therefore not a departure from the sale basis.
Completed-contract method	Use on short-term contracts, and whenever percentage-of-completion cannot be used on long-term contracts.	Existence of inherent hazards in the contract beyond the normal, recurring business risks; conditions for using the percentage-of-completion method are absent.
Completion-of-production basis	Immediate marketability at quoted prices; unit interchangeability; difficulty of determining costs; and no significant distribution costs.	Known or determinable revenues; inability to determine costs and thereby defer expense recognition until sale.
Installment-sales method and cost-recovery method	Absence of reasonable basis for estimating degree of collectibility and costs of collection.	Collectibility of the receivable is so uncertain that the seller does not recognize gross profit (or income) until cash is actually received.
Deposit method	Cash received before the sales transaction is completed.	No recognition of revenue and income because there is not sufficient transfer of the risks and rewards of ownership.

---

[24]Adapted from Henry R. Jaenicke, *Survey of Present Practices in Recognizing Revenues, Expenses, Gains, and Losses, A Research Report* (Stamford, Conn.: FASB, 1981), p. 11.

Suppose you purchased a gift card for spa services at Sundara Spa for $300. The gift card expires at the end of 6 months. When should Sundara record the revenue? Here are two choices:

1　At the time Sundara receives the cash for the gift card.
2　At the time Sundara provides the service to the gift-card holder.

If you answered number 2, you would be right. Companies should recognize revenue when the obligation is satisfied—which is when Sundara performs the service.

Now let's add a few more facts. Suppose that the gift-card holder fails to use the card in the 6-month period. Statistics show that between 2 and 15 percent of gift-card holders never redeem their cards. Do you still believe that Sundara should record the revenue at the expiration date?

If you say you are not sure, you are probably right. Here is why: Certain states (such as California) do not recognize expiration dates, and therefore the customer has the right to redeem an otherwise expired gift card at any time. Let's for the moment say we are in California. Because the card holder may never redeem, when can Sundara recognize the revenue? Sundara would have to show statistically that after a certain period of time, the likelihood of redemption is remote. If it can make that case, it can recognize the revenue. Otherwise it may have to wait a long time.

Unfortunately, Sundara may still have a problem. It may be required to pay to the state the value of the spa service. The treatment for unclaimed gift cards may fall under the state abandoned-and-unclaimed-property laws. Most common unclaimed items are required to be remitted to the states after a 5-year period. Failure to report and remit the property can result in additional fines and penalties. So if Sundara is in a state where unclaimed property must be sent to the state, Sundara should report a liability on its balance sheet.

Source: PricewaterhouseCoopers, "Issues Surrounding the Recognition of Gift Card Sales and Escheat Liabilities," *Quick Brief* (December 2004).

Beyond the Numbers

As indicated in the story, companies must estimate gift card expiration dates to determine if they can recognize gift card receipts as revenue. Could companies use the accounting for gift cards to manage earnings? Explain.

Observations

The accounting profession is giving considerable attention to the issue of the proper time to recognize revenue. As indicated earlier, a series of highly publicized cases of companies prematurely recognizing revenue has caused the SEC to increase its enforcement actions in this area. In some of these cases, companies made significant adjustments to previously issued financial statements. In addition, the FASB has on its agenda a project to develop a comprehensive statement on revenue recognition. The planned statement will do the following: (a) eliminate the inconsistencies between existing authoritative literature and accepted practices, (b) fill the voids that have emerged in revenue recognition guidance in recent years,

You will want to read the
CONVERGENCE CORNER
on the next page for
discussion of how international
convergence efforts relate to
revenue recognition.

and (c) provide a conceptual basis for addressing revenue recognition issues that arise in the future. The SEC has made it clear that it will not tolerate abuses of the financial reporting process and that it will prosecute those who fail to adhere to "certain standards."

For our capital markets to be efficient, investors must have confidence that the financial information is both relevant and reliable. As a result, it is imperative that companies eliminate aggressive revenue recognition practices. Recent efforts by the SEC and the accounting profession should lead to higher-quality reporting in this area.

CONVERGENCE CORNER

Revenue Recognition

The general concepts and principles used for revenue recognition are similar between U.S. GAAP and international GAAP (iGAAP). Where they differ is in the detail. As indicated in the chapter, U.S. GAAP provides specific guidance related to revenue recognition for many different industries. That is not the case for iGAAP. Also the SEC has issued broad and specific guidance for public companies in the United States related to revenue recognition. Again, the IASB does not have a regulatory body that provides additional guidance.

RELEVANT FACTS

- The IASB defines revenue to include both revenues and gains. U.S. GAAP provides separate definitions for revenues and gains.

- Revenue recognition fraud is a major issue in U.S. financial reporting. The same situation occurs overseas as evidenced by revenue recognition breakdowns at Dutch software company **Baan NV**, Japanese electronics giant **NEC**, and Dutch grocer **AHold NV**.

- A specific standard exists for revenue recognition under iGAAP (*IAS 18*). In general, the standard is based on the probability that the economic benefits associated with the transaction will flow to the company selling the goods, rendering the service, or receiving investment income. In addition, the revenues and costs must be capable of being measured reliably. U.S. GAAP uses concepts such as realized, realizable, and earned as a basis for revenue recognition.

- iGAAP prohibits the use of the completed-contract method of accounting for long-term construction contracts (*IAS 13*). Companies must use the percentage-of-completion method. If revenues and costs are difficult to estimate, then companies recognize revenue only to the extent of the cost incurred—a zero-profit approach.

- In long-term construction contracts, iGAAP requires recognition of a loss immediately if the overall contract is going to be unprofitable. In other words, U.S. GAAP and iGAAP are the same regarding this issue.

ABOUT THE NUMBERS

As mentioned, iGAAP does not permit the completed-contract method of accounting for long-term construction contracts. If costs or revenues cannot be reliably determined, then how does a company report revenues related to its construction contracts using iGAAP? To illustrate, assume the following facts for England Construction Co. for a contract to build a dam at Windswept Canyon.

- The contract price to construct the dam is $400 million.

- Estimated incurred costs are $54 million in 2007, $180,000 in 2008, and $126 million in 2009.

- England uses iGAAP but is uncertain as regards these cost numbers.

In this situation, England recognizes revenue up to the cost incurred until the cost numbers can be more reliably determined. For example, assume that England incurred $55 million in costs in 2007. The presentation on its income statement would be as follows.

England Construction Co. Income Statement (partial) for 2007	
Revenue from long-term contracts	$55,000,000
Costs of construction	55,000,000
Gross profit	$ –0–

Under iGAAP, zero profit is recognized. Once costs can be reliably determined, the percentage-of-completion method is used in future periods.

ON THE HORIZON

The FASB and IASB are now involved in a joint project on revenue recognition. The purpose of this project is to develop comprehensive guidance on when to recognize revenue. Presently the Boards are considering an approach that focuses on *changes* in assets and liabilities (rather than on *earned* and *realized*) as the basis for revenue recognition. It is hoped that this approach will lead to more consistent accounting in this area. For more on this topic, see *http://www.fasb.org/project/revenue_recognition.shtml*.

ACCOUNTING, ANALYSIS, PRINCIPLES

Diversified Products, Inc. operates in several lines of business including the construction and real estate industries. While the majority of its revenues are recognized at point of sale, Diversified appropriately recognizes revenue on long-term construction contracts using the percentage-of-completion method. It recognizes sales of some properties using the installment-sales approach. Income data for 2008 from operations other than construction and real estate are as follows.

Revenues	$9,500,000
Expenses	7,750,000

1 Diversified started a construction project during 2007. The total contract price is $1,000,000, and $200,000 in costs were incurred in both 2007 and 2008. In 2007 Diversified recognized $50,000 gross profit on the project. Estimated costs to complete the project in 2009 are $400,000.

2 During this year, Diversified sold real estate parcels at a price of $630,000. Gross profit at a 25% rate is recognized when cash is received. Diversified collected $500,000 during the year on these sales.

Accounting

Determine net income for Diversified Products for 2008. Ignore taxes.

Analysis

Determine free cash flow for Diversified Products for 2008. In 2008 Diversified had depreciation expense of $175,000 and a net increase in working capital (changes in accounts receivable and accounts payable) of $250,000. In 2008, capital expenditures were $500,000; Diversified paid dividends of $120,000.

Principles

"Application of the percentage-of-completion and installment-sales method revenue recognition approaches illustrates the tradeoff between relevance and reliability of accounting information." Explain.

Solution

Accounting

Revenues	$9,500,000
Expenses	7,750,000
	1,750,000
Gross profit on construction contract*	50,000
Gross profit on installment sales**	125,000
Net income	$1,925,000

$$* \quad \frac{\$200,000 + \$200,000}{\$200,000 + \$200,000 + \$400,000} = 50\%$$

($1,000,000 − $800,000) × 50%	$100,000
Less: Gross profit recognized in 2007	50,000
Gross profit recognized in 2008	$50,000

**$500,000 × 25% = $125,000

Analysis

Net income	$1,925,000
Depreciation expense (non-cash expense)	175,000
Increase in working capital	(250,000)
Cash flow from operations	1,850,000
Capital expenditures	(500,000)
Dividends	(120,000)
Free cash flow	$1,230,000

Principles

Both methods attempt to report revenues that faithfully represent the operations of the company so that future earnings and cash flows can be predicted (*relevance*). With percentage-of-completion, companies use subjective estimates (based on prior experience) of the percent completed to measure the amount of gross profit to recognize in the periods before completion. Thus, it would appear that relevance takes precedence in this case.

In contrast, under the installment method, there is no reliable basis to determine collectibility of installment sales (high degree of unreliability as to the realizability criterion). Therefore, companies do not recognize gross profit until cash is collected. This delay in recognition suggests that *reliability* carries the day in the case of installment-sales accounting.

Key Terms

completed-contract method, 316
completion-of-production basis, 317
cost-recovery method, 322
cost-to-cost basis, 313
deposit method, 322
earned (revenues), 307
high rate of returns, 309

installment-sales method, 319
percentage-of-completion method, 313
point of sale (delivery), 309
realizable (revenues), 307
realized (revenues), 306
revenue recognition principle, 306

Summary of Learning Objectives

1 Apply the revenue recognition principle. The revenue recognition principle provides that revenue is recognized (1) when it is realized or realizable and (2) when it is earned. Companies recognize revenues at the time when they exchange goods and services for cash or claims to cash. Revenues are realizable when assets received in exchanges are readily convertible to known amounts of cash or claims to cash. A company earns revenues when it has substantially accomplished what it must do to be entitled to the benefits represented by the revenues—that is, when the earnings process is complete or virtually complete.

2 Describe accounting issues involved with revenue recognition at point of sale. The two conditions for

recognizing revenue are usually met by the time a company delivers a product or merchandise or renders services to customers. Companies commonly recognize revenues from manufacturing and selling activities at time of sale.

3 Apply the percentage-of-completion method for long-term contracts. To apply the percentage-of-completion method to long-term contracts, a company must have some basis for measuring the progress toward completion at particular interim dates. One of the most popular measures used to determine the progress toward completion is the cost-to-cost basis. Using this basis, companies measure the percentage of completion by comparing costs incurred to date with the most recent estimate of the total costs to complete the contract. The company measures the percentage of costs incurred to total estimated costs, and then applies that percentage to the total revenue or the estimated total gross profit on the contract, to arrive at the revenue or the gross profit amounts to be recognized to date.

4 Apply the completed-contract method for long-term contracts. Under the completed-contract method, companies recognize revenue and gross profit only at point of sale—that is, when the contract is completed. Under both the percentage-of-completion and the completed-contract methods, companies must recognize the entire expected contract loss in the current period.

5 Describe the installment-sales and cost-recovery methods of accounting. The *installment-sales method* recognizes income in the periods of collection rather than in the period of sale. The accounting profession justifies the installment-sales method on the basis that when there is no reasonable approach for estimating the degree of collectibility, companies should not recognize revenue until cash is collected. Under the *cost-recovery method*, companies do not recognize profit until the buyer's cash payments exceed the seller's cost of the merchandise sold. After all costs have been recovered, companies include in income any additional cash collections.

BEHIND THE NUMBERS · APPENDIX 7A

REVENUE RECOGNITION PROCEDURES

Long-Term Contracts

> OBJECTIVE 6
>
> **Prepare the journal entries to record long-terms contracts.**

We can illustrate the percentage-of-completion method using journal entries. Assume that Hardhat Construction Company has a contract to construct a $4,500,000 bridge, at an estimated cost of $4,000,000. The contract is to start in July 2007. The following data pertain to the construction period. (Note that by the end of 2008, the estimated total cost has increased from $4,000,000 to $4,050,000.)

	2007	2008	2009
Costs to date	$1,000,000	$2,916,000	$4,050,000
Estimated costs to complete	3,000,000	1,134,000	–
Progress billings during the year	900,000	2,400,000	1,200,000
Cash collected during the year	750,000	1,750,000	2,000,000

The percent complete would be computed as follows.

Illustration 7A-1

Application of Percentage-of-Completion Method, Cost-to-Cost Basis

	2007	2008	2009
Contract price	$4,500,000	$4,500,000	$4,500,000
Less estimated cost			
Costs to date	1,000,000	2,916,000	4,050,000
Estimated costs to complete	3,000,000	1,134,000	–
Estimated total costs	4,000,000	4,050,000	4,050,000
Estimated total gross profit	$ 500,000	$ 450,000	$ 450,000
Percent complete	25% $\left(\dfrac{\$1,000,000}{\$4,000,000}\right)$	72% $\left(\dfrac{\$2,916,000}{\$4,050,000}\right)$	100% $\left(\dfrac{\$4,050,000}{\$4,050,000}\right)$

On the basis of the information provided, Hardhat would prepare the following entries to record (1) the costs of construction, (2) progress billings, and (3) collections. These entries appear as summaries of the many transactions that the company would enter individually as they occur during the year.

Illustration 7A-2
Journal Entries—
Percentage-of-Completion
Method, Cost-to-Cost
Basis

	2007		2008		2009	
(1) To record costs of construction:						
Construction in Process	1,000,000		1,916,000		1,134,000	
Materials, Cash,						
Payables, etc.		1,000,000		1,916,000		1,134,000
(2) To record progress billings:						
Accounts Receivable	900,000		2,400,000		1,200,000	
Billings on Construction						
in Process		900,000		2,400,000		1,200,000
(3) To record collections:						
Cash	750,000		1,750,000		2,000,000	
Accounts Receivable		750,000		1,750,000		2,000,000

In Illustration 7A-2, the costs incurred to date as a proportion of the estimated total costs to be incurred on the project are a measure of the extent of progress toward completion. Illustration 7A-3 shows calculation of the estimated revenue and gross profit to be recognized for each year.

		2007	2008	2009
Revenue recognized in:				
2007	$4,500,000 × 25%	$1,125,000		
2008	$4,500,000 × 72%		$3,240,000	
	Less: Revenue recognized in 2007		1,125,000	
	Revenue in 2008		$2,115,000	
2009	$4,500,000 × 100%			$4,500,000
	Less: Revenue recognized in			
	2007 and 2008			3,240,000
	Revenue in 2009			$1,260,000
Gross profit recognized in:				
2007	$500,000 × 25%	$ 125,000		
2008	$450,000 × 72%		$ 324,000	
	Less: Gross profit recognized in 2007		125,000	
	Gross profit in 2008		$ 199,000	
2009	$450,000 × 100%			$ 450,000
	Less: Gross profit recognized in			
	2007 and 2008			324,000
	Gross profit in 2009			$ 126,000

Illustration 7A-3
Percentage-of-Completion,
Revenue and Gross Profit
by Year

Illustration 7A-4 (page 330) shows the entries to recognize revenue and gross profit each year and to record completion and final approval of the contract.

	2007		2008		2009	
To recognize revenue and gross profit:						
Construction in Process (gross profit)	125,000		199,000		126,000	
Construction Expenses	1,000,000		1,916,000		1,134,000	
Revenue from Long-Term Contract		1,125,000		2,115,000		1,260,000
To record completion of the contract:						
Billings on Construction in Process					4,500,000	
Construction in Process						4,500,000

Illustration 7A-4

Journal Entries to Recognize Revenue and Gross Profit and to Record Contract Completion—Percentage-of-Completion Method, Cost-to-Cost Basis

Note that Hardhat debits to Construction in Process the gross profit computed in Illustration 7A-3 (page 329), and it credits to Revenue from Long-Term Contract the amounts computed. It debits to a nominal account, Construction Expenses, the difference between the amounts recognized each year for revenue and for gross profit. Similar to cost of goods sold in a manufacturing enterprise, Hardhat reports this account in the income statement which represents the actual cost of construction incurred in that period. For example, in the cost-to-cost illustration, Hardhat uses the actual costs of $1,000,000 in 2007 to compute both the gross profit of $125,000 and the percent complete (25%).

To maintain a record of total costs incurred (plus recognized profit) to date, companies must continue to accumulate costs in the Construction in Process account. Although theoretically a series of "sales" takes place using the percentage-of-completion method, the company cannot remove inventory cost until it completes the construction and transfers the bridge to the new owner. The Construction in Process account would include the following summarized entries over the term of the construction project.

Construction in Process			
2007 construction costs	$1,000,000	12/31/09 to close completed project	$4,500,000
2007 recognized gross profit	125,000		
2008 construction costs	1,916,000		
2008 recognized gross profit	199,000		
2009 construction costs	1,134,000		
2009 recognized gross profit	126,000		
Total	$4,500,000	Total	$4,500,000

Illustration 7A-5

Content of Construction in Process Account—Percentage-of-Completion Method

The Hardhat Construction illustration contained a **change in estimate** in the second year, 2008, when the estimated total costs increased from $4,000,000 to $4,050,000. The company adjusts the percent completed to the new estimate of total costs and then deducts the amount of revenues and gross profit recognized in prior periods from revenues and gross profit computed for progress to date. In this way, Hardhat accounts for the change in estimate in a **cumulative catch-up manner** (see year 2008 in Illustration 7A-3) **in the period of change**. Therefore the balance sheet at the end of the period of change and the accounting in subsequent periods are as they would have been if the revised estimate had been the original estimate.

Financial Statement Presentation—Percentage-of-Completion

Generally, when a company records a receivable from a sale, it reduces the Inventory account. In this case, however, the company continues to carry both the receivable and the inventory. Subtracting the balance in the **Billings account** from Construction in Process avoids double-counting the inventory. During the life of the contract, the company reports in the balance sheet the difference between the Construction in Process and the Billings on Construction in Process accounts. This difference is **a current asset if a debit, and a current liability if a credit**.

Hardhat can at any time calculate the unbilled portion of revenue recognized to date by subtracting the billings to date from the revenue recognized to date for 2007, as Illustration 7A-6 shows. When the costs incurred plus the gross profit recognized to date (the balance in Construction in Process) exceed the billings, the company reports this excess as a current asset entitled "Cost and recognized profit in excess of billings" (sometimes referred to as "unbilled revenue"). When the billings exceed costs incurred and gross profit to date, the company reports this excess as a current liability entitled "Billings in excess of costs and recognized profit."

Contract revenue recognized to date: $4,500,000 × $\dfrac{\$1,000,000}{\$4,000,000}$ =	$1,125,000
Billings to date	900,000
Cost and recognized profit in excess of billings	$ 225,000

Illustration 7A-6
Computation of Unbilled Contract Price at 12/31/07

When a company has a number of projects, and costs exceed billings on some contracts and billings exceed costs on others, the company should segregate the contracts. It should include on the asset side those contracts on which costs and recognized profit exceed billings. It should include on the liability side those contracts on which billings exceed costs and recognized profit. Separate disclosures of the dollar volume of billings and costs are preferable to a summary presentation of the net difference.

Using data from the previous illustration, Hardhat Construction Company would report the status and results of its long-term construction activities under the percentage-of-completion method as follows.

Hardhat Construction Company

	2007	2008	2009
Income Statement			
Revenue from long-term contracts	$1,125,000	$2,115,000	$1,260,000
Costs of construction	1,000,000	1,916,000	1,134,000
Gross profit	$ 125,000	$ 199,000	$ 126,000

Illustration 7A-7
Financial Statement Presentation—Percentage-of-Completion Method

Balance Sheet (12/31)				
Current assets		2007	2008	
Accounts receivable		$150,000	$800,000	
Inventories				
Construction in process	$1,125,000			
Less: Billings	900,000			
Costs and recognized profit in excess of billings		225,000		
Current liabilities				
Billings ($3,300,000) in excess of costs and recognized profit ($3,240,000)			60,000	

Note 1. Summary of Significant Accounting Policies

Long-term construction contracts. The company recognizes revenues and reports profits from long-term construction contracts, its principal business, under the percentage-of-completion method of accounting. These contracts generally extend for periods in excess of one year. The amounts of revenues and profits recognized each year are based on the ratio of costs incurred to the total estimated costs. Costs included in construction in process include direct materials, direct labor, and project-related overhead. Corporate general and administrative expenses are charged to the periods as incurred and are not allocated to construction contracts.

Completed-Contract Method

Under the completed-contract method, the **annual entries** to record costs of construction, progress billings, and collections from customers would be identical to those illustrated above, with the significant exclusion of the recognition of revenue and gross profit. For the bridge project illustrated, on the preceding pages, Hardhat would make the following entries in 2009 under the completed-contract method to recognize revenue and costs and to close out the inventory and billings accounts.

	2009	
Billings on Construction in Process	4,500,000	
Revenue from Long-Term Contract		4,500,000
Costs of Construction	4,050,000	
Construction in Process		4,050,000

Comparing the two methods in relation to the same bridge project, Hardhat Construction Company would have recognized gross profit as follows.

Illustration 7A-8
Comparison of Gross Profit Recognized under Different Methods

	Percentage-of-Completion	Completed-Contract
2007	$125,000	$ 0
2008	199,000	0
2009	126,000	450,000

Under the completed-contract method, Hardhat Construction would report its long-term construction activities as follows.

Illustration 7A-9
Financial Statement Presentation—Completed-Contract Method

Hardhat Construction Company

	2007	2008	2009
Income Statement			
Revenue from long-term contract	—	—	$4,500,000
Costs of construction	—	—	4,050,000
Gross profit	—	—	$ 450,000

Balance Sheet (12/31)		2007	2008
Current assets			
Accounts receivable		$150,000	$800,000
Inventories			
Construction in process	$1,000,000		
Less: Billings	900,000		
Unbilled contract costs		100,000	
Current liabilities			
Billings ($3,300,000) in excess of contract			
costs ($2,916,000)			384,000

Note 1. Summary of Significant Accounting Policies
Long-term construction contracts. The company recognizes revenues and reports profits from long-term construction contracts, its principal business, under the completed-contract method. These contracts generally extend for periods in excess of one year. Contract costs and billings are accumulated during the periods of construction, but no revenues or profits are recognized until completion of the contract. Costs included in construction in process include direct material, direct labor, and project-related overhead. Corporate general and administrative expenses are charged to the periods as incurred.

Installment Sales

The steps to record installment sales are as follows.

OBJECTIVE 7

Prepare the journal entries to record installment sales.

For the sales in any one year:

1 During the year, record both sales and cost of sales in the regular way, using the special accounts described later, and compute the rate of gross profit on installment-sales transactions.

2 At the end of the year, apply the rate of gross profit to the cash collections of the current year's installment sales to arrive at the realized gross profit.

3 Defer to future years the gross profit not realized.

For sales made in prior years:

• Apply the gross profit rate of each year's sales against cash collections of accounts receivable resulting from that year's sales to arrive at the realized gross profit.

Companies should use special accounts in recording income from installment sales. These accounts provide certain special information required to determine the realized and unrealized gross profit in each year of operations. The requirements for special accounts are as follows.

1 Companies must keep installment-sales transactions separate in the accounts from all other sales.

2 Companies must be able to determine gross profit on sales sold on installment.

3 The amount of cash collected on installment-sales accounts receivable must be known, and, further, the total collected on the current year's sales and on each preceding year's sales must be determinable.

4 Companies must make provision for carrying forward each year's deferred gross profit.

In each year, the company charges ordinary operating expenses to expense accounts and closes those accounts to Income Summary, as under customary accounting procedure. Thus, the only peculiarity in computing net income under the installment-sales method as generally applied is **the deferral of gross profit until realized by accounts receivable collection**.

To illustrate the installment-sales method in accounting for the sales of merchandise, assume the following data.

	2007	2008	2009
Installment sales	$200,000	$250,000	$240,000
Cost of installment sales	150,000	190,000	168,000
Gross profit	$ 50,000	$ 60,000	$ 72,000
Rate of gross profit on sales	25%[a]	24%[b]	30%[c]
Cash receipts			
2007 sales	$ 60,000	$100,000	$ 40,000
2008 sales		100,000	125,000
2009 sales			80,000

[a] $\dfrac{\$50,000}{\$200,000}$ [b] $\dfrac{\$60,000}{\$250,000}$ [c] $\dfrac{\$72,000}{\$240,000}$

Illustration 7A-10
Installment Sales Data

To simplify the illustration, we have excluded interest charges. Summary entries in general journal form for the year 2007 are shown on page 334.

2007

Installment Accounts Receivable, 2007	200,000	
Installment Sales		200,000
(To record sales made on installment in 2007)		
Cash	60,000	
Installment Accounts Receivable, 2007		60,000
(To record cash collected on installment receivables)		
Cost of Installment Sales	150,000	
Inventory (or Purchases)		150,000
(To record cost of goods sold on installment in 2007 on		
either a perpetual or a periodic inventory basis)		
Installment Sales	200,000	
Cost of Installment Sales		150,000
Deferred Gross Profit, 2007		50,000
(To close installment sales and cost of installment sales		
for the year)		
Deferred Gross Profit, 2007	15,000	
Realized Gross Profit on Installment Sales		15,000
(To remove from deferred gross profit the profit realized		
through cash collections; $60,000 \times 25\%$)		
Realized Gross Profit on Installment Sales	15,000	
Income Summary		15,000
(To close profits realized by collections)		

Illustration 7A-11 shows computation of the realized and deferred gross profit for the year 2007.

Illustration 7A-11
Computation of Realized and Deferred Gross Profit, Year 1

2007	
Rate of gross profit current year	25%
Cash collected on current year's sales	$60,000
Realized gross profit (25% of $60,000)	15,000
Gross profit to be deferred ($50,000 − $15,000)	35,000

Summary entries in journal form for year 2 (2008) are shown below.

2008

Installment Accounts Receivable, 2008	250,000	
Installment Sales		250,000
(To record sales made on installment in 2008)		
Cash	200,000	
Installment Accounts Receivable, 2007		100,000
Installment Accounts Receivable, 2008		100,000
(To record cash collected on installment receivables)		
Cost of Installment Sales	190,000	
Inventory (or Purchases)		190,000
(To record cost of goods sold on installment in 2008)		
Installment Sales	250,000	
Cost of Installment Sales		190,000
Deferred Gross Profit, 2008		60,000
(To close installment sales and cost of installment sales		
for the year)		
Deferred Gross Profit, 2007 ($100,000 \times 25\%$)	25,000	
Deferred Gross Profit, 2008 ($100,000 \times 24\%$)	24,000	
Realized Gross Profit on Installment Sales		49,000
(To remove from deferred gross profit the profit realized		
through collections)		
Realized Gross Profit on Installment Sales	49,000	
Income Summary		49,000
(To close profits realized by collections)		

Illustration 7A-12 shows computation of the realized and deferred gross profit for the year 2008.

2008	
Current year's sales	
Rate of gross profit	24%
Cash collected on current year's sales	$100,000
Realized gross profit (24% of $100,000)	24,000
Gross profit to be deferred ($60,000 − $24,000)	36,000
Prior year's sales	
Rate of gross profit—2007	25%
Cash collected on 2007 sales	$100,000
Gross profit realized in 2008 on 2007 sales (25% of $100,000)	25,000
Total gross profit realized in 2008	
Realized on collections of 2007 sales	$ 25,000
Realized on collections of 2008 sales	24,000
Total	$ 49,000

Illustration 7A-12
Computation of Realized and Deferred Gross Profit, Year 2

The entries in 2009 would be similar to those of 2008, and the total gross profit realized would be $64,000, as shown by the computations in Illustration 7A-13.

2009	
Current year's sales	
Rate of gross profit	30%
Cash collected on current year's sales	$ 80,000
Gross profit realized on 2009 sales (30% of $80,000)	24,000
Gross profit to be deferred ($72,000 − $24,000)	48,000
Prior years' sales	
2007 sales	
Rate of gross profit	25%
Cash collected	$ 40,000
Gross profit realized in 2009 on 2007 sales (25% of $40,000)	10,000
2008 sales	
Rate of gross profit	24%
Cash collected	$125,000
Gross profit realized in 2009 on 2008 sales (24% of $125,000)	30,000
Total gross profit realized in 2009	
Realized on collections of 2007 sales	$ 10,000
Realized on collections of 2008 sales	30,000
Realized on collections of 2009 sales	24,000
Total	$ 64,000

Illustration 7A-13
Computation of Realized and Deferred Gross Profit, Year 3

Additional Problems of Installment-Sales Accounting

In addition to computing realized and deferred gross profit currently, other problems are involved in accounting for installment-sales transactions. These problems are related to:

1 Interest on installment contracts.
2 Uncollectible accounts.
3 Defaults and repossessions.

Interest on Installment Contracts.   Because the collection of installment receivables is spread over a long period, it is customary to charge the buyer interest on the unpaid balance. Companies set up a schedule of equal payments consisting of interest and principal. They attribute each successive payment to a smaller amount of interest and a correspondingly larger amount attributable to principal, as shown in Illustration 7A-14. This illustration assumes that a company sells for $3,000 an asset costing $2,400; the three installments of $1,164.10 include interest of 8 percent.

Illustration 7A-14
Installment Payment
Schedule

Date	Cash (Debit)	Interest Earned (Credit)	Installment Receivables (Credit)	Installment Unpaid Balance	Realized Gross Profit (20%)
1/2/07	—	—	—	$3,000.00	—
1/2/08	$1,164.10^a	$240.00^b	$ 924.10^c	2,075.90^d	$184.82^e
1/2/09	1,164.10	166.07	998.03	1,077.87	199.61
1/2/10	1,164.10	86.23	1,077.87	–0–	215.57
					$600.00

^{a}Periodic payment = Original unpaid balance ÷ PV of an annuity of $1.00 for three periods at 8% (Appendix A, Table 4); $1,164.10 = $3,000 ÷ 2.57710.
^{b}$3,000.00 × .08 = $240.
^{c}$1,164.10 − $240.00 = $924.10.
^{d}$3,000.00 − $924.10 = $2,075.90.
^{e}$924.10 × .20 = $184.82.

Companies should account for interest separate from the gross profit recognized on the installment-sales collections during the period. They recognize interest payments as interest revenue at the time of the cash receipt.

Uncollectible Accounts.   Installment contracts commonly include a repossession feature in the sales agreement. This feature gives the selling company an opportunity to recoup any uncollectible accounts through repossession and resale of repossessed merchandise. As a result, the problem of bad debts or uncollectible accounts receivable is somewhat different for concerns selling on an installment basis. If the experience of the company indicates that repossessions do not, as a rule, compensate for uncollectible balances, it may be advisable to provide for such losses through charges to a special bad-debt expense account just as is done for other credit sales.

Defaults and Repossessions.   Depending on the terms of the sales contract and the policy of the credit department, the seller can repossess merchandise sold under an installment arrangement if the purchaser fails to meet payment requirements. The company may then recondition the repossessed merchandise and resell it for cash or installment payments.

The accounting for **repossessions** recognizes that the related installment receivable account is not collectible and that the company should write off the uncollectible account. In such a case, the seller would remove both the account receivable and the applicable deferred gross profit from the ledger using the following entry:

Repossessed Merchandise (an inventory account)	xx	
Deferred Gross Profit	xx	
Installment Accounts Receivable		xx

This entry assumes that the company would record the repossessed merchandise at exactly the amount of the uncollected account less the deferred gross profit applicable. This assumption may or may not be proper. In determining the amount, the company should consider various issues: the condition of the merchandise repossessed, the cost of reconditioning, and the market for second-hand merchandise of that particular type. **The objective should be to put any repossessed asset on the books at its fair value or, when fair value is not ascertainable, at the best possible approximation of fair value.** If the fair value of the merchandise repossessed is less than the uncollected balance less the deferred gross profit, the company should record a "loss on repossession" at the date of repossession.

Some contend that a company should enter repossessed merchandise at a valuation that will permit the company to make its regular rate of gross profit on resale. If the company enters the merchandise at its approximated cost to purchase, the regular rate of gross profit could be provided for upon its ultimate sale, but that is completely a secondary consideration. It is more important that the company record at fair value the repossessed asset in accordance with the general practice of carrying assets at acquisition price, as represented by the fair market value at the date of acquisition.

To illustrate the required entry, assume that Leeburg Appliances sells a refrigerator to Marilyn Hunt for $1,500 on September 1, 2008. Terms require a down payment of $600 and $60 on the first of every month for 15 months, starting October 1, 2008. It is further assumed that the refrigerator cost $900 and that Leeburg prices the product to provide a 40 percent rate of gross profit on selling price. At the year-end, December 31, 2008, Leeburg should have collected a total of $180 in addition to the original down payment.

If Hunt makes her January and February payments in 2009 and then defaults, the account balances applicable to Hunt at time of default are as shown in Illustration 7A-15.

Installment accounts receivable (September 1, 2008)		$1,500
Less: Down payment:	$600	
Payments to date ($60 × 5)	300	900
Installment accounts receivable (March 1, 2009)		$ 600
Installment accounts receivable (March 1, 2009)		$600
Gross profit rate		× 40%
Deferred gross profit		$240

Illustration 7A-15
Computation of Installment Receivable Balances

As indicated, Leeburg can compute the balance of deferred gross profit applicable to Hunt's account by applying the gross profit rate for the year of sale to the 2009 balance of Hunt's account receivable, 40 percent of $600, or $240. The account balances are therefore:

Installment Account Receivable, 2008	600 (dr.)
Deferred Gross Profit, 2008	240 (cr.)

Leeburg repossesses the refrigerator following Hunt's default. If Leeburg estimates the fair value of the inventory repossessed is $150, Leeburg would make the following entry to record the repossession:

Deferred Gross Profit, 2008	240	
Repossessed Merchandise	150	
Loss on Repossession	210	
Installment Account Receivable (Hunt)		600

Companies determine the amount of the loss by the following two steps:

1 Subtract the deferred gross profit from the amount of the account receivable, to determine the unrecovered cost (or book value) of the merchandise repossessed.

2 Subtract the estimated fair value of the merchandise repossessed from the unrecovered cost, to get the amount of the loss on repossession.

Illustration 7A-16 shows computation of the loss on the refrigerator.

Balance of account receivable (representing uncollected selling price)	$600
Less: Deferred gross profit	240
Unrecovered cost	360
Less: Estimated fair value of merchandise repossessed	150
Loss (Gain) on repossession	$210

As pointed out earlier, Leeburg (the selling company) may charge the loss on repossession to Allowance for Doubtful Accounts if it maintains such an account.

Financial Statement Presentation of Installment-Sales Transactions

If installment-sales transactions represent a significant part of total sales, companies should fully disclose installment sales, the cost of installment sales, and any expenses allocable to installment sales. If installment sales constitute an insignificant part of total sales, it may be satisfactory to include only the realized gross profit in the income statement as a special item following the gross profit on sales, as shown in Illustration 7A-17.

Health Machine Company
Income Statement
For the Year Ended December 31, 2008

Sales	$620,000
Cost of goods sold	490,000
Gross profit on sales	130,000
Gross profit realized on installment sales	51,000
Total gross profit on sales	$181,000

If more complete disclosure of installment-sales transactions is desired, companies may use a presentation similar to that shown in Illustration 7A-18.

Health Machine Company
Income Statement
For the Year Ended December 31, 2008

	Installment Sales	Other Sales	Total
Sales	$248,000	$620,000	$868,000
Cost of goods sold	182,000	490,000	672,000
Gross profit on sales	66,000	130,000	196,000
Less: Deferred gross profit on installment sales of this year	47,000		47,000
Realized gross profit on this year's sales	19,000	130,000	149,000
Add: Gross profit realized on installment sales of prior years	32,000		32,000
Gross profit realized this year	$ 51,000	$130,000	$181,000

This method of presentation is somewhat awkward. However, the awkwardness is difficult to avoid if companies want to provide full disclosure of installment-sales transactions in the income statement. One solution, of course, is to prepare a separate schedule showing installment-sales transactions, with only the final figure carried into the income statement.

In the balance sheet it is generally desirable to classify installment accounts receivable by year of collectibility. There is some question as to whether companies should include in current assets installment accounts that are not collectible for two or more years. If installment sales are part of normal operations, companies may consider such sales as current assets because they are collectible within the operating cycle of the business. Little confusion should result from this practice if companies fully disclose maturity dates, as illustrated in Illustration 7A-19.

Current Assets		
Notes and accounts receivable		
Trade customers	$78,800	
Less: Allowance for doubtful accounts	3,700	
	75,100	
Installment accounts collectible in 2008	22,600	
Installment accounts collectible in 2009	47,200	$144,900

Illustration 7A-19
Disclosure of Installment Accounts Receivable, by Year

On the other hand, companies should report in the "Other assets" section receivables from an installment contract (or contracts), resulting from a transaction not related to normal operations if due beyond one year.

If repossessed merchandise is a part of inventory, companies should include it as such in the current assets section of the balance sheet. They should include any gain or loss on repossessions in the "Other revenues and gains" or "Other expenses and losses" section of the income statement.

Companies generally treat **deferred gross profit on installment sales** as unearned revenue and classify it as a current liability. Theoretically, deferred gross profit consists of three elements:

1 income tax liability to be paid when the company reports sales as realized revenue (current liability);

2 allowance for collection expense, bad debts, and repossession losses (deduction from installment accounts receivable); and

3 net income (retained earnings, restricted as to dividend availability).

Because of the difficulty in allocating deferred gross profit among these three elements, however, companies frequently report the whole amount as unearned revenue.

Key Terms

repossessions, 336

Summary of Learning Objectives for Appendix 7A

6   Prepare the journal entries to record long-term contracts. Companies should make entries to record (1) costs of construction, (2) progress billings, and (3) collections.

At the end of the period, they also record revenue and gross profit. The annual entries to record costs of construction, progress billings, and collections from customers under the completed-contract method would be identical to those for the percentage-of-completion method, with the significant exclusion of the recognition of revenue and gross profit.

7 Prepare the journal entries to record installment sales. During the year, record both sales and cost of

sales in the regular way. At the end of the year, apply the rate of gross profit to the cash collections of the current year's installment sales to arrive at the realized gross profit. Defer to future years the gross profit not realized.

REVIEW EXERCISE

Outback Industries manufactures power-distribution equipment, builds power plants, and develops real estate. While the company recognizes the majority of its revenues at point of sale, Outback appropriately recognizes revenue on long-term construction projects using the percentage-of-completion method. It recognizes sales of some properties using the installment-sales approach. Income data for 2008 from operations other than construction and real estate are as follows.

Revenues	$6,500,000
Expenses	4,350,000

Other information:

1 Outback started a construction project during 2007. The total contract price is $1,000,000, and $100,000 in costs were incurred in 2008. Estimated costs to complete the project in 2009 are $400,000. In 2007 Outback incurred $200,000 of costs and recognized $50,000 gross profit on this project.

2 During this year, Outback sold real estate parcels at a price of $400,000. It recognizes gross profit at a 35% rate when cash is received. Outback collected $200,000 during the year on these sales.

3 The reported revenues include an order for power relays valued at $150,000. This new customer is not ready to take delivery. At year-end Outback billed the customer and shipped the relays to an Outback warehouse close to the customer for quick delivery when needed.

Instructions

a Determine net income for Outback Industries for 2008. Ignore taxes.

b Some year-end audit work discovered that in 2008 Outback made installment sales in the amount of $80,000 (cost of sales $52,000) to customers with very questionable credit backgrounds. The company accounted for these sales using the cost-recovery method. Outback collected $20,000 from these customers in 2008. Determine the effect of this change in accounting on the income computed in part (a).

Solution

a

Revenues	$6,350,000*
Expenses	4,350,000
	2,000,000
Gross profit on construction contract**	78,571
Gross profit on installment sales***	70,000
Net income	$2,148,571

*$6,500,000 − $150,000. Outback should not recognize this revenue until the customer takes delivery.

$$\frac{\$200,000 + \$100,000}{\$200,000 + \$100,000 + \$400,000} = 42.857\% \times (\$1,000,000 - \$700,000) = \$128,571$$

** (the above)

Less gross profit recognized in 2007   (50,000)

$ 78,571

***$200,000 × 35% = $70,000

b   Cash received on these sales was $20,000 × 35% = 7,000, which Outback recognized in (a) under the installment method. Income would be $7,000 lower under cost recovery; the company would recognize no gross profit until collections exceed cost. Thus, Outback will not recognize any gross profit on these sales until it collects another $45,000 ($52,000 − $7,000).

Questions

Note: All **asterisked** assignment materials relate to material contained in the appendix to the chapter.

1 When is revenue conventionally recognized? What conditions should exist for the recognition at date of sale of all or part of the revenue and income of any sale transaction?

2 When is revenue recognized in the following situations: (a) Revenue from selling products? (b) Revenue from services rendered? (c) Revenue from permitting others to use enterprise assets? (d) Revenue from disposing of assets other than products?

3 Identify several types of sales transactions and indicate the types of business for which that type of transaction is common.

4 Barnaby Inc. is exposed to continued risks of a high rate of return of its products sold. Under what conditions may Barnaby recognize sales transactions as current revenue?

5 What are the two basic methods of accounting for long-term construction contracts? Indicate the circumstances that determine when one or the other of these methods should be used.

6 F. Scott Fitzgerald Construction Co. has a $60 million contract to construct a highway overpass and cloverleaf. The total estimated cost for the project is $50 million. Costs incurred in the first year of the project are $9 million. F. Scott Fitzgerald Construction Co. appropriately uses the percentage-of-completion method. How much revenue and gross profit should F. Scott Fitzgerald recognize in the first year of the project?

7 For what reasons should the percentage-of-completion method be used over the completed-contract method whenever possible?

8 What is a common technique used to determine the extent of progress in long-term construction projects?

9 How are losses on the total long-term contracts accounted for?

10 Describe the installment-sales method of accounting.

11 Explain the differences between the installment-sales method and the cost-recovery method.

12 Identify and briefly describe the two methods generally employed to account for the cash received in situations where the collection of the sales price is not reasonably assured.

13 What is the deposit method, and when might companies use it?

14 What is the nature of an installment sale? How do installment sales differ from ordinary credit sales?

15 Jack London sold his condominium for $500,000 on September 14, 2007; he had paid $310,000 for it in 1999. London collected the selling price as follows: 2007, $80,000; 2008, $320,000; and 2009, $100,000. London appropriately uses the installment-sales method. Prepare a schedule to determine the gross profit for 2007, 2008, and 2009 from the installment sale.

16 When is revenue recognized under the cost-recovery method?

17 When is revenue recognized under the deposit method? How does the deposit method differ from the installment-sales and cost-recovery methods?

*18 Under the percentage-of-completion method, how are the Construction in Process and the Billings on Construction in Process accounts reported in the balance sheet?

Brief Exercises

(LO 1, 2)   **BE7-1**   Scooby Doo Music sold CDs to retailers and recorded sales revenue of $800,000. During 2008, retailers returned CDs to Scooby Doo and were granted credit of $78,000. Past experience indicates that the normal return rate is 15%. Prepare Scooby Doo's entries to record (a) the $78,000 of returns and (b) estimated returns at December 31, 2008.

(LO 1, 3)   **BE7-2**   Shock Wave, Inc. began work on a $7,000,000 contract in 2008 to construct an office building. During 2008, Shock Wave, Inc. incurred costs of $1,715,000. At December 31, 2008, the estimated future costs to complete the project total $3,185,000. Compute the estimated revenue and gross profit to be recognized in 2008.

(LO 1, 4)   **BE7-3**   Use the information from BE7-2, but assume Shock Wave uses the completed-contract method. Compute the estimated revenue and gross profit to be recognized in 2008.

(LO 1, 3, 4)   **BE7-4**   Shaq Fu Construction Company began work on a $420,000 construction contract in 2008. During 2008, Shaq Fu incurred costs of $288,000, billed its customer for $215,000, and collected $175,000. At December 31, 2008, the estimated future costs to complete the project total $162,000. Determine Shaq Fu's profit or loss for 2008 using (a) the percentage-of-completion method and (b) the completed-contract method, if any.

(LO 1, 5)   **BE7-5**   Thunder Paradise Corporation began selling goods on an installment basis on January 1, 2008. During 2008, Thunder Paradise had installment sales of $150,000; cash collections of $54,000; cost of installment sales of $105,000. Determine the gross profit recognized, using the installment-sales method.

(LO 1, 5)   **BE7-6**   Yogi Bear Corporation sold equipment to Magilla Company for $20,000. The equipment is on Yogi's books at a net amount of $14,000. Yogi collected $10,000 in 2007, $5,000 in 2008, and $5,000 in 2009. If Yogi uses the installment-sales method, what amount of gross profit will be recognized in each year?

(LO 1, 5)   **BE7-7**   Use the information from BE7-6. If Yogi uses the cost-recovery method, what amount of gross profit will be recognized in each year?

(LO 6)   *__BE7-8__   Using the information from BE7-2, prepare Shock Wave's 2008 journal entries using the percentage-of-completion method.

(LO 6)   *__BE7-9__   Using the information from BE7-2, prepare Shock Wave's 2008 journal entries using the completed-contract method.

(LO 7)   *__BE7-10__   Using the information in BE7-5, prepare Thunder Paradise's entries to record installment sales, cash collected, cost of installment sales, deferral of gross profit, and gross profit recognized.

Exercises

(LO 1, 3, 4)   **E7-1**   **(Recognition of Profit on Long-Term Contracts)**   During 2007 Pierson Company started a construction job with a contract price of $1,500,000. The job was completed in 2009. The following information is available.

	2007	2008	2009
Costs incurred to date	$400,000	$935,000	$1,070,000
Estimated costs to complete	600,000	165,000	–0–

Instructions

(a) Compute the amount of gross profit to be recognized each year assuming the percentage-of-completion method is used.

(b) Compute the amount of gross profit to be recognized each year assuming the completed-contract method is used.

(AICPA adapted)

(LO 1, 3)   **E7-2**   **(Gross Profit on Uncompleted Contract)**   On April 1, 2008, Brad Bridgewater Inc. entered into a cost-plus-fixed-fee contract to construct an electric generator for Tom Dolan Corporation. At the contract date, Bridgewater estimated that it would take 2 years to complete the project at a cost of $2,000,000. The fixed fee stipulated in the contract is $450,000. Bridgewater appropriately accounts for this contract under the percentage-of-completion method. During 2008 Bridgewater incurred costs of $700,000 related to the project. The estimated cost at December 31, 2008, to complete the contract is $1,300,000. Dolan was billed $600,000 under the contract.

Instructions

Prepare a schedule to compute the amount of gross profit to be recognized by Bridgewater under the contract for the year ended December 31, 2008. Show supporting computations in good form.

(AICPA adapted)

E7-3 (Recognition of Profit, Percentage-of-Completion) In 2007 Jeff Rouse Construction Company agreed to construct an apartment building at a price of $1,000,000. The information relating to the costs and billings for this contract is as follows.

	2007	2008	2009
Costs incurred to date	$280,000	$600,000	$ 785,000
Estimated costs yet to be incurred	520,000	200,000	–0–
Customer billings to date	150,000	400,000	1,000,000
Collection of billings to date	120,000	320,000	940,000

(LO 1, 3)

Instructions

Assuming that the percentage-of-completion method is used, compute the amount of gross profit to be recognized in 2007 and 2008.

E7-4 (Recognition of Revenue on Long-Term Contract) Amy Van Dyken Construction Company uses the percentage-of-completion method of accounting. In 2008, Van Dyken began work under contract #E2-D2, which provided for a contract price of $2,200,000. Other details follow:

	2008	2009
Costs incurred to date	$ 480,000	$1,425,000
Estimated costs to complete, as of December 31	1,120,000	–0–
Billings during the year	420,000	1,680,000

(LO 1, 3, 4)

Instructions

(a) What portion of the total contract price would be recognized as revenue in 2008? In 2009?
(b) Assuming the same facts as those above except that Van Dyken uses the completed-contract method of accounting, what portion of the total contract price would be recognized as revenue in 2009?

E7-5 (Recognition of Profit for Long-Term Contracts) Andre Agassi Construction Company began operations January 1, 2008. During the year, Andre Agassi Construction entered into a contract with Lindsey Davenport Corp. to construct a manufacturing facility. At that time, Agassi estimated that it would take 5 years to complete the facility at a total cost of $4,500,000. The total contract price for construction of the facility is $6,300,000. During the year, Agassi incurred $1,185,800 in construction costs related to the construction project. The estimated cost to complete the contract is $4,204,200. Lindsey Davenport Corp. was billed and paid 30% of the contract price.

(LO 1, 3, 4)

Instructions

Prepare schedules to compute the amount of gross profit to be recognized for the year ended December 31, 2008, under each of the following methods.

(a) Completed-contract method.
(b) Percentage-of-completion method.

Show supporting computations in good form.

(AICPA adapted)

E7-6 (Long-Term Contract Reporting) Derrick Adkins Construction Company began operations in 2008. Construction activity for the first year is shown below. All contracts are with different customers, and any work remaining at December 31, 2008, is expected to be completed in 2009.

(LO 1, 5

Project	Total Contract Price	Billings through 12/31/08	Cash Collections through 12/31/08	Contract Costs Incurred through 12/31/08	Estimated Additional Costs to Complete
1	$ 560,000	$ 360,000	$340,000	$450,000	$140,000
2	670,000	220,000	210,000	126,000	504,000
3	500,000	500,000	440,000	330,000	–0–
	$1,730,000	$1,080,000	$990,000	$906,000	$644,000

Instructions

Derrick Adkins Construction Company uses the completed-contract method. Determine the amount of income or loss to be reported for each of the three projects in 2008.

(LO 1, 5) **E7-7** **(Installment-Sales Method Calculations)** Austin Corporation appropriately uses the installment-sales method of accounting to recognize income in its financial statements. The following information is available for 2008 and 2009.

	2008	2009
Installment sales	$900,000	$1,000,000
Cost of installment sales	630,000	680,000
Cash collections on 2008 sales	370,000	350,000
Cash collections on 2009 sales	–0–	475,000

Instructions

Compute the amount of realized gross profit recognized in each year.

(AICPA adapted)

(LO 1, 5) **E7-8** **(Installment-Sales and Cost-Recovery Methods)** Kenny Harrison Corp., a capital goods manufacturing business that started on January 4, 2008, and operates on a calendar-year basis, uses the installment-sales method of profit recognition in accounting for all its sales. The following data were taken from the 2008 and 2009 records.

	2008	2009
Installment sales	$480,000	$620,000
Gross profit as a percent of costs	25%	28%
Cash collections on sales of 2008	$140,000	$240,000
Cash collections on sales of 2009	–0–	$180,000

The amounts given for cash collections exclude amounts collected for interest charges.

Instructions

(a) Compute the amount of realized gross profit to be recognized on the 2009 income statement, using the installment-sales method.
(b) Compute the amount of realized gross profit to be recognized on the income statement, using the cost-recovery method.

(CIA adapted)

(LO 1, 5) **E7-9** **(Installment-Sales Method and Cost-Recovery Method)** On January 1, 2008, Barkley Company sold property for $200,000. The sale price will be collected as follows: $100,000 in 2008, $60,000 in 2009, and $40,000 in 2010. The property had cost Barkley $150,000 when it was purchased in 2006.

Instructions

(a) Compute the amount of gross profit realized each year assuming Barkley uses the cost-recovery method.
(b) Compute the amount of gross profit realized each year assuming Barkley uses the installment-sales method.

(LO 1, 5) **E7-10** **(Cost-Recovery Method)** On January 1, 2008, Tom Brands sells 200 acres of farmland for $600,000. Tom Brands purchased the farmland in 1995 at a cost of $500,000. The sale price will be paid in three installments of $200,000 each on December 31, 2008, 2009, and 2010. Collectibility of the payments is uncertain; Tom, therefore, uses the cost-recovery method.

Instructions

Determine the realized gross profit that Tom should recognize on December 31, 2008, 2009, and 2010.

(LO 6) ***E7-11** **(Entries for Long-Term Contracts)** Assume the same information as in E7-4. Prepare a complete set of journal entries for Amy Van Dyken Construction for 2008, using the percentage-of-completion method.

(LO 7) ***E7-12** **(Entries for Installment Sales)** Assume the same information as in E7-7. Prepare all journal entries required for Austin Corporation in 2009.

(LO 1, 3, 6) ***E7-13** **(Analysis of Percentage-of-Completion Financial Statements)** In 2008, Beth Botsford Construction Corp. began construction work under a 3-year contract. The contract price was $1,000,000. Beth Botsford uses the percentage-of-completion method for financial accounting purposes. The income to be recognized each year is based on the proportion of cost incurred to total estimated costs for completing the contract. The financial statement presentations relating to this contract at December 31, 2008, follow.

Balance Sheet

Accounts receivable—construction contract billings		$21,500
Construction in process	$65,000	
Less contract billings	61,500	
Cost of uncompleted contract in excess of billings		3,500

Income Statement

Income (before tax) on the contract recognized in 2008	$18,200

Instructions

(a) How much cash was collected in 2008 on this contract?

(b) What was the initial estimated total income before tax on this contract?

(AICPA adapted)

---

*E7-14 (**Gross Profit Calculations and Repossessed Merchandise**)   Randy Barnes Corporation, which began business on January 1, 2007, appropriately uses the installment-sales method of accounting. The following data were obtained for the years 2007 and 2008.

(LO 2, 5, 7)

	2007	2008
Installment sales	$750,000	$840,000
Cost of installment sales	525,000	604,800
General & administrative expenses	70,000	84,000
Cash collections on sales of 2007	310,000	300,000
Cash collections on sales of 2008	–0–	400,000

Instructions

(a) Compute the balance in the deferred gross profit accounts on December 31, 2007, and on December 31, 2008.

(b) A 2007 sale resulted in default in 2009. At the date of default, the balance on the installment receivable was $12,000, and the repossessed merchandise had a fair value of $8,000. Prepare the entry to record the repossession.

(AICPA adapted)

---

*E7-15 (**Interest Revenue from Installment Sale**)   Gail Devers Corporation sells farm machinery on the installment plan. On July 1, 2008, Devers entered into an installment sale contract with Gwen Torrence Inc. for a 10-year period. Equal annual payments under the installment sale are $100,000 and are due on July 1. The first payment was made on July 1, 2008.

(LO 2, 5, 7)

Additional Information

1. The amount that would be realized on an outright sale of similar farm machinery is $676,000.

2. The cost of the farm machinery sold to Gwen Torrence Inc. is $500,000.

3. The finance charges relating to the installment period are $324,000 based on a stated interest rate of 10%, which is appropriate.

4. Circumstances are such that the collection of the installments due under the contract is reasonably assured.

Instructions

What income or loss before income taxes should Devers record for the year ended December 31, 2008, as a result of the transaction above?

(AICPA adapted)

See the book's companion website, at www.wiley.com/college/warfield, for Additional Exercises.

Problems

(LO 1, 2, 3, 4, 5)

P7-1 (**Comprehensive Two-Part Revenue Recognition**) Simona Amanar Industries has two operating divisions—Gina Construction Division and Chorkina Securities Division. Each division maintains its own accounting system and method of revenue recognition.

Gina Construction Division

During the fiscal year ended November 30, 2008, Gina Construction Division had one construction project in process. A $30,000,000 contract for construction of a civic center was granted on June 19, 2008, and construction began on August 1, 2008. Estimated costs of completion at the contract date were $25,000,000 over a 2-year time period from the date of the contract. On November 30, 2008, construction costs of $7,800,000 had been incurred and progress billings of $9,500,000 had been made. The construction costs to complete the remainder of the project were reviewed on November 30, 2008, and were estimated to amount to only $16,200,000 because of an expected decline in raw materials costs. Revenue recognition is based upon a percentage-of-completion method.

Chorkina Securities Division

Chorkina Securities Division works through manufacturers' agents in various cities. Orders for alarm systems and down payments are forwarded from agents, and the division ships the goods f.o.b. factory directly to customers (usually police departments and security guard companies). Customers are billed directly for the balance due plus actual shipping costs. The company received orders for $6,000,000 of goods during the fiscal year ended November 30, 2008. Down payments of $600,000 were received and $5,200,000 of goods were billed and shipped. Actual freight costs of $100,000 were also billed. Commissions of 10% on product price are paid to manufacturing agents after goods are shipped to customers. Such goods are warranted for 90 days after shipment, and warranty returns have been about 1% of sales. Revenue is recognized at the point of sale by this division.

Instructions

(a) There are a variety of methods of revenue recognition. Define and describe each of the following methods of revenue recognition and indicate whether each is in accordance with generally accepted accounting principles.

  (1) Point of sale.
  (2) Completed-contract.
  (3) Percentage-of-completion.
  (4) Installment-sales.

(b) Compute the revenue to be recognized in fiscal year 2008 for the two operating divisions of Simona Amanar Industries in accordance with generally accepted accounting principles.

(LO 1, 3, 4)

P7-2 (**Recognition of Profit on Long-Term Contract**) Jenny Thompson Construction Company has entered into a contract beginning January 1, 2007, to build a parking complex. It has been estimated that the complex will cost $600,000 and will take 3 years to construct. The complex will be billed to the purchasing company at $900,000. The following data pertain to the construction period.

	2007	2008	2009
Costs to date	$270,000	$420,000	$600,000
Estimated costs to complete	330,000	180,000	–0–
Progress billings to date	270,000	550,000	900,000
Cash collected to date	240,000	500,000	900,000

Instructions

(a) Using the percentage-of-completion method, compute the estimated gross profit that would be recognized during each year of the construction period.

(b) Using the completed-contract method, compute the estimated gross profit that would be recognized during each year of the construction period.

(LO 1, 3)

P7-3 (**Recognition of Profit on Long-Term Contract**) On March 1, 2007, Winter Company entered into a contract to build an apartment building. It is estimated that the building will cost $2,000,000 and will take 3 years to complete. The contract price was $3,000,000. The information on page 347 pertains to the construction period.

	2007	2008	2009
Costs to date	$ 600,000	$1,560,000	$2,100,000
Estimated costs to complete	1,400,000	390,000	–0–
Progress billings to date	1,050,000	2,100,000	3,000,000
Cash collected to date	950,000	1,950,000	2,750,000

Instructions

Compute the amount of gross profit to be recognized each year assuming the percentage-of-completion method is used.

P7-4 **(Recognition of Profit, Percentage-of-Completion)** On February 1, 2007, Amanda Beard Construction Company obtained a contract to build an athletic stadium. The stadium was to be built at a total cost of $5,400,000 and was scheduled for completion by September 1, 2009. One clause of the contract stated that Beard was to deduct $15,000 from the $6,600,000 billing price for each week that completion was delayed. Completion was delayed 6 weeks, which resulted in a $90,000 penalty. Below are the data pertaining to the construction period.

(LO 1, 3)

	2007	2008	2009
Costs to date	$1,782,000	$3,850,000	$5,500,000
Estimated costs to complete	3,618,000	1,650,000	–0–
Progress billings to date	1,200,000	3,100,000	6,510,000
Cash collected to date	1,000,000	2,800,000	6,510,000

Instructions

Using the percentage-of-completion method, compute the estimated gross profit recognized in the years 2007–2009.

P7-5 **(Long-Term Contract with an Overall Loss)** On July 1, 2007, Kim Kyung-wook Construction Company Inc. contracted to build an office building for Fu Mingxia Corp. for a total contract price of $1,950,000. On July 1, Kyung-wook estimated that it would take between 2 and 3 years to complete the building. On December 31, 2009, the building was deemed substantially completed. Following are accumulated contract costs incurred, estimated costs to complete the contract, and accumulated billings to Mingxia for 2007, 2008, and 2009.

(LO 1, 3, 4)

	At 12/31/07	At 12/31/08	At 12/31/09
Contract costs incurred to date	$ 150,000	$1,200,000	$2,100,000
Estimated costs to complete the contract	1,350,000	800,000	–0–
Billings to Mingxia	300,000	1,100,000	1,850,000

Instructions

(a) Using the percentage-of-completion method, prepare schedules to compute the gross profit or loss to be recognized as a result of this contract for the years ended December 31, 2007, 2008, and 2009. (Ignore income taxes.)

(b) Using the completed-contract method, prepare schedules to compute the gross profit or loss to be recognized as a result of this contract for the years ended December 2007, 2008, and 2009. (Ignore income taxes.)

P7-6 **(Installment-Sales Computations)** Presented below is summarized information for Deng Yaping Co., which sells merchandise on the installment basis.

(LO 1, 5)

	2007	2008	2009
Sales (on installment plan)	$250,000	$260,000	$280,000
Cost of sales	150,000	163,800	182,000
Gross profit	$100,000	$ 96,200	$ 98,000
Collections from customers on:			
2007 installment sales	$ 75,000	$100,000	$ 50,000
2008 installment sales		100,000	120,000
2009 installment sales			110,000

Instructions

Compute the realized gross profit for each of the years 2007, 2008, and 2009.

(LO 1, 5)

P7-7 **(Installment-Sales Income Statements)** Laura Flessel Stores sells merchandise on open account as well as on installment terms.

	2007	2008	2009
Sales on account	$385,000	$426,000	$525,000
Installment sales	320,000	275,000	380,000
Collections on installment sales			
Made in 2007	110,000	90,000	40,000
Made in 2008		110,000	140,000
Made in 2009			125,000
Cost of sales			
Sold on account	270,000	277,000	341,000
Sold on installment	214,400	167,750	224,200
Selling expenses	77,000	87,000	92,000
Administrative expenses	50,000	51,000	52,000

Instructions

From the data above, which cover the 3 years since Laura Flessel Stores commenced operations, determine the net income for each year, applying the installment-sales method of accounting.

(LO 1, 4)

P7-8 **(Completed-Contract Method)** Mauer Construction Company, Inc., entered into a firm fixed-price contract with Giovanna Trillini Clinic on July 1, 2007, to construct a four-story office building. At that time, Mauer estimated that it would take between 2 and 3 years to complete the project. The total contract price for construction of the building is $4,500,000. Mauer appropriately accounts for this contract under the completed-contract method in its financial statements and for income tax reporting. The building was deemed substantially completed on December 31, 2009. Estimated percentage of completion, accumulated contract costs incurred, estimated costs to complete the contract, and accumulated billings to the Trillini Clinic under the contract were as follows.

	At December 31, 2007	At December 31, 2008	At December 31, 2009
Percentage of completion	30%	65%	100%
Contract costs incurred	$1,140,000	$3,055,000	$4,800,000
Estimated costs to complete the contract	$2,660,000	$1,645,000	–0–
Billings to Trillini Clinic	$1,500,000	$2,500,000	$4,300,000

Instructions

Prepare schedules to compute the profit or loss to be recognized as a result of this contract for the years ended December 31, 2007, 2008, and 2009. Ignore income taxes. Show supporting computations in good form.

(AICPA adapted)

(LO 1, 3, 4)

P7-9 **(Revenue Recognition Methods—Comparison)** Joy's Construction is in its fourth year of business. Joy performs long-term construction projects and accounts for them using the completed-contract method. Joy built an apartment building at a price of $1,000,000. The costs and billings for this contract for the first 3 years are as follows.

	2007	2008	2009
Costs incurred to date	$320,000	$600,000	$ 790,000
Estimated costs yet to be incurred	480,000	200,000	–0–
Customer billings to date	150,000	410,000	1,000,000
Collection of billings to date	120,000	340,000	950,000

Joy has contacted you, a certified public accountant, about the following concern. She would like to attract some investors, but she believes that in order to recognize revenue she must first "deliver" the product. Therefore, on her income statement she did not recognize any gross profits from the above contract until 2009, when she recognized the entire $210,000. That looked good for 2009, but the preceding years looked grim by comparison. She wants to know about an alternative to this completed-contract revenue recognition.

Instructions

Draft a letter to Joy, telling her about the percentage-of-completion method of recognizing revenue. Compare it to the completed-contract method. Explain the idea behind the percentage-of-completion method. In addition, illustrate how much revenue she could have recognized in 2007, 2008, and 2009 if she had used this method.

P7-10 (**Comprehensive Problem—Long-Term Contracts**) You have been engaged by Rich Mathre Construction Company to advise it concerning the proper accounting for a series of long-term contracts. Rich Mathre Construction Company commenced doing business on January 1, 2008. Construction activities for the first year of operations are shown below. All contract costs are with different customers, and any work remaining at December 31, 2008, is expected to be completed in 2009.

(LO 1, 3, 4)

Project	Total Contract Price	Billings Through 12/31/08	Cash Collections Through 12/31/08	Contract Costs Incurred Through 12/31/08	Estimated Additional Costs to Complete
A	$ 300,000	$200,000	$180,000	$248,000	$ 67,000
B	350,000	110,000	105,000	67,800	271,200
C	280,000	280,000	255,000	186,000	–0–
D	200,000	35,000	25,000	123,000	87,000
E	240,000	205,000	200,000	185,000	15,000
	$1,370,000	$830,000	$765,000	$809,800	$440,200

Instructions

(a) Prepare a schedule to compute gross profit (loss) to be reported, using the percentage-of-completion method.
(b) Repeat the requirements for part (a) assuming Rich Mathre uses the completed-contract method.
(c) Using the responses above for illustrative purposes, prepare a brief report comparing the conceptual merits (both positive and negative) of the two revenue recognition approaches.

*P7-11 (**Entries for Long-Term Contract**) Assume the same information as P7-3. (a) Prepare all necessary journal entries for Winter Company for 2009. (b) Prepare a partial balance sheet for December 31, 2008, showing the balances in the receivables and inventory accounts.

(LO 6)

*P7-12 (**Installment-Sales Entries**) Assume the same information as P7-6. Prepare the journal entries required by Deng Yaping Co. in 2009, applying the installment-sales method of accounting. (Ignore interest charges.)

(LO 7)

*P7-13 (**Installment-Sales Computations and Entries**) Isabell Werth Stores sell appliances for cash and also on the installment plan. Entries to record cost of sales are made monthly.

(LO 7)

Isabell Werth Stores
Trial Balance
December 31, 2008

	Dr.	Cr.
Cash	$153,000	
Installment Accounts Receivable, 2007	48,000	
Installment Accounts Receivable, 2008	91,000	
Inventory—New Merchandise	123,200	
Inventory—Repossessed Merchandise	24,000	
Accounts Payable		$ 98,500
Deferred Gross Profit, 2007		45,600
Capital Stock		170,000
Retained Earnings		93,900
Sales		343,000
Installment Sales		200,000
Cost of Sales	255,000	
Cost of Installment Sales	128,000	
Gain or Loss on Repossessions	800	
Selling and Administrative Expenses	128,000	
	$951,000	$951,000

The accounting department has prepared the following analysis of cash receipts for the year.

Cash sales (including repossessed merchandise)	$424,000
Installment accounts receivable, 2007	104,000
Installment accounts receivable, 2008	109,000
Other	36,000
Total	$673,000

Repossessions recorded during the year are summarized as follows.

	2007
Uncollected balance	$8,000
Loss on repossession	800
Repossessed merchandise	4,800

Instructions

From the trial balance and accompanying information:

(a) Compute the rate of gross profit for 2007 and 2008.

(b) Prepare closing entries as of December 31, 2008, under the installment-sales method of accounting.

(c) Prepare an income statement for the year ended December 31, 2008. Include only the realized gross profit in the income statement.

(LO 7)

*P7-14 (Installment-Sales Entries) The following summarized information relates to the installment-sales activity of Lisa Jacob Stores Inc. for the year 2008.

Instalment sales during 2008	$500,000
Cost of goods sold on installment basis	330,000
Collections from customers	200,000
Unpaid balances on merchandise repossessed	24,000
Estimated value of merchandise repossessed	9,200

Instructions

(a) Prepare journal entries at the end of 2008 to record on the books of Lisa Jacob Stores, Inc. the summarized data above.

(b) Prepare the entry to record the gross profit realized during 2008.

ACCOUNTING IN ACTION

Financial Reporting and Analysis

 ■ **Financial Reporting Issues: The Procter & Gamble Company**

AIA7-1 The financial statements of **Procter & Gamble (P&G)** can be accessed at the book's website.

Instructions

Refer to P&G's financial statements and the accompanying notes to answer the following questions.

(a) What were P&G's sales for 2006?

(b) What was the percentage of increase or decrease in P&G's sales from 2005 to 2006? From 2004 to 2005? What trend is evident?

(c) In its notes to the financial statements, what criteria does P&G use to recognize revenue?

(d) How does P&G account for trade promotions? Does the accounting conform to accrual accounting concepts? Explain.

■ Comparative Analysis: The Coca-Cola Company and PepsiCo, Inc.

AIA7-2 The financial statements of **The Coca-Cola Company** and **PepsiCo, Inc.** can be accessed at the book's website.

Instructions

Use information found at the book's website to answer the following questions.

(a) What were Coca-Cola's and PepsiCo's net revenues (sales) for the year 2006? Which company increased its revenues more (dollars and percentage) from 2005 to 2006?

(b) Are the revenue recognition policies of Coca-Cola and PepsiCo similar? Explain.

(c) In which foreign countries (geographic areas) did Coca-Cola and PepsiCo experience significant revenues in 2006? Compare the amounts of foreign revenues to U.S. revenues for both Coca-Cola and PepsiCo.

■ Financial Statement Analysis

AIA7-3 The following note appears in the "Summary of Significant Accounting Policies" section of the annual report of **Westinghouse Electric Corporation**.

Westinghouse Electric Corporation
Summary of Significant Accounting Policies

Note 1 (in part): Revenue Recognition. Sales are primarily recorded as products are shipped and services are rendered. The percentage-of-completion method of accounting is used for nuclear steam supply system orders with delivery schedules generally in excess of five years and for certain construction projects where this method of accounting is consistent with industry practice.

WFSI revenues are generally recognized on the accrual method. When accounts become delinquent for more than two payment periods, usually 60 days, income is recognized only as payments are received. Such delinquent accounts for which no payments are received in the current month, and other accounts on which income is not being recognized because the receipt of either principal or interest is questionable, are classified as nonearning receivables.

Instructions

(a) Identify the revenue recognition methods used by Westinghouse Electric as discussed in its note on significant accounting policies.

(b) Under what conditions are the revenue recognition methods identified in the first paragraph of Westinghouse's note above acceptable?

(c) From the information provided in the second paragraph of Westinghouse's note, identify the type of operation being described and defend the acceptability of the revenue recognition method.

AIA7-4 On December 31, 2007, LAS1 Construction entered into a major long-term construction project with the following terms.

Total contract price $3,000,000

Total expected cost $2,4000,000

Construction is expected to take 3 years. Production costs and cash flows are shown in the following table.

Projected Production Costs and Cash Flows		
Year	Costs Incurred	Cash Received
2007	$ 900,000	$1,000,000
2008	800,000	1,000,000
2009	700,000	1,000,000
Totals	$2,400,000	$3,000,000

(a) Show the gross profit for each year under *both* the percentage-of-completion and completed-contract methods.

(b) Assume that total projected costs increase by $100,000, and the company makes the change in estimate at December 31, 2008. Compute the gross profit for 2008 under the revised assumption.

(CFA adapted)

AIA7-5 Provide responses to the following.

(a) Compare the volatility of reported earnings over the life of a contract of both the completed-contract and percentage-of-completion accounting methods. (Assume that under percentage-of-completion, the income is earned evenly.)

(b) Discuss the difference in volatility when a company has many contracts.

(CFA adapted)

Concepts for Analysis

AIA7-6 **(Revenue Recognition—Alternative Methods)** Alexsandra Isosev Industries has three operating divisions—Falilat Mining, Mourning Paperbacks, and Osygus Protection Devices. Each division maintains its own accounting system and method of revenue recognition.

Falilat Mining

Falilat Mining specializes in the extraction of precious metals such as silver, gold, and platinum. During the fiscal year ended November 30, 2008, Falilat entered into contracts worth $2,250,000 and shipped metals worth $2,000,000. A quarter of the shipments were made from inventories on hand at the beginning of the fiscal year, and the remainder were made from metals that were mined during the year. Mining totals for the year, valued at market prices, were: silver at $750,000, gold at $1,300,000, and platinum at $490,000. Falilat uses the completion-of-production method to recognize revenue, because its operations meet the specified criteria (i.e., reasonably assured sales prices, interchangeable units, and insignificant distribution costs).

Mourning Paperbacks

Mourning Paperbacks sells large quantities of novels to a few book distributors that in turn sell to several national chains of bookstores. Mourning allows distributors to return up to 30% of sales, and distributors give the same terms to bookstores. While returns from individual titles fluctuate greatly, the returns from distributors have averaged 20% in each of the past 5 years. A total of $8,000,000 of paperback novel sales were made to distributors during the fiscal year. On November 30, 2008, $3,200,000 of fiscal 2008 sales were still subject to return privileges over the next 6 months. The remaining $4,800,000 of fiscal 2008 sales had actual returns of 21%. Sales from fiscal 2008 totaling $2,500,000 were collected in fiscal 2008, with less than 18% of sales returned. Mourning records revenue according to the method referred to as revenue recognition when the right of return exits, because all applicable criteria for use of this method are met by Mourning's operations.

Osygus Protection Devices

Osygus Protection Devices works through manufacturers' agents in various cities. Orders for alarm systems and down payments are forwarded from agents, and Osygus ships the goods f.o.b. shipping point. Customers are billed for the balance due plus actual shipping costs. The firm received orders for $6,000,000 of goods during the fiscal year ended November 30, 2008. Down payments of $600,000 were received, and $5,000,000 of goods were billed and shipped. Actual freight costs of $100,000 were also billed. Commissions of 10% on product price were paid to manufacturers' agents after the goods were shipped to customers. Such goods are warranted for 90 days after shipment, and warranty returns have been about 1% of sales. Revenue is recognized at the point of sale by Osygus.

Instructions

(a) There are a variety of methods for revenue recognition. Define and describe each of the following methods of revenue recognition, and indicate whether each is in accordance with generally accepted accounting principles.
  (1) Completion-of-production method.
  (2) Percentage-of-completion method.
  (3) Installment-sales method.

(b) Compute the revenue to be recognized in the fiscal year ended November 30, 2008, for:
  (1) Falilat Mining.
  (2) Mourning Paperbacks.
  (3) Osygus Protection Devices.

(CMA adapted)

AIA7-7 **(Recognition of Revenue—Theory)** Revenue is usually recognized at the point of sale. Under special circumstances, however, bases other than the point of sale are used for the timing of revenue recognition.

Instructions

(a) Why is the point of sale usually used as the basis for the timing of revenue recognition?

(b) Disregarding the special circumstances when bases other than the point of sale are used, discuss the merits of each of the following objections to the sales basis of revenue recognition.

    (1) It is too conservative because revenue is earned throughout the entire process of production.

    (2) It is not conservative enough because accounts receivable do not represent disposable funds, sales returns and allowances may be made, and collection and bad debt expenses may be incurred in a later period.

(c) Revenue may also be recognized (1) during production and (2) when cash is received. For each of these two bases of timing revenue recognition, give an example of the circumstances in which it is properly used and discuss the accounting merits of its use in lieu of the sales basis.

(AICPA adapted)

AIA7-8 **(Recognition of Revenue—Theory)** The earning of revenue by a business enterprise is recognized for accounting purposes when the transaction is recorded. In some situations, revenue is recognized approximately as it is earned in the economic sense. In other situations, however, accountants have developed guidelines for recognizing revenue by other criteria, such as at the point of sale.

Instructions

(Ignore income taxes.)

(a) Explain and justify why revenue is often recognized as earned at time of sale.

(b) Explain in what situations it would be appropriate to recognize revenue as the productive activity takes place.

(c) At what times, other than those included in (a) and (b) above, may it be appropriate to recognize revenue? Explain.

AIA7-9 **(Recognition of Revenue—Bonus Dollars)** Alexei & Nemov Inc. was formed early this year to sell merchandise credits to merchants who distribute the credits free to their customers. For example, customers can earn additional credits based on the dollars they spend with a merchant (e.g., airlines and hotels). Accounts for accumulating the credits and catalogs illustrating the merchandise for which the credits may be exchanged are maintained online. Centers with inventories of merchandise premiums have been established for redemption of the credits. Merchants may not return unused credits to Alexei & Nemov.

The following schedule expresses Alexei & Nemov's expectations as to percentages of a normal month's activity that will be attained. For this purpose, a "normal month's activity" is defined as the level of operations expected when expansion of activities ceases or tapers off to a stable rate. The company expects that this level will be attained in the third year and that sales of credits will average $6,000,000 per month throughout the third year.

Month	Actual Credit Sales Percent	Merchandise Premium Purchases Percent	Credit Redemptions Percent
6th	30%	40%	10%
12th	60	60	45
18th	80	80	70
24th	90	90	80
30th	100	100	95

Alexei & Nemov plans to adopt an annual closing date at the end of each 12 months of operation.

Instructions

(a) Discuss the factors to be considered in determining when revenue should be recognized in measuring the income of a business enterprise.

(b) Discuss the accounting alternatives that should be considered by Alexei & Nemov Inc. for the recognition of its revenues and related expenses.

(c) For each accounting alternative discussed in (b), give balance sheet accounts that should be used and indicate how each should be classified.

(AICPA adapted)

AIA7-10 **(Recognition of Revenue from Subscriptions)** *Cutting Edge* is a monthly magazine that has been on the market for 18 months. It currently has a circulation of 1.4 million copies. Currently negotiations are underway to obtain a bank loan in order to update their facilities. They are producing close to capacity and expect to grow at an average of 20% per year over the next 3 years.

After reviewing the financial statements of *Cutting Edge*, Gary Hall, the bank loan officer, had indicated that a loan could be offered to *Cutting Edge* only if it could increase its current ratio and decrease its debt to equity ratio to a specified level.

Alexander Popov, the marketing manager of *Cutting Edge*, has devised a plan to meet these requirements. Popov indicates that an advertising campaign can be initiated to immediately increase circulation. The potential customers would be contacted after the purchase of another magazine's mailing list. The campaign would include:

1. An offer to subscribe to *Cutting Edge* at three-fourths the normal price.
2. A special offer to all new subscribers to receive the most current world atlas whenever requested at a guaranteed price of $2.
3. An unconditional guarantee that any subscriber will receive a full refund if dissatisfied with the magazine.

Although the offer of a full refund is risky, Popov claims that few people will ask for a refund after receiving half of their subscription issues. Popov notes that other magazine companies have tried this sales promotion technique and experienced great success. Their average cancellation rate was 25%. On the average, each company increased its initial circulation threefold and in the long run had increased circulation to twice that which existed before the promotion. In addition, 60% of the new subscribers are expected to take advantage of the atlas premium. Popov feels confident that the increased subscriptions from the advertising campaign will increase the current ratio and decrease the debt to equity ratio.

You are the controller of *Cutting Edge* and must give your opinion of the proposed plan.

Instructions

(a) When should revenue from the new subscriptions be recognized?
(b) How would you classify the estimated sales returns stemming from the unconditional guarantee?
(c) How should the atlas premium be recorded? Is the estimated premium claims a liability? Explain.
(d) Does the proposed plan achieve the goals of increasing the current ratio and decreasing the debt to equity ratio?

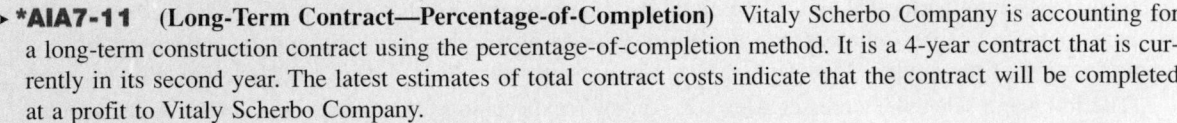 ***AIA7-11** (**Long-Term Contract—Percentage-of-Completion**) Vitaly Scherbo Company is accounting for a long-term construction contract using the percentage-of-completion method. It is a 4-year contract that is currently in its second year. The latest estimates of total contract costs indicate that the contract will be completed at a profit to Vitaly Scherbo Company.

Instructions

(a) What theoretical justification is there for Vitaly Scherbo Company's use of the percentage-of-completion method?
(b) How would progress billings be accounted for? Include in your discussion the classification of progress billings in Vitaly Scherbo Company financial statements.
(c) How would the income recognized in the second year of the 4-year contract be determined using the cost-to-cost method of determining percentage of completion?
(d) What would be the effect on earnings per share in the second year of the 4-year contract of using the percentage-of-completion method instead of the completed-contract method? Discuss.

(AICPA adapted)

*AIA7-12 (**Revenue Recognition—Real Estate Development**) Pankratov Lakes is a new recreational real estate development which consists of 500 lake-front and lake-view lots. As a special incentive to the first 100 buyers of lake-view lots, the developer is offering 3 years of free financing on 10-year, 12% notes, no down payment, and one week at a nearby established resort—"a $1,200 value." The normal price per lot is $12,000. The cost per lake-view lot to the developer is an estimated average of $2,000. The development costs continue to be incurred; the actual average cost per lot is not known at this time. The resort promotion cost is $700 per lot. The notes are held by Davis Corp., a wholly owned subsidiary.

Instructions

(a) Discuss the revenue recognition and gross profit measurement issues raised by this situation.
(b) How would the developer's past financial and business experience influence your decision concerning the recording of these transactions?
(c) Assume 50 persons have accepted the offer, signed 10-year notes, and have stayed at the local resort. Prepare the journal entries that you believe are proper.
(d) What should be disclosed in the notes to the financial statements?

Professional Tools

■ Ethical Decision Making

AIA7-13 **(Revenue Recognition)**   Nimble Health and Racquet Club (NHRC), which operates eight clubs in the Chicago metropolitan area, offers one-year memberships. The members may use any of the eight facilities but must reserve racquetball court time and pay a separate fee before using the court. As an incentive to new customers, NHRC advertised that any customers not satisfied for any reason could receive a refund of the remaining portion of unused membership fees. Membership fees are due at the beginning of the individual membership period. However, customers are given the option of financing the membership fee over the membership period at a 9% interest rate.

Some customers have expressed a desire to take only the regularly scheduled aerobic classes without paying for a full membership. During the current fiscal year, NHRC began selling coupon books for aerobic classes to accommodate these customers. Each book is dated and contains 50 coupons that may be redeemed for any regularly scheduled aerobics class over a one-year period. After the one-year period, unused coupons are no longer valid.

During 2005, NHRC expanded into the health equipment market by purchasing a local company that manufactures rowing machines and cross-country ski machines. These machines are used in NHRC's facilities and are sold through the clubs and mail order catalogs. Customers must make a 20% down payment when placing an equipment order; delivery is 60–90 days after order placement. The machines are sold with a 2-year unconditional guarantee. Based on past experience, NHRC expects the costs to repair machines under guarantee to be 4% of sales.

NHRC is in the process of preparing financial statements as of May 31, 2008, the end of its fiscal year. James Hogan, corporate controller, expressed concern over the company's performance for the year and decided to review the preliminary financial statements prepared by Barbara Hardy, NHRC's assistant controller. After reviewing the statements, Hogan proposed that the following changes be reflected in the May 31, 2008, published financial statements.

1. Membership revenue should be recognized when the membership fee is collected.
2. Revenue from the coupon books should be recognized when the books are sold.
3. Down payments on equipment purchases and expenses associated with the guarantee on the rowing and cross-country machines should be recognized when paid.

Hardy indicated to Hogan that the proposed changes are not in accordance with generally accepted accounting principles, but Hogan insisted that the changes be made. Hardy believes that Hogan wants to manipulate income to forestall any potential financial problems and increase his year-end bonus. At this point, Hardy is unsure what action to take.

Instructions

(a) (1) Describe when Nimble Health and Racquet Club (NHRC) should recognize revenue from membership fees, court rentals, and coupon book sales.
     (2) Describe how NHRC should account for the down payments on equipment sales, explaining when this revenue should be recognized.
     (3) Indicate when NHRC should recognize the expense associated with the guarantee of the rowing and cross-country machines.
(b) Discuss why James Hogan's proposed changes and his insistence that the financial statement changes be made is unethical. Structure your answer around or to include the following aspects of ethical conduct: competence, confidentiality, integrity, and/or objectivity.
(c) Identify some specific actions Barbara Hardy could take to resolve this situation.

(CMA adapted)

AIA7-14 **(Revenue Recognition—Membership Fees)**   Midwest Health Club offers one-year memberships. Membership fees are due in full at the beginning of the individual membership period. As an incentive to new customers, MHC advertised that any customers not satisfied for any reason could receive a refund of the remaining portion of unused membership fees. As a result of this policy, Stanley Hack, corporate controller, recognized revenue ratably over the life of the membership.

MHC is in the process of preparing its year-end financial statements. Phyllis Cavaretta, MHC's treasurer, is concerned about the company's lackluster performance this year. She reviews the financial statements Hack prepared and tells Hack to recognize membership revenue when the fees are received.

Instructions

Answer the following questions.

(a) What are the ethical issues involved?
(b) What should Hack do?

■ Financial Accounting Research (FARS)

AIA7-15 Employees at your company disagree about the accounting for returns. The sales manager believes that granting more generous returns provisions can give the company a competitive edge and increase sales revenue. The controller cautions that, depending on the terms granted, loose returns provisions might lead to non-GAAP recording of revenue. The company CFO would like you to research the issue to provide an authoritative answer.

Instructions

Using the **Financial Accounting Research System (FARS)** database, respond to the following items. (Provide text strings used in your search.)

(a) Which statement addresses revenue recognition when right of return exists?

(b) What is meant by "right of return"?

(c) When there is a right of return, what conditions must the company meet to recognize the revenue at the time of sale?

(d) What factors may impair the ability to make a reasonable estimate of future returns?

■ Professional Simulation

AIA7-16 Go to the book's website, at **www.wiley.com/college/warfield**, to find an interactive problem that simulates the computerized CPA exam. The professional simulation for this chapter asks you to address questions related to revenue recognition issues.

| What do the numbers mean? | Guideline Answers to Beyond the Numbers Questions |

Grossed Out, p. 308

Q: What qualitative characteristic of accounting information is affected when Priceline reports its gross bookings in a unique fashion? Explain.

A: Comparability. If Priceline "grosses up" its bookings while other companies are reporting net, then statement readers will not be able to compare the revenues reported by the companies. By reporting gross, Priceline will report a much higher revenue number, implying much higher sales volume. It is like comparing apples to oranges.

No Take-Backs, Revisited p. 311

Q: Explain how the Lucent and Diebold cases illustrate violation of revenue recognition criteria.

A: In both cases, the earned criterion is not met. This is because the customers have the right to return the product at their option. That is, the sale is not final. If the compa- nies stuffed the goods in the channel on credit, the realized or realizability criterion also is not met: Neither Lucent nor Diebold has been paid, and neither will be paid if the customers are allowed to return the products.

Less Conservative, p. 317

Q: How does the Halliburton case illustrate the qualitative characteristic of consistency? Explain the importance of the full disclosure principle in this case.

A: When a company changes its accounting methods or the way it applies an accounting method, it is difficult to compare the reported results from one period to the next— that is, it is difficult to maintain *consistency*. In this case, Halliburton, could have helped financial statement users compare its results across periods if it had provided better disclosure of the change in accounting for disputed claims.

Guideline Answers, continued

The Check Is in the Mail, p. 319

Q: To get better control of its revenue recognition policies, a company like Datapoint Corp. could tighten up its policies on credit sales to require customers to pay more cash before the company ships its product. Discuss some of the pros and cons of such a strategy.

A: From an accounting standpoint, a cash-only policy would improve the reliability of Datapoint's revenue measures, since the company would recognize all revenue on a cash basis with little uncertainty as to realizability. However, changing to cash-only may not be a good business decision, especially if granting credit terms is a common practice in this industry. Thus, Datapoint will have more reliable revenue numbers, but the numbers will be lower due to the business lost from customers who want to buy on credit.

Liability or Revenue?, p. 324

Q: As indicated in the story, companies must estimate gift card expiration dates to determine if they can recognize gift card receipts as revenue. Could companies use the accounting for gift cards to manage earnings? Explain.

A: Any time an estimate is needed to determine accounting numbers, companies could use it to manage earnings. In this case, when needing a "bump" in earnings, the retailer could change its estimates for gift card expirations, thereby recognizing more of the liability as revenue. That is, the gift card liability could be used as a "cookie jar" reserve (recall our discussion in Chapter 5).

It can also be difficult to compare expiration rates across retailers to sort out such earnings management. For example, Circuit City defers all revenue on gift cards until they are redeemed. But when cards go unused for more than 2 years, it deducts $2 per month from the value of the card. Expiration assumptions may differ across retailers, making it difficult to compare the impact of such programs on company performance and possible earnings management. See R. Berner, "Gift Cards: No Gift to Investors," *Business Week* (March 14, 2005), pp. 86-87.

Remember to check the book's companion website to find additional resources for this chapter.

CHAPTER 8
CASH AND RECEIVABLES

No-Tell Nortel

In 2003, **Nortel** announced that its net income for the year was really half what it originally reported. In addition, the company had understated net income for 2002. How could this happen? One reason: It appears that Nortel set up "cookie jar" reserves, using the allowance for doubtful accounts as the cookie jar. As the following chart shows, in 2002 Nortel overestimated the amount of bad debt expense (with a sizable allowance for doubtful accounts). Then, in 2003 Nortel slashed the amount of bad debt expense, even though the total money owed by customers remained nearly unchanged. In 2002, its allowance was 19 percent of receivables compared to 10 percent in 2003—quite a difference.

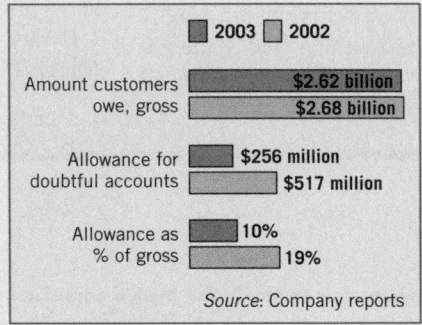

	2003	2002
Amount customers owe, gross	$2.62 billion	$2.68 billion
Allowance for doubtful accounts	$256 million	$517 million
Allowance as % of gross	10%	19%

Source: Company reports

It is difficult to determine if the allowance was too high in 2002 or too low in 2003, or both. What-ever the case, the use of the allowance cookie jar permitted Nortel to report higher operating margins and net income in 2003.

This analysis suggests the importance of looking carefully at the amount of bad debt expense re-ported in annual reports. Sometimes companies use it to artificially *decrease* income. Others under-state bad debt expense to *increase* income. For example, analysts have noted that many large hos-pitals, such as **Tenet Healthcare** and **HCA**, may be facing increasing uncollectible accounts that are presently not fully reflected in their balance sheets.

Source: Adapted from J. Weil, "At Nortel, Warning Signs Existed Months Ago, *Wall Street Journal* (May 18, 2004), p. C3; and B. McLean, "Reality Checkup," *Fortune* (January 12, 2004), p. 140.

Preview of Chapter 8

As our opening story indicates, estimating the collectibility of accounts receivable has important implications for accurate reporting of operating profits, net income, and assets. In this chapter we discuss cash and receivables—two assets that are important to companies as diverse as **Nortel** and **Tenet Healthcare**. *The content and organization of the chapter are as follows.*

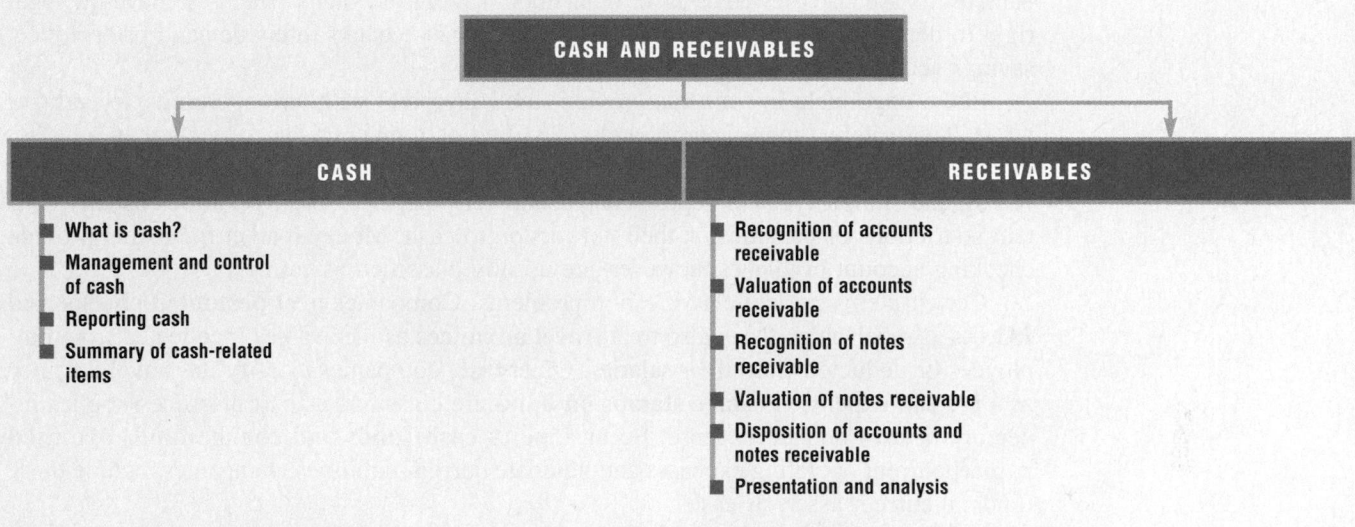

CASH AND RECEIVABLES

CASH

- What is cash?
- Management and control of cash
- Reporting cash
- Summary of cash-related items

RECEIVABLES

- Recognition of accounts receivable
- Valuation of accounts receivable
- Recognition of notes receivable
- Valuation of notes receivable
- Disposition of accounts and notes receivable
- Presentation and analysis

Learning Objectives

After studying this chapter, you should be able to:

1. Identify items considered cash.
2. Indicate how to report cash and related items.
3. Define receivables and identify the different types of receivables.
4. Explain accounting issues related to recognition of accounts receivable.
5. Explain accounting issues related to valuation of accounts receivable.
6. Explain accounting issues related to recognition of notes receivable.
7. Explain accounting issues related to valuation of notes receivable.
8. Explain accounting issues related to disposition of accounts and notes receivable.
9. Describe how to report and analyze receivables.

Inside Chapter 8

- **What Do the Numbers Mean?**
  Too much of a good thing? (p. 359)
  Going for broke (p. 369)
  Collection is a click away (p. 370)
  Ugly ducklings (p. 381)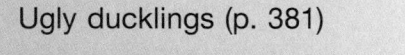
- **What's the Principle?** (p. 365, 367, 381, 382)
- **Convergence Corner** (p. 384)
- **Accounting, Analysis, Principles** (p. 385)
  Record receivables, prepare balance sheet.
  Evaluate liquidity.
  Apply concepts to bad debts.

WHAT IS CASH?

OBJECTIVE 1

Identify items considered cash.

Cash, the most liquid of assets, is the standard medium of exchange and the basis for measuring and accounting for all other items. Companies generally classify cash as a current asset. Cash consists of coin, currency, and available funds on deposit at the bank. Negotiable instruments such as money orders, certified checks, cashier's checks, personal checks, and bank drafts are also viewed as cash. What about savings accounts? Banks do have the legal right to demand notice before withdrawal. But, because banks rarely demand prior notice, savings accounts nevertheless are considered cash.

Some negotiable instruments provide small investors with an opportunity to earn interest. These items, more appropriately classified as temporary investments than as cash, include money market funds, money market savings certificates, certificates of deposit (CDs), and similar types of deposits and "short-term paper."[1] These securities usually contain restrictions or penalties on their conversion to cash. Money market funds that provide checking account privileges, however, are usually classified as cash.

Certain items present classification problems: Companies treat **postdated checks and I.O.U.s** as receivables. They also treat **travel advances** as receivables if collected from employees or deducted from their salaries. Otherwise, companies classify the travel advance as a prepaid expense. **Postage stamps on hand** are classified as part of office supplies inventory or as a prepaid expense. Because **petty cash funds and change funds are used** to meet current operating expenses and liquidate current liabilities, companies include these funds in current assets as cash.

MANAGEMENT AND CONTROL OF CASH

Cash is the asset most susceptible to improper diversion and use. Management faces two problems in accounting for cash transactions: (1) to establish proper controls to prevent any unauthorized transactions by officers or employees, and (2) to provide information necessary to properly manage cash on hand and cash transactions. Yet even with sophisticated control devices, errors can and do happen. For example, the *Wall Street Journal* ran a story entitled "A $7.8 Million Error Has a Happy Ending for a Horrified Bank." The story described how **Manufacturers Hanover Trust Co.** mistakenly overpaid about $7.8 million in cash dividends to its stockholders. (As implied in the headline, most stockholders returned the monies.)

[1]A variety of "short-term paper" is available for investment. For example, **certificates of deposit** (CDs) represent formal evidence of indebtedness, issued by a bank, subject to withdrawal under the specific terms of the instrument. Issued in $1,000 to $100,000 denominations, they have maturities anywhere from 7 days to 10 years and generally pay interest at the short-term interest rate in effect at the date of issuance.

Banks and savings and loan associations issue **money-market savings certificates** generally in denominations of $10,000 or more for 6-month periods (6 to 48 months). The interest rate is tied to the 26-week Treasury bill rate.

In **money-market funds**, a variation of the mutual fund, the mix of Treasury bills and commercial paper making up the fund's portfolio determines the yield. Most money-market funds require an initial minimum investment of $1,000; many allow withdrawal by check or wire transfer.

Treasury bills are U.S. government obligations generally issued with 4-, 13-, and 26-week maturities; they are sold in $10,000 denominations at weekly government auctions.

Commercial paper is a short-term note issued by corporations with good credit ratings. Often issued in $5,000 and $10,000 denominations, these notes generally yield a higher rate than Treasury bills.

To safeguard cash and to ensure the accuracy of the accounting records for cash, companies need effective **internal control** over cash. Provisions of the Sarbanes-Oxley Act of 2002 call for enhanced efforts to increase the quality of internal control (for cash and other assets). Such efforts are expected to result in improved financial reporting.

However, the increasing volume of transactions conducted with the swipe of a debit or credit card presents new challenges to the effort to maintain control over liquid assets. As one writer noted, "In 5,000 years there have been only four times that we have changed the way we pay—there was barter to coinage; coins to paper; paper to checks; and then cards. Just since 1995, the amount of stuff that American consumers buy using plastic has increased 430 percent."[2] In 2003, for the first time, Americans bought more using cards than cash.[3] In addition, electronic commerce conducted over the Internet continues to grow.

Each of these trends contributes to the shift from cold cash to digital cash, and poses new challenges for the control of cash. In the appendix to this chapter, we discuss some of the basic control procedures used to ensure the correct reporting of cash.

What do the numbers mean?   Too Much of a Good Thing?

Can it ever be a bad thing to have too much cash on hand? Maybe so. As the data in the following table indicate, **General Motors** and some other major companies have been stockpiling cash at levels not recently seen.

Company	Total Cash (in billions)
General Motors	$54.8
Berkshire Hathaway	$36.0
Ford Motor Company	$33.6
Hewlett-Packard	$13.9
Intel	$13.5

Given the low returns on cash, investors may ask why companies maintain such large cash balances. Some companies with good growth prospects plan to use these resources to fuel growth. They intend to step up spending on property, plant, and equipment or on research and development. Or they may hold cash in order to acquire other companies that have growth prospects. However, without good use for stockpiled cash, stockholders would be better served by a payout in the form of a cash dividend.

Beyond the Numbers

As an investor, what factors would you consider in evaluating whether a company has too much cash on hand?

REPORTING CASH

Although the reporting of cash is relatively straightforward, a number of issues merit special attention. These issues relate to the reporting of:

1 Restricted cash.

2 Bank overdrafts.

3 Cash equivalents.

OBJECTIVE 2

Indicate how to report cash and related items.

[2]K. Brooker, "Just One Word: Plastic," *Fortune* (February 23, 2004), p. 130.

[3]Ibid, p. 132. Non-U.S. consumers are even bigger users of digital cash than U.S. consumers. For example, non-check payments in Japan and Europe comprise over 70 percent of all payment transactions. U.S. consumers' continued use of checks and cash for payment raises fraud concerns, though, as duplication technology makes it easier to forge checks and currency.

Restricted Cash

Petty cash, payroll, and dividend funds are examples of cash set aside for a particular purpose. In most situations, these fund balances are not material. Therefore, companies do not segregate them from cash in the financial statements. When material in amount, companies segregate **restricted cash** from "regular" cash for reporting purposes. Companies classify restricted cash either in the current assets or in the long-term assets section, depending on the date of availability or disbursement. Classification in the current section is appropriate if using the cash for payment of existing or maturing obligations (within a year or the operating cycle, whichever is longer). On the other hand, companies show the restricted cash in the long-term section of the balance sheet if holding the cash for a longer period of time.

Cash classified in the long-term section is frequently set aside for plant expansion, retirement of long-term debt or, in the case of **International Thoroughbred Breeders**, for entry fee deposits.

Illustration 8-1
Disclosure of
Restricted Cash

International Thoroughbred Breeders

Restricted cash and investments (See Note)	$3,730,000

Note: Restricted Cash. At year-end, the Company had approximately $3,730,000, which was classified as restricted cash and investments. These funds are primarily cash received from horsemen for nomination and entry fees to be applied to upcoming racing meets, purse winnings held in trust for horsemen, and amounts held for unclaimed ticketholder winnings.

INTERNATIONAL INSIGHT

Among other potential restrictions, companies need to determine whether any of the cash in accounts outside the U.S. is restricted by regulations against exportation of currency.

Banks and other lending institutions often require customers to maintain minimum cash balances in checking or savings accounts. The SEC defines these minimum balances, called **compensating balances**, as "that portion of any demand deposit (or any time deposit or certificate of deposit) maintained by a corporation which constitutes support for existing borrowing arrangements of the corporation with a lending institution. Such arrangements would include both outstanding borrowings and the assurance of future credit availability."[4]

To avoid misleading investors about the amount of cash available to meet recurring obligations, the SEC recommends that companies state separately **legally restricted deposits** held as compensating balances against **short-term** borrowing arrangements among the "Cash and cash equivalent items" in current assets. Companies should classify separately restricted deposits held as compensating balances against **long-term** borrowing arrangements as noncurrent assets in either the investments or other assets sections, using a caption such as "Cash on deposit maintained as compensating balance." In cases where compensating balance arrangements exist without agreements that restrict the use of cash amounts shown on the balance sheet, companies should describe the arrangements and the amounts involved in the notes.

Bank Overdrafts

Bank overdrafts occur when a company writes a check for more than the amount in its cash account. Companies should report bank overdrafts in the current liabilities section, adding them to the amount reported as accounts payable. If material, companies should disclose these items separately, either on the face of the balance sheet or in the related notes.[5]

---

[4]*Accounting Series Release No. 148,* "Amendments to Regulations S-X and Related Interpretations and Guidelines Regarding the Disclosure of Compensating Balances and Short-Term Borrowing Arrangements," Securities and Exchange Commission (November 13, 1973). The SEC defines 15 percent of liquid assets (current cash balances, whether restricted or not, plus marketable securities) as being material, thereby requiring additional reporting.

[5]Bank overdrafts usually occur because of a simple oversight by the company writing the check. Banks often expect companies to have overdrafts from time to time and therefore negotiate a fee as payment for this possible occurrence. However, at one time, **E. F. Hutton** (a large brokerage firm) began intentionally overdrawing its accounts by astronomical amounts—on some days exceeding $1 billion—thus obtaining interest-free loans that it could invest. Because the amounts were so large and fees were not negotiated in advance, E. F. Hutton came under criminal investigation for its actions.

Bank overdrafts are generally not offset against the cash account. A major exception is when available cash is present in another account in the same bank on which the overdraft occurred. Offsetting in this case is required.

Cash Equivalents

A current classification that has become popular is "Cash and cash equivalents."[6] **Cash equivalents** are short-term, highly liquid investments that are both (a) readily convertible to known amounts of cash, and (b) so near their maturity that they present insignificant risk of changes in interest rates. Generally, only investments with original maturities of three months or less qualify under these definitions. Examples of cash equivalents are Treasury bills, commercial paper, and money market funds. Some companies combine cash with temporary investments on the balance sheet. In these cases, they describe the amount of the short-term investments either parenthetically or in the notes.

Additional Disclosures of Restricted Cash

SUMMARY OF CASH-RELATED ITEMS

Cash and cash equivalents include the medium of exchange and most negotiable instruments. If the item cannot be quickly converted to coin or currency, a company separately classifies it as an investment, receivable, or prepaid expense. Companies segregate and classify cash that is unavailable for payment of currently maturing liabilities in the long-term assets section. Illustration 8-2 summarizes the classification of cash-related items.

Classification of Cash, Cash Equivalents, and Noncash Items

Item	Classification	Comment
Cash	Cash	If unrestricted, report as cash. If restricted, identify and classify as current and noncurrent assets.
Petty cash and change funds	Cash	Report as cash.
Short-term paper	Cash equivalents	Investments with maturity of less than 3 months, often combined with cash.
Short-term paper	Short-term investments	Investments with maturity of 3 to 12 months.
Postdated checks and IOU's	Receivables	Assumed to be collectible.
Travel advances	Receivables	Assumed to be collected from employees or deducted from their salaries.
Postage on hand (as stamps or in postage meters)	Prepaid expenses	May also be classified as office supplies inventory.
Bank overdrafts	Current liability	If right of offset exists, reduce cash.
Compensating balances	Cash separately classified as a deposit maintained as compensating balance	Classify as current or noncurrent in the balance sheet. Disclose separately in notes details of the arrangement.

Illustration 8-2
Classification of Cash-Related Items

[6]*Accounting Trends and Techniques—2006,* indicates that approximately 4 percent of the companies surveyed use the caption "Cash," 88 percent use "Cash and cash equivalents," and 3 percent use a caption such as "Cash and marketable securities" or similar terminology.

Try it out! Richardson Company has collected the following information related to determining its cash balance at December 31, 2008.

1   Richardson has a savings account balance of $400,000 and a checking account balance of $210,750. Richardson maintains a petty cash fund of $2,000.

2   The company has made travel advances of $15,000 for employee travel in the first quarter of the next year. The employees will reimburse the company through salary reduction.

3   Postage stamps on hand amount to $740.

4   A separate cash fund of $250,000 is restricted for future office expansion.

5   Richardson holds a check dated January 12, 2009, for $1,000 and a certified check from a customer for $750.

6   Currency and coin on hand total $5,245.

Instructions

Determine the amount of cash to be reported on Richardson's balance sheet at December 31, 2008.

Solution

Cash includes the following:

Savings account	$400,000
Checking account	210,750
Petty cash	2,000
Certified check from customer	750
Currency and coin on hand	5,245
Cash reported on December 31, 2008, balance sheet	$618,745

Other items would be classified as follows.

1   Travel advances (to be reimbursed by employees) should be reported as "Receivables—employees" in the amount of $15,000.

2   Cash restricted in the amount of $250,000 for the office expansion should be reported as a noncurrent asset.

3   The postage stamps should be classified as office supplies or as a prepaid expense.

4   The postdated check of $1,000 should be reported as accounts receivable.

SECTION TWO RECEIVABLES

Receivables are claims held against customers and others for money, goods, or services. For financial statement purposes, companies classify receivables as either **current** (short-term) or **noncurrent** (long-term). Companies expect to collect **current receivables** within a year or during the current operating cycle, whichever is longer. They classify all other receivables as **noncurrent**. Receivables are further classified in the balance sheet as either trade or nontrade receivables.

Customers often owe a company amounts for goods bought or services rendered. A company may subclassify these **trade receivables**, usually the most significant item it possesses, into accounts receivable and notes receivable. **Accounts receivable** are oral promises of the purchaser to pay for goods and services sold. They represent "open accounts" resulting from short-term extensions of credit. A company normally collects them within 30 to 60 days. **Notes receivable** are written promises to pay a certain sum of money on a specified future date. They may arise from sales, financing, or other transactions. Notes may be short-term or long-term.

Nontrade receivables arise from a variety of transactions. Some examples of nontrade receivables are:

1 Advances to officers and employees.

2 Advances to subsidiaries.

3 Deposits paid to cover potential damages or losses.

4 Deposits paid as a guarantee of performance or payment.

5 Dividends and interest receivable.

6 Claims against:

    a Insurance companies for casualties sustained.

    b Defendants under suit.

    c Governmental bodies for tax refunds.

    d Common carriers for damaged or lost goods.

    e Creditors for returned, damaged, or lost goods.

    f Customers for returnable items (crates, containers, etc.).

Because of the peculiar nature of nontrade receivables, companies generally report them as separate items in the balance sheet. Illustration 8-3 shows the reporting of trade and nontrade receivables in the balance sheets of **Adolph Coors Company** and **Seaboard Corporation**.

> **OBJECTIVE 3**
> **Define receivables and identify the different types of receivables.**

Illustration 8-3
Receivables Balance
Sheet Presentations

Adolph Coors Company
(in thousands)

Current assets	
Cash and cash equivalents	$160,038
Short-term investments	96,190
Accounts and notes receivable	
Trade, less allowance for	
doubtful accounts of $299	106,962
Subsidiaries	11,896
Other, less allowance for certain	
claims of $584	7,751
Inventories	102,660
Other supplies, less allowance for	
obsolete supplies of $3,968	27,729
Prepaid expenses and other assets	12,848
Deferred tax asset	22,917
Total current assets	$548,991

Seaboard Corporation
(in thousands)

Current assets		
Cash and cash equivalents		$ 19,760
Short-term investments		91,375
Receivables		
Trade	$194,966	
Due from foreign affiliates	36,662	
Other	41,816	
		273,444
Allowance for doubtful		
receivables		(29,801)
Net receivables		243,643
Inventories		218,030
Deferred income taxes		14,132
Prepaid expenses and deposits		23,760
Total current assets		$610,700

The basic issues in accounting for accounts and notes receivable are the same: **recognition**, **valuation**, and **disposition**. We discuss these basic issues for accounts and notes receivable next.

RECOGNITION OF ACCOUNTS RECEIVABLE

In most receivables transactions, the amount to be recognized is the exchange price between the two parties. **The exchange price is the amount due from the debtor** (a customer or a borrower). Some type of business document, often an invoice, serves as evidence of the exchange price. Two factors may complicate the measurement of the exchange price: (1) the availability of discounts (trade and cash discounts), and (2) the length of time between the sale and the due date of payments (the interest element).

Trade Discounts

Prices may be subject to a trade or quantity discount. Companies use such **trade discounts** to avoid frequent changes in catalogs, to alter prices for different quantities purchased, or to hide the true invoice price from competitors.

Trade discounts are commonly quoted in percentages. For example, say your textbook has a list price of $90, and the publisher sells it to college bookstores for list less a 30 percent trade discount. The publisher then records the receivable at $63 per textbook. The publisher, per normal practice, simply deducts the trade discount from the list price and bills the customer net.

As another example, **Maxwell House** at one time sold a 10-ounce jar of its instant coffee listing at $5.85 to supermarkets for $5.05, a trade discount of approximately 14 percent. The supermarkets in turn sold the instant coffee for $5.20 per jar. Maxwell House records the receivable and related sales revenue at $5.05 per jar, not $5.85.

Cash Discounts (Sales Discounts)

Companies offer **cash discounts** (**sales discounts**) to induce prompt payment. Cash discounts generally read in terms such as 2/10, n/30 (2 percent if paid within 10 days, gross amount due in 30 days), or 2/10, E.O.M., net 30, E.O.M. (2 percent if paid any time before the tenth day of the following month, with full payment received by the thirtieth of the following month).

Companies usually take sales discounts unless their cash is severely limited. Why? A company that receives a 1 percent reduction in the sales price for payment within 10 days, total payment due within 30 days, effectively earns 18.25 percent ($.01 \div [20/365]$), or at least avoids that rate of interest cost.

Companies usually record sales and related sales discount transactions by entering the receivable and sale at the gross amount. Under this method, companies recognize sales discounts only when they receive payment within the discount period. The income statement shows sales discounts as a deduction from sales to arrive at net sales.

Some contend that sales discounts not taken reflect penalties added to an established price to encourage prompt payment. That is, the seller offers sales on account at a slightly higher price than if selling for cash. The cash discount offered offsets the increase. Thus, customers who pay within the discount period actually purchase at the cash price. Those who pay after expiration of the discount period pay a penalty for the delay—an amount in excess of the cash price. Per this reasoning, companies record sales and receivables net. They subsequently debit any discounts not taken to Accounts Receivable and credit to Sales Discounts Forfeited. The entries in Illustration 8-4 (page 365) show the difference between the gross and net methods.

If using the gross method, a company reports sales discounts as a deduction from sales in the income statement. Proper matching dictates that the company also reasonably estimates the expected discounts to be taken and charge that amount against sales. If using the net method, a company considers Sales Discounts Forfeited as an "Other revenue" item.[7]

---

[7]To the extent that discounts not taken reflect a short-term financing, some argue that companies could use an interest revenue account to record these amounts.

Gross Method			Net Method		
Sales of $10,000, terms 2/10, n/30					
Accounts Receivable	10,000		Accounts Receivable	9,800	
Sales		10,000	Sales		9,800
Payment of $4,000 received within discount period					
Cash	3,920		Cash	3,920	
Sales Discounts	80		Accounts Receivable		3,920
Accounts Receivable		4,000			
Payment of $6,000 received after discount period					
Cash	6,000		Accounts Receivable	120	
Accounts Receivable		6,000	Sales Discounts		
			Forfeited		120
			Cash	6,000	
			Accounts Receivable		6,000

Illustration 8-4
Entries under Gross and Net Methods of Recording Cash (Sales) Discounts

Theoretically, the recognition of Sales Discounts Forfeited is correct. The receivable is stated closer to its realizable value, and the net sales figure measures the revenue earned from the sale. As a practical matter, however, companies seldom use the net method because it requires additional analysis and bookkeeping. For example, the net method requires adjusting entries to record sales discounts forfeited on accounts receivable that have passed the discount period.

Nonrecognition of Interest Element

Ideally, a company should measure receivables in terms of their present value, that is, the discounted value of the cash to be received in the future. When expected cash receipts require a waiting period, the receivable face amount is not worth the amount that the company ultimately receives.

To illustrate, assume that **Best Buy** makes a sale on account for $1,000 with payment due in four months. The applicable annual rate of interest is 12 percent, and payment is made at the end of four months. The present value of that receivable is not $1,000 but $961.54 ($1,000 × .96154). In other words, the $1,000 Best Buy receives four months from now is not the same as the $1,000 received today.

Theoretically, any revenue after the period of sale is interest revenue. In practice, companies ignore interest revenue related to accounts receivable because the amount of the discount is not usually material in relation to the net income for the period. The profession specifically excludes from present value considerations "receivables arising from transactions with customers in the normal course of business which are due in customary trade terms not exceeding approximately one year."[8]

WHAT'S THE PRINCIPLE?

Materiality means it must make a difference to a decision maker. The FASB believes that present value concepts can be ignored for short-term receivables.

VALUATION OF ACCOUNTS RECEIVABLE

Reporting of receivables involves (1) classification and (2) valuation on the balance sheet. Classification involves determining the length of time each receivable will be outstanding. Companies classify receivables intended to be collected within a year or the operating cycle, whichever is longer, as current. All other receivables are classified as long-term.

---

[8]"Interest on Receivables and Payables," *Opinions of the Accounting Principles Board No. 21* (New York: AICPA, 1971), par. 3(a).

Companies value and report short-term receivables at net realizable value—the net amount they expect to receive in cash. Determining net realizable value requires estimating both uncollectible receivables and any returns or allowances to be granted.

Uncollectible Accounts Receivable

As one revered accountant aptly noted, the credit manager's idea of heaven probably would be a place where everyone (eventually) paid his or her debts.[9] The recent experiences of **Circuit City**, **Sears** (now **Sears Holdings**), **Target**, and **Kohls**, as shown in Illustration 8-5, indicate the importance of credit sales for many companies. Note that for Sears, increased bad debt expense led to a lower stock price, which prompted Sears to sell its credit card portfolio to **Citigroup** in 2003.

Illustration 8-5
Credit and Its Costs

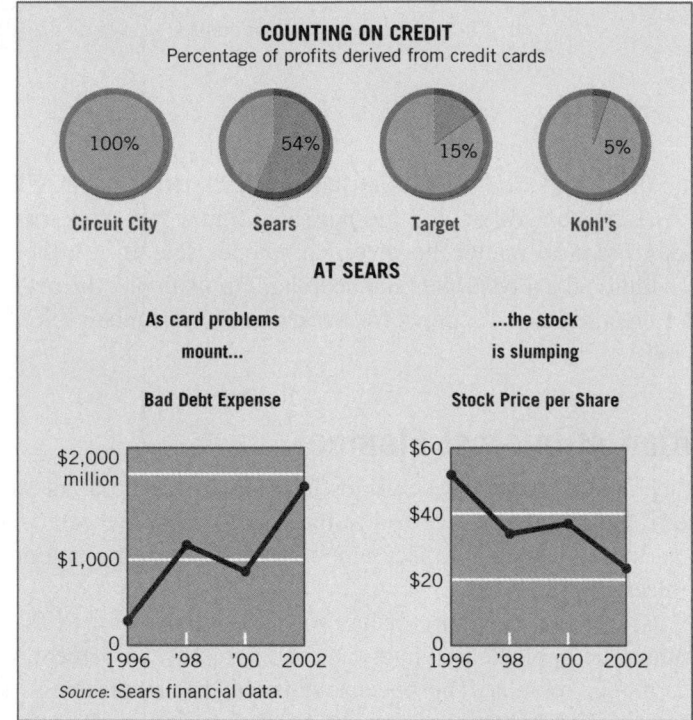

Sales on any basis other than cash make uncertain the possibility of collecting the account. An uncollectible account receivable is a loss of revenue that requires, through proper entry in the accounts, a decrease in the asset accounts receivable and a related decrease in income and stockholders' equity. Companies recognize the loss in revenue and the decrease in income by recording bad debt expense.

Companies use two procedures to record uncollectible accounts:

METHODS FOR RECORDING UNCOLLECTIBLES

1 DIRECT WRITE-OFF METHOD. No entry is made until a specific account has definitely been established as uncollectible. Then the loss is recorded by crediting Accounts Receivable and debiting Bad Debt Expense.

2 ALLOWANCE METHOD. An estimate is made of the expected uncollectible accounts from all sales made on account or from the total of outstanding receivables. This estimate is entered as an expense and an indirect reduction in accounts receivable (via an increase in the allowance account) in the period in which the sale is recorded.

[9]William J. Vatter, *Managerial Accounting* (Englewood Cliffs, N.J.: Prentice Hall, 1950), p. 60.

The **direct write-off method** records the bad debt in the period in which a company determines that it cannot collect a specific receivable. In contrast, the **allowance method** enters the expense on an estimated basis in the accounting period in which the sales on account occur.

Supporters of the **direct write-off method** (which is used for tax purposes) contend that it records facts, not estimates. It assumes that a good account receivable resulted from each sale, and that later events revealed certain accounts to be uncollectible and worthless. From a practical standpoint this method is simple and convenient to apply. But the direct write-off method is theoretically deficient: It usually fails to match costs with revenues of the period. Nor does it result in receivables being stated at estimated realizable value on the balance sheet. **As a result, using the direct write-off method is not considered appropriate, except when the amount uncollectible is immaterial.**

Advocates of the **allowance method** believe that companies should record bad debt expense in the same period as the sale, to properly match expenses and revenues and to achieve a proper carrying value for accounts receivable. They contend that although estimates are involved, companies can predict the percentage of uncollectible receivables from past experiences, present market conditions, and an analysis of the outstanding balances. Many companies set their credit policies to provide for a certain percentage of uncollectible accounts. (In fact, many feel that failure to reach that percentage means that they are losing sales due to overly restrictive credit policies.)

The FASB considers the collectibility of receivables a loss contingency. Thus, the allowance method is appropriate in situations where it is probable that an asset has been impaired and that the amount of the loss can be reasonably estimated.[10]

A receivable is a prospective cash inflow. The probability of its collection must be considered in valuing cash flows. These estimates normally are based either on (1) percentage of sales or (2) outstanding receivables.

Percentage-of-Sales (Income Statement) Approach

If there is a fairly stable relationship between previous years' credit sales and bad debts, then a company can convert that relationship into a percentage and use it to determine this year's bad debt expense.

WHAT'S THE PRINCIPLE?

The percentage-of-sales method illustrates the *matching principle*, which relates expenses to revenues earned.

The **percentage-of-sales approach** matches costs with revenues because it relates the charge to the period in which a company records the sale. To illustrate, assume that Chad Shumway Corp. estimates from past experience that about 2 percent of credit sales become uncollectible. If Chad Shumway has credit sales of $400,000 in 2008, it records bad debt expense using the percentage-of-sales method as follows.

Bad Debt Expense	8,000	
Allowance for Doubtful Accounts		8,000

The Allowance for Doubtful Accounts is a valuation account (i.e., a contra asset), subtracted from trade receivables on the balance sheet.[11] The amount of bad debt expense and the related credit to the allowance account are unaffected by any balance currently existing in the allowance account. Because the bad debt expense estimate is related to a nominal account (Sales), any balance in the allowance is ignored. Therefore, the percentage-of-sales method achieves a proper matching of cost and revenues. This method is frequently referred to as the **income statement approach**.

Percentage-of-Receivables (Balance Sheet) Approach

Using past experience, a company can estimate the percentage of its outstanding receivables that will become uncollectible, without identifying specific accounts. This procedure

[10]"Accounting for Contingencies," *Statement of Financial Accounting Standards No. 5* (Stamford, Conn.: FASB, 1975), par. 8.

[11]The account description employed for the allowance account is usually Allowance for Doubtful Accounts or simply Allowance. *Accounting Trends and Techniques—2006,* for example, indicates that approximately 84 percent of the companies surveyed used "allowance" in their description.

provides a reasonably accurate estimate of the receivables' realizable value. But, it does not fit the concept of matching cost and revenues. Rather, it simply reports receivables in the balance sheet at net realizable value. Hence it is referred to as the **percentage-of-receivables** (or **balance sheet**) **approach**.

Companies may apply this method using one **composite rate** that reflects an estimate of the uncollectible receivables. Or, companies may set up an **aging schedule** of accounts receivable, which applies a different percentage based on past experience to the various age categories. An aging schedule also identifies which accounts require special attention by indicating the extent to which certain accounts are past due. The following schedule of Wilson & Co. is an example.

Illustration 8-6
Accounts Receivable
Aging Schedule

Wilson & Co.
Aging Schedule

Name of Customer	Balance Dec. 31	Under 60 days	60–90 days	91–120 days	Over 120 days
Western Stainless Steel Corp.	$ 98,000	$ 80,000	$18,000		
Brockway Steel Company	320,000	320,000			
Freeport Sheet & Tube Co.	55,000				$55,000
Allegheny Iron Works	74,000	60,000		$14,000	
	$547,000	$460,000	$18,000	$14,000	$55,000

Summary

Age	Amount	Percentage Estimated to be Uncollectible	Required Balance in Allowance
Under 60 days old	$460,000	4%	$18,400
61–90 days old	18,000	15%	2,700
91–120 days old	14,000	20%	2,800
Over 120 days	55,000	25%	13,750
Year-end balance of allowance for doubtful accounts			$37,650

Wilson reports bad debt expense of $37,650 for this year, assuming that no balance existed in the allowance account.

To change the illustration slightly, **assume that the allowance account had a credit balance of $800 before adjustment**. In this case, Wilson adds $36,850 ($37,650 – $800) to the allowance account, and makes the following entry.

Bad Debt Expense	36,850	
Allowance for Doubtful Accounts		36,850

Wilson therefore states the balance in the Allowance account at $37,650. **If the Allowance balance before adjustment had a debit balance of $200,** then Wilson records bad debt expense of $37,850 ($37,650 desired balance + $200 debit balance). In the percentage-of-receivables method, Wilson **cannot ignore** the balance in the allowance account, because the percentage is related to a real account (Accounts Receivable).

Companies usually do not prepare an aging schedule to determine bad debt expense. Rather, they prepare it as a control device to determine the composition of receivables and to identify delinquent accounts. Companies base the estimated loss percentage developed for each category on previous loss experience and the advice of credit department personnel.

Whether using a composite rate or an aging schedule, the primary objective of the percentage-of-outstanding-receivables method for financial statement purposes is to report

**Tutorial on Recording
Uncollectible Accounts**

receivables in the balance sheet at net realizable value. However, it is deficient in that it may not match the bad debt expense to the period in which the sale takes place.

The allowance for doubtful accounts as a percentage of receivables will vary, depending on the industry and the economic climate. Companies such as **Eastman Kodak**, **General Electric**, and **Monsanto** have recorded allowances ranging from $3 to $6 per $100 of accounts receivable. Other large companies, such as **CPC International** ($1.48), **Texaco** ($1.23), and **USX Corp.** ($0.78), have had bad debt allowances of less than $1.50 per $100. At the other extreme are hospitals that allow for $15 to $20 per $100 of accounts receivable.[12]

What do the numbers mean?   Going for Broke

The start of the new millennium has been a tough one for companies and their investors, creditors, and employees. **Enron**, **Kmart**, and **WorldCom** all declared bankruptcy—with WorldCom representing the largest bankruptcy ever. The trend seems to be continuing.

It is not surprising that banks and other creditors are raising their lending standards to guard against future loan defaults. Even so, some question whether creditors have set up reasonable bad debt allowances to ensure that financial performance is reported accurately. Indeed, one recent analysis for hospitals (mentioned in our opening story) indicates that additional bad debt expense needed to properly reflect future write-offs could result in an earnings hit of as much as 18 percent for some hospitals. That will be tough medicine for these companies to swallow.

Source: Adapted from: Julie Creswell, "First Going for Broke," *Fortune* (February 18, 2002), pp. 24–25; Bethany McLean, "Reality Check-up," *Fortune* (January 12, 2004), pp. 140.

Beyond the Numbers

What are some factors that would explain high uncollectible account rates for hospitals versus other businesses?

In summary, the percentage-of-receivables method results in a more accurate valuation of receivables on the balance sheet. From a matching viewpoint, the percentage-of-sales approach provides the better results. Illustration 8-7 relates these methods to the basic theory.

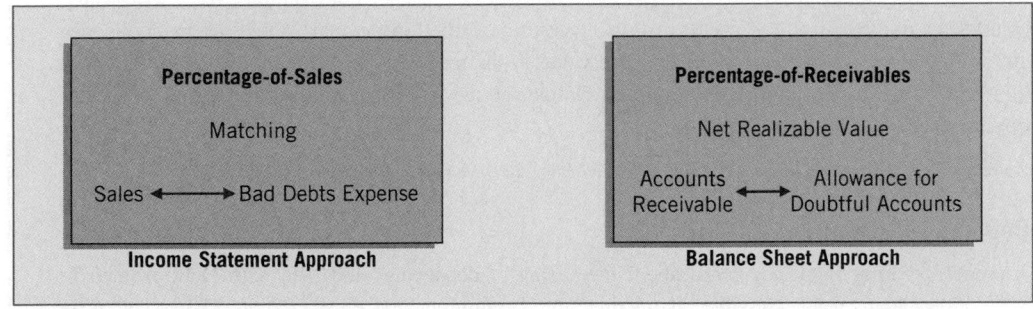

Illustration 8-7
Comparison of Methods for Estimating Uncollectibles

[12]A U.S. Department of Commerce study indicated, as a general rule, the following relationships between the age of accounts receivable and their uncollectibility.

30 days or less	4% uncollectible
31–60 days	10% uncollectible
61–90 days	17% uncollectible
91–120 days	26% uncollectible

After 120 days, an approximate 3–4 percent increase in uncollectibles for every 30 days outstanding occurs for the remainder of the first year.

The account title employed for the allowance account is usually Allowance for Doubtful Accounts or simply Allowance.

Regardless of the method chosen, determining the expense associated with uncollectible accounts requires a large degree of judgment. Recent concern exists that, similar to **Nortel** in our opening story, some banks use this judgment to manage earnings. By overestimating the amounts of uncollectible loans in a good earnings year, the bank can "save for a rainy day" in a future period. In future (less-profitable) periods, banks can reduce the overly conservative allowance for loan loss account to increase earnings. In this regard, the SEC brought action against **Suntrust Banks**, requiring a reversal of $100 million of bad debt expense. This reversal increased aftertax profit by $61 million.[13]

Collection of Accounts Receivable Written Off

When a company determines a particular account receivable to be uncollectible, it removes the balance from the books by debiting Allowance for Doubtful Accounts and crediting Accounts Receivable. If it eventually collects on a receivable that it previously wrote off, it first reestablishes the receivable by debiting Accounts Receivable and crediting Allowance for Doubtful Accounts. The company then debits Cash and credits the customer's account for the amount received.

If using the direct write-off approach, the company debits the amount collected to Cash and credits a revenue account entitled Uncollectible Amounts Recovered, with proper notation in the customer's account.

What do the numbers mean?   Collection Is a Click Away

What do lenders do with uncollectible receivables? After they record bad debts on their books, they next try to collect what they can from the deadbeat customers. Some lenders auction their bad loans in the market for distressed debt, usually paying a fee of 5–15 percent to a distressed debt broker, who arranges the sale.

Recently, several Web sites have sprung up to provide a meeting place between lenders with bad loans and collectors. These sites are sort of an "eBay of deadbeats." For example, **Bank One Corp.** listed $211 million of unpaid credit card receivables on **DebtforSale.com**. While the lenders generally recover less than 10 percent of the face value of the receivables in an auction, by going online they can reduce the costs of their bad debts. Online services charge just 0.5–1 percent for their auction services.

Source: Adapted from P. Gogoi, "An eBay of Deadbeats," *Business Week* (September 18, 2000), p. 124.

Beyond the Numbers

Assume that First Bank has heard about the "eBay of deadbeats" and lists with DebtforSale.com $200,000 of loans it has classified as uncollectible. Assuming First Bank collects 25 percent of the loans listed online and pays DebtforSale a 1 percent collection fee, prepare the journal entry(ies) to record the recoveries.

---

[13]Recall from our earnings management discussion in Chapter 5 that increasing or decreasing income through management manipulation can reduce the quality of financial reports.

Try it out! Modest Mouse Co. had net sales of $600,000 in 2008. At December 31, 2008, before adjusting entries, the balances in selected accounts were: Accounts Receivable $125,000 debit; Allowance for Doubtful Accounts $1,150 credit.

Instructions

Prepare the journal entries for the following items affecting the allowance for doubtful accounts.

a   Record bad debt expense. Modest Mouse estimates that 2% of its net sales will prove to be uncollectible.

b   Record bad debt expense. Modest Mouse prepares an aging schedule that estimates total uncollectible accounts to be $12,300.

c   The company collects an account with a balance of $450, which was written off in a previous period. Prepare the journal entry(ies) to record the collection.

Solution

a   Bad Debt Expense   12,000*
        Allowance for Doubtful Accounts   12,000
    *$600,000 × .02 = $12,000

b   Bad Debt Expense   11,150
        Allowance for Doubtful Accounts   11,150*
    *$12,300 (amount needed in allowance) − $ 1,150 (amount recorded) = $11,150

c   Accounts Receivable   450
        Allowance for Doubtful Accounts   450
    Cash   450
        Accounts Receivable   450

RECOGNITION OF NOTES RECEIVABLE

A note receivable is supported by a formal **promissory note**, a written promise to pay a certain sum of money at a specific future date. Such a note is a negotiable instrument that a **maker** signs in favor of a designated **payee** who may legally and readily sell or otherwise transfer the note to others. Although notes contain an interest element because of the time value of money, companies classify them as interest-bearing or noninterest-bearing. **Interest-bearing notes** have a stated rate of interest. **Zero-interest-bearing notes** (noninterest-bearing) include interest as part of their face amount. Notes receivable are considered fairly liquid, even if long-term, because companies may easily convert them to cash (although they might pay a fee to do so).

Companies frequently accept notes receivable from customers who need to extend the payment period of an outstanding receivable. Or they require notes from high-risk or new customers. In addition, companies often use notes in loans to employees and subsidiaries, and in the sales of property, plant, and equipment. In some industries (e.g., the pleasure and sport boat industry) notes support all credit sales. The majority of notes, however, originate from lending transactions. The basic issues in accounting for notes receivable are the same as those for accounts receivable: **recognition**, **valuation**, and **disposition**.

Companies generally record short-term notes at face value (less allowances) because the interest implicit in the maturity value is immaterial. A general rule is that notes treated as cash equivalents (maturities of three months or less and easily converted to cash) are not subject to premium or discount amortization.

However, companies should record and report long-term notes receivable at the **present value of the cash they expect to collect**. When the interest stated on an interest-bearing note equals the effective (market) rate of interest, the note sells at face value.[14] When the stated rate differs from the market rate, the cash exchanged (present value) differs from the face value of the note. Companies then record this difference, either a discount or a premium, and amortize it over the life of a note to approximate the effective-interest rate. This illustrates one of the many situations in which time value of money concepts are applied to accounting measurement. (Appendix A provides a more complete discussion of time value of money concepts and applications.)

Note Issued at Face Value

To illustrate the discounting of a note issued at face value, assume that Bigelow Corp. lends Scandinavian Imports $10,000 in exchange for a $10,000, three-year note bearing interest at 10 percent annually. The market rate of interest for a note of similar risk is also 10 percent. We show the time diagram depicting both cash flows in Illustration 8-8.

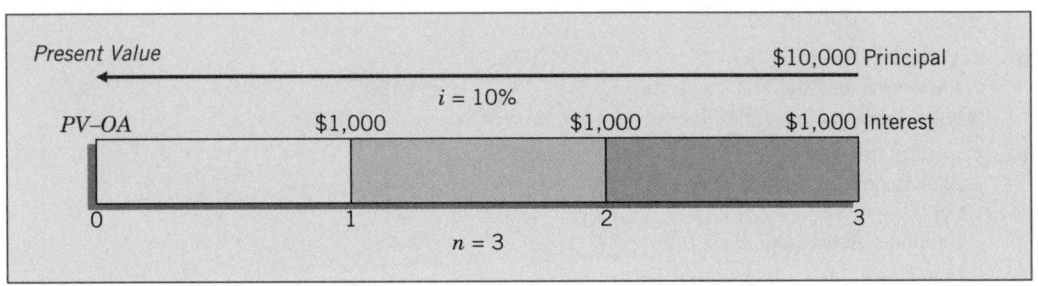

Bigelow computes the present value or exchange price of the note as follows.

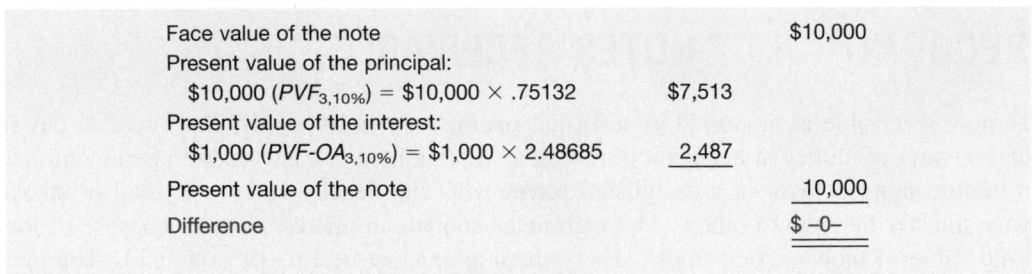

Face value of the note		$10,000
Present value of the principal:		
$10,000 ($PVF_{3,10\%}$) = $10,000 × .75132	$7,513	
Present value of the interest:		
$1,000 ($PVF\text{-}OA_{3,10\%}$) = $1,000 × 2.48685	2,487	
Present value of the note		10,000
Difference		$ –0–

In this case, the present value of the note equals its face value, because the effective and stated rates of interest are also the same. Bigelow records the receipt of the note as follows.

Notes Receivable	10,000	
Cash		10,000

---

[14]The **stated interest rate**, also referred to as the face rate or the coupon rate, is the rate contracted as part of the note. The **effective-interest rate**, also referred to as the *market rate* or the *effective yield*, is the rate used in the market to determine the value of the note—that is, the discount rate used to determine present value.

Bigelow recognizes the interest earned each year as follows.

Cash	1,000	
Interest Revenue		1,000

Note Not Issued at Face Value

Zero-Interest-Bearing Notes

If a company receives a zero-interest-bearing note, its present value is the cash paid to the issuer. Because the company knows both the future amount and the present value of the note, it can compute the interest rate. This rate is often referred to as the **implicit interest rate**. Companies record the difference between the future (face) amount and the present value (cash paid) as a discount and amortize it to interest revenue over the life of the note.

To illustrate, Jeremiah Company receives a three-year, $10,000 zero-interest-bearing note, the present value of which is $7,721.80. The implicit rate that equates the total cash to be received ($10,000 at maturity) to the present value of the future cash flows ($7,721.80) is 9 percent (the present value of 1 for three periods at 9 percent is .77218). We show the time diagram depicting the one cash flow in Illustration 8-10.

You can use a financial calculator to solve this problem.

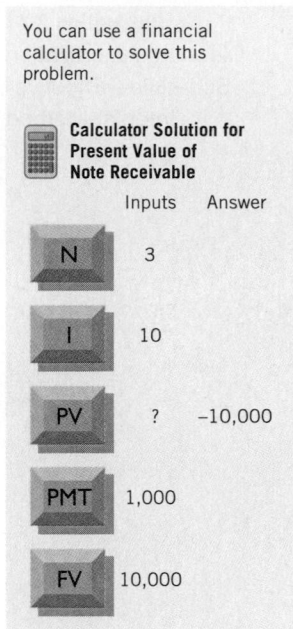

Calculator Solution for Present Value of Note Receivable

	Inputs	Answer
N	3	
I	10	
PV	?	−10,000
PMT	1,000	
FV	10,000	

Illustration 8-10
Time Diagram for Zero-Interest-Bearing Note

Expanded Discussion of Using Calculators to Solve Present-Value Problems

Jeremiah records the transaction as follows:

Notes Receivable	10,000.00	
Discount on Notes Receivable ($10,000 − $7,721.80)		2,278.20
Cash		7,721.80

Discount on Notes Receivable is a valuation account. Companies report it on the balance sheet as a contra-asset account to notes receivable. They then amortize the discount, and recognize interest revenue annually using the **effective-interest method**. Illustration 8-11 (page 376) shows the three-year discount amortization and interest revenue schedule.

Jeremiah records interest revenue at the end of the first year using the effective-interest method as follows.

Discount on Notes Receivable	694.96	
Interest Revenue ($7,721.80 × 9%)		694.96

The amount of the discount, $2,278.20 in this case, represents the interest revenue Jeremiah will receive from the note over the three years.

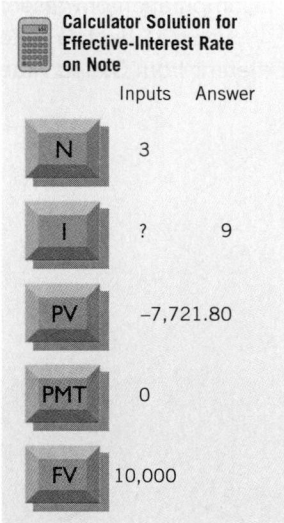

Calculator Solution for Effective-Interest Rate on Note

	Inputs	Answer
N	3	
I	?	9
PV	−7,721.80	
PMT	0	
FV	10,000	

Interest-Bearing Notes

Often the stated rate and the effective rate differ. The zero-interest-bearing note is one example.

Illustration 8-11
Discount Amortization
Schedule—Effective-
Interest Method

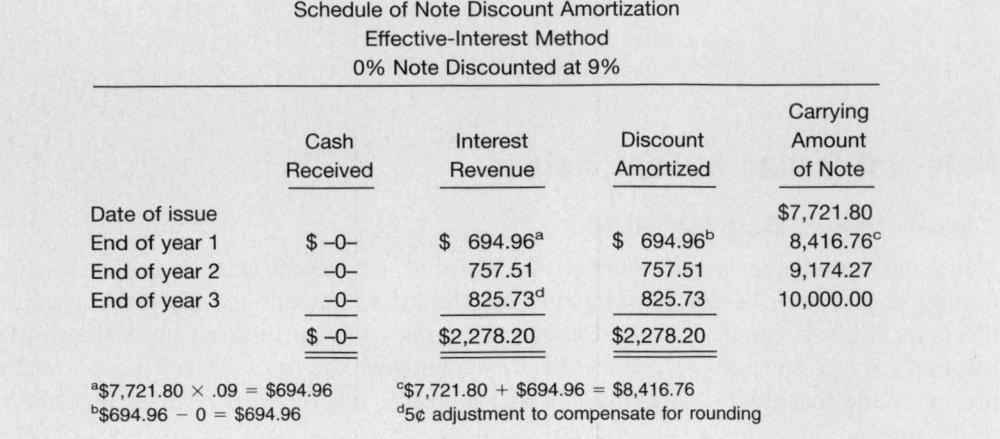

Schedule of Note Discount Amortization
Effective-Interest Method
0% Note Discounted at 9%

	Cash Received	Interest Revenue	Discount Amortized	Carrying Amount of Note
Date of issue				$7,721.80
End of year 1	$ –0–	$ 694.96[a]	$ 694.96[b]	8,416.76[c]
End of year 2	–0–	757.51	757.51	9,174.27
End of year 3	–0–	825.73[d]	825.73	10,000.00
	$ –0–	$2,278.20	$2,278.20	

[a]$7,721.80 × .09 = $694.96   [c]$7,721.80 + $694.96 = $8,416.76
[b]$694.96 – 0 = $694.96   [d]5¢ adjustment to compensate for rounding

To illustrate a more common situation, assume that Morgan Corp. makes a loan to Marie Co. and receives in exchange a three-year, $10,000 note bearing interest at 10 percent annually. The market rate of interest for a note of similar risk is 12 percent. We show the time diagram depicting both cash flows in Illustration 8-12.

Illustration 8-12
Time Diagram for Interest-
Bearing Note

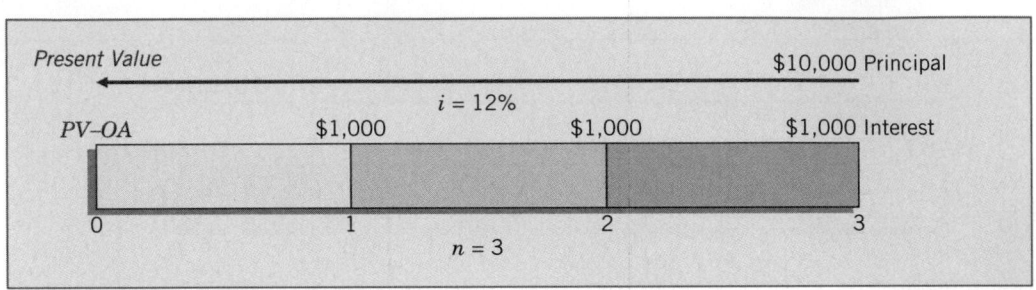

Morgan computes the present value of the two cash flows as follows.

Illustration 8-13
Computation of Present
Value—Effective Rate
Different from Stated Rate

Face value of the note		$10,000
Present value of the principal:		
$10,000 ($PVF_{3,12\%}$) = $10,000 × .71178	$7,118	
Present value of the interest:		
$1,000 ($PVF\text{-}OA_{3,12\%}$) = $1,000 × 2.40183	2,402	
Present value of the note		9,520
Difference (Discount)		$ 480

In this case, because the effective rate of interest (12 percent) exceeds the stated rate (10 percent), the present value of the note is less than the face value. That is, Morgan exchanged the note at a **discount**. Morgan records the receipt of the note at a discount as follows.

Notes Receivable	10,000	
Discount on Notes Receivable		480
Cash		9,520

Morgan then amortizes the discount and recognizes interest revenue annually using the **effective-interest method**. Illustration 8-14 shows the three-year discount amortization and interest revenue schedule. On the date of issue, the note has a present value of $9,520. Its unamortized discount—additional interest revenue spread over the three-year life of the note—is $480.

Illustration 8-14
Discount Amortization
Schedule—Effective-
Interest Method

Schedule of Note Discount Amortization
Effective-Interest Method
10% Note Discounted at 12%

	Cash Received	Interest Revenue	Discount Amortized	Carrying Amount of Note
Date of issue				$ 9,520
End of year 1	$1,000[a]	$1,142[b]	$142[c]	9,662[d]
End of year 2	1,000	1,159	159	9,821
End of year 3	1,000	1,179	179	10,000
	$3,000	$3,480	$480	

[a]$10,000 × 10% = $1,000   [c]$1,142 − $1,000 = $142
[b]$9,520 × 12% = $1,142   [d]$9,520 + $142 = $9,662

At the end of year 1, Morgan receives $1,000 in cash. But its interest revenue is $1,142 ($9,520 × 12%). The difference between $1,000 and $1,142 is the amortized discount, $142. Morgan records receipt of the annual interest and amortization of the discount for the first year as follows (amounts per amortization schedule).

Cash	1,000	
Discount on Notes Receivable	142	
Interest Revenue		1,142

The carrying amount of the note is now $9,662 ($9,520 + $142). Morgan repeats this process until the end of year 3.

When the present value exceeds the face value, the note is exchanged at a premium. Companies record the premium on a note receivable as a debit and amortize it using the effective-interest method over the life of the note as annual reductions in the amount of interest revenue recognized.

Notes Received for Property, Goods, or Services

When a **note is received in exchange for property**, **goods**, **or services** in a bargained transaction entered into at arm's length, the stated interest rate is presumed to be fair unless:

1   No interest rate is stated, or

2   The stated interest rate is unreasonable, or

3   The face amount of the note is materially different from the current cash sales price for the same or similar items or from the current market value of the debt instrument.[15]

In these circumstances, the company measures the present value of the note by the fair value of the property, goods, or services or by an amount that reasonably approximates the market value of the note.

To illustrate, Oasis Development Co. sold a corner lot to Rusty Pelican as a restaurant site. Oasis accepted in exchange a five-year note having a maturity value of $35,247 and no stated interest rate. The land originally cost Oasis $14,000. At the date of sale the land had a fair market value of $20,000. Given the criterion above, Oasis uses the fair market value of the land, $20,000, as the present value of the note. Oasis therefore records the sale as:

Notes Receivable	35,247	
Discount on Notes Receivable ($35,247 − $20,000)		15,247
Land		14,000
Gain on Sale of Land ($20,000 − $14,000)		6,000

Oasis amortizes the discount to interest revenue over the five-year life of the note using the effective-interest method.

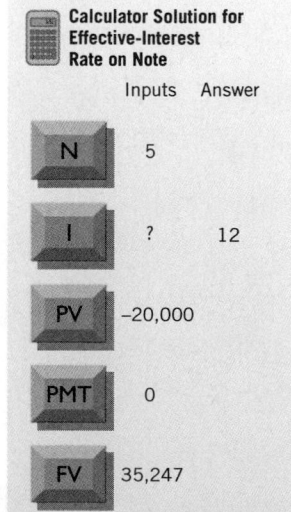

Calculator Solution for
Effective-Interest
Rate on Note

	Inputs	Answer
N	5	
I	?	12
PV	−20,000	
PMT	0	
FV	35,247	

[15]"Interest on Receivables and Payables," *Opinions of the Accounting Principles Board No. 21* (New York: AICPA, 1971), par. 12.

Choice of Interest Rate

In note transactions, other factors involved in the exchange, such as the fair market value of the property, goods, or services, determine the effective or real interest rate. But, if a company cannot determine that fair value, and if the note has no ready market, determining the present value of the note is more difficult. To estimate the present value of a note under such circumstances, the company must approximate an applicable interest rate that may differ from the stated interest rate. This process of interest-rate approximation is called **imputation**. The resulting interest rate is called an **imputed interest rate**.

The prevailing rates for similar instruments, from issuers with similar credit ratings, affect the choice of a rate. Restrictive covenants, collateral, payment schedule, and the existing prime interest rate also impact the choice. A company determines the imputed interest rate when it receives the note. It ignores any subsequent changes in prevailing interest rates.

VALUATION OF NOTES RECEIVABLE

OBJECTIVE 7

Explain accounting issues related to valuation of notes receivable.

Expanded Discussion of Loan Impairments and Restructurings

Like accounts receivable, companies record and report short-term notes receivable at their net realizable value—that is, at their face amount less all necessary allowances. The primary notes receivable allowance account is Allowance for Doubtful Accounts. The computations and estimations involved in valuing short-term notes receivable and in recording bad debt expense and the related allowance **exactly parallel that for trade accounts receivable**. Companies estimate the amount of uncollectibles by using either a percentage of sales revenue or an analysis of the receivables.

Long-term note receivables involve additional estimation problems. For example, the value of a note receivable can change significantly over time from its original cost. That is, with the passage of time, historical numbers become less and less relevant. To address this issue, the FASB required that for financial instruments such as receivables, companies disclose not only their cost but also their fair value in the notes to the financial statements.

Recently the Board has taken the additional step of giving companies the option to use fair value as the basis of measurement in the financial statements.[16] The Board believes that fair value measurement for financial instruments provides more relevant and understandable information than historical cost. It considers fair value to be more relevant because it reflects the current cash equivalent value of financial instruments. As a result, companies now have the option to record fair value in their accounts for most financial instruments, including receivables.

If companies choose the **fair value option**, the receivables are recorded at fair value, with unrealized gains or losses reported as part of net income. A **holding gain or loss** is the net change in the fair value of the receivable from one period to another, exclusive of interest revenue recognized but not recorded. As a result, the company reports the receivable at fair value each reporting date. In addition, it reports the change in value as part of net income.

To illustrate, assume that Hardy Company has long-term receivables that have a cost basis of $1,200,000 at December 31, 2008. The fair value of the receivable is determined to be $1,450,000, and Hardy elects to use the fair value option. At December 31, 2008, Hardy makes an adjusting entry to a valuation allowance, referred to as Receivables Fair Value Adjustment, to record the increase in value of $250,000 ($1,450,000 − $1,200,000) and to record the unrealized holding gain.

December 31, 2008

Receivables Fair Value Adjustment	250,000	
Unrealized Holding Gain or Loss		250,000

---

[16]*Statement of Financial Accounting Standards No. 159*, "The Fair Value Option for Financial Assets and Financial Liabilities—Including an amendment of FASB Statement No. 115" (Norwalk, Conn.: FASB, 2007).

Because the Receivables Fair Value Adjustment account is a debit, it is added to the cost basis of the receivables account to arrive at the fair value for the receivables. The fair value of the receivable is the amount reported on the balance sheet. The company reports the unrealized holding gain or loss in the "Other income or gain" section of the income statement.

Another issue that sometimes develops with receivables relates to the impairment of the receivable.[17] A note receivable is considered **impaired** when it is probable that the creditor will be unable to collect all amounts due (both principal and interest) according to the contractual terms of the receivable. In this case the receivable should be written off and a loss recorded.

Expanded Discussion of Impairments and Troubled Debt Restructuring (Appendix G)

DISPOSITION OF ACCOUNTS AND NOTES RECEIVABLE

In the normal course of events, companies collect accounts and notes receivable when due and then remove them from the books. However, the growing size and significance of credit sales and receivables has led to changes in this "normal course of events." **In order to accelerate the receipt of cash from receivables, the owner may transfer accounts or notes receivables to another company for cash.**

There are various reasons for this early transfer. First, for competitive reasons, providing sales financing for customers is virtually mandatory in many industries. In the sale of durable goods, such as automobiles, trucks, industrial and farm equipment, and appliances, most sales are on an installment-contract basis. Many companies in these industries have created wholly-owned subsidiaries specializing in receivables financing. For example, **Ford Motor Co.** has **Ford Motor Credit Co.**, and **John Deere** has **John Deere Credit**.

Second, the **holder** may sell receivables because money is tight and access to normal credit is unavailable or too expensive. Also, a firm may sell its receivables, instead of borrowing, to avoid violating existing lending agreements.

Finally, billing and collection of receivables are often time-consuming and costly. Credit card companies such as **MasterCard**, **VISA**, **American Express**, **Diners Club**, **Discover**, and others take over the collection process and provide merchants with immediate cash.

Conversely, some **purchasers** of receivables buy them to obtain the legal protection of ownership rights afforded a purchaser of assets versus the lesser rights afforded a secured creditor. In addition, banks and other lending institutions may need to purchase receivables because of legal lending limits. That is, they cannot make any additional loans but they can buy receivables and charge a fee for this service.

The transfer of receivables to a third party for cash happens in one of two ways: (1) secured borrowing and (2) sales of receivables.

OBJECTIVE 8
Explain accounting issues related to disposition of accounts and notes receivable.

Secured Borrowing

A company often uses receivables as collateral in a borrowing transaction. In fact, a creditor often requires that the debtor designate (assign) or pledge[18] receivables as security for the loan. If the loan is not paid when due, the creditor can convert the collateral to cash— that is, to collect the receivables.

To illustrate, on March 1, 2008, Howat Mills, Inc. provides (assigns) $700,000 of its accounts receivable to Citizens Bank as collateral for a $500,000 note. Howat Mills continues to collect the accounts receivable; the account debtors are not notified of the

---

[17]For example, we need only look at the problems our financial institutions, most notably the big money center banks, have had in collecting from energy loans, real estate loans, and loans in less-developed countries. As one wise person noted, a bank lending money to a Third World country is like lending money to one's children: You should never expect to get the interest, let alone the principal.

[18]If a company transfers the receivables for custodial purposes, the custodial arrangement is often referred to as a **pledge**.

arrangement. Citizens Bank assesses a finance charge of 1 percent of the accounts receivable and interest on the note of 12 percent. Howat Mills makes monthly payments to the bank for all cash it collects on the receivables. Illustration 8-15 shows the entries for the secured borrowing for Howatt Mills and Citizens Bank.

Howat Mills, Inc.			Citizens Bank		
Transfer of accounts receivable and issuance of note on March 1, 2008					
Cash	493,000		Notes Receivable	500,000	
Finance Charge	7,000*		Finance Revenue		7,000*
Notes Payable		500,000	Cash		493,000
*1% × $700,000					
Collection in March of $440,000 of accounts less cash discounts of $6,000 plus receipt of $14,000 sales returns					
Cash	434,000				
Sales Discounts	6,000				
Sales Returns	14,000		(No entry)		
Accounts Receivable		454,000*			
$440,000 + $14,000					
Remitted March collections plus accrued interest to the bank on April 1					
Interest Expense	5,000*		Cash	439,000	
Notes Payable	434,000		Interest Revenue		5,000*
Cash		439,000	Notes Receivable		434,000
*$500,000 × .12 × 1/12					
Collection in April of the balance of accounts less $2,000 written off as uncollectible					
Cash	244,000				
Allowance for Doubtful Accounts	2,000		(No entry)		
Accounts Receivable		246,000*			
*$700,000 − $454,000					
Remitted the balance due of $66,000 ($500,000 − $434,000) on the note plus interest on May 1					
Interest Expense	660*		Cash	66,660	
Notes Payable	66,000		Interest Revenue		660*
Cash		66,660	Notes Receivable		66,000
*$66,000 × .12 × 1/12					

Illustration 8-15
Entries for Transfer of Receivables—Secured Borrowing

In addition to recording the collection of receivables, Howat Mills must recognize all discounts, returns and allowances, and bad debts. Each month Howat Mills uses the proceeds from the collection of the accounts receivable to retire the note obligation. In addition, it pays interest on the note.[19]

Sales of Receivables

Sales of receivables have increased substantially in recent years. A common type is a sale to a factor. **Factors** are finance companies or banks that buy receivables from businesses for a fee and then collect the remittances directly from the customers. **Factoring receivables** is traditionally associated with the textile, apparel, footwear, furniture, and home furnishing industries.[20] Illustration 8-16 shows a typical factoring arrangement.

[19]What happens if Citizens Bank collected the transferred accounts receivable rather than Howat Mills? Citizens Bank would simply remit the cash proceeds to Howat Mills, and Howat Mills would make the same entries shown in Illustration 8-15. As a result, Howat Mills reports these "collaterized" receivables as an asset on the balance sheet.

[20]Credit cards like **MasterCard** and **VISA** are a type of factoring arrangement. Typically the purchaser of the receivable charges a ¾–1½ percent commission of the receivables purchased (the commission is 4–5 percent for credit card factoring).

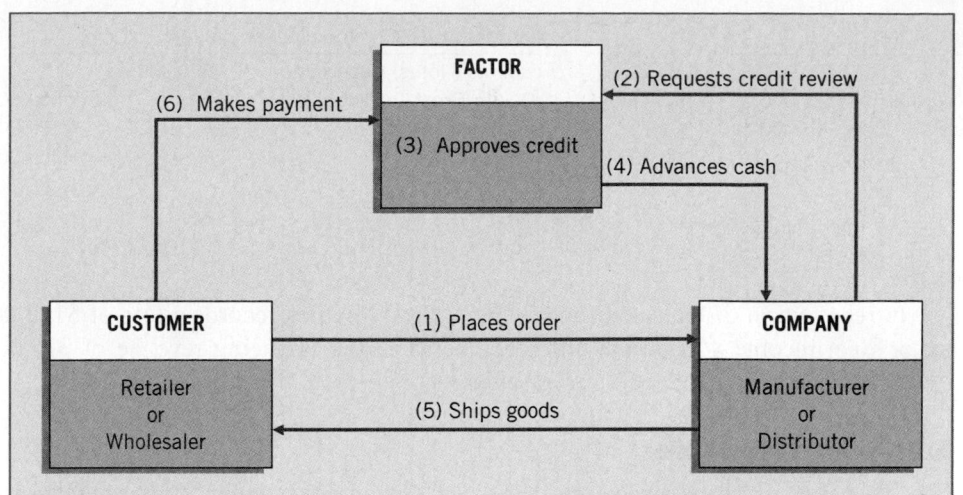

Illustration 8-16
Basic Procedures in
Factoring

A recent phenomenon in the sale (transfer) of receivables is securitization. **Securitization** takes a pool of assets such as credit card receivables, mortgage receivables, or car loan receivables, and sells shares in these pools of interest and principal payments. This, in effect, creates securities backed by these pools of assets. Virtually every asset with a payment stream and a long-term payment history is a candidate for securitization.

What are the differences between factoring and securitization? Factoring usually involves sale to only one company, fees are high, the quality of the receivables is low, and the seller afterward does not service the receivables. In a securitization, many investors are involved, margins are tight, the receivables are of higher quality, and the seller usually continues to service the receivables.

In either a factoring or a securitization transaction, a company sells receivables on either a **without recourse** or a **with recourse** basis.[21]

Sale without Recourse

When buying receivables **without recourse**, the purchaser assumes the risk of collectibility and absorbs any credit losses. The transfer of accounts receivable in a nonrecourse transaction is an outright sale of the receivables both in form (transfer of title) and substance (transfer of control). In nonrecourse transactions, as in any sale of assets, the seller debits Cash for the proceeds and credits Accounts Receivable for the face value of the receivables. The seller recognizes the difference, reduced by any provision for probable adjustments (discounts, returns, allowances, etc.), as a Loss on the Sale of Receivables. The seller uses a Due from Factor account (reported as a receivable) to account for the proceeds retained by the factor to cover probable sales discounts, sales returns, and sales allowances.

To illustrate, Crest Textiles, Inc. factors $500,000 of accounts receivable with Commercial Factors, Inc., on a **without recourse** basis. Crest Textiles transfers the receivable records to Commercial Factors, which will receive the collections. Commercial Factors assesses a finance charge of 3 percent of the amount of accounts receivable and retains an amount equal to 5 percent of the accounts receivable (for probable adjustments). Crest Textiles and Commercial Factors make the following journal entries (shown on page 380) for the receivables transferred without recourse.

**Comprehensive Illustration
of Sale Without Recourse**

---

[21]**Recourse** is the right of a transferee of receivables to receive payment from the transferor of those receivables for (1) failure of the debtors to pay when due, (2) the effects of prepayments, or (3) adjustments resulting from defects in the eligibility of the transferred receivables. See "Accounting for Transfers and Servicing of Financial Assets and Extinguishments of Liabilities," *Statement of Financial Accounting Standards No. 140* (Stamford, Conn.: FASB, 2000), p. 155.

Crest Textiles, Inc.		
Cash	460,000	
Due from Factor	25,000*	
Loss on Sale of Receivables	15,000**	
Accounts (Notes) Receivable		500,000
*5% × $500,000		
**3% × $500,000		

Commercial Factors, Inc.		
Accounts (Notes) Receivable	500,000	
Due to Crest Textiles		25,000
Financing Revenue		15,000
Cash		460,000

Illustration 8-17
Entries for Sale of
Receivables Without
Recourse

In recognition of the sale of receivables, Crest Textiles records a loss of $15,000. The factor's net income will be the difference between the financing revenue of $15,000 and the amount of any uncollectible receivables.

Sale with Recourse

For receivables sold **with recourse**, the seller guarantees payment to the purchaser in the event the debtor fails to pay. To record this type of transaction, the seller uses a **financial components approach**, because the seller has a continuing involvement with the receivable.[22] In this approach, each party to the sale only recognizes the assets and liabilities that it controls after the sale.

To illustrate, assume the same information as in Illustration 8-17 for Crest Textiles and for Commercial Factors, except that Crest Textiles sold the receivables on a with-recourse basis. Crest Textiles determines that this recourse obligation has a fair value of $6,000. To determine the loss on the sale of the receivables, Crest Textiles computes the net proceeds from the sale as follows.

Illustration 8-18
Net Proceeds
Computation

Cash received	$460,000	
Due from factor	25,000	$485,000
Less: Recourse obligation		6,000
Net proceeds		$479,000

Net proceeds are cash or other assets received in a sale less any liabilities incurred. Crest Textiles then computes the loss as follows.

Illustration 8-19
Loss on Sale
Computation

Carrying (book) value	$500,000
Net proceeds	479,000
Loss on sale of receivables	$ 21,000

Illustration 8-20 (next page) shows the journal entries for both Crest Textiles and Commercial Factors for the receivables sold with recourse.

In this case, Crest Textiles recognizes a loss of $21,000. In addition, it records a liability of $6,000 to indicate the probable payment to Commercial Factors for uncollectible receivables. If Commercial Factors collects all the receivables, Crest Textiles eliminates its recourse liability and increases income. Commercial Factors' net income is the financing revenue of $15,000. It will have no bad debts related to these receivables.

**Tutorial on the Disposition
of Receivables**

---

[22]Accounting standards before *SFAS No. 140* generally required that the transferor account for financial assets transferred as an inseparable unit that had been entirely sold or entirely retained. Those standards were difficult to apply and produced inconsistent and arbitrary results. Values are now assigned to such components as the recourse provision, servicing rights, and agreement to reacquire.

Illustration 8-20
Entries for Sale of
Receivables with
Recourse

Crest Textiles, Inc.		
Cash	460,000	
Due from Factor	25,000	
Loss on Sale of		
Receivables	21,000	
Accounts (Notes)		
Receivable		500,000
Recourse Liability		6,000

Commercial Factors, Inc.		
Accounts Receivable	500,000	
Due to Crest Textiles		25,000
Financing Revenue		15,000
Cash		460,000

What do the numbers mean?

Ugly Ducklings

Ugly Duckling is a used-car dealer that has carved out a niche by selling cars to customers with questionable credit histories. Ugly Duckling and other "subprime lenders" earn a profit by loaning money to riskier borrowers so they can purchase automobiles or homes. To compensate for the higher probability of default of these customers, subprime lenders charge higher rates of interest on these high-risk loans. In many instances these companies package their subprime loans and sell them as securities. However, recognition of gains on these transfers of receivables is appropriate only if Ugly Duckling can reasonably estimate the proportion of the loans that borrowers will not repay (the receivables are sold with recourse).

However, estimating loan defaults is difficult. If subprime lenders fail to set rates high enough to cover unexpected higher rates of default, a severe cash squeeze will result. In addition, if too many of the loans that it sells then default, Ugly Duckling will have to take them back, thereby eliminating any gain it recorded on the original sale. Indeed, in one year alone, **ContiFinancial** had to write off over $654 million in subprime loans. Similarly, bank regulators had to step in and take over **Superior Bank FSB**, which specialized in subprime loans, because it overestimated the value of its subprime loans.

Thus, the subprime lending business is a risky one. Depending on default and interest rate assumptions on these receivables, companies like Ugly Duckling may not survive to grow into lending swans.

Beyond the Numbers

Recently, the market values of the securities backed by subprime loans have declined significantly. Can these declines in value be related to the collectibility of the subprime loans? Explain.

Secured Borrowing versus Sale

The FASB concluded that a sale occurs only if the seller surrenders control of the receivables to the buyer. The following three conditions must be met before a company can record a sale:

1 The transferred asset has been isolated from the transferor (put beyond reach of the transferor and its creditors).

2 The transferees have obtained the right to pledge or exchange either the transferred assets or beneficial interests in the transferred assets.

3 The transferor does not maintain effective control over the transferred assets through an agreement to repurchase or redeem them before their maturity.

WHAT'S THE PRINCIPLE?

Application of these securitization rules should result in recording financial components that meet the definitions of assets and liabilities.

If the three conditions are met, a sale occurs. Otherwise, the transferor should record the transfer as a secured borrowing. If sale accounting is appropriate, a company must still consider assets obtained and liabilities incurred in the transaction. Illustration 8-21 (page 382) shows the rules of accounting for transfers of receivables. As it shows, if there is continuing involvement in a sale transaction, a company must record the assets obtained and liabilities incurred.

Illustration 8-21
Accounting for Transfers
of Receivables

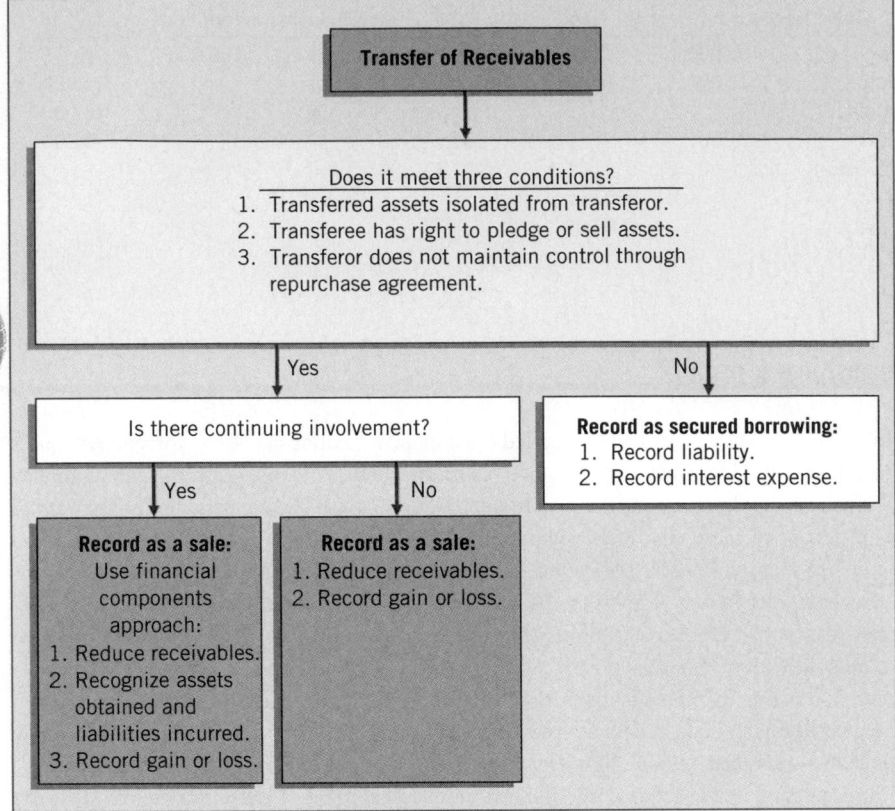

INTERNATIONAL INSIGHT

The IASB has a similar conceptual approach to the sale of receivables, although it provides more flexibility in implementation.

PRESENTATION AND ANALYSIS

Presentation of Receivables

OBJECTIVE 9

Describe how to report and analyze receivables.

WHAT'S THE PRINCIPLE?

Providing information that will help users assess a company's current liquidity and prospective cash flows is a primary objective of accounting.

The general rules in classifying receivables are:

1 Segregate the different types of receivables that a company possesses, if material.

2 Appropriately offset the valuation accounts against the proper receivable accounts.

3 Determine that receivables classified in the current assets section will be converted into cash within the year or the operating cycle, whichever is longer.

4 Disclose any loss contingencies that exist on the receivables.

5 Disclose any receivables designated or pledged as collateral.

6 Disclose all significant concentrations of credit risk arising from receivables.[23]

The assets sections of Colton Corporation's balance sheet in Illustration 8-22 show many of the disclosures required for receivables.

[23]Concentrations of credit risk exist when receivables have common characteristics that may affect their collection. These common characteristics might be companies in the same industry or same region of the country. For example, **Quantum Corporation** reported that sales of its disk drives to its top five customers (including **Hewlett-Packard**) represented nearly 40 percent of its revenues in 2003. Financial statements users want to know if a substantial amount of receivables from such sales are to customers facing uncertain economic conditions. No numerical guidelines are provided as to what is meant by a "concentration of credit risk."

Three items should be disclosed with an identified concentration: (1) information on the characteristic that determines the concentration, (2) the amount of loss that could occur upon nonperformance, and (3) information on any collateral related to the receivable. "Disclosures about Fair Value of Financial Instruments," *Statement of Financial Accounting Standards No. 107* (Norwalk, Conn.: FASB, 1991), par. 15.

Illustration 8-22
Disclosure of Receivables

Colton Corporation
Balance Sheet (partial)
As Of December 31, 2008

Current assets
Cash and cash equivalents ... $ 1,870,250
Accounts receivable (Note 2) ... $8,977,673
  Less: Allowance for doubtful accounts ... 500,226
  ... 8,477,447
Advances to subsidiaries due 9/30/09 ... 2,090,000
Notes receivable—trade (Note 2) ... 1,532,000
Federal income taxes refundable ... 146,704
Dividends and interest receivable ... 75,500
Other receivables and claims (including debit
  balances in accounts payable) ... 174,620 ... 12,496,271
  Total current assets ... 14,366,521
Noncurrent receivables
Notes receivable from officers and key employees ... 376,090
Claims receivable (litigation settlement to be collected
  over four years) ... 585,000

Note 2: Accounts and Notes Receivable. In November 2008, the Company arranged with a finance company to refinance a part of its indebtedness. The loan is evidenced by a 12% note payable. The note is payable on demand and is secured by substantially all the accounts receivable.

Additional Disclosures of Receivables

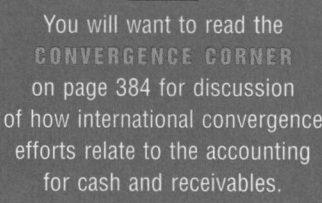

INTERNATIONAL INSIGHT

Holding receivables that it will pay in a foreign currency represents risk that the exchange rate may move against the company. This results in a decrease in the amount collected in terms of U.S. dollars. Companies engaged in cross-border transactions often "hedge" these receivables by buying contracts to exchange currencies at specified amounts at future dates.

Analysis of Receivables
Accounts Receivable Turnover Ratio

Analysts frequently compute financial ratios to evaluate the liquidity of a company's accounts receivable. To assess the liquidity of the receivables, they use the **accounts receivable turnover ratio**. This ratio measures the number of times, on average, a company collects receivables during the period. The ratio is computed by dividing net sales by average (net) accounts receivable outstanding during the year. Theoretically, the numerator should include only net credit sales, but this information is frequently unavailable. However, if the relative amounts of credit and cash sales remain fairly constant, the trend indicated by the ratio will still be valid. Barring significant seasonal factors, average receivables outstanding can be computed from the beginning and ending balances of net trade receivables.

To illustrate, **Circuit City** reported 2006 net sales of $11,598 million, its beginning and ending accounts receivable balances were $231 million and $221 million, respectively. Illustration 8-23 shows the computation of its accounts receivables turnover ratio.

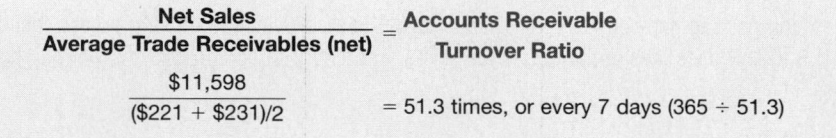

ILLUSTRATION 8-23
Computation of Accounts Receivable Turnover

This information[24] shows how successful the company is in collecting its outstanding receivables. If possible, an aging schedule should also be prepared to help determine how long receivables have been outstanding. A satisfactory accounts receivable turnover may have resulted because certain receivables were collected quickly though others have been outstanding for a relatively long period. An aging schedule would reveal such patterns.

You will want to read the CONVERGENCE CORNER on page 384 for discussion of how international convergence efforts relate to the accounting for cash and receivables.

[24]Often the accounts receivable turnover is transformed to **days to collect accounts receivable** or **days outstanding**—an average collection period. In this case, 51.3 is divided into 365 days, resulting in 7 days. Several figures other than 365 could be used. A common alternative is 360 days because it is divisible by 30 (days) and 12 (months). *Use 365 days in any homework computations.*

CONVERGENCE CORNER

Cash and Receivables

iGAAP and U.S. GAAP are very similar in accounting for cash and receivables. *AIS No. 1* ("Presentation of Financial Statements") is the only standard that discusses issues specifically related to cash. *IFRS No. 7* ("Financial Instruments: Disclosures") and *IAS No. 39* ("Financial Instruments: Recognition and Measurement") are the two international standards that address issues related to financial instruments and more specifically receivables.

RELEVANT FACTS

• The accounting and reporting related to cash is essentially the same under both iGAAP and U.S. GAAP. In addition, the definition used for cash equivalents is the same.

• The basic accounting and reporting issues related to recognition and measurement of receivables, such as the use of allowance accounts, how to record trade and sales discounts, use of percentage-of-sales and receivables methods, pledging, and factoring are essentially the same between iGAAP and U.S. GAAP.

• Although iGAAP implies that receivables with different characteristics should be reported separately, there is no standard that mandates this segregation. In addition, there is no specific standard related to pledging, assignment, or factoring.

• Like the FASB, the IASB has worked to implement fair value measurement for all financial instruments, but both Boards have faced bitter opposition from various factions. As a consequence, the Boards have adopted a piecemeal approach in which disclosure of fair value information in the notes is the first step. The second step is the *fair value option* which permits companies to record fair values in the financial statements. Both Boards have indicated that they believe all financial instruments should be recorded and reported at fair value.

• iGAAP and U.S. GAAP standards on the fair value option are similar but not identical. The international standard related to the fair value option is subject to certain qualifying criteria not in the U.S. standard. In addition, there is some difference in the financial instruments covered.

• iGAAP and U.S. GAAP differ in the criteria used to derecognize a receivable. iGAAP is a combination of an approach focused on risks and rewards and loss of control. U.S. GAAP uses loss of control as the primary criterion. In addition, iGAAP permits partial derecognition; U.S. GAAP does not.

ABOUT THE NUMBERS

In the accounting for loans and receivables, iGAAP permits the reversal of impairment losses, with the reversal limited to the asset's amortized cost before the impairment. To illustrate, Zirbel Company has a loan receivable with a carrying value of $10,000 at December 31, 2008. On January 2, 2009, the borrower declares bankruptcy, and Zirbel estimates that it will collect only one-half of the loan balance. Zirbel makes the following entry to record the impairment.

Impairment Loss	5,000	
Loan Receivable		5,000

On January 10, 2010, Zirbel learns that the customer has emerged from bankruptcy. Zirbel now estimates that all but $1,000 will be repaid on the loan. Under iGAAP, Zirbel records this reversal as follows.

Loan Receivable	4,000	
Recovery of Impairment Loss		4,000

Zirbel reports the recovery in 2010 income. Under U.S. GAAP, reversal of impairment is not permitted. Rather, the balance on the loan after the impairment becomes the new basis for the loan.

ON THE HORIZON

It appears likely that the question of recording fair values for financial instruments will continue to be an important issue to resolve as the Boards work toward convergence. Both the IASB and the FASB have indicated that they believe that financial statements would be more transparent and understandable if companies recorded and reported all financial instruments at fair value.

The fair value option for recording financial instruments such as receivables is an important step in moving closer to fair value recording. However, we hope that this is only an intermediate step and that the Boards continue to work toward the adoption of comprehensive fair value accounting for financial instruments.

ACCOUNTING, ANALYSIS, PRINCIPLES

The Flatiron Pub provides catering services to local businesses. The following information was available for The Flatiron for the years ended December 31, 2007 and 2008.

	December 31, 2007	December 31, 2008
Cash	$ 2,000	$ 1,610
Accounts receivable	46,000	63,000
Allowance for doubtful accounts	550	?
Other current assets	8,500	8,000
Current liabilities	37,000	44,600
Total credit sales	205,000	255,000
Collections on accounts receivable	190,000	228,000

(handwritten margin notes): AR 46 000 + 255000 − 228000 − 10 000 = 63 000; −110; Allowance 1600 | 550, x = 2625, 1575; Cash 5000 N/R 5000; Cash 9500 Due from Factor 200 Loss on Sale 700 A/R 10000 Recourse L 400

Flatiron management is preparing for a meeting with its bank concerning renewal of a loan and has collected the following information related to the above balances.

1 The cash reported at December 31, 2008, reflects the following items: cash on hand $1,500 and postage stamps $110. Other cash-related items include: checking account $4,000; and petty cash $75.

2 On November 30, The Flatiron agreed to accept a 6-month, $5,000 note bearing 12% interest, payable at maturity, from a major client in settlement of a $5,000 bill.

3 The Flatiron factors some accounts receivable at the end of the year. It transferred accounts totaling $10,000 to Final Factor, Inc. with recourse. Final Factor will receive the collections from Flatiron's customers and will retain 2% of the balances. Final Factor assesses The Flatiron a finance charge of 3% on this transfer. The fair value of the recourse obligation is $400.

4 The Flatiron charged off uncollectible accounts with balances of $1,600. On the basis of the latest available information, the 2008 provision for bad debts is estimated to be 2.5% of accounts receivable.

Accounting

a Based on the above transactions, determine the balance for (1) Accounts Receivable and (2) the Allowance for Doubtful Accounts at December 31, 2008.

b Prepare the current assets section of The Flatiron's balance sheet at December 31, 2008.

Analysis

c Compute the current ratio and the accounts receivable turnover ratio for December 31, 2008. Use these measures to analyze The Flatiron's liquidity. The accounts receivable turnover ratio in 2007 was 4.37.

d Discuss how the analysis in part **(c)** would be affected if The Flatiron had transferred the receivables in a secured borrowing transaction.

Principles

e What is the conceptual basis for recording bad debt expense based on the percentage-of-receivables at December 31, 2008?

Solution

Accounting

a (1) Accounts Receivable

Beginning balance	$46,000
Credit sales during 2008	255,000
Collections during 2008	(228,000)
Factored receivables	(10,000)
Ending balance	$63,000

(2) Allowance for Doubtful Accounts

Beginning balance	$550
Charge-offs	(1,600)
2008 bad debt expense	2,625*
Ending balance ($63,000 × 2.5%)	$1,575

*This is a plug figure to bring the allowance to the correct balance.

b Current assets section of balance sheet

Cash		$ 5,465*
Accounts receivable	$63,000	
Allowance for doubtful accounts	(1,575)	61,425
Interest receivable ($5,000 × 12%) × 1/12		50
Due from factor ($10,000 × 2%)		200
Note receivable		5,000
Postage stamps		110
Other current assets		8,000
Total current assets		$80,250

*	Cash as reported	$1,610
	Checking account	4,000
	Petty cash	75
	Postage stamps	(110)
	Reported cash	$5,465

Analysis

c

	2007	2008
Current ratio	1.51	1.80
	($55,950 ÷ $37,000)	($80,250 ÷ $44,600)
Accounts receivable turnover ratio	4.37	4.77
		$255,000 ÷ [($45,450 + $61,425) ÷ 2]

Both ratios indicate that The Flatiron's liquidity has improved.

d With a secured borrowing, the receivables would stay on The Flatiron's books and a note payable would be recorded. This would reduce both the current ratio and accounts receivable turnover ratio.

Principles

e The matching principle requires that bad debt expense be recorded in the period of the sale. Otherwise, income will be overstated by the amount of bad debt expense. In addition, reporting the receivables net of the allowance provides a more representationally faithful reporting (at net realizable value) of this asset.

Key Terms

Summary of Learning Objectives

1 Identify items considered cash. To be reported as "cash," an asset must be readily available for the payment of current obligations and free from contractual restrictions that limit its use in satisfying debts. Cash consists of coin, currency, and available funds on deposit at the bank. Negotiable instruments such as money orders, certified checks, cashier's checks, personal checks, and bank drafts are also viewed as cash. Savings accounts are usually classified as cash.

2 Indicate how to report cash and related items. Companies report cash as a current asset in the balance sheet. The reporting of other related items are: (1) *Restricted cash:* The SEC recommends that companies state separately legally restricted deposits held as compensating balances against short-term borrowing among the "Cash and cash equivalent items" in current assets. Restricted deposits held against long-term borrowing arrangements should be separately classified as noncurrent assets in either the investments or other assets sections. (2) *Bank overdrafts:* Companies should report overdrafts in the current liabilities section and usually add them to the amount reported as accounts payable. If material, these items should be separately disclosed either on the face of the balance sheet or in the related notes. (3) *Cash equivalents:* Companies often report this item together with cash as "Cash and cash equivalents."

3 Define receivables and identify the different types of receivables. Receivables are claims held against customers and others for money, goods, or services. The receivables are classified into three types: (1) current or noncurrent, (2) trade or nontrade, (3) accounts receivable or notes receivable.

4 Explain accounting issues related to recognition of accounts receivable. Two issues that may complicate the measurement of accounts receivable are: (1) The availability of discounts (trade and cash discounts), and (2) the length of time between the sale and the payment due dates (the interest element).

Ideally, companies should measure receivables in terms of their present value—that is, the discounted value of the cash to be received in the future. The profession specifically excludes from the present-value considerations receivables arising from normal business transactions that are due in customary trade terms within approximately one year.

5 Explain accounting issues related to valuation of accounts receivable. Companies value and report short-term receivables at net realizable value—the net amount expected to be received in cash, which is not necessarily the amount legally receivable. Determining net realizable value requires estimating uncollectible receivables.

6 Explain accounting issues related to recognition of notes receivable. Companies record short-term notes at face value and long-term notes receivable at the present value of the cash they expect to collect. When the interest stated on an interest-bearing note equals the effective (market) rate of interest, the note sells at face value. When the stated rate differs from the effective rate, a company records either a discount or premium.

7 Explain accounting issues related to valuation of notes receivable. Like accounts receivable, companies record and report short-term notes receivable at their net realizable value. The same is also true of long-term receivables. Special issues relate to uncollectibles and impairments.

8   Explain accounting issues related to disposition of accounts and notes receivable.   To accelerate the receipt of cash from receivables, the owner may transfer the receivables to another company for cash in one of two ways: (1) *Secured borrowing:* A creditor often requires that the debtor designate or pledge receivables as security for the loan. (2) *Sales (factoring) of receivables:* Factors are finance companies or banks that buy receivables from businesses and then collect the remittances directly from the customers. In many cases, transferors may have some continuing involvement with the receivable sold. Companies use a financial components approach to record this type of transaction.

9   Describe how to report and analyze receivables.   Companies should report receivables with appropriate offset of valuation accounts against receivables, classify receivables as current or noncurrent, identify pledged or designated receivables, and identify concentrations of risks arising from receivables. Analysts assess receivables based on accounts receivable turnover and the days outstanding.

BEHIND THE NUMBERS APPENDIX 8A

CASH CONTROLS

As we indicated in the chapter, cash creates many management and control problems. In this appendix, we discuss some of the basic control issues related to cash.

Using Bank Accounts

OBJECTIVE 10

Explain common techniques employed to control cash.

To obtain desired control objectives, a company can vary the number and location of banks and the types of bank accounts. For large companies operating in multiple locations, the location of bank accounts can be important. Establishing collection accounts in strategic locations can accelerate the flow of cash into the company by shortening the time between a customer's mailing of a payment and the company's use of the cash. Multiple collection centers generally reduce the size of a company's **collection float**. This is the difference between the amount on deposit according to the company's records and the amount of collected cash according to the bank record.

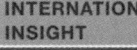

INTERNATIONAL INSIGHT

Multinational corporations often have cash accounts in more than one currency. For financial statement purposes, these corporations typically translate these currencies into U.S. dollars, using the exchange rate in effect at the balance sheet date.

Large, multilocation companies frequently use **lockbox accounts** to collect in cities with heavy customer billing. The company rents a local post office box and authorizes a local bank to pick up the remittances mailed to that box number. The bank empties the box at least once a day and immediately credits the company's account for collections. The greatest advantage of a lockbox is that it accelerates the availability of collected cash. Generally, in a lockbox arrangement the bank microfilms the checks for record purposes and provides the company with a deposit slip, a list of collections, and any customer correspondence. Thus, a lockbox system improves the control over cash and accelerates collection of cash. If the income generated from accelerating the receipt of funds exceeds the cost of the lockbox system, then it is a worthwhile undertaking.

The **general checking account** is the principal bank account in most companies and frequently the only bank account in small businesses. A company deposits in and disburses cash from this account. A company cycles all transactions through it. For example, a company deposits from and disburses to all other bank accounts through the general checking account.

Companies use **imprest bank accounts** to make a specific amount of cash available for a limited purpose. The account acts as a clearing account for a large volume of checks or for a specific type of check. To clear a specific and intended amount through the imprest account, a company transfers that amount from the general checking account or other source. Companies often use imprest bank accounts for disbursing payroll checks, dividends, commissions, bonuses, confidential expenses (e.g., officers' salaries), and travel expenses.

The Imprest Petty Cash System

Almost every company finds it necessary to pay small amounts for miscellaneous expenses such as taxi fares, minor office supplies, and employee's lunches. Disbursements by check for such items is often impractical, yet some control over them is important. A simple method of obtaining reasonable control, while adhering to the rule of disbursement by check, is the **imprest system for petty cash** disbursements. This is how the system works:

1   The company designates a petty cash custodian, and gives the custodian a small amount of currency from which to make payments. It records transfer of funds to petty cash as:

Petty Cash	300	
Cash		300

2   The petty cash custodian obtains signed receipts from each individual to whom he or she pays cash, attaching evidence of the disbursement to the petty cash receipt. Petty cash transactions are not recorded until the fund is reimbursed; someone other than the petty cash custodian records those entries.

3   When the supply of cash runs low, the custodian presents to the general cashier a request for reimbursement supported by the petty cash receipts and other disbursement evidence. The custodian receives a company check to replenish the fund. At this point, the company records transactions based on petty cash receipts.

Office Supplies Expense	42	
Postage Expense	53	
Entertainment Expense	76	
Cash Over and Short	2	
Cash		173

4   If the company decides that the amount of cash in the petty cash fund is excessive, it lowers the fund balance as follows.

Cash	50	
Petty Cash		50

A company makes entries to the Petty Cash account only to increase or decrease the size of the fund.

A company uses a **Cash Over and Short** account when the petty cash fund fails to prove out. That is, an error occurs such as incorrect change, overpayment of expense, or lost receipt. If cash proves out **short** (i.e., the sum of the receipts and cash in the fund is less than the imprest amount), the company debits the shortage to the Cash Over and Short account. If cash proves out **over**, it credits the overage to Cash Over and Short. The company closes Cash Over and Short only at the end of the year. It generally shows Cash Over and Short on the income statement as an "Other expense or revenue."

There are usually expense items in the fund except immediately after reimbursement. Therefore, to maintain accurate financial statements, a company must reimburse the funds at the end of each accounting period and also when nearly depleted.

Under the imprest system the petty cash custodian is responsible at all times for the amount of the fund on hand either as cash or in the form of signed receipts. These receipts provide the evidence required by the disbursing officer to issue a reimbursement check. Further, a company follows two additional procedures to obtain more complete control over the petty cash fund:

1   A superior of the petty cash custodian makes surprise counts of the fund from time to time to determine that a satisfactory accounting of the fund has occurred.

2   The company cancels or mutilates petty cash receipts after they have been submitted for reimbursement, so that they cannot be used to secure a second reimbursement.

Physical Protection of Cash Balances

Not only must a company safeguard cash receipts and cash disbursements through internal control measures, but it must also protect the cash on hand and in banks. Because receipts become cash on hand and disbursements are made from cash in banks, adequate control of receipts and disbursements is part of the protection of cash balances, along with certain other procedures.

Physical protection of cash is so elementary a necessity that it requires little discussion. A company should make every effort to minimize the cash on hand in the office. It should only have on hand a petty cash fund, the current day's receipts, and perhaps funds for making change. Insofar as possible, it should keep these funds in a vault, safe, or locked cash drawer. The company should transmit intact each day's receipts to the bank as soon as practicable. Accurately stating the amount of available cash both in internal management reports and in external financial statements is also extremely important.

Every company has a record of cash received, disbursed, and the balance. Because of the many cash transactions, however, errors or omissions may occur in keeping this record. Therefore, a company must periodically prove the balance shown in the general ledger. It can count cash actually present in the office—petty cash, change funds, and undeposited receipts—for comparison with the company records. For cash on deposit, a company prepares a bank reconciliation—a reconciliation of the company's record and the bank's record of the company's cash.

Reconciliation of Bank Balances

At the end of each calendar month the bank supplies each customer with a **bank statement** (a copy of the bank's account with the customer) together with the customer's checks that the bank paid during the month.[1] If neither the bank nor the customer made any errors, if all deposits made and all checks drawn by the customer reached the bank within the same month, and if no unusual transactions occurred that affected either the company's or the bank's record of cash, the balance of cash reported by the bank to the customer equals that shown in the customer's own records. This condition seldom occurs for one or more of the reconciling items presented below.

RECONCILING ITEMS

1 DEPOSITS IN TRANSIT. End-of-month deposits of cash recorded on the depositor's books in one month are received and recorded by the bank in the following month.

2 OUTSTANDING CHECKS. Checks written by the depositor are recorded when written but may not be recorded by (may not "clear") the bank until the next month.

3 BANK CHARGES. Charges recorded by the bank against the depositor's balance for such items as bank services, printing checks, **not-sufficient-funds (NSF) checks**, and safe-deposit box rentals. The depositor may not be aware of these charges until the receipt of the bank statement.

4 BANK CREDITS. Collections or deposits by the bank for the benefit of the depositor that may be unknown to the depositor until receipt of the bank statement. Examples are note collection for the depositor and interest earned on interest-bearing checking accounts.

5 BANK OR DEPOSITOR ERRORS. Errors on either the part of the bank or the part of the depositor cause the bank balance to disagree with the depositor's book balance.

---

[1]As we mentioned in the chapter, paper checks continue to be used as a means of payment. However, ready availability of desktop publishing software and hardware has created new opportunities for check fraud in the form of duplicate, altered, and forged checks. At the same time, new fraud-fighting technologies, such as ultraviolet imaging, high-capacity barcodes, and biometrics, are being developed. These technologies convert paper documents into electronically processed document files, thereby reducing the risk of fraud.

A company expects differences between its record of cash and the bank's record. Therefore, it must reconcile the two to determine the nature of the differences between the two amounts. A **bank reconciliation** is a schedule explaining any differences between the bank's and the company's records of cash. If the difference results only from transactions not yet recorded by the bank, the company's record of cash is considered correct. But, if some part of the difference arises from other items, either the bank or the company must adjust its records.

A company may prepare two forms of a bank reconciliation. One form reconciles from the bank statement balance to the book balance or vice versa. The other form reconciles both the bank balance and the book balance to a correct cash balance. Most companies use this latter form. Illustration 8A-1 shows a sample of that form and its common reconciling items.

Balance per bank statement (end of period)		$$$
Add: Deposits in transit	$$	
Undeposited receipts (cash on hand)	$$	
Bank errors that understate the bank statement balance	$$	$$
		$$$
Deduct: Outstanding checks	$$	
Bank errors that overstate the bank statement balance	$$	$$
Correct cash balance		$$$
Balance per depositor's books		$$$
Add: Bank credits and collections not yet recorded in the books	$$	
Book errors that understate the book balance	$$	$$
		$$$
Deduct: Bank charges not yet recorded in the books	$$	
Book errors that overstate the book balance	$$	$$
Correct cash balance		$$$

Illustration 8A-1
Bank Reconciliation Form and Content

This form of reconciliation consists of two sections: (1) "Balance per bank statement" and (2) "Balance per depositor's books." Both sections end with the same "Correct cash balance." The correct cash balance is the amount to which the books must be adjusted and is the amount reported on the balance sheet. **Companies prepare adjusting journal entries for all the addition and deduction items appearing in the "Balance per depositor's books" section.** Companies should immediately call to the bank's attention any errors attributable to it.

To illustrate, Nugget Mining Company's books show a cash balance at the Denver National Bank on November 30, 2008, of $20,502. The bank statement covering the month of November shows an ending balance of $22,190. An examination of Nugget's accounting records and November bank statement identified the following reconciling items.

1 A deposit of $3,680 that Nugget mailed November 30 does not appear on the bank statement.

2 Checks written in November but not charged to the November bank statement are:

Check #7327	$ 150
#7348	4,820
#7349	31

3 Nugget has not yet recorded the $600 of interest collected by the bank November 20 on Sequoia Co. bonds held by the bank for Nugget.

4 Bank service charges of $18 are not yet recorded on Nugget's books.

5 The bank returned one of Nugget's customer's checks for $220 with the bank statement, marked "NSF." The bank treated this bad check as a disbursement.

6 Nugget discovered that it incorrectly recorded check #7322, written in November for $131 in payment of an account payable, as $311.

7 A check for Nugent Oil Co. in the amount of $175 that the bank incorrectly charged to Nugget accompanied the statement.

Nugget reconciled the bank and book balances to the correct cash balance of $21,044 as shown in Illustration 8A-2.

Illustration 8A-2
Sample Bank
Reconciliation

Nugget Mining Company Bank Reconciliation Denver National Bank, November 30, 2008			
Balance per bank statement (end of period)			$22,190
Add: Deposit in transit	(1)	$3,680	
Bank error—incorrect check charged to account by bank	(7)	175	3,855
			26,045
Deduct: Outstanding checks	(2)		5,001
Correct cash balance			$21,044
Balance per books			$20,502
Add: Interest collected by the bank	(3)	$ 600	
Error in recording check #7322	(6)	180	780
			21,282
Deduct: Bank service charges	(4)	18	
NSF check returned	(5)	220	238
Correct cash balance			$21,044

The journal entries required to adjust and correct Nugget's books in early December 2008 are taken from the items in the "Balance per books" section and are as follows.

Cash	600	
Interest Revenue		600
(To record interest on Sequoia Co. bonds, collected by bank)		
Cash	180	
Accounts Payable		180
(To correct error in recording amount of check #7322)		
Office Expense—Bank Charges	18	
Cash		18
(To record bank service charges for November)		
Accounts Receivable	220	
Cash		220
(To record customer's check returned NSF)		

**Expanded Discussion of a
Four-Column Bank
Reconciliation**

After posting the entries, Nugget's cash account will have a balance of $21,044. Nugget should return the Nugent Oil Co. check to Denver National Bank, informing the bank of the error.

Key Terms

bank reconciliation, 391
imprest system for petty cash, 389

not-sufficient-funds (NSF) checks, 390

Summary of Learning Objective for Appendix 8A

10 Explain common techniques employed to control cash.
The common techniques employed to control cash are:
(1) *Using bank accounts:* A company can vary the number and location of banks and the types of accounts to obtain desired control objectives. (2) *The imprest petty cash system:* It may be impractical to require small amounts of various expenses be paid by check, yet some control over them is important. (3) *Physical*

protection of cash balances: Adequate control of receipts and disbursements is a part of the protection of cash balances. Every effort should be made to minimize the cash on hand in the office. (4) *Reconciliation of bank balances:* Cash on deposit is not available for count and is proved by preparing a bank reconciliation.

REVIEW EXERCISE

The trial balance before adjustment for Slamar Company shows the following balances.

	Debit	Credit
Net sales		$860,000
Accounts receivable	$338,000	
Allowance for doubtful accounts	4,240	

Instructions

a Using the data above, give the journal entries required to record each of the following cases. (Each situation is independent.)

1 To obtain additional cash, Slamar factors without recourse $50,000 of accounts receivable with Pierce Finance. The finance charge is 11% of the amount factored.

2 To obtain a one-year loan of $75,000, Slamar assigns $80,000 of specific receivable accounts to Milo Financial. The finance charge is 9% of the loan; the cash is received and the accounts turned over to Milo Financial.

3 The company wants to maintain the Allowance for Doubtful Accounts at 6% of gross accounts receivable.

4 The company wishes to increase the allowance account by 2% of net sales.

b Discuss how analysis based on the current ratio and the accounts receivable turnover ratio would be affected if Slamar had transferred the receivables in situation 1 using a secured borrowing.

Solution

a	**1**	Cash	44,500	
		Loss on Sale of Receivables ($50,000 × 11%)	5,500	
		Accounts Receivable		50,000
	2	Cash	68,250	
		Finance Charge ($75,000 × 9%)	6,750	
		Notes Payable		75,000

3	Bad Debt Expense	24,520	
	Allowance for Doubtful Accounts		
	[($338,000 × 6%) + $4,240]		24,520
4	Bad Debt Expense	17,200	
	Allowance for Doubtful Accounts ($860,000 × 2%)		17,200

b With a secured borrowing, the receivables would stay on Slamar's books, and Slamar would record a note payable. This would reduce the current ratio and accounts receivable turnover ratio.

Questions

Note: All **asterisked** assignment materials relate to material covered in appendix to the chapter.

1 What may be included under the heading of "cash"?

2 In what accounts should the following items be classified?

(a) Coins and currency.

(b) U.S. Treasury (government) bonds.

(c) Certificate of deposit.

(d) Cash in a bank that is in receivership.

(e) NSF check (returned with bank statement).

(f) Deposit in foreign bank (exchangeability limited).

(g) Postdated checks.

(h) Cash to be used for retirement of long-term bonds.

(i) Deposits in transit.

(j) 100 shares of **Dell** stock (intention is to sell in one year or less).

(k) Savings and checking accounts.

(l) Petty cash.

(m) Stamps.

(n) Travel advances.

3 Define a "compensating balance." How should a compensating balance be reported?

4 Michael Tilsen Thomas Inc. reported in a recent annual report "Restricted cash for debt redemption." What section of the balance sheet would report this item?

5 What are the reasons that a company gives trade discounts? Why are trade discounts not recorded in the accounts like cash discounts?

6 What are two methods of recording accounts receivable transactions when a cash discount situation is involved? Which is more theoretically correct? Which is used in practice more of the time? Why?

7 What are the basic problems that occur in the valuation of accounts receivable?

8 What is the theoretical justification of the allowance method as contrasted with the direct write-off method of accounting for bad debts?

9 Indicate how well the percentage-of-sales method and the aging method accomplish the objectives of the allowance method of accounting for bad debts.

10 Of what merit is the contention that the allowance method lacks the objectivity of the direct write-off method? Discuss in terms of accounting's measurement function.

11 Explain how the accounting for bad debts can be used for earnings management.

12 Because of calamitous earthquake losses, Kishwaukee Company, one of your client's oldest and largest customers, suddenly and unexpectedly became bankrupt. Approximately 30% of your client's total sales have been made to Kishwaukee Company during each of the past several years. The amount due from Kishwaukee Company—none of which is collectible—equals 22% of total accounts receivable, an amount that is considerably in excess of what was determined to be an adequate provision for doubtful accounts at the close of the preceding year. How would your client record the write-off of the Kishwaukee Company receivable if it is using the allowance method of accounting for bad debts? Justify your suggested treatment.

13 What is the normal procedure for handling the collection of accounts receivable previously written off using the direct write-off method? The allowance method?

14 On January 1, 2008, John Singer Co. sells property for which it had paid $690,000 to Sargent Company, receiving in return Sargent's zero-interest-bearing note for $1,000,000 payable in 5 years. What entry would John Singer make to record the sale, assuming that John Singer frequently sells similar items of property for a cash sales price of $620,000?

15 What is "imputed interest"? In what situations is it necessary to impute an interest rate for notes receivable? What are the considerations in imputing an appropriate interest rate?

16 What is the fair value option? Where do companies that elect the fair value option report unrealized gains and losses?

17 Indicate three reasons why a company might sell its receivables to another company.

18 When is the financial components approach to recording the transfers of receivables used? When should a transfer of receivables be recorded as a sale?

19 Hale Hardware is planning to factor some of its receivables. The cash received will be used to pay for inventory purchases. The factor has indicated that it will require "recourse" on the sold receivables. Explain to the controller of Hale Hardware what "recourse" is and how the recourse will be reflected in Hale's financial statements after the sale of the receivables.

20 Outkast Outfitters Company includes in its trial balance for December 31 an item for Accounts Receivable $769,000. This balance consists of the following items:

Due from regular customers	$523,000
Refund receivable on prior year's income taxes (an established claim)	15,500
Travel advance to employees	22,000
Loan to wholly owned subsidiary	45,500
Advances to creditors for goods ordered	61,000
Accounts receivable assigned as security for loans payable	75,000
Notes receivable past due plus interest on these notes	27,000
Total	$769,000

Illustrate how these items should be shown in the balance sheet as of December 31.

21 What is the accounts receivable turnover ratio, and what type of information does it provide?

22 You are evaluating Hawthorn Downs Racetrack for a potential loan. An examination of the notes to the financial statements indicates restricted cash at year-end amounts to $100,000. Explain how you would use this information in evaluating Hawthorn's liquidity.

*23 Distinguish among the following: (1) a general checking account, (2) an imprest bank account, and (3) a lockbox account.

Brief Exercises

BE8-1 Stowe Enterprises owns the following assets at December 31, 2008. **(LO 1)**

Cash in bank—savings account	63,000	Checking account balance	17,000
Cash on hand	9,300	Postdated checks	750
Cash refund due from IRS	31,400	Certificates of deposit (180-day)	90,000

What amount should be reported as cash?

BE8-2 Montoya Co. uses the gross method to record sales made on credit. On June 1, 2008, it made sales of $40,000 with terms 3/15, n/45. On June 12, 2008, Montoya received full payment for the June 1 sale. Prepare the required journal entries for Montoya Co. **(LO 4)**

BE8-3 Use the information from BE8-2, assuming Montoya Co. uses the net method to account for cash discounts. Prepare the required journal entries for Montoya Co. **(LO 4)**

BE8-4 Battle Tank, Inc. had net sales in 2008 of $1,200,000. At December 31, 2008, before adjusting entries, the balances in selected accounts were: Accounts Receivable $250,000 debit, and Allowance for Doubtful Accounts $2,100 credit. If Battle Tank estimates that 2% of its net sales will prove to be uncollectible, prepare the December 31, 2008, journal entry to record bad debt expense. **(LO 5)**

BE8-5 Use the information presented in BE8-4 for Battle Tank, Inc. **(LO 5)**

(a) Instead of estimating the uncollectibles at 2% of net sales, assume that 10% of accounts receivable will prove to be uncollectible. Prepare the entry to record bad debts expense.

(b) Instead of estimating uncollectibles at 2% of net sales, assume Battle Tank prepares an aging schedule that estimates total uncollectible accounts at $24,600. Prepare the entry to record bad debts expense.

BE8-6 Addams Family Importers sold goods to Acme Decorators for $20,000 on November 1, 2008, accepting Acme's $20,000, 6-month, 6% note. Prepare Addams's November 1 entry, December 31 annual adjusting entry, and May 1 entry for the collection of the note and interest. **(LO 6)**

BE8-7 Aero Acrobats lent $15,944 to Afterburner, Inc., accepting Afterburner's 2-year, $20,000, zero-interest-bearing note. The implied interest rate is 12%. Prepare Aero's journal entries for the initial transaction, recognition of interest each year, and the collection of $20,000 at maturity. **(LO 6)**

(LO 8)   **BE8-8**   On October 1, 2008, Akira, Inc. assigns $1,000,000 of its accounts receivable to Alisia National Bank as collateral for a $700,000 note. The bank assesses a finance charge of 2% of the receivables assigned and interest on the note of 9%. Prepare the October 1 journal entries for both Akira and Alisia.

(LO 8)   **BE8-9**   CRC Incorporated factored $100,000 of accounts receivable with Fredrick Factors Inc. on a without recourse basis. Fredrick assesses a 2% finance charge of the amount of accounts receivable and retains an amount equal to 6% of accounts receivable for possible adjustments. Prepare the journal entry for CRC Incorporated and Fredrick Factors to record the factoring of the accounts receivable to Fredrick.

(LO 8)   **BE8-10**   Use the information in BE8-9 for CRC. Assume that the receivables are sold with recourse. Prepare the journal entry for CRC to record the sale, assuming that the recourse obligation has a fair value of $7,500.

(LO 8)   **BE8-11**   Keyser Woodcrafters sells $200,000 of receivables to Commercial Factors, Inc. on a with recourse basis. Commercial assesses a finance charge of 5% and retains an amount equal to 4% of accounts receivable. Keyser estimates the fair value of the recourse obligation to be $8,000. Prepare the journal entry for Keyser to record the sale.

(LO 8)   **BE8-12**   Use the information presented in BE8-11 for Keyser Woodcrafters but assume that the recourse obligation has a fair value of $4,000, instead of $8,000. Prepare the journal entry and discuss the effects of this change in the value of the recourse obligation on Keyser's financial statements.

(LO 9)   **BE8-13**   The financial statements of **General Mills, Inc.** report net sales of $5,416,000,000. Accounts receivable are $277,300,000 at the beginning of the year and $337,800,000 at the end of the year. Compute General Mills's accounts receivable turnover ratio and the average collection period for accounts receivable in days.

(LO 10)   ***BE8-14**   Genesis Company designated Alex Kidd as petty cash custodian and established a petty cash fund of $200. The fund is reimbursed when the cash in the fund is at $17. Petty cash receipts indicate funds were disbursed for office supplies $94 and miscellaneous expenses $87. Prepare journal entries for the establishment of the fund and the reimbursement.

(LO 10)   ***BE8-15**   Jaguar Corporation is preparing a bank reconciliation and has identified the following potential reconciling items. For each item, indicate if it is (1) added to balance per bank statement, (2) deducted from balance per bank statement, (3) added to balance per books, or (4) deducted from balance per books.

(a) Deposit in transit $5,500.   (d) Outstanding checks $7,422.
(b) Interest credited to Jaguar's account $31.   (e) NSF check returned $377.
(c) Bank service charges $25.

(LO 10)   ***BE8-16**   Use the information presented in BE8-15 for Jaguar Corporation. Prepare any entries necessary to make Jaguar's accounting records correct and complete.

Exercises

(LO 1)   **E8-1**   **(Determining Cash Balance)**   The controller for Clint Eastwood Co. is attempting to determine the amount of cash to be reported on its December 31, 2008, balance sheet. The following information is provided.

1. Commercial savings account of $600,000 and a commercial checking account balance of $900,000 are held at First National Bank of Yojimbo.

2. Money market fund account held at Volonte Co. (a mutual fund organization) permits Eastwood to write checks on this balance, $5,000,000.

3. Travel advances of $180,000 for executive travel for the first quarter of next year (employee to reimburse through salary reduction).

4. A separate cash fund in the amount of $1,500,000 is restricted for the retirement of long-term debt.

5. Petty cash fund of $1,000.

6. An I.O.U. from Marianne Koch, a company customer, in the amount of $190,000.

7. A bank overdraft of $110,000 has occurred at one of the banks the company uses to deposit its cash receipts. At the present time, the company has no deposits at this bank.

8. The company has two certificates of deposit, each totaling $500,000. These CDs have a maturity of 120 days.

9. Eastwood has received a check that is dated January 12, 2009, in the amount of $125,000.

10. Eastwood has agreed to maintain a cash balance of $500,000 at all times at First National Bank of Yojimbo to ensure future credit availability.

11. Eastwood has purchased $2,100,000 of commercial paper of Sergio Leone Co. which is due in 60 days.

12. Currency and coin on hand amounted to $7,700.

Instructions

(a) Compute the amount of cash to be reported on Eastwood Co.'s balance sheet at December 31, 2008.

(b) Indicate the proper reporting for items that are not reported as cash on the December 31, 2008, balance sheet.

E8-2   (Determine Cash Balance)   Presented below are a number of independent situations.   **(LO 1)**

Instructions

For each individual situation, determine the amount that should be reported as cash. If the item(s) is not reported as cash, explain the rationale.

1. Checking account balance $925,000; certificate of deposit $1,400,000; cash advance to subsidiary of $980,000; utility deposit paid to gas company $180.

2. Checking account balance $600,000; an overdraft in special checking account at same bank as normal checking account of $17,000; cash held in a bond sinking fund $200,000; petty cash fund $300; coins and currency on hand $1,350.

3. Checking account balance $590,000; postdated check from customer $11,000; cash restricted due to maintaining compensating balance requirement of $100,000; certified check from customer $9,800; postage stamps on hand $620.

4. Checking account balance at bank $37,000; money market balance at mutual fund (has checking privileges) $48,000; NSF check received from customer $800.

5. Checking account balance $700,000; cash restricted for future plant expansion $500,000; short-term Treasury bills $180,000; cash advance received from customer $900 (not included in checking account balance); cash advance of $7,000 to company executive, payable on demand; refundable deposit of $26,000 paid to federal government to guarantee performance on construction contract.

E8-3   (Financial Statement Presentation of Receivables)   Jim Carrie Company shows a balance of $181,140   **(LO 3, 4)**
in the Accounts Receivable account on December 31, 2008. The balance consists of the following.

Installment accounts due in 2009	$23,000
Installment accounts due after 2009	34,000
Overpayments to creditors	2,640
Due from regular customers, of which $40,000 represents	
accounts pledged as security for a bank loan	79,000
Advances to employees	1,500
Advance to subsidiary company (made in 2003)	81,000

Instructions

Illustrate how the information above should be shown on the balance sheet of Jim Carrie Company on December 31, 2008.

E8-4   (Determine Ending Accounts Receivable)   Your accounts receivable clerk, Mitra Adams, to whom you   **(LO 3, 4)**
pay a salary of $1,500 per month, has just purchased a new BMW. You decided to test the accuracy of the accounts receivable balance of $82,000 as shown in the ledger.

The following information is available for your *first year* in business.

(1) Collections from customers	$198,000
(2) Merchandise purchased	320,000
(3) Ending merchandise inventory	90,000
(4) Goods are marked to sell at 40% above cost	

Instructions

Compute an estimate of the ending balance of accounts receivable from customers that should appear in the ledger and any apparent shortages. Assume that all sales are made on account.

(LO 4) **E8-5 (Record Sales Gross and Net)** On June 3, Arnold Company sold to Chester Company merchandise having a sale price of $3,000 with terms of 2/10, n/60, f.o.b. shipping point. An invoice totaling $90, terms n/30, was received by Chester on June 8 from John Booth Transport Service for the freight cost. On June 12, the company received a check for the balance due from Chester Company.

Instructions

(a) Prepare journal entries on the Arnold Company books to record all the events noted above under each of the following bases.
  (1) Sales and receivables are entered at gross selling price.
  (2) Sales and receivables are entered at net of cash discounts.

(b) Prepare the journal entry under basis 2, assuming that Chester Company did not remit payment until July 29.

(LO 4) **E8-6 (Recording Sales Transactions)** Presented below is information from Perez Computers Incorporated.

July 1 Sold $20,000 of computers to Robertson Company with terms 3/15, n/60. Perez uses the gross method to record cash discounts.
  10 Perez received payment from Robertson for the full amount owed from the July transactions.
  17 Sold $200,000 in computers and peripherals to The Clark Store with terms of 2/10, n/30.
  30 The Clark Store paid Perez for its purchase of July 17.

Instructions

Prepare the necessary journal entries for Perez Computers.

(LO 5) **E8-7 (Recording Bad Debts)** Duncan Company reports the following financial information before adjustments.

	Dr.	Cr.
Accounts Receivable	$100,000	
Allowance for Doubtful Accounts		$ 2,000
Sales (all on credit)		900,000
Sales Returns and Allowances	50,000	

Instructions

Prepare the journal entry to record Bad Debt Expense assuming Duncan Company estimates bad debts at (a) 1% of net sales and (b) 5% of accounts receivable.

(LO 5) **E8-8 (Recording Bad Debts)** At the end of 2007 Aramis Company has accounts receivable of $800,000 and an allowance for doubtful accounts of $40,000. On January 16, 2008, Aramis Company determined that its receivable from Ramirez Company of $6,000 will not be collected, and management authorized its write-off.

Instructions

(a) Prepare the journal entry for Aramis Company to write off the Ramirez receivable.

(b) What is the net realizable value of Aramis Company's accounts receivable before the write-off of the Ramirez receivable?

(c) What is the net realizable value of Aramis Company's accounts receivable after the write-off of the Ramirez receivable?

(LO 5) **E8-9 (Computing Bad Debts and Preparing Journal Entries)** The trial balance before adjustment of Reba McIntyre Inc. shows the following balances.

	Dr.	Cr.
Accounts Receivable	$90,000	
Allowance for Doubtful Accounts	1,750	
Sales (all on credit)		$680,000

Instructions

Prepare the entry for estimated bad debts assuming that the allowance is to provide for doubtful accounts on the basis of (a) 4% of gross accounts receivable and (b) 1% of net sales.

(LO 5) **E8-10 (Bad-Debt Reporting)** The chief accountant for Emily Dickinson Corporation provides you with the following (shown on page 399) list of accounts receivable written off in the current year.

Date	Customer	Amount
March 31	E. L. Masters Company	$7,800
June 30	Stephen Crane Associates	6,700
September 30	Amy Lowell's Dress Shop	7,000
December 31	R. Frost, Inc.	9,830

Emily Dickinson Corporation follows the policy of debiting Bad Debt Expense as accounts are written off. The chief accountant maintains that this procedure is appropriate for financial statement purposes because the Internal Revenue Service will not accept other methods for recognizing bad debts.

All of Emily Dickinson Corporation's sales are on a 30-day credit basis. Sales for the current year total $2,200,000, and research has determined that bad debt losses approximate 2% of sales.

Instructions

(a) Do you agree or disagree with Dickinson's policy concerning recognition of bad debt expense? Why or why not?

(b) By what amount would net income differ if bad debt expense was computed using the percentage-of-sales approach? 12 670

E8-11 (Bad Debts—Aging) Danica Patrick, Inc. includes the following account among its trade receivables. **(LO 5)**

Hopkins Co.

1/1	Balance forward	700	1/28	Cash (#1710)	1,100
1/20	Invoice #1710	1,100	4/2	Cash (#2116)	1,350
3/14	Invoice #2116	1,350	4/10	Cash (1/1 Balance)	155
4/12	Invoice #2412	1,710	4/30	Cash (#2412)	1,000
9/5	Invoice #3614	490	9/20	Cash (#3614 and	
10/17	Invoice #4912	860		part of #2412)	790
11/18	Invoice #5681	2,000	10/31	Cash (#4912)	860
12/20	Invoice #6347	800	12/1	Cash (#5681)	1,250
			12/29	Cash (#6347)	800

Instructions

Age the balance and specify any items that apparently require particular attention at year-end.

E8-12 (Journalizing Various Receivable Transactions) Presented below is information related to James Garfield Corp. **(LO 4, 5, 8)**

July	1	James Garfield Corp. sold to Warren Harding Co. merchandise having a sales price of $8,000 with terms 2/10, net/60. Garfield records its sales and receivables net.
	5	Accounts receivable of $9,000 (gross) are factored with Andrew Jackson Credit Corp. without recourse at a financing charge of 9%. Cash is received for the proceeds; collections are handled by the finance company. (These accounts were all past the discount period.)
	9	Specific accounts receivable of $9,000 (gross) are pledged to Alf Landon Credit Corp. as security for a loan of $6,000 at a finance charge of 6% of the amount of the loan. The finance company will make the collections. (All the accounts receivable are past the discount period.)
Dec.	29	Warren Harding Co. notifies Garfield that it is bankrupt and will pay only 10% of its account. Give the entry to write off the uncollectible balance using the allowance method. (*Note:* First record the increase in the receivable on July 11 when the discount period passed.)

Instructions

Prepare all necessary entries in general journal form for Garfield Corp.

E8-13 (Assigning Accounts Receivable) On April 1, 2008, Rasheed Company assigns $400,000 of its accounts receivable to the Third National Bank as collateral for a $200,000 loan due July 1, 2008. The assignment agreement calls for Rasheed Company to continue to collect the receivables. Third National Bank assesses a finance charge of 2% of the accounts receivable, and interest on the loan is 10% (a realistic rate of interest for a note of this type). **(LO 8)**

Instructions

(a) Prepare the April 1, 2008, journal entry for Rasheed Company.

(b) Prepare the journal entry for Rasheed's collection of $350,000 of the accounts receivable during the period from April 1, 2008, through June 30, 2008.

(c) On July 1, 2008, Rasheed paid Third National all that was due from the loan it secured on April 1, 2008. Prepare the journal entry to record this payment.

(LO 5, 8)   **E8-14** **(Journalizing Various Receivable Transactions)**   The trial balance before adjustment for Phil Collins Company shows the following balances.

	Dr.	Cr.
Accounts Receivable	$82,000	
Allowance for Doubtful Accounts	2,120	
Sales (net)		$430,000

Instructions

Using the data above, prepare the journal entries required to record each of the following cases. (Each situation is independent.)

1. To obtain additional cash, Collins factors without recourse $25,000 of accounts receivable with Stills Finance. The finance charge is 10% of the amount factored.

2. To obtain a one-year loan of $55,000, Collins assigns $65,000 of specific receivable accounts to Crosby Financial. The finance charge is 8% of the loan; the cash is received and the accounts turned over to Crosby Financial.

3. The company wants to maintain the Allowance for Doubtful Accounts at 5% of gross accounts receivable.

4. The company wishes to increase the allowance account by 1½% of net sales.

(LO 8)   **E8-15** **(Transfer of Receivables with Recourse)**   Ames Quartet Inc. factors receivables with a carrying amount of $200,000 to Joffrey Company for $160,000 on a with recourse basis.

Instructions

The recourse provision has a fair value of $1,000. This transaction should be recorded as a sale. Prepare the appropriate journal entry to record this transaction on the books of Ames Quartet Inc.

(LO 8)   **E8-16** **(Transfer of Receivables with Recourse)**   Beyoncé Corporation factors $175,000 of accounts receivable with Kathleen Battle Financing, Inc. on a with recourse basis. Kathleen Battle Financing will collect the receivables. The receivables records are transferred to Kathleen Battle Financing on August 15, 2008. Kathleen Battle Financing assesses a finance charge of 2% of the amount of accounts receivable and also reserves an amount equal to 4% of accounts receivable to cover probable adjustments.

Instructions

(a) What conditions must be met for a transfer of receivables with recourse to be accounted for as a sale?

(b) Assume the conditions from part (a) are met. Prepare the journal entry on August 15, 2008, for Beyoncé to record the sale of receivables, assuming the recourse obligation has a fair value of $2,000.

(LO 8)   **E8-17** **(Transfer of Receivables without Recourse)**   JFK Corp. factors $300,000 of accounts receivable with LBJ Finance Corporation on a without recourse basis on July 1, 2008. The receivables records are transferred to LBJ Finance, which will receive the collections. LBJ Finance assesses a finance charge of 1½% of the amount of accounts receivable and retains an amount equal to 4% of accounts receivable to cover sales discounts, returns, and allowances. The transaction is to be recorded as a sale.

Instructions

(a) Prepare the journal entry on July 1, 2008, for JFK Corp. to record the sale of receivables without recourse.

(b) Prepare the journal entry on July 1, 2008, for LBJ Finance Corporation to record the purchase of receivables without recourse.

E8-18 (Note Transactions at Unrealistic Interest Rates)   On July 1, 2008, Agincourt Inc. made two sales.   (LO 8, 7)

1. It sold land having a fair market value of $700,000 in exchange for a 4-year zero-interest-bearing promissory note in the face amount of $1,101,460. The land is carried on Agincourt's books at a cost of $590,000.

2. It rendered services in exchange for a 3%, 8-year promissory note having a face value of $400,000 (interest payable annually).

Agincourt Inc. recently had to pay 8% interest for money that it borrowed from British National Bank. The customers in these two transactions have credit ratings that require them to borrow money at 12% interest.

Instructions

(a) Record the two journal entries that should be recorded by Agincourt Inc. for the sales transactions above that took place on July 1, 2008. (Round to the nearest dollar.)

(b) Assume that Agincourt uses the fair value option for the note issued in exchange for the land. Prepare the entry at December 31, 2008, if the fair value of the note is $720,000.

E8-19 (Notes Receivable with Unrealistic Interest Rate)   On December 31, 2008, Ed Abbey Co. performed   (LO 6, 7)
environmental consulting services for Hayduke Co. Hayduke was short of cash, and Abbey Co. agreed to accept a $200,000 zero-interest-bearing note due December 31, 2010, as payment in full. Hayduke is somewhat of a credit risk and typically borrows funds at a rate of 10%. Abbey is much more creditworthy and has various lines of credit at 6%.

Instructions

(a) Prepare the journal entry to record the transaction of December 31, 2008, for the Ed Abbey Co.

(b) Assuming Ed Abbey Co.'s fiscal year-end is December 31, prepare the journal entry for December 31, 2009.

(c) Assuming Ed Abbey Co.'s fiscal year-end is December 31, prepare the journal entry for December 31, 2010.

(d) Assume that Ed Abbey Co. elects the fair value option for this note. Prepare the journal entry at December 31, 2009, if the fair value of the note is $185,000.

E8-20 (Basic Note and Accounts Receivable Transactions)   (LO 5, 6, 7)
Part 1
On July 1, 2008, John Depp Company, a calendar-year company, sold special-order merchandise on credit and
received in return an interest-bearing note receivable from the customer. John Depp Company will receive interest at the prevailing rate for a note of this type. Both the principal and interest are due in one lump sum on June 30, 2009.

Instructions

(a) When should John Depp Company report interest revenue from the note receivable? Discuss the rationale for your answer.

(b) Briefly explain how Depp will apply the fair value option, if it is used to account for this note receivable.

Part 2
On December 31, 2008, John Depp Company had significant amounts of accounts receivable as a result of credit sales to its customers. Depp uses the allowance method based on credit sales to estimate bad debts. Past experience indicates that 2% of credit sales normally will not be collected. This pattern is expected to continue.

Instructions

(a) Discuss the rationale for using the allowance method based on credit sales to estimate bad debts. Contrast this method with the allowance method based on the balance in the trade receivables accounts.

(b) How should John Depp Company report the allowance for doubtful accounts on its balance sheet at December 31, 2008? Also, describe the alternatives, if any, for presentation of bad debt expense in John Depp Company's 2008 income statement.

(AICPA adapted)

E8-21 (Sale of Notes Receivable)   Sergey Luzov Wholesalers Co. sells industrial equipment for a standard   (LO 7, 8)
3-year note receivable. Revenue is recognized at time of sale. Each note is secured by a lien on the equipment

and has a face amount equal to the equipment's list price. Each note's stated interest rate is below the customer's market rate at date of sale. All notes are to be collected in three equal annual installments beginning one year after sale. Some of the notes are subsequently sold to a bank with recourse, some are subsequently sold without recourse, and some are retained by Luzov. At year end, Luzov evaluates all outstanding notes receivable and provides for estimated losses arising from defaults.

Instructions

(a) What is the appropriate valuation basis for Luzov's notes receivable at the date it sells equipment?

(b) How should Luzov account for the sale, without recourse, of a February 1, 2008, note receivable sold on May 1, 2008? Why is it appropriate to account for it in this way?

(c) At December 31, 2008, how should Luzov measure and account for the impact of estimated losses resulting from notes receivable that it

    (1) Retained and did not sell?

    (2) Sold to bank with recourse?

(AICPA adapted)

(LO 6, 7, 8)

E8-22 **(Reporting of Notes Receivable, Interest, and Sale of Receivables)** On July 1, 2008, Gale Sondergaard Company sold special-order merchandise on credit and received in return an interest-bearing note receivable from the customer. Sondergaard will receive interest at the prevailing rate for a note of this type. Both the principal and interest are due in one lump sum on June 30, 2009.

On September 1, 2008, Sondergaard sold special-order merchandise on credit and received in return a zero-interest-bearing note receivable from the customer. The prevailing rate of interest for a note of this type is determinable. The note receivable is due in one lump sum on August 31, 2010.

Sondergaard also has significant amounts of trade accounts receivable as a result of credit sales to its customers. On October 1, 2008, some trade accounts receivable were assigned to Irene Dunne Finance Company on a non-notification (Sondergaard handles collections) basis for an advance of 75% of their amount at an interest charge of 8% on the balance outstanding.

On November 1, 2008, other trade accounts receivable were sold on a without recourse basis. The factor withheld 5% of the trade accounts receivable factored as protection against sales returns and allowances and charged a finance charge of 3%.

Instructions

(a) How should Sondergaard determine the interest revenue for 2008 on the:

    (1) Interest-bearing note receivable? Why?

    (2) Zero-interest-bearing note receivable? Why?

(b) How should Sondergaard report the interest-bearing note receivable and the zero-interest-bearing note receivable on its balance sheet at December 31, 2008?

(c) How should Sondergaard account for subsequent collections on the trade accounts receivable assigned on October 1, 2008, and the payments to Irene Dunne Finance? Why?

(d) How should Sondergaard account for the trade accounts receivable factored on November 1, 2008? Why?

(AICPA adapted)

(LO 9)

E8-23 **(Analysis of Receivables)** Presented below is information for Jones Company.

1. Beginning-of-the-year Accounts Receivable balance was $15,000.
2. Net sales (all on account) for the year were $100,000. Jones does not offer cash discounts.
3. Collections on accounts receivable during the year were $70,000.

Instructions

(a) Prepare summary journal entries to record the items noted above.

(b) Compute Jones's accounts receivable turnover ratio and its days to collect accounts receivable for the year. The company does not believe it will have any bad debts.

(c) Use the turnover ratio computed in (b) to analyze Jones's liquidity. The turnover ratio last year was 6.0.

(LO 8)

E8-24 **(Transfer of Receivables)** Use the information for Jones Company as presented in E8-23. Jones is planning to factor some accounts receivable at the end of the year. Accounts totaling $25,000 will be transferred to Credit Factors, Inc. with recourse. Credit Factors will retain 5% of the balances for probable adjustments and assesses a finance charge of 4%. The fair value of the recourse obligation is $1,200.

Instructions

(a) Prepare the journal entry to record the sale of the receivables.

(b) Compute Jones's accounts receivables turnover ratio for the year, assuming the receivables are sold, and discuss how factoring of receivables affects the turnover ratio.

*E8-25 (Petty Cash) Carolyn Keene, Inc. decided to establish a petty cash fund to help ensure internal control over its small cash expenditures. The following information is available for the month of April.   **(LO 10)**

1. On April 1, it established a petty cash fund in the amount of $200.
2. A summary of the petty cash expenditures made by the petty cash custodian as of April 10 is as follows.

Delivery charges paid on merchandise purchased	$60
Supplies purchased and used	25
Postage expense	33
I.O.U. from employees	17
Miscellaneous expense	36

The petty cash fund was replenished on April 10. The balance in the fund was $27.

3. The petty cash fund balance was increased $100 to $300 on April 20.

Instructions

Prepare the journal entries to record transactions related to petty cash for the month of April.

*E8-26 (Petty Cash) The petty cash fund of Fonzarelli's Auto Repair Service, a sole proprietorship, contains the following.   **(LO 10)**

1. Coins and currency		$ 15.20
2. Postage stamps		2.90
3. An I.O.U. from Richie Cunningham, an employee, for cash advance		40.00
4. Check payable to Fonzarelli's Auto Repair from Pottsie Weber, an employee, marked NSF		34.00
5. Vouchers for the following:		
Stamps	$ 20.00	
Two Rose Bowl tickets for Nick Fonzarelli	170.00	
Printer cartridge	14.35	204.35
		$296.45

The general ledger account Petty Cash has a balance of $300.

Instructions

Prepare the journal entry to record the reimbursement of the petty cash fund.

*E8-27 (Bank Reconciliation and Adjusting Entries) Angela Lansbury Company deposits all receipts and makes all payments by check. The following information is available from the cash records.   **(LO 10)**

June 30 Bank Reconciliation

Balance per bank	$ 7,000
Add: Deposits in transit	1,540
Deduct: Outstanding checks	(2,000)
Balance per books	$ 6,540

Month of July Results

	Per Bank	Per Books
Balance July 31	$8,650	$9,250
July deposits	5,000	5,810
July checks	4,000	3,100
July note collected (not included in July deposits)	1,000	—
July bank service charge	15	—
July NSF check from a customer, returned by the bank (recorded by bank as a charge)	335	—

Instructions

(a) Prepare a bank reconciliation going from balance per bank and balance per books to correct cash balance.

(b) Prepare the general journal entry or entries to correct the Cash account.

(LO 10) ***E8-28 (Bank Reconciliation and Adjusting Entries)** Logan Bruno Company has just received the August 31, 2008, bank statement, which is summarized below.

County National Bank	Disbursements	Receipts	Balance
Balance, August 1			$9,369
Deposits during August		$32,200	41,569
Note collected for depositor, including $40 interest		1,040	42,609
Checks cleared during August	$34,500		8,109
Bank service charges	20		8,089
Balance, August 31			8,089

The general ledger Cash account contained the following entries for the month of August.

Cash			
Balance, August 1	10,050	Disbursements in August	34,903
Receipts during August	35,000		

Deposits in transit at August 31 are $3,800, and checks outstanding at August 31 total $1,050. Cash on hand at August 31 is $310. The bookkeeper improperly entered one check in the books at $146.50 which was written for $164.50 for supplies (expense); it cleared the bank during the month of August.

Instructions

(a) Prepare a bank reconciliation dated August 31, 2008, proceeding to a correct balance.

(b) Prepare any entries necessary to make the books correct and complete.

(c) What amount of cash should be reported in the August 31 balance sheet?

 **See the book's companion website, at www.wiley.com/college/warfield, for Additional Exercises.**

Problems

(LO 2) **P8-1 (Determine Proper Cash Balance)** Dumaine Equipment Co. closes its books regularly on December 31, but at the end of 2008 it held its cash book open so that a more favorable balance sheet could be prepared for credit purposes. Cash receipts and disbursements for the first 10 days of January were recorded as December transactions. The following information is given.

1. January cash receipts recorded in the December cash book totaled $39,640, of which $22,000 represents cash sales, and $17,640 represents collections on account for which cash discounts of $360 were given.

2. January cash disbursements recorded in the December check register liquidated accounts payable of $26,450 on which discounts of $250 were taken.

3. The ledger has not been closed for 2008.

4. The amount shown as inventory was determined by physical count on December 31, 2008.

The company uses the periodic method of inventory.

Instructions

(a) Prepare any entries you consider necessary to correct Dumaine's accounts at December 31.

(b) To what extent was Dumaine Equipment Co. able to show a more favorable balance sheet at December 31 by holding its cash book open? (Compute working capital and the current ratio.) Assume that the balance sheet that was prepared by the company showed the following amounts:

	Debit	Credit
Cash	$39,000	
Receivables	42,000	
Inventories	67,000	
Accounts payable		$45,000
Other current liabilities		14,200

P8-2 **(Bad-Debt Reporting)** Presented below are a series of unrelated situations.

(LO 5)

1. Spock Company's unadjusted trial balance at December 31, 2008, included the following accounts.

	Debit	Credit
Allowance for doubtful accounts	$4,000	
Net sales		$1,500,000

Spock Company estimates its bad debt expense to be 1½% of net sales. Determine its bad debt expense for 2008.

2. An analysis and aging of Scotty Corp. accounts receivable at December 31, 2008, disclosed the following.

Amounts estimated to be uncollectible	$ 180,000
Accounts receivable	1,750,000
Allowance for doubtful accounts (per books)	125,000

What is the net realizable value of Scotty's receivables at December 31, 2008?

3. Uhura Co. provides for doubtful accounts based on 3% of credit sales. The following data are available for 2008.

Credit sales during 2008	$2,100,000
Allowance for doubtful accounts 1/1/08	17,000
Collection of accounts written off in prior years	
(customer credit was reestablished)	8,000
Customer accounts written off as uncollectible during 2008	30,000

What is the balance in the Allowance for Doubtful Accounts at December 31, 2008?

4. At the end of its first year of operations, December 31, 2008, Chekov Inc. reported the following information.

Accounts receivable, net of allowance for doubtful accounts	$950,000
Customer accounts written off as uncollectible during 2008	24,000
Bad debt expense for 2008	84,000

What should be the balance in accounts receivable at December 31, 2008, before subtracting the allowance for doubtful accounts?

5. The following accounts were taken from Chappel Inc.'s trial balance at December 31, 2008.

	Debit	Credit
Net credit sales		$750,000
Allowance for doubtful accounts	$ 14,000	
Accounts receivable	410,000	

If doubtful accounts are 3% of accounts receivable, determine the bad debt expense to be reported for 2008.

Instructions

Answer the questions relating to each of the five independent situations as requested.

P8-3 **(Bad-Debt Reporting—Aging)** Mary Pierce Corporation operates in an industry that has a high rate of bad debts. Before any year-end adjustments, the balance in Pierce's Accounts Receivable account was $555,000 and the Allowance for Doubtful Accounts had a credit balance of $35,000. The year-end balance reported in the balance sheet for the Allowance for Doubtful Accounts will be based on the aging schedule shown below.

(LO 5)

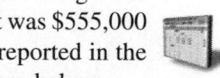

Days Account Outstanding	Amount	Probability of Collection	*Estimated uncollectible*
Less than 16 days	$300,000	.98	*6 000*
Between 16 and 30 days	100,000	.90	*10 000*
Between 31 and 45 days	80,000	.85	*12 000*
Between 46 and 60 days	40,000	.75	*10 000*
Between 61 and 75 days	20,000	.40	*12 000*
Over 75 days	15,000	.00	*15 000*

Allowance for DA   65 000

Instructions

(a) What is the appropriate balance for the Allowance for Doubtful Accounts at year-end?

(b) Show how accounts receivable would be presented on the balance sheet.

(c) What is the dollar effect of the year-end bad debt adjustment on the before-tax income?

(CMA adapted)

(LO 5)

P8-4 (Bad-Debt Reporting) From inception of operations to December 31, 2008, Blaise Pascal Corporation provided for uncollectible accounts receivable under the allowance method: provisions were made monthly at 2% of credit sales; bad debts written off were charged to the allowance account; recoveries of bad debts previously written off were credited to the allowance account; and no year-end adjustments to the allowance account were made. Pascal's usual credit terms are net 30 days.

The balance in the Allowance for Doubtful Accounts was $154,000 at January 1, 2008. During 2008 credit sales totaled $9,000,000, interim provisions for doubtful accounts were made at 2% of credit sales, $95,000 of bad debts were written off, and recoveries of accounts previously written off amounted to $15,000. Pascal installed a computer facility in November 2008, and an aging of accounts receivable was prepared for the first time as of December 31, 2008. A summary of the aging is as follows.

Classification by Month of Sale	Balance in Each Category	Estimated % Uncollectible
November–December 2008	$1,080,000	2%
July–October	650,000	10%
January–June	420,000	25%
Prior to 1/1/08	150,000	70%
	$2,300,000	

Based on the review of collectibility of the account balances in the "Prior to 1/1/08" aging category, additional receivables totaling $60,000 were written off as of December 31, 2008. The 70% uncollectible estimate applies to the remaining $90,000 in the category. Effective with the year ended December 31, 2008, Pascal adopted a new accounting method for estimating the allowance for doubtful accounts at the amount indicated by the year-end aging analysis of accounts receivable.

Instructions

(a) Prepare a schedule analyzing the changes in the Allowance for Doubtful Accounts for the year ended December 31, 2008. Show supporting computations in good form. (*Hint*: In computing the 12/31/08 allowance, subtract the $60,000 write-off).

(b) Prepare the journal entry for the year-end adjustment to the Allowance for Doubtful Accounts balance as of December 31, 2008.

(AICPA adapted)

(LO 5)

P8-5 (Bad-Debt Reporting) Presented below is information related to the Accounts Receivable accounts of Gulistan Inc. during the current year 2008.

1. An aging schedule of the accounts receivable as of December 31, 2008, is as follows.

Age	Net Debit Balance	% to Be Applied after Correction Is Made
Under 60 days	$172,342	1%
60–90 days	136,490	3%
91–120 days	39,924*	6%
Over 120 days	23,644	$4,200 definitely uncollectible; estimated remainder uncollectible is 25%
	$372,400	

*The $2,740 write-off of receivables is related to the 91-to-120 day category.

2. The Accounts Receivable control account has a debit balance of $372,400 on December 31, 2008.

3. Two entries were made in the Bad Debt Expense account during the year: (1) a debit on December 31 for the amount credited to Allowance for Doubtful Accounts, and (2) a credit for $2,740 on November 3, 2008, and a debit to Allowance for Doubtful Accounts because of a bankruptcy.

4. The Allowance for Doubtful Accounts is as follows for 2008.

Allowance for Doubtful Accounts					
Nov. 3	Uncollectible accounts written off	2,740	Jan. 1	Beginning balance	8,750
			Dec. 31	5% of $372,400	18,620

5. A credit balance exists in the Accounts Receivable (60–90 days) of $4,840, which represents an advance on a sales contract.

Instructions

Assuming that the books have not been closed for 2008, make the necessary correcting entries. (Round to nearest dollar.)

P8-6 **(Journalize Various Accounts Receivable Transactions)** The balance sheet of Antonio Vivaldi Company at December 31, 2007, includes the following.

Notes receivable		$ 36,000
Accounts receivable	182,100	
Less: Allowance for doubtful accounts	17,300	200,800

Transactions in 2008 include the following.

1. Accounts receivable of $138,000 were collected including accounts of $40,000 on which 2% sales discounts were allowed.
2. $6,300 was received in payment of an account which was written off the books as worthless earlier in 2008. (*Hint:* Reestablish the receivable account.)
3. Customer accounts of $17,500 were written off during the year.
4. At year-end the Allowance for Doubtful Accounts was estimated to need a balance of $20,000. This estimate is based on an analysis of aged accounts receivable.

Instructions

Prepare all journal entries necessary to reflect the transactions above.

P8-7 **(Assigned Accounts Receivable—Journal Entries)** Nikos Company finances some of its current operations by assigning accounts receivable to a finance company. On July 1, 2008, it assigned, under guarantee, specific accounts amounting to $100,000. The finance company advanced to Nikos 80% of the accounts assigned (20% of the total to be withheld until the finance company has made its full recovery), less a finance charge of ½% of the total accounts assigned.

On July 31 Nikos Company received a statement that the finance company had collected $55,000 of these accounts and had made an additional charge of ½% of the total accounts outstanding as of July 31. This charge is to be deducted at the time of the first remittance due Nikos Company from the finance company. (*Hint*: Make entries at this time.) On August 31, 2008, Nikos Company received a second statement from the finance company, together with a check for the amount due. The statement indicated that the finance company had collected an additional $30,000 and had made a further charge of ½% of the balance outstanding as of August 31.

Instructions

Make all entries on the books of Nikos Company that are involved in the transactions above.

(AICPA adapted)

P8-8 **(Notes Receivable with Realistic Interest Rate)** On October 1, 2008, Jeppo Farm Equipment Company sold a pecan-harvesting machine to Lujan Brothers Farm, Inc. In lieu of a cash payment Lujan Brothers Farm gave Jeppo a 2-year, $100,000, 8% note (a realistic rate of interest for a note of this type). The note required interest to be paid annually on October 1. Jeppo's financial statements are prepared on a calendar-year basis.

Instructions

Assuming Lujan Brothers Farm fulfills all the terms of the note, prepare the necessary journal entries for Jeppo Farm Equipment Company for the entire term of the note.

P8-9 **(Notes Receivable Journal Entries)** On December 31, 2008, Menachem Inc. rendered services to Begin Corporation at an agreed price of $91,844.10, accepting $36,000 down and agreeing to accept the balance in four equal installments of $18,000 receivable each December 31. An assumed interest rate of 11% is imputed.

Instructions

Prepare the entries that would be recorded by Menachem Inc. for the sale and for the receipts and interest on the following dates. (Assume that the effective interest method is used for amortization purposes.)

(a) December 31, 2008.   (c) December 31, 2010.   (e) December 31, 2012.

(b) December 31, 2009.   (d) December 31, 2011.

(LO 6, 7)   **P8-10 (Comprehensive Receivables Problem)** Connecticut Inc. had the following long-term receivable account balances at December 31, 2007.

Note receivable from sale of division	$1,800,000
Note receivable from officer	400,000

Transactions during 2008 and other information relating to Connecticut's long-term receivables were as follows.

1. The $1,800,000 note receivable is dated May 1, 2007, bears interest at 9%, and represents the balance of the consideration received from the sale of Connecticut's electronics division to New York Company. Principal payments of $600,000 plus appropriate interest are due on May 1, 2008, 2009, and 2010. The first principal and interest payment was made on May 1, 2008. Collection of the note installments is reasonably assured.

2. The $400,000 note receivable is dated December 31, 2007, bears interest at 8%, and is due on December 31, 2010. The note is due from Sean May, president of Connecticut Inc. and is collateralized by 10,000 shares of Connecticut's common stock. Interest is payable annually on December 31, and all interest payments were paid on their due dates through December 31, 2008. The quoted market price of Connecticut's common stock was $45 per share on December 31, 2008.

3. On April 1, 2008, Connecticut sold a patent to Pennsylvania Company in exchange for a $200,000 zero-interest-bearing note due on April 1, 2010. There was no established exchange price for the patent, and the note had no ready market. The prevailing rate of interest for a note of this type at April 1, 2008, was 12%. The present value of $1 for two periods at 12% is 0.797 (use this factor). The patent had a carrying value of $40,000 at January 1, 2008, and the amortization for the year ended December 31, 2008, would have been $8,000. The collection of the note receivable from Pennsylvania is reasonably assured.

4. On July 1, 2008, Connecticut sold a parcel of land to Harrisburg Company for $200,000 under an installment sale contract. Harrisburg made a $60,000 cash down payment on July 1, 2008, and signed a 4-year 11% note for the $140,000 balance. The equal annual payments of principal and interest on the note will be $45,125 payable on July 1, 2009, through July 1, 2012. The land could have been sold at an established cash price of $200,000. The cost of the land to Connecticut was $150,000. Circumstances are such that the collection of the installments on the note is reasonably assured.

Instructions

(a) Prepare the long-term receivables section of Connecticut's balance sheet at December 31, 2008.

(b) Prepare a schedule showing the current portion of the long-term receivables and accrued interest receivable that would appear in Connecticut's balance sheet at December 31, 2008.

(c) Prepare a schedule showing interest revenue from the long-term receivables that would appear on Connecticut's income statement for the year ended December 31, 2008.

(LO 8, 9)   **P8-11 (Income Effects of Receivables Transactions)** Radisson Company requires additional cash for its business. Radisson has decided to use its accounts receivable to raise the additional cash and has asked you to determine the income statement effects of the following contemplated transactions.

1. On July 1, 2008, Radisson assigned $400,000 of accounts receivable to Stickum Finance Company. Radisson received an advance from Stickum of 85% of the assigned accounts receivable less a commission of 3% on the advance. Prior to December 31, 2008, Radisson collected $220,000 on the assigned accounts receivable, and remitted $232,720 to Stickum, $12,720 of which represented interest on the advance from Stickum.

2. On December 1, 2008, Radisson sold $300,000 of net accounts receivable to Wunsch Company for $250,000. The receivables were sold outright on a without recourse basis.

3. On December 31, 2008, an advance of $120,000 was received from First Bank by pledging $160,000 of Radisson's accounts receivable. Radisson's first payment to First Bank is due on January 30, 2009.

Instructions

Prepare a schedule showing the income statement effects for the year ended December 31, 2008, as a result of the above facts.

P8-12 **(Bad-Debt Reporting Issues)** Rosita Arenas Company sells office equipment and supplies to many organizations in the city and surrounding area on contract terms of 2/10, n/30. In the past, over 75% of the credit customers have taken advantage of the discount by paying within 10 days of the invoice date.

(LO 5)

The number of customers taking the full 30 days to pay has increased within the last year. Current indications are that less than 60% of the customers are now taking the discount. Bad debts as a percentage of gross credit sales have risen from the 1.5% provided in past years to about 4% in the current year.

The controller has responded to a request for more information on the deterioration in collections of accounts receivable with the report reproduced below.

Rosita Arenas Company
Finance Committee Report—Accounts Receivable Collections
May 31, 2008

The fact that some credit accounts will prove uncollectible is normal. Annual bad debt write-offs have been 1.5% of gross credit sales over the past five years. During the last fiscal year, this percentage increased to slightly less than 4%. The current Accounts Receivable balance is $1,600,000. The condition of this balance in terms of age and probability of collection is as follows.

Proportion of Total	Age Categories	Probability of Collection	
68%	not yet due	99%	8 400
15%	less than 30 days past due	96½%	6 400
8%	30 to 60 days past due	95%	6 400
5%	61 to 120 days past due	91%	12 000
2½%	121 to 180 days past due	70%	19 200
1½%	over 180 days past due	20%	63 280

The Allowance for Doubtful Accounts had a credit balance of $43,300 on June 1, 2007. Rosita Arenas Company has provided for a monthly bad debts expense accrual during the current fiscal year based on the assumption that 4% of gross credit sales will be uncollectible. Total gross credit sales for the 2007–2008 fiscal year amounted to $4,000,000. Write-offs of bad accounts during the year totaled $145,000.

Instructions

(a) Prepare an accounts receivable aging schedule for Rosita Arenas Company using the age categories identified in the controller's report to the finance committee showing:
   (1) The amount of accounts receivable outstanding for each age category and in total.
   (2) The estimated amount that is uncollectible for each category and in total.
(b) Compute the amount of the year-end adjustment necessary to bring Allowance for Doubtful Accounts to the balance indicated by the age analysis. Then prepare the necessary journal entry to adjust the accounting records.
(c) In a recessionary environment with tight credit and high interest rates:
   (1) Identify steps Rosita Arenas Company might consider to improve the accounts receivable situation.
   (2) Then evaluate each step identified in terms of the risks and costs involved.

(CMA adapted)

*P8-13 **(Petty Cash, Bank Reconciliation)** Bill Howe is reviewing the cash accounting for Kappeler, Inc., a local mailing service. Howe's review will focus on the petty cash account and the bank reconciliation for the month ended May 31, 2008. He has collected the following information from Kappeler's book-keeper for this task.

(LO 10)

Petty Cash

1. The petty cash fund was established on May 10, 2008, in the amount of $250.
2. Expenditures from the fund by the custodian as of May 31, 2008, were evidenced by approved receipts for the following.

Postage expense	$33.00
Mailing labels and other supplies	75.00
I.O.U. from employees	30.00
Shipping charges	57.45
Newspaper advertising	22.80
Miscellaneous expense	15.35

On May 31, 2008, the petty cash fund was replenished and increased to $300; currency and coin in the fund at that time totaled $16.40.

Bank Reconciliation

Third National Bank Bank Statement			
	Disbursements	Receipts	Balance
Balance, May 1, 2008			$8,769
Deposits		$28,000	
Note payment direct from customer (interest of $30)		930	
Checks cleared during May	$31,150		
Bank service charges	27		
Balance, May 31, 2008			6,522

Kappeler's Cash Account	
Balance, May 1, 2008	$ 9,150
Deposits during May 2008	31,000
Checks written during May 2008	(31,835)

Deposits in transit are determined to be $3,000, and checks outstanding at May 31 total $550. Cash on hand (besides petty cash) at May 31, 2008, is $246.

Instructions

(a) Prepare the journal entries to record the transactions related to the petty cash fund for May.

(b) Prepare a bank reconciliation dated May 31, 2008, proceeding to a correct cash balance, and prepare the journal entries necessary to make the books correct and complete.

(c) What amount of cash should be reported in the May 31, 2008, balance sheet?

(LO 10) ***P8-14 (Bank Reconciliation and Adjusting Entries)** The cash account of Jose Orozco Co. showed a ledger balance of $3,969.85 on June 30, 2008. The bank statement as of that date showed a balance of $4,150. Upon comparing the statement with the cash records, the following facts were determined.

1. There were bank service charges for June of $25.

2. A bank memo stated that Bao Dai's note for $900 and interest of $36 had been collected on June 29, and the bank had made a charge of $5.50 on the collection. (No entry had been made on Orozco's books when Bao Dai's note was sent to the bank for collection.)

3. Receipts for June 30 for $2,890 were not deposited until July 2.

4. Checks outstanding on June 30 totaled $2,136.05.

5. The bank had charged the Orozco Co.'s account for a customer's uncollectible check amounting to $453.20 on June 29.

6. A customer's check for $90 had been entered as $60 in the cash receipts journal by Orozco on June 15.

7. Check no. 742 in the amount of $491 had been entered in the cash journal as $419, and check no. 747 in the amount of $58.20 had been entered as $582. Both checks had been issued to pay for purchases of equipment.

Instructions

(a) Prepare a bank reconciliation dated June 30, 2008, proceeding to a correct cash balance.

(b) Prepare any entries necessary to make the books correct and complete.

(LO 10) ***P8-15 (Bank Reconciliation and Adjusting Entries)** Presented below is information related to Tanizaki Inc.

Balance per books at October 31, $41,847.85; receipts $173,523.91; disbursements $166,193.54. Balance per bank statement November 30, $56,274.20.

The following checks were outstanding at November 30.

1224	$1,635.29
1230	2,468.30
1232	3,625.15
1233	482.17

Included with the November bank statement and not recorded by the company were a bank debit memo for $27.40 covering bank charges for the month, a debit memo for $572.13 for a customer's check returned and marked

NSF, and a credit memo for $1,400 representing bond interest collected by the bank in the name of Tanizaki Inc. Cash on hand at November 30 recorded and awaiting deposit amounted to $1,915.40.

Instructions

(a) Prepare a bank reconciliation (to the correct balance) at November 30, for Tanizaki Inc. from the information above.
(b) Prepare any journal entries required to adjust the cash account at November 30.

ACCOUNTING IN ACTION

Financial Reporting and Analysis

■ Financial Reporting Issues: The Procter & Gamble Company

AIA8-1 The financial statements of **Procter & Gamble (P&G)** can be accessed at the book's website.

Instructions

Refer to P&G's financial statements and the accompanying notes to answer the following questions.

(a) What criteria does P&G use to classify "Cash and cash equivalents" as reported in its balance sheet?
(b) As of June 30, 2006, what balances did P&G have in cash and cash equivalents? What were the major uses of cash during the year?
(c) P&G reports no allowance for doubtful accounts, suggesting that bad debt expense is not material for this company. Is it reasonable that a company like P&G would not have material bad debt expense? Explain.

■ Comparative Analysis: The Coca-Cola Company and PepsiCo, Inc.   **PEPSICO**

AIA8-2 The financial statements of The Coca-Cola Company and PepsiCo, Inc. can be accessed at the book's website.

Instructions

Use information found at the book's website to answer the following questions.

(a) What were the cash and cash equivalents reported by Coca-Cola and PepsiCo at the end of 2006? What does each company classify as cash equivalents?
(b) What were the accounts receivable (net) for Coca-Cola and PepsiCo at the end of 2006? Which company reports the greater allowance for doubtful accounts receivable (amount and percentage of gross receivable) at the end of 2006?
(c) Assuming that all "net operating revenues" (Coca-Cola) and all "net sales" (PepsiCo) were net *credit* sales, compute the accounts receivable turnover ratio for 2006 for Coca-Cola and PepsiCo; also compute the days outstanding for receivables. What is your evaluation of the difference?

■ Financial Statement Analysis

AIA8-3 Occidental Petroleum Corporation reported the following information in a recent annual report.

Occidental Petroleum Corporation
Consolidated Balance Sheets
(in millions)

Assets at December 31	Current Year	Prior Year
Current assets		
Cash and cash equivalents	$ 683	$ 146
Trade receivables, net of allowances	804	608
Receivables from joint ventures, partnerships, and other	330	321
Inventories	510	491
Prepaid expenses and other	147	307
Total current assets	2,474	1,873
Long-term receivables, net	264	275

Notes to Consolidated Financial Statements

Cash and Cash Equivalents.   Cash equivalents consist of highly liquid investments. Cash equivalents totaled approximately $661 million and $116 million at the current and prior year-ends, respectively.

Trade Receivables.   Occidental has agreement to sell, under a revolving sale program, an undivided percentage ownership interest in a designated pool of non-interest-bearing receivables. Under this program, Occidental serves as the collection agent with respect to the receivables sold. An interest in new receivables is sold as collections are made from customers. The balance sold at the current year-end, was $360 million.

Instructions

(a) What items other than coin and currency may be included in "cash"?

(b) What items may be included in "cash equivalents"?

(c) What are compensating balance arrangements, and how should they be reported in financial statements?

(d) What are the possible differences between cash equivalents and short-term (temporary) investments?

(e) Assuming that the sale agreement meets the criteria for sale accounting, cash proceeds were $345 million, the carrying value of the receivables sold was $360 million, and the fair value of the recourse obligation was $15 million, what was the effect on income from the sale of receivables?

(f) Briefly discuss the impact of the transaction in (e) on Occidental's liquidity.

AIA8-4   **Microsoft** is the leading developer of software in the world. To continue to be successful Microsoft must generate new products, which requires significant amounts of cash. Shown below is the current asset and current liability information from Microsoft's balance sheet (in millions). Following the Microsoft data is the current asset and current liability information for **Oracle** (in millions), another major software developer.

Microsoft Corporation
Balance Sheets (partial)
As of June 30
(in millions)

Current assets	2006	2005
Cash and equivalents	$ 6,714	$ 4,851
Short-term investments	27,447	32,900
Accounts receivable	9,316	7,180
Other	5,533	3,806
Total current assets	$49,010	$48,737
Total current liabilities	$22,442	$16,877

Oracle
Balance Sheets (partial)
As of May 31
(in millions)

Current assets	2006	2005
Cash and equivalents	$6,659	$3,894
Short-term investments	946	877
Receivables	3,022	2,570
Other current assets	1,347	1,107
Total current assets	11,974	8,448
Current liabilities	$6,930	$8,063

Part 1 (Cash and Cash Equivalents)

Instructions

(a) What is the definition of a cash equivalent? Give some examples of cash equivalents. How do cash equivalents differ from other types of short-term investments?

(b) Calculate (1) the current ratio and (2) working capital for each company for 2006 and discuss your results.

(c) Is it possible to have too many liquid assets?

Part 2 (Accounts Receivables)

Microsoft provided the following disclosure related to its accounts receivable.

Microsoft Corporation

Notes to the Financial Statements

Allowance for Doubtful Accounts. The allowance for doubtful accounts reflects our best estimate of probable losses inherent in the accounts receivable balance. We determine the allowance based on known troubled accounts, historical experience, and other currently available evidence. Activity in the allowance for doubtful accounts is as follows:

(in millions)

Year Ended June 30	Balance at beginning of period	Charged to costs and expenses	Write-offs and other	Balance at end of period
2004	$242	$44	$(120)	$166
2005	166	48	(43)	171
2006	171	40	(69)	142

Instructions

(a) Compute Microsoft's accounts receivable turnover ratio for 2006 and discuss your results. Microsoft had sales revenue of $44,282 million in 2006 and an accounts receivable turnover ratio of 6.65 in 2005.

(b) Reconstruct the summary journal entries for 2006 based on the information in the disclosure.

(c) Briefly discuss how the accounting for bad debts affects the analysis in Part 2 (a).

AIA8-5 The following information is taken from the 2006 financial statements and accompanying notes of **The Scotts Miracle-Gro Company**, a manufacturer of lawn-care products.

The Scotts Miracle-Gro Company

(in millions)	2006	2005
Accounts receivable	$391.7	$334.7
Allowance for uncollectible accounts	11.3	11.4
Sales	2,697.1	2,369.3
Total current assets	942.0	787.8

Note 17. Concentrations of Credit Risk (partial)

Financial Instruments which potentially subject the Company to concentration of credit risk consist principally of trade accounts receivable. The company sells its consumer products to a wide variety lof retailers, including mass merchandisers, home centers, independent hardware stores, nurseries, garden outlets, warehouse clubs and local and regional chains. Professional products are sold to commercial nurseries, greenhouses, landscape services, and growers of specialty agriculture crops.

At September 30, 2006, 76% of the Company's accounts receivable were due from customers geographically located in North America. Approximately 79% of these receivables were generated from the consumer business with the remaining 21% due from customers of Scotts LawnService®, the professional businesses (primarily distributors), Smith & Hawken®, and Morning Song®. Our top 3 customers within the consumer business accounted for 53% of total consumer accounts receivable.

The remainder of the Company's accounts receivable at September 30, 2006 were generated from customers located outside of North America, primarily retailers, distributors, nurseries and growers in Europe. No concentrations of customers or individual customers within this group account for more than 10% of the Company's accounts receivable at either balance sheet date.

The Company's three largest customers accounted for the following percentage of net sales in each respective period:

	Largest Customer	2nd-Largest Customer	3rd-Largest Customer
2006	21.5%	11.2%	10.5%
2005	23.5%	11.9%	9.7%
2004	25.0%	12.9%	9.4%

Sales to the Company's three largest customers are reported within the Company's North America segment. No other customers accounted for more than 10% of fiscal 2006, fiscal 2005 or fiscal 2004 net sales.

Instructions

Answer each of the following questions.

(a) Calculate the accounts receivable turnover ratio and average collection period for 2006 for the company.

(b) Is accounts receivable a material component of the company's total current assets?

(c) Scotts sells seasonal products. How might this affect the accuracy of your answer to part (a)?

(d) Evaluate the credit risk of Scotts' concentrated receivables.

(e) Comment on the informational value of Scotts' Note 17 on concentrations of credit risk.

Concepts for Analysis

AIA8-6 **(Bad-Debt Accounting)** Ariel Company has significant amounts of trade accounts receivable. Ariel uses the allowance method to estimate bad debts instead of the direct write-off method. During the year, some specific accounts were written off as uncollectible, and some that were previously written off as uncollectible were collected.

Instructions

(a) What are the deficiencies of the direct write-off method?

(b) What are the two basic allowance methods used to estimate bad debts, and what is the theoretical justification for each?

(c) How should Ariel account for the collection of the specific accounts previously written off as uncollectible?

AIA8-7 **(Various Receivable Accounting Issues)** Anne Archer Company uses the net method of accounting for sales discounts. Anne Archer also offers trade discounts to various groups of buyers.

On August 1, 2008, Archer sold some accounts receivable on a without recourse basis. Archer incurred a finance charge.

Archer also has some notes receivable bearing an appropriate rate of interest. The principal and total interest are due at maturity. The notes were received on October 1, 2008, and mature on September 30, 2010. Archer's operating cycle is less than one year.

Instructions

(a) (1) Using the net method, how should Archer account for the sales discounts at the date of sale? What is the rationale for the amount recorded as sales under the net method?

   (2) Using the net method, what is the effect on Archer's sales revenues and net income when customers do not take the sales discounts?

(b) What is the effect of trade discounts on sales revenues and accounts receivable? Why?

(c) How should Archer account for the accounts receivable factored on August 1, 2008? Why?

(d) How should Archer account for the note receivable and the related interest on December 31, 2008? Why?

AIA8-8 **(Bad-Debt Reporting Issues)** Orlando Bloom conducts a wholesale merchandising business that sells approximately 5,000 items per month with a total monthly average sales value of $250,000. Its annual bad debt ratio has been approximately 1½% of sales. In recent discussions with his bookkeeper, Mr. Bloom has become confused by all the alternatives apparently available in handling the Allowance for Doubtful Accounts balance. The following information has been shown.

1. An allowance can be set up (a) on the basis of a percentage of sales or (b) on the basis of a valuation of all past due or otherwise questionable accounts receivable. Those considered uncollectible can be charged to such allowance at the close of the accounting period, or specific items can be charged off directly against (1) Gross Sales or to (2) Bad Debt Expense in the year in which they are determined to be uncollectible.

2. Collection agency and legal fees, and so on, incurred in connection with the attempted recovery of bad debts can be charged to (a) Bad Debt Expense, (b) Allowance for Doubtful Accounts, (c) Legal Expense, or (d) General Expense.

3. Debts previously written off in whole or in part but currently recovered can be credited to (a) Other Revenue, (b) Bad Debt Expense, or (c) Allowance for Doubtful Accounts.

Instructions

Which of the foregoing methods would you recommend to Mr. Bloom in regard to (1) allowances and charge-offs, (2) collection expenses, and (3) recoveries? State briefly and clearly the reasons supporting your recommendations.

AIA8-9 (Zero-Interest-Bearing Note Receivable) On September 30, 2007, Tiger Machinery Co. sold a machine and accepted the customer's zero-interest-bearing note. Tiger normally makes sales on a cash basis. Since the machine was unique, its sales price was not determinable using Tiger's normal pricing practices.

After receiving the first of two equal annual installments on September 30, 2008, Tiger immediately sold the note with recourse. On October 9, 2009, Tiger received notice that the note was dishonored, and it paid all amounts due. At all times prior to default, the note was reasonably expected to be paid in full.

Instructions

(a) (1) How should Tiger determine the sales price of the machine?
   (2) How should Tiger report the effects of the zero-interest-bearing note on its income statement for the year ended December 31, 2007? Why is this accounting presentation appropriate?
(b) What are the effects of the sale of the note receivable with recourse on Tiger's income statement for the year ended December 31, 2008, and its balance sheet at December 31, 2008?
(c) How should Tiger account for the effects of the note being dishonored?

AIA8-10 (Accounting for Zero-Interest-Bearing Note) Soon after beginning the year-end audit work on  March 10 at Engone Company, the auditor has the following conversation with the controller.

CONTROLLER: The year ended March 31st should be our most profitable in history and, as a consequence, the board of directors has just awarded the officers generous bonuses.

AUDITOR: I thought profits were down this year in the industry, according to your latest interim report.

CONTROLLER: Well, they were down, but 10 days ago we closed a deal that will give us a substantial increase for the year.

AUDITOR: Oh, what was it?

CONTROLLER: Well, you remember a few years ago our former president bought stock in Rocketeer Enterprises because he had those grandiose ideas about becoming a conglomerate. For 6 years we have not been able to sell this stock, which cost us $3,000,000 and has not paid a nickel in dividends. Thursday we sold this stock to Campbell Inc. for $4,000,000. So, we will have a gain of $700,000 ($1,000,000 pretax) which will increase our net income for the year to $4,000,000, compared with last year's $3,800,000. As far as I know, we'll be the only company in the industry to register an increase in net income this year. That should help the market value of the stock!

AUDITOR: Do you expect to receive the $4,000,000 in cash by March 31st, your fiscal year-end?

CONTROLLER: No. Although Campbell Inc. is an excellent company, they are a little tight for cash because of their rapid growth. Consequently, they are going to give us a $4,000,000 zero-interest-bearing note with payments of $400,000 per year for the next 10 years. The first payment is due on March 31 of next year.

AUDITOR: Why is the note zero-interest-bearing?

CONTROLLER: Because that's what everybody agreed to. Since we don't have any interest-bearing debt, the funds invested in the note do not cost us anything and besides, we were not getting any dividends on the Rocketeer Enterprises stock.

Instructions

Do you agree with the way the controller has accounted for the transaction? If not, how should the transaction be accounted for?

AIA8-11 (Receivables Management) As the manager of the accounts receivable department for Vicki Maher Leather Goods, Ltd., you recently noticed that Percy Shelley, your accounts receivable clerk who is paid $1,200 per month, has been wearing unusually tasteful and expensive clothing. (This is Vicki Maher's first year in business.) This morning, Shelley drove up to work in a brand new Lexus.

Naturally suspicious by nature, you decide to test the accuracy of the accounts receivable balance of $132,000 as shown in the ledger. The following information is available for your first year (precisely 9 months ended September 30, 2008) in business.

(1) Collections from customers	$198,000
(2) Merchandise purchased	360,000
(3) Ending merchandise inventory	90,000
(4) Goods are marked to sell at 40% above cost.	

Instructions

Assuming all sales were made on account, compute the ending accounts receivable balance that should appear in the ledger, noting any apparent shortage. Then, draft a memo dated October 3, 2008, to John Castle, the branch manager, explaining the facts in this situation. Remember that this problem is serious, and you do not want to make hasty accusations.

Professional Tools

■ Ethical Decision Making

AIA8-12   (Bad-Debt Reporting)   Santo Company is a subsidiary of Hughes Corp. The controller believes that the yearly allowance for doubtful accounts for Santo should be 2% of net credit sales. The president, nervous that the parent company might expect the subsidiary to sustain its 10% growth rate, suggests that the controller increase the allowance for doubtful accounts to 3% yearly. The supervisor thinks that the lower net income, which reflects a 6% growth rate, will be a more sustainable rate for Santo Company.

Instructions

(a) Should the controller be concerned with Santo Company's growth rate in estimating the allowance? Explain your answer.

(b) Does the president's request pose an ethical dilemma for the controller? Give your reasons.

■ Financial Accounting Research (FARS)

AIA8-13   As the new staff person in your company's treasury department, you have been asked to conduct research related to a proposed transfer of receivables. Your supervisor wants the authoritative sources for the following items that are discussed in the securitization agreement.

Instructions

Using the **Financial Accounting Research System (FARS)** database, respond to the following items. (Provide text strings used in your search.)

(a) List the current statement and the previous statement that addressed transfers of receivables.

(b) Provide definitions for the following:
   (1) Transfer.
   (2) Recourse.
   (3) Collateral.

(c) Provide other examples (besides recourse and collateral) that qualify as continuing involvement.

■ Professional Simulation

AIA8-14   Go to the book's companion website, at **www.wiley.com/college/warfield**, to find an interactive problem that simulates the computerized CPA exam. The professional simulation for this chapter asks you to address questions related to the accounting for receivables.

What do the numbers mean?

Too Much of a Good Thing?, p. 359

Q: As an investor, what factors would you consider in evaluating whether a company has too much cash on hand?

A: Because cash likely will be used to pay current obligations, you should review the level of current liabilities (those due within one year). In addition, an investor should look at the company's growth prospects, including any expansion plans. For example, in a recent year **Walgreens** reported over $1 billion in cash on hand but also discussed an aggressive plan to open over 450 new stores in the coming year. No doubt the cash on hand will help finance this store growth.

Going for Broke, p. 369

Q: What are some factors that would explain high uncollectible account rates for hospitals versus other businesses?

A: Collectibility of the accounts receivable is primarily affected by the creditworthiness of the customer and the nature of the product being sold. In the case of hospitals, the product being sold is medical services. Unlike an automobile or other products purchased on credit, if the patient does not pay the bill, it is difficult for a hospital to repossess the service provided. In addition, these customers' abilities to pay their bills may have been negatively affected by the illness being treated. Furthermore, although many hospital customers have health insurance to help cover the cost of their treatments, rising medical costs combined with reductions in medical insurance benefits have increased collection risk for many hospitals.

Collection Is a Click Away, p. 370

Q: Assume that First Bank has heard about the "eBay of deadbeats" and lists with DebtforSale.com $200,000 of loans it has classified as uncollectible. Assuming First Bank collects 25 percent of the loans listed online and pays DebtforSale a 1 percent collection fee, prepare the journal entry(ies) to record the recoveries.

A: The entry to record the collections would be:

Cash	49,500*	
Allowance for Doubtful Accounts	151,500	
Accounts Receivable		200,000

*$200,000 × 25% × (1 − .01)

Ugly Ducklings, p. 381

Q: Recently, the market values of the securities backed by subprime loans have declined significantly. Can these declines in value be related to the collectibility of the subprime loans? Explain.

A: It is likely that the decline of these bonds is associated with a decline in the collectibility of the subprime loans. Recently, for example, interest rates have increased and the economy has slowed, which has led to increased delinquencies on subprime mortgages. As indicated in the story, the principal and interest payments collected on the subprime loans provide the cash flow to pay the investors in the securities backed by these loans. When the loans default, the securities drop in value. For further discussion, see B. Vikas, "Freddie Mac Tightens Standards," *The New York Times, nytimes.com*, accessed February 28, 2007.

Remember to check the book's companion website to find additional resources for this chapter.

CHAPTER 9
ACCOUNTING FOR INVENTORIES

Inventories in the Crystal Ball

A substantial increase in inventory may be a leading indicator of an upcoming decline in profit margins. The auto industry is an example. Detroit's inventories have been growing for several years because the domestic manufacturers like to run factories at full capacity, even if they are not selling cars as fast as they can make them. That arrangement is particularly tough for **General Motors**. It overproduces and then tries to push vehicle sales with incentives and month-long "blow-out" events. GM's hope is that an ever-growing market will cover the problem until customer demand grows to the point where the cars are purchased without so many incentives.

But recently, all that was growing was GM inventories. Not too long ago, the average sticker on a Cadillac DeVille was $54,193, but the net price after incentives was $42,211. This meant that the factory was giving up a substantial amount of profit through rebates, dealer cash, or lease or interest-rate subsidies. A similar deal could be had at **Ford**, which was selling Explorers for $25,745 net, a 24 percent reduction for various factory incentives. But inventories at GM and Ford continued to grow, even with these significant incentives.

These data concern investors. As one analyst remarked, "When inventory grows faster than sales, profits drop." That is, when companies face slowing sales and growing inventory, then markdowns in prices usually result. These markdowns, in turn, lead to lower sales revenue and income, thereby squeezing profit margins on sales.

Research supporting these observations (Bernard and Noel, 1991) indicates that increases in retailers' inventory translate into lower prices and lower net income. Interestingly, the same research found that for manufacturers, only increases in finished goods inventory lead to future profit declines. Increases in raw materials and work-in-process inventories signal that the company is building its inventory to meet increased demand. Therefore, future sales and income will be higher. These research results reinforce the usefulness of the GAAP requirement for manufacturers to disclose their inventory components on the balance sheet or in related notes.

Sources: J. Flint, "Inventories: Too Much of a Good Thing," *Forbes.com* (September 21, 2004); S. Pulliam, "Heard on the Street," *Wall Street Journal* (May 21, 1997), p. C1; and Victor Bernard and J. Noel, "Do Inventory Disclosures Predict Sales and Earnings?" *Journal of Accounting, Auditing, and Finance* (March 1991), pp. 145–182.

Preview of Chapter 9

As our opening story indicates, information on inventories and changes in inventory helps to predict financial performance. *In this chapter we discuss the basic issues related to accounting and reporting for the costs of inventory, as follows.*

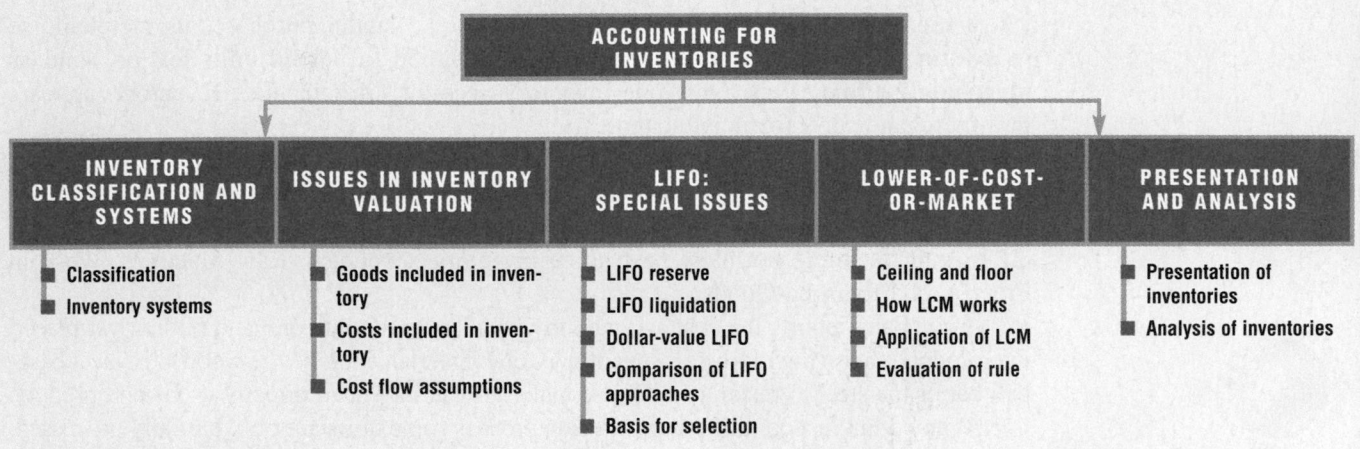

		ACCOUNTING FOR INVENTORIES		
INVENTORY CLASSIFICATION AND SYSTEMS	**ISSUES IN INVENTORY VALUATION**	**LIFO: SPECIAL ISSUES**	**LOWER-OF-COST-OR-MARKET**	**PRESENTATION AND ANALYSIS**
■ Classification ■ Inventory systems	■ Goods included in inventory ■ Costs included in inventory ■ Cost flow assumptions	■ LIFO reserve ■ LIFO liquidation ■ Dollar-value LIFO ■ Comparison of LIFO approaches ■ Basis for selection	■ Ceiling and floor ■ How LCM works ■ Application of LCM ■ Evaluation of rule	■ Presentation of inventories ■ Analysis of inventories

Learning Objectives

After studying this chapter, you should be able to:

1. Identify major classifications of inventory.
2. Distinguish between perpetual and periodic inventory systems.
3. Understand the items to include as inventory cost.
4. Describe and compare the cost flow assumptions used to account for inventories.
5. Explain the significance and use of a LIFO reserve.
6. Understand the effect of LIFO liquidations.
7. Explain the dollar-value LIFO method.
8. Identify the major advantages and disadvantages of LIFO.
9. Describe and apply the lower-of-cost-or-market rule.
10. Explain how to report and analyze inventory.

Inside Chapter 9

■ **What Do the Numbers Mean?**
Staying lean (p. 421)
It was the Wild West (p. 424)
Comparability, please (p. 426)
Comparing apples to apples (p. 440)
Put it in reverse (p. 447)
The squeeze (p. 457)

■ **What's the Principle?** (pp. 423, 425, 430, 442, 443, 446)

■ **Convergence Corner** (p. 450)

■ **Accounting, Analysis, Principles** (p. 451)
Determine ending inventory and apply lower-of-cost-or-market.
Compare LIFO and FIFO companies.
Consider consistency/reliability of lower-of-cost-or-market.

INVENTORY CLASSIFICATION AND SYSTEMS

Classification

Inventories are asset items that a company holds for sale in the ordinary course of business, or goods that it will use or consume in the production of goods to be sold. The description and measurement of inventory require careful attention. The investment in inventories is frequently the largest current asset of merchandising (retail) and manufacturing businesses.

A **merchandising concern**, such as **Wal-Mart**, usually purchases its merchandise in a form ready for sale. It reports the cost assigned to unsold units left on hand as **merchandise inventory**. Only one inventory account, Merchandise Inventory, appears in a merchandiser's financial statements.

Manufacturing concerns, on the other hand, produce goods to sell to the merchandising firms. Many of the largest U.S. businesses are manufacturers, such as **Boeing, IBM, Exxon-Mobil, Procter & Gamble, Ford**, and **Motorola**. Although the products they produce may differ, manufacturers normally have three inventory accounts—Raw Materials, Work in Process, and Finished Goods.

**Additional Inventory
Disclosures**

A company reports the cost assigned to goods and materials on hand but not yet placed into production as **raw materials inventory**. Raw materials include the wood to make a baseball bat or the steel to make a car. These materials can be traced directly to the end product.

At any point in a continuous production process some units are only partially processed. The cost of the raw material for these unfinished units, plus the direct labor cost applied specifically to this material and a ratable share of manufacturing overhead costs, constitute the **work-in-process inventory**.

Illustration 9-1

Comparison of Current
Assets Presentation for
Merchandising and
Manufacturing Companies

Companies report the costs identified with the completed but unsold units on hand at the end of the fiscal period as **finished goods inventory**. Illustration 9-1 contrasts the financial statement presentation of inventories of a merchandising company with those of a manufacturing company. The remainder of the balance sheet is essentially similar for the two types of companies.

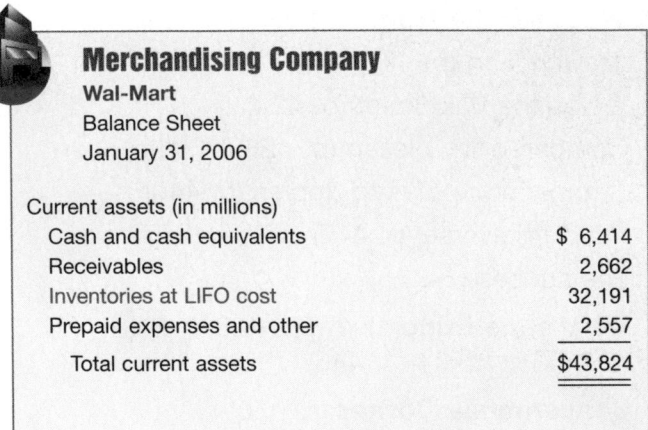

Merchandising Company	
Wal-Mart	
Balance Sheet	
January 31, 2006	
Current assets (in millions)	
Cash and cash equivalents	$ 6,414
Receivables	2,662
Inventories at LIFO cost	32,191
Prepaid expenses and other	2,557
Total current assets	$43,824

Manufacturing Company		
Caterpillar Inc.		
Balance Sheet		
December 31, 2005		
Current assets (in millions)		
Cash and short-term investments		$1,108
Receivables, net		13,968
Inventories		
Raw materials	$1,689	
Work-in-process	814	
Finished goods	2,493	
Supplies	228	
Total inventories		5,224
Other current assets		2,490
Total current assets		$22,790

Inventory Systems

Whether a company manufactures or merchandises goods, it needs an accurate accounting system with up-to-date records. It may lose sales and customers if it does not stock products in the desired style, quality, and quantity. Further, companies must monitor inventory levels carefully to limit the financing costs of carrying large amounts of inventory. Companies use one of two types of systems for maintaining accurate inventory records—the perpetual system or the periodic system.

Perpetual System

A **perpetual inventory system** continuously tracks changes in the Inventory account. That is, a company records all purchases and sales (issues) of goods directly in the Inventory account **as they occur**. The accounting features of a perpetual inventory system are as follows.

1 Debit purchases of merchandise for resale or raw materials for production to Inventory rather than to Purchases.

2 Record freight-in, purchase returns and allowances, and purchase discounts in Inventory rather than in separate accounts.

3 Recognize cost of goods sold for each sale by debiting Cost of Goods Sold and crediting Inventory.

4 Maintain a subsidiary ledger of individual inventory records as a control measure. The subsidiary records show the quantity and cost of each type of inventory on hand.

> OBJECTIVE 2
> **Distinguish between perpetual and periodic inventory systems.**

The perpetual inventory system provides a **continuous record** of the balances in both the Inventory account and the Cost of Goods Sold account.

A computerized recordkeeping system records nearly instantaneously any additions to and issuances from inventory. The popularity and affordability of computerized accounting software makes the perpetual system cost-effective for many kinds of businesses. Many retail stores now incorporate the recording of sales with optical scanners at the cash register into perpetual inventory systems.

What do the numbers mean?   Staying Lean

With the introduction and use of "just-in-time" (JIT) inventory order systems and better supplier relationships, many companies have leaner inventory levels.

Wal-Mart provides a classic example of the use of tight inventory controls. Department managers use a scanner that when placed over the bar code corresponding to a particular item, will tell them how many of the items the store sold yesterday, last week, and over the same period last year. It will tell them how many of those items are in stock, how many are on the way, and how many the neighboring Wal-Mart stores are carrying (in case one store runs out). Such practices have helped Wal-Mart become one of the top-ranked companies on the Fortune 500 in terms of sales.

Beyond the Numbers

Where would you look in the financial statements to uncover the benefits of JIT inventory systems?

Periodic System

Under a **periodic inventory system**, a company only periodically determines the quantity of inventory on hand, as the name implies. It records all acquisitions of inventory during the accounting period by debiting the Purchases account. A company then adds the total in the Purchases account at the end of the accounting period to the cost of the inventory on hand at the beginning of the period. This sum determines the total cost of the goods available for sale during the period. To compute the cost of goods sold, the company subtracts the ending inventory from the cost of goods available for sale. Note that under a periodic inventory system, the cost of goods sold is a residual amount that depends on a physically counted ending inventory.

No matter what type of inventory records companies use, or how well organized their procedures for recording purchases and requisitions, they all face the danger of loss and error. Waste, breakage, theft, improper entry, failure to prepare or record requisitions, and other similar possibilities may cause the inventory records to differ from the actual inventory on hand. Thus all companies need periodic verification of the inventory records by actual count, weight, or measurement; they compare the counts with the detailed inventory records. A company corrects the records to agree with the quantities actually on hand.

Insofar as possible, companies should take the physical inventory near the end of the fiscal year, to reflect correct inventory quantities in their annual accounting reports. Because this is not always possible, however, physical inventories taken within two or three months of the year's end are satisfactory, if a company maintains detailed inventory records with a fair degree of accuracy.[1]

To illustrate the difference between a perpetual and a periodic system, assume that Fesmire Company had the following transactions during the current year.

Beginning inventory	100 units at $6	= $ 600
Purchases	900 units at $6	= $5,400
Sales	600 units at $12	= $7,200
Ending inventory	400 units at $6	= $2,400

Fesmire records these transactions during the current year as shown in Illustration 9-2.

Illustration 9-2
Comparative Entries—
Perpetual vs. Periodic

Perpetual Inventory System			Periodic Inventory System		
1. Beginning inventory, 100 units at $6:					
The inventory account shows the inventory on hand at $600.			The inventory account shows the inventory on hand at $600.		
2. Purchase 900 units at $6:					
Inventory	5,400		Purchases	5,400	
Accounts Payable		5,400	Accounts Payable		5,400
3. Sale of 600 units at $12:					
Accounts Receivable	7,200		Accounts Receivable	7,200	
Sales		7,200	Sales		7,200
Cost of Goods Sold	3,600		(No entry)		
(600 at $6)					
Inventory		3,600			
4. End-of-period entries for inventory accounts, 400 units at $6:					
No entry necessary.			Inventory (ending, by count)	2,400	
The account, Inventory, shows the ending			Cost of Goods Sold	3,600	
balance of $2,400			Purchases		5,400
($600 + $5,400 − $3,600)			Inventory (beginning)		600

When a company uses a perpetual inventory system and a difference exists between the perpetual inventory balance and the physical inventory count, it needs a separate entry to adjust the perpetual inventory account. To illustrate, assume that at the end of the reporting period, Fesmire's perpetual inventory account reports an inventory balance of $4,000. However, a physical count indicates inventory worth $3,800 is actually on hand. Fesmire records the necessary writedown as follows.

Inventory Over and Short	200	
Inventory		200

---

[1]In recent years, some companies have developed methods of determining inventories, including statistical sampling, that are sufficiently reliable to make unnecessary an annual physical count of each item of inventory. However, most companies need more current information regarding their inventory levels to protect against stockouts or overpurchasing, and to aid in the preparation of monthly or quarterly financial data. As a result, many companies use a **modified perpetual inventory system**, in which they track increases and decreases in quantities only—not dollar amounts—in a detailed inventory record. It is merely a memorandum device outside the double-entry system, which helps in determining the level of inventory at any point in time.

Perpetual inventory overages and shortages generally represent a misstatement of cost of goods sold. The difference results from normal and expected shrinkage, breakage, shoplifting, incorrect recordkeeping, and the like. Inventory Over and Short is therefore an adjustment to Cost of Goods Sold. In practice, companies sometimes report Inventory Over and Short in the "Other revenues and gains" or "Other expenses and losses" section of the income statement, depending on its balance.

Note that a company using the periodic inventory system does not report the account Inventory Over and Short. The periodic method thus lacks accounting records against which to compare the physical count. Instead, a company buries inventory overages and shortages in cost of goods sold.

BASIC ISSUES IN INVENTORY VALUATION

The valuation of inventories can be a complex process. It requires determining the following.

1 **The physical goods to include in inventory** (who owns the goods?—goods in transit, consigned goods, special sales agreements).

2 **The costs to include in inventory** (product vs. period costs).

3 **The cost flow assumption to adopt** (specific identification, average cost, FIFO, LIFO, retail, etc.).

We explore these basic issues in the next three sections.

Physical Goods Included in Inventory

Technically, a company should record purchases when it obtains legal title to the goods. In practice, however, a company records acquisitions when it **receives** the goods. Why? Because it is difficult to determine the exact time of legal passage of title for every purchase. In addition, no material error likely results from such a practice if consistently applied. Exceptions to the general rule can arise for goods in transit and consigned goods.

WHAT'S THE PRINCIPLE?

Regardless of the system used—periodic or perpetual—companies must determine two things: (1) Do all of the goods included in the inventory count belong to the company? (2) Does the company own any goods that are not included in the count?

Goods in Transit

Sometimes purchased merchandise remains in transit—is not yet received—at the end of a fiscal period. The accounting for these shipped goods depends on who owns them. Companies determine ownership by applying the "passage of title" rule. If companies ship the goods **f.o.b. shipping point**, title passes to the buyer when the seller delivers the goods to the common carrier, who acts as an agent for the buyer. (The abbreviation f.o.b. stands for free on board.) If companies ship the goods **f.o.b. destination**, title passes to the buyer when the buyer receives the goods from the common carrier. "Shipping point" and "destination," are often designated by a particular location, for example, f.o.b. Denver.

When a company obtains legal title to goods, it must record them as purchases in that fiscal period. Goods shipped f.o.b. shipping point that are in transit at the end of the period belong to the buyer. The buyer should show the purchase in its records, because legal title to these goods passed to the buyer upon shipment of the goods. To disregard such purchases results in understating inventories and accounts payable in the balance sheet, and understating purchases and ending inventories in the income statement.

Consigned Goods

Companies market certain products through a **consignment** shipment. Under this arrangement, one party (the consignor) ships merchandise to another (the consignee), who acts as the consignor's agent in selling the goods. The consignee agrees to accept the **consigned goods** without any liability, except to exercise due care and reasonable protection from loss or damage, until it sells the goods to a third party. When the consignee sells the goods, it remits the revenue to the consignor, less a selling commission and expenses incurred in accomplishing the sale.

Goods out on consignment remain the property of the consignor. The consignor thus includes the goods in its inventory (at purchase price or production cost). Occasionally, and only when the inventory has a significant value the consignor shows the inventory out on consignment as a separate item. Sometimes a consignor reports the inventory on consignment in the notes to the financial statements. For example, **Eagle Clothes, Inc.** reported the following related to consigned goods: "Inventories consist of finished goods shipped on consignment to customers of the Company's subsidiary **April-Marcus, Inc.**" The consignee makes no entry to the inventory account for goods received. Remember, these goods remain the property of the consignor until sold. In fact, the consignee should be extremely careful *not* to include any of the goods consigned as a part of inventory.

Costs Included in Inventory

OBJECTIVE 3

Understand the items to include as inventory cost.

One of the most important problems in dealing with inventories concerns the dollar amount at which to carry the inventory in the accounts. **Companies generally account for the acquisition of inventories, like other assets, on a cost basis.**

Product Costs

Product costs are those costs that "attach" to the inventory. As a result, a company records product costs in its Inventory account. These costs are directly connected with bringing the goods to the buyer's place of business and converting such goods to a salable condition. Such charges include freight charges on goods purchased, other direct costs of acquisition, and labor and other production costs incurred in processing the goods up to the time of sale.

It seems proper also to allocate to inventories a share of any buying costs or expenses of a purchasing department, storage costs, and other costs incurred in storing or handling the goods before their sale. However, because of the practical difficulties involved in allocating such costs and expenses, companies usually exclude these items in valuing inventories.

A manufacturing company's costs include direct materials, direct labor, and manufacturing overhead costs. Manufacturing overhead costs include indirect materials, indirect labor, and various costs incurred in the manufacturing process. These various costs include such items as depreciation, taxes, insurance, and heat and electricity.

What do the numbers mean?   It Was the Wild West

The practice of promotional payments, also known as vendor allowances, is widespread in the retail world. Eager to meet sales targets or to promote their products through shelf placements and in store advertisements, vendors have been happy to grease the palms of retailers with rebates, allowances, and price breaks.

The question is, "How should retailers account for these payments?" Until recently some retailers recorded the payments as a reduction of selling expense. Unfortunately, in some of these cases the retailers had not actually sold the goods. Others accounted for them as a reduction of cost of goods sold.

Recently the SEC sued three executives of **Kmart Holding** and some Kmart vendors for their role in a $24 million accounting fraud that booked vendor allowances early. The scheme apparently allowed some Kmart managers to meet internal profit-margin targets. Similarly, **Royal Ahold** (a large Dutch supermarket operator) discovered that its **U.S. Foodservice** unit had improperly accounted for vendor payments, resulting in overstated earnings of at least $500 million. In addition, it found inflated profits at two of its other subsidiaries, also caused by improper accounting for vendor payments.

One analyst noted that it was like "the Wild West out there" because the lack of rules about when to recognize these payments and how to classify them allowed a certain amount of lawlessness. As a result, the FASB recently ruled that unless certain conditions are met, these payments must reduce cost of goods sold on the income statement. The accounting now appears right, but it took some frauds to close the accounting gap in this area.

Source: C. Schneider, "Retailers and Vendor Allowances," *CFO.com* (August 13, 2003).

Beyond the Numbers

How does the requirement to record vendor allowances in Cost of Goods Sold address the problem of retailers' early recognition of vendor allowances?

Period Costs

Period costs are those costs that are indirectly related to the acquisition or production of goods. Period costs such as selling expenses and, under ordinary circumstances, general and administrative expenses are therefore **not included as part as part of inventory cost.**

Yet, conceptually, these expenses are as much a cost of the product as the initial purchase price and related freight charges attached to the product. Why then do companies exclude these costs from inventoriable items? Because companies generally consider selling expenses as more directly related to the cost of goods sold than to the unsold inventory. In addition, period costs, especially administrative expenses, are so unrelated or indirectly related to the immediate production process that any allocation is purely arbitrary.[2]

Companies usually expense as incurred **interest costs** associated with getting inventories ready for sale. Supporters of this approach argue that interest costs are really a cost of financing. Others contend that interest costs incurred to finance activities associated with readying inventories for sale are as much a cost of the asset as materials, labor, and overhead. Therefore, they reason, companies should capitalize interest costs.

The FASB ruled that companies should capitalize interest costs related to assets constructed for internal use or assets produced as discrete projects (such as ships or real estate projects) for sale or lease.[3] The FASB emphasized that these discrete projects should take considerable time, entail substantial expenditures, and be likely to involve significant amounts of interest cost. A company should not capitalize interest costs for inventories that it routinely manufactures or otherwise produces in large quantities on a repetitive basis. In this case, the informational benefit does not justify the cost.

Illustration 9-3 summarizes the guidelines for determining the physical goods and costs to include in inventory.

Discussion of Inventory Errors

WHAT'S THE PRINCIPLE?

In capitalizing interest, companies apply both constraints— materiality and cost/benefit.

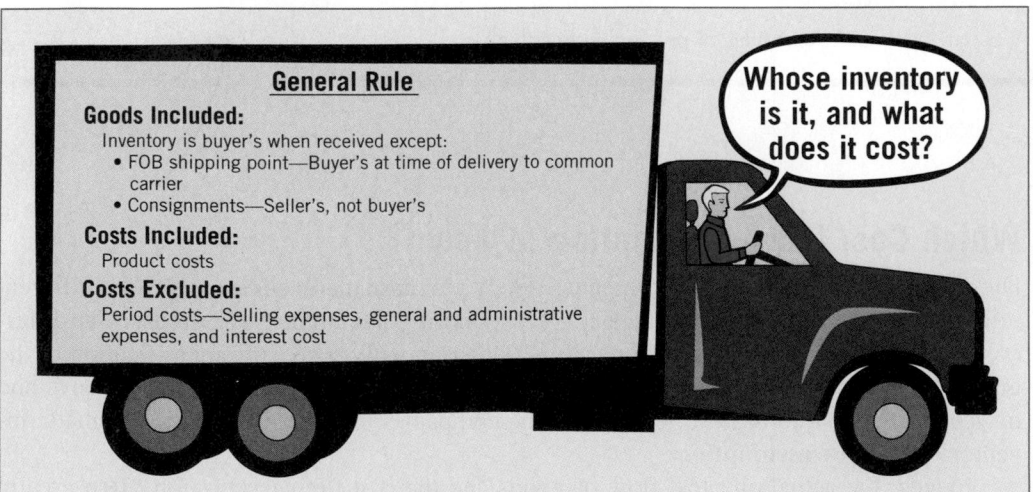

Illustration 9-3
Goods and Costs Included in Inventory

---

[2]Abnormal freight, handling costs, and amounts of wasted materials (spoilage) should not be recorded as inventory costs. If the costs associated with the actual level of spoilage or product defects are greater than the costs associated with normal spoilage or defects, the excess should be charged as an expense in the current period. "Inventory Costs: An Amendment of ARB No. 43, Chapter 4," *Statement of Financial Accounting Standards No. 151* (Norwalk, Conn.: FASB 2004.)

[3]"Capitalization of Interest Cost," *Statement of Financial Accounting Standards No. 34* (Stamford, Conn.: FASB, 1979). The reporting rules related to interest-cost capitalization have their greatest impact in accounting for long-term assets. We therefore discuss them in Chapter 10.

Does it really matter *where* a company reports certain costs in its income statement, as long as it includes them all as expenses in computing income?

For e-tailers, such as **Amazon.com** or **Drugstore.com**, *where* they report certain selling costs does appear to be important. Contrary to well-established retailer practices, these companies insist on reporting some selling costs—fulfillment costs related to inventory shipping and warehousing—as part of administrative expenses, instead of as cost of goods sold. This practice, an example of pro-forma reporting, is allowable within GAAP, *if* applied consistently and adequately disclosed. Although the practice doesn't affect the bottom line, it does make the e-tailers' gross margins look better. For example, at one time Amazon.com reported $265 million of selling costs in one quarter. Some experts thought Amazon.com should have included those charges in costs of goods sold, which would substantially have lowered its gross profit, as shown below.

(in millions)	E-tailer Reporting	Traditional Reporting
Sales	$2,795	$2,795
Cost of goods sold	2,132	2,397
Gross profit	$ 663	$ 398
Gross margin %	24%	14%

Similarly, if **Drugstore.com** and **eToys.com** made similar adjustments, their gross margins would go from positive to negative.

Thus, if you want to be able to compare the operating results of e-tailers to other traditional retailers, it might be a good idea to have a good accounting map in order to navigate their income statements and how they report certain selling costs.

Source: Adapted from P. Elstrom, "The End of Fuzzy Math?" *Business Week,* e.Biz—Net Worth (December 11, 2000). See also *EITF No. 00–10,* "Accounting for Shipping and Handling Fees and Costs." Under this standard, companies must disclose the accounting policy for classifying these selling costs in income.

Beyond the Numbers

What are some other examples of pro-forma reporting?

OBJECTIVE 4
Describe and compare the cost flow assumptions used to account for inventories.

Which Cost Flow Assumption to Adopt?

During any given fiscal period, companies likely purchase merchandise at several different prices. If a company prices inventories at cost and it made numerous purchases at different unit costs, which cost price should it use? Conceptually, a specific identification of the given items sold and unsold seems optimal. But this measure often proves expensive and may be impossible to achieve. Consequently, companies use one of several systematic inventory **cost flow assumptions**.

Indeed, the actual physical flow of goods and the cost flow assumption often greatly differ. **There is no requirement that the cost flow assumption adopted be consistent with the physical movement of goods.** A company's major objective in selecting a method should be to choose the one that, under the circumstances, most clearly reflects periodic income.[4]

To illustrate, assume that Call-Mart Inc. had the following transactions in its first month of operations.

---

[4]"Restatement and Revision of Accounting Research Bulletins," *Accounting Research Bulletin No. 43* (New York: AICPA, 1953), Ch. 4, Statement 4.

Date	Purchases	Sold or Issued	Balance
March 2	2,000 @ $4.00		2,000 units
March 15	6,000 @ $4.40		8,000 units
March 19		4,000 units	4,000 units
March 30	2,000 @ $4.75		6,000 units

From this information, Call-Mart computes the ending inventory of 6,000 units and the cost of goods available for sale (beginning inventory + purchases) of $43,900 [(2,000 @ $4.00) + (6,000 @ $4.40) + (2,000 @ $4.75)]. The question is, which price or prices should it assign to the 6,000 units of ending inventory? The answer depends on which cost flow assumption it uses.

Specific Identification

Specific identification calls for identifying each item sold and each item in inventory. A company includes in its cost of goods sold calculations the costs of the specific items sold. It also includes the costs of the specific items on hand in the inventory. This method should be used only in instances where it is practical to physically separate the different purchases made. As a result, most companies use this method only when handling a relatively small number of costly, easily distinguishable items. In the retail trade this includes some types of jewelry, fur coats, automobiles, and some furniture. In manufacturing it includes special orders and many products manufactured under a job cost system.

To illustrate, assume that Call-Mart Inc.'s 6,000 units of inventory consists of 1,000 units from the March 2 purchase, 3,000 from the March 15 purchase, and 2,000 from the March 30 purchase. Illustration 9-4 shows how Call-Mart computes the ending inventory and cost of goods sold.

Date	No. of Units	Unit Cost	Total Cost
March 2	1,000	$4.00	$ 4,000
March 15	3,000	4.40	13,200
March 30	2,000	4.75	9,500
Ending inventory	6,000		$26,700

Cost of goods available for sale (computed in previous section)	$43,900
Deduct: Ending inventory	26,700
Cost of goods sold	$17,200

Illustration 9-4
Specific Identification Method

This method appears ideal. Specific identification matches actual costs against actual revenue. Thus, a company reports ending inventory at actual cost. In other words, **under specific identification the cost flow matches the physical flow of the goods**. On closer observation, however, this method has certain deficiencies.

Some argue that specific identification allows a company to manipulate net income. For example, assume that a wholesaler purchases identical plywood early in the year at three different prices. When it sells the plywood, the wholesaler can select either the lowest or the highest price to charge to expense. It simply selects the plywood from a specific lot for delivery to the customer. A business manager, therefore, can manipulate net income by delivering to the customer the higher- or lower-priced item, depending on whether the company seeks higher or lower reported earnings for the period.

Another problem relates to the arbitrary allocation of costs that sometimes occurs with specific inventory items. For example, a company often faces difficulty in relating shipping charges, storage costs, and discounts directly to a given inventory item. This results in allocating these costs somewhat arbitrarily, leading to a "breakdown" in the precision of the specific identification method.[5]

Average-Cost

As the name implies, the **average-cost method** prices items in the inventory on the basis of the average cost of all similar goods available during the period. To illustrate use of the periodic inventory method, Call-Mart computes the ending inventory and cost of goods sold using a **weighted-average method** as follows.

Illustration 9-5
Weighted-Average
Method—Periodic
Inventory

Date of Invoice	No. Units	Unit Cost	Total Cost
March 2	2,000	$4.00	$ 8,000
March 15	6,000	4.40	26,400
March 30	2,000	4.75	9,500
Total goods available	10,000		$43,900

Weighted-average cost per unit $\dfrac{\$43,900}{10,000} = \$4.39$

Inventory in units   6,000 units
Ending inventory   6,000 × $4.39 = $26,340

Cost of goods available for sale	$43,900
Deduct: Ending inventory	26,340
Cost of goods sold	$17,560

In computing the average cost per unit, Call-Mart includes the beginning inventory, if any, both in the total units available and in the total cost of goods available.

Companies use the **moving-average method** with perpetual inventory records. Illustration 9-6 shows the application of the moving-average method for perpetual records.

Illustration 9-6
Moving-Average
Method—Perpetual
Inventory

Date	Purchased		Sold or Issued	Balance	
March 2	(2,000 @ $4.00)	$ 8,000		(2,000 @ $4.00)	$ 8,000
March 15	(6,000 @ 4.40)	26,400		(8,000 @ 4.30)	34,400
March 19			(4,000 @ $4.30)		
			$17,200	(4,000 @ 4.30)	17,200
March 30	(2,000 @ 4.75)	9,500		(6,000 @ 4.45)	26,700

---

[5]The motion picture industry provides a good illustration of the cost allocation problem. Often actors receive a percentage of net income for a given movie or television program. Some actors, however, have alleged that their films or programs have been extremely profitable to the studios but that they have received little in the way of profit sharing. Actors contend that the studios allocate additional costs to unsuccessful projects to avoid sharing profits.

In this method, a company computes a new average unit cost *each time* it makes a purchase. For example, on March 15, after purchasing 6,000 units for $26,400, Call-Mart has 8,000 units costing $34,400 ($8,000 + $26,400) on hand. The average unit cost is $34,400 divided by 8,000, or $4.30. Call-Mart uses this unit cost in costing withdrawals from inventory until it makes another purchase. At that point, Call-Mart computes a new average unit cost. Accordingly, the company shows the cost of the 4,000 units withdrawn on March 19 at $4.30, for a total cost of goods sold of $17,200. On March 30, following the purchase of 2,000 units for $9,500, Call-Mart determines a new unit cost of $4.45, for an ending inventory of $26,700.

Companies often use the average-cost methods for practical rather than conceptual reasons. These methods are simple to apply and are objective. They are not as subject to income manipulation as some of the other inventory pricing methods. In addition, proponents of the average-cost methods reason that measuring a specific physical flow of inventory is often impossible. Therefore, it is better to cost items on an average-price basis. This argument is particularly persuasive when dealing with similar inventory items.

First-In, First-Out (FIFO)

The **FIFO method** assumes that a company uses goods in the order in which it purchases them. In other words, the FIFO method assumes that **the first goods purchased are the first used** (in a manufacturing concern) **or the first sold** (in a merchandising concern). The inventory remaining must therefore represent the most recent purchases.

To illustrate, assume that Call-Mart uses the periodic inventory system (and so computes the amount of inventory only at the end of the month). It determines its cost of the ending inventory by taking the cost of the most recent purchase and working back until it accounts for all units in the inventory. Call-Mart determines its ending inventory and cost of goods sold, as shown in Illustration 9-7

Date	No. Units	Unit Cost	Total Cost
March 30	2,000	$4.75	$ 9,500
March 15	4,000	4.40	17,600
Ending inventory	6,000		$27,100

Cost of goods available for sale	$43,900
Deduct: Ending inventory	27,100
Cost of goods sold	$16,800

Illustration 9-7
FIFO Method—Periodic Inventory

If Call-Mart instead uses a perpetual inventory system in quantities and dollars, it attaches a cost figure to each withdrawal. Then the cost of the 4,000 units removed on March 19 consists of the items purchased on March 2 and March 15. Illustration 9-8 shows the inventory on a FIFO-basis perpetual system for Call-Mart.

Date	Purchased	Sold or Issued	Balance
March 2	(2,000 @ $4.00)　$ 8,000		2,000 @ $4.00　$ 8,000
March 15	(6,000 @　4.40)　26,400		2,000 @　4.00⎤ 6,000 @　4.40⎦　34,400
March 19		2,000 @ $4.00⎤ 2,000 @　4.40⎦ ($16,800)	4,000 @　4.40　17,600
March 30	(2,000 @　4.75)　9,500		4,000 @　4.40⎤ 2,000 @　4.75⎦　27,100

Illustration 9-8
FIFO Method—Perpetual Inventory

Here, the ending inventory is $27,100, and the cost of goods sold is $16,800 [(2,000 @ 4.00) + (2,000 @ $4.40)].

Notice that in these two FIFO examples, the cost of goods sold ($16,800) and ending inventory ($27,100) are the same. **In all cases where FIFO is used, the inventory and cost of goods sold would be the same at the end of the month whether a perpetual or periodic system is used.** Why? Because the same costs will always be first in and, therefore, first out. This is true whether a company computes cost of goods sold as it sells goods throughout the accounting period (the perpetual system) or as a residual at the end of the accounting period (the periodic system).

One advantage of FIFO is that it often approximates the physical flow of goods. When the physical flow of goods is actually first-in, first-out, the FIFO method is similar to specific identification. At the same time, it prevents manipulation of income. With FIFO, a company cannot pick a certain cost item to charge to expense.

Another advantage of the FIFO method is that the ending inventory is close to current cost. Because the first goods in are the first goods out, the ending inventory amount consists of the most recent purchases. This is particularly true with rapid inventory turnover. This approach generally approximates replacement cost on the balance sheet when price changes have not occurred since the most recent purchases.

However, the FIFO method fails to match current costs against current revenues on the income statement. A company charges the oldest costs against the more current revenue, possibly distorting gross profit and net income.

Last-In, First-Out (LIFO)

WHAT'S THE PRINCIPLE?

Remember—there is no requirement under GAAP that the cost flow assumption adopted be consistent with the physical movement of goods.

The **LIFO method** matches the cost of the last goods purchased against revenue. If Call-Mart Inc. uses a periodic inventory system, it assumes that **the cost of the total quantity sold or issued during the month comes from the most recent purchases**. Call-Mart prices the ending inventory by using the total units as a basis of computation and disregards the exact dates of sales or issuances. For example, assume that the cost of the 4,000 units withdrawn absorbed the 2,000 units purchased on March 30 and 2,000 of the 6,000 units purchased on March 15. Illustration 9-9 shows how the company computes the inventory and related cost of goods sold.

Illustration 9-9
LIFO Method—Periodic Inventory

Date of Invoice	No. Units	Unit Cost	Total Cost
March 2	2,000	$4.00	$ 8,000
March 15	4,000	4.40	17,600
Ending inventory	6,000		$25,600

Goods available for sale		$43,900
Deduct: Ending inventory		25,600
Cost of goods sold		$18,300

Tutorial on Inventory Methods

The month-end periodic inventory computation presented in Illustration 9-9 (inventory $25,600 and cost of goods sold $18,300) shows a different amount from the perpetual inventory computation (inventory $26,300 and cost of goods sold $17,600) as shown in Illustration 9-10 (next page). The periodic system matches the **total withdrawals** for the month with the total purchases for the month in applying the last-in, first-out method. In contrast, the perpetual system matches **each withdrawal** with the immediately preceding purchases. In effect, the periodic computation assumed that Call-Mart included the cost of the goods that it purchased on March 30 in the sale on March 19.

If a company keeps a perpetual inventory record in quantities and dollars, compared to the periodic record, applying the last-in, first-out method results in **different ending inventory and cost of goods sold amounts**.

Date	Purchased	Sold or Issued	Balance	
March 2	(2,000 @ $4.00) $ 8,000		2,000 @ $4.00 $ 8,000	
March 15	(6,000 @ 4.40) 26,400		2,000 @ 4.00 } 6,000 @ 4.40 } 34,400	
March 19		(4,000 @ $4.40) $17,600	2,000 @ 4.00 } 2,000 @ 4.40 } 16,800	
March 30	(2,000 @ 4.75) 9,500		2,000 @ 4.00 } 2,000 @ 4.40 } 26,300 2,000 @ 4.75 }	

Illustration 9-10
LIFO Method—Perpetual
Inventory

Try it out! Harper Company uses a periodic inventory system. The following information is available for June, when the company sold 1,200 units.

Date	Units	Unit Cost	Total Cost
June 1 Inventory	500	$7	$ 3,500
June 12 Purchase	800	8	6,400
June 25 Purchase	700	9	6,300
	2,000		$16,200

Instructions

Compute the June 30 inventory using each of the following methods:

a   Average-cost.

b   FIFO.

c   LIFO.

Solution

a   Average-cost method

Date	Units	Unit Cost	Total Cost
June 1	500	$7	$ 3,500
June 12	800	8	6,400
June 25	700	9	6,300
	2,000		$16,200

Weighted-average cost per unit = $16,200 ÷ 2,000 = $8.10
Ending inventory = (2,000 − 1,200) × $8.10 = $6,480

b   FIFO method

Date	Units	Unit Cost	Total Cost
June 25	700	$9	$6,300
June 12	100	8	800
Ending inventory	800		$7,100

c LIFO method

Date	Units	Unit Cost	Total Cost
June 1	500	$7	$3,500
June 12	300	8	2,400
Ending inventory	800		$5,900

SPECIAL ISSUES RELATED TO LIFO

LIFO Reserve

OBJECTIVE 5

Explain the significance and use of a LIFO reserve.

Many companies use LIFO for tax and external reporting purposes. However, they maintain a FIFO, average-cost, or standard-cost system for internal reporting purposes. There are several reasons to do so:

1 Companies often base their pricing decisions on a FIFO, average-, or standard-cost assumption, rather than on a LIFO basis.

2 Recordkeeping on some other basis is easier because the LIFO assumption usually does not approximate the physical flow of the product.

3 Profit-sharing and other bonus arrangements often depend on a non-LIFO inventory assumption.

4 The use of a pure LIFO system is troublesome for interim periods, which require estimates of year-end quantities and prices.

Companies record the difference between the inventory method used for internal reporting purposes and LIFO in an account titled Allowance to Reduce Inventory to LIFO. More simply, it is also called the **LIFO reserve**. The change in the allowance balance from one period to the next is the **LIFO effect**. The LIFO effect is the adjustment that companies must make to the accounting records in a given year.

To illustrate, assume that Acme Boot Company uses the FIFO method for internal reporting purposes and LIFO for external reporting purposes. At January 1, 2008, the Allowance to Reduce Inventory to LIFO balance is $20,000. The ending balance should be $50,000. As a result, Acme Boot realizes a LIFO effect of $30,000 and makes the following entry at year-end.

Cost of Goods Sold	30,000	
Allowance to Reduce Inventory to LIFO		30,000

Acme Boot deducts the Allowance to Reduce Inventory to LIFO from inventory to ensure that it states the inventory on a LIFO basis at year-end.

The AICPA Task Force on LIFO Inventory Problems concluded that companies should disclose either the LIFO reserve or the replacement cost of the inventory.[6] Illustration 9-11 shows an example of this kind of disclosure.

---

[6]The AICPA Task Force on LIFO Inventory Problems, *Issues Paper* (New York: AICPA, November 30, 1984), pars. 2–24. The SEC has endorsed this issues paper, and therefore it has authoritative status for GAAP purposes.

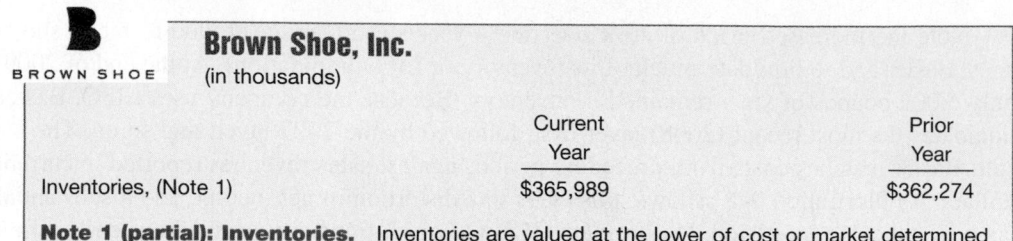

Brown Shoe, Inc.
(in thousands)

	Current Year	Prior Year
Inventories, (Note 1)	$365,989	$362,274

Note 1 (partial): Inventories. Inventories are valued at the lower of cost or market determined principally by the last-in, first-out (LIFO) method. If the first-in, first-out (FIFO) cost method had been used, inventories would have been $11,709 higher in the current year and $13,424 higher in the previous year.

Illustration 9-11
Note Disclosure of LIFO Reserve

Additional LIFO Reserve Disclosures

LIFO Liquidation

Up to this point, we have emphasized a **specific-goods approach** to costing LIFO inventories. (This approach is also called traditional LIFO or unit LIFO.) The specific-goods approach is often unrealistic for two reasons:

> OBJECTIVE **6**
> **Understand the effect of LIFO liquidations.**

1 When a company has many different inventory items, the accounting cost of tracking each inventory item is expensive.

2 Erosion of the LIFO inventory can easily occur. Referred to as **LIFO liquidation**, this erosion often distorts net income and leads to substantial tax payments.

To understand the LIFO liquidation problem, assume that Basler Co. has 30,000 pounds of steel in its inventory on December 31, 2008, costed on a specific-goods LIFO approach, as follows:

Ending Inventory (2008)			
	Pounds	Unit Cost	LIFO Cost
2005	8,000	$ 4	$ 32,000
2006	10,000	6	60,000
2007	7,000	9	63,000
2008	5,000	10	50,000
	30,000		$205,000

As indicated, the ending 2008 inventory of $205,000 for Basler comprises costs from past periods. These costs are called **layers** (increases from period to period). The first layer is identified as the base layer. Illustration 9-12 shows the layers for Basler.

Illustration 9-12
Layers of LIFO Inventory

2008 Layer	$50,000 (5,000 × $10)
2007 Layer	$63,000 (7,000 × $9)
2006 Layer	$60,000 (10,000 × $6)
2005 Base layer	$32,000 (8,000 × $4)

Note the increased price of steel over the 4-year period. In 2009, due to metal shortages, Basler had to liquidate much of its inventory (a LIFO liquidation). At the end of 2009, only 6,000 pounds of steel remained in inventory. Because the company uses LIFO, Basler liquidates the most recent (2008) layer first, followed by the 2007 layer, and so on. The result: Basler matches costs from preceding periods against sales revenues reported in current dollars. As Illustration 9-13 shows, this leads to a distortion in net income and a substantial tax bill in the current period. Unfortunately **LIFO liquidations can occur frequently when companies use a specific-goods LIFO approach**.

Illustration 9-13
LIFO Liquidation

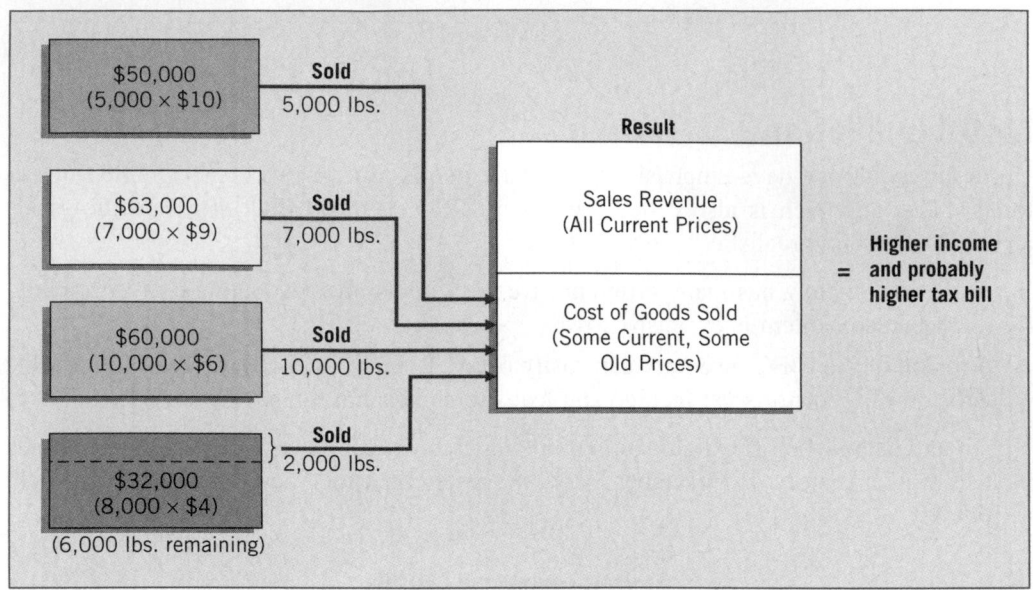

To alleviate the LIFO liquidation problems and to simplify the accounting, companies can combine goods into pools. A **pool** groups items of a similar nature. Thus, instead of only identical units, a company combines, and accounts for together, a number of similar units or products. This method, the **specific-goods pooled-LIFO approach**, usually results in fewer LIFO liquidations. Why? Because the reduction of one quantity in the pool may be offset by an increase in another.

The specific-goods pooled-LIFO approach eliminates some of the disadvantages of the specific-goods (traditional) accounting for LIFO inventories. This pooled approach, using quantities as its measurement basis, however, creates other problems.

First, most companies continually change the mix of their products, materials, and production methods. As a result, in employing a pooled approach using quantities, companies must continually redefine the pools. This can be time-consuming and costly.

Second, even when practical, the approach often results in an erosion ("LIFO liquidation") of the layers, thereby losing much of the LIFO-costing benefit. An erosion of the layers results due to replacement of a specific good or material in the pool with another good or material. The new item may not be similar enough to be treated as part of the old pool. Therefore a company may need to recognize any inflationary profit deferred on the old goods as it replaces them.

Dollar-Value LIFO

OBJECTIVE 7
Explain the dollar-value LIFO method.

The dollar-value LIFO method overcomes the problems of redefining pools and eroding layers. **The dollar-value LIFO method determines and measures any increases and decreases in a pool in terms of total dollar value, not the physical quantity of the goods in the inventory pool.**

Such an approach has two important advantages over the specific-goods pooled approach. First, companies may include a broader range of goods in a dollar-value LIFO pool. Second, a dollar-value LIFO pool permits replacement of goods that are similar, similar in use, or interchangeable. (In contrast, a specific-goods LIFO pool allows only replacement of items that are substantially identical.)

Thus, dollar-value LIFO techniques help protect LIFO layers from erosion. Because of this advantage, companies frequently use the dollar-value LIFO method in practice.[7] Companies use the more traditional LIFO approaches only when dealing with few goods and expecting little change in product mix.

Under the dollar-value LIFO method, one pool may contain the entire inventory. However, companies generally use several pools.[8] In general, the more goods included in a pool, the more likely that increases in the quantities of some goods will offset decreases in other goods in the same pool. Thus, companies avoid liquidation of the LIFO layers. It follows that having fewer pools means less cost and less chance of a reduction of a LIFO layer.

Dollar-Value LIFO Example

To illustrate how the dollar-value LIFO method works, assume that Enrico Company first adopts dollar-value LIFO on December 31, 2007 (base period). The inventory at current prices on that date was $20,000. The inventory on December 31, 2008, at current prices is $26,400.

Can we conclude that Enrico's inventory quantities increased 32 percent ($26,400 ÷ $20,000 = 132%) during the year? First, we need to ask: What is the value of the ending inventory in terms of beginning-of-the-year prices? Assuming that prices have increased 20 percent during the year, the ending inventory at beginning-of-the-year prices amounts to $22,000 ($26,400 ÷ 120%). Therefore, the inventory quantity has increased only 10 percent, or from $20,000 to $22,000 in terms of beginning-of-the-year prices.

The next step is to price this real-dollar quantity increase. This real-dollar quantity increase of $2,000 valued at year-end prices is $2,400 (120% × $2,000). This increment (layer) of $2,400, when added to the beginning inventory of $20,000, totals $22,400 for the December 31, 2008, inventory, as shown below.

First layer—(beginning inventory) in terms of 100	$20,000
Second layer—(2008 increase) in terms of 120	2,400
Dollar-value LIFO inventory, December 31, 2008	$22,400

Note that a layer forms only when the ending inventory at base-year prices exceeds the beginning inventory at base-year prices. Only when a new layer forms must Enrico compute a new index.

Comprehensive Dollar-Value LIFO Example

To illustrate the use of the dollar-value LIFO method in a more complex situation, assume that Bismark Company develops the following information.

[7]A study by James M. Reeve and Keith G. Stanga disclosed that the vast majority of respondent companies applying LIFO use the dollar-value method or the dollar-value retail method. Only a small minority of companies uses the specific-goods (unit-LIFO) approach or the specific-goods pooling approach. See J. M. Reeve and K. G. Stanga, "The LIFO Pooling Decision," *Accounting Horizons* (June 1987), p. 27.

[8]The Reeve and Stanga study (ibid.) reports that most companies have only a few pools—the median is six for retailers and three for nonretailers. But the distributions are highly skewed; some companies have 100 or more pools. Retailers that use LIFO have significantly more pools than nonretailers. About a third of the nonretailers (mostly manufacturers) use a single pool for their entire LIFO inventory.

December 31		Inventory at End-of-Year Prices	÷	Price Index (percentage)	=	End-of-Year Inventory at Base-Year Prices
(Base year)	2005	$200,000		100%		$200,000
	2006	299,000		115		260,000
	2007	300,000		120		250,000
	2008	351,000		130		270,000

At December 31, 2005, Bismark computes the ending inventory under dollar-value LIFO as $200,000, as Illustration 9-14 shows.

Illustration 9-14
Computation of 2005
Inventory at LIFO Cost

Ending Inventory at Base-Year Prices	Layer at Base-Year Prices		Price Index (percentage)		Ending Inventory at LIFO Cost
$200,000	$200,000	×	100	=	$200,000

At December 31, 2006, a comparison of the ending inventory at base-year prices ($260,000) with the beginning inventory at base-year prices ($200,000) indicates that the quantity of goods has increased $60,000 ($260,000 − $200,000). Bismark then prices this increment (layer) at the 2006 index of 115 percent to arrive at a new layer of $69,000. Ending inventory for 2006 is $269,000, composed of the beginning inventory of $200,000 and the new layer of $69,000. Illustration 9-15 shows the computations.

Illustration 9-15
Computation of 2006
Inventory at LIFO Cost

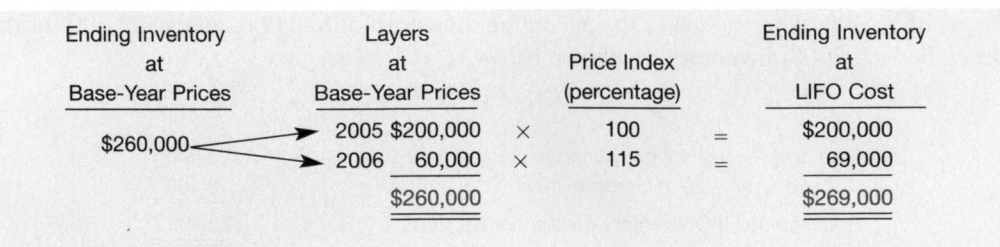

Ending Inventory at Base-Year Prices	Layers at Base-Year Prices		Price Index (percentage)		Ending Inventory at LIFO Cost
$260,000	2005 $200,000	×	100	=	$200,000
	2006 60,000	×	115	=	69,000
	$260,000				$269,000

At December 31, 2007, a comparison of the ending inventory at base-year prices ($250,000) with the beginning inventory at base-year prices ($260,000) indicates a decrease in the quantity of goods of $10,000 ($250,000 − $260,000). If the ending inventory at base-year prices is less than the beginning inventory at base-year prices, **a company must subtract the decrease from the most recently added layer. When a decrease occurs, the company "peels off" previous layers at the prices in existence when it added the layers.**

In Bismark's situation, this means that it removes $10,000 in base-year prices from the 2006 layer of $60,000 at base-year prices. It values the balance of $50,000 ($60,000 − $10,000) at base-year prices at the 2006 price index of 115 percent. As a result, it now values this 2006 layer at $57,500 ($50,000 × 115%). Therefore, Bismark computes the ending inventory at $257,500, consisting of the beginning inventory of $200,000 and the second layer of $57,500. Illustration 9-16 (next page) shows the computations for 2007. Note that if Bismark eliminates a layer or base (or portion thereof), it cannot rebuild it in future periods. That is, the layer is gone forever.

At December 31, 2008, a comparison of the ending inventory at base-year prices ($270,000) with the beginning inventory at base-year prices ($250,000) indicates that an increase in the dollar quantity of goods of $20,000 ($270,000 − $250,000) in terms of base-year prices. After converting the $20,000 increase to the 2008 price index, the ending

Illustration 9-16
Computation of 2007
Inventory at LIFO Cost

Ending Inventory at Base-Year Prices	Layers at Base-Year Prices		Price Index (percentage)		Ending Inventory at LIFO Cost
$250,000	2005 $200,000	×	100	=	$200,000
	2006 50,000	×	115	=	57,500
	$250,000				$257,500

inventory is $283,500, composed of the beginning layer of $200,000, a 2006 layer of $57,500, and a 2008 layer of $26,000 ($20,000 × 130%). Illustration 9-17 shows this computation.

Illustration 9-17
Computation of 2008
Inventory at LIFO Cost

Ending Inventory at Base-Year Prices	Layers at Base-Year Prices		Price Index (percentage)		Ending Inventory at LIFO Cost
$270,000	2005 $200,000	×	100	=	$200,000
	2006 50,000	×	115	=	57,500
	2008 20,000	×	130	=	26,000
	$270,000				$283,500

The ending inventory at base-year prices must always equal the total of the layers at base-year prices. Checking that this situation exists will help to ensure correct dollar-value computations.

Comparison of LIFO Approaches

We presented three different approaches to computing LIFO inventories in this chapter—specific-goods LIFO, specific-goods pooled-LIFO, and dollar-value LIFO. As we indicated earlier, the use of the specific-goods LIFO is unrealistic. Most companies have numerous goods in inventory at the end of a period. Costing (pricing) them on a unit basis is extremely expensive and time-consuming.

The specific-goods pooled-LIFO approach reduces recordkeeping and clerical costs. In addition, it is more difficult to erode the layers because the reduction of one quantity in the pool may be offset by an increase in another. Nonetheless, the pooled approach using quantities as its measurement basis can lead to untimely LIFO liquidations.

As a result, **most companies using a LIFO system employ dollar-value LIFO.** Although the approach appears complex, the logic and the computations are actually quite simple, after determining an appropriate index.

However, problems do exist with the dollar-value LIFO method. The selection of the items to be put in a pool can be subjective.[9] Such a determination, however, is extremely important because manipulation of the items in a pool without conceptual justification can affect reported net income. For example, the SEC noted that some companies have set up pools that are easy to liquidate. As a result, to increase income, a company simply decreases inventory, thereby matching low-cost inventory items to current revenues.

To curb this practice, the SEC has taken a much harder line on the number of pools that companies may establish. In the well-publicized case of **Stauffer Chemical Company**, the company had increased the number of LIFO pools from 8 to 280, boosting its net income by $16,515,000 or approximately 13 percent.[10] Stauffer justified the change in its Annual

Tutorial on LIFO Inventory Issues

---

[9]Companies should analyze how inventory purchases are affected by price changes, how goods are stocked, how goods are used, and if future liquidations are likely. See William R. Cron and Randall Hayes, "The Dollar Value LIFO Pooling Decision: The Conventional Wisdom Is Too General," *Accounting Horizons* (December 1989), p. 57.

[10]Commerce Clearing House, *SEC Accounting Rules* (Chicago: CCH, 1983), par. 4035.

report on the basis of "achieving a better matching of cost and revenue." The SEC required Stauffer to reduce the number of its inventory pools, contending that some pools were inappropriate and alleging income manipulation.

Try it out!

Truman Company uses the dollar-value LIFO method of computing its inventory. Inventory for the last three years is as shown below:

Year Ended December 31	Inventory at Current-Year Cost	Price Index
2007	$60,000	100
2008	84,000	105
2009	87,000	116

Instructions

Compute the value of the 2008 and 2009 inventories using the dollar-value LIFO method.

Solution

Year	Inventory at End-of-Year Prices	Inventory at Base-Year Prices	Layers at Base-Year Prices	×	Price-Index Layers at LIFO Cost	Dollar-Value LIFO Inventory
2007	$60,000	$60,000 ÷ 100 = $60,000	2007 $60,000	×	100 = $60,000	$60,000
2008	84,000	$84,000 ÷ 105 = $80,000	2007 $60,000	×	100 = $60,000	
			2008 20,000	×	105 = $21,000	$81,000
2009	87,000	$87,000 ÷ 116 = $75,000	2007 $60,000	×	100 = $60,000	
			2008 15,000	×	105 = $15,750	$75,750

Note: Consistent with LIFO costing in times of rising prices, the dollar-value LIFO inventory amount is less than inventory stated at end-of-year prices. The company did not add layers at the 2009 prices. This is because the increase in inventory at end-of-year (current) prices was primarily due to higher prices. Also, establishing the LIFO layers based on price-adjusted dollars relative to base-year layers reduces the likelihood of a LIFO liquidation.

Basis for Selection of Inventory Method

How does a company choose among the various inventory methods? Although no absolute rules can be stated, preferability for LIFO usually occurs in either of two circumstances: (1) LIFO is generally preferred if selling prices and revenues have been increasing faster than costs, thereby distorting income. (2) LIFO is generally preferred in situations where its use is traditional, such as department stores and industries where a fairly constant "base stock" is present (such as refining, chemicals, and glass).[11]

Conversely, LIFO is probably inappropriate in certain situations: (1) where prices tend to lag behind costs; (2) where specific identification is traditional, such as in the sale of automobiles, farm equipment, art, and antique jewelry; or (3) where unit costs tend to decrease as production increases, thereby nullifying the tax benefit that LIFO might provide.[12]

[11]*Accounting Trends and Techniques—2006* (New York: AICPA) reports that of 799 inventory method disclosures, 229 used LIFO, 349 used FIFO, 155 used average cost, and 30 used other methods.

[12]See Barry E. Cushing and Marc J. LeClere, "Evidence on the Determinants of Inventory Accounting Policy Choice," *The Accounting Review* (April 1992), pp. 355–366, Table 4, p. 363, for a list of factors hypothesized to affect FIFO–LIFO choices.

Major Advantages of LIFO

One obvious advantage of LIFO approaches is that the LIFO cost flow often approximates the physical flow of the goods in and out of inventory. For instance, in the case of a coal pile, the last coal in is the first coal out because it is on the top of the pile. The coal remover is not going to take the coal from the bottom of the pile! The coal taken first is the coal placed on the pile last.

> **OBJECTIVE 8**
> Identify the major advantages and disadvantages of LIFO.

However, this is one of only a few situations where the actual physical flow corresponds to LIFO. Therefore most adherents of LIFO use other arguments for its widespread use, as follows.

Matching. LIFO matches the more recent costs against current revenues to provide a better measure of current earnings. During periods of inflation, many challenge the quality of non-LIFO earnings, noting that failing to match current costs against current revenues **creates transitory or "paper profits" ("inventory profits")**. Inventory profits occur when the inventory costs matched against sales are less than the inventory replacement cost. This results in understating the cost of goods sold and overstating profit. Using LIFO (rather than a method such as FIFO) matches current costs against revenues, thereby reducing inventory profits.

Tax Benefits/Improved Cash Flow. LIFO's popularity mainly stems from its tax benefits. As long as the price level increases and inventory quantities do not decrease, a deferral of income tax occurs. Why? Because a company matches the items it most recently purchased (at the higher price level) against revenues. For example, when **Fuqua Industries** switched to LIFO, it realized a tax savings of about $4 million. Even if the price level decreases later, the company still temporarily deferred its income taxes. Thus, use of LIFO in such situations improves a company's cash flow.[13]

The tax law requires that if a company uses LIFO for tax purposes, it must also use LIFO for financial accounting purposes[14] (although neither tax law nor GAAP requires a company to pool its inventories in the same manner for book and tax purposes). This requirement is often referred to as the **LIFO conformity rule**. Other inventory valuation methods do not have this requirement.

Major Disadvantages of LIFO Approaches

Despite its advantages, LIFO has the following drawbacks.

Reduced Earnings. Many corporate managers view the lower profits reported under the LIFO method in inflationary times as a distinct disadvantage. They would rather have higher reported profits than lower taxes. Some fear that investors may misunderstand an accounting change to LIFO, and that the lower profits may cause the price of the company's stock to fall. In fact, though, there is evidence to refute this contention.

It is questionable whether companies should switch from LIFO to FIFO for the sole purpose of increasing reported earnings.[15] Intuitively we assume that companies with higher

---

[13]In periods of rising prices, the use of fewer pools will translate into greater income tax benefits through the use of LIFO. The use of fewer pools allows inventory reductions of some items to be offset by inventory increases in others. In contrast, the use of more pools increases the likelihood of liquidating old, low-cost inventory layers and incurring negative tax consequences. See Reeve and Stanga, ibid., pp. 28–29.

[14]Management often selects an accounting procedure because a lower tax results from its use, instead of an accounting method that is conceptually more appealing. Throughout this textbook, we identify accounting procedures that provide income tax benefits to the user.

[15]Because of steady or falling raw materials costs and costs savings from electronic data interchange and just-in-time technologies in recent years, many businesses using LIFO no longer experience substantial tax benefits. Even some companies for which LIFO is creating a benefit are finding that the administrative costs associated with LIFO are higher than the LIFO benefit obtained. As a result, some companies are moving to FIFO or average-cost.

reported earnings would have a higher share valuation (common stock price). Some studies have indicated, however, that the users of financial data exhibit a much higher sophistication than expected. Share prices are the same and, in some cases, even higher under LIFO in spite of lower reported earnings.[16]

The concern about reduced income resulting from adoption of LIFO has even less substance now. The IRS has relaxed the LIFO conformity rule such that companies may provide non-LIFO income numbers as supplementary information. As a result, the profession now permits supplemental non-LIFO disclosures. While not intended to override the basic LIFO method adopted for financial reporting, the supplemental disclosure may be useful in comparing operating income and working capital with companies not on LIFO.

Inventory Understated. LIFO may have a distorting effect on a company's balance sheet. The inventory valuation is normally outdated because the oldest costs remain in inventory. This understatement makes the working capital position of the company appear worse than it really is.

The magnitude and direction of this variation between the carrying amount of inventory and its current price depend on the degree and direction of the price changes and the amount of inventory turnover. The combined effect of rising product prices and avoidance of inventory liquidations increases the difference between the inventory carrying value at LIFO and current prices of that inventory. This magnifies the balance sheet distortion attributed to the use of LIFO.

What do the numbers mean?   Comparing Apples to Apples

Investors commonly use the current ratio to evaluate a company's liquidity. They compute the current ratio as current assets divided by current liabilities. A higher current ratio indicates that a company is better able to meet its current obligations when they come due. However, it is not meaningful to compare the current ratio for a company using LIFO to one for a company using FIFO. It would be like comparing apples to oranges, since the two companies measure inventory (and cost of goods sold) differently.

To make the current ratio comparable on an apples-to-apples basis, analysts use the LIFO reserve. The following inventory adjustment should do the trick:

LIFO inventory + LIFO reserve = FIFO inventory

(For cost of goods sold, add the *change* in the LIFO reserve to LIFO cost of goods sold to yield the comparable FIFO amount.)

For example, for **Brown Shoe, Inc.** (see Illustration 9-11), with current assets of $487.8 million and current liabilities of $217.8 million, the current ratio using LIFO is: $487.8 ÷ $217.8 = 2.2. After adjusting for the LIFO reserve, Brown's current ratio under FIFO would be: ($487.8 + $11.7) ÷ $217.8 = 2.3. Without the LIFO adjustment, the Brown Shoe current ratio is understated.

Beyond the Numbers

What are some reasons a company like Brown Shoe might change from the LIFO to the FIFO method?

[16]See, for example, Shyam Sunder, "Relationship Between Accounting Changes and Stock Prices: Problems of Measurement and Some Empirical Evidence," *Empirical Research in Accounting: Selected Studies, 1973* (Chicago: University of Chicago), pp. 1–40. But see Robert Moren Brown, "Short-Range Market Reaction to Changes to LIFO Accounting Using Preliminary Earnings Announcement Dates," *The Journal of Accounting Research* (Spring 1980), which found that companies that do change to LIFO suffer a short-run decline in the price of their stock.

Physical Flow. LIFO does not approximate the physical flow of the items except in specific situations (such as the coal pile). Originally companies could use LIFO only in certain circumstances. This situation has changed over the years. Now, physical flow characteristics no longer determine whether a company may employ LIFO.

Involuntary Liquidation/Poor Buying Habits. If a company eliminates the base or layers of old costs, it may match old, irrelevant costs against current revenues. A distortion in reported income for a given period may result, as well as detrimental income-tax consequences.[17]

Because of the liquidation problem, LIFO may cause poor buying habits. A company may simply purchase more goods and match these goods against revenue to avoid charging the old costs to expense. Furthermore, recall that with LIFO, a company may attempt to manipulate its net income at the end of the year simply by altering its pattern of purchases.[18]

One survey uncovered the following reasons why companies reject LIFO.[19]

Reasons to Reject LIFO	Number	% of Total*
No expected tax benefits		
No required tax payment	34	16%
Declining prices	31	15
Rapid inventory turnover	30	14
Immaterial inventory	26	12
Miscellaneous tax related	38	17
	159	74%
Regulatory or other restrictions	26	12%
Excessive cost		
High administrative costs	29	14%
LIFO liquidation–related costs	12	6
	41	20%
Other adverse consequences		
Lower reported earnings	18	8%
Bad accounting	7	3
	25	11%

*Percentage totals more than 100% as some companies offered more than one explanation.

Illustration 9-18
Why Do Companies Reject LIFO? Summary of Responses

Companies often combine inventory methods. For example, most companies use LIFO in combination with other valuation approaches. One reason is that certain product lines can be highly susceptible to deflation instead of inflation. In addition, if the level of inventory is unstable, unwanted involuntary liquidations may result in certain product lines if using LIFO. Finally, for high inventory turnover in certain product lines, a company cannot justify LIFO's additional recordkeeping and expense. In such cases, a company often uses average-cost because it is easy to compute.[20]

INTERNATIONAL INSIGHT

LIFO is not permitted under international accounting standards.

[17]The AICPA Task Force on LIFO Inventory Problems recommends that companies disclose the effects on income of LIFO inventory liquidations in the notes to the financial statements, but that they do not afford special treatment to the effects in the income statement. *Issues Paper* (New York: AICPA, 1984), pp. 36–37.

[18]For example, **General Tire and Rubber** accelerated raw material purchases at the end of the year to minimize the book profit from a liquidation of LIFO inventories and to minimize income taxes for the year.

[19]Michael H. Granof and Daniel Short, "Why Do Companies Reject LIFO?" *Journal of Accounting, Auditing, and Finance* (Summer 1984), pp. 323–333, Table 1, p. 327.

[20]For an interesting discussion of the reasons for and against the use of FIFO and average cost, see Michael H. Granof and Daniel G. Short, "For Some Companies, FIFO Accounting Makes Sense," *Wall Street Journal* (August 30, 1982), and the subsequent rebuttal by Gary C. Biddle "Taking Stock of Inventory Accounting Choices," *Wall Street Journal* (September 15, 1982).

Although a company may use a variety of inventory methods to assist in accurate computation of net income, once it selects a pricing method, it must apply it consistently thereafter. If conditions indicate that the inventory pricing method in use is unsuitable, the company must seriously consider all other possibilities before selecting another method. It should clearly explain any change and disclose its effect in the financial statements.

To improve comparability of its LIFO inventory amounts, **JC Penney, Inc.** presented the following information in its annual report.

Illustration 9-19
Supplemental Non-LIFO
Disclosure

JC Penney, Inc.

Some companies in the retail industry use the FIFO method in valuing part or all of their inventories. Had JC Penney used the FIFO method and made no other assumptions with respect to changes in income resulting therefrom, income and income per share from continuing operations would have been:

Income from continuing operations (in millions)	$325
Income from continuing operations per share	$4.63

LOWER-OF-COST-OR-MARKET

OBJECTIVE 9

Describe and apply the lower-of-cost-or-market rule.

Inventories are recorded at their cost. However, if inventory declines in value below its original cost, a major departure from the historical cost principle occurs. Whatever the reason for a decline—obsolescence, price-level changes, damaged goods, and so forth—a company should write down the inventory to reflect this loss. **A company abandons the historical cost principle when the future utility (revenue-producing ability) of the asset drops below its original cost.**

Companies with a declining inventory utility therefore value inventory on the basis of the lower-of-cost-or-market instead. Recall that **cost** is the acquisition price of inventory computed using one of the historical cost-based methods—specific identification, average-cost, FIFO, or LIFO. The term **market** in the phrase "the lower-of-cost-or-market" (LCM) generally means the cost to replace the item by purchase or reproduction. In a retailing business the term "market" refers to the market in which a company *purchases* goods, not the market in which it sells them. In manufacturing, the term "market" refers to the cost to reproduce. Thus the rule really means that **companies value goods at cost or cost to replace, whichever is lower.**

For example, say a retailer purchased a **Casio** calculator wristwatch for $30. The retailer can sell the wristwatch for $48.95 and can replace it for $25. The retailer should therefore value the wristwatch at $25 for inventory purposes under the lower-of-cost-or-market rule. A company can use the lower-of-cost-or-market rule of valuation after applying any of the cost flow methods discussed above to determine the inventory cost.

A departure from cost is justified because **a company should charge a loss of utility against revenues in the period in which the loss occurs**, not in the period of sale. In addition, the lower-of-cost-or-market method is **a conservative approach to inventory valuation**. That is, when doubt exists about the value of an asset, a company should undervalue, not overvalue, it.

WHAT'S THE PRINCIPLE?

The use of the lower-of-cost-or-market rule is an excellent example of the conservatism constraint.

Lower-of-Cost-or-Market—Ceiling and Floor

Why use replacement cost to represent market value? Because a decline in the replacement cost of an item usually reflects or predicts a decline in selling price. Using replacement cost allows a company to maintain a consistent rate of gross profit on sales (normal profit margin). Sometimes, however, a reduction in the replacement cost of an item fails to indicate a corresponding reduction in its utility. This requires using two additional valuation limitations to value ending inventory—net realizable value and net realizable value less a normal profit margin.

Net realizable value (NRV) is the estimated selling price in the ordinary course of business, less reasonably predictable costs of completion and disposal. A normal profit margin is subtracted from that amount to arrive at **net realizable value less a normal profit margin**.

To illustrate, assume that Jerry Mander Corp. has unfinished inventory with a sales value of $1,000, estimated cost of completion of $300, and a normal profit margin of 10 percent of sales. The company determines the net realizable value as shown in Illustration 9-20.

Inventory—sales value		$1,000
Less: Estimated cost of completion and disposal		300
Net realizable value		700
Less: Allowance for normal profit margin (10% of sales)		100
Net realizable value less a normal profit margin		$ 600

Illustration 9-20
Computation of Net Realizable Value

The general **lower-of-cost-or-market (LCM)** rule is: **A company values inventory at the lower-of-cost-or-market, with *market* limited to an amount that is not more than net realizable value or less than net realizable value less a normal profit margin.**[21]

What is the rationale for these two limitations? The **upper (ceiling)** and **lower (floor) limits** for the value of the inventory prevent companies from reporting inventory at an amount in excess of the net selling price or at an amount less than the net selling price less a normal profit margin. The maximum limitation, **not to exceed the net realizable value (ceiling)**, covers obsolete, damaged, or shopworn material. It prevents overstatement of inventories and understatement of the loss in the current period. That is, if the replacement cost of an item exceeds its net realizable value, a company should not report inventory at replacement cost. The company can receive only the selling price less cost of disposal. To report the inventory at replacement cost would result in an overstatement of inventory and an understated loss in the current period.

To illustrate, assume that **Staples** paid $1,000 for a laser printer that it can now replace for $900. The printer's net realizable value is $700. At what amount should Staples report the laser printer in the financial statements? To report the replacement cost of $900 overstates the ending inventory and understates the loss for the period. Therefore, Staples should report the printer at $700.

The minimum limitation is **not to be less than net realizable value reduced by an allowance for an approximately normal profit margin (floor)**. This deters understatement of inventory and overstatement of the loss in the current period. It establishes a floor below which a company should price inventory, regardless of replacement cost. It makes no sense to price inventory below net realizable value less a normal margin. This minimum amount (floor) measures what the company can receive for the inventory and still earn a normal profit. Illustration 9-21 (page 444) graphically presents these guidelines.

WHAT'S THE PRINCIPLE?

Setting a floor and a ceiling increases the relevancy of the inventory presentation. The inventory figure provides a better understanding of how much revenue the inventory will generate.

How Lower-of-Cost-or-Market Works

The **designated market value** is the amount that a company compares to cost. It is **always the middle value of three amounts**: replacement cost, net realizable value, and net realizable value less a normal profit margin.

[21]"Restatement and Revision of Accounting Research Bulletins," *Accounting Research Bulletin No. 43* (New York: AICPA, 1953), Ch. 4, par. 8.

Illustration 9-21
Inventory Valuation—
Lower-of-Cost-or-Market

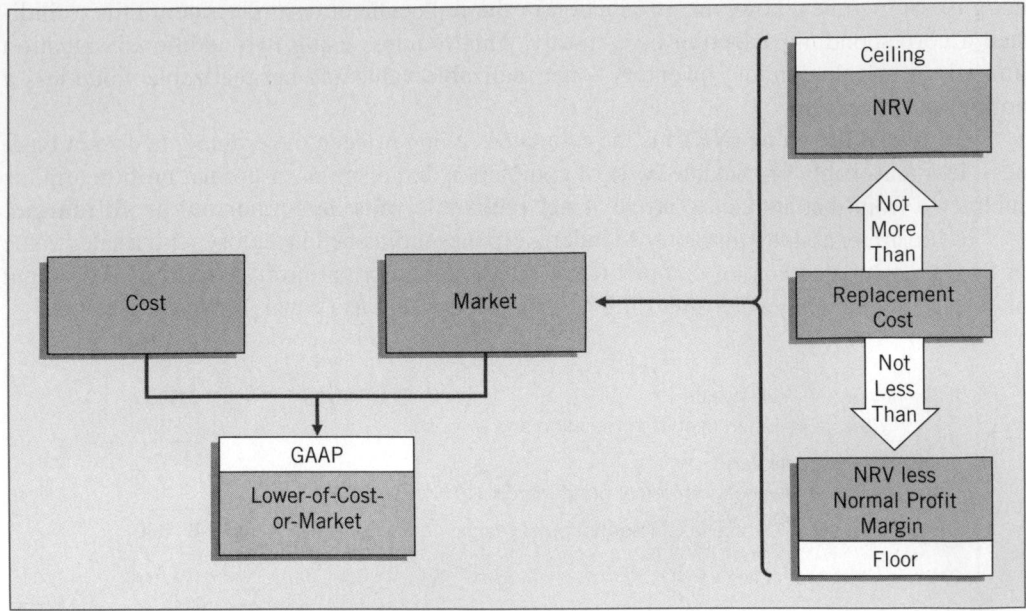

To illustrate how to compute designated market value, assume the following information relative to the inventory of Regner Foods, Inc.

Illustration 9-22
Computation of
Designated Market Value

Food	Replacement Cost	Net Realizable Value (Ceiling)	Net Realizable Value Less a Normal Profit Margin (Floor)	Designated Market Value
Spinach	$ 88,000	$120,000	$104,000	$104,000
Carrots	90,000	100,000	70,000	90,000
Cut beans	45,000	40,000	27,500	40,000
Peas	36,000	72,000	48,000	48,000
Mixed vegetables	105,000	92,000	80,000	92,000

Designated Market Value Decision:

Spinach	Net realizable value less a normal profit margin is selected because it is the middle value.
Carrots	Replacement cost is selected because it is the middle value.
Cut beans	Net realizable value is selected because it is the middle value.
Peas	Net realizable value less a normal profit margin is selected because it is the middle value.
Mixed vegetables	Net realizable value is selected because it is the middle value.

Regner Foods then compares designated market value to cost to determine the lower-of-cost-or-market. It determines the final inventory value as shown in Illustration 9-23 (next page).

The application of the lower-of-cost-or-market rule incorporates only losses in value that occur in the normal course of business from such causes as style changes, shift in demand, or regular shop wear. A company reduces damaged or deteriorated goods to net realizable value. When material, it may carry such goods in separate inventory accounts.

Illustration 9-23
Determining Final
Inventory Value

Food	Cost	Replacement Cost	Net Realizable Value (Ceiling)	Net Realizable Value Less a Normal Profit Margin (Floor)	Designated Market Value	Final Inventory Value
Spinach	$ 80,000	$ 88,000	$120,000	$104,000	$104,000	$ 80,000
Carrots	100,000	90,000	100,000	70,000	90,000	90,000
Cut beans	50,000	45,000	40,000	27,500	40,000	40,000
Peas	90,000	36,000	72,000	48,000	48,000	48,000
Mixed vegetables	95,000	105,000	92,000	80,000	92,000	92,000
						$350,000

Final Inventory Value:

Spinach — Cost ($80,000) is selected because it is lower than designated market value (net realizable value less a normal profit margin).

Carrots — Designated market value (replacement cost, $90,000) is selected because it is lower than cost.

Cut beans — Designated market value (net realizable value, $40,000) is selected because it is lower than cost.

Peas — Designated market value (net realizable value less a normal profit margin, $48,000) is selected because it is lower than cost.

Mixed vegetables — Designated market value (net realizable value, $92,000) is selected because it is lower than cost.

Methods of Applying Lower-of-Cost-or-Market

In the Regner Foods illustration, we assumed that the company applied the lower-of-cost-or-market rule to each individual type of food. However, companies may apply the lower-of-cost-or-market rule either directly to each item, to each category, or to the total of the inventory. If a company follows a major-category or total-inventory approach in applying the lower-of-cost-or-market rule, increases in market prices tend to offset decreases in market prices.

To illustrate, assume that Regner Foods separates its food products into two major categories, frozen and canned, as shown in Illustration 9-24.

Illustration 9-24
Alternative Applications of
Lower-of-Cost-or-Market

	Cost	Designated Market	Lower-of-Cost-or-Market by: Individual Items	Major Categories	Total Inventory
Frozen					
Spinach	$ 80,000	$104,000	$ 80,000		
Carrots	100,000	90,000	90,000		
Cut beans	50,000	40,000	40,000		
Total frozen	230,000	234,000		$230,000	
Canned					
Peas	90,000	48,000	48,000		
Mixed vegetables	95,000	92,000	92,000		
Total canned	185,000	140,000		140,000	
Total	$415,000	$374,000	$350,000	$370,000	$374,000

If Regner Foods applied the lower-of-cost-or-market rule to individual items, the amount of inventory is $350,000. If it applies the rule to major categories, inventory jumps to $370,000. If it applies LCM to the total inventory, inventory totals $374,000. Why this difference? When a company uses a major-categories or total-inventory approach, market values higher than cost offset market values lower than cost. For Regner Foods, using the major-categories approach partially offsets the high market value for spinach. Using the total-inventory approach totally offsets it.

Companies usually price inventory on an item-by-item basis. In fact, tax rules require that companies use an individual-item basis barring practical difficulties. In addition, the individual-item approach gives the most conservative valuation for balance sheet purposes.[22] Often, a company prices inventory on a total-inventory basis when it offers only one end product (comprised of many different raw materials). If it produces several end products, a company might use a category approach instead. The method selected should be the one that most clearly reflects income. **Whichever method a company selects, it should apply the method consistently from one period to another.**[23]

Evaluation of the Lower-of-Cost-or-Market Rule

The lower-of-cost-or-market rule suffers some conceptual deficiencies:

1 A company recognizes decreases in the value of the asset and the charge to expense in the period in which the loss in utility occurs—not in the period of sale. On the other hand, it recognizes increases in the value of the asset only at the point of sale. This inconsistent treatment can distort income data.

2 Application of the rule results in inconsistency because a company may value the inventory at cost in one year and at market in the next year.

3 Lower-of-cost-or-market values the inventory in the balance sheet conservatively, but its effect on the income statement may or may not be conservative. Net income for the year in which a company takes the loss is definitely lower. Net income of the subsequent period may be higher than normal if the expected reductions in sales price do not materialize.

4 Application of the lower-of-cost-or-market rule uses a "normal profit" in determining inventory values. Since companies estimate "normal profit" based on past experience (and which they may not attain in the future), this subjective measure presents an opportunity for income manipulation.

Many financial statement users appreciate the lower-of-cost-or-market rule because they know that it at least prevents overstatement of inventory. In addition, recognizing all losses but anticipating no gains generally results in lower income.

WHAT'S THE PRINCIPLE?

The inconsistency in the presentation of inventory is an example of the trade-off between *relevancy* and *reliability*. Market is more relevant than cost, and cost is more reliable than market. Apparently, relevance takes precedence in a down market, while reliability is more important in an up market.

---

[22]If a company uses dollar-value LIFO, determining the LIFO cost of an individual item may be more difficult. The company might decide that it is more appropriate to apply the lower-of-cost-or-market rule to the total amount of each pool. The AICPA Task Force on LIFO Inventory Problems concluded that the most reasonable approach to applying the lower-of-cost-or-market provisions to LIFO inventories is to base the determination on reasonable groupings of items. A pool constitutes a reasonable grouping.

[23]Inventory accounting for financial statement purposes can be different from income-tax purposes. For example, companies cannot use the lower-of-cost-or-market rule with LIFO for tax purposes. However, companies may use of the lower-of-cost-or-market and LIFO for financial accounting purposes.

What do the numbers mean?

The lower-of-cost-or-market rule is designed to provide timely information about the decline in the value of inventory. And income takes a hit in the period of the write-down.

What happens in the periods after the write-down? For some companies, gross margins and bottom lines get a boost when the company sells inventory that was written down in a previous period. As the following table shows, three companies, **Vishay Intertechnology**, **Transwitch**, and **Cisco Systems** reported gains from selling inventory written down in a previous period. The table describes the extent of the company's disclosure of the gain from the reversal of the write-down.

Company	Gain from Reversal	Disclosure
Vishay Intertechnology	Not available	Poor—The semi-conductor company did not mention the gain in its earnings announcement. In an SEC filing two weeks later, it disclosed the gain on the inventory it had written down.
Transwitch	$600,000	Poor—The company did not mention the gain in its earnings announcement. In an SEC filing three weeks later, it disclosed the gain on the written-down inventory.
Cisco Systems	$525 million	Full—The networking giant detailed the gains from selling inventory it had previously written off in its earnings release and SEC filings.

For Transwitch, the reversal of fortunes amounted to 23 percent of net income. The problem is that the $600,000 credit had little to do with the company's ongoing operations, and the company did not do a good job disclosing the effect of the reversal on current-year profitability.

Even when companies do disclose a reversal, it is sometimes hard to determine the impact on income. For example, **Intel** disclosed that it had sold inventory that it had written down in prior periods but did not specify how much reserved inventory was sold.

After the recent accounting scandals, transparency of financial reporting has become a top priority. With better disclosure of the reversals that boost profits in the current period, financial transparency would also get a boost.

Source: Adapted from S. E. Ante, "The Secret Behind Those Profit Jumps," *BusinessWeek Online* (December 8, 2003).

Beyond the Numbers

Describe the economic conditions that give rise to inventory write-downs followed by reversals.

PRESENTATION AND ANALYSIS

Presentation of Inventories

Accounting standards require financial statement disclosure of the composition of the inventory, inventory financing arrangements, and the inventory costing methods employed. The standards also require the consistent application of costing methods from one period to another.

OBJECTIVE 10

Explain how to report and analyze inventory.

Manufacturers should report the inventory composition either in the balance sheet or in a separate schedule in the notes. The relative mix of raw materials, work-in-process, and finished goods helps in assessing liquidity and in computing the stage of inventory completion.

Significant or unusual financing arrangements relating to inventories may require note disclosure. Examples include transactions with related parties, product financing arrangements, firm-purchase commitments, involuntary liquidation of LIFO inventories, and pledging of inventories as collateral. Companies should present inventories pledged as collateral for a loan in the current assets section rather than as an offset to the liability.

A company should also report the basis on which it states inventory amounts (lower-of-cost-or-market) and the method used in determining cost (LIFO, FIFO, average-cost, etc.). For example, the annual report of **Mumford of Wyoming** contains the following disclosures.

Additional Inventory Disclosures

Mumford of Wyoming

Note A: Significant Accounting Policies

Live feeder cattle and feed—last-in, first-out (LIFO) cost, which is below approximate market	$854,800
Live range cattle—lower of principally identified cost or market	$1,240,500
Live sheep and supplies—lower of first-in, first-out (FIFO) cost or market	$674,000
Dressed meat and by-products—principally at market less allowances for distribution and selling expenses	$362,630

Illustration 9-25

Disclosure of Inventory Methods

The preceding illustration shows that a company can use different costing methods for different elements of its inventory. If Mumford changes the method of costing any of its inventory elements, it must report a change in accounting principle. For example, if Mumford changes its method of accounting for live sheep from FIFO to average-cost, it should separately report this change, along with the effect on income, in the financial statements. Changes in accounting principle require an explanatory paragraph in the auditor's report describing the change in method.

Fortune Brands, Inc. reported its inventories in its annual report as shown in Illustration 9-26. (Note the "trade practice" followed in classifying inventories among the current assets.)

Fortune Brands, Inc.
($000S)

Current assets	
Inventories (Note 2)	
Leaf tobacco	$ 563,424
Bulk whiskey	232,759
Other raw materials, supplies and work in process	238,906
Finished products	658,326
	1,693,415

Illustration 9-26

Disclosure of Trade Practice in Valuing Inventories

Note 2: Inventories

Inventories are priced at the lower of cost (average; first-in, first-out; and minor amounts at last-in, first-out) or market. In accordance with generally recognized trade practice, the leaf tobacco and bulk whiskey inventories are classified as current assets, although part of such inventories due to the duration of the aging process, ordinarily will not be sold within one year.

Analysis of Inventories

As our opening story illustrates, the amount of inventory that a company carries can have significant economic consequences. As a result, companies must manage inventories. But inventory management is a two-edged sword. It requires constant attention. On the one hand, management wants to stock a great variety and quantity of items, to provide customers with the greatest selection. However, such an inventory policy may incur excessive carrying costs (e.g., investment, storage, insurance, taxes, obsolescence, and damage). On the other hand, low inventory levels lead to stockouts, lost sales, and disgruntled customers.

Using financial ratios helps to chart a middle course between these two dangers. Common ratios used in the management and evaluation of inventory levels are inventory turnover and a related measure, average days to sell the inventory.

Inventory Turnover Ratio

The **inventory turnover ratio** measures the number of times on average a company sells the inventory during the period. It measures the liquidity of the inventory. To compute inventory turnover, divide the cost of goods sold by the average inventory on hand during the period. Barring seasonal factors, analysts compute average inventory from beginning and ending inventory balances. For example, in its 2005 annual report **Kellogg Company** reported a beginning inventory of $681 million, an ending inventory of $717 million, and cost of goods sold of $5,611.6 million for the year. Illustration 9-27 shows the inventory turnover formula and Kellogg Company's 2005 ratio computation.

$$\text{Inventory Turnover} = \frac{\text{Cost of Goods Sold}}{\text{Average Inventory}}$$

$$= \left[\frac{\$5,611.6}{\dfrac{\$681 + \$717}{2}} \right] = 8 \text{ times}$$

Illustration 9-27
Inventory Turnover Ratio for Kellogg Company, 2005

Average Days to Sell Inventory

A variant of the inventory turnover ratio is the **average days to sell inventory**. This measure represents the average number of days' sales for which inventory is on hand. For example, the inventory turnover for Kellogg Company of 8 times divided into 365 is approximately 45.6 days.

There are typical levels of inventory in every industry. However, companies that keep their inventory at lower levels with higher turnovers than those of their competitors, and still satisfy customer needs, are the most successful.

You will want to read the CONVERGENCE CORNER on page 450 for discussion of how international convergence efforts relate to the accounting for inventories.

CONVERGENCE CORNER

Inventories

The major iGAAP requirements related to accounting and reporting for inventories are found in *IAS 2* ("Inventories"), *IAS 18* ("Revenue"), and *IAS 41* ("Agriculture"). In most cases, iGAAP and U.S. GAAP are the same. The major differences are that iGAAP prohibits the use of the LIFO cost flow assumption and records market in the lower-of-cost-or-market differently.

RELEVANT FACTS

- The requirements for accounting for and reporting inventories are more principles-based under iGAAP. That is, U.S. GAAP provides more detailed guidelines in inventory accounting.

- Who owns the goods—goods in transit, consigned goods, special sales agreements—as well as the costs to include in inventory are essentially accounted for the same under iGAAP and U.S. GAAP.

- A major difference between iGAAP and U.S. GAAP relates to the LIFO cost flow assumption. U.S. GAAP permits the use of LIFO for inventory valuation. iGAAP prohibits its use. FIFO and average-cost are the only two acceptable cost flow assumptions permitted under iGAAP. Both sets of GAAP permit specific identification where appropriate.

- In the lower-of-cost-or-market test for inventory valuation, iGAAP defines market as net realizable value. U.S. GAAP, on the other hand, defines market as replacement cost subject to the constraints of net realizable value (the ceiling) and net realizable value less a normal markup (the floor). That is, iGAAP does not use a ceiling or a floor to determine market.

ABOUT THE NUMBERS

Presented below is a disclosure under iGAAP related to inventories for **Nokia Corporation**, which reflects application of iGAAP to its inventories.

Nokia Corporation
Notes to the Consolidated Financial Statements (in part)
Note 1.   Accounting principles

Inventories

Inventories are stated at the lower of cost or net realizable value. Cost is determined using standard cost, which approximates actual cost on a FIFO basis. Net realizable value is the amount that can be realized from the sale of the inventory in the normal course of business after allowing for the costs of realization. In addition to the cost of materials and direct labor, an appropriate proportion of production overhead is included in the inventory values. An allowance is recorded for excess inventory and obsolescence based on the lower of cost or net realizable value.

Note 18.   Inventories (000,000 euros)

	2006	2005
Raw materials, supplies, and other	360	361
Work in progress	600	685
Finished goods	594	622
Total	1,554	1,668

- In U.S. GAAP, if inventory is written down under the lower-of-cost-or-market valuation, the new basis is now considered its cost. As a result, the inventory may not be written back up to its original cost in a subsequent period. Under iGAAP, the write-down may be reversed in a subsequent period up to the amount of the previous write-down. Both the write-down and any subsequent reversal should be reported on the income statement.

- Unlike property, plant, and equipment, iGAAP does not permit the option of valuing inventories at fair value. As indicated above, iGAAP requires inventory to be written down, but inventory cannot be written up above its original cost.

- Similar to U.S. GAAP, certain agricultural products and mineral products can be reported at net realizable value using iGAAP.

ON THE HORIZON

One convergence issue that will be difficult to resolve relates to the use of the LIFO cost flow assumption. As indicated, iGAAP specifically prohibits its use. Conversely, the LIFO cost flow assumption is widely used in the United States because of its favorable tax advantages. In addition, many argue that LIFO from a financial reporting point of view provides a better matching of current costs against revenue and therefore enables companies to compute a more realistic income.

The problem is compounded in the Unites States because LIFO cannot be used for tax purposes unless it is used for financial reporting purposes. As a result, unless the tax law changes, it is unlikely that U.S. GAAP will eliminate the use of the LIFO cost flow assumption because of its substantial tax advantages for many companies.

Also, U.S. GAAP has more detailed rules related to accounting and reporting of inventories than iGAAP. We expect that these more detailed rules will be used internationally because they provide practical guidance for some inventory accounting and reporting issues.

ACCOUNTING, ANALYSIS, PRINCIPLES

Englehart Company has the following inventory, purchases, and sales data for the month of March.

Inventory:

March 1	200 units @ $4.00	$ 800

Purchases:

March 10	500 units @ $4.50	2,250
March 20	400 units @ $4.75	1,900
March 30	300 units @ $5.00	1,500

Sales:

March 15	500 units
March 25	400 units

The physical inventory count on March 31 shows 500 units on hand.

Accounting

a Assuming Englehart uses a perpetual inventory system, determine the cost of inventory on hand at March 31 and the cost of goods sold for March under (1) first-in, first-out (FIFO) and (2) last-in, first-out (LIFO).

b Shortly after the end of the month, there is a severe downturn in the market for Englehart's product. The company determines the following: the replacement cost for the ending inventory is $2,400; net realizable value is $2,300; and net realizable value less a normal profit margin is $2,250. Is a lower-of-cost-or-market write-down required (assume the FIFO cost flow assumption)? Explain.

Analysis

Most of Englehart's competitors use LIFO inventory costing. How can an analyst compare the results of companies in an industry, when some use LIFO and others use FIFO?

Principles

How does application of the lower-of-cost-or-market rule affect the (1) consistency and (2) the reliability of accounting information?

Solution

Accounting

a The cost of goods available for sale is $6,450, as follows:

Inventory:		200 units @ $4.00	$ 800
Purchases:	March 10	500 units @ $4.50	2,250
	March 20	400 units @ $4.75	1,900
	March 30	300 units @ $5.00	1,500
Total cost of good available for sale			$6,450

Under a **perpetual inventory system**, the cost of goods sold under each cost flow methods is as follows.

FIFO Method

Date	Purchases	Sales	Balance
March 1			(200 @ $4.00) $800
March 10	(500 @ $4.50) $2,250		(200 @ $4.00)
			(500 @ $4.50) $3,050
March 15		(200 @ $4.00)	
		(300 @ $4.50)	(200 @ $4.50) $900
		$2,150	
March 20	(400 @ $4.75) $1,900		(200 @ $4.50)
			(400 @ $4.75) $2,800
March 25		(200 @ $4.50)	
		(200 @ $4.75)	
		$1,850	
March 30	(300 @ $5.00) $1,500		(200 @ $4.75)
			(300 @ $5.00) $2,450

Ending inventory = $2,450   Cost of good sold = $6,450 − $2,450 = $4,000

LIFO Method

Date	Purchases	Sales	Balance
March 1			(200 @ $4.00) $800
March 10	(500 @ $4.50) $2,250		(200 @ $4.00)
			(500 @ $4.50) $3,050
March 15		(500 @ $4.50) $2,250	(200 @ $4.00) $800
March 20	(400 @ $4.75) $1,900		(200 @ $4.00)
			(400 @ $4.75) $2,700
March 25		(400 @ $4.75) $1,900	(200 @ $4.00) $800
March 30	(300 @ $5.00) $1,500		(200 @ $4.00)
			(300 @ $5.00) $2,300

Ending inventory = $2,300   Cost of good sold = $6,450 − $2,300 = $4,150

b   Yes, a lower-of-cost-or-market write-down is needed. The designated market value is $2,300 (net realizable value), which is greater than net realizable value less normal profit margin (floor) and less than replacement cost (ceiling). Thus, there would be a write-down of $150 ($2,450 − $2,300).

Analysis

Companies that use LIFO report the LIFO reserve, which measures the difference between inventory values based on LIFO relative to FIFO. Thus, by adding the LIFO reserve to the inventories under LIFO, analysts obtain a FIFO-based inventory measure. They can use this measure in any analysis involving inventories (e.g., inventory turnover).

Principles

Use of the lower-of-cost-or-market rule can result in inconsistent results because the inventory may be valued at cost one year but at market in the next year. Application of the LCM rule requires estimates of the normal profit margin in determining designated market value. These estimates are based on past results, which may not be attained in the future. Such estimation reduces the reliability of inventory valuations based on lower-of-cost-or-market.

Key Terms

average-cost method, 428
average days to sell inventory, 449
consigned goods, 423
cost flow assumptions, 426
designated market value, 443
dollar-value LIFO, 434
finished goods inventory, 420
first-in, first-out (FIFO) method, 429
f.o.b. destination, 423
f.o.b. shipping point, 423
inventories, 420
inventory turnover ratio, 449
last-in, first-out (LIFO) method, 430
LIFO effect, 432
LIFO liquidation, 433
LIFO reserve, 432
lower (floor) limit, 443

lower-of-cost-or-market (LCM), 443
market (for LCM), 442
merchandise inventory, 420
moving-average method, 428
net realizable value (NRV), 443
net realizable value less a normal profit margin, 443
period costs, 425
periodic inventory system, 421
perpetual inventory system, 421
product costs, 424
raw materials inventory, 420
specific-goods pooled-LIFO approach, 434
specific identification, 427
upper (ceiling) limit, 443
weighted-average method, 428
work-in-process inventory, 420

Summary of Learning Objectives

1 Identify major classifications of inventory. Only one inventory account, Merchandise Inventory, appears in the financial statements of a merchandising concern. A manufacturer normally has three inventory accounts: Raw Materials, Work in Process, and Finished Goods. Companies report as raw materials inventory the cost assigned to goods and materials on hand but not yet placed into production. They report as work-in-process inventory the cost of the raw materials on which production has been started but not completed, plus the direct labor cost applied specifically to this material and a ratable share of manufacturing overhead costs. Finally, they report as finished goods inventory the costs identified with the completed but unsold units on hand at the end of the fiscal period.

2 Distinguish between perpetual and periodic inventory systems. A perpetual inventory system maintains a continuous record of changes in inventory in the Inventory account. That is, a company records all purchases and sales (issues) of goods directly in the Inventory account as they occur. Under a periodic inventory system, companies determine the quantity of inventory on hand only periodically. A company debits a Purchases account, but the Inventory account remains the same. It determines cost of goods sold at the end of the period using a formula. Companies using a periodic system ascertain ending inventory by physical count.

3 Understand the items to include as inventory cost. Product costs are those costs that attach to the inventory and are recorded in the inventory account. Such charges include freight charges on goods purchased, other direct costs of acquisition, and labor and other production costs incurred in processing the goods up to the time of sale. Period costs are those costs that are indirectly related the acquisition or production of the goods. These changes, such as selling expense and general and administrative expenses, are therefore not included as part of inventory cost.

4 Describe and compare the cost flow assumptions used to account for inventories. (1) *Average-cost* prices items in the inventory on the basis of the average cost of all similar goods available during the period. (2) *First-in, first-out (FIFO)* assumes that a company uses goods in the order in which it purchases them. The inventory remaining must therefore represent the most recent purchases. (3) *Last-in, first-out (LIFO)* matches the cost of the last goods purchased against revenue.

5 Explain the significance and use of a LIFO reserve. The difference between the inventory method used for internal reporting purposes and LIFO is referred to as the Allowance to Reduce Inventory to LIFO, or the LIFO reserve. Companies should disclose either the LIFO reserve or the replacement cost of the inventory in the financial statements.

6 Understand the effect of LIFO liquidations. LIFO liquidations match costs from preceding periods against sales revenues reported in current dollars. This distorts net income and results in a substantial tax bill in the current period. LIFO liquidations can occur frequently when using a specific-goods LIFO approach.

7 Explain the dollar-value LIFO method. For the dollar-value LIFO method, companies determine and measure increases and decreases in a pool in terms of total dollar value, not the physical quantity of the goods in the inventory pool.

8 Identify the major advantages and disadvantages of LIFO. The major *advantages* of LIFO are as follows: (1) LIFO matches recent costs against current revenues to provide a better measure of current earnings. (2) As long as the price level increases and inventory quantities do not decrease, a deferral of income tax occurs in LIFO. (3) Because of the deferral of income tax, cash flow improves. Major *disadvantages* are: (1) reduced earnings, (2) understated inventory, (3) no approximated

physical flow of the items except in peculiar situations, and (4) involuntary liquidation issues.

9 Describe and apply the lower-of-cost-or-market rule. If inventory declines in value below its original cost for whatever reason, a company should write down the inventory to reflect this loss. The general rule is to abandon the historical cost principle when the future utility (revenue-producing ability) of the asset drops below its original cost.

10 Explain how to report and analyze inventory. Accounting standards require financial statement disclosure of: (1) the composition of the inventory (in the balance sheet or a separate schedule in the notes); (2) significant or unusual inventory financing arrangements; and (3) inventory costing methods employed (which may differ for different elements of inventory). Accounting standards also require the consistent application of costing methods from one period to another. Common ratios used to manage and evaluate of inventory levels are inventory turnover and a related measure, average days to sell the inventory.

BEHIND THE NUMBERS APPENDIX 9A   GROSS PROFIT METHOD

OBJECTIVE 11

Determine ending inventory by applying the gross profit method.

Companies take a physical inventory to verify the accuracy of the perpetual inventory records or, if no records exist, to arrive at an inventory amount. Sometimes, however, taking a physical inventory is impractical. In such cases, companies use substitute measures to approximate inventory on hand.

One substitute method of verifying or determining the inventory amount is the **gross profit method** (also called the gross margin method).[1] Auditors widely use this method in situations where they need only an estimate of the company's inventory (e.g., interim reports). Companies also use this method when fire or other catastrophe destroys either inventory or inventory records. The gross profit method relies on three assumptions:

1 The beginning inventory plus purchases equal total goods to be accounted for.

2 Goods not sold must be on hand.

3 The sales, reduced to cost, deducted from the sum of the opening inventory plus purchases, equal ending inventory.

To illustrate, assume that Cetus Corp. has a beginning inventory of $60,000 and purchases of $200,000, both at cost. Sales at selling price amount to $280,000. The gross profit on selling price is 30 percent. Cetus applies the gross margin method as follows.

---

[1]We discuss an estimation method used in the retail industry, the retail method, in Appendix D at the book companion website, **www.wiley.com/warfield**.

Beginning inventory (at cost)		$ 60,000
Purchases (at cost)		200,000
Goods available (at cost)		260,000
Sales (at selling price)	$280,000	
Less: Gross profit (30% of $280,000)	84,000	
Sales (at cost)		196,000
Approximate inventory (at cost)		$ 64,000

The current period's records contain all the information Cetus needs to compute inventory at cost, except for the gross profit percentage. Cetus determines the gross profit percentage by reviewing company policies or prior-period records. In some cases, companies must adjust this percentage if they consider prior periods unrepresentative of the current period.[2]

Computation of Gross Profit Percentage

In most situations, the **gross profit percentage** is stated as a percentage of selling price. The previous illustration, for example, used a 30 percent gross profit on sales. Gross profit on selling price is the common method for quoting the profit for several reasons: (1) Most companies state goods on a retail basis, not a cost basis. (2) A profit quoted on selling price is lower than one based on cost. This lower rate gives a favorable impression to the consumer. (3) The gross profit based on selling price can never exceed 100 percent.[3]

In Illustration 9A-1, the gross profit was a given. But how did Cetus derive that figure? To see how to compute a gross profit percentage, assume that an article cost $15 and sells for $20, a gross profit of $5. This markup is $\frac{1}{4}$ or 25 percent of retail, and $\frac{1}{3}$ or 33 $\frac{1}{3}$ percent of cost.

$$\frac{\text{Markup}}{\text{Retail}} = \frac{\$5}{\$20} = 25\% \text{ at retail} \qquad \frac{\text{Markup}}{\text{Cost}} = \frac{\$5}{\$15} = 33\frac{1}{3}\% \text{ on cost}$$

[2]An alternative method of estimating inventory using the gross profit percentage, considered by some to be less complicated than the traditional method, uses the standard income statement format as follows. (Assume the same data as in the Cetus illustration above.)

Sales		$280,000		$280,000
Cost of sales				
Beginning inventory	$ 60,000		$ 60,000	
Purchases	200,000		200,000	
Goods available for sale	260,000		260,000	
Ending inventory	(3) ?		(3) 64,000 Est.	
Cost of goods sold		(2) ?		(2)196,000 Est.
Gross profit on sales (30%)		(1) ?		(1) 84,000 Est.

Compute the unknowns as follows: first the gross profit amount, then cost of goods sold, and then the ending inventory, as shown below.

(1) $280,000 × 30% = $84,000 (gross profit on sales).
(2) $280,000 − $84,000 = $196,000 (cost of goods sold).
(3) $260,000 − $196,000 = $64,000 (ending inventory).

[3]The terms *gross margin percentage*, *rate of gross profit*, and *percentage markup* are synonymous, although companies more commonly use *markup* in reference to cost and *gross profit* in reference to sales.

Although companies normally compute the gross profit on the basis of selling price, you should understand the basic relationship between markup on cost and markup on selling price.

For example, assume that a company marks up a given item by 25 percent. What, then, is the **gross profit on selling price**? To find the answer, assume that the item sells for $1. In this case, the following formula applies.

$$
\begin{aligned}
\textbf{Cost + Gross Profit} &= \textbf{Selling Price} \\
C + .25C &= SP \\
(1 + .25)C &= SP \\
1.25C &= \$1.00 \\
C &= \$0.80
\end{aligned}
$$

The gross profit equals $0.20 ($1.00 − $0.80). The rate of gross profit on selling price is therefore 20 percent ($0.20/$1.00).

Conversely, assume that the gross profit on selling price is 20 percent. What is the **markup on cost**? To find the answer, again assume that the item sells for $1.00. Again, the same formula holds:

$$
\begin{aligned}
\textbf{Cost + Gross Profit} &= \textbf{Selling Price} \\
C + .20SP &= SP \\
C &= (1 - .20)SP \\
C &= .80SP \\
C &= .80(\$1.00) \\
C &= \$0.80
\end{aligned}
$$

As in the previous example, the markup equals $0.20 ($1.00 − $0.80). The markup on cost is 25 percent ($0.20/$0.80).

Retailers use the following formulas to express these relationships:

Illustration 9A-3
Formulas Relating to
Gross Profit

1. Gross Profit on Selling Price = $\dfrac{\text{Percentage Markup on Cost}}{100\% + \text{Percentage Markup on Cost}}$

2. Percentage Markup on Cost = $\dfrac{\text{Gross Profit on Selling Price}}{100\% - \text{Gross Profit on Selling Price}}$

To understand how to use these formulas, consider the following calculations.

Illustration 9A-4
Application of Gross Profit
Formulas

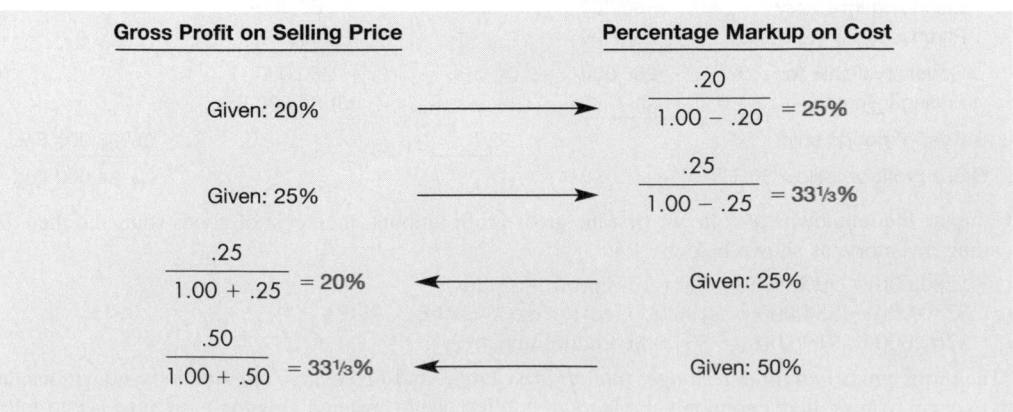

Because selling price exceeds cost, and with the gross profit amount the same for both, **gross profit on selling price will always be less than the related percentage based on cost**. Note that companies may not multiply sales by a cost-based markup percentage. Instead, company must convert the gross profit percentage to a percentage based on selling price.

What do the numbers mean?   The Squeeze

Managers and analysts closely follow gross profits. A small change in the gross profit rate can significantly affect the bottom line. For example, in 1993 **Apple Computer** suffered a textbook case of shrinking gross profits. In response to pricing wars in the personal computer market, Apple had to quickly reduce the price of its signature Macintosh computers—reducing prices more quickly than it could reduce its costs. As a result, its gross profit rate fell from 44 percent in 1992 to 40 percent in 1993. Though the drop of 4 percent seems small, its impact on the bottom line caused Apple's stock price to drop from $57 per share on June 1, 1993, to $27.50 by mid-July 1993.

As another example, **Debenham**, the second largest department store in the United Kingdom, experienced a 14 percentage share price decline. The cause? Mark-downs on slow-moving inventory reduced its gross margin.

Source: Alison Smith, "Debenham's Shares Hit by Warning," *Financial Times* (July 24, 2002), p. 21.

Beyond the Numbers

How does the change in accounting for vendor allowances (see "It Was the Wild West" on p. 424) affect the reported gross profits of retailers?

Evaluation of Gross Profit Method

What are the major disadvantages of the gross profit method? One major disadvantage is that **it provides an estimate**. As a result, companies *must* take a physical inventory once a year to verify the inventory. Second, the gross profit method **uses past percentages** in determining the markup. Although the past often provides answers to the future, a current rate is more appropriate. Note that whenever significant fluctuations occur, companies should adjust the percentage as appropriate. Third, companies must be careful when **applying a blanket gross profit rate**. Frequently, a store or department handles merchandise with widely varying rates of gross profit. In these situations, the company may need to apply the gross profit method by subsections, lines of merchandise, or a similar basis that classifies merchandise according to the products' respective rates of gross profit.

The gross profit method is normally unacceptable for financial reporting purposes because it provides only an estimate. GAAP requires a physical inventory as additional verification of the inventory indicated in the records. Nevertheless, GAAP permits the gross profit method to determine ending inventory for interim reporting purposes (generally quarterly), provided a company discloses the use of this method. Note that the results of the gross profit method will follow closely the inventory method used (FIFO, LIFO, average cost) because it relies on historical records.

Key Terms

gross profit method, 454
gross profit percentage, 455

Summary of Learning Objective for Appendix 9A

11 Determine ending inventory by applying the gross profit method. To determine ending inventory by applying the gross profit method, follow these steps: (1) Compute the gross profit percentage on selling price. (2) Compute gross profit by multiplying net sales by the gross profit percentage. (3) Compute cost of goods sold by subtracting gross profit from net sales. (4) Compute ending inventory by subtracting cost of goods sold from total goods available for sale.

REVIEW EXERCISE

Norwood Company makes miniature circuit boards that are components of wireless phones and personal organizers. The company has experienced strong growth, and you are especially interested in how well Norwood is managing its inventory balances. You have collected the following information for the current year.

Inventory at the beginning of year	$125.5 million
Inventory at the end of year, before any adjustments	$116.7 million
Total cost of goods sold, before any adjustments	$1,776.4 million

The company values inventory at lower-of-cost-(using LIFO cost flow assumption) or-market.

Instructions

a Compute Norwood's inventory turnover ratio.

b Recompute the inventory turnover ratio after adjusting Norwood's inventory information for the following items.

1 During the year, Norwood recorded sales and costs of goods sold on $2 million of units shipped to various wholesalers on consignment. At year-end, none of these units have been sold by wholesalers.

2 Shipping contracts changed 2 months ago from f.o.b. shipping point to f.o.b. destination point. At the end of the year, $5 million of products are en route to China and will not arrive until after financial statements are released. Current inventory balances do not reflect this change in policy.

3 At the end of the year, Norwood determined that a certain section of inventory with an historical cost of $12 million has a replacement cost of $10.8 million, net realizable value of $10.0 million, and net realizable value less a normal profit margin of $9.4 million.

4 To be more consistent with industry inventory valuation practices, Norwood changed from LIFO to FIFO for its inventory of high-speed circuit boards. This inventory is currently carried at $724 million (cost of goods sold, $941 million). Data for this item of inventory for the year are as follows (units in millions).

Month	Units Purchased	Inventory Sold	Price per Unit	Units Balance
January 1	100		$3.10	100
April 10	150		3.20	250
October 20		130		120
November 20	250		3.50	370
December 15		150		220

Solution

a $\dfrac{\$1,776.4}{(\$125.5 + \$116.7)/2} = 14.7$ times

b Adjustments to ending inventory

Item	Adjustment to Ending Inventory ($000,000)	Explanation
1. Consigned goods	$2	Norwood should count the goods it has consigned in other stores.
2. Goods in transit	$5	Goods officially change hands at the point of destination. Norwood should still show these goods in inventory (not cost of goods sold), until they reach the destination.
3. Lower-of-cost-or-market	$(2)	The correct valuation is $10.0 million since the market designation of $10.0 million is less than the original cost.
4. Change to FIFO	$46[a]	FIFO results in higher inventory (lower cost of goods sold) in times of rising prices.

[a]Circuit board ending inventory under LIFO: $724
 Circuit board ending inventory under FIFO: 220 @ $3.50 = $770
   Difference: $46 ($770 − $724)

Adjusted inventory turnover ratio: $= \dfrac{\$1,725.4^{b}}{(\$125.5 + \$167.7)^{c}/2}$
$= 11.8$ times

[b]Cost of goods sold: $1,776.40 − $2 − $5 + $2 − $46 = $1,725.40
[c]Ending inventory: $116.7 + $2 + $5 − $2 + $46 = $167.7

Questions

Note: All **asterisked** assignment materials relate to material covered in the appendix to the chapter.

1 In what ways are the inventory accounts of a retailing concern different from those of a manufacturing enterprise?

2 Why should inventories be included in (a) a statement of financial position and (b) the computation of net income?

3 What is the difference between a perpetual inventory and a physical inventory? If a company maintains a perpetual inventory, should its physical inventory at any date be equal to the amount indicated by the perpetual inventory records? Why?

4 Mariah Carey Inc. indicated in a recent annual report that approximately $19 million of merchandise was received on consignment. Should Mariah Carey Inc. report this amount on its balance sheet? Explain.

5 Where, if at all, should the following items be classified on a balance sheet?

(a) Goods out on approval to customers.

(b) Goods in transit that were recently purchased f.o.b. destination.

(c) Land held by a realty firm for sale.

(d) Raw materials.

(e) Goods received on consignment.

(f) Manufacturing supplies.

6 Define "cost" as applied to the valuation of inventories.

7 Specific identification is sometimes said to be the ideal method of assigning cost to inventory and to cost of goods sold. Briefly indicate the arguments for and against this method of inventory valuation.

8 First-in, first-out; weighted-average; and last-in, first-out methods are often used instead of specific identification for inventory valuation purposes. Compare these methods with the specific identification method, discussing the theoretical propriety of each method in the determination of income and asset valuation.

9 As compared with the FIFO method of costing inventories, does the LIFO method result in a larger or smaller net income in a period of rising prices? What is the comparative effect on net income in a period of falling prices?

10 What is the dollar-value method of LIFO inventory valuation? What advantage does the dollar-value method have over the specific goods approach of LIFO inventory valuation? Why will the traditional LIFO inventory costing method and the dollar-value LIFO inventory costing method produce different inventory valuations if the composition of the inventory base changes?

11 Explain the following terms:

(a) LIFO layer.

(b) LIFO reserve.

(c) LIFO effect.

12 On December 31, 2007, the inventory of Alando Company amounts to $800,000. During 2008, the company decides to use the dollar-value LIFO method of costing inventories. On December 31, 2008, the inventory is $1,026,000 at December 31, 2008, prices. Using the December 31, 2007, price level of 100 and the December 31, 2008, price level of 108, compute the inventory value at December 31, 2008, under the dollar-value LIFO method.

13 An article in the *Wall Street Journal* used the phrases "phantom (paper) profits" and "high LIFO profits" through involuntary liquidation. Explain these phrases.

14 Where there is evidence that the utility of inventory goods, as part of their disposal in the ordinary course of business, will be less than cost, what is the proper accounting treatment?

15 Explain the rationale for the ceiling and floor in the lower-of-cost-or-market method of valuing inventories.

16 What approaches may be employed in applying the lower-of-cost-or-market procedure? Which approach is normally used and why?

17 In some instances accounting principles require a departure from valuing inventories at cost alone. Determine the proper unit inventory price in the following cases.

	Cases				
	1	2	3	4	5
Cost	$15.90	$16.10	$15.90	$15.90	$15.90
Net realizable value	14.30	19.20	15.20	10.40	16.40
Net realizable value less normal profit	12.80	17.60	13.75	8.80	14.80
Market (replacement cost)	14.80	17.20	12.80	9.70	16.80

18 White Stripes Company reported inventory in its balance sheet as follows:

Inventories $115,756,800

What additional disclosures might be necessary to present the inventory fairly?

19 Of what significance is inventory turnover to a retail store?

*20 What are the major uses of the gross profit method?

*21 A fire destroys all of the merchandise of Rosanna Arquette Company on February 10, 2008. Presented below is information compiled up to the date of the fire.

Inventory, January 1, 2008	$ 400,000
Sales to February 10, 2008	1,750,000
Purchases to February 10, 2008	1,140,000
Freight-in to February 10, 2008	60,000
Rate of gross profit on selling price	40%

What is the approximate inventory on February 10, 2008?

Brief Exercises

(LO 1)   **BE9-1** Included in the December 31 trial balance of Billie Joel Company are the following assets.

Cash	$ 190,000	Work in process	$200,000
Equipment (net)	1,100,000	Receivables (net)	400,000
Prepaid insurance	41,000	Patents	110,000
Raw materials	335,000	Finished goods	150,000

Prepare the current assets section of the December 31 balance sheet.

(LO 1, 2)   **BE9-2** Alanis Morrissette Company uses a perpetual inventory system. Its beginning inventory consists of 50 units that cost $30 each. During June, the company purchased 150 units at $30 each, returned 6 units for credit, and sold 125 units at $50 each. Journalize the June transactions.

BE9-3 Mayberry Company took a physical inventory on December 31 and determined that goods costing $200,000 were on hand. Not included in the physical count were $15,000 of goods purchased from Taylor Corporation, f.o.b. shipping point; and $22,000 of goods sold to Mount Pilot Company for $30,000, f.o.b. destination. Both the Taylor purchase and the Mount Pilot sale were in transit at year-end. What amount should Mayberry report as its December 31 inventory? **(LO 3)**

BE9-4 Jose Zorilla Company uses a periodic inventory system. For April, when the company sold 700 units, the following information is available. **(LO 2, 4)**

	Units	Unit Cost	Total Cost
April 1 inventory	250	$10	$ 2,500
April 15 purchase	400	12	4,800
April 23 purchase	350	13	4,550
	1,000		$11,850

Compute the April 30 inventory and the April cost of goods sold using the average-cost method.

BE9-5 Data for Jose Zorilla Company are presented in BE9-4. Compute the April 30 inventory and the April cost of goods sold using the FIFO method. **(LO 2, 4)**

BE9-6 Data for Jose Zorilla Company are presented in BE9-4. Compute the April 30 inventory and the April cost of goods sold using the LIFO method. **(LO 2, 4)**

BE9-7 Easy-E Company had ending inventory at end-of-year prices of $100,000 at December 31, 2006; $123,200 at December 31, 2007; and $134,560 at December 31, 2008. The year-end price indexes were 100 for 2006; 110 for 2007; and 116 for 2008. Compute the ending inventory for Easy-E Company for 2006 through 2008 using the dollar-value LIFO method. **(LO 7)**

BE9-8 Wingers uses the dollar-value LIFO method of computing its inventory. Data for the past 3 years follow. Compute the value of the 2008 and 2009 inventories using the dollar-value LIFO method. **(LO 7)**

Year Ended December 31	Inventory at Current-year Cost	Price Index
2007	$19,750	100
2008	21,708	108
2009	25,935	114

BE9-9 Presented below is information related to Alstott Inc.'s inventory. **(LO 9)**

(per unit)	Skis	Boots	Parkas
Historical cost	$190.00	$106.00	$53.00
Selling price	217.00	145.00	73.75
Cost to distribute	19.00	8.00	2.50
Current replacement cost	203.00	105.00	51.00
Normal profit margin	32.00	29.00	21.25

Determine the following: (a) the two limits to market value (i.e., the ceiling and the floor) that should be used in the lower-of-cost-or-market computation for skis; (b) the cost amount that should be used in the lower-of-cost-or-market comparison of boots; and (c) the market amount that should be used to value parkas on the basis of the lower-of-cost-or-market.

BE9-10 Robin Corporation has the following four items in its ending inventory. **(LO 9)**

Item	Cost	Replacement Cost	Net Realizable Value (NRV)	NRV Less Normal Profit Margin
Jokers	$2,000	$1,900	$2,100	$1,600
Penguins	5,000	5,100	4,950	4,100
Riddlers	4,400	4,550	4,625	3,700
Scarecrows	3,200	2,990	3,830	3,070

Determine the final lower-of-cost-of-market inventory value for each item.

(LO 10) **BE9-11** In its 2006 annual report, **Deere and Company** reported inventory of $1,957.3 million on October 31, 2006, and $2,134.9 million on October 31, 2005, cost of goods sold of $15,362 million for the year ended October 31, 2006, and net sales of $19,884 million. Compute Deere and Company's inventory turnover and the average days to sell inventory for the fiscal year 2006.

(LO 11) ***BE9-12** Big Hurt Corporation's April 30 inventory was destroyed by fire. January 1 inventory was $150,000, and purchases for January through April totaled $500,000. Sales for the same period were $700,000. Big Hurt's normal gross profit percentage is 31%. Using the gross profit method, estimate Big Hurt's April 30 inventory that was destroyed by fire.

Exercises

(LO 1, 3) **E9-1** **(Inventoriable Costs)** Presented below is a list of items that may or may not be reported as inventory in a company's December 31 balance sheet.

1. Goods out on consignment at another company's store.
 ? , 2. Goods sold on an installment basis. Y if bad debts cannot be estimated
3. Goods purchased f.o.b. shipping point that are in transit at December 31.
4. Goods purchased f.o.b. destination that are in transit at December 31.
 5. Goods sold to another company, for which our company has signed an agreement to repurchase at a set price that covers all costs related to the inventory.
6. Goods sold f.o.b. shipping point that are in transit at December 31.
7. Freight charges on goods purchased.
8. Factory labor costs incurred on goods still unsold.
 ? 9. Interest costs incurred for inventories that are routinely manufactured. Y
10. Costs incurred to advertise goods held for resale.
11. Materials on hand not yet placed into production by a manufacturing firm.
 ? 12. Office supplies.
13. Raw materials on which a manufacturing firm has started production, but which are not completely processed.
 ? 14. Factory supplies.
15. Goods held on consignment from another company.
16. Costs identified with units completed by a manufacturing firm, but not yet sold.
17. Goods sold f.o.b. destination that are in transit at December 31.
18. Temporary investments in stocks and bonds that will be resold in the near future.

Instructions

Indicate which of these items would typically be reported as inventory in the financial statements. If an item should **not** be reported as inventory, indicate how it should be reported in the financial statements.

(LO 1, 3) **E9-2** **(Inventoriable Costs)** In your audit of Jose Oliva Company, you find that a physical inventory on December 31, 2008, showed merchandise with a cost of $441,000 was on hand at that date. You also discover the following items were all excluded from the $441,000.

1. Merchandise of $61,000 which is held by Oliva on consignment. The consignor is the Max Suzuki Company.
2. Merchandise costing $38,000 which was shipped by Oliva f.o.b. destination to a customer on December 31, 2008. The customer was expected to receive the merchandise on January 6, 2009.
3. Merchandise costing $46,000 which was shipped by Oliva f.o.b. shipping point to a customer on December 29, 2008. The customer was scheduled to receive the merchandise on January 2, 2009.
4. Merchandise costing $83,000 shipped by a vendor f.o.b. destination on December 30, 2008, and received by Oliva on January 4, 2009.
5. Merchandise costing $51,000 shipped by a vendor f.o.b. seller on December 31, 2008, and received by Oliva on January 5, 2009.

Instructions

Based on the above information, calculate the amount that should appear on Oliva's balance sheet at December 31, 2008, for inventory.

E9-3 **(Inventoriable Costs)** In an annual audit of Jan Matejko Company at December 31, 2008, you find the following transactions near the closing date.

(LO 1, 3)

1. A special machine, fabricated to order for a customer, was finished and specifically segregated in the back part of the shipping room on December 31, 2008. The customer was billed on that date and the machine excluded from inventory although it was shipped on January 4, 2009.

2. Merchandise costing $2,800 was received on January 3, 2009, and the related purchase invoice recorded January 5. The invoice showed the shipment was made on December 29, 2008, f.o.b. destination.

3. A packing case containing a product costing $3,400 was standing in the shipping room when the physical inventory was taken. It was not included in the inventory because it was marked "Hold for shipping instructions." Your investigation revealed that the customer's order was dated December 18, 2008, but that the case was shipped and the customer billed on January 10, 2009. The product was a stock item of your client.

4. Merchandise received on January 6, 2009, costing $680 was entered in the purchase journal on January 7, 2009. The invoice showed shipment was made f.o.b. supplier's warehouse on December 31, 2008. Because it was not on hand at December 31, it was not included in inventory.

5. Merchandise costing $720 was received on December 28, 2008, and the invoice was not recorded. You located it in the hands of the purchasing agent; it was marked "on consignment."

Instructions

Assuming that each of the amounts is material, state whether the merchandise should be included in the client's inventory. Give your reason for your decision on each item.

E9-4 **(Inventoriable Costs)** Alonzo Spellman, an inventory control specialist, is interested in better understanding the accounting for inventories. Although Alonzo understands the more sophisticated computer inventory control systems, he has little knowledge of how inventory cost is determined. In studying the records of Ditka Enterprises, which sells normal brand-name goods from its own store and on consignment through Wannstedt Inc., he asks you to answer the following questions.

(LO 1, 3)

Instructions

(a) Should Ditka Enterprises include in its inventory normal brand-name goods purchased from its suppliers but not yet received if the terms of purchase are f.o.b. shipping point (manufacturer's plant)? Why?

(b) Should Ditka Enterprises include freight-in expenditures as an inventory cost? Why?

(c) What are products on consignment? How should they be reported in the financial statements?

(AICPA adapted)

E9-5 **(Inventoriable Costs—Perpetual)** Colin Davis Machine Company maintains a general ledger account for each class of inventory, debiting such accounts for increases during the period and crediting them for decreases. The transactions below relate to the Raw Materials inventory account, which is debited for materials purchased and credited for materials requisitioned for use.

(LO 2, 3) 

1. An invoice for $8,100, terms f.o.b. destination, was received and entered January 2, 2008. The receiving report shows that the materials were received December 28, 2007.

2. Materials costing $28,000, shipped f.o.b. destination, were not entered by December 31, 2007, "because they were in a railroad car on the company's siding on that date and had not been unloaded."

3. Materials costing $7,300 were returned to the creditor on December 29, 2007, and were shipped f.o.b. shipping point. The return was entered on that date, even though the materials are not expected to reach the creditor's place of business until January 6, 2008.

4. An invoice for $7,500, terms f.o.b. shipping point, was received and entered December 30, 2007. The receiving report shows that the materials were received January 4, 2008, and the bill of lading shows that they were shipped January 2, 2008.

5. Materials costing $19,800 were received December 30, 2007, but no entry was made for them because "they were ordered with a specified delivery of no earlier than January 10, 2008."

Instructions

Prepare correcting general journal entries required at December 31, 2007, assuming that the books have not been closed.

(LO 2, 3)   **E9-6 (Determining Merchandise Amounts—Periodic)** Two or more items are omitted in each of the following tabulations of income statement data. Fill in the amounts that are missing.

	2006	2007	2008
Sales	$290,000	*360 800?* $?	$410,000
Sales returns	11,000	13,000	*20,000?*
Net sales	*279,000?* ?	347,000	*380,000?*
Beginning inventory	20,000	32,000	*37,000?*
Ending inventory	*32,000?*	*37,000?*	*44,000?*
Purchases	*242,000?*	260,000	298,000
Purchase returns and allowances	5,000	8,000	10,000
Transportation-in	8,000	9,000	12,000
Cost of goods sold	233,000	*256,000?*	293,000
Gross profit on sales	46,000	91,000	97,000

(LO 1, 2, 3)   **E9-7 (Financial Statement Presentation of Manufacturing Amounts—Periodic)** Navajo Company is a manufacturing firm. Presented below is selected information from its 2008 accounting records.

Raw materials inventory, 1/1/08	$ 30,800	Transportation-out	$ 8,000
Raw materials inventory, 12/31/08	37,400	Selling expenses	300,000
Work in process inventory, 1/1/08	72,600	Administrative expenses	180,000
Work in process inventory, 12/31/08	61,600	Purchase discounts	10,640
Finished goods inventory, 1/1/08	35,200	Purchase returns and allowances	6,460
Finished goods inventory, 12/31/08	22,000	Interest expense	15,000
Purchases	278,600	Direct labor	440,000
Transportation-in	6,600	Manufacturing overhead	330,000

Instructions

(a) Compute raw materials used.

(b) Compute the cost of goods manufactured.

(c) Compute cost of goods sold.

(d) Indicate how inventories would be reported in the December 31, 2008, balance sheet.

(LO 2, 4)   **E9-8 (Periodic versus Perpetual Entries)** Fong Sai-Yuk Company sells one product. Presented below is information for January for Fong Sai-Yuk Company.

Jan.	2	Inventory	100 units at $5 each
	4	Sale	80 units at $8 each
	11	Purchase	150 units at $6 each
	13	Sale	120 units at $8.75 each
	20	Purchase	160 units at $7 each
	27	Sale	100 units at $9 each

Fong Sai-Yuk uses the FIFO cost flow assumption. All purchases and sales are on account.

Instructions

(a) Assume Fong Sai-Yuk uses a periodic system. Prepare all necessary journal entries, including the end-of-month closing entry to record cost of goods sold. A physical count indicates that the ending inventory for January is 110 units.

(b) Compute gross profit using the periodic system.

(c) Assume Fong Sai-Yuk uses a perpetual system. Prepare all necessary journal entries.

(d) Compute gross profit using the perpetual system.

(LO 2, 4)   **E9-9 (FIFO and LIFO—Periodic and Perpetual)** Inventory information for Part 311 of Monique Aaron Corp. discloses the following information for the month of June.

June	1	Balance	300 units @ $10	June 10	Sold	200 units @ $24
	11	Purchased	800 units @ $12	15	Sold	500 units @ $25
	20	Purchased	500 units @ $13	27	Sold	300 units @ $27

Instructions

(a) Assuming that the periodic inventory method is used, compute the cost of goods sold and ending inventory under (1) LIFO and (2) FIFO.

(b) Assuming that the perpetual inventory record is kept in dollars and costs are computed at the time of each withdrawal, what is the value of the ending inventory at LIFO?

(c) Assuming that the perpetual inventory record is kept in dollars and costs are computed at the time of each withdrawal, what is the gross profit if the inventory is valued at FIFO?

(d) Why is it stated that LIFO usually produces a lower gross profit than FIFO?

E9-10 (FIFO, LIFO and Average-Cost Determination)   John Adams Company's record of transactions for the month of April was as follows.   (LO 4)

Purchases				Sales		
April 1 (balance on hand)	600 @ $6.00		April 3	500 @ $10.00		
4	1,500 @ 6.08		9	1,400 @ 10.00		
8	800 @ 6.40		11	600 @ 11.00		
13	1,200 @ 6.50		23	1,200 @ 11.00		
21	700 @ 6.60		27	900 @ 12.00		
29	500 @ 6.79			4,600		
	5,300					

Instructions

(a) Assuming that perpetual inventory records are kept in units only, compute the inventory at April 30 using (1) LIFO and (2) average-cost.

(b) Assuming that perpetual inventory records are kept in dollars, determine the inventory using (1) FIFO and (2) LIFO.

(c) Compute cost of goods sold assuming periodic inventory procedures and inventory priced at FIFO.

(d) In an inflationary period, which inventory method—FIFO, LIFO, average-cost—will show the highest net income?

E9-11 (FIFO, LIFO, Average-Cost Inventory)   Petrova Company was formed on December 1, 2007. The following information is available from Petrova's inventory records for Product BAP.   (LO 4)

	Units	Unit Cost
January 1, 2008 (beginning inventory)	600	$ 8
Purchases in 2008		
January 5	1,200	9
January 25	1,300	10
February 16	800	11
March 26	600	12

A physical inventory on March 31, 2008, shows 1,600 units on hand.

Instructions

Prepare schedules to compute the ending inventory at March 31, 2008, under each of the following inventory methods.

(a) FIFO.   **(b)** LIFO.   **(c)** Weighted-average.

E9-12 (Compute FIFO, LIFO, Average-Cost—Periodic)   Presented below is information related to Blow-fish radios for Hootie Company for the month of July.   (LO 4)

Date	Transaction	Units In	Unit Cost	Total	Units Sold	Selling Price	Total
July 1	Balance	100	$4.10	$ 410			
6	Purchase	800	4.20	3,360			
7	Sale				300	$7.00	$ 2,100
10	Sale				300	7.30	2,190
12	Purchase	400	4.50	1,800			
15	Sale				200	7.40	1,480
18	Purchase	300	4.60	1,380			
22	Sale				400	7.40	2,960
25	Purchase	500	4.58	2,290			
30	Sale				200	7.50	1,500
	Totals	2,100		$9,240	1,400		$10,230

Instructions

(a) Assuming that the periodic inventory method is used, compute the inventory cost at July 31 under each of the following cost flow assumptions.

   (1) FIFO.

   (2) LIFO.

   (3) Weighted-average. (Round the weighted-average unit cost to the nearest one-tenth of one cent.)

(b) Answer the following questions.

   (1) Which of the methods used above will yield the lowest figure for gross profit for the income statement? Explain why.

   (2) Which of the methods used above will yield the lowest figure for ending inventory for the balance sheet? Explain why.

(LO 2, 4)   **E9-13 (FIFO and LIFO—Periodic and Perpetual)** The following is a record of Pervis Ellison Company's transactions for Boston teapots for the month of May 2008.

May 1	Balance 400 units @ $20	May 10	Sale 300 units @ $38
12	Purchase 600 units @ $25	20	Sale 540 units @ $38
28	Purchase 400 units @ $30		

Instructions

(a) Assuming that perpetual inventories are **not** maintained and that a physical count at the end of the month shows 560 units on hand, what is the cost of the ending inventory using (1) FIFO and (2) LIFO?

(b) Assuming that perpetual records are maintained and they tie into the general ledger, calculate the ending inventory using (1) FIFO and (2) LIFO.

(LO 4, 10)   **E9-14 (FIFO and LIFO; Income Statement Presentation)** The board of directors of Deion Sanders Corporation is considering whether or not it should instruct the accounting department to shift from a first-in, first-out (FIFO) basis of pricing inventories to a last-in, first-out (LIFO) basis. The following information is available.

Sales	21,000 units @ $50
Inventory, January 1	6,000 units @ 20
Purchases	6,000 units @ 22
	10,000 units @ 25
	7,000 units @ 30
Inventory, December 31	8,000 units @ ?
Operating expenses	$200,000

Instructions

(a) Prepare a condensed income statement for the year on both bases for comparative purposes.

(b) Advise the Board: Should the company switch to LIFO? Explain.

(LO 4)   **E9-15 (FIFO and LIFO Effects)** You are the vice-president of finance of Sandy Alomar Corporation, a retail company. The company prepared two different schedules of gross margin for the first quarter ended March 31, 2008. These schedules appear below.

	Sales ($5 per unit)	Cost of Goods Sold	Gross Margin
Schedule 1	$150,000	$124,900	$25,100
Schedule 2	150,000	129,400	20,600

The computation of cost of goods sold in each schedule is based on the following data.

	Units	Cost per Unit	Total Cost
Beginning inventory, January 1	10,000	$4.00	$40,000
Purchase, January 10	8,000	4.20	33,600
Purchase, January 30	6,000	4.25	25,500
Purchase, February 11	9,000	4.30	38,700
Purchase, March 17	11,000	4.40	48,400

Jane Torville, the president of the corporation, cannot understand how two different gross margins can be computed from the same set of data. As the vice-president of finance, you have explained to Ms. Torville that the two schedules are based on different assumptions concerning the flow of inventory costs, i.e., first-in, first-out, and last-in, first-out. Schedules 1 and 2 were not necessarily prepared in this sequence of cost flow assumptions.

Instructions

Prepare two separate schedules computing cost of goods sold and supporting schedules showing the composition of the ending inventory under both cost flow assumptions.

E9-16 (FIFO and LIFO—Periodic) Howie Long Shop began operations on January 2, 2008. The following stock record card for footballs was taken from the records at the end of the year.   **(LO 3, 4, 8)**

Date	Voucher	Terms	Units Received	Unit Invoice Cost	Gross Invoice Amount
1/15	10624	Net 30	50	$20	$1,000
3/15	11437	1/5, net 30	65	16	1,040 2⁵⁷,6
6/20	21332	1/10, net 30	90	15	1,350
9/12	27644	1/10, net 30	84	12	1,008 3162.06
11/24	31269	1/10, net 30	76	11	836
	Totals		365		$5,234

A physical inventory on December 31, 2008, reveals that 100 footballs were in stock. The bookkeeper informs you that all the discounts were taken. Assume that Howie Long Shop uses the invoice price less discount for recording purchases.

Instructions

(a) Compute the December 31, 2008, inventory using the FIFO method. 1135
(b) Compute the 2008 cost of goods sold using the LIFO method. 3400
(c) What method would you recommend to the owner to minimize income taxes in 2008, using the inventory information for footballs as a guide? FIFO

E9-17 (LIFO Effect) One of the accounting staff of Timber Lake Co. developed the following example to encourage the use of the LIFO method.   **(LO 4, 5)**

In a nutshell, LIFO subtracts inflation from inventory costs, deducts it from taxable income, and records it in a LIFO reserve account on the books. The LIFO benefit grows as inflation widens the gap between current-year and past-year (minus inflation) inventory costs. This gap is:

	With LIFO	Without LIFO
Revenue	$3,200,000	$3,200,000
Cost of goods sold	2,800,000	2,800,000
Operating expenses	150,000	150,000
Operating income	250,000	250,000
LIFO adjustment	40,000	0
Taxable income	$210,000	$250,000
Income taxes @ 36%	$75,600	$90,000
Cash flow	$174,400	$160,000
Extra cash	$14,400	0
Increased cash flow	9%	0%

Instructions

(a) Explain what is meant by the LIFO reserve account.
(b) How does LIFO subtract inflation from inventory costs?
(c) Explain how the cash flow of $174,400 in this example was computed. Explain why this amount may not be correct.
(d) Why does a company that uses LIFO have extra cash? Explain whether this situation will always exist.

(LO 4, 7)   **E9-18** **(Alternative Inventory Methods—Comprehensive)** Tori Amos Corporation began operations on December 1, 2007. The only inventory transaction in 2007 was the purchase of inventory on December 10, 2007, at a cost of $20 per unit. None of this inventory was sold in 2007. Relevant information is as follows.

Ending inventory units		
December 31, 2007		100
December 31, 2008, by purchase date		
December 2, 2008	100	
July 20, 2008	50	150

During the year the company made the following purchases and sales.

Purchases		Sales	
March 15	300 units at $24	April 10	200
July 20	300 units at 25	August 20	300
September 4	200 units at 28	November 18	150
December 2	100 units at 30	December 12	200

The company uses the periodic inventory method.

Instructions

(a) Determine ending inventory under (1) specific identification, (2) FIFO, (3) LIFO, and (4) average-cost.

(b) Determine ending inventory using dollar-value LIFO. Assume that the December 2, 2008, purchase cost is the current cost of inventory. (*Hint*: The beginning inventory is the base layer priced at $20 per unit; the relevant price index is 1.4667.)

(LO 7)   **E9-19** **(Dollar-Value LIFO)** Oasis Company has used the dollar-value LIFO method for inventory cost determination for many years. The following data were extracted from Oasis's records.

Date	Price Index	Ending Inventory at Base Prices	Ending Inventory at Dollar-Value LIFO
December 31, 2007	105	$92,000	$92,600
December 31, 2008	?	97,000	98,350

Instructions

Calculate the index used for 2008 that yielded the above results.

(LO 7)   **E9-20** **(Dollar-Value LIFO)** Enya Corp. adopted the dollar-value LIFO method on January 1, 2008. Its inventory on that date was $160,000. On December 31, 2008, the inventory at prices existing on that date amounted to $140,000. The price level at January 1, 2008, was 100, and the price level at December 31, 2008, was 112.

Instructions

(a) Compute the amount of the inventory at December 31, 2008, under the dollar-value LIFO method.

(b) On December 31, 2009, the inventory at prices existing on that date was $172,500, and the price level was 115. Compute the inventory on that date under the dollar-value LIFO method.

(LO 7)   **E9-21** **(Dollar-Value LIFO)** Presented below is information related to Dino Radja Company.

Date	Ending Inventory (End-of-Year Prices)	Price Index
December 31, 2005	$ 80,000	100
December 31, 2006	115,500	105
December 31, 2007	108,000	120
December 31, 2008	122,200	130
December 31, 2009	154,000	140
December 31, 2010	176,900	145

Instructions

Compute the ending inventory for Dino Radja Company for 2005 through 2010 using the dollar-value LIFO method.

E9-22 (Lower-of-Cost-or-Market) The inventory of 3T Company on December 31, 2008, consists of these items.

Part No	Quantity	Cost per Unit	Market per Unit
110	600	$ 90	$100
111	1,000	60	52
112	500	80	76
113	200	170	180
120	400	205	208
121ª	1,600	16	14
122	300	240	235

ªPart No. 121 is obsolete and has a realizable value of $0.20 each as scrap.

Instructions

(a) Determine the inventory as of December 31, 2008, by the lower-of-cost-or-market method, applying this method directly to each item.
(b) Determine the inventory by the lower-of-cost-or-market method, applying the method to the total of the inventory.

E9-23 (Lower-of-Cost-or-Market) Smashing Pumpkins Company uses the lower-of-cost-or-market method, on an individual-item basis, in pricing its inventory items. The inventory at December 31, 2008, consists of products D, E, F, G, H, and I. Relevant per-unit data for these products appear below.

	Item D	Item E	Item F	Item G	Item H	Item I
Estimated selling price	$120	$110	$95	$90	$110	$90
Cost	75	80	80	80	50	36
Replacement cost	120	72	70	30	70	30
Estimated selling expense	30	30	30	25	30	30
Normal profit	20	20	20	20	20	20

Instructions

Using the lower-of-cost-or-market rule, determine the proper unit value for balance sheet reporting purposes at December 31, 2008, for each of the inventory items above.

E9-24 (Lower-of-Cost-or-Market) Michael Bolton Company follows the practice of pricing its inventory at the lower-of-cost-or-market, on an individual-item basis.

Item No.	Quantity	Cost per Unit	Cost to Replace	Estimated Selling Price	Cost of Completion and Disposal	Normal Profit
1320	1,200	$3.20	$3.00	$4.50	$.35	$1.25
1333	900	2.70	2.30	3.50	.50	.50
1426	800	4.50	3.70	5.00	.40	1.00
1437	1,000	3.60	3.10	3.20	.25	.90
1510	700	2.25	2.00	3.25	.80	.60
1522	500	3.00	2.70	3.80	.40	.50
1573	3,000	1.80	1.60	2.50	.75	.50
1626	1,000	4.70	5.20	6.00	.50	1.00

Instructions

From the information above, determine the amount of Bolton Company inventory.

(LO 10)   **E9-25** **(Analysis of Inventories)** The financial statements of **General Mills, Inc.**'s 2006 annual report disclose the following information.

(in millions)	May 28, 2006	May 29, 2005	May 28, 2004
Inventories	$1,055	$1,037	$1,063

	Fiscal Year	
	2006	2005
Sales	$11,640	$11,244
Cost of sales	6,966	6,834
Net earnings	1,090	1,240

Instructions

Compute General Mills's **(a)** inventory turnover, and **(b)** the average days to sell inventory for 2006 and 2005.

(LO 11)   ***E9-26** **(Gross Profit Method)** Rasheed Wallace Company lost most of its inventory in a fire in December just before the year-end physical inventory was taken. The corporation's books disclosed the following.

Beginning inventory	$170,000	Sales	$650,000
Purchases for the year	390,000	Sales returns	24,000
Purchase returns	30,000	Rate of gross margin on sales	40%

Merchandise with a selling price of $21,000 remained undamaged after the fire. Damaged merchandise with an original selling price of $15,000 had a net realizable value of $5,300.

Instructions

Compute the amount of the loss as a result of the fire, assuming that the corporation had no insurance coverage.

See the book's companion website, at www.wiley.com/college/warfield, for Additional Exercises.

Problems

(LO 3, 4, 7)   **P9-1** **(Various Inventory Issues)** The following independent situations relate to inventory accounting.

1. Jag Co. purchased goods with a list price of $150,000, subject to trade discounts of 20% and 10% with no cash discounts allowable. How much should Jag Co. record as the cost of these goods?

2. Francis Company's inventory of $1,100,000 at December 31, 2008, was based on a physical count of goods priced at cost and before any year-end adjustments relating to the following items.
    a. Goods shipped f.o.b. shipping point on December 24, 2008, from a vendor at an invoice cost of $69,000 to Francis Company were received on January 4, 2009.
    b. The physical count included $29,000 of goods billed to Sakic Corp. f.o.b. shipping point on December 31, 2008. The carrier picked up these goods on January 3, 2009.
    What amount should Francis report as inventory on its balance sheet?

3. Mark Messier Corp. had 1,500 units of part M.O. on hand May 1, 2008, costing $21 each. Purchases of part M.O. during May were as follows.

	Units	Unit Cost
May 9	2,000	$22
17	3,500	23
26	1,000	24

A physical count on May 31, 2008, shows 2,100 units of part M.O. on hand. Using the FIFO method, what is the cost of part M.O. inventory at May 31, 2008? Using the LIFO method, what is the inventory cost? Using the average-cost method, what is the inventory cost?

4. Forsberg Company adopted the dollar-value LIFO method on January 1, 2008 (using internal price indexes and multiple pools). The following data are available for inventory pool A for the 2 years following adoption of LIFO.

Inventory	At Base-Year Cost	At Current-Year Cost	Price Index
1/1/08	$200,000	$200,000	100
12/31/08	240,000	252,000	105 *242 000*
12/31/09	256,000	286,720	112 *257 680*

Using the dollar-value LIFO method, at what amount should the inventory be reported at December 31, 2009?

5. Eric Lindros Inc., a retail store chain, had the following information in its general ledger for the year 2009.

Merchandise purchased for resale	$909,400
Interest on notes payable to vendors	8,700
Purchase returns	16,500 —
Freight-in	22,000 +
Freight-out	17,100

What is Lindros' inventoriable cost for 2009?

Instructions

Answer each of the questions about inventories and explain your answers.

P9-2 **(Compute FIFO, LIFO, and Average-Cost—Periodic and Perpetual)** Taos Company's record of transactions concerning part X for the month of April was as follows. **(LO 2, 4)**

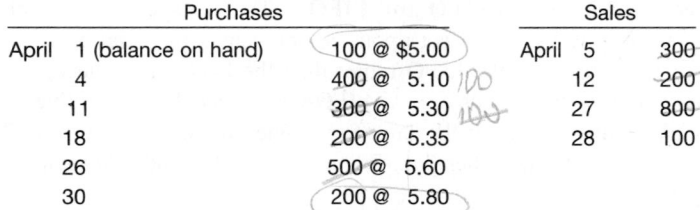

Purchases		Sales	
April 1 (balance on hand)	100 @ $5.00	April 5	300
4	400 @ 5.10 *100*	12	200
11	300 @ 5.30 *100*	27	800
18	200 @ 5.35	28	100
26	500 @ 5.60		
30	200 @ 5.80		

Instructions

(a) Compute the inventory at April 30 on each of the following bases. Assume that perpetual inventory records are kept in units only. Carry unit costs to the nearest cent.
  (1) First-in, first-out (FIFO).
  (2) Last-in, first-out (LIFO).
  (3) Average-cost.
(b) If the perpetual inventory record is kept in dollars, and costs are computed at the time of each withdrawal, what amount would be shown as ending inventory in 1, 2, and 3 above? Carry average unit costs to four decimal places.

P9-3 **(Compute FIFO, LIFO and Average-Cost—Periodic and Perpetual)** Some of the information found on a detail inventory card for David Letterman Inc. for the first month of operations is as follows. **(LO 2, 4)**

	Received		Issued,	Balance,
Date	No. of Units	Unit Cost	No. of Units	No. of Units
January 2	1,200	$3.00		1,200
7			700	500
10	600	3.20		1,100
13			500	600
18	1,000	3.30	300	1,300
20			1,100	200
23	1,300	3.40		1,500
26			800	700
28	1,500	3.60		2,200
31			1,300	900

Instructions

(a) From these data compute the ending inventory on each of the following bases. Assume that perpetual inventory records are kept in units only. Carry unit costs to the nearest cent and ending inventory to the nearest dollar.

   (1) First-in, first-out (FIFO).
   (2) Last-in, first-out (LIFO).
   (3) Average-cost.

(b) If the perpetual inventory record is kept in dollars, and costs are computed at the time of each withdrawal, would the amounts shown as ending inventory in 1, 2, and 3 above be the same? Explain and compute.

(LO 2, 4) **P9-4** **(Compute FIFO, LIFO, Average-Cost—Periodic and Perpetual)**   Iowa Company is a multi-product firm. Presented below is information concerning one of its products, the Hawkeye.

Date	Transaction	Quantity	Price/Cost
1/1	Beginning inventory	1,000 *500*	$12
2/4	Purchase	2,000	18
2/20	Sale	2,500	30
4/2	Purchase	3,000 *1000*	23
11/4	Sale	2,000	33

sale 4500
end 1500

Instructions

Compute cost of goods sold, assuming Iowa uses:

(a) Periodic system, FIFO cost flow.
(b) Perpetual system, FIFO cost flow.
(c) Periodic system, LIFO cost flow.
(d) Perpetual system, LIFO cost flow.
(e) Periodic system, weighted-average cost flow.
(f) Perpetual system, moving-average cost flow.

(LO 2, 4, 10) **P9-5** **(Financial Statement Effects of FIFO and LIFO)**   The management of Maine Company has asked its accounting department to describe the effect upon the company's financial position and its income statements of accounting for inventories on the LIFO rather than the FIFO basis during 2008 and 2009. The accounting department is to assume that the change to LIFO would have been effective on January 1, 2008, and that the initial LIFO base would have been the inventory value on December 31, 2007. Presented below are the company's financial statements and other data for the years 2008 and 2009 when the FIFO method was employed.

	Financial Position as of		
	12/31/07	12/31/08	12/31/09
Cash	$ 90,000	$130,000	$ 141,600
Accounts receivable	80,000	100,000	120,000
Inventory	120,000	140,000	180,000
Other assets	160,000	170,000	200,000
Total assets	$450,000	$540,000	$ 641,600
Accounts payable	$ 40,000	$ 60,000	$ 80,000
Other liabilities	70,000	80,000	110,000
Common stock	200,000	200,000	200,000
Retained earnings	140,000	200,000	251,600
Total equities	$450,000	$540,000	$ 641,600

	Income for Years Ended	
	12/31/08	12/31/09
Sales	$900,000	$1,350,000
Less: Cost of goods sold	505,000	770,000
Other expenses	205,000	304,000
	710,000	1,074,000
Net income before income taxes	190,000	276,000
Income taxes (40%)	76,000	110,400
Net income	$114,000	$ 165,600

Other data:

1. Inventory on hand at 12/31/07 consisted of 40,000 units valued at $3 each.

2. Sales (all units sold at the same price in a given year):

   2008—150,000 units @ $6 each   2009—180,000 units @ $7.50 each

3. Purchases (all units purchased at the same price in given year):

   2008—150,000 units @ $3.50 each   2009—180,000 units @ $4.50 each

4. On December 31 each year, the company pays income taxes at the effective rate of 40%.

Instructions

Name the account(s) presented in the financial statements that would have different amounts for 2009 if the company had used LIFO rather than FIFO, and state the new amount for each account that is named. Show computations.

(CMA adapted)

P9-6 (Dollar-Value LIFO) Falcon's Televisions produces television sets in three categories: portable, mid-size, and flatscreen. On January 1, 2007, Falcon adopted dollar-value LIFO and decided to use a single inventory pool. The company's January 1 inventory consists of:

(LO 6, 7)

Category	Quantity	Cost per Unit	Total Cost
Portable	6,000	$100	$ 600,000
Midsize	8,000	250	2,000,000
Flatscreen	3,000	400	1,200,000
	17,000		$3,800,000

During 2007, the company had the following purchases and sales.

Category	Quantity Purchased	Cost per Unit	Quantity Sold	Selling Price per Unit
Portable	15,000	$120	14,000	$150
Midsize	20,000	300	24,000	405
Flatscreen	10,000	460	6,000	600
	45,000		44,000	

Instructions

(Round to four decimals.)

(a) Compute ending inventory, cost of goods sold, and gross profit.
(b) Assume the company uses three inventory pools instead of one. Repeat instruction (a).

P9-7 (LIFO Effect on Income) Michelle Kwan Inc. sells two products: figure skates and speed skates. At December 31, 2008, Kwan used the first-in, first-out (FIFO) inventory method. Effective January 1, 2009, Kwan changed to the last-in, first-out (LIFO) inventory method. It is impracticable to determine the prior-year effects. As a result, the ending inventory of 2008 for which the FIFO method was used is also the beginning inventory for 2009 for the LIFO method. Any layers added during 2009 should be costed by reference to the first acquisitions of 2009 and any layers liquidated during 2009 should be considered a permanent liquidation.

(LO 4, 6)

The following information was available from Kwan's inventory records for the 2 most recent years.

	Figure Skates		Speed Skates	
	Units	Unit Cost	Units	Unit Cost
2008 purchases				
January 7	7,000	$40	22,000	$20
April 16	12,000	45		
November 8	17,000	54	18,500	34
December 13	9,000	62		

	Figure Skates		Speed Skates	
	Units	Unit Cost	Units	Unit Cost
2009 purchases				
February 11	3,000	$66	23,000	$36
May 20	8,000	75		
October 15	20,000	81		
December 23			15,500	42
Units on hand				
December 31, 2008	15,100		15,000	
December 31, 2009	18,000		13,200	

Instructions

Compute the effect on income before income taxes for the year ended December 31, 2009, resulting from the change from the FIFO to the LIFO inventory method.

(AICPA adapted)

(LO 7)

P9-8 (Dollar-Value LIFO) Warren Dunn Company cans a variety of vegetable-type soups. Recently, the company decided to value its inventories using dollar-value LIFO pools. The clerk who accounts for inventories does not understand how to value the inventory pools using this new method, so, as a private consultant, you have been asked to teach him how this new method works.

He has provided you with the following information about purchases made over a 6-year period.

Date	Ending Inventory (End-of-Year Prices)	Price Index	Date	Ending Inventory (End-of-Year Prices)	Price Index
Dec. 31, 2003	$ 80,000	100	Dec. 31, 2006	131,300	130
Dec. 31, 2004	115,500	105	Dec. 31, 2007	154,000	140
Dec. 31, 2005	108,000	120	Dec. 31, 2008	174,000	145

You have already explained to him how this inventory method is maintained, but he would feel better about it if you were to leave him detailed instructions explaining how these calculations are done and why he needs to put all inventories at a base-year value.

Instructions

(a) Compute the ending inventory for Warren Dunn Company for 2003 through 2008 using dollar-value LIFO.

(b) Using your computation schedules as your illustration, write a step-by-step set of instructions explaining how the calculations are done. Begin your explanation by briefly explaining the theory behind this inventory method, including the purpose of putting all amounts into base-year price levels.

(LO 9)

P9-9 (Lower-of-Cost-or-Market) Grant Wood Company manufactures desks. Most of the company's desks are standard models and are sold on the basis of catalog prices. At December 31, 2008, the following finished desks appear in the company's inventory.

Finished Desks	A	B	C	D
2008 catalog selling price	$450	$480	$900	$1,050
FIFO cost per inventory list 12/31/08	470	450	830	960
Estimated current cost to manufacture (at December 31, 2008, and early 2009)	460	440	610	1,000
Sales commissions and estimated other costs of disposal	45	60	90	130
2009 catalog selling price	500	540	900	1,200

The 2008 catalog was in effect through November 2008, and the 2009 catalog is effective as of December 1, 2008. All catalog prices are net of the usual discounts. Generally, the company attempts to obtain a 20% gross margin on selling price and has usually been successful in doing so.

Instructions

At what amount should each of the four desks appear in the company's December 31, 2008, inventory, assuming that the company has adopted a lower-of-FIFO-cost-or-market approach for valuation of inventories on an individual-item basis?

(LO 9) **P9-10 (Lower-of-Cost-or-Market)** Jonathan Brandis Company is a food wholesaler that supplies independent grocery stores in the region. The company has a perpetual inventory system for all of its food products. The

FIFO method of inventory valuation is used to determine the cost of the inventory at the end of each month. Transactions and other related information regarding two of the items (instant coffee and sugar) carried by Brandis are given below for October 2008, the last month of Brandis's fiscal year.

	Instant Coffee	Sugar
Standard unit of packaging	Case containing 24, one-pound jars.	Baler containing 12, five-pound bags.
Inventory, 10/1/08	1,000 cases @ $60.20 per case	500 balers @ $6.50 per baler
Purchases	1. 10/10/08—1,600 cases @ $62.10 per case plus freight of $480. 2. 10/20/08—2,400 cases @ $64.00 per case plus freight of $480.	1. 10/5/08—850 balers @ $5.76 per baler plus freight of $320. 2. 10/16/08—640 balers @ $6.00 per baler plus freight of $320. 3. 10/24/08—600 balers @ $6.20 per baler plus freight of $360.
Purchase terms	2/10, net/30, f.o.b. shipping point	Net 30 days, f.o.b. shipping point
October sales	3,600 cases @ $76.00 per case	1,950 balers @ $8.00 per baler
Returns and allowances	A customer returned 50 cases that had been shipped in error. The customer's account was credited for $3,800.	As the October 16 purchase was unloaded, 20 balers were discovered damaged. A representative of the trucking firm confirmed the damage and the balers were discarded. Credit of $120 for the merchandise and $10 for the freight was received by Brandis.
Inventory values 10/31/08		
Net realizable value	$66.00 per case	$6.60 per baler

Net realizable value less a
    normal profit of 15%
    of net realizable value
	$56.10 per case	$5.61 per baler

Brandis's sales terms are 1/10, net/30, f.o.b. shipping point. Brandis records all purchases net of purchase discounts and takes all purchase discounts. The most recent quoted price for coffee is $60 per case and for sugar $6.10 per baler, before freight and purchase discounts.

Instructions

(a) Calculate the number of units in inventory and the FIFO unit cost for instant coffee and sugar as of October 31, 2008.

(b) Brandis Company applies the lower-of-cost-or-market rule in valuing its year-end inventory. Calculate the total dollar amount of the inventory for instant coffee and sugar applying the lower-of-cost-or-market rule on an individual-product basis.

(c) Could Brandis Company apply the lower-of-cost-or-market rule to groups of products or the inventory as a whole rather than on an individual-product basis? Explain your answer.

(CMA adapted)

P9-11 (**Statement and Note Disclosure, and LCM**) Garth Brooks Specialty Company, a division of Fresh Horses Inc., manufactures three models of gear shift components for bicycles that are sold to bicycle manufacturers, retailers, and catalog outlets. Since beginning operations in 1973, Brooks has assumed a first-in, first-out cost flow in its perpetual inventory system. Except for overhead, manufacturing costs are accumulated using actual costs. Overhead is applied to production using predetermined overhead rates. The balances of the inventory accounts at the end of Brooks's fiscal year, November 30, 2008, are shown below. The inventories are stated at cost before any year-end adjustments. **(LO 9, 10)**

Finished goods	$647,000
Work-in-process	112,500
Raw materials	240,000
Factory supplies	69,000

The information shown on page 476 relates to Brooks's inventory and operations.

1. The finished goods inventory consists of the items analyzed below.

	Cost	Market
Down-tube shifter		
Standard model	$ 67,500	$ 67,000
Click adjustment model	94,500	87,000
Deluxe model	108,000	110,000
Total down-tubeshifters	270,000	264,000
Bar-end shifter		
Standard model	83,000	90,050
Click adjustment model	99,000	97,550
Total bar-end shifters	182,000	187,600
Head-tube shifter		
Standard model	78,000	77,650
Click adjustment model	117,000	119,300
Total head-tube shifters	195,000	196,950
Total finished goods	$647,000	$648,550

2. One-half of the head-tube shifter finished goods inventory is held by catalog outlets on consignment.

3. Three-quarters of the bar-end shifter finished goods inventory has been pledged as collateral for a bank loan.

4. One-half of the raw materials balance represents derailleurs acquired at a contracted price 20 percent above the current market price. The market value of the rest of the raw materials is $127,400.

5. The total market value of the work-in-process inventory is $108,700.

6. Included in the cost of factory supplies are obsolete items with an historical cost of $4,200. The market value of the remaining factory supplies is $65,900.

7. Brooks applies the lower-of-cost-or-market method to each of the three types of shifters in finished goods inventory. For each of the other three inventory accounts, Brooks applies the lower-of-cost-or-market method to the total of each inventory account.

8. Consider all amounts presented above to be material in relation to Brooks's financial statements taken as a whole.

Instructions

(a) Prepare the inventory section of Brooks's statement of financial position as of November 30, 2008, including any required note(s).

(b) Without prejudice to your answer to requirement (a), assume that the market value of Brooks's inventories is less than cost. Explain how this decline would be presented in Brooks's income statement for the fiscal year ended November 30, 2008.

(CMA adapted)

(LO 11)   ***P9-12   (Gross Profit Method)**   David Hasselholf Company lost most of its inventory in a fire in December just before the year-end physical inventory was taken. Corporate records disclose the following.

Inventory (beginning)	$ 80,000	Sales		$415,000
Purchases	280,000	Sales returns		21,000
Purchase returns	28,000	Gross profit % based on selling price		34%

Merchandise with a selling price of $30,000 remained undamaged after the fire, and damaged merchandise has a salvage value of $7,150. The company does not carry fire insurance on its inventory.

Instructions

Prepare a formal labeled schedule computing the fire loss incurred, using the gross profit method.

ACCOUNTING IN ACTION

Financial Reporting and Analysis

■ Financial Reporting Issues: The Procter & Gamble Company

AIA9-1 The financial statements of **Procter & Gamble (P&G)** can be accessed at the book's website.

Instructions

Refer to P&G's financial statements and the accompanying notes to answer the following questions.

(a) How does P&G value its inventories? Which inventory costing method does P&G use as a basis for reporting its inventories?

(b) How does P&G report its inventories in the balance sheet? In the notes to its financial statements, what three descriptions are used to classify its inventories?

(c) What costs does P&G include in inventory?

(d) What was P&G's inventory turnover ratio in 2006? What is its gross profit percentage? Evaluate P&G's inventory turnover ratio and its gross profit percentage.

■ Comparative Analysis: The Coca-Cola Company and PepsiCo, Inc.

PEPSICO

AIA9-2 The financial statements of **The Coca-Cola Company** and **PepsiCo, Inc.** can be accessed at the book's website.

Instructions

Use information found at the book's website to answer the following questions.

(a) What is the amount of inventory reported by Coca-Cola at December 31, 2006, and by PepsiCo at December 31, 2006? What percent of total assets is invested in inventory by each company?

(b) What inventory costing methods are used by Coca-Cola and PepsiCo? How does each company value its inventories?

(c) In the notes, what classifications (description) are used by Coca-Cola and PepsiCo to categorize their inventories?

(d) Compute and compare the inventory turnover ratios and days to sell inventory for 2006 for Coca-Cola and PepsiCo. Indicate why there might be a significant difference between the two companies.

■ Financial Statement Analysis

AIA9-3 Assume the following:

Quarter	Units Purchased	Per Unit Cost	Dollar Purchases	Unit Sales
1	200	$22	$ 4,400	200
2	300	24	7,200	200
3	300	26	7,800	200
4	200	28	5,600	200
Year	1,000		$25,000	800

Inventory at beginning of Quarter 1: 400 units at $20 per unit = $8,000
Inventory at end of Quarter 4: 600 units

(a) Calculate reported inventory at the end of the year under *each* of the following inventory methods.
  (1) FIFO.
  (2) LIFO.
  (3) Average-cost.

(b) Calculate the cost of goods sold for the year under each method listed in part a.

(c) Discuss the effect of the differences among the three methods on:
  (1) Reported income for the year.
  (2) Stockholders' equity at the end of the year.

(CFA adapted)

AIA9-4 Compare the effect of the use of the LIFO inventory method with use of the FIFO method on each of the following, assuming rising prices and stable inventory quantities.

(a) Gross profit margin.

(b) Net income.

(c) Cash from operations.

(d) Inventories.

(e) Inventory turnover ratio.

(f) Working capital.

(g) Total assets.

(h) Debt-to-equity ratio.

(CFA adapted)

AIA9-5 Albertson's reported that its inventory turnover ratio increased from 8.2 times in 2003 to 8.4 times in 2004. The following data appear in Albertson's annual report.

Albertson's

	Jan.31, 2002	Jan. 30, 2003	Jan. 29, 2004
Total revenues	$36,605	$35,626	$35,436
Cost of sales (using LIFO)	26,179	25,248	25,306
Year-end inventories at FIFO	3,793	3,256	3,611
Year-end inventories at LIFO	3,196	2,973	3,035

(a) Compute Albertson's inventory turnover ratios for 2003 and 2004, using:

(1) Cost of sales and LIFO inventory.

(2) Cost of sales and FIFO inventory.

(b) Some firms calculate inventory turnover using sales rather than cost of goods sold in the numerator. Calculate Albertson's 2003 and 2004 turnover, using:

(1) Sales and LIFO inventory.

(2) Sales and FIFO inventory.

(c) Describe the method that Albertson's appears to use.

(d) State which method you would choose to evaluate Albertson's performance. Justify your choice.

AIA9-6 Supersonic Inc. reported the following information regarding 2007–2008 inventory.

Supersonic Inc.

	2008	2007
Current assets		
Cash	$ 153,010	$ 538,489
Accounts receivable, net of allowance for doubtful accounts		
of $46,000 in 2005 and $160,000 in 2007	1,627,980	2,596,291
Inventories (Note 2)	1,340,494	1,734,873
Other current assets	123,388	90,592
Assets of discontinued operations	—	32,815
Total current assets	3,244,872	4,993,060

Notes to Consolidated Financial Statements

Note 1 (in part): Nature of Business and Significant Accounting Policies

Inventories—Inventories are stated at the lower of cost or market. Cost is determined by the last-in, first-out (LIFO) method by the parent company and by the first-in, first-out (FIFO) method by its subsidiaries.

Note 2:   Inventories

Inventories consist of the following:

	2008	2007
Raw materials	$1,264,646	$2,321,178
Work in process	240,988	171,222
Finished goods and display units	129,406	711,252
Total inventories	1,635,040	3,203,652
Less: Amount classified as long-term	294,546	1,468,779
Current portion	$1,340,494	$1,734,873

Inventories are stated at the lower of cost determined by the LIFO method or market for Supersonic Inc. Inventories for the two wholly-owned subsidiaries, Supersonic Command Inc. (U.S.) and Supersonic Limited (U.K.) are stated on the FIFO method which amounted to $566,000 at October 31, 2007. No inventory is stated on the FIFO method at October 31, 2008. Included in inventory stated at FIFO cost was $32,815 at October 31, 2007, of Supersonic Command inventory classified as an asset from discontinued operations (see Note 14). If the FIFO method had been used for the entire consolidated group, inventories after an adjustment to the lower-of-cost-or-market, would have been approximately $2,000,000 and $3,800,000 at October 31, 2008 and 2007, respectively.

Inventory has been written down to estimated net realizable value, and results of operations for 2008, 2007, and 2006 include a corresponding charge of approximately $868,000, $960,000, and $273,000, respectively, which represents the excess of LIFO cost over market.

Inventory of $294,546 and $1,468,779 at October 31, 2008 and 2007, respectively, shown on the balance sheet as a noncurrent asset represents that portion of the inventory that is not expected to be sold currently.

Reduction in inventory quantities during the years ended October 31, 2008, 2007, and 2006 resulted in liquidation of LIFO inventory quantities carried at a lower cost prevailing in prior years as compared with the cost of fiscal 2006 purchases. The effect of these reductions was to decrease the net loss by approximately $24,000, $157,000 and $90,000 at October 31, 2008, 2007, and 2006, respectively.

Instructions

(a) Why might Supersonic Inc. use two different methods for valuing inventory?

(b) Comment on why Supersonic Inc. might disclose how its LIFO inventories would be valued under FIFO.

(c) Why does the LIFO liquidation reduce operating costs?

(d) Comment on whether Supersonic would report more or less income if it had been on a FIFO basis for all its inventory.

AIA9-7   **Barrick Gold Corporation**, with headquarters in Toronto, Canada, is the world's most profitable and largest gold mining company outside South Africa. Part of the key to Barrick's success has been due to its ability to maintain cash flow while improving production and increasing its reserves of gold-containing property. During 2005, Barrick achieved record growth in cash flow, production, and reserves.

The company maintains an aggressive policy of developing previously identified, but undeveloped, target areas that have the possibility of a large amount of gold ore. Barrick limits the riskiness of this development by choosing only properties that are located in politically stable regions and by the company's use of internally generated funds, rather than debt, to finance growth. Barrick's inventories are as follows.

Barrick Gold Corporation

Inventories (in millions, US dollars)

Current	
Ore in stockpiles	$360
Gold in process	160
Mine operating supplies	133
	$653
Non-current (included in other assets)	
Ore in stockpiles	$251

Instructions

(a) Why do you think that there are no finished goods inventories? Why do you think the raw material, ore in stockpiles, is considered both a current and a noncurrent asset?

(b) Consider that Barrick has no finished goods inventories. What journal entries would it make to record a sale?

(c) Suppose that gold bullion that cost $1.8 million to produce was sold for $2.4 million. The journal entry was made to record the sale, but no entry was made to remove the gold from the gold-in-process inventory. How would this error affect the following?

Balance Sheet		Income Statement	
Inventory	?	Cost of goods sold	?
Retained earnings	?	Net income	?
Accounts payable	?		
Working capital	?		
Current ratio	?		

AIA9-8 **T J International** was founded in 1969 as Trus Joist International. The firm, a manufacturer of specialty building products, has its headquarters in Boise, Idaho. Through its partnership in the Trus Joist MacMillan joint venture, the company develops and manufactures engineered lumber. This product is a high-quality substitute for structural lumber, and uses lower-grade wood and materials formerly considered waste. The company also is majority owner of the Outlook Window Partnership, which is a consortium of three wood and vinyl window manufacturers. Following is T J International's adapted income statement and information concerning inventories from a recent annual report.

T J International

Sales	$618,876,000
Cost of goods sold	475,476,000
Gross profit	143,400,000
Selling and administrative expenses	102,112,000
Income from operations	41,288,000
Other expense	24,712,000
Income before income tax	16,576,000
Income taxes	7,728,000
Net income	$ 8,848,000

Inventories. Inventories are valued at the lower of cost or market and include material, labor, and production overhead costs. Inventories consisted of the following:

	Current Year	Prior Year
Finished goods	$27,512,000	$23,830,000
Raw materials and work-in-progress	34,363,000	33,244,000
	61,875,000	57,074,000
Reduction to LIFO cost	(5,263,000)	(3,993,000)
	$56,612,000	$53,081,000

The last-in, first-out (LIFO) method is used for determining the cost of lumber, veneer, Microllam lumber, TJI joists, and open web joists. Approximately 35 percent of total inventories at the end of the current year were valued using the LIFO method. The first-in, first-out (FIFO) method is used to determine the cost of all other inventories.

Instructions

(a) How much would income before taxes have been if TJ International had used FIFO costing to value all inventories?

(b) If the income tax rate is 46.6%, what would income tax have been if the company had used FIFO costing to value all inventories? In your opinion, is this difference in net income between the two methods material? Explain.

(c) Does the use of a different costing system for different types of inventory mean that there is a different physical flow of goods among the different types of inventory? Explain.

AIA9-9 As indicated in the chapter, the FIFO and LIFO inventory methods can result in significantly different income statement and balance sheet figures. However, it is possible to convert income for a LIFO firm to its FIFO-based equivalent. To assist financial statement users in this task, companies using LIFO are required to disclose in their footnotes the "LIFO reserve" (LR). That is, they must disclose the difference between the inventory balance shown on the balance sheet and the amount that would have been reported had the firm used current cost (or FIFO), as illustrated for **Brown Shoe Company** on page 433.

The following equation converts LIFO cost of goods sold (COGS) to FIFO cost of goods sold.

$$COGS_{FIFO} = COGS_{LIFO} - \text{LIFO effect}$$

where

$$\text{LIFO effect} = [LR_{ending} - LR_{beginning}]$$

The following equation converts LIFO net income (NI) to FIFO net income.

$$NI_{FIFO} = NI_{LIFO} + (\text{LIFO effect}) (1 - \text{tax rate})$$

Instructions

Obtain the annual report of a firm that reports a LIFO reserve in its footnotes.

(a) Identify the LIFO reserve at the two most recent balance sheet dates.
(b) Determine the LIFO effect during the most recent year.
(c) By how much would cost of goods sold during the most recent year change if the firm used FIFO?
(d) By how much would net income during the most recent year change if the firm used FIFO? (*Hint:* To estimate the tax rate, divide income tax expense by income before taxes.)

Concepts for Analysis

AIA9-10 **(Inventoriable Costs)** Your company asks you to travel to Milwaukee to observe and verify the inventory of the Milwaukee branch of one of your clients. You arrive on Thursday, December 30, and find that the client has just started the inventory procedures. You spot a railway car on the sidetrack at the unloading door and ask the warehouse superintendent, Predrag Danilovic, how he plans to inventory the contents of the car. He responds, "We are not going to include the contents in the inventory."

Later in the day, you ask the bookkeeper for the invoice on the carload and the related freight bill. The invoice lists the various items, prices, and extensions of the goods in the car. You note that the carload was shipped December 24 from Albuquerque, f.o.b. Albuquerque, and that the total invoice price of the goods in the car was $35,300. The freight bill called for a payment of $1,500. Terms were net 30 days. The bookkeeper affirms the fact that this invoice is to be held for recording in January.

Instructions

(a) Does your client have a liability that should be recorded at December 31? Discuss.
(b) Prepare a journal entry(ies), if required, to reflect any accounting adjustment required. Assume a perpetual inventory system is used by your client.
(c) For what possible reason(s) might your client wish to postpone recording the transaction?

AIA9-11 **(Inventoriable Costs)** Jack McDowell, the controller for McDowell Lumber Company, has recently hired you as assistant controller. He wishes to determine your expertise in the area of inventory accounting, and he therefore asks you to answer the following unrelated questions.

(a) A company is involved in the wholesaling and retailing of automobile tires for foreign cars. Most of the inventory is imported, and the company values the inventory at the actual inventory cost plus freight-in. At year-end, the warehousing costs are prorated over cost of goods sold and ending inventory. Are warehousing costs considered a product cost or a period cost?
(b) A certain portion of a company's "inventory" is composed of obsolete items. Should obsolete items that are not currently consumed in the production of "goods or services to be available for sale" be classified as part of inventory?

(c) A company purchases airplanes for sale to others. However, until they are sold, the company charters and services the planes. What is the proper way to report these airplanes in the company's financial statements?

AIA9-12 **(General Inventory Issues)** In January 2008, Wesley Crusher Inc. requested and secured permission from the commissioner of the Internal Revenue Service to compute inventories under the last-in, first-out (LIFO) method and elected to determine inventory cost under the dollar-value method. Crusher Inc. satisfied the commissioner that cost could be accurately determined by use of an index number computed from a representative sample selected from the company's single inventory pool.

Instructions

(a) Why should inventories be included in (1) a balance sheet and (2) the computation of net income?

(b) The Internal Revenue Code allows some accountable events to be considered differently for income tax reporting purposes and financial accounting purposes, while other accountable events must be reported the same for both purposes. Discuss why it might be desirable to report some accountable events differently for financial accounting purposes than for income tax reporting purposes.

(c) Discuss the ways and conditions under which the FIFO and LIFO inventory costing methods produce different inventory valuations. Do not discuss procedures for computing inventory cost.

(AICPA adapted)

AIA9-13 **(LIFO Inventory Advantages)** Jean Honore, president of Fragonard Co., recently read an article that claimed that at least 100 of the country's largest 500 companies were either adopting or considering adopting the last-in, first-out (LIFO) method for valuing inventories. The article stated that the firms were switching to LIFO to (1) neutralize the effect of inflation in their financial statements, (2) eliminate inventory profits, and (3) reduce income taxes. Ms. Honore wonders if the switch would benefit her company.

Fragonard currently uses the first-in, first-out (FIFO) method of inventory valuation in its periodic inventory system. The company has a high inventory turnover rate, and inventories represent a significant proportion of the assets.

Ms. Honore has been told that the LIFO system is more costly to operate and will provide little benefit to companies with high turnover. She intends to use the inventory method that is best for the company in the long run rather than selecting a method just because it is the current fad.

Instructions

(a) Explain to Ms. Honore what "inventory profits" are and how the LIFO method of inventory valuation could reduce them.

(b) Explain to Ms. Honore the conditions that must exist for Fragonard Co. to receive tax benefits from a switch to the LIFO method.

AIA9-14 **(LIFO Application and Advantages)** Neshki Corporation is a medium-sized manufacturing company with two divisions and three subsidiaries, all located in the United States. The Metals Division manufactures metal castings for the automotive industry, and the Plastics Division produces small plastic items for electrical products and other uses. The three subsidiaries manufacture various products for other industrial users.

Neshki Corporation plans to change from the lower of first-in, first-out (FIFO) cost or market method of inventory valuation to the last-in, first-out (LIFO) method of inventory valuation to obtain tax benefits. To make the method acceptable for tax purposes, the change also will be made for its annual financial statements.

Instructions

(a) Describe the establishment of and subsequent pricing procedures for each of the following LIFO inventory methods.

   (1) LIFO applied to units of product when the periodic inventory system is used.

   (2) Application of the dollar-value method to LIFO units of product.

(b) Discuss the specific advantages and disadvantages of using the dollar-value LIFO application as compared to specific goods LIFO (unit LIFO). Ignore income tax considerations.

(c) Discuss the general advantages and disadvantages claimed for LIFO methods.

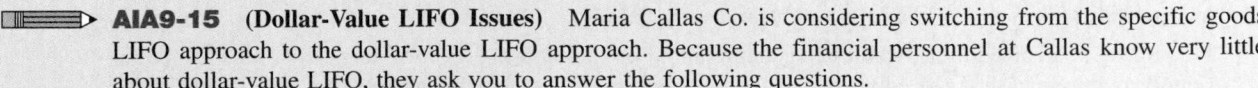

AIA9-15 **(Dollar-Value LIFO Issues)** Maria Callas Co. is considering switching from the specific goods LIFO approach to the dollar-value LIFO approach. Because the financial personnel at Callas know very little about dollar-value LIFO, they ask you to answer the following questions.

(a) What is a LIFO pool?

(b) Is it possible to use a LIFO pool concept and not use dollar-value LIFO? Explain.

(c) What is a LIFO liquidation?

(d) How are price indexes used in the dollar-value LIFO method?

(e) What are the advantages of dollar-value LIFO over specific goods LIFO?

AIA9-16 (FIFO and LIFO) Günter Grass Company is considering changing its inventory valuation method  from FIFO to LIFO because of the potential tax savings. However, the management wishes to consider all of the effects on the company, including its reported performance, before making the final decision.

The inventory account, currently valued on the FIFO basis, consists of 1,000,000 units at $7 per unit on January 1, 2008. There are 1,000,000 shares of common stock outstanding as of January 1, 2008, and the cash balance is $400,000. The company has made the following forecasts for the period 2008–2010.

	2008	2009	2010
Unit sales (in millions of units)	1.1	1.0	1.3
Sales price per unit	$10	$10	$12
Unit purchases (in millions of units)	1.0	1.1	1.2
Purchase price per unit	$7	$8	$9
Annual depreciation (in thousands of dollars)	$300	$300	$300
Cash dividends per share	$0.15	$0.15	$0.15
Cash payments for additions to and replacement of plant and equipment (in thousands of dollars)	$350	$350	$350
Income tax rate	40%	40%	40%
Operating expenses (exclusive of depreciation) as a percent of sales	15%	15%	15%
Common shares outstanding (in millions)	1	1	1

Instructions

(a) Prepare a schedule that illustrates and compares the following data for Günter Grass Company under the FIFO and the LIFO inventory method for 2008–2010. Assume the company would begin LIFO at the beginning of 2008.

(1) Year-end inventory balances.   **(3)** Earnings per share.
(2) Annual net income after taxes.   **(4)** Cash balance.

Assume all sales are collected in the year of sale and all purchases, operating expenses, and taxes are paid during the year incurred.

(b) Using the data above, your answer to (a), and any additional issues you believe need to be considered, prepare a report that recommends whether or not Günter Grass Company should change to the LIFO inventory method. Support your conclusions with appropriate arguments.

(CMA adapted)

AIA9-17 (Lower-of-Cost-or-Market) You have been asked by the financial vice president to develop a short presentation on the lower-of-cost-or-market method for inventory purposes. The financial VP needs to explain this method to the president, because it appears that a portion of the company's inventory has declined in value.

Instructions

The financial VP asks you to answer the following questions.

(a) What is the purpose of the lower-of-cost-or-market method?
(b) What is meant by market? (*Hint*: Discuss the ceiling and floor constraints.)
(c) Do you apply the lower-of-cost-or-market method to each individual item, to a category, or to the total of the inventory? Explain.
(d) What are the potential disadvantages of the lower-of-cost-or-market method?

***AIA9-18 (Gross Profit Method)** Presented below is information related to Joey Harrington Corporation for the current year.

Beginning inventory	$ 600,000	
Purchases	1,500,000	
Total goods available for sale		$2,100,000
Sales		2,500,000

Instructions

(a) Compute the ending inventory, assuming that (1) gross profit is 45% of sales; (2) gross profit is 60% of cost; (3) gross profit is 35% of sales; and (4) gross profit is 25% of cost.
(b) Harrington would like to use the gross profit method to value its inventories for financial reporting purposes. Prepare a brief memorandum to Harrington explaining why use of the gross profit method would not be permitted for financial reporting.

Professional Tools

■ Ethical Decision Making

AIA9-19 Gamble Company uses the LIFO method for inventory costing. In an effort to lower net income, company president Oscar Gamble tells the plant accountant to take the unusual step of recommending to the purchasing department a large purchase of inventory at year-end. The price of the item to be purchased has nearly doubled during the year, and the item represents a major portion of inventory value.

Instructions

Answer the following questions.

(a) Identify the major stakeholders. If the plant accountant recommends the purchase, what are the consequences?
(b) If Gamble Company were using the FIFO method of inventory costing, would Oscar Gamble give the same order? Why or why not?

■ Financial Accounting Research (FARS)

AIA9-20 In conducting year-end inventory counts, your audit team is debating the impact of the client's "right of return" policy both on inventory valuation and revenue recognition. The assistant controller argues that there is no need to worry about the return policies since they have not changed in a while. The audit senior wants a more authoritative answer, and she has asked you to conduct some research of the authoritative literature before she presses the point with the client.

Instructions

Using the **Financial Accounting Research System (FARS)** database, respond to the following items. (Provide text strings used in the search.)

(a) Which statement addresses revenue recognition when right of return exists?
(b) When is this statement important for a company?
(c) Sales with high rates of return can ultimately cause inventory to be misstated. Why are returns allowed? Should different industries be able to make different types of return policies?
(d) In what situations would a reasonable estimate of returns be difficult to make?

AIA9-21 Jones Co. is in a technology-intensive industry. Recently, one of its competitors introduced a new product with technology that might render obsolete some of Jones's inventory. The accounting staff wants to follow the appropriate authoritative literature in determining the accounting for this significant market event.

Instructions

Using the **Financial Accounting Research System (FARS)** database, respond to the following items. (Provide text strings used in the search.)

(a) Identify the authoritative literature addressing inventory pricing. (*Hint*: Do not ignore the literature issued by predecessors to the FASB.)
(b) List three types of goods that are classified as inventory. What characteristic will automatically exclude an item from being classified as inventory?
(c) Define "market" as used in the phrase "lower-of-cost-or-market."
(d) Explain when it is acceptable to state inventory above cost and which industries allow this practice.

■ Professional Simulations

AIA9-22 and AIA9-23 Go to the book's companion website, at **www.wiley.com/college/warfield**, to find interactive problems that simulate the computerized CPA exam. The professional simulations for this chapter ask you to address questions related to the accounting for inventories.

What do the numbers mean?

Staying Lean, p. 421

Q: Where would you look in the financial statements to uncover the benefits of JIT inventory systems?

A: There are two places where financial statements may reflect just-in-time effects. The first is in inventory levels, which should be lower, given the same level of sales. Thus, inventory turnover ratios should be higher. Second, if there are fewer inventories on hand, the company will have less need for short-term borrowings to finance the inventory, resulting in lower interest expense.

It Was the Wild West, p. 424

Q: How does the requirement to record vendor allowances in Cost of Goods Sold address the problem of retailers' early recognition of vendor allowances?

A: The requirement to report vendor allowances in Cost of Goods Sold means that when the retailer receives the vendor allowance, it will record it as a reduction in the cost of the inventory. Rather than recording the payment as a reduction in selling expense, which would be reflected in income immediately, the lower cost is not reflected in income until the inventory is sold.

Comparability, Please, p. 426

Q: What are some other examples of pro-forma reporting?

A: As we discussed in Chapter 5, companies commonly use pro-forma reporting for one-time items such as restructuring charges or impairments. Some companies report a pro-forma income number after adding back amortization expense on certain intangible assets. Recall from the discussion in Chapter 5 that the SEC has issued Regulation G, which requires companies to reconcile pro-forma numbers to GAAP income.

Comparing Apples to Apples, p. 440

Q: What are some reasons a company like Brown Shoe might change from the LIFO to the FIFO method?

A: One reason to change is to better match the flow of inventory. In addition, FIFO costing results in higher reported income. Some companies have found that with low inflation, the tax benefits of LIFO may not exceed the cost of its additional recordkeeping. Finally, Brown may want to use the same cost flow assumption used by other companies in its industry. This would make it easier for investors to compare Brown's results to those of its competitors.

Put It in Reverse, p. 447

Q: Describe the economic conditions that give rise to inventory write-downs followed by reversals.

A: As alluded to in the story, the general economic conditions motivating the lower-of-cost-or-market write-down are those of slow growth or recession. In this situation, there will be pressure to discount prices in order to sell the goods. Additionally, a market in which products rapidly become obsolete would increase the likelihood of an inventory write-down. Reversals occur in periods when the general economic conditions create a new demand for the previously written-down products. It is unlikely that inventory written down due to technological obsolescence would experience a reversal.

The Squeeze, p. 457

Q: How does the change in accounting for vendor allowances (see "It Was the Wild West" on p. 424) affect the reported gross profits of retailers?

A: The change in vendor-allowance accounting reclassified the vendor allowance payments from reductions in Selling Expense to reductions in Cost of Goods Sold. The result is an increase in the gross profit.

 **Remember to check the book's companion website to find additional resources for this chapter.**

CHAPTER 10

ACCOUNTING FOR PROPERTY, PLANT, AND EQUIPMENT

Where Have All the Assets Gone?

Investments in long-lived assets, such as property, plant, and equipment, are important elements in many companies' balance sheets. As the chart below indicates, major companies, such as **Southwest Airlines** and **Wal-Mart,** recently reported property, plant, and equipment (PP&E) as a percent of total assets ranging from 54 percent up to nearly 77 percent.

However, for various strategic reasons, many companies are now shedding property, plant, and equipment. Instead, they are paying others to manufacture and assemble products—functions they previously performed in their own facilities. Companies are also reducing fixed assets by outsourcing warehousing and distribution. Such logistics outsourcing can cut companies' own costs for keeping and managing inventories, and spare them the need to invest in advanced tracking technologies increasingly required by retailers. In a recent year more than 80 percent of the country's 100 biggest companies used third-party logistics providers. As a result, some companies such as **Nortel** and **Lucent** are decreasing their investment in long-lived assets, as the following chart shows.

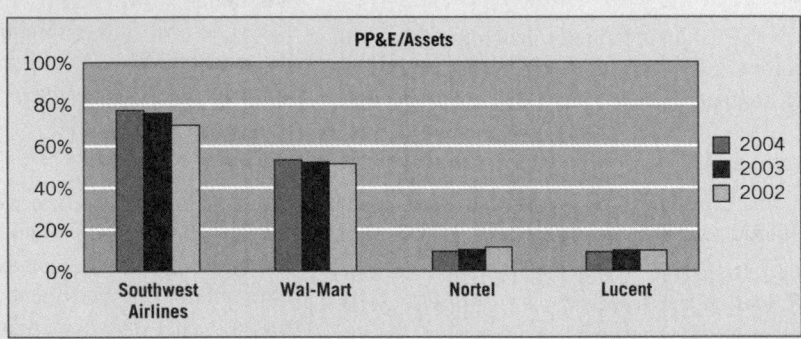

Nortel is a good example of these strategies. It has sold and outsourced certain facilities in order to reduce its direct manufacturing activities and costs. Nortel also sold its training and headset businesses. Further, it has aggressively outsourced other operations to reduce costs. Reductions in these areas will enable Nortel and other outsourcing companies to concentrate on their core operations and better manage investments in property, plant and equipment.

Sources: Adapted from Chapter 1 in Grady Means and David Schneider, *MetaCapitalism: The e-Business Revolution and the Design of 21st-Century Companies and Markets* (New York: John Wiley and Sons, 2000); and Kris Maher, "Global Goods Jugglers," *Wall Street Journal Online* (July 5, 2005).

Preview of Chapter 10

As we indicate in the opening story, a company like **Southwest Airlines** has a substantial investment in property, plant, and equipment. Conversely, other companies, such as **Nortel,** have a minor investment in these types of assets. In this chapter, we discuss the proper accounting for the acquisition, use, and disposition of property, plant, and equipment. *The content and organization of the chapter are as follows.*

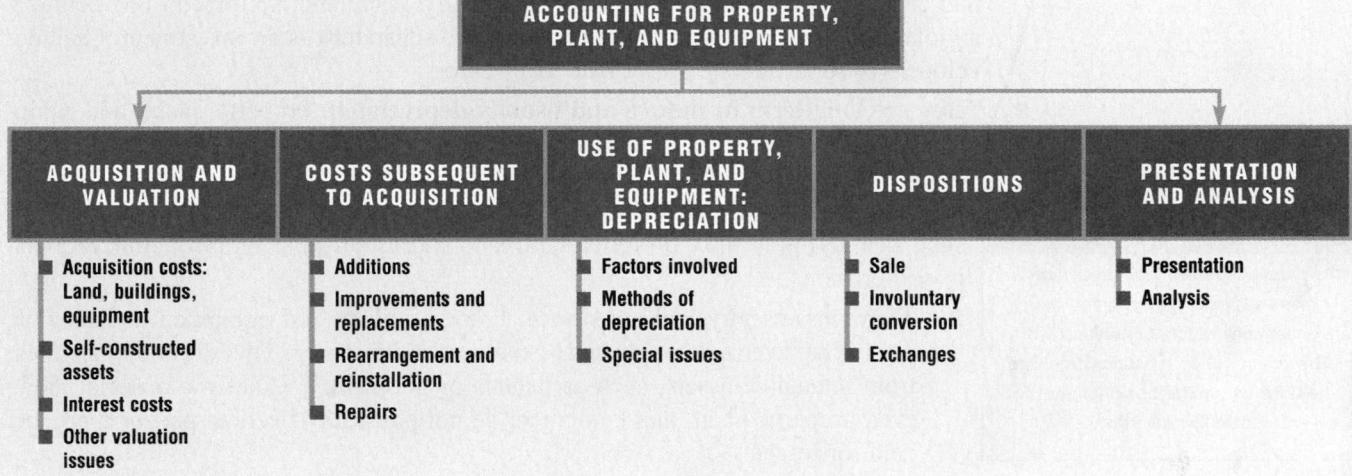

ACCOUNTING FOR PROPERTY, PLANT, AND EQUIPMENT

ACQUISITION AND VALUATION	COSTS SUBSEQUENT TO ACQUISITION	USE OF PROPERTY, PLANT, AND EQUIPMENT: DEPRECIATION	DISPOSITIONS	PRESENTATION AND ANALYSIS
■ Acquisition costs: Land, buildings, equipment ■ Self-constructed assets ■ Interest costs ■ Other valuation issues	■ Additions ■ Improvements and replacements ■ Rearrangement and reinstallation ■ Repairs	■ Factors involved ■ Methods of depreciation ■ Special issues	■ Sale ■ Involuntary conversion ■ Exchanges	■ Presentation ■ Analysis

Learning Objectives

After studying this chapter, you should be able to:

1. Describe property, plant, and equipment and costs to include in its initial valuation.
2. Describe the accounting problems associated with interest capitalization.
3. Understand accounting issues related to acquiring and valuing plant assets.
4. Describe the accounting treatment for costs subsequent to acquisition.
5. Explain the concept of depreciation.
6. Identify the factors involved in the depreciation process.
7. Compare activity, straight-line, and decreasing-charge methods of depreciation.
8. Describe the accounting treatment for the disposal of property, plant, and equipment.
9. Explain how to report and analyze property, plant, and equipment.

Inside Chapter 10

■ **What Do the Numbers Mean?**
What's in your interest? (p. 492)
Disconnected (p. 496)
Decelerating depreciation (p. 505)
Depreciation choices (p. 508)

■ **What's the Principle?** (pp. 488, 496, 502, 503, 504)

■ **Convergence Corner** (p. 519)

■ **Accounting, Analysis, Principles** (p. 520)
Record exchange of nonmonetary assets.
Evaluate return on assets.
Discuss commercial substance.

Describe property, plant, and equipment and costs to include in its initial valuation.

Companies like **Boeing**, **Target**, and **Starbucks** use assets of a durable nature. Such assets are called **property, plant, and equipment**. Other terms commonly used are **plant assets** and **fixed assets**. We use these terms interchangeably throughout this textbook.

Property, plant, and equipment include land, building structures (offices, factories, warehouses), and equipment (machinery, furniture, tools). The major characteristics of property, plant, and equipment are as follows.

1 They are acquired for use in operations and not for resale. Only assets used in normal business operations are classified as property, plant, and equipment. For example, an idle building is more appropriately classified separately as an investment. Land developers or subdividers classify land as inventory.

2 They are long-term in nature and usually depreciated. Property, plant, and equipment yield services over a number of years. Companies allocate the cost of the investment in these assets to future periods through periodic depreciation charges. The exception is land, which is depreciated only if a material decrease in value occurs, such as a loss in fertility of agricultural land because of poor crop rotation, drought, or soil erosion.

3 They possess physical substance. Property, plant, and equipment are tangible assets characterized by physical existence or substance. This differentiates them from intangible assets, such as patents or goodwill. Unlike raw material, however, property, plant, and equipment do not physically become part of a product held for resale.

WHAT'S THE PRINCIPLE?

Fair value is relevant to inventory but less so for property, plant, and equipment which, consistent with the going-concern assumption, are held for use in the business, not for sale like inventory.

ACQUISITION AND VALUATION OF PROPERTY, PLANT, AND EQUIPMENT

Most companies use historical cost as the basis for valuing property, plant, and equipment. **Historical cost measures the cash or cash equivalent price of obtaining the asset and bringing it to the location and condition necessary for its intended use.** For example, companies like **Kellogg Co.** consider the purchase price, freight costs, sales taxes, and installation costs of a productive asset as part of the asset's cost. It then allocates these costs to future periods through depreciation. Further, Kellogg **adds to the asset's cost** any related costs incurred **after the asset's acquisition**, such as additions, improvements, or replacements, **if they provide future service potential.** Otherwise, Kellogg expenses these costs immediately.

Disagreement does exist concerning differences between historical cost and other valuation methods (such as replacement cost or fair market value) **arising after acquisition**. *APB Opinion No. 6* states, "property, plant, and equipment should not be written up to reflect appraisal, market, or current values which are above cost." Although the opinion notes minor exceptions, current standards indicate that departures from historical cost are rare. The main reasons for this position are as follows:

1 At the date of acquisition, cost reflects fair value.

2 Historical cost involves actual, not hypothetical, transactions and so is the most reliable.

3 Companies should not anticipate gains and losses but should recognize gains and losses only when the asset is sold.

Cost of Land

All expenditures made to acquire land and ready it for use are considered part of the land cost. Thus, when **Wal-Mart** or **Home Depot** purchases land on which to build a new store,

Expanded Discussion of Alternative Valuation Methods

its land costs typically include (1) the purchase price; (2) closing costs, such as title to the land, attorney's fees, and recording fees; (3) costs incurred in getting the land in condition for its intended use, such as grading, filling, draining, and clearing; (4) assumption of any liens, mortgages, or encumbrances on the property; and (5) any additional land improvements that have an indefinite life.

For example, when Home Depot purchases land for the purpose of constructing a building, it considers all costs incurred up to the excavation for the new building as land costs. **Removal of old buildings—clearing, grading, and filling—is a land cost because this activity is necessary to get the land in condition for its intended purpose.** Home Depot treats any proceeds from getting the land ready for its intended use, such as salvage receipts on the demolition of an old building or the sale of cleared timber, as **reductions in the price of the land**.

In some cases, when Home Depot purchases land, it may assume certain obligations on the land such as back taxes or liens. In such situations, the cost of the land is the cash paid for it, plus the encumbrances. In other words, if the purchase price of the land is $50,000 cash, but Home Depot assumes accrued property taxes of $5,000 and liens of $10,000, its land cost is $65,000.

Home Depot also might incur **special assessments** for local improvements, such as pavements, street lights, sewers, and drainage systems. It should charge these costs to the Land account because they are relatively permanent in nature. That is, after installation, they are maintained by the local government. In addition, Home Depot should charge any permanent improvements it makes, such as landscaping, to the Land account. It records separately any **improvements with limited lives**, such as private driveways, walks, fences, and parking lots, as Land Improvements. These costs are depreciated over their estimated lives.

Generally, land is part of property, plant, and equipment. However, if the major purpose of acquiring and holding land is speculative, a company more appropriately classifies the land as an **investment**. If a real estate concern holds the land for resale, it should classify the land as **inventory**.

In cases where land is held as an investment, what accounting treatment should be given for taxes, insurance, and other direct costs incurred while holding the land? Many believe these costs should be capitalized. The reason: They are not generating revenue from the investment at this time. Companies generally use this approach except when the asset is currently producing revenue (such as rental property).

Cost of Buildings

The cost of buildings should include all expenditures related directly to their acquisition or construction. These costs include (1) materials, labor, and overhead costs incurred during construction and (2) professional fees and building permits. Generally, companies contract others to construct their buildings. Companies consider all costs incurred, from excavation to completion, as part of the building costs.

But how should companies account for an old building that is on the site of a newly proposed building? Is the cost of removal of the old building a cost of the land or a cost of the new building? Recall that **if a company purchases land with an old building on it, then the cost of demolition less its salvage value is a cost of getting the land ready for its intended use and relates to the land rather than to the new building**. In other words, all costs of getting an asset ready for its intended use are costs of that asset.

Cost of Equipment

The term "equipment" in accounting includes delivery equipment, office equipment, machinery, furniture and fixtures, furnishings, factory equipment, and similar fixed assets. The cost of such assets includes the purchase price, freight and handling charges incurred, insurance on the equipment while in transit, cost of special foundations if required, assembling

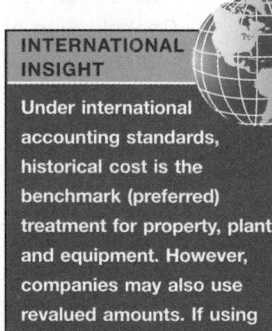

INTERNATIONAL INSIGHT

Under international accounting standards, historical cost is the benchmark (preferred) treatment for property, plant, and equipment. However, companies may also use revalued amounts. If using revaluation, companies must revalue the class of assets regularly.

and installation costs, and costs of conducting trial runs. Costs thus include all expenditures incurred in acquiring the equipment and preparing it for use.

Self-Constructed Assets

Occasionally companies construct their own assets. Determining the cost of such machinery and other fixed assets can be a problem. Without a purchase price or contract price, the company must allocate costs and expenses to arrive at the cost of the **self-constructed asset**. Materials and direct labor used in construction pose no problem; companies can trace these costs directly to work and material orders related to the fixed assets constructed.

However, the assignment of indirect costs of manufacturing creates special problems. These indirect costs, called **overhead** or **burden**, include power, heat, light, insurance, property taxes on factory buildings and equipment, factory supervisory labor, depreciation of fixed assets, and supplies.

To account for overhead, a company assigns a portion of all overhead to the construction process. The reason: These costs are attached to all products and assets manufactured or constructed. Failure to allocate overhead costs understates the initial cost of the asset and results in an inaccurate future allocation.

If the allocated overhead results in recording construction costs in excess of the costs that an outside independent producer would charge, the company should charge the excess overhead as a period loss rather than capitalize it. This avoids capitalizing the asset at more than its probable fair value.

Interest Costs During Construction

The proper accounting for interest costs has been a long-standing controversy. Some argue that companies should not charge interest to construction costs. They contend that if a company had used stock (equity) financing rather than debt, it would not record this cost. Others argue that companies should record all costs of funds, whether identifiable or not. They reason that whether actual or imputed, interest is a cost of the building and companies should record it as such. Illustration 10-1 indicates the different ways that interest costs might be added to the cost of the asset.

Illustration 10-1
Capitalization of
Interest Costs

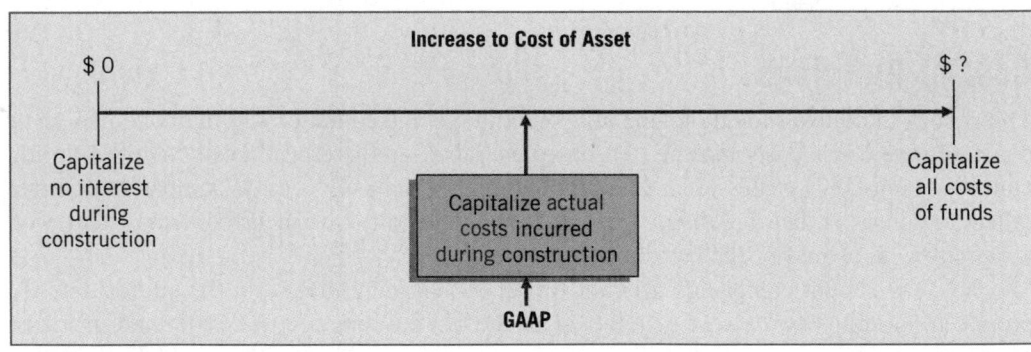

GAAP requires the capitalization of actual interest (with modification). This method follows from the concept that the **historical cost of acquiring an asset includes all costs (including interest) incurred to bring the asset to the condition and location necessary for its intended use.** The rationale for this approach is that during construction the asset is not generating revenues, and therefore interest costs should be deferred (capitalized).[1] Once construction is completed, the asset is ready for its intended use and the company can earn revenues. At this point a company should report interest as an expense and match it

[1]"Capitalization of Interest Cost," *Statement of Financial Accounting Standards No. 34* (Stamford, Conn.: FASB, 1979).

to these revenues. It follows that the company should expense any interest cost incurred in purchasing an asset that is ready for its intended use.

To illustrate the impact of interest capitalization on financial statements, assume that Richards Company begins construction on a building early in 2008 and completes construction by the end of the year. Richards incurred total interest costs on borrowing during 2008 in the amount of $325,000. It determines that $165,000 of these total interest costs is attributable to expenditures on the new building. (See Appendix 10A for a comprehensive illustration of the procedures for determining the amount of capitalized interest.) The following summary journal entry shows how Richards would record capitalized interest and interest expense in 2008.

Building (Capitalized Interest)	165,000	
Interest Expense	160,000	
Cash		325,000

At December 31, 2008, Richards would disclose the amount of interest capitalized, either as part of the nonoperating section of the income statement or in the notes accompanying the financial statements. Illustrations 10-2 and 10-3 show both forms of disclosure.

Income from operations		XXXX
Other expenses and losses		
Interest expense	$325,000	
Less: Capitalized interest	165,000	160,000
Income before taxes on income		XXXX
Income taxes		XXX
Net income		XXXX

Illustration 10-2
Capitalized Interest Reported in the Income Statement

Note 1: Accounting Policies. *Capitalized Interest.* During 2008 total interest cost was $325,000, of which $165,000 was capitalized and $160,000 was charged to expense.

Illustration 10-3
Capitalized Interest Disclosed in a Note

Special Issues Related to Interest Capitalization

Two issues related to interest capitalization merit special attention:

1 Expenditures for land.

2 Interest revenue.

Expenditures for Land. When a company purchases land with the intention of developing it for a particular use, interest costs associated with those expenditures qualify for interest capitalization. If it purchases land as a site for a structure (such as a plant site), **interest costs capitalized during the period of construction are part of the cost of the plant, not the land**. Conversely, if the company develops land for lot sales, it includes any capitalized interest cost as part of the acquisition cost of the developed land. However, it should **not** capitalize interest costs involved in purchasing land held **for speculation** because the asset is ready for its intended use.

Interest Revenue. Companies frequently borrow money to finance construction of assets. They temporarily invest the excess borrowed funds in interest-bearing securities until they need the funds to pay for construction. During the early stages of construction, interest revenue earned may exceed the interest cost incurred on the borrowed funds.

Should companies offset interest revenue against interest cost when determining the amount of interest to capitalize as part of the construction cost of assets? In general, **companies should not net or offset interest revenue against interest cost**. Temporary or short-term investment decisions are not related to the interest incurred as part of the acquisition

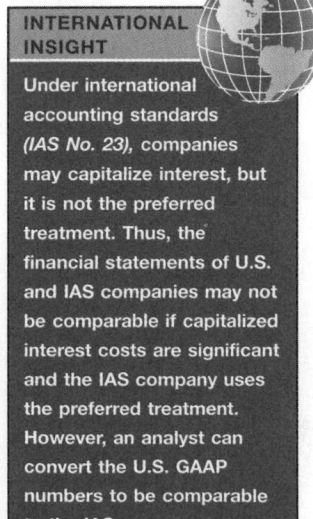

INTERNATIONAL INSIGHT

Under international accounting standards *(IAS No. 23)*, companies may capitalize interest, but it is not the preferred treatment. Thus, the financial statements of U.S. and IAS companies may not be comparable if capitalized interest costs are significant and the IAS company uses the preferred treatment. However, an analyst can convert the U.S. GAAP numbers to be comparable to the IAS company.

cost of assets. Therefore, companies should capitalize the interest incurred on qualifying assets whether or not they temporarily invest excess funds in short-term securities. Some criticize this approach because a company can defer the interest cost but report the interest revenue in the current period.

What do the numbers mean? | What's in Your Interest?

The requirement to capitalize interest can significantly impact financial statements. For example, when earnings of building manufacturer **Jim Walter's Corporation** dropped from $1.51 to $1.17 per share, the company offset 11 cents per share of the decline by capitalizing the interest on coal mining projects and several plants under construction.

How do statement users determine the impact of interest capitalization on a company's bottom line? They examine the notes to the financial statements. Companies with material interest capitalization must disclose the amounts of capitalized interest relative to total interest costs. For example, **Anadarko Petroleum Corporation** capitalized nearly 30 percent of its total interest costs in a recent year and provided the following footnote related to capitalized interest.

Financial Footnotes
Total interest costs incurred during the year were $82,415,000. Of this amount, the Company capitalized $24,716,000. Capitalized interest is included as part of the cost of oil and gas properties. The capitalization rates are based on the Company's weighted-average cost of borrowings used to finance the expenditures.

Beyond the Numbers
Recently, interest rates have been rising. What are the implications of rising interest rates for the amount of interest capitalized by a company like Anardarko?

Other Valuation Issues

Like other assets, **companies should record property, plant, and equipment at the fair value of what they give up or at the fair value of the asset received, whichever is more clearly evident**. However, the process of asset acquisition sometimes obscures fair value. For example, if a company buys land and buildings together for one price, how does it determine separate values for the land and buildings? We examine these types of accounting problems in the following sections.

Cash Discounts

OBJECTIVE 3

Understand accounting issues related to acquiring and valuing plant assets.

When a company purchases plant assets subject to cash discounts for prompt payment, how should it report the discount? If it takes the discount, the company should consider the discount as a reduction in the purchase price of the asset. But should the company reduce the asset cost even if it does not take the discount?

Two points of view exist on this question. One approach considers the discount—whether taken or not—as a reduction in the cost of the asset. The rationale for this approach is that the real cost of the asset is the cash or cash equivalent price of the asset. In addition, some argue that the terms of cash discounts are so attractive that failure to take them indicates management error or inefficiency.

Proponents of the other approach argue that failure to take the discount should not always be considered a loss. The terms may be unfavorable, or it might not be prudent for the company to take the discount. At present, companies use both methods, though most prefer the former method.

Lump-Sum Purchases

A special problem of pricing fixed assets arises when a company purchases a group of plant assets at a single **lump-sum price**. When this common situation occurs, the company allocates the total cost among the various assets on the basis of their relative fair market values.

The assumption is that costs will vary in direct proportion to fair value. This is the same principle that companies apply to allocate a lump-sum cost among different inventory items.

To determine fair market value, a company should use valuation techniques that are appropriate in the circumstances. In some cases, a single valuation technique will be appropriate. In other cases, multiple valuation approaches might have to be used.

To illustrate, Norduct Homes, Inc. decides to purchase several assets of a small heating concern, Comfort Heating, for $80,000. Comfort Heating is in the process of liquidation. Its assets sold are:

	Book Value	Fair Market Value
Inventory	$30,000	$ 25,000
Land	20,000	25,000
Building	35,000	50,000
	$85,000	$100,000

Norduct Homes allocates the $80,000 purchase price on the basis of the relative fair market values (assuming specific identification of costs is impracticable) in the following manner.

		Illustration 10-4
Inventory	$\dfrac{\$25,000}{\$100,000} \times \$80,000 = \$20,000$	Allocation of Purchase Price—Relative Fair Market Value Basis
Land	$\dfrac{\$25,000}{\$100,000} \times \$80,000 = \$20,000$	
Building	$\dfrac{\$50,000}{\$100,000} \times \$80,000 = \$40,000$	

Issuance of Stock

When companies acquire property by issuing securities, such as common stock, the par or stated value of such stock fails to properly measure the property cost. If trading of the stock is active, **the market value of the stock issued is a fair indication of the cost of the property acquired. The stock is a good measure of the current cash equivalent price.**

For example, Upgrade Living Co. decides to purchase some adjacent land for expansion of its carpeting and cabinet operation. In lieu of paying cash for the land, the company issues to Deedland Company 5,000 shares of common stock (par value $10) that have a fair market value of $12 per share. Upgrade Living Co. records the following entry.

Land (5,000 × $12)	60,000	
Common Stock		50,000
Additional Paid-In Capital		10,000

If the company cannot determine the market value of the common stock exchanged, it establishes the market value of the property. It then uses the value of the property as the basis for recording the asset and issuance of the common stock.[2]

---

[2]The valuation approaches that should be used are the market, income, or cost approach, or a combination of these approaches. The *market approach* uses observable prices and other relevant information generated by market transactions involving comparable assets. The *income approach* uses valuation techniques to convert future amounts (for example, cash flows or earnings) to a single present value amount (discounted). The *cost approach* is based on the amount that currently would be required to replace the service capacity of an asset (often referred to as current replacement cost). In determining the fair value, the company should assume the highest and best use of the asset ("Fair Value Measurement," *Statement of Financial Accounting Standard No. 157* (Norwalk, Conn.: FASB, September 2006).

Accounting for Contributions

Companies sometimes receive or make contributions (donations or gifts). Such contributions, **nonreciprocal transfers**, transfer assets in one direction. A contribution is often some type of asset (such as cash, securities, land, buildings, or use of facilities), but it also could be the forgiveness of a debt.

When companies acquire assets as donations, a strict cost concept dictates that the valuation of the asset should be zero. However, a departure from the cost principle seems justified; the only costs incurred (legal fees and other relatively minor expenditures) are not a reasonable basis of accounting for the assets acquired. To record nothing is to ignore the economic realities of an increase in wealth and assets. Therefore, companies use the **fair value of the asset** to establish its value on the books.

What then is the proper accounting for the credit in this transaction? Some believe the credit should be made to Donated Capital (an additional paid-in capital account). This approach views the increase in assets from a donation as contributed capital, rather than as earned revenue.

Others argue that companies should report donations as revenues from contributions. Their reasoning is that only the owners of a business contribute capital. At issue in this approach is whether the company should report revenue immediately or over the period that the asset is employed. For example, to attract new industry a city may offer land, but the receiving enterprise may incur additional costs in the future (e.g., transportation or higher state income taxes) because the location is not the most desirable. As a consequence, some argue that company should defer the revenue and recognize it as the costs are incurred.

The FASB's position is that **in general, companies should recognize contributions received as revenues in the period received.**[3] Companies measure contributions at the fair value of the assets received.[4] To illustrate, Max Wayer Meat Packing, Inc. has recently accepted a donation of land with a fair value of $150,000 from the Memphis Industrial Development Corp. In return Max Wayer Meat Packing promises to build a packing plant in Memphis. Max Wayer's entry is:

Land	150,000	
Contribution Revenue		150,000

When a company contributes a nonmonetary asset, it should record the amount of the donation as an expense at the fair value of the donated asset. If a difference exists between the fair value of the asset and its book value, the company should recognize a gain or loss. To illustrate, Kline Industries donates land to the city of Los Angeles for a city park. The land cost $80,000 and has a fair market value of $110,000. Kline Industries records this donation as follows:

Contribution Expense	110,000	
Land		80,000
Gain on Disposal of Land		30,000

In some cases, companies promise to give (pledge) some type of asset in the future. Should companies record this promise immediately or when they give the assets? If the promise is **unconditional** (depends only on the passage of time or on demand by the recipient for performance), the company should report the contribution expense and related payable immediately. If the promise is **conditional**, the company recognizes expense in the period benefited by the contribution, generally when it transfers the asset.

---

[3]"Accounting for Contributions Received and Contributions Made," *Statement of Financial Accounting Standards No. 116* (Norwalk, Conn.: FASB, 1993). The scope of this standard excludes transfers of assets from governmental units to business enterprises. However, we believe that the basic requirements should hold also for these types of contributions. Therefore, companies should record all assets at fair value and all credits as revenue.

[4]"Accounting for Nonmonetary Transactions," op. cit., par. 18. Also, *FASB No. 116* indicates that companies should record expenses on contributions made at the fair value of the assets given up.

Summary

In summary, historical cost is generally used as the basis for recording the acquisition of property, plant, and equipment. Historical cost is measured by the cash or cash-equivalent price of obtaining an asset and bringing it to the location and condition for its intended use. Modifications to the general rule arise in a number of special situations, as summarized in Illustration 10-5.

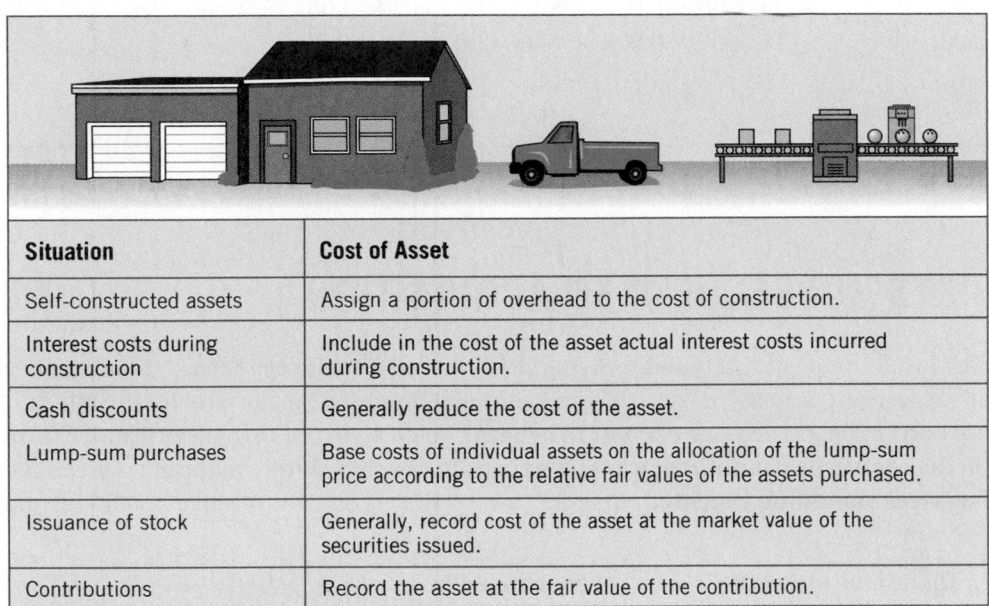

Illustration 10-5
Accounting for Acquisition of Property, Plant, and Equipment in Special Situations

Situation	Cost of Asset
Self-constructed assets	Assign a portion of overhead to the cost of construction.
Interest costs during construction	Include in the cost of the asset actual interest costs incurred during construction.
Cash discounts	Generally reduce the cost of the asset.
Lump-sum purchases	Base costs of individual assets on the allocation of the lump-sum price according to the relative fair values of the assets purchased.
Issuance of stock	Generally, record cost of the asset at the market value of the securities issued.
Contributions	Record the asset at the fair value of the contribution.

Try it out! Garcia Company made two major purchases of property, plant, and equipment during the year.

1 Garcia purchased land for $37,000. Closing costs were $2,800. A dilapidated warehouse was removed at a cost of $21,000.

2 The company purchased a building, land, and machinery for a cash payment of $460,000. The estimated fair values of the assets are: building $330,000; land $99,000; and machinery $121,000.

Instructions

Compute the amount at which Garcia should record the land in transaction 1 and each of the assets in transaction 2.

Solution

Purchase transaction 1:

Purchase price	$37,000
Closing cost	2,800
Removal cost	21,000
Land cost	$60,800

330 000 √
99 000 √
121 000 √
550 000

Purchase transaction 2:

	Fair Values
Building	$330,000
Land	99,000
Machinery	121,000
	$550,000

Building	$330,000/$550,000 × $460,000 = $276,000
Land	$ 99,000/$550,000 × $460,000 = 82,800
Machinery	$121,000/$550,000 × $460,000 = 101,200
	$460,000

COSTS SUBSEQUENT TO ACQUISITION

OBJECTIVE 4

Describe the accounting treatment for costs subsequent to acquisition.

After installing plant assets and readying them for use, a company incurs additional costs that range from ordinary repairs to significant additions. The major problem is allocating these costs to the proper time periods. **In general, costs incurred to achieve greater future benefits should be capitalized, whereas expenditures that simply maintain a given level of services should be expensed.** In order to capitalize costs, one of three conditions must be present:

1 The useful life of the asset must be increased.

2 The quantity of units produced from the asset must be increased.

3 The quality of the units produced must be enhanced.

WHAT'S THE PRINCIPLE?

Expensing long-lived ashtrays and waste baskets is an application of the *materiality constraint.*

For example, a company like **Boeing** should expense expenditures that do not increase an asset's future benefits. That is, it expenses immediately ordinary repairs that maintain the existing condition of the asset or restore it to normal operating efficiency.

Companies expense most expenditures below an established arbitrary minimum amount, say, $100 or $500. Although conceptually this treatment may be incorrect, expediency demands it. Otherwise, companies would set up depreciation schedules for such items as wastepaper baskets and ashtrays.

What do the numbers mean?   Disconnected

It all started with a check of the books by an internal auditor for **WorldCom Inc**. The telecom giant's newly installed chief executive had asked for a financial review, and the auditor was spot-checking records of capital expenditures. She found the company was using an unorthodox technique to account for one of its biggest expenses: charges paid to local telephone networks to complete long-distance calls.

Instead of recording these charges as operating expenses, WorldCom recorded a significant portion as capital expenditures. The maneuver was worth hundreds of millions of dollars to WorldCom's bottom line. It effectively turned a loss for all of 2001 and the first quarter of 2002 into a profit. The graph below compares WorldCom's accounting to that under GAAP. Soon after this discovery, WorldCom filed for bankruptcy.

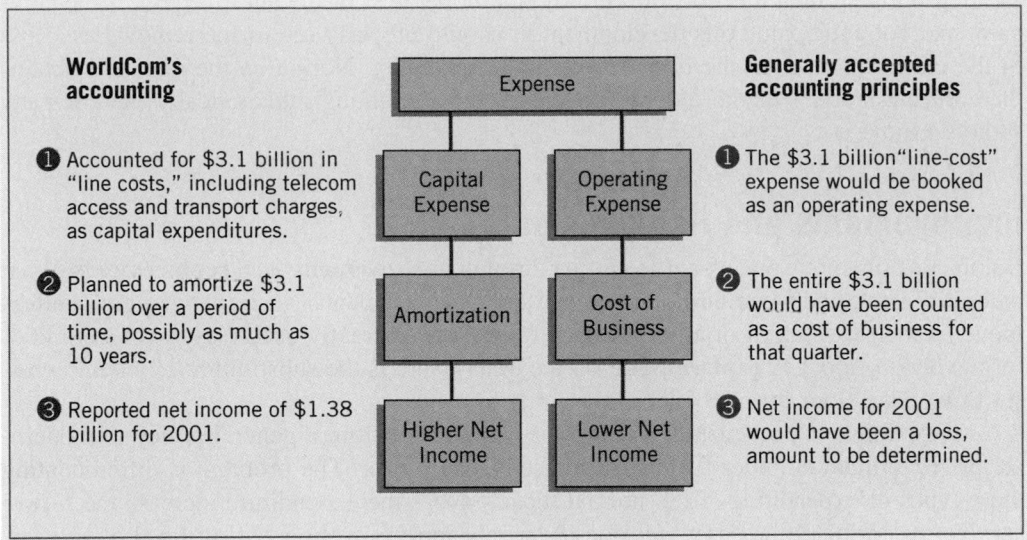

WorldCom's accounting		Generally accepted accounting principles
1 Accounted for $3.1 billion in "line costs," including telecom access and transport charges, as capital expenditures.	Expense → Capital Expense / Operating Expense → Amortization / Cost of Business → Higher Net Income / Lower Net Income	**1** The $3.1 billion "line-cost" expense would be booked as an operating expense.
2 Planned to amortize $3.1 billion over a period of time, possibly as much as 10 years.		**2** The entire $3.1 billion would have been counted as a cost of business for that quarter.
3 Reported net income of $1.38 billion for 2001.		**3** Net income for 2001 would have been a loss, amount to be determined.

Source: Adapted from Jared Sandberg, Deborah Solomon, and Rebecca Blumenstein, "Inside WorldCom's Unearthing of a Vast Accounting Scandal," *Wall Street Journal* (June 27, 2002,), p. A1.

Beyond the Numbers

WorldCom's accounting for line changes also resulted in improper reporting of its "Cash flow provided by operations." Explain how.

The distinction between a **capital (asset) expenditure** and a **revenue (expense) expenditure** is not always clear-cut. Yet, in most cases, **consistent application of a capital/expense policy** is more important than attempting to provide general theoretical guidelines for each transaction. Generally, companies incur four major types of expenditures related to existing assets.

MAJOR TYPES OF EXPENDITURES

ADDITIONS. Increase or extension of existing assets.

IMPROVEMENTS AND REPLACEMENTS. Substitution of an improved asset for an existing one.

REARRANGEMENT AND REINSTALLATION. Movement of assets from one location to another.

REPAIRS. Expenditures that maintain assets in condition for operation.

Additions

Additions should present no major accounting problems. By definition, **companies capitalize any addition to plant assets because a new asset is created**. For example, the addition of a wing to a hospital, or of an air conditioning system to an office, increases the service potential of that facility. Companies should capitalize such expenditures and match them against the revenues that will result in future periods.

One problem that arises in this area is the accounting for any changes related to the existing structure as a result of the addition. Is the cost incurred to tear down an old wall to make room for the addition, a cost of the addition or an expense or loss of the period? The answer is that it depends on the original intent. If the company had anticipated building an addition later, then this cost of removal is a proper cost of the addition. But if the company had not anticipated this development, it should properly report the removal as a loss in the current period on the basis of inefficient planning. Normally, the company retains the carrying amount of the old wall in the accounts, although theoretically the company should remove it.

Improvements and Replacements

Companies substitute one asset for another through **improvements** and **replacements**. What is the difference between an improvement and a replacement? An **improvement (betterment)** is the substitution of a **better asset** for the one currently used (say, a concrete floor for a wooden floor). A **replacement**, on the other hand, is the substitution of a **similar asset** (a wooden floor for a wooden floor).

Many times, improvements and replacements result from a general policy to modernize or rehabilitate an older building or piece of equipment. The problem is differentiating these types of expenditures from normal repairs. Does the expenditure increase the **future service potential** of the asset? Or does it merely **maintain the existing level** of service? Frequently, the answer is not clear-cut. Good judgment is required to correctly classify these expenditures.

If the expenditure increases the future service potential of the asset, a company should capitalize it. The accounting is therefore handled in one of three ways, depending on the circumstances:

1 ***Use the substitution approach.*** Conceptually, the substitution approach is correct if the carrying amount of the old asset is available. It is then a simple matter to remove the cost of the old asset and replace it with the cost of the new asset.

To illustrate, Instinct Enterprises decides to replace the pipes in its plumbing system. A plumber suggests that the company use plastic tubing in place of the cast iron pipes and copper tubing. The old pipe and tubing have a book value of \$15,000 (cost of \$150,000 less accumulated depreciation of \$135,000), and a scrap value of \$1,000. The plastic tubing system costs \$125,000. If Instinct pays \$124,000 for the new tubing after exchanging the old tubing, it makes the following entry:

Plumbing System	125,000	
Accumulated Depreciation	135,000	
Loss on Disposal of Plant Assets	14,000	
Plumbing System		150,000
Cash (\$125,000 − \$1,000)		124,000

The problem is determining the book value of the old asset. Generally, the components of a given asset depreciate at different rates. However, generally no separate accounting is made. For example, the tires, motor, and body of a truck depreciate at different rates, but most companies use one rate for the entire truck. Companies can set separate depreciation rates, but it is often impractical. If a company cannot determine the carrying amount of the old asset, it adopts one of two other approaches.

2 ***Capitalize the new cost.*** Another approach capitalizes the improvement and keeps the carrying amount of the old asset on the books. The justification for this approach is that the item is sufficiently depreciated to reduce its carrying amount almost to zero. Although this assumption may not always be true, the differences are often insignificant. Companies usually handle improvements in this manner.

3 ***Charge to accumulated depreciation.*** In cases when a company does not improve the quantity or quality of the asset itself, but instead extends its useful life, the company debits the expenditure to Accumulated Depreciation rather than to an asset account. The theory behind this approach is that the replacement extends the useful life of the asset

and thereby recaptures some or all of the past depreciation. The net carrying amount of the asset is the same whether debiting the asset or accumulated depreciation.

Rearrangement and Reinstallation

Companies incur **rearrangement and reinstallation costs** to benefit future periods. An example is the rearrangement and reinstallation of machines to facilitate future production.

If a company like **Eastman Kodak** can determine or estimate the original installation cost and the accumulated depreciation to date, it handles the rearrangement and reinstallation cost as a replacement. If not, which is generally the case, Eastman Kodak should capitalize the new costs (if material in amount) as an asset to be amortized over future periods expected to benefit. If these costs are immaterial, if they cannot be separated from other operating expenses, or if their future benefit is questionable, the company should immediately expense them.

Repairs

A company makes **ordinary repairs** to maintain plant assets in operating condition. It charges ordinary repairs to an expense account in the period incurred, on the basis that **it is the primary period benefited**. Maintenance charges that occur regularly include replacing minor parts, lubricating and adjusting equipment, repainting, and cleaning. A company treats these as ordinary operating expenses.

It is often difficult to distinguish a repair from an improvement or replacement. The major consideration is whether the expenditure benefits more than one year or one operating cycle, whichever is longer. If a **major repair** (such as an overhaul) occurs, several periods will benefit. A company should handle the cost as an addition, improvement, or replacement.[5]

If companies prepare income statements for short periods of time, say, monthly or quarterly, the same principles apply. Ordinary repairs and other regular maintenance charges for an annual period may benefit several quarters, and companies may need to allocate the cost among those periods. A company will often find it advantageous to concentrate its repair program at a certain time of the year, perhaps during the period of least activity or when the plant is shut down for vacation. Short-term comparative statements might be misleading if the company shows such expenditures as expenses of the quarter in which they were incurred. To give comparability to monthly or quarterly income statements, a company might use an account such as Allowance for Repairs so that it can better assign repair costs to the periods benefited.

Summary of Costs Subsequent to Acquisition

Illustration 10-6 (next page) summarizes the accounting treatment for various costs incurred subsequent to the acquisition of capitalized assets.

---

[5]The Accounting Standards Executive Committee (AcSEC) of the AICPA has proposed that companies expense as incurred the costs involved for planned major expenditures unless they represent an *additional* component or the *replacement* of an existing component. The "expense as incurred" approach is justified on the basis that these costs are relatively consistent from period to period, that they are not separately identifiable assets or property units in and of themselves, and that they serve only to restore assets to their original operating condition. See Accounting Standards Executive Committee, "Accounting for Certain Costs and Activities Related to Property, Plant, and Equipment," Exposure Draft (New York: AICPA, June 29, 2001).

Illustration 10-6
Summary of Costs Subsequent to Acquisition of Property, Plant, and Equipment

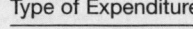

Type of Expenditure	Normal Accounting Treatment
Additions	Capitalize cost of addition to asset account.
Improvements and replacements	(a) **Carrying value known:** Remove cost of and accumulated depreciation on old asset, recognizing any gain or loss. Capitalize cost of improvement/replacement.
	(b) **Carrying value unknown:**
	1. If the asset's useful life is extended, debit accumulated depreciation for cost of improvement/replacement.
	2. If the quantity or quality of the asset's productivity is increased, capitalize cost of improvement/replacement to asset account.
Rearrangement and reinstallation	(a) If original installation cost is **known,** account for cost of rearrangement/reinstallation as a replacement (carrying value known).
	(b) If original installation cost is **unknown** and rearrangement/reinstallation cost is **material** in amount and benefits future periods, capitalize as an asset.
	(c) If original installation cost is **unknown** and rearrangement/reinstallation cost is **not material or future benefit is questionable,** expense the cost when incurred.
Repairs	(a) **Ordinary:** Expense cost of repairs when incurred.
	(b) **Major:** As appropriate, treat as an addition, improvement, or replacement.

USE OF PROPERTY, PLANT, AND EQUIPMENT: DEPRECIATION

OBJECTIVE 5

Explain the concept of depreciation.

Most individuals at one time or another purchase and trade in an automobile. The automobile dealer and the buyer typically discuss what the trade-in value of the old car is. Also, they may talk about what the trade-in value of the new car will be in several years. In both cases a decline in value is considered to be an example of depreciation.

To accountants, however, depreciation is not a matter of valuation. Rather, **depreciation is a means of cost allocation. Depreciation is the accounting process of allocating the cost of tangible assets to expense in a systematic and rational manner to those periods expected to benefit from the use of the asset.** For example, a company like **Goodyear** (one of the world's largest tire manufacturers) does not depreciate assets on the basis of a decline in their fair market value. Instead, it depreciates through systematic charges to expense.

This approach is employed because the value of the asset may fluctuate between the time the asset is purchased and the time it is sold or junked. Attempts to measure these interim value changes have not been well received because values are difficult to measure objectively. Therefore, Goodyear charges the asset's cost to depreciation expense over its estimated life. It makes no attempt to value the asset at fair market value between acquisition and disposition. Companies use the cost allocation approach because it matches costs with revenues and because fluctuations in market value are uncertain and difficult to measure.

Factors Involved in the Depreciation Process

OBJECTIVE 6

Identify the factors involved in the depreciation process.

Before establishing a pattern of charges to revenue, a company must answer three basic questions:

1 What depreciable base is to be used for the asset?

2 What is the asset's useful life?

3 What method of cost apportionment is best for this asset?

The answers to these questions involve combining several estimates into one single figure. Note the calculations assume perfect knowledge of the future, which is never attainable.

Depreciable Base for the Asset

The base established for depreciation is a function of two factors: the original cost, and salvage or disposal value. We discussed historical cost earlier in the chapter. **Salvage value** is the estimated amount that a company will receive when it sells the asset or removes it from service. It is the amount to which a company writes down or depreciates the asset during its useful life. If an asset has a cost of $10,000 and a salvage value of $1,000, its **depreciation base** is $9,000.

Tutorial on Depreciation Methods

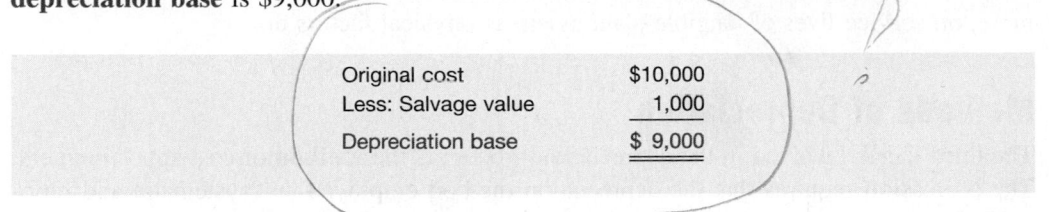

Original cost	$10,000
Less: Salvage value	1,000
Depreciation base	$ 9,000

Illustration 10-7
Computation of Depreciation Base

From a practical standpoint, companies often assign a zero salvage value. Some long-lived assets, however, have substantial salvage values.

Estimation of Service Lives

The service life of an asset often differs from its physical life. A piece of machinery may be physically capable of producing a given product for many years beyond its service life. But a company may not use the equipment for all that time because the cost of producing the product in later years may be too high. For example, the old Slater cotton mill in Pawtucket, Rhode Island, is preserved in remarkable physical condition as an historic landmark in U.S. industrial development, although its service life was terminated many years ago.[6]

Companies retire assets for two reasons: **physical factors** (such as casualty or expiration of physical life) and **economic factors** (obsolescence). Physical factors are the wear and tear, decay, and casualties that make it difficult for the asset to perform indefinitely. These physical factors set the outside limit for the service life of an asset.

We can classify the economic or functional factors into three categories:

1 **Inadequacy** results when an asset ceases to be useful to a company because the demands of the firm have changed. An example would be the need for a larger building to handle increased production. Although the old building may still be sound, it may have become inadequate for the company's purpose.

2 **Supersession** is the replacement of one asset with another more efficient and economical asset. Examples would be the replacement of the mainframe computer with a PC network, or the replacement of the Boeing 767 with the Boeing 787.

3 **Obsolescence** is the catchall for situations not involving inadequacy and supersession.

Because the distinction between these categories appears artificial, it is probably best to consider economic factors collectively instead of trying to make distinctions that are not clear-cut.

To illustrate the concepts of physical and economic factors, consider a new nuclear power plant. Which is more important in determining the useful life of a nuclear power plant—physical factors or economic factors? The limiting factors seem to be (1) ecological considerations, (2) competition from other power sources, and (3) safety concerns. Physical life does not appear to be the primary factor affecting useful life. Although the plant's physical life may be far from over, the plant may become obsolete in 10 years.

For a house, physical factors undoubtedly are more important than the economic or functional factors relative to useful life. Whenever the physical nature of the asset primarily

[6]Taken from J. D. Coughlan and W. K. Strand, *Depreciation Accounting, Taxes and Business Decisions* (New York: The Ronald Press, 1969), pp. 10–12.

determines useful life, maintenance plays an extremely vital role. The better the maintenance, the longer the life of the asset.[7]

In most cases, a company estimates the useful life of an asset based on its past experience with the same or similar assets. Others use sophisticated statistical methods to establish a useful life for accounting purposes. And in some cases, companies select arbitrary service lives. In a highly industrial economy such as that of the United States, where research and innovation are so prominent, technological factors have as much effect, if not more, on service lives of tangible plant assets as physical factors do.

Methods of Depreciation

The third factor involved in the depreciation process is the **method** of cost apportionment. The profession requires that the depreciation method employed be "systematic and rational." Companies may use a number of depreciation methods, as follows.

WHAT'S THE PRINCIPLE?

Depreciation attempts to match the cost of an asset to the periods that benefit from the use of that asset.

1 Activity method (units of use or production).

2 Straight-line method.

3 Decreasing charge methods (accelerated):

    a Sum-of-the-years'-digits.

    b Declining-balance method.[8]

To illustrate these depreciation methods, assume that Stanley Coal Mines recently purchased an additional crane for digging purposes. The following data relate to this purchase.

Cost of crane	$500,000
Estimated useful life	5 years
Estimated salvage value	$ 50,000
Productive life in hours	30,000 hours

Activity Method

OBJECTIVE 7

Compare activity, straight-line, and decreasing-charge methods of depreciation.

The **activity method** (also called the **variable-charge** or **units-of-production approach**) assumes that depreciation is **a function of use or productivity, instead of the passage of time**. A company considers the life of the asset in terms of either the **output** it provides (units it produces), or an **input** measure such as the number of hours it works. Conceptually, the proper cost association relies on output instead of hours used, but often the output is not easily measurable. In such cases, an input measure such as machine hours is a more appropriate method of measuring the dollar amount of depreciation charges for a given accounting period.

The crane poses no particular depreciation problem. Stanley can measure the usage (hours) relatively easily. If Stanley uses the crane for 4,000 hours the first year, the depreciation charge is:

[7]The airline industry also illustrates the type of problem involved in estimation. In the past, aircraft were assumed not to wear out—they just became obsolete. However, some jets have been in service as long as 20 years, and maintenance of these aircraft has become increasingly expensive. In addition, some recent air disasters have heightened the public's concern about worn-out aircraft. As a result, some airlines now replace aircraft not because of obsolescence but because of physical deterioration.

[8]*Accounting Trends and Techniques—2006* reports that of its 600 surveyed companies, for reporting purposes, 592 used straight-line, 14 used declining-balance, 4 used sum-of-the-years'-digits, 30 used an accelerated method (not specified), and 24 used units of production.

$$\frac{(\text{Cost less Salvage}) \times \text{Hours This Year}}{\text{Total Estimated Hours}} = \text{Depreciation Charge}$$

$$\frac{(\$500,000 - \$50,000) \times 4,000}{30,000} = \$60,000$$

Illustration 10-8
Depreciation Calculation,
Activity Method—Crane
Example

The major limitation of this method is that it is inappropriate in situations in which depreciation is a function of time instead of activity. For example, a building steadily deteriorates due to the elements (time) regardless of its use. In addition, where economic or functional factors affect an asset, independent of its use, the activity method loses much of its significance. For example, if a company is expanding rapidly, a particular building may soon become obsolete for its intended purposes. In both cases, activity is irrelevant. Another problem in using an activity method is the difficulty of estimating units of output or service hours received.

In cases where loss of services results from activity or productivity, the activity method matches costs and revenues the best. Companies that desire low depreciation during periods of low productivity, and high depreciation during high productivity, either adopt or switch to an activity method. In this way, a plant running at 40 percent of capacity generates 60 percent lower depreciation charges. **Inland Steel**, for example, switched to units-of-production depreciation at one time and reduced its losses by $43 million, or $1.20 per share.[9]

Straight-Line Method

The **straight-line method** considers depreciation a **function of time rather than a function of usage**. Companies widely use this method because of its simplicity. The straight-line procedure is often the most conceptually appropriate, too. When creeping obsolescence is the primary reason for a limited service life, the decline in usefulness may be constant from period to period. Stanley computes the depreciation charge for the crane as follows.

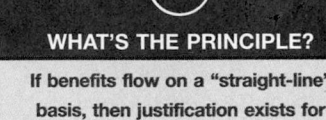

WHAT'S THE PRINCIPLE?
If benefits flow on a "straight-line" basis, then justification exists for matching the cost of the asset on a straight-line basis with these benefits.

$$\frac{\text{Cost less Salvage}}{\text{Estimated Service Life}} = \text{Depreciation Charge}$$

$$\frac{\$500,000 - \$50,000}{5} = \$90,000$$

Illustration 10-9
Depreciation Calculation,
Straight-Line Method—
Crane Example

The major objection to the straight-line method is that it rests on two tenuous assumptions: (1) The asset's economic usefulness is the same each year, and (2) the repair and maintenance expense is essentially the same each period.

One additional problem that occurs in using straight-line—as well as some others—is that distortions in the rate of return analysis (income/assets) develop. Illustration 10-10 indicates how the rate of return increases, given constant revenue flows, because the asset's book value decreases.

Illustration 10-10
Depreciation and Rate of Return Analysis—Crane Example

Year	Depreciation Expense	Undepreciated Asset Balance (book value)	Income (after depreciation expense)	Rate of Return (Income ÷ Assets)
0		$500,000		
1	$90,000	410,000	$100,000	24.4%
2	90,000	320,000	100,000	31.2%
3	90,000	230,000	100,000	43.5%
4	90,000	140,000	100,000	71.4%
5	90,000	50,000	100,000	200.0%

[9]"Double Standard," *Forbes* (November 22, 1982), p. 178.

Decreasing-Charge Methods

The **decreasing-charge methods** provide for a higher depreciation cost in the earlier years and lower charges in later periods. Because these methods allow for higher early-year charges than in the straight-line method, they are often called **accelerated depreciation methods**.

What is the main justification for this approach? The rationale is that companies should charge more depreciation in earlier years because the asset is most productive in its earlier years. Furthermore, the accelerated methods provide a constant cost because the depreciation charge is lower in the later periods, at the time when the repair and maintenance costs are often higher. Generally, companies use one of two decreasing-charge methods: the sum-of-the-years'-digits method, or the declining-balance method.

Sum-of-the-Years'-Digits.   The **sum-of-the-years'-digits method** results in a decreasing depreciation charge based on a decreasing fraction of depreciable cost (original cost less salvage value). Each fraction uses the sum of the years as a denominator $(5 + 4 + 3 + 2 + 1 = 15)$. The numerator is the number of years of estimated life remaining as of the beginning of the year. In this method, the numerator decreases year by year, and the denominator remains constant (5/15, 4/15, 3/15, 2/15, and 1/15). At the end of the asset's useful life, the balance remaining should equal the salvage value. Illustration 10-11 shows this method of computation.[10]

Illustration 10-11
Sum-of-the-Years'-Digits
Depreciation
Schedule—Crane
Example

Year	Depreciation Base	Remaining Life in Years	Depreciation Fraction	Depreciation Expense	Book Value, End of Year
1	$450,000	5	5/15	$150,000	$350,000
2	450,000	4	4/15	120,000	230,000
3	450,000	3	3/15	90,000	140,000
4	450,000	2	2/15	60,000	80,000
5	450,000	1	1/15	30,000	50,000[a]
		15	15/15	$450,000	

[a]Salvage value.

Declining-Balance Method.   The **declining-balance method** utilizes a depreciation rate (expressed as a percentage) that is some multiple of the straight-line method. For example, the double-declining rate for a 10-year asset is 20 percent (double the straight-line rate, which is 1/10 or 10 percent). Companies apply the constant rate to the declining book value each year. Unlike other methods, the declining-balance method **does not deduct the salvage value** in computing the depreciation base. The declining-balance rate is multiplied by the book value of the asset at the beginning of each period. Since the depreciation charge reduces the book value of the asset each period, applying the constant-declining-balance rate to a successively lower book value results in lower depreciation charges each year. This process continues until the book value of the asset equals its estimated salvage value. At that time the company discontinues depreciation.

Companies use various multiples in practice. For example, the **double-declining-balance method** depreciates assets at twice (200 percent) the straight-line rate. Illustration 10-12 shows Stanley's depreciation charges if using the double-declining approach.

[10]What happens if the estimated service life of the asset is, let us say, 51 years? How would we calculate the sum-of-the-years'-digits? Fortunately mathematicians have developed the following formula that permits easy computation:

$$\frac{n(n + 1)}{2} = \frac{51(51 + 1)}{2} = 1,326$$

Year	Book Value of Asset First of Year	Rate on Declining Balance[a]	Depreciation Expense	Balance Accumulated Depreciation	Book Value, End of Year
1	$500,000	40%	$200,000	$200,000	$300,000
2	300,000	40%	120,000	320,000	180,000
3	180,000	40%	72,000	392,000	108,000
4	108,000	40%	43,200	435,200	64,800
5	64,800	40%	14,800[b]	450,000	50,000

[a]Based on twice the straight-line rate of 20% ($90,000/$450,000 = 20%; 20% × 2 = 40%).
[b]Limited to $14,800 because book value should not be less than salvage value.

Illustration 10-12
Double-Declining
Depreciation
Schedule—Crane
Example

Companies often switch from the declining-balance method to the straight-line method near the end of the asset's useful life to ensure that they depreciate the asset only to its salvage value.[11]

What do the numbers mean?   Decelerating Depreciation

Which depreciation method should management select? Many believe that companies should use the method that best matches revenues with expenses. For example, if revenues generated by the asset are constant over its useful life, select straight-line depreciation. On the other hand, if revenues are higher (or lower) at the beginning of the asset's life, then use a decreasing (or increasing) method. Thus, if revenues from the asset can be reliably estimated, selecting a depreciation method that best matches costs with those revenues would seem to provide the most useful information to investors and creditors for assessing the future cash flows from the asset.

Managers in the real estate industry face a different challenge when considering depreciation choices. Real estate managers are frustrated with depreciation accounting because in their view, real estate often does not decline in value. In addition, because real estate is highly debt-financed, most real estate concerns report losses in earlier years of operations when the sum of depreciation and interest exceeds the revenue from the real estate project. As a result, real estate companies, like **Kimco Realty**, argue for some form of increasing-charge method of depreciation (lower depreciation at the beginning and higher depreciation at the end). Such a method would report higher total assets and net income in the earlier years of the project.[12]

Beyond the Numbers

Under what conditions might increasing-charge depreciation *not* result in better matching?

[11]A pure form of the declining-balance method (sometimes appropriately called the "fixed percentage of book value method") has also been suggested as a possibility. This approach finds a rate that depreciates the asset exactly to salvage value at the end of its expected useful life. The formula for determination of this rate is as follows:

$$\text{Depreciation rate} = 1 - \sqrt[n]{\frac{\text{Salvage value}}{\text{Acquisition cost}}}$$

The life in years is n. After computing the depreciation rate, a company applies it on the declining book value of the asset from period to period, which means that depreciation expense will be successively lower. This method is not used extensively in practice due to cumbersome computations. Further, it is not permitted for tax purposes.

[12]In this regard, real estate investment trusts (REITs) often report (in addition to net income) an earnings measure, funds from operations (FFO), that adjusts income for depreciation expense and other noncash expenses. This method is not GAAP, and there is mixed empirical evidence about whether FFO or GAAP income is more useful to real estate investment trust investors. See, for example, Richard Gore and David Stott, "Toward a More Informative Measure of Operating Performance in the REIT Industry: Net Income vs. FFO," *Accounting Horizons* (December 1998); and Linda Vincent, "The Information Content of FFO for REITs," *Journal of Accounting and Economics* (January 1999).

Special Depreciation Issues

Two special issues related to depreciation remain to be discussed. The major issues are:

1 How should depreciation be computed for partial periods?

2 How are revisions in depreciation rates handled?

Depreciation and Partial Periods

Companies seldom purchase plant assets on the first day of a fiscal period or dispose of them on the last day of a fiscal period. A practical question is: How much depreciation should a company charge for the partial periods involved?

In computing depreciation expense for partial periods, companies must determine the depreciation expense for the full year and then prorate this depreciation expense between the two periods involved. This process should continue throughout the useful life of the asset.

Assume, for example, that Steeltex Company purchases an automated drill machine with a 5-year life for $45,000 (no salvage value) on June 10, 2006. The company's fiscal year ends December 31. Steeltex therefore charges depreciation for only $6\frac{2}{3}$ months during that year. The total depreciation for a full year (assuming straight-line depreciation) is $9,000 ($45,000/5). The depreciation for the first, partial year is therefore:

$$\frac{6\frac{2}{3}}{12} \times \$9,000 = \$5,000$$

The partial-period calculation is relatively simple when Steeltex uses straight-line depreciation. But how is partial-period depreciation handled when it uses an accelerated method such as sum-of-the-years'-digits or double-declining balance? As an illustration, assume that Steeltex purchased another machine for $10,000 on July 1, 2006, with an estimated useful life of five years and no salvage value. Illustration 10-13 shows the depreciation figures for 2006, 2007, and 2008.

Illustration 10-13
Calculation of Partial-
Period Depreciation,
Two Methods

	Sum-of-the-Years'-Digits	Double-Declining Balance
1st full year	(5/15 × $10,000) = $3,333.33	(40% × $10,000) = $4,000
2nd full year	(4/15 × 10,000) = 2,666.67	(40% × 6,000) = 2,400
3rd full year	(3/15 × 10,000) = 2,000.00	(40% × 3,600) = 1,440

Depreciation from July 1, 2006, to December 31, 2006

6/12 × $3,333.33 = $1,666.67	6/12 × $4,000 = $2,000

Depreciation for 2007

6/12 × $3,333.33 = $1,666.67	6/12 × $4,000 = $2,000
6/12 × 2,666.67 = 1,333.33	6/12 × 2,400 = 1,200
$3,000.00	$3,200

or ($10,000 − $2,000) × 40% = $3,200

Depreciation for 2008

6/12 × $2,666.67 = $1,333.33	6/12 × $2,400 = $1,200
6/12 × 2,000.00 = 1,000.00	6/12 × 1,440 = 720
$2,333.33	$1,920

or ($10,000 − $5,200) × 40% = $1,920

Sometimes a company like Steeltex modifies the process of allocating costs to a partial period to handle acquisitions and disposals of plant assets more simply. It may compute depreciation for the full period on the opening balance in the asset account and not charge depreciation on acquisitions during the year. It then charges a full year of depreciation in the year of disposal. Other variations charge one-half year's depreciation both in the year of acquisition and in the year of disposal (referred to as the **half-year convention**), or charge a full year in the year of acquisition and none in the year of disposal.

In fact, Steeltex may adopt any one of these several fractional-year policies in allocating cost to the first and last years of an asset's life so long as it applies the method consistently. However, **unless otherwise stipulated, companies normally compute depreciation on the basis of the nearest full month**.

Illustration 10-14 shows depreciation allocated under five different fractional-year policies using the straight-line method on the $45,000 automated drill machine purchased by Steeltex Company on June 10, 2006, discussed earlier.

Machine Cost = $45,000	Depreciation Allocated per Period Over 5-Year Life*					
Fractional-Year Policy	2006	2007	2008	2009	2010	2011
1. Nearest fraction of a year.	$5,000[a]	$9,000	$9,000	$9,000	$9,000	$4,000[b]
2. Nearest full month.	5,250[c]	9,000	9,000	9,000	9,000	3,750[d]
3. Half year in period of acquisition and disposal.	4,500	9,000	9,000	9,000	9,000	4,500
4. Full year in period of acquisition, none in period of disposal.	9,000	9,000	9,000	9,000	9,000	–0–
5. None in period of acquisition, full year in period of disposal.	–0–	9,000	9,000	9,000	9,000	9,000

*Rounded to nearest dollar.
[a]6.667/12 ($9,000)   [b]5.333/12 ($9,000)   [c]7/12 ($9,000)   [d]5/12 ($9,000)

Illustration 10-14
Fractional-Year
Depreciation Policies

Revision of Depreciation Rates

When purchasing a plant asset, companies carefully determine depreciation rates based on past experience with similar assets and other pertinent information. The provisions for depreciation are only estimates, however. They may need to revise them during the life of the asset. Unexpected physical deterioration or unforeseen obsolescence may decrease the estimated useful life of the asset. Improved maintenance procedures, revision of operating procedures, or similar developments may prolong the life of the asset beyond the expected period.[13]

For example, assume that **International Paper Co.** purchased machinery with an original cost of $90,000. It estimates a 20-year life with no salvage value. However, during year 11, International Paper estimates that it will use the machine for an additional 20 years. Its total life, therefore, will be 30 years instead of 20. Depreciation has been recorded at the rate of 1/20 of $90,000, or $4,500 per year by the straight-line method. On the basis of a 30-year life, International Paper should have recorded depreciation as 1/30 of $90,000, or $3,000 per year. It has therefore overstated depreciation, and understated net income, by $1,500 for each of the past 10 years, or a total amount of $15,000. Illustration 10-15 shows this computation.

	Per Year	For 10 Years
Depreciation charged per books (1/20 × $90,000)	$4,500	$45,000
Depreciation based on a 30-year life (1/30 × $90,000)	3,000	30,000
Excess depreciation charged	$1,500	$15,000

Illustration 10-15
Computation of
Accumulated Difference
Due to Revisions

[13]As an example of a change in operating procedures, **General Motors (GM)** used to write off its tools—such as dies and equipment used to manufacture car bodies—over the life of the body type. Through this procedure, it expensed tools twice as fast as **Ford** and three times as fast as **Daimler-Chrysler**. However, it slowed the depreciation process on these tools and lengthened the lives on its plant and equipment. These revisions reduced depreciation and amortization charges by approximately $1.23 billion, or $2.55 per share, in the year of the change. In Chapter 18, we provide a more complete discussion of changes in estimates.

International Paper should report this change in estimate in the current and prospective periods. It should not make any changes in previously reported results. And it does not adjust opening balances nor attempt to "catch up" for prior periods. The reason? Changes in estimates are a continual and inherent part of any estimation process. Continual restatement of prior periods would occur for revisions of estimates unless handled prospectively. Therefore, no entry is made at the time the change in estimate occurs. Charges for depreciation in subsequent periods (assuming use of the straight-line method) are determined by **dividing the remaining book value less any salvage value by the remaining estimated life**.

Illustration 10-16
Computing Depreciation after Revision of Estimated Life

Machinery	$90,000
Less: Accumulated depreciation	45,000
Book value of machinery at end of 10th year	$45,000

Depreciation (future periods) = $45,000 book value ÷ 20 years remaining life = $2,250

The entry to record depreciation for each of the remaining 20 years is:

Depreciation Expense	2,250	
Accumulated Depreciation—Machinery		2,250

What do the numbers mean?   Depreciation Choices

The amount of depreciation expense recorded depends on both the depreciation method used and estimates of service lives and salvage values of the assets. Differences in these choices and estimates can have a significant impact on a company's reported results and can make it difficult to compare the depreciation numbers of different companies. For example, when **DuPont** switched its depreciation method from accelerated to straight-line, it reported a $250 million decrease in depreciation expense (and an increase in income) in the year of the change. And when **Willamette Industries** extended by 5 years the estimated service lives of its machinery and equipment, the effect on income was an increase of nearly $54 million.

An analyst can determine the impact of these management choices and judgments on the amount of depreciation expense by examining the notes to financial statements. For example, Willamette Industries provided the following note to its financial statements to explain the rationale for the change in estimated useful lives and to provide information that can be used to compare the useful lives of its assets to those of other companies.

Note 4: Property, Plant, and Equipment (partial)	
	Range of useful lives
Land	—
Buildings1	5–35
Machinery & equipment	5–25
Furniture & fixtures	3–15

During the year, the estimated service lives for most machinery and equipment were extended five years. The change was based upon a study performed by the company's engineering department, comparisons to typical industry practices, and the effect of the company's extensive capital investments which have resulted in a mix of assets with longer productive lives due to technological advances. As a result of the change, net income was increased by $54,000,000.

**Expanded Discussion—
Special Depreciation
Methods**

Beyond the Numbers

Do the changes in useful lives by Willamette reveal information about how well assets are being managed? Explain.

Try it out! Hasz Company purchased a building for $275,000 and machinery with a cost of $100,000. The building is to be depreciated using the double-declining-balance method with a 25-year useful life and a $50,000 salvage value. The machinery is to be depreciated using the sum-of-the-years'-digits method with a 5-year useful life and a $10,000 salvage value.

Instructions

a Compute depreciation expense for the first 2 years for the building and the machinery.

b Hasz management is preparing budgeted financial statements and is curious how depreciation on a straight-line basis for the machinery in year 3 would compare to depreciation expense computed in part **a**. Would depreciation be higher or lower under straight-line?

Solution

a Depreciation expense—Years 1 and 2:

Building depreciation:

Year 1: ($275,000 − $0)   × 0.08* = $22,000

Year 2: ($275,000 − $22,000) × 0.08* = $20,240

*(1/25) × 2

Machinery depreciation:

Year 1: ($100,000 − $10,000) × 5/15* = $30,000

Year 2: ($100,000 − $10,000) × 4/15 = $24,000

*5 + 4 + 3 + 2 + 1 **or** [5 × (5 + 1)] ÷ 2

b Comparison to straight-line depreciation—Year 3:

Machinery depreciation, straight-line:

Year 3 (and all years): ($100,000 − $10,000) ÷ 5 = $18,000

Machinery depreciation, sum-of-the-years'-digits:

Year 3: ($100,000 − $10,000) × 3/15 = $18,000

For year 3, depreciation expense under this accelerated method and straight-line is the same. Beginning in year 4, straight-line depreciation will be higher.

DISPOSITIONS OF PLANT ASSETS

A company, like **Intel**, may retire plant assets voluntarily or dispose of them by sale, exchange, involuntary conversion, or abandonment. Regardless of the type of disposal, depreciation must be taken up to the date of disposition. Then, Intel should remove all accounts related to the retired asset. Generally, the book value of the specific plant asset does not equal its disposal value. As a result, a gain or loss develops. The reason: Depreciation is an estimate of cost allocation and not a process of valuation. **The gain or loss is really a correction of net income** for the years during which Intel used the fixed asset.

OBJECTIVE 8
Describe the accounting treatment for the disposal of property, plant, and equipment.

Intel should show gains or losses on the disposal of plant assets in the income statement along with other items from customary business activities. However, if it sold, abandoned, spun off, or otherwise disposed of the "operations of a component of a business," then it should report the results separately in the discontinued operations section of the income statement. That is, Intel should report any gain or loss from disposal of a business component with the related results of discontinued operations.

Sale of Plant Assets

Companies record depreciation for the period of time between the date of the last depreciation entry and the date of sale. To illustrate, assume that Barret Company recorded depreciation on a machine costing $18,000 for 9 years at the rate of $1,200 per year. If it sells the machine in the middle of the tenth year for $7,000, Barret records depreciation to the date of sale as:

Depreciation Expense	600	
Accumulated Depreciation—Machinery		600

The entry for the sale of the asset then is:

Cash	7,000	
Accumulated Depreciation—Machinery	11,400	
[($1,200 × 9)+ $600]		
Machinery		18,000
Gain on Disposal of Machinery		400

The book value of the machinery at the time of the sale is $6,600 ($18,000 − $11,400). Because the machinery sold for $7,000, the amount of the gain on the sale is $400.

Involuntary Conversion

Sometimes an asset's service is terminated through some type of **involuntary conversion** such as fire, flood, theft, or condemnation. Companies report the difference between the amount recovered (e.g., from a condemnation award or insurance recovery), if any, and the asset's book value as a gain or loss. They treat these gains or losses like any other type of disposition. In some cases, these gains or losses may be reported as extraordinary items in the income statement, **if the conditions of the disposition are unusual and infrequent in nature**.

To illustrate, Camel Transport Corp. had to sell a plant located on company property that stood directly in the path of an interstate highway. For a number of years the state had sought to purchase the land on which the plant stood, but the company resisted. The state ultimately exercised its right of eminent domain, which the courts upheld. In settlement, Camel received $500,000, which substantially exceeded the $200,000 book value of the plant and land (cost of $400,000 less accumulated depreciation of $200,000). Camel made the following entry.

Cash	500,000	
Accumulated Depreciation—Plant Assets	200,000	
Plant Assets		400,000
Gain on Disposal of Plant Assets		300,000

If the conditions surrounding the condemnation are judged to be unusual and infrequent, Camel's gain of $300,000 is reported as an extraordinary item.

Some object to the recognition of a gain or loss in certain *involuntary* conversions. For example, the federal government often condemns forests for national parks. The paper companies that owned these forests must report a gain or loss on the condemnation. However, companies such as **Georgia-Pacific** contend that no gain or loss should be reported because they must replace the condemned forest land immediately and so are in the same economic position as they were before. The issue is whether condemnation and subsequent purchase should be viewed as one or two transactions. *FASB Interpretation No. 30* rules against the companies by requiring "that gain or loss be recognized when a nonmonetary asset is involuntarily converted to monetary assets even though an enterprise reinvests or is obligated to reinvest the monetary assets in replacement nonmonetary assets."[14]

Exchanges

The proper accounting for exchanges of nonmonetary assets, such as property, plant, and equipment, is controversial.[15] Some argue that companies should account for these types of exchanges based on the fair value of the asset given up or the fair value of the asset received, with a gain or loss recognized. Others believe that they should account for exchanges based on the recorded amount (book value) of the asset given up, with no gain or loss recognized. Still others favor an approach that recognizes losses in all cases, but defers gains in special situations.

Ordinarily companies account for the exchange of **nonmonetary assets** on the basis of **the fair value of the asset given up or the fair value of the asset received, whichever is clearly more evident**.[16] Thus, companies **should recognize immediately** any gains or losses on the exchange. The rationale for immediate recognition is that most transactions have **commercial substance**, and therefore gains and losses should be recognized.

Meaning of Commercial Substance

As indicated above, fair value is the basis for measuring an asset acquired in a nonmonetary exchange if the transaction has commercial substance. An exchange has **commercial substance** if the future cash flows change as a result of the transaction. That is, if the two parties' economic positions change, the transaction has commercial substance.

For example, Andrew Co. exchanges some if its equipment for land held by Roddick Inc. It is likely that the timing and amount of the cash flows arising for the land will differ significantly from the cash flows arising from the equipment. As a result, both Andrew Co. and Roddick Inc. are in different economic positions. Therefore, the exchange has commercial substance, and the companies recognize a gain or loss on the exchange.

What if companies exchange similar assets, such as one truck for another truck?[17] Even in an exchange of similar assets, a change in the economic position of the company can result. For example, let's say the useful life of the truck received is significantly longer than that of the truck given up. The cash flows for the trucks can differ significantly. As a result, the transaction has commercial substance, and the company should use fair value as a basis for measuring the asset received in the exchange.

---

[14]"Accounting for Involuntary Conversions of Nonmonetary Assets to Monetary Assets," *FASB Interpretation No. 30* (Stamford, Conn.: FASB, 1979), summary paragraph.

[15]Nonmonetary assets are items whose price in terms of the monetary unit may change over time. Monetary assets—cash and short- or long-term accounts and notes receivable—are fixed in terms of units of currency by contract or otherwise.

[16]"Accounting for Nonmonetary Transactions," *Opinions of the Accounting Principles Board No. 29* (New York: AICPA, 1973), par 18, and "Exchanges of Nonmonetary Assets, an Amendment of *APB Opinion No. 29*," *Statement of Financial Accounting Standards No. 153* (Norwalk, Conn: FASB, 2004).

[17]In previous accounting standards, the primary factor in determining whether to recognize gains on exchanges was whether the assets were "similar" in nature. This approach was problematic due to the subjectivity of determining similarity in the assets being exchanged. The new commercial-substance condition addresses this concern and contributes to international accounting convergence. With the commercial-substance approach, U.S. GAAP and iGAAP are now in agreement.

However, it is possible to exchange similar assets but not have a significant difference in cash flows. That is, the company is in the same economic position as before the exchange. In that case, the company recognizes a loss but generally defers a gain.

As we will see in the examples below, use of fair value generally results in recognizing a gain or loss at the time of the exchange. Consequently companies must determine if the transaction has commercial substance. To make this determination, they must carefully evaluate the cash flow characteristics of the assets exchanged.[18]

Illustration 10-17 summarizes asset exchange situations and the related accounting.

Illustration 10-17
Accounting for
Exchanges

Type of Exchange	Accounting Guidance
Exchange has commercial substance.	Recognize gains and losses immediately.
Exchange lacks commercial substance—no cash received.	Defer gains; recognize losses immediately.
Exchange lacks commercial substance—cash received.	Recognize partial gain; recognize losses immediately.*

*If cash is 25% or more of the fair value of the exchange, recognize entire gain because earnings process is complete.

As Illustration 10-17 indicates, companies immediately recognize losses they incur on all exchanges. The accounting for gains depends on whether the exchange has commercial substance. If the exchange has commercial substance, the company recognizes the gain immediately. However, the profession modifies the rule for immediate recognition of a gain when an exchange lacks commercial substance: If the company receives no cash in such an exchange, it defers recognition of a gain. If the company receives cash in such an exchange, it recognizes part of the gain immediately.

To illustrate the accounting for these different types of transactions, we examine various loss and gain exchange situations.

Exchanges—Loss Situation

When a company exchanges nonmonetary assets and a loss results, the company recognizes the loss immediately. The rationale: Companies should not value assets at more than their cash equivalent price; if the loss were deferred, assets would be overstated. Therefore, companies recognize a loss immediately whether the exchange has commercial substance or not.

For example, Information Processing, Inc. trades its used machine for a new model at Jerrod Business Solutions Inc. The exchange has commercial substance. The used machine has a book value of $8,000 (original cost $12,000 less $4,000 accumulated depreciation) and a fair value of $6,000. The new model lists for $16,000. Jerrod gives Information Processing a trade-in allowance of $9,000 for the used machine. Information Processing computes the cost of the new asset as follows.

Illustration 10-18
Computation of Cost of
New Machine

List price of new machine	$16,000
Less: Trade-in allowance for used machine	9,000
Cash payment due	7,000
Fair value of used machine	6,000
Cost of new machine	$13,000

[18]The determination of the commercial substance of a transaction requires significant judgment. In determining whether future cash flows change, it is necessary to do one of two things: (1) Determine whether the risk, timing, and amount of cash flows arising for the asset received differ from the cash flows associated with the outbound asset. Or, (2) evaluate whether cash flows are affected with the exchange versus without the exchange. Also note that if companies cannot determine fair values of the assets exchanged, then they should use recorded book values in accounting for the exchange.

Information Processing records this transaction as follows:

Equipment	13,000	
Accumulated Depreciation—Equipment	4,000	
Loss on Disposal of Equipment	2,000	
Equipment		12,000
Cash		7,000

We verify the loss on the disposal of the used machine as follows:

Fair value of used machine	$6,000
Book value of used machine	8,000
Loss on disposal of used machine	$2,000

Illustration 10-19
Computation of Loss on Disposal of Used Machine

Why did Information Processing not use the trade-in allowance or the book value of the old asset as a basis for the new equipment? The company did not use the trade-in allowance because it included a price concession (similar to a price discount). Few individuals pay list price for a new car. Dealers such as Jerrod often inflate trade-in allowances on the used car so that actual selling prices fall below list prices. To record the car at list price would state it at an amount in excess of its cash equivalent price because of the new car's inflated list price. Similarly, use of book value in this situation would overstate the value of the new machine by $2,000.[19]

Exchanges—Gain Situation

Has Commercial Substance. Now let's consider the situation in which a nonmonetary exchange has commercial substance and a gain is realized. In such a case, a company usually records the cost of a nonmonetary asset acquired in exchange for another nonmonetary asset at the **fair value of the asset given up**, and immediately recognizes a gain. The company should use the **fair value of the asset received** only if it is more clearly evident than the fair value of the asset given up.

To illustrate, Interstate Transportation Company exchanged a number of used trucks plus cash for a semi-truck. The used trucks have a combined book value of $42,000 (cost $64,000 less $22,000 accumulated depreciation). Interstate's purchasing agent, experienced in the second-hand market, indicates that the used trucks have a fair market value of $49,000. In addition to the trucks, Interstate must pay $11,000 cash for the semi-truck. Interstate computes the cost of the semi-truck as follows.

Fair value of trucks exchanged	$49,000
Cash paid	11,000
Cost of semi-truck	$60,000

Illustration 10-20
Computation of Semi-Truck Cost

Interstate records the exchange transaction as follows:

Semi-truck	60,000	
Accumulated Depreciation—Trucks	22,000	
Trucks		64,000
Gain on Disposal of Used Trucks		7,000
Cash		11,000

The gain is the difference between the fair value of the used trucks and their book value. We verify the computation as follows.

---

[19]Recognize that for Jerrod (the dealer), the asset given up in the exchange is considered inventory. As a result, Jerrod records a sale and related cost of goods sold. The used machine received by Jerrod is recorded at fair value.

Illustration 10-21
Computation of Gain on
Disposal of Used Trucks

Fair value of used trucks		$49,000
Cost of used trucks	$64,000	
Less: Accumulated depreciation	22,000	
Book value of used trucks		42,000
Gain on disposal of used trucks		$ 7,000

In this case, Interstate is in a different economic position, and therefore the transaction has commercial substance. Thus, it **recognizes a gain**.

Lacks Commercial Substance—No Cash Received. We now assume that the Interstate Transportation Company exchange lacks commercial substance. That is, the economic position of Interstate did not change significantly as a result of this exchange. In this case, Interstate defers the gain of $7,000 and reduces the basis of the semi-truck. Illustration 10-22 shows two different but acceptable computations to illustrate this reduction.

Illustration 10-22
Basis of Semi-Truck—Fair
Value vs. Book Value

Fair value of semi-truck	$60,000		Book value of used trucks	$42,000
Less: Gain deferred	7,000	OR	Plus: Cash paid	11,000
Basis of semi-truck	$53,000		Basis of semi-truck	$53,000

Interstate records this transaction as follows:

Semi-truck	53,000	
Accumulated Depreciation—Trucks	22,000	
Trucks		64,000
Cash		11,000

If the exchange lacks commercial substance, the company recognizes the gain (reflected in the basis of the semi-truck) when it later sells the semi-truck, not at the time of the exchange.

Lacks Commercial Substance—Some Cash Received. When a company receives cash (sometimes referred to as "boot") in an exchange that lacks commercial substance, it may immediately recognize a portion of the gain.[20] Illustration 10-23 shows the general formula for gain recognition when an exchange includes some cash.

Illustration 10-23
Formula for Gain
Recognition, Some Cash
Received

$$\frac{\text{Cash Received (Boot)}}{\text{Cash Received (Boot)} + \text{Fair Value of Other Assets Received}} \times \text{Total Gain} = \frac{\text{Recognized}}{\text{Gain}}$$

To illustrate, assume that Queenan Corporation traded in used machinery with a book value of $60,000 (cost $110,000 less accumulated depreciation $50,000) and a fair value of $100,000. It receives in exchange a machine with a fair value of $90,000 plus cash of $10,000. Illustration 10-24 shows calculation of the total gain on the exchange.

Illustration 10-24
Computation of Total Gain

Fair value of machine exchanged	$100,000
Book value of machine exchanged	60,000
Total gain	$ 40,000

---

[20]When the monetary consideration is significant, i.e., **25 percent or more** of the fair value of the exchange, both parties consider the transaction a **monetary exchange**. Such "monetary" exchanges rely on the fair values to measure the gains or losses that are recognized in their entirety. *EITF Issue No. 86-29*, "Nonmonetary Transactions: Magnitude of Boot and the Exception to the Use of Fair Value," *Emerging Issues Task Force Abstracts* (October 1, 1987).

Generally, when a transaction lacks commercial substance, a company defers any gain. But because Queenan received $10,000 in cash, it recognizes a partial gain. The portion of the gain a company recognizes is the ratio of monetary assets (cash in this case) to the total consideration received. Queenan computes the partial gain as follows:

$$\frac{\$10,000}{\$10,000 + \$90,000} \times \$40,000 = \$4,000$$

Illustration 10-25
Computation of Gain Based on Ratio of Cash Received

Because Queenan recognizes only a gain of $4,000 on this transaction, it defers the remaining $36,000 ($40,000 − $4,000) and reduces the basis (recorded cost) of the new machine. Illustration 10-26 shows the computation of the basis.

Fair value of new machine	$90,000		Book value of old machine	$60,000
Less: Gain deferred	36,000	OR	Portion of book value presumed sold	6,000*
Basis of new machine	$54,000		Basis of new machine	$54,000

$$^*\frac{\$10,000}{\$100,000} \times \$60,000 = \$6,000$$

Illustration 10-26
Computation of Gain Based on Ratio of Cost Received

Queenan records the transaction with the following entry.

Cash	10,000	
Machine	54,000	
Accumulated Depreciation—Machine	50,000	
Machine		110,000
Gain on Disposal of Machine		4,000

The rationale for the treatment of a partial gain is as follows: Before a nonmonetary exchange that includes some cash, a company has an unrecognized gain, which is the difference between the book value and the fair value of the old asset. When the exchange occurs, a portion of the fair value is converted to a more liquid asset. The ratio of this liquid asset to the total consideration received is the portion of the total gain that the company realizes. Thus, the company recognizes and records that amount.

Illustration 10-27 presents in summary form the accounting requirements for recognizing gains and losses on exchanges of nonmonetary assets.[21]

1. Compute the total gain or loss on the transaction. This amount is equal to the difference between the fair value of the asset given up and the book value of the asset given up.
2. If a loss is computed in step 1, always recognize the entire loss.
3. If a gain is computed in step 1,
   (a) and the exchange has commercial substance, recognize the entire gain.
   (b) and the exchange lacks commercial substance,
      (1) and no cash is involved, no gain is recognized.
      (2) and some cash is given, no gain is recognized.
      (3) and some cash is received, the following portion of the gain is recognized:

$$\frac{\text{Cash Received (Boot)}}{\text{Cash Received (Boot)} + \text{Fair Value of Other Assets Received}} \times \text{Total Gain}^*$$

*If the amount of cash exchanged is 25% or more, recognize entire gain.

Illustration 10-27
Summary of Gain and Loss Recognition on Exchanges of Nonmonetary Assets

[21]Adapted from an article by Robert Capettini and Thomas E. King, "Exchanges of Nonmonetary Assets: Some Changes," *The Accounting Review* (January 1976).

Companies disclose in their financial statements nonmonetary exchanges during a period. Such disclosure indicates the nature of the transaction(s), the method of accounting for the assets exchanged, and gains or losses recognized on the exchanges.[22]

PRESENTATION AND ANALYSIS

Presentation of Property, Plant, and Equipment

<table>
<tr><td>

OBJECTIVE 9

Explain how to report and analyze property, plant, and equipment.

</td></tr>
</table>

A company should disclose the basis of valuation—usually historical cost—for property, plant, equipment, and natural resources along with pledges, liens, and other commitments related to these assets. It should not offset any liability secured by property, plant, equipment, and natural resources against these assets. Instead, this obligation should be reported in the liabilities section. The company should segregate property, plant, and equipment not currently employed as producing assets in the business (such as idle facilities or land held as an investment) from assets used in operations.

When depreciating assets, a company credits a valuation account normally called Accumulated Depreciation. Using an Accumulated Depreciation account permits the user of the financial statements to see the original cost of the asset and the amount of depreciation that the company charged to expense in past years.

When depleting natural resources, some companies use an Accumulated Depletion account. Many, however, simply credit the natural resource account directly. The rationale for this approach is that the natural resources are physically consumed, making direct reduction of the cost of the natural resources appropriate.

Because of the significant impact on the financial statements of the depreciation method(s) used, companies should disclose the following.

a Depreciation expense for the period.

b Balances of major classes of depreciable assets, by nature and function.

c Accumulated depreciation, either by major classes of depreciable assets or in total.

d A general description of the method or methods used in computing depreciation with respect to major classes of depreciable assets.[23]

Expanded Discussion of Natural Resources

Special disclosure requirements relate to the oil and gas industry. Companies engaged in these activities must disclose the following in their financial statements: (1) the basic method of accounting for those costs incurred in oil and gas producing activities (e.g., full-cost versus successful-efforts), and (2) how the company disposes of costs relating to extractive activities (e.g., dispensing immediately versus depreciation and depletion.)[24]

The 2005 annual report of **International Paper Company** in Illustration 10-28 shows an acceptable disclosure. It uses condensed balance sheet data supplemented with details and policies in notes to the financial statements.

---

[22]"Accounting for Nonmonetary Transactions," op. cit., par. 28.

[23]"Omnibus Opinion—1967," *Opinions of the Accounting Principles Board No. 12* (New York: AICPA, 1967), par. 5. Some believe that companies should disclose the average useful life of the assets or the range of years of asset life to help users understand the age and life of property, plant, and equipment.

[24]Public companies, in addition to these two required disclosures, must include as supplementary information numerous schedules reporting reserve quantities; capitalized costs; acquisition, exploration, and development activities; and a standardized measure of discounted future net cash flows related to proved oil and gas reserve quantities. See "Disclosures about Oil and Gas Producing Activities," *Statement of Financial Accounting Standards Board No. 69* (Stamford, Conn.: FASB, 1982).

International Paper Company

Illustration 10-28
Disclosures for
Property, Plant,
Equipment, and Natural
Resources

Consolidated Balance Sheet (partial)

In millions at December 31	2005	2004
Assets		
Total current assets	$ 7,409	$12,586
Plants, properties and equipment, net	11,801	12,216
Forestlands	2,190	2,157
Investments	625	655
Goodwill	5,043	4,994
Deferred charges and other assets	1,703	1,609
Total assets	$28,771	$34,217

Note 1 (partial)

Plants, Properties and Equipment Plants, properties and equipment are stated at cost, less accumulated depreciation. Expenditures for betterments are capitalized whereas normal repairs and maintenance are expensed as incurred. The units-of-production method of depreciation is used for major pulp and paper mills and certain wood products facilities and the straight-line method for other plants and equipment. Annual straight-line depreciation rates are, for buildings, 2 1/2% to 8 1/2%, and, for machinery and equipment, 5% to 33%.

Forestlands At December 31, 2005, International Paper and its subsidiaries owned or controlled about 6.8 million acres of forestlands in the United States and 1.3 million acres in Brazil, and had, through licenses and forest management agreements, harvesting rights on government owned forestlands in Russia. Forestlands include owned property as well as certain timber harvesting rights with terms of one or more years, and are stated at cost, less cost of timber harvested (COTH). Costs attributable to timber are charged against income as trees are cut. The rate charged is determined annually based on the relationship of incurred costs to estimated current merchantable volume.

Note 11 (partial)

Plants, properties and equipment by major classification were:

In millions at December 31	2005	2004
Pulp, paper and packaging facilities		
Mills	$19,865	$20,895
Packaging plants	5,685	5,633
Wood products facilities	978	974
Other plants, properties and equipment	1,886	1,824
Gross cost	28,414	29,326
Less: Accumulated depreciation	16,613	17,110
Plants, properties and equipment, net	$11,801	$12,216

Analysis of Property, Plant, Equipment

Analysts evaluate assets relative to activity (turnover) and profitability.

Asset Turnover Ratio

How efficiently a company uses its assets to generate sales is measured by the **asset turnover ratio**. This ratio divides net sales by average total assets for the period. The resulting number is the dollars of sales produced by each dollar invested in assets. To illustrate, we use the following data from the **Tootsie Roll Industries** 2005 annual report. Illustrations 10-29 and 10-30 (page 518) show, respectively, financial data for Tootsie Roll and computation of its asset turnover ratio.

Additional Property, Plant, and Equipment Disclosures

Illustration 10-29
Financial Data for
Tootsie Roll Industries

Tootsie Roll Industries

2005 Financial Data

	(in millions)
Net sales	$487.8
Total assets, December 31, 2005	813.7
Total assets, December 31, 2004	811.8
Net income	77.2

Illustration 10-30
Asset Turnover Ratio

$$\text{Asset Turnover} = \frac{\text{Net Sales}}{\text{Average Total Assets}}$$
$$= \frac{\$487.8}{(\$813.7 + \$811.8)}$$
$$= .60$$

You will want to read the
CONVERGENCE CORNER
on the next page for
discussion of how
international convergence
efforts relate to the
accounting for property,
plant, and equipment.

The asset turnover ratio shows that Tootsie Roll generated sales of $0.60 per dollar of assets in the year ended December 31, 2005.

Asset turnover ratios vary considerably among industries. For example, a large utility like **Ameren** has a ratio of 0.32 times. A large grocery chain like **Kroger** has a ratio of 2.73 times. Thus, in comparing performance among companies based on the asset turnover ratio, you need to consider the ratio within the context of the industry in which a company operates.

Profit Margin on Sales Ratio

Another measure for analyzing the use of property, plant, and equipment is the **profit margin on sales ratio** (rate of return on sales). Calculated as net income divided by net sales, this profitability ratio does not, by itself, answer the question of how profitably a company uses its assets. But by relating the profit margin on sales to the asset turnover during a period of time, we can ascertain how profitably the company used assets during that period of time in a measure of the rate of return on assets. Using the Tootsie Roll Industries data shown above, we compute the profit margin on sales ratio and the rate of return on assets as follows.

Illustration 10-31
Profit Margin on Sales

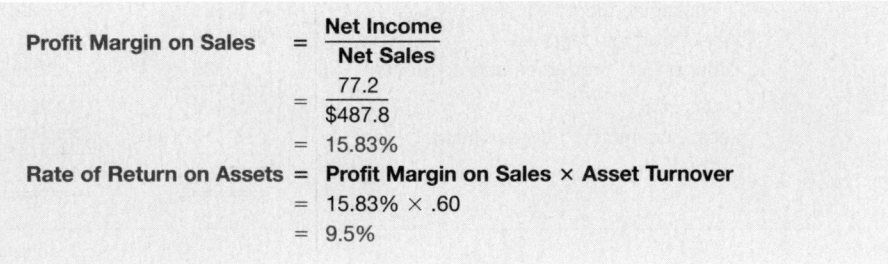

$$\text{Profit Margin on Sales} = \frac{\text{Net Income}}{\text{Net Sales}}$$
$$= \frac{77.2}{\$487.8}$$
$$= 15.83\%$$
$$\text{Rate of Return on Assets} = \text{Profit Margin on Sales} \times \text{Asset Turnover}$$
$$= 15.83\% \times .60$$
$$= 9.5\%$$

Rate of Return on Assets

The rate of return a company achieves through use of its assets is the **rate of return on assets (ROA)**. Rather than using the profit margin on sales, we can compute it directly by dividing net income by average total assets. Using Tootsie Roll's financial data, we compute the ratio as follows.

Illustration 10-32
Rate of Return on Assets

$$\text{Rate of Return on Assets} = \frac{\text{Net Income}}{\text{Average Total Assets}}$$
$$= \frac{77.2}{(\$813.7 + \$811.8)/2}$$
$$= 9.5\%$$

The 9.5 percent rate of return computed in this manner equals (with rounding) the 9.5 percent rate computed by multiplying the profit margin on sales by the asset turnover. The rate of return on assets measures profitability well because it combines the effects of profit margin and asset turnover.

CONVERGENCE CORNER

Property, Plant, and Equipment

iGAAP adheres to many of the same principles of U.S. GAAP in the accounting for property, plant, and equipment. iGAAP related to property, plant, and equipment is found in *IAS 16* ("Property, Plant and Equipment") and *IAS 23* ("Borrowing Costs").

RELEVANT FACTS

- Under iGAAP, capitalization of interest or borrowing costs incurred during construction of assets can be either expensed or capitalized. No such choice exists in U.S. GAAP; once certain criteria are met, interest must be capitalized.

- iGAAP, like U.S. GAAP, capitalizes all direct costs in self-constructed assets. iGAAP does not address the capitalization of fixed overhead, although in practice these costs are generally capitalized.

- The accounting for exchanges of nonmonetary assets has recently converged between iGAAP and U.S. GAAP. U.S GAAP, per *SFAS No.153*, now requires that gains on exchanges of nonmonetary assets be recognized if the exchange has commercial substance. This is the same framework used in iGAAP.

- iGAAP also views depreciation as allocation of cost over an asset's life. iGAAP permits the same depreciation methods (straight-line, accelerated, units-of-production) as U.S. GAAP.

- As discussed in the Chapter 4 Convergence Corner, iGAAP permits asset revaluations (which are not permitted in U.S. GAAP). Consequently, companies that use the revaluation framework must follow revaluation depreciation procedures. We illustrate revaluation depreciation in the "About the Numbers" discussion.

ABOUT THE NUMBERS

As indicated, iGAAP permits companies to carry assets at historical cost or use a revaluation model for fixed assets. According to *IAS 16*, if revaluation is used, it must be applied to all assets in a class of assets and assets must be revalued on an annual basis. What about depreciation? To illustrate, assume Pernice Company applies revaluation accounting to plant assets with a carrying value of $1,000,000, a useful life of 5 years, and no salvage value. At the end of year 1, independent appraisers determine that the asset has a fair value of $900,000. Pernice makes the following journal entries in year 1, assuming straight-line depreciation.

To record depreciation expense in Year I

Depreciation Expense	200,000	
Accumulated Depreciation—Plant Assets		200,000

To adjust the plant assets to fair value and record revaluation surplus

Accumulated Depreciation—Plant Assets	200,000	
Plant Assets		100,000
Revaluation Surplus		100,000

Thus, there is a two-step process. First, Pernice records depreciation based on the cost basis of $1,000,000. As a result, it reports depreciation expense of $200,000 on the income statement. Second, it records the revaluation of $100,000, which is the difference between the fair value of $900,000 and the book value of $800,000. Recall that the revaluation surplus is reported in stockholders' equity as a component of "Other comprehensive income." Pernice now reports the following information at the end of year 1 for its plant assets.

Plant assets ($1,000,000 − $100,000)	$900,000
Accumulated depreciation—Plant assets	–0–
Book value	$900,000
Revaluation surplus (Equity)	$100,000

As indicated, $900,000 is the new basis of the asset. Pernice reports depreciation expense of $200,000 in the income statement and $100,000 in "Other comprehensive income." Assuming no change in the useful life, depreciation in year 2 will be $225,000 ($900,000 ÷ 4).

ON THE HORIZON

The IASB is working on a project to amend *IAS 23* ("Borrowing Costs") that converges to the FASB standard in this area. That amendment is due to be published in 2007. With respect to revaluations, as part of the conceptual framework project, the Boards will examine the measurement bases used in accounting. It is too early to say whether a converged conceptual framework will recommend fair value measurement (and revaluation accounting) for property, plant, and equipment. However, this is likely to be one of the more contentious issues, given the long-standing use of historical cost as a measurement basis in U.S. GAAP.

ACCOUNTING, ANALYSIS, PRINCIPLES

Accounting

Durler Company purchased equipment on January 2, 2005, for $112,000. The equipment had an estimated useful life of 5 years with an estimated salvage value of $12,000. Durler uses straight-line depreciation on all assets. On January 2, 2009, Durler exchanged this equipment plus $12,000 in cash for newer equipment. The old equipment has a fair market value of $50,000.

Prepare the journal entry to record the exchange on the books of Durler Company. Assume that the exchange has commercial substance.

Analysis

How will this exchange affect comparisons of the return on asset ratio for Durler in the year of the exchange compared to prior years?

Principles

How does the concept of commercial substance affect the accounting and analysis of this exchange?

Solution

Accounting

Equipment ($50,000 + $12,000)	62,000	
Accumulated Depreciation—Equipment	80,000*	
Equipment		112,000
Cash		12,000
Gain on Disposal of Equipment		18,000**

*Accumulated depreciation to January 2, 2009:
[($112,000 − $12,000) ÷ 5] × 4 = $80,000

**Computation of gain on disposal of equipment:

Fair value of equipment exchanged	$50,000
Book value of equipment exchanged ($112,000 − $80,000)	32,000
Gain on disposal of equipment	$18,000

Analysis

The gain on the disposal increases income, leading to a one-time increase in the return on assets in the year of the exchange. In essence, the gain reflects the extent to which prior years' depreciation was overstated related to the decline in the fair value of the asset traded in. As a result, in the year of the exchange, Durler's ROA will appear higher than in prior years. Some analysts will adjust these nonrecurring gains out of income when conducting analysis using ROA.

Principles

The concept of commercial substance is a fundamental element in the accounting for exchanges. If the transaction above lacked commercial substance, the gain on the exchange would be deferred. That is, if the expected cash flows arising from the assets exchanged are not significantly different, Durler is in the same economic position after the exchange with respect to exchanged assets. As a result, no gain is reported, and the nonrecurring time gain will not affect analysts' comparisons of a company's ROA across years with and without exchanges.

Key Terms

accelerated depreciation method, 504
activity method, 502
additions, 497
asset turnover ratio, 517
capital expenditure, 497
commercial substance, 511
declining-balance method, 504
decreasing-charge method, 504
depreciation, 500
depreciation base, 501
double-declining-balance method, 504
fixed assets, 488
historical cost, 488
inadequacy 501
improvements (betterments), 498
involuntary conversion, 510
lump sum price, 492

major repairs, 499
nonmonetary assets, 511
nonreciprocal transfers, 494
obsolescence, 501
ordinary repairs, 499
plant assets, 488
profit margin on sales ratio, 518
property, plant, and equipment, 488
rate of return on assets (ROA), 518
rearrangement and reinstallation costs, 499
replacements, 498
revenue expenditure, 497
salvage value, 501
self-constructed asset, 490
straight-line method, 503
sum-of-the-years'-digits method, 504
supersession, 501

Summary of Learning Objectives

1 Describe property, plant, and equipment and costs included in its initial valuation. The major characteristics of property, plant, and equipment are: (1) They are acquired for use in operations and not for resale. (2) They are long-term in nature and usually subject to depreciation. (3) They possess physical substance.

The costs included in initial valuation of property, plant, and equipment are as follows:

Cost of land: Includes all expenditures made to acquire land and to ready it for use. Land costs typically include (1) the purchase price; (2) closing costs, such as title to the land, attorney's fees, and recording fees; (3) costs incurred in getting the land in condition for its intended use, such as grading, filling, draining, and clearing; (4) assumption of any liens, mortgages, or encumbrances on the property; and (5) any additional land improvements that have an indefinite life.

Cost of buildings: Includes all expenditures related directly to their acquisition or construction. These costs include (1) materials, labor, and overhead costs incurred during construction, and (2) professional fees and building permits.

Cost of equipment: Includes the purchase price, freight and handling charges incurred, insurance on the equipment while in transit, cost of special foundations if required, assembling and installation costs, and costs of conducting trial runs.

2 Describe the accounting problems associated with interest capitalization. Companies should capitalize only actual interest (with modifications). The rationale for this approach is that during construction, the asset is not generating revenue, and therefore companies should defer (capitalize) interest cost. Once construction is completed, the asset is ready for its intended use, and revenues can be earned. Companies should expense any interest cost incurred in purchasing an asset that is ready for its intended use.

3 Understand accounting issues related to acquiring and valuing plant assets. The following issues relate to acquiring and valuing plant assets: (1) *Cash discounts:* Whether taken or not, cash discounts are generally considered a reduction in the cost of the asset; the real cost of the asset is the cash or cash equivalent price of the asset. (2) *Lump-sum purchase:* Allocate the total cost among the various assets on the basis of their relative fair market values. (3) *Issuance of stock:* If the stock is actively traded, the market value of the stock issued is a fair indication of the cost of the property acquired. If the market value of the common stock exchanged is not determinable, establish the value of the property and use it as the basis for recording the asset and issuance of the common stock. (4) *Contributions:* Record at the fair value of the asset received and credit revenue for the same amount.

4 Describe the accounting treatment for costs subsequent to acquisition. Illustration 10-6 (page 500) provides a summary of how to account for costs subsequent to acquisition.

5 Explain the concept of depreciation. Depreciation allocates the cost of tangible assets to expense in a systematic and rational manner to those periods expected to benefit from the use of the asset.

6 Identify the factors involved in the depreciation process. Three factors involved in the depreciation process are: (1) determining the depreciation base for the asset, (2) estimating service lives, and (3) selecting a method of cost apportionment (depreciation).

7 Compare activity, straight-line, and decreasing-charge methods of depreciation. (1) *Activity method:* Assumes that depreciation is a function of use or productivity instead of the passage of time. Considers the life of the asset in terms of either the output it provides or an input measure such as the number of hours it works. (2) *Straight-line method:* Considers depreciation a function of time instead of a function of usage. This simple straight-line procedure is often the most conceptually appropriate when the decline in usefulness is constant from period to period. (3) *Decreasing-charge methods:* Provide for a higher depreciation cost in the earlier years and lower charges in later periods. The main justification for this approach is that the asset suffers the greatest loss of services in its early years.

8 Describe the accounting treatment for the disposal of property, plant, and equipment. Regardless of the time of disposal, companies take depreciation up to the date of disposition, and then remove all accounts related to the retired asset. Companies report gains or losses on the retirement of plant assets in the income statement along with other items that arise from customary business activities. Illustrations 10-17 (page 512) and 10-27 (page 515) summarize how to account for disposals through exchange.

9 Explain how to report and analyze property, plant, and equipment. Companies should disclose the basis of valuation for property, plant, and equipment along with pledges, liens, and other commitments related to these assets. Companies should not offset any liability secured by property, plant, and equipment against these assets, but should report it in the liabilities section. When assets are depreciated, companies normally credit a valuation account called Accumulated Depreciation. Analysis may be performed to evaluate the asset turnover ratio, profit margin on sales, and rate of return on assets.

BEHIND THE NUMBERS APPENDIX 10A — INTEREST-CAPITALIZATION PROCEDURES

Interest Capitalization

In this appendix, we illustrate the specific steps for determining the amount of interest capitalization under the approach recognized as GAAP. To implement this general approach, companies must consider three items:

OBJECTIVE 10
Understand the procedures for determining capitalized interest amounts.

1 Qualifying assets.

2 Capitalization period.

3 Amount to capitalize.

Qualifying Assets

To qualify for interest capitalization, assets must require a period of time to get them ready for their intended use. A company capitalizes interest costs starting with the first expenditure related to the asset. Capitalization continues until the company substantially readies the asset for its intended use.

Assets that qualify for interest capitalization include assets under construction for a company's own use (including buildings, plants, and large machinery) and assets intended for sale or lease that are constructed or otherwise produced as discrete projects (e.g., ships or real estate developments).

Examples of assets that do not qualify for interest capitalization are (1) assets that are in use or ready for their intended use, and (2) assets that the company does not use in its earnings activities and that are not undergoing the activities necessary to get them ready for use. Examples of this second type include land remaining undeveloped and assets not used because of obsolescence, excess capacity, or need for repair.

Capitalization Period

The **capitalization period** is the period of time during which a company must capitalize interest. It begins with the presence of three conditions:

1 Expenditures for the asset have been made.

2 Activities that are necessary to get the asset ready for its intended use are in progress.

3 Interest cost is being incurred.

Interest capitalization **continues as long as these three conditions are present**. The capitalization period ends when the asset is substantially complete and ready for its intended use.

> **INTERNATIONAL INSIGHT**
>
> Under international accounting standards, companies may capitalize interest, but it is not the preferred treatment. The benchmark treatment is to expense interest in the period incurred.

Amount to Capitalize

The amount of interest to capitalize is limited to the lower of actual interest cost incurred during the period or avoidable interest. **Avoidable interest** is the amount of interest cost during the period that a company could theoretically avoid if it had not made expenditures for the asset. If the actual interest cost for the period is $90,000 and the avoidable interest is $80,000, the company capitalizes only $80,000. Or, if the actual interest cost is $80,000 and the avoidable interest is $90,000, it still capitalizes only $80,000. In no situation should interest cost include a cost of capital charge for stockholders' equity. Furthermore, GAAP requires interest capitalization for a qualifying asset only if its effect, compared with the effect of expensing interest, is material.[1]

To apply the avoidable interest concept, a company determines the potential amount of interest that it may capitalize during an accounting period by multiplying the interest rate(s) by the **weighted-average accumulated expenditures** for qualifying assets during the period.

Weighted-Average Accumulated Expenditures. In computing the weighted-average accumulated expenditures, a company weights the construction expenditures by the amount of time (fraction of a year or accounting period) that it can incur interest cost on the expenditure.

To illustrate, assume a 17-month bridge construction project with current-year payments to the contractor of $240,000 on March 1, $480,000 on July 1, and $360,000 on November 1. The company computes the weighted-average accumulated expenditures for the year ended December 31 as follows.

[1]"Capitalization of Interest Cost," *Statement of Financial Accounting Standards No. 34* (Stamford, Conn.: FASB, 1979), summary paragraph.

Expenditures			Capitalization		Weighted-Average
Date	Amount	×	Period*	=	Accumulated Expenditures
March 1	$ 240,000		10/12		$200,000
July 1	480,000		6/12		240,000
November 1	360,000		2/12		60,000
	$1,080,000				$500,000

*Months between date of expenditure and date interest capitalization stops or end of year, whichever comes first (in this case December 31).

To compute the weighted-average accumulated expenditures, a company weights the expenditures by the amount of time that it can incur interest cost on each one. For the March 1 expenditure, the company associates 10 months' interest cost with the expenditure. For the expenditure on July 1, it incurs only 6 months' interest costs. For the expenditure made on November 1, the company incurs only 2 months of interest cost.

Interest Rates. Companies follow these principles in selecting the appropriate interest rates to be applied to the weighted-average accumulated expenditures:

1 For the portion of weighted-average accumulated expenditures that is less than or equal to any amounts borrowed specifically to finance construction of the assets, use the interest rate incurred on the specific borrowings.

2 For the portion of weighted-average accumulated expenditures that is greater than any debt incurred specifically to finance construction of the assets, use a weighted average of interest rates incurred on all other outstanding debt during the period.[2]

Illustration 10A-2 shows the computation of a weighted-average interest rate for debt greater than the amount incurred specifically to finance construction of the assets.

	Principal	Interest
12%, 2-year note	$ 600,000	$ 72,000
9%, 10-year bonds	2,000,000	180,000
7.5%, 20-year bonds	5,000,000	375,000
	$7,600,000	$627,000

$$\text{Weighted-average Interest Rate} = \frac{\text{Total Interest}}{\text{Total Principal}} = \frac{\$627,000}{\$7,600,000} = 8.25\%$$

Comprehensive Example of Interest Capitalization

To illustrate the issues related to interest capitalization, assume that on November 1, 2007, Shalla Company contracted Pfeifer Construction Co. to construct a building for $1,400,000 on land costing $100,000 (purchased from the contractor and included in the first payment). Shalla made the following payments to the construction company during 2008.

January 1	March 1	May 1	December 31	Total
$210,000	$300,000	$540,000	$450,000	$1,500,000

[2]The interest rate to be used may rely exclusively on an average rate of all the borrowings, if desired. For our purposes, we use the specific borrowing rate followed by the average interest rate because we believe it to be more conceptually consistent. Either method can be used; *FASB Statement No. 34* does not provide explicit guidance on this measurement. For a discussion of this issue and others related to interest capitalization, see Kathryn M. Means and Paul M. Kazenski, "SFAS 34: Recipe for Diversity," *Accounting Horizons* (September 1988); and Wendy A. Duffy, "A Graphical Analysis of Interest Capitalization," *Journal of Accounting Education* (Fall 1990).

Pfeifer Construction completed the building, ready for occupancy, on December 31, 2008. Shalla had the following debt outstanding at December 31, 2008.

Specific Construction Debt

1. 15%, 3-year note to finance purchase of land and construction of the building, dated December 31, 2007, with interest payable annually on December 31 $750,000

Other Debt

2. 10%, 5-year note payable, dated December 31, 2004, with interest payable annually on December 31 $550,000
3. 12%, 10-year bonds issued December 31, 2005, with interest payable annually on December 31 $600,000

Shalla computed the weighted-average accumulated expenditures during 2008 as shown in Illustration 10A-3.

Expenditures			Current Year Capitalization		Weighted-Average
Date	Amount	×	Period	=	Accumulated Expenditures
January 1	$ 210,000		12/12		$210,000
March 1	300,000		10/12		250,000
May 1	540,000		8/12		360,000
December 31	450,000		0		0
	$1,500,000				$820,000

Illustration 10A-3
Computation of Weighted-Average Accumulated Expenditures

Note that the expenditure made on December 31, the last day of the year, does not have any interest cost.

Shalla computes the avoidable interest as shown in Illustration 10A-4.

Weighted-Average Accumulated Expenditures	×	Interest Rate	=	Avoidable Interest
$750,000		.15 (construction note)		$112,500
70,000[a]		.1104 (weighted average of other debt)[b]		7,728
$820,000				$120,228

Illustration 10A-4
Computation of Avoidable Interest

[a]The amount by which the weighted-average accumulated expenditures exceeds the specific construction loan.

[b]Weighted-average interest rate computation:

	Principal	Interest
10%, 5-year note	$ 550,000	$ 55,000
12%, 10-year bonds	600,000	72,000
	$1,150,000	$127,000

$$\text{Weighted-average Interest Rate} = \frac{\text{Total Interest}}{\text{Total Principal}} = \frac{\$127,000}{\$1,150,000} = 11.04\%$$

The company determines the actual interest cost, which represents the maximum amount of interest that it may capitalize during 2008, as shown in Illustration 10A-5.

Construction note	$750,000 ×.15	=	$112,500
5-year note	$550,000 ×.10	=	55,000
10-year bonds	$600,000 ×.12	=	72,000
Actual interest			$239,500

Illustration 10A-5
Computation of Actual Interest Cost

The interest cost that Shalla capitalizes is the lesser of $120,228 (avoidable interest) and $239,500 (actual interest), or $120,228.

Shalla records the following journal entries during 2008:

**Tutorial on Interest
Capitalization**

January 1

Land	100,000	
Building (or Construction in Process)	110,000	
Cash		210,000

March 1

Building	300,000	
Cash		300,000

May 1

Building	540,000	
Cash		540,000

December 31

Building	450,000	
Cash		450,000

Building (Capitalized Interest)	120,228	
Interest Expense ($239,500 − $120,228)	119,272	
Cash ($112,500 + $55,000 + $72,000)		239,500

Shalla should write off capitalized interest cost as part of depreciation over the useful life of the assets involved and not over the term of the debt. It should disclose the total interest cost incurred during the period, with the portion charged to expense and the portion capitalized indicated.

At December 31, 2008, Shalla discloses the amount of interest capitalized either as part of the nonoperating section of the income statement or in the notes accompanying the financial statements. We illustrate both forms of disclosure, in Illustrations 10A-6 and 10A-7.

Illustration 10A-6
Capitalized Interest
Reported in the Income
Statement

Income from operations		XXXX
Other expenses and losses:		
Interest expense	$239,500	
Less: Capitalized Interest	120,228	119,272
Income before taxes on income		XXXX
Income taxes		XXX
Net income		XXXX

Illustration 10A-7
Capitalized Interest
Disclosed in a Note

Note 1: Accounting Policies. *Capitalized Interest.* During 2008 total interest cost was $239,500, of which $120,228 was capitalized and $119,272 was charged to expense.

Key Terms

avoidable interest, 523
capitalization period, 523
weighted-average accumulated expenditures, 523

Summary of Learning Objective for Appendix 10A

10 Understand the procedures for determining capitalized interest amounts. The amount of avoidable interest is determined by applying interest rates (either on specific construction borrowing or rates on other outstanding debt) to weighted-average accumulated expenditures. Weights on expenditures are based on the amount of time during the period that interest cost could be incurred on the expenditure. The amount capitalized in the cost of the asset is the lower of the avoidable or actual interest.

REVIEW EXERCISE

Norwel Company manufactures miniature circuit boards used in wireless phones and personal organizers. On June 5, 2008, Norwel purchased a circuit board stamping machine at a retail price of $12,000. Norwel paid 5% sales tax on this purchase. Norwel paid a contractor $1,400 for a specially wired platform for the machine, to ensure noninterrupted power to the machine. Norwel estimates the machine will have a 4-year useful life, with a salvage value of $2,000 at the end of 4 years. Norwel uses straight-line depreciation and employs the "half-year" convention in accounting for partial-year depreciation. Norwel's fiscal year ends on December 31.

Instructions

a   At what amount should Norwel record the acquisition cost of the machine?

b   How much depreciation expense should Norwel record in 2008 and in 2009?

c   At what amount will the machine be reported in Norwel's balance sheet at December 31, 2009?

d   On July 1, 2010, Norwel decides to outsource its circuit board operations to Boards-R-Us Inc. As part of this plan, Norwel sells the machine (and the platform) to Boards-R-Us for $7,000. What is the impact of this disposal on Norwel's 2010 income before taxes?

Solution

a   Historical cost is measured by the cash or cash-equivalent price of obtaining the asset and bringing it to the location and condition for its intended use. For Norwel, this is:

Price	$12,000
Tax ($12,000 × .05)	600
Platform	1,400
Total	$14,000

b   Depreciable base: $14,000 − $2,000 = $12,000

Depreciation expense: $12,000 ÷ 4 = $3,000 per year

2008: 1/2 year = $3,000 × .50 = $1,500

2009: full year = $3,000

c   The amount reported on the balance sheet is the cost of the asset less accumulated depreciation:

Machine	$14,000
Accumulated depreciation	(4,500)
Book value	$ 9,500

d   The income effect is a gain or loss, determined by comparing the book value of the asset to the disposal value:

Cost	$14,000
Less: Accumulated depreciation ($1,500 + $3,000 + $1,500)	6,000
Book value of machine and platform	8,000
Cash received for machine and platform	7,000
Loss before income taxes	$ 1,000

Questions

Note: All **asterisked** assignment materials relate to material covered in the appendix to the chapter.

1 What are the major characteristics of plant assets?

2 Esplanade Inc. owns land that it purchased on January 1, 2001, for $420,000. At December 31, 2008, its current value is $770,000 as determined by appraisal. At what amount should Esplanade report this asset on its December 31, 2008, balance sheet? Explain.

3 Name the items, in addition to the amount paid to the former owner or contractor, that may properly be included as part of the acquisition cost of the following plant assets.

   (a) Land.

   (b) Machinery and equipment.

   (c) Buildings.

4 Indicate where the following items would be shown on a balance sheet.

   (a) A lien that was attached to the land when purchased.

   (b) Landscaping costs.

   (c) Attorney's fees and recording fees related to purchasing land.

   (d) A parking lot servicing employees in the building.

   (e) Cost of temporary building for workers during construction of building.

   (f) Interest expense on bonds payable incurred during construction of a building.

   (g) Assessments for sidewalks that are maintained by the city.

   (h) The cost of demolishing an old building that was on the land when purchased.

5 What is the rationale for assigning a portion of overhead to the cost of an asset?

6 The Buildings account of Denis Leary Inc. includes the following items that were used in determining the basis for depreciating the cost of a building.

   (a) Architect's fees.

   (b) Interest and taxes during construction.

   (c) Commission paid on the sale of capital stock.

   (d) Bond discount.

Do you agree with these charges? If not, how would you deal with each of the items above in the corporation's books and in its annual financial statements?

7 Jones Company has purchased two tracts of land. One tract will be the site of its new manufacturing plant. The other is being purchased with the hope that it will be sold in the next year at a profit. How should these two tracts of land be reported in the balance sheet?

8 One financial accounting issue encountered when a company constructs its own plant is whether the interest cost on funds borrowed to finance construction should be capitalized and then amortized over the life of the assets constructed. What is a common accounting justification for capitalizing such interest?

9 How should the amount of interest capitalized be disclosed in the footnotes to the financial statements? How should interest revenue from temporarily invested excess funds borrowed to finance the construction of assets be accounted for?

10 Discuss the basic accounting problem that arises in handling each of the following situations.

   (a) Assets purchased by issuance of capital stock.

   (b) Acquisition of plant assets by gift or donation.

   (c) Purchase of a plant asset subject to a cash discount.

   (d) A group of assets acquired for a lump sum.

   (e) An asset traded in or exchanged for another asset.

11 Yukio Mishima Industries acquired equipment this year to be used in its operations. The equipment was delivered by the suppliers, installed by Mishima, and placed into operation. Some of it was purchased for cash with discounts available for prompt payment. What costs should Mishima capitalize for the new equipment purchased this year? Explain.

12 Adam Dunn Co. purchased for $2,200,000 property that included both land and a building to be used in operations. The seller's book value was $300,000 for the land and $900,000 for the building. By appraisal, the fair market value was estimated to be $500,000 for the land and $2,000,000 for the building. At what amount should Dunn report the land and the building at the end of the year?

13 Richardson Co. acquires machinery by paying $10,000 cash. Richardson purchased a similar machine last month for $13,500. At what cost should the new equipment be recorded?

14 Michael Bennett is evaluating two recent transactions involving exchanges of equipment. In one case, the exchange has commercial substance; in the second situation, the exchange lacks commercial substance. Explain to Bennett the differences in accounting for these two situations.

15 Identify the factors that are relevant in determining the annual depreciation charge, and explain whether these factors are determined objectively or whether they are based on judgment.

16 Some believe that accounting depreciation measures the decline in the value of fixed assets. Do you agree? Explain.

17 Explain how estimation of service lives can result in unrealistically high valuations of fixed assets.

18 The plant manager of a manufacturing firm suggested in a conference of the company's executives that accountants should speed up depreciation on the machinery in the finishing department because improvements were rapidly making those machines obsolete and a depreciation fund big enough to cover their replacement is needed. Discuss the accounting concept of depreciation and the effect on a business concern of the depreciation recorded for plant assets, paying particular attention to the issues raised by the plant manager.

19 Elizabeth Ashley Company purchased a machine on January 2, 2008, for $600,000. The machine has an estimated useful life of 5 years and a salvage value of $100,000. Depreciation was computed by the 150% declining-balance method. What is the amount of accumulated depreciation at the end of December 31, 2009?

20 JLo Company purchased machinery for $120,000 on January 1, 2008. It is estimated that the machinery will have a useful life of 20 years, scrap value of $15,000, production of 84,000 units, and working hours of 42,000. During 2008 the company uses the machinery for 14,300 hours, and the machinery produces 20,000 units. Compute depreciation under the straight-line, units-of-output, working-hours, sum-of-the-years'-digits, and declining-balance (use 10% as the annual rate) methods.

21 A building that was purchased December 31, 1983, for $2,400,000 was originally estimated to have a life of 50 years with no salvage value at the end of that time. Depreciation has been recorded through 2007. During 2008 an examination of the building by an engineering firm discloses that its estimated useful life is 15 years after 2007. What should be the amount of depreciation for 2008?

22 Melanie Mayron purchased a computer for $6,000 on July 1, 2008. She intends to depreciate it over 4 years using the double-declining balance method. Salvage value is $1,000. Compute depreciation for 2009.

23 Saadi Company purchased a heavy-duty truck on July 1, 2005, for $30,000. It was estimated that it would have a useful life of 10 years and then would have a trade-in value of $6,000. It was traded on August 1, 2009, for a another truck costing $39,000; $13,000 was allowed as trade-in value (also fair value) on the old truck and $26,000 was paid in cash. What is the entry to record the trade-in? Assume the exchange has commercial substance. The company uses the straight-line method.

24 Once equipment has been installed and placed in operation, subsequent expenditures relating to this equipment are frequently thought of as repairs or general maintenance and, hence, chargeable to operations in the period in which the expenditure is made. Actually, determination of whether such an expenditure should be charged to operations or capitalized involves a much more careful analysis of the character of the expenditure. What are the factors that should be considered in making such a decision? Discuss fully.

25 What accounting treatment is normally given to the following items in accounting for plant assets?

(a) Additions.

(b) Major repairs.

(c) Improvements and replacements.

26 New machinery, which replaced a number of employees, was installed and put in operation in the last month of the fiscal year. The employees had been dismissed after payment of an extra month's wages, and this amount was added to the cost of the machinery. Discuss the propriety of the charge and, if it was improper, describe the proper treatment.

27 To what extent do you consider the following items to be proper costs of the fixed asset? Give reasons for your opinions.

(a) Overhead of a business that builds its own equipment.

(b) Cost of constructing new models of machinery.

(c) Cash discounts on purchases of equipment.

(d) Interest paid during construction of a building.

(e) Cost of a safety device installed on a machine.

(f) Freight on equipment returned before installation, for replacement by other equipment of greater capacity.

(g) Cost of plywood partitions erected as part of the remodeling of the office.

(h) Replastering of a section of the building.

(i) Cost of a new motor for one of the trucks.

28 Recently, Michelangelo Manufacturing Co. presented the account "Allowance for Repairs" in the long-term liabilities section. Evaluate this procedure.

29 What are the general rules for how gains or losses on retirement of plant assets should be reported in income?

*30 What interest rate should be used in determining the amount of interest to be capitalized? How should the amount to be capitalized be determined?

Brief Exercises

BE10-1 Bonanza Brothers Inc. purchased land at a price of $27,000. Closing costs were $1,400. An old building was removed at a cost of $12,200. What amount should be recorded as the cost of the land?

(LO 1)

BE10-2 Chavez Corporation purchased a truck with a price of $60,000. Chavez signed a 6-month note for the purchase, subject to a 2% cash discount if paid in 60 days. Prepare the journal entry to record the purchase of this truck.

(LO 3)

(LO 3)   **BE10-3**   Cool Spot Inc. purchased land, building, and equipment from Pinball Wizard Corporation for a cash payment of $306,000. The estimated fair values of the assets are land $60,000; building $220,000; and equipment $80,000. At what amounts should each of the three assets be recorded?

(LO 3)   **BE10-4**   Dark Wizard Company obtained land by issuing 2,000 shares of its $10 par value common stock. The land was recently appraised at $85,000. The common stock is actively traded at $41 per share. Prepare the journal entry to record the acquisition of the land.

(LO 4)   **BE10-5**   Indicate which of the following costs should be expensed when incurred.
(a) $13,000 paid to rearrange and reinstall machinery.
(b) $200 paid for tune-up and oil change on delivery truck.
(c) $200,000 paid for addition to building.
(d) $7,000 paid to replace a wooden floor with a concrete floor.
(e) $2,000 paid for a major overhaul on a truck, which extends useful life.

(LO 6, 7)   **BE10-6**   Cheetah Company purchased machinery on January 1, 2008, for $60,000. The machinery is estimated to have a salvage value of $6,000 after a useful life of 8 years. (a) Compute 2008 depreciation expense using the straight-line method. (b) Compute 2008 depreciation expense using the straight-line method assuming the machinery was purchased on September 1, 2008.

(LO 6, 7)   **BE10-7**   Use the information for Cheetah Company given in BE10-6. (a) Compute 2008 depreciation expense using the sum-of-the-years'-digits method. (b) Compute 2008 depreciation expense using the sum-of-the-years'-digits method assuming the machinery was purchased on April 1, 2008.

(LO 6, 7)   **BE10-8**   Use the information for Cheetah Company given in BE10-6. (a) Compute 2008 depreciation expense using the double-declining balance method. (b) Compute 2008 depreciation expense using the double-declining balance method assuming the machinery was purchased on October 1, 2008.

(LO 6, 7)   **BE10-9**   Garfield Company purchased a machine on July 1, 2008, for $25,000. Garfield paid $200 in title fees and county property tax of $125 on the machine. In addition, Garfield paid $500 shipping charges for delivery, and paid $475 to a local contractor to build and wire a platform for the machine on the plant floor. The machine has an estimated useful life of 6 years with a scrap value of $3,000. Determine the depreciation base of Garfield's new machine. Garfield uses straight-line depreciation.

(LO 6, 7)   **BE10-10**   Myst Company purchased a computer for $7,000 on January 1, 2007. Straight-line depreciation is used, based on a 5-year life and a $1,000 salvage value. In 2009, the estimates are revised. Myst now feels the computer will be used until December 31, 2010, when it can be sold for $500. Compute the 2009 depreciation.

(LO 6, 7, 8)   **BE10-11**   Sim City Corporation owns machinery that cost $20,000 when purchased on January 1, 2005. Depreciation has been recorded at a rate of $3,000 per year, resulting in a balance in accumulated depreciation of $9,000 at December 31, 2007. The machinery is sold on September 1, 2008, for $10,500. Prepare journal entries to (a) update depreciation for 2008 and (b) record the sale.

(LO 6, 7, 8)   **BE10-12**   Use the information presented for Sim City Corporation in BE10-11, but assume the machinery is sold for $5,200 instead of $10,500. Prepare journal entries to (a) update depreciation for 2008, and (b) record the sale.

(LO 8)   **BE10-13**   Strider Corporation traded a used truck (cost $20,000, accumulated depreciation $18,000) for a small computer worth $3,700. Strider also paid $1,000 in the transaction. Prepare the journal entry to record the exchange, assuming it has commercial substance.

(LO 8)   **BE10-14**   Sloan Company traded a used welding machine (cost $9,000, accumulated depreciation $3,000) for office equipment with an estimated fair value of $5,000. Sloan also paid $2,000 cash in the transaction. Prepare the journal entry to record the exchange. The exchange has commercial substance.

(LO 8)   **BE10-15**   Bubey Company traded a used truck for a new truck. The used truck cost $30,000 and has accumulated depreciation of $27,000. The new truck is worth $35,000. Bubey also made a cash payment of $33,000. Prepare Bubey's entry to record the exchange. The exchange has commercial substance.

(LO 8)   **BE10-16**   Buck Rogers Corporation traded a used truck for a new truck. The used truck cost $20,000 and has accumulated depreciation of $17,000. The new truck is worth $35,000. Rogers also made a cash payment of $33,000. Prepare Rogers' entry to record the exchange. The exchange has commercial substance.

(LO 9)   **BE10-17**   In ts 2006 annual report **Campbell Soup Company** reports beginning-of-the-year total assets of $6,776 million, end-of-the-year total assets of $7,870 million, total sales of $7,343 million, and net income of $766 million. (a) Compute Campbell's asset turnover ratio. (b) Compute Campbell's profit margin on sales. (c) Compute Cambell's rate of return on plant assets (1) using assets turnover and profit margin and (2) using net income.

Exercises

E10-1 (Acquisition Costs of Realty) The following expenditures and receipts are related to land, land improvements, and buildings acquired for use in a business enterprise. The receipts are enclosed in parentheses.

(LO 3)

(a) Money borrowed to pay building contractor (signed a note) $(275,000)
(b) Payment for construction from note proceeds   275,000
(c) Cost of land fill and clearing   8,000
(d) Delinquent real estate taxes on property assumed by purchaser   7,000
(e) Premium on 6-month insurance policy during construction   6,000
(f) Refund of 1-month insurance premium because construction completed early   (1,000)
(g) Architect's fee on building   22,000
(h) Cost of real estate purchased as a plant site (land $200,000 and building $50,000)   250,000
(i) Commission fee paid to real estate agency   9,000
(j) Installation of fences around property   4,000
(k) Cost of razing and removing building   11,000
(l) Proceeds from salvage of demolished building   (5,000)
(m) Interest paid during construction on money borrowed for construction   13,000
(n) Cost of parking lots and driveways   19,000
(o) Cost of trees and shrubbery planted (permanent in nature)   14,000
(p) Excavation costs for new building   3,000

Instructions

Identify each item by letter and list the items in columnar form, as shown below. All receipt amounts should be reported in parentheses. For any amounts entered in the Other Accounts column also indicate the account title.

Item	Land	Land Improvements	Building	Other Accounts

E10-2 (Acquisition Costs of Realty) Martin Buber Co. purchased land as a factory site for $400,000. The process of tearing down two old buildings on the site and constructing the factory required 6 months.

(LO 2, 3)

The company paid $42,000 to raze the old buildings and sold salvaged lumber and brick for $6,300. Legal fees of $1,850 were paid for title investigation and drawing the purchase contract. Payment to an engineering firm was made for a land survey, $2,200, and for drawing the factory plans, $68,000. The land survey had to be made before definitive plans could be drawn. Title insurance on the property cost $1,500, and a liability insurance premium paid during construction was $900. The contractor's charge for construction was $2,740,000. The company paid the contractor in two installments: $1,200,000 at the end of 3 months and $1,540,000 upon completion. Interest costs of $170,000 were incurred to finance the construction.

Instructions

Determine the cost of the land and the cost of the building as they should be recorded on the books of Martin Buber Co. Assume that the land survey was for the building.

E10-3 (Acquisition Costs of Trucks) Alexei Urmanov Corporation operates a retail computer store. To improve delivery services to customers, the company purchases three new trucks on April 1, 2008. The terms of acquisition for each truck are described below.

(LO 3)

1. Truck #1 has a list price of $15,000 and is acquired for a cash payment of $13,900.
2. Truck #2 has a list price of $16,000. It is acquired in exchange for a computer system that Urmanov carries in inventory. The computer system cost $12,000 and is normally sold by Urmanov for $15,200. Urmanov uses a perpetual inventory system.
3. Truck #3 has a list price of $14,000. It is acquired in exchange for 1,000 shares of common stock in Urmanov Corporation. The stock has a par value per share of $10 and a market value of $13 per share.

Instructions

Prepare the appropriate journal entries for the foregoing transactions for Urmanov Corporation.

E10-4 (Treatment of Various Costs) Ben Sisko Supply Company, a newly formed corporation, incurred the following expenditures related to Land, to Buildings, and to Machinery and Equipment.

(LO 3)

Abstract company's fee for title search		$ 520 B
Architect's fees		2,800 B
Cash paid for land and dilapidated building thereon		87,000 L
Removal of old building	$20,000	
Less: Salvage	5,500	14,500 L
Surveying before construction		370 B
Interest on short-term loans during construction		7,400
Excavation before construction for basement		19,000 B
Machinery purchased (subject to 2% cash discount, which was not taken)		55,000 M
Freight on machinery purchased		1,340 M
Storage charges on machinery, necessitated by noncompletion of building when machinery was delivered		2,180
New building constructed (building construction took 6 months from date of purchase of land and old building)		485,000 B
Assessment by city for drainage project		1,600
Hauling charges for delivery of machinery from storage to new building		620
Installation of machinery		2,000 M
Trees, shrubs, and other landscaping after completion of building (permanent in nature)		5,400 L

Instructions

Determine the amounts that should be debited to Land, to Buildings, and to Machinery and Equipment. Assume the benefits of capitalizing interest during construction exceed the cost of implementation. Indicate how any costs not debited to these accounts should be recorded.

(LO 3)   **E10-5** **(Correction of Improper Cost Entries)**   Plant acquisitions for selected companies are as follows.

1. Belanna Industries Inc. acquired land, buildings, and equipment from a bankrupt company, Torres Co., for a lump sum price of $700,000. At the time of purchase, Torres assets had the following book and appraisal values.

	Book Values	Appraisal Values
Land	$200,000	$150,000
Buildings	250,000	350,000
Equipment	300,000	300,000

To be conservative, the company decided to take the lower of the two values for each asset acquired. The following entry was made.

Land	150,000	
Buildings	250,000	
Equipment	300,000	
Cash		700,000

2. Harry Enterprises purchased store equipment by making a $2,000 cash down payment and signing a 1-year, $23,000, 10% note payable. The purchase was recorded as follows.

Store Equipment	27,300	
Cash		2,000
Note Payable		23,000
Interest Payable		2,300

3. Kim Company purchased office equipment for $20,000, terms 2/10, n/30. Because the company intended to take the discount, it made no entry until it paid for the acquisition. The entry was:

Office Equipment	20,000	
Cash		19,600
Purchase Discounts		400

4. Kaisson Inc. recently received at zero cost land from the Village of Cardassia as an inducement to locate its business in the Village. The appraised value of the land is $27,000. The company made no entry to record the land because it had no cost basis.

5. Zimmerman Company built a warehouse for $600,000. It could have purchased the building for $740,000. The controller made the following entry.

600

Warehouse	740,000	
Cash		600,000
~~Profit on Construction~~		140,000

Instructions

Prepare the entry that should have been made at the date of each acquisition.

E10-6 **(Entries for Equipment Acquisitions)** Jane Geddes Engineering Corporation purchased conveyor equipment with a list price of $10,000. The vendor's credit terms were 2/10, n/30. Presented below are two independent cases related to the equipment. Assume that the purchases of equipment are recorded gross. (Round to nearest dollar.)

(LO 3, 8)

(a) Geddes paid cash for the equipment 8 days after the purchase.
(b) Geddes traded in equipment with a book value of $2,000 (initial cost $8,000), and paid $9,500 in cash one month after the purchase. The old equipment could have been sold for $400 at the date of trade. Assume the exchange has commercial substance.

Instructions

Prepare the general journal entries required to record the acquisition and payment in each of the independent cases above. Round to the nearest dollar.

E10-7 **(Entries for Asset Acquisition, Including Self-Construction)** Below are transactions related to Michelle Wie Company.

(LO 1, 3)

Land 81000
Contrib Rev 81000

(a) The City of Pebble Beach gives the company 5 acres of land as a plant site. The market value of this land is determined to be $81,000.

Land 180000
Bldg 630000
Com Stock 810 000

(b) 13,000 shares of common stock with a par value of $50 per share are issued in exchange for land and buildings. The property has been appraised at a fair market value of $810,000, of which $180,000 has been allocated to land and $630,000 to buildings. The stock of Michelle Wie Company is not listed on any exchange, but a block of 100 shares was sold by a stockholder 12 months ago at $65 per share, and a block of 200 shares was sold by another stockholder 18 months ago at $58 per share.
(c) No entry has been made to remove from the accounts for Materials, Direct Labor, and Overhead the amounts properly chargeable to plant asset accounts for machinery constructed during the year. The following information is given relative to costs of the machinery constructed.

Materials used	$12,500
Factory supplies used	900
Direct labor incurred	15,000
Additional overhead (over regular) caused by construction of machinery, excluding factory supplies used	2,700
Fixed overhead rate applied to regular manufacturing operations	60% of direct labor cost
Cost of similar machinery if it had been purchased from outside suppliers	44,000

Instructions

Prepare journal entries on the books of Michelle Wie Company to record these transactions.

E10-8 **(Entries for Acquisition of Assets)** Presented below is information related to Bucky Katt Company.

(LO 1, 3)

1. On July 6 Bucky Katt Company acquired the plant assets of Satchel Company, which had discontinued operations. The appraised value of the property is:

Land	$ 400,000
Building	1,200,000
Machinery and equipment	800,000
Total	$2,400,000

Com. St. 1250000
Ad. Pd Cap

Bucky Katt Company gave 12,500 shares of its $100 par value common stock in exchange. The stock had a market value of $168 per share on the date of the purchase of the property.
2. Bucky Katt Company expended the following amounts in cash between July 6 and December 15, the date when it first occupied the building.

Repairs to building	$105,000
Construction of bases for machinery to be installed later	135,000
Driveways and parking lots	122,000
Remodeling of office space in building, including new partitions and walls	161,000
Special assessment by city on land	18,000

3. On December 20, the company paid cash for machinery, $260,000, subject to a 2% cash discount, and freight on machinery of $10,500.

Instructions

Prepare entries on the books of Bucky Katt Company for these transactions.

(LO 4)

E10-9 (Analysis of Subsequent Expenditures) Queen Kelly Resources Group has been in its plant facility for 15 years. Although the plant is quite functional, numerous repair costs are incurred to maintain it in sound working order. The company's plant asset book value is currently $800,000, as indicated below.

Original cost	$1,200,000
Accumulated depreciation	400,000
	$ 800,000

During the current year, the following expenditures were made to the plant facility.

(a) Because of increased demands for its product, the company increased its plant capacity by building a new addition at a cost of $270,000.

(b) The entire plant was repainted at a cost of $23,000.

(c) The roof was an asbestos cement slate. For safety purposes it was removed and replaced with a wood shingle roof at a cost of $61,000. Book value of the old roof was $41,000.

(d) The electrical system was completely updated at a cost of $22,000. The cost of the old electrical system was not known. It is estimated that the useful life of the building will not change as a result of this updating.

(e) A series of major repairs were made at a cost of $47,000, because parts of the wood structure were rotting. The cost of the old wood structure was not known. These extensive repairs are estimated to increase the useful life of the building.

Instructions

Indicate how each of these transactions would be recorded in the accounting records.

(LO 4)

E10-10 (Analysis of Subsequent Expenditures) The following transactions occurred during 2009. Assume that depreciation of 10% per year is charged on all machinery and 5% per year on buildings, on a straight-line basis, with no estimated salvage value. Depreciation is charged for a full year on all fixed assets acquired during the year, and no depreciation is charged on fixed assets disposed of during the year.

Jan. 30	A building that cost $132,000 in 1992 is torn down to make room for a new building. The wrecking contractor was paid $5,100 and was permitted to keep all materials salvaged.
Mar. 10	Machinery that was purchased in 2002 for $16,000 is sold for $2,900 cash, f.o.b. purchaser's plant. Freight of $300 is paid on this machinery.
Mar. 20	A gear breaks on a machine that cost $9,000 in 2004, and is replaced at a cost of $385. The replacement does not extend the useful life of the machine.
May 18	A special base installed for a machine in 2003 when the machine was purchased has to be replaced at a cost of $5,500 because of defective workmanship on the original base. The cost of the machinery was $14,200 in 2003. The cost of the base was $3,500, and this amount was charged to the Machinery account in 2003.
June 23	One of the buildings is repainted at a cost of $6,900. It had not been painted since it was constructed in 2005.

Instructions

Prepare general journal entries for the transactions. (Round to nearest dollar.)

(LO 4)

E10-11 (Analysis of Subsequent Expenditures) Plant assets often require expenditures subsequent to acquisition. It is important that they be accounted for properly. Any errors will affect both the balance sheets and income statements for a number of years.

Instructions

For each of the following items, indicate whether the expenditure should be capitalized (C) or expensed (E) in the period incurred.

(a) _____C_____ Improvement.
(b) _____E_____ Replacement of a minor broken part on a machine.
(c) _____C_____ Expenditure that increases the useful life of an existing asset.
(d) _____C_____ Expenditure that increases the efficiency and effectiveness of a productive asset but does
not increase its salvage value.
(e) _____C_____ Expenditure that increases the efficiency and effectiveness of a productive asset and
increases the asset's salvage value.
(f) _____C_____ Expenditure that increases the quality of the output of the productive asset.
(g) _____C_____ Improvement to a machine that increased its fair market value and its production capacity
by 30% without extending the machine's useful life.
(h) _____E_____ Ordinary repairs.
(i) _____C_____ Addition.
(j) _____E_____ Interest on borrowing necessary to finance a major overhaul of machinery. The overhaul
extended the life of the machinery.

E10-12 **(Depreciation Computations—SL, SYD, DDB)** Montoni Company purchases equipment on January 1, year 1, at a cost of $469,000. The asset is expected to have a service life of 12 years and a salvage value of $40,000.   **(LO 6, 7)**

Instructions

(a) Compute the amount of depreciation for each of years 1 through 3 using the straight-line depreciation method.
(b) Compute the amount of depreciation for each of years 1 through 3 using the sum-of-the-years'-digits method.
(c) Compute the amount of depreciation for each of years 1 through 3 using the double-declining balance method.
(In performing your calculations, round constant percentage to the nearest one-hundredth of a point and round answers to the nearest dollar.)

E10-13 **(Depreciation—Conceptual Understanding)** Warhol Company acquired a plant asset at the beginning of year 1. The asset has an estimated service life of 5 years. An employee has prepared depreciation schedules for this asset using three different methods to compare the results of using one method with the results of using other methods. You are to assume that the following schedules have been correctly prepared for this asset using (1) the straight-line method, (2) the sum-of-the-years'-digits method, and (3) the double-declining balance method.   **(LO 5, 6, 7)**

Year	Straight-line	Sum-of-the-Years'-Digits	Double-declining Balance
1	$ 9,000	$15,000	$20,000
2	9,000	12,000	12,000
3	9,000	9,000	7,200
4	9,000	6,000	4,320
5	9,000	3,000	1,480
Total	$45,000	$45,000	$45,000

Instructions

Answer the following questions.

(a) What is the cost of the asset being depreciated? 50000
(b) What amount, if any, was used in the depreciation calculations for the salvage value for this asset? 5000
(c) Which method will produce the highest charge to income in year 1? SL
(d) Which method will produce the highest charge to income in year 4? DDB
(e) Which method will produce the highest book value for the asset at the end of year 3? SL
(f) If the asset is sold at the end of year 3, which method would yield the highest gain (or lowest loss) on disposal of the asset?

E10-14 **(Depreciation Computations—SYD, DDB—Partial Periods)** Judds Company purchased a new plant asset on April 1, 2008, at a cost of $711,000. It was estimated to have a service life of 20 years and a salvage value of $60,000. Judds' accounting period is the calendar year.   **(LO 6, 7)**

Instructions

(a) Compute the depreciation for this asset for 2008 and 2009 using the sum-of-the-years'-digits method.
(b) Compute the depreciation for this asset for 2008 and 2009 using the double-declining balance method.

E10-15 **(Depreciation Computations—Five Methods)** Jon Seceda Furnace Corp. purchased machinery for $315,000 on May 1, 2008. It is estimated that it will have a useful life of 10 years, scrap value of $15,000, production of 240,000 units, and working hours of 25,000. During 2009 Seceda Corp. uses the machinery for 2,650 hours, and the machinery produces 25,500 units.   **(LO 6, 7)**

Instructions

From the information given, compute the depreciation charge for 2009 under each of the following methods (round to three decimal places).

(a) Straight-line   (c) Working hours.   (e) Declining-balance
(b) Units-of-output.   (d) Sum-of-the-years'-digits.   (use 20% as the annual rate).

(LO 6, 7)   **E10-16** **(Depreciation Computations—Four Methods)** Billips Corporation purchased a new machine for its assembly process on August 1, 2008. The cost of this machine was $117,900. The company estimated that the machine would have a trade-in value of $12,900 at the end of its service life. Its life is estimated at 5 years and its working hours are estimated at 21,000 hours. Year-end is December 31.

Instructions

Compute the depreciation expense under the following methods: (a) straight-line depreciation for 2008, (b) activity method for 2008, assuming that machine usage was 800 hours, (c) sum-of-the-years'-digits for 2009, and (d) double-declining balance for 2009. (Round to nearest dollar.) Each of the foregoing should be considered unrelated.

(LO 6, 7)   **E10-17** **(Depreciation Computations—Five Methods, Partial Periods)** Dawayne Wade Company purchased equipment for $212,000 on October 1, 2008. It is estimated that the equipment will have a useful life of 8 years and a salvage value of $12,000. Estimated production is 40,000 units and estimated working hours 20,000. During 2008, Wade uses the equipment for 525 hours and the equipment produces 1,000 units.

Instructions

Compute depreciation expense under each of the following methods. Wade is on a calendar-year basis ending December 31. (Round to nearest dollar.)

(a) Straight-line method for 2008.   (d) Sum-of-the-years'-digits method for 2010.
(b) Activity method (units of output) for 2008.   (e) Double-declining balance method for 2009.
(c) Activity method (working hours) for 2008.

(LO 6, 7)   **E10-18** **(Different Methods of Depreciation)** Jackel Industries presents you with the following information.

Description	Date Purchased	Cost	Salvage Value	Life in Years	Depreciation Method	Accumulated Depreciation to 12/31/08	Depreciation for 2009
Machine A	2/12/07	$142,500	$16,000	10	(a)	$33,350	(b)
Machine B	8/15/06	(c)	21,000	5	SL	29,000	(d)
Machine C	7/21/05	75,400	23,500	8	DDB	(e)	(f)
Machine D	10/12/(g)	219,000	69,000	5	SYD	70,000	(h)

Instructions

Complete the table for the year ended December 31, 2009. The company depreciates all assets using the half-year convention.

(LO 4, 6, 7)   **E10-19** **(Depreciation Computation—Addition, Change in Estimate)** In 1981, Manning Company completed the construction of a building at a cost of $2,000,000 and first occupied it in January 1982. It was estimated that the building will have a useful life of 40 years, and a salvage value of $60,000 at the end of that time.

Early in 1992, an addition to the building was constructed at a cost of $500,000. At that time it was estimated that the remaining life of the building would be, as originally estimated, an additional 30 years, and that the addition would have a life of 30 years, and a salvage value of $20,000.

In 2010, it is determined that the probable life of the building and addition will extend to the end of 2041 or 20 years beyond the original estimate.

Instructions

(a) Using the straight-line method, compute the annual depreciation that would have been charged from 1982 through 1991.
(b) Compute the annual depreciation that would have been charged from 1992 through 2009.
(c) Prepare the entry, if necessary, to adjust the account balances because of the revision of the estimated life in 2010.
(d) Compute the annual depreciation to be charged beginning with 2010.

E10-20 (**Depreciation — Replacement, Change in Estimate**) Randy Johnson Company constructed a building   (LO 4, 6, 7)
at a cost of $2,200,000 and occupied it beginning in January 1989. It was estimated at that time that its life would
be 40 years, with no salvage value.

In January 2009, a new roof was installed at a cost of $300,000, and it was estimated then that the building
would have a useful life of 25 years from that date. The cost of the old roof was $160,000.

Instructions

(a) What amount of depreciation should have been charged annually from the years 1989 to 2008? (Assume
straight-line depreciation.)
(b) What entry should be made in 2009 to record the replacement of the roof?
(c) Prepare the entry in January 2009 to record the revision in the estimated life of the building, if necessary.
(d) What amount of depreciation should be charged for the year 2009?

E10-21 (**Nonmonetary Exchange**) Busytown Corporation, which manufactures shoes, hired a recent college   (LO 8)
graduate to work in its accounting department. On the first day of work, the accountant was assigned to total a batch
of invoices with the use of an adding machine. Before long, the accountant, who had never before seen such a
machine, managed to break the machine. Busytown Corporation gave the machine plus $340 to Dick Tracy Business
Machine Company (dealer) in exchange for a new machine. Assume the following information about the machines.

	Busytown Corp. (Old Machine)	Dick Tracy Co. (New Machine)
Machine cost	$290	$270
Accumulated depreciation	140	–0–
Fair value	85	425

Instructions

For each company, prepare the necessary journal entry to record the exchange. (The exchange has commercial
substance.)

E10-22 (**Nonmonetary Exchange**) Carlos Arruza Company exchanged equipment used in its manufacturing   (LO 8)
operations plus $3,000 in cash for similar equipment used in the operations of Tony LoBianco Company. The fol-
lowing information pertains to the exchange.

	Carlos Arruza Co.	Tony LoBianco Co.
Equipment (cost)	$28,000	$28,000
Accumulated depreciation	19,000	10,000
Fair value of equipment	12,500	15,500
Cash given up	3,000	

Instructions

(a) Prepare the journal entries to record the exchange on the books of both companies. Assume that the exchange
has commercial substance.
(b) Prepare the journal entries to record the exchange on the books of both companies. Assume that the exchange
lacks commercial substance.

E10-23 (**Nonmonetary Exchange**) Dana Ashbrook Inc. has negotiated the purchase of a new piece of   (LO 8)
automatic equipment at a price of $8,000 plus trade-in, f.o.b. factory. Dana Ashbrook Inc. paid $8,000 cash and
traded in used equipment. The used equipment had originally cost $62,000; it had a book value of $42,000 and
a secondhand market value of $47,800, as indicated by recent transactions involving similar equipment. Freight
and installation charges for the new equipment required a cash payment of $1,100.

Instructions

(a) Prepare the general journal entry to record this transaction, assuming that the exchange has commercial
substance.
(b) Assume the same facts as in (a) except that the exchange lacks commercial substance. Prepare the general
journal entry to record this transaction.

E10-24 (**Entries for Disposition of Assets**) On December 31, 2008, Travis Tritt Inc. has a machine with a   (LO 8)
book value of $940,000. The original cost and related accumulated depreciation at this date are as follows.

Machine	$1,300,000
Accumulated depreciation	360,000
	$ 940,000

Depreciation is computed at $60,000 per year on a straight-line basis.

Instructions

Presented below is a set of independent situations. For each independent situation, indicate the journal entry to be made to record the transaction. Make sure that depreciation entries are made to update the book value of the machine prior to its disposal.

(a) A fire completely destroys the machine on August 31, 2009. An insurance settlement of $430,000 was received for this casualty. Assume the settlement was received immediately.

(b) On April 1, 2009, Tritt sold the machine for $1,040,000 to Dwight Yoakam Company.

(c) On July 31, 2009, the company donated this machine to the Mountain King City Council. The fair market value of the machine at the time of the donation was estimated to be $1,100,000.

E10-25 **(Disposition of Assets)** On April 1, 2008, Yellow Card Company received a condemnation award of $430,000 cash as compensation for the forced sale of the company's land and building, which stood in the path of a new state highway. The land and building cost $60,000 and $280,000, respectively, when they were acquired. At April 1, 2008, the accumulated depreciation relating to the building amounted to $160,000. On August 1, 2008, Yellow Card purchased a piece of replacement property for cash. The new land cost $90,000, and the new building cost $400,000.

Instructions

Prepare the journal entries to record the transactions on April 1 and August 1, 2008.

(LO 9)

E10-26 **(Ratio Analysis)** The 2006 annual report of **Walgreens** contains the following information.

Walgreens

(in millions)	2006	2005
Total assets	$17,131.1	$14,608.8
Total liabilities	7,015.3	5,719.1
Net sales	47,409.0	42,201.6
Net income	1,750.6	1,559.5

Instructions

Compute the following ratios for Walgreens for 2006.

(a) Asset turnover ratio.

(b) Rate of return on assets.

(c) Profit margin on sales.

(d) How can the asset turnover ratio be used to compute the rate of return on assets?

*E10-27 **(Capitalization of Interest)** Harrisburg Furniture Company started construction of a combination office and warehouse building for its own use at an estimated cost of $5,000,000 on January 1, 2008. Harrisburg expected to complete the building by December 31, 2008. Harrisburg has the following debt obligations outstanding during the construction period.

Construction loan—12% interest, payable semiannually, issued December 31, 2007	$2,000,000
Short-term loan—10% interest, payable monthly, and principal payable at maturity on May 30, 2009	1,400,000
Long-term loan—11% interest, payable on January 1 of each year. Principal payable on January 1, 2012	1,000,000

Instructions

(Carry all computations to two decimal places.)

(a) Assume that Harrisburg completed the office and warehouse building on December 31, 2008, as planned, at a total cost of $5,200,000. The weighted average of accumulated expenditures was $3,600,000. Compute the avoidable interest on this project.

(b) Compute the depreciation expense for the year ended December 31, 2009. Harrisburg elected to depreciate the building on a straight-line basis and determined that the asset has a useful life of 30 years and a salvage value of $300,000.

*E10-28 **(Capitalization of Interest)** On December 31, 2007, Alma-Ata Inc. borrowed $3,000,000 at 12% payable annually to finance the construction of a new building. In 2008, the company made the following expenditures related to this building: March 1, $360,000; June 1, $600,000; July 1, $1,500,000; December 1, $1,500,000. Additional information is provided as follows. **(LO 10)**

1. Other debt outstanding

10-year, 13% bond, December 31, 2001, interest payable annually	$4,000,000
6-year, 10% note, dated December 31, 2005, interest payable annually	$1,600,000

2. March 1, 2008, expenditure included land costs of $150,000
3. Interest revenue earned in 2008 — $ 49,000

Instructions

(a) Determine the amount of interest to be capitalized in 2008 in relation to the construction of the building.

(b) Prepare the journal entry to record the capitalization of interest and the recognition of interest expense, if any, at December 31, 2008.

See the book's companion website, at www.wiley.com/college/warfield, for Additional Exercises.

Problems

P10-1 **(Classification of Acquisition Costs)** Selected accounts included in the property, plant, and equipment section of Jim Thome Corporation's balance sheet at December 31, 2007, had the following balances. **(LO 1, 3, 7, 8)**

Land	$ 300,000
Land improvements	140,000
Buildings	1,100,000
Machinery and equipment	960,000

During 2008 the following transactions occurred.

1. A tract of land was acquired for $150,000 as a potential future building site.
2. A plant facility consisting of land and building was acquired from Ichiro Company in exchange for 20,000 shares of Thorne's common stock. On the acquisition date, Thorne's stock had a closing market price of $37 per share on a national stock exchange. The plant facility was carried on Ichiro books at $110,000 for land and $320,000 for the building at the exchange date. Current appraised values for the land and building, respectively, are $230,000 and $690,000.
3. Items of machinery and equipment were purchased at a total cost of $400,000. Additional costs were incurred as follows.

Freight and unloading	$13,000
Sales taxes	20,000
Installation	26,000

4. Expenditures totaling $95,000 were made for new parking lots, streets, and sidewalks at the corporation's various plant locations. These expenditures had an estimated useful life of 15 years.
5. A machine costing $80,000 on January 1, 2000, was scrapped on June 30, 2008. Double-declining-balance depreciation has been recorded on the basis of a 10-year life.
6. A machine was sold for $20,000 on July 1, 2008. Original cost of the machine was $44,000 on January 1, 2005, and it was depreciated on the straight-line basis over an estimated useful life of 7 years and a salvage value of $2,000.

Instructions

(a) Prepare a detailed analysis of the changes in each of the following balance sheet accounts for 2008.

Land
Land improvements
Buildings
Machinery and equipment

(Hint: Disregard the related accumulated depreciation accounts.)

(b) List the items in the fact situation that were not used to determine the answer to (a), showing the pertinent amounts and supporting computations in good form for each item. In addition, indicate where, or if, these items should be included in Jim Thome's income statement and balance sheet.

(AICPA adapted)

(LO 1, 3)

P10-2 (Classification of Land and Building Costs) Steve Nash Company was incorporated on January 2, 2009, but was unable to begin manufacturing activities until July 1, 2009, because new factory facilities were not completed until that date.

The Land and Building account at December 31, 2009, was as follows.

January 31, 2009	Land and building	$160,000
February 28, 2009	Cost of removal of building	9,800
May 1, 2009	Partial payment of new construction	60,000
May 1, 2009	Legal fees paid	3,770
June 1, 2009	Second payment on new construction	40,000
June 1, 2009	Insurance premium	2,280
June 1, 2009	Special tax assessment	4,000
June 30, 2009	General expenses	36,300
July 1, 2009	Final payment on new construction	40,000
December 31, 2009	Asset write-up	43,800
		399,950
December 31, 2009	Depreciation—2009 at 1%	4,000
	Account balance	$395,950

The following additional information is to be considered.

1. To acquire land and building the company paid $80,000 cash and 800 shares of its 8% cumulative preferred stock, par value $100 per share. Fair market value of the stock is $107 per share.
2. Cost of removal of old buildings amounted to $9,800, and the demolition company retained all materials of the building.
3. Legal fees covered the following.

Examination of title covering purchase of land	$1,910
Legal work in connection with construction contract	1,860
	$3,770

4. Insurance premium covered the building for a 2-year term beginning May 1, 2009.
5. The special tax assessment covered street improvements that are permanent in nature.
6. General expenses covered the following for the period from January 2, 2009, to June 30, 2009.

President's salary	$32,100
Plant superintendent covering supervision of new building	4,200
	$36,300

7. Because of a general increase in construction costs after entering into the building contract, the board of directors increased the value of the building $43,800, believing that such an increase was justified to reflect the current market at the time the building was completed. Retained earnings was credited for this amount.
8. Estimated life of building—50 years.
   Depreciation for 2009—1% of asset value (1% of $400,000, or $4,000).

Instructions

(a) Prepare entries to reflect correct land, building, and accumulated depreciation accounts at December 31, 2009.
(b) Show the proper presentation of land, building, and accumulated depreciation on the balance sheet at December 31, 2009.

(AICPA adapted)

(LO 1, 3) **P10-3** (Costs of Self-Constructed Assets) George Fayne Mining Co. received a $760,000 low bid from a reputable manufacturer for the construction of special production equipment needed by Fayne in an expansion program. Because the company's own plant was not operating at capacity, Fayne decided to construct the equipment and recorded the following production costs related to the construction.

Services of consulting engineer	$ 40,000
Work subcontracted	31,000
Materials	300,000
Plant labor normally assigned to production	114,000
Plant labor normally assigned to maintenance	160,000
Total	$645,000

Management prefers to record the cost of the equipment under the incremental cost method. Approximately 40% of the company's production is devoted to government supply contracts which are all based in some way on cost. The contracts require that any self-constructed equipment be allocated its full share of all costs related to the construction.

The following information is also available.

1. The production labor was for partial fabrication of the equipment in the plant. Skilled personnel were required and were assigned from other projects. The maintenance labor would have been idle time of nonproduction plant employees who would have been retained on the payroll whether or not their services were utilized.
2. Payroll taxes and employee fringe benefits are approximately 35% of labor cost and are included in manufacturing overhead cost. Total manufacturing overhead for the year was $6,084,000, including the $160,000 maintenance labor used to construct the equipment.
3. Manufacturing overhead is approximately 60% variable and is applied on the basis of production labor cost. Production labor cost for the year for the corporation's normal products totaled $8,286,000.
4. General and administrative expenses include $27,000 of allocated executive salary cost and $13,750 of postage, telephone, supplies, and miscellaneous expenses identifiable with this equipment construction.

Instructions

(a) Prepare a schedule computing the amount that should be reported as the full cost of the constructed equipment to meet the requirements of the government contracts. Any supporting computations should be in good form.
(b) Prepare a schedule computing the incremental cost of the constructed equipment.
(c) What is the greatest amount that should be capitalized as the cost of the equipment? Why?

(AICPA adapted)

P10-4 (**Lump-sum Purchase and Nonmonetary Exchange**) Kent Adamson Company is a manufacturer of ballet shoes and is experiencing a period of sustained growth. In an effort to expand its production capacity to meet the increased demand for its product, the company recently made several acquisitions of plant and equipment. Tod Mullinger, newly hired in the position of fixed-assets accountant, requested that Watt Kaster, Adamson's controller, review the following transactions.

(LO 3, 8)

Transaction 1

On December 1, 2008, Adamson Company purchased several assets of Haukap Shoes Inc., a small shoe manufacturer whose owner was retiring. The purchase amounted to $210,000 and included the assets listed below. Adamson Company engaged the services of Tennyson Appraisal Inc., an independent appraiser, to determine the fair market values of the assets which are also presented below.

	Haukap Book Value	Fair Market Value
Inventory	$ 60,000	$ 50,000
Land	40,000	80,000
Building	70,000	120,000
	$170,000	$250,000

During its fiscal year ended May 31, 2009, Adamson incurred $8,000 for interest expense in connection with the financing of these assets.

Transaction 2

On March 1, 2009, Adamson Company exchanged a number of used trucks plus cash for vacant land adjacent to its plant site. Adamson intends to use the land for a parking lot. The trucks had a combined book value of $35,000, as Adamson had recorded $20,000 of accumulated depreciation against these assets. Adamson's purchasing agent, who has had previous dealings in the second-hand market, indicated that the trucks had a fair market value of $46,000 at the time of the transaction. In addition to the trucks, Adamson Company paid $19,000 cash for the land. The exchange has commercial substance.

Instructions

(a) Plant assets such as land, buildings, and equipment receive special accounting treatment. Describe the major characteristics of these assets that differentiate them from other types of assets.

(b) For each of the transactions described above, determine the value at which Adamson Company should record the acquired assets. Support your calculations with an explanation of the underlying rationale.

(c) The books of Adamson Company show the following additional transactions for the fiscal year ended May 31, 2009. For each of these transactions, indicate whether the asset should be classified as a plant asset. If it is a plant asset, explain why it is. If it is not a plant asset, explain why not, and identify the proper classification.

1. Acquisition of a building for speculative purposes.
2. Purchase of a 2-year insurance policy covering plant equipment.
3. Purchase of the rights for the exclusive use of a process used in the manufacture of ballet shoes.

(CMA adapted)

(LO 6, 7)

P10-5 (Depreciation for Partial Period—SL, SYD, and DDB) Beckham Company purchased Machine #201 on May 1, 2008. The following information relating to Machine #201 was gathered at the end of May.

Price	$73,500
Credit terms	2/10, n/30
Freight-in costs	$ 970
Preparation and installation costs	$ 3,800
Labor costs during regular production operations	$10,500

It was expected that the machine could be used for 10 years, after which the salvage value would be zero. Beckham intends to use the machine for only 8 years, however, after which it expects to be able to sell it for $1,200. The invoice for Machine #201 was paid May 5, 2008. Beckham uses the calendar year as the basis for the preparation of financial statements.

Instructions

(a) Compute the depreciation expense for the years indicated using the following methods. (Round to the nearest dollar.)
  (1) Straight-line method for 2008.
  (2) Sum-of-the-years'-digits method for 2009.
  (3) Double-declining balance method for 2008.

(b) Suppose Jen David, the president of Beckham, tells you that because the company is a new organization, she expects it will be several years before production and sales reach optimum levels. She asks you to recommend a depreciation method that will allocate less of the company's depreciation expense to the early years and more to later years of the assets' lives. What method would you recommend?

(LO 6, 7)

P10-6 (Depreciation—Partial Periods, Machinery) Goran Tool Company records depreciation annually at the end of the year. Its policy is to take a full year's depreciation on all assets used throughout the year, and depreciation for one-half a year on all machines acquired or disposed of during the year. The depreciation rate for the machinery is 10% applied on a straight-line basis, with no estimated scrap value.

The balance of the Machinery account at the beginning of 2008 was $172,300; the Accumulated Depreciation on Machinery account had a balance of $72,900. The following transactions affecting the machinery accounts took place during the year.

Jan. 15 Machine No. 38, which cost $9,600 when acquired June 3, 2001, was retired and sold as scrap metal for $600.

Feb. 27 Machine No. 81 was purchased. The fair market value of this machine was $12,500. It replaces Machines No. 12 and No. 27, which were traded in on the new machine. Machine No. 12 was acquired February 4, 1996, at a cost of $5,500 and is still carried in the accounts although fully depreciated and not in use. Machine No. 27 was acquired June 11, 2001, at a cost of $8,200. In addition to these two used machines, $9,000 was paid in cash. (Assume the exchange lacks commercial substance.)

Apr. 7 Machine No. 54 was equipped with electric control equipment at a cost of $940. This machine, originally equipped with simple hand controls, was purchased December 11, 2004, for $1,800. The new electric controls can be attached to any one of several machines in the shop.

12 Machine No. 24 was repaired at a cost of $720 after a fire caused by a short circuit in the wiring burned out the motor and damaged certain essential parts.

July 22 Machines No. 25, 26, and 41 are sold for $3,100 cash. The purchase dates and cost of these machines are:

No. 25	$4,000	May 8, 2000
No. 26	3,200	May 8, 2000
No. 41	2,800	June 1, 2002

Instructions

(a) Record each transaction in general journal entry form.

(b) Compute and record depreciation for the year. No machines now included in the balance of the account were acquired before January 1, 1999.

P10-7 (Depreciation—SYD, Act., SL, and DDB) The following data relate to the Plant Assets account of Faith Hill, Inc. at December 31, 2008.

(LO 6, 7)

Plant Assets

	A	B	C	D
Original cost	$35,000	$51,000	$80,000	$80,000
Year purchased	2003	2004	2005	2007
Useful life	10 years	15,000 hours	15 years	10 years
Salvage value	$3,100	$3,000	$5,000	$5,000
Depreciation method	Sum-of-the-years'-digits	Activity	Straight-line	Double-declining balance
Accum. Depr. through 2008[a]	$23,200	$35,200	$15,000	$16,000

[a]In the year an asset is purchased, Hill, Inc. does not record any depreciation expense on the asset. In the year an asset is retired or traded in, Hill, Inc. takes a full year's depreciation on the asset.

The following transactions occurred during 2009.

(a) On May 5, Asset A was sold for $13,000 cash. The company's bookkeeper recorded this retirement in the following manner in the cash receipts journal:

Cash	13,000	
Asset A		13,000

(b) On December 31, it was determined that Asset B had been used 2,100 hours during 2009.

(c) On December 31, before computing depreciation expense on Asset C, the management of Faith Hill, Inc. decided the useful life remaining from January 1, 2009, was 10 years.

(d) On December 31, it was discovered that a plant asset purchased in 2008 had been expensed completely in that year. This asset cost $22,000 and has a useful life of 10 years and no salvage value. Management has decided to use the double-declining balance method for this asset, which can be referred to as "Asset E."

Instructions

Prepare the necessary correcting entries for the year 2009. Record the appropriate depreciation expense on the above-mentioned assets.

P10-8 (Nonmonetary Exchanges) Susquehanna Corporation wishes to exchange a machine used in its operations. Susquehanna has received the following offers from other companies in the industry.

(LO 8)

1. Choctaw Company offered to exchange a similar machine plus $23,000. (The exchange has commercial substance for both parties.)

2. Powhatan Company offered to exchange a similar machine. (The exchange lacks commercial substance for both parties.)

3. Shawnee Company offered to exchange a similar machine, but wanted $8,000 in addition to Susquehanna's machine. (The exchange has commercial substance for both parties.)

In addition, Susquehanna contacted Seminole Corporation, a dealer in machines. To obtain a new machine, Susquehanna must pay $93,000 in addition to trading in its old machine.

	Susquehanna	Choctaw	Powhatan	Shawnee	Seminole
Machine cost	$160,000	$120,000	$147,000	$160,000	$130,000
Accumulated depreciation	50,000	45,000	71,000	75,000	–0–
Fair value	92,000	69,000	92,000	100,000	185,000

Instructions

For each of the four independent situations, prepare the journal entries to record the exchange on the books of each company. (Round to nearest dollar.)

(LO 8)   **P10-9** **(Nonmonetary Exchanges)**   During the current year, Garrison Construction trades an old crane that has a book value of $80,000 (original cost $140,000 less accumulated depreciation $60,000) for a new crane from Keillor Manufacturing Co. The new crane cost Keillor $165,000 to manufacture and is classified as inventory. The following information is also available.

	Garrison Const.	Keillor Mfg. Co.
Fair market value of old crane	$ 72,000	
Fair market value of new crane		$190,000
Cash paid	118,000	
Cash received		118,000

Instructions

(a) Assuming that this exchange is considered to have commercial substance, prepare the journal entries on the books of (1) Garrison Construction and (2) Keillor Manufacturing.

(b) Assuming that this exchange lacks commercial substance for Garrison, prepare the journal entries on the books of Garrison Construction.

(c) Assuming the same facts as those in (a), except that the fair market value of the old crane is $98,000 and the cash paid is $92,000, prepare the journal entries on the books of (1) Garrison Construction and (2) Keillor Manufacturing.

(d) Assuming the same facts as those in (b), except that the fair market value of the old crane is $87,000 and the cash paid $103,000, prepare the journal entries on the books of (1) Garrison Construction and (2) Keillor Manufacturing.

(LO 8)      **P10-10** **(Dispositions, Including Condemnation, and Demolition)**   Presented below is a schedule of property dispositions for Frank Thomas Co.

Schedule of Property Dispositions

	Cost	Accumulated Depreciation	Cash Proceeds	Fair Market Value	Nature of Disposition
Land	$40,000	—	$31,000	$31,000	Condemnation
Building	15,000	—	3,600	—	Demolition
Warehouse	70,000	$11,000	74,000	74,000	Destruction by fire
Furniture	10,000	7,850	—	3,100	Contribution
Automobile	8,000	3,460	2,960	2,960	Sale

The following additional information is available.

Land

On February 15, a condemnation award was received as consideration for unimproved land held primarily as an investment, and on March 31, another parcel of unimproved land to be held as an investment was purchased at a cost of $35,000.

Building

On April 2, land and building were purchased at a total cost of $75,000, of which 20% was allocated to the building on the corporate books. The real estate was acquired with the intention of demolishing the building, and this was accomplished during the month of November. Cash proceeds received in November represent the net proceeds from demolition of the building.

Warehouse

On June 30, the warehouse was destroyed by fire. The warehouse was purchased January 2, 1995, and had depreciated $11,000. On December 27, the insurance proceeds and other funds were used to purchase a replacement warehouse at a cost of $90,000.

Furniture

On August 15, furniture was contributed to a qualified charitable organization. No other contributions were made or pledged during the year.

Automobile

On November 3, the automobile was sold to Ozzie Guillen, a stockholder.

Instructions

Indicate how these items would be reported on the income statement of Frank Thomas Co.

(AICPA adapted)

*P10-11 (**Comprehensive Fixed Asset Problem**) Selig Sporting Goods Inc. has been experiencing growth in the demand for its products over the last several years. The Olympic Games have greatly increased the popularity of basketball around the world. As a result, a European sports retailing consortium entered into an agreement with Selig's Roundball Division to purchase basketballs and other accessories on an increasing basis over the next 5 years.

(LO 3, 6, 7, 10)

To be able to meet the quantity commitments of this agreement, Selig had to obtain additional manufacturing capacity. A real estate firm located an available factory in close proximity to Selig's Roundball manufacturing facility, and Selig agreed to purchase the factory and used machinery from Lebron Athletic Equipment Company on October 1, 2007. Renovations were necessary to convert the factory for Selig's manufacturing use.

The terms of the agreement required Selig to pay Lebron $50,000 when renovations started on January 1, 2008, with the balance to be paid as renovations were completed. The overall purchase price for the factory and machinery was $400,000. The building renovations were contracted to Malone Construction at $100,000. The payments made, as renovations progressed during 2008, are shown below. The factory was placed in service on January 1, 2009.

	1/1	4/1	10/1	12/31
Lebron	$50,000	$100,000	$100,000	$150,000
Malone		30,000	30,000	40,000

On January 1, 2008, Selig secured a $500,000 line-of-credit with a 12% interest rate to finance the purchase cost of the factory and machinery, and the renovation costs. Selig drew down on the line-of-credit to meet the payment schedule shown above; this was Selig's only outstanding loan during 2003.

Rob Stewart, Selig's controller, will capitalize the maximum allowable interest costs for this project. Selig's policy regarding purchases of this nature is to use the appraisal value of the land for book purposes and prorate the balance of the purchase price over the remaining items. The building had originally cost Lebron $300,000 and had a net book value of $50,000. The machinery originally cost $125,000 and had a net book value of $40,000 on the date of sale. The land was recorded on Lebron's books at $40,000. An appraisal conducted by independent appraisers at the time of acquisition valued the land at $280,000, the building at $105,000, and the machinery at $45,000.

Linda Safford, chief engineer, estimated that the renovated plant would be used for 15 years, with an estimated salvage value of $30,000. Safford estimated that the productive machinery would have a remaining useful life of 5 years and a salvage value of $3,000. Selig's depreciation policy specifies the 200% declining-balance method for machinery and the 150% declining-balance method for the plant. One-half year's depreciation is taken in the year the plant is placed in service and one-half year is allowed when the property is disposed of or retired. Selig uses a 360-day year for calculating interest costs.

Instructions

(a) Determine the amounts to be recorded on the books of Selig Sporting Goods Inc. as of December 31, 2008, for each of the following properties acquired from Lebron Athletic Equipment Company.
   (1) Land.   (2) Building.   (3) Machinery.
(b) Calculate Selig Sporting Goods Inc.'s 2009 depreciation expense, for book purposes, for each of the properties acquired from Lebron Athletic Equipment Company.
(c) Discuss the arguments for and against the capitalization of interest costs.

(CMA adapted)

*P10-12 (**Interest During Construction**) Jerry Landscaping began construction of a new plant on December 1, 2007. On this date the company purchased a parcel of land for $142,000 in cash. In addition, it paid $2,000 in surveying costs and $4,000 for a title insurance policy. An old dwelling on the premises was demolished at a cost of $3,000, with $1,000 being received from the sale of materials.

(LO 1, 2, 10)

Architectural plans were also formalized on December 1, 2007, when the architect was paid $30,000. The necessary building permits costing $3,000 were obtained from the city and paid for on December 1 as well. The excavation work began during the first week in December with payments made to the contractor as follows.

Date of Payment	Amount of Payment
March 1	$240,000
May 1	360,000
July 1	60,000

The building was completed on July 1, 2008.

To finance construction of this plant, Jerry borrowed $600,000 from the bank on December 1, 2007. Jerry had no other borrowings. The $600,000 was a 10-year loan bearing interest at 8%.

Instructions

Compute the balance in each of the following accounts at December 31, 2007, and December 31, 2008.

(a) Land.
(b) Buildings.
(c) Interest Expense.

(LO 10)

*P10-13 (Capitalization of Interest) Wordcrafters Inc. is a book distributor that had been operating in its original facility since 1978. The increase in certification programs and continuing education requirements in several professions has contributed to an annual growth rate of 15% for Wordcrafters since 2003. Wordcrafters' original facility became obsolete by early 2008 because of the increased sales volume and the fact that Wordcrafters now carries tapes and disks in addition to books.

On June 1, 2008, Wordcrafters contracted with Favre Construction to have a new building constructed for $5,000,000 on land owned by Wordcrafters. Construction commenced on June 2, 2008. The payments made by Wordcrafters to Favre Construction are shown in the schedule below.

Date	Amount
July 30, 2008	$1,200,000
January 30, 2009	1,500,000
May 30, 2009	1,300,000
Total payments	$4,000,000

Construction was completed and the building was ready for occupancy on May 27, 2009. Wordcrafters had no new borrowings directly associated with the new building but had the following debt outstanding at May 31, 2009, the end of its fiscal year.

14 $\frac{1}{2}$%, 5-year note payable of $2,000,000, dated April 1, 2005, with interest payable annually on April 1.
12%, 10-year bond issue of $3,000,000 sold at par on June 30, 2001, with interest payable annually on June 30.

The new building qualifies for interest capitalization. The effect of capitalizing the interest on the new building, compared with the effect of expensing the interest, is material.

Instructions

(a) Compute the weighted average accumulated expenditures on Wordcrafters' new building during the capitalization period.
(b) Compute the avoidable interest on Wordcrafters' new building.
(c) Some interest cost of Wordcrafters Inc. is capitalized for the year ended May 31, 2008.
  (1) Identify the items relating to interest costs that must be disclosed in Wordcrafters' financial statements.
  (2) Compute the amount of each of the items that must be disclosed.

(CMA adapted)

ACCOUNTING IN ACTION

Financial Reporting and Analysis

 ■ **Financial Reporting Issues: The Procter & Gamble Company**

AIA10-1 The financial statements of **Procter & Gamble (P&G)** can be accessed at the book's website.

Instructions

Refer to P&G's financial statements and the accompanying notes to answer the following questions.

(a) What descriptions does P&G use in its balance sheet to classify its property, plant, and equipment?
(b) What method or methods of depreciation does P&G use to depreciate its property, plant, and equipment?
(c) Over what estimated useful lives does P&G depreciate its property, plant, and equipment?

(d) What amounts for depreciation and amortization expense did P&G record in its income statement in 2006, 2005, and 2004?

(e) What were the capital expenditures for property, plant, and equipment made by P&G in 2006, 2005, and 2004?

■ Comparative Analysis: The Coca-Cola Company and PepsiCo, Inc.   **PEPSICO**

AIA10-2 The financial statements of **The Coca-Cola Company** and **PepsiCo, Inc.** can be accessed at the book's website.

Instructions

Use information found at the book's website to answer the following questions.

(a) What amount is reported in the balance sheets as property, plant, and equipment (net) of Coca-Cola at December 31, 2006, and of PepsiCo at December 30, 2006? What percentage of total assets is invested in property, plant, and equipment by each company?

(b) What depreciation methods are used by Coca-Cola and PepsiCo for property, plant, and equipment? How much depreciation was reported by Coca-Cola and PepsiCo in 2006, 2005, and 2004?

(c) Compute and compare the following ratios for Coca-Cola and PepsiCo for 2006.
  (1) Asset turnover.
  (2) Profit margin on sales.
  (3) Rate of return on assets.

(d) What amount was spent in 2006 for capital expenditures by Coca-Cola and PepsiCo? What amount of interest was capitalized in 2006?

■ Financial Statement Analysis

AIA10-3 **McDonald's** is the largest and best-known global food service retailer, with more than 30,000 restaurants in 121 countries. On any day, McDonald's serves approximately 1 percent of the world's population. Presented below is information related to McDonald's property and equipment.

McDonald's Corporation

Summary of Significant Accounting Policies Section

Property and Equipment. Property and equipment are stated at cost, with depreciation and amortization provided on the straight-line method over the following estimated useful lives: buildings—up to 40 years; leasehold improvements—lesser of useful lives of assets or lease terms including option periods; and equipment—3 to 12 years.

[In the notes to the financial statements:]

Property and Equipment

Net property and equipment consisted of:

(in millions)	December 31, 2005	December 31, 2004
Land	$ 4,486.9	$ 4,661.1
Buildings and improvements on owned land	10,104.5	10,260.3
Buildings and improvements on leased land	10,243.9	10,520.7
Equipment, signs, and seating	4,468.2	4,426.1
Other	593.7	639.6
	29,897.2	30,507.8
Accumulated depreciation and amortization	(9,989.2)	(9,804.7)
Net property and equipment	$19,908.0	$20,703.1

Depreciation and amortization expense was (in millions):
2005: $1,186.7; 2004—$1,138.3; 2003—$1,113.3

[In the management discussion and analysis section, McDonald's provides the following schedule.]

Cash Provided by Operations

(dollars in millions)	2005	2004	2003
Cash provided by operations	$4,337	$3,904	$3,269
Cash provided by operations as a percent of capital expenditures	270%	275%	250%

Instructions

(a) What method of depreciation does McDonald's use?

(b) Does depreciation and amortization expense cause cash flow from operations to increase? Explain.

(c) What does the schedule of cash flow measures indicate?

AIA10-4 **Boeing** and **McDonnell Douglas** were two leaders in the manufactures of aircraft. In the mid-1990s Boeing announced intentions to acquire McDonnell Douglas and create one huge corporation. Competitors, primarily **Airbus of Europe**, were very concerned that they would not be able to compete with such a huge rival. In addition, customers were concerned that this merger would reduce the number of suppliers to a point where Boeing would be able to dictate prices. Provided below are figures taken from the pre-merger financial statements of Boeing and McDonnell Douglas, which allow a comparison of the operations of the two corporations prior to their merger.

($ in millions)	Boeing	McDonnell Douglas
Total revenue	$19,515	$14,322
Net income (loss)	393	(416)
Total assets (average)	22,098	10,466
Land (average)	404	91
Buildings and fixtures	5,791	1,647
Machinery and equipment	7,251	2,161
Average property, plant, and equipment (at cost)	13,744	3,899
Accumulated depreciation	7,288	2,541
Depreciation expense	976	196

Instructions

(a) Which company used a longer average estimated useful life for its assets?

(b) Based on the asset turnover ratio, which company used its assets more effectively to generate sales?

(c) Which company generated a better return on assets?

(d) Besides an increase in size, what other factors might have motivated this merger?

■ International Reporting Issues

AIA10-5 Companies following international accounting standards are permitted to revalue fixed assets above the assets' historical costs. Such revaluations are allowed under various countries' standards and the standards issued by the International Accounting Standards Board (IASB). **Liberty International**, a real estate company, headquartered in United Kingdom (U.K.), follows U.K. standards. In a recent year, Liberty disclosed the following information on revaluations of its tangible fixed assets. The revaluation reserve measures the amount by which tangible fixed assets are recorded above historical cost and is reported in Liberty's stockholders' equity.

 **Liberty International**

Completed Investment Properties

Completed investment properties are professionally valued on a market value basis by external valuers at the balance sheet data. Surpluses and deficits arising during the year are reflected in the revaluation reserve.

Liberty reported the following additional data. Amounts for **Kimco Realty** (which follows U.S. GAAP) in the same year are provided for comparison.

	Liberty	Kimco
	(pounds sterling in thousands)	(dollars, in millions)
Total revenues	£ 741	$ 517
Average total assets	5,577	4,696
Net income	125	297

Instructions

(a) Compute the following ratios for Liberty and Kimco.

(1) Return on assets.

(2) Profit margin.

(3) Asset turnover.

How do these companies compare on these performance measures?

(b) Liberty reports a revaluation reserve of 1,952 pounds. Assume that 1,550 of this amount arose from an increase in the net replacement value of investment properties during the year. Prepare the journal entry to record this increase. (*Hint:* Credit the Revaluation Reserve account.)

(c) Under U.K. (and IASB) standards, are Liberty's assets and equity overstated? If so, why? When comparing Liberty to U.S. companies, like Kimco, what adjustments would you need to make in order to have valid comparisons of ratios such as those computed in (a) above?

Concepts for Analysis

AIA10-6 (**Options to Purchase Property**)   Your client, Salvador Plastics Co., found three suitable sites, each having certain unique advantages, for a new plant facility. In order to thoroughly investigate the advantages and disadvantages of each site, 1-year options were purchased for an amount equal to 6% of the contract price of each site. The costs of the options cannot be applied against the contracts. Before the options expired, one of the sites was purchased at the contract price of $400,000. The option on this site had cost $24,000. The two options not exercised had cost $16,000 each.

Instructions

Present arguments in support of recording the cost of the land at each of the following amounts.

(a) $400,000.
(b) $424,000.
(c) $456,000.

(AICPA adapted)

AIA10-7 (**Acquisition, Improvements, and Sale of Realty**)   William Bradford Company purchased land for use as its corporate headquarters. A small factory that was on the land when it was purchased was torn down before construction of the office building began. Furthermore, a substantial amount of rock blasting and removal had to be done to the site before construction of the building foundation began. Because the office building was set back on the land far from the public road, Bradford Company had the contractor construct a paved road that led from the public road to the parking lot of the office building.

Three years after the office building was occupied, Bradford Company added four stories to the office building. The four stories had an estimated useful life of 5 years more than the remaining estimated useful life of the original office building.

Ten years later the land and building were sold at an amount more than their net book value, and Bradford Company had a new office building constructed in another state for use as its new corporate headquarters.

Instructions

(a) Which of the expenditures above should be capitalized? How should each be depreciated or amortized? Discuss the rationale for your answers.
(b) How would the sale of the land and building be accounted for? Include in your answer an explanation of how to determine the net book value at the date of sale. Discuss the rationale for your answer.

AIA10-8 (**Accounting for Self-Constructed Assets**)   Shanette Medical Labs, Inc. began operations 5 years ago producing stetrics, a new type of instrument it hoped to sell to doctors, dentists, and hospitals. The demand for stetrics far exceeded initial expectations, and the company was unable to produce enough stetrics to meet demand.

The company was manufacturing its product on equipment that it built at the start of its operations. To meet demand, more efficient equipment was needed. The company decided to design and build the equipment, because the equipment currently available on the market was unsuitable for producing stetrics.

In 2008, a section of the plant was devoted to development of the new equipment and a special staff was hired. Within 6 months a machine developed at a cost of $714,000 increased production dramatically and reduced labor costs substantially. Elated by the success of the new machine, the company built three more machines of the same type at a cost of $441,000 each.

Instructions

(a) In general, what costs should be capitalized for self-constructed equipment?
(b) Discuss the propriety of including in the capitalized cost of self-constructed assets:
  (1) The increase in overhead caused by the self-construction of fixed assets.
  (2) A proportionate share of overhead on the same basis as that applied to goods manufactured for sale.

(c) Discuss the proper accounting treatment of the $273,000 ($714,000 − $441,000) by which the cost of the first machine exceeded the cost of the subsequent machines. This additional cost should not be considered research and development costs.

AIA10-9 **(Depreciation Basic Concepts)** Prophet Manufacturing Company was organized January 1, 2008. During 2008 it has used in its reports to management the straight-line method of depreciating its plant assets.

On November 8 you are having a conference with Prophet's officers to discuss the depreciation method to be used for income tax and stockholder reporting. Frank Peretti, president of Prophet, has suggested the use of a new method, which he feels is more suitable than the straight-line method for the needs of the company during the period of rapid expansion of production and capacity that he foresees. Following is an example in which the proposed method is applied to a fixed asset with an original cost of $248,000, an estimated useful life of 5 years, and a scrap value of approximately $8,000.

Year	Years of Life Used	Fraction Rate	Depreciation Expense	Accumulated Depreciation at End of Year	Book Value at End of Year
1	1	1/15	$16,000	$ 16,000	$232,000
2	2	2/15	32,000	48,000	200,000
3	3	3/15	48,000	96,000	152,000
4	4	4/15	64,000	160,000	88,000
5	5	5/15	80,000	240,000	8,000

The president favors the new method because he has heard that:

1. It will increase the funds recovered during the years near the end of the assets' useful lives when maintenance and replacement disbursements are high.
2. It will result in increased write-offs in later years and thereby will reduce taxes.

Instructions

(a) What is the purpose of accounting for depreciation?
(b) Is the president's proposal within the scope of generally accepted accounting principles? In making your decision discuss the circumstances, if any, under which use of the method would be reasonable and those, if any, under which it would not be reasonable.
(c) The president wants your advice on the following questions.
  (1) Do depreciation charges recover or create funds? Explain.
  (2) Assume that the Internal Revenue Service accepts the proposed depreciation method in this case. If the proposed method were used for stockholder and tax reporting purposes, how would it affect the availability of funds generated by operations?

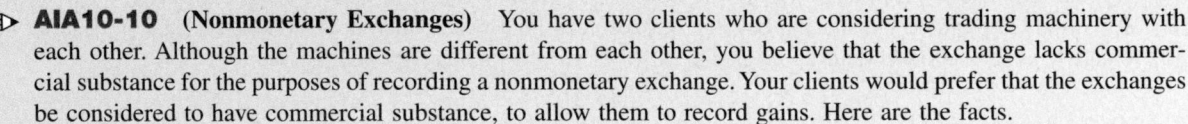 **AIA10-10** **(Nonmonetary Exchanges)** You have two clients who are considering trading machinery with each other. Although the machines are different from each other, you believe that the exchange lacks commercial substance for the purposes of recording a nonmonetary exchange. Your clients would prefer that the exchanges be considered to have commercial substance, to allow them to record gains. Here are the facts.

	Client A	Client B
Original cost	$100,000	$150,000
Accumulated depreciation	40,000	80,000
Market value	95,000	125,000
Cash received (paid)	(30,000)	30,000

Instructions

(a) Record the trade-in on Client A's books assuming the exchange has commercial substance.
(b) Record the trade-in on Client A's books assuming the exchange lacks commercial substance.
(c) Write a memo to the controller of Company A indicating and explaining the dollar impact on current and future statements of treating the exchange as having versus lacking commercial substance.
(d) Record the entry on Client B's books assuming the exchange has commercial substance.
(e) Record the entry on Client B's books assuming the exchange lacks commercial substance.
(f) Write a memo to the controller of Company B indicating and explaining the dollar impact on current and future statements of treating the exchange as having versus lacking commercial substance.

AIA10-11 **(Assets Acquired through Issuance of Stock)** You have been engaged to examine the financial statements of Richard Corporation for the year ending December 31, 2008. Richard was organized in January 2008 by Messrs. Dean and Anderson, original owners of options to acquire oil leases on 5,000 acres of land for $1,200,000. They expected that (1) the oil leases would be acquired by the corporation and (2) subsequently 180,000 shares of the corporation's common stock would be sold to the public at $20 per share. In February 2009, they exchanged their options, $400,000 cash, and $200,000 of other assets for 75,000 shares of common stock of the corporation. The corporation's board of directors appraised the leases at $2,100,000, basing its appraisal on the price of other acreage recently leased in the same area. The options were, therefore, recorded at $900,000 ($2,100,000 − $1,200,000 option price).

The options were exercised by the corporation in March 2009, prior to the sale of common stock to the public in April 2009. Leases on approximately 500 acres of land were abandoned as worthless during the year.

Instructions

(a) Why is the valuation of assets acquired by a corporation in exchange for its own common stock sometimes difficult?

(b) (1) What reasoning might Richard Corporation use to support valuing the leases at $2,100,000, the amount of the appraisal by the board of directors?

(2) Assuming that the board's appraisal was sincere, what steps might Richard Corporation have taken to strengthen its position to use the $2,100,000 value and to provide additional information if questions were raised about possible overvaluation of the leases?

(c) Discuss the propriety of charging one-tenth of the recorded value of the leases to expense at December 31, 2009, because leases on 500 acres of land were abandoned during the year.

(AICPA adapted)

Professional Tools

■ Ethical Decision Making

AIA10-12 Field Company purchased a warehouse in a downtown district where land values are rapidly increasing. Adolph Phillips, controller, and Wilma Smith, financial vice president, are trying to allocate the cost of the purchase between the land and the building. Phillips, noting that depreciation can be taken only on the building, favors placing a very high proportion of the cost on the warehouse itself, thus reducing taxable income and income taxes. Smith, his supervisor, argues that the allocation should recognize the increasing value of the land, regardless of the depreciation potential of the warehouse. Besides, she says, net income is negatively impacted by additional depreciation and will cause the company's stock price to go down.

Instructions

(a) What stakeholder interests are in conflict?
(b) What ethical issues does Phillips face?
(c) How should these costs be allocated?

■ Financial Accounting Research (FARS)

AIA10-13 Your client is in the planning phase for a major plant expansion, which will involve the construction of a new warehouse. The assistant controller does not believe that interest cost can be included in the cost of the warehouse, because it is a financing expense. Others on the planning team believe that some interest cost can be included in the cost of the warehouse, but no one could identify the specific authoritative guidance for this issue. Your supervisor asks you to research this issue.

Instructions

Using the **Financial Accounting Research System (FARS)** database, respond to the following items. (Provide text strings used in your search.)

(a) Is it permissible to capitalize interest into the cost of assets? What standard addresses this issue?
(b) What are the objectives for capitalizing interest?
(c) Discuss which assets qualify for interest capitalization.
(d) Is there a limit to the amount of interest that may be capitalized in a period?
(e) What disclosures are required, if interest capitalization is allowed?

■ Professional Simulation

AIA10-14 Go to the book's companion website, at **www.wiley.com/college/warfield**, to find an interactive problem that simulates the computerized CPA exam. The professional simulation for this chapter asks you to address questions related to the accounting for property, plant, and equipment.

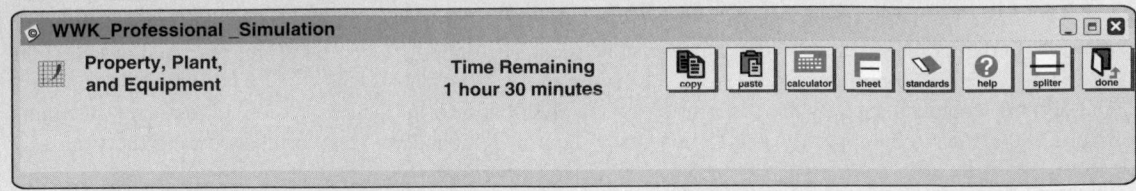

What do the numbers mean?　　　Guideline Answers to Beyond the Numbers Questions

What's in Your Interest?, p. 492

Q: Recently, interest rates have been rising. What are the implications of rising interest rates for the amount of interest capitalized by a company like Anardarko?

A: In general, for a company with ongoing construction projects, rising interest rates will result in higher amounts of capitalized interest. However, as discussed in more detail in Appendix 10A, if the company had already borrowed money before interest rates increased, it would use the lower rates on the outstanding debt to determine the amount of interest to capitalize. In this case, the amount of interest capitalized would not increase.

Disconnected, p. 496

Q: WorldCom's accounting for line charges also resulted in improper reporting of its "Cash flow provided by operations." Explain how.

A: The expenses for local telephone charges should have been treated as normal operating costs. Cash payments for such operating expenses reduce cash flow from operations. Cash flow from operations is an important measure of a company's financial strength.

When WorldCom treated these payments as capital expenditures, it showed them as an outflow of cash for investing activities rather than as operating expenses. Investors would have seen such investments as favorable expenditures. Thus, the improper reporting both overstated "Cash flow from operations" and misstated the company's investing activities.

Decelerating Depreciation, p. 505

Q: Under what conditions might increasing-charge depreciation *not* result in better matching?

A: Better matching might not result for two reasons: First, the properties might not generate higher revenues (e.g., due to competition or changes in demand for certain properties), as predicted by the real estate companies. As a result, when combined with the higher depreciation charges, lower income will be reported in later years. Alternatively (or in addition), older properties may also have higher maintenance costs. If the real estate companies cannot charge higher rent (increased revenue), these higher costs combined with higher depreciation in later years will result in lower income. In both scenarios, by using increasing-charge depreciation, the real estate companies might end up deferring losses.

Depreciation Choices, p. 508

Q: Do the changes in useful lives by Willamette reveal information about how well assets are being managed? Explain.

A: Assuming the changes were not made simply to increase earnings (that is, for purposes of earnings management), and given that others in the industry have similar useful-life assumptions, these changes likely reflect favorably on how assets are being managed. For example, longer useful lives could imply that the company has good maintenance programs for its equipment and/or that it has found more efficient ways to use the equipment with the help of the newer technology. Nonetheless, it would be a good idea to check on the useful lives of competitors' assets and to verify the investments in newer equipment (in the investing section of the statement of cash flows).

Remember to check the book's companion website to find additional resources for this chapter.

CHAPTER 11

INTANGIBLE ASSETS

Untouchable

As shown in the graph below, tangible assets as a percent of all assets have declined dramatically in the last 50 years. Consequently, companies today increasingly derive value from intangible assets—intellectual property, technology, or reputation. Many well-known companies make most of their money from intangible assets: **Microsoft Corp.**'s software, **Pfizer Inc.**'s drug patents, and **Walt Disney Co.**'s film and television productions.

However, the experience at **Winstar Communications** illustrates how quickly the value of intangible assets can erode. Just before Winstar filed for bankruptcy, it listed $5 billion in assets, a large share comprised of questionable intangible assets related to its customer base. Within just a few months, its assets fetched just $42 *million.* Winstar's investors and creditors learned the shocking speed at which the value of such assets can decline.

Perhaps former Federal Reserve Chairman Alan Greenspan's remarks are relevant in these turbulent times: ". . . a firm is inherently fragile if its value-added emanates more from conceptual as distinct from physical assets. Trust and reputation can vanish overnight. A factory cannot."

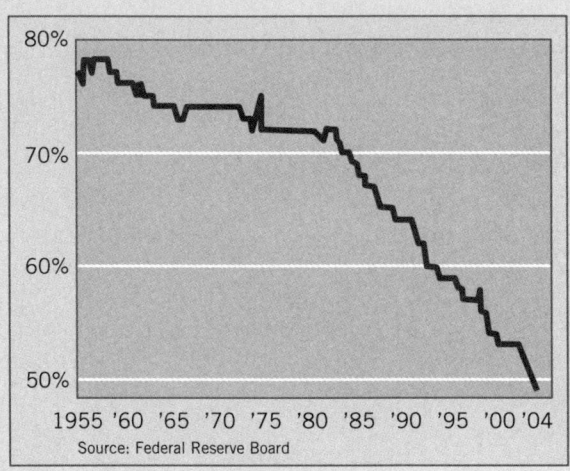

Tangible assets as a percentage of all assets of nonfinancial businesses

Sources: Adapted from Greg Ip, "The Rise and Fall of Intangible Assets Leads to Shorter Company Life Spans," *Wall Street Journal Online* (April 4, 2002).

Preview of Chapter 11

As our opening story indicates, the accounting and reporting of intangibles is taking on increasing importance in this information age, especially for companies like **Microsoft Corp.**, **Pfizer Inc.**, and **Walt Disney Co.** In this chapter we explain the basic conceptual and reporting issues related to intangible assets. *The content and organization of this chapter are as follows.*

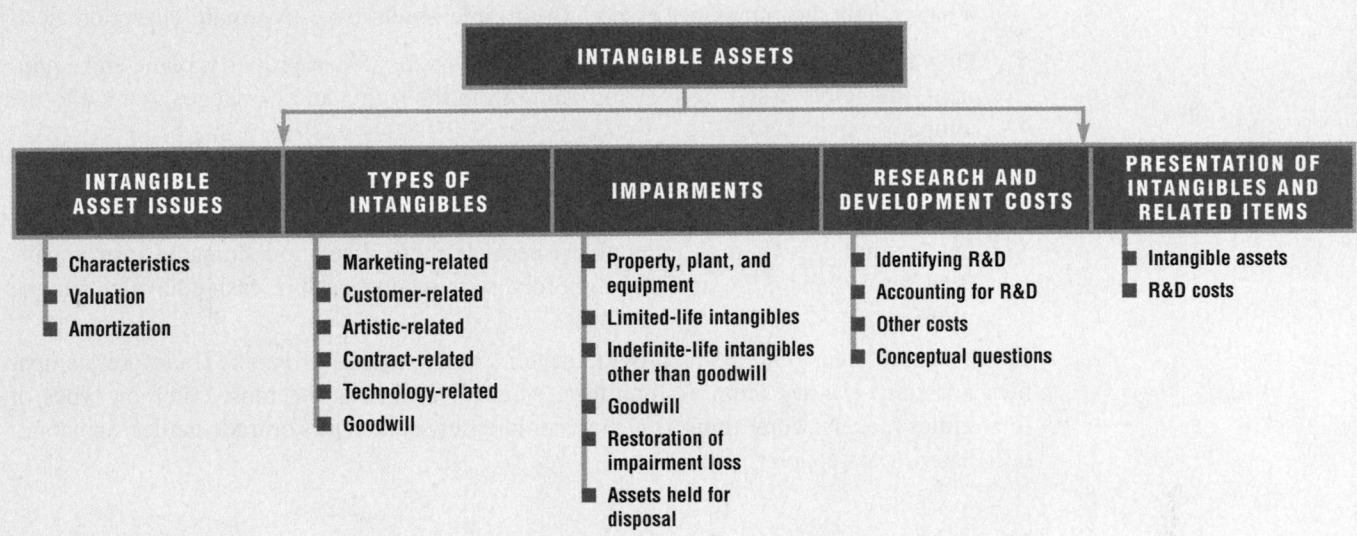

INTANGIBLE ASSETS

INTANGIBLE ASSET ISSUES	TYPES OF INTANGIBLES	IMPAIRMENTS	RESEARCH AND DEVELOPMENT COSTS	PRESENTATION OF INTANGIBLES AND RELATED ITEMS
▪ Characteristics	▪ Marketing-related	▪ Property, plant, and equipment	▪ Identifying R&D	▪ Intangible assets
▪ Valuation	▪ Customer-related	▪ Limited-life intangibles	▪ Accounting for R&D	▪ R&D costs
▪ Amortization	▪ Artistic-related	▪ Indefinite-life intangibles other than goodwill	▪ Other costs	
	▪ Contract-related	▪ Goodwill	▪ Conceptual questions	
	▪ Technology-related	▪ Restoration of impairment loss		
	▪ Goodwill	▪ Assets held for disposal		

Learning Objectives

After studying this chapter, you should be able to:

1. Describe the characteristics of intangible assets.
2. Identify the costs to include in the initial valuation of intangible assets.
3. Explain the procedure for amortizing intangible assets.
4. Describe the types of intangible assets.
5. Explain the conceptual issues related to goodwill.
6. Describe the accounting procedures for recording goodwill.
7. Explain the accounting issues related to impairments.
8. Identify the conceptual issues related to research and development costs.
9. Describe the accounting for research and development and similar costs.
10. Indicate the presentation of intangible assets and related items.

Inside Chapter 11

▪ **What Do the Numbers Mean?**
Sweet to sour (p. 561)
Patent battles (p. 562)
The value of a secret formula (p. 563)
Real news, or just bookkeeping? (p. 572)

▪ **What's the Principle?**
(pp. 556, 565, 577)

▪ **Accounting, Analysis, Principles** (p. 580)
Record intangible assets.
Analyze income volatility of impairments.
Evaluate tradeoff between relevance and reliability.

▪ **Convergence Corner** (582)

INTANGIBLE ASSET ISSUES

Characteristics

OBJECTIVE 1

Describe the characteristics of intangible assets.

Gap Inc.'s most important asset is its brand image, not its store fixtures. **Coca-Cola**'s success comes from its secret formula for making Coke, not its plant facilities. **America Online**'s subscriber base provides its most important asset, not its Internet connection equipment. As these examples show, we have an economy dominated today by information and service providers. For these companies, their major assets are often intangible in nature. Accounting for these intangibles is difficult.

What exactly are intangible assets? **Intangible assets** have two main characteristics.[1]

1 **They lack physical existence.** Unlike tangible assets such as property, plant, and equipment, intangible assets derive their value from the rights and privileges granted to the company using them.

2 **They are not financial instruments.** Assets such as bank deposits, accounts receivable, and long-term investments in bonds and stocks also lack physical substance. However, they are not classified as intangibles, because these assets are financial instruments. They derive their value from the right (claim) to receive cash or cash equivalents in the future.

In most cases, intangible assets provide benefits over a period of years. Therefore, companies normally classify them as long-term assets. We discuss the most common types of intangibles (patents, copyrights, franchises or licenses, trademarks or trade names, and goodwill) later in the chapter.

Valuation

Purchased Intangibles

OBJECTIVE 2

Identify the costs to include in the initial valuation of intangible assets.

Intangibles purchased from another party are **recorded at cost**. Cost includes all costs of acquisition and expenditures necessary to make the intangible asset ready for its intended use. Typical costs include purchase price, legal fees, and other incidental expenses.

If a company acquires intangibles for stock or in exchange for other assets, **the cost of the intangible is the fair value of the consideration given or the fair value of the intangible received, whichever is more clearly evident**. When a company buys several intangibles, or a combination of intangibles and tangibles, in a "basket purchase," it should allocate the cost on the basis of fair values. Essentially the accounting treatment for purchased intangibles closely parallels that for purchased tangible assets.

WHAT'S THE PRINCIPLE?

The basic attributes of intangibles, their uncertainty as to future benefits, and their uniqueness have discouraged valuation in excess of cost.

Internally Created Intangibles

Costs incurred internally to create intangibles are generally expensed. Thus, even though a company may incur substantial research and development costs to create an intangible, it expenses these costs.

How do companies justify this approach? Some argue that the costs incurred internally to create intangibles bear no relationship to their real value. Therefore, expensing these costs is appropriate. Others note that it is difficult to associate internal costs with a specific intangible. And others contend that due to the underlying subjectivity related to intangibles, companies should follow a conservative approach—that is, expense as incurred. As a result, **companies only capitalize direct costs** incurred in developing the intangible, such as legal costs.

---

[1]"Goodwill and Other Intangible Assets," *Statement of Financial Accounting Standards No. 142* (Norwalk, Conn.: FASB, 2001).

Amortization of Intangibles

Intangibles have either a **limited (finite) useful life** or an **indefinite useful life**. For example, a company like **Walt Disney** has both types of intangibles. Walt Disney **amortizes** its **limited life** intangible assets. It **does not amortize** intangible assets with an **indefinite life**.

Limited-Life Intangibles

The allocation of the cost of intangible assets in a systematic way is called **amortization**. Walt Disney amortizes its limited-life intangibles by systematic charges to expense over their useful life. The useful life should reflect the periods over which these assets will contribute to cash flows. Walt Disney considers these factors in determining useful life:

1 The expected use of the asset by the company.

2 The expected useful life of another asset or a group of assets to which the useful life of the intangible asset may relate (such as lease rights to a studio lot).

3 Any legal, regulatory, or contractual provisions that may limit the useful life.

4 Any legal, regulatory, or contractual provisions that enable renewal or extension of the asset's legal or contractual life without substantial cost. This factor assumes that there is evidence to support renewal or extension. Disney also must be able to accomplish renewal or extension without material modifications of the existing terms and conditions.

5 The effects of obsolescence, demand, competition, and other economic factors. Examples include the stability of the industry, known technological advances, legislative action that results in an uncertain or changing regulatory environment, and expected changes in distribution channels.

6 The level of maintenance expenditure required to obtain the expected future cash flows from the asset. For example, a material level of required maintenance in relation to the carrying amount of the asset may suggest a very limited useful life.[2]

The amount of amortization expense for a limited-life intangible asset should reflect the pattern in which the company consumes or uses up the asset, if the company can reliably determine that pattern. For example, assume that Second Wave, Inc. purchases a license to provide a limited quantity of a gene product, called Mega. Second Wave should amortize the cost of the license following the pattern of use of Mega. If it cannot determine the pattern of production or consumption, Second Wave should use the straight-line method of amortization. (*For homework problems, assume the use of the straight-line method unless stated otherwise.*)

When Second Wave amortizes these licenses, it should show the charges as expenses. It should credit either the appropriate asset accounts or separate accumulated amortization accounts.

The amount of an intangible asset to be amortized should be its cost less residual value. The residual value is assumed to be zero unless at the end of its useful life the intangible asset has value to another company. For example, if Hardy Co. commits to purchasing an intangible asset from U2D Co. at the end of the asset's useful life, U2D Co. should reduce the cost of its intangible asset by the residual value. Similarly, U2D Co. should consider market values, if reliably determined, for residual values.

What happens if the life of a limited-life intangible asset changes? In that case the remaining carrying amount should be amortized over the revised remaining useful life.

Indefinite-Life Intangibles

If no legal, regulatory, contractual, competitive, or other factors limit the useful life of an intangible asset, a company considers its useful life indefinite. **Indefinite** means that there is no foreseeable limit on the period of time over which the intangible asset is

---

[2]Ibid, par. 11.

expected to provide cash flows. A company does not amortize an intangible asset with an indefinite life.

To illustrate, assume that Double Clik, Inc. acquired a trademark that it uses to distinguish a leading consumer product. It renews the trademark every 10 years at minimal cost. All evidence indicates that this trademark product will generate cash flows for an indefinite period of time. In this case, the trademark has an indefinite life; Double Clik does not record any amortization.

Illustration 11-1 summarizes the accounting treatment for intangible assets.

Illustration 11-1
Accounting Treatment for Intangibles

	Manner Acquired		
Type of Intangible	Purchased	Internally Created	Amortization
Limited-life intangibles	Capitalize	Expense*	Over useful life
Indefinite-life intangibles	Capitalize	Expense*	Do not amortize

*Except for direct costs, such as legal costs.

TYPES OF INTANGIBLE ASSETS

OBJECTIVE 4
Describe the types of intangible assets.

As indicated, the accounting for intangible assets depends on whether the intangible has a limited or an indefinite life. There are many different types of intangibles, often classified into the following six major categories.[3]

1 Marketing-related intangible assets.
2 Customer-related intangible assets.
3 Artistic-related intangible assets.
4 Contract-related intangible assets.
5 Technology-related intangible assets.
6 Goodwill.

Marketing-Related Intangible Assets

Companies primarily use **marketing-related intangible assets** in the marketing or promotion of products or services. Examples are trademarks or trade names, newspaper mastheads, Internet domain names, and noncompetition agreements.

A common form of a marketing-related intangible asset is a trademark or trade name. A **trademark** or **trade name** is a word, phrase, or symbol that distinguishes or identifies a particular company or product. Under common law, the right to use a trademark or trade name, whether registered or not, rests exclusively with the original user as long as the original user continues to use it. Registration with the U.S. Patent and Trademark Office provides legal protection for an **indefinite number of renewals for periods of 10 years each**. Therefore a company that uses an established trademark or trade name may properly consider it to have an indefinite life. Trade names like Kleenex, Pepsi-Cola, Buick, Excedrin, Wheaties, and iPhone create immediate product identification in our minds, thereby enhancing marketability.

---

[3]This classification framework is based on "Business Combinations," *Statement of Financial Accounting Standards No. 141* (Norwalk, Conn.: FASB, 2001).

If a company acquires a trademark or trade name, it capitalizes the cost at the purchase price. If a company develops a trademark or trade name, it capitalizes costs related to securing it, such as attorney fees, registration fees, design costs, consulting fees, and successful legal defense costs. However, it excludes research and development costs. When the total cost of a trademark or trade name is insignificant, a company may simply expense it. In most cases, the life of a trademark or trade name is indefinite. Therefore companies do not amortize its cost.

The value of a marketing-related intangible can be substantial. Consider Internet domain names. The name **Drugs.com** recently sold for $800,000. The bidding for the name **Loans.com** approached $500,000.

Company names themselves identify qualities and characteristics that companies work hard and spend much to develop. In a recent year an estimated 1,230 companies took on new names in an attempt to forge new identities, and paid over $250 million to corporate-identity consultants. Among these were **Primerica** (formerly American Can), **Navistar** (formerly International Harvester), and **Nissan** (formerly Datsun).[4]

Customer-Related Intangible Assets

Customer-related intangible assets result from interactions with outside parties. Examples include customer lists, order or production backlogs, and both contractual and noncontractual customer relationships.

To illustrate, assume that We-Market Inc. acquires the customer list of a large newspaper for $6,000,000 on January 1, 2008. This customer database includes name, contact information, order history, and demographic information. We-Market expects to benefit evenly from the information over a three-year period. In this case, the customer list is a limited-life intangible that We-Market should amortize on a straight-line basis over the three-year period.

We-Market records the purchase of the customer list and the amortization of the customer list at the end of each year as follows.

January 1, 2008

Customer List	6,000,000	
Cash		6,000,000
(To record purchase of customer list)		

December 31, 2008, 2009, 2010

Customer List Amortization Expense	2,000,000	
Customer List (or Accumulated Customer		
List Amortization)		2,000,000
(To record amortization expense)		

The preceding example assumed no residual value for the customer list. But what if We-Market determines that it can sell the list for $60,000 to another company at the end of three years? In that case We-Market should subtract this residual value from the cost in order to determine the proper amortization expense for each year. Amortization expense would therefore be $1,980,000, as shown in Illustration 11-2 (page 560).

Companies should assume a zero residual value unless the asset's useful life is less than the economic life and reliable evidence is available concerning the residual value.[5]

---

[4]To illustrate how various intangibles arise from a given product, consider how the creators of the highly successful game Trivial Pursuit protected their creation. First, they copyrighted the 6,000 questions that are at the heart of the game. Then they shielded the Trivial Pursuit name by applying for a registered trademark. As a third mode of protection, they obtained a design patent on the playing board's design as a unique graphic creation.

[5]"Goodwill and Other Intangible Assets," *Statement of Financial Accounting Standards No. 142* (Norwalk, Conn.: FASB, 2001), par. B55.

Illustration 11-2
Calculation of
Amortization Expense
with Residual Value

Cost	$6,000,000
Residual value	60,000
Amortization base	$5,940,000

Amortization expense per period: $1,980,000 ($5,940,000 ÷ 3)

Artistic-Related Intangible Assets

Artistic-related intangible assets involve ownership rights to plays, literary works, musical works, pictures, photographs, and video and audiovisual material. Copyrights protect these ownership rights.

A **copyright** is a federally granted right that all authors, painters, musicians, sculptors, and other artists have in their creations and expressions. A copyright is granted for the **life of the creator plus 70 years**. It gives the owner, or heirs, the exclusive right to reproduce and sell an artistic or published work. Copyrights are not renewable. Companies may capitalize the costs of acquiring and defending a copyright. However, they must expense the research and development costs involved as incurred.

Copyrights can be valuable. For example, the **Walt Disney Company** faced the loss of its copyright on Mickey Mouse, which could have affected sales of billions of dollars of Mickey-related goods and services (including theme parks). This copyright was so valuable that Disney and many other big entertainment companies fought all the way to the Supreme Court (and won) an extension of copyright lives from 50 to 70 years. Another example of the value of these intangibles is **Really Useful Group**, which owns copyrights on the musicals of Andrew Lloyd Webber—*Cats, Phantom of the Opera, Jesus Christ-Superstar,* and others. It has little hard assets, yet analysts value it at over $300 million.

Generally, the useful life of the copyright is less than its legal life (life of the creator plus 70 years). Thus, Really Useful Group should allocate the costs of its copyrights to the years in which it expects to receive the benefits. The difficulty of determining the number of years over which it will receive benefits normally encourages a company like Really Useful Group to write off these costs over a fairly short period of time.

Contract-Related Intangible Assets

Contract-related intangible assets represent the value of rights that arise from contractual arrangements. Examples are franchise and licensing agreements, construction permits, broadcast rights, and service or supply contracts. A common form of contract-based intangible asset is a franchise.

A **franchise** is a contractual arrangement under which the franchisor grants the franchisee the right to sell certain products or services, to use certain trademarks or trade names, or to perform certain functions, usually within a designated geographical area. We deal with franchises everyday, from driving in an automobile purchased from a **Toyota** dealer, to eating lunch at **McDonald's**, to living in a home purchased through a **Century 21** real estate broker, or to vacationing at a **Marriott** resort.

The franchisor, having developed a unique concept or product, protects its concept or product through a patent, copyright, or trademark or trade name. The franchisee acquires the right to exploit the franchisor's idea or product by signing a franchise agreement.

A municipality (or other governmental body) and a company that uses public property often enter into another type of franchise arrangement. In such cases, a municipality allows a privately owned company to use public property in performing its services. Examples are the use of public waterways for a ferry service, the use of public land for telephone or electric lines, the use of phone lines for cable TV, the use of city streets for a bus line, or the use of the airwaves for radio or TV broadcasting. Such operating rights, obtained through agreements with governmental units or agencies, are frequently referred to as **licenses** or **permits**.

Franchises and licenses may be for a definite period of time, for an indefinite period of time, or perpetual. The company securing the franchise or license carries an intangible asset account entitled Franchise or License on its books, only when it can identify costs (such as a lump-sum payment in advance or legal fees and other expenditures) with the acquisition of the operating right. **A company should amortize the cost of a franchise (or license) with a limited life as operating expense over the life of the franchise.** It should not amortize a franchise with an indefinite life, or a perpetual franchise, but instead should carry it at cost.

Annual payments made under a franchise agreement should be entered as operating expenses in the period in which they are incurred. The payments do not represent an asset since they do not relate to future rights to use public property.

What do the numbers mean? | Sweet to Sour

Krispy Kreme, the doughnut maker once dubbed the "hottest brand in the land," has taken a series of beatings. The latest: a formal inquiry by the Securities and Exchange Commission in October 2004 into its accounting. The problem seems to be with franchises Krispy Kreme reacquired a few years ago from owners who wanted to exit the business. Krispy Kreme decided to book most of the purchase price as an intangible asset called "reacquired franchise rights," which it does not amortize, or write-down, over time.

Management justified the accounting based on its belief that reacquired franchise rights have "indefinite lives." But critics charge that this artificially inflates profits and doesn't reflect the cost of the stores on its balance sheet. To compound its woes, some of the reacquired franchises were purchased from related parties, at prices some allege were too generous.

Accounting experts say it's unclear whether Krispy Kreme's method violates GAAP. One research firm found that all of the companies it follows with reacquired franchise rights amortize the costs over time. Krispy Kreme's methods are "definitely not conservative," according to one analyst.

The SEC probe couldn't have come at a worse time. Krispy Kreme's profits have plunged, and the stock lost about 75 percent of its value in the last year. Given the company's tumbling profits and hyper-aggressive accounting, investors should expect restatements and a big write-down when its auditor performs its annual impairment test. In other words, Krispy Kreme's outlook has gone from sweet to sour.

Source: Adapted from David Stires, "Accounting," *Fortune* (November 1, 2004), p. 42.

Beyond the Numbers

Is Krispy Kreme's accounting for reacquired franchise rights a form of earnings management? Explain.

Technology-Related Intangible Assets

Technology-related intangible assets relate to innovations or technological advances. Examples are patented technology and trade secrets granted by the U.S. Patent and Trademark Office. A **patent** gives the holder exclusive right to use, manufacture, and sell a product or process **for a period of 20 years** without interference or infringement by others. With this exclusive right, fortunes can be made. For example, companies such as **Merck**,

Polaroid, and **Xerox** were founded on patents.[6] The two principal kinds of patents are **product patents**, which cover actual physical products, and **process patents**, which govern the process of making products.

If a company like **Qualcomm** purchases a patent from an inventor (or other owner), the purchase price represents its cost. Qualcomm can capitalize other costs incurred in connection with securing a patent, as well as attorneys' fees and other unrecovered costs of a successful legal suit to protect the patent, as part of the patent cost. However, it **must expense as incurred** any research and development costs related to the **development** of the product, process, or idea that it subsequently patents. We discuss accounting for research and development costs in more detail on pages 574–577.

Qualcomm should amortize the cost of a patent over its legal life or its useful life (the period benefits are received), whichever is **shorter**. If it owns a patent from the date it is granted, and Qualcomm expects the patent to be useful during its entire legal life, the company should amortize it over 20 years. If it appears that the patent will be useful for a shorter period of time, say, for five years, it should amortize its cost over five years.

Changing demand, new inventions superseding old ones, inadequacy, and other factors often limit the useful life of a patent to less than the legal life. For example, the useful life of patents in the pharmaceutical and drug industry is frequently less than the legal life because of the testing and approval period that follows their issuance. A typical drug patent has 5 to 11 years knocked off its 20-year legal life. Why? Because a drug-maker spends one to four years on animal tests, four to six years on human tests, and two to three years for the Food and Drug Administration to review the tests. All this time occurs after issuing the patent but before the product goes on a pharmacist's shelves.

What do the numbers mean? Patent Battles

From bioengineering to software design to the Internet, global competition is bringing battles over patents to the boiling point. For example, **Priceline.com** filed suit against **Microsoft** for launching Hotel Price Matcher, a service that operates much like the name-your-own-price-system Priceline pioneered.

Do you ever wonder who thought of the technology that saves your shipping and credit card information when you shop online? It was **Amazon.com**, which patented "one-click" shopping. To protect its technology, Amazon.com filed a complaint against **Barnesandnoble.com**, its rival in the Web-retailing wars, alleging infringement on its patent for one-click shopping. Even though Amazon.com and Barnesandnoble.com settled their dispute, patent battles continue between online retailers and independent software developers, claiming that companies like Amazon.com are unfairly undercutting its competition through these "business-method" patents.

Source: Adapted from "Battle over Patents Threatens to Damp Web's Innovative Spirit," *Wall Street Journal* (November 8, 1999); and L. Rohde, "Amazon, Barnes and Noble Settle Patent Dispute, *CNN.com* (March 8, 2002).

Beyond the Numbers

Does society benefit from patent protection on business methods, as it presumably does on patents on drugs?

A company charges all legal fees and other costs incurred in successfully defending a patent suit to Patents, an asset account, because such a suit establishes the legal rights of the holder of the patent. Such costs should be amortized along with acquisition cost, over the remaining useful life of the patent.

---

[6]Consider the opposite result: Sir Alexander Fleming, who discovered penicillin, decided not to use a patent to protect his discovery. He hoped that companies would produce it more quickly to help save sufferers. Companies, however, refused to develop it because they did not have the patent shield and, therefore, were afraid to make the investment.

Amortization expense should reflect the pattern, if reliably determined, in which a company uses up the patent.[7] A company may credit amortization of patents directly to the Patents account or to an Accumulated Patent Amortization account. To illustrate, assume that Harcott Co. incurs $180,000 in legal costs on January 1, 2008 to successfully defend a patent. The patent's useful life is 20 years, amortized on a straight-line basis. Harcott records the legal fees and the amortization at the end of 2008 as follows.

January 1, 2008

Patents	180,000	
Cash		180,000
(To record legal fees related to patent)		

December 31, 2008

Patent Amortization Expense	9,000	
Patents (or Accumulated Patent Amortization)		9,000
(To record amortization of patent)		

We've said that a patent's useful life should not extend beyond its legal life of 20 years. However, companies often make small modifications or additions that lead to a new patent. For example, **Astra Zeneca Plc** filed for additional patents on minor modifications to its heartburn drug, Prilosec. The effect may be to extend the life of the old patent. In that case Astra Zeneca can apply the unamortized costs of the old patent to the new patent if the new patent provides essentially the same benefits.[8] Alternatively, if a patent becomes impaired because demand drops for the product, the asset should be written down or written off immediately to expense.

What do the numbers mean?   The Value of a Secret Formula

The nuclear secrets contained within the Los Alamos nuclear lab seem easier to check out than a library book. But **The Coca-Cola Company** has managed to keep the recipe for the world's best-selling soft drink under wraps for more than 100 years. How has it done so?

Coca-Cola offers almost no information about its lifeblood. The only written copy of the formula resides in a bank vault in Atlanta. This handwritten sheet is available to no one except by vote of Coca-Cola's board of directors.

Can't science offer some clues? Coke purportedly contains 17 to 18 ingredients. That includes the usual caramel color and corn syrup, as well as a blend of oils known as 7X (rumored to be a mix of orange, lemon, cinnamon, and others). Distilling natural products like these is complicated, since they're made of thousands of compounds. One ingredient you will not find is cocaine. Although the original formula did contain trace amounts, today's Coke doesn't. When was it removed? That too is a secret.

Some experts estimate the power of the Coca-Cola formula and related brand image at $67.5 billion, or more than 60 percent of Coke's stock value.

Sources: Adapted from R. Tucker, "How Has Coke's Formula Stayed a Secret?" *Fortune* (June 24, 2000), p. 42; and P. Berner and D. Kiley, "Global Brands," *Business Week* (August 1, 2005), p. 90.

Beyond the Numbers

Where in Coca-Cola's financial statements could you find some indication of the value of its secret formula?

---

[7]Companies may compute amortization on a units-of-production basis in a manner similar to that described for depreciation on property, plant, and equipment. See Chapter 10, page 502–503.

[8]Another example is **Eli Lilly**'s drug Prozac (prescribed to treat depression). In 1998 this product accounted for 43 percent of Eli Lilly's sales. The patent on Prozac expired in 2001, and the company was unable to extend its protection with a second-use patent for the use of Prozac to treat appetite disorders. Sales of the product slipped substantially as generic equivalents entered the market.

Try it out! During 2008, Brenly Company spent $110,000 in research and development costs. As a result, it patented a new product on July 1, 2008. Legal costs of $24,000 related to the patent were incurred as of July 1, 2008. The patent had a legal life of 20 years and a useful life of 12 years. In 2010, Brenly determined that a competitor's product would make its product worthless at the end of 2012.

Instructions

a Prepare all necessary journal entries for Brenly for 2008.
b Compute patent amortization expense for 2010.

Solution

a During 2008

Research and Development Expense	110,000	
Cash		110,000

July 1, 2008

Patents	24,000	
Cash		24,000

December 31, 2008

Patent Amortization Expense	1,000	
Patents ($24,000 ÷ 12) × 6/12		1,000

b 2010 patent amortization expense: $[\$24,000 - (\$2,000 \times 1\ \frac{1}{2})] \div 3 \text{ years} = \underline{\$7,000}$

Goodwill

Explain the conceptual issues related to goodwill.

Although companies may capitalize certain costs to develop specifically identifiable assets such as patents and copyrights, the amounts capitalized are generally insignificant. But companies do record material amounts of intangible assets when purchasing intangible assets, particularly in situations involving the purchase of another business (often referred to as a business combination).

In a business combination, a company assigns the cost (purchase price), where possible, to the identifiable tangible and intangible net assets. It records the remainder in an intangible asset account called **Goodwill**. Goodwill is often referred to as the most intangible of intangible assets, because it is only identified with the business as a whole. The only way to sell it is to sell the business.

The problem of determining the proper cost to allocate to intangible assets in a business combination is complex. Many different types of intangibles may be considered, such as those we discussed earlier. It is extremely difficult not only to identify certain types of intangibles but also to assign a value to them in a business combination. As a result, companies only record identifiable intangible assets that they can reliably measure. They record all other intangible assets, too difficult to identify or measure, as goodwill.[9]

[9]*SFAS No. 141* provides detailed guidance regarding the recognition of identifiable intangible assets in a business combination. Using this guidance, it was expected that companies would recognize more identifiable intangible assets, and less goodwill, in the financial statements as a result of business combinations. According to *Accounting Trends and Techniques* (AICPA, 2004), companies surveyed reported nearly twice as many identifiable intangible assets compared to the survey in 2001. There was little change in the number of survey companies reporting goodwill.

Recording Goodwill

Internally Created Goodwill. **Goodwill generated internally should not be capitalized in the accounts.** The reason? Measuring the components of goodwill is simply too complex, and associating any costs with future benefits is too difficult. The future benefits of goodwill may have no relationship to the costs incurred in the development of that goodwill. To add to the mystery, goodwill may even exist in the absence of specific costs to develop it. Finally, because no objective transaction with outside parties takes place, a great deal of subjectivity—even misrepresentation—may occur.

Purchased Goodwill. Goodwill is recorded only when an entire business is purchased. Because goodwill is a "going concern" valuation, it cannot be separated from the business as a whole. To record goodwill, a company compares the fair value of the net tangible and identifiable intangible assets with the purchase price of the acquired business. The difference is considered goodwill. This is why goodwill is sometimes referred to as a "plug," or "gap filler," or **master valuation** account. **Goodwill is the residual—the excess of cost over fair value of the identifiable net assets acquired.**

To illustrate, Multi-Diversified, Inc. decides that it needs a parts division to supplement its existing tractor distributorship. The president of Multi-Diversified is interested in buying a small concern in Chicago (Tractorling Company). Illustration 11-3 presents the balance sheet of Tractorling Company.

> OBJECTIVE 6
> Describe the accounting procedures for recording goodwill.

> **WHAT'S THE PRINCIPLE?**
> Capitalizing goodwill only when it is purchased in an arm's-length transaction, and not capitalizing any goodwill generated internally, is another example of *reliability* winning out over *relevance*.

Tractorling Co.
Balance Sheet
As of December 31, 2008

Assets		Equities	
Cash	$ 25,000	Current liabilities	$ 55,000
Receivables	35,000	Capital stock	100,000
Inventories	42,000	Retained earnings	100,000
Property, plant, and equipment, net	153,000		
Total assets	$255,000	Total equities	$255,000

Illustration 11-3
Tractorling Balance Sheet

After considerable negotiation, Tractorling Company decides to accept Multi-Diversified's offer of $400,000. What, then, is the value of the goodwill, if any?

The answer is not obvious. Tractorling's historical cost-based balance sheet does not disclose the fair values of its identifiable assets. Suppose, though, that as the negotiations progress, Multi-Diversified investigates Tractorling's underlying assets to determine their fair values. Such an investigation may be accomplished either through a purchase audit undertaken by Multi-Diversified's auditors or by an independent appraisal from some other source. The investigation determines the valuations shown in Illustration 11-4.

Expanded Discussion—
Valuing Goodwill

Fair Values

Cash	$ 25,000
Receivables	35,000
Inventories	122,000
Property, plant, and equipment, net	205,000
Patents	18,000
Liabilities	(55,000)
Fair value of net assets	$350,000

Illustration 11-4
Fair Value of Tractorling's Net Assets

Normally, differences between current fair value and book value are more common among long-term assets than in the current assets category. Cash obviously poses no problems as to value. And receivables normally are fairly close to current valuation, although they may at times need certain adjustments due to inadequate bad debt provisions. Liabilities usually are stated at book value. However, if interest rates have changed since the company incurred the liabilities, a different valuation (such as present value based on expected cash flows) might be appropriate. Careful analysis must be made to determine that no unrecorded liabilities are present.

The $80,000 difference in Tractorling's inventories ($122,000 − $42,000) could result from a number of factors, the most likely being that the company uses LIFO. Recall that during periods of inflation, LIFO better matches expenses against revenues. However, it also creates a balance sheet distortion. Ending inventory consists of older layers costed at lower valuations.

In many cases, the values of long-term assets such as property, plant, and equipment, and intangibles may have increased substantially over the years. This difference could be due to inaccurate estimates of useful lives, continual expensing of small expenditures (say, less than $300), inaccurate estimates of salvage values, and the discovery of some unrecorded assets (as in Tractorling's case, where analysis determines Patents have a fair value of $18,000). Or, fair values may have substantially increased.

Since the investigation now determines the fair value of net assets to be $350,000, why would Multi-Diversified pay $400,000? Undoubtedly, Tractorling points to its established reputation, good credit rating, top management team, well-trained employees, and so on. These factors make the value of the business greater than $350,000. At the same time, Multi-Diversified places a premium on the future earning power of these attributes as well as the basic asset structure of the company today. At this point in the negotiations, price can be a function of many factors. The most important is probably sheer skill at the bargaining table.

Multi-Diversified labels the difference between the purchase price of $400,000 and the fair market value of $350,000 as goodwill. Goodwill is viewed as one or a group of unidentifiable values (intangible assets), the cost of which "is measured by the difference between the cost of the group of assets or enterprise acquired and the sum of the assigned costs of individual tangible and identifiable intangible assets acquired less liabilities assumed."[10] This procedure for valuation, a **master valuation approach**, assumes goodwill covers all the values that cannot be specifically identified with any identifiable tangible or intangible asset. Illustration 11-5 shows this approach. Multi-Diversified records this transaction as follows.

Illustration 11-5
Determination of
Goodwill—Master
Valuation Approach

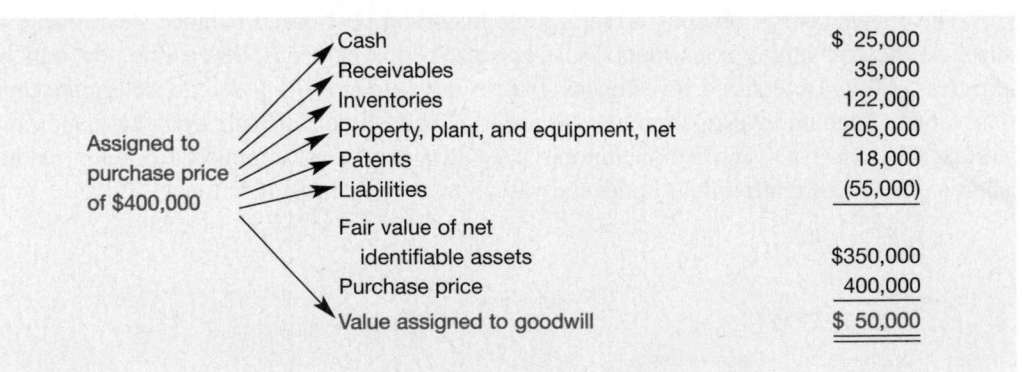

Cash	$ 25,000
Receivables	35,000
Inventories	122,000
Property, plant, and equipment, net	205,000
Patents	18,000
Liabilities	(55,000)
Fair value of net identifiable assets	$350,000
Purchase price	400,000
Value assigned to goodwill	$ 50,000

Assigned to purchase price of $400,000

---

[10]The FASB expressed concern about measuring goodwill as a residual, but noted that there is no real measurement alternative since goodwill is not separable from the company as a whole. "Business Combinations," *Statement of Financial Accounting Standards No. 141* (Norwalk, Conn.: FASB, 2001), par. B145.

Cash	25,000	
Receivables	35,000	
Inventories	122,000	
Property, Plant, and Equipment	205,000	
Patents	18,000	
Goodwill	50,000	
Liabilities		55,000
Cash		400,000

Companies often identify goodwill on the balance sheet as the **excess of cost over the fair value** of the net assets acquired.

Goodwill Write-off

Companies that recognize goodwill in a business combination **consider it to have an indefinite life and therefore should not amortize it**. The reason: Investors find the amortization charge of little use in evaluating financial performance. In addition, although goodwill may decrease over time, predicting the actual life of goodwill and an appropriate pattern of amortization is extremely difficult.

Furthermore, goodwill often is the largest intangible asset on a company's balance sheet and the investment community wants to know the amount invested in goodwill. Therefore, **companies only adjust its carrying value when goodwill is impaired**. This approach significantly impacts the income statements of some companies. For example, **AOL Time Warner** (now **Time Warner**), **AT&T**, and other companies wrote off $750 billion of goodwill in a recent year. (See "What Do the Numbers Mean?" discussion on page 572.)

Some believe that goodwill's value eventually disappears. Therefore, they argue companies should charge goodwill to expense over the periods affected. Amortizing goodwill better matches expense with revenues. Others note that the accounting treatment for purchased goodwill and goodwill created internally should be consistent. They point out that companies immediately expense goodwill created internally and thus it does not appear as an asset. Companies should follow the same treatment, they argue, for purchased goodwill. Even though these arguments may have some merit, nonamortization of goodwill combined with an adequate impairment test should provide the most useful financial information to the investment community.

Negative Goodwill—Badwill

Negative goodwill (often referred to as a **bargain purchase** or **badwill**) arises when the fair value of the assets acquired exceeds the purchase price of the assets. This situation results from a market imperfection. In this case, the seller would have been better off to sell the assets individually than in total. However, situations do occur (e.g., a forced liquidation or distressed sale due to the death of a company founder), in which the purchase price is less than the value of the net identifiable assets. This results in a credit, which is referred to as **negative goodwill** or, alternatively, as **excess of fair value over the cost acquired**, **badwill**, or **bargain purchase**.

The FASB requires that companies recognize this remaining excess as an extraordinary gain. The Board noted that extraordinary gain treatment is appropriate in order to highlight the excess, and to reflect the unusual nature and infrequent occurrence of the item. Some disagree with the approach, as it results in a gain at the time of the purchase. However, we believe that the Board took a practical approach, given that this transaction rarely occurs.[11]

---

[11]"Business Combinations," *Statement of Financial Accounting Standards No. 141* (Norwalk, Conn.: FASB, 2001), pars. B187–B192.

IMPAIRMENTS

As we discussed, in some cases, the carrying amount of a long-lived asset (property, plant, and equipment or intangible assets) is not recoverable. Therefore a company needs a write-off. This write-off is referred to as an **impairment**. Illustration 11-6 shows the reporting rules for impairments.

Illustration 11-6
Impairment Tests

Type of Long-Lived Asset	Impairment Test
Property, plant, and equipment	Recoverability test, then fair value test
Limited-life intangible	Recoverability test, then fair value test
Indefinite-life intangible other than goodwill	Fair value test
Goodwill	Fair value test on reporting unit, then fair value test on implied goodwill

---

OBJECTIVE 7

Explain the accounting issues related to impairments.

As the illustration indicates, a company uses a **recoverability test** to determine whether an impairment has occurred for property, plant, and equipment and for limited-life intangibles. If the asset's cost is not recoverable, the company then uses a **fair value test** to measure the impairment loss. For indefinite-life intangibles other than goodwill, only the fair value test is employed. Goodwill requires a more complex fair value test.

In the following sections, we look at impairments of the various types of long-lived assets shown in Illustration 11-6, above.

Impairment of Property, Plant, and Equipment

As noted above, if events or changes in circumstances indicate that the carrying amount of property, plant, or equipment may not be recoverable, companies use a **recoverability test** to determine whether an impairment has occurred. To apply the first step of the recoverability test, a company estimates the future net cash flows expected from the **use of that asset and its eventual disposition**. If the sum of the expected future net cash flows (undiscounted) is **less than the carrying amount** of the asset, the asset is considered impaired. Conversely, if the sum of the expected future net cash flows (undiscounted) is **equal to or greater than the carrying amount** of the asset, no impairment has occurred.[12]

The recoverability test screens for asset impairments. For example, if the expected future net cash flows from an asset are $400,000 and its carrying amount is $350,000, no impairment has occurred. However, if its expected future net cash flows are $300,000, an impairment has occurred. The rationale for the recoverability test relies on a basic presumption that a balance sheet should report long-lived assets at no more than the carrying amounts that are recoverable.

If the recoverability test indicates that an impairment has occurred, the company computes a loss. **The impairment loss is the amount by which the carrying amount of the asset exceeds its fair value.** The fair value of an asset is measured by its market value if an active market for it exists. If no active market exists, the **present value of expected future net cash flows** should be used. The company should use its market rate of interest

---

[12]"Accounting for the Impairment or Disposal of Long-lived Assets," *Statement of Financial Accounting Standards No. 144* (Norwalk, Conn.: 2001).

in discounting to present value. We summarize the process of determining an impairment loss as follows.

1 Review events or changes in circumstances for possible impairment.[13]

2 If the review indicates impairment, apply the recoverability test. If the sum of the expected future net cash flows from the long-lived asset is less than the carrying amount of the asset, an impairment has occurred.

3 Assuming an impairment, the impairment loss is the amount by which the carrying amount of the asset exceeds the fair value of the asset. The fair value is the market value or the present value.

Example 1: No Impairment

M. Alou Inc. has equipment that, due to changes in its use, Alou reviews for possible impairment. The asset's carrying amount is $600,000 ($800,000 cost less $200,000 accumulated depreciation). M. Alou determines that the expected future net cash flows (undiscounted) from the use of the asset and its eventual disposition are $650,000.

The recoverability test indicates that the $650,000 of expected future net cash flows from the asset's use exceed its carrying amount of $600,000. As a result, no impairment is assumed to have occurred. Recall that the undiscounted future net cash flows must be less than the asset's carrying amount for a company to deem the asset impaired and to measure the impairment loss. Therefore, M. Alou Inc. will not recognize an impairment loss in this case.

Example 2: With Impairment

Assume the same facts as Example 1, except that the expected future net cash flows from Alou's equipment are $580,000 (instead of $650,000). The recoverability test indicates that the expected future net cash flows of $580,000 from the use of the asset are less than its carrying amount of $600,000. Therefore an impairment has occurred.

The difference between the carrying amount of Alou's asset and its fair value is the **impairment loss**. This asset has a fair value of $525,000. Illustration 11-7 shows the loss computation.

Carrying amount of the equipment	$600,000
Fair value of equipment (fair value)	525,000
Loss on impairment	$ 75,000

Illustration 11-7
Computation of Impairment Loss

M. Alou records the impairment loss as follows.

Loss on Impairment	75,000	
Accumulated Depreciation		75,000

Alou reports the impairment loss as part of income from continuing operations, generally in the "Other expenses and losses" section. Alou should **not report the loss as an**

---

[13]Examples of various events or changes in circumstances are:
  a. A significant decrease in the market value of an asset.
  b. A significant change in the extent or manner in which an asset is used.
  c. A significant adverse change in legal factors or in the business climate that affects the value of an asset.
  d. An accumulation of costs significantly in excess of the amount originally expected to acquire or construct an asset.
  e. A projection or forecast that demonstrates continuing losses associated with an asset.

extraordinary item. Costs associated with an impairment loss are the same costs that would flow through operations, and Alou reports them as part of continuing operations, since these assets will continue to be used in operations. Therefore, Alou should not report the loss below "Income from continuing operations."

A company that recognizes an impairment loss should disclose the asset(s) impaired, the events leading to the impairment, the amount of the loss, and how it determined fair value (disclosing the interest rate used, if appropriate).

Impairment of Limited-Life Intangibles

The rules that apply to impairments of property, plant, and equipment also apply to limited-life intangibles. To illustrate, assume that Lerch, Inc. has a patent on how to extract oil from shale rock. Unfortunately, more efficient competing technologies have made the shale oil technology somewhat unprofitable, and the patent has provided little income to date. As a result, Lerch performs a **recoverability test**. It finds that the expected net future cash flows from this patent are $35 million, and the patent has a carrying amount of $60 million. Because the expected future net cash flows of $35 million are less than the carrying amount of $60 million, Lerch must measure an impairment loss.

Discounting the expected net future cash flows at its market rate of interest, Lerch determines the fair value of its patent to be $20 million. Illustration 11-8 shows the impairment loss computation (fair value test).

Illustration 11-8
Computation of Loss on
Impairment of Patent

Carrying amount of patent	$60,000,000
Fair value (based on present value computation)	20,000,000
Loss on impairment	$40,000,000

The journal entry to record this loss is:

Loss on Impairment	40,000,000	
Patents		40,000,000

After recognizing the impairment, the reduced carrying amount of the patents is its new cost basis. Lerch should amortize the patent's new cost over its useful life or legal life, whichever is shorter. Even if oil prices increase in subsequent periods, and the value of the patent increases, **restoration of the previously recognized impairment loss is not permitted**.

Impairment of Indefinite-Life Intangibles Other Than Goodwill

Companies should test indefinite-life intangibles other than goodwill for impairment at least annually. The impairment test for an indefinite-life asset other than goodwill is a **fair value test**. This test compares the fair value of the intangible asset with the asset's carrying amount. If the fair value of the intangible asset is less than the carrying amount, a company recognizes an impairment. This one-step test is used because it would be relatively easy for many indefinite-life assets to meet the recoverability test (because cash flows may extend many years into the future). **As a result, companies do not use the recoverability test.**

To illustrate, assume that Arcon Radio purchased a broadcast license for $2,000,000. The license is renewable every 10 years if the company provides appropriate service and does not violate Federal Communications Commission (FCC) rules and procedures. Arcon has renewed the license with the FCC twice, at a minimal cost. Because it expects cash flows to last indefinitely, Arcon reported the license as an indefinite-life intangible asset. Recently the FCC decided to no longer renew broadcast licenses, but to auction these licenses to the highest bidder. Arcon's existing license has two years remaining, and cash flows are expected for these two years. Arcon performs an impairment test and determines that the fair value of the intangible asset is $1,500,000. It therefore reports an impairment loss of $500,000, computed as follows.

Carrying amount of broadcast license	$2,000,000
Fair value of broadcast license	1,500,000
Loss on impairment	$ 500,000

Illustration 11-9
Computation of Loss on Impairment of Broadcast License

Arcon Radio now reports the license at $1,500,000, its fair value. Even if the value of the license increases in the remaining two years, Arcon may not restore the previously recognized impairment loss.

Impairment of Goodwill

The impairment rule for goodwill is a two-step process. First, a company should compare the fair value of the reporting unit to its carrying amount including goodwill. If the fair value of the reporting unit exceeds the carrying amount, the company does not consider the goodwill to be impaired. The company does not have to do anything else.

To illustrate, assume that Kohlbuy Corporation has three divisions in its company. It purchased one division, Pritt Products, four years ago for $2 million. Unfortunately, Pritt experienced operating losses over the last three quarters, and Kohlbuy management is reviewing the division for purposes of recognizing an impairment. Illustration 11-10 lists the Pritt Division's net assets, including the associated goodwill of $900,000 from purchase.

Cash	$ 200,000
Receivables	300,000
Inventory	700,000
Property, plant, and equipment (net)	800,000
Goodwill	900,000
Less: Accounts and notes payable	(500,000)
Net assets	$2,400,000

Illustration 11-10
Net Assets of Pritt Division, Including Goodwill

Kohlbuy determines that the fair value of Pritt Division is $2,800,000. **As a result, no impairment is recognized, because the fair value of the division is greater than the carrying amount of the net assets.**

However, if the fair value of Pritt Division is less than the carrying amount of the net assets, then Kohlbuy performs a second step to determine whether impairment has occurred. In the second step, Kohlbuy determines the fair value of the goodwill (referred to as *the implied value of goodwill*) and compares this amount to its carrying amount. To illustrate, assume that the fair value of Pritt's Division was $1,900,000 instead of $2,800,000. Illustration 11-11 shows the implied value of the goodwill in this case.[14]

Illustration 11-11
Determination of Implied
Value of Goodwill

Fair value of Pritt Division	$1,900,000
Net identifiable assets (excluding goodwill) ($2,400,000 − $900,000)	1,500,000
Implied value of goodwill	$ 400,000

Kohlbuy then compares the implied value of the goodwill to the recorded goodwill, to determine whether an impairment has occurred, as shown in Illustration 11-12.

Illustration 11-12
Measurement of Goodwill
Impairment

Carrying amount of goodwill	$900,000
Implied value of goodwill	400,000
Loss on impairment	$500,000

What do the numbers mean?   Real News, or Just Bookkeeping?

Companies used 2002 to take massive write-offs. As Chief Investment Strategist Abby Joseph Cohen of **Goldman Sachs** noted, "Simply stated, many companies are writing off not only the kitchen sink but the bathtub as well." For instance, **AOL Time Warner Inc.** (now **Time Warner**) had a goodwill write-down in the first quarter of that year that—by itself—reduced S&P 500 earnings by $2 to $4 on an after-tax basis, Ms. Cohen said.

In her investment letter, Ms. Cohen attributed companies' massive write-downs to "the air"— that is, a confluence of the impacts from the September 11, 2001, terrorist attacks, the official announcement that the country is in a recession, and new rules for the write-down of goodwill.

Though earnings hits can be tough to swallow in the quarter in which they are taken, they often are not of lasting impact psychologically or operationally. "The quarter in which the write-offs are recorded typically bears the statistical brunt, but may not be reflective of performance in future quarters," according to Ms. Cohen.

Goodwill impairment issues continue to grab their share of business headlines. For example, **Hewlett-Packard** has received a fair amount of criticism for it failure to take goodwill impairment charges on goodwill arising from its merger with **Compaq**. HP's chief financial officer acknowledges the issue, but plays down its significance: "There's no question that if profitability doesn't improve, there will be an impairment charge." He makes the case that it wouldn't matter much, given that it would be just a bookkeeping entry.

Source: Carol J. Loomis, "Why Carly's Big Bet Is Failing," *Fortune* (February 7, 2005), p. 50.

Beyond the Numbers

What do you think: Is an impairment charge just an entry, or can it provide some new information about management decisions, like H-P's merger with Compaq?

[14]Illustration 11-11 assumes that the carrying amount and the fair value of net identifiable assets (excluding goodwill) are the same. If different, the fair value of the net identifiable assets (excluding goodwill) is used to determine the implied value of goodwill.

Restoration of Impairment Loss

After recording an impairment loss, the reduced carrying amount of an asset held for use becomes its new cost basis. A company does not change the new cost basis except for depreciation or amortization in future periods or for additional impairments.

To illustrate, assume that Ortiz Company at December 31, 2007, has a patent with a carrying amount of $500,000. Ortiz determines the patent is impaired and writes it down to its fair value of $400,000. At the end of 2008, assume that the fair value of this asset is $480,000. The carrying amount of the patent should not change in 2008 except for the amortization taken in 2008. Ortiz **may not restore the impairment loss for an asset held for use**. The rationale for not writing the asset up in value is that the new cost basis puts the impaired asset on an equal basis with other assets that are not impaired.

Impairment of Assets Held for Disposal

What happens if a company intends to dispose of the impaired asset, instead of holding it for use? In this case, the company reports the impaired asset at the lower of cost or net realizable-value (fair value less cost to sell). Because the company intends to dispose of the asset in a short period of time, it uses net realizable value in order to provide a better measure of the net cash flows that it will receive from this asset.

A company does not depreciate or amortize assets held for disposal during the period it holds them. The rationale is that depreciation is inconsistent with the notion of assets to be disposed of and with the use of the lower of cost or net realizable value. In other words, **assets held for disposal are like inventory; companies should report them at the lower of cost or net realizable value**.

Because a company will recover assets held for disposal through sale rather than through operations, it continually revalues them. Each period, a company reports them at the lower of cost or net realizable value. Thus **a company can write up or write down an asset held for disposal in future periods, as long as the value after the writeup never exceeds the carrying amount of the asset before the impairment**. Companies should report losses or gains related to these impaired assets as part of "**Income from continuing operations**."

INTERNATIONAL INSIGHT

International accounting standards permit write-ups for subsequent recoveries of impairment, whereas U.S. GAAP prohibits those write-ups, except for assets to be disposed of.

Try it out! Presented below is information related to a copyright owned by Hastings Corporation at December 31, 2008.

Cost	$3,400,000
Carrying amount	1,700,000
Expected future net cash flows	1,600,000
Fair value	1,300,000

Assume that Hastings Corporation will continue using this copyright in the future. As of December 31, 2008, the copyright is estimated to have a remaining useful life of 8 years.

Instructions

a   Prepare the necessary journal entry to record an impairment of the copyright (if any) at December 31, 2008.

b   Compute the copyright amortization expense for 2009.

Loss on Impairment	400,000	
Copyrights ($1,700,000 − $1,300,000)		400,000

b Copyright amortization expense: $1,300,000 ÷ 8 years = $162,500

RESEARCH AND DEVELOPMENT COSTS

OBJECTIVE 8

Identify the conceptual issues related to research and development costs.

Research and development (R&D) costs are not in themselves intangible assets. However we present the accounting for R&D costs here, because research and development activities frequently result in the development of something that a company patents or copyrights (such as a new product, process, idea, formula, composition, or literary work).

Many companies spend considerable sums of money on research and development to create new products or processes, to improve present products, and to discover new knowledge that may be valuable at some future date. Illustration 11-13 shows the outlays for R&D made by selected U.S. companies.

Illustration 11-13
R&D Outlays, as a Percentage of Sales and Profits

Company	R&D ($ million)	R&D/Sales	R&D/Net Income
Caterpillar	$ 928.0	3.07%	45.60%
Deere & Co.	611.6	3.06%	43.50%
Dell	463.0	0.94%	15.22%
General Mills	158.0	1.43%	14.98%
Hewlett-Packard	3,506.0	4.39%	100.26%
Johnson & Johnson	5,203.0	10.99%	61.15%
Kellogg	148.9	1.55%	16.72%

INTERNATIONAL INSIGHT

International accounting standards require the capitalization of appropriate development expenditures. This conflicts with U.S. GAAP.

Two difficulties arise in accounting for these research and development (R&D) expenditures: (1) identifying the costs associated with particular activities, projects, or achievements, and (2) determining the magnitude of the future benefits and length of time over which such benefits may be realized. Because of these latter uncertainties, the accounting practice in this area has been simplified. **Companies must expense all research and development costs when incurred.**[15]

Identifying R&D Activities

Illustration 11-14 (page 575) shows the definitions for **research activities** and **development activities**. These definitions differentiate research and development costs from similar costs.[16]

Note that R&D activities do not include routine or periodic alterations to existing products, production lines, manufacturing processes, and other ongoing operations, even

[15]"Accounting for Research and Development Costs," *Statement of Financial Accounting Standards No. 2* (Stamford, Conn.: FASB, 1974), par. 12.
[16]Ibid., par. 8.

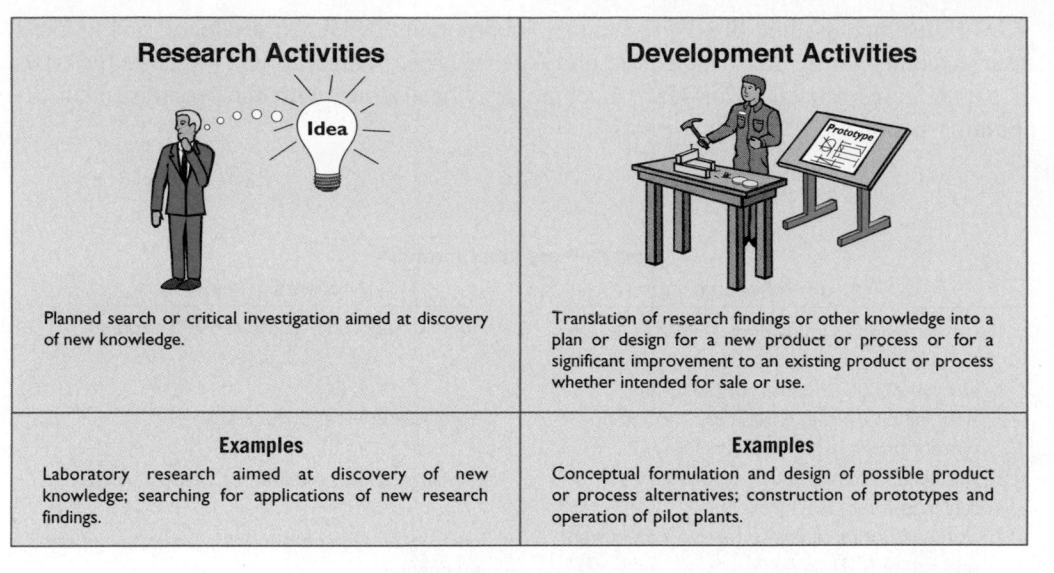

Illustration 11-14
R&D Activities

though these alterations may represent improvements. For example, routine ongoing efforts to refine, enrich, or improve the qualities of an existing product are not considered R&D activities.

Accounting for R&D Activities

The costs associated with R&D activities and the accounting treatments accorded them are as follows.

1   *Materials, Equipment, and Facilities.* Expense the entire costs, **unless the items have alternative future uses** (in other R&D projects or otherwise), in which case carry as inventory and allocate as consumed; or capitalize and depreciate as used.

2   *Personnel.* Expense salaries, wages, and other related costs of personnel engaged in R&D as incurred.

3   *Purchased Intangibles.* Expense the **entire cost, unless the items have alternative future uses** (in other R&D projects or otherwise), in which case capitalize and amortize.

4   *Contract Services.* Expense the costs of services performed by others in connection with the R&D as incurred.

5   *Indirect Costs.* Include a reasonable allocation of indirect costs in R&D costs, except for general and administrative cost, which must be clearly related in order to be included in R&D.[17]

Consistent with item 1 above, if a company owns a research facility consisting of buildings, laboratories, and equipment that conducts R&D activities and that has alternative future uses (in other R&D projects or otherwise), it should capitalize the facility as an operational asset. The company accounts for depreciation and other costs related to such research facilities as R&D expenses.[18]

[17]Ibid., par. 11.

[18]Companies in **the extractive industries** can use the following accounting treatment for the unique costs of research, exploration, and development activities and for those costs that are similar to but not classified as R&D costs: (1) expense as incurred, (2) capitalize and either depreciate or amortize over an appropriate period of time, or (3) accumulate as part of inventoriable costs. Choice of the appropriate accounting treatment for such costs is based on the degree of certainty of future benefits and the principle of matching revenues and expenses.

OBJECTIVE 9
Describe the accounting for research and development and similar costs.

To illustrate, assume that Next Century Incorporated develops, produces, and markets laser machines for medical, industrial, and defense uses.[19] Illustration 11-15 lists the types of expenditures related to its laser machine activities, along with the recommended accounting treatment.

Illustration 11-15

Sample R&D Expenditures and Their Accounting Treatment

Next Century Incorporated

Type of Expenditure	Accounting Treatment
1. Construction of long-range research facility for use in current and future projects (three-story, 400,000-square-foot building).	Capitalize and depreciate as R&D expense.
2. Acquisition of R&D equipment for use on current project only.	Expense immediately as R&D.
3. Acquisition of machinery to be used on current and future R&D projects.	Capitalize and depreciate as R&D expense.
4. Purchase of materials to be used on current and future R&D projects.	Inventory and allocate to R&D projects; expense as consumed.
5. Salaries of research staff designing new laser bone scanner.	Expense immediately as R&D.
6. Research costs incurred under contract with New Horizon, Inc., and billable monthly.	Record as a receivable (reimbursable expenses).
7. Material, labor, and overhead costs of prototype laser scanner.	Expense immediately as R&D.
8. Costs of testing prototype and design modifications.	Expense immediately as R&D.
9. Legal fees to obtain patent on new laser scanner.	Capitalize as patent and amortize to overhead as part of cost of goods manufactured.
10. Executive salaries.	Expense as operating expense (general and administrative).
11. Cost of marketing research to promote new laser scanner.	Expense as operating expense (selling).
12. Engineering costs incurred to advance the laser scanner to full production stage.	Expense immediately as R&D.
13. Costs of successfully defending patent on laser scanner.	Capitalize as patent and amortize to overhead as part of cost of goods manufactured.
14. Commissions to sales staff marketing new laser scanner.	Expense as operating expense (selling).

Other Costs Similar to R&D Costs

Many costs have characteristics similar to research and development costs. Examples are start-up costs, initial operating losses, and advertising costs. For the most part these costs are expensed as incurred. Illustration 11-16 presents a brief explanation of costs and the accounting for them.

---

[19]Sometimes companies conduct R&D activities for other companies under a contractual arrangement. In this case, the contract usually specifies that the company performing the R&D work be reimbursed for all direct costs and certain specific indirect costs, plus a profit element. Because reimbursement is expected, the company doing the R&D work records the R&D costs as a receivable. The company for whom the work has been performed reports these costs as R&D and expenses them as incurred.

For a more complete discussion of how an enterprise should account for funding of its R&D by others, see "Research and Development Arrangements," *Statement of Financial Accounting Standards No. 68* (Stamford, Conn.: FASB, 1982).

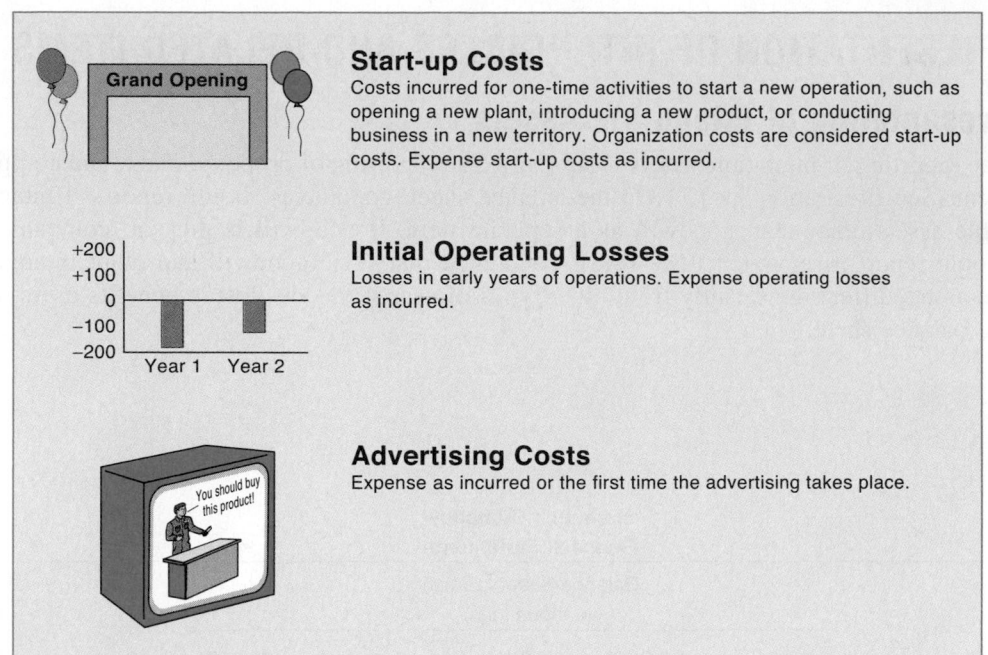

Illustration 11-16
Accounting for Other
Costs Similar to
R&D Costs

Note that it is not uncommon for start-up activities to occur at the same time as other activities, such as the acquisition or development of assets. For example, in opening a new plant, the cost of the plant is an asset and should be depreciated using appropriate GAAP reporting guidelines. Similarly, tangible assets used in advertising, such as billboards or blimps, are recorded as assets because they have alternative future uses.[20]

Conceptual Questions

The requirement that companies expense immediately all R&D costs (as well as start-up and other similar costs) incurred internally is a conservative, practical solution. It ensures consistency in practice and uniformity among companies. But the practice of immediately writing off expenditures made in the expectation of benefiting future periods is conceptually incorrect.

Proponents of immediate expensing contend that from an income statement standpoint, long-run application of this standard frequently makes little difference. They argue that because of the ongoing nature of most companies' R&D activities, the amount of R&D cost charged to expense each accounting period is about the same, whether there is immediate expensing or capitalization and subsequent amortization. Others criticize this practice. They believe that the balance sheet should report an intangible asset related to expenditures that have future benefit. To preclude capitalization of all R&D expenditures removes from the balance sheet what may be a company's most valuable asset. This standard represents one of the many trade-offs made among relevance, reliability, and cost-benefit considerations.[21]

WHAT'S THE PRINCIPLE?

The requirement that companies expense all R&D costs as incurred is an example of the conflict between *relevance* and *reliability*. Here, this requirement leans strongly in support of *reliability*, as well as *conservatism*, *consistency*, and *comparability*. No attempt is made to match costs and revenues.

---

[20]"Reporting on the Costs of Start-up Activities," *Statement of Position 98-5* (New York: AICPA, 1998).

[21]Research findings indicate that capitalizing R&D costs may be helpful to investors. For example, one study showed a significant relationship between R&D outlays and subsequent benefits in the form of increased productivity, earnings, and shareholder value for R&D–intensive companies. Baruch Lev and Theodore Sougiannis, "The Capitalization, Amortization, and Value-Relevance of R&D," *Journal of Accounting and Economics* (February 1996).

Another study found that there was a significant decline in earnings usefulness for companies that were forced to switch from capitalizing to expensing R&D costs, and that the decline appears to persist over time. Martha L. Loudder and Bruce K. Behn, "Alternative Income Determination Rules and Earnings Usefulness: The Case of R&D Costs," *Contemporary Accounting Research* (Fall 1995).

PRESENTATION OF INTANGIBLES AND RELATED ITEMS

Presentation of Intangible Assets

OBJECTIVE **10**

Indicate the presentation of intangible assets and related items.

The reporting of intangible assets is similar to the reporting of property, plant, and equipment (See Illustration 11-17.) On the balance sheet, companies should report all intangible assets other than goodwill as a separate item. If goodwill is present, companies should report it separately. The FASB concluded that since goodwill and other intangible assets differ significantly from other types of assets, this disclosure benefits users of the balance sheet.

Illustration 11-17
Intangible Asset
Disclosures

Harbaugh Company
Financial Statements

Balance Sheet (partial)
(in thousands)

Intangible assets (Note C)	$3,840
Goodwill (Note D)	2,575

Income Statement (partial)
(in thousands)

Continuing operations (partial)

Amortization expense	$380
Impairment losses (goodwill)	46

Notes to the Financial Statements

Note C: Acquired Intangible Assets

	As of December 31, 2008	
	Gross Carrying Amount	Accumulated Amortization
Amortized intangible assets		
Trademark	$2,000	$(100)
Customer list	500	(310)
Other	60	(10)
Total	$2,560	$(420)
Unamortized intangible assets		
Licenses	$1,300	
Trademark	400	
Total	$1,700	

Aggregate Amortization Expense

For year ended 12/31/08	$380

Estimated Amortization Expense

For year ended 12/31/09	$200
For year ended 12/31/10	90
For year ended 12/31/11	70
For year ended 12/31/12	60
For year ended 12/31/13	50

Note D: Goodwill

The changes in the carrying amount of goodwill for the year ended December 31, 2008, are as follows:

($000s)	Technology Segment	Communications Segment	Total
Balance as of January 1, 2008	$1,413	$904	$2,317
Goodwill acquired during year	189	115	304
Impairment losses	—	(46)	(46)
Balance as of December 31, 2008	$1,602	$973	$2,575

The Communications segment is tested for impairment in the third quarter, after the annual forecasting process. Due to an increase in competition in the Texas and Louisiana cable industry, operating profits and cash flows were lower than expected in the fourth quarter of 2007 and the first and second quarters of 2008. Based on that trend, the earnings forecast for the next 5 years was revised. In September 2008, a goodwill impairment loss of $46 was recognized in the Communications reporting unit. The fair value of that reporting unit was estimated using the expected present value of future cash flows.

On the income statement, companies should present amortization expense and impairment losses for intangible assets other than goodwill as part of continuing operations. Goodwill impairment losses should also be presented as a separate line item in the continuing operations section, unless the goodwill impairment is associated with a discontinued operation.

The notes to the financial statements should include information about acquired intangible assets, including the aggregate amortization expense for each of the succeeding five years. If companies do not use separate accumulated amortization accounts, they should disclose accumulated amortization in the notes. The notes should include information about changes in the carrying amount of goodwill during the period. As noted earlier, Illustration 11-17 shows the type of disclosure made related to intangible assets in the financial statements and related notes for Harbaugh Company.

Presentation of Research and Development Costs

Acceptable accounting practice requires that companies disclose in the financial statements (generally in the notes) the total R&D costs charged to expense each period for which they present an income statement. **Merck & Co., Inc.**, a global research pharmaceutical company, reported both internal and acquired research and development in its recent income statement, as shown in Illustration 11-18.

Additional Disclosures of Intangibles and R&D Costs

Merck & Co., Inc.
(in millions)

	Years Ended December 31		
	2006	2005	2004
Sales	$22,636.0	$22,011.9	$22,972.8
Costs, Expenses, and Other			
Materials and production	6,001.1	5,149.6	4,965.7
Marketing and administrative	8,165.4	7,155.5	7,238.7
Research and development	4,782.9	3,848.0	4,010.2
Restructuring costs	142.3	322.2	107.6
Equity income from affiliates	(2,294.4)	(1,717.1)	(1,008.2)
Other (income) expense, net	(382.7)	(110.2)	(344.0)
	$16,414.6	$14,648.0	$14,970.0

Illustration 11-18
Income Statement Disclosure of R&D Costs

In addition, Merck provides a discussion about R&D expenditures in its annual report, as shown in Illustration 11-19.

Illustration 11-19
Merck's R&D
Disclosure

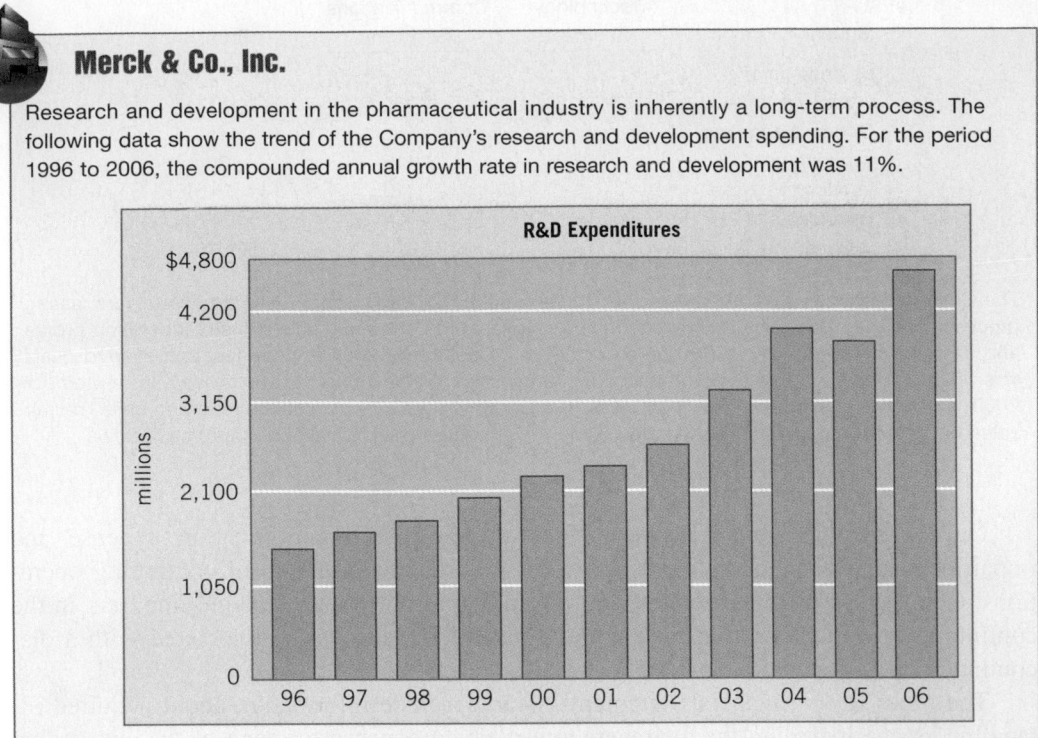

Merck & Co., Inc.

Research and development in the pharmaceutical industry is inherently a long-term process. The following data show the trend of the Company's research and development spending. For the period 1996 to 2006, the compounded annual growth rate in research and development was 11%.

You will want to read the CONVERGENCE CORNER
on page 582 for discussion of how international convergence efforts relate to the accounting for intangible assets.

ACCOUNTING, ANALYSIS, PRINCIPLES

Accounting

On January 2, 2008, Raconteur Corp. reported the following intangible assets: (1) copyright with a carrying value of $15,000; and (2) a trade name with a carrying value of $8,500. The trade name has a remaining life of 5 years and can be renewed at nominal cost indefinitely. The copyright has a remaining life of 10 years.

At December 31, 2008, Raconteur assessed the intangible assets for possible impairment and developed the following information.

	Estimated Expected Cash Flows (Undiscounted)	Fair Value
Copyright	$20,000	$16,000
Trade name	10,000	5,000

Prepare any journal entries required for Raconteur's intangible assets at December 31, 2008.

Analysis

Many stock analysts indicate a preference for less-volatile operating income measures. Such measures make it easier to predict future income and cash flows, using reported income measures. How does the accounting for impairments of intangible assets affect the volatility of operating income?

Principles

Many accounting issues involve a tradeoff between the primary characteristics of relevance and reliability of information. How does the accounting for intangible asset impairments reflect this tradeoff?

Solution

Accounting

Copyright Amortization Expense	1,500	
Copyright ($15,000 ÷ 10)		1,500

There is a full year of amortization on the copyright. There is no amortization for the trade name, which is considered an indefinite-life intangible.

Loss on Impairment (Trade name)	3,500	
Trade name ($8,500 − $5,000)		3,500

The recoverability test for the copyright indicates that the copyright is not impaired: The expected cash flows (undiscounted) of $20,000 are greater than the carrying value of $13,500 ($15,000 − $1,500).

The trade name is tested for impairment using a fair value test. Thus, Raconteur writes it down to the fair value of $5,000.

Analysis

Impairment losses are recorded in operating income. Because impairments tend to be non-recurring items, their recognition can make operating income more volatile from year to year. This volatility effect can be particularly severe for indefinite-life intangibles, such as a trade name or goodwill. The higher carrying values (due to no amortization), combined with the annual fair-value impairment test, can result in impairment losses having a significant impact on operating income.

Principles

The accounting for impairments provides relevant information about intangible assets by indicating in a timely fashion that intangible assets have declined in value. However, providing this timely information requires significant subjective judgments related to estimating (1) expected cash flows for the cash flow recovery test and (2) fair values in determining the amount of the impairment to be recognized. These estimates may raise concerns about the reliability of impairment-loss amounts.

CONVERGENCE CORNER

Intangible Assets

There are some significant differences between iGAAP and U.S. GAAP in the accounting for both intangible assets and impairments. iGAAP related to intangible assets is presented in *IAS 38* ("Intangible Assets"). iGAAP related to impairments is found in *IAS 36* ("Impairment of Assets").

 RELEVANT FACTS

• As in U.S. GAAP, under iGAAP the costs associated with research and development are segregated into the two components. Costs in the research phase are always expensed under both iGAAP and U.S. GAAP. Under iGAAP, however, costs in the development phase are capitalized once technological feasibility is achieved.

• iGAAP permits some capitalization of internally generated intangible assets (e.g., brand value), if it is probable there will be a future benefit and the amount can be reliably measured. U.S. GAAP requires expensing of all costs associated with internally generated intangibles.

• iGAAP requires an impairment test at each reporting date for long-lived assets and intangibles and records an impairment if the asset's carrying amount exceeds its recoverable amount. The recoverable amount is the higher of the asset's fair value less costs to sell and its value in use. *Value in use* is the future cash flows to be derived from the particular assets, discounted to present value. Under U.S. GAAP, impairment loss is measured as the excess of the carrying amount over the asset's fair value.

• iGAAP allows reversal of impairment losses when there has been a change in economic conditions or in the expected use of the asset. Under U.S. GAAP, impairment losses cannot be reversed for assets to be held and used; the impairment loss results in a new cost basis for the asset. iGAAP and U.S. GAAP are similar in the accounting for impairments of assets held for disposal.

• iGAAP and U.S. GAAP are similar for intangibles acquired in a business combination. That is, companies recognize an intangible asset separately from goodwill if the intangible represents contractual or legal rights or is capable of being separated or divided and sold, transferred, licensed, rented, or exchanged. Under iGAAP, companies recognize acquired *in-process research and development* (IPR&D) as a separate intangible asset if it meets the definition of an intangible asset and its fair value can be measured reliably. U.S. GAAP currently requires companies to write off acquired IPR&D.

 ABOUT THE NUMBERS

To illustrate the effect of differences in the accounting for brands and IPR&D, consider the following disclosure by GlaxoSmithKline plc in its 2006 annual report.

Notes to the Financial Statements

Intangible assets (in part):
The following table sets out the iGAAP to U.S. GAAP adjustments required to the iGAAP income statement for amortisation of brands:

Income Statement

	2006 (£ million)
Amortisation charge under iGAAP	139
Amortisation charge under US GAAP	1,454
iGAAP to U.S. GAAP adjustment	1,315

In addition to the above adjustments for amortisation and impairments, further iGAAP to U.S. GAAP adjustments arose during the year of £125 million in respect of the acquisition and disposal of in-process R&D, licences, patents etc. which are capitalised under iGAAP but charged directly to research and development expense under U.S. GAAP.

Thus, GlaxoSmithKline would report lower income by £1.3 billion if it accounted for its brands under U.S. GAAP. In addition, its assets and income would be lower under U.S. GAAP by £125 million due to the write-off of in-process R&D.

ON THE HORIZON

The IASB and FASB have identified a project relating to the accounting for research and development that could possibly converge iGAAP and U.S. GAAP on the issue of in-process R&D. One possibility is to amend U.S. GAAP to allow capitalization of in-process R&D similar to the provisions in iGAAP. A second project, in a very preliminary stage, would consider expanded recognition of internally generated intangible assets. As indicated, iGAAP permits more recognition of intangibles compared to U.S. GAAP. Thus, it will be challenging to develop converged standards for intangible assets, given the long-standing prohibition on capitalizing internally generated intangible assets and research and development in U.S. GAAP. Learn more about the timeline for the intangible asset project at the IASB website: *http://www.iasb.org/Current+Projects/IASB+Projects/IASB+Work+Plan.htm.*

Key Terms

amortization, 557
copyright, 560
development activities, 574
fair value test, 570
franchise, 560
goodwill, 564
impairment, 568
indefinite-life intangibles, 557
intangible assets, 556

license (permit), 561
limited-life intangibles, 557
master valuation approach, 566
negative goodwill (badwill), 567
patent, 561
recoverability test, 568
research activities, 574
research and development (R&D) costs, 574
trademark, trade name, 558

Summary of Learning Objectives

1 Describe the characteristics of intangible assets. Intangible assets have two main characteristics: (1) They lack physical existence, and (2) they are not financial instruments. In most cases, intangible assets provide services over a period of years. As a result, they are normally classified as long-term assets.

2 Identify the costs to include in the initial valuation of intangible assets. Intangibles are recorded at cost. Cost includes all costs of acquisition and expenditures necessary to make the intangible asset ready for its intended use. If intangibles are acquired for stock or in exchange for other assets, the cost of the intangible is the fair value of the consideration given or the fair value of the intangible received, whichever is more clearly evident. When a company buys several intangibles, or a combination of intangibles and tangibles, in a "basket purchase," it should allocate the cost on the basis of fair values.

3 Explain the procedure for amortizing intangible assets. Intangibles have either a limited useful life or an indefinite useful life. Companies amortize intangible assets with a limited life. They do not amortize intangible assets with indefinite lives. Limited-life intangibles should be amortized by systematic charges to expense over their useful life. The useful life should reflect the period over which these assets will contribute to cash flows. The amount to report for amortization expense should reflect the pattern in which a company consumes or uses up the asset, if it can reliably determine that pattern. Otherwise the company should use a straight-line approach.

4 Describe the types of intangible assets. Major types of intangibles are: (1) *marketing-related intangibles*, used in the marketing or promotion of products or services; (2) *customer-related intangibles*, resulting from interactions with outside parties; (3) *artistic-related intangibles*, giving ownership rights to such items as plays and literary works; (4) *contract-related intangibles*, repre-senting the value of rights that arise from contractual arrangements; (5) *technology-related intangibles*, relating to innovations or technological advances; and (6) *goodwill*, arising from business combinations.

5 Explain the conceptual issues related to goodwill. Goodwill is unique because unlike receivables, inventories, and patents that a company can sell or exchange individually in the marketplace, goodwill can be identified only with the company as a whole. Goodwill is a "going concern" valuation and is recorded only when an entire business is purchased. A company should not capitalize goodwill generated internally in the accounts, because measuring the components of goodwill is too complex and associating any costs with future benefits too difficult. The future benefits of goodwill may have no relationship to the costs incurred in the development of that goodwill. Goodwill may exist even in the absence of specific costs to develop it.

6 Describe the accounting procedures for recording goodwill. To record goodwill, a company compares the fair value of the net tangible and identifiable intangible assets with the purchase price of the acquired business. The difference is considered goodwill. Goodwill is the residual—the excess of cost over fair value of the identifiable net assets acquired. Goodwill is often identified on the balance sheet as the excess of cost over the fair value of the net assets acquired.

7 Explain the accounting issues related to impairments. Impairment of a long-lived asset occurs when the carrying amount of the asset is not recoverable. Impairments for property, plant, and equipment and for limited-life intangible assets are based on a recoverability test and a fair value test. Indefinite-life intangibles use only a fair value test. Goodwill impairment uses a two-step process: First, test the fair value of the reporting unit, then do the fair value test on implied goodwill.

8 Identify the conceptual issues related to research and development costs. R&D costs are not in themselves intangible assets, but R&D activities frequently result in the development of something a company patents or copyrights. The difficulties in accounting for R&D expenditures are: (1) identifying the costs associated with particular activities, projects, or achievements, and (2) determining the magnitude of the future benefits and length of time over which a company may realize such benefits. Because of these latter uncertainties, companies are required to expense all research and development costs when incurred.

9 Describe the accounting for research and development and similar costs. Pages 575–576 show the costs associated with R&D activities and the accounting treatment accorded them. Many costs have characteristics similar to R&D costs. Examples are start-up costs, initial operating losses, and advertising costs. For the most part, these costs are expensed as incurred, similar to the accounting for R&D costs.

10 Indicate the presentation of intangible assets and related items. The reporting of intangibles differs from the reporting of property, plant, and equipment in that contra accounts are not normally shown. On the balance sheet, companies should report all intangible assets other than goodwill as a separate item. If goodwill is present, it too should be reported as a separate item. On the income statement, companies should report amortization expense and impairment losses in continuing operations. The notes to the financial statements have additional detailed information. Financial statements must disclose the total R&D costs charged to expense each period for which an income statement is presented.

REVIEW EXERCISE

Argot Co., organized in 2007, provided you with the following information.

1 Purchased a franchise for $42,000 on July 1, 2007. The rights to the franchise will expire on July 1, 2015.

2 Incurred a net loss of $33,000 in 2007, including a state incorporation fee of $2,000 and related legal fees of organizing, $5,000. (All fees were incurred in 2007.)

3 Purchased a patent on January 2, 2008, for $80,000. It is estimated to have a 10-year life.

4 Costs incurred to develop a secret formula as of March 1, 2008, were $90,000. The secret formula has an indefinite life.

5 On April 1, 2008, Argot Co. purchased a small manufacturing concern for $700,000. Goodwill recorded in the transaction was $180,000.

6 On July 1, 2008, legal fees for successful defense of the patent purchased on January 2, 2008, were $11,400.

7 Research and development costs incurred as of September 1, 2008, were $110,000.

Instructions

a Prepare the journal entries to record all the entries related to the patent during 2008.

b At December 31, 2008, an impairment test is performed on the franchise purchased in 2007. It is estimated that the net cash flows to be received from the franchise will be $25,000, and its fair value is $13,000. Compute the amount of impairment, if any, to be recorded on December 31, 2008.

c What is the amount to be reported for intangible assets on the balance sheet at December 31, 2007? At December 31, 2008?

Solution

a January 2, 2008

Patents	80,000	
Cash		80,000

July 1, 2008

Patents	11,400	
Cash		11,400

December 31, 2008

Patent Amortization Expense	8,600	
Patents		8,600

Computation of patent expense:

$80,000 × 12/120 =	$8,000
$11,400 × 6/114 =	600
Total	$8,600

b Computation of impairment loss:

Cost	$42,000
Less: Accumulated amortization ($42,000 × 18/96)	7,875
Book value	$34,125

Book value of $34,125 is greater than net cash flows of $25,000. Therefore the franchise is impaired. The impairment loss is computed as follows.

Book value	$34,125
Fair value	13,000
Loss on impairment	$21,125

c Intangible assets as of December 31, 2007:

Franchise	$39,375*

*Cost	$42,000
Less: Accumulated amortization ($42,000 × 6/96)	2,625
Total	$39,375

The net loss and all organization costs are deducted in 2007.

Intangible assets as of December 31, 2008:

Franchise	$ 13,000
Patents ($80,000 + $11,400 − $8,600)	$ 82,800
Goodwill	$180,000

All the costs to develop the secret formula and the research and development costs are expensed as incurred.

Questions

1 What are the two main characteristics of intangible assets?

2 If intangibles are acquired for stock, how is the cost of the intangible determined?

3 Intangibles have either a limited useful life or an indefinite useful life. How should these two different types of intangibles be amortized?

4 Why does the accounting profession make a distinction between internally created intangibles and purchased intangibles?

5 In 2008 Sheila Wright Corp. spent $420,000 for "goodwill" visits by sales personnel to key customers. The purpose of these visits was to build a solid, friendly relationship for the future and to gain insight into the problems and needs of the companies served. How should this expenditure be reported?

6 What are factors to be considered in estimating the useful life of an intangible asset?

7 What should be the pattern of amortization for a limited-life intangible?

8 **Columbia Sportswear Company** acquired a trademark that is helpful in distinguishing one of its new products. The trademark is renewable every 10 years at minimal cost. All evidence indicates that this trademark product will generate cash flows for an indefinite period of time. How should this trademark be amortized?

9 Michael Redd Company spent $190,000 developing a new process, $45,000 in legal fees to obtain a patent, and $91,000 to market the process that was patented, all in the year 2008. How should these costs be accounted for in 2008?

10 No Doubt purchased a patent for $450,000 which has an estimated useful life of 10 years. Its pattern of use or consumption cannot be reliably determined. Prepare the entry to record the amortization of the patent in its first year of use.

11 Explain the difference between artistic-related intangible assets and contract-related intangible assets.

12 What is goodwill? What is negative goodwill?

13 Under what circumstances is it appropriate to record goodwill in the accounts? How should goodwill, properly recorded on the books, be written off in order to conform with generally accepted accounting principles?

14 In examining financial statements, financial analysts often write off goodwill immediately. Evaluate this procedure.

15 Astaire Inc. is considering the write-off of a limited life intangible because of its lack of profitability. Explain to the management of Astaire how to determine whether a write-off is permitted.

16 Assume the same information as question 15, except that an indefinite-life intangible other than goodwill is being considered for write-off. How would this situation be recorded?

17 Kuga Co. has equipment with a carrying amount of $700,000. The expected future net cash flows from the equipment is $705,000, and its fair value is $590,000. The equipment is expected to be used in operations in the future. What amount (if any) should Kuga report as an impairment to its equipment?

18 Last year Blair Company recorded an impairment on an intangible asset held for use. Recent appraisals indicate that the asset has increased in value. Should Blair record this recovery in value?

19 Explain how losses on impaired assets should be reported in income.

20 Mills Company determines that its goodwill is impaired. It finds that its implied goodwill is $380,000 and its recorded goodwill is $400,000. The fair value of its identifiable assets is $1,450,000. What is the amount of goodwill impaired?

21 What is the nature of research and development costs?

22 Research and development activities may include (a) personnel costs, (b) materials and equipment costs, and (c) indirect costs. What is the recommended accounting treatment for these three types of R&D costs?

23 Which of the following activities should be expensed currently as R&D costs?

(a) Testing in search for or evaluation of product or process alternatives.

(b) Engineering follow-through in an early phase of commercial production.

(c) Legal work in connection with patent applications or litigation, and the sale or licensing of patents.

24 Indicate the proper accounting for the following items.

(a) Organization costs.

(b) Advertising costs.

(c) Operating losses.

25 In 2007, Cassie Logan Corporation developed a new product that will be marketed in 2008. In connection with the development of this product, the following costs were incurred in 2007: research and development costs $420,000; materials and supplies consumed $60,000; and compensation paid to research consultants $125,000. It is anticipated that these costs will be recovered in 2010. What is the amount of research and development costs that Cassie Logan should record in 2007 as a charge to expense?

26 Recently, a group of university students decided to incorporate for the purposes of selling a process to recycle the waste product from manufacturing cheese. Some of the initial costs involved were legal fees and office expenses incurred in starting the business, state incorporation fees, and stamp taxes. One student wishes to charge these costs against revenue in the current period. Another wishes to defer these costs and amortize them in the future. Which student is correct?

27 An intangible asset with an estimated useful life of 30 years was acquired on January 1, 1998, for $450,000. On January 1, 2008, a review was made of intangible assets and their expected service lives, and it was determined that this asset had an estimated useful life of 30 more years from the date of the review. What is the amount of amortization for this intangible in 2008?

Brief Exercises

(LO 2, 3) **BE11-1** Doom Troopers Corporation purchases a patent from Judge Dredd Company on January 1, 2008, for $64,000. The patent has a remaining legal life of 16 years. Doom Troopers feels the patent will be useful for 10 years. Prepare Doom Troopers' journal entries to record the purchase of the patent and 2008 amortization.

BE11-2 Use the information provided in BE11-1. Assume that at January 1, 2010, the carrying amount of the patent on Doom Troopers' books is $51,200. In January, Doom Troopers spends $24,000 successfully defending a patent suit. Doom Troopers still feels the patent will be useful until the end of 2017. Prepare the journal entries to record the $24,000 expenditure and 2010 amortization. **(LO 2, 3)**

BE11-3 Dr. Robotnik's, Inc., spent $60,000 in attorney fees while developing the trade name of its new product, the Mean Bean Machine. Prepare the journal entries to record the $60,000 expenditure and the first year's amortization, using an 8-year life. **(LO 2, 3)**

BE11-4 Spidey Corporation commenced operations in early 2008. The corporation incurred $70,000 of costs such as fees to underwriters, legal fees, state fees, and promotional expenditures during its formation. Prepare journal entries to record the $70,000 expenditure and 2008 amortization, if any. **(LO 9)**

BE11-5 Knuckles Corporation obtained a franchise from Sonic Hedgehog Inc. for a cash payment of $100,000 on April 1, 2008. The franchise grants Knuckles the right to sell certain products and services for a period of 8 years. Prepare Knuckles' April 1 journal entry and December 31 adjusting entry. **(LO 2, 3)**

BE11-6 On September 1, 2008, Dungeon Corporation acquired Dragon Enterprises for a cash payment of $750,000. At the time of purchase, Dragon's balance sheet showed assets of $620,000, liabilities of $200,000, and stockholders' equity of $420,000. The fair value of Dragon's assets is estimated to be $800,000. Compute the amount of goodwill acquired by Dungeon. **(LO 6)**

BE11-7 Kinoland Company owns machinery that cost $900,000 and has accumulated depreciation of $360,000. The expected future net cash flows from the use of this asset are expected to be $500,000. The fair value of the equipment is $400,000. Prepare the journal entry, if any, to record the impairment loss. **(LO 7)**

BE11-8 Nobunaga Corporation owns a patent that has a carrying amount of $330,000. Nobunaga expects future net cash flows from this patent to total $190,000. The fair value of the patent is $110,000. Prepare Nobunaga's journal entry, if necessary, to record the loss on impairment. **(LO 7)**

BE11-9 Evander Corporation purchased Holyfield Company 3 years ago and at that time recorded goodwill of $400,000. The Holyfield Division's net assets, including the goodwill, have a carrying amount of $800,000. The fair value of the division is estimated to be $1,000,000. Prepare Evander's journal entry, if necessary, to record impairment of the goodwill. **(LO 7)**

BE11-10 Use the information provided in BE11-9. Assume that the fair value of the division is estimated to be $750,000 and the implied goodwill is $325,000. Prepare Evander's journal entry, if necessary, to record impairment of the goodwill. **(LO 7)**

BE11-11 Dorsett Corporation incurred the following costs in 2008. **(LO 9)**

Cost of laboratory research aimed at discovery of new knowledge	$140,000
Cost of testing in search for product alternatives	100,000
Cost of engineering activity required to advance the design of a product to the manufacturing stage	210,000
	$450,000

Prepare the necessary 2008 journal entry or entries for Dorsett.

BE11-12 Indicate whether the following items are capitalized or expensed in the current year. **(LO 9)**

(a) Purchase cost of a patent from a competitor.
(b) Research and development costs.
(c) Organizational costs.
(d) Costs incurred internally to create goodwill.

BE11-13 Langer Industries had one patent recorded on its books as of January 1, 2008. This patent had a book value of $240,000 and a remaining useful life of 8 years. During 2008, Langer incurred research and development costs of $96,000 and brought a patent infringement suit against a competitor. On December 1, 2008, Langer received the good news that its patent was valid and that its competitor could not use the process Langer had patented. The company incurred $85,000 to defend this patent. At what amount should patent(s) be reported on the December 31, 2008, balance sheet, assuming monthly amortization of patents? **(LO 3, 10)**

BE11-14 Wiggens Industries acquired two copyrights during 2008. One copyright related to a textbook that was developed internally at a cost of $9,900. This textbook is estimated to have a useful life of 3 years from September 1, 2008, the date it was published. The second copyright (a history research textbook) was purchased from University Press on December 1, 2008, for $19,200. This textbook has an indefinite useful life. How should Wiggens report these two copyrights on its balance sheet as of December 31, 2008? **(LO 3, 10)**

Exercises

(LO 1, 4) **E11-1** **(Classification Issues—Intangibles)** Presented below is a list of items that could be included in the intangible assets section of the balance sheet.

1. Investment in a subsidiary company. no
2. Timberland. no
3. Cost of engineering activity required to advance the design of a product to the manufacturing stage. no
4. Lease prepayment (6 months' rent paid in advance). no
5. Cost of equipment obtained. no
6. Cost of searching for applications of new research findings.
7. Costs incurred in the formation of a corporation. no
8. Operating losses incurred in the start-up of a business. no
9. Training costs incurred in start-up of new operation. no
10. Purchase cost of a franchise. yes
11. Goodwill generated internally. no
12. Cost of testing in search for product alternatives. no
13. Goodwill acquired in the purchase of a business. yes
14. Cost of developing a patent. no
15. Cost of purchasing a patent from an inventor. yes
16. Legal costs incurred in securing a patent. yes
17. Unrecovered costs of a successful legal suit to protect the patent. no
18. Cost of conceptual formulation of possible product alternatives. no
19. Cost of purchasing a copyright. yes
20. Research and development costs. no
21. Long-term receivables. no
22. Cost of developing a trademark. no
23. Cost of purchasing a trademark. yes

Instructions

(a) Indicate which items on the list above would generally be reported as intangible assets in the balance sheet.
(b) Indicate how, if at all, the items not reportable as intangible assets would be reported in the financial statements.

(LO 1, 4) **E11-2** **(Classification Issues—Intangibles)** Presented below is selected account information related to Martin Burke Inc. as of December 21, 2008. All these accounts have debit balances.

Cable television franchises Y	Film contract rights Y
Music copyrights Y	Customer lists Y
Research and development costs N	Prepaid expenses N
Goodwill Y	Covenants not to compete N
Cash N	Brand names Y
Discount on notes payable N	Notes receivable (due in 12 months) N
Accounts receivable N	Investments in affiliated companies N
Property, plant, and equipment N	Organization costs N
Internet domain name Y	Land N

Instructions

Identify which items should be classified as an intangible asset. For those items not classified as an intangible asset, indicate where they would be reported in the financial statements.

(LO 1, 4) **E11-3** **(Classification Issues—Intangible Asset)** Joni Hyde Inc. has the following amounts included in its general ledger at December 31, 2008.

Organization costs	$24,000 N
Trademarks	15,000 Y
Discount on bonds payable	35,000 N
Deposits with advertising agency for ads to promote goodwill of company	10,000 N
Excess of cost over fair value of net identifiable assets of acquired subsidiary	75,000 Y
Cost of equipment acquired for research and development projects; the equipment has an alternative future use	90,000 N
Costs of developing a secret formula for a product that is expected to be marketed for at least 20 years	80,000 N

Instructions

(a) On the basis of the information above, compute the total amount to be reported by Hyde for intangible assets on its balance sheet at December 31, 2008.

(b) If an item is not to be included in intangible assets, explain its proper treatment for reporting purposes.

E11-4 **(Intangible Amortization)** Presented below is selected information for Alatorre Company. **(LO 3, 9)**

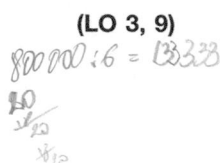

1. Alatorre purchased a patent from Vania Co. for $1,000,000 on January 1, 2006. The patent is being amortized over its remaining legal life of 10 years, expiring on January 1, 2016. During 2008, Alatorre determined that the economic benefits of the patent would not last longer than 6 years from the date of acquisition. What amount should be reported in the balance sheet for the patent, net of accumulated amortization, at December 31, 2008?

2. Alatorre bought a franchise from Alexander Co. on January 1, 2007, for $400,000. The carrying amount of the franchise on Alexander's books on January 1, 2007, was $500,000. The franchise agreement had an estimated useful life of 30 years. Because Alatorre must enter a competitive bidding at the end of 2016, it is unlikely that the franchise will be retained beyond 2016. What amount should be amortized for the year ended December 31, 2008?

3. On January 1, 2008, Alatorre incurred organization costs of $275,000. What amount of organization expense should be reported in 2008?

4. Alatorre purchased the license for distribution of a popular consumer product on January 1, 2008, for $150,000. It is expected that this product will generate cash flows for an indefinite period of time. The license has an initial term of 5 years but by paying a nominal fee, Alatorre can renew the license indefinitely for successive 5-year terms. What amount should be amortized for the year ended December 31, 2008?

Instructions

Answer the questions asked about each of the factual situations.

E11-5 **(Correct Intangible Asset Account)** As the recently appointed auditor for William J. Bryan Corporation, you have been asked to examine selected accounts before the 6-month financial statements of June 30, 2008, are prepared. The controller for William J. Bryan Corporation mentions that only one account is kept for Intangible Assets. The account is shown below. **(LO 2, 3, 8)**

Intangible Assets

		Debit	Credit	Balance
Jan. 4	Research and development costs	940,000		940,000 X
Jan. 5	Legal costs to obtain patent	75,000		1,015,000
Jan. 31	Payment of 7 months' rent on property leased by Bryan	91,000		1,106,000 X
Feb. 11	Premium on common stock		250,000	856,000 X
March 31	Unamortized bond discount on bonds due March 31, 2028	84,000		940,000 X
April 30	Promotional expenses related to start-up of business	207,000		1,147,000
June 30	Operating losses for first 6 months	241,000		1,388,000 X

Instructions

Prepare the entry or entries necessary to correct this account. Assume that the patent has a useful life of 10 years.

E11-6 **(Recording and Amortization of Intangibles)** Rolanda Marshall Company, organized in 2007, has set up a single account for all intangible assets. The following summary discloses the debit entries that have been recorded during 2008. **(LO 3, 9)**

1/2/08	Purchased patent (8-year life)	$ 350,000
4/1/08	Purchased goodwill (indefinite life)	360,000
7/1/08	Purchased franchise with 10-year life; expiration date 7/1/18	450,000
8/1/08	Payment of copyright (5-year life)	156,000
9/1/08	Research and development costs	215,000 ×
		$1,531,000

Instructions

Prepare the necessary entries to clear the Intangible Assets account and to set up separate accounts for distinct types of intangibles. Make the entries as of December 31, 2008, recording any necessary amortization and reflecting all balances accurately as of that date. (Use straight-line amortization.)

(LO 2, 3) **E11-7 (Accounting for Trade Name)** In early January 2007, Outkast Corporation applied for a trade name, incurring legal costs of $16,000. In January of 2008, Outkast incurred $7,800 of legal fees in a successful defense of its trade name.

Instructions

(a) Compute 2007 amortization, book value as of December 31, 2007, 2008 amortization, and book value as of December 31, 2008, if the company amortizes the trade name over 10 years.

(b) Compute the 2008 amortization and the December 31, 2008, book value, assuming that at the beginning of 2008, Outkast determines that the trade name will provide no future benefits beyond December 31, 2011.

(c) Ignoring the response for part (b), compute the 2009 amortization and the December 31, 2009 book value, assuming that at the beginning of 2009, based on new market research, Outkast determines that the fair value of the trade name is $15,000. Estimated total future cash flows from the trade name is $16,000 on January 3, 2009.

(LO 9) **E11-8 (Accounting for Organization Costs)** Lovett Corporation was organized in 2007 and began operations at the beginning of 2008. The company is involved in interior design consulting services. The following costs were incurred prior to the start of operations.

Attorney's fees in connection with organization of the company	$15,000 _dexp under GAAP_
Purchase of drafting and design equipment	10,000
Costs of meetings of incorporators to discuss organizational activities	7,000
State filing fees to incorporate	1,000
	$33,000

Instructions

(a) Compute the total amount of organization costs incurred by Lovett.

(b) Prepare the journal entry to record organization costs for 2008.

(LO 2, 3, 8) **E11-9 (Accounting for Patents, Franchises, and R&D)** Clinton Company has provided information on intangible assets as follows.

Patent 'Dec 31 '08
_1,440 000_
Franchise
_432 000_

A patent was purchased from Reagan Company for $2,000,000 on January 1, 2007. Clinton estimated the remaining useful life of the patent to be 10 years. The patent was carried in Reagan's accounting records at a net book value of $2,000,000 when Reagan sold it to Clinton. _Jan 1 '08 1800 000 / 5 = 360 000_

During 2008, a franchise was purchased from Bush Company for $480,000. In addition, 5% of revenue from the franchise must be paid to Bush. Revenue from the franchise for 2008 was $2,500,000. Clinton estimates the useful life of the franchise to be 10 years and takes a full year's amortization in the year of purchase.

Clinton incurred research and development costs in 2008 as follows.

Materials and equipment	$142,000
Personnel	189,000
Indirect costs	102,000
	$433,000

Clinton estimates that these costs will be recouped by December 31, 2011. The materials and equipment purchased have no alternative uses.

On January 1, 2008, because of recent events in the field, Clinton estimates that the remaining life of the patent purchased on January 1, 2007, is only 5 years from January 1, 2008.

Instructions

(a) Prepare a schedule showing the intangibles section of Clinton's balance sheet at December 31, 2008. Show supporting computations in good form.

(b) Prepare a schedule showing the income statement effect for the year ended December 31, 2008, as a result of the facts above. Show supporting computations in good form.

(AICPA adapted)

E11-10 **(Accounting for Patents)** During 2004, Wonder Corporation spent $170,000 in research and development costs. As a result, a new product called the New Age Piano was patented. The patent was obtained on October 1, 2004, and had a legal life of 20 years and a useful life of 10 years. Legal costs of $18,000 related to the patent were incurred as of October 1, 2004.

(LO 2, 3)

Instructions

(a) Prepare all journal entries required in 2004 and 2005 as a result of the transactions above.

(b) On June 1, 2006, Wonder spent $9,480 to successfully prosecute a patent infringement suit. As a result, the estimate of useful life was extended to 12 years from June 1, 2006. Prepare all journal entries required in 2006 and 2007.

(c) In 2008, Wonder determined that a competitor's product would make the New Age Piano obsolete and the patent worthless by December 31, 2009. Prepare all journal entries required in 2008 and 2009.

E11-11 **(Accounting for Patents)** Tones Industries has the following patents on its December 31, 2007, balance sheet.

(LO 2, 3)

Patent Item	Initial Cost	Date Acquired	Useful Life at Date Acquired
Patent A	$30,600	3/1/04	17 years
Patent B	$15,000	7/1/05	10 years
Patent C	$14,400	9/1/06	4 years

The following events occurred during the year ended December 31, 2008.

1. Research and development costs of $245,700 were incurred.

2. Patent D was purchased on July 1 for $36,480. This patent has a useful life of 9½ years.

3. As a result of reduced demands for certain products protected by Patent B, a possible impairment of Patent B's value may have occurred at December 31, 2008. The controller for Tones estimates the expected future cash flows from Patent B will be as follows.

Year	Expected Future Cash Flows
2009	$2,000
2010	2,000
2011	2,000

The proper discount rate to be used for these flows is 8%. (Assume that the cash flows occur at the end of the year.)

Instructions

(a) Compute the total carrying amount of Tones's patents on its December 31, 2007, balance sheet.

(b) Compute the total carrying amount of Tones's patents on its December 31, 2008, balance sheet.

E11-12 **(Accounting for Goodwill)** Fred Moss, owner of Moss Interiors, is negotiating for the purchase of Zweifel Galleries. The balance sheet of Zweifel is given in an abbreviated form below.

(LO 5, 6)

Zweifel Galleries
Balance Sheet
As of December 31, 2008

Assets		Liabilities and Stockholders' Equity		
Cash	$100,000	Accounts payable		$ 50,000
Land	70,000	Long-term notes payable		300,000
Building (net)	200,000	Total liabilities		350,000
Equipment (net)	175,000	Common stock	$200,000	
Copyright (net)	30,000	Retained earnings	25,000	225,000
Total assets	$575,000	Total liabilities and stockholders' equity		$575,000

Moss and Zweifel agree that:

1. Land is undervalued by $30,000.
2. Equipment is overvalued by $5,000.

Zweifel agrees to sell the gallery to Moss for $350,000.

Instructions

Prepare the entry to record the purchase of Zweifel Galleries on Moss's books.

(LO 3, 5, 6)   **E11-13** **(Accounting for Goodwill)**   On July 1, 2007, Brigham Corporation purchased Young Company by paying $250,000 cash and issuing a $100,000 note payable to Steve Young. At July 1, 2007, the balance sheet of Young Company was as follows.

Cash	$ 50,000	Accounts payable	$200,000
Receivables	90,000	Stockholders' equity	235,000
Inventory	100,000		$435,000
Land	40,000		
Buildings (net)	75,000		
Equipment (net)	70,000		
Trademarks	10,000		
	$435,000		

The recorded amounts all approximate current values except for land (fair value of $60,000), inventory (fair value of $125,000), and trademarks (fair value of $15,000).

Instructions

(a) Prepare the July 1 entry for Brigham Corporation to record the purchase.
(b) Prepare the December 31 entry for Brigham Corporation to record amortization of intangibles. The trademark has an estimated useful life of 4 years with a residual value of $3,000.

(LO 7)   **E11-14** **(Impairment)**   Presented below is information related to equipment owned by Suarez Company at December 31, 2007.

Cost	$9,000,000
Accumulated depreciation to date	1,000,000
Expected future net cash flows	7,000,000
Fair value	4,800,000

Assume that Suarez will continue to use this asset in the future. As of December 31, 2007, the equipment has a remaining useful life of 4 years.

Instructions

(a) Prepare the journal entry (if any) to record the impairment of the asset at December 31, 2007.
(b) Prepare the journal entry to record depreciation expense for 2008.
(c) The fair value of the equipment at December 31, 2008, is $5,100,000. Prepare the journal entry (if any) necessary to record this increase in fair value.

(LO 7)   **E11-15** **(Impairment)**   Assume the same information as E11-14, except that Suarez intends to dispose of the equipment in the coming year. It is expected that the cost of disposal will be $20,000.

Instructions

(a) Prepare the journal entry (if any) to record the impairment of the asset at December 31, 2007.
(b) Prepare the journal entry (if any) to record depreciation expense for 2008.
(c) The asset was not sold by December 31, 2008. The fair value of the equipment on that date is $5,300,000. Prepare the journal entry (if any) necessary to record this increase in fair value. It is expected that the cost of disposal is still $20,000.

(LO 7)   **E11-16** **(Impairment)**   The management of Luis Andujar Inc. was discussing whether certain equipment should be written off as a charge to current operations because of obsolescence. This equipment has a cost of $900,000, with depreciation to date of $400,000 as of December 31, 2007. On December 31, 2007, management projected its future net cash flows from this equipment to be $300,000 and its fair value to be $230,000. The company intends to use this equipment in the future.

Instructions

(a) Prepare the journal entry (if any) to record the impairment at December 31, 2007.
(b) Where should the gain or loss (if any) on the write-down be reported in the income statement?
(c) At December 31, 2008, the equipment's fair value increased to $260,000. Prepare the journal entry (if any) to record this increase in fair value.
(d) What accounting issues did management face in accounting for this impairment?

E11-17 **(Copyright Impairment)** Presented below is information related to copyrights owned by Tom Holder Company at December 31, 2008.   **(LO 7)**

Cost	$8,600,000
Carrying amount	4,300,000
Expected future net cash flows	4,000,000
Fair value	3,200,000

Assume that Holder will continue to use this copyright in the future. As of December 31, 2008, the copyright is estimated to have a remaining useful life of 10 years.

Instructions

(a) Prepare the journal entry (if any) to record the impairment of the asset at December 31, 2008. The company does not use accumulated amortization accounts.
(b) Prepare the journal entry to record amortization expense for 2009 related to the copyrights.
(c) The fair value of the copyright at December 31, 2009, is $3,400,000. Prepare the journal entry (if any) necessary to record the increase in fair value.

E11-18 **(Goodwill Impairment)** Presented below is net asset information related to the Carlos Division of Santana, Inc.   **(LO 6, 7)**

Carlos Division Net Assets As of December 31, 2008 (in millions)	
Cash	$ 50
Receivables	200
Property, plant, and equipment (net)	2,600
Goodwill	200
Less: Notes payable	(2,700)
Net assets	$ 350

The purpose of the Carlos division is to develop a nuclear-powered aircraft. If successful, traveling delays associated with refueling could be substantially reduced. Many other benefits would also occur. To date, management has not had much success and is deciding whether a write-down at this time is appropriate. Management estimated its future net cash flows from the project to be $400 million. Management has also received an offer to purchase the division for $335 million. All identifiable assets' and liabilities' book and fair value amounts are the same.

Instructions

(a) Prepare the journal entry (if any) to record the impairment at December 31, 2008.
(b) At December 31, 2009, it is estimated that the division's fair value increased to $345 million. Prepare the journal entry (if any) to record this increase in fair value.

E11-19 **(Accounting for R&D Costs)** Leontyne Price Company from time to time embarks on a research program when a special project seems to offer possibilities. In 2007 the company expends $325,000 on a research project, but by the end of 2007 it is impossible to determine whether any benefit will be derived from it.   **(LO 9)**

Instructions

(a) What account should be charged for the $325,000, and how should it be shown in the financial statements?
(b) The project is completed in 2008, and a successful patent is obtained. The R&D costs to complete the project are $110,000. The administrative and legal expenses incurred in obtaining patent number 472-1001-84 in 2008 total $16,000. The patent has an expected useful life of 5 years. Record these costs in journal entry form. Also, record patent amortization (full year) in 2008.

(c) In 2009, the company successfully defends the patent in extended litigation at a cost of $47,200, thereby extending the patent life to December 31, 2016. What is the proper way to account for this cost? Also, record patent amortization (full year) in 2009.

(d) Additional engineering and consulting costs incurred in 2009 required to advance the design of a product to the manufacturing stage total $60,000. These costs enhance the design of the product considerably. Discuss the proper accounting treatment for this cost.

(LO 9)   **E11-20   (Accounting for R&D Costs)**   Thomas More Company incurred the following costs during 2008 in connection with its research and development activities.

Cost of equipment acquired that will have alternative uses in future R&D projects over the next 5 years (uses straight-line depreciation)	$280,000
Materials consumed in R&D projects	59,000
Consulting fees paid to outsiders for R&D projects	100,000
Personnel costs of persons involved in R&D projects	128,000
Indirect costs reasonably allocable to R&D projects	50,000
Materials purchased for future R&D projects	34,000

Instructions

Compute the amount to be reported as research and development expense by More on its income statement for 2008. Assume equipment is purchased at the beginning of the year.

*

See the book's website, at www.wiley.com/college/warfield, for Additional Exercises.

Problems

(LO 2, 3)

P11-1   (Correct Intangible Asset Account)   Esplanade Co., organized in 2007, has set up a single account for all intangible assets. The following summary discloses the debit entries that have been recorded during 2007 and 2008.

Intangible Assets

7/1/07	8-year franchise; expiration date 6/30/15	$ 42,000
10/1/07	Advance payment on laboratory space (2-year lease)	28,000
12/31/07	Net loss for 2007 including state incorporation fee, $1,000, and related legal fees of organizing, $5,000 (all fees incurred in 2007)	16,000
1/2/08	Patent purchased (10-year life)	74,000
3/1/08	Cost of developing a secret formula (indefinite life)	75,000
4/1/08	Goodwill purchased (indefinite life)	278,400
6/1/08	Legal fee for successful defense of patent purchased above	12,650
9/1/08	Research and development costs	160,000

Instructions

Prepare the necessary entries to clear the Intangible Assets account and to set up separate accounts for distinct types of intangibles. Make the entries as of December 31, 2008, recording any necessary amortization and reflecting all balances accurately as of that date. (Ignore income tax effects.)

(LO 2, 3)

P11-2   (Accounting for Patents)   Ankara Laboratories holds a valuable patent (No. 758-6002-1A) on a precipitator that prevents certain types of air pollution. Ankara does not manufacture or sell the products and processes it develops. Instead, it conducts research and develops products and processes which it patents, and then assigns the patents to manufacturers on a royalty basis. Occasionally it sells a patent. The history of Ankara patent number 758-6002-1A is as follows.

Date	Activity	Cost
1998–1999	Research conducted to develop precipitator	$384,000
Jan. 2000	Design and construction of a prototype	87,600
March 2000	Testing of models	42,000
Jan. 2001	Fees paid engineers and lawyers to prepare patent application; patent granted June 30, 2001	62,050
Nov. 2002	Engineering activity necessary to advance the design of the precipitator to the manufacturing stage	81,500
Dec. 2003	Legal fees paid to successfully defend precipitator patent	35,700
April 2004	Research aimed at modifying the design of the patented precipitator	43,000
July 2008	Legal fees paid in unsuccessful patent infringement suit against a competitor	34,000

Ankara assumed a useful life of 17 years when it received the initial precipitator patent. On January 1, 2006, it revised its useful life estimate downward to 5 remaining years. Amortization is computed for a full year if the cost is incurred prior to July 1, and no amortization for the year if the cost is incurred after June 30. The company's year ends December 31.

Instructions

Compute the carrying value of patent No. 758-6002-1A on each of the following dates:

(a) December 31, 2001.
(b) December 31, 2005.
(c) December 31, 2008.

P11-3 (**Accounting for Franchise, Patents, and Trade Name**) Information concerning Haerhpin Corporation's intangible assets is as follows. **(LO 2, 3)**

1. On January 1, 2008, Haerhpin signed an agreement to operate as a franchisee of Hsian Copy Service, Inc. for an initial franchise fee of $75,000. Of this amount, $15,000 was paid when the agreement was signed, and the balance is payable in 4 annual payments of $15,000 each, beginning January 1, 2009. The agreement provides that the down payment is not refundable and no future services are required of the franchisor. The present value at January 1, 2008, of the 4 annual payments discounted at 14% (the implicit rate for a loan of this type) is $43,700. The agreement also provides that 5% of the revenue from the franchise must be paid to the franchisor annually. Haerhpin's revenue from the franchise for 2008 was $950,000. Haerhpin estimates the useful life of the franchise to be 10 years.

2. Haerhpin incurred $65,000 of experimental and development costs in its laboratory to develop a patent that was granted on January 2, 2008. Legal fees and other costs associated with registration of the patent totaled $13,600. Haerhpin estimates that the useful life of the patent will be 8 years.

3. A trademark was purchased from Shanghai Company for $32,000 on July 1, 2005. Expenditures for successful litigation in defense of the trademark totaling $8,160 were paid on July 1, 2008. Haerhpin estimates that the useful life of the trademark will be 20 years from the date of acquisition.

Instructions

(a) Prepare a schedule showing the intangible assets section of Haerhpin's balance sheet at December 31, 2008. Show supporting computations in good form.
(b) Prepare a schedule showing all expenses resulting from the transactions that would appear on Haerhpin's income statement for the year ended December 31, 2008. Show supporting computations in good form.

(AICPA adapted)

P11-4 (**Accounting for R&D Costs**) During 2005, Bloom Tool Company purchased a building site for its proposed research and development laboratory at a cost of $60,000. Construction of the building was started in 2006. The building was completed on December 31, 2007, at a cost of $280,000 and was placed in service on January 2, 2008. The estimated useful life of the building for depreciation purposes was 20 years. The straight-line method of depreciation was to be employed, and there was no estimated salvage value. **(LO 9, 10)**

Management estimates that about 50% of the projects of the research and development group will result in long-term benefits (i.e., at least 10 years) to the corporation. The remaining projects either benefit the current period or are abandoned before completion. A summary of the number of projects and the direct costs incurred in conjunction with the research and development activities for 2008 appears on the next page.

	Number of Projects	Salaries and Employee Benefits	Other Expenses (excluding Building Depreciation Charges)
Completed projects with long-term benefits	15	$ 90,000	$50,000
Abandoned projects or projects that benefit the current period	10	65,000	15,000
Projects in process—results indeterminate	5	40,000	12,000
Total	30	$195,000	$77,000

Upon recommendation of the research and development group, Bloom Tool Company acquired a patent for manufacturing rights at a cost of $80,000. The patent was acquired on April 1, 2007, and has an economic life of 10 years.

Instructions

If generally accepted accounting principles were followed, how would the items above relating to research and development activities be reported on the following financial statements?

(a) The company's income statement for 2008.
(b) The company's balance sheet as of December 31, 2008.

Be sure to give account titles and amounts, and briefly justify your presentation.

(CMA adapted)

(LO 7)

P11-5 (Impairment) Olsson Company uses special strapping equipment in its packaging business. The equipment was purchased in January 2008 for $8,000,000 and had an estimated useful life of 8 years with no salvage value. At December 31, 2009, new technology was introduced that would accelerate the obsolescence of Olsson's equipment. Olsson's controller estimates that expected future net cash flows on the equipment will be $5,300,000 and that the fair value of the equipment is $4,400,000. Olsson intends to continue using the equipment, but it is estimated that the remaining useful life is 4 years. Olsson uses straight-line depreciation.

Instructions

(a) Prepare the journal entry (if any) to record the impairment at December 31, 2009.
(b) Prepare any journal entries for the equipment at December 31, 2010. The fair value of the equipment at December 31, 2010, is estimated to be $4,600,000.
(c) Repeat the requirements for (a) and (b), assuming that Olsson intends to dispose of the equipment and that it has not been disposed of as of December 31, 2010.

(LO 5, 6, 7)

P11-6 (Goodwill, Impairment) On July 31, 2008, Postera Company paid $3,000,000 to acquire all of the common stock of Mendota Incorporated, which became a division of Postera. Mendota reported the following balance sheet at the time of the acquisition.

Current assets	$ 800,000	Current liabilities	$ 600,000
Noncurrent assets	2,700,000	Long-term liabilities	500,000
Total assets	$3,500,000	Stockholders' equity	2,400,000
		Total liabilities and stockholders' equity	$3,500,000

It was determined at the date of the purchase that the fair value of the identifiable net assets of Mendota was $2,650,000. Over the next 6 months of operations, the newly purchased division experienced operating losses. In addition, it now appears that it will generate substantial losses for the foreseeable future. At December 31, 2008, Mendota reports the following balance sheet information.

Current assets	$ 450,000
Noncurrent assets (including goodwill recognized in purchase)	2,400,000
Current liabilities	(700,000)
Long-term liabilities	(500,000)
Net assets	$1,650,000

It is determined that the fair value of the Mendota Division is $1,850,000. The recorded amount for Mendota's net assets (excluding goodwill) is the same as fair value, except for property, plant, and equipment, which has a fair value $150,000 above the carrying value.

Instructions

(a) Compute the amount of goodwill recognized, if any, on July 31, 2008.

(b) Determine the impairment loss, if any, to be recorded on December 31, 2008.

(c) Assume that fair value of the Mendota Division is $1,500,000 instead of $1,850,000. Determine the impairment loss, if any, to be recorded on December 31, 2008.

(d) Prepare the journal entry to record the impairment loss, if any, and indicate where the loss would be reported in the income statement.

P11-7 **(Comprehensive Intangible Assets)** Montana Matt's Golf Inc. was formed on July 1, 2007, when Matt Magilke purchased the Old Master Golf Company. Old Master provides video golf instruction at kiosks in shopping malls. Magilke plans to integrate the instruction business into his golf equipment and accessory stores. Magilke paid $750,000 cash for Old Master. At the time Old Master's balance sheet reported assets of $650,000 and liabilities of $200,000 (thus owners' equity was $450,000). The fair value of Old Master's assets is estimated to be $800,000. Included in the assets is the Old Master trade name with a fair value of $10,000 and a copyright on some instructional books with a fair value of $20,000. The trade name has a remaining life of 5 years and can be renewed at nominal cost indefinitely. The copyright has a remaining life of 40 years.

(LO 2, 3, 6, 7, 10)

Instructions

(a) Prepare the intangible assets section of Montana Matt's Golf Inc. at December 31, 2007. How much amortization expense is included in Montana Matt's income for the year ended December 31, 2007? Show all supporting computations.

(b) Prepare the journal entry to record amortization expense for 2008. Prepare the intangible assets section of Montana Matt's Golf Inc. at December 31, 2008. (No impairments are required to be recorded in 2008.)

(c) At the end of 2009, Magilke is evaluating the results of the instructional business. Due to fierce competition from online and television (e.g., the Golf Channel), the Old Master reporting unit has been losing money. Its book value is now $500,000. The fair value of the Old Master reporting unit is $430,000. The implied value of goodwill is $80,000. Magilke has collected the following information related to the company's intangible assets.

Intangible Asset	Expected Cash Flows (undiscounted)	Fair Values
Trade name	$ 9,000	$ 3,000
Copyright	30,000	25,000

Prepare the journal entries required, if any, to record impairments on Montana Matt's intangible assets. (Assume that any amortization for 2009 has been recorded.) Show supporting computations.

ACCOUNTING IN ACTION

Financial Reporting and Analysis

■ Financial Reporting Issues: The Procter & Gamble Company

AIA11-1 The financial statements of **Procter & Gamble (P&G)** can be accessed at the book's website.

Instructions

Refer to P&G's financial statements and the accompanying notes to answer the following questions.

(a) Does P&G report any intangible assets, especially goodwill, in its 2006 financial statements and accompanying notes?

(b) How much research and development (R&D) cost was expensed by P&G in 2006 and 2005? What percentage of sales revenue and net income did P&G spend on R&D in 2006 and 2005?

■ Comparative Analysis: The Coca-Cola Company and PepsiCo, Inc.

AIA11-2 The financial statements of **The Coca-Cola Company** and **PepsiCo, Inc.** can be accessed at the book's website.

Instructions

Use information found at the book's website to answer the following questions.

(a) (1) What amounts for intangible assets were reported in their respective balance sheets by Coca-Cola and PepsiCo?

(2) What percentage of total assets is each of these reported amounts?

(3) What was the change in the amount of intangibles from 2005 to 2006 for Coca-Cola and PepsiCo?

(b) (1) On what basis and over what periods of time did Coca-Cola and PepsiCo amortize their intangible assets?

(2) What were the amounts of accumulated amortization reported by Coca-Cola and PepsiCo at the end of 2006 and 2005?

(3) What was the composition of the identifiable and unidentifiable intangible assets reported by Coca-Cola and PepsiCo at the end of 2006?

■ Financial Statement Analysis

AIA11-3 **Merck & Co., Inc.** and **Johnson & Johnson** are two leading producers of health care products. Each has considerable assets, and each expends considerable funds each year toward the development of new products. The development of a new health care product is often very expensive, and risky. New products frequently must undergo considerable testing before approval for distribution to the public. For example, it took Johnson & Johnson 4 years and $200 million to develop its 1-DAY ACUVUE contact lenses. Below are some basic data compiled from the financial statements of these two companies.

($ in millions)	Johnson & Johnson	Merck
Total assets	$53,317	$42,573
Total revenue	47,348	22,939
Net income	8,509	5,813
Research and development expense	5,203	4,010
Intangible assets	11,842	2,765

Instructions

(a) What kinds of intangible assets might a health care products company have? Does the composition of these intangibles matter to investors—that is, would it be perceived differently if all of Merck's intangibles were goodwill, than if all of its intangibles were patents?

(b) Suppose the president of Merck has come to you for advice. He has noted that by eliminating research and development expenditures the company could have reported $1.3 billion more in net income. He is frustrated because much of the research never results in a product, or the products take years to develop. He says shareholders are eager for higher returns, so he is considering eliminating research and development expenditures for at least a couple of years. What would you advise?

(c) The notes to Merck's financial statements note that Merck has goodwill of $1.1 billion. Where does recorded goodwill come from? Is it necessarily a good thing to have a lot of goodwill on your books?

AIA11-4 Furtado Company owns machinery that, due to changes in industry conditions, may be impaired. Furtado intends to continue to use this machinery in its operations.

Instructions

(a) Briefly describe the procedure that Furtado should follow in determining if it should record an impairment on the machinery.

(b) On what basis should Furtado measure any impairment loss?

(c) Discuss the effect of impairment recognition on each of the following measures in (1) the year of impairment and (2) the year following the impairment.

1. Net income
2. Income from operations
3. Cash from operations
4. Stockholders' equity
5. Return on equity
6. Asset turnover

(d) Assume now that Furtado plans to dispose of this machinery and appropriately classifies the assets as "held-for-disposal." Repeat the analysis in part (c).

■ International Reporting Issues

AIA11-5 Presented below are data and accounting policy notes for the goodwill of three international drug companies. **Bayer**, a German company, prepares its statements in accordance with International Financial

Reporting Standards (IFRS); **Glaxo SmithKline** follows United Kingdom (U.K.) rules; and **Merck**, a U.S. company, prepares its financial statements in accordance with U.S. GAAP.

Related Information	Bayer (€ millions)	Glaxo SmithKline (£ millions)	Merck ($ millions)
Research and development expense	€2,107	£2,839	$4,010
Amortization expense	0	12	0
Net income	603	4,302	5,813
Accumulated goodwill amortization	0	84	0
Stockholders' equity	12,268	10,091	17,288

Both U.S. GAAP and IFRS do not allow amortization of goodwill. Under U.K. standards, goodwill is amortized over useful lives not to exceed 20 years.

Instructions

(a) Compute the return on equity for each of these companies, and use this analysis to briefly discuss the relative profitability of the three companies.

(b) Assume that each of the companies uses the maximum allowable amortization period for goodwill (if any). Discuss how these companies' goodwill amortization policies affect your ability to compare their amortization expense and income.

(c) Some analysts believe that the only valid way to compare companies that follow different goodwill accounting practices is to treat all goodwill as an asset and record expense only if the goodwill is impaired.* Using the data above, make these adjustments as appropriate, and compare the profitability of the three drug companies, comparing this information to your analysis in (a).

(d) IFRS requires that development costs must be capitalized if technical and commercial feasibility of the resulting product has been established. Assume that Bayer recorded €1 million of development costs in the year reported above. Discuss briefly how this accounting affects your ability to compare the financial results of Bayer and Merck.

Concepts for Analysis

AIA11-6 **(Accounting for Pollution Expenditure)** Phil Mickelson Company operates several plants at which limestone is processed into quicklime and hydrated lime. The Eagle Ridge plant, where most of the equipment was installed many years ago, continually deposits a dusty white substance over the surrounding countryside. Citing the unsanitary condition of the neighboring community of Scales Mound, the pollution of the Galena River, and the high incidence of lung disease among workers at Eagle Ridge, the state's Pollution Control Agency has ordered the installation of air pollution control equipment. Also, the Agency has assessed a substantial penalty, which will be used to clean up Scales Mound.

After considering the costs involved (which could not have been reasonably estimated prior to the Agency's action), Phil Mickelson Company decides to comply with the Agency's orders, the alternative being to cease operations at Eagle Ridge at the end of the current fiscal year. The officers of Mickelson agree that the air pollution control equipment should be capitalized and depreciated over its useful life, but they disagree over the period(s) to which the penalty should be charged.

Instructions

Discuss the conceptual merits and reporting requirements of accounting for the penalty in each of the following ways.

(a) As a charge to the current period.

(b) As a correction of prior periods.

(c) As a capitalizable item to be amortized over future periods.

(AICPA adapted)

AIA11-7 **(Accounting for Pre-Opening Costs)** After securing lease commitments from several major stores, Lobo Shopping Center, Inc. was organized and built a shopping center in a growing suburb.

*Trevor Harris, *Apples to Apples: Accounting for Value in World Markets* (New York: Morgan Stanley Dean Witter, February 1998).

The shopping center would have opened on schedule on January 1, 2008, if it had not been struck by a severe tornado in December. Instead, it opened for business on October 1, 2008. All of the additional construction costs that were incurred as a result of the tornado were covered by insurance.

In July 2007, in anticipation of the scheduled January opening, a permanent staff had been hired to promote the shopping center, obtain tenants for the uncommitted space, and manage the property.

A summary of some of the costs incurred in 2007 and the first 9 months of 2008 follows.

	2007	January 1, 2008 through September 30, 2008
Interest on mortgage bonds	$720,000	$540,000
Cost of obtaining tenants	300,000	360,000
Promotional advertising	540,000	557,000

The promotional advertising campaign was designed to familiarize shoppers with the center. Had it been known in time that the center would not open until October 2008, the 2007 expenditure for promotional advertising would not have been made. The advertising had to be repeated in 2008.

All of the tenants who had leased space in the shopping center at the time of the tornado accepted the October occupancy date on condition that the monthly rental charges for the first 9 months of 2008 be canceled.

Instructions

Explain how each of the costs for 2007 and the first 9 months of 2008 should be treated in the accounts of the shopping center corporation. Give the reasons for each treatment.

(AICPA adapted)

AIA11-8 (Accounting for Patents) On June 30, 2008, your client, Bearcat Company, was granted two patents covering plastic cartons that it had been producing and marketing profitably for the past 3 years. One patent covers the manufacturing process, and the other covers the related products.

Bearcat executives tell you that these patents represent the most significant breakthrough in the industry in the past 30 years. The products have been marketed under the registered trademarks Evertight, Duratainer, and Sealrite. Licenses under the patents have already been granted by your client to other manufacturers in the United States and abroad and are producing substantial royalties.

On July 1, Bearcat commenced patent infringement actions against several companies whose names you recognize as those of substantial and prominent competitors. Bearcat's management is optimistic that these suits will result in a permanent injunction against the manufacture and sale of the infringing products as well as collection of damages for loss of profits caused by the alleged infringement.

The financial vice-president has suggested that the patents be recorded at the discounted value of expected net royalty receipts.

Instructions

(a) What is the meaning of "discounted value of expected net receipts"? Explain.

(b) How would such a value be calculated for net royalty receipts?

(c) What basis of valuation for Bearcat's patents would be generally accepted in accounting? Give supporting reasons for this basis.

(d) Assuming no practical problems of implementation, and ignoring generally accepted accounting principles, what is the preferable basis of valuation for patents? Explain.

(e) What would be the preferable theoretical basis of amortization? Explain.

(f) What recognition, if any, should be made of the infringement litigation in the financial statements for the year ending September 30, 2008? Discuss.

(AICPA adapted)

AIA11-9 (Accounting for Research and Development Costs) Indiana Jones Co. is in the process of developing a revolutionary new product. A new division of the company was formed to develop, manufacture, and market this new product. As of year-end (December 31, 2008), the new product has not been manufactured for resale. However, a prototype unit was built and is in operation.

Throughout 2008 the new division incurred certain costs. These costs include design and engineering studies, prototype manufacturing costs, administrative expenses (including salaries of administrative personnel), and market research costs. In addition, approximately $900,000 in equipment (with an estimated useful life of 10 years) was purchased for use in developing and manufacturing the new product. Approximately $315,000 of this equipment was built specifically for the design development of the new product.

The remaining $585,000 of equipment was used to manufacture the pre-production prototype and will be used to manufacture the new product once it is in commercial production.

Instructions

(a) How are "research" and "development" defined in *Statement of Financial Accounting Standards No. 2*?

(b) Briefly indicate the practical and conceptual reasons for the conclusion reached by the Financial Accounting Standards Board on accounting and reporting practices for research and development costs.

(c) In accordance with *Statement of Financial Accounting Standards No. 2*, how should the various costs of Indiana Jones described above be recorded on the financial statements for the year ended December 31, 2008?

(AICPA adapted)

Professional Tools

■ Ethical Decision Making

AIA11-10 (Accounting for R and D Costs) Waveland Corporation's research and development department has an idea for a project it believes will culminate in a new product that would be very profitable for the company. Because the project will be very expensive, the department requests approval from the company's controller, Ron Santo.

Santo recognizes that corporate profits have been down lately and is hesitant to approve a project that will incur significant expenses that cannot be capitalized due to the requirements of *FASB Statement No. 2*. He knows that if they hire an outside firm that does the work and obtains a patent for the process, Waveland Corporation can purchase the patent from the outside firm and record the expenditure as an asset. Santo knows that the company's own R&D department is first-rate, and he is confident they can do the work well.

Instructions

Answer the following questions.

(a) Who are the stakeholders in this situation?

(b) What are the ethical issues involved?

(c) What should Santo do?

■ Financial Accounting Research (FARS)

AIA11-11 Mills Company is contemplating the purchase of a smaller company, which is a distributor of Mills's products. Top management of Mills is convinced that the acquisition will result in significant synergies in its selling and distribution functions. The financial management group (of which you are a part) has been asked to prepare some analysis of the effects of the acquisition on the combined company's financial statements. This is the first acquisition for Mills, and some of the senior staff insist that based on their recollection of goodwill accounting, any goodwill recorded on the acquisition will result in a "drag" on future earnings for goodwill amortization. Other younger members on the staff argue that goodwill accounting has changed. Your supervisor asks you to research this issue.

Instructions

Using the **Financial Accounting Research System (FARS)** database, respond to the following items. (Provide text strings used in your search.)

(a) Identify the accounting standard that addresses goodwill and other intangible assets. When was it issued? Might this explain the disagreement among the accounting staff? Explain.

(b) Define goodwill.

(c) Is goodwill subject to amortization? Explain.

(d) When goodwill is recognized by a subsidiary, should it be tested for impairment at the consolidated level or the subsidiary level? Discuss.

■ Professional Simulation

AIA11-12 Go to the book's companion website, at **www.wiley.com/college/warfield**, to find an interactive problem that simulates the computerized CPA exam. The professional simulation for this chapter asks you to address questions related to intangible assets and similar costs.

What do the numbers mean?

Sweet to Sour, p. 561

Q: Is Krispy Kreme's accounting for reacquired franchise rights a form of earnings management? Explain.

A: By classifying the reacquired franchise rights as an indefinite-life intangible asset, this intangible asset is not subject to annual amortization charges. As a result, Krispy Kreme's income is overstated, at least until the intangible assets are subjected to an impairment test. If Krispy Kreme is using this unique classification for the purpose of increasing its earnings, this accounting would represent earnings management.

Patent Battles, p. 562

Q: Does society benefit from patent protection on business methods, as it presumably does on patents on drugs?

A: A commonly invoked rationale for patent protection for drugs is that, without the protection, drugmakers might not make the significant investment required to develop drugs that would benefit society. Although business-method patents may not convey the same societal benefits as those related to patents, they nonetheless provide incentives for companies to innovate—innovation that might not occur in the absence of patent protection. To the extent that these innovations benefit consumers through better service, then an argument for societal benefits can be supported. However, if the patent serves primarily to protect the patentholder from competition, consumers might be harmed by the higher prices for the services covered by the patent.

The Value of a Secret Formula, p. 563

Q: Where in Coca-Cola's financial statements could you find some indication of the value of its secret formula?

A: Because The Coca-Cola Company developed the secret formula internally, any costs associated with its secret formula were charged to expense as incurred (as research and development costs). Thus, the value of the secret formula is not directly represented in Coca-Cola's balance sheet. Some indirect information about the value of the secret formula can be drawn from the sales and profits generated from the sales of Coca-Cola products.

Real News, or Just Bookkeeping?, p. 572

Q: What do you think: Is an impairment charge just an entry, or can it provide some new information about management decisions, like H-P's merger with Compaq?

A: Recall that the measurement of the impairment is based on an evaluation of the carrying value of the goodwill compared to the implied fair value. Generally, companies estimate the fair value based on discounting of expected future cash flows. As a result, the impairment charge provides relevant information about the future cash flows and hence the fair value of the goodwill. Possibly it also indicates (1) whether management paid too much when it purchased the reporting unit, and/or (2) how well the company has managed the reporting unit since it was acquired.

 Remember to check the book's companion website to find additional resources for this chapter.

CHAPTER 12
ACCOUNTING FOR LIABILITIES

Now You See It, Now You Don't

A look at the liability side of the balance sheet of the German company **Beru Aktiengesellschaft**, Ludwigsburg, dated March 31, 2003, shows how international standards are changing the reporting of financial information. On this date, the company showed one liability this way:

Anticipated losses arising from pending transactions 3,285,000 euros

Do you believe a liability should be reported for pending transactions? *Anticipated losses* means they have not yet occurred; *pending transactions* means the condition that might cause the loss also has not occurred. So where is the liability? Who does the company owe? Where is the obligation?

U.S. GAAP provides guidance on this subject. A company can accrue a liability for a contingency only if an obligation has arisen from a past event, if payment is probable, and if a reasonable estimate of the obligation can be made. In short, under U.S. GAAP, companies cannot accrue anticipated future losses today.

German accounting, however, is more permissive. Companies are permitted to report liabilities for possible future events. In essence, establishing this general-purpose "liability" provides a buffer for Beru if losses do materialize. If you take a more skeptical view, you might say it lets Beru smooth its income by charging expenses in good years and reducing expenses in bad years.

We should note that the story has a happy ending. As indicated earlier in the text, European companies switched to International Financial Reporting Standards (IFRS) in 2005. Because IFRS are similar to U.S. GAAP, liabilities like "Anticipated losses from pending transactions" disappear. Now when we look at Beru's 2005 financial statements, we find a note stating that it reports as liabilities only obligations arising from past transactions that can be reasonably estimated.

Preview of Chapter 12

As our opening story indicates, investors pay considerable attention to a company's liabilities. The stock market severely punishes companies with high debt levels and the related impact of higher interest costs on income performance. In this chapter we explain the accounting issues related to liabilities as follows.

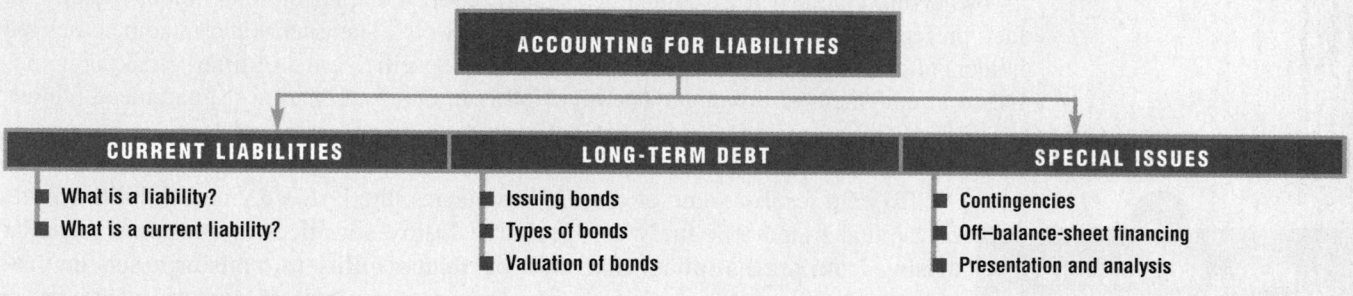

ACCOUNTING FOR LIABILITIES		
CURRENT LIABILITIES	**LONG-TERM DEBT**	**SPECIAL ISSUES**
■ What is a liability? ■ What is a current liability?	■ Issuing bonds ■ Types of bonds ■ Valuation of bonds	■ Contingencies ■ Off–balance-sheet financing ■ Presentation and analysis

Learning Objectives

After studying this chapter, you should be able to:

1. Describe the nature, type, and valuation of current liabilities.
2. Identify various types of bond issues.
3. Describe the accounting valuation for bonds at date of issuance.
4. Describe the accounting procedures for the extinguishment of debt.
5. Identify the criteria used to account for and disclose gain and loss contingencies.
6. Explain the accounting for different types of loss contingencies.
7. Explain the reporting of off–balance-sheet financing arrangements.
8. Indicate how to present and analyze liabilities and contingencies.

Inside Chapter 12

■ **What Do the Numbers Mean?**
Frequent buyers (p. 611)
All about bonds (p. 614)
"How's my rating?" (p. 616)
Gift cards: Handle with care (p. 626)
More disclosure, please (p. 633)

■ **What's the Principle?** (pp. 606, 610, 625, 628)

■ **Convergence Corner** (p. 636)

■ **Accounting, Analysis, Principles** (p. 637)
Record current and long-term liabilities.
Assess liquidity and solvency.
Apply the definition of a liability.

WHAT IS A LIABILITY?

The question "What is a liability?" is not easy to answer. For example, is preferred stock a liability or an ownership claim? The first reaction is to say that preferred stock is in fact an ownership claim. If it is, companies should report it as part of stockholders' equity. In fact, preferred stock has many elements of debt as well.[1] The issuer (and in some cases the holder) often has the right to call the stock within a specific period of time—making it similar to a repayment of principal. The dividend is in many cases almost guaranteed (cumulative provision)—making it look like interest. As a result, preferred stock is but one of many financial instruments that are difficult to classify.[2]

To help resolve some of these controversies, the FASB defined **liabilities** in its conceptual framework study as **"probable future sacrifices of economic benefits arising from present obligations of a particular entity to transfer assets or provide services to other entities in the future as a result of past transactions or events."**[3] In other words, a liability has three essential characteristics:

1 It is a present obligation that entails settlement by probable future transfer or use of cash, goods, or services.

2 It is an unavoidable obligation.

3 The transaction or other event creating the obligation has already occurred.

Because liabilities involve future disbursements of assets or services, one of their most important features is the date on which they are payable. A company must satisfy currently maturing obligations in the ordinary course of business to continue operating. Liabilities with a more distant due date do not, as a rule, represent a claim on the company's current resources. They are therefore in a slightly different category. This feature gives rise to the basic division of liabilities into two categories: current liabilities and long-term debt.

WHAT'S THE PRINCIPLE?

To determine the appropriate classification of specific financial instruments, companies need proper definitions of assets, liabilities, and equities. They often use the conceptual framework definitions as the basis for resolving controversial classification issues.

WHAT IS A CURRENT LIABILITY?

OBJECTIVE 1

Describe the nature, type, and valuation of current liabilities.

Recall that current assets are cash or other assets that companies reasonably expect to convert into cash, sell, or consume in operations within a single operating cycle or within a year (if the company completes more than one cycle per year). **Current liabilities** are **"obligations whose liquidation is reasonably expected to require use of existing resources properly classified as current assets, or the creation of other current**

---

[1]This illustration is not just a theoretical exercise. In practice, a number of preferred stock issues have all the characteristics of a debt instrument, except that they are called and legally classified preferred stock. In some cases, the IRS has even permitted companies to treat the dividend payments as interest expense for tax purposes.

[2]The FASB has addressed this issue in part in *"Accounting for Certain Financial Instruments with Characteristics of both Liabilities and Equity," Statement of Financial Accounting Standards No. 150* (Norwalk, Conn.: FASB, 2003).

[3]"Elements of Financial Statements of Business Enterprises," *Statement of Financial Accounting Concepts No. 6* (Stamford, Conn.: FASB, 1980). The FASB and IASB liability definitions are similar. The Boards are working on a joint conceptual framework project, which will likely change the definition of a liability (and assets.) See *http://fasb.org/project/conceptual_framework.shtml* for the current status of this project.

Landscape credits the Notes Payable account for the face value of the note, which is $2,000 more than the actual cash it received. It debits the difference between the cash received and the face value of the note to Discount on Notes Payable. **Discount on Notes Payable is a contra account to Notes Payable, and therefore is subtracted from Notes Payable on the balance sheet**. Illustration 12-1 shows the balance sheet presentation on March 1.

Current liabilities		
Notes payable	102,000	
Less: Discount on notes payable	2,000	100,000

Illustration 12-1
Balance Sheet
Presentation of Discount

The amount of the discount, $2,000 in this case, represents the cost of borrowing $100,000 for four months. Accordingly, Landscape charges the discount to interest expense over the life of the note. That is, the Discount on Notes Payable balance **represents interest expense chargeable to future periods**. Thus, Landscape should not debit Interest Expense for $2,000 at the time of obtaining the loan.

Current Maturities of Long-Term Debt

PepsiCo reports as a current liability the portion of bonds, mortgage notes, and other long-term indebtedness that matures within the next fiscal year. It categorizes this amount as **current maturities of long-term debt**. When a company like PepsiCo pays only a part of a long-term debt within the next 12 months, as in the case of serial bonds that it retires through a series of annual installments, **it reports the maturing portion of long-term debt as a current liability** and the balance as a long-term debt. However, it **excludes** long-term debts maturing currently as current liabilities if they are to be:

1 retired by assets accumulated for this purpose that properly have not been shown as current assets,

2 refinanced, or retired from the proceeds of a new debt issue, or

3 converted into capital stock.

In these situations, the use of current assets or the creation of other current liabilities does not occur. Therefore, classification as a current liability is inappropriate. A company should disclose the plan for liquidation of such a debt either parenthetically or by a note to the financial statements.

However, a company should classify as a current liability one that is **due on demand** (callable by the creditor) or will be due on demand within a year (or operating cycle, if longer). Creditors often call liabilities due to a violation of the debt agreement. For example, most debt agreements specify that a borrower must maintain a given level of equity to debt, or a minimum amount of working capital. If the company violates such an agreement, it must classify the debt as current because it is a reasonable expectation that the company will use existing working capital to satisfy the debt. Only if a company can show that it is **probable** that it will cure (satisfy) the violation within the grace period usually given in these agreements can it classify the debt as noncurrent.[7]

Dividends Payable

A **cash dividend payable** is an amount a corporation owes to its stockholders as a result of the board of directors' authorization. At the date of declaration the corporation assumes a liability that places the stockholders in the position of creditors in the amount of dividends

---

[7]"Classification of Obligations That Are Callable by the Creditor," *Statement of Financial Accounting Standards No. 78* (Stamford, Conn.: FASB, 1983).

WHAT'S THE PRINCIPLE?

Preferred dividends in arrears do represent a probable future economic sacrifice, but the expected sacrifice does not result from a past transaction or past event. The sacrifice will result from a future event (declaration by the board of directors). Note disclosure improves the predictive value of the financial statements in this situation.

declared. Because companies always pay cash dividends within one year of declaration (generally within three months), they classify them as current liabilities.

On the other hand, companies do not recognize accumulated but undeclared dividends on cumulative preferred stock as a liability. Why? Because **preferred dividends in arrears** are not an obligation until the board of directors authorizes the distribution of earnings. Nevertheless, companies should disclose the amount of cumulative dividends unpaid in a note, or show it parenthetically in the capital stock section.

Companies also do not recognize dividends payable in the form of additional shares of stock as a liability. Such **stock dividends** (as we discuss in Chapter 13) do not require future outlays of assets or services. Further, the board of directors may recover them at any time prior to issuance. Even so, companies generally report such undistributed stock dividends in the stockholders' equity section because they represent retained earnings in the process of transfer to paid-in capital.

Unearned Revenues

A magazine publisher, such as **Golf Digest**, receives payment when a customer subscribes to its magazines. An airline company, such as **American Airlines**, sells tickets for future flights. Software companies, like **Microsoft**, issue coupons that allow customers to upgrade to the next version of their software. How do these companies account for **unearned revenues** that they receive before delivering goods or rendering services?

1 Upon receipt of the advance, debit Cash, and credit a current liability account identifying the source of the unearned revenue.

2 Upon earning the revenue, debit the unearned revenue account, and credit an earned revenue account.

To illustrate, assume that Allstate University sells 10,000 season football tickets at $50 each for its five-game home schedule. Allstate University records the sales of season tickets as follows.

August 6

Cash	500,000	
Unearned Football Ticket Revenue		500,000
(To record sale of 10,000 season tickets)		

After each game, Allstate University makes the following entry.

September 7

Unearned Football Ticket Revenue	100,000	
Football Ticket Revenue		100,000
(To record football ticket revenues earned)		

Unearned Football Ticket Revenue is, therefore, unearned revenue. Allstate University would report it as a current liability in the balance sheet. As revenue is earned, a transfer from unearned revenue to earned revenue occurs. Unearned revenue is material for some companies: In the airline industry, tickets sold for future flights represent almost 50 percent of total current liabilities.

Illustration 12-2 shows specific unearned and earned revenue accounts used in selected types of businesses.

Illustration 12-2

Unearned and Earned Revenue Accounts

	Account Title	
Type of Business	Unearned Revenue	Earned Revenue
Airline	Unearned Passenger Ticket Revenue	Passenger Revenue
Magazine publisher	Unearned Subscription Revenue	Subscription Revenue
Hotel	Unearned Rental Revenue	Rental Revenue
Auto dealer	Unearned Warranty Revenue	Warranty Revenue
Retailers	Unearned Gift Card Revenue	Sales Revenue

The balance sheet should report obligations for any commitments that are redeemable in goods and services. The income statement should report revenues earned during the period.

What do the numbers mean?

Numerous companies offer premiums to customers in the form of a promise of future goods or services as an incentive for purchases today. A premium plan that has widespread adoption is the frequent-flyer programs used by all major airlines. On the basis of mileage accumulated, frequent-flyer members receive discounted or free airline tickets. Airline customers can earn miles toward free travel by making long-distance phone calls, staying in hotels, and charging gasoline and groceries on a specified credit card. Those free tickets represent an enormous potential liability because people using them may displace paying passengers.

When airlines first started offering frequent-flyer bonuses, everyone assumed that the airlines could accommodate the free-ticket holders with otherwise-empty seats. That made the additional cost of the program so minimal that airlines didn't accrue it or report the small liability. But, as more and more paying passengers were crowded off flights by frequent-flyer awardees, the loss of revenues grew enormously. For example, **United Airlines** at one time reported a liability of $1.4 billion for advance ticket sales, a good portion of which pertained to free frequent-flyer tickets.

Although the profession has studied the accounting for this transaction, no authoritative guidelines have been issued.

Beyond the Numbers

Some companies, like **Microsoft** report unearned revenue related to future upgrades of its programs. Briefly discuss how a decline in the level of these unearned revenues can provide a signal about Microsoft's current sales.

Try it out! The following are selected 2008 transactions of Alston Company.

Sept. 1   Borrowed $90,000 by signing a $90,000, 8%, 6-month note.

Oct. 1   Sold 1,000 annual subscriptions to its monthly basketball magazine for $20 each.

Instructions

a Prepare the necessary annual adjusting entries for the preceding transactions at December 31, 2008.

b Prepare the entry on March 1, 2009 for payment of the note and interest.

Solution

a   **December 31, 2008**

Interest Expense ($90,000 × .08 × 4/12)	2,400	
Interest Payable		2,400
Unearned Subscription Revenue	5,000	
Subscription Revenue (1,000 × $20 × 3/12)		5,000

b	March 1, 2009		
Notes Payable		90,000	
Interest Payable		2,400	
Interest Expense ($90,000 × .08 × 2/12)		1,200	
Cash			93,600

SECTION TWO   LONG-TERM DEBT

Long-term debt consists of probable future sacrifices of economic benefits arising from present obligations that are not payable within a year or the operating cycle of the company, whichever is longer. Bonds payable, long-term notes payable, mortgages payable, pension liabilities, and lease liabilities are examples of long-term debt.

A company often incurs long-term debt through a formal process. For example, a corporation, per its bylaws, usually requires approval by the board of directors and the stockholders before it contracts long-term debt arrangements.

Generally, long-term note agreements or bond indentures state **covenants** or **restrictions** that protect both lenders and borrowers. The indenture or agreement often includes the amounts authorized to be issued, interest rate, due date(s), call provisions, property pledged as security, sinking fund requirements, working capital and dividend restrictions, and limitations concerning the assumption of additional debt. Companies should describe these stipulations in the body of the financial statements or the notes if important for a complete understanding of the financial position and the results of operations.[8]

ISSUING BONDS

Bonds are the most common type of long-term debt that companies report on the balance sheet. The main purpose of bonds is to borrow for the long term when the amount of capital needed is too large for one lender to supply. By issuing bonds in $100, $1,000, or $10,000 denominations, a company can divide a large amount of long-term indebtedness into many small investing units, thus enabling more than one lender to participate in the loan.

A bond arises from a contract known as a **bond indenture**. A bond represents a promise to pay: (1) a sum of money at a designated maturity rate, plus (2) periodic interest at a specified rate on the maturity amount (face value). Individual bonds are evidenced by a paper certificate and typically have a $1,000 face value. Companies usually make bond interest payments semiannually, although the interest rate is generally expressed as an annual rate.

---

[8]Although it would seem that these covenants provide adequate protection to the long-term debtholder, many bondholders suffer considerable losses when companies add more debt to the capital structure. Consider what can happen to bondholders in leveraged buyouts (LBOs), which are usually led by management. In an LBO of **RJR Nabisco**, for example, solidly rated 9⅜ percent bonds due in 2016 plunged 20 percent in value when management announced the leveraged buyout. Such a loss in value occurs because the additional debt added to the capital structure increases the likelihood of default. Although covenants protect bondholders, interpretations of the covenants can easily differ.

A company may sell an entire bond issue to an investment bank which acts as a selling agent in the process of marketing the bonds. In such arrangements, investment banks may either *underwrite* the entire issue by guaranteeing a certain sum to the company, thus taking the risk of selling the bonds for whatever price they can get (a procedure called *firm underwriting*). Or they may sell the bond issue for a commission on the proceeds of the sale (a procedure called *best-efforts underwriting*). Alternatively, the issuing company may sell the bonds directly to a large institution, financial or otherwise, without the aid of an underwriter (a *private placement*).

TYPES OF BONDS

Below, we define some of the more common types of bonds found in practice.

OBJECTIVE 2
Identify various types of bond issues.

TYPES OF BONDS

SECURED AND UNSECURED BONDS. **Secured bonds** are backed by a pledge of some sort of collateral. For example, *mortgage bonds* are secured by a claim on real estate; *collateral trust bonds* are secured by stocks and bonds of other corporations. Bonds not backed by collateral are **unsecured.** A **debenture bond** is unsecured. A so-called *junk bond* is unsecured and also very risky, and therefore pays a high interest rate. Companies often use junk bonds to finance leveraged buyouts.

TERM, SERIAL BONDS, AND CALLABLE BONDS. Bond issues that mature on a single date are called **term bonds.** Issues that mature in installments are called **serial bonds.** School or sanitary districts, municipalities, or other local taxing bodies that receive money through a special levy frequently use serially maturing bonds. **Callable bonds** give the issuer the right to call and retire the bonds prior to maturity.

CONVERTIBLE, COMMODITY-BACKED, AND DEEP DISCOUNT BONDS. Bonds that are convertible into other securities of a corporation for a specified time after issuance are **convertible bonds**.

Companies have developed two similar types of bonds in an attempt to attract capital in a tight money market—commodity-backed bonds and deep discount bonds. **Commodity-backed bonds** (also called **asset-linked bonds**) are redeemable in measures of a commodity, such as barrels of oil, tons of coal, or ounces of rare metal. To illustrate, **Sunshine Mining**, a silver-mining company, sold two issues of bonds redeemable with either $1,000 in cash or 50 ounces of silver, whichever is greater at maturity, and that have a stated interest rate of $8\frac{1}{2}$ percent. The accounting problem for such bonds is to project their maturity value; silver has fluctuated between $4 and $40 an ounce since the bonds were issued.

JCPenney Company sold the first publicly marketed long-term debt securities in the United States that do not bear interest. These **deep-discount bonds**, also referred to as **zero-interest debenture bonds**, are sold at a discount that provides the buyer's total interest payoff at maturity.

REGISTERED AND BEARER (COUPON) BONDS. Bonds issued in the name of the owner are **registered bonds.** They require surrender of the certificate and issuance of a new certificate to complete a sale. A **bearer** or **coupon bond**, however, is not recorded in the name of the owner and may be transferred from one owner to another by mere delivery.

INCOME AND REVENUE BONDS. **Income bonds** pay no interest unless the issuing company is profitable. **Revenue bonds** pay interest from specified revenue sources. Airports, school districts, counties, toll-road authorities, and governmental bodies most frequently issue revenue bonds.

How do investors monitor their bond investments? One way is to review the bond listings found in the newspaper or online. Corporate bond listings show the coupon (interest) rate, maturity date, and last price. However, because corporate bonds are more actively held by large institutional investors, the listings also indicate the current yield and the volume traded. Corporate bond listings would look like those below.

Issuer	Coupon Maturity	Price: High Low	Yield: High Low	Volume ($,000)
BellSouth Corp.	6.000	102.190	5.839	
	11/15/2034	95.370	6.357	23,125
General Motors Corp	8.375	96.426	8.721	
	07/15/2033	86.781	9.779	923,072

The companies issuing the bonds are listed in the first column, in this case, a telecommunications company **BellSouth Corp.**, and the automaker **General Motors Corp.**. Immediately after the names is a column with the interest rate paid by the bond as a percentage of its par value, with its maturity date below. The BellSouth bonds, for example, pay 6 percent and mature on November 15, 2034. The General Motors bonds pay quite a bit more at 8.375 percent.

The BellSouth bonds have a current yield of 6.3 percent based on its closing low price of 95.370 per $1,000. The high/low prices are based on trading in a five-day period, in which the volume traded on the exchange amounted to $23,125 million. For General Motors, at the high price of 96.426, its bonds yield 8.721 percent. The GM bonds had volume of nearly $1 billion dollars.

Also, as indicated in the chapter, interest rates and the bond's term to maturity have a real effect on bond prices. For example, an increase in interest rates will lead to a decline in bond values. Similarly, a decrease in interest rates will lead to a rise in bond values. The data reported below, based on three different bond funds, demonstrates these relationships between interest rate changes and bond values.

Bond Price Changes in Response to Interest Rate Changes	1% Interest Rate Increase	1% Interest Rate Decrease
Short-term fund (2–5 years)	−2.5%	+2.5%
Intermediate-term fund (5 years)	−5%	+5%
Long-term fund (10 years)	−10%	+10%

Data source: The Vanguard Group.

Another factor that affects bond prices is the call feature, which decreases the value of the bond. Investors must be rewarded for the risk that the issuer will call the bond if interest rates decline, which forces the investor to reinvest at lower rates.

Source: The Bond Market Association (*www.investinginbonds.com*) (accessed March 2007).

Beyond the Numbers

Some bonds are convertible. That is, the bondholders have the option to exchange their bonds for common shares, which could be quite valuable for the bonds issued by a growth company. What effect does a conversion have on the coupon rate of a bond?

VALUATION OF BONDS PAYABLE—DISCOUNT AND PREMIUM

The selling price of a bond issue is set by the supply and demand of buyers and sellers, relative risk, market conditions, and the state of the economy. The investment community values a bond at the present value of its future cash flows, which consist of (1) interest and (2) principal. The rate used to compute the present value of these cash flows is the interest rate that provides an acceptable return on an investment commensurate with the issuer's risk characteristics.

The interest rate written in the terms of the bond indenture (and often printed on the bond certificate) is known as the **stated, coupon,** or **nominal rate.** The issuer of the bonds sets this rate, expressed as a percentage of the **face value.** The rate is also called the **par value, principal amount,** or **maturity value** of the bonds.

If the rate employed by the investment community (buyers) differs from the stated rate, the present value of the bonds computed by the buyers (and the current purchase price) will differ from the face value of the bonds. **The difference between the face value and the present value of the bonds is either a discount or premium:**[9]

- If the bonds sell for *less than face value*, they sell at a **discount.**
- If the bonds sell for *more than face value*, they sell at a **premium.**

The rate of interest the bondholders actually earn is called the **effective yield** or the **market rate.** If bonds sell at a discount, the effective yield exceeds the stated rate. Conversely, if bonds sell at a premium, the effective yield is lower than the stated rate. While a bond is outstanding, several variables affect its price, most notably the market rate of interest. **There is an inverse relationship between the market interest rate and the price of the bond.**

Here we consider an example to illustrate the computation of the **present value of a bond issue.** Assume that ServiceMaster issues $100,000 in bonds, due in five years with 9 percent interest payable annually at year-end. At the time of issue, the market rate for such bonds is 11 percent. The following time diagram depicts both the interest and the principal cash flows.

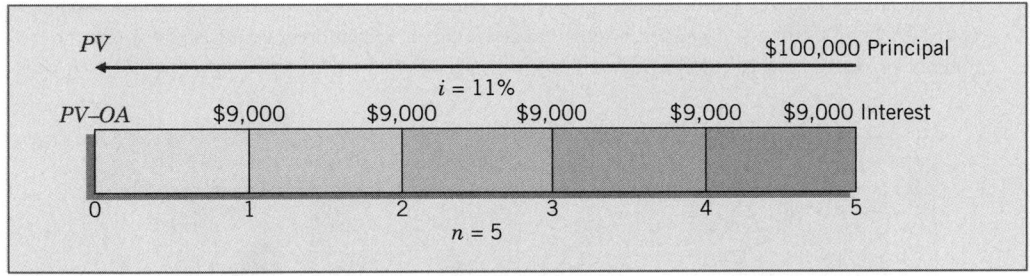

The actual principal and interest cash flows are discounted at an 11 percent rate for five periods as shown in Illustration 12-3.

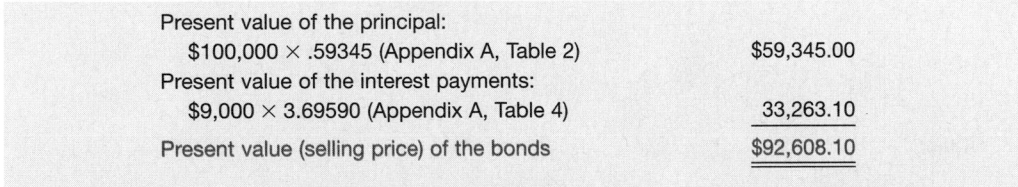

Present value of the principal:	
$100,000 × .59345 (Appendix A, Table 2)	$59,345.00
Present value of the interest payments:	
$9,000 × 3.69590 (Appendix A, Table 4)	33,263.10
Present value (selling price) of the bonds	$92,608.10

Illustration 12-3
Present Value Computation of Bond Selling at a Discount

By paying $92,608.10 at the date of issue, investors realize an effective rate or yield of 11 percent over the five-year term of the bonds. These bonds would sell at a discount of $7,391.90 ($100,000 − $92,608.10). The price at which the bonds sell is typically stated as a percentage of the face or par value of the bonds. For example, the ServiceMaster bonds sold for 92.6 (92.6% of par). If ServiceMaster had received $102,000, then the bonds sold for 102 (102% of par).

---

[9]Until the 1950s corporations commonly issued bonds with low, even-percentage coupons (such as 4 percent) to demonstrate their financial solidity. Frequently, large discounts resulted. More recently, it has become acceptable to set the stated rate of interest on bonds in rather precise amounts (such as 10.65 percent). Companies usually attempt to align the stated rate as closely as possible with the market or effective rate at the time of issue.

When bonds sell *below face value*, it means that investors demand a rate of interest **higher** than the stated rate. Usually this occurs because the investors can earn a greater rate on alternative investments of equal risk. They cannot change the stated rate, so they refuse to pay face value for the bonds. Thus, by changing the amount invested, they alter the effective rate of return. The investors receive interest at the stated rate computed on the face value, but they actually earn at **an effective rate that exceeds the stated rate because they paid less than face value for the bonds**.

What do the numbers mean?   "How's My Rating?"

Two major publication companies, **Moody's Investors Service** and **Standard & Poor's Corporation**, issue quality ratings on every public debt issue. The following table summarizes the ratings issued by Standard & Poor's, along with historical default rates on bonds with different ratings. As expected, bonds receiving the highest quality rating of AAA have the lowest historical default rates. Bonds rated below BBB, which are considered below investment grade ("junk bonds"), experience default rates ranging from 20 to 50 percent.

Original rating	AAA	AA	A	BBB	BB	B	CCC
Default rate*	0.52%	1.31	2.32	6.64	19.52	35.76	54.38

*Percentage of defaults by issuers recently rated by Standard & Poor's; based on rating they were initially assigned.
Data source: Standard & Poor's Corp.

Debt ratings reflect credit quality. The market closely monitors these ratings when determining the required yield and pricing of bonds at issuance and in periods after issuance, especially if a bond's rating is upgraded or downgraded. Data on recent downgrades suggest that the number of "fallen angels" (downgraded debt) is on the rise.

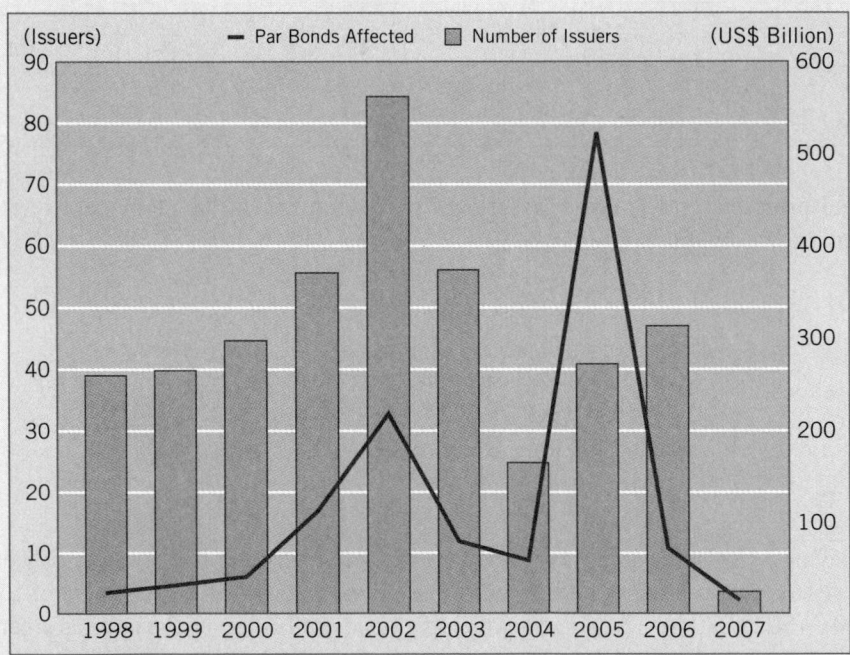

Data as of Feb. 1, 2007.
Source: Standard & Poor's Global Fixed Income Research (February 6, 2007).

As recently as 1999, the number and amount of upgrades exceeded downgrades. However, following a decline in 2003, the number of fallen angels has increased from 2004–2006, and 2007 was off to a good start. It is not surprising, then, that bond investors and companies who issue bonds keep a close watch on debt ratings—both when bonds are issued and while the bonds are outstanding.

Source: A. Borrus, M. McNamee, and H. Timmons, "The Credit Raters: How They Work and How They Might Work Better," *Business Week* (April 8, 2002), pp. 38–40; Standard and Poors, *Global Fixed Income Research*, "Fallen Angel Activity" (February 6, 2007.)

Beyond the Numbers

What effect will a ratings downgrade or upgrade have on a company's profitability?

Bonds Issued at Par on Interest Date

When a company issues bonds on an interest payment date at par (at face value), it accrues no interest. No premium or discount exists. The company simply records the cash proceeds and the face value of the bonds.

To illustrate, if Buchanan Company issues at par 10-year term bonds with a par value of $800,000, dated January 1, 2008, and bearing interest at an annual rate of 10 percent payable semiannually on January 1 and July 1, it records the following entry:

Cash	800,000	
Bonds Payable		800,000

Buchanan records the first semiannual interest payment of $40,000 ($800,000 × .10 × 1/2) on July 1, 2008, as follows.

Bond Interest Expense	40,000	
Cash		40,000

It records accrued interest expense at December 31, 2008 (year-end) as follows.

Bond Interest Expense	40,000	
Bond Interest Payable		40,000

Bonds Issued at Discount or Premium on Interest Date

If Buchanan Company issues the $800,000 of bonds described above, at 97 (meaning 97% of par), it records the issuance as follows.

Cash ($800,000 × .97)	776,000	
Discount on Bonds Payable	24,000	
Bonds Payable		800,000

Recall from our earlier discussion that because of its relation to interest, **companies amortize the discount and charge it to interest expense over the period of time that the bonds are outstanding**. We discuss the methods used to amortize the discount or premium in Appendix 12A.

Classification of Discount and Premium

Discount on bonds payable is **not an asset**. It does not provide any future economic benefit. A bond discount means that the company borrowed less than the face or maturity value of the bond. It therefore faces an actual (effective) interest rate higher than the stated (nominal) rate. Conceptually, discount on bonds payable is a liability valuation account. That is, it reduces the face or maturity amount of the related liability. This account is referred to as a **contra account**.

Premium on bonds payable has no existence apart from the related debt. The lower interest cost results because the proceeds of borrowing exceed the face or maturity amount of the debt. Conceptually, premium on bonds payable also is a liability valuation account.

It adds to the face or maturity amount of the related liability. This account is referred to as an **adjunct account.** As a result of such an account, **companies report bond discounts and bond premiums as a direct deduction from or addition to the face amount of the bond**.

Costs of Issuing Bonds

The issuance of bonds involves engraving and printing costs, legal and accounting fees, commissions, promotion costs, and other similar charges. According to *APB Opinion No. 21*, companies debit these items to a **deferred charge account** (asset) for Unamortized Bond Issue Costs; companies then amortize these items over the life of the debt, in a manner similar to that used for discount on bonds.

We disagree with this approach. Unamortized bond-issue cost, in our view is an expense (or a reduction in the value of the related liability). Apparently, the FASB also has some concern with current GAAP treatment; it notes in *Concepts Statement No. 6* that debt-issue cost is not considered an asset because it provides no future economic benefit. The cost of issuing bonds, in effect, reduces the proceeds of the bonds issued and increases the effective interest rate. Companies may thus account for it the same as the unamortized discount.

There is an obvious difference between GAAP and *Concepts Statement No. 6*'s view of debt-issue costs. However, until an issued standard supersedes *Opinion No. 21*, **acceptable GAAP for debt-issue costs is to treat them as a deferred charge and amortize them over the life of the debt**.

To illustrate the accounting for costs of issuing bonds, assume that Microchip Corporation issued and sold $20,000,000 of 10-year debenture bonds for $20,795,000 on January 1, 2008. Costs of issuing the bonds were $245,000. Microchip records the issuance of the bonds as follows.

January 1, 2008

Cash	20,550,000	
Unamortized Bond Issue Costs	245,000	
Premium on Bonds Payable		795,000
Bonds Payable		20,000,000
(To record issuance of bonds)		

Microchip amortizes the bond-issue costs over the life of the bonds.

Extinguishment of Debt

<table>
<tr><td>

OBJECTIVE **4**

Describe the accounting procedures for the extinguishment of debt.

</td></tr>
</table>

How do companies record the payment of debt—often referred to as **extinguishment of debt**? If a company holds the bonds (or any other form of debt security) to maturity, the answer is straightforward: The company does not compute any gains or losses. It will have fully amortized any premium or discount and any issue costs at the date the bonds mature. As a result, the carrying amount will equal the maturity (face) value of the bond. As the maturity or face value will also equal to the bond's market value at that time, no gain or loss exists.

In some cases, a company extinguishes debt before its maturity date. The amount paid on extinguishment or redemption before maturity, including any call premium and expense of reacquisition, is called the **reacquisition price**. On any specified date, the **net carrying amount** of the bonds is the amount payable at maturity, adjusted for unamortized premium or discount and cost of issuance. Any excess of the net carrying amount over the reacquisition price is a **gain from extinguishment**. If the reacquisition price exceeds the net carrying amount, the company experiences a **loss from extinguishment**. At the time of reacquisition, **companies must amortize the unamortized**

premium or discount, and any costs of issue applicable to the bonds, up to the reacquisition date.

To illustrate, assume that on January 1, 2000, General Bell Corp. issued at 97 bonds with a par value of $800,000, due in 20 years. It incurred bond issue costs totaling $16,000. Eight years after the issue date, General Bell calls the entire issue at 101 and cancels it.[10] At that time, the unamortized discount balance is $14,400, and the unamortized bond issue cost balance is $9,600. Illustration 12-4 indicates how General Bell computes the loss on redemption (extinguishment).

Reacquisition price ($800,000 × 1.01)		$808,000
Net carrying amount of bonds redeemed:		
Face value	$800,000	
Unamortized discount	(14,400)	
Unamortized issue costs	(9,600)	776,000
Loss on redemption		$ 32,000

Illustration 12-4
Computation of Loss on Redemption of Bonds

General Bell records the reacquisition and cancellation of the bonds as follows.

Bonds Payable	800,000	
Loss on Redemption of Bonds	32,000	
Discount on Bonds Payable		14,400
Unamortized Bond Issue Costs		9,600
Cash		808,000

It is often advantageous for the issuing corporation to acquire the **entire** outstanding bond issue and replace it with a new bond issue bearing a lower rate of interest. The replacement of an existing issuance with a new one is called **refunding**. Whether the early redemption or other extinguishment of outstanding bonds is a nonrefunding or a refunding situation, a company should recognize the difference (gain or loss) between the reacquisition price and the net carrying amount of the redeemed bonds in income of the period of redemption.

Try it out!

Jordan Company issued $400,000 of 9% bonds on January 1, 2008. The bonds are due January 1, 2013, with interest payable each July 1 and January 1. The bonds were issued at 102. On January 1, 2011, Jordan retired the bonds at 99. At the time of retirement, the unamortized premium was $3,200.

Instructions

Prepare Jordan's journal entries for:

a January 1, 2008.

b December 31, 2008. (Ignore bond premium amortization.)

c January 1, 2011.

---

[10]The issuer of callable bonds must generally exercise the call on an interest date. Therefore, the amortization of any discount or premium will be up to date, and there will be no accrued interest. However, early extinguishments through purchases of bonds in the open market are more likely to be on other than an interest date. If the purchase is not made on an interest date, the company must amortize the discount or premium, and it must accrue the interest payable from the last interest date to the date of purchase.

Solution

a January 1, 2008

Cash ($400,000 × 1.02)	408,000	
Bonds Payable		400,000
Premium on Bonds Payable		8,000

b December 31, 2008

Bond Interest Expense ($400,000 × 0.9 × 6/12)	18,000	
Bond Interest Payable		18,000

c January 1, 2011

Bonds Payable	400,000	
Premium on Bonds Payable	3,200	
Cash ($400,000 × .99)		396,000
Gain on Redemption of Bonds ($403,200 − $396,000)		7,200

SECTION THREE SPECIAL ISSUES

In this section we present three important issues related to liability accounting and presentation:

1 Contingencies.

2 Off–balance-sheet financing.

3 Presentation and analysis.

CONTINGENCIES

A **contingency** is "an existing condition, situation, or set of circumstances involving uncertainty as to possible gain or loss to an enterprise that will ultimately be resolved when one or more future events occur or fail to occur."[11]

Gain Contingencies

> OBJECTIVE **5**
>
> Identify the criteria used to account for and disclose gain and loss contingencies.

Gain contingencies are claims or rights to receive assets (or have a liability reduced) whose existence is uncertain but which may become valid eventually. The typical gain contingencies are:

1 Possible receipts of monies from gifts, donations, bonuses, and so on.

2 Possible refunds from the government in tax disputes.

3 Pending court cases with a probable favorable outcome.

4 Tax loss carryforwards (discussed in Chapter 15).

Companies follow a conservative policy in this area. **They do not record gain contingencies**. A company discloses gain contingencies in the notes only when a high probability

---

[11]"Accounting for Contingencies," *Statement of Financial Accounting Standards No. 5* (Stamford, Conn.: FASB, 1975), par. 1.

exists for realizing them. As a result, it is unusual to find information about contingent gains in the financial statements and the accompanying notes. Illustration 12-5 presents an example of a disclosure of a gain contingency.

BMC Industries, Inc.

Note 13: Legal Matters.   In the first quarter, a U.S. District Court in Miami, Florida, awarded the Company a $5.1 million judgment against Barth Industries (Barth) of Cleveland, Ohio and its parent, Nesco Holdings, Inc. (Nesco). The judgment relates to an agreement under which Barth and Nesco were to help automate the plastic lens production plant in Fort Lauderdale, Florida. The Company has not recorded any income relating to this judgment because Barth and Nesco have filed an appeal.

Illustration 12-5
Disclosure of Gain
Contingency

Loss Contingencies

Loss contingencies involve possible losses. A liability incurred as a result of a loss contingency is by definition a contingent liability. **Contingent liabilities** depend on the occurrence of one or more future events to confirm either the amount payable, the payee, the date payable, or its existence. That is, these factors depend on a contingency.

When a loss contingency exists, the likelihood that the future event or events will confirm the incurrence of a liability can range from probable to remote. The FASB uses the terms **probable**, **reasonably possible**, and **remote** to identify three areas within that range and assigns the following meanings.

> **Probable**. The future event or events are likely to occur.
>
> **Reasonably possible**. The chance of the future event or events occurring is more than remote but less than likely.
>
> **Remote**. The chance of the future event or events occurring is slight.

Companies should accrue an estimated loss from a loss contingency by a charge to expense and a liability recorded only if **both** of the following conditions are met.[12]

1 Information available prior to the issuance of the financial statements indicates that it is **probable that the company has incurred a liability** at the date of the financial statements. A company does not need to know the exact payee nor the exact date payable. **What it must know, though, is whether it is probable that it incurred a liability**.

2 The company can **reasonably estimate** the amount of the loss.

To determine a reasonable estimate of the liability, a company may use its own experience, experience of other companies in the industry, engineering or research studies, legal advice, or educated guesses by qualified personnel.

Use of the terms *probable, reasonably possible,* and *remote* to classify contingencies involves judgment and subjectivity. Illustration 12-6 (page 622) lists examples of loss contingencies and the general accounting treatment accorded them.

Practicing accountants express concern over the diversity that now exists in the interpretation of *probable, reasonably possible*, and *remote*. Current practice relies heavily on the exact language used in responses received from lawyers; such language is necessarily

---

[12]We discuss loss contingencies that result in the incurrence of a liability in this chapter. We discuss loss contingencies that result in the impairment of an asset (e.g., collectibility of receivables or threat of expropriation of assets) in other sections of this textbook.

Illustration 12-6
Accounting Treatment of
Loss Contingencies

Usually Accrued

Loss Related to:

1. Collectibility of receivables
2. Obligations related to product warranties and product defects
3. Premiums offered to customers

Not Accrued

Loss Related to:

4. Risk of loss or damage of enterprise property by fire, explosion, or other hazards
5. General or unspecified business risks
6. Risk of loss from catastrophes assumed by property and casualty insurance companies, including reinsurance companies

May Be Accrued*

Loss Related to:

7. Threat of expropriation of assets
8. Pending or threatened litigation
9. Actual or possible claims and assessments**
10. Guarantees of indebtedness of others
11. Obligations of commercial banks under "standby letters of credit"
12. Agreements to repurchase receivables (or the related property) that have been sold

*Should be accrued when both criteria—probable and reasonably estimable—are met.
**Estimated amounts of losses incurred prior to the balance sheet date but settled subsequently should be accrued as of the balance sheet date.

biased and protective rather than predictive. As a result, accruals and disclosures of contingencies vary considerably in practice. Some of the more common loss contingencies are the following.[13]

1 Litigation, claims, and assessments.

2 Guarantee and warranty costs.

3 Environmental liabilities.

4 Self-insurance risks.

Below, we examine these types of loss contingencies. Note that companies do not report in the notes to the financial statements those general risk contingencies inherent in business operations, such as the possibility of war, strike, uninsurable catastrophes, or a business recession.

Litigation, Claims, and Assessments

OBJECTIVE 6

Explain the accounting for different types of loss contingencies.

Companies must consider the following factors, among others, in determining whether to record a liability with respect to **pending or threatened litigation** and actual or possible **claims** and **assessments**.

1 The **time period** in which the underlying cause of action occurred.

2 The **probability** of an unfavorable outcome.

3 The ability to make a **reasonable estimate** of the amount of loss.

To report a loss and a liability in the financial statements, **the cause for litigation must have occurred on or before the date of the financial statements**. It does not matter that the company became aware of the existence or possibility of the lawsuit or claims after the date of the financial statements but before issuing them.

[13]*Accounting Trends and Techniques—2006* reports that of the 600 companies surveyed, companies reported loss contingencies as follows: litigation, 521; environmental, 254; insurance, 154; possible tax assessments, 134; governmental investigation, 127; and others, 80.

To evaluate the probability of an unfavorable outcome, a company considers the following: the nature of the litigation; the progress of the case; the opinion of legal counsel; its own and others' experience in similar cases; and any management response to the lawsuit.

However, companies can seldom predict the outcome of pending litigation with any assurance. And, even if the evidence available at the balance sheet date does not favor the company, it is hardly reasonable to expect the company to publish in its financial statements a dollar estimate of the probable negative outcome. Such specific disclosures might weaken the company's position in the dispute and encourage the plaintiff to intensify its efforts.

A typical example of the wording of such a litigation disclosure is the note to the financial statements of **Apple Computer, Inc.**, relating to litigation over repetitive stress injuries, as shown in Illustration 12-7.

Apple Computer, Inc.

"Repetitive Stress Injury" Litigation.   The Company is named in numerous lawsuits (fewer than 100) alleging that the plaintiff incurred so-called "repetitive stress injury" to the upper extremities as a result of using keyboards and/or mouse input devices sold by the Company. On October 4, in a trial of one of these cases (*Dorsey v. Apple*) in the United States District Court for the Eastern District of New York, the jury rendered a verdict in favor of the Company, and final judgment in favor of the Company has been entered. The other cases are in various stages of pretrial activity. These suits are similar to those filed against other major suppliers of personal computers. Ultimate resolution of the litigation against the Company may depend on progress in resolving this type of litigation in the industry overall.

Illustration 12-7
Disclosure of Litigation

With respect to **unfiled suits** and **unasserted claims and assessments**, a company must determine (1) the degree of **probability** that a suit may be filed or a claim or assessment may be asserted, and (2) the **probability** of an unfavorable outcome. For example, assume that the Federal Trade Commission investigates the Nawtee Company for restraint of trade and institutes enforcement proceedings. Private claims of triple damages for redress often follow such proceedings. In this case, Nawtee must determine the probability of the claims being asserted **and** the probability of triple damages being awarded. If both are probable, if the loss is reasonably estimable, and if the cause for action is dated on or before the date of the financial statements, then Nawtee should accrue the liability.[14]

Guarantee and Warranty Costs

A **warranty (product guarantee)** is a seller's promise to a buyer to make good on a deficiency of quantity, quality, or performance in a product. Manufacturers commonly use it as a sales promotion technique. Some automakers, for instance, "hyped" their sales by extending their new-car warranty to seven years or 100,000 miles. For a specified period of time following the date of sale to the consumer, manufacturers may promise to bear all or part of the cost of replacing defective parts, to perform any necessary repairs or servicing without charge, to refund the purchase price, or even to "double your money back."

Warranties and guarantees involve future costs. These additional costs, sometimes called "after costs" or "post-sale costs," frequently are significant. Although the future cost is

---

[14]Companies need not disclose contingencies involving an unasserted claim or assessment when no claimant has come forward unless (1) it is considered probable that a claim will be asserted, and (2) there is a reasonable possibility that the outcome will be unfavorable.

indefinite as to amount, due date, and even customer, a liability is probable in most cases. Companies should recognize this probable liability in the accounts if they can reasonably estimate it. The estimated amount of the liability includes all the costs that the company will incur after sale and delivery and that are incident to the correction of defects or deficiencies required under the warranty provisions. Warranty costs are a classic example of a loss contingency.

Companies use two basic methods of accounting for warranty costs: (1) the cash-basis method and (2) the accrual method.

Cash Basis. Under the **cash-basis method**, companies expense warranty costs as incurred. In other words, a **seller or manufacturer charges warranty costs to the period in which it complies with the warranty**. The company does not record a liability for future costs arising from warranties, nor does it charge the period of sale.

Companies frequently justify use of this method, the only one recognized for income tax purposes, on the basis of expediency when warranty costs are immaterial or when the warranty period is relatively short. A company must use the cash-basis method when it does not accrue a warranty liability in the year of sale either because:

1 it is not probable that a liability has been incurred, or

2 it cannot reasonably estimate the amount of the liability.

Accrual Basis. If it is probable that customers will make warranty claims *and* a company can reasonably estimate the costs involved, the company must use the accrual method. Under the **accrual method**, companies charge warranty costs to operating expense **in the year of sale**.

The accrual method is the generally accepted method. Companies should use it whenever the warranty is an integral and inseparable part of the sale and is viewed as a loss contingency. We refer to this approach as the **expense-warranty approach**.

Example of Expense-Warranty Approach. To illustrate the expense-warranty method, assume that Denson Machinery Company begins production on a new machine in July 2008, and sells 100 units at $5,000 each by its year-end, December 31, 2008. Each machine is under warranty for one year. the company estimates, based on past experience with a similar machine, that the warranty cost will average $200 per unit. Further, as a result of parts replacements and services rendered in compliance with machinery warranties, the company incurs $4,000 in warranty costs in 2008 and $16,000 in 2009. Entries to record the sale and servicing of machines would be as follows.

1 Sale of 100 machines at $5,000 each, July through December 2008:

Cash or Accounts Receivable	500,000	
Sales		500,000

2 Recognition of warranty expense, July through December 2008:

Warranty Expense	4,000	
Cash, Inventory, Accrued Payroll		4,000
(Warranty costs incurred)		
Warranty Expense	16,000	
Estimated Liability under Warranties		16,000
(To accrue estimated warranty costs)		

The December 31, 2008, balance sheet reports Estimated Liability Under Warranties as a current liability of $16,000, and the income statement for 2008 reports Warranty Expense of $20,000.

3 Recognition of warranty costs incurred in 2009 (on 2008 machinery sales):

Estimated Liability under Warranties	16,000	
Cash, Inventory, or Accrued Payroll		16,000
(Warranty costs incurred)		

If Denson Machinery applies the cash-basis method, it reports $4,000 as warranty expense in 2008 and $16,000 as warranty expense in 2009. It records all of the sale price as revenue in 2008. In many instances, application of the cash-basis method fails to match the warranty costs relating to the products sold during a given period with the revenues derived from such products. As such, **it violates the matching principle**. Where ongoing warranty policies exist year after year, the differences between the cash- and the expense- warranty basis probably would not be so great.

Sales-Warranty Approach. Companies sometimes sell a warranty **separately from the product**. For example, when you purchase a television set, you are entitled to the manufacturer's warranty. You also will undoubtedly be offered an extended warranty on the product at an additional cost.[15]

In this case, the seller should recognize separately the sale of the television with the manufacturer's warranty and the sale of the extended warranty.[16] This approach is referred to as the **sales-warranty approach**. **Companies defer revenue on the sale of the extended warranty** and generally recognize it on a straight-line basis over the life of the contract. The seller of the warranty defers revenue because it has an obligation to perform services over the life of the contract. The seller should defer and amortize only those costs that vary with and are directly related to the sale of the contracts (mainly commissions). It expenses costs such as employees' salaries, advertising, and general and administrative expenses that it would have incurred even if it did not sell a contract.

To illustrate, assume you purchase a new automobile from Hanlin Auto for $20,000. In addition to the regular warranty on the car (the manufacturer will pay for all repairs for the first 36,000 miles or three years, whichever comes first), you purchase at a cost of $600 an extended warranty that protects you for an additional three years or 36,000 miles. Hanlin Auto records the sale of the automobile (with the regular warranty) and the sale of the extended warranty on January 2, 2008, as follows.

Cash	20,600	
Sales		20,000
Unearned Warranty Revenue		600

At the end of the fourth year, it recognizes revenue (using straight-line amortization) as follows.

Unearned Warranty Revenue	200	
Warranty Revenue		200

> **WHAT'S THE PRINCIPLE?**
>
> Warranties are loss contingencies that satisfy the conditions necessary for a liability. Regarding the income statement, the *matching principle* requires that companies report the related expense in the period in which the sale occurs.

Because the extended warranty contract starts only after the regular warranty expires, Hanlin Auto defers revenue recognition until the fourth year. If it incurs the costs of performing services under the extended warranty contract on other than a straight-line basis (as historical evidence might indicate), Hanlin Auto should recognize revenue over the contract period in proportion to the costs it expected to incur in performing services under the contract.[17]

---

[15]A company separately prices a contract **if the customer has the option to purchase** the services provided under the contract for an expressly stated amount separate from the price of the product. An extended warranty or product maintenance contract usually meets these conditions.

[16]"Accounting for Separately Extended Warranty and Product Maintenance Contracts," *FASB Technical Bulletin No. 90–1* (Stamford, Conn.: FASB, 1990).

[17]Ibid, par. 3.

Do you wonder how companies like **Home Depot**, **Starbucks**, or **The Gap** account for the gift cards they issue? Evidently, a number of companies who recently got in trouble with their accounting for gift cards should have thought about it a bit more.

Here is how it works: When a company sells a gift card (or a gift certificate), there is some probability that the card or certificate will never be redeemed. Unredeemed gift cards are called *breakage*. An estimated 2 percent to 15 percent of gift cards go unredeemed.

The question is, when can a company recognize revenue on gift cards? For example, assume **Best Buy** sells a $100 gift card today for a cash receipt of $100. One common accounting for the gift card is to record on the sale date income of $10 and $90 of an unearned revenue liability. This approach assumes that that typically 10 percent of gift cards will never be redeemed based on historical experience (i.e., a 10% breakage rate).

The SEC disagrees. It says that the appropriate accounting on the date of the gift card sale would be to increase cash by $100 and to record an unearned revenue of $100. The company should not immediately record any income related to unredeemed gift cards. Generally, unearned revenue becomes earned when the seller is legally released from its obligation due to redemption or expiration. And since gift cards may be presented to a retailer at any time, the deferred revenue liability is classified as current on a company's balance sheet. It is easy to see why some companies want to recognize some of the breakage income earlier.

Indeed, they can recognize some breakage income earlier, but only if they can reasonably and objectively estimate the amount of breakage and time period of actual gift card redemption. If a retailer meets those criteria, then it can recognize some breakage revenue earlier but must allocate it over the breakage period. In our example above, if **Best Buy** has a four-year breakage period, it could recognize $2.50 ($10 ÷ 4) in the year of the sale. So handle the accounting for gift cards with care, or you risk a call from the SEC.

Source: "SEC Spurns Immediate Recognition of Gift Card 'Breakage,'" Bear Stearns Equity Research—Accounting & Tax Policy (December 6, 2005).

Beyond the Numbers

Even though an increase in gift card unearned revenue increases current liabilities (and may indicate reduced liquidity), what signal about future profitability do changes in unearned revenue provide?

Environmental Liabilities

Estimates to clean up existing toxic waste sites total upward of $752 billion over a 30-year period. In addition, cost estimates of cleaning our air and preventing future deterioration of the environment run even higher. Consider some of the average environmental costs per company in various industries:

	Amount in Dollars	Percentage of Revenues
High-tech companies	$2 million	6.1%.
Utilities	$340 million	6.1%
Steel and metals	$50 million	2.9%
Oil companies	$430 million	1.9%

Given that the average pretax profit of the 500 largest U.S. manufacturing companies recently was 7.7 percent of sales, these figures are staggering!

These costs will only grow when we take into account federal "Superfund legislation." This legislation provides not only a government-supported fund to clean up pollution, but also a mandate to clean up existing waste sites. Further, it provided the Environmental Protection Agency (EPA) with the power to clean up waste sites and charge the clean-up costs to parties the EPA deems responsible for contaminating the site. These potentially responsible parties have an onerous liability. The EPA estimates that it will likely cost an average of $25 million to clean up each polluted site. For the most troublesome sites, the cost could easily reach $100 million or more.

In many industries, the construction and operation of long-lived assets involves obligations associated with the retirement of those assets. For example, when a mining company opens a strip mine, it may also commit to restore the land once it completes mining. Similarly, when an oil company erects an offshore drilling platform, it may be legally obligated to dismantle and remove the platform at the end of its useful life.

Accounting Recognition of Asset Retirement Obligations. A company must recognize an **asset retirement obligation (ARO)** when it has an existing legal obligation associated with the retirement of a long-lived asset and when it can reasonably estimate the amount of the liability. Companies should record the ARO at fair value.[18]

Obligating Events. Examples of existing legal obligations, which require recognition of a liability include, but are not limited to:

- decommissioning nuclear facilities,
- dismantling, restoring, and reclamation of oil and gas properties,
- certain closure, reclamation, and removal costs of mining facilities,
- closure and post-closure costs of landfills.

In order to capture the benefits of these long-lived assets, **the company is generally legally obligated for the costs associated with retirement of the asset, whether the company hires another party to perform the retirement activities or performs the activities with its own workforce and equipment.** AROs give rise to various recognition patterns. For example, the obligation may arise at the outset of the asset's use (e.g., erection of an oil-rig), or it may build over time (e.g., a landfill that expands over time).

Measurement. A company initially measures an ARO at **fair value,** which is defined as the amount that the company would pay in an active market to settle the ARO. While active markets do not exist for many AROs, companies should estimate fair value based on the best information available. Such information could include market prices of similar liabilities, if available. Alternatively, companies may use present value techniques to estimate fair value.

Recognition and Allocation. To record an ARO in the financial statements, a company includes the cost associated with the ARO in the carrying amount of the related long-lived asset, and it records a liability for the same amount. It records an asset retirement cost as part of the related asset because these costs are tied to operating the asset and are necessary to prepare the asset for its intended use. Therefore, the value of the specific asset (e.g., mine, drilling platform, nuclear power plant) should be increased because the future economic benefit comes from the use of this productive asset. **Companies should not record the capitalized asset retirement costs in a separate account because there is no future economic benefit that can be associated with these costs alone.**

In subsequent periods, companies allocate the cost of the ARO to expense over the period of the related asset's useful life. Companies may use the straight-line method for this allocation, as well as other systematic and rational allocations.

Illustration of ARO Accounting Provisions. To illustrate the accounting for AROs, assume that on January 1, 2008, Wildcat Oil Company erected an oil platform in the Gulf of Mexico. Wildcat is legally required to dismantle and remove the platform at the end of its useful life, estimated to be five years. Wildcat estimates that dismantling and removal will

---

[18]"Accounting for Asset Retirement Obligations," *Statement of Financial Accounting Standards No. 143* (Norwalk, Conn.: FASB, 2001).

cost $1,000,000. Based on a 10 percent discount rate, the present value of the asset retirement obligation is $620,920 ($1,000,000 × .62092). Wildcat records this ARO as follows.

January 1, 2008

Drilling Platform	620,920	
Asset Retirement Obligation		620,920

During the life of the asset, Wildcat allocates the asset retirement cost to expense. Using the straight-line method, Wildcat makes the following entries to record this expense.

December 31, 2008, 2009, 2010, 2011, 2012

Depreciation Expense ($620,920 ÷ 5)	124,184	
Accumulated Depreciation		124,184

In addition, Wildcat must accrue interest expense each period. Wildcat records interest expense and the related increase in the asset retirement obligation on December 31, 2008, as follows.

December 31, 2008

Interest Expense ($620,920 × 10%)	62,092	
Asset Retirement Obligation		62,092

On January 10, 2013, Wildcat contracts with Rig Reclaimers, Inc. to dismantle the platform at a contract price of $995,000. Wildcat makes the following journal entry to record settlement of the ARO.

January 10, 2013

Asset Retirement Obligation	1,000,000	
Gain on Settlement of ARO		5,000
Cash		995,000

WHAT'S THE PRINCIPLE?

Even if companies can estimate the amount of losses with a high degree of certainty, the losses are not liabilities because they result from a future event and not from a past event.

Generally, companies need to provide more extensive disclosure regarding environmental liabilities. In addition, companies should record more of these liabilities. The SEC believes that companies should not delay recognition of a liability due to significant uncertainty. The SEC argues that if the liability is within a range, and no amount within the range is the best estimate, then management should recognize the minimum amount of the range. That treatment is in accordance with *FASB Interpretation No. 14*, "Reasonable Estimation of the Amount of a Loss." The SEC also believes that companies should report environmental liabilities in the balance sheet independent of recoveries from third parties. Thus, companies may not net possible insurance recoveries against liabilities but must show them separately. Because there is much litigation regarding recovery of insurance proceeds, these "assets" appear to be gain contingencies. Therefore, companies will not be reporting these on the balance sheet.[19]

Self-Insurance

A company may take out insurance policies against many contingencies such as fire, flood, storm, and accident. Some contingencies, however, are not insurable, or the insurance rates are prohibitive (e.g., earthquakes and riots). For such contingencies, some companies adopt a self-insurance policy.

---

[19]As we indicated earlier, the FASB pronouncements on this topic require that when some amount within the range appears at the time to be a better estimate than any other amount within the range, a company accrues that amount. When no amount within the range is a better estimate than any other amount, the company **accrues** the dollar amount at the low end of the range and **discloses** the dollar amount at the high end of the range. See *FASB Interpretation No. 14*, "Reasonable Estimation of the Amount of a Loss" (Stamford, Conn.: FASB, 1976), par. 3, and *FASB Statement No. 5*, "Accounting for Contingencies" (Stamford, Conn.: FASB, 1975).

Despite its name, **self-insurance** is **not insurance**, but **risk assumption**. Any company that assumes its own risks puts itself in the position of incurring expenses or losses as they occur. There is little theoretical justification for the establishment of a liability based on a hypothetical charge to insurance expense. This is "as if" accounting. The conditions for accrual stated in *FASB Statement No. 5* are not satisfied prior to the occurrence of the event. Until that time there is no diminution in the value of the property. And unlike an insurance company, which has contractual obligations to reimburse policyholders for losses, a company can have no such obligation to itself and, hence, no liability either before or after the occurrence of damage.[20]

The note shown in Illustration 12-8 from the annual report of **Adolph Coors Company** is typical of the self-insurance disclosure.

INTERNATIONAL INSIGHT

In Switzerland, companies may make provisions for general (nonspecified) contingencies to the extent allowed by tax regulations.

Illustration 12-8
Disclosure of Self-Insurance

Adolph Coors Company

Notes to Financial Statements

Note 4: Commitments and Contingencies. It is generally the policy of the Company to act as a self-insurer for certain insurable risks consisting primarily of physical loss to corporate property, business interruption resulting from such loss, employee health insurance programs, and workers' compensation. Losses and claims are accrued as incurred.

Exposure to **risks of loss resulting from uninsured past injury to others**, however, is an existing condition involving uncertainty about the amount and timing of losses that may develop. In such a case, a contingency does exist. A company with a fleet of vehicles for example, would have to accrue uninsured losses resulting from injury to others or damage to the property of others that took place prior to the date of the financial statements (if the experience of the company or other information enables it to make a reasonable estimate of the liability). However, it should not establish a liability for **expected future injury** to others or damage to the property of others, even if it can reasonably estimate the amount of losses.

OFF–BALANCE-SHEET FINANCING

What do **Krispy Kreme**, **Cisco Systems**, **Enron**, and **Adelphia Communications** have in common? All have been accused of using off–balance-sheet financing to minimize the reporting of debt on their balance sheets. **Off–balance-sheet financing** is an attempt to borrow monies is such a way that prevents the recording of obligations. It has become an issue of extreme importance. Many allege, for example, that Enron, in one of the largest corporate failures on record, hid a considerable amount of its debt off the balance sheet. As a result, given the public's concerns about what happened at Enron, any company that uses off–balance-sheet financing today risks having investors dump their stock, and having the share price fall as a result.

Nevertheless, a considerable amount of off–balance-sheet financing continues to exist. As one writer noted, "The basic drives of humans are few: to get enough food, to find shelter, and to keep debt off the balance sheet."

OBJECTIVE 7

Explain the reporting of off–balance-sheet financing arrangements.

---

[20]"Accounting for Contingencies," *FASB Statement No. 5,* op. cit., par. 28. A commentary in *Forbes* (June 15, 1974), p. 42, stated its position on this matter quite succinctly: "The simple and unquestionable fact of life is this: Business is cyclical and full of unexpected surprises. Is it the role of accounting to disguise this unpleasant fact and create a fairyland of smoothly rising earnings? Or, should accounting reflect reality, warts and all—floods, expropriations and all manner of rude shocks?"

Different Forms

Off–balance-sheet financing can take many different forms:

1 **Nonconsolidated Subsidiary:** Under GAAP, a parent company does not have to consolidate a subsidiary company that is less than 50 percent owned. In such cases, the parent therefore does not report the assets and liabilities of the subsidiary. All the parent reports on its balance sheet is the investment in the subsidiary. As a result, users of the financial statements may not understand that the subsidiary has considerable debt for which the parent may ultimately be liable if the subsidiary runs into financial difficulty.

2 **Special Purpose Entity (SPE):** A company creates a **special purpose entity** to perform a special project. To illustrate, assume that Clarke Company decides to build a new factory, but management does not want to report on its balance sheet the borrowing used to fund the construction. Instead, it creates an SPE whose sole purpose is to build the plant. The SPE finances and builds the plant. In return, Clarke guarantees that it or some outside party will purchase all the products produced by the plant. (Some refer to this as a **take-or-pay contract**). As a result, Clarke does not report the asset or liability on its books. Although the accounting rules in this area are complex, a company can achieve this objective with relative ease.

3 **Operating Leases:** Another way that companies keep debt off the balance sheet is by leasing. Instead of owning the assets, companies lease them. Again, by meeting certain conditions, the company has to report only rent expense each period and to provide note disclosure of the transaction. Note that SPEs often use leases to accomplish off–balance-sheet treatment. We discuss accounting for lease transactions in Chapter 17.

Expanded Discussion of Special Purpose Entities

Rationale

Why do companies engage in off–balance-sheet financing? A major reason is that many believe that **removing debt enhances the quality of the balance sheet** and permits credit to be obtained more readily and at less cost.

Second, loan covenants often limit the amount of debt a company may have. As a result, the company uses off–balance-sheet financing because **these types of commitments might not be considered in computing the debt limitation**.

Third, some argue that companies severely understate the asset side of the balance sheet. For example, companies that use LIFO costing for inventories and depreciate assets on an accelerated basis will often have carrying amounts for inventories and property, plant, and equipment that are much lower than their current values. As an offset to these lower values, some believe that part of the debt does not have to be reported. In other words, **if companies report assets at current values**, less pressure would undoubtedly exist for off–balance-sheet financing arrangements.

Whether the arguments above have merit is debatable. The general idea of "out of sight, out of mind" may not be true in accounting. Many users of financial statements indicate that they factor these off–balance-sheet financing arrangements into their computations when assessing debt to equity relationships. Many loan covenants also attempt to account for these complex arrangements. Nevertheless, many companies still believe that benefits will accrue if they omit certain obligations from the balance sheet.

As a response to off–balance-sheet financing arrangements, the FASB has increased disclosure (note) requirements. This response is consistent with an "efficient markets" philosophy: The important question is not whether the presentation is off–balance-sheet or not, but whether the items are disclosed at all. In addition, the SEC, in response to the Sarbanes-Oxley Act of 2002, now requires companies to provide related information in the management discussion and analysis section of their annual report. Specifically, companies must disclose (1) all contractual obligations in a tabular format and (2) contingent liabilities and commitments in either a textual or tabular format. We believe that recording more obligations on the balance sheet would enhance financial reporting. Given the problems with companies such as **Enron, Dynergy, Williams Company, Adelphia Communications**, and **Calpine**, our expectation is that less off–balance-sheet financing will occur in the future.[21]

PRESENTATION AND ANALYSIS

Presentation of Current Liabilities

Companies commonly present the current liabilities accounts as the first classification in the liabilities and stockholders' equity section of the balance sheet. Within the current liabilities section, companies have a choice of the sequence in which they list accounts: They may list current liabilities accounts in order of maturity, in descending order of amount, or in order of liquidation preference.

Detail and supplemental information concerning current liabilities should be sufficient to meet the requirement of full disclosure. Companies should clearly identify secured liabilities, as well as indicate the related assets pledged as collateral. If the due date of any liability can be extended, a company should disclose the details. Finally, a company should not offset current liabilities against assets that it will apply to their liquidation.

Presentation of Long-Term Debt

Companies that have large amounts and numerous issues of long-term debt frequently report only one amount in the balance sheet, supported with comments and schedules in the accompanying notes. Companies should report long-term debt that **matures within one year** as a current liability, unless they are using noncurrent assets to accomplish retirement. If the company plans to refinance debt, convert it into stock, or retire it from a bond retirement fund, it should continue to report the debt as noncurrent. However, the company should disclose the method it will use in its liquidation.

Note disclosures generally indicate the nature of the liabilities, maturity dates, interest rates, call provisions, conversion privileges, restrictions imposed by the creditors, and assets designated or pledged as security. Companies should show in the assets section of the balance sheet any assets pledged as security for the debt. Companies should also disclose the fair value of the long-term debt if it is practical to estimate fair value. Finally, companies must disclose future payments for sinking fund requirements and maturity amounts of long-term debt for each of the next five years. These disclosures aid financial statement users in evaluating the amounts and timing of future cash flows. Illustration 12-9 (page 632) shows the type of information provided for **Best Buy Co.** If the company has any off–balance-sheet financing, it must provide extensive note disclosure.

Presentation of Contingencies

A company records a loss contingency and a liability if the loss is *both* probable and estimable. But, if the loss is *either* probable or estimable **but not both**, and if there is at least a **reasonable possibility** that a company may have incurred a liability, it must disclose the information shown in the notes at the top of page 633.

OBJECTIVE **8**

Indicate how to present and analyze liabilities and contingencies.

Additional Disclosures of Current Liabilities

---

[21]It is unlikely that the FASB will be able to stop all types of off–balance-sheet transactions. Financial information is the Holy Grail of Wall Street. Developing new financial instruments and arrangements to sell and market to customers is not only profitable but also adds to the prestige of the investment firms that create them. Thus, new financial products will continue to appear that will test the ability of the FASB to develop appropriate accounting standards for them.

Illustration 12-9
Liability Disclosure

BEST BUY CO.
(dollars in millions)

Assets	February 25, 2006	February 26, 2005
Current Assets		
Cash and cash equivalents	$ 681	$ 354
Short-term investments	3,051	2,994
Receivables	506	375
Merchandise inventories	3,338	2,851
Other current assets	409	329
Total current assets	$7,985	$6,903
Current Liabilities		
Accounts payable	$3,234	$2,824
Unredeemed gift card liabilities	469	410
Accrued compensation and related expenses	354	234
Accrued liabilities	878	844
Accured income taxes	703	575
Current portion of long-term debt	418	72
Total current liabilities	$6,056	$4,959
Long-Term Liabilities	$ 373	$ 358
Long-Term Debt	$ 178	$ 528

Note 4. Debt

Long-term debt consists of the following:

	Feb. 25, 2006	Feb. 26, 2005
Convertible subordinated debentures, unsecured, due 2022, initial interest rate 2.25%	$ 402	$ 402
Financing lease obligations, due 2009 to 2026, interest rates ranging from 3.0% to 6.1%	157	107
Capital lease obligations, due 2007 to 2026, interest rates ranging from 1.8% to 8.9%	27	13
Other debt, due 2010. interest rates ranging from 8.4% to 8.8%	10	23
Master lease obligations, due 2006, interest rate 5.9%	—	55
Total debt	596	600
Less: current portion[1]	(418)	(72)
Total long-term debt	$ 178	$ 528

[1]Since holders of our debentures due in 2022 may require us to purchase all or a portion of their debentures on January 15, 2007, we have classified our debentures in the current portion of long-term debt at February 25, 2006.

Lease obligations and other debt are secured by certain property and equipment with a net book value of $41 and $98 at February 25, 2006, and February 26, 2005, respectively.

The future maturities of long-term debt, including capitalized leases, consist of the following:

Fiscal Year	
2007[1]	$418
2008	16
2009	16
2010	25
2011	17
Thereafter	104
	$596

[1]Holders of our debentures due in 2022 may require us to purchase all or a portion of their debentures on January 15, 2007. The table above assumes that all holders of our debentures exercise thier redemption options.

1 The nature of the contingency.

2 An estimate of the possible loss or range of loss or a statement that an estimate cannot be made.

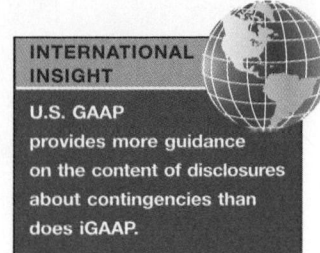

Companies should disclose certain other contingent liabilities, even though the possibility of loss may be remote, as follows.

1 Guarantees of indebtedness of others.

2 Obligations of commercial banks under "stand-by letters of credit."

3 Guarantees to repurchase receivables (or any related property) that have been sold or assigned.

Disclosure should include the nature and amount of the guarantee and, if estimable, the amount that the company can recover from outside parties.

What do the numbers mean? More Disclosure, Please

On November 19, 2001, **Enron** filed its third-quarter financial statements and reported debt on its balance sheet of approximately $13 billion. Yet on the same day, Enron informed its bankers that its debt was approximately $38 billion. The company explained the $25 billion difference as being either off–balance-sheet or on the balance sheet other than debt. Congress subsequently passed the Sarbanes-Oxley Act of 2002, one of whose provisions mandates that the SEC conduct a study to determine the extent of off–balance-sheet transactions that are occurring.

Table 1 below indicates the extent of disclosure and recognition of contingent liabilities discussed in this chapter, classified into three categories. The statistics provided relate to the 10,100 companies listed on the U.S. stock exchanges.

Table 1

Type of Contingency	Companies Disclosing	Companies Recording
Litigation-contingent liabilities	46.3%	5.1%
Environmental contingent liabilities	10.2%	5.1%
Guarantees	35.4%	10.2%

As Table 1 indicates, approximately 46 percent of companies disclose litigation-contingent liabilities, but only 5.1 percent record any liability related to these contingencies. On the other hand, 35 percent of the companies disclose guarantees but less than a third of these companies (10.2%) record a liability for these contingencies. Table 2 shows the dollar amount of these contingent liabilities as disclosed and recorded.

Table 2

Type of Contingency	Companies Disclosing ($ millions)	Companies Recording ($ millions)
Litigation-contingent liabilities	$52,354	$11,814
Environmental contingent liabilities	$23,414	$18,723
Guarantees	$46,535,399	$123,949

As Table 2 indicates, companies disclosed litigation-contingent liabilities of approximately $52 billion, but recorded as liabilities only $11.8 billion. Incredibly, companies disclosed more than $46 *trillion*, but recorded only a small fraction (just $124 billion) of that amount as liabilities.

These tables suggest that the FASB must continue to address the issue of contingencies to ensure that companies provide relevant and reliable information for this type of financial event.

Source: "Report and Recommendations Pursuant to Section 401(c) of the Sarbanes-Oxley Act of 2002 on Arrangements with Off-Balance Sheet Implications, Special Purpose Entities, and Transparency of Filings by Issuers," United States Securities and Exchange Commission—Office of Chief Accountant, Office of Economic Analyses, Division of Corporation Finance, June 2005.

Beyond the Numbers

What are some of the drawbacks of requiring more recognition (as opposed to disclosure) of contingencies, such as those related to litigation or environmental costs?

Analysis of Current Liabilities

The distinction between current liabilities and long-term debt is important. It provides information about the liquidity of the company. Liquidity regarding a liability is the expected time to elapse before its payment. In other words, a liability soon to be paid is a current liability. A liquid company is better able to withstand a financial downturn. Also, it has a better chance of taking advantage of investment opportunities that develop.

Analysts use certain basic ratios such as net cash flow provided by operating activities to current liabilities, and the turnover ratios for receivables and inventory, to assess liquidity. Two other ratios used to examine liquidity are the current ratio and the acid-test ratio.

The **current ratio** is the ratio of total current assets to total current liabilities. Illustration 12-10 shows its formula.

Illustration 12-10
Formula for Current Ratio

$$\text{Current Ratio} = \frac{\text{Current Assets}}{\text{Current Liabilities}}$$

The ratio is frequently expressed as a coverage of so many times. Sometimes it is called the **working capital ratio** because working capital is the excess of current assets over current liabilities.

A satisfactory current ratio does not disclose that a portion of the current assets may be tied up in slow-moving inventories. With inventories, especially raw materials and work in process, there is a question of how long it will take to transform them into the finished product and what amount the company ultimately will realize in the sale of the merchandise. Eliminating the inventories, along with any prepaid expenses, from the amount of current assets might provide better information for short-term creditors. Many analysts favor an **acid-test** or **quick ratio** that relates total current liabilities to cash, short-term investments, and receivables. Illustration 12-11 shows the formula for this ratio.

Illustration 12-11
Formula for Acid-Test Ratio

$$\text{Acid-test Ratio} = \frac{\text{Cash} + \text{Short-term Investments} + \text{Net Receivables}}{\text{Current Liabilities}}$$

To illustrate the computation of these two ratios, refer to the information for **Best Buy Co.** in Illustration 12-9. Illustration 12-12 shows the computation of the current and acid-test ratios for Best Buy.

Illustration 12-12
Computation of Current and Acid-Test Ratios for Best Buy

$$\text{Current Ratio} = \frac{\text{Current Assets}}{\text{Current Liabilities}} = \frac{\$7,985}{\$6,056} = 1.32 \text{ times}$$

$$\text{Acid-test Ratio} = \frac{\text{Cash} + \text{Short-term Investments} + \text{Net Receivables}}{\text{Current Liabilities}} = \frac{\$4,238}{\$6,056} = 0.70 \text{ times}$$

Best Buy's current position is adequate. At 0.70, Best Buy's acid-test ratio is well below 1. A comparison to another retailer, **Circuit City**, whose acid-test ratio is 0.66 indicates that Best Buy may be carrying less inventory than its industry counterparts.

Analysis of Long-Term Debt

Long-term creditors and stockholders are interested in a company's long-run solvency, particularly its ability to pay interest as it comes due and to repay the face value of the debt at maturity. Two ratios that provide information about debt-paying ability and long-run solvency are debt to total assets and times interest earned.

The **debt to total assets ratio** measures the percentage of the total assets provided by creditors. The higher the percentage of debt to total assets, the greater the risk that the company may be unable to meet its maturing obligations. To compute it, divide total debt (both current and long-term liabilities) by total assets, as Illustration 12-13 shows.

$$\text{Debt to Total Assets} \; = \; \frac{\text{Total Debt}}{\text{Total Assets}}$$

Illustration 12-13
Computation of Debt to Total Assets Ratio

The **times interest earned ratio** indicates the company's ability to meet interest payments as they come due. As Illustration 12-14 shows, this ratio is computed by dividing income before interest expense and income taxes by interest expense.

$$\text{Times Interest Earned} \; = \; \frac{\text{Income before Income Taxes and Interest Expense}}{\text{Interest Expense}}$$

Illustration 12-14
Computation of Times Interest Earned Ratio

To illustrate these long-term debt ratios, we use data from **Best Buy**'s 2006 annual report, which disclosed total liabilities of $6,607 million, total assets of $11,864 million, interest expense of $16 million, income taxes of $581 million, and net income of $1,140 million. We compute Best Buy's debt to total assets and times interest earned ratios as follows.

$$\text{Debt to Total Assets} \; = \; \frac{\$6,607}{\$11,864} \; = \; 55.7\%$$

$$\text{Times Interest Earned} \; = \; \frac{(\$1,140 + \$16 + \$581)}{\$16} \; = \; 109 \text{ times}$$

Illustration 12-15
Computation of Long-Term Debt Ratios for Best Buy

Even though Best Buy has a relatively high debt to total assets percentage of 55.7 percent, its interest coverage of 109 times indicates it can easily meet its interest payments.

You will want to read the CONVERGENCE CORNER on page 636 for discussion of how international convergence efforts relate to the accounting for liabilities.

CONVERGENCE CORNER

Liabilities

iGAAP and U.S. GAAP have similar definitions for liabilities. iGAAP related to reporting and recognition of liabilities is found in *IAS 1* ("Presentation of Financial Statements") and *IAS 37* ("Provisions, Contingent Liabilities, and Contingent Assets").

RELEVANT FACTS

• Similar to U.S. practice, iGAAP requires that companies present current and noncurrent liabilities on the face of the balance sheet, with current liabilities generally presented in order of liquidity.

• Under iGAAP, the measurement of a provision related to a contingency is based on the best estimate of the expenditure required to settle the obligation. If a range of estimates is predicted and no amount in the range is more likely than any other amount in the range, the "mid-point" of the range is used to measure the liability. In U.S GAAP, the minimum amount in a range is used.

• Both GAAPs prohibit the recognition of liabilities for future losses. However, iGAAP permits recognition of a restructuring liability, once a company has committed to a restructuring plan. U.S. GAAP has additional criteria (i.e., related to communicating the plan to employees) before a restructuring liability can be established.

• iGAAP and U.S. GAAP are similar in the treatment of asset retirement obligations (AROs). However, the recognition criteria for an ARO are more stringent under U.S. GAAP: The ARO is not recognized unless there is a present legal obligation and the fair value of the obligation can be reasonably estimated.

• iGAAP and U.S. GAAP are similar in their treatment of contingencies. However, the criteria for recognizing contingent assets are less stringent in the U.S. Under U.S. GAAP, contingent assets for insurance recoveries are recognized if probable; iGAAP requires the recovery be "virtually certain" before recognition of an asset is permitted.

ABOUT THE NUMBERS

As indicated, iGAAP and U.S. GAAP differ as the criteria to be used in recording restructuring liabilities. The following disclosure by **Nestlé Group** in its 2006 annual report reflects application of iGAAP to a restructuring situation.

Notes to the Financial Statements	
23 provisions (in part) (in millions of CHF)	
	Restructuring
At 1 January, 2006	950
Provisions made in the period	437
Amounts used	(326)
Unused amounts reversed	(34)
Modification—translation, consolidation	7
At 31 December, 2006	1,034

Restructuring
Restructuring provisions arise from a number of projects across the Group. These include plans to optimise industrial manufacturing capacities by closing inefficient production facilities and reorganising others, mainly in Europe. . . . Restructuring provisions are expected to result in future cash outflows when implementing the plans (usually over the following two to three years) and are consequently not discounted.

As indicated in the chapter, the establishment of restructuring liabilities for future costs can be used as a "cookie jar" to manage net income. That is, companies can set up a liability and related expense charge in one period to reduce income and then reduce the liability in future periods to increase net income. For example, when Nestlé makes the following entry for the unused amounts reversed in 2006, it is able to increase its income by 34 million CHE.

Restructuring Liability	34	
Gain from Reversal of Restructuring Liability		34

We are not implying that Nestlé is using its reserve in inappropriate ways. Our point is that less-stringent iGAAP rules for establishing restructuring liabilities could be used as an earnings management tool.

ON THE HORIZON

As indicated in the Convergence Corner for Chapter 2, the IASB and FASB are working on a conceptual framework project, part of which will examine the definition of a liability. In addition, this project will address the difference in measurements used between iGAAP and U.S. GAAP for contingent liabilities. Also, in its project on business combinations, the IASB is considering changing it definition of a contingent asset to converge with U.S. GAAP.

ACCOUNTING, ANALYSIS, PRINCIPLES

Accounting

YellowCard Company manufactures accessories for iPods. It had the following selected transactions during 2008.

1 YellowCard provides a 2-year warranty on its docking stations, which it began selling in 2008. During 2008 YellowCard spent $6,000 servicing warranty claims. At year-end, YellowCard estimates that an additional $45,000 will be spent in the future to service warranties related to 2008 sales.

2 On July 1, 2008, YellowCard issued $200,000 of 8 percent bonds at 100. The bonds mature on July 1, 2013, with interest payable July 1 and January 1. Under the bond indenture, YellowCard is required to make a sinking fund payment of $40,000 every July 1.

Prepare any journal entries in 2008 related to YellowCard's warranties and bonds. Yellow-Card has a December 31 year-end.

Analysis

How does introduction of the warranty and issuance of the bonds affect common ratios used to assess YellowCard's liquidity and solvency?

Principles

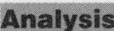

YellowCard is contemplating offering an extended warranty, under which customers can get 3 years' service on YellowCard and iPod products for an up-front payment of $30. Since the company gets paid up-front, YellowCard management does not believe it should record a liability related to this warranty program. Briefly explain how this new warranty meets the definition of a liability.

Solution

Accounting

1

2008

Warranty Expense	6,000	
Cash, Inventory, etc.		6,000

December 31, 2008

Warranty Expense	45,000	
Estimated Liability Under Warranties		45,000

2

July 1, 2008

Cash ($200,000 × 100%)	200,000	
Bonds Payable		200,000

December 31, 2008

Interest Expense ($200,000 × 8% × 1/2)	8,000	
Interest Payable		8,000

Analysis

Companies generally classify warranty liabilities as current. The warranty amounts recorded will increase current liabilities, thereby decreasing common liquidity measures (such as the current ratio and the acid-test ratio), which have current liabilities in the denominator. The amounts related to the bond payable will affect both liquidity and solvency measures. Yellow-Card should classify as current liabilities the interest payable of $8,000. This classification will decrease common liquidity measures (such as the current ratio and the acid-test ratio), which have current liabilities in the denominator. The sinking fund payment of $40,000 due on July 1, 2009, reduces current assets (and liquidity ratios). The remaining Bonds Payable balance will be classified as a long-term liability and will reflect unfavorably on such solvency measures as the debt to total assets ratio, which include total liabilities in the numerator.

Principles

According to FASB *Concepts Statement No. 6*, liabilities are probable future sacrifices of economic benefits arising from present obligations of a particular entity to transfer assets or provide services to other entities in the future as a result of past transactions or events. With respect to the new warranty plan, YellowCard would be currently obligated to provide repair service to its customers, arising from the prior sales of its products. So even though customers are making an upfront payment, YellowCard still has an obligation to provide services in the future. Thus the company should record the payments as unearned revenue until it is no longer obligated to make repairs. That is, the current accounting reflects application of the expense-warranty approach. The new plan would be accounted for under the sales-warranty approach, which defers a certain percentage of the original sales price until some future time when the company incurs actual costs or the warranty expires.

Key Terms

acid-test (quick) ratio, 634
asset retirement obligation (ARO), 627
bearer (coupon) bonds, 613
bond discount, 615
bond indenture, 612
bond premium, 615
callable bonds, 613
cash dividend payable, 609
commodity-backed bonds, 613
contingency, 620
contingent liabilities, 621
convertible bonds, 613
current liabilities, 607
current maturities of long-term debt, 609
current ratio, 634
debenture bonds, 613
debt to total assets ratio, 635
deep-discount (zero-interest) debenture bonds, 613
effective yield, or market rate, 615
expense-warranty approach, 624
extinguishment of debt, 618
face, par, principal or maturity value, 615
gain contingencies, 620
income bonds, 613
liabilities, 606
litigation, claims, and assessments, 622
long-term debt, 612

loss contingencies, 621
notes payable (trade notes payable), 607
off–balance-sheet financing, 629
operating cycle, 607
preferred dividends in arrears, 610
present value of a bond issue, 615
probable (contingency), 621
reasonably possible (contingency), 621
refunding, 619
registered bonds, 613
remote (contingency), 621
revenue bonds, 613
sales-warranty approach, 625
secured bonds, 613
self-insurance, 629
serial bonds, 613
special purpose entity (SPE), 630
stated, coupon, or nominal rate, 615
take-or-pay contract, 630
term bonds, 613
times interest earned ratio, 635
trade accounts payable, 607
trade notes payable, 607
unearned revenues, 610
warranty, 623
working capital ratio, 634
zero-interest debenture bonds, 613

Summary of Learning Objectives

1 Describe the nature, type, and valuation of current liabilities. Current liabilities are obligations whose liquidation a company reasonably expects will require the use of current assets or the creation of other current liabilities. Theoretically, companies should measure liabilities by the present value of the future outlay of cash required to liquidate them. In practice, companies usually record and report current liabilities at their full maturity value.

There are several types of current liabilities, such as: (1) accounts payable, (2) notes payable, (3) current maturities of long-term debt, (4) dividends payable, (5) unearned revenues, (6) taxes payable, and (7) employee-related liabilities.

2 Identify various types of bond issues. Various types of bond issues are: (1) Secured and unsecured bonds. (2) Term, serial bonds, and callable bonds. (3) Convertible, commodity-backed, and deep discount bonds. (4) Registered and bearer (coupon) bonds. (5) Income and revenue bonds. The variety in the types of bonds results from attempts to attract capital from different investors and risk takers and to satisfy the cash flow needs of the issuers.

3 Describe the accounting valuation for bonds at date of issuance. The investment community values a bond at the present value of its future cash flows, which consist of interest and principal. The rate used to compute the present value of these cash flows is the interest rate that provides an acceptable return on an investment commensurate with the issuer's risk characteristics. The interest rate written in the terms of the bond indenture and ordinarily appearing on the bond certificate is the stated, coupon, or nominal rate. The issuer of the bonds sets the rate and expresses it as a percentage of the face value (also called the par value, principal amount, or maturity value) of the bonds. If the rate employed by the buyers differs from the stated rate, the present value of the bonds computed by the buyers will differ from the face value of the bonds. The difference between the face value and the present value of the bonds is either a discount or premium.

4 Describe the accounting procedures for the extinguishment of debt. At the time of reacquisition, a company must amortize the unamortized premium or discount and any costs of issue applicable to the debt up to the reacquisition date. The amount paid on extinguishment or redemption before maturity, including any call premium and expense of reacquisition, is the reacquisition price. On any specified date, the net carrying amount of the debt is the amount payable at maturity,

adjusted for unamortized premium or discount, and cost of issuance. Any excess of the net carrying amount over the reacquisition price is a gain from extinguishment, whereas the excess of the reacquisition price over the net carrying amount is a loss from extinguishment. Companies recognize gains and losses on extinguishments in income.

5 Identify the criteria used to account for and disclose gain and loss contingencies. Companies do not record gain contingencies. Instead, they disclose them in the notes only when the probabilities are high that a gain contingency will occur. A company should accrue an estimated loss from a loss contingency by charging expense and recording a liability only if both of the following conditions are met: (1) Information available prior to the issuance of the financial statements indicates that it is probable that a liability has been incurred at the date of the financial statements, *and* (2) the amount of the loss can be reasonably estimated.

6 Explain the accounting for different types of loss contingencies. (1) Companies must consider the following factors in determining whether to record a liability with respect to pending or threatened litigation and actual or possible claims and assessments: (a) the time period in which the underlying cause for action occurred; (b) the probability of an unfavorable outcome; and (c) the ability to reasonably estimate the amount of loss.

(2) If it is probable that customers will make claims under warranties relating to goods or services that have been sold and it can reasonably estimate the costs involved, the company uses the accrual method. It charges warranty costs under the accrual basis to operating expense in the year of sale.

(3) A company must recognize asset retirement obligations when it has an existing legal obligation related to the retirement of a long-lived asset and it can reasonably estimate the amount.

7 Explain the reporting of off–balance-sheet financing arrangements. Off–balance-sheet financing is an attempt to borrow funds in such a way to prevent recording of obligations. Examples of off–balance-sheet arrangements are (1) nonconsolidated subsidiaries, (2) special purpose entities, and (3) operating leases.

8 Indicate how to present and analyze liabilities and contingencies. Companies commonly present the current liability accounts as the first classification in the liabilities and stockholders' equity section of the balance sheet. Within the current liabilities section, companies may list the accounts in order of maturity, in descending order of amount, or in order of liquidation preference. Detail and supplemental information concerning current liabilities should be sufficient to meet the requirement of full disclosure. If the loss is either probable or estimable but not both, and if there is at least a reasonable possibility that a company may have incurred a liability, it should disclose in the notes both the nature of the contingency and estimate the possible loss. Two ratios used to analyze liquidity are the current and acid-test ratios.

Companies that have large amounts and numerous issues of long-term debt frequently report only one amount in the balance sheet and support this with comments and schedules in the accompanying notes. Companies should show any assets pledged as security for the debt in the assets section of the balance sheet. Companies should report long-term debt that matures within one year as a current liability, unless retirement is to be accomplished with other than current assets. If a company plans to refinance the debt, convert it into stock, or retire it from a bond retirement fund, it should continue to report it as noncurrent, accompanied with a note explaining the method it will use in the debt's liquidation. Disclosure is required of future payments for sinking fund requirements and maturity amounts of long-term debt during each of the next five years. Debt to total assets and times interest earned are two ratios that provide information about debt-paying ability and long-run solvency.

BEHIND THE NUMBERS APPENDIX 12A | EFFECTIVE-INTEREST AMORTIZATION

OBJECTIVE 9

Compute amortization of bond discount and premium using the effective-interest method.

The preferred procedure for amortization of a discount or premium is the **effective-interest method** (also called **present value amortization**). Under the effective-interest method, companies:

1 Compute bond interest expense first by multiplying the **carrying value** of the bonds at the beginning of the period by the effective-interest rate. (The carrying value is the face amount minus any unamortized discount, or plus any unamortized premium. The term *carrying value* is synonymous with *book value*.)

2 Next, determine the bond discount or premium amortization by comparing the bond interest expense with the interest to be paid.

Illustration 12A-1 depicts graphically the computation of the amortization.

Illustration 12A-1
Bond Discount and Premium Amortization Computation

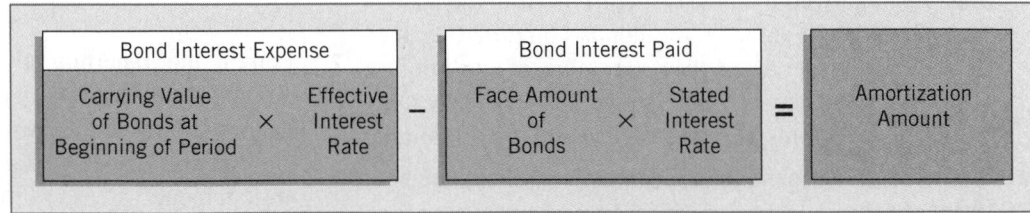

The effective-interest method produces a periodic interest expense equal to **a constant percentage of the carrying value of the bonds**. Since the percentage is the effective rate of interest incurred by the borrower at the time of issuance, the effective-interest method matches expenses with revenues better than the straight-line method. **Amortization of a discount increases bond interest expense, and amortization of a premium decreases it.**

Some bonds are callable by the issuer after a certain date at a stated price. This allows the issuing corporation to reduce its bonded indebtedness or take advantage of lower interest rates. **Whether callable or not, companies must amortize any premium or discount over the bond's life to maturity date because early redemption (call of the bond) is not a certainty.**

Bonds Issued at a Discount

To illustrate amortization of a discount, Evermaster Corporation issued $100,000 of 8 percent term bonds on January 1, 2008, due on January 1, 2013, with interest payable each July 1 and January 1. Because the investors required an effective-interest rate of 10 percent, they paid $92,278 for the $100,000 of bonds, creating a $7,722 discount. Evermaster computes the $7,722 discount as follows.[1]

Maturity value of bonds payable		$100,000
Present value of $100,000 due in 5 years at 10%, interest payable semiannually (Appendix A, Table 2);		
$FV(PVF_{10,5\%})$; ($100,000 × .61391)	$61,391	
Present value of $4,000 interest payable semiannually for 5 years at 10% annually (Appendix A, Table 4);		
$R(PVF\text{-}OA_{10,5\%})$; ($4,000 × 7.72173)	30,887	
Proceeds from sale of bonds		92,278
Discount on bonds payable		$ 7,722

Illustration 12A-2
Computation of Discount on Bonds Payable

The five-year amortization schedule appears in Illustration 12A-3.

Cash 92,278
Discount 7722
Bond 100 000

Illustration 12A-3
Bond Discount Amortization Schedule

Schedule of Bond Discount Amortization
Effective Interest Method—Semiannual Interest Payments
5-Year, 8% Bonds Sold to Yield 10%

Date	Cash Paid	Interest Expense	Discount Amortized	Carrying Value
1/1/08				$ 92,278
7/1/08	$ 4,000[a]	$ 4,614[b]	$ 614[c]	92,892[d]
1/1/09	4,000	4,645	645	93,537
7/1/09	4,000	4,677	677	94,214
1/1/10	4,000	4,711	711	94,925
7/1/10	4,000	4,746	746	95,671
1/1/11	4,000	4,783	783	96,454
7/1/11	4,000	4,823	823	97,277
1/1/12	4,000	4,864	864	98,141
7/1/12	4,000	4,907	907	99,048
1/1/13	4,000	4,952	952	100,000
	$40,000	$47,722	$7,722	

[a]$4,000 = $100,000 × .08 × 6/12
[b]$4,614 = $92,278 × .10 × 6/12
[c]$614 = $4,614 − $4,000
[d]$92,892 = $92,278 + $614

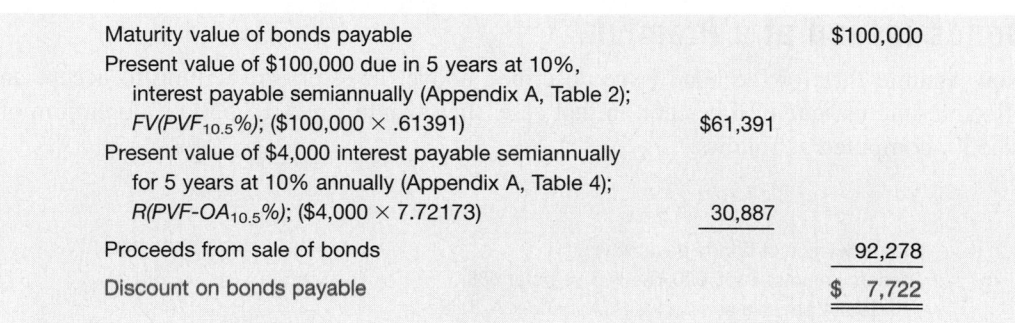

Calculator Solution for Present Value of Bonds:

	Inputs	Answer
N	10	
I/YR	5	
PV	?	92,278
PMT	−4,000	
FV	−100,000	

Evermaster records the issuance of its bonds at a discount on January 1, 2008, as follows.

Cash	92,278	
Discount on Bonds Payable	7,722	
Bonds Payable		100,000

[1]Because companies pay interest semiannually, the interest rate used is 5% (10% × 6/12). The number of periods is 10 (5 years × 2).

It records the first interest payment on July 1, 2008, and amortization of the discount as follows.

Bond Interest Expense	4,614	
Discount on Bonds Payable		614
Cash		4,000

Evermaster records the interest expense accrued at December 31, 2008 (year-end) and amortization of the discount as follows.

Bond Interest Expense	4,645	
Bond Interest Payable		4,000
Discount on Bonds Payable		645

Bonds Issued at a Premium

Now assume that for the bond issue described above, investors are willing to accept an effective-interest rate of 6 percent. In that case, they would pay $108,530 or a premium of $8,530, computed as follows.

Illustration 12A-4
Computation of Premium on Bonds Payable

Maturity value of bonds payable		$100,000
Present value of $100,000 due in 5 years at 6%,		
interest payable semiannually (Appendix A, Table 2);		
$FV(PVF_{10,3\%})$; ($100,000 × .74409)	$74,409	
Present value of $4,000 interest payable semiannually		
for 5 years at 6% annually (Appendix A, Table 4);		
$R(PVF\text{-}OA_{10,3\%})$; ($4,000 × 8.53020)	34,121	
Proceeds from sale of bonds		108,530
Premium on bonds payable		$ 8,530

The five-year amortization schedule appears in Illustration 12A-5.

Illustration 12A-5
Bond Premium Amortization Schedule

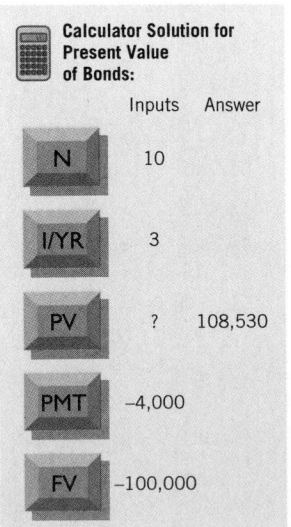

Calculator Solution for Present Value of Bonds:

	Inputs	Answer
N	10	
I/YR	3	
PV	?	108,530
PMT	−4,000	
FV	−100,000	

Schedule of Bond Premium Amortization
Effective Interest Method—Semiannual Interest Payments
5-Year, 8% Bonds Sold to Yield 6%

Date	Cash Paid	Interest Expense	Premium Amortized	Carrying Value
1/1/08				$108,530
7/1/08	$ 4,000[a]	$ 3,256[b]	$ 744[c]	107,786[d]
1/1/09	4,000	3,234	766	107,020
7/1/09	4,000	3,211	789	106,231
1/1/10	4,000	3,187	813	105,418
7/1/10	4,000	3,162	838	104,580
1/1/11	4,000	3,137	863	103,717
7/1/11	4,000	3,112	888	102,829
1/1/12	4,000	3,085	915	101,914
7/1/12	4,000	3,057	943	100,971
1/1/13	4,000	3,029	971	100,000
	$40,000	$31,470	$8,530	

[a]$4,000 = $100,000 × .08 × 6/12   [c]$744 = $4,000 − $3,256
[b]$3,256 = $108,530 × .06 × 6/12   [d]$107,786 = $108,530 − $744

Evermaster records the issuance of its bonds at a premium on January 1, 2008, as follows:

Cash	108,530	
Premium on Bonds Payable		8,530
Bonds Payable		100,000

Evermaster records the first interest payment on July 1, 2008, and amortization of the premium as follows.

Bond Interest Expense	3,256	
Premium on Bonds Payable	744	
Cash		4,000

Evermaster should amortize the discount or premium as an adjustment to interest expense over the life of the bond in such a way as to result in a **constant rate of interest** when applied to the carrying value of debt outstanding at the beginning of any given period.[2]

Although the FASB recommends the effective-interest method, companies may use a **straight-line method** if the results obtained are not materially different from those produced by the effective interest method. Under the straight-line method, companies amortize a constant amount each year. If using straight-line amortization, Evermaster would record the first interest payment on its bonds issued at a premium, as follows.

July 1, 2008

Bond Interest Expense	3,147	
Premium on Bonds Payable ($8,530 ÷ 10)	853	
Cash		4,000

Accruing Interest

In our previous examples, the interest payment dates and the date the financial statements were issued were the same. For example, when Evermaster sold bonds at a premium, the two interest payment dates coincided with the financial reporting dates. However, what happens if Evermaster wishes to report financial statements at the end of February 2008? In this case, the company prorates the premium by the appropriate number of months, to arrive at the proper interest expense as follows.

Interest accrual ($4,000 × 2/6)	$1,333.33
Premium amortized ($744 × 2/6)	(248.00)
Interest expense (Jan.–Feb.)	$1,085.33

Illustration 12A-6
Computation of Interest Expense

Evermaster records this accrual as follows.

Bond Interest Expense	1,085.33	
Premium on Bonds Payable	248.00	
Bond Interest Payable		1,333.33

If the company prepares financial statements six months later, it follows the same procedure. That is, the premium amortized would be as follows.

Premium amortized (March–June) ($744 × 4/6)	$496.00
Premium amortized (July–August) ($766 × 2/6)	255.33
Premium amortized (March–August, 2008)	$751.33

Illustration 12A-7
Computation of Premium Amortization

---

[2]"Interest on Receivables and Payables," *Opinions of the Accounting Principles Board No. 21* (New York: AICPA, 1971), par. 16.

Key Terms for Appendix 12A

carrying value, 640
effective-interest method of amortization, 640
straight-line method of amortization, 643

Summary of Learning Objective for Appendix 12A

9 Compute amortization of bond discount and premium using the effective-interest method. Companies amortize the discount (premium) and charge (credit) it to interest expense over the period of time that the bonds are outstanding. Amortization of a discount increases bond interest expense and amortization of a premium decreases it. The preferred procedure for amortization of a discount or premium is the effective-interest method. Under the effective-interest method, companies (1) compute bond interest expense by multiplying the carrying value of the bonds at the beginning of the period by the effective-interest rate, and (2) determine the bond discount or premium amortization by comparing the bond interest expense with the interest to be paid.

REVIEW EXERCISE

Timberlake Inc. has been producing quality children's apparel for more than 25 years. The company's fiscal year runs from April 1 to March 31. The following information relates to the obligations of Timberlake as of March 31, 2008.

Bonds Payable

Timberlake issued $5,000,000 of 11% bonds on July 1, 2002, at par. The bonds will mature on July 1, 2012. Interest is paid semiannually on July 1 and January 1.

Notes Payable

Timberlake has signed several long-term notes with financial institutions and insurance companies. The maturities of these notes are given in the schedule below. The total unpaid interest for all of these notes amounts to $210,000 on March 31, 2008.

Due Date	Amount Due
April 1, 2008	$ 200,000
July 1, 2008	300,000
October 1, 2008	150,000
January 1, 2009	150,000
April 1, 2009–March 31, 2010	600,000
April 1, 2010–March 31, 2011	500,000
	$1,900,000

Estimated Warranties

Timberlake has a one-year product warranty on some selected items in its product line. The estimated warranty liability on sales made during the 2006–2007 fiscal year and still outstanding as of March 31, 2007, amounted to $84,000. The warranty costs on sales made from April 1, 2007, through March 31, 2008, are estimated at $210,000. The actual warranty costs incurred during the current 2007–2008 fiscal year are as follows.

Warranty claims honored on 2006–2007 sales	$ 84,000
Warranty claims honored on 2007–2008 sales	95,000
Total warranty claims honored	$179,000

210 000
– 95 000
115 000

Other Information

1 *Trade payables.* Accounts payable for supplies, goods, and services purchased on open account amount to $370,000 as of March 31, 2008.

2 *Miscellaneous accruals.* Other accruals not separately classified amount to $75,000 as of March 31, 2008.

3 *Dividends.* On March 15, 2008, Timberlake's board of directors declared a cash dividend of $0.40 per common share and a 10% common stock dividend. Both dividends were to be distributed on April 12, 2008, to the common stockholders of record at the close of business on March 31, 2008. Data regarding Timberlake common stock are as follows.

Par value	$5 per share
Number of shares issued and outstanding	3,000,000 shares
Market values of common stock:	
March 15, 2008	$22.00 per share
March 31, 2008	21.50 per share
April 12, 2008	22.50 per share

4 Timberlake purchased a warehouse in 2004 for $300,000. In February 2008, due to the passage of a new wetlands restoration law, Timberlake will be required to restore the wetlands surrounding the warehouse site when the warehouse is abandoned in 2008. Timberlake has estimated that the fair value of the cost to restore the site is $35,000.

Instructions

Prepare the liabilities section of the balance sheet and appropriate notes to the statement for Timberlake Inc. as of March 31, 2008, as they should appear in its annual report.

Solution

Timberlake Inc.
Balance Sheet (partial)
March 31, 2008

Current liabilities
Notes payable ($200,000 + $300,000 + $150,000 + $150,000)		$ 800,000
Accounts payable		370,000
Estimated warranty payables ($84,000 + $210,000 − $179,000)		115,000
Cash dividends payable (3,000,000 × $0.40) (Note A)		1,200,000
Accrued interest [($5,000,000 × .11 × ¼) + $210,000]		347,500
Miscellaneous accruals		75,000
Total current liabilities		2,907,500

Long-term liabilities
11% bonds payable (Note B)	$5,000,000	
Asset retirement obligation, warehouse site	35,000	
Notes payable (Note C)	1,100,000	
Total long-term liabilities		6,135,000
Total liabilities		$9,042,500

Notes to the Financial Statements

Note A—Cash Dividends On March 15, 2008, the Board of Directors declared a cash dividend of $0.40 per common share to common stockholders of record on March 31, 2008. The dividend is payable on April 12, 2008.

Note B—Bonds The 11% bonds call for semiannual interest payments on each January 1 and July 1. The bonds mature on July 1, 2012.

Note C—Notes Payable The current liabilities include current maturities of several notes payable. The long-term notes payable mature as follows.

Due Date	Amount Due
April 1, 2009–March 31, 2010	$600,000
April 1, 2010–March 31, 2011	500,000

Questions

Note: All **asterisked** assignment materials relate to material covered in the appendix to the chapter.

1 Distinguish between a current liability and a long-term debt.

2 Assume that your friend Greg Jonas, who is a music major, asks you to define and discuss the nature of a liability. Assist him by preparing a definition of a liability and by explaining to him what you believe are the elements or factors inherent in the concept of a liability.

3 Why is the liability section of the balance sheet of primary significance to bankers?

4 How are current liabilities related by definition to current assets? How are current liabilities related to a company's operating cycle?

5 Jon Bryant, a newly hired loan analyst, is examining the current liabilities of a corporate loan applicant. He observes that unearned revenues have declined in the current year compared to the prior year. Is this a positive indicator about the client's liquidity? Explain.

6 How is present value related to the concept of a liability?

7 What is the nature of a "discount" on notes payable?

8 How should a debt callable by the creditor be reported in the debtor's financial statements?

9 Discuss the accounting treatment or disclosure that should be accorded a declared but unpaid cash dividend; an accumulated but undeclared dividend on cumulative preferred stock; a stock dividend distributable.

10 How does unearned revenue arise? Why can it be classified properly as a current liability? Give several examples of business activities that result in unearned revenues.

11 (a) From what sources might a corporation obtain funds through long-term debt? (b) What is a bond indenture? What does it contain? (c) What is a mortgage?

12 Differentiate between term bonds, mortgage bonds, collateral trust bonds, debenture bonds, income bonds, callable bonds, registered bonds, bearer or coupon bonds, convertible bonds, commodity-backed bonds, and deep-discount bonds.

13 Distinguish between the following interest rates for bonds payable:

  (a) yield rate   **(d)** market rate

  (b) nominal rate   **(e)** effective rate

  (c) stated rate

14 Distinguish between the following values relative to bonds payable:

  (a) maturity value   **(c)** market value

  (b) face value   **(d)** par value

15 Under what conditions of bond issuance does a discount on bonds payable arise? Under what conditions of bond issuance does a premium on bonds payable arise?

16 How should discount on bonds payable be reported on the financial statements? Premium on bonds payable?

17 How should the costs of issuing bonds be accounted for and classified in the financial statements?

18 Why would a company wish to reduce its bond indebtedness before its bonds reach maturity? Indicate how this can be done and the correct accounting treatment for such a transaction.

19 Define (a) a contingency and (b) a contingent liability.

20 Under what conditions should a contingent liability be recorded?

21 Distinguish between a current liability and a contingent liability. Give two examples of each type.

22 How are the terms probable, reasonably possible, and remote related to contingent liabilities?

23 Contrast the cash-basis method and the accrual method of accounting for warranty costs.

24 How does the expense warranty approach differ from the sales warranty approach?

25 Should a liability be recorded for risk of loss due to lack of insurance coverage? Discuss.

26 What factors must be considered in determining whether or not to record a liability for pending litigation? For threatened litigation?

27 What is off-balance-sheet financing? Why might a company be interested in off-balance-sheet financing?

28 What disclosures are required relative to long-term debt and sinking fund requirements?

29 Within the current liabilities section, how do you believe the accounts should be listed? Defend your position.

30 How does the acid-test ratio differ from the current ratio? How are they similar?

31 When should liabilities for each of the following items be recorded on the books of an ordinary business corporation?

(a) Acquisition of goods by purchase on credit.

(b) Officers' salaries.

(c) Special bonus to employees.

(d) Dividends.

*32 Zeno Company sells its bonds at a premium and applies the effective interest method in amortizing the premium. Will the annual interest expense increase or decrease over the life of the bonds? Explain.

Brief Exercises

BE12-1 Congo Corporation uses a periodic inventory system and the gross method of accounting for purchase discounts. On July 1, Congo purchased $40,000 of inventory, terms 2/10, n/30, FOB shipping point. Congo paid freight costs of $1,200. On July 3, Congo returned damaged goods and received credit of $6,000. On July 10, Congo paid for the goods. Prepare all necessary journal entries for Congo.   **(LO 1)**

BE12-2 Shin's Company borrowed $50,000 on November 1, 2008, by signing a $50,000, 9%, 3-month note. Prepare Shin's November 1, 2008, entry; the December 31, 2008, annual adjusting entry; and the February 1, 2009, entry.   **(LO 1)**

BE12-3 Kawasaki Corporation borrowed $50,000 on November 1, 2008, by signing a $51,125, 3-month, zero-interest-bearing note. Prepare Kawasaki's November 1, 2008, entry; the December 31, 2008, annual adjusting entry; and the February 1, 2009, entry.   **(LO 1)**

BE12-4 Game Pro Magazine sold 10,000 annual subscriptions on August 1, 2008, for $18 each. Prepare Game Pro's August 1, 2008, journal entry and the December 31, 2008, annual adjusting entry.   **(LO 1)**

BE12-5 Ghostbusters Corporation issues $300,000 of 9% bonds, due in 10 years, with interest payable semi-annually. At the time of issue, the market rate for such bonds is 10%. Compute the issue price of the bonds.   **(LO 3)**

BE12-6 The Goofy Company issued $200,000 of 10% bonds on January 1, 2009. The bonds are due January 1, 2009, with interest payable each July 1 and January 1. The bonds are issued at face value. Prepare Goofy's journal entries for (a) the January issuance, (b) the July 1 interest payment, and (c) the December 31 adjusting entry.   **(LO 3)**

BE12-7 Assume the bonds in BE12-6 were issued at 98. Prepare the journal entry at January 1, 2009.   **(LO 3)**

BE12-8 Assume the bonds in BE12-6 were issued at 103. Prepare the journal entry at January 1, 2009.   **(LO 3)**

BE12-9 At December 31, 2009, Treasure Land Corporation has the following account balances.   **(LO 8)**

Bonds payable, due January 1, 2017	$2,000,000
Discount on bonds payable	98,000
Bond interest payable	80,000

Show how the above accounts should be presented on the December 31, 2009, balance sheet, including the proper classifications.

BE12-10 On January 1, 2009, Uncharted Waters Corporation retired $600,000 of bonds at 99. At the time of retirement, the unamortized premium was $15,000 and unamortized bond issue costs were $5,250. Prepare the corporation's journal entry to record the reacquisition of the bonds.   **(LO 4)**

(LO 6)   **BE12-11**   Justice League Inc. is involved in a lawsuit at December 31, 2008. (a) Prepare the December 31 entry assuming it is probable that Justice League will be liable for $700,000 as a result of this suit. (b) Prepare the December 31 entry, if any, assuming it is *not* probable that Justice League will be liable for any payment as a result of this suit.

(LO 6)   **BE12-12**   Kohlbeck Company recently was sued by a competitor for patent infringement. Attorneys have determined that it is probable that Kohlbeck will lose the case and that a reasonable estimate of damages to be paid by Kohlbeck is $200,000. In light of this case, Kohlbeck is considering establishing a $100,000 self-insurance allowance. What entry(ies), if any, should Kohlbeck record to recognize this loss contingency?

(LO 6)   **BE12-13**   Frantic Factory provides a 2-year warranty with one of its products which was first sold in 2008. In that year, Frantic spent $70,000 servicing warranty claims. At year-end, Frantic estimates that an additional $500,000 will be spent in the future to service warranty claims related to 2008 sales. Prepare Frantic's journal entry to record the $70,000 expenditure, and the December 31 adjusting entry.

(LO 6)   **BE12-14**   Herzog Zwei Corporation sells DVD players. The corporation also offers its customers a 2-year warranty contract. During 2008, Herzog Zwei sold 15,000 warranty contracts at $99 each. The corporation spent $180,000 servicing warranties during 2008, and it estimates that an additional $900,000 will be spent in the future to service the warranties. Prepare Herzog Zwei's journal entries for (a) the sale of contracts, (b) the cost of servicing the warranties, and (c) the recognition of warranty revenue.

(LO 6)   **BE12-15**   Darby's Drillers erects and places into service an off-shore oil platform on January 1, 2008, at a cost of $10,000,000. Darby is legally required to dismantle and remove the platform at the end of its useful life in 10 years. The estimated fair value of the dismantling and removal costs at January 1, 2008, is $500,000. Prepare the entry to record the asset retirement obligation.

(LO 9)   ***BE12-16**   On January 1, 2009, Qix Corporation issued $400,000 of 7% bonds, due in 10 years. The bonds were issued for $372,816, and pay interest each July 1 and January 1. Qix uses the effective interest method. Prepare the company's journal entries for (a) the January 1 issuance, (b) the July 1 interest payment, and (c) the December 31 adjusting entry. Assume an effective interest rate of 8%.

(LO 9)   ***BE12-17**   Assume the bonds in BE12-16 were issued for $429,757 and the effective interest rate is 6%. Prepare the company's journal entries for (a) the January 1 issuance, (b) the July 1 interest payment, and (c) the December 31 adjusting entry.

(LO 9)   ***BE12-18**   Izzy Corporation issued $400,000 of 7% bonds on November 1, 2009, for $429,757. The bonds were dated November 1, 2009, and mature in 10 years, with interest payable each May 1 and November 1. Izzy uses the effective interest method with an effective rate of 6%. Prepare Izzy's December 31, 2009, adjusting entry.

Exercises

(LO 1, 8)   **E12-1**   **(Balance Sheet Classification of Various Liabilities)**   How would each of the following items be reported on the balance sheet?

   (a) Accrued vacation pay. CL
   (b) Estimated taxes payable. CL
   (c) Service warranties on appliance sales. CL
   (d) Bank overdraft. CL
   (e) Employee payroll deductions unremitted. CL
   (f) Unpaid bonus to officers. CL
   (g) Deposit received from customer to guarantee performance of a contract. Un. Rev   CL
   (h) Sales taxes payable. CL
   (i) Gift certificates sold to customers but not yet redeemed. CL
   (j) Premium offers outstanding. CL
   (k) Discount on notes payable. w/ NP
   (l) Personal injury claim pending. footnote
   (m) Current maturities of long-term debts to be paid from current assets. CL
   (n) Cash dividends declared but unpaid. CL
   (o) Dividends in arrears on preferred stock. footnote
   (p) Loans from officers. N/P

E12-2 (Accounts and Notes Payable) The following are selected 2008 transactions of Sean Astin Corporation. **(LO 1)**

Sept. 1 Purchased inventory from Encino Company on account for $50,000. Astin records purchases gross and uses a periodic inventory system.

Oct. 1 Issued a $50,000, 12-month, 12% note to Encino in payment of account.

Oct. 1 Borrowed $50,000 from the Shore Bank by signing a 12-month, zero-interest-bearing $56,000 note.

Instructions

(a) Prepare journal entries for the selected transactions above.
(b) Prepare adjusting entries at December 31.
(c) Compute the total net liability to be reported on the December 31 balance sheet for:
  (1) the interest-bearing note.
  (2) the zero-interest-bearing note.

E12-3 (Classification of Liabilities) Presented below are various account balances of K.D. Lang Inc. **(LO 1, 8)**

(a) Unamortized premium on bonds payable, of which $3,000 will be amortized during the next year.
(b) Bank loans payable of a winery, due March 10, 2012. (The product requires aging for 5 years before sale.)
(c) Serial bonds payable, $1,000,000, of which $200,000 are due each July 31.
(d) Amounts withheld from employees' wages for income taxes.
(e) Notes payable due January 15, 2011.
(f) Credit balances in customers' accounts arising from returns and allowances after collection in full of account.
(g) Bonds payable of $2,000,000 maturing June 30, 2010.
(h) Overdraft of $1,000 in a bank account. (No other balances are carried at this bank.)
(i) Deposits made by customers who have ordered goods.

Instructions

Indicate whether each of the items above should be classified on December 31, 2009, as a current liability, a long-term liability, or under some other classification. Consider each one independently from all others; that is, do not assume that all of them relate to one particular business. If the classification of some of the items is doubtful, explain why in each case.

E12-4 (Classification) The following items are found in the financial statements. **(LO 1, 8)**

(a) Discount on bonds payable
(b) Unamortized bond issue costs
(c) Gain on repurchase of debt
(d) Mortgage payable (payable in equal amounts over next 3 years)
(e) Debenture bonds payable (maturing in 5 years)
(f) Notes payable (due in 4 years)
(g) Premium on bonds payable
(h) Income bonds payable (due in 3 years)

Instructions

Indicate how each of these items should be classified in the financial statements.

E12-5 (Entries for Bond Transactions) Presented below are two independent situations. **(LO 3)**

1. On January 1, 2008, Paul Simon Company issued $200,000 of 9%, 10-year bonds at par. Interest is payable quarterly on April 1, July 1, October 1, and January 1.

2. On January 1, 2008, Graceland Company issued $100,000 of 12%, 10-year bonds dated June 1 at par. Interest is payable semiannually on July 1 and January 1.

Instructions

For each of these two independent situations, prepare journal entries to record:

(a) The issuance of the bonds.
(b) The payment of interest on July 1.
(c) The accrual of interest on December 31.

(LO 6)

E12-6 (Warranties) Soundgarden Company sold 200 copymaking machines in 2008 for $4,000 apiece, together with a one-year warranty. Maintenance on each machine during the warranty period averages $330.

Instructions

(a) Prepare entries to record the sale of the machines and the related warranty costs, assuming that the accrual method is used. Actual warranty costs incurred in 2008 were $17,000.

(b) On the basis of the data above, prepare the appropriate entries, assuming that the cash basis method is used.

(LO 6)

E12-7 (Warranties) Sheryl Crow Equipment Company sold 500 Rollomatics during 2008 at $6,000 each. During 2008, Crow spent $20,000 servicing the 2-year warranties that accompany the Rollomatic. All applicable transactions are on a cash basis.

Instructions

(a) Prepare 2008 entries for Crow using the expense warranty approach. Assume that Crow estimates the total cost of servicing the warranties will be $120,000 for 2 years.

(b) Prepare 2008 entries for Crow assuming that the warranties are not an integral part of the sale. Assume that of the sales total, $150,000 relates to sales of warranty contracts. Crow estimates the total cost of servicing the warranties will be $120,000 for 2 years. Estimate revenues earned on the basis of costs incurred and estimated costs.

(LO 3, 4)

E12-8 (Entry for Retirement of Bond; Bond Issue Costs) On January 2, 2003, Banno Corporation issued $1,500,000 of 10% bonds at 97 due December 31, 2012. Legal and other costs of $24,000 were incurred in connection with the issue. Interest on the bonds is payable annually each December 31. The $24,000 bond issue costs are being deferred and amortized. The discount on the bonds is also being amortized.

The bonds are callable at 101 (i.e., at 101% of face amount), and on January 2, 2008, Banno called $900,000 face amount of the bonds and retired them. For the bonds called, unamortized bond discount at retirement was $13,500, and unamortized bond issue cost was $7,200.

Instructions

Ignoring income taxes, compute the amount of loss, if any, to be recognized by Banno as a result of retiring the $900,000 of bonds in 2008, and prepare the journal entry to record the retirement.

(AICPA adapted)

(LO 3, 4)

E12-9 (Entries for Retirement and Issuance of Bonds) Eddie Haskel, Inc. had outstanding $6,000,000 of 11% bonds (interest payable July 31 and January 31) due in 10 years. On July 1, it issued $9,000,000 of 10%, 15-year bonds (interest payable July 1 and January 1) at 98. A portion of the proceeds was used to call the 11% bonds at 102 on August 1. Unamortized bond discount and bond issue cost applicable to the 11% bonds were $120,000 and $30,000, respectively.

Instructions

Prepare the journal entries necessary to record issuance of the new bonds and the refunding of the bonds.

(LO 3, 4)

E12-10 (Entries for Retirement and Issuance of Bonds) Katie Couric Company had bonds outstanding with a maturity value of $300,000. On April 30, 2009, when these bonds had an unamortized discount of $10,000, they were called in at 104. To pay for these bonds, Couric had issued other bonds a month earlier bearing a lower interest rate. The newly issued bonds had a life of 10 years. The new bonds were issued at 103 (face value $300,000). Bond issue costs related to the new bonds were $3,000.

Instructions

Ignoring interest, compute the gain or loss and record this refunding transaction.

(AICPA adapted)

(LO 5, 6)

E12-11 (Contingencies) Presented below are three independent situations. Answer the question at the end of each situation.

1. During 2008, Salt-n-Pepa Inc. became involved in a tax dispute with the IRS. Salt-n-Pepa's attorneys have indicated that they believe it is probable that Salt-n-Pepa will lose this dispute. They also believe that Salt-n-Pepa will have to pay the IRS between $900,000 and $1,400,000. After the 2008 financial statements were issued, the case was settled with the IRS for $1,200,000. What amount, if any, should be reported as a liability for this contingency as of December 31, 2008?

2. On October 1, 2008, Alan Jackson Chemical was identified as a potentially responsible party by the Environmental Protection Agency. Jackson's management along with its counsel have concluded that it is probable that Jackson will be responsible for damages, and a reasonable estimate of these damages is $5,000,000. Jackson's insurance policy of $9,000,000 has a deductible clause of $500,000, but it is uncertain whether the policy will apply to these damages. How should Alan Jackson Chemical report this information in its financial statements at December 31, 2008?

3. Melissa Etheridge Inc. had a manufacturing plant in Bosnia, which was destroyed in the civil war. It is not certain who will compensate Etheridge for this destruction, but Etheridge has been assured by governmental officials that it will receive a definite amount for this plant. The amount of the compensation will be less than the fair value of the plant, but more than its book value. How should the contingency be reported in the financial statements of Etheridge Inc.?

E12-12 (Asset Retirement Obligation) Oil Products Company purchases an oil tanker depot on January 1, 2009, at a cost of $600,000. Oil Products expects to operate the depot for 10 years, at which time it is legally required to dismantle the depot and remove the underground storage tanks. It is estimated that it will cost $75,000 to dismantle the depot and remove the tanks at the end of the depot's useful life.   **(LO 6)**

Instructions

(a) Prepare the journal entries to record the depot and the asset retirement obligation for the depot on January 1, 2009. Based on an effective interest rate of 6%, the fair value of the asset retirement obligation on January 1, 2009, is $41,879.

(b) Prepare any journal entries required for the depot and the asset retirement obligation at December 31, 2009. Oil Products uses straight-line depreciation; the estimated residual value for the depot is zero.

(c) On December 31, 2018, Oil Products pays a demolition firm $80,000 to dismantle the depot and remove the tanks. Prepare the journal entry for the settlement of the asset retirement obligation.

E12-13 (Financial Statement Impact of Liability Transactions) Presented below is a list of possible transactions.   **(LO 1, 8)**

1. Purchased inventory for $80,000 on account (assume perpetual system is used).
2. Issued an $80,000 note payable in payment on account (see item 1 above).
3. Recorded accrued interest on the note from item 2 above.
4. Borrowed $100,000 from the bank by signing a 6-month, $112,000, zero-interest-bearing note.
5. Recognized 4 months' interest expense on the note from item 4 above.
6. Recorded cash sales of $75,260, which includes 6% sales tax.
7. Recorded accrued property taxes payable.
8. Recorded bonuses due to employees.
9. Recorded a contingent loss on a lawsuit that the company will probably lose.
10. Accrued warranty expense (assume expense warranty approach).
11. Paid warranty costs that were accrued in item 10 above.
12. Recorded sales of product and related warranties (assume sales warranty approach).
13. Paid warranty costs under contracts from item 12 above.
14. Recognized warranty revenue (see item 12 above).

Instructions

Set up a table using the format shown below and analyze the effect of the 14 transactions on the financial statement categories indicated.

#	Assets	Liabilities	Stockholders' Equity	Net Income
1				

Use the following code:

I: Increase   D: Decrease   NE: No net effect

E12-14 (Ratio Computations and Discussion) Sprague Company has been operating for several years, and on December 31, 2008, presented the following balance sheet.   **(LO 8)**

<table>
<tr><td colspan="4">**Sprague Company**
Balance Sheet
December 31, 2008</td></tr>
<tr><td>Cash</td><td>$ 40,000</td><td>Accounts payable</td><td>$ 80,000</td></tr>
<tr><td>Receivables</td><td>75,000</td><td>Mortgage payable</td><td>140,000</td></tr>
<tr><td>Inventories</td><td>95,000</td><td>Common stock ($1.00 par)</td><td>150,000</td></tr>
<tr><td>Plant assets (net)</td><td>220,000</td><td>Retained earnings</td><td>60,000</td></tr>
<tr><td></td><td>$430,000</td><td></td><td>$430,000</td></tr>
</table>

The net income for 2008 was $25,000. Assume that total assets are the same in 2007 and 2008.

Instructions

Compute each of the following ratios. For each of the four indicate the manner in which it is computed and its significance as a tool in the analysis of the financial soundness of the company.

(a) Current ratio. (c) Debt to total assets.
(b) Acid-test ratio. (d) Rate of return on assets.

(LO 8) **E12-15** (**Long-Term Debt Disclosure**) At December 31, 2007, Zeta-James Company has outstanding three long-term debt issues. The first is a $2,000,000 note payable which matures June 30, 2010. The second is a $6,000,000 bond issue which matures September 30, 2011. The third is a $17,500,000 sinking fund debenture with annual sinking fund payments of $3,500,000 in each of the years 2009 through 2013.

Instructions

Prepare the note disclosure required for the long-term debt at December 31, 2007.

(LO 8) **E12-16** (**Ratio Computations and Analysis**) Hood Company's condensed financial statements provide the following information.

Hood Company **Balance Sheet**	Dec. 31, 2008	Dec. 31, 2007
Cash	$ 52,000	$ 60,000
Accounts receivable (net)	198,000	80,000
Marketable securities (short-term)	80,000	40,000
Inventories	440,000	360,000
Prepaid expenses	3,000	7,000
Total current assets	$ 773,000	$ 547,000
Property, plant, and equipment (net)	857,000	853,000
Total assets	$1,630,000	$1,400,000
Current liabilities	240,000	160,000
Bonds payable	400,000	400,000
Common stockholders' equity	990,000	840,000
Total liabilities and stockholders' equity	$1,630,000	$1,400,000

Income Statement **For the Year Ended December 31, 2008**	
Sales	$1,640,000
Cost of goods sold	(800,000)
Gross profit	840,000
Selling and administrative expense	(440,000)
Interest expense	(40,000)
Net income	$ 360,000

Instructions

(a) Determine the following for 2008.
   (1) Current ratio at December 31.
   (2) Acid-test ratio at December 31.
   (3) Accounts receivable turnover.
   (4) Inventory turnover.
   (5) Rate of return on assets.
   (6) Profit margin on sales.

(b) Prepare a brief evaluation of the financial condition of Hood Company and of the adequacy of its profits.

E12-17 **(Ratio Computations and Effect of Transactions)** Presented below is information related to Carver Inc.

Carver Inc.
Balance Sheet
December 31, 2008

Cash		$ 45,000	Notes payable (short-term)	$ 50,000
Receivables	$110,000		Accounts payable	32,000
Less: Allowance	15,000	95,000	Accrued liabilities	5,000
Inventories		170,000	Capital stock (par $5)	260,000
Prepaid insurance		8,000	Retained earnings	141,000
Land		20,000		$488,000
Equipment (net)		150,000		
		$488,000		

Income Statement
For the Year Ended December 31, 2008

Sales		$1,400,000
Cost of goods sold		
Inventory, Jan. 1, 2008	$200,000	
Purchases	790,000	
Cost of goods available for sale	990,000	
Inventory, Dec. 31, 2008	170,000	
Cost of goods sold		820,000
Gross profit on sales		580,000
Operating expenses		170,000
Net income		$ 410,000

Instructions

(a) Compute the following ratios or relationships of Carver Inc. Assume that the ending account balances are representative unless the information provided indicates differently.

   (1) Current ratio.
   (2) Inventory turnover.
   (3) Receivables turnover.
   (4) Earnings per share.
   (5) Profit margin on sales.
   (6) Rate of return on assets on December 31, 2008.

(b) Indicate for each of the following transactions whether the transaction would improve, weaken, or have no effect on the current ratio of Carver Inc. at December 31, 2008.

   (1) Write off an uncollectible account receivable, $2,200.
   (2) Purchased its own common stock for cash.
   (3) Pay $40,000 on notes payable (short-term).
   (4) Collect $23,000 on accounts receivable.
   (5) Buy equipment on account.
   (6) Give an existing creditor a short-term note in settlement of account.

(LO 9)   ***E12-18   (Entries for Bond Transactions—Effective-Interest)**   Celine Dion Company issued $600,000 of 10%, 20-year bonds on January 1, 2009, at 102. Interest is payable semiannually on July 1 and January 1. Dion Company uses the effective interest method of amortization for bond premium or discount. Assume an effective yield of 9.75%.

Instructions

Prepare the journal entries to record the following. (Round to the nearest dollar.)

(a) The issuance of the bonds.
(b) The payment of interest and related amortization on July 1, 2009.
(c) The accrual of interest and the related amortization on December 31, 2009.

(LO 9)   ***E12-19   (Amortization Schedule—Straight-line Interest)**   Dan Majerle Company sells 10% bonds having a maturity value of $2,000,000 for $1,855,816. The bonds are dated January 1, 2008, and mature January 1, 2013. Interest is payable annually on January 1.   *Eff Rate 11.96*

Instructions

Set up a schedule of interest expense and discount amortization under the straight-line method.

(LO 3, 9)   ***E12-20   (Determine Proper Amounts in Account Balances)**   Presented below are two independent situations.

(a) CeCe Winans Corporation incurred the following costs in connection with the issuance of bonds: (1) printing and engraving costs, $12,000; (2) legal fees, $49,000, and (3) commissions paid to underwriter, $60,000. What amount should be reported as Unamortized Bond Issue Costs, and where should this amount be reported on the balance sheet?
(b) Ron Kenoly Inc. issued $600,000 of 9%, 10-year bonds on June 30, 2008, for $562,500. This price provided a yield of 10% on the bonds. Interest is payable semiannually on December 31 and June 30. If Kenoly uses the effective interest method, determine the amount of interest expense to record if financial statements are issued on October 31, 2008.

(LO 9)   ***E12-21   (Entries and Questions for Bond Transactions)**   On June 30, 2009, Mischa Auer Company issued $4,000,000 face value of 13%, 20-year bonds at $4,300,920, a yield of 12%. Auer uses the effective interest method to amortize bond premium or discount. The bonds pay semiannual interest on June 30 and December 31.

Instructions

(a) Prepare the journal entries to record the following transactions.
   (1) The issuance of the bonds on June 30, 2009.
   (2) The payment of interest and the amortization of the premium on December 31, 2009.
   (3) The payment of interest and the amortization of the premium on June 30, 2010.
   (4) The payment of interest and the amortization of the premium on December 31, 2010.
(b) Show the proper balance sheet presentation for the liability for bonds payable on the December 31, 2010, balance sheet.
(c) Provide the answers to the following questions.
   (1) What amount of interest expense is reported for 2010?
   (2) Will the bond interest expense reported in 2010 be the same as, greater than, or less than the amount that would be reported if the straight-line method of amortization were used?
   (3) Determine the total cost of borrowing over the life of the bond.
   (4) Will the total bond interest expense for the life of the bond be greater than, the same as, or less than the total interest expense if the straight-line method of amortization were used?

(LO 9)   ***E12-22   (Entries for Bond Transactions)**   On January 1, 2008, Aumont Company sold 12% bonds having a maturity value of $500,000 for $537,907.37, which provides the bondholders with a 10% yield. The bonds

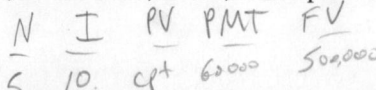

are dated January 1, 2008, and mature January 1, 2013, with interest payable December 31 of each year. Aumont Company allocates interest and unamortized discount or premium on the effective interest basis.

Instructions

(a) Prepare the journal entry at the date of the bond issuance.
(b) Prepare a schedule of interest expense and bond amortization for 2008–2010.
(c) Prepare the journal entry to record the interest payment and the amortization for 2008.
(d) Prepare the journal entry to record the interest payment and the amortization for 2010.

*E12-23 (Information Related to Various Bond Issues) Karen Austin Inc. has issued three types of debt on January 1, 2008, the start of the company's fiscal year.   (LO 9)

(a) $10 million, 10-year, 15% unsecured bonds, interest payable quarterly. Bonds were priced to yield 12%.
(b) $25 million par of 10-year, zero-coupon bonds at a price to yield 12% per year.
(c) $20 million, 10-year, 10% mortgage bonds, interest payable annually to yield 12%.

Instructions

Prepare a schedule that identifies the following items for each bond: (1) maturity value, (2) number of interest periods over life of bond, (3) stated rate per each interest period, (4) effective interest rate per each interest period, (5) payment amount per period, and (6) present value of bonds at date of issue.

See the book's companion website, at www.wiley.com/college/warfield, for Additional Exercises.

Problems

P12-1 (Current Liability Entries and Adjustments) Described below are certain transactions of James Edwards Corporation.   (LO 1)

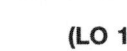

1. On February 2, the corporation purchased goods from Jack Haley Company for $50,000 subject to cash discount terms of 2/10, n/30. Purchases and accounts payable are recorded by the corporation at net amounts after cash discounts. The invoice was paid on February 26.
2. On April 1, the corporation bought a truck for $40,000 from General Motors Company, paying $4,000 in cash and signing a one-year, 12% note for the balance of the purchase price.
3. On May 1, the corporation borrowed $80,000 from Chicago National Bank by signing a $92,000 zero-interest-bearing note due one year from May 1.
4. On August 1, the board of directors declared a $300,000 cash dividend that was payable on September 10 to stockholders of record on August 31.

Instructions

(a) Make all the journal entries necessary to record the transactions above using appropriate dates.
(b) James Edwards Corporation's year-end is December 31. Assuming that no adjusting entries relative to the transactions above have been recorded, prepare any adjusting journal entries concerning interest that are necessary to present fair financial statements at December 31. Assume straight-line amortization of discounts.

P12-2 (Comprehensive Problem; Issuance, Classification, Reporting) Presented below are four independent situations.   (LO 1, 3, 8)

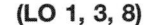

(a) On March 1, 2008, Heide Co. issued at 103 plus accrued interest $3,000,000, 9% bonds. The bonds are dated January 1, 2008, and pay interest semiannually on July 1 and January 1. In addition, Heide Co. incurred $27,000 of bond issuance costs. Compute the net amount of cash received by Heide Co. as a result of the issuance of these bonds.
(b) On January 1, 2008, Reymont Co. issued 9% bonds with a face value of $500,000 for $469,280 to yield 10%. The bonds are dated January 1, 2008, and pay interest annually. What amount is reported as bond discount on the issue date?

(c) Czeslaw Building Co. has a number of long-term bonds outstanding at December 31, 2009. These long-term bonds have the following sinking fund requirements and maturities for the next 6 years.

	Sinking Fund	Maturities
2010	$300,000	$100,000
2011	100,000	250,000
2012	100,000	100,000
2013	200,000	—
2014	200,000	150,000
2015	200,000	100,000

Indicate how this information should be reported in the financial statements at December 31, 2009.

(d) In the long-term debt structure of Marie Curie Inc., the following three bonds were reported: mortgage bonds payable $10,000,000; collateral trust bonds $5,000,000; bonds maturing in installments, secured by plant equipment $4,000,000. Determine the total amount, if any, of debenture bonds outstanding.

(LO 6)

P12-3 **(Warranties, Accrual, and Cash Basis)** Willy Randolph Corporation sells portable computers under a 2-year warranty contract that requires the corporation to replace defective parts and to provide the necessary repair labor. During 2008 the corporation sells for cash 300 computers at a unit price of $3,500. On the basis of past experience, the 2-year warranty costs are estimated to be $155 for parts and $185 for labor per unit. (For simplicity, assume that all sales occurred on December 31, 2008.) The warranty is not sold separately from the computer.

Instructions

(a) Record any necessary journal entries in 2008, applying the cash basis method.
(b) Record any necessary journal entries in 2008, applying the expense warranty accrual method.
(c) What liability relative to these transactions would appear on the December 31, 2008, balance sheet, and how would it be classified if the cash basis method is applied?
(d) What liability relative to these transactions would appear on the December 31, 2008, balance sheet, and how would it be classified if the expense warranty accrual method is applied?

In 2009 the actual warranty costs to Willy Randolph Corporation were $21,400 for parts and $24,900 for labor.

(e) Record any necessary journal entries in 2009, applying the cash basis method.
(f) Record any necessary journal entries in 2009, applying the expense warranty accrual method.

(LO 6)

P12-4 **(Warranties, Accrual, and Cash Basis)** Albert Pujols Company sells a machine for $7,400 under a 12-month warranty agreement that requires the company to replace all defective parts and to provide the repair labor at no cost to the customers. With sales being made evenly throughout the year, the company sells 650 machines in 2008 (warranty expense is incurred half in 2008 and half in 2009). As a result of product testing, the company estimates that the warranty cost is $370 per machine ($170 parts and $200 labor).

Instructions

Assuming that actual warranty costs are incurred exactly as estimated, what journal entries would be made relative to these facts.

(a) Under application of the expense warranty accrual method for:
   (1) Sale of machinery in 2008?
   (2) Warranty costs incurred in 2008?
   (3) Warranty expense charged against 2008 revenues?
   (4) Warranty costs incurred in 2009?
(b) Under application of the cash basis method for:
   (1) Sale of machinery in 2008?
   (2) Warranty costs incurred in 2008?
   (3) Warranty expense charged against 2008 revenues?
   (4) Warranty costs incurred in 2009?
(c) What amount, if any, is disclosed in the balance sheet as a liability for future warranty costs as of December 31, 2008, under each method?
(d) Which method best reflects the income in 2008 and 2009 of Albert Pujols Company? Why?

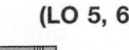

P12-5 **(Loss Contingencies: Entries and Essay)** On November 24, 2008, 26 passengers on Tom Paris Airlines Flight No. 901 were injured upon landing when the plane skidded off the runway. Personal injury suits for damages totaling $5,000,000 were filed on January 11, 2009, against the airline by 18 injured passengers. The airline carries no insurance. Legal counsel has studied each suit and advised Paris that it can reasonably expect to pay 60% of the damages claimed. The financial statements for the year ended December 31, 2008, were issued February 27, 2009.

(LO 5, 6)

Instructions

(a) Prepare any disclosures and journal entries required by the airline in preparation of the December 31, 2008, financial statements.

(b) Ignoring the Nov. 24, 2008, accident, what liability due to the risk of loss from lack of insurance coverage should Tom Paris Airlines record or disclose? During the past decade the company has experienced at least one accident per year and incurred average damages of $3,200,000. Discuss fully.

P12-6 **(Loss Contingencies: Entries and Essays)** Shoyo Corporation, in preparation of its December 31, 2008, financial statements, is attempting to determine the proper accounting treatment for each of the following situations.

(LO 5, 6)

1. As a result of uninsured accidents during the year, personal injury suits for $350,000 and $60,000 have been filed against the company. It is the judgment of Shoyo's legal counsel that an unfavorable outcome is unlikely in the $60,000 case but that an unfavorable verdict approximating $225,000 will probably result in the $350,000 case.

2. Shoyo Corporation owns a subsidiary in a foreign country that has a book value of $5,725,000 and an estimated fair value of $8,700,000. The foreign government has communicated to Shoyo its intention to expropriate the assets and business of all foreign investors. On the basis of settlements other firms have received from this same country, Shoyo expects to receive 40% of the fair value of its properties as final settlement. *gain contingencies - only disclose*

3. Shoyo's chemical product division consisting of five plants is uninsurable because of the special risk of injury to employees and losses due to fire and explosion. The year 2008 is considered one of the safest (luckiest) in the division's history because no loss due to injury or casualty was suffered. Having suffered an average of three casualties a year during the rest of the past decade (ranging from $60,000 to $700,000), management is certain that next year the company will probably not be so fortunate.

Instructions

(a) Prepare the journal entries that should be recorded as of December 31, 2008, to recognize each of the situations above.

(b) Indicate what should be reported relative to each situation in the financial statements and accompanying notes. Explain why.

P12-7 **(Liability Errors)** You are the independent auditor engaged to audit Christine Agazzi Corporation's December 31, 2008, financial statements. Christine Agazzi manufactures household appliances. During the course of your audit, you discovered the following contingent liabilities.

(LO 5, 6)

1. Christine Agazzi began production on a new dishwasher in June 2008 and, by December 31, 2008, sold 100,000 to various retailers for $500 each. Each dishwasher is under a one-year warranty. The company estimates that its warranty expense per dishwasher will amount to $25. At year-end, the company had already paid out $1,000,000 in warranty expenses. Christine Agazzi's income statement shows warranty expenses of $1,000,000 for 2008. Agazzi accounts for warranty costs on the accrual basis.

2. In response to your attorney's letter, Robert Sklodowski, Esq., has informed you that Agazzi has been cited for dumping toxic waste into the Kishwaukee River. Clean-up costs and fines amount to $3,330,000. Although the case is still being contested, Sklodowski is certain that Agazzi will most probably have to pay the fine and clean-up costs. No disclosure of this situation was found in the financial statements.

3. Christine Agazzi is the defendant in a patent infringement lawsuit by Heidi Goldman over Agazzi's use of a hydraulic compressor in several of its products. Sklodowski claims that, if the suit goes against Agazzi, the loss may be as much as $5,000,000; however, Sklodowski believes the loss of this suit to be only reasonably possible. Again, no mention of this suit occurs in the financial statements.

As presented, these contingencies are not reported in accordance with GAAP which may create problems in issuing a clean audit report. You feel the need to note these problems in the work papers.

Instructions

Heading each page with the name of the company, balance sheet date, and a brief description of the problem, write a brief narrative for each of the above issues in the form of **a memorandum** to be incorporated in the audit work papers. Explain what led to the discovery of each problem and what the problem really is. In addition, indicate the proper accounting (along with any appropriate journal entries) to record these contingencies in accordance with GAAP.

(LO 1, 5, 6)

P12-8 (**Various Current Liabilities**)   Alex Rodriguez Inc., a publishing company, is preparing its December 31, 2008, financial statements and must determine the proper accounting treatment for the following situations; they have retained your group to assist them in this task.

(a) Rodriguez sells subscriptions to several magazines for a 1-year, 2-year, or 3-year period. Cash receipts from subscribers are credited to magazine subscriptions collected in advance, and this account had a balance of $2,300,000 at December 31, 2008. Outstanding subscriptions at December 31, 2008, expire as follows.

> During 2009—$600,000
> During 2010—   500,000
> During 2011—   800,000

(b) On January 2, 2008, Rodriguez discontinued collision, fire, and theft coverage on its delivery vehicles and became self-insured for these risks. Actual losses of $50,000 during 2007 were charged to delivery expense. The 2006 premium for the discontinued coverage amounted to $80,000 and the controller wants to set up a reserve for self-insurance by a debit to delivery expense of $30,000 and a credit to the reserve for self-insurance of $30,000.

(c) A suit for breach of contract seeking damages of $1,000,000 was filed by an author against Rodriguez on July 1, 2008. The company's legal counsel believes that an unfavorable outcome is probable. A reasonable estimate of the court's award to the plaintiff is in the range between $300,000 and $700,000. No amount within this range is a better estimate of potential damages than any other amount.

(d) During December 2008, a competitor company filed suit against Rodriguez for industrial espionage claiming $1,500,000 in damages. In the opinion of management and company counsel, it is reasonably possible that damages will be awarded to the plaintiff. However, the amount of potential damages awarded to the plaintiff cannot be reasonably estimated.

Instructions

For each of the above situations, provide the journal entry that should be recorded as of December 31, 2008, or explain why an entry should not be recorded.

(AICPA adapted)

(LO 3, 9)

P12-9 (**Comprehensive Bond Problem**)   In each of the following independent cases the company closes its books on December 31.

1. Billips Co. sells $250,000 of 10% bonds on March 1, 2008. The bonds pay interest on September 1 and March 1. The due date of the bonds is September 1, 2011. The bonds yield 12%. Give entries through December 31, 2009.

2. Bogut Co. sells $600,000 of 12% bonds on June 1, 2008. The bonds pay interest on December 1 and June 1. The due date of the bonds is June 1, 2012. The bonds yield 10%. On October 1, 2009, Dougherty buys back $120,000 worth of bonds for $126,000 (includes accrued interest). Give entries through December 1, 2010.

Instructions

(Round to the nearest dollar.)

For the two cases above prepare all of the relevant journal entries from the time of sale until the date indicated. Use the effective interest method for discount and premium amortization (construct amortization tables where applicable). Amortize premium or discount on interest dates and at year-end. (Assume that no reversing entries were made.)

(LO 3, 9)

P12-10 (**Analysis of Amortization Schedule and Interest Entries**)   The following amortization and interest schedule reflects the issuance of 10-year bonds by Terrel Brandon Corporation on January 1, 2001, and the subsequent interest payments and charges. The company's year-end is December 31, and financial statements are prepared annually.

Amortization Schedule

12 %

Year	Cash	Interest Expense	Amount Unamortized	Carrying Value
1/1/01			$5,651	$ 94,349
2001	$11,000	$11,322	5,329	94,671
2002	11,000	11,361	4,968	95,032
2003	11,000	11,404	4,564	95,436
2004	11,000	11,452	4,112	95,888
2005	11,000	11,507	3,605	96,395
2006	11,000	11,567	3,038	96,962
2007	11,000	11,635	2,403	97,597
2008	11,000	11,712	1,691	98,309
2009	11,000	11,797	894	99,106
2010	11,000	11,894		100,000

Instructions

(a) Indicate whether the bonds were issued at a premium or a discount and how you can determine this fact from the schedule.

(b) Indicate whether the amortization schedule is based on the straight-line method or the effective interest method and how you can determine which method is used.

(c) Determine the stated interest rate and the effective interest rate. 12 %.

(d) On the basis of the schedule above, prepare the journal entry to record the issuance of the bonds on January 1, 2001.

(e) On the basis of the schedule above, prepare the journal entry or entries to reflect the bond transactions and accruals for 2001. (Interest is paid January 1.)

(f) On the basis of the schedule above, prepare the journal entry or entries to reflect the bond transactions and accruals for 2008. Brandon Corporation does not use reversing entries.

ACCOUNTING IN ACTION

Financial Reporting and Analysis

■ Financial Reporting Issues: The Procter & Gamble Company

AIA12-1 The financial statements of **Procter & Gamble (P&G)** can be accessed at the book's website.

Instructions

Refer to P&G's financial statements and the accompanying notes to answer the following questions.

(a) What was P&G's 2006 short-term debt and related weighted average interest rate on this debt?

(b) What was P&G's 2006 working capital, acid-test ratio, and current ratio? Comment on P&G's liquidity.

(c) What types of commitments and contingencies has P&G's reported in its financial statements? What is management's reaction to these contingencies?

(d) What cash outflow obligations related to the repayment of long-term debt does P&G have over the next 5 years?

(e) P&G indicates that it believes that it has the ability to meet business requirements in the foreseeable future. Prepare an assessment of its solvency and financial flexibility using ratio analysis.

■ Comparative Analysis: The Coca-Cola Company and PepsiCo, Inc.

AIA12-2 The financial statements of **The Coca-Cola Company** and **PepsiCo, Inc.** can be accessed at the book's website.

Instructions

Use information found at the book's website to answer the following questions.

(a) How much working capital does each of these companies have at the end of 2006? Comment on the appropriateness of the working capital they maintain.

(b) Compute both company's (a) current cash debt coverage ratio, (b) cash debt coverage ratio, (c) current ratio, (d) acid-test ratio, (e) receivable turnover ratio and (f) inventory turnover ratio for 2006. Comment on each company's overall liquidity.

(c) What types of loss or gain contingencies do these two companies have at December 31, 2006?

(d) Compute the debt to total assets ratio and the times interest earned ratio for these two companies. Comment on the quality of these two ratios for both Coca-Cola and PepsiCo.

(e) What is the difference between the fair value and the historical cost (carrying amount) of each company's debt at year-end 2006? Why might a difference exist in these two amounts?

(f) Both companies have debt issued in foreign countries. Speculate as to why these companies may use foreign debt to finance their operations. What risks are involved in this strategy, and how might they adjust for this risk?

■ Financial Statement Analysis

AIA12-3 Despite being a publicly traded company only since 1987, **Northland Cranberries** of Wisconsin Rapids, Wisconsin, is one of the world's largest cranberry growers. Despite its short life as a publicly traded corporation, it has engaged in an aggressive growth strategy. As a consequence, the company has taken on significant amounts of both short-term and long-term debt. The following information is taken from recent annual reports of the company.

Northland Cranberries

	Current Year	Prior Year
Current assets	$ 6,745,759	$ 5,598,054
Total assets	107,744,751	83,074,339
Current liabilities	10,168,685	4,484,687
Total liabilities	73,118,204	49,948,787
Stockholders' equity	34,626,547	33,125,552
Net sales	21,783,966	18,051,355
Cost of goods sold	13,057,275	8,751,220
Interest expense	3,654,006	2,393,792
Income tax expense	1,051,000	1,917,000
Net income	1,581,707	2,942,954

Instructions

(a) Evaluate the company's liquidity by calculating and analyzing working capital and the current ratio.

(b) The following discussion of the company's liquidity was provided by the company in the Management Discussion and Analysis section of the company's annual report. Comment on whether you agree with management's statements, and what might be done to remedy the situation.

The lower comparative current ratio in the current year was due to $3 million of short-term borrowing then outstanding which was incurred to fund the Yellow River Marsh acquisitions last year. As a result of the extreme seasonality of its business, the company does not believe that its current ratio or its underlying stated working capital at the current, fiscal year-end is a meaningful indication of the Company's liquidity. As of March 31 of each fiscal year, the Company has historically carried no significant amounts of inventories and by such date all of the Company's accounts receivable from its crop sold for processing under the supply agreements have been paid in cash, with the resulting cash received from such payments used to reduce indebtedness. The Company utilizes its revolving bank credit facility, together with cash generated from operations, to fund its working capital requirements throughout its growing season.

AIA12-4 Presented on the next page is the current liabilities section and related note of **Mohican Company**.

Mohican Company

(dollars in thousands)

	Current Year	Prior Year
Current liabilities		
Current portion of long-term debt	$ 15,000	$ 10,000
Short-term debt	2,668	405
Accounts payable	29,495	42,427
Accrued warranty	16,843	16,741
Accrued marketing programs	17,512	16,585
Other accrued liabilities	35,653	33,290
Accrued and deferred income taxes	16,206	17,348
Total current liabilities	$133,377	$136,796

Notes to Consolidated Financial Statements

Note 1 (in part): Summary of Significant Accounting Policies and Related Data Accrued Warranty The company provides an accrual for future warranty costs based upon the relationship of prior years' sales to actual warranty costs.

Instructions

Answer the following questions.

(a) What is the difference between the cash basis and the accrual basis of accounting for warranty costs?

(b) Under what circumstance, if any, would it be appropriate for Mohican Company to recognize deferred revenue on warranty contracts?

(c) If Mohican Company recognized deferred revenue on warranty contracts, how would it recognize this revenue in subsequent periods?

AIA12-5 **(Working Capital—Accounts Payable Days)** As discussed in the chapter, an important consideration in evaluating current liabilities is a company's operating cycle. The operating cycle is the average time required to go from cash-to-cash in generating revenue. To determine the length of the operating cycle, two measures are used: the average days to sell inventory (inventory days) and the average days to collect receivables (receivable days). The inventory-days computation measures the average number of days it takes to move an item from raw materials or purchase to final sale (from the day it comes in the company's door to the point it is converted to cash or an account receivable). The receivable-days computation measures the average number of days it takes to collect an account.

Most businesses must then determine how to finance the period of time when the liquid assets are tied up in inventory and accounts receivable. To determine how much to finance, companies first determine how long it takes to pay their creditors, or *accounts payable days*. Accounts payable days measures the number of days it takes to pay a supplier invoice. Consider the following operating cycle worksheet for BOP Clothing Co. shown below.

	2008	2009
Cash	$ 45,000	$ 30,000
Accounts Receivable	250,000	325,000
Inventory	830,000	800,000
Accounts Payable	720,000	775,000
Purchases	1,100,000	1,425,000
Cost of Goods Sold	1,145,000	1,455,000
Sales	1,750,000	1,950,000
Operating Cycle		
Inventory days[1]	264.6	200.7
Receivable days[2]	52.1	60.8
Operating cycle	316.7	261.5
Less: Accounts payable days[3]	238.9	198.5
Days to be financed	77.8	63.0

	2008	2009
Working capital	$405,000	$380,000
Current ratio	1.56	1.49
Acid-test ratio	0.41	0.46

[1] Inventory Days = (Inventory × 365)/Cost of Goods Sold
[2] Receivable Days = (Accounts Receivable × 365)/Sales
[3] Accounts Payable Days = (Accounts Payable × 365)/Purchases
Purchases = Cost of Goods Sold + Ending Inventory − Beginning Inventory. The ratios above assume that other current assets and liabilities are negligible.

These data indicate that BOP has reduced its overall operating cycle (to 261.5 days) as well as the number of days to be financed with sources of funds other than accounts payable (from 78 to 63 days). Most businesses cannot finance the operating cycle with accounts payable financing alone, so working capital financing, usually short-term interest-bearing loans, is needed to cover the shortfall. In this case, BOP would need to borrow less money to finance its operating cycle in 2009 than in 2008.

Instructions

(a) Use the BOP analysis to briefly discuss how the operating cycle data relate to the amount of working capital and the current and acid-test ratios.

(b) Select two other real companies that are in the same industry and complete the operating cycle worksheet on page 661, along with the working capital and ratio analysis. Briefly summarize and interpret the results. To simplify the analysis, you may use ending balances to compute turnover ratios.

[Adapted from Operating Cycle Worksheet at *www.entrepreneur.com*]

AIA12-6 The following article appeared in the *Wall Street Journal*.

Bond Markets

Giant Commonwealth Edison Issue Hits Resale Market With $70 Million Left Over

NEW YORK—**Commonwealth Edison Co.**'s slow-selling new 91/4% bonds were tossed onto the resale market at a reduced price with about $70 million still available from the $200 million offered Thursday, dealers said.

The Chicago utility's bonds, rated double-A by Moody's and double-A-minus by Standard & Poor's, originally had been priced at 99.803, to yield 9.3% in 5 years. They were marked down yesterday the equivalent of about $5.50 for each $1,000 face amount, to about 99.25, where their yield jumped to 9.45%.

Instructions

(a) How will the development above affect the accounting for Commonwealth Edison's bond issue?

(b) Provide several possible explanations for the markdown and the slow sale of Commonwealth Edison's bonds.

PEPSICO AIA12-7 **PepsiCo, Inc.** based in Purchase, New York, is a leading company in the beverage industry. Assume that the following events occurred relating to PepsiCo's long-term debt in a recent year.

1. The company decided on February 1 to refinance $500 million in short-term 7.4% debt to make it long-term 6%.
2. $780 million of long-term zero-coupon bonds with an effective interest rate of 10.1% matured July 1 and were paid.
3. On October 1, the company issued $200 million Australian-dollar 6.3% bonds at 102 and €95 million in 11.4% Italian bonds at 99.
4. The company holds $100 million in perpetual foreign interest payment bonds that were issued in 1989, and presently have a rate of interest of 5.3%. These bonds are called perpetual because they have no stated due date. Instead, at the end of every 10-year period after the bond's issuance, the bondholders and PepsiCo have the option of redeeming the bonds. If either party desires to redeem the bonds, the bonds must be redeemed. If the bonds are not redeemed, a new interest rate is set, based on the then-prevailing interest rate for 10-year bonds. The company does not intend to cause redemption of the bonds, but will reclassify this debt to current next year, since the bondholders could decide to redeem the bonds.

Instructions

(a) Consider event 1. What are some of the reasons the company may have decided to refinance this short-term debt, besides lowering the interest rate?

(b) What do you think are the benefits to the investor in purchasing zero-coupon bonds, such as those described in event 2? What journal entry would be required to record the payment of these bonds? If financial statements are prepared each December 31, in which year would the bonds have been included in short-term liabilities?

(c) Make the journal entry to record the bond issue described in event 3. Note that the bonds were issued on the same day, yet one was issued at a premium and the other at a discount. What are some of the reasons that this may have happened?

(d) What are the benefits to PepsiCo in having perpetual bonds as described in event 4? Suppose that in the current year the bonds are not redeemed and the interest rate is adjusted to 6% from 7.5%. Make all necessary journal entries to record the renewal of the bonds and the change in rate.

Concepts for Analysis

AIA12-8 **(Nature of Liabilities)** Presented below is the current liabilities section of Nizami Corporation.

	($000)	
	2008	2007
Current liabilities		
Notes payable	$ 68,713	$ 7,700
Accounts payable	179,496	101,379
Compensation to employees	60,312	31,649
Accrued liabilities	158,198	77,621
Income taxes payable	10,486	26,491
Current maturities of long-term debt	16,592	6,649
Total current liabilities	$493,797	$251,489

Instructions

Answer the following questions.

(a) What are the essential characteristics that make an item a liability?

(b) How does one distinguish between a current liability and a long-term liability?

(c) What are accrued liabilities? Give three examples of accrued liabilities that Nizami might have.

(d) What is the theoretically correct way to value liabilities? How are current liabilities usually valued?

(e) Why are notes payable reported first in the current liability section?

AIA12-9 **(Current versus Noncurrent Classification)** D'Annunzio Corporation includes the following items in its liabilities at December 31, 2008.

1. Notes payable, $25,000,000, due June 30, 2009.

2. Deposits from customers on equipment ordered by them from D'Annunzio, $6,250,000.

3. Salaries payable, $3,750,000, due January 14, 2009.

Instructions

Indicate in what circumstances, if any, each of the three liabilities above would be excluded from current liabilities.

AIA12-10 **(Current versus Noncurrent Classification)** The following items are listed as liabilities on the balance sheet of Eleutherios Company on December 31, 2008.

Accounts payable	$ 420,000
Notes payable	750,000
Bonds payable	2,250,000

The accounts payable represent obligations to suppliers that are due in January 2009. The notes payable mature on various dates during 2009. The bonds payable mature on July 1, 2009.

These liabilities must be reported on the balance sheet in accordance with generally accepted accounting principles governing the classification of liabilities as current and noncurrent.

Instructions

(a) What is the general rule for determining whether a liability is classified as current or noncurrent?

(b) Under what conditions may any of Eleutherios Company's liabilities be classified as noncurrent? Explain your answer.

(CMA adapted)

AIA12-11 **(Bond Theory: Balance Sheet Presentations, Interest Rate, Premium)** On January 1, 2009, Branagh Company issued for $1,075,230 its 20-year, 13% bonds that have a maturity value of $1,000,000 and pay interest semiannually on January 1 and July 1. Bond issue costs were not material in amount. On the next page are three presentations of the long-term liability section of the balance sheet that might be used for these bonds at the issue date.

1. Bonds payable (maturing January 1, 2029)	$1,000,000
Unamortized premium on bonds payable	75,230
Total bond liability	$1,075,230

2. Bonds payable—principal (face value $1,000,000 maturing January 1, 2029)	$ 97,220[a]
Bonds payable—interest (semiannual payment $65,000)	978,010[b]
Total bond liability	$1,075,230

3. Bonds payable—principal (maturing January 1, 2029)	$1,000,000
Bonds payable—interest ($65,000 per period for 40 periods)	2,600,000
Total bond liability	$3,600,000

[a]The present value of $1,000,000 due at the end of 40 (6-month) periods at the yield rate of 6% per period.
[b]The present value of $65,000 per period for 40 (6-month) periods at the yield rate of 6% per period.

Instructions

(a) Discuss the conceptual merit(s) of each of the date-of-issue balance sheet presentations shown above for these bonds.

(b) Explain why investors would pay $1,075,230 for bonds that have a maturity value of only $1,000,000.

(c) Assuming that a discount rate is needed to compute the carrying value of the obligations arising from a bond issue at any date during the life of the bonds, discuss the conceptual merit(s) of using for this purpose:
  (1) The coupon or nominal rate.
  (2) The effective or yield rate at date of issue.

(d) If the obligations arising from these bonds are to be carried at their present value computed by means of the current market rate of interest, how would the bond valuation at dates subsequent to the date of issue be affected by an increase or a decrease in the market rate of interest?

(AICPA adapted)

AIA12-12 **(Various Long-Term Liability Conceptual Issues)** Emma Thompson Company has completed a number of transactions during 2008. In January the company purchased under contract a machine at a total price of $1,200,000, payable over 5 years with installments of $240,000 per year. The seller has considered the transaction as an installment sale with the title transferring to Thompson at the time of the final payment.

On March 1, 2008, Thompson issued $10 million of general revenue bonds priced at 99 with a coupon of 10% payable July 1 and January 1 of each of the next 10 years. The July 1 interest was paid and on December 30 the company transferred $500,000 to the trustee, Hollywood Trust Company, for payment of the January 1, 2009, interest.

Due to the depressed market for the company's stock, Thompson purchased $500,000 par value of their 6% convertible bonds for a price of $455,000. It expects to resell the bonds when the price of its stock has recovered.

As the accountant for Emma Thompson Company, you have prepared the balance sheet as of December 31, 2008, and have presented it to the president of the company. You are asked the following questions about it.

1. Why has depreciation been charged on equipment being purchased under contract? Title has not passed to the company as yet and, therefore, they are not our assets. Why should the company not show on the left side of the balance sheet only the amount paid to date instead of showing the full contract price on the left side and the unpaid portion on the right side? After all, the seller considers the transaction an installment sale.

2. What is bond discount? As a debit balance, why is it not classified among the assets?

3. Bond interest is shown as a current liability. Did we not pay our trustee, Hollywood Trust Company, the full amount of interest due this period?

Instructions

Outline your answers to these questions by writing a brief paragraph that will justify your treatment.

AIA12-13 **(Loss Contingencies)** Animaniacs Company is a manufacturer of toys. During the year, the following situations arose.

1. A safety hazard related to one of its toy products was discovered. It is considered probable that liabilities have been incurred. On the basis of past experience, a reasonable estimate of the amount of loss can be made.

2. One of its small warehouses is located on the bank of a river and could no longer be insured against flood losses. No flood losses have occurred after the date that the insurance became unavailable.

3. This year, Animaniacs began promoting a new toy by including a coupon, redeemable for a movie ticket, in each toy's carton. The movie ticket, which cost Animaniacs $3, is purchased in advance and then mailed to the customer when the coupon is received by Animaniacs. Animaniacs estimated, based on past experience, that 60% of the coupons would be redeemed. Forty-five percent of the coupons were actually redeemed this year, and the remaining 15% of the coupons are expected to be redeemed next year.

Instructions

(a) How should Animaniacs report the safety hazard? Why?
(b) How should Animaniacs report the noninsurable flood risk? Why?
(c) How should Animaniacs account for the toy promotion campaign in this year?

AIA12-14 (Loss Contingencies) On February 1, 2008, one of the huge storage tanks of Paunee Manufacturing Company exploded. Windows in houses and other buildings within a one-mile radius of the explosion were severely damaged, and a number of people were injured. As of February 15, 2008 (when the December 31, 2007, financial statements were completed and sent to the publisher for printing and public distribution), no suits had been filed or claims asserted against the company as a consequence of the explosion. The company fully anticipates that suits will be filed and claims asserted for injuries and damages. Because the casualty was uninsured and the company considered at fault, Paunee Manufacturing will have to cover the damages from its own resources.

Instructions

Discuss fully the accounting treatment and disclosures that should be accorded the casualty and related contingent losses in the financial statements dated December 31, 2007.

AIA12-15 (Loss Contingency) Presented below is a note disclosure for Ralph Ellison Corporation.

Litigation and Environmental: The Company has been notified, or is a named or a potentially responsible party in a number of governmental (federal, state and local) and private actions associated with environmental matters, such as those relating to hazardous wastes, including certain sites which are on the United States EPA National Priorities List ("Superfund"). These actions seek cleanup costs, penalties and/or damages for personal injury or to property or natural resources.

In 2008, the Company recorded a pre-tax charge of $56,229,000, included in the "Other Expense (Income)—Net" caption of the Company's Consolidated Statements of Income, as an additional provision for environmental matters. These expenditures are expected to take place over the next several years and are indicative of the Company's commitment to improve and maintain the environment in which it operates. At December 31, 2008, environmental accruals amounted to $69,931,000, of which $61,535,000 are considered noncurrent and are included in the "Deferred Credits and Other Liabilities" caption of the Company's Consolidated Balance Sheets.

While it is impossible at this time to determine with certainty the ultimate outcome of environmental matters, it is management's opinion, based in part on the advice of independent counsel (after taking into account accruals and insurance coverage applicable to such actions) that when the costs are finally determined they will not have a material adverse effect on the financial position of the Company.

Instructions

Answer the following questions.

(a) What conditions must exist before a loss contingency can be recorded in the accounts?
(b) Suppose that Ralph Ellison Corporation could not reasonably estimate the amount of the loss, although it could establish with a high degree of probability the minimum and maximum loss possible. How should this information be reported in the financial statements?
(c) If the amount of the loss is uncertain, how would the loss contingency be reported in the financial statements?

AIA12-16 (Loss Contingencies) The following three independent sets of facts relate to (1) the possible accrual or (2) the possible disclosure of a loss contingency.

Situation I

Subsequent to the date of a set of financial statements, but prior to the issuance of the financial statements, a company enters into a contract that will probably result in a significant loss to the company. The amount of the loss can be reasonably estimated.

Situation II

A company offers a one-year warranty for the product that it manufactures. A history of warranty claims has been compiled and the probable amount of claims related to sales for a given period can be determined.

Situation III

A company has adopted a policy of recording self-insurance for any possible losses resulting from injury to others by the company's vehicles. The premium for an insurance policy for the same risk from an independent insurance company would have an annual cost of $4,000. During the period covered by the financial statements, there were no accidents involving the company's vehicles that resulted in injury to others.

Instructions

Discuss the accrual or type of disclosure necessary (if any) and the reason(s) why such disclosure is appropriate for each of the three independent sets of facts above.

(AICPA adapted)

Professional Tools

■ Ethical Decision Making

AIA12-17 (**Debt Issue**) Roland Carlson is the president, founder, and majority owner of Thebeau Medical Corporation, an emerging medical technology products company. Thebeau is in dire need of additional capital to keep operating and to bring several promising products to final development, testing, and production. Roland, as owner of 51% of the outstanding stock, manages the company's operations. He places heavy emphasis on research and development and long-term growth. The other principal stockholder is Jana Kingston who, as a non-employee investor, owns 40% of the stock. Jana would like to deemphasize the R & D functions and emphasize the marketing function to maximize short-run sales and profits from existing products. She believes this strategy would raise the market price of Thebeau's stock.

All of Roland's personal capital and borrowing power is tied up in his 51% stock ownership. He knows that any offering of additional shares of stock will dilute his controlling interest because he won't be able to participate in such an issuance. But, Jana has money and would likely buy enough shares to gain control of Thebeau. She then would dictate the company's future direction, even if it meant replacing Roland as president and CEO.

The company already has considerable debt. Raising additional debt will be costly, will adversely affect Thebeau's credit rating, and will increase the company's reported losses due to the growth in interest expense. Jana and the other minority stockholders express opposition to the assumption of additional debt, fearing the company will be pushed to the brink of bankruptcy. Wanting to maintain his control and to preserve the direction of "his" company, Roland is doing everything to avoid a stock issuance and is contemplating a large issuance of bonds, even if it means the bonds are issued with a high effective-interest rate.

Instructions

(a) Who are the stakeholders in this situation?
(b) What are the ethical issues in this case?
(c) What would you do if you were Roland?

■ Financial Accounting Research (FARS)

AIA12-18 Hincapie Co. manufactures specialty bike accessories. The company is known for product quality, and it has offered one of the best warranties in the industry on its higher-priced products—a lifetime guarantee, performing all the warranty work in its own shops. The warranty on these products is included in the sales price.

Due to the recent introduction and growth in sales of some products targeted to the low-price market, Hincapie is considering partnering with another company to do the warranty work on this line of products, if customers purchase a service contract at the time of original product purchase. Hincapie has called you to advise the company on the accounting for this new warranty arrangement.

Instructions

Using the **Financial Accounting Research System (FARS)** database, respond to the following items. (Provide text strings used in your search.)

(a) Identify the accounting literature that addresses the accounting for the type of separately priced warranty that Hincapie is considering.
(b) When are warranty contracts considered separately priced?
(c) What are incremental direct acquisition costs and how should they be treated?
(d) How many letters of comment were received on this proposed Technical Bulletin? Why did some of the respondents feel that the effective date of this Technical Bulletin should be delayed?

AIA12-19 Wie Company has been operating for just 2 years, producing specialty golf equipment for women golfers. To date, the company has been able to finance its successful operations with investments from its principal owner, Michelle Wie, and cash flows from operations. However, current expansion plans will require some borrowing to expand the company's production line.

As part of the expansion plan, Wie will acquire some used equipment by signing a zero-interest-bearing note. The note has a maturity value of $50,000 and matures in 5 years. A reliable fair value measure for the equipment is not available, given the age and specialty nature of the equipment. As a result, Wie's accounting staff is unable to determine an established exchange price for recording the equipment (nor the interest rate to be used to record interest expense on the long-term note). They have asked you to conduct some accounting research on this topic.

Instructions

Using the **Financial Accounting Research System (FARS) database**, respond to the following items. (Provide text strings used in your search.)

(a) Identify the accounting standard that provides guidance on the zero-interest-bearing note. Use some of the examples to explain how the standard applies in this setting.

(b) How is present value determined when an established exchange price is not determinable and a note has no ready market? What is the resulting interest rate often called?

(c) Where should a discount or premium appear in the financial statements? What about issue costs?

■ Professional Simulations

AIA12-20 and AIA12-21 Go to the book's companion website, at **www.wiley.com/college/warfield**, to find interactive problems that simulate the computerized CPA exam. The professional simulations for this chapter ask you to address questions related to the accounting for current liabilities and long-term debt.

What Do the Numbers Mean?

Frequent Buyers, p. 611

Q: Some companies, like Microsoft report unearned revenue related to future upgrades of its programs. Briefly discuss how a decline in the level of these unearned revenues can provide a signal about Microsoft's current sales.

A: The amount of unearned revenue will increase based on sales of products such as Windows and Office. That is, at the time of a sale, customers are paying not only for the current version of the software but also for future upgrades. In this case, Microsoft recognizes sales revenue from the current version of the software and records as a liability (unearned revenue) the value of future upgrades to the software that are "owed" to customers.

Market analysts read such an increase in unearned revenue as a positive signal about Microsoft's sales and profitability. When Microsoft's sales are growing, its unearned revenue account increases. Thus, an *increase* in a liability is good news about Microsoft sales. Alternatively, a decline in unearned revenue is bad news.

All About Bonds, p. 614

Q: Some bonds are convertible. That is, the bondholders have the option to exchange their bonds for common shares, which could be quite valuable for the bonds issued by a growth company. What effect does a conversion have on the coupon rate of a bond?

A: The conversion feature is valuable to investors because it gives them an option to share in the upside potential in the value of the stock (if they convert the bonds). Note that with a "straight" bond, the investor receives only principal repayment and interest. As a result, investors are willing to accept a lower coupon rate on a convertible compared to a bond of similar risk without the conversion feature. For example, Amazon.com at one time issued convertible bonds that pay interest at an effective yield of 4.75 percent. This rate was much lower than Amazon.com would have had to pay by issuing straight debt. For this lower interest rate, the investor receives the right to buy Amazon.com's common stock at a fixed price until the bond's maturity.

(*continued*)

Guideline Answers, continued

"How's My Rating?," p. 616

Q: What effect will a ratings downgrade or upgrade have on a company's profitability?

A: The primary effect will be on a company's interest costs on any new loans. When ratings are upgraded, the interest rate on borrowings will decrease; when ratings are downgraded, the interest rate on borrowing will increase. Thus, with a rating increase, interest expense will decrease, and income will be higher. Similarly, if a company's debt rating declines, its interest costs will increase, and income will be lower.

Gift Cards: Handle with Care, p. 626

Q: Even though an increase in gift card unearned revenue increases current liabilities (and may indicate reduced liquidity), what signal about future profitability do changes in unearned revenue provide?

A: Similar to the discussion of frequent buyers (see page 613), the amount of unearned revenue for gift cards is an indicator of future sales when the gift card holders redeem the cards. In addition, to the extent that these customers make additional purchases, purchases of gift cards can drive additional sales increases and cash flows in future periods. Thus, retail analysts follow gift card balances to get a read on future store traffic that could lead to sales growth. At the same time, a decline in the unearned revenue from gift cards is bad news.

More Disclosure, Please, p. 633

Q: What are some of the drawbacks of requiring more recognition (as opposed to disclosure) of contingencies, such as those related to litigation or environmental costs?

A: One drawback concerns the lack of reliability associated with the estimates inherent in these contingencies. According to the conceptual framework (*SFAC No. 5*), items recognized in financial statements should be *both* relevant and reliable. While information on these items is relevant, determining the amount to recognize requires a number of subjective judgments that could negatively affect the representational faithfulness, verifiability, and neutrality (the elements of reliability) of the recorded amounts.

A second drawback is the possible negative impact on contracts (e.g., debt agreements, compensation plans). When the currently disclosed amounts are recognized, it could lead to violation of loan covenants or reduced bonuses paid to managers, when these items are based on income statement and balance sheet amounts.

These are examples of the "economic consequences" arising from accounting standards. Note that required disclosures of certain litigation contingencies could have negative economic consequences if the information in the disclosures can be used against the company in the legal proceeding.

Remember to check the book's companion website to find additional resources for this chapter.

CHAPTER 13

STOCKHOLDERS' EQUITY

Everything Else Equal?

Not all dividend payers are created equal. Some stocks provide a good dividend yield but also promise strong earnings growth. These stocks could provide a healthy one-two punch for investors. A good example is Seattle's **Plum Creek Timber**. It pays a dividend of close to 4.2 percent, and it also expects earnings to expand about 6 percent in the next year.

General Motors has a seemingly healthy dividend of 5.8 percent. But the big automaker had a loss of $1.1 billion in a recent quarter, and it is having trouble reducing its onerous health-care benefits. There is concern that GM may be forced to trim its dividend at some point to conserve cash. The following chart shows that dividends are an important part of total stock returns.

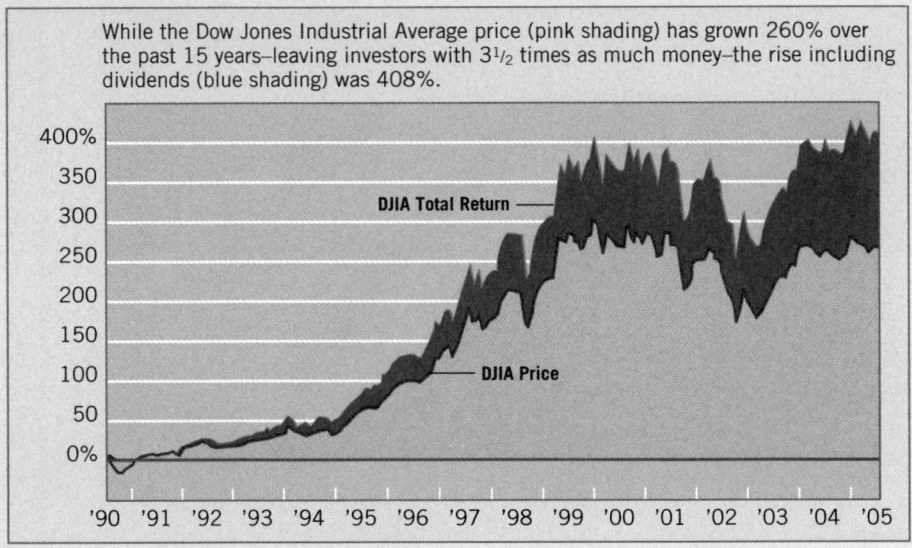

While the Dow Jones Industrial Average price (pink shading) has grown 260% over the past 15 years–leaving investors with $3^1/_2$ times as much money–the rise including dividends (blue shading) was 408%.

Source: WSJ Marketing Data Group

As one analyst noted, "Investors have consistently underappreciated the value of compounding dividends in a portfolio. And dividends usually provide a strong degree of downside protection for a portfolio." But be wary when focusing on high-dividend stocks. Those with problems may find it difficult to keep their dividend payments going in the future.

Source: Adapted from Gary Zuckerman, "When Dividends Are Sweet, Be Choosy," *Wall Street Journal Online* (July 3, 2005).

Preview of Chapter 13

As our opening story indicates, dividends combined with other information about a company can provide useful information to investors. In this chapter we explain the accounting issues for dividend transactions, as well as other transactions related to the stockholders' equity of a corporation. *The content and organization of the chapter are as follows.*

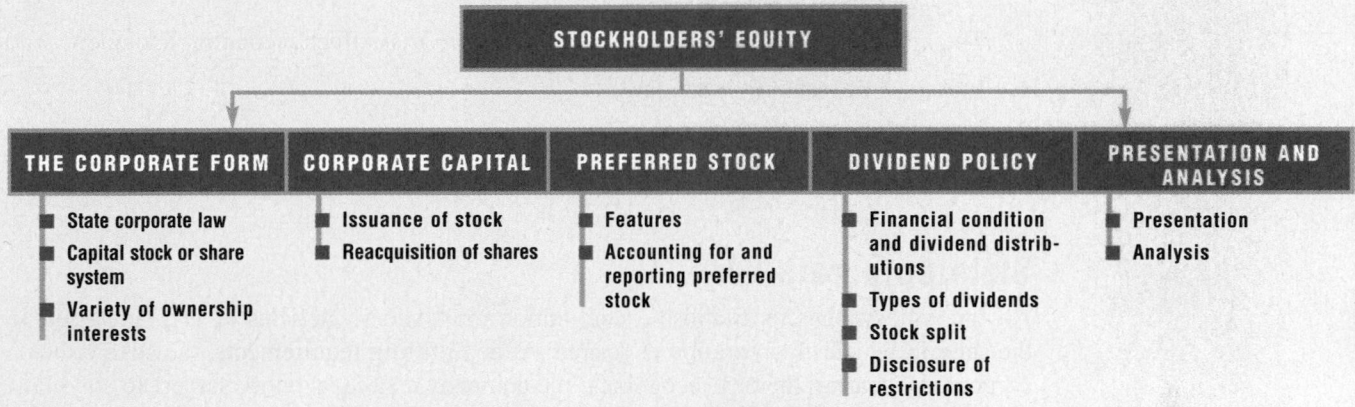

STOCKHOLDERS' EQUITY				
THE CORPORATE FORM	**CORPORATE CAPITAL**	**PREFERRED STOCK**	**DIVIDEND POLICY**	**PRESENTATION AND ANALYSIS**
▪ State corporate law ▪ Capital stock or share system ▪ Variety of ownership interests	▪ Issuance of stock ▪ Reacquisition of shares	▪ Features ▪ Accounting for and reporting preferred stock	▪ Financial condition and dividend distributions ▪ Types of dividends ▪ Stock split ▪ Disclosure of restrictions	▪ Presentation ▪ Analysis

Learning Objectives

After studying this chapter, you should be able to:

1. Discuss the characteristics of the corporate form of organization.
2. Identify the key components of stockholders' equity.
3. Explain the accounting procedures for issuing shares of stock.
4. Describe the accounting for treasury stock.
5. Explain the accounting for and reporting of preferred stock.
6. Describe the policies used in distributing dividends.
7. Identify the various forms of dividend distributions.
8. Explain the accounting for small and large stock dividends, and for stock splits.
9. Indicate how to present and analyze stockholders' equity.

Inside Chapter 13

■ **What Do the Numbers Mean?**
Classy stock (p. 674)
The case of the disappearing receivable (p. 678)
Signals to buy? (p. 681)
Splitsville (p. 693)

■ **What's the Principle?**
(pp. 680, 691, 694, 708)

■ **Convergence Corner** (p. 701)

■ **Accounting, Analysis, Principles** (p. 702)
Record stockholders' equity transactions.
Assess performance based on stockholders' equity ratios.
Explain the conceptual basis for treasury stock accounting.

THE CORPORATE FORM OF ORGANIZATION

OBJECTIVE 1

Discuss the characteristics of the corporate form of organization.

Of the three **primary forms of business organization**—the proprietorship, the partnership, and the corporation—the corporate form dominates. The corporation is by far the leader in terms of the aggregate amount of resources controlled, goods and services produced, and people employed. All of the Fortune 500 largest industrial firms are corporations. Although the corporate form has a number of advantages (as well as disadvantages) over the other two forms, its principal advantage is its facility for attracting and accumulating large amounts of capital.

The special characteristics of the corporate form that affect accounting include:

1 Influence of state corporate law.

2 Use of the capital stock or share system.

3 Development of a variety of ownership interests.

State Corporate Law

Anyone who wishes to establish a corporation must submit **articles of incorporation** to the state in which incorporation is desired. After fulfilling requirements, the state issues a corporation charter, thereby recognizing the company as a legal entity subject to state law. Regardless of the number of states in which a corporation has operating divisions, it is incorporated in only one state.

It is to the company's advantage to incorporate in a state whose laws favor the corporate form of business organization. **General Motors**, for example, is incorporated in Delaware; **U.S. Steel** is a New Jersey corporation. Some corporations have increasingly been incorporating in states with laws favorable to existing management. For example, to thwart possible unfriendly takeovers, at one time, **Gulf Oil** changed its state of incorporation to Delaware. There, the board of directors alone, without a vote of the shareholders, may approve certain tactics against takeovers.

Each state has its own business incorporation act. The accounting for stockholders' equity follows the provisions of these acts. In many cases states have adopted the principles contained in the Model Business Corporate Act prepared by the American Bar Association. State laws are complex and vary both in their provisions and in their definitions of certain terms. Some laws fail to define technical terms. As a result, terms often mean one thing in one state and another thing in a different state. These problems may be further compounded because legal authorities often interpret the effects and restrictions of the laws differently.

INTERNATIONAL INSIGHT

In the United States, stockholders are treated equally as far as access to financial information. That is not always the case in other countries. For example, in Mexico, foreign investors as well as minority investors often have difficulty obtaining financial data. These restrictions are rooted in the habits of companies that, for many years, were tightly controlled by a few stockholders and managers.

Capital Stock or Share System

Stockholders' equity in a corporation generally consists of a large number of units or shares. Within a given class of stock each share exactly equals every other share. The number of shares possessed determines each owner's interest. If a company has one class of stock divided into 1,000 shares, a person who owns 500 shares controls one-half of the ownership interest. One holding 10 shares has a one-hundredth interest.

Each share of stock has certain rights and privileges. Only by special contract can a company restrict these rights and privileges at the time it issues the shares. Owners must examine the articles of incorporation, stock certificates, and the provisions of the state law to ascertain such restrictions on or variations from the standard rights and privileges. In the absence of restrictive provisions, each share carries the following rights:

1 To share proportionately in profits and losses.

2 To share proportionately in management (the right to vote for directors).

3   To share proportionately in corporate assets upon liquidation.

4   To share proportionately in any new issues of stock of the same class—called the **preemptive right**.[1]

The first three rights are self explanatory. The last right is used to protect each stockholder's proportional interest in the company. **The preemptive right protects an existing stockholder from involuntary dilution of ownership interest**. Without this right, stockholders might find their interest reduced by the issuance of additional stock without their knowledge, and at prices unfavorable to them. However, many corporations have eliminated the preemptive right. Why? Because this right makes it inconvenient for corporations to issue large amounts of additional stock, as they frequently do in acquiring other companies.

The share system easily allows one individual to transfer an interest in a company to another investor. For example, individuals owning shares in **Circuit City may sell them to others at any time and at any price without obtaining the consent of the company or other stockholders**. Each share is personal property of the owner, who may dispose of it at will. Circuit City simply maintains a list or subsidiary ledger of stockholders as a guide to dividend payments, issuance of stock rights, voting proxies, and the like. Because owners freely and frequently transfer shares, Circuit City must revise the subsidiary ledger of stockholders periodically, generally in advance of every dividend payment or stockholders' meeting.

In addition, the major stock exchanges require ownership controls that the typical corporation finds uneconomic to provide. Thus, corporations often use **registrars and transfer agents** who specialize in providing services for recording and transferring stock. The Uniform Stock Transfer Act and the Uniform Commercial Code govern the negotiability of stock certificates.

Variety of Ownership Interests

In every corporation one class of stock must represent the basic ownership interest. That class is called common stock. **Common stock** is the residual corporate interest that bears the ultimate risks of loss and receives the benefits of success. It is guaranteed neither dividends nor assets upon dissolution. But common stockholders generally control the management of the corporation and tend to profit most if the company is successful. In the event that a corporation has only one authorized issue of capital stock, that issue is by definition common stock, whether so designated in the charter or not.

In an effort to broaden investor appeal, corporations may offer two or more classes of stock, each with different rights or privileges. In the preceding section we pointed out that each share of stock of a given issue has the same four inherent rights as other shares of the same issue. By special stock contracts between the corporation and its stockholders, however, the stockholder may sacrifice certain of these rights in return for other special rights or privileges. Thus special classes of stock, usually called **preferred stock**, are created. In return for any special preference, the preferred stockholder always sacrifices some of the inherent rights of common stock ownership.

A common type of preference is to give the preferred stockholders a prior claim on earnings. The corporation thus assures them a dividend, usually at a stated rate, before it distributes any amount to the common stockholders. In return for this preference the preferred stockholders may sacrifice their right to a voice in management or their right to share in profits beyond the stated rate.

INTERNATIONAL INSIGHT

The U.S. and British systems of corporate governance and finance depend to a large extent on equity financing and the widely dispersed ownership of shares traded in highly liquid markets. The German and Japanese systems have relied more on debt financing, interlocking stock ownership, banker/directors, and worker/shareholder rights.

---

[1]This privilege is referred to as a **stock right** or **warrant**. The warrants issued in these situations are of short duration, unlike the warrants issued with other securities.

What do the numbers mean?   **Classy Stock**

Some companies grant preferences to different shareholders by issuing different classes of common stock. Blue-chip newspaper companies, such as **The New York Times, Dow Jones,** and **The Washington Post,** have two classes of stock. Also, **Ford** and **Comcast** are two-class companies.

Sometimes these different classes of shares trade at dramatically different prices. For example, **Molex** has issued both common shares and Class A common stock, with the common shares trading at up to a 15 percent premium over the Class A shares. Why the difference in price? The most common explanation is voting rights. In the Molex case, the common shareholders get one vote per share; Class A shares don't get to vote.

For most retail investors, voting rights are not that important. But for family-controlled companies, issuing newer classes of lower or non-voting stock effectively creates currency for acquisitions, increases liquidity, or puts a public value on the company without diluting the family's voting control. Thus, investors must carefully compare the apparent bargain prices for some classes of stock—they may end up as second-class citizens with no voting rights.

Source: Adapted from Lauren Rublin, "Separate but Equal," *Barron's Online* (August 16, 1999); and Andy Serwer, "Dual-Listed Companies Aren't Fair or Balanced," *Fortune* (September 20, 2004), p. 83.

Beyond the Numbers

Assume that you are considering investing in the bonds of a company like Molex. Should you be concerned that the company has a two-class share structure? Explain.

CORPORATE CAPITAL

OBJECTIVE 2

Identify the key components of stockholders' equity.

Owner's equity in a corporation is defined as stockholders' equity, shareholders' equity, or corporate capital. The following three categories normally appear as part of stockholders' equity:

1 Capital stock.

2 Additional paid-in capital.

3 Retained earnings.

The first two categories, capital stock and additional paid-in capital, constitute contributed (paid-in) capital. **Retained earnings** represents the earned capital of the company. **Contributed capital (paid-in capital)** is the total amount paid in on capital stock—the amount provided by stockholders to the corporation for use in the business. Contributed capital includes items such as the par value of all outstanding stock and premiums less discounts on issuance. **Earned capital** is the capital that develops from profitable operations. It consists of all undistributed income that remains invested in the company.

Stockholders' equity is the difference between the assets and the liabilities of the company. That is, the owners' or stockholders' interest in a company like **Walt Disney Co.** is a **residual interest.**[2] **Stockholders' (owners') equity** represents the cumulative net contributions by stockholders plus retained earnings. As a residual interest, stockholders' equity has no existence apart from the assets and liabilities of Disney—stockholders' equity equals net assets. Stockholders' equity is not a claim to specific assets but a claim against a portion of the total assets. Its amount is not specified or fixed; it depends on Disney's profitability. Stockholders' equity grows if it is profitable. It shrinks, or may disappear entirely, if Disney loses money.

[2]"Elements of Financial Statements," *Statement of Financial Accounting Concepts No. 6* (Stamford, Conn.: FASB, 1985), par. 60.

Issuance of Stock

In issuing stock, companies follow these procedures: First, the state must authorize the stock, generally in a certificate of incorporation or charter. Next, the corporation offers shares for sale, entering into contracts to sell stock. Then, after receiving amounts for the stock, the corporation issues shares. The corporation generally makes no entry in the general ledger accounts when it receives its stock authorization from the state of incorporation.

OBJECTIVE **3**

Explain the accounting procedures for issuing shares of stock.

We discuss the accounting problems involved in the issuance of stock under the following topics.

1 Accounting for par value stock.

2 Accounting for no-par stock.

3 Accounting for stock issued in combination with other securities (lump-sum sales).

4 Accounting for stock issued in noncash transactions.

5 Accounting for costs of issuing stock.

Par Value Stock

The par value of a stock has no relationship to its fair market value. At present, the par value associated with most capital stock issuances is very low. For example, **PepsiCo**'s par value is 1⅔ ¢, **Kellogg**'s is $0.25, and **Hershey**'s is $1. Such values contrast dramatically with the situation in the early 1900s, when practically all stock issued had a par value of $100. Low par values help companies avoid the contingent liability associated with stock sold below par.[3]

To show the required information for issuance of par value stock, corporations maintain accounts for each class of stock as follows.

1 *Preferred Stock or Common Stock.* Together, these two stock accounts reflect the par value of the corporation's issued shares. The company credits these accounts when it originally issues the shares. It makes no additional entries in these accounts unless it issues additional shares or retires them.

2 *Additional Paid-in Capital (also called Paid-in Capital in Excess of Par).* The **Additional Paid-in Capital** account indicates any excess over par value paid in by stockholders in return for the shares issued to them. Once paid in, the excess over par becomes a part of the corporation's additional paid-in capital. The individual stockholder has no greater claim on the excess paid in than all other holders of the same class of shares.

No-Par Stock

Many states permit the issuance of capital stock without par value, called **no-par stock**. The reasons for issuance of no-par stock are twofold: First, issuance of no-par stock **avoids the contingent liability** (see footnote 3) that might occur if the corporation issued par value stock at a discount. Second, some confusion exists over the relationship (or rather the absence of a relationship) between the par value and fair market value. If shares have no par value, **the questionable treatment of using par value as a basis for fair value never arises**. This is particularly advantageous whenever issuing stock for property items such as tangible or intangible fixed assets.

A major disadvantage of no-par stock is that some states levy a high tax on these issues. In addition, in some states the total issue price for no-par stock may be considered legal capital, which could reduce the flexibility in paying dividends.

---

[3]Companies rarely, if ever, issue stock at a value below par value. If issuing stock below par, the company records the discount as a debit to Additional Paid-in Capital. In addition, the corporation may call on the original purchaser or the current holder of the shares issued below par to pay in the amount of the discount to prevent creditors from sustaining a loss upon liquidation of the corporation.

Corporations sell no-par shares, like par value shares, for whatever price they will bring. However, unlike par value shares, corporations issue them without a premium or a discount. The exact amount received represents the credit to common or preferred stock. For example, Video Electronics Corporation is organized with authorized common stock of 10,000 shares without par value. Video Electronics makes only a memorandum entry for the authorization, inasmuch as no amount is involved. If Video Electronics then issues 500 shares for cash at $10 per share, it makes the following entry:

Cash	5,000	
Common Stock—No-Par Value		5,000

If it issues another 500 shares for $11 per share, Video Electronics makes this entry:

Cash	5,500	
Common Stock—No-Par Value		5,500

True no-par stock should be carried in the accounts at issue price without any additional paid-in capital or discount reported. But some states require that no-par stock have a **stated value**. The stated value is a minimum value below which a company cannot issue it. Thus, instead of being no-par stock, such stated-value stock becomes, in effect, stock with a very low par value. It thus is open to all the criticism and abuses that first encouraged the development of no-par stock.[4]

If no-par stock has a stated value of $5 per share but sells for $11, all such amounts in excess of $5 are recorded as additional paid-in capital, which in many states is fully or partially available for dividends. Thus, no-par value stock, with a low stated value, permits a new corporation to commence its operations with additional paid-in capital that may exceed its stated capital. For example, if a company issued 1,000 of the shares with a $5 stated value at $15 per share for cash, it makes the following entry.

Cash	15,000	
Common Stock		5,000
Paid-in Capital in Excess of Stated Value		10,000

Most corporations account for no-par stock with a stated value as if it were par value stock with par equal to the stated value.

Stock Issued with Other Securities (Lump-Sum Sales)

Generally, corporations sell classes of stock separately from one another. The reason to do so is to track the proceeds relative to each class, as well as relative to each lot. Occasionally, a corporation issues two or more classes of securities for a single payment or lump sum, in the acquisition of another company. The accounting problem in such **lump-sum sales** is how to allocate the proceeds among the several classes of securities. Companies use one of two methods of allocation: (1) the proportional method and (2) the incremental method.

Proportional Method. If the fair market value or other sound basis for determining relative value is available for each class of security, **the company allocates the lump sum received among the classes of securities on a proportional basis**. For instance, assume a company issues 1,000 shares of $10 stated value common stock having a market value of $20 a share, and 1,000 shares of $10 par value preferred stock having a market value of $12 a share, for a lump sum of $30,000. Illustration 13-1 shows how the company allocates the $30,000 to the two classes of stock.

---

[4]*Accounting Trends and Techniques—2006* indicates that its 600 surveyed companies reported 649 issues of outstanding common stock, 576 par value issues, and 61 no-par issues; 7 of the no-par issues were shown at their stated (assigned) values.

Fair market value of common (1,000 × $20) = $20,000
Fair market value of preferred (1,000 × $12) = 12,000

Aggregate fair market value $32,000

Allocated to common: $\frac{\$20,000}{\$32,000}$ × $30,000 = $18,750

Allocated to preferred: $\frac{\$12,000}{\$32,000}$ × $30,000 = 11,250

Total allocation $30,000

Illustration 13-1
Allocation in Lump-Sum
Securities Issuance—
Proportional Method

Incremental Method. In instances where a company cannot determine the fair market value of all classes of securities, it may use the incremental method. It uses the market value of the securities as a basis for those classes that it knows, and allocates the remainder of the lump sum to the class for which it does not know the market value. For instance, if a company issues 1,000 shares of $10 stated value common stock having a market value of $20, and 1,000 shares of $10 par value preferred stock having no established market value, for a lump sum of $30,000, it allocates the $30,000 to the two classes as shown in Illustration 13-2.

Lump-sum receipt $30,000
Allocated to common (1,000 × $20)   20,000

Balance allocated to preferred $10,000

Illustration 13-2
Allocation in Lump-Sum
Securities Issuance—
Incremental Method

If a company cannot determine fair value for any of the classes of stock involved in a lump-sum exchange, it may need to use other approaches. It may rely on an expert's appraisal. Or, if the company knows that one or more of the classes of securities issued will have a determinable market value in the near future, it may use a best estimate basis with the intent to adjust later, upon establishment of the future market value.

Stock Issued in Noncash Transactions

Accounting for the issuance of shares of stock for property or services involves an issue of valuation. **The general rule is: Companies should record stock issued for services or property other than cash at either the fair value of the stock issued or the fair value of the noncash consideration received, whichever is more clearly determinable.**

If a company can readily determine both, and the transaction results from an arm's-length exchange, there will probably be little difference in their fair values. In such cases the basis for valuing the exchange should not matter.

If a company cannot readily determine either the fair value of the stock it issues or the property or services it receives, it should employ an appropriate valuation technique. Depending on available data, the valuation may be based on market transactions involving comparable assets or the use of discounted expected future cash flows. Companies should avoid the use of the book, par, or stated values as a basis of valuation for these transactions.

A company may exchange unissued stock or treasury stock (issued shares that it has reacquired but not retired) for property or services. If it uses treasury shares, the cost of the treasury shares should not be considered the decisive factor in establishing the fair value of the property or services. Instead, it should use the fair value of the treasury stock, if known, to value the property or services. Otherwise, if it does not know the fair value of the treasury stock, it should use the fair value of the property or services received, if determinable.

The following series of transactions illustrates the procedure for recording the issuance of 10,000 shares of $10 par value common stock for a patent for Marlowe Company, in various circumstances.

1 Marlowe cannot readily determine the fair value of the patent, but it knows the fair value of the stock is $140,000.

Patent	140,000	
Common Stock (10,000 shares × $10 per share)		100,000
Paid-in Capital in Excess of Par		40,000

2 Marlowe cannot readily determine the fair value of the stock, but it determines the fair value of the patent is $150,000.

Patent	150,000	
Common Stock (10,000 shares × $10 per share)		100,000
Paid-in Capital in Excess of Par		50,000

3 Marlowe cannot readily determine the fair value of the stock nor the fair value of the patent. An independent consultant values the patent at $125,000 based on discounted expected cash flows.

Patent	125,000	
Common Stock (10,000 shares × $10 share)		100,000
Paid-in Capital in Excess of Par		25,000

In corporate law, the board of directors has the power to set the value of noncash transactions. However, boards sometimes abuse this power. The issuance of stock for property or services has resulted in cases of overstated corporate capital through intentional overvaluation of the property or services received. The overvaluation of the stockholders' equity resulting from inflated asset values creates watered stock. The corporation should eliminate the "water" by simply writing down the overvalued assets.

What do the numbers mean? The Case of the Disappearing Receivable

Sometimes companies issue stock but may not receive cash in return. As a result, a company records a receivable. Controversy existed regarding the presentation of this receivable on the balance sheet. Some argued that the company should report the receivable as an asset similar to other receivables. Others argued that the company should report the receivable as a deduction from stockholders' equity (similar to the treatment of treasury stock). The SEC settled this issue: It requires companies to use the contra-equity approach because the risk of collection in this type of transaction is often very high.

This accounting issue surfaced in **Enron**'s accounting. Starting in early 2000, Enron issued shares of its common stock to four "special-purpose entities," in exchange for which it received a note receivable. Enron then increased its assets (by recording a receivable) and stockholders' equity, a move the company now calls an accounting error. As a result of this accounting treatment, Enron overstated assets and stockholders' equity by $172 million in its 2000 audited financial statements and by $828 million in its unaudited 2001 statements. This $1 billion overstatement was 8.5 percent of Enron's previously reported stockholders' equity at that time.

As Lynn Turner, former chief accountant of the SEC, noted, "It is a basic accounting principle that you don't record equity until you get cash, and a note doesn't count as cash." Situations like this led investors, creditors, and suppliers to lose faith in Enron's numbers, which led to its bankruptcy.

Source: Adapted from Jonathan Weil, "Basic Accounting Tripped Up Enron—Financial Statements Didn't Add Up—Auditors Overlook a Simple Rule," *Wall Street Journal* (November 11, 2001), p. C1.

Beyond the Numbers

As we have learned, companies record receivables and increases in equity (sales revenue) when they make sales on credit. (Recall our revenue recognition discussion in Chapter 7.) Describe the differences in the facts and circumstances for credit sales that support recognition of the receivable in the sales context but not for stock issued on credit.

If, as a result of the issuance of stock for property or services, a corporation undervalues the recorded assets, it creates secret reserves. An understated corporate structure (secret reserve) may also result from other methods: excessive depreciation or amortization charges, expensing capital expenditures, excessive write-downs of inventories or receivables, or any other understatement of assets or overstatement of liabilities. An example of a liability overstatement is an excessive provision for estimated product warranties that ultimately results in an understatement of owners' equity, thereby creating a secret reserve.

Costs of Issuing Stock

When a company like **Walgreens** issues stock, it should report direct costs incurred to sell stock, such as underwriting costs, accounting and legal fees, printing costs, and taxes, as a reduction of the amounts paid in. Walgreens therefore debits issue costs to Additional Paid-in Capital because they are unrelated to corporate operations. In effect, **issue costs are a cost of financing**. As such, issue costs should reduce the proceeds received from the sale of the stock.

Walgreens should expense management salaries and other indirect costs related to the stock issue because it is difficult to establish a relationship between these costs and the sale proceeds. In addition, Walgreens expenses recurring costs, primarily registrar and transfer agents' fees, as incurred.

Reacquisition of Shares

Companies often buy back their own shares. In fact, share buybacks now exceed dividends as a form of distribution to stockholders.[5] For example, **Dell, Yahoo!**, and **Home Depot** had buybacks recently of $10 billion, $3 billion, and $2 billion, respectively. Illustration 13-3 indicates that buybacks are increasing dramatically.

> **OBJECTIVE 4**
> **Describe the accounting for treasury stock.**

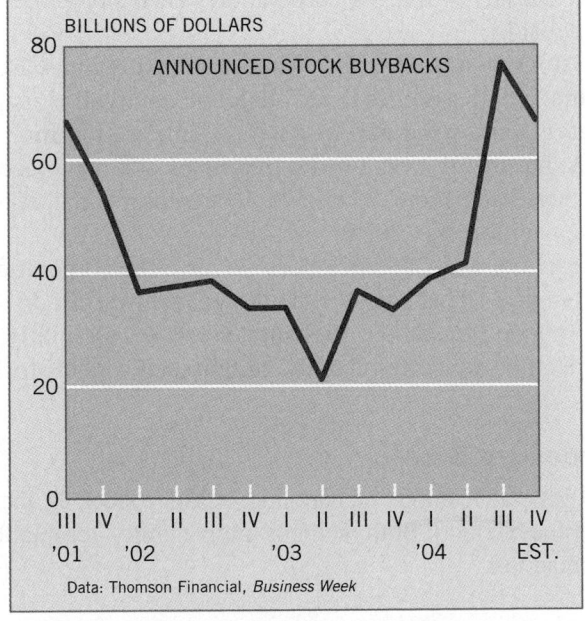

Illustration 13-3
Stock Buybacks on the Rise

Source: *Business Week* (November 29, 2004), p.116.

---

[5]At the beginning of the 1990s the situation was just the opposite. That is, share buybacks were less than half the level of dividends. Companies are extremely reluctant to reduce or eliminate their dividends, because they believe that the market negatively views this action.

Corporations purchase their outstanding stock for several reasons:

1 *To provide tax-efficient distributions of excess cash to shareholders.* Capital gain rates on sales of stock to the company by the stockholders have been approximately half the ordinary tax rate for many investors. This advantage has been somewhat diminished by recent changes in the tax law related to dividends.

2 *To increase earnings per share and return on equity.* Reducing both shares outstanding and stockholders' equity often enhances certain performance ratios. However, strategies to hype performance measures might increase performance in the short-run, but these tactics add no real long-term value.

3 *To provide stock for employee stock compensation contracts or to meet potential merger needs.* **Honeywell Inc.** reported that it would use part of its purchase of one million common shares for employee stock option contracts. Other companies acquire shares to have them available for business acquisitions.

4 *To thwart takeover attempts or to reduce the number of stockholders.* By reducing the number of shares held by the public, existing owners and managements bar "outsiders" from gaining control or significant influence. When Ted Turner attempted to acquire **CBS**, CBS started a substantial buyback of its stock. Companies may also use stock purchases to eliminate dissident stockholders.

5 *To make a market in the stock.* As one company executive noted, "Our company is trying to establish a floor for the stock." Purchasing stock in the marketplace creates a demand. This may stabilize the stock price or, in fact, increase it.

Some publicly held corporations have chosen to "go private," that is, to eliminate public (outside) ownership entirely by purchasing all of their outstanding stock. Companies often accomplish such a procedure through a **leveraged buyout (LBO)**, in which the company borrows money to finance the stock repurchases.

After reacquiring shares, a company may either retire them or hold them in the treasury for reissue. If not retired, such shares are referred to as **treasury stock** (**treasury shares**). Technically, treasury stock is a corporation's own stock, reacquired after having been issued and fully paid.

Treasury stock is not an asset. When a company purchases treasury stock, a reduction occurs in both assets and stockholders' equity. It is inappropriate to imply that a corporation can own a part of itself. A corporation may sell treasury stock to obtain funds, but that does not make treasury stock a balance sheet asset. When a corporation buys back some of its own outstanding stock, it has not acquired an asset; it reduces net assets.

The possession of treasury stock does not give the corporation the right to vote, to exercise preemptive rights as a stockholder, to receive cash dividends, or to receive assets upon corporate liquidation. **Treasury stock is essentially the same as unissued capital stock.** No one advocates classifying unissued capital stock as an asset in the balance sheet.[6]

WHAT'S THE PRINCIPLE?

As we indicated in Chapter 2, an asset should have probable future economic benefits. Treasury stock simply reduces common stock outstanding.

Discussion of Using Par or
Stated Value for Treasury
Stock Transactions

Purchase of Treasury Stock

Companies use two general methods of handling treasury stock in the accounts: the cost method and the par-value method. Both methods are generally acceptable. The cost method enjoys more widespread use.[7]

---

[6]The possible justification for classifying these shares as assets is that the company will use them to liquidate a specific liability that appears on the balance sheet. *Accounting Trends and Techniques—2006* reported that out of 600 companies surveyed, 388 disclosed treasury stock, but none classified it as an asset.

[7]*Accounting Trends and Techniques—2006* indicates that of its selected list of 600 companies, 373 carried common stock in treasury at cost and only 9 at par or stated value; 2 companies carried preferred stock in treasury at cost and none at par or stated value.

What do the numbers mean?

Market analysts sometimes look to stock buybacks as a buy signal for a stock. That strategy is not that surprising if you look at the performance of companies that did buybacks. For example, in one study, buyback companies outperformed similar companies without buybacks by an average of 23 percent. In a recent three-year period, companies followed by **Buybackletter.com** were up 16.4 percent, while the S&P 500 Stock Index was up just 7.1 percent in that period. Why the premium? Well, the conventional wisdom is that companies who buy back shares believe their shares are undervalued. Thus, analysts view the buyback announcement as an important piece of inside information about future company prospects.

On the other hand, buybacks can actually hurt businesses and their shareholders over the long-run. Whether the buyback is a good thing appears to depend a lot on why the company did the buyback and what the repurchased shares were used for. One study found that companies often increased their buybacks when earnings growth slowed. This allowed the companies to prop up earnings per share (based on fewer shares outstanding). Furthermore, many buybacks do not actually result in a net reduction in shares outstanding. For example, companies, such as **Microsoft,** bought back shares to meet share demands for stock option exercises, resulting in higher net shares outstanding when it re-issued the repurchased shares to the option holders upon exercise. In this case the buyback actually indicated a further dilution in the share ownership in the buyback company.

This does not mean you should never trust a buyback signal. But if the buyback is intended to manage the company's earnings or if the buyback results in dilution, take a closer look.

Source: Adapted from Ann Tergesen, "When Buybacks Are Signals to Buy," *Business Week Online* (October 1, 2001); and Rachel Beck, "Stock BuyBacks Not Always Good for the Company, Shareholders," *Naples [FL] Daily News* (March 7, 2004). p. I1.

Beyond the Numbers

Assume you are an investor in a company that has offered to buy back your shares. What factors would you consider is deciding whether to tender (sell) your shares?

- The **cost method** results in debiting the Treasury Stock account for the reacquisition cost and in reporting this account as a deduction from the total paid-in capital **and** retained earnings on the balance sheet.

- The **par-** or **stated-value method** records all transactions in treasury shares at their par value and reports the treasury stock as a deduction from capital stock only.

No matter which method a company uses, most states consider the cost of the treasury shares acquired as a restriction on retained earnings.

Companies generally use the cost method to account for treasury stock. This method derives its name from the fact that a company maintains the Treasury Stock account at the cost of the shares purchased.[8] Under the cost method, the company debits the Treasury Stock account for the cost of the shares acquired. Upon reissuance of the shares, it credits the account for this same cost. The original price received for the stock does not affect the entries to record the acquisition and reissuance of the treasury stock.

To illustrate, assume that Pacific Company issued 100,000 shares of $1 par value common stock at a price of $10 per share. In addition, it has retained earnings of $300,000. Illustration 13-4 (page 682) shows the stockholders' equity section on December 31, 2008, before purchase of treasury stock.

---

[8]If making numerous acquisitions of blocks of treasury shares at different prices, a company may use inventory costing methods—such as specific identification, average, or FIFO—to identify the cost at date of reissuance.

Illustration 13-4
Stockholders' Equity with
No Treasury Stock

Stockholders' equity	
Paid-in capital	
Common stock, $1 par value, 100,000 shares issued and outstanding	$ 100,000
Additional paid-in capital	900,000
Total paid-in capital	1,000,000
Retained earnings	300,000
Total stockholders' equity	$1,300,000

On January 20, 2009, Pacific acquires 10,000 shares of its stock at $11 per share. Pacific records the reacquisition as follows:

January 20, 2009

Treasury Stock	110,000	
Cash		110,000

Note that Pacific debited Treasury Stock for the cost of the shares purchased. The original paid-in capital account, Common Stock, is not affected because the number of issued shares does not change. The same is true for the Additional Paid-in Capital account. Pacific deducts treasury stock from total paid-in capital and retained earnings in the stockholders' equity section.

Illustration 13-5 shows the stockholders' equity section for Pacific after purchase of the treasury stock.

Illustration 13-5
Stockholders' Equity with
Treasury Stock

Stockholders' equity	
Paid-in capital	
Common stock, $1 par value, 100,000 shares issued and 90,000 outstanding	$ 100,000
Additional paid-in capital	900,000
Total paid-in capital	1,000,000
Retained earnings	300,000
Total paid-in capital and retained earnings	1,300,000
Less: Cost of treasury stock (10,000 shares)	110,000
Total stockholders' equity	$1,190,000

Pacific subtracts the cost of the treasury stock from the total of common stock, additional paid-in capital, and retained earnings. It therefore reduces stockholders' equity. Many states require a corporation to restrict retained earnings for the cost of treasury stock purchased. The restriction keeps intact the corporation's legal capital that it temporarily holds as treasury stock. When the corporation sells the treasury stock, it lifts the restriction.

Pacific discloses both the number of shares issued (100,000) and the number in the treasury (10,000). The difference is the number of shares of stock outstanding (90,000). The term **outstanding stock** means the number of shares of issued stock that stockholders own.

Sale of Treasury Stock

Companies usually reissue or retire treasury stock. When selling treasury shares, the accounting for the sale depends on the price. If the selling price of the treasury stock equals its cost, the company records the sale of the shares by debiting Cash and crediting Treasury Stock. In cases where the selling price of the treasury stock is not equal to cost, then accounting for treasury stock sold **above cost** differs from the accounting for treasury stock sold **below cost**. However, the sale of treasury stock either above or below cost increases both total assets and stockholders' equity.

Sale of Treasury Stock above Cost. When the selling price of shares of treasury stock exceeds its cost, a company credits the difference to Paid-in Capital from Treasury Stock. To illustrate, assume that Pacific acquired 10,000 shares of its treasury stock at $11 per share. It now sells 1,000 shares at $15 per share on March 10. Pacific records the entry as follows.

March 10, 2008

Cash	15,000	
Treasury Stock		11,000
Paid-in Capital from Treasury Stock		4,000

There are two reasons why Pacific does not credit $4,000 to Gain on Sale of Treasury Stock: (1) Gains on sales occur when selling assets; treasury stock is not an asset. (2) A gain or loss should not be recognized from stock transactions with its own stockholders. Thus, Pacific should not include paid-in capital arising from the sale of treasury stock in the measurement of net income. Instead, it lists paid-in capital from treasury stock separately on the balance sheet, as a part of paid-in capital.

Sale of Treasury Stock below Cost. When a corporation sells treasury stock below its cost, it usually debits the excess of the cost over selling price to Paid-in Capital from Treasury Stock. Thus, if Pacific sells an additional 1,000 shares of treasury stock on March 21 at $8 per share, it records the sale as follows.

March 21, 2008

Cash	8,000	
Paid-in Capital from Treasury Stock	3,000	
Treasury Stock		11,000

We can make several observations based on the two sale entries (sale above cost and sale below cost): (1) Pacific credits Treasury Stock at cost in each entry. (2) Pacific uses Paid-in Capital from Treasury Stock for the difference between the cost and the resale price of the shares. (3) Neither entry affects the original paid-in capital account, Common Stock.

After eliminating the credit balance in Paid-in Capital from Treasury Stock, the corporation debits any additional excess of cost over selling price to Retained Earnings. To illustrate, assume that Pacific sells an additional 1,000 shares at $8 per share on April 10. Illustration 13-6 shows the balance in the Paid-in Capital from Treasury Stock account (before the April 10 purchase).

Paid-in Capital from Treasury Stock

Mar. 21	3,000	Mar. 10	4,000
		Balance	1,000

Illustration 13-6
Treasury Stock Transactions in Paid-in Capital Account

In this case, Pacific debits $1,000 of the excess to Paid-in Capital from Treasury Stock. It debits the remainder to Retained Earnings. The entry is:

April 10, 2008

Cash	8,000	
Paid-in Capital from Treasury Stock	1,000	
Retained Earnings	2,000	
Treasury Stock		11,000

Retiring Treasury Stock

The board of directors may approve the retirement of treasury shares. This decision results in cancellation of the treasury stock and a reduction in the number of shares of issued stock. Retired treasury shares have the status of authorized and unissued shares. The accounting effects are similar to the sale of treasury stock except that corporations debit the **paid-in capital accounts applicable to the retired shares** instead of cash. For example, if a corporation originally sells the shares at par, it debits Common Stock for the par value per share. If it originally sells the shares at $3 above par value, it also debits Paid-in Capital in Excess of Par Value for $3 per share at retirement.

Try it out! On May 1, 2008, Penton Corporation reacquired 200 shares of its $5 par value common stock at $40 per share. On July 1, Penton reissued 125 shares at $42 per share. On October 1, Penton reissued 75 shares at $36 per share.

Instructions

Prepare Penton's journal entries to record these transactions using the cost method.

Solution

May 1, 2008

Treasury Stock	8,000	
Cash (200 × $40)		8,000

July 1, 2008

Cash (125 × $42)	5,250	
Treasury Stock (125 × $40)		5,000
Paid-in Capital from Treasury Stock		250

October 1, 2008

Cash (75 × $36)	2,700	
Paid-in Capital from Treasury Stock	250	
Retained Earnings	50	
Treasury Stock (75 × $40)		3,000

PREFERRED STOCK

OBJECTIVE 5

Explain the accounting for and reporting of preferred stock.

As noted earlier, **preferred stock** is a special class of shares that possesses certain preferences or features not possessed by the common stock.[9] The following features are those most often associated with preferred stock issues.

1 Preference as to dividends.

2 Preference as to assets in the event of liquidation.

3 Convertible into common stock.

4 Callable at the option of the corporation.

5 Nonvoting.

The features that distinguish preferred from common stock may be of a more restrictive and negative nature than preferences. For example, the preferred stock may be nonvoting, noncumulative, and nonparticipating.

[9]"*Accounting Trends and Techniques—2006* reports that of its 600 surveyed companies, 52 had preferred stock outstanding; 42 had one class of preferred, and 10 had two or more classes.

Companies usually issue preferred stock with a par value, expressing the dividend preference as a **percentage of the par value**. Thus, holders of 8 percent preferred stock with a $100 par value are entitled to an annual dividend of $8 per share. This stock is commonly referred to as 8 percent preferred stock. In the case of no-par preferred stock, a corporation expresses a dividend preference as a **specific dollar amount** per share, for example, $7 per share. This stock is commonly referred to as $7 preferred stock.

A preference as to dividends does not assure the payment of dividends. It merely assures that the corporation must pay the stated dividend rate or amount applicable to the preferred stock before paying any dividends on the common stock.

A company often issues preferred stock (instead of debt) because of a high debt-to-equity ratio. In other instances, it issues preferred stock through private placements with other corporations at a lower-than-market dividend rate because the acquiring corporation receives largely tax-free dividends (due to the IRS's 70 percent or 80 percent dividends received deduction).

Features of Preferred Stock

A corporation may attach whatever preferences or restrictions, in whatever combination it desires, to a preferred stock issue, as long as it does not specifically violate its state incorporation law. Also, it may issue more than one class of preferred stock. We discuss the most common features attributed to preferred stock below.

Cumulative Preferred Stock

Cumulative preferred stock requires that if a corporation fails to pay a dividend in any year, it must make it up in a later year before paying any dividends to common stockholders. If the directors fail to declare a dividend at the normal date for dividend action, the dividend is said to have been "passed." Any passed dividend on cumulative preferred stock constitutes a **dividend in arrears**. Because no liability exists until the board of directors declares a dividend, a corporation does not record a dividend in arrears as a liability but discloses it in a note to the financial statements. A corporation seldom issues noncumulative preferred stock because a passed dividend is lost forever to the preferred stockholder. As a result, this stock issue would be less marketable.

Participating Preferred Stock

Holders of **participating preferred stock** share ratably with the common stockholders in any profit distributions beyond the prescribed rate. That is, 5 percent preferred stock, if fully participating, will receive not only its 5 percent return, but also dividends at the same rates as those paid to common stockholders if paying amounts in excess of 5 percent of par or stated value to common stockholders. Note that participating preferred stock may be only partially participating. Although seldom used, examples of companies that have issued participating preferreds are **LTV Corporation, Southern California Edison,** and **Allied Products Corporation**.

Convertible Preferred Stock

Convertible preferred stock allows stockholders, at their option, to exchange preferred shares for common stock at a predetermined ratio. The convertible preferred stockholder not only enjoys a preferred claim on dividends but also has the option of converting into a common stockholder with unlimited participation in earnings.

Callable Preferred Stock

Callable preferred stock permits the corporation at its option to call or redeem the outstanding preferred shares at specified future dates and at stipulated prices. Many preferred issues are callable. The corporation usually sets the call or redemption price slightly above the original issuance price and commonly states it in terms related to the par value. The callable feature permits the corporation to use the capital obtained through the issuance of such stock until the need has passed or it is no longer advantageous.

The existence of a call price or prices tends to set a ceiling on the market value of the preferred shares unless they are convertible into common stock. When a corporation redeems preferred stock, it must pay any dividends in arrears.

Redeemable Preferred Stock

Recently, more and more issuances of preferred stock have features that make the security more like debt (legal obligation to pay) than an equity instrument. For example, **redeemable preferred stock** has a mandatory redemption period or a redemption feature that the issuer cannot control.

Previously, public companies were not permitted to report these debt-like preferreds in equity, but they were not required to report them as a liability either. There were concerns about classification of these debt-like securities, which may have been reported as equity or in the "mezzanine" section of balance sheets between debt and equity. There also was diversity in practice as to how dividends on these securities were reported. The FASB recently issued a standard that affects the accounting for certain hybrid instruments and requires debt-like securities, like redeemable preferred stock to be classified as liabilities and be measured and accounted for similar to liabilities.[10]

Accounting for and Reporting Preferred Stock

The accounting for preferred stock at issuance is similar to that for common stock. A corporation allocates proceeds between the par value of the preferred stock and additional paid-in capital. To illustrate, assume that Bishop Co. issues 10,000 shares of $10 par value preferred stock for $12 cash per share. Bishop records the issuance as follows:

Cash	120,000	
Preferred Stock		100,000
Paid-in Capital in Excess of Par		20,000

Thus, Bishop maintains separate accounts for these different classes of shares.

In contrast to convertible bonds (recorded as a liability on the date of issue) corporations consider convertible preferred stock as a part of stockholders' equity. In addition, when exercising convertible preferred stocks, there is no theoretical justification for recognition of a gain or loss. A company recognizes no gain or loss when dealing with stockholders in their capacity as business owners. Instead, the company **employs the book value method**: debit Preferred Stock, along with any related Additional Paid-in Capital; credit Common Stock and Additional Paid-in Capital (if an excess exists).

Preferred stock generally has no maturity date. Therefore, no legal obligation exists to pay the preferred stockholder. As a result, companies classify preferred stock as part of stockholders' equity. Companies generally report preferred stock at par value as the first item in the stockholders' equity section. They report any excess over par value as part of additional paid-in capital. They also consider dividends on preferred stock as a distribution of income and not an expense. Companies must disclose the pertinent rights of the preferred stock outstanding.[11]

---

[10]"Accounting for Certain Financial Instruments with Characteristics of Both Liabilities and Equity," *Statement of Financial Accounting Standards No. 150* (Norwalk Conn.: FASB, 2003). *SFAS No. 150* represents completion of the first phase in a broader project on liabilities and equity. In phase two, the FASB will deal with the accounting for compound financial instruments (e.g., convertible debt, covered in Appendix 13A) that have characteristics of liabilities and equity, the definition of an ownership relationship, and the definition of liabilities (an amendment to *FASB Concepts Statement No. 6*, "Elements of Financial Statements.")

[11]"Disclosure of Information about Capital Structure," *Statement of Financial Accounting Standards No. 129* (Norwalk, Conn.: FASB, 1997).

DIVIDEND POLICY

OBJECTIVE 6
**Describe the policies
used in distributing
dividends.**

As indicated in the opening story, dividend payouts can be important signals to the market. The practice of paying dividends declined sharply in the 1980s and 1990s as companies focused on growth and plowed profits back into the business. A resurgence in dividend payouts is due in large part to the dividend tax cut of 2003, which reduced the rate of tax on dividends to 15 percent (quite a bit lower than the ordinary income rate charged in the past). In addition, investors who were burned by accounting scandals in recent years began demanding higher payouts in the form of dividends. Why? A dividend check provides proof that at least some portion of a company's profits is genuine.[12]

Determining the proper amount of dividends to pay is a difficult financial management decision. Companies that are paying dividends are extremely reluctant to reduce or eliminate their dividend. They fear that the securities market might negatively view this action. As a consequence, companies that have been paying cash dividends will make every effort to continue to do so. In addition, the type of shareholder the company has (taxable or nontaxable, retail investor or institutional investor) plays a large role in determining dividend policy.

Very few companies pay dividends in amounts equal to their legally available retained earnings. The major reasons are as follows.

1 To maintain agreements (bond covenants) with specific creditors, to retain all or a portion of the earnings, in the form of assets, to build up additional protection against possible loss.

2 To meet state corporation requirements, that earnings equivalent to the cost of treasury shares purchased be restricted against dividend declarations.

3 To retain assets that would otherwise be paid out as dividends, to finance growth or expansion. This is sometimes called internal financing, reinvesting earnings, or "plowing" the profits back into the business.

4 To smooth out dividend payments from year to year by accumulating earnings in good years and using such accumulated earnings as a basis for dividends in bad years.

5 To build up a cushion or buffer against possible losses or errors in the calculation of profits.

The reasons above are self-explanatory except for the second. The laws of some states require that the corporation restrict its legal capital from distribution to stockholders, to protect against loss for creditors.[13] The applicable state law determines the legality of a dividend.

Financial Condition and Dividend Distributions

Effective management of a company requires attention to more than the legality of dividend distributions. Management must also consider economic conditions, most importantly, liquidity. Assume an extreme situation as shown in Illustration 13-7.

Fielder Company			
Balance Sheet			
Plant assets	$500,000	Capital stock	$400,000
	$500,000	Retained earnings	100,000
			$500,000

Illustration 13-7
Balance Sheet, Showing a
Lack of Liquidity

[12]Jeff Opdyke, "Tax Cut, Shareholder Pressure Stoke Surge in Dividends," *Wall Street Journal Online* (January 18, 2005).

[13]If the corporation buys its own outstanding stock, it reduces its legal capital and distributes assets to stockholders. If permitted, the corporation could, by purchasing treasury stock at any price desired, return to the stockholders their investments and leave creditors with little or no protection against loss.

Fielder Company has a retained earnings credit balance. Unless retained earnings are restricted, the company can declare a dividend of $100,000. But because all its assets are plant assets used in operations, payment of a cash dividend of $100,000 would require the sale of plant assets or borrowing.

Even if a balance sheet shows current assets, as in Illustration 13-8, the question remains as to whether Sheets Company needs those cash assets for other purposes.

Illustration 13-8
Balance Sheet, Showing
Cash but Minimal Working
Capital

Sheets Company Balance Sheet				
Cash	$100,000	Current liabilities		$ 60,000
Plant assets	460,000	Capital stock	$400,000	
	$560,000	Retained earnings	100,000	500,000
				$560,000

The existence of current liabilities strongly implies that the company needs some of the cash to meet current debts as they mature. In addition, day-by-day cash requirements for payrolls and other expenditures not included in current liabilities also require cash.

Thus, before declaring a dividend, management must consider **availability of funds to pay the dividend**. A company should not pay a dividend unless both the present and future financial position warrant the distribution.

The SEC encourages companies to disclose their dividend policy in their annual report, especially those that (1) have earnings but fail to pay dividends, or (2) do not expect to pay dividends in the foreseeable future. In addition, the SEC encourages companies that consistently pay dividends to indicate whether they intend to continue this practice in the future.

Types of Dividends

OBJECTIVE 7

Identify the various
forms of dividend
distributions.

Companies generally base dividend distributions either on accumulated profits (that is, retained earnings) or on some other capital item such as additional paid-in capital. Dividends are of the following types.

1 Cash dividends.
2 Property dividends.
3 Liquidating dividends.
4 Stock dividends.

Although commonly paid in cash, companies occasionally pay dividends in stock or some other asset.[14] **All dividends, except for stock dividends, reduce the total stockholders' equity in the corporation.** When declaring a stock dividend, the corporation does not pay out assets or incur a liability. It issues additional shares of stock to each stockholder and nothing more.

The natural expectation of any stockholder who receives a dividend is that the corporation has operated successfully. As a result, he or she is receiving a share of its profits. A company should disclose a **liquidating dividend**—that is, a dividend not based on retained earnings—to the stockholders so that they will not misunderstand its source.

---

[14]*Accounting Trends and Techniques—2006* reported that of its 600 surveyed companies, 389 paid a cash dividend on common stock, 46 paid a cash dividend on preferred stock, 2 issued stock dividends, and 3 issued or paid dividends in kind. Some companies declare more than one type of dividend in a given year.

Cash Dividends

The board of directors votes on the declaration of **cash dividends**. Upon approval of the resolution, the board declares a dividend. Before paying it, however, the company must prepare a current list of stockholders. For this reason there is usually a time lag between declaration and payment. For example, the board of directors might approve a resolution at the January 10 (**date of declaration**) meeting, and declare it payable February 5 (**date of payment**) to all stockholders of record January 25 (**date of record**).[15] In this example, the period from January 10 to January 25 gives time for the company to complete and register any transfers in process. The time from January 25 to February 5 provides an opportunity for the transfer agent or accounting department, depending on who does this work, to prepare a list of stockholders as of January 25 and to prepare and mail dividend checks.

A declared cash dividend is a liability. Because payment is generally required very soon, it is usually a current liability. Companies use the following entries to record the declaration and payment of an ordinary dividend payable in cash. For example, Roadway Freight Corp. on June 10 declared a cash dividend of 50 cents a share on 1.8 million shares payable July 16 to all stockholders of record June 24.

At date of declaration (June 10)

Retained Earnings (Cash Dividends Declared)	900,000	
Dividends Payable		900,000

At date of record (June 24)

No entry

At date of payment (July 16)

Dividends Payable	900,000	
Cash		900,000

To set up a ledger account that shows the amount of dividends declared during the year, Roadway Freight might debit Cash Dividends Declared instead of Retained Earnings at the time of declaration. It then closes this account to Retained Earnings at year-end.

A company may declare dividends either as a certain percent of par, such as a 6 percent dividend on preferred stock, or as an amount per share, such as 60 cents per share on no-par common stock. In the first case, the rate multiplied by the par value of outstanding shares equals the total dividend. In the second, the dividend equals the amount per share multiplied by the number of shares outstanding. **Companies do not declare or pay cash dividends on treasury stock.**

Dividend policies vary among corporations. Some companies, such as **Bank of America**, **Clorox Co.**, and **Tootsie Roll Industries**, take pride in a long, unbroken string of quarterly dividend payments. They would lower or pass the dividend only if forced to do so by a sustained decline in earnings or a critical shortage of cash.

"Growth" companies, on the other hand, pay little or no cash dividends because their policy is to expand as rapidly as internal and external financing permit. For example, **Questcor Pharmaceuticals Inc.** has never paid cash dividends to its common stockholders. These investors hope that the price of their shares will appreciate in value. The investors will then realize a profit when they sell their shares. Many companies focus more on increasing share price, stock repurchase programs, and corporate earnings than on dividend payout.

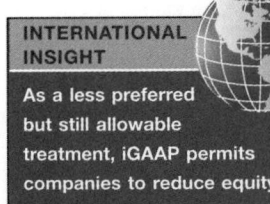

INTERNATIONAL INSIGHT

As a less preferred but still allowable treatment, iGAAP permits companies to reduce equity by the amount of proposed dividends prior to their legal declaration.

---

[15]Theoretically, the ex-dividend date is the day after the date of record. However, to allow time for transfer of the shares, the stock exchanges generally advance the ex-dividend date two to four days. Therefore, the party who owns the stock on the day prior to the expressed ex-dividend date receives the dividends. The party who buys the stock on and after the ex-dividend date does not receive the dividend. Between the declaration date and the ex-dividend date, the market price of the stock includes the dividend.

Property Dividends

Dividends payable in assets of the corporation other than cash are called **property dividends** or **dividends in kind**. Property dividends may be merchandise, real estate, or investments, or whatever form the board of directors designates. **Ranchers Exploration and Development Corp.** reported one year that it would pay a fourth-quarter dividend in gold bars instead of cash. Because of the obvious difficulties of divisibility of units and delivery to stockholders, the usual property dividend is in the form of securities of other companies that the distributing corporation holds as an investment.

For example, after ruling that **DuPont**'s 23 percent stock interest in **General Motors** violated antitrust laws, the Supreme Court ordered DuPont to divest itself of the GM stock within 10 years. The stock represented 63 million shares of GM's 281 million shares then outstanding. DuPont could not sell the shares in one block of 63 million. Further, it could not sell 6 million shares annually for the next 10 years without severely depressing the value of the GM stock. DuPont solved its problem by declaring a property dividend and distributing the GM shares as a dividend to its own stockholders.

When declaring a property dividend, the corporation should **restate at fair value the property it will distribute**, **recognizing any gain or loss** as the difference between the property's fair value and carrying value at date of declaration. The corporation may then record the declared dividend as a debit to Retained Earnings (or Property Dividends Declared) and a credit to Property Dividends Payable, at an amount equal to the fair value of the distributed property. Upon distribution of the dividend, the corporation debits Property Dividends Payable and credits the account containing the distributed asset (restated at fair value).

For example, Trendler, Inc. transferred to stockholders some of its investments in marketable securities costing $1,250,000 by declaring a property dividend on December 28, 2007, to be distributed on January 30, 2008, to stockholders of record on January 15, 2008. At the date of declaration the securities have a market value of $2,000,000. Trendler makes the following entries.

At date of declaration (December 28, 2007)

Investments in Securities	750,000	
Gain on Appreciation of Securities		750,000
Retained Earnings (Property Dividends Declared)	2,000,000	
Property Dividends Payable		2,000,000

At date of distribution (January 30, 2008)

Property Dividends Payable	2,000,000	
Investments in Securities		2,000,000

Liquidating Dividends

Some corporations use paid-in capital as a basis for dividends. Without proper disclosure of this fact, stockholders may erroneously believe the corporation has been operating at a profit. To avoid this type of deception, intentional or unintentional, a clear statement of the source of every dividend should accompany the dividend check.

Dividends based on other than retained earnings are sometimes described as **liquidating dividends**. This term implies that such dividends are a return of the stockholder's investment rather than of profits. In other words, **any dividend not based on earnings reduces corporate paid-in capital and to that extent, it is a liquidating dividend**. Companies in the extractive industries may pay dividends equal to the total of accumulated income and depletion. The portion of these dividends in excess of accumulated income represents a return of part of the stockholder's investment.

For example, McChesney Mines Inc. issued a "dividend" to its common stockholders of $1,200,000. The cash dividend announcement noted that stockholders should consider $900,000 as income and the remainder a return of capital. McChesney Mines records the dividend as follows:

At date of declaration

Retained Earnings	900,000	
Additional Paid-in Capital	300,000	
Dividends Payable		1,200,000

At date of payment

Dividends Payable	1,200,000	
Cash		1,200,000

In some cases, management simply decides to cease business and declares a liquidating dividend. In these cases, liquidation may take place over a number of years to ensure an orderly and fair sale of assets. For example, when **Overseas National Airways** dissolved, it agreed to pay a liquidating dividend to its stockholders over a period of years equivalent to $8.60 per share. Each liquidating dividend payment in such cases reduces paid-in capital.

Stock Dividends

If management wishes to "capitalize" part of the earnings (i.e., reclassify amounts from earned to contributed capital), and thus retain earnings in the business on a permanent basis, it may issue a stock dividend. In this case, **the company distributes no assets**. Each stockholder maintains exactly the same proportionate interest in the corporation and the same total book value after the company issues the stock dividend. Of course, the book value per share is lower because each stockholder holds more shares.

A **stock dividend** therefore is the issuance by a corporation of its own stock to its stockholders on a pro rata basis, without receiving any consideration. In recording a stock dividend, some believe that the company should transfer the **par value of the stock issued** as a dividend from retained earnings to capital stock. Others believe that it should transfer the **fair value of the stock issued**—its market value at the declaration date—from retained earnings to capital stock and additional paid-in capital.

The fair value position was adopted, at least in part, in order to influence the stock dividend policies of corporations. Evidently in 1941 both the New York Stock Exchange and many in the accounting profession regarded periodic stock dividends as objectionable. They believed that the term dividend when used with a distribution of additional stock was misleading because investors' net assets did not increase as a result of this "dividend." As a result, these groups decided to make it more difficult for corporations to sustain a series of such stock dividends out of their accumulated earnings, by requiring the use of fair market value when it substantially exceeded book value.[16]

When the stock dividend is less than 20–25 percent of the common shares outstanding at the time of the dividend declaration, the company is therefore required to transfer the **fair market value** of the stock issued from retained earnings. Stock dividends of less than 20–25 percent are often referred to as **small (ordinary) stock dividends**. This method of handling stock dividends is justified on the grounds that "many recipients of stock dividends look upon them as distributions of corporate earnings and usually in an amount equivalent to the fair value of the additional shares received."[17] We consider this argument unconvincing. It is generally agreed that stock dividends are not income to the recipients.

WHAT'S THE PRINCIPLE?

By requiring fair value, the intent was to punish companies that used stock dividends. This approach violates the neutrality concept (that is, that standards-setting should be even-handed).

OBJECTIVE 8

Explain the accounting for small and large stock dividends, and for stock splits.

---

[16]This was perhaps the earliest instance of "economic consequences" affecting an accounting pronouncement. The Committee on Accounting Procedure described its action as required by "proper accounting and corporate policy." See Stephen A. Zeff, "The Rise of 'Economic Consequences,'" *The Journal of Accountancy* (December 1978), pp. 53–66.

[17]American Institute of Certified Public Accountants, *Accounting Research and Terminology Bulletins,* No. 43 (New York: AICPA, 1961), Ch. 7, par. 10. One study concluded that *small* stock dividends do not always produce significant amounts of extra value on the date after issuance (ex date) and that *large* stock dividends almost always fail to generate extra value on the ex-dividend date. Taylor W. Foster III and Don Vickrey, "The Information Content of Stock Dividend Announcements," *The Accounting Review,* Vol. LIII, No. 2 (April 1978), pp. 360–370.

Therefore, sound accounting should not recommend procedures simply because some recipients think they are income.

To illustrate a small stock dividend, assume that Vine Corporation has outstanding 1,000 shares of $100 par value capital stock and retained earnings of $50,000. If Vine declares a 10 percent stock dividend, it issues 100 additional shares to current stockholders. If the fair value of the stock at the time of the stock dividend is $130 per share, the entry is:

At date of declaration

Retained Earnings (Stock Dividend Declared)	13,000	
Common Stock Dividend Distributable		10,000
Paid-in Capital in Excess of Par		3,000

Note that the stock dividend does not affect any asset or liability. The entry merely reflects a reclassification of stockholders' equity. If Vine prepares a balance sheet between the dates of declaration and distribution, it should show the common stock dividend distributable in the stockholders' equity section as an addition to capital stock (whereas it shows cash or property dividends payable as current liabilities).

When issuing the stock, the entry is:

At date of distribution

Common Stock Dividend Distributable	10,000	
Common Stock		10,000

No matter what the fair value is at the time of the stock dividend, each stockholder retains the same proportionate interest in the corporation.

Some state statutes specifically prohibit the issuance of stock dividends on treasury stock. In those states that permit treasury shares to participate in the distribution accompanying a stock dividend or stock split, the planned use of the treasury shares influences corporate practice. For example, if a corporation issues treasury shares in connection with employee stock options, the treasury shares may participate in the distribution because the corporation usually adjusts the number of shares under option for any stock dividends or splits. But no useful purpose is served by issuing additional shares to the treasury stock without a specific purpose, since they are essentially equivalent to authorized but unissued shares.

To continue with our example of the effect of the small stock dividend, note in Illustration 13-9 that the stock dividend does not change the total stockholders' equity. Also note that it does not change the proportion of the total shares outstanding held by each stockholder.

Illustration 13-9
Effects of a Small (10%)
Stock Dividend

Before dividend	
Capital stock, 1,000 shares of $100 par	$100,000
Retained earnings	50,000
Total stockholders' equity	$150,000
Stockholders' interests:	
A. 400 shares, 40% interest, book value	$ 60,000
B. 500 shares, 50% interest, book value	75,000
C. 100 shares, 10% interest, book value	15,000
	$150,000
After declaration but before distribution of 10% stock dividend	
If fair value ($130) is used as basis for entry:	
Capital stock, 1,000 shares at $100 par	$100,000
Common stock distributable, 100 shares at $100 par	10,000
Paid-in capital in excess of par	3,000
Retained earnings ($50,000 − $13,000)	37,000
Total stockholders' equity	$150,000

Illustration 13-9
(continued)

After declaration and distribution of 10% stock dividend

If fair value ($130) is used as basis for entry:

Capital stock, 1,100 shares at $100 par	$110,000
Paid-in capital in excess of par	3,000
Retained earnings ($50,000 − $13,000)	37,000
Total stockholders' equity	$150,000

Stockholders' interest:

A. 440 shares, 40% interest, book value	$ 60,000
B. 550 shares, 50% interest, book value	75,000
C. 110 shares, 10% interest, book value	15,000
	$150,000

Stock Split

If a company has undistributed earnings over several years, and accumulates a sizable balance in retained earnings, the market value of its outstanding shares likely increases. Stock issued at prices less than $50 a share can easily attain a market value in excess of $200 a share. The higher the market price of a stock, however, the less readily some investors can purchase it.

The managements of many corporations believe that better public relations depend on wider ownership of the corporation stock. They therefore target a market price sufficiently low to be within range of the majority of potential investors. To reduce the market value of shares, they use the common device of a **stock split**. For example, after its stock price increased by 25-fold, **Qualcomm Inc.** split its stock 4-for-1. Qualcomm's stock had risen above $500 per share, raising concerns that Qualcomm could not meet an analyst target of $1,000 per share. The split reduced the analysts' target to $250, which it could better meet with wider distribution of shares at lower trading prices.

From an accounting standpoint, Qualcomm **records no entry for a stock split**. However, it enters a memorandum note to indicate the changed par value of the shares and the increased number of shares. Illustration 13-10 shows the lack of change in stockholders' equity for a 2-for-1 stock split on 1,000 shares of $100 par value stock with the par being halved upon issuance of the additional shares.

Illustration 13-10
Effects of a Stock Split

Stockholders' Equity before 2-for-1 Split		Stockholders' Equity after 2-for-1 Split	
Common stock, 1,000 shares		Common stock, 2,000 shares	
at $100 par	$100,000	at $50 par	$100,000
Retained earnings	50,000	Retained earnings	50,000
	$150,000		$150,000

What do the numbers mean?   Splitsville

Stock splits were all the rage in the booming stock market of the 1990s. Of major companies on the **New York Stock Exchange**, fewer than 80 companies split shares in 1990. By 1998, with stock prices soaring, over 200 companies split shares. Although the split does not increase a stockholder's proportionate ownership of the company, studies show that split shares usually outperform those that don't split, as well as the market as a whole, for several years after the split. In addition, the splits help the company keep the shares in more attractive price ranges.

(*continued*)

Splitsville, continued

What about when the market "turns south"? A number of companies who split their shares in the boom markets of the 1990s have since seen their share prices decline to a point considered too low. For example, since **Ameritrade**'s 12-for-1 split in 1999, its stock price declined over 74 percent, so that it was trading around $6 per share in March 2002. And **Lucent** traded at less than $5 a share following a 4-for-1 split. For some investors, these low-priced stocks are unattractive because some brokerage commissions rely on the number of shares traded, not the dollar amount. Others are concerned that low-priced shares are easier for would-be scamsters to manipulate.

Some companies execute reverse stock splits in which, say, five shares are consolidated into one. Thus, a stock previously trading at $5 per share would be part of an unsplit share trading at $25. Unsplitting might thus avoid some of the negative consequences of a low trading price. The downside to this strategy is that analysts might view reverse splits as additional bad news about the direction of the stock price. For example, **Webvan**, a failed Internet grocer, did a 1-for-25 reverse split just before it entered bankruptcy.

Source: Adapted from David Henry, "Stocks: The Case for Unsplitting," *BusinessWeek Online* (April 1, 2002).

Beyond the Numbers

Many people play the stock market through investments in mutual funds. Do you think these investors are influenced by the trading ranges of individual stocks? Explain.

Stock Split and Stock Dividend Differentiated

From a legal standpoint, a stock split differs from a stock dividend. How? A stock split increases the number of shares outstanding and decreases the par or stated value per share. **A stock dividend, although it increases the number of shares outstanding, does not decrease the par value; thus it increases the total par value of outstanding shares.**

The reasons for issuing a stock dividend are numerous and varied. Stock dividends can be primarily a publicity gesture, **because many consider stock dividends as dividends**. Another reason is that the corporation may simply wish to retain profits in the business by capitalizing a part of retained earnings. In such a situation, it makes a transfer on declaration of a stock dividend from earned capital to contributed capital.

A corporation may also use a stock dividend, like a stock split, to increase the marketability of the stock, although marketability is often a secondary consideration. If the stock dividend is large, it has the same effect on market price as a stock split. **Whenever corporations issue additional shares for the purpose of reducing the unit market price, then the distribution more closely resembles a stock split than a stock dividend. This effect usually results only if the number of shares issued is more than 20–25 percent of the number of shares previously outstanding.**[18] A stock dividend of more than 20–25 percent of the number of shares previously outstanding is called a **large stock dividend**.[19] Such a distribution should not be called a stock dividend but instead "a split-up effected in the form of a dividend" or "stock split."

Also, since a split-up effected in the form of a dividend does not alter the par value per share, companies generally are required to transfer the par value amount from retained earnings. In other words, companies transfer from retained earnings to capital stock **the par value of the stock issued**, as opposed to a transfer of the mar-

---

WHAT'S THE PRINCIPLE?

The reporting guidelines for large stock dividends are based on the *substance* rather than the form of the transaction. This contributes to financial reports that are representationally faithful.

---

[18]*Accounting Research and Terminology Bulletin No. 43,* par. 13.

[19]The SEC has added more precision to the 20–25 percent rule. Specifically, the SEC indicates that companies should consider distributions of 25 percent or more as a "split-up effected in the form of a dividend." Companies should account for distributions of less than 25 percent as a stock dividend. The SEC more precisely defined GAAP here. As a result, public companies follow the SEC rule.

ket value of the shares issued as in the case of a small stock dividend.[20] For example, **Brown Group, Inc.** at one time authorized a 2-for-1 split, effected in the form of a stock dividend. As a result of this authorization, it distributed approximately 10.5 million shares, and transferred more than $39 million representing the par value of the shares issued from Retained Earnings to the Common Stock account.

To illustrate a large stock dividend (stock split-up effected in the form of a dividend), Rockland Steel, Inc. declared a 30 percent stock dividend on November 20, payable December 29 to stockholders of record December 12. At the date of declaration, 1,000,000 shares, par value $10, are outstanding and with a fair market value of $200 per share. The entries are:

At date of declaration (November 20)

Retained Earnings	3,000,000	
Common Stock Dividend Distributable		3,000,000

Computation: 1,000,000 shares	300,000 additional shares	
$\times$ 30%	$\times$ $10 par value	
300,000	$3,000,000	

At date of distribution (December 29)

Common Stock Dividend Distributable	3,000,000	
Common Stock		3,000,000

Illustration 13-11 summarizes and compares the effects in the balance sheet and related items of various types of dividends and stock splits.

Effect on:	Declaration of Cash Dividend	Payment of Cash Dividend	Declaration and Distribution of		
			Small Stock Dividend	Large Stock Dividend	Stock Split
Retained earnings	Decrease	–0–	Decrease[a]	Decrease[b]	–0–
Capital stock	–0–	–0–	Increase[b]	Increase[b]	–0–
Additional paid-in capital	–0–	–0–	Increase[c]	–0–	–0–
Total stockholders' equity	Decrease	–0–	–0–	–0–	–0–
Working capital	Decrease	–0–	–0–	–0–	–0–
Total assets	–0–	Decrease	–0–	–0–	–0–
Number of shares outstanding	–0–	–0–	Increase	Increase	Increase

[a]Market value of shares. [b]Par or stated value of shares. [c]Excess of market value over par.

Illustration 13-11
Effects of Dividends and Stock Splits on Financial Statement Elements

Disclosure of Restrictions on Retained Earnings

Many corporations restrict retained earnings or dividends, without any formal journal entries. Such restrictions are **best disclosed by note**. Parenthetical notations are sometimes used, but restrictions imposed by bond indentures and loan agreements commonly require an extended explanation. Notes provide a medium for more complete explanations and free the financial statements from abbreviated notations. The note disclosure should reveal the

---

[20]Often, a company records a split-up effected in the form of a dividend as a debit to Paid-in Capital instead of Retained Earnings to indicate that this transaction should affect only paid-in capital accounts. No reduction of retained earnings is required except as indicated by legal requirements. For homework purposes, assume that the debit is to Retained Earnings. See, for example, Taylor W. Foster III and Edmund Scribner, "Accounting for Stock Dividends and Stock Splits: Corrections to Textbook Coverage," *Issues in Accounting Education* (February 1998).

source of the restriction, pertinent provisions, and the amount of retained earnings subject to restriction, or the amount not restricted.

Restrictions may be based on the retention of a certain retained earnings balance, the ability to maintain certain working capital requirements, additional borrowing, and other considerations. The example from the annual report of **Alberto-Culver Company** in Illustration 13-12 shows a note disclosing potential restrictions on retained earnings and dividends.

Illustration 13-12
Disclosure of Restrictions
on Retained Earnings and
Dividends

Alberto-Culver Company

Note 3 (in part): The $200 million revolving credit facility, the term note..., and the receivables agreement impose restrictions on such items as total debt, working capital, dividend payments, treasury stock purchases, and interest expense. At year-end, the company was in compliance with these arrangements, and $220 million of consolidated retained earnings was not restricted as to the payment of dividends.

Try it out! The following data are from the balance sheet accounts of Newton Company on December 31, 2007.

Available-for-sale securities	$210,000
Common stock ($5 par value)	100,000
Paid-in capital in excess of par	50,000
Retained earnings	250,000

Instructions

Prepare the necessary journal entries for the following independent items:

a Newton declared a dividend on July 1, 2008, and paid the dividend on August 1, 2008, in available-for-sale securities. The securities had a carrying value of $70,000 and a market value of $85,000.

b Newton declared a 10% stock dividend on September 15 when the stock's market value was $15 per share and distributed it on October 15.

Solution

a

July 1, 2008

Available-for-Sale Securities	15,000	
Gain on Appreciation of Securities		15,000
Retained Earnings	85,000	
Property Dividends Payable		85,000

August 1, 2008

Property Dividends Payable	85,000	
Available-for-Sale Securities		85,000

b

September 15, 2008

Retained Earnings [($100,000/$5) × .10 × $15]	30,000	
Common Stock Dividend Distributable (2,000 × $5)		10,000
Paid-in Capital in Excess of Par		20,000

October 15, 2008

Common Stock Dividend Distributable	10,000	
Common Stock		10,000

PRESENTATION AND ANALYSIS OF STOCKHOLDERS' EQUITY

Presentation

Balance Sheet

Illustration 13-13 shows a comprehensive stockholders' equity section from the balance sheet of Frost Company that includes most of the equity items we discussed in this chapter.

OBJECTIVE 9

Indicate how to present and analyze stockholders' equity.

Illustration 13-13
Comprehensive Stockholders' Equity Presentation

Frost Corporation
Stockholders' Equity
December 31, 2008

Capital stock		
Preferred stock, $100 par value, 7% cumulative, 100,000 shares authorized, 30,000 shares issued and outstanding	$3,000,000	
Common stock, no par, stated value $10 per share, 500,000 shares authorized, 400,000 shares issued	4,000,000	
Common stock dividend distributable, 20,000 shares	200,000	
Total capital stock		$ 7,200,000
Additional paid-in capital[21]		
Excess over par—preferred	$ 150,000	
Excess over stated value—common	840,000	990,000
Total paid-in capital		8,190,000
Retained earnings		4,360,000
Total paid-in capital and retained earnings		12,550,000
Less: Cost of treasury stock (2,000 shares, common)		(190,000)
Accumulated other comprehensive loss[22]		(360,000)
Total stockholders' equity		$12,000,000

Frost should disclose the pertinent rights and privileges of the various securities outstanding. For example, companies must disclose all of the following dividend and liquidation preferences, participation rights, call prices and dates, conversion or exercise prices and pertinent dates, sinking fund requirements, unusual voting rights, and significant terms

---

[21]*Accounting Trends and Techniques—2006* reports that of its 600 surveyed companies, 543 had additional paid-in capital; 330 used the caption "Additional paid-in capital"; 106 used "Capital in excess of par or stated value" as the caption; 80 used "Paid-in capital" or "Additional capital"; and 27 used other captions.

[22]Companies may include a number of items in the "Accumulated other comprehensive loss." Among these items are "Foreign currency translation adjustments," "Unrealized holding gains and losses for available-for-sale securities," "Changes in fair value of derivatives," "Guarantees of employee stock option plan (ESOP) debt," "Unearned or deferred compensation related to employee stock award plans," and others.

Accounting Trends and Techniques—2006 reports that of its 600 surveyed companies reporting other items in the equity section, 46 reported cumulative translation adjustments, 26 reported unrealized losses/gains on certain investments, and 32 reported changes in the fair value of derivatives. A number of companies had more than one item.

of contracts to issue additional shares. Liquidation preferences should be disclosed in the equity section of the balance sheet, rather than in the notes to the financial statements, to emphasize the possible effect of this restriction on future cash flows.[23]

Statement of Stockholders' Equity

Reporting of Stockholders' Equity in Eastman-Kodak's Annual Report

The **statement of stockholders' equity** is frequently presented in the following basic format.

1 Balance at the beginning of the period.

2 Additions.

3 Deductions.

4 Balance at the end of the period.

Companies must disclose changes in the separate accounts comprising stockholders' equity, to make the financial statements sufficiently informative.[24] Such changes may be disclosed in separate statements or in the basic financial statements or notes thereto.[25]

A **columnar format** for the presentation of changes in stockholders' equity items in published annual reports is gaining in popularity. An example is **Kellogg Company**'s statement of stockholders' equity, shown in Illustration 13-14.

Illustration 13-14
Columnar Format for Statement of Stockholders' Equity

Kellogg Company and Subsidiaries

Consolidated Statement of Stockholders' Equity

(millions)	Common Stock Shares	Common Stock Amount	Capital in Excess of Par Value	Retained Earnings	Treasury Stock Shares	Treasury Stock Amount	Accumulated Other Comprehensive Income	Total Shareholders' Equity	Total Comprehensive Income
Balance October 31, 2005	418.5	$104,6	$160.3	$3,164.7	13.1	$ (569.8)	$ (576.1)	$2,283.7	$ 844.2
Common stock repurchases					14.9	(649.8)		(649.8)	
Net earnings				1,004.1				1,004.1	1,004.1
Dividends				(449.9)				(449.9)	
Other comprehensive income							121.8	121.8	121.8
Stock compensation			85.7					85.7	
Stock options exercised and other			46.3		(88.5)	(7.2)	307.5	265.3	
Impact of adoption of *SFAS No. 158*							(591.9)	(591.9)	
Balance, December 30, 2006	418.5	$104.6	$292.3	$3,630.4	20.8	$(912.1)	$(1,046.2)	$2,069.0	$1,125.9

[23]"Disclosure of Information about Capital Structure," *Statement of Financial Accounting Standards No. 129* (Norwalk, Conn.: FASB, February 1997), par. 4.

[24]If a company has other comprehensive income, and computes total comprehensive income only in the statement of stockholders' equity, it must display the statement of stockholders' equity with the same prominence as other financial statements. "Reporting Comprehensive Income," *Statement of Financial Accounting Standards No. 130* (Norwalk, Conn.: FASB, June 1997).

[25]*Accounting Trends and Techniques—2006* reports that of the 600 companies surveyed, 586 presented statements of stockholders' equity, 4 presented separate statements of retained earnings only, 3 presented combined statements of income and retained earnings, and 7 presented changes in equity items in the notes only.

Analysis

Analysts use stockholders' equity ratios to evaluate a company's profitability and long-term solvency. We discuss and illustrate the following three ratios below.

1 Rate of return on common stock equity.

2 Payout ratio.

3 Book value per share.

Rate of Return on Common Stock Equity

The **rate of return on common stock equity** measures profitability from the common stockholders' viewpoint. This ratio shows how many dollars of net income the company earned for each dollar invested by the owners. Return on equity (ROE) also helps investors judge the worthiness of a stock when the overall market is not doing well. For example, **Best Buy** shares dropped nearly 40 percent, along with the broader market in 2001–2002. But a review of its return on equity during this period and since shows a steady return of 20 to 22 percent while the overall market ROE declined from 16 percent to 8 percent. More importantly, Best Buy and other stocks, such as **3M** and **Procter & Gamble**, recovered their lost market value, while other stocks with less robust ROEs stayed in the doldrums.

Financial Analysis Primer

Return on equity equals net income less preferred dividends, divided by average common stockholders' equity. For example, assume that Gerber's Inc. had net income of $360,000, declared and paid preferred dividends of $54,000, and average common stockholders' equity of $2,550,000. Illustration 13-15 shows how to compute Gerber's ratio.

$$\text{Rate of Return on Common Stock Equity} = \frac{\text{Net Income} - \text{Preferred Dividends}}{\text{Average Common Stockholders' Equity}}$$

$$= \frac{\$360,000 - \$54,000}{\$2,550,000}$$

$$= 12\%$$

Illustration 13-15
Computation of Rate of Return on Common Stock Equity

As shown in Illustration 13-15, when preferred stock is present, income available to common stockholders equals net income less preferred dividends. Similarly, the amount of common stock equity used in this ratio equals total stockholders' equity less the par value of preferred stock.

A company can improve its return on common stock equity through the prudent use of debt or preferred stock financing. **Trading on the equity** describes the practice of using borrowed money or issuing preferred stock in hopes of obtaining a higher rate of return on the money used. Shareholders win if return on the assets is higher than the cost of financing these assets. When this happens, the rate of return on common stock equity will exceed the rate of return on total assets. In short, the company is "trading on the equity at a gain." In this situation, the money obtained from bondholders or preferred stockholders earns enough to pay the interest or preferred dividends and leaves a profit for the common stockholders. On the other hand, if the cost of the financing is higher that the rate earned on the assets, the company is trading on equity at a loss and stockholders lose.

Payout Ratio

Another ratio of interest to investors, the **payout ratio**, is the ratio of cash dividends to net income. If preferred stock is outstanding, this ratio equals cash dividends paid to common stockholders, divided by net income available to common stockholders. For example, assume that Troy Co. has cash dividends of $100,000 and net income of $500,000, and no preferred stock outstanding. Illustration 13-16 shows the payout ratio computation.

Illustration 13-16
Computation of Payout Ratio

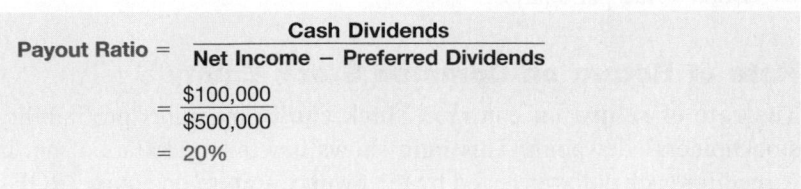

$$\text{Payout Ratio} = \frac{\text{Cash Dividends}}{\text{Net Income} - \text{Preferred Dividends}}$$

$$= \frac{\$100,000}{\$500,000}$$

$$= 20\%$$

As discussed in the opening story, it is important to some investors that the payout be sufficiently high to provide a good yield on the stock.[26]

Book Value per Share

A much-used basis for evaluating net worth is found in the book value or equity value per share of stock. **Book value per share** of stock is the amount each share would receive if the company were liquidated **on the basis of amounts reported on the balance sheet**. However, the figure loses much of its relevance if the valuations on the balance sheet fail to approximate fair market value of the assets. Book value per share equals common stockholders' equity divided by outstanding common shares. Assume that Chen Corporation's common stockholders' equity is $1,000,000 and it has 100,000 shares of common stock outstanding. Illustration 13-17 shows its book value per share computation.

Illustration 13-17
Computation of Book Value Per Share

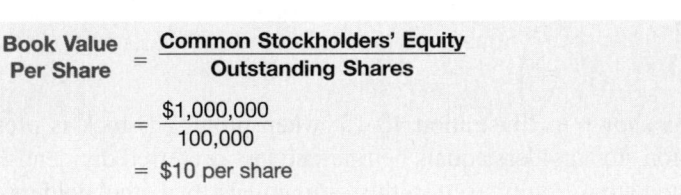

$$\frac{\text{Book Value}}{\text{Per Share}} = \frac{\text{Common Stockholders' Equity}}{\text{Outstanding Shares}}$$

$$= \frac{\$1,000,000}{100,000}$$

$$= \$10 \text{ per share}$$

[26]Analysts also closely watch the **dividend yield**—the cash dividend per share divided by the market price of the stock. This ratio indicates the rate of return that investors will receive in cash dividends from their investment.

You will want to read the CONVERGENCE CORNER
on the next page for discussion of how
international convergence efforts relate to stockholders' equity.

CONVERGENCE CORNER

Stockholders' Equity

The primary iGAAP reporting standards related to stockholders' equity are *IAS 1* ("Presentation of Financial Statements"), *IAS 32* ("Financial Instruments: Presentation"), and *IAS 39* ("Financial Instruments: Recognition and Measurement"). The accounting for transactions related to stockholders' equity, such as issuance of shares, purchase of treasury stock, and declaration and payment of dividends, are similar under both iGAAP and U.S. GAAP. Major differences relate to terminology used, introduction of items such as revaluation surplus, and presentation of stockholders' equity information.

 RELEVANT FACTS

• Many countries have different investor groups than the United States. For example, in Germany, financial institutions like banks are not only the major creditors but often are the largest stockholders as well. In the United States and the United Kingdom, many companies rely on substantial investment from private investors.

• The accounting for treasury stock retirements differs between iGAAP and U.S. GAAP. Under U.S. GAAP a company has three options: (1) charge the excess of the cost of treasury stock over par value to retained earnings, (2) allocate the difference between paid-in capital and retained earnings, or (3) charge the entire amount to paid-in capital. Under iGAAP, the excess may have to be charged to paid-in capital, depending on the original transaction related to the issuance of the stock.

• A major difference between iGAAP and U.S. GAAP relates to the account Revaluation Surplus. Revaluation surplus arises under iGAAP because companies are permitted to revalue their property, plant, and equipment to fair value under certain circumstances. This account is part of general reserves under iGAAP and is not considered contributed capital.

 ABOUT THE NUMBERS

A significant difference in iGAAP and U.S. GAAP is the accounting for securities with characteristics of debt and equity, such as convertible debt. As discussed in Appendix 13A, under U.S. GAAP all of the proceeds of convertible debt are recorded as long-term debt. To illustrate, assume **Amazon.com** issued at par $10 million of 10-year bonds with a coupon rate of 4.75%. Amazon makes the following entry to record the issuance under U.S. GAAP.

Cash	10,000,000	
Bonds Payable		10,000,000

Under iGAAP (*IAS 39*, "Financial Instruments: Recognition and Measurement), Amazon must "bifurcate" (split out) the equity component—the value of the conversion option—of the bond issue. The equity component can be estimated using option pricing models. Assume that Amazon estimates the value of the equity option embedded in the bond to be $1,575,000. Under iGAAP, the convertible bond issue is recorded as follows.

Cash	10,000,000	
Bonds Payable		8,425,000
Additional Paid-in Capital—Convertible Bonds		1,575,000

Thus, iGAAP provides a more faithful representation of the impact of the bond issue, by recording separately its debt and equity components. However, there are concerns about reliability of the models used to estimate the equity component of the bond.

• Both iGAAP and U.S. GAAP consider the statement of stockholders' equity a primary financial statement. However, under iGAAP a company has the option of preparing a statement of stockholders' equity similar to U.S. GAAP or preparing a statement of recognized income and expense (SoRIE). The SoRIE reports the items that were charged directly to equity such as revaluation surplus and then adds the net income for the period to arrive at total recognized income and expense. In this situation, additional note disclosure is required to provide reconciliations of other equity items.

 ON THE HORIZON

As indicated in earlier discussions, the IASB and the FASB are currently working on a project related to financial statement presentation. An important part of this study is to determine whether certain line items, subtotals, and totals should be clearly defined and required to be displayed in the financial statements. For example, it is likely that the statement of stockholders' equity and its presentation will be examined closely. The statement of recognized income and expense now permitted under iGAAP will probably be eliminated. In addition, the options of how to present other comprehensive income under U.S. GAAP will change in any converged standard. Also, the FASB has been working on a standard that will likely converge to iGAAP in the area of hybrid financial instruments.

ACCOUNTING, ANALYSIS, PRINCIPLES

On January 1, 2008, Agassi Corporation had the following stockholders' equity accounts.

Common Stock ($10 par value, 60,000 shares issued and outstanding)	$600,000
Paid-in Capital in Excess of Par Value ↓6,000	500,000
Retained Earnings	620,000

‑ 63,000
‑ 84,000

During the year, the following transactions occurred.

Jan. 15   Declared and paid a $1.05 cash dividend per share to stockholders.
Apr. 15   Declared and paid a 10% stock dividend. The market price of the stock
was $14 per share.
May 15   Reacquired 2,000 common shares at a market price of $15 per share.
Nov. 15   Reissued 1,000 shares held in treasury at a price of $18 per share.
Dec. 31   Determined that net income for the year was $370,000.

Accounting

Journalize the transactions. (Include entries to close net income to Retained Earnings.) Determine the ending balances for Paid-in Capital, Retained Earnings, and Stockholders' Equity.

Analysis

Calculate the payout ratio and the return on common stock equity ratio.

Principles

R. Federer is examining Agassi's financial statements and wonders whether the "gains" or "losses" on Agassi's treasury stock transactions should be included in income for the year. Briefly explain whether, and the conceptual reasons why, gains or losses on treasury stock transactions should be recorded in income.

Solution

Accounting

January 15, 2008

Retained Earnings ($1.05 × 60,000)	63,000	
Cash		63,000

April 15, 2008

Retained Earnings [(10% × 60,000) × $14]	84,000	
Common Stock		60,000
Paid-in Capital in Excess of Par Value		24,000

May 15, 2008

Treasury Stock (2,000 × $15)	30,000	
Cash		30,000

November 15, 2008

Cash ($18 × 1,000)	18,000	
Paid-in Capital from Treasury Stock		3,000
Treasury Stock		15,000

December 31, 2008

Income Summary	370,000	
Retained Earnings		370,000

The balances are indicated in the following partial balance sheet.

Agassi Corporation
Balance Sheet (partial)
December 31, 2008

Stockholders' equity
  Paid-in capital
    Capital stock
      Common stock, $10 par value,

66,000 shares issued and outstanding, (1)	$660,000
Additional paid-in capital (2)	527,000
Total paid-in capital	1,187,000
Retained earnings (3)	843,000
Total paid-in capital and retained earnings	2,030,000
Less: Treasury stock (4)	15,000
Total stockholders' equity	$2,015,000

(1) $600,000 + $60,000
(2) $500,000 + $24,000 + $3,000
(3) $620,000 − $63,000 − $ 84,000 + $370,000
(4) $30,000 − $15,000

Analysis

Payout ratio: $63,000 ÷ $ 370,000 = 17%
Return on common stock equity: $370,000 ÷ [($1,720,000 + $2,105,000) ÷ 2] = 19.3%

Principles

Treasury stock sold above or below cost does not result in gains or losses because treasury stock does not meet the definition of an asset. Rather, it is unissued equity. Furthermore, gains or losses should not be recorded, because share repurchases and reissues are transactions with its own stockholders; the effects of such transactions should not be recorded in income.

Key Terms

Summary of Learning Objectives

1 Discuss the characteristics of the corporate form of organization. Among the specific characteristics of the corporate form that affect accounting are the: (1) influence of state corporate law, (2) use of the capital stock or share system, and (3) development of a variety of ownership interests. In the absence of restrictive provisions, each share of stock carries the right to share proportionately in: (1) profits and losses; (2) management (the right to vote for directors); (3) corporate assets upon liquidation; (4) any new issues of stock of the same class (called the preemptive right).

2 Identify the key components of stockholders' equity. Stockholders' or owners' equity is classified into two categories: contributed capital and earned capital. Contributed capital (paid-in capital) describes the total amount paid in on capital stock. Put another way, it is the amount that stockholders advance to the corporation for use in the business. Contributed capital includes items such as the par value of all outstanding capital stock and premiums less any discounts on issuance. Earned capital is the capital that develops if the business operates profitably; it consists of all undistributed income that remains invested in the company.

3 Explain the accounting procedures for issuing shares of stock. Accounts are kept for the following different types of stock: *Par value stock:* (a) preferred stock or common stock; (b) paid-in capital in excess of par or additional paid-in capital; and (c) discount on stock. *No-par stock:* common stock or common stock and additional paid-in capital, if stated value is used. Stock issued in combination with other securities (lump-sum sales): The two methods of allocation available are (a) the proportional method; and (b) the incremental method. Stock issued in noncash transactions: When issuing stock for services or property other than cash, the company should record the property or services at either the fair market value of the stock issued, or the fair value of the noncash consideration received, whichever is more clearly determinable.

4 Describe the accounting for treasury stock. The cost method is generally used in accounting for treasury stock. This method derives its name from the fact that a company maintains the Treasury Stock account at the cost of the shares purchased. Under the cost method, a company debits the Treasury Stock account for the cost of the shares acquired and credits it for this same cost upon reissuance. The price received for the stock when originally issued does not affect the entries to record the acquisition and reissuance of the treasury stock.

5 Explain the accounting for and reporting of preferred stock. Preferred stock is a special class of shares that possesses certain preferences or features not possessed by the common stock. The features that are most often associated with preferred stock issues are: (1) preference as to dividends; (2) preference as to assets in the event of liquidation; (3) convertible into common stock; (4) callable at the option of the corporation; (5) nonvoting. At issuance, the accounting for preferred stock is similar to that for common stock. When convertible preferred stock is converted, a company uses the book value method: It debits Preferred Stock, along with any related Additional Paid-in Capital, and credits Common Stock and Additional Paid-in Capital (if an excess exists).

6 Describe the policies used in distributing dividends. The state incorporation laws normally provide information concerning the legal restrictions related to the payment of dividends. Corporations rarely pay dividends in an amount equal to the legal limit. This is due, in part, to the fact that companies use assets represented by undistributed earnings to finance future operations of the business. If a company is considering declaring a dividend, it must ask two preliminary questions: (1) Is the condition of the corporation such that the dividend is **legally permissible**? (2) Is the condition of the corporation such that a dividend is **economically sound**?

7 Identify the various forms of dividend distributions. Dividends are of the following types: (1) cash dividends, (2) property dividends, (3) liquidating dividends (dividends based on other than retained earnings), (4) stock dividends (the issuance by a corporation of its own stock to its stockholders on a pro rata basis, but without receiving consideration).

8 Explain the accounting for small and large stock dividends, and for stock splits. Generally accepted accounting principles require that the accounting for small stock dividends (less than 20 or 25 percent) rely on the fair market value of the stock issued. When declaring a stock dividend, a company debits Retained Earnings at the fair market value of the stock it distributes. The entry includes a credit to Common Stock Dividend Distributable at par value times the number of shares, with any excess credited to Paid-in Capital in Excess of Par. If the number of shares issued exceeds 20 or 25 percent of the shares outstanding (large stock dividend), it debits Retained Earnings at par value and credits Common Stock Distributable—there is no additional paid-in capital.

A stock dividend is a capitalization of retained earnings that reduces retained earnings and increases certain contributed capital accounts. The par value per share and total stockholders' equity remain unchanged with a stock dividend, and all stockholders retain their same proportionate share of ownership. A stock split results in an increase or decrease in the number of shares outstanding, with a corresponding decrease or increase in the par or stated value per share. No accounting entry is required for a stock split.

9 Indicate how to present and analyze stockholders' equity. The stockholders' equity section of a balance sheet includes capital stock, additional paid-in capital, and retained earnings. A company might also present additional items such as treasury stock and accumulated other comprehensive income. Companies often provide a statement of stockholders' equity. Common ratios that use stockholders' equity amounts are: rate of return on common stock equity, payout ratio, and book value per share.

Expanded Discussion of Quasi-Reorganization

BEHIND THE NUMBERS APPENDIX 13A	ACCOUNTING FOR FINANCIAL INSTRUMENTS WITH BOTH DEBT AND EQUITY CHARACTERISTICS

As we indicated in both the liability and stockholders' equity chapters, it is sometimes difficult to determine whether a financial instrument is debt or equity, or a combination of both. As a result, the FASB has issued a standard on this subject.[1] In this appendix we discuss the accounting for two financial instruments that have both debt and equity characteristics:

1 Convertible debt.

2 Stock warrants issued with other securities.

Convertible Debt

Convertible bonds can be converted into other corporate securities during some specified period of time after issuance. **A convertible bond combines the benefits of a bond with the privilege of exchanging it for stock at the holder's option.** Investors who purchase it desire the security of a bond holding—guaranteed interest—plus the added option of conversion if the value of the stock appreciates significantly.

Corporations issue convertibles for two main reasons. One is to raise equity capital without giving up more ownership control than necessary. A second reason to issue convertibles is to obtain debt financing at cheaper rates. Many companies could issue debt only at high interest rates unless they attach a convertible covenant. The conversion privilege entices the investor to accept a lower interest rate than would normally be the case on a straight debt issue. For example, **Amazon.com** at one time issued convertible bonds that pay interest at an effective yield of 4.75 percent. This rate was much lower than Amazon.com would have had to pay by issuing straight debt. For this lower interest rate, the investor receives the right to buy Amazon.com's common stock at a fixed price until the bond's maturity.[2]

> OBJECTIVE 10
> Understand the accounting issues related to financial instruments with both debt and equity characteristics.

[1]"Accounting for Certain Financial Instruments with Characteristics of Both Liabilities and Equity," *Statement of Financial Accounting Standards No. 150* (Norwalk Conn.: FASB, 2003).

[2]As with any investment, a buyer must be careful. For example, **Wherehouse Entertainment Inc.**, which had 6¼ percent convertibles outstanding, was taken private in a leveraged buyout. As a result, the convertible was suddenly as risky as a junk bond of a highly leveraged company with a coupon of only 6¼ percent. As one holder of the convertibles noted, "What's even worse is that the company will be so loaded down with debt that it probably won't have enough cash flow to make its interest payments. And the convertible debt we hold is subordinated to the rest of Wherehouse's debt." These types of situations have made convertibles less attractive and have led to the introduction of takeover protection covenants in some convertible bond offerings.

At Time of Issuance

Presently, the method for recording convertible bonds at the date of issue follows the method used to record straight debt issues (with none of the proceeds recorded as equity). Companies amortize any discount or premium that results from the issuance of convertible bonds to its maturity date because it is difficult to predict when, if at all, conversion will occur.

At Time of Conversion

If converting bonds into other securities, a company uses the book value method to record the conversion. The book value method records the securities exchanged for the bond at the carrying amount (book value) of the bond.

To illustrate, assume that Hilton, Inc. has a $1,000 bond that is convertible into 10 shares of common stock (par value $10). At the time of conversion, the unamortized premium is $50. Hilton records the conversion of the bonds as follows:

Bonds Payable	1,000	
Premium on Bonds Payable	50	
Common Stock		100
Paid-in Capital in Excess of Par		950

If Hilton retires the bonds instead, it reports a gain or loss on the transaction if the book value differs from cash paid.

Stock Warrants Issued with Other Securities

Warrants issued with other securities are basically long-term options to buy common stock at a fixed price. Although sometimes traded, generally the life on perpetual warrants is five years, occasionally 10.

A warrant works like this: **Tenneco, Inc.** offered a unit comprising one share of stock and one detachable warrant. As its name implies, the **detachable stock warrant** can be "detached" from the warrant and traded as a separate security. The Tenneco warrant in this example is exercisable at $24.25 per share and good for five years. The unit (share of stock plus detachable warrant) sold for 22.75 ($22.75). Since the price of the common stock the day before the sale was 19.88 ($19.88), the difference suggests a price of 2.87 ($2.87) for the warrant.

In this situation, the warrant had an apparent value of 2.87 ($2.87), even though it would not be profitable at present for the purchaser to exercise the warrant and buy the stock, because the price of the stock was much below the exercise price of $24.25.[3] The investor pays for the warrant in order to receive a possible future call on the stock at a fixed price when the price rises significantly. For example, if the price of the stock rises to $30, the investor gains $2.88 ($30 − $24.25 − $2.87) on an investment of $2.87, a 100 percent increase! But, if the price never rises, the investor loses the full $2.87.[4]

A company should allocate the proceeds from the sale of debt with detachable stock warrants between the two securities.[5] The profession takes the position that two separable instruments are involved—(1) a bond and (2) a warrant giving the holder the right to purchase common stock at a certain price. Companies can trade warrants that are detachable separately from the debt. This allows the determination of a market value. The two methods of allocation available are:

1 The proportional method.

2 The incremental method.

---

[3] We show later in this discussion that a company normally determines the value of the warrant on the basis of a relative market value approach because of the difficulty of imputing a warrant value in any other manner.

[4] From the illustration, note that buying warrants can be an "all or nothing" proposition.

[5] A detachable warrant means that the warrant can sell separately from the bond. *APB Opinion No. 14* makes a distinction between detachable and nondetachable warrants. A company must sell nondetachable warrants with the security as a complete package, which prevents any allocation.

Proportional Method

AT&T's offering of detachable five-year warrants to buy one share of common stock (par value $5) at $25 (at a time when a share was selling for approximately $50) enabled it to price its offering of bonds at par with a moderate 8¾ percent yield. To place a value on the two securities, investors determine (1) the value of the bonds without the warrants, and (2) the value of the warrants.

For example, assume that AT&T's bonds (par $1,000) sold for 99 without the warrants soon after their issue. The market value of the warrants at that time was $30. (Prior to sale the warrants will not have a market value.) The allocation relies on an estimate of market value, generally as established by an investment banker, or on the relative market value of the bonds and the warrants soon after the company issues and trades them. The price paid for 10,000, $1,000 bonds with the warrants attached was par, or $10,000,000. Illustration 13A-1 shows the allocation between the bonds and warrants.

Fair market value of bonds (without warrants) ($10,000,000 × .99)	=	$ 9,900,000
Fair market value of warrants (10,000 × $30)	=	300,000
Aggregate fair market value		$10,200,000
Allocated to bonds:	$\dfrac{\$9,900,000}{\$10,200,000} \times \$10,000,000 =$	$ 9,705,882
Allocated to warrants:	$\dfrac{\$300,000}{\$10,200,000} \times \$10,000,000 =$	294,118
Total allocation		$10,000,000

Illustration 13A-1
Proportional Allocation of Proceeds between Bonds and Warrants

In this situation the bonds sell at a discount. The company records the sale as follows.

Cash	9,705,882	
Discount on Bonds Payable	294,118	
Bonds Payable		10,000,000

In addition, the company sells warrants that it credits to paid-in capital. It makes the following entry.

Cash	294,118	
Paid-in Capital—Stock Warrants		294,118

The company may combine the entries if desired. Here, we show them separately to indicate that the purchaser of the bond is buying not only a bond but also a possible future claim on common stock.

Assuming investors exercise all 10,000 warrants (one warrant per one share of stock), the company makes the following entry.

Cash (10,000 × $25)	250,000	
Paid-in Capital—Stock Warrants	294,118	
Common Stock (10,000 × $5)		50,000
Paid-in Capital in Excess of Par		494,118

What if investors fail to exercise the warrants? In that case, the company debits Paid-in Capital—Stock Warrants for $294,118, and credits Paid-in Capital from Expired Warrants for a like amount. The additional paid-in capital reverts to the former stockholders.

Incremental Method

In instances where a company cannot determine the fair value of either the warrants or the bonds, it applies the incremental method used in lump-sum security purchases (as explained on page 677). That is, the company uses the security for which it *can* determine the market value. It allocates the remainder of the purchase price to the security for which it does not know the market value.

For example, assume that the market price of the AT&T warrants is $300,000, but the company cannot determine the market price of the bonds without the warrants. Illustration 13A-2 shows the amount allocated to the warrants and the stock in this case.

Illustration 13A-2

Incremental Allocation of Proceeds between Bonds and Warrants

Lump-sum receipt	$10,000,000
Allocated to the warrants	300,000
Balance allocated to bonds	$ 9,700,000

Conceptual Questions

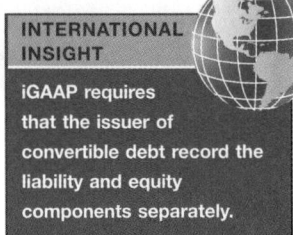

The question arises whether the allocation of value to the warrants is consistent with the handling accorded convertible debt, in which companies allocate no value to the conversion privilege. The FASB stated that the features of a convertible security are **inseparable** in the sense that choices are mutually exclusive: The holder either converts or redeems the bonds for cash, but cannot do both. No basis, therefore, exists for recognizing the conversion value in the accounts.

The Board, however, indicated that the issuance of bonds with **detachable warrants** involves two securities, one a debt security that will remain outstanding until maturity, and the other a warrant to purchase common stock. At the time of issuance, separable instruments exist. This therefore justifies separate treatment. **Nondetachable warrants**, however, **do not require an allocation of the proceeds between the bonds and the warrants**. Companies record the entire proceeds as debt.

Many argue that the conversion feature is not significantly different in nature from the call represented by a warrant.

The question is whether, although the legal forms differ, sufficient similarities of substance exist to support the same accounting treatment. Some contend that inseparability *per se* is an insufficient basis for restricting allocation between identifiable components of a transaction. Examples of allocation between assets of value in a single transaction do exist, such as allocation of values in basket purchases and separation of principal and interest in capitalizing long-term leases. Critics of the current accounting for convertibles say that to deny recognition of value to the conversion feature merely looks to the form of the instrument and does not deal with the substance of the transaction.

In its current deliberations on this subject, the FASB is considering whether companies should separate the debt and equity components of these securities (such as convertible debt or bonds issued with nondetachable warrants). However, until the profession officially reverses its stand in this area, companies will continue to report convertible debt and bonds issued with nondetachable warrants solely as debt.

Key Terms

convertible bond, 705
detachable stock warrants, 706
warrants, 706

Summary of Learning Objective for Appendix 13A

10 Understand the accounting issues related to financial instruments with both debt and equity characteristics.
Two securities that have both debt and equity characteristics are convertible debt and debt issued with stock warrants. Companies account for convertible debt and debt issued with nondetachable warrants as debt. A company separates debt issued with detachable warrants into debt and equity, using either the proportional method or the incremental method. It appears likely that the FASB will soon require that companies separate securities with both debt and equity characteristics into their debt and equity components.

REVIEW EXERCISE

D'Ouville Company was formed on July 1, 2005. It was authorized to issue 500,000 shares of $10 par value common stock and 100,000 shares of 8%, $25 par value, cumulative and nonparticipating preferred stock. D'Ouville Company has a July 1–June 30 fiscal year. The following information relates to the stockholders' equity accounts of D'Ouville Company.

Common Stock

Prior to the 2007–2008 fiscal year, D'Ouville Company had 110,000 shares of outstanding common stock issued as follows.

1 95,000 shares were issued for cash on July 1, 2005, at $31 per share.

2 On July 24, 2005, 5,000 shares were exchanged for a plot of land which cost the seller $70,000 in 1999 and had an estimated market value of $220,000 on July 24, 2005.

3 10,000 shares were issued on March 1, 2007, for $42 per share.

During the 2007–2008 fiscal year, the following transactions regarding common stock took place.

November 30, 2007	D'Ouville purchased 2,000 shares of its own stock on the open market at $39 per share. D'Ouville uses the cost method for treasury stock.
December 15, 2007	D'Ouville declared a 5% stock dividend for stockholders of record on January 15, 2008, to be issued on January 31, 2008. D'Ouville was having a liquidity problem and could not afford a cash dividend at the time. D'Ouville's common stock was selling at $52 per share on December 15, 2007.
June 20, 2008	D'Ouville sold 500 shares of its own common stock that it had purchased on November 30, 2007, for $21,000.

Preferred Stock

D'Ouville issued 100,000 shares of preferred stock at $44 per share on July 1, 2006.

Cash Dividends

D'Ouville has followed a schedule of declaring cash dividends in December and June, with payment being made to stockholders of record in the following month. The cash dividends which have been declared since inception of the company through June 30, 2008, are shown below.

Declaration Date	Common Stock	Preferred Stock
12/15/06	$0.30 per share	$1.00 per share
6/15/07	$0.30 per share	$1.00 per share
12/15/07	—	$1.00 per share

No cash dividends were declared during June 2008 due to the company's liquidity problems.

Retained Earnings

As of June 30, 2007, D'Ouville retained earnings account had a balance of $650,000. For the fiscal year ending June 30, 2008, D'Ouville reported net income of $80,000.

Instructions

Prepare the stockholders' equity section of the balance sheet, including appropriate notes, for D'Ouville Company as of June 30, 2008, as it should appear in its annual report to the shareholders.

Solution

D'Ouville Company
Stockholders' Equity
June 30, 2008

Capital stock		
8% preferred stock, $25 par value, cumulative and nonparticipating, 100,000 shares authorized, 100,000 shares issued and outstanding—Note A		$2,500,000
Common stock, $10 par value, 500,000 shares authorized, 115,400 shares issued, with 1,500 shares held in the treasury		1,154,000
Additional paid-in capital		
On preferred stock	$1,900,000	
On common stock	2,711,800*	
On treasury stock	1,500	4,613,300
Total paid-in capital		8,267,300
Retained earnings		349,200**
Total paid-in capital and retained earnings		8,616,500
Less: Treasury stock, 1,500 shares at cost		58,500
Total stockholders' equity		$8,558,000

Note A: D'Ouville Company is in arrears on the preferred stock in the amount of $100,000.

*Premium on Common Stock:

Issue of 95,000 shares × ($31 − $10)	$1,995,000
Issue of 5,000 shares for plot of land ($220,000 − $50,000)	170,000
10,000 shares issued (3/1/00) [10,000 × ($42 − $10)]	320,000
5,400 shares as dividend [5,400 × ($52 − $10)]	226,800
	$2,711,800

**Retained Earnings:

Beginning Balance	+	Income	−	Stock Dividend	−	Preferred Dividend	=	Ret. Earnings, Ending Balance
$650,000	+	$80,000	−	$280,800	−	$100,000	=	$349,200

Questions

Note: All **asterisked** assignment materials relate to content in the appendix to the chapter.

1 In the absence of restrictive provisions, what are the basic rights of stockholders of a corporation?

2 Why is a preemptive right important?

3 Distinguish between common and preferred stock.

4 Why is the distinction between paid-in capital and retained earnings important?

5 Explain each of the following terms: authorized capital stock, unissued capital stock, issued capital stock, outstanding capital stock, and treasury stock.

6 What is meant by par value, and what is its significance to stockholders?

7 Describe the accounting for the issuance for cash of no-par value common stock at a price in excess of the stated value of the common stock.

8 Explain the difference between the proportional method and the incremental method of allocating the proceeds of lump sum sales of capital stock.

9 What are the different bases for stock valuation when assets other than cash are received for issued shares of stock?

10 Explain how underwriting costs and accounting and legal fees associated with the issuance of stock should be recorded.

11 For what reasons might a corporation purchase its own stock?

12 Discuss the propriety of showing:

(a) Treasury stock as an asset.

(b) "Gain" or "loss" on sale of treasury stock as additions to or deductions from income.

(c) Dividends received on treasury stock as income.

13 What features or rights may alter the character of preferred stock?

14 Little Texas Inc. recently noted that its 4% preferred stock and 4% participating second preferred stock, which are both cumulative, have priority as to dividends up to 4% of their par value. Its participating preferred stock participates equally with the common stock in any dividends in excess of 4%. What is meant by the term participating? Cumulative?

15 Where in the financial statements is preferred stock normally reported?

16 List possible sources of additional paid-in capital.

17 Pleasant Dolls Inc. purchases 10,000 shares of its own previously issued $10 par common stock for $290,000. Assuming the shares are held in the treasury with intent to reissue, what effect does this transaction have on (a) net income, (b) total assets, (c) total paid-in capital, and (d) total stockholders' equity?

18 Indicate how each of the following accounts should be classified in the stockholders' equity section.

(a) Common Stock.

(b) Retained Earnings.

(c) Paid-in Capital in Excess of Par.

(d) Treasury Stock.

(e) Paid-in Capital from Treasury Stock.

(f) Paid-in Capital in Excess of Stated Value

(g) Preferred Stock

19 What factors influence the dividend policy of a company?

20 What are the principal considerations of a board of directors in making decisions involving dividend declarations? Discuss briefly.

21 Dividends are sometimes said to have been paid "out of retained earnings." What is the error, if any, in that statement?

22 Distinguish among: cash dividends, property dividends, liquidating dividends, and stock dividends.

23 Describe the accounting entry for a stock dividend, if any. Describe the accounting entry for a stock split, if any.

24 Stock splits and stock dividends may be used by a corporation to change the number of shares of its stock outstanding.

(a) What is meant by a stock split effected in the form of a dividend?

(b) From an accounting viewpoint, explain how the stock split effected in the form of a dividend differs from an ordinary stock dividend.

(c) How should a stock dividend that has been declared but not yet issued be classified in a statement of financial position? Why?

25 The following comment appeared in the notes of Alvarado Corporation's annual report: "Such distributions, representing proceeds from the sale of James Buchanan, Inc. were paid in the form of partial liquidating dividends and were in lieu of a portion of the Company's ordinary cash dividends." How would a partial liquidating dividend be accounted for in the financial records?

26 This comment appeared in the annual report of Rodriguez Lopez Inc.: "The Company could pay cash or property dividends on the Class A common stock without paying cash or property dividends on the Class B common stock. But if the Company pays any cash or property dividends on the Class B common stock, it would be required to pay at least the same dividend on the Class A common stock." How is a property dividend accounted for in the financial records?

27 For what reasons might a company restrict a portion of its retained earnings?

28 How are restrictions of retained earnings reported?

*29 On July 1, 2008, Roberts Corporation issued $3,000,000 of 9% bonds payable in 20 years. The bonds include detachable warrants giving the bondholder the right to purchase for $30 one share of $1 par value common stock at any time during the next 10 years. The bonds were sold for $3,000,000. The value of the warrants at the time of issuance was $200,000. Prepare the journal entry to record this transaction.

Brief Exercises

(LO 3)   **BE13-1**   Lost Vikings Corporation issued 300 shares of $10 par value common stock for $4,100. Prepare Lost Vikings' journal entry.

(LO 3)   **BE13-2**   Shinobi Corporation issued 600 shares of no-par common stock for $10,200. Prepare Shinobi's journal entry if (a) the stock has no stated value, and (b) the stock has a stated value of $2 per share.

(LO 4, 9)   **BE13-3**   Lufia Corporation has the following account balances at December 31, 2008.

Common stock, $5 par value	$ 210,000
Treasury stock	90,000
Retained earnings	2,340,000
Paid-in capital in excess of par	1,320,000

Prepare Lufia's December 31, 2008, stockholders' equity section.

(LO 3)   **BE13-4**   Primal Rage Corporation issued 300 shares of $10 par value common stock and 100 shares of $50 par value preferred stock for a lump sum of $14,200. The common stock has a market value of $20 per share, and the preferred stock has a market value of $90 per share. Prepare the journal entry to record the issuance.

(LO 3)   **BE13-5**   On February 1, 2008, Mario Andretti Corporation issued 2,000 shares of its $5 par value common stock for land worth $31,000. Prepare the February 1, 2008, journal entry.

(LO 3)   **BE13-6**   Powerdrive Corporation issued 2,000 shares of its $10 par value common stock for $70,000. Powerdrive also incurred $1,500 of costs associated with issuing the stock. Prepare Powerdrive's journal entry to record the issuance of the company's stock.

(LO 4)   **BE13-7**   Maverick Inc. has outstanding 10,000 shares of $10 par value common stock. On July 1, 2008, Maverick reacquired 100 shares at $85 per share. On September 1, Maverick reissued 60 shares at $90 per share. On November 1, Maverick reissued 40 shares at $83 per share. Prepare Maverick's journal entries to record these transactions using the cost method.

(LO 4)   **BE13-8**   Power Rangers Corporation has outstanding 20,000 shares of $5 par value common stock. On August 1, 2008, Power Rangers reacquired 200 shares at $75 per share. On November 1, Power Rangers reissued the 200 shares at $70 per share. Power Rangers had no previous treasury stock transactions. Prepare Power Rangers' journal entries to record these transactions using the cost method.

(LO 5)   **BE13-9**   Popeye Corporation issued 450 shares of $100 par value preferred stock for $61,500. Prepare Popeye's journal entry.

(LO 6)   **BE13-10**   Micro Machines Inc. declared a cash dividend of $1.50 per share on its 2 million outstanding shares. The dividend was declared on August 1, payable on September 9 to all stockholders of record on August 15. Prepare all journal entries necessary on those three dates.

(LO 6, 7)   **BE13-11**   Ren Inc. owns shares of Stimpy Corporation stock classified as available-for-sale securities. At December 31, 2007, the available-for-sale securities were carried in Ren's accounting records at their cost of $875,000, which equals their market value. On September 21, 2008, when the market value of the securities was $1,400,000, Ren declared a property dividend whereby the Stimpy securities are to be distributed on October 23, 2008, to stockholders of record on October 8, 2008. Prepare all journal entries necessary on those three dates.

(LO 6, 7)   **BE13-12**   Radical Rex Mining Company declared, on April 20, a dividend of $700,000 payable on June 1. Of this amount, $125,000 is a return of capital. Prepare the April 20 and June 1 entries for Radical Rex.

(LO 8)   **BE13-13**   Mike Holmgren Football Corporation has outstanding 200,000 shares of $10 par value common stock. The corporation declares a 5% stock dividend when the fair value of the stock is $65 per share. Prepare the journal entries for Mike Holmgren Football Corporation for both the date of declaration and the date of distribution.

(LO 8)   **BE13-14**   Use the information from BE13-13, but assume Mike Holmgren Football Corporation declared a 100% stock dividend rather than a 5% stock dividend. Prepare the journal entries for both the date of declaration and the date of distribution.

(LO 10)   *****BE13-15**   Divac Corporation issued 1,000 $1,000 bonds at 101. Each bond was issued with one detachable stock warrant. After issuance, the bonds were selling in the market at 98, and the warrants had a market value of $40. Use the proportional method to record the issuance of the bonds and warrants.

*BE13-16 Ceballos Corporation issued 1,000 $1,000 bonds at 101. Each bond was issued with one detachable stock warrant. After issuance, the bonds were selling separately at 98. The market price of the warrants without the bonds cannot be determined. Use the incremental method to record the issuance of the bonds and warrants. **(LO 10)**

*BE13-17 Malik Sealy Corporation issued 2,000 shares of $10 par value common stock upon conversion of 1,000 shares of $50 par value preferred stock. The preferred stock was originally issued at $55 per share. The common stock is trading at $26 per share at the time of conversion. Record the conversion of the preferred stock. **(LO 10)**

Exercises

E13-1 (Recording the Issuances of Common Stock) During its first year of operations, Collin Raye Corporation had the following transactions pertaining to its common stock. **(LO 3)**

Jan. 10	Issued 80,000 shares for cash at $6 per share.
Mar. 1	Issued 5,000 shares to attorneys in payment of a bill for $35,000 for services rendered in helping the company to incorporate.
July 1	Issued 30,000 shares for cash at $8 per share.

Instructions

(a) Prepare the journal entries for these transactions, assuming that the common stock has a par value of $5 per share.

(b) Prepare the journal entries for these transactions, assuming that the common stock is no par with a stated value of $3 per share.

E13-2 (Recording the Issuance of Common and Preferred Stock) Kathleen Battle Corporation was organized on January 1, 2008. It is authorized to issue 10,000 shares of 8%, $100 par value preferred stock, and 500,000 shares of no par common stock with a stated value of $1 per share. The following stock transactions were completed during the first year. **(LO 3)**

Jan. 10	Issued 80,000 shares of common stock for cash at $5 per share.
Mar. 1	Issued 5,000 shares of preferred stock for cash at $108 per share.
Apr. 1	Issued 24,000 shares of common stock for land. The asking price of the land was $90,000; the fair market value of the land was $80,000.
May 1	Issued 80,000 shares of common stock for cash at $7 per share.
Aug. 1	Issued 10,000 shares of common stock to attorneys in payment of their bill of $50,000 for services rendered in helping the company organize.
Nov. 1	Issued 1,000 shares of preferred stock for cash at $112 per share.

Instructions

Prepare the journal entries to record the above transactions.

E13-3 (Stock Issued for Land) Twenty-five thousand shares reacquired by Elixir Corporation for $53 per share were exchanged for undeveloped land that has an appraised value of $1,700,000. At the time of the exchange the common stock was trading at $62 per share on an organized stock exchange. **(LO 3)**

Instructions

(a) Prepare the journal entry to record the acquisition of land assuming that the purchase of the stock was originally recorded using the cost method.

(b) Briefly identify the possible alternatives (including those that are totally unacceptable) for quantifying the cost of the land and briefly support your choice.

E13-4 (Lump-Sum Sale of Stock with Bonds) Faith Evans Corporation is a regional company which is an SEC registrant. The corporation's securities are thinly traded on NASDAQ (National Association of Securities Dealers Quotes). Faith Evans Corp. has issued 10,000 units. Each unit consists of a $500 par, 12% subordinated debenture and 10 shares of $5 par common stock. The investment banker has retained 400 units as the underwriting fee. The other 9,600 units were sold to outside investors for cash at $880 per unit. Prior to this sale the 2-week asking price of common stock was $40 per share. Twelve percent is a reasonable market yield for the debentures, and therefore the par value of the bonds is equal to the fair value. **(LO 3)**

Instructions

(a) Prepare the journal entry to record Evans' transaction, under the following conditions.

    (1) Employing the incremental method.

    (2) Employing the proportional method, assuming the recent price quote on the common stock reflects fair value.

(b) Briefly explain which method is, in your opinion, the better method.

(LO 3, 5)   **E13-5 (Lump-Sum Sales of Stock with Preferred Stock)** Dave Matthew Inc. issues 500 shares of $10 par value common stock and 100 shares of $100 par value preferred stock for a lump sum of $100,000.

Instructions

(a) Prepare the journal entry for the issuance when the market value of the common shares is $165 each and market value of the preferred is $230 each. (Round to nearest dollar.)

(b) Prepare the journal entry for the issuance when only the market value of the common stock is known and it is $170 per share.

(LO 3, 4)   **E13-6 (Stock Issuances and Repurchase)** Lindsey Hunter Corporation is authorized to issue 50,000 shares of $5 par value common stock. During 2008, Lindsey Hunter took part in the following selected transactions.

1. Issued 5,000 shares of stock at $45 per share, less costs related to the issuance of the stock totaling $7,000.

2. Issued 1,000 shares of stock for land appraised at $50,000. The stock was actively traded on a national stock exchange at approximately $46 per share on the date of issuance.

3. Purchased 500 shares of treasury stock at $43 per share. The treasury shares purchased were issued in 2003 at $40 per share.

Instructions

(a) Prepare the journal entry to record item 1.
(b) Prepare the journal entry to record item 2.
(c) Prepare the journal entry to record item 3 using the cost method.

(LO 4)   **E13-7 (Effect of Treasury Stock Transactions on Financials)** Chauncy Company has outstanding 40,000 shares of $5 par common stock which had been issued at $30 per share. Chauncy then entered into the following transactions.

1. Purchased 5,000 treasury shares at $45 per share.

2. Resold 2,000 of the treasury shares at $49 per share.

3. Resold 500 of the treasury shares at $40 per share.

Instructions

Use the following code to indicate the effect each of the three transactions has on the financial statement categories listed in the table below, assuming Chauncy Company uses the cost method: (I = Increase; D = Decrease; NE = No effect).

#	Assets	Liabilities	Stockholders' Equity	Paid-in Capital	Retained Earnings	Net Income
1						
2						
3						

(LO 3, 10)   **E13-8 (Preferred Stock Entries and Dividends)** Otis Thorpe Corporation has 10,000 shares of $100 par value, 8%, preferred stock and 50,000 shares of $10 par value common stock outstanding at December 31, 2008.

Instructions

Answer the questions in each of the following independent situations.

(a) If the preferred stock is cumulative and dividends were last paid on the preferred stock on December 31, 2005, what are the dividends in arrears that should be reported on the December 31, 2008, balance sheet? How should these dividends be reported?

(b) If the preferred stock is convertible into seven shares of $10 par value common stock and 4,000 shares are converted, what entry is required for the conversion assuming the preferred stock was issued at par value?

(c) If the preferred stock was issued at $107 per share, how should the preferred stock be reported in the stockholders' equity section?

E13-9 (Correcting Entries for Equity Transactions) Pistons Inc. recently hired a new accountant with extensive experience in accounting for partnerships. Because of the pressure of the new job, the accountant was unable to review what he had learned earlier about corporation accounting. During the first month, he made the following entries for the corporation's capital stock.

(LO 3, 4)

May 2	Cash	192,000	
	Capital Stock		192,000
	(Issued 12,000 shares of $5 par value common stock at $16 per share)		
10	Cash	600,000	
	Capital Stock		600,000
	(Issued 10,000 shares of $30 par value preferred stock at $60 per share)		
15	Capital Stock	15,000	
	Cash		15,000
	(Purchased 1,000 shares of common stock for the treasury at $15 per share)		
31	Cash	8,500	
	Capital Stock		5,000
	Gain on Sale of Stock		3,500
	(Sold 500 shares of treasury stock at $17 per share)		

Handwritten annotations:
Com Stock 60 000
APIC 132 000
Pre Stk 300 000
APIC 30 000
Tres. Stock
cash
Tres Stck 500 × 17
APIC 500 × 2

Instructions

On the basis of the explanation for each entry, prepare the entries that should have been made for the capital stock transactions.

E13-10 (Analysis of Equity Data and Equity Section Preparation) For a recent 2-year period, the balance sheet of Santana Dotson Company showed the following stockholders' equity data at December 31 in millions.

(LO 3, 4)

	2008	2007
Additional paid-in capital	$ 931	$ 817
Common stock—par	545	540
Retained earnings	7,167	5,226
Treasury stock	1,564	918
Total stockholders' equity	$7,079	$5,665
Common stock shares issued	218	216
Common stock shares authorized	500	500
Treasury stock shares	34	27

Handwritten: 46   34

Instructions

(a) Answer the following questions.
   (1) What is the par value of the common stock? *2.5*
   (2) What is the cost per share of treasury stock at December 31, 2008, and at December 31, 2007?
(b) Prepare the stockholders' equity section at December 31, 2008.

E13-11 (Equity Items on the Balance Sheet) The following are selected transactions that may affect stockholders' equity.

(LO 7, 8)

1. Recorded accrued interest earned on a note receivable. *AT RET. NIT SEI*
2. Declared a cash dividend. *LT SEl . REV*
3. Declared and distributed a stock split.
4. Recorded a retained earnings restriction.
5. Recorded the expiration of insurance coverage that was previously recorded as prepaid insurance. *AV REL NIU SEU*
6. Paid the cash dividend declared in item 2 above. *AV L.V*

LT NI RECISED

7. Recorded accrued interest expense on a note payable.
8. Declared a stock dividend. *REV PIC*
9. Distributed the stock dividend declared in item 8.

Instructions

In the table below, indicate the effect each of the nine transactions has on the financial statement elements listed. Use the following code:

I = Increase   D = Decrease   NE = No effect

Item	Assets	Liabilities	Stockholders' Equity	Paid-in Capital	Retained Earnings	Net Income

(LO 7, 8)   **E13-12   (Cash Dividend and Liquidating Dividend)**   Lotoya Davis Corporation has ten million shares of common stock issued and outstanding. On June 1 the board of directors voted an 80 cents per share cash dividend to stockholders of record as of June 14, payable June 30. *800,000)*

Instructions

(a) Prepare the journal entry for each of the dates above assuming the dividend represents a distribution of earnings.

(b) How would the entry differ if the dividend were a liquidating dividend?

(LO 8)   **E13-13   (Stock Split and Stock Dividend)**   The common stock of Alexander Hamilton Inc. is currently selling at $120 per share. The directors wish to reduce the share price and increase share volume prior to a new issue. The per share par value is $10; book value is $70 per share. Nine million shares are issued and outstanding.

Instructions

Prepare the necessary journal entries assuming the following.

(a) The board votes a 2-for-1 stock split. *none*

(b) The board votes a 100% stock dividend.

(c) Briefly discuss the accounting and securities market differences between these two methods of increasing the number of shares outstanding.

(LO 8)   **E13-14   (Entries for Stock Dividends and Stock Splits)**   The stockholders' equity accounts of G.K. Chesterton Company have the following balances on December 31, 2008.

Common stock, $10 par, 300,000 shares issued and outstanding	$3,000,000
Paid-in capital in excess of par	1,200,000
Retained earnings	5,600,000

Shares of G.K. Chesterton Company stock are currently selling on the Midwest Stock Exchange at $37.

Instructions

Prepare the appropriate journal entries for each of the following cases.

(a) A stock dividend of 5% is declared and issued.   *Com. Stock*

(b) A stock dividend of 100% is declared and issued.

(c) A 2-for-1 stock split is declared and issued.

E13-15 **(Dividend Entries)** The following data were taken from the balance sheet accounts of Masefield Corporation on December 31, 2007.

Current assets	$540,000
Investments	624,000
Common stock (par value $10)	500,000
Paid-in capital in excess of par	150,000
Retained earnings	840,000

Instructions

Prepare the required journal entries for the following unrelated items.

(a) A 5% stock dividend is declared and distributed at a time when the market value of the shares is $39 per share.

(b) The par value of the capital stock is reduced to $2 with a 5-for-1 stock split.

(c) A dividend is declared January 5, 2008, and paid January 25, 2008, in bonds held as an investment. The bonds have a book value of $100,000 and a fair market value of $135,000.

E13-16 **(Computation of Retained Earnings)** The following information has been taken from the ledger accounts of Isaac Stern Corporation.

Total income since incorporation	$317,000
Total cash dividends paid	60,000
Total value of stock dividends distributed	30,000
Gains on treasury stock transactions	18,000
Unamortized discount on bonds payable	32,000

Instructions

Determine the current balance of retained earnings.

E13-17 **(Stockholders' Equity Section)** Bruno Corporation's post-closing trial balance at December 31, 2008, was as follows.

Bruno Corporation
Post-Closing Trial Balance
December 31, 2008

	Dr.	Cr.
Accounts payable		$ 310,000
Accounts receivable	$ 480,000	
Accumulated depreciation—building and equipment		185,000
Additional paid-in capital—common		
In excess of par value		1,300,000
From sale of treasury stock		160,000
Allowance for doubtful accounts		30,000
Bonds payable		300,000
Building and equipment	1,450,000	
Cash	190,000	
Common stock ($1 par value)		200,000
Dividends payable on preferred stock—cash		4,000
Inventories	560,000	
Land	400,000	
Preferred stock ($50 par value)		500,000
Prepaid expenses	40,000	
Retained earnings		301,000
Treasury stock—common at cost	170,000	
Totals	$3,290,000	$3,290,000

At December 31, 2008, Bruno had the following number of common and preferred shares.

	Common	Preferred
Authorized	600,000	60,000
Issued	200,000	10,000
Outstanding	190,000	10,000

The dividends on preferred stock are $4 cumulative. In addition, the preferred stock has a preference in liquidation of $50 per share.

Instructions

Prepare the stockholders' equity section of Bruno's balance sheet at December 31, 2008.

(AICPA adapted)

(LO 4, 7, 8)

E13-18 **(Dividends and Stockholders' Equity Section)** Anne Cleves Company reported the following amounts in the stockholders' equity section of its December 31, 2007, balance sheet.

Preferred stock, 10%, $100 par (10,000 shares authorized, 2,000 shares issued)	$200,000
Common stock, $5 par (100,000 shares authorized, 20,000 shares issued)	100,000
Additional paid-in capital	125,000
Retained earnings	450,000
Total	$875,000

During 2008, Cleves took part in the following transactions concerning stockholders' equity.

1. Paid the annual 2007 $10 per share dividend on preferred stock and a $2 per share dividend on common stock. These dividends had been declared on December 31, 2007.

2. Purchased 1,700 shares of its own outstanding common stock for $40 per share. Cleves uses the cost method.

3. Reissued 700 treasury shares for land valued at $30,000.

4. Issued 500 shares of preferred stock at $105 per share.

5. Declared a 10% stock dividend on the outstanding common stock when the stock is selling for $45 per share.

6. Issued the stock dividend.

7. Declared the annual 2008 $10 per share dividend on preferred stock and the $2 per share dividend on common stock. These dividends are payable in 2009.

Instructions

(a) Prepare journal entries to record the transactions described above.

(b) Prepare the December 31, 2008, stockholders' equity section. Assume 2008 net income was $330,000.

(LO 9)

E13-19 **(Comparison of Alternative Forms of Financing)** Shown below is the liabilities and stockholders' equity section of the balance sheet for Jana Kingston Company and Mary Ann Benson Company. Each has assets totaling $4,200,000.

Jana Kingston Co.		Mary Ann Benson Co.	
Current liabilities	$ 300,000	Current liabilities	$ 600,000
Long-term debt, 10%	1,200,000	Common stock ($20 par)	2,900,000
Common stock ($20 par)	2,000,000	Retained earnings (Cash	
Retained earnings (Cash		dividends, $328,000)	700,000
dividends, $220,000)	700,000		
	$4,200,000		$4,200,000

For the year each company has earned the same income before interest and taxes.

	Jana Kingston Co.	Mary Ann Benson Co.
Income before interest and taxes	$1,200,000	$1,200,000
Interest expense	120,000	–0–
	1,080,000	1,200,000
Income taxes (45%)	486,000	540,000
Net income	$ 594,000	$ 660,000

At year end, the market price of Kingston's stock was $101 per share, and Benson's was $63.50.

Instructions

(a) Which company is more profitable in terms of return on total assets?

(b) Which company is more profitable in terms of return on common stock equity?

(c) Which company has the greater net income per share of stock? Neither company issued or reacquired shares during the year.

(d) From the point of view of net income, is it advantageous to the stockholders of Jana Kingston Co. to have the long-term debt outstanding? Why?

(e) What is the book value per share for each company?

E13-20 (Trading on the Equity Analysis) Presented below is information from the annual report of Emporia Plastics, Inc.

(LO 9)

Operating income	$ 532,150
Bond interest expense	135,000
	397,150
Income taxes	183,432
Net income	$ 213,718
Bonds payable	$1,000,000
Common stock	875,000
Retained earnings	375,000

Instructions

(a) Compute the return on common stock equity and the rate of interest paid on bonds. (Assume balances for debt and equity accounts approximate averages for the year.)

(b) Is Emporia Plastics, Inc. trading on the equity successfully? Explain.

*E13-21 (Issuance of Bonds with Detachable Warrants) On September 1, 2008, Sands Company sold at 104 (plus accrued interest) 4,000 of its 9%, 10-year, $1,000 face value, nonconvertible bonds with detachable stock warrants. Each bond carried two detachable warrants; each warrant was for one share of common stock at a specified option price of $15 per share. Shortly after issuance, the warrants were quoted on the market for $3 each. No market value can be determined for the bonds above. Interest is payable on December 1 and June 1. Bond issue costs of $30,000 were incurred.

(LO 10)

Instructions

Prepare in general journal format the entry to record the issuance of the bonds.

(AICPA adapted)

*E13-22 (Issuance of Bonds with Stock Warrants) On May 1, 2008, Friendly Company issued 2,000 $1,000 bonds at 102. Each bond was issued with one detachable stock warrant. Shortly after issuance, the bonds were selling at 98, but the market value of the warrants cannot be determined.

(LO 10)

Instructions

(a) Prepare the entry to record the issuance of the bonds and warrants.

(b) Assume the same facts as part (a), except that the warrants had a fair value of $30. Prepare the entry to record the issuance of the bonds and warrants.

*E13-23 (Issuance and Conversion of Bonds) For each of the unrelated transactions described below, present the entry(ies) required to record each transaction.

1. Grand Corp. issued $20,000,000 par value 10% convertible bonds at 99. If the bonds had not been convertible, the company's investment banker estimates they would have been sold at 95. Expenses of issuing the bonds were $70,000.

2. Hoosier Company issued $20,000,000 par value 10% bonds at 98. One detachable stock purchase warrant was issued with each $100 par value bond. At the time of issuance, the warrants were selling for $4.

3. On July 1, 2008, Trady Company called its 11% convertible debentures for conversion. The $10,000,000 par value bonds were converted into 1,000,000 shares of $1 par value common stock. On July 1, there was $55,000 of unamortized discount applicable to the bonds, and the company paid an additional $75,000 to the bondholders to induce conversion of all the bonds. The company records the conversion using the book value method.

*E13-24 **(Conversion of Bonds)** Vargo Company has bonds payable outstanding in the amount of $500,000, and the Premium on Bonds Payable account has a balance of $7,500. Each $1,000 bond is convertible into 20 shares of preferred stock of par value of $50 per share. All bonds are converted into preferred stock.

Instructions

Using the book value method, what entry would be made?

See the book's companion website, at www.wiley.com/college/warfield, for Additional Exercises.

Problems

(LO 3, 4, 9)

P13-1 **(Equity Transactions and Statement Preparation)** On January 5, 2008, Drabek Corporation received a charter granting the right to issue 5,000 shares of $100 par value, 8% cumulative and nonparticipating preferred stock, and 50,000 shares of $5 par value common stock. It then completed these transactions.

Jan. 11 Issued 20,000 shares of common stock at $16 per share.
Feb. 1 Issued to Robb Nen Corp. 4,000 shares of preferred stock for the following assets: machinery with a fair market value of $50,000; a factory building with a fair market value of $110,000; and land with an appraised value of $270,000.
July 29 Purchased 1,800 shares of common stock at $19 per share. (Use cost method.)
Aug. 10 Sold the 1,800 treasury shares at $14 per share.
Dec. 31 Declared a $0.25 per share cash dividend on the common stock and declared the preferred dividend.
Dec. 31 Closed the Income Summary account. There was a $175,700 net income.

Instructions

(a) Record the journal entries for the transactions listed above.
(b) Prepare the stockholders' equity section of Drabek Corporation's balance sheet as of December 31, 2008.

(LO 4, 9)

P13-2 **(Treasury Stock Transactions and Presentation)** Andruw Jones Company had the following stockholders' equity as of January 1, 2008.

Common stock, $5 par value, 20,000 shares issued	$100,000
Paid-in capital in excess of par	300,000
Retained earnings	320,000
Total stockholders' equity	$720,000

During 2008, the following transactions occurred.

Feb. 1 Jones repurchased 2,000 shares of treasury stock at a price of $18 per share.
Mar. 1 800 shares of treasury stock repurchased above were reissued at $17 per share.
Mar. 18 500 shares of treasury stock repurchased above were reissued at $14 per share.
Apr. 22 600 shares of treasury stock repurchased above were reissued at $20 per share.

Instructions

(a) Prepare the journal entries to record the treasury stock transactions in 2008, assuming Jones uses the cost method.
(b) Prepare the stockholders' equity section as of April 30, 2008. Net income for the first 4 months of 2008 was $110,000.

(LO 3, 4, 7, 8)

P13-3 **(Equity Transactions and Statement Preparation)** Amado Company has two classes of capital stock outstanding: 8%, $20 par preferred and $5 par common. At December 31, 2007, the accounts shown on page 721 were included in stockholders' equity.

Preferred Stock, 150,000 shares	$ 3,000,000
Common Stock, 2,000,000 shares	10,000,000
Paid-in Capital in Excess of Par—Preferred	200,000
Paid-in Capital in Excess of Par—Common	27,000,000
Retained Earnings	4,500,000

The following transactions affected stockholders' equity during 2008.

Jan.	1	25,000 shares of preferred stock issued at $22 per share.
Feb.	1	40,000 shares of common stock issued at $20 per share.
June	1	2-for-1 stock split (par value reduced to $2.50).
July	1	30,000 shares of common treasury stock purchased at $9 per share. Amado uses the cost method.
Sept.	15	10,000 shares of treasury stock reissued at $11 per share.
Dec.	31	The preferred dividend is declared, and a common dividend of 50¢ per share is declared.
Dec.	31	Net income is $2,100,000.

Instructions

Prepare the stockholders' equity section for Amado Company at December 31, 2008. Show all supporting computations.

P13-4 **(Stock Transactions—Lump Sum)** Matsui Corporation's charter authorized issuance of 100,000 shares of $10 par value common stock and 50,000 shares of $50 preferred stock. The following transactions involving the issuance of shares of stock were completed. Each transaction is independent of the others. **(LO 3, 5)**

1. Issued a $10,000, 9% bond payable at par and gave as a bonus one share of preferred stock, which at that time was selling for $106 a share.
2. Issued 500 shares of common stock for machinery. The machinery had been appraised at $7,100; the seller's book value was $6,200. The most recent market price of the common stock is $15 a share.
3. Issued 375 shares of common stock and 100 shares of preferred stock for a lump sum amounting to $11,300. The common stock had been selling at $14 and the preferred stock at $65.
4. Issued 200 shares of common stock and 50 shares of preferred stock for furniture and fixtures. The common stock had a fair market value of $16 per share; the furniture and fixtures have a fair value of $6,200.

Instructions

Record the transactions listed above in journal entry form.

P13-5 **(Treasury Stock—Cost Method)** Before Polska Corporation engages in the treasury stock transactions listed below, its general ledger reflects, among others, the following account balances (par value of its stock is $30 per share). **(LO 4)**

Paid-in Capital in Excess of Par	Common Stock	Retained Earnings
$99,000	$270,000	$80,000

Instructions

Record the treasury stock transactions (given below) under the cost method of handling treasury stock; use the FIFO method for purchase-sale purposes.

(a) Bought 380 shares of treasury stock at $39 per share.
(b) Bought 300 shares of treasury stock at $43 per share.
(c) Sold 350 shares of treasury stock at $42 per share.
(d) Sold 120 shares of treasury stock at $38 per share.

P13-6 **(Treasury Stock—Cost Method—Equity Section Preparation)** Constantine Company has the following stockholders' equity accounts at December 31, 2007. **(LO 4, 7, 9)**

Common Stock—$100 par value, authorized 8,000 shares	$480,000
Retained Earnings	294,000

Instructions

(a) Prepare entries in journal form to record the following transactions, which took place during 2008.

(1) 240 shares of outstanding stock were purchased at $97 per share. (These are to be accounted for using the cost method.)

(2) A $20 per share cash dividend was declared.

    (3) The dividend declared in No. 2 was paid.

    (4) The treasury shares purchased in No. 1 were resold at $102 per share.

    (5) 500 shares of outstanding stock were purchased at $103 per share.

    (6) 330 of the shares purchased in No. 5 were resold at $96 per share.

(b) Prepare the stockholders' equity section of Constantine Company's balance sheet after giving effect to these transactions, assuming that the net income for 2008 was $94,000. State law requires restriction of retained earnings for the amount of treasury stock.

(LO 4, 7)   **P13-7**   **(Cash Dividend Entries)**   The books of John Dos Passos Corporation carried the following account balances as of December 31, 2007.

Cash	$ 195,000
Preferred stock, 6% cumulative, nonparticipating, $50 par	200,000
Common stock, no par value, 300,000 shares issued	1,500,000
Paid-in capital in excess of par (preferred)	150,000
Treasury stock (common 4,200 shares at cost)	33,600
Retained earnings	105,000

The company decided not to pay any dividends in 2007.

    The board of directors, at their annual meeting on December 21, 2008, declared the following: "The current year dividends shall be 6% on the preferred and $.30 per share on the common. The dividends in arrears shall be paid by issuing 1,500 shares of treasury stock." At the date of declaration, the preferred is selling at $80 per share, and the common at $8 per share. Net income for 2008 is estimated at $77,000.

Instructions

(a) Prepare the journal entries required for the dividend declaration and payment, assuming that they occur simultaneously.

(b) Could John Dos Passos Corporation give the preferred stockholders 2 years' dividends and common stockholders a 30 cents per share dividend, all in cash?

(LO 7, 8)   **P13-8**   **(Dividends and Splits)**   Gutsy Company provides you with the following condensed balance sheet information.

Assets		Liabilities and Stockholders' Equity		
Current assets	$ 40,000	Current and long-term liabilities		$100,000
Investments in ABC stock		Stockholders' equity		
(10,000 shares at cost)	60,000	Common stock ($2 par)	$ 20,000	
Equipment (net)	250,000	Paid-in capital in excess of par	110,000	
Intangibles	60,000	Retained earnings	180,000	310,000
Total assets	$410,000	Total liabilities and		
		stockholders' equity		$410,000

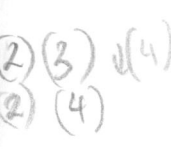

Instructions

For each transaction below, indicate the dollar impact (if any) on the following five items: (1) total assets, (2) common stock, (3) paid-in capital in excess of par, (4) retained earnings, and (5) stockholders' equity. (Each situation is independent.)

(a) Gutsy declares and pays a $0.50 per share cash dividend.

(b) Gutsy declares and issues a 10% stock dividend when the market price of the stock is $14 per share.

(c) Gutsy declares and issues a 40% stock dividend when the market price of the stock is $15 per share.

(d) Gutsy declares and distributes a property dividend. Gutsy gives one share of ABC stock for every two shares of Gutsy Company stock held. ABC is selling for $10 per share on the date the property dividend is declared.

(e) Gutsy declares a 2-for-1 stock split and issues new shares.

(LO 3, 4, 7, 9)   **P13-9**   **(Stockholders' Equity Section of Balance Sheet)**   The following is a summary of all relevant transactions of Jackson Day Corporation since it was organized in 2008.

    In 2008, 15,000 shares were authorized and 7,000 shares of common stock ($50 par value) were issued at a price of $57. In 2009, 1,000 shares were issued as a stock dividend when the stock was selling for $62. Three hundred shares of common stock were bought in 2010 at a cost of $66 per share. These 300 shares are still in the company treasury.

In 2009, 10,000 preferred shares were authorized and the company issued 4,000 of them ($100 par value) at $113. Some of the preferred stock was reacquired by the company and later reissued for $4,700 more than it cost the company.

The corporation has earned a total of $610,000 in net income after income taxes and paid out a total of $312,600 in cash dividends since incorporation.

Instructions

Prepare the stockholders' equity section of the balance sheet in proper form for Jackson Day Corporation as of December 31, 2010. Account for treasury stock using the cost method.

P13-10 **(Stock Dividends and Stock Split)** Jenny Dill Inc.'s $10 par common stock is selling for $120 per share. Five million shares are currently issued and outstanding. The board of directors wishes to stimulate interest in Jenny Dill common stock before a forthcoming stock issue but does not wish to distribute capital at this time. The board also believes that too many adjustments to the stockholders' equity section, especially retained earnings, might discourage potential investors. **(LO 8)**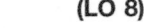

The board has considered three options for stimulating interest in the stock:

1. A 20% stock dividend. _Small_

2. A 100% stock dividend.

3. A 2-for-1 stock split.

Instructions

Acting as financial advisor to the board, you have been asked to report briefly on each option and, considering the board's wishes, make a recommendation. Discuss the effects of each of the foregoing options.

P13-11 **(Stock and Cash Dividends)** Gul Ducat Corporation has outstanding 2,000,000 shares of common stock of a par value of $10 each. The balance in Retained Earnings at January 1, 2008, was $24,000,000, and it then had additional paid-in capital of $5,000,000. During 2008, the company's net income was $5,700,000. A cash dividend of $0.60 a share was paid June 30, 2008, and a 6% stock dividend was declared on November 30, 2008, and distributed to stockholders of record at the close of business on December 31, 2008. You have been asked to advise on the proper accounting treatment of the stock dividend. **(LO 7, 8)**

The existing stock of the company is actively traded on a national stock exchange. The market price of the stock has been as follows.

October 31, 2008	$31
November 30, 2008	$35
December 31, 2008	$38

Instructions

(a) Prepare the journal entry to record the cash dividend.
(b) Prepare the journal entry to record the stock dividend.
(c) Prepare the stockholders' equity section (including schedules of retained earnings and additional paid-in capital) of the balance sheet of Gul Ducat Corporation for the year 2008 on the basis of the foregoing information. Draft a note to the financial statements setting forth the basis of the accounting for the stock dividend, and add separately appropriate comments or explanations regarding the basis chosen.

P13-12 **(Analysis and Classification of Equity Transactions)** Ohio Company was formed on July 1, 2005. It was authorized to issue 300,000 shares of $10 par value common stock and 100,000 shares of 8% $25 par value, cumulative and nonparticipating preferred stock. Ohio Company has a July 1–June 30 fiscal year. **(LO 3, 4, 7, 8, 9)**

The following information relates to the stockholders' equity accounts of Ohio Company.

Common Stock

Prior to the 2007–2008 fiscal year, Ohio Company had 110,000 shares of outstanding common stock issued as follows.

1. 95,000 shares were issued for cash on July 1, 2005, at $31 per share.

2. On July 24, 2005, 5,000 shares were exchanged for a plot of land which cost the seller $70,000 in 1999 and had an estimated market value of $220,000 on July 24, 2005.

3. 10,000 shares were issued on March 1, 2006, for $42 per share.

During the 2007–2008 fiscal year, the following transactions regarding common stock took place.

November 30, 2007	Ohio purchased 2,000 shares of its own stock on the open market at $39 per share. Ohio uses the cost method for treasury stock.

| December 15, 2007 | Ohio declared a 5% stock dividend for stockholders of record on January 15, 2008, to be issued on January 31, 2008. Ohio was having a liquidity problem and could not afford a cash dividend at the time. Ohio's common stock was selling at $52 per share on December 15, 2007. |
| June 20, 2008 | Ohio sold 500 shares of its own common stock that it had purchased on November 30, 2007, for $21,000. |

Preferred Stock

Ohio issued 50,000 shares of preferred stock at $44 per share on July 1, 2006.

Cash Dividends

Ohio has followed a schedule of declaring cash dividends in December and June, with payment being made to stockholders of record in the following month. The cash dividends which have been declared since inception of the company through June 30, 2008, are shown below.

Declaration Date	Common Stock	Preferred Stock
12/15/06	$0.30 per share	$1.00 per share
6/15/07	$0.30 per share	$1.00 per share
12/15/07	—	$1.00 per share

No cash dividends were declared during June 2008 due to the company's liquidity problems.

Retained Earnings

As of June 30, 2007, Ohio's retained earnings account had a balance of $690,000. For the fiscal year ending June 30, 2008, Ohio reported net income of $40,000.

Instructions

Prepare the stockholders' equity section of the balance sheet, including appropriate notes, for Ohio Company as of June 30, 2008, as it should appear in its annual report to the shareholders.

(CMA adapted)

(LO 10)

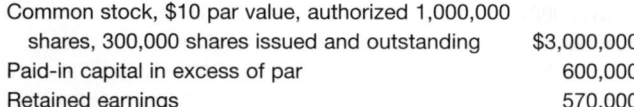

*P13-13 **(Entries for Various Dilutive Securities)** The stockholders' equity section of McLean Inc. at the beginning of the current year appears below.

Common stock, $10 par value, authorized 1,000,000 shares, 300,000 shares issued and outstanding	$3,000,000
Paid-in capital in excess of par	600,000
Retained earnings	570,000

During the current year the following transactions occurred.

1. The company sold to the public a $200,000, 10% bond issue at 102. The company also issued with each $100 bond one detachable stock purchase warrant, which provided for the purchase of common stock at $30 per share. Shortly after issuance, similar bonds without warrants were selling at 96 and the warrants at $8.

2. At the end of the year, 80% of the warrants in (1) had been exercised, and the remaining were outstanding and in good standing.

Instructions

(a) Prepare general journal entries for the current year to record the transactions listed above.

(b) Prepare the stockholders' equity section of the balance sheet at the end of the current year. Assume that retained earnings at the end of the current year is $750,000.

(LO 10)

*P13-14 **(Entries for Conversion, Amortization, and Interest of Bonds)** Counter Inc. issued $1,500,000 of convertible 10-year bonds on July 1, 2008. The bonds provide for 12% interest payable semiannually on January 1 and July 1. The discount in connection with the issue was $34,000, which is being amortized monthly on a straight-line basis.

The bonds are convertible after one year into 8 shares of Counter Inc.'s $100 par value common stock for each $1,000 of bonds.

On August 1, 2009, $150,000 of bonds were turned in for conversion into common. Interest has been accrued monthly and paid as due. At the time of conversion any accrued interest on bonds being converted is paid in cash. Unamortized discount on the converted bonds is $3,032.

Instructions

Prepare the journal entries to record the conversion, amortization, and interest in connection with the bonds as of the following dates.

(a) July 1, 2008.
(b) August 1, 2009. (Assume the book value method is used.)

(AICPA adapted)

ACCOUNTING IN ACTION

Financial Reporting and Analysis

■ Financial Reporting Issues: The Procter & Gamble Company

AIA13-1 The financial statements of **Procter & Gamble (P&G)** can be accessed at the book's website.

Instructions

Refer to P&G's financial statements and the accompanying notes to answer the following questions.

(a) What is the par or stated value of P&G's preferred stock?
(b) What is the par or stated value of P&G's common stock?
(c) What percentage of P&G's authorized common stock was issued at June 30, 2006?
(d) How many shares of common stock were outstanding at June 30, 2006, and June 30, 2005?
(e) What was the dollar amount effect of the cash dividends on P&G's stockholders' equity for 2006?
(f) What is P&G's rate of return on common stock equity for 2006 and 2005?
(g) What is P&G's payout ratio for 2006 and 2005?
(h) What was the market price range (high/low) of P&G's common stock during the quarter ended June 30, 2006?

■ Comparative Analysis: The Coca-Cola Company and PepsiCo, Inc.

AIA13-2 The financial statements of **The Coca-Cola Company** and **PepsiCo, Inc.** can be accessed at the book's website.

Instructions

Use information found at the book's website to answer the following questions.

(a) What is the par or stated value of Coca-Cola's and PepsiCo's common or capital stock?
(b) What percentage of authorized shares was issued by Coca-Cola at December 31, 2006, and by PepsiCo at December 30, 2006?
(c) How many shares are held as treasury stock by Coca-Cola at December 31, 2006, and by PepsiCo at December 30, 2006?
(d) How many Coca-Cola common shares are outstanding at December 31, 2006? How many PepsiCo shares of capital stock are outstanding at December 30, 2006?
(e) What were the dollar amount effects of the cash dividends on each company's stockholders' equity in 2006?
(f) What are Coca-Cola's and PepsiCo's rate of return on common/capital stock equity for 2006 and 2005? Which company gets the higher return on the equity of its shareholders?
(g) What are Coca-Cola's and PepsiCo's payout ratios for 2006?
(h) What was the market price range (high/low) for Coca-Cola's common stock and PepsiCo's capital stock during the fourth quarter of 2006? Which company's (Coca-Cola's or PepsiCo's) stock price increased more (%) during 2006?

■ Financial Statement Analysis

AIA13-3 **Kellogg Corporation** is the world's leading producer of ready-to-eat cereal products. In recent years the company has taken numerous steps aimed at improving its profitability and earnings per share. Following are some basic facts for Kellogg Corporation.

Kellogg Corporation

(all dollars in millions)

	Current Year	Prior Year
Net sales	$9,614	$8,812
Net earnings	891	787
Total assets	10,790	10,143
Total liabilities	8,533	8,699
Common stock, $0.25 par value	104	104
Capital in excess of par value		25
Retained earnings	2,701	2,248
Treasury stock, at cost	108	204
Number of shares outstanding (in millions)	413	410

Instructions

(a) What are some of the reasons that management purchases its own stock?

(b) Explain how earnings per share might be affected by treasury stock transactions.

(c) Calculate the ratio of debt to total assets for the current and prior year, and discuss the implications of the change.

AIA13-4 The following note related to stockholders' equity was reported in **Wiebold, Inc.**'s annual report.

On February 1, the Board of Directors declared a 3-for-2 stock split, distributed on February 22 to shareholders of record on February 10. Accordingly, all numbers of common shares, except unissued shares and treasury shares, and all per share data have been restated to reflect this stock split.

On the basis of amounts declared and paid, the annualized quarterly dividends per share were $0.80 in the current year and $0.75 in the prior year.

Instructions

(a) What is the significance of the date of record and the date of distribution?

(b) Why might Weibold have declared a 3-for-2 for stock split?

(c) What impact does Wiebold's stock split have on (1) total stockholders' equity, (2) total par value, (3) outstanding shares, and (4) book value per share?

Concepts for Analysis

AIA13-5 (**Preemptive Rights and Dilution of Ownership**) Alvarado Computer Company is a small, closely held corporation. Eighty percent of the stock is held by Eduardo Alvarado, president. Of the remainder, 10% is held by members of his family and 10% by Shaunda Jones, a former officer who is now retired. The balance sheet of the company at June 30, 2008, was substantially as shown below.

Assets		Liabilities and Stockholders' Equity	
Cash	$ 22,000	Current liabilities	$ 50,000
Other	450,000	Capital stock	250,000
	$472,000	Retained earnings	172,000
			$472,000

Additional authorized capital stock of $300,000 par value had never been issued. To strengthen the cash position of the company, Eduardo Alvarado issued capital stock with a par value of $100,000 to himself at par for cash. At the next stockholders' meeting, Jones objected and claimed that her interests had been injured.

Instructions

(a) Which stockholders' right was ignored in the issue of shares to Eduardo Alvarado?

(b) How may the damage to Jones's interests be repaired most simply?

(c) If Eduardo Alvarado offered Jones a personal cash settlement and they agreed to employ you as an impartial arbitrator to determine the amount, what settlement would you propose? Present your calculations with sufficient explanation to satisfy both parties.

AIA13-6 **(Issuance of Stock for Land)** Crosby Corporation is planning to issue 3,000 shares of its own $10 par value common stock for two acres of land to be used as a building site.

Instructions

(a) What general rule should be applied to determine the amount at which the land should be recorded?
(b) Under what circumstances should this transaction be recorded at the fair market value of the land?
(c) Under what circumstances should this transaction be recorded at the fair market value of the stock issued?
(d) Assume Crosby intentionally records this transaction at an amount greater than the fair market value of the land and the stock. Discuss this situation.

AIA13-7 **(Conceptual Issues—Equity)** Statements of Financial Accounting Concepts set forth financial ac-  counting and reporting objectives and fundamentals that will be used by the Financial Accounting Standards Board in developing standards. *Concepts Statement No. 6* defines various elements of financial statements.

Instructions

Answer the following questions based on *SFAC No. 6*.

(a) Define and discuss the term "equity."
(b) What transactions or events change owners' equity?
(c) Define "investments by owners" and provide examples of this type of transaction. What financial statement element other than equity is typically affected by owner investments?
(d) Define "distributions to owners" and provide examples of this type of transaction. What financial statement element other than equity is typically affected by distributions?
(e) What are examples of changes within owners' equity that do not change the total amount of owners' equity?

AIA13-8 **(Stock Dividends and Splits)** The directors of Amman Corporation are considering the issuance of a stock dividend. They have asked you to discuss the proposed action by answering the following questions.

Instructions

(a) What is a stock dividend? How is a stock dividend distinguished from a stock split (1) from a legal standpoint, and (2) from an accounting standpoint?
(b) For what reasons does a corporation usually declare a stock dividend? A stock split?
(c) Discuss the amount, if any, of retained earnings to be capitalized in connection with a stock dividend.

(AICPA adapted)

AIA13-9 **(Stock Dividends)** Kitakyushu Inc., a client, is considering the authorization of a 10% common stock dividend to common stockholders. The financial vice president of Kitakyushu wishes to discuss the accounting implications of such an authorization with you before the next meeting of the board of directors.

Instructions

(a) The first topic the vice president wishes to discuss is the nature of the stock dividend to the recipient. Discuss the case against considering the stock dividend as income to the recipient.
(b) The other topic for discussion is the propriety of issuing the stock dividend to all "stockholders of record" or to "stockholders of record exclusive of shares held in the name of the corporation as treasury stock." Discuss the case against issuing stock dividends on treasury shares.

(AICPA adapted)

AIA13-10 **(Stock Dividend, Cash Dividend, and Treasury Stock)** AROD Company has 30,000 shares of $10 par value common stock authorized and 20,000 shares issued and outstanding. On August 15, 2008, AROD purchased 1,000 shares of treasury stock for $16 per share. AROD uses the cost method to account for treasury stock. On September 14, 2008, AROD sold 500 shares of the treasury stock for $20 per share.

In October 2008, AROD declared and distributed 1,950 shares as a stock dividend from unissued shares when the market value of the common stock was $21 per share.

On December 20, 2008, AROD declared a $1 per share cash dividend, payable on January 10, 2009, to shareholders of record on December 31, 2008.

Instructions

(a) How should AROD account for the purchase and sale of the treasury stock, and how should the treasury stock be presented in the balance sheet at December 31, 2008?
(b) How should AROD account for the stock dividend, and how would it affect the stockholders' equity at December 31, 2008? Why?

(c) How should AROD account for the cash dividend, and how would it affect the balance sheet at December 31, 2008? Why?

(AICPA adapted)

Professional Tools

■ Ethical Decision Making

AIA13-11 (Treasury Stock) Jean Loptien, president of Sycamore Corporation, is concerned about several large stockholders who have been very vocal lately in their criticisms of her leadership. She thinks they might mount a campaign to have her removed as the corporation's CEO. She decides that buying them out by purchasing their shares could eliminate them as opponents, and she is confident they would accept a "good" offer. Loptien knows the corporation's cash position is decent, so it has the cash to complete the transaction. She also knows the purchase of these shares will increase earnings per share, which should make other investors quite happy. (Earnings per share is calculated by dividing net income available for the common shareholders by the weighted-average number of shares outstanding. Therefore, if the number of shares outstanding is decreased by purchasing treasury shares, earnings per share increases.)

Instructions

Answer the following questions.

(a) Who are the stakeholders in this situation?
(b) What are the ethical issues involved?
(c) Should Loptien authorize the transaction?

■ Financial Accounting Research (FARS)

AIA13-12 Recall from Chapter 12 that Hincapie Co. (a specialty bike-accessory manufacturer) is expecting growth in sales of some products targeted to the low-price market. Hincapie is contemplating a preferred stock issue to help finance this expansion in operations. The company is leaning toward participating preferred stock because ownership will not be diluted, but the investors will get an extra dividend if the company does well. The company management wants to be certain that its reporting of this transaction is transparent to its current shareholders and wants you to research the disclosure requirements related to its captial structure.

Instructions

Using the **Financial Accounting Research System (FARS)** database, respond to the following items. (Provide text strings used in your search.)

(a) Identity the FASB standard that addresses disclosure of information about capital structure.
(b) Find definitions for the following:
   (1) Securities
   (2) Participation rights.
   (3) Preferred stock.
(c) What information about securities must be disclosed? Discuss how the proposed Hincapie preferred stock issue will be reported.

■ Professional Simulation

AIA13-13 Go to the book's companion website, at **www.wiley.com/college/warfield**, to find an interactive problem that simulates the computerized CPA exam. The professional simulation for this chapter asks you to address questions related to the accounting for stockholders' equity.

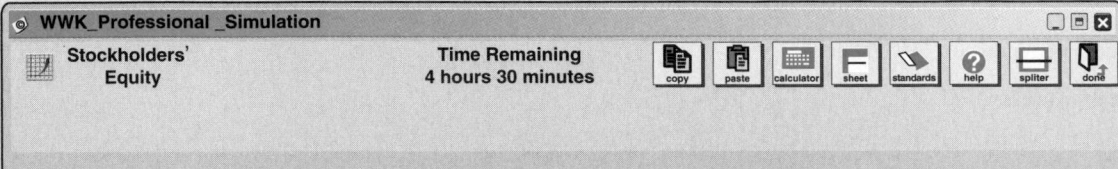

What do the numbers mean?

Classy Stock, p. 674

Q: Assume that you are considering investing in the bonds of a company like Molex. Should you be concerned that the company has a two-class share structure? Explain.

A: Generally, a bond investor should not be concerned about a two-class structure. As we learned in Chapter 12, bond in- vestors, through the bond indenture agreement, are insured receipt of interest and principal payments before any class of shareholders are paid. Because bond investors do not have voting rights, they should not be concerned with differential voting rights among different classes of equity investors.

The Case of the Disappearing Receivable, p. 678

Q: As we have learned, companies allowably record re- ceivables and increases in equity when they make sales on credit. (Recall our revenue recognition discussion in Chap- ter 7.) Describe the differences in the facts and circumstances for credit sales that support recognition of the receivable in the sales context but not for stock issued on credit.

A: As alluded to in the story, the key difference is the high risk of collection of the receivable associated with the stock issue. Recall that companies can recognize credit sales and the associated accounts receivable only when they can reli- ably estimate the accounts that will not be repaid (usually based on past experience). Using this approach, sales rev- enue is offset with bad debt expense. Apparently, there is no similar reliable basis to estimate the collectibilty of stock is- sue receivables.

Signals to Buy?, p. 681

Q: Assume you are an investor in a company that has of- fered to buy back your shares. What factors would you consider is deciding whether to tender (sell) your shares?

A: In addition to the factors mentioned in the story (how the repurchased shares will be used and possible EPS man- agement objectives), you might also investigate whether the company's risk has changed. For example, if the company has entered a phase of slowing growth such that it does not have a lot of good investment or other growth opportunities for which the cash used to repurchase your shares could be used, then you might consider selling. You could then use the proceeds to invest in other stocks with a growth and investment profile more similar to the prior investment.

Splitsville, p. 693

Q: Many people play the stock market through investments in mutual funds. Do you think these investors are influenced by the trading ranges of individual stocks? Explain.

A: The trading ranges of individual stocks should not be that important to mutual fund investors. This is because one of the benefits of the mutual fund is that an investor with a smaller amount to invest can achieve diversification objectives at lower cost without investing in a large number of individual stocks. One rule of thumb is that a random selection of 10 stocks for your portfolio will achieve significant diversification. If trading commissions are discounted for trades in at least 100 share lots and average share prices are $50 per share, a 10-stock portfolio would require an investment of $50,000 (10 stocks × 100 shares each × $50). You could achieve a similar level of diversi- fication by making smaller investments in several mutual funds. For example, many no-load funds (funds with no trading commissions) require an initial investment of just $2,500. So a fairly diversified portfolio of, say, five funds could be built with an investment of just $12,500. Fewer funds can be purchased because each mutual fund invests in numerous stocks.

Remember to check the book's companion website to find additional resources for this chapter.

CHAPTER 14

INVESTMENTS

Who's in Control Here?

The Coca-Cola Company (Coke) owns 36 percent of the shares of **Coca-Cola Enterprises** (a U.S. bottling business); **PepsiCo Inc.** owns 46 percent of **The Pepsi Bottling Group (PBG)** and 41 percent of **PepsiAmericas**. These bottling businesses are very important to Coca-Cola and PepsiCo, because they are the primary distributors of Coke and Pepsi products. In return, these companies depend on Coca-Cola and PepsiCo to provide significant marketing and distribution development support. Indeed, it can be said that Coca-Cola and PepsiCo control the bottling companies, who would not exist without their support.

However, because The Coca-Cola Company and PepsiCo own less than 50 percent of the shares in these companies, they do not prepare consolidated financial statements. Instead, Coca-Cola and PepsiCo account for these investments using the *equity method*. Under the equity method, for example, Coca-Cola reports a single income item for its profits from the bottlers, and only the net amount of its investment in the balance sheet.

Equity-method accounting gives Coca-Cola and PepsiCo pristine balance sheets and income statements, by separating the assets and liabilities and the profit margins of these bottlers from its beverage-making business. What's more, the International Accounting Standards Board (IASB) has issued *IAS No. 28* which requires that companies use the equity method. Previously, many international companies were permitted to use either the equity method or proportional consolidation for investments similar to Coke's and Pepsi's. It is good news that both U.S. and international companies are following the same rules. (On negative side, however, some of these companies should be consolidated but are not.)

A final point: In response to a recent FASB interpretation, companies are now starting to consolidate more 20 to 50 percent–owned investments. According to *Financial Accounting Standards Interpretation No. 46(R)*, consolidation of entities, such as the Coke and Pepsi bottlers, may be required if the risks and rewards of those investments accrue primarily to Coke and Pepsi. In fact, Coke has consolidated some of its bottling companies, which should result in the reporting of more complete information on these affiliated companies.

Preview of Chapter 14

As our opening story indicates, U.S. and international standard-setters are studying the measurement, recognition, and disclosure for certain investments. In this chapter we address the accounting for debt and equity investments. *The content and organization of the chapter are as follows.*

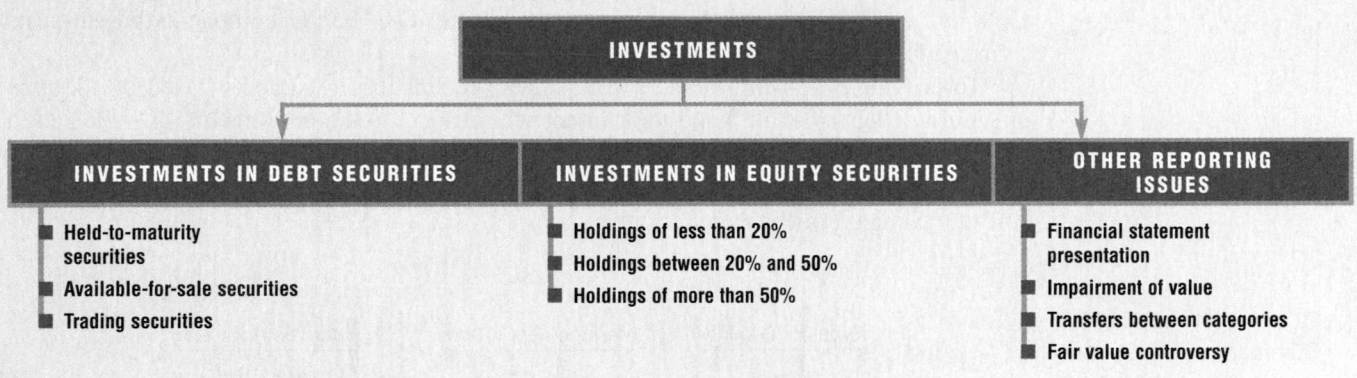

```
                              ┌─────────────────────┐
                              │     INVESTMENTS     │
                              └─────────────────────┘
```

INVESTMENTS IN DEBT SECURITIES	INVESTMENTS IN EQUITY SECURITIES	OTHER REPORTING ISSUES
■ Held-to-maturity securities ■ Available-for-sale securities ■ Trading securities	■ Holdings of less than 20% ■ Holdings between 20% and 50% ■ Holdings of more than 50%	■ Financial statement presentation ■ Impairment of value ■ Transfers between categories ■ Fair value controversy

Learning Objectives

After studying this chapter, you should be able to:

1. Identify the three categories of debt securities and describe the accounting and reporting treatment for each category.

2. Understand the procedures for discount and premium amortization on bond investments.

3. Identify the categories of equity securities and describe the accounting and reporting treatment for each category.

4. Explain the equity method of accounting and compare it to the fair value method for equity securities.

5. Describe the disclosure requirements for investments in debt and equity securities.

6. Discuss the accounting for impairments of debt and equity investments.

7. Describe the accounting for transfer of investment securities between categories.

Inside Chapter 14

- **What Do the Numbers Mean?**
  What is fair value? (p. 739)
  Consolidate this! (p. 749)
  More disclosure, please (p. 750)
  The irony of it all (p. 755)

- **What's the Principle?**
  (pp. 733, 734, 736, 748, 750, 755)

- **Accounting, Analysis, Principles** (p. 758)
  Account for investment securities.
  Analyze effect of investment securities on net income.
  Explain bases of measurement of investment securities.

- **Convergence Corner** (p. 760)

WHO'S IN CONTROL HERE?

Companies have different motivations for investing in securities issued by other companies.[1] **One motivation is to earn a high rate of return.** For example, companies like **Coca-Cola** and **PepsiCo** can receive interest revenue from a debt investment or dividend revenue from an equity investment. In addition, they can realize capital gains on both types of securities. **Another motivation for investing (in equity securities) is to secure certain operating or financing arrangements with another company.** As in the opening story, **Coca-Cola** and **PepsiCo** are able to exercise some control over bottler companies based on its significant (but not controlling) equity investments.

To provide useful information, companies account for investments based on the type of security (debt or equity) and their intent with respect to the investment. As indicated in Illustration 14-1, we organize our study of investments by type of security. Within each section, we explain how the accounting for investments in debt and equity securities varies according to management intent.

Illustration 14-1
Summary of Investment
Accounting Approaches

Types of Security	Management Intent	Valuation Approach
Debt (Section 1)	No plans to sell	Amortized cost
	Plan to sell	Fair value
Equity (Section 2)	Plan to sell	Fair value
	Exercise some control	Equity method

SECTION ONE INVESTMENTS IN DEBT SECURITIES

Debt securities represent a creditor relationship with another entity. Debt securities include U.S. government securities, municipal securities, corporate bonds, convertible debt, and commercial paper. Trade accounts receivable and loans receivable are not debt securities because they do not meet the definition of a security.

Companies group investments in debt securities into three separate categories for accounting and reporting purposes:

OBJECTIVE 1
Identify the three categories of debt securities and describe the accounting and reporting treatment for each category.

- **Held-to-maturity**: Debt securities that the company has the positive intent and ability to hold to maturity.

- **Trading**: Debt securities bought and held primarily for sale in the near term to generate income on short-term price differences.

- **Available-for-sale**: Debt securities not classified as held-to-maturity or trading securities.

[1]A **security** is a share, participation, or other interest in property or in an enterprise of the issuer or an obligation of the issuer that has the following three characteristics: (a) It either is represented by an instrument issued in bearer or registered form or, if not represented by an instrument, is registered in books maintained to record transfers by or on behalf of the issuer. (b) It is of a type commonly traded on securities exchanges or markets or, when represented by an instrument, is commonly recognized in any area in which it is issued or dealt in as a medium for investment. (c) It either is one of a class or series or by its terms is divisible into a class or series of shares, participations, interests, or obligations. From "Accounting for Certain Investments in Debt and Equity Securities," *Statement of Financial Accounting Standards No. 115* (Norwalk, Conn.: FASB, 1993), p. 48, par. 137.

Illustration 14-2 identifies these categories, along with the accounting and reporting treatments required for each.

Category	Valuation	Unrealized Holding Gains or Losses	Other Income Effects
Held-to-maturity	Amortized cost	Not recognized	Interest when earned; gains and losses from sale.
Trading securities	Fair value	Recognized in net income	Interest when earned; gains and losses from sale.
Available-for-sale	Fair value	Recognized as other comprehensive income and as separate component of stockholders' equity	Interest when earned; gains and losses from sale.

Illustration 14-2
Accounting for Debt Securities by Category

Amortized cost is the acquisition cost adjusted for the amortization of discount or premium, if appropriate. **Fair value** is the amount at which a company can exchange a financial instrument in a current transaction between willing parties, other than in a forced or liquidation sale.[2]

HELD-TO-MATURITY SECURITIES

Only debt securities can be classified as held-to-maturity. By definition, equity securities have no maturity date. A company like **Starbucks** should classify a debt security as **held-to-maturity** only if it has **both (1) the positive intent** and **(2) the ability to hold those securities to maturity**. It should not classify a debt security as held-to-maturity if it intends to hold the security for an indefinite period of time. Likewise, if Starbucks anticipates that a sale may be necessary due to changes in interest rates, foreign currency risk, liquidity needs, or other asset-liability management reasons, it should not classify the security as held-to-maturity.[3]

Companies account for held-to-maturity securities **at amortized cost**, not fair value. If management intends to hold certain investment securities to maturity and has no plans to sell them, fair values (selling prices) are not relevant for measuring and evaluating the cash flows associated with these securities. Finally, because companies do not adjust held-to-maturity securities to fair value, these securities do not increase the volatility of either reported earnings or reported capital as do trading securities and available-for-sale securities.

To illustrate the accounting for held-to-maturity debt securities, assume that Robinson Company purchased $100,000 of 8 percent bonds of Evermaster

OBJECTIVE 2
Understand the procedures for discount and premium amortization on bond investments.

WHAT'S THE PRINCIPLE?
Companies generally report debt securities at fair value not only because the information is relevant but also because it is reliable.

[2]Under *SFAS No. 159* ("The Fair Value Option for Financial Assets and Financial Liabilities, Including an amendment of FASB Statement No. 115," Norwalk, Conn.: FASB, 2007), companies may choose to use the fair value option for any held-to-maturity or available-for-sale security. If the fair value option is chosen, the securities selected are reported at fair value and the change in fair value is recognized in income. Companies may report some held-to-maturity or available-for-sale securities using the fair value option, while other securities in the same category are reported using the guidelines in Illustration 14-2. All trading securities are required to be reported at fair value, and changes in fair value are recognized in income.

[3]The FASB defines situations where, even though a company sells a security before maturity, it has constructively held the security to maturity, and thus does not violate the held-to-maturity requirement. These include selling a security close enough to maturity (such as three months) so that interest rate risk is no longer an important pricing factor.

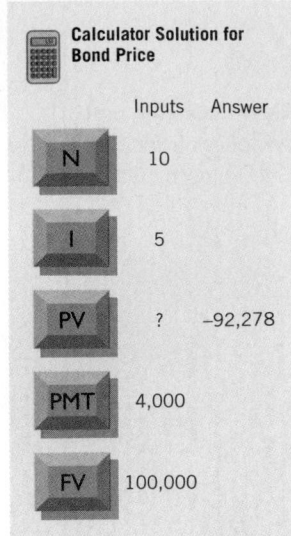

Calculator Solution for Bond Price

Inputs	Answer
N	10
I	5
PV	? −92,278
PMT	4,000
FV	100,000

Corporation on January 1, 2008, at a discount, paying $92,278. The bonds mature January 1, 2013; interest is payable each July 1 and January 1. Robinson records the investment as follows:

January 1, 2008

Held-to-Maturity Securities	92,278	
Cash		92,278

Robinson uses a Held-to-Maturity Securities account to indicate the type of debt security purchased.

As indicated in Chapter 12, companies must amortize premium or discount using the **effective-interest method** unless some other method—such as the straight-line method—yields a similar result. They apply the effective-interest method to bond investments in a way similar to that for bonds payable. To compute interest revenue, companies compute the effective-interest rate or yield at the time of investment and apply that rate to the beginning carrying amount (book value) for each interest period. The investment carrying amount is increased by the amortized discount or decreased by the amortized premium in each period.

Illustration 14-3 shows the effect of the discount amortization on the interest revenue that Robinson records each period for its investment in Evermaster bonds.

Illustration 14-3
Schedule of Interest
Revenue and Bond
Discount Amortization—
Effective-Interest Method

			8% Bonds Purchased to Yield 10%	
Date	Cash Received	Interest Revenue	Bond Discount Amortization	Carrying Amount of Bonds
1/1/08				$ 92,278
7/1/08	$ 4,000ᵃ	$ 4,614ᵇ	$ 614ᶜ	92,892ᵈ
1/1/09	4,000	4,645	645	93,537
7/1/09	4,000	4,677	677	94,214
1/1/10	4,000	4,711	711	94,925
7/1/10	4,000	4,746	746	95,671
1/1/11	4,000	4,783	783	96,454
7/1/11	4,000	4,823	823	97,277
1/1/12	4,000	4,864	864	98,141
7/1/12	4,000	4,907	907	99,048
1/1/13	4,000	4,952	952	100,000
	$40,000	$47,722	$7,722	

ᵃ$4,000 = $100,000 × .08 × ⁶⁄₁₂
ᵇ$4,614 = $92,278 × .10 × ⁶⁄₁₂
ᶜ$614 = $4,614 − $4,000
ᵈ$92,892 = $92,278 + $614

Robinson records the receipt of the first semiannual interest payment on July 1, 2008 (using the data in Illustration 14-3) as follows:

July 1, 2008

Cash	4,000	
Held-to-Maturity Securities	614	
Interest Revenue		4,614

WHAT'S THE PRINCIPLE?

The use of some simpler method that yields results similar to the effective-interest method is an application of the materiality concept.

Because Robinson is on a calendar-year basis, it accrues interest and amortizes the discount at December 31, 2008, as follows.

December 31, 2008

Interest Receivable	4,000	
Held-to-Maturity Securities	645	
Interest Revenue		4,645

Robinson reports its investment in Evermaster bonds in its December 31, 2008, financial statements, as follows.

Illustration 14-4
Reporting of
Held-to-Maturity
Securities

Balance Sheet	
Current assets	
Interest receivable	$ 4,000
Long-term investments	
Held-to-maturity securities, at amortized cost	$93,537
Income Statement	
Other revenues and gains	
Interest revenue	$ 9,259

Sometimes a company sells a held-to-maturity debt security so close to its maturity date that a change in the market interest rate would not significantly affect the security's fair value. Such a sale may be considered a sale at maturity and would not call into question the company's original intent to hold the investment to maturity. Let's assume, as an example, that Robinson Company sells its investment in Evermaster bonds on November 1, 2012, at 99¾ plus accrued interest. The discount amortization from July 1, 2012, to November 1, 2012, is $635 (⁴⁄₆ × $952). Robinson records this discount amortization as follows.

November 1, 2012

Held-to-Maturity Securities	635	
Interest Revenue		635

Illustration 14-5 shows the computation of the realized gain on the sale.

Illustration 14-5
Computation of Gain on
Sale of Bonds

Selling price of bonds (exclusive of accrued interest)		$99,750
Less: Book value of bonds on November 1, 2012:		
Amortized cost, July 1, 2012	$99,048	
Add: Discount amortized for the period July 1, 2012, to November 1, 2012	635	
		99,683
Gain on sale of bonds		$ 67

Robinson records the sale of the bonds as:

November 1, 2012

Cash	102,417	
Interest Revenue (4/6 × $4,000)		2,667
Held-to-Maturity Securities		99,683
Gain on Sale of Securities		67

The credit to Interest Revenue represents accrued interest for four months, for which the purchaser pays cash. The debit to Cash represents the selling price of the bonds plus accrued interest ($99,750 + $2,667). The credit to Held-to-Maturity Securities represents the book value of the bonds on the date of sale. The credit to Gain on Sale of Securities represents the excess of the selling price over the book value of the bonds.

> **Try it out!** Larry White Company purchases $1,750,000, 10-year, 12% bonds on January 1, 2008, at $1,820,000 to yield 10%. White will receive semiannual interest July 1 and January 1. White uses the effective-interest method of amortization. The company intends to hold these bonds to maturity.

Instructions

a Prepare the entry to record the purchase of the bonds on January 1, 2008.

b Prepare the journal entry to record the receipt of interest on July 1, 2008,

Solution

a   **January 1, 2008**

Held-to-Maturity Securities   1,820,000
   Cash   1,820,000

b   **July 1, 2008**

Cash [($1,750,000 × 12%) × ½]   105,000
   Held-to-Maturity Securities ($105,000 − $91,000)   14,000
   Interest Revenue [($1,820,000 × 10%) × ½]   91,000

AVAILABLE-FOR-SALE SECURITIES

WHAT'S THE PRINCIPLE?

Recognizing unrealized gains and losses is an application of the concept of comprehensive income.

Companies, like **Amazon.com**, report **available-for-sale** securities at fair value. It records the unrealized gains and losses related to changes in the fair value of available-for-sale debt securities in an unrealized holding gain or loss account. Amazon adds (subtracts) this amount to other comprehensive income for the period. Other comprehensive income is then added to (subtracted from) accumulated other comprehensive income, which is shown as a separate component of stockholders' equity until realized. Thus, **companies report available-for-sale securities at fair value on the balance sheet, but do not report changes in fair value as part of net income until after selling the security**. This approach reduces the volatility of net income.

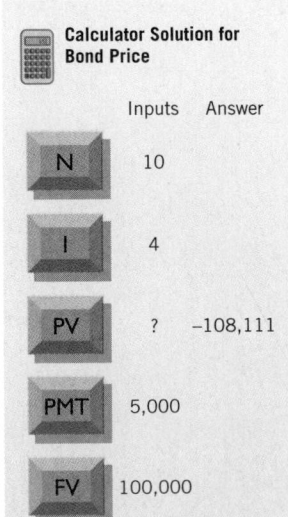

Calculator Solution for Bond Price

	Inputs	Answer
N	10	
I	4	
PV	?	−108,111
PMT	5,000	
FV	100,000	

Example: Single Security

To illustrate the accounting for available-for-sale securities, assume that Graff Corporation purchases $100,000, 10 percent, five-year bonds on January 1, 2008, with interest payable on July 1 and January 1. The bonds sell for $108,111, which results in a bond premium of $8,111 and an effective interest rate of 8 percent.

Graff records the purchase of the bonds as follows.[4]

January 1, 2008

Available-for-Sale Securities   108,111
   Cash   108,111

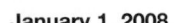

[4]Companies generally record investments acquired at par, at a discount, or at a premium in the accounts at cost, including brokerage and other fees but excluding the accrued interest. They generally do not record investments at maturity value. The use of a separate discount or premium account as a valuation account is acceptable procedure for investments, but in practice companies do not widely use it.

Illustration 14-6 discloses the effect of the premium amortization on the interest revenue Graff records each period using the effective-interest method.

10% Bonds Purchased to Yield 8%

Date	Cash Received	Interest Revenue	Bond Premium Amortization	Carrying Amount of Bonds
1/1/08				$108,111
7/1/08	$ 5,000ª	$ 4,324ᵇ	$ 676ᶜ	107,435ᵈ
1/1/09	5,000	4,297	703	106,732
7/1/09	5,000	4,269	731	106,001
1/1/10	5,000	4,240	760	105,241
7/1/10	5,000	4,210	790	104,451
1/1/11	5,000	4,178	822	103,629
7/1/11	5,000	4,145	855	102,774
1/1/12	5,000	4,111	889	101,885
7/1/12	5,000	4,075	925	100,960
1/1/13	5,000	4,040	960	100,000
	$50,000	$41,889	$8,111	

ª$5,000 = $100,000 × .10 × $^{6}\!/\!_{12}$
ᵇ$4,324 = $108,111 × .08 × $^{6}\!/\!_{12}$
ᶜ$676 = $5,000 − $4,324
ᵈ$107,435 = $108,111 − $676

The entry to record interest revenue on July 1, 2008, is as follows.

July 1, 2008

Cash	5,000	
Available-for-Sale Securities		676
Interest Revenue		4,324

At December 31, 2008, Graff makes the following entry to recognize interest revenue.

December 31, 2008

Interest Receivable	5,000	
Available-for-Sale Securities		703
Interest Revenue		4,297

As a result, Graff reports revenue for 2008 of $8,621 ($4,324 + $4,297).

To apply the fair value method to these debt securities, assume that at year-end the fair value of the bonds is $105,000 and that the carrying amount of the investments is $106,732. Comparing this fair value with the carrying amount (amortized cost) of the bonds at December 31, 2008, Graff recognizes an unrealized holding loss of $1,732 ($106,732 − $105,000). It reports this loss as other comprehensive income. Graff makes the following entry.

December 31, 2008

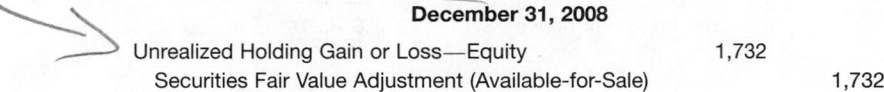

Unrealized Holding Gain or Loss—Equity	1,732	
Securities Fair Value Adjustment (Available-for-Sale)		1,732

Graff uses a valuation account instead of crediting the Available-for-Sale Securities account. The use of the **Securities Fair Value Adjustment (Available-for-Sale) account** enables the company to maintain a record of its amortized cost. Because the adjustment account has a credit balance in this case, Graff subtracts it from the balance of the Available-for-Sale Securities account to determine fair value. Graff reports this fair value amount on the balance sheet. At each reporting date, Graff reports the bonds at fair value with an adjustment to the Unrealized Holding Gain or Loss—Equity account.

Example: Portfolio of Securities

To illustrate the accounting for a portfolio of securities, assume that Webb Corporation has two debt securities classified as available-for-sale. Illustration 14-7 identifies the amortized cost, fair value, and the amount of the unrealized gain or loss.

Illustration 14-7
Computation of Securities
Fair Value Adjustment—
Available-for-Sale
Securities (2007)

| | | **Available-for-Sale Debt Security Portfolio** | | |
| | | **December 31, 2007** | | |
Investments	Amortized Cost	Fair Value	Unrealized Gain (Loss)
Watson Corporation 8% bonds	$ 93,537	$103,600	$ 10,063
Anacomp Corporation 10% bonds	200,000	180,400	(19,600)
Total of portfolio	$293,537	$284,000	(9,537)
Previous securities fair value adjustment balance			–0–
Securities fair value adjustment—Cr.			$ (9,537)

The fair value of Webb's available-for-sale portfolio totals $284,000. The gross unrealized gains are $10,063, and the gross unrealized losses are $19,600, resulting in a net unrealized loss of $9,537. That is, the fair value of available-for-sale securities is $9,537 lower than its amortized cost. Webb makes an adjusting entry to a valuation allowance to record the decrease in value and to record the loss as follows.

December 31, 2007

Unrealized Holding Gain or Loss—Equity	9,537	
Securities Fair Value Adjustment (Available-for-Sale)		9,537

Webb reports the unrealized holding loss of $9,537 as other comprehensive income and a reduction of stockholders' equity. Recall that companies exclude from net income any unrealized holding gains and losses related to available-for-sale securities.

Sale of Available-for-Sale Securities

If a company sells bonds carried as investments in available-for-sale securities before the maturity date, it must make entries to remove from the Available-for-Sale Securities account the amortized cost of bonds sold. To illustrate, assume that Webb Corporation sold the Watson bonds (from Illustration 14-7) on July 1, 2008, for $90,000, at which time it had an amortized cost of $94,214. Illustration 14-8 shows the computation of the realized loss.

Illustration 14-8
Computation of Loss on
Sale of Bonds

Amortized cost (Watson bonds)	$94,214
Less: Selling price of bonds	90,000
Loss on sale of bonds	$ 4,214

Webb records the sale of the Watson bonds as follows.

July 1, 2008

Cash	90,000	
Loss on Sale of Securities	4,214	
Available-for-Sale Securities		94,214

Webb reports this realized loss in the "Other expenses and losses" section of the income statement. Assuming no other purchases and sales of bonds in 2008, Webb on December 31, 2008, prepares the information shown in Illustration 14-9.

Illustration 14-9
Computation of Securities
Fair Value Adjustment—
Available-for-Sale (2008)

2009

Available-for-Sale Debt Security Portfolio **December 31, 2008**			
Investments	Amortized Cost	Fair Value	Unrealized Gain (Loss)
Anacomp Corporation 10% bonds (total portfolio)	$200,000	$195,000	$(5,000)
Previous securities fair value adjustment balance—Cr.			(9,537)
Securities fair value adjustment—Dr.			$ 4,537

Webb has an unrealized holding loss of $5,000. However, the Securities Fair Value Adjustment account already has a credit balance of $9,537. To reduce the adjustment account balance to $5,000, Webb debits it for $4,537, as follows.

December 31, 2008

Securities Fair Value Adjustment (Available-for-Sale)	4,537	
Unrealized Holding Gain or Loss—Equity		4,537

What do the numbers mean?

What Is Fair Value?

In the fall of 2000, Wall Street brokerage firm **Morgan Stanley** told investors that rumor of big losses in its bond portfolio were "greatly exaggerated." As it turns out, Morgan Stanley also was exaggerating.

Recently, the SEC accused Morgan Stanley of violating securities laws by overstating the value of certain bonds by $75 million. The overvaluations stemmed more from wishful thinking than reality, in violation of generally accepted accounting principles, the SEC said. "In effect, Morgan Stanley valued its positions at the price at which it thought a willing buyer and seller should enter into an exchange, rather than at a price at which a willing buyer and a willing seller would enter into a current exchange," the SEC wrote.

Especially egregious, stated one accounting expert, were the SEC's findings that Morgan Stanley in some instances used its own more optimistic assumptions as a substitute for external pricing sources. "What that is saying is: 'Fair value is what you want the value to be. Pick a number...' That's especially troublesome."

As indicated in the text, the FASB has been working on a new standard for assessing what is fair and what isn't when it comes to assigning valuations. Concerns over the issue caught fire after the collapses of **Enron Corp.** and other energy traders that abused the wide discretion given them under fair-value accounting. Investors have expressed similar worries about some financial companies, which use internal— and subjectively designed—mathematical models to come up with valuations when market quotes aren't available.

Source: Adapted from Susanne Craig and Jonathan Weil, "SEC Targets Morgan Stanley Values," *Wall Street Journal* (November 8, 2004), p. C3.

Beyond the Numbers

What type of measurement methods are used to determine fair value? Which measurement method is the most reliable?

Financial Statement Presentation

Webb's December 31, 2008, balance sheet and the 2008 income statement include the following items and amounts (the Anacomp bonds are long-term investments but are not intended to be held to maturity).

Illustration 14-10
Reporting of Available-
for-Sale Securities

Balance Sheet		
Current assets		
Interest receivable	$	xxx
Investments		
Available-for-sale securities, at fair value	$195,000	
Stockholders' equity		
Accumulated other comprehensive loss	$	5,000
Income Statement		
Other revenues and gains		
Interest revenue	$	xxx
Other expenses and losses		
Loss on sale of securities	$	4,214

Some favor including the unrealized holding gain or loss in net income rather than showing it as other comprehensive income.[5] However, some companies, particularly financial institutions, note that recognizing gains and losses on assets, but not liabilities, introduces substantial volatility in net income. They argue that hedges often exist between assets and liabilities so that gains in assets are offset by losses in liabilities, and vice versa. In short, to recognize gains and losses only on the asset side is unfair and not representative of the economic activities of the company.

This argument convinced the FASB. As a result, companies **do not include in net income** these unrealized gains and losses. However, even this approach solves only some of the problems, because **volatility of capital** still results. This is of concern to financial institutions because regulators restrict financial institutions' operations based on their level of capital. In addition, companies can still manage their net income by engaging in **gains trading** (i.e., selling the winners and holding the losers).

TRADING SECURITIES

Companies hold **trading securities** with the intention of selling them in a short period of time. "Trading" in this context means frequent buying and selling. Companies thus use trading securities to generate profits from short-term differences in price. Companies generally hold these securities for less than three months, some for merely days or hours.

Companies report trading securities at fair value, with unrealized holding gains and losses reported as part of net income. Similar to held-to-maturity or available-for-sale investments, they are required to amortize any discount or premium. A **holding gain or loss** is the net change in the fair value of a security from one period to another, exclusive of dividend or interest revenue recognized but not received. In short, the FASB says to adjust the trading securities to fair value, at each reporting date. In addition, companies report the change in value as part of net income, not other comprehensive income.

---

[5]In Chapter 5, we discussed the reporting of other comprehensive income and the concept of comprehensive income. "Reporting Comprehensive Income," *Statement of Financial Accounting Standards No. 130* (Norwalk, Conn.: FASB, 1997).

To illustrate, assume that on December 31, 2007, Western Publishing Corporation determined its trading securities portfolio to be as shown in Illustration 14-11. (Assume that 2007 is the first year that Western Publishing held trading securities.) At the date of acquisition, Western Publishing recorded these trading securities at cost, including brokerage commissions and taxes, in the account entitled Trading Securities. This is the first valuation of this recently purchased portfolio.

Trading Debt Security Portfolio
December 31, 2007

Investments	Cost	Fair Value	Unrealized Gain (Loss)
Burlington Northern 10% bonds	$ 43,860	$ 51,500	$ 7,640
GM Corporation 11% bonds	184,230	175,200	(9,030)
Time Warner 8% bonds	86,360	91,500	5,140
Total of portfolio	$314,450	$318,200	3,750
Previous securities fair value adjustment balance			–0–
Securities fair value adjustment—Dr.			$3,750

Illustration 14-11
Computation of Securities Fair Value Adjustment—Trading Securities Portfolio (2007)

The total cost of Western Publishing's trading portfolio is $314,450. The gross unrealized gains are $12,780 ($7,640 + $5,140), and the gross unrealized losses are $9,030, resulting in a net unrealized gain of $3,750. The fair value of trading securities is $3,750 greater than its cost.

At December 31, Western Publishing makes an adjusting entry to a valuation allowance, referred to as Securities Fair Value Adjustment (Trading), to record the increase in value and to record the unrealized holding gain.

INTERNATIONAL INSIGHT

iGAAP provides for classification as trading, available for sale, or held-to-maturity for all types of financial assets. U.S. GAAP applies these classifications only to securities.

December 31, 2007

Securities Fair Value Adjustment (Trading)	3,750	
Unrealized Holding Gain or Loss—Income		3,750

Because the Securities Fair Value Adjustment account balance is a debit, Western Publishing adds it to the cost of the Trading Securities account to arrive at a fair value for the trading securities. Western Publishing reports this fair value amount on the balance sheet.

When securities are actively traded, the FASB believes that the investments should be reported at fair value on the balance sheet. In addition, changes in fair value (unrealized gains and losses) should be reported in income. Such reporting on trading securities provides more relevant information to existing and prospective stockholders.

Try it out! At December 31, 2007, the trading security portfolio for Harper Company is as follows:

Security	Cost	Fair Value	Unrealized Gain (Loss)
A	$24,500	$21,000	$(3,500)
B	17,500	19,500	2,000
C	32,000	36,000	4,000
Total	$74,000	$76,500	2,500
Previous securities fair value adjustment balance—Cr.			(1,200)
Securities fair value adjustment—Dr.			$ 3,700

During 2008 Harper sold security B for $18,400. The fair value of the securities on December 31, 2008, was security A $20,500 and security C $35,200.

Instructions

Prepare journal entries for each of the following.

a   The December 31, 2007, adjusting entry.
b   The sale of security B during 2008.
c   The December 31, 2008, adjusting entry.

Solution

a   **December 31, 2007**

Securities Fair Value Adjustment (Trading)	3,700	
Unrealized Holding Gain or Loss—Income		3,700

b   **During 2008**

Cash	18,400	
Gain on Sale of Securities		900
Trading Securities		17,500

c   **December 31, 2008**

Unrealized Holding Gain or Loss—Income	3,300	
Securities Fair Value Adjustment (Trading)		3,300*

*[$2,500 + ($24,500 + $32,000) − ($20,500 + $35,200)]

SECTION TWO — INVESTMENTS IN EQUITY SECURITIES

OBJECTIVE 3

Identify the categories of equity securities and describe the accounting and reporting treatment for each category.

Equity securities represent ownership interests such as common, preferred, or other capital stock. They also include rights to acquire or dispose of ownership interests at an agreed-upon or determinable price, such as in warrants, rights, and call or put options. Companies do not treat convertible debt securities as equity securities. Nor do they treat as equity securities redeemable preferred stock (which must be redeemed for common stock). The cost of equity securities includes the purchase price of the security plus broker's commissions and other fees incidental to the purchase.

The degree to which one corporation **(investor)** acquires an interest in the common stock of another corporation **(investee)** generally determines the accounting treatment for the investment subsequent to acquisition. The classification of such investments depends on the percentage of the investee voting stock that is held by the investor:

1   Holdings of less than 20 percent (**fair value method**)—investor has passive interest.

2   Holdings between 20 percent and 50 percent (**equity method**)—investor has significant influence.

3   Holdings of more than 50 percent (**consolidated statements**)—investor has controlling interest.

Illustration 14-12 lists these levels of interest or influence and the corresponding valuation and reporting method that companies must apply to the investment.

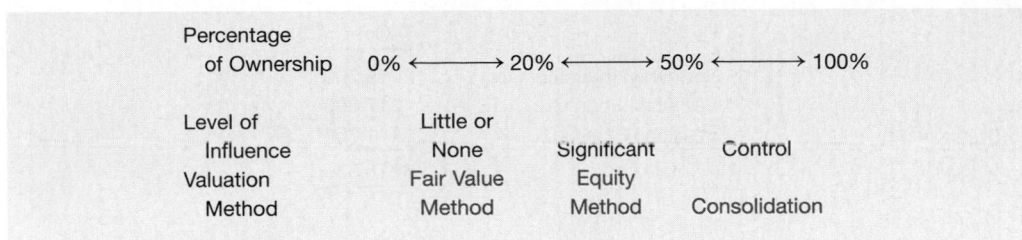

Illustration 14-12
Levels of Influence
Determine Accounting
Methods

The accounting and reporting for equity securities therefore depends upon the level of influence and the type of security involved, as shown in Illustration 14-13.

Illustration 14-13
Accounting and Reporting
for Equity Securities by
Category

Category	Valuation	Unrealized Holding Gains or Losses	Other Income Effects
Holdings less than 20%			
1. Available-for-sale	Fair value	Recognized in "Other comprehensive income" and as separate component of stockholders' equity	Dividends declared; gains and losses from sale.
2. Trading	Fair value	Recognized in net income	Dividends declared; gains and losses from sale.
Holdings between 20% and 50%	Equity	Not recognized	Proportionate share of investee's net income.
Holdings more than 50%	Consolidation	Not recognized	Not applicable.

HOLDINGS OF LESS THAN 20%

When an investor has an interest of less than 20 percent, it is presumed that the investor has little or no influence over the investee. In such cases, if market prices are available subsequent to acquisition, the company values and reports the investment using the **fair value method**.[6] The fair value method requires that companies classify equity securities at acquisition as **available-for-sale securities** or **trading securities**. Because equity securities have no maturity date, companies cannot classify them as held-to-maturity.

Available-for-Sale Securities

Upon acquisition, companies record available-for-sale securities at cost.[7] To illustrate, assume that on November 3, 2008 Republic Corporation purchased common stock of three companies, each investment representing less than a 20 percent interest.

---

[6]When market prices are unavailable, a company values the investment and reports it at cost in periods subsequent to acquisition. This approach is often referred to as the **cost method**. Companies recognize dividends when received. They value the portfolio and report it at acquisition cost. Companies only recognize gains or losses after selling the securities.

[7]Companies should record equity securities acquired in **exchange for noncash consideration** (property or services) at (1) the fair value of the consideration given, or (2) the fair value of the security received, whichever is more clearly determinable. Accounting for numerous purchases of securities requires the preservation of information regarding the cost of individual purchases, as well as the dates of purchases and sales. If **specific identification** is not possible, companies may use an **average cost** for multiple purchases of the same class of security. The **first-in, first-out method** (FIFO) of assigning costs to investments at the time of sale is also acceptable and normally employed.

	Cost
Northwest Industries, Inc.	$259,700
Campbell Soup Co.	317,500
St. Regis Pulp Co.	141,350
Total cost	$718,550

Republic records these investments as follows.

November 3, 2008

| Available-for-Sale Securities | 718,550 | |
| Cash | | 718,550 |

On December 6, 2008, Republic receives a cash dividend of $4,200 on its invest-ment in the common stock of Campbell Soup Co. It records the cash dividend as follows.

December 6, 2008

| Cash | 4,200 | |
| Dividend Revenue | | 4,200 |

All three of the investee companies reported net income for the year, but only Camp-bell Soup declared and paid a dividend to Republic. But, recall that when an investor owns less than 20 percent of the common stock of another corporation, it is presumed that the investor has relatively little influence on the investee. As a result, **net income earned by the investee is not a proper basis for recognizing income from the invest-ment by the investor**. Why? Because the increased net assets resulting from profitable operations may be permanently retained for use in the investee's business. Therefore, **the investor earns net income only when the investee declares cash dividends**.

At December 31, 2008, Republic's available-for-sale equity security portfolio has the cost and fair value shown in Illustration 14-14.

Illustration 14-14
Computation of Securities Fair Value Adjustment—Available-for-Sale Equity Security Portfolio (2008)

Available-for-Sale Equity Security Portfolio
December 31, 2008

Investments	Cost	Fair Value	Unrealized Gain (Loss)
Northwest Industries, Inc.	$259,700	$275,000	$ 15,300
Campbell Soup Co.	317,500	304,000	(13,500)
St. Regis Pulp Co.	141,350	104,000	(37,350)
Total of portfolio	$718,550	$683,000	(35,550)
Previous securities fair value adjustment balance			–0–
Securities fair value adjustment—Cr.			$(35,550)

For Republic's available-for-sale equity securities portfolio, the gross unrealized gains are $15,300, and the gross unrealized losses are $50,850 ($13,500 + $37,350), resulting in a net unrealized loss of $35,550. The fair value of the available-for-sale securities portfo-lio is below cost by $35,550.

As with available-for-sale **debt** securities, Republic records the net unrealized gains and losses related to changes in the fair value of available-for-sale **equity** securities in an Unre-alized Holding Gain or Loss—Equity account. Republic reports this amount as a **part of other comprehensive income and as a component of accumulated other comprehensive**

income (reported in stockholders' equity) until realized. In this case, Republic prepares an adjusting entry debiting the Unrealized Holding Gain or Loss—Equity account and crediting the Securities Fair Value Adjustment account to record the decrease in fair value and to record the loss as follows.

December 31, 2008

Unrealized Holding Gain or Loss—Equity	35,550	
Securities Fair Value Adjustment (Available-for-Sale)		35,550

On January 23, 2009, Republic sold all of its Northwest Industries, Inc. common stock receiving net proceeds of $287,220. Illustration 14-15 shows the computation of the realized gain on the sale.

Net proceeds from sale	$287,220
Cost of Northwest shares	259,700
Gain on sale of stock	$ 27,520

Illustration 14-15
Computation of Gain on Sale of Stock

Republic records the sale as follows.

January 23, 2009

Cash	287,220	
Available-for-Sale Securities		259,700
Gain on Sale of Stock		27,520

In addition, assume that on February 10, 2009, Republic purchased 20,000 shares of Continental Trucking at a market price of $12.75 per share plus brokerage commissions of $1,850 (total cost, $256,850).

Illustration 14-16 lists Republic's portfolio of available-for-sale securities, as of December 31, 2009.

Available-for-Sale Equity Security Portfolio
December 31, 2009

Investments	Cost	Fair Value	Unrealized Gain (Loss)
Continental Trucking	$256,850	$278,350	$ 21,500
Campbell Soup Co.	317,500	362,550	45,050
St. Regis Pulp Co.	141,350	139,050	(2,300)
Total of portfolio	$715,700	$779,950	64,250
Previous securities fair value adjustment balance—Cr.			(35,550)
Securities fair value adjustment—Dr.			$ 99,800

Illustration 14-16
Computation of Securities Fair Value Adjustment— Available-for-Sale Equity Security Portfolio (2009)

At December 31, 2009, the fair value of Republic's available-for-sale equity securities portfolio exceeds cost by $64,250 (unrealized gain). The Securities Fair Value Adjustment account had a credit balance of $35,550 at December 31, 2009. To adjust its December 31, 2009, available-for-sale portfolio to fair value, the company debits the Securities Fair Value Adjustment account for $99,800 ($35,550 + $64,250). Republic records this adjustment as follows.

December 31, 2009

Securities Fair Value Adjustment (Available-for-Sale)	99,800	
Unrealized Holding Gain or Loss—Equity		99,800

Trading Securities

The accounting entries to record trading equity securities are the same as for available-for-sale equity securities, except for recording the unrealized holding gain or loss. For trading equity securities, companies **report the unrealized holding gain or loss as part of net income**. Thus, the account titled Unrealized Holding Gain or Loss—Income is used.

HOLDINGS BETWEEN 20% AND 50%

An investor corporation may hold an interest of less than 50 percent in an investee corporation and thus not possess legal control. However, as shown in our opening story about **Coca-Cola**, an investment in voting stock of less than 50 percent can still give Coke (the investor) the ability to exercise significant influence over the operating and financial policies of its bottlers.[8] **Significant influence** may be indicated in several ways. Examples include representation on the board of directors, participation in policy-making processes, material intercompany transactions, interchange of managerial personnel, or technological dependency.

Another important consideration is the extent of ownership by an investor in relation to the concentration of other shareholdings. To achieve a reasonable degree of uniformity in application of the "significant influence" criterion, the profession concluded that an investment (direct or indirect) of 20 percent or more of the voting stock of an investee should lead to a presumption that in the absence of evidence to the contrary, an investor has the ability to exercise significant influence over an investee.[9]

In instances of "significant influence" (generally an investment of 20 percent or more), the investor must account for the investment using the **equity method**.

Equity Method

OBJECTIVE 4

Explain the equity method of accounting and compare it to the fair value method for equity securities.

Under the **equity method** the investor and the investee acknowledge a substantive economic relationship. The company originally records the investment at the cost of the shares acquired but subsequently adjusts the amount each period for changes in the investee's net assets. That is, the **the investor's proportionate share of the earnings (losses) of the investee periodically increases (decreases) the investment's carrying amount. All dividends received by the investor from the investee also decrease the investment's carrying amount.** The equity method recognizes that investee's earnings increase investee's net assets, and that investee's losses and dividends decrease these net assets.

To illustrate the equity method and compare it with the fair value method, assume that Maxi Company purchases a 20 percent interest in Mini Company. To apply the fair value method in this example, assume that Maxi does not have the ability to exercise significant

---

[8]"The Equity Method of Accounting for Investments in Common Stock," *Opinions of the Accounting Principles Board No. 18* (New York: AICPA, 1971), par. 17.

[9]Cases in which an investment of 20 percent or more might not enable an investor to exercise significant influence include:

   (1) The investee opposes the investor's acquisition of its stock.

   (2) The investor and investee sign an agreement under which the investor surrenders significant shareholder rights.

   (3) The investor's ownership share does not result in "significant influence" because majority ownership of the investee is concentrated among a small group of shareholders who operate the investee without regard to the views of the investor.

   (4) The investor tries and fails to obtain representation on the investee's board of directors.

"Criteria for Applying the Equity Method of Accounting for Investments in Common Stock," *Interpretations of the Financial Accounting Standards Board No. 35* (Stamford, Conn.: FASB, 1981).

influence, and classifies the securities as available-for-sale. Where this example applies the equity method, assume that the 20 percent interest permits Maxi to exercise significant influence. Illustration 14-17 shows the entries.

Illustration 14-17
Comparison of Fair Value Method and Equity Method

Entries by Maxi Company			
Fair Value Method		**Equity Method**	
On January 2, 2007, Maxi Company acquired 48,000 shares (20% of Mini Company common stock) at a cost of $10 a share.			
Available-for-Sale-Securities	480,000	Investment in Mini Stock	480,000
Cash	480,000	Cash	480,000
For the year 2007, Mini Company reported net income of $200,000; Maxi Company's share is 20%, or $40,000.			
No entry		Investment in Mini Stock	40,000
		Revenue from Investment	40,000
At December 31, 2007, the 48,000 shares of Mini Company have a fair value (market price) of $12 a share, or $576,000.			
Securities Fair Value Adjustment		No entry	
(Available-for-Sale)	96,000		
Unrealized Holding Gain			
or Loss—Equity	96,000		
On January 28, 2008, Mini Company announced and paid a cash dividend of $100,000; Maxi Company received 20%, or $20,000.			
Cash	20,000	Cash	20,000
Dividend Revenue	20,000	Investment in Mini Stock	20,000
For the year 2008, Mini reported a net loss of $50,000; Maxi Company's share is 20%, or $10,000.			
No entry		Loss on Investment	10,000
		Investment in Mini Stock	10,000
At December 31, 2008, the Mini Company 48,000 shares have a fair value (market price) of $11 a share, or $528,000.			
Unrealized Holding Gain			
or Loss—Equity	48,000	No entry	
Securities Fair Value Adjustment			
(Available-for-Sale)	48,000		

Note that under the fair value method, Maxi reports as revenue only the cash dividends received from Mini. **The earning of net income by Mini (the investee) is not considered a proper basis for recognition of income from the investment by Maxi (the investor).** Why? Mini may permanently retain in the business any increased net assets resulting from its profitable operation. Therefore, Maxi only earns revenue when it receives dividends from Mini.

Under the equity method, Maxi reports as revenue its share of the net income reported by Mini. Maxi records the cash dividends received from Mini as a decrease in the investment carrying value. As a result, Maxi records its share of the net income of Mini in the year when it is earned. With significant influence, Maxi can ensure that Mini will pay dividends, if desired, on any net asset increases resulting from net income. To wait until receiving a dividend ignores the fact that Maxi is better off if the investee has earned income.

Using dividends as a basis for recognizing income poses an additional problem. For example, assume that the investee reports a net loss. However, the investor exerts influence to force a dividend payment from the investee. In this case, the investor reports income, even though the investee is experiencing a loss. **In other words, using dividends as a basis for recognizing income fails to report properly the economics of the situation.**

For some companies, equity accounting can be a real pain to the bottom line. For example, **Amazon.com**, the pioneer of Internet retailing, at one time struggled to turn a profit. Furthermore, some of Amazon's equity investments had resulted in Amazon's earnings performance going from bad to worse. In a recent year, Amazon.com disclosed equity stakes in such companies as **Altera International**, **Basis Technology**, **Drugstore.com**, and **Eziba.com**. These equity investees reported losses that made Amazon's already bad bottom line even worse, accounting for up to 22 percent of its reported loss in one year alone.

Investee Losses Exceed Carrying Amount

If an investor's share of the investee's losses exceeds the carrying amount of the investment, should the investor recognize additional losses? Ordinarily the investor should discontinue applying the equity method and not recognize additional losses.

If the investor's potential loss is not limited to the amount of its original investment (by guarantee of the investee's obligations or other commitment to provide further financial support), or if imminent return to profitable operations by the investee appears to be assured, the investor should recognize additional losses.[10]

Try it out! On December 31, 2007, Grandon Corporation acquired 20% of the outstanding common stock of Nickels Company. The purchase price was $900,000 for 30,000 shares. Nickels declared and paid a $0.70 per share cash dividend on June 30 and on December 31, 2008. Nickels reported net income of $500,000 for 2008. The fair value of Nickels' stock was $29 per share at December 31, 2008.

Instructions

Determine (1) the amount at which Grandon reports the investment on the balance sheet at December 31, 2008, and (2) the total income from the investment reported in 2008, assuming the following.

a Grandon cannot exercise significant influence over Nickels. The securities are classified as available-for-sale.

b Grandon can exercise significant influence over Nickels.

Solution

		(a) No Significant Influence	(b) Significant Influence
1	Reported investment amount	$870,000 (30,000 × $29/share)	$958,000 [$900,000 − ($1.40 × 30,000) + ($500,000 × .20)]
2	Investment income reported	$42,000 ($1.40 × 30,000)	$100,000 ($500,000 × .20)

HOLDINGS OF MORE THAN 50%

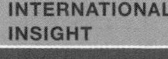

When one corporation acquires a voting interest of more than 50 percent in another corporation, it is said to have a **controlling interest**. In such a relationship, the investor corporation is referred to as the **parent** and the investee corporation as the **subsidiary**. Companies present the investment in the common stock of the subsidiary as a long-term investment on the separate financial statements of the parent.

When the parent treats the subsidiary as an investment, the parent generally prepares **consolidated financial statements**. Consolidated financial statements treat the parent and subsidiary corporations as a single economic entity. (Advanced accounting courses extensively discuss the subject of when and how to prepare consolidated financial statements.) Whether or not consolidated financial statements are prepared, the parent company generally accounts for the investment in the subsidiary **using the equity method** as explained in this chapter.

---

[10]"The Equity Method of Accounting for Investments in Common Stock," op. cit., par. 19(i).

What do the numbers mean?

Presently the rules for consolidation seem very straightforward: If a company owns more than 50 percent of another company, it generally should be consolidated. If it owns less than 50 percent, it is generally not consolidated. However the FASB recognizes the artificiality of the present test. Determination of who really has control often relies on factors other than stock ownership.

In fact, specific guidelines force consolidation even though stock ownership is not above 50 percent in certain limited situations. For example, **Enron**'s failure to consolidate three special-purpose entities (SPEs) that it effectively controlled led to an overstatement of income of $569 million and overstatement of equity of $1.2 billion. In each of Enron's three SPEs, the GAAP guidelines would have led to consolidation. That is, the following factors indicate that consolidation should have occurred: the majority owner of the special-purpose entity (SPE) made only a modest investment; the activities of the SPE primarily benefited Enron; and the substantive risks and rewards related to the assets or debt of the SPE rested directly or indirectly with Enron.

The FASB has issued new guidelines related to SPEs, given all the reporting problems that have surfaced related to SPEs at Enron and other companies.

Beyond the Numbers

Why is it important to determine who really has control for accounting purposes?

OTHER REPORTING ISSUES SECTION THREE

We have identified the basic issues involved in accounting for investments in debt and equity securities. In addition, the following issues relate to both of these types of securities.

1 Financial statement presentation.

2 Impairment of value.

3 Transfers between categories.

4 Fair value controversy.

FINANCIAL STATEMENT PRESENTATION OF INVESTMENTS

Companies must present individual amounts for the three categories of investments either on the balance sheet or in the related notes. Illustration 14-18 (page 750) summarizes the valuation and balance sheet classification of investments.

For securities classified as available-for-sale and separately for securities classified as held-to-maturity, a company should describe:

1 Aggregate fair value, gross unrealized holding gains, gross unrealized losses, and amortized cost basis by major security type (debt and equity).

2 Information about the contractual maturities of debt securities. The company may group maturity information, for example (a) within one year, (b) after one year through five years, (c) after five years through ten years, and (d) after ten years.

In classifying investments, evidence should support management's expressed intent, such as the history of the company's investment activities, events subsequent to the balance sheet date, and the nature and purpose of the investment.

OBJECTIVE 5

Describe the disclosure requirements for investments in debt and equity securities.

Actual Company Disclosures Related to Investments and Comprehensive Income

Illustration 14-18
Investment Valuation and
Classification

Investment Category	Valuation	Classification
Trading securities (debt and equity)	Fair value	Current asset.
Held-to-maturity (debt)	Amortized cost	Current or noncurrent based on maturity date of individual security.
Available-for-sale debt	Fair value	Depends on the circumstances. Current or noncurrent based on maturities and expectations as to sales and redemptions in the following year.
Available-for-sale equity	Fair value	Depends on the circumstances. Current or noncurrent based on expectations as to sales in the following year.

Companies must be extremely careful with debt securities held to maturity. If a company prematurely sells a debt security in this category, the sale may "taint" the entire held-to-maturity portfolio. That is, a management's statement regarding "intent" is no longer credible. Therefore the company may have to reclassify the securities. This could lead to unfortunate consequences. An interesting by-product of this situation is that companies that wish to retire their debt securities early are finding it difficult to do so. The holder will not sell because the securities are classified as held-to-maturity.

Disclosures Required Under the Equity Method

The significance of an investment to the investor's financial position and operating results should determine the extent of disclosures. The following disclosures in the investor's financial statements generally apply to the equity method.

**Disclosures Related to
Equity Investments**

1 The name of each investee and the percentage of ownership of common stock.

2 The accounting policies of the investor with respect to investments in common stock.

3 The difference, if any, between the amount in the investment account and the amount of underlying equity in the net assets of the investee.

4 The aggregate value of each identified investment based on quoted market price (if available).

5 When equity-method investments are, in the aggregate, material in relation to the financial position and operating results of an investor, the company may need to present summarized information concerning assets, liabilities, and results of operations of the investees, either individually or in groups, as appropriate.

WHAT'S THE PRINCIPLE?

The consolidation of financial results of different companies follows the economic entity assumption and disregards legal entities. The key objective is to provide useful information to financial statement users.

What do the numbers mean? | **More Disclosure, Please**

As indicated in the last two sections, the level of disclosure for investment securities is extensive. How to account for investment securities is a particularly sensitive area, given the large amounts of equity investments involved. And presently companies report investments in equity securities at cost, equity, fair value, and full consolidation, depending on the circumstances. As a recent SEC study noted, "there are so many different accounting treatments for investments that it raises the question of whether they are all needed."

Presented on the next page is an estimate of the percentage of companies on the major exchanges that have investments in the equity of other entities.

Investments in the Equity of Other Companies

Categorized by Accounting Treatment	Percent of Companies
Presenting consolidated financial statements	91.1%
Reporting equity method investments	23.5
Reporting cost method investments*	17.4
Reporting available-for-sale investments	37.4
Reporting trading investments	6.2

*If the equity investments are not publicly traded, the company often accounts for the investment under the cost method. Changes in value are therefore not recognized unless there is impairment.

As the table indicates, many companies have equity investments of some type. These investments can be substantial. For example, based on the table above, the total amount of equity-method investments appearing on company balance sheets is approximately $403 billion and the amount shown in the income statements in any one year for all companies is approximately $38 billion.

Source: "Report and Recommendations Pursuant to Section 401(c) of the Sarbanes-Oxley Act of 2002 on Arrangements with Off-Balance Sheet Implications, Special Purpose Entities, and Transparency of Filings by Issuers," United States Securities and Exchange Commission—Office of Chief Accountant, Office of Economic Analyses, Division of Corporation Finance (June 2005), pp. 36–39.

Beyond the Numbers

Explain the rational for the different accounting treatment for investments in the equity of other companies.

In addition, the investor should disclose the reasons for not using the equity method in cases of 20 percent or more ownership interest, and for using the equity method in cases of less than 20 percent ownership interest.

Reclassification Adjustments

As we indicated in Chapter 5, companies report changes in unrealized holding gains and losses related to available-for-sale securities as part of other comprehensive income. Companies may display the components of other comprehensive income in one of three ways: (1) in a combined statement of income and comprehensive income, (2) in a separate statement of comprehensive income that begins with net income, or (3) in a statement of stockholders' equity.

The reporting of changes in unrealized gains or losses in comprehensive income is straightforward unless a company sells securities during the year. In that case, double counting results when the company reports realized gains or losses as part of net income but also shows the amounts as part of other comprehensive income in the current period or in previous periods.

To ensure that gains and losses are not counted twice when a sale occurs, a **reclassification adjustment** is necessary. To illustrate, assume that Open Company has the following two available-for-sale securities in its portfolio at the end of 2007 (its first year of operations).

Investments	Cost	Fair Value	Unrealized Holding Gain (Loss)
Lehman Inc. common stocks	$ 80,000	$105,000	$25,000
Woods Co. common stocks	120,000	135,000	15,000
Total of portfolio	$200,000	$240,000	40,000
Previous securities fair value adjustment balance			–0–
Securities fair value adjustment—Dr.			$40,000

Illustration 14-19
Available-for-Sale Security Portfolio (2007)

If Open Company reports net income in 2007 of $350,000, it presents a statement of comprehensive income as follows.

Illustration 14-20
Statement of Comprehensive Income (2007)

Open Company Statement of Comprehensive Income For the Year Ended December 31, 2007	
Net income	$350,000
Other comprehensive income	
Holding gains arising during period	40,000
Comprehensive income	$390,000

During 2008, Open Company sold the Lehman Inc. common stock for $105,000 and realized a gain on the sale of $25,000 ($105,000 − $80,000). At the end of 2008, the fair value of the Woods Co. common stock increased an additional $20,000, to $155,000. Illustration 14-21 shows the computation of the change in the securities fair value adjustment account.

Illustration 14-21
Available-for-Sale Security Portfolio (2008)

Investments	Cost	Fair Value	Unrealized Holding Gain (Loss)
Woods Co. common stocks	$120,000	$155,000	$35,000
Previous securities fair value adjustment balance—Dr.			(40,000)
Securities fair value adjustment—Cr.			$ (5,000)

Illustration 14-21 indicates that Open should report an unrealized holding loss of $5,000 in comprehensive income in 2008. In addition, Open realized a gain of $25,000 on the sale of the Lehman common stock. **Comprehensive income includes both realized and unrealized components.** Therefore Open recognizes a total holding gain (loss) in 2008 of $20,000, computed as follows.

Illustration 14-22
Computation of Total Holding Gain (Loss)

Unrealized holding gain (loss)	$ (5,000)
Realized holding gain	25,000
Total holding gain recognized	$20,000

Open reports net income of $720,000 in 2008, which includes the realized gain on sale of the Lehman securities. Illustration 14-23 shows a statement of comprehensive income for 2008, indicating how Open reported the components of holding gains (losses).

Illustration 14-23
Statement of Comprehensive Income (2008)

Open Company Statement of Comprehensive Income For the Year Ended December 31, 2008		
Net income (includes $25,000 realized gain on Lehman shares)		$720,000
Other comprehensive income		
Total holding gains arising during period [$(5,000) + $25,000]	$20,000	
Less: Reclassification adjustment for gains included in net income	(25,000)	(5,000)
Comprehensive income		$715,000

In 2007, Open included the unrealized gain on the Lehman Co. common stock in comprehensive income. In 2008, Open sold the stock. It reported the realized gain in net income, which increased comprehensive income again. To avoid double counting this gain, Open makes a reclassification adjustment to eliminate the realized gain from the computation of comprehensive income in 2008.

A company may display reclassification adjustments on the face of the financial statement in which it reports comprehensive income. Or it may disclose these reclassification adjustments in the notes to the financial statements.

Comprehensive Example

To illustrate the reporting of investment securities and related gain or loss on available-for-sale securities, assume that on January 1, 2008, Hinges Co. had cash and common stock of $50,000.[11] At that date the company had no other asset, liability, or equity balance. On January 2, Hinges purchased for cash $50,000 of equity securities classified as available-for-sale. On June 30, Hinges sold part of the available-for-sale security portfolio, realizing a gain as shown in Illustration 14-24.

Fair value of securities sold	$22,000
Less: Cost of securities sold	20,000
Realized gain	$ 2,000

Illustration 14-24
Computation of Realized Gain

Hinges did not purchase or sell any other securities during 2008. It received $3,000 in dividends during the year. At December 31, 2008, the remaining portfolio is as shown in Illustration 14-25.

Fair value of portfolio	$34,000
Less: Cost of portfolio	30,000
Unrealized gain	$ 4,000

Illustration 14-25
Computation of Unrealized Gain

Illustration 14-26 shows the company's income statement for 2008.

Hinges Company	
Income Statement	
For the Year Ended December 31, 2008	
Dividend revenue	$3,000
Realized gains on investment in securities	2,000
Net income	$5,000

Illustration 14-26
Income Statement

The company reports its change in the unrealized holding gain in a statement of comprehensive income as shown in Illustration 14-27 (page 754).

---

[11]We adapted this example from Dennis R. Beresford, L. Todd Johnson, and Cheri L. Reither, "Is a Second Income Statement Needed?" *Journal of Accountancy* (April 1996), p. 71.

Illustration 14-27
Statement of
Comprehensive Income

Hinges Company
Statement of Comprehensive Income
For the Year Ended December 31, 2008

Net income		$5,000
Other comprehensive income:		
Holding gains arising during the period	$6,000	
Less: Reclassification adjustment for gains included		
in net income	2,000	4,000
Comprehensive income		$9,000

Its statement of stockholders' equity appears in Illustration 14-28.

Illustration 14-28
Statement of
Stockholders' Equity

Hinges Company
Statement of Stockholders' Equity
For the Year Ended December 31, 2008

	Common Stock	Retained Earnings	Accumulated Other Comprehensive Income	Total
Beginning balance	$50,000	$ –0–	$ –0–	$50,000
Add: Net income		5,000		5,000
Other comprehensive income			4,000	4,000
Ending balance	$50,000	$5,000	$4,000	$59,000

The comparative balance sheet is shown in Illustration 14-29.

Illustration 14-29
Comparative Balance
Sheet

Hinges Company
Comparative Balance Sheet

	1/1/08	12/31/08
Assets		
Cash	$50,000	$25,000
Available-for-sale securities		34,000
Total assets	$50,000	$59,000
Stockholders' equity		
Common stock	$50,000	$50,000
Retained earnings		5,000
Accumulated other comprehensive income		4,000
Total stockholders' equity	$50,000	$59,000

This example indicates how an unrealized gain or loss on available-for-sale securities affects all the financial statements. Note that a company must disclose the components that comprise accumulated other comprehensive income.

IMPAIRMENT OF VALUE

A company should evaluate every investment, at each reporting date, to determine if it has suffered **impairment**—a loss in value that is other than temporary. For example, if an investee experiences a bankruptcy or a significant liquidity crisis, the investor may suffer a permanent loss. **If the decline is judged to be other than temporary, a company writes**

down the cost basis of the individual security to a new cost basis. The company accounts for the write-down as a realized loss. Therefore, it includes the amount in net income.

For debt securities, a company uses the impairment test to determine whether "it is probable that the investor will be unable to collect all amounts due according to the contractual terms."

For equity securities, the guideline is less precise. Any time realizable value is lower than the carrying amount of the investment, a company must consider an impairment. Factors involved include the length of time and the extent to which the fair value has been less than cost; the financial condition and near-term prospects of the issuer; and the intent and ability of the investor company to retain its investment to allow for any anticipated recovery in fair value.

To illustrate an impairment, assume that Strickler Company holds available-for-sale bond securities with a par value and amortized cost of $1 million. The fair value of these securities is $800,000. Strickler has previously reported an unrealized loss on these securities of $200,000 as part of other comprehensive income. In evaluating the securities, Strickler now determines that it probably will not collect all amounts due. In this case, it reports the unrealized loss of $200,000 as a loss on impairment of $200,000. Strickler includes this amount in income, with the bonds stated at their new cost basis. It records this impairment as follows.

Loss on Impairment	200,000	
Securities Fair Value Adjustment (Available-for-Sale)	200,000	
Unrealized Holding Gain or Loss—Equity		200,000
Available-for-Sale Securities		200,000

The new cost basis of the investment in debt securities is $800,000. Strickler includes subsequent increases and decreases in the fair value of impaired available-for-sale securities as other comprehensive income.[12]

Companies base impairment for debt and equity securities on a fair value test. The FASB rejected the discounted cash flow alternative for securities because of the availability of market price information.

OBJECTIVE **6**

Discuss the accounting for impairments of debt and equity investments.

WHAT'S THE PRINCIPLE?

If the assumption of being able to recover the carrying value of the investment is not valid, then a company should report a reduction in value and a realized loss.

What do the numbers mean?

The Irony of It All

The **Federal National Mortgage Association** (FNMA)—known as "Fannie Mae"—is a government-sponsored company that owns or guarantees about 25 percent of all the mortgages in the United States. Recently numerous articles have detailed accounting abuses by Fannie Mae. For example, Fannie Mae has acknowledged that some of its accounting polices do not comply with GAAP. It is now preparing to restate its financial statements back to 2001 and possibly to recognize at least $9 billion in losses related to derivatives.

Interestingly, Fannie Mae has caused much hardship for many of its brethren in the financial community (such as **DNB Financial, Independent Bank Corporation,** and **Wilmington Trust**). The reason: Many are holding security investments in Fannie Mae. And now the institutions are taking permanent write-downs on these securities because the losses appear to be other than temporary. (In other words, the Fannie Mae securities are impaired.) The irony is that a number of the companies that are taking impairment losses are the very ones that recently fought hard to make sure the FASB did not tighten up impairment accounting rules. Even more ironic is the fact the one of their fellow lobbyers (FNMA) is the source of their impairments!

Beyond the Numbers

When is a loss in value other than temporary?

---

[12]Companies may not amortize any discount related to the debt securities after recording the impairment. The new cost basis of impaired held-to-maturity securities does not change unless additional impairment occurs.

TRANSFERS BETWEEN CATEGORIES

Companies account for transfers between any of the categories at fair value. Thus, if a company transfers available-for-sale securities to held-to-maturity investments, it records the new investment (held-to-maturity) at the date of transfer at **fair value** in the new category. Similarly, if it transfers held-to-maturity investments to available-for-sale investments, it records the new investments (available-for-sale) at **fair value**. This **fair value** rule assures that a company cannot omit recognition of fair value simply by transferring securities to the held-to-maturity category. Illustration 14-30 summarizes the accounting treatment for transfers.

Illustration 14-30
Accounting for Transfers

Examples of the Entries for Recording Transfers Between Categories

Type of Transfer	Measurement Basis	Impact of Transfer on Stockholders' Equity*	Impact of Transfer on Net Income*
Transfer from trading to available-for-sale	Security transferred at fair value at the date of transfer, which is the new cost basis of the security.	The unrealized gain or loss at the date of transfer increases or decreases stockholders' equity.	The unrealized gain or loss at the date of transfer is recognized in income.
Transfer from available-for-sale to trading	Security transferred at fair value at the date of transfer, which is the new cost basis of the security.	The unrealized gain or loss at the date of transfer increases or decreases stockholders' equity.	The unrealized gain or loss at the date of transfer is recognized in income.
Transfer from held-to-maturity to available-for-sale**	Security transferred at fair value at the date of transfer.	The separate component of stockholders' equity is increased or decreased by the unrealized gain or loss at the date of transfer.	None
Transfer from available-for-sale to held-to-maturity	Security transferred at fair value at the date of transfer.	The unrealized gain or loss at the date of transfer carried as a separate component of stockholders' equity is amortized over the remaining life of the security.	None

*Assumes that adjusting entries to report changes in fair value for the current period are not yet recorded.
**Statement No. 115 states that these types of transfers should be rare.

FAIR VALUE CONTROVERSY

The reporting of investment securities is controversial. Some believe that all securities should be reported at fair value; others believe they all should be stated at amortized cost. Others favor the present approach. In this section we look at some of the major unresolved issues.

Measurement Based on Intent

Companies classify debt securities as held-to-maturity, available-for-sale, or trading. As a result, companies can report three identical debt securities in three different ways in the financial statements. Some argue such treatment is confusing. Furthermore, the held-to-maturity category relies solely on intent, a subjective evaluation. What is not subjective is the market price of the debt instrument. In other words, the three classifications are subjective, resulting in arbitrary classifications.

Gains Trading

Companies can classify certain debt securities as held-to-maturity and therefore report them at amortized cost. Companies can classify other debt and equity securities as available-for-sale and report them at fair value with the unrealized gain or loss reported as other comprehensive income. In either case, a company can become involved in "gains trading" (also referred to as "cherry picking," "snacking," or "sell the best and keep the rest"). In **gains trading**, companies sell their "winners," reporting the gains in income, and hold on to the losers.

Liabilities Not Fairly Valued

Many argue that if companies report investment securities at fair value, they also should report liabilities at fair value. Why? By recognizing changes in value on only one side of the balance sheet (the asset side), a high degree of volatility can occur in the income and stockholders' equity amounts. Further, financial institutions are involved in asset and liability management (not just asset management). Viewing only one side may lead managers to make uneconomic decisions as a result of the accounting.

The Board sympathizes with this view and now permits companies to measure many liabilities at fair value.[13] As a result, companies have the opportunity to reduce volatility in reported income caused by measuring related assets and liabilities at fair value.

Subjectivity of Fair Values

Some question the relevance of fair value measures for investments in securities, arguing in favor of reporting based on amortized cost. They believe that amortized cost provides relevant information: it focuses on the decision to acquire the asset, the earning effects of that decision that will be realized over time, and the ultimate recoverable value of the asset. They argue that fair value ignores those concepts. Instead, fair value focuses on the effects of transactions and events that do not involve the company, reflecting opportunity gains and losses whose recognition in the financial statements is, in their view, not appropriate until realized.

SUMMARY OF REPORTING TREATMENT OF SECURITIES

Illustration 14-31 (page 758) summarizes the major debt and equity securities and their reporting treatment.

---

[13]In a recent standard concerning valuation of financial assets and financial liabilities, the FASB indicates its support for valuing liabilitities at fair value. See "The Fair Value Option for Financial Assets and Liabilities," *Statement of Financial Accounting Standards No. 159* (Norwalk, Conn.: FASB, February 2007).

Illustration 14-31
Summary of Treatment of Major Debt and Equity Securities

Category	Balance Sheet	Income Statement
Trading (debt and equity securities)	Investments shown at fair value. Current assets.	Interest and dividends are recognized as revenue. Unrealized holding gains and losses are included in net income.
Available-for-sale (debt and equity securities)	Investments shown at fair value. Current or long-term assets. Unrealized holding gains and losses are a separate component of stockholders' equity.	Interest and dividends are recognized as revenue. Unrealized holding gains and losses are **not** included in net income but in other comprehensive income.
Held-to-maturity (debt securities)	Investments shown at amortized cost. Current or long-term assets.	Interest is recognized as revenue.
Equity method and/or consolidation (equity securities)	Investments originally are carried at cost, are periodically adjusted by the investor's share of the investee's earnings or losses, and are decreased by all dividends received from the investee. Classified as long-term.	Revenue is recognized to the extent of the investee's earnings or losses reported subsequent to the date of investment.

You will want to read the CONVERGENCE CORNER on page 760 for discussion of how international convergence efforts relate to investments.

ACCOUNTING, ANALYSIS, PRINCIPLES

Presented below are the following investment securities that Ogden Company has at December 31, 2008.

Situation 1: Held-to-maturity securities have an amortized cost of $320,000 and a fair value of $400,000 at December 31, 2008.

Situation 2: Trading securities have a cost basis of $800,000 and a fair value of $920,000 at December 31, 2008.

Situation 3: Available-for-sale securities have a cost basis of $1,400,000 and a fair value of $1,600,000. One of the available-for-sale securities has a cost basis of $200,000 and fair value of $50,000. Ogden decides that the decline in value associated with this security is other than temporary.

Situation 4: Ogden Company purchased 25% of the stock of Skolnick Company for $900,000. Ogden Company is deemed to have significant influence over the operating activities of Skolnick Company. During 2008, Skolnick Company reported net income of $300,000 and paid a dividend of $100,000.

Accounting

Prepare the journal entry (if necessary) at December 31, 2008, for Ogden Company for each of these situations. Assume that Ogden's first year of operations is 2008.

Analysis

Explain the effect on net income for each of these situations.

Principles

Explain why these investment securities may have different bases of measurement such as cost or fair value.

Solution

Accounting

Situation 1: Ogden Company would not make any entry to adjust to fair value because these securities are assumed to be held-to-maturity.

Situation 2: The entry to record the increase in value at December 31, 2008, would be:

Securities Fair Value Adjustment (Trading Securities)	120,000	
Unrealized Holding Gain or Loss—Income ($920,000 − $800,000)		120,000

Situation 3: The entry to record the impairment on December 31, 2008, would be:

Loss on Impairment	150,000	
Available-for-Sale Securities ($200,000 − $50,000)		150,000

The entry to record the increase in value at December 31, 2008, would be:

Securities Fair Value Adjustment (Available-for-Sale Securities)	350,000*	
Unrealized Holding Gain or Loss—Equity		350,000

*$1,600,000 − ($1,400,000 − $150,000)

Situation 4: The entry to record the increase in the equity investment due to Skolnick Company's net income would be:

Investment in Skolnick Stock	75,000	
Revenues from Investment ($300,000 × 25%)		75,000

The entry to record the dividend payment would be:

Cash	25,000	
Investment in Skolnick Stock ($100,000 × 25%)		25,000

Analysis

Situation 1: No effect on net income at December 31, 2008.
Situation 2: Net income increased $120,000 at December 31, 2008.
Situation 3: Net income decreased $150,000 at December 31, 2008.
Situation 4: Net income increased $75,000 at December 31, 2008.

Principles

The rationale for reporting held-to-maturity securities at amortized cost is that if management intends to hold the securities to maturity, fair values are not relevant for evaluating the cash flows associated with these securities.

On the other hand, if the securities are trading or available-for-sale, they may be sold before maturity or have such short maturities that information on their fair value is relevant for determining future cash flows.

When a company exercises significant influence over the operations of another company, it is argued that the investor company should use the equity method of accounting. The rationale for this measurement basis is that the investor company should report the net income at the time the investee company earns it. Under the fair value method for available-for-sale securities, the company does not report income until it receives a dividend or sells the security (although it can increase or decrease other comprehensive income).

CONVERGENCE CORNER

Investments

The accounting for investment securities is discussed in *IAS 27* ("Consolidated and Separate Financial Statements"), *IAS 28* ("Accounting for Investments in Associates"), and *IAS 39* ("Financial Instruments: Recognition and Measurement"). The accounting and reporting under iGAAP and U.S. GAAP are for the most part very similar, although the criteria used to determine the accounting is often different.

RELEVANT FACTS

- The accounting for trading, available-for-sale, and held-to-maturity securities is essentially the same between iGAAP and U.S. GAAP.

- Gains and losses related to available-for-sale securities are reported in other comprehensive income under U.S. GAAP. Under iGAAP, these gains and losses are reported directly in equity.

- Both iGAAP and U.S. GAAP use the same test to determine whether the equity method of accounting should be used—that is, significant influence with a general guide of over 20% ownership. iGAAP uses the term *associate investment* rather than *equity investment* to describe its investment under the equity method.

- Reclassifications of securities from one category to another generally follow the same accounting under the two GAAP systems. Reclassification in and out of trading securities is prohibited under iGAAP. It is not prohibited under U.S. GAAP, but this type of reclassification should be rare.

 ### ABOUT THE NUMBERS

The following example illustrates the accounting for investment impairments under iGAAP. Belerus Company has an available-for-sale investment in the 8%, 10-year bonds stock of Wimbledon Company. The investment has a carrying value of 2,300,000 euros at December 31, 2008. Early in January 2009, Belerus learns that Wimbledon has lost a major customer. As a result, Belerus determines that this investment is impaired and now has a fair value of 1,500,000 euros. Belerus makes the following entry to record the impairment.

Loss on Impairment (€2,300,000 − €1,500,000)	800,000	
Available-for-Sale Investment		800,000

Early in 2010, Wimbledon secures several new customers, and its prospects have improved considerably. Belerus determines the fair value of its investment is now 2,000,000 euros and makes the following entry under iGAAP.

Available-for-Sale Impairment (€2,000,000 − €1,500,000)	500,000	
Recovery of Loss on Investment		500,000

Under U.S. GAAP, Belerus is prohibited from recording the recovery in value of the impaired investment. That is, once an investment is impaired, the impaired value becomes the new basis for the investment.

- Under iGAAP, both the investor and an associate company should follow the same accounting policies. As a result, in order to prepare financial information, adjustments are made to the associate's policies to conform to the investor's books.

- The basis for consolidation under iGAAP is control. Under U.S. GAAP, a bipolar approach is used, which is a risk-and-reward model (often referred to as a *variable-entity approach*) and a voting-interest approach. However, under both systems, for consolidation to occur, the investor company must generally own 50% of another company.

- U.S. GAAP does not permit the reversal of an impairment charge related to available-for-sale debt and equity investments. iGAAP follows the same approach for available-for-sale equity investments but permits reversal for available-for-sale debt securities and held-to-maturity securities.

 ### ON THE HORIZON

As indicated earlier, both the FASB and IASB have indicated that they believe that all financial instruments should be reported at fair value and that changes in fair value should be reported as part of net income. It seems likely as more companies choose the fair value option for financial instruments, we will eventually arrive at fair value measurement for all financial instruments.

Key Terms

Summary of Learning Objectives

1 Identify the three categories of debt securities and describe the accounting and reporting treatment for each category. (1) Carry and report *held-to-maturity debt securities* at amortized cost. (2) Value *trading debt securities* for reporting purposes at fair value, with unrealized holding gains or losses included in net income. (3) Value *available-for-sale debt securities* for reporting purposes at fair value, with unrealized holding gains or losses reported as other comprehensive income and as a separate component of stockholders' equity.

2 Understand the procedures for discount and premium amortization on bond investments. Similar to bonds payable, companies should amortize discount or premium on bond investments using the effective-interest method. They apply the effective interest rate or yield to the beginning carrying value of the investment for each interest period in order to compute interest revenue.

3 Identify the categories of equity securities and describe the accounting and reporting treatment for each category. The degree to which one corporation (investor) acquires an interest in the common stock of another corporation (investee) generally determines the accounting treatment for the investment. Long-term investments by one corporation in the common stock of another can be classified according to the percentage of the voting stock of the investee held by the investor.

4 Explain the equity method of accounting and compare it to the fair value method for equity securities.

Under the equity method the investor and the investee acknowledge a substantive economic relationship. The company originally records the investment at cost but subsequently adjusts the amount each period for changes in the net assets of the investee. That is, the investor's proportionate share of the earnings (losses) of the investee periodially increases (decreases) the investment's carrying amount. All dividends received by the investor from the investee decrease the investment's carrying amount. Under the fair value method a company reports the equity investment at fair value each reporting period irrespective of the investee's earnings or dividends paid to it. A company applies the equity method to investment holdings between 20 percent and 50 percent of ownership. It applies the fair value method to holdings below 20 percent.

5 Describe the disclosure requirements for investments in debt and equity securities. Companies should report trading securities at aggregate fair value as current assets. They should classify individual held-to-maturity and available-for-sale securities as current or noncurrent, depending on the circumstances. For available-for-sale and held-to-maturity securities, a company should describe: aggregate fair value, gross unrealized holding gains, gross unrealized losses, amortized cost basis by type (debt and equity), and information about the contractual maturity of debt securities. A company needs a reclassification adjustment when it reports realized gains or losses as part of net income but also shows the amounts as part of other comprehensive income in the current or in previous periods. Companies should report unrealized holding gains or losses related to available-for-sale securities in other comprehensive income and the aggregate balance as accumulated comprehensive income on the balance sheet.

6 Discuss the accounting for impairments of debt and equity investments. Impairments of debt and equity

securities are losses in value that are determined to be other than temporary, are based on a fair value test, and are charged to income.

7 Describe the accounting for transfer of investment securities between categories. Transfers of securities between categories of investments should be accounted for at fair value, with unrealized holding gains or losses treated in accordance with the nature of the transfer.

REVIEW EXERCISE

Powerpuff Corp. carries an account in its general ledger called Investments, which contained the following debits for investment purchases and no credits.

Feb. 1, 2007	Blossom Company common stock, $100 par 200 shares	$ 37,400
April 1	U.S. government bonds, 11%, due April 1, 2017, interest payable April 1 and October 1, 100 bonds of $1,000 par each	100,000
July 1	Buttercup Company 12% bonds, par $50,000, dated March 1, 2003 purchased at par plus accrued interest, interest payable annually on March 1, due March 1, 2027	52,000

Instructions

a Prepare entries necessary to classify the amounts into proper accounts, assuming that all the securities are classified as available-for-sale.

b Prepare the entry to record the accrued interest on December 31, 2007.

c The fair values of the securities on December 31, 2007, were:

Blossom Company common stock	$ 33,800 (1% of total shares)
U.S. government bonds	124,700
Buttercup Company bonds	58,600

What entry or entries, if any, would you recommend be made?

d The U.S. government bonds were sold on July 1, 2008, for $119,200 plus accrued interest. Give the proper entry.

e Now assume Powerpuff's investment in Blossom Company represents 30% of Blossom's shares. Prepare the 2007 entries for the investment in Blossom stock. In 2007, Blossom declared and paid dividends of $9,000 (on September 30) and reported net income of $30,000.

Solution

a

Available-for-Sale Securities	187,400*	
Interest Revenue ($50,000 × .12 × 4/12)	2,000	
Investments		189,400

*$37,400 + $100,000 + $50,000

b

December 31, 2007

Interest Receivable	7,750	
Interest Revenue		7,750**

**Accrued interest: $50,000 × .12 × 10/12 = $5,000
Accrued interest: $100,000 × .11 × 3/12 = 2,750
$7,750

c

**Available-for-Sale Portfolio
December 31, 2007**

Securities	Cost	Fair Value	Unrealized Gain (Loss)
Blossom Company stock	$ 37,400	$ 33,800	$ (3,600)
U.S. government bonds	100,000	124,700	24,700
Buttercup Company bonds	50,000	58,600	8,600
Total	$187,400	$217,100	29,700
Previous securities fair value adjustment balance			0
Securities fair value adjustment—Dr.			$29,700

Securities Fair Value Adjustment (Available-for-Sale)	29,700	
Unrealized Holding Gain or Loss — Equity		29,700

d

July 1, 2008

Cash ($119,200 + $2,750)	121,950	
Available-for-Sale Securities		100,000
Interest Revenue ($100,000 × .11 × 3/12)		2,750
Gain on Sale of Securities		19,200

e

February 1, 2007

Investment in Blossom Stock	37,400	
Cash		37,400

September 30, 2007

Cash	2,700	
Investment in Blossom Stock (30% × $9,000)		2,700

December 31, 2007

Investment in Blossom stock	9,000	
Revenue from Investment (30% × $30,000)		9,000

Questions

1 Distinguish between a debt security and an equity security.

2 What purpose does the variety in bond features (types and characteristics) serve?

3 What is the cost of a long-term investment in bonds?

4 Identify and explain the three types of classifications for investments in debt securities.

5 When should a debt security be classified as held-to-maturity?

6 Explain how trading securities are accounted for and reported.

7 At what amount should trading, available-for-sale, and held-to-maturity securities be reported on the balance sheet?

8 On July 1, 2008, Ingalls Company purchased $2,000,000 of Wilder Company's 8% bonds, due on July 1, 2015. The bonds, which pay interest semiannually on January 1 and July 1, were purchased for $1,750,000 to yield 10%. Determine the amount of interest revenue Ingalls should report on its income statement for year ended December 31, 2008.

9 If the bonds in Question 8 are classified as available-for-sale and they have a fair value at December 31, 2008, of $1,802,000, prepare the journal entry (if any) at December 31, 2008, to record this transaction.

10 Indicate how unrealized holding gains and losses should be reported for investment securities classified as trading, available-for-sale, and held-to-maturity.

11 (a) Assuming no Securities Fair Value Adjustment (Available-for-Sale) account balance at the beginning of the year, prepare the adjusting entry at the end of the year if Laura Company's available-for-sale securities have a market value $70,000 below cost. (b) Assume the same information as part (a), except that Laura Company has a debit balance in its Securities Fair Value Adjustment (Available-for-Sale) account of $10,000 at the beginning of the year. Prepare the adjusting entry at year-end.

12 Identify and explain the different types of classifications for investment in equity securities.

13 Why are held-to-maturity investments applicable only to debt securities?

14 Harry Company sold 10,000 shares of Potter Co. common stock for $27.50 per share, incurring $1,770 in brokerage commissions. These securities were classified as trading and originally cost $250,000. Prepare the entry to record the sale of these securities.

15 Distinguish between the accounting treatment for available-for-sale equity securities and trading equity securities.

16 What constitutes "significant influence" when an investor's financial interest is below the 50% level?

17 Explain how the investment account is affected by investee activities under the equity method.

18 When the equity method is applied, what disclosures should be made in the investor's financial statements?

19 Hatch Co. uses the equity method to account for investments in common stock. What accounting should be made for dividends received in excess of Hatch's share of investee's earnings subsequent to the date of investment?

20 Elizabeth Corp. has an investment with a carrying value (equity method) on its books of $170,000 representing a 40% interest in Dole Company, which suffered a $620,000 loss this year. How should Elizabeth Corp. handle its proportionate share of Dole's loss?

21 Where on the asset side of the balance sheet are trading securities, available-for-sale securities, and held-to-maturity securities reported? Explain.

22 Explain why reclassification adjustments are necessary.

23 Briefly discuss how a transfer of securities from the available-for-sale category to the trading category affects stockholders' equity and income.

24 When is a debt security considered impaired? Explain how to account for the impairment of an available-for-sale debt security.

Brief Exercises

(LO 2)   **BE14-1**   Moonwalker Company purchased, as a held-to-maturity investment, $50,000 of the 9%, 5-year bonds of Prime Time Corporation for $46,304, which provides an 11% return. Prepare Moonwalker's journal entries for (a) the purchase of the investment, and (b) the receipt of annual interest and discount amortization. Assume effective-interest amortization is used.

(LO 2)   **BE14-2**   Use the information from BE14-1, but assume the bonds are purchased as an available-for-sale security. Prepare Moonwalker's journal entries for (a) the purchase of the investment, (b) the receipt of annual interest and discount amortization, and (c) the year-end fair value adjustment. The bonds have a year-end fair value of $47,200.

(LO 2)   **BE14-3**   Mask Corporation purchased, as a held-to-maturity investment, $40,000 of the 8%, 5-year bonds of Phantasy Star, Inc. for $43,412, which provides a 6% return. The bonds pay interest semiannually. Prepare Mask's journal entries for (a) the purchase of the investment, and (b) the receipt of semiannual interest and premium amortization. Assume effective-interest amortization is used.

(LO 2)   **BE14-4**   Pete Sampras Corporation purchased trading investment bonds for $40,000 at par. At December 31, Sampras received annual interest of $2,000, and the fair value of the bonds was $38,400. Prepare Sampras' journal entries for (a) the purchase of the investment, (b) the interest received, and (c) the fair value adjustment.

BE14-5 Buttercup Corporation purchased 300 shares of Bubbles Inc. common stock as an available-for-sale investment for $9,900. During the year, Bubbles paid a cash dividend of $3.25 per share. At year-end, Bubbles stock was selling for $34.50 per share. Prepare Buttercup's journal entries to record (a) the purchase of the investment, (b) the dividends received, and (c) the fair value adjustment. **(LO 3)**

BE14-6 Use the information from BE14-5 but assume the stock was purchased as a trading security. Prepare Buttercup's journal entries to record (a) the purchase of the investment, (b) the dividends received, and (c) the fair value adjustment. **(LO 3)**

BE14-7 Penn Corporation purchased for $300,000 a 25% interest in Teller, Inc. This investment enables Penn to exert significant influence over Teller. During the year Teller earned net income of $180,000 and paid dividends of $60,000. Prepare Penn's journal entries related to this investment. **(LO 4)**

BE14-8 Swartentruber Company has a stock portfolio valued at $4,000. Its cost was $3,500. If the Securities Fair Value Adjustment (Available-for-Sale) account has a debit balance of $200, prepare the journal entry at year-end. **(LO 3)**

BE14-9 The following information relates to **Starbucks** for 2006: net income $564.259 million; unrealized holding gain of $1.767 million related to available-for-sale securities during the year; accumulated other comprehensive income of $20.914 million on January 1, 2006. Assuming no other changes in accumulated other comprehensive income, determine (a) other comprehensive income for 2006, (b) comprehensive income for 2006, and (c) accumulated other comprehensive income at December 31, 2006. **(LO 5)**

BE14-10 Raveonette Co. has an available-for-sale investment in the bonds of No Doubt Corp. with a carrying (and fair) value of $75,000. Raveonette determined that due to poor economic prospects for No Doubt, the bonds have decreased in value to $60,000. It is determined that this loss in value is other-than-temporary. Prepare the journal entry, if any, to record the reduction in value. **(LO 6)**

Exercises

E14-1 **(Investment Classifications)** For the following investments identify whether they are: **(LO 1, 3)**

1. Trading Securities
2. Available-for-Sale Securities
3. Held-to-Maturity Securities

Each case is independent of the other.

(a) A bond that will mature in 4 years was bought 1 month ago when the price dropped. As soon as the value increases, which is expected next month, it will be sold.   *TS*

(b) 10% of the outstanding stock of Farm-Co was purchased. The company is planning on eventually getting a total of 30% of its outstanding stock.   *AS*

(c) 10-year bonds were purchased this year. The bonds mature at the first of next year.   *TS ?*

(d) Bonds that will mature in 5 years are purchased. The company would like to hold them until they mature, but money has been tight recently and they may need to be sold.   *AS*

(e) Preferred stock was purchased for its constant dividend. The company is planning to hold the preferred stock for a long time.   *AS*

(f) A bond that matures in 10 years was purchased. The company is investing money set aside for an expansion project planned 10 years from now.   *HM*

E14-2 **(Entries for Held-to-Maturity Securities)** On January 1, 2008, Dagwood Company purchased at par 12% bonds having a maturity value of $300,000. They are dated January 1, 2008, and mature January 1, 2013, with interest receivable December 31 of each year. The bonds are classified in the held-to-maturity category. **(LO 2)**

Instructions

(a) Prepare the journal entry at the date of the bond purchase.
(b) Prepare the journal entry to record the interest received for 2008.
(c) Prepare the journal entry to record the interest received for 2009.

E14-3 **(Entries for Held-to-Maturity Securities)** On January 1, 2008, Hi and Lois Company purchased 12% bonds, having a maturity value of $300,000, for $322,744.44. The bonds provide the bondholders with a 10% **(LO 2)**

yield. They are dated January 1, 2008, and mature January 1, 2013, with interest receivable December 31 of each year. Hi and Lois Company uses the effective-interest method to allocate unamortized discount or premium. The bonds are classified in the held-to-maturity category.

Instructions

(a) Prepare the journal entry at the date of the bond purchase.
(b) Prepare a bond amortization schedule.
(c) Prepare the journal entry to record the interest received and the amortization for 2008.
(d) Prepare the journal entry to record the interest received and the amortization for 2009.

(LO 2)   **E14-4   (Entries for Available-for-Sale Securities)**   Assume the same information as in E14-3 except that the securities are classified as available-for-sale. The fair value of the bonds at December 31 of each year-end is as follows.

2008	$320,500	2011	$310,000
2009	$309,000	2012	$300,000
2010	$308,000		

Instructions

(a) Prepare the journal entry at the date of the bond purchase.
(b) Prepare the journal entries to record the interest received and recognition of fair value for 2008.
(c) Prepare the journal entry to record the recognition of fair value for 2009.

(LO 2)   **E14-5   (Effective-Interest versus Straight-Line Bond Amortization)**   On January 1, 2008, Phantom Company acquires $200,000 of Spiderman Products, Inc., 9% bonds at a price of $185,589. The interest is payable each December 31, and the bonds mature December 31, 2010. The investment will provide Phantom Company a 12% yield. The bonds are classified as held-to-maturity.

? HTM

Instructions

(a) Prepare a 3-year schedule of interest revenue and bond discount amortization, applying the straight-line method.
(b) Prepare a 3-year schedule of interest revenue and bond discount amortization, applying the effective-interest method.
(c) Prepare the journal entry for the interest receipt of December 31, 2009, and the discount amortization under the straight-line method.
(d) Prepare the journal entry for the interest receipt of December 31, 2009, and the discount amortization under the effective-interest method.

(LO 3)   **E14-6   (Entries for Available-for-Sale and Trading Securities)**   The following information is available for Barkley Company at December 31, 2008, regarding its investments.

Securities	Cost	Fair Value
3,000 shares of Myers Corporation Common Stock	$40,000	$48,000
1,000 shares of Cole Incorporated Preferred Stock	25,000	22,000
	$65,000	$70,000

Instructions

(a) Prepare the adjusting entry (if any) for 2008, assuming the securities are classified as trading.
(b) Prepare the adjusting entry (if any) for 2008, assuming the securities are classified as available-for-sale.
(c) Discuss how the amounts reported in the financial statements are affected by the entries in (a) and (b).

(LO 3)   **E14-7   (Trading Securities Entries)**   On December 21, 2008, Bucky Katt Company provided you with the following information regarding its trading securities.

December 31, 2008

Investments (Trading)	Cost	Fair Value	Unrealized Gain (Loss)
Clemson Corp. stock	$20,000	$19,000	$(1,000)
Colorado Co. stock	10,000	9,000	(1,000)
Buffaloes Co. stock	20,000	20,600	600
Total of portfolio	$50,000	$48,600	(1,400)
Previous securities fair value adjustment balance			–0–
Securities fair value adjustment—Cr.			$(1,400)

During 2009, Colorado Company stock was sold for $9,400. The fair value of the stock on December 31, 2009, was: Clemson Corp. stock—$19,100; Buffaloes Co. stock—$20,500.

Instructions

(a) Prepare the adjusting journal entry needed on December 31, 2008.
(b) Prepare the journal entry to record the sale of the Colorado Company stock during 2009.
(c) Prepare the adjusting journal entry needed on December 31, 2009.

E14-8 **(Available-for-Sale Securities Entries and Reporting)** Satchel Corporation purchases equity securities costing $73,000 and classifies them as available-for-sale securities. At December 31, the fair value of the port-folio is $65,000.

(LO 3)

Instructions

Prepare the adjusting entry to report the securities properly. Indicate the statement presentation of the accounts in your entry.

E14-9 **(Available-for-Sale Securities Entries and Financial Statement Presentation)** At December 31, 2008, the available-for-sale equity portfolio for Steffi Graf, Inc. is as follows.

(LO 3)

Security	Cost	Fair Value	Unrealized Gain (Loss)
A	$17,500	$15,000	($2,500)
B	12,500	14,000	1,500
C	23,000	25,500	2,500
Total	$53,000	$54,500	1,500
Previous securities fair value adjustment balance—Dr.			400
Securities fair value adjustment—Dr.			$1,100

On January 20, 2009, Steffi Graf, Inc. sold security A for $15,100. The sale proceeds are net of brokerage fees.

Instructions

(a) Prepare the adjusting entry at December 31, 2008, to report the portfolio at fair value.
(b) Show the balance sheet presentation of the investment related accounts at December 31, 2008. (Ignore notes presentation.)
(c) Prepare the journal entry for the 2009 sale of security A.

E14-10 **(Comprehensive Income Disclosure)** Assume the same information as E14-9 and that Steffi Graf Inc. reports net income in 2008 of $120,000 and in 2009 of $140,000. Total holding gains (including any realized holding gain or loss) arising during 2009 total $40,000.

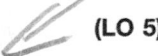 **(LO 5)**

Instructions

(a) Prepare a statement of comprehensive income for 2008 starting with net income.
(b) Prepare a statement of comprehensive income for 2009 starting with net income.

E14-11 **(Equity Securities Entries)** Arantxa Corporation made the following cash purchases of securities during 2008, which is the first year in which Arantxa invested in securities.

(LO 3)

1. On January 15, purchased 10,000 shares of Sanchez Company's common stock at $33.50 per share plus commission $1,980.

2. On April 1, purchased 5,000 shares of Vicario Co.'s common stock at $52.00 per share plus commission $3,370.

3. On September 10, purchased 7,000 shares of WTA Co.'s preferred stock at $26.50 per share plus commission $4,910.

On May 20, 2008, Arantxa sold 4,000 shares of Sanchez Company's common stock at a market price of $35 per share less brokerage commissions, taxes, and fees of $3,850. The year-end fair values per share were: Sanchez $30, Vicario $55, and WTA $28. In addition, the chief accountant of Arantxa told you that Arantxa Corporation plans to hold these securities for the long term but may sell them in order to earn profits from appreciation in prices.

Instructions

(a) Prepare the journal entries to record the above three security purchases.
(b) Prepare the journal entry for the security sale on May 20.
(c) Compute the unrealized gains or losses and prepare the adjusting entry for Arantxa on December 31, 2008.

(LO 3, 4)   **E14-12** (Journal Entries for Fair Value and Equity Methods) Presented below are two independent situations.

Situation 1

Conchita Cosmetics acquired 10% of the 200,000 shares of common stock of Martinez Fashion at a total cost of $13 per share on March 18, 2008. On June 30, Martinez declared and paid a $75,000 cash dividend. On December 31, Martinez reported net income of $122,000 for the year. At December 31, the market price of Martinez Fashion was $15 per share. The securities are classified as available-for-sale.

Situation 2

Monica, Inc. obtained significant influence over Seles Corporation by buying 30% of Seles's 30,000 outstanding shares of common stock at a total cost of $9 per share on January 1, 2008. On June 15, Seles declared and paid a cash dividend of $36,000. On December 31, Seles reported a net income of $85,000 for the year.

Instructions

Prepare all necessary journal entries in 2008 for both situations.

(LO 4)   **E14-13** (Equity Method) Parent Co. invested $1,000,000 in Sub Co. for 25% of its outstanding stock. Sub Co. pays out 40% of net income in dividends each year.

Instructions

Use the information in the following T-account for the investment in Sub to answer the following questions.

Investment in Sub Co.	
1,000,000	
110,000	
	44,000

(a) How much was Parent Co.'s share of Sub Co.'s net income for the year?
(b) How much was Parent Co.'s share of Sub Co.'s dividends for the year?
(c) What was Sub Co.'s total net income for the year?
(d) What was Sub Co.'s total dividends for the year?

(LO 3)   **E14-14** (Equity Investment—Trading) Oregon Co. had purchased 200 shares of Washington Co. for $40 each this year and classified the investment as a trading security. Oregon Co. sold 100 shares of the stock for $45 each. At year end the price per share of the Washington Co. stock had dropped to $35.

Instructions

Prepare the journal entries for these transactions and any year-end adjustments.

(LO 3)   **E14-15** (Equity Investments—Trading) Kenseth Company has the following securities in its trading portfolio of securities on December 31, 2008.

Investments (Trading)	Cost	Fair Value
1,500 shares of Gordon, Inc., Common	$ 73,500	$ 69,000
5,000 shares of Wallace Corp., Common	180,000	175,000
400 shares of Martin, Inc., Preferred	60,000	61,600
	$313,500	$305,600

All of the securities were purchased in 2008.
In 2009, Kenseth completed the following securities transactions.

      March 1   Sold the 1,500 shares of Gordon, Inc., Common, @ $45 less fees of $1,200.
      April 1   Bought 700 shares of Earnhart Corp., Common, @ $75 plus fees of $1,300.

Kenseth Company's portfolio of trading securities appeared as follows on December 31, 2009.

Investments (Trading)	Cost	Fair Value
5,000 shares of Wallace Corp., Common	$180,000	$175,000
700 shares of Earnhart Corp., Common	53,800	50,400
400 shares of Martin, Inc., Preferred	60,000	58,000
	$293,800	$283,400

Instructions

Prepare the general journal entries for Kenseth Company for:

(a) The 2008 adjusting entry.
(b) The sale of the Gordon stock.
(c) The purchase of the Earnhart stock.
(d) The 2009 adjusting entry for the trading portfolio.

E14-16 **(Fair Value and Equity Method Compared)** Jaycie Phelps Inc. acquired 20% of the outstanding com **(LO 3, 4)**
mon stock of Theresa Kulikowski Inc. on December 31, 2008. The purchase price was $1,200,000 for 50,000
shares. Kulikowski Inc. declared and paid an $0.85 per share cash dividend on June 30 and on December 31,
2009. Kulikowski reported net income of $730,000 for 2009. The fair value of Kulikowski's stock was $27 per
share at December 31, 2009.

Instructions

(a) Prepare the journal entries for Jaycie Phelps Inc. for 2008 and 2009, assuming that Phelps cannot exercise significant influence over Kulikowski. The securities should be classified as available-for-sale.
(b) Prepare the journal entries for Jaycie Phelps Inc. for 2008 and 2009, assuming that Phelps can exercise significant influence over Kulikowski.
(c) At what amount is the investment in securities reported on the balance sheet under each of these methods at
December 31, 2009? What is the total net income reported in 2009 under each of these methods?

E14-17 **(Equity Method)** On January 1, 2008, Pennington Corporation purchased 30% of the common shares **(LO 4)**
of Edwards Company for $180,000. During the year, Edwards earned net income of $80,000 and paid dividends
of $20,000.

Instructions

Prepare the entries for Pennington to record the purchase and any additional entries related to this investment in
Edwards Company in 2008.

E14-18 **(Impairment of Debt Securities)** Hagar Corporation has municipal bonds classified as available-for **(LO 6)**
sale at December 31, 2008. These bonds have a par value of $800,000, an amortized cost of $800,000, and a fair
value of $720,000. The unrealized loss of $80,000 previously recognized as other comprehensive income and as a
separate component of stockholders' equity is now determined to be other than temporary. That is, the company believes that impairment accounting is now appropriate for these bonds.

Instructions

(a) Prepare the journal entry to recognize the impairment.
(b) What is the new cost basis of the municipal bonds? Given that the maturity value of the bonds is $800,000,
should Hagar Corporation amortize the difference between the carrying amount and the maturity value over
the life of the bonds?
(c) At December 31, 2009, the fair value of the municipal bonds is $760,000. Prepare the entry (if any) to record
this information.

See the book's companion website, at www.wiley.com/college/warfield, for
Additional Exercises.

Problems

P14-1 **(Debt Securities)** Presented below is an amortization schedule related to Kathy Baker Company's 5-year, **(LO 2)**
$100,000 bond with a 7% interest rate and a 5% yield, purchased on December 31, 2008, for $108,660.

Date	Cash Received	Interest Revenue	Bond Premium Amortization	Carrying Amount of Bonds
12/31/08				$108,660
12/31/09	$7,000	$5,433	$1,567	107,093
12/31/10	7,000	5,354	1,646	105,447
12/31/11	7,000	5,272	1,728	103,719
12/31/12	7,000	5,186	1,814	101,905
12/31/13	7,000	5,095	1,905	100,000

The following schedule presents a comparison of the amortized cost and fair value of the bonds at year-end.

	12/31/09	12/31/10	12/31/11	12/31/12	12/31/13
Amortized cost	$107,093	$105,447	$103,719	$101,905	$100,000
Fair value	$106,500	$107,500	$105,650	$103,000	$100,000

Instructions

(a) Prepare the journal entry to record the purchase of these bonds on December 31, 2008, assuming the bonds are classified as held-to-maturity securities.

(b) Prepare the journal entry(ies) related to the held-to-maturity bonds for 2009.

(c) Prepare the journal entry(ies) related to the held-to-maturity bonds for 2011.

(d) Prepare the journal entry(ies) to record the purchase of these bonds, assuming they are classified as available-for-sale.

(e) Prepare the journal entry(ies) related to the available-for-sale bonds for 2009.

(f) Prepare the journal entry(ies) related to the available-for-sale bonds for 2011.

(LO 2)   **P14-2 (Available-for-Sale Debt Securities)**   On January 1, 2008, Rob Wilco Company purchased $200,000, 8% bonds of Mercury Co. for $184,557. The bonds were purchased to yield 10% interest. Interest is payable semiannually on July 1 and January 1. The bonds mature on January 1, 2013. Rob Wilco Company uses the effective-interest method to amortize discount or premium. On January 1, 2010, Rob Wilco Company sold the bonds for $185,363 after receiving interest to meet its liquidity needs.

Instructions

(a) Prepare the journal entry to record the purchase of bonds on January 1. Assume that the bonds are classified as available-for-sale.

(b) Prepare the amortization schedule for the bonds.

(c) Prepare the journal entries to record the semiannual interest on July 1, 2008, and December 31, 2008.

(d) If the fair value of Mercury bonds is $186,363 on December 31, 2009, prepare the necessary adjusting entry. (Assume the securities fair value adjustment balance on January 1, 2009, is a debit of $3,375.)

(e) Prepare the journal entry to record the sale of the bonds on January 1, 2010.

(LO 2, 3)   **P14-3 (Available-for-Sale Investments)**   Octavio Paz Corp. carries an account in its general ledger called Investments, which contained debits for investment purchases, and no credits. These debits are described as follows.

Feb. 1, 2008	Chiang Kai-shek Company common stock, $100 par, 200 shares	$ 37,400
April 1	U.S. government bonds, 11%, due April 1, 2018, interest payable April 1 and October 1, 100 bonds of $1,000 par each	100,000
July 1	Claude Monet Company 12% bonds, par $50,000, dated March 1, 2008 purchased at 104 plus accrued interest, interest payable annually on March 1, due March 1, 2028	54,000

Instructions

(Round all computations to the nearest dollar.)

(a) Prepare entries necessary to classify the amounts into proper accounts, assuming that all the securities are classified as available-for-sale.

(b) Prepare the entry to record the accrued interest and the amortization of premium on December 31, 2008, using the straight-line method.

(c) The fair values of the securities on December 31, 2008, were:

Chiang Kai-shek Company common stock	$ 33,800
U.S. government bonds	124,700
Claude Monet Company bonds	58,600

What entry or entries, if any, would you recommend be made?

(d) The U.S. government bonds were sold on July 1, 2009, for $119,200 plus accrued interest. Give the proper entry.

(LO 2)   **P14-4 (Available-for-Sale Debt Securities)**   Presented below is information taken from a bond investment amortization schedule with related fair values provided. These bonds are classified as available-for-sale.

	12/31/08	12/31/09	12/31/10
Amortized cost	$491,150	$519,442	$550,000
Fair value	$499,000	$506,000	$550,000

Instructions

(a) Indicate whether the bonds were purchased at a discount or at a premium.

(b) Prepare the adjusting entry to record the bonds at fair value at December 31, 2008. The Securities Fair Value Adjustment account has a debit balance of $1,000 prior to adjustment.

(c) Prepare the adjusting entry to record the bonds at fair value at December 31, 2009.

P14-5 (Equity Securities Entries and Disclosures) Incognito Company has the following securities in its investment portfolio on December 31, 2007 (all securities were purchased in 2007): (1) 3,000 shares of Green Day Co. common stock which cost $58,500, (2) 10,000 shares of David Sanborn Ltd. common stock which cost $580,000, and (3) 6,000 shares of Abba Company preferred stock which cost $255,000. The Securities Fair Value Adjustment account shows a credit of $10,100 at the end of 2007.

(LO 3)

In 2008, Incognito completed the following securities transactions.

1. On January 15, sold 3,000 shares of Green Day's common stock at $23 per share less fees of $2,150.

2. On April 17, purchased 1,000 shares of Tractors' common stock at $31.50 per share plus fees of $1,980.

On December 31, 2008, the market values per share of these securities were: Green Day $20, Sanborn $62, Abba $40, and Tractors $29. In addition, the accounting supervisor of Incognito told you that, even though all these securities have readily determinable fair values, Incognito will not actively trade these securities because the top management intends to hold them for more than one year.

Instructions

(a) Prepare the entry for the security sale on January 15, 2008.

(b) Prepare the journal entry to record the security purchase on April 17, 2008.

(c) Compute the unrealized gains or losses and prepare the adjusting entry for Incognito on December 31, 2008.

(d) How should the unrealized gains or losses be reported on Incognito's balance sheet? — ?

P14-6 (Trading and Available-for-Sale Securities Entries) Loxley Company has the following portfolio of investment securities at September 30, 2008, its last reporting date.

(LO 3)

Trading Securities	Cost	Fair Value
Dan Fogelberg, Inc. common (5,000 shares)	$225,000	$200,000
Petra, Inc. preferred (3,500 shares)	133,000	140,000
Tim Weisberg Corp. common (1,000 shares)	180,000	179,000

On October 10, 2008, the Fogelberg shares were sold at a price of $54 per share. In addition, 3,000 shares of Los Tigres common stock were acquired at $59.50 per share on November 2, 2008. The December 31, 2008, fair values were: Petra $96,000, Los Tigres $132,000, and the Weisberg common $193,000. All the securities are classified as trading.

Instructions

(a) Prepare the journal entries to record the sale, purchase, and adjusting entries related to the trading securities in the last quarter of 2008.

(b) How would the entries in part (a) change if the securities were classified as available-for-sale?

P14-7 (Available-for-Sale and Held-to-Maturity Debt Securities Entries) The following information relates to the debt securities investments of Yellowjackets Company.

(LO 2)

1. On February 1, the company purchased 12% bonds of Hilton Paris Co. having a par value of $500,000 at 100 plus accrued interest. Interest is payable April 1 and October 1.

2. On April 1, semiannual interest is received.

3. On July 1, 9% bonds of Chieftains, Inc. were purchased. These bonds with a par value of $200,000 were purchased at 100 plus accrued interest. Interest dates are June 1 and December 1.

4. On September 1, bonds with a par value of $100,000, purchased on February 1, are sold at 99 plus accrued interest.

5. On October 1, semiannual interest is received.

6. On December 1, semiannual interest is received.

7. On December 31, the fair value of the bonds purchased February 1 and July 1 are 95 and 93, respectively.

Instructions

(a) Prepare any journal entries you consider necessary, including year-end entries (December 31), assuming these are available-for-sale securities.

(b) If Yellowjackets classified these as held-to-maturity securities, explain how the journal entries would differ from those in part (a).

(LO 3, 4, 5) **P14-8** **(Fair Value and Equity Methods)** Pacers Corp. is a medium-sized corporation specializing in quarrying stone for building construction. The company has long dominated the market, at one time achieving a 70% market penetration. During prosperous years, the company's profits, coupled with a conservative dividend policy, resulted in funds available for outside investment. Over the years, Pacers has had a policy of investing idle cash in equity securities. In particular, Pacers has made periodic investments in the company's principal supplier, Pierce Industries. Although the firm currently owns 12% of the outstanding common stock of Pierce Industries, Pacers does not have significant influence over the operations of Pierce Industries.

Cheryl Miller has recently joined Pacers as assistant controller, and her first assignment is to prepare the 2008 year-end adjusting entries for the accounts that are valued by the "fair value" rule for financial reporting purposes. Miller has gathered the following information about Pacers' pertinent accounts.

1. Pacers has trading securities related to Dale Davis Motors and Rik Smits Electric. During this fiscal year, Pacers purchased 100,000 shares of Davis Motors for $1,400,000; these shares currently have a market value of $1,600,000. Pacers' investment in Smits Electric has not been profitable; the company acquired 50,000 shares of Smits in April 2008 at $20 per share, a purchase that currently has a value of $620,000.

2. Prior to 2008, Pacers invested $22,500,000 in Pierce Industries and has not changed its holdings this year. This investment in Pierce Industries was valued at $21,500,000 on December 31, 2007. Pacers' 12% ownership of Pierce Industries has a current market value of $22,275,000.

Instructions

(a) Prepare the appropriate adjusting entries for Pacers as of December 31, 2008, to reflect the application of the "fair value" rule for both classes of securities described above.

(b) For both classes of securities presented above, describe how the results of the valuation adjustments made in (a) would be reflected in the body of and notes to Pacers' 2008 financial statements.

(c) Prepare the entries for the Pierce investment, assuming that Pacers owns 30% of Pierce's shares. Pierce reported income of $500,000 in 2008 and paid cash dividends of $100,000.

(LO 3, 5) **P14-9** **(Financial Statement Presentation of Available-for-Sale Investments)** Woolford Company has the following portfolio of available-for-sale securities at December 31, 2008.

Security	Quantity	Percent Interest	Per Share Cost	Per Share Market
Favre, Inc.	2,000 shares	8%	$11	$16
Brady Corp.	5,000 shares	14%	23	17
McNabb Company	4,000 shares	2%	31	24

Instructions

(a) What should be reported on Woolford's December 31, 2008, balance sheet relative to these long-term available-for-sale securities?

On December 31, 2009, Woolford's portfolio of available-for-sale securities consisted of the following common stocks.

Security	Quantity	Percent Interest	Per Share Cost	Per Share Market
Brady Corp.	5,000 shares	14%	$23	$30
McNabb Company	4,000 shares	2%	31	23
McNabb Company	2,000 shares	1%	25	23

At the end of year 2009, Woolford Company changed its intent relative to its investment in Favre, Inc. and reclassified the shares to trading securities status when the shares were selling for $9 per share.

(b) What should be reported on the face of Woolford's December 31, 2009, balance sheet relative to available-for-sale securities investments? What should be reported to reflect the transactions above in Woolford's 2009 income statement?

(c) Assuming that comparative financial statements for 2008 and 2009 are presented, draft the footnote necessary for full disclosure of Woolford's transactions and position in equity securities.

(LO 3, 5) **P14-10** **(Gain on Sale of Securities and Comprehensive Income)** On January 1, 2008, Enid Inc. had the following balance sheet.

Enid Inc.
Balance Sheet
As of January 1, 2008

Assets		Equity	
Cash	$ 50,000	Common stock	$250,000
Available-for-sale securities	240,000	Accumulated other comprehensive income	40,000
Total	$290,000	Total	$290,000

The accumulated other comprehensive income related to unrealized holding gains on available-for-sale securities. The fair value of Enid Inc.'s available-for-sale securities at December 31, 2008, was $190,000; its cost was $120,000. No securities were purchased during the year. Enid Inc.'s income statement for 2008 was as follows. (Ignore income taxes.)

Enid Inc.
Income Statement
For the Year Ended December 31, 2008

Dividend revenue	$15,000
Gain on sale of available-for-sale securities	20,000
Net income	$35,000

Instructions

(Assume all transactions during the year were for cash.)
(a) Prepare the journal entry to record the sale of the available-for-sale securities in 2008.
(b) Prepare a statement of comprehensive income for 2008.
(c) Prepare a balance sheet as of December 31, 2008.

P14-11 **(Equity Investments—Available for Sale)**   Big Brother Holdings, Inc. had the following available-for-sale investment portfolio at January 1, 2008.   **(LO 3)**

Earl Company	1,000 shares @ $15 each	$15,000
Josie Company	900 shares @ $20 each	18,000
David Company	500 shares @ $9 each	4,500
Available-for-sale securities @ cost		37,500
Securities fair value adjustment—Available-for-sale		(7,500)
Available-for-sale securities @ fair value		$30,000

During 2008, the following transactions took place.

1. On March 1, Josie Company paid a $2 per share dividend.
2. On April 30, Big Brother Holdings, Inc. sold 300 shares of David Company for $10 per share.
3. On May 15, Big Brother Holdings, Inc. purchased 50 more shares of Earl Co. stock at $16 per share.
4. At December 31, 2008, the stocks had the following price per share values: Earl $17, Josie $19, and David $8.

During 2009, the following transactions took place.

5. On February 1, Big Brother Holdings, Inc. sold the remaining David shares for $7 per share.
6. On March 1, Josie Company paid a $2 per share dividend.
7. On December 21, Earl Company declared a cash dividend of $3 per share to be paid in the next month.
8. At December 31, 2009, the stocks had the following price per shares values: Earl $19 and Josie $21.

Instructions

(a) Prepare journal entries for each of the above transactions.
(b) Prepare a partial balance sheet showing the Investments account at December 31, 2008 and 2009.

(LO 3, 5) **P14-12** **(Available-for-Sale Securities—Statement Presentation)** Alvarez Corp. invested its excess cash in available-for-sale securities during 2008. As of December 31, 2008, the portfolio of available-for-sale securities consisted of the following common stocks.

Security	Quantity	Cost	Fair Value
Keesha Jones, Inc.	1,000 shares	$ 15,000	$ 21,000
Eola Corp.	2,000 shares	50,000	42,000
Yevette Aircraft	2,000 shares	72,000	60,000
	Totals	$137,000	$123,000

−14 000

Instructions

(a) What should be reported on Alvarez's December 31, 2008, balance sheet relative to these securities? What should be reported on Alvarez's 2008 income statement?

On December 31, 2009, Alvarez's portfolio of available-for-sale securities consisted of the following common stocks.

Security	Quantity	Cost	Fair Value
Keesha Jones, Inc.	1,000 shares	$ 15,000	$20,000
Keesha Jones, Inc.	2,000 shares	38,000	40,000
King Company	1,000 shares	16,000	12,000
Yevette Aircraft	2,000 shares	72,000	22,000
	Totals	$141,000	$94,000

During the year 2009, Alvarez Corp. sold 2,000 shares of Eola Corp. for $38,200 and purchased 2,000 more shares of Keesha Jones, Inc. and 1,000 shares of King Company.

(b) What should be reported on Alvarez's December 31, 2009, balance sheet? What should be reported on Alvarez's 2009 income statement?

On December 31, 2010, Alvarez's portfolio of available-for-sale securities consisted of the following common stocks.

Security	Quantity	Cost	Fair Value
Yevette Aircraft	2,000 shares	$72,000	$82,000
King Company	500 shares	8,000	6,000
	Totals	$80,000	$88,000

During the year 2010, Alvarez Corp. sold 3,000 shares of Keesha Jones, Inc. for $39,900 and 500 shares of King Company at a loss of $2,700.

(c) What should be reported on the face of Alvarez's December 31, 2010, balance sheet? What should be reported on Alvarez's 2010 income statement?

(d) What would be reported in a statement of comprehensive income at (1) December 31, 2008, and (2) December 31, 2009?

ACCOUNTING IN ACTION

Financial Reporting and Analysis

■ **Financial Reporting Issues: The Procter & Gamble Company**

AIA14-1 The financial statements of **Procter & Gamble (P&G)** can be accessed at the book's website.

Instructions

Refer to P&G's financial statements and the accompanying notes to answer the following questions.

(a) What investments does P&G report in 2006, and where are these investments reported in its financial statements?

(b) How are P&G's investments valued?

(c) How does P&G determine fair value?

■ Comparative Analysis: The Coca-Cola Company and PepsiCo, Inc.

AIA14-2 The financial statements of **The Coca-Cola Company** and **PepsiCo, Inc.** can be accessed at the book's website.

Instructions

Use information found at the book's website to answer the following questions.

(a) Based on the information contained in these financial statements, determine each of the following for each company.

    (1) Cash used in (for) investing activities during 2006 (from the statement of cash flows).

    (2) Cash used for acquisitions and investments in unconsolidated affiliates (or principally bottling companies) during 2006.

    (3) Total investment in unconsolidated affiliates (or investments and other assets) at the end of 2006.

    (4) What conclusions concerning the management of investments can be drawn from these data?

(b) (1) Briefly identify from Coca-Cola's December 31, 2006, balance sheet the investments it reported as being accounted for under the equity method. (2) What is the amount of investments that Coca-Cola reported in its 2006 balance sheet as "cost method investments," and what is the nature of these investments?

(c) In its Note 11 on Financial Instruments, what total amounts did Coca-Cola report at December 31, 2006, as: (1) trading securities, (2) available-for-sale securities, and (3) held-to-maturity securities?

■ Financial Statement Analysis

AIA14-3 **Union Planters** is a Tennessee bank holding company (that is, a corporation that owns banks). (Union Planters is now part of **Regions Bank**.) Union Planters manages $32 billion in assets, the largest of which is its loan portfolio of $19 billion. In addition to its loan portfolio, however, like other banks it has significant debt investments. The nature of these investments varies from short-term in nature to long-term in nature. As a consequence, consistent with the requirements of accounting rules, Union Planters reports its investments in two different categories—trading and available-for-sale. The following facts were found in a recent Union Planters' annual report.

Union Planters
(all dollars in millions)

	Amortized Cost	Gross Unrealized Gains	Gross Unrealized Losses	Fair Value
Trading account assets	$ 275	—	—	$ 275
Securities available for sale	8,209	$108	$15	8,302
Net income				224
Net securities gains (losses)				(9)

Instructions

(a) Why do you suppose Union Planters purchases investments, rather than simply making loans? Why does it purchase investments that vary in nature both in terms of their maturities and in type (debt versus stock)?

(b) How must Union Planters account for its investments in each of the two categories?

(c) In what ways does classifying investments into two different categories assist investors in evaluating the profitability of a company like Union Planters?

(d) Suppose that the management of Union Planters was not happy with its net income for the year. What step could it have taken with its investment portfolio that would have definitely increased reported profit? How much could it have increased reported profit? Why do you suppose it chose not to do this?

Concepts for Analysis

AIA14-4 **(Issues Raised about Investment Securities)** You have just started work for Andre Love Co. as part of the controller's group involved in current financial reporting problems. Jackie Franklin, controller for Love, is interested in your accounting background because the company has experienced a series of financial reporting surprises over the last few years. Recently, the controller has learned from the company's auditors that an FASB *Statement* may apply to its investment in securities. She assumes that you are familiar with this pronouncement and asks how the following situations should be reported in the financial statements.

Situation 1
Trading securities in the current assets section have a fair value that is $4,200 lower than cost.

Situation 2
A trading security whose fair value is currently less than cost is transferred to the available-for-sale category.

Situation 3
An available-for-sale security whose fair value is currently less than cost is classified as noncurrent but is to be reclassified as current.

Situation 4
A company's portfolio of available-for-sale securities consists of the common stock of one company. At the end of the prior year the fair value of the security was 50% of original cost, and this reduction in market value was reported as an other than temporary impairment. However, at the end of the current year the fair value of the security had appreciated to twice the original cost.

Situation 5
The company has purchased some convertible debentures that it plans to hold for less than a year. The fair value of the convertible debentures is $7,700 below its cost.

Instructions
What is the effect upon carrying value and earnings for each of the situations above? Assume that these situations are unrelated.

AIA14-5 **(Equity Securities)** James Joyce Co. has the following available-for-sale securities outstanding on December 31, 2008 (its first year of operations).

	Cost	Fair Value
Anna Wickham Corp. Stock	$20,000	$19,000
D. H. Lawrence Company Stock	10,000	8,800
Edith Sitwell Company Stock	20,000	20,600
	$50,000	$48,400

During 2009 D. H. Lawrence Company stock was sold for $9,200, the difference between the $9,200 and the "fair value" of $8,800 being recorded as a "Gain on Sale of Securities." The market price of the stock on December 31, 2009, was: Anna Wickham Corp. stock $19,900; Edith Sitwell Company stock $20,500.

Instructions
(a) What justification is there for valuing available-for-sale securities at fair value and reporting the unrealized gain or loss as part of stockholders' equity?

(b) How should James Joyce Company apply this rule on December 31, 2008? Explain.

(c) Did James Joyce Company properly account for the sale of the D. H. Lawrence Company stock? Explain.

(d) Are there any additional entries necessary for James Joyce Company at December 31, 2009, to reflect the facts on the financial statements in accordance with generally accepted accounting principles? Explain.

(AICPA adapted)

AIA14-6 **(Financial Statement Effect of Equity Securities)** Presented below are three unrelated situations involving equity securities.

Situation 1
An equity security, whose market value is currently less than cost, is classified as available-for-sale but is to be reclassified as trading.

Situation 2

A noncurrent portfolio with an aggregate market value in excess of cost includes one particular security whose market value has declined to less than one-half of the original cost. The decline in value is considered to be other than temporary.

Situation 3

The portfolio of trading securities has a cost in excess of fair value of $13,500. The available-for-sale portfolio has a fair value in excess of cost of $28,600.

Instructions

What is the effect upon carrying value and earnings for each of the situations above?

AIA14-7 **(Equity Securities)** The Financial Accounting Standards Board issued its *Statement No. 115* to clarify accounting methods and procedures with respect to certain debt and all equity securities. An important part of the statement concerns the distinction between held-to-maturity, available-for-sale, and trading securities.

Instructions

(a) Why does a company maintain an investment portfolio of held-to-maturity, available-for-sale, and trading securities?

(b) What factors should be considered in determining whether investments in securities should be classified as held-to-maturity, available-for-sale, and trading? How do these factors affect the accounting treatment for unrealized losses?

AIA14-8 **(Investment Accounted for under the Equity Method)** On July 1, 2008, Sylvia Warner Company purchased for cash 40% of the outstanding capital stock of Robert Graves Company. Both Sylvia Warner Company and Robert Graves Company have a December 31 year-end. Graves Company, whose common stock is actively traded in the over-the-counter market, reported its total net income for the year to Warner Company and also paid cash dividends on November 15, 2008, to Warner Company and its other stockholders.

Instructions

How should Warner Company report the above facts in its December 31, 2008, balance sheet and its income statement for the year then ended? Discuss the rationale for your answer.

(AICPA adapted)

AIA14-9 **(Equity Investment)** On July 1, 2008, Munns Company purchased for cash 40% of the outstanding capital stock of Huber Corporation. Both Munns and Huber have a December 31 year-end. Huber Corporation, whose common stock is actively traded on the American Stock Exchange, paid a cash dividend on November 15, 2008, to Munns Company and its other stockholders. It also reported its total net income for the year of $920,000 to Munns Company.

Instructions

Prepare a one-page memorandum of instructions on how Munns Company should report the above facts in its December 31, 2008, balance sheet and its 2008 income statement. In your memo, identify and describe the method of valuation you recommend. Provide rationale where you can. Address your memo to the chief accountant at Munns Company.

Professional Tools

■ Ethical Decision Making

AIA14-10 **(Fair Value)** Addison Manufacturing holds a large portfolio of debt and equity securities as an investment. The fair value of the portfolio is greater than its original cost, even though some securities have decreased in value. Ted Abernathy, the financial vice president, and Donna Nottebart, the controller, are near year-end in the process of classifying for the first time this securities portfolio in accordance with *FASB Statement No. 115*. Abernathy wants to classify those securities that have increased in value during the period as trading securities in order to increase net income this year. He wants to classify all the securities that have decreased in value as available-for-sale (the equity securities) and as held-to-maturity (the debt securities).

Nottebart disagrees. She wants to classify those securities that have decreased in value as trading securities and those that have increased in value as available-for-sale (equity) and held-to-maturity (debt). She contends that the company is having a good earnings year and that recognizing the losses will help to smooth the income this year. As a result, the company will have built-in gains for future periods when the company may not be as profitable.

Instructions

Answer the following questions.

(a) Will classifying the portfolio as each proposes actually have the effect on earnings that each says it will?

(b) Is there anything unethical in what each of them proposes? Who are the stakeholders affected by their proposals?

(c) Assume that Abernathy and Nottebart properly classify the entire portfolio into trading, available-for-sale, and held-to-maturity categories. But then each proposes to sell just before year-end the securities with gains or with losses, as the case may be, to accomplish their effect on earnings. Is this unethical?

■ Financial Accounting Research System (FARS)

AIA14-11 Your client, Cascade Company, is planning to invest some of its excess cash in 5-year revenue bonds issued by the county and in the stock of one of its suppliers, Teton Co. Teton's shares trade on the over-the-counter market. Cascade plans to classify these investments as available-for-sale. They would like you to conduct some research on the accounting for these investments.

Instructions

Using the **Financial Accounting Research System (FARS)** database, respond to the following items. (Provide text strings used in your search.)

(a) Since the Teton shares do not trade on one of the large stock markets, Cascade argues that the fair value of this investment is not readily available. According to the authoritative literature, when is the fair value of a security "readily determinable"?

(b) How is an impairment of a security accounted for?

(c) To avoid volatility in their financial statements due to fair value adjustments, Cascade debated whether the bond investment could be classified as held-to-maturity; Cascade is pretty sure it will hold the bonds for 5 years. How close to maturity could Cascade sell an investment and still classify it as held-to-maturity?

(d) What disclosures must be made for any sale or transfer from securities classified as held-to-maturity?

■ Professional Simulation

AIA14-12 Go to the book's companion website, at **www.wiley.com/college/warfield**, to find an interactive problem that simulates the computerized CPA exam. The professional simulation for this chapter asks you to address questions related to investments.

WWK_Professional_Simulation		
Investments	Time Remaining 4 hour 10 minutes	copy paste calculator sheet standards help spliter done

---

What do the numbers mean?

What Is Fair Value?, p. 739

Q: What types of measurements are used to determine fair value? Which measurement method is the most reliable?

A: Fair value is the price that would be received to sell an asset or would be paid to transfer a liability in an orderly transaction between market participants at the measurement date. The most reliable measure of fair value relates to quoted prices in active markets for identical assets or liabilities that a company has the ability to access. Another determination of fair value can be made from similar-type assets or liabilities in active markets, often referred to as *significant other observable inputs*. Another level would be significant unobservable inputs such as the use of present value techniques to determine fair value.

Consolidate This!, p. 749

Q: Why is it important to determine who really has control for accounting purposes?

A: Companies that do not consolidate the financial information of companies they control fail to provide a clear picture of the risks and rewards of their ownership. Enron is an example.

More Disclosure, Please, p. 750

Q: Explain the rationale for different accounting treatment for investments in the equity of other companies.

A: The rationale for different accounting treatment generally relates to the level of control the company has over its investment in another company. For example, if a company has little or no control, the investment is generally reported at fair value, and the company reports the unrealized gain or loss in other comprehensive income (if an available-for-sale security) or in income (if a trading security).

If the investment is significant but the company does not control the other company, then the investor company uses the equity method of accounting. Significant influence may be indicated by representation on the board of directors, participation in policy-making processes, material intercompany transactions, interchange of managerial personnel, or technological dependency. Under this method, the investor company will recognize income from the investee company at the time it is reported. The investor's investment is reduced when a cash dividend is paid to it by the investee company.

A company will consolidate the financial information into their financial statements when it controls the other company. Control is often defined as owning more than 50 percent of another company. In this case it is assumed that the investor has all the risks and rewards of ownership.

The Irony of It All, p. 755

Q: When is a loss in value other than temporary?

A: A company should evaluate every investment, at each reporting date, to determine if it has suffered impairment—a loss in value that is other than temporary. For example, if an investee experiences a bankruptcy or a significant liquidity crisis, the investor may suffer a permanent loss. In this case the company should write down its investment and establish a new cost basis. Attempting to determine when the loss is permanent in nature involves the use of good judgment.

Remember to check the book's companion website to find additional resources for this chapter.

CHAPTER 15

ACCOUNTING FOR INCOME TAXES

Tax Uncertainty

One set of costs that companies manage are those related to taxes. In fact, in today's competitive markets, managers are expected to look for places in the tax code that a company can exploit to pay less tax to state and federal governments. By paying less in taxes, companies have more cash available to fund operations, finance expansion, and create new jobs. What happens, though, when companies push the tax saving envelop? Well, they may face a tax audit, the results of which could hurt their financial statements.

A notable example of corporate maneuvering to reduce taxable income involved **Limited Brands Inc.** It managed state-tax costs downward by locating part of its business in low-tax-rate states while operating retail outlets elsewhere. For example, by basing a subsidiary (which does nothing more than hold the trademarks for Bath and Body Works and Victoria's Secret) in Delaware, it is able to transfer hundreds of millions of dollars from Limited's retail outlets in high-tax states into Delaware, which has a state tax rate of zero.

However, the IRS and some states have been increasing their scrutiny of transactions that seem done only to avoid taxes and that do not serve a legitimate business purpose. In one case, an attorney for North Carolina alleged that Limited Brands Inc. ". . . engaged in hocus pocus bookkeeping and deceptive accounting," the sole purpose of which was to reduce its state-tax bill. The court agreed, and Limited Inc. had to pay millions of dollars in taxes dating back to 1994.

Limited Brands shareholders likely got an unpleasant surprise when they learned the company also had a big tax obligation from its "uncertain tax position" related to off-shore locations. The same can be said for many other companies that take tax deductions that may not hold up under the scrutiny of the tax court or an IRS audit. Current accounting rules are not very specific on when companies have to record an obligation for taxes that will be owed on uncertain tax positions. This is changing because the SEC and the FASB are concerned about non-recognition of significant tax obligations. As this text is being written, the FASB is working on a rule that would require companies to record loss contingencies for more uncertain tax provisions in their financial statements.

Source: See Glenn Simpson, "A Tax Maneuver in Delaware Puts Squeeze on States," *Wall Street Journal* (August 9, 2002), p. A1; and FASB, "Uncertain Tax Positions: Recognition of Tax Benefits," (July 14, 2005), *www.fasb.org/project/uncertain_tax_positions.shtml*.

Preview of Chapter 15

As our opening story indicates, companies spend a considerable amount of time and effort to minimize their income tax payments. And with good reason, as income taxes are a major cost of doing business for most corporations. Yet, at the same time, companies must present financial information to the investment community that provides a clear picture of present and potential tax obligations and tax benefits. In this chapter, we discuss the basic guidelines that companies must follow in reporting income taxes. *The content and organization of the chapter are as follows.*

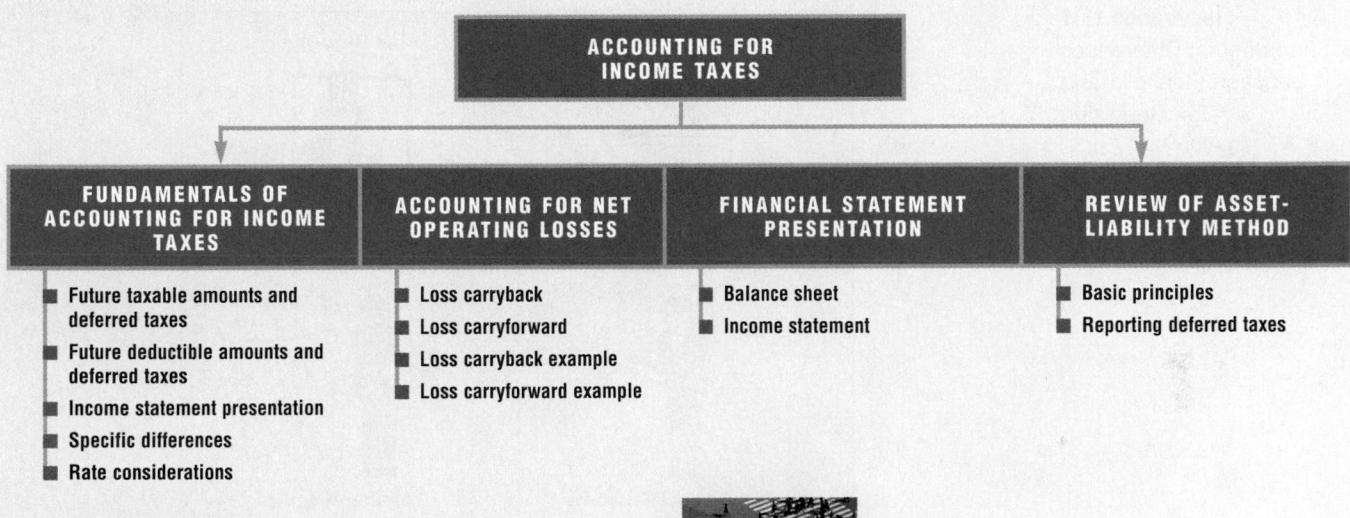

```
                        ┌─────────────────────────┐
                        │   ACCOUNTING FOR         │
                        │   INCOME TAXES           │
                        └─────────────────────────┘
```

FUNDAMENTALS OF ACCOUNTING FOR INCOME TAXES	ACCOUNTING FOR NET OPERATING LOSSES	FINANCIAL STATEMENT PRESENTATION	REVIEW OF ASSET-LIABILITY METHOD
■ Future taxable amounts and deferred taxes	■ Loss carryback	■ Balance sheet	■ Basic principles
■ Future deductible amounts and deferred taxes	■ Loss carryforward	■ Income statement	■ Reporting deferred taxes
■ Income statement presentation	■ Loss carryback example		
■ Specific differences	■ Loss carryforward example		
■ Rate considerations			

Learning Objectives

After studying this chapter, you should be able to:

1. Identify differences between pretax financial income and taxable income.

2. Describe a temporary difference that results in future taxable amounts.

3. Describe a temporary difference that results in future deductible amounts.

4. Explain the purpose of a deferred tax asset valuation allowance.

5. Describe the presentation of income tax expense in the income statement.

6. Describe various temporary and permanent differences.

7. Explain the effect of various tax rates and tax rate changes on deferred income taxes.

8. Apply accounting procedures for a loss carryback and a loss carryforward.

9. Describe the presentation of deferred income taxes in financial statements.

10. Indicate the basic principles of the asset-liability method.

Inside Chapter 15

- **What Do the Numbers Mean?**
  Real liabilities (p. 786)
  Real assets (p. 789)
  Read those notes (p. 802)
  NOLs: Good news or bad? (p. 808)

- **What's the Principle?** (pp. 786, 787, 789, 790, 795)

- **Accounting, Analysis, Principles** (p. 811)
  Prepare the journal entry for deferred taxes.
  Analyze effects of taxes.
  Determine impact of conceptual framework on deferred taxes.

- **Convergence Corner** (p. 814)

FUNDAMENTALS OF ACCOUNTING FOR INCOME TAXES

Up to this point, you have learned the basic guidelines that corporations use to report information to investors and creditors. Corporations also must file income tax returns following the guidelines developed by the Internal Revenue Service (IRS). Because GAAP and tax regulations differ in a number of ways, so frequently do pretax financial income and taxable income. Consequently, the amount that a company reports as tax expense will differ from the amount of taxes payable to the IRS. Illustration 15-1 highlights these differences.

Illustration 15-1
Fundamental Differences
between Financial and
Tax Reporting

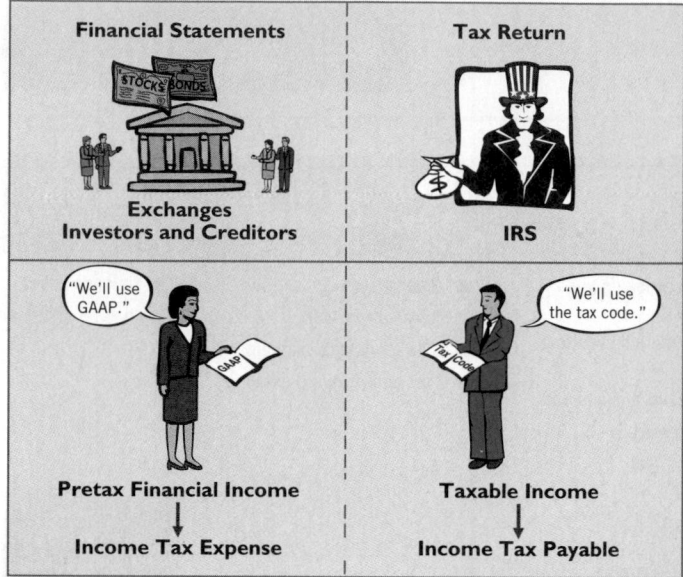

Pretax financial income is a *financial reporting* term. It also is often referred to as *income before taxes*, *income for financial reporting purposes*, or *income for book purposes*. Companies determine pretax financial income according to GAAP. They measure it with the objective of providing useful information to investors and creditors.

Taxable income (income for tax purposes) is a *tax accounting* term. It indicates the amount used to compute income tax payable. Companies determine taxable income according to the Internal Revenue Code (the tax code). Income taxes provide money to support government operations.

To illustrate how differences in GAAP and IRS rules affect financial reporting and taxable income, assume that Chelsea Inc. reported revenues of $130,000 and expenses of $60,000 in each of its first three years of operations. Illustration 15-2 shows the (partial) income statement over these three years.

Illustration 15-2
Financial Reporting
Income

Chelsea Inc. GAAP Reporting				
	2008	2009	2010	Total
Revenues	$130,000	$130,000	$130,000	
Expenses	60,000	60,000	60,000	
Pretax financial income	$ 70,000	$ 70,000	$ 70,000	$210,000
Income tax expense (40%)	$ 28,000	$ 28,000	$ 28,000	$ 84,000

For tax purposes (following the tax code), Chelsea reported the same expenses to the IRS in each of the years. But, as Illustration 15-3 (page 783) shows, Chelsea reported taxable revenues of $100,000 in 2008, $150,000 in 2009, and $140,000 in 2010.

Illustration 15-3
Tax Reporting Income

Chelsea Inc. Tax Reporting				
	2008	2009	2010	Total
Revenues	$100,000	$150,000	$140,000	
Expenses	60,000	60,000	60,000	
Taxable income	$ 40,000	$ 90,000	$ 80,000	$ 210,000
Income tax payable (40%)	$ 16,000	$ 36,000	$ 32,000	$ 84,000

Income tax expense and income tax payable differed over the three years, but were equal **in total**, as Illustration 15-4 shows.

Illustration 15-4
Comparison of Income
Tax Expense to Income
Tax Payable

Chelsea inc. Income Tax Expense and Income Tax Payable				
	2008	2009	2010	Total
Income tax expense	$28,000	$28,000	$28,000	$84,000
Income tax payable	16,000	36,000	32,000	84,000
Difference	$12,000	$ (8,000)	$ (4,000)	$ 0

The differences between income tax expense and income tax payable in this example arise for a simple reason. For financial reporting, companies use the full accrual method to report revenues. For tax purposes, they use a modified cash basis. As a result, Chelsea reports pretax financial income of $70,000 and income tax expense of $28,000 for each of the three years. However, taxable income fluctuates. For example, in 2008 taxable income is only $40,000, so Chelsea owes just $16,000 to the IRS that year. Chelsea classifies the income tax payable as a current liability on the balance sheet.

As Illustration 15-4 indicates, for Chelsea the $12,000 ($28,000 − $16,000) difference between income tax expense and income tax payable in 2008 reflects taxes that it will pay in future periods. This $12,000 difference is often referred to as a **deferred tax amount**. In this case it is a **deferred tax liability**. In cases where taxes will be lower in the future, Chelsea records a **deferred tax asset**. We explain the measurement and accounting for deferred tax liabilities and assets in the following two sections.

Future Taxable Amounts and Deferred Taxes

The example summarized in Illustration 15-4 shows how income tax payable can differ from income tax expense. This can happen when there are temporary differences between the amounts reported for tax purposes and those reported for book purposes. A **temporary difference** is the difference between the tax basis of an asset or liability and its reported (carrying or book) amount in the financial statements, which will result in taxable amounts or deductible amounts in future years. **Taxable amounts** increase taxable income in future years. **Deductible amounts** decrease taxable income in future years.

In Chelsea's situation, the only difference between the book basis and tax basis of the assets and liabilities relates to accounts receivable that arose from revenue recognized for book purposes. Illustration 15-5 (page 784) indicates that Chelsea reports accounts receivable at $30,000 in the December 31, 2008, GAAP-basis balance sheet. However, the receivables have a zero tax basis.

OBJECTIVE 2

Describe a temporary difference that results in future taxable amounts.

Illustration 15-5
Temporary Difference,
Sales Revenue

Per Books	12/31/08	Per Tax Return	12/31/08
Accounts receivable	$30,000	Accounts receivable	$–0–

What will happen to the $30,000 temporary difference that originated in 2008 for Chelsea? Assuming that Chelsea expects to collect $20,000 of the receivables in 2009 and $10,000 in 2010, this collection results in future taxable amounts of $20,000 in 2009 and $10,000 in 2010. These future taxable amounts will cause taxable income to exceed pretax financial income in both 2009 and 2010.

An assumption inherent in a company's GAAP balance sheet is that companies recover and settle the assets and liabilities at their reported amounts (carrying amounts). This assumption creates a requirement under accrual accounting to recognize *currently* the deferred tax consequences of temporary differences. That is, companies recognize the amount of income taxes that are payable (or refundable) when they recover and settle the reported amounts of the assets and liabilities, respectively. Illustration 15-6 shows the reversal of the temporary difference described in Illustration 15-5 and the resulting taxable amounts in future periods.

Illustration 15-6
Reversal of Temporary
Difference, Chelsea Inc.

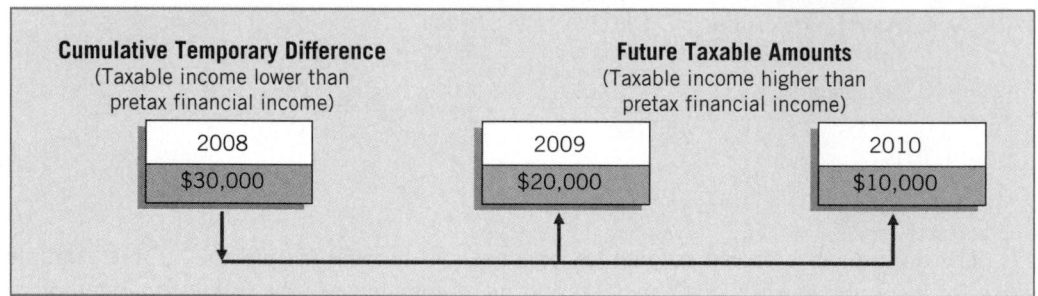

Chelsea assumes that it will collect the accounts receivable and report the $30,000 collection as taxable revenues in future tax returns. A payment of income tax in both 2009 and 2010 will occur. Chelsea should therefore record in its books in 2008 the deferred tax consequences of the revenue and related receivables reflected in the 2008 financial statements. Chelsea does this by recording a deferred tax liability.

Deferred Tax Liability

A **deferred tax liability** is the deferred tax consequences attributable to taxable temporary differences. In other words, **a deferred tax liability represents the increase in taxes payable in future years as a result of taxable temporary differences existing at the end of the current year**.

Recall from the Chelsea example that income tax payable is $16,000 ($40,000 × 40%) in 2008 (Illustration 15-4). In addition, a temporary difference exists at year-end because Chelsea reports the revenue and related accounts receivable differently for book and tax purposes. The book basis of accounts receivable is $30,000, and the tax basis is zero. Thus, the total deferred tax liability at the end of 2008 is $12,000, computed as shown in Illustration 15-7.

Illustration 15-7
Computation of Deferred
Tax Liability, End of 2008

Book basis of accounts receivable	$30,000
Tax basis of accounts receivable	–0–
Cumulative temporary difference at the end of 2008	30,000
Tax rate	40%
Deferred tax liability at the end of 2008	$12,000

Chelsea may also compute the deferred tax liability by preparing a schedule that indicates the future taxable amounts due to existing temporary differences. Such a schedule, as shown in Illustration 15-8, is particularly useful when the computations become more complex.

	Future Years		
	2009	2010	Total
Future taxable amounts	$20,000	$10,000	$30,000
Tax rate	40%	40%	
Deferred tax liability at the end of 2008	$ 8,000	$ 4,000	$12,000

Illustration 15-8
Schedule of Future
Taxable Amounts

Because it is the first year of operations for Chelsea, there is no deferred tax liability at the beginning of the year. Chelsea computes the income tax expense for 2008 as shown in Illustration 15-9.

Deferred tax liability at end of 2008	$12,000
Deferred tax liability at beginning of 2008	–0–
Deferred tax expense for 2008	12,000
Current tax expense for 2008 (Income tax payable)	16,000
Income tax expense (total) for 2008	$28,000

Illustration 15-9
Computation of Income
Tax Expense, 2008

This computation indicates that income tax expense has two components—**current tax expense** (the amount of income tax payable for the period) and deferred tax expense. **Deferred tax expense** is the increase in the deferred tax liability balance from the beginning to the end of the accounting period.

Companies credit taxes due and payable to Income Tax Payable, and credit the increase in deferred taxes to Deferred Tax Liability. They then debit the sum of those two items to Income Tax Expense. For Chelsea, it makes the following entry at the end of 2008.

Income Tax Expense	28,000	
Income Tax Payable		16,000
Deferred Tax Liability		12,000

At the end of 2009 (the second year), the difference between the book basis and the tax basis of the accounts receivable is $10,000. Chelsea multiplies this difference by the applicable tax rate to arrive at the deferred tax liability of $4,000 ($10,000 × 40%), which it reports at the end of 2009. Income tax payable for 2009 is $36,000 (Illustration 15-3), and the income tax expense for 2009 is as shown in Illustration 15-10.

Deferred tax liability at end of 2009	$ 4,000
Deferred tax liability at beginning of 2009	12,000
Deferred tax expense (benefit) for 2009	(8,000)
Current tax expense for 2009 (Income tax payable)	36,000
Income tax expense (total) for 2009	$28,000

Illustration 15-10
Computation of Income
Tax Expense, 2009

Chelsea records income tax expense, the change in the deferred tax liability, and income tax payable for 2009 as follows.

Income Tax Expense	28,000	
Deferred Tax Liability	8,000	
Income Tax Payable		36,000

The entry to record income taxes at the end of 2010 reduces the Deferred Tax Liability by $4,000. The Deferred Tax Liability account appears as follows at the end of 2010.

Illustration 15-11
Deferred Tax Liability
Account after Reversals

Deferred Tax Liability			
2009	8,000	2008	12,000
2010	4,000		

The Deferred Tax Liability account has a zero balance at the end of 2010.

What do the numbers mean?

Real Liabilities

Some analysts dismiss deferred tax liabilities when assessing the financial strength of a company. But the FASB indicates that the deferred tax liability meets the definition of a liability established in *Statement of Financial Accounting Concepts No. 6*, "Elements of Financial Statements" because:

1 *It results from a past transaction.* In the Chelsea example, the company performed services for customers and recognized revenue in 2008 for financial reporting purposes but deferred it for tax purposes.

2 *It is a present obligation.* Taxable income in future periods will exceed pretax financial income as a result of this temporary difference. Thus, a present obligation exists.

3 *It represents a future sacrifice.* Taxable income and taxes due in future periods will result from past events. The payment of these taxes when they come due is the future sacrifice.

A study by B. Ayers indicates that the market views deferred tax assets and liabilities similarly to other assets and liabilities. Further, the study concludes that *SFAS No. 109* increased the usefulness of deferred tax amounts in financial statements.

Source: B. Ayers, "Deferred Tax Accounting Under *SFAS No. 109*: An Empirical Investigation of Its Incremental Value-Relevance Relative to *APB No. 11*," *The Accounting Review* (April 1998).

Beyond the Numbers

What is the importance of *Statement of Financial Concepts No. 6* to the conceptual framework, and how does it help to resolve various accounting and financial reporting issues?

Summary of Income Tax Accounting Objectives

WHAT'S THE PRINCIPLE?

Recognizing a deferred tax liability is a good example of accrual accounting. The deferred tax liability is reported when incurred, rather than when paid.

One objective of accounting for income taxes is to recognize the amount of taxes payable or refundable for the current year. In Chelsea's case, income tax payable is $16,000 for 2008.

A **second objective** is to recognize deferred tax liabilities and assets for the future tax consequences of events already recognized in the financial statements or tax returns. For example, Chelsea sold services to customers that resulted in accounts receivable of $30,000 in 2008. It reported that amount on the 2008 income statement, but not on the tax return as income. That amount will appear on future tax returns as income for the period **when collected**. As a result, a $30,000 temporary difference exists at the end of 2008, which will cause future taxable amounts. Chelsea reports a deferred tax liability of $12,000 on the balance sheet at the end of 2008, which represents the increase in taxes payable in future years ($8,000 in 2009 and $4,000 in 2010) as a result of a temporary difference existing at the end of the current year. The related deferred tax liability is reduced by $8,000 at the end of 2009 and by another $4,000 at the end of 2010.

In addition to affecting the balance sheet, deferred taxes impact income tax expense in each of the three years affected. In 2008, taxable income ($40,000) is less than pretax financial income ($70,000). Income tax payable for 2008 is therefore $16,000 (based on taxable income). Deferred tax expense of $12,000 results from the increase in the Deferred Tax Liability account on the balance sheet. Income tax expense is then $28,000 for 2008.

In 2009 and 2010, however, taxable income will exceed pretax financial income, due to the reversal of the temporary difference ($20,000 in 2009 and $10,000 in 2010). Income tax payable will therefore exceed income tax expense in 2009 and 2010. Chelsea will debit the Deferred Tax Liability account for $8,000 in 2009 and $4,000 in 2010. It records credits for these amounts in Income Tax Expense. These credits are often referred to as a **deferred tax benefit** (which we discuss again later on).

Future Deductible Amounts and Deferred Taxes

Assume that during 2008, Cunningham Inc. estimated its warranty costs related to the sale of microwave ovens to be $500,000, paid evenly over the next two years. For book purposes, in 2008 Cunningham reported warranty expense and a related estimated liability for warranties of $500,000 in its financial statements. For tax purposes, **the warranty tax deduction is not allowed until paid**. Therefore, Cunningham recognizes no warranty liability on a tax-basis balance sheet. Illustration 15-12 shows the balance sheet difference at the end of 2008.

OBJECTIVE 3
Describe a temporary difference that results in future deductible amounts.

Per Books	12/31/08	Per Tax Return	12/31/08
Estimated liability for warranties	$500,000	Estimated liability for warranties	$–0–

Illustration 15-12
Temporary Difference, Warranty Liability

When Cunningham pays the warranty liability, it reports an expense (deductible amount) for tax purposes. Because of this temporary difference, Cunningham should recognize in 2008 the tax benefits (positive tax consequences) for the tax deductions that will result from the future settlement of the liability. Cunningham reports this future tax benefit in the December 31, 2008, balance sheet as a **deferred tax asset**.

We can think about this situation another way. Deductible amounts occur in future tax returns. These **future deductible amounts** cause taxable income to be less than pretax financial income in the future as a result of an existing temporary difference. Cunningham's temporary difference originates (arises) in one period (2008) and reverses over two periods (2009 and 2010). Illustration 15-13 diagrams this situation.

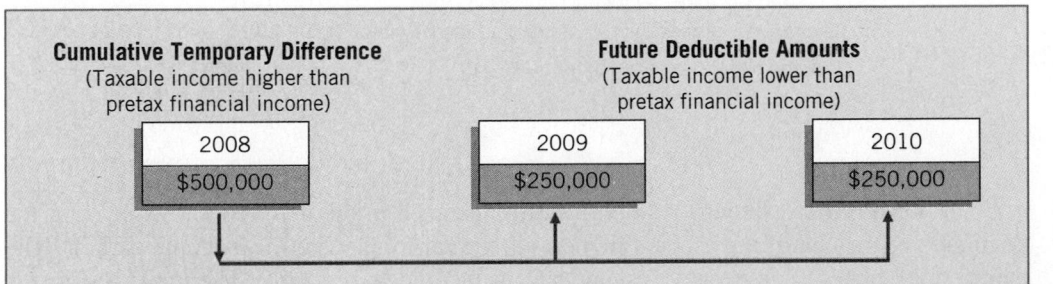

Cumulative Temporary Difference (Taxable income higher than pretax financial income)	Future Deductible Amounts (Taxable income lower than pretax financial income)	
2008	2009	2010
$500,000	$250,000	$250,000

Illustration 15-13
Reversal of Temporary Difference, Cunningham Inc.

Deferred Tax Asset

A **deferred tax asset** is the deferred tax consequence attributable to deductible temporary differences. In other words, a **deferred tax asset represents the increase in taxes refundable (or saved) in future years as a result of deductible temporary differences existing at the end of the current year**.

To illustrate, assume that Hunt Co. accrues a loss and a related liability of $50,000 in 2008 for financial reporting purposes because of pending litigation. Hunt cannot

WHAT'S THE PRINCIPLE?
Recognizing a deferred tax asset is another good example accrual accounting. The deferred tax asset is reported when the benefit occurs, rather than when the tax payments are reduced.

deduct this amount for tax purposes until the period it pays the liability, expected in 2009. As a result, a deductible amount will occur in 2009 when Hunt settles the liability (Estimated Litigation Liability), causing taxable income to be lower than pretax financial income. Illustration 15-14 shows the computation of the deferred tax asset at the end of 2008 (assuming a 40 percent tax rate).

Illustration 15-14
Computation of Deferred
Tax Asset, End of 2008

Book basis of litigation liability	$50,000
Tax basis of litigation liability	–0–
Cumulative temporary difference at the end of 2008	50,000
Tax rate	40%
Deferred tax asset at the end of 2008	$20,000

Hunt can also compute the deferred tax asset by preparing a schedule that indicates the future deductible amounts due to deductible temporary differences. Illustration 15-15 shows this schedule.

Illustration 15-15
Schedule of Future
Deductible Amounts

	Future Years
Future deductible amounts	$50,000
Tax rate	40%
Deferred tax asset at the end of 2008	$20,000

Assuming that 2008 is Hunt's first year of operations, and income tax payable is $100,000, Hunt computes its income tax expense as follows.

Illustration 15-16
Computation of Income
Tax Expense, 2008

Deferred tax asset at end of 2008	$ 20,000
Deferred tax asset at beginning of 2008	–0–
Deferred tax expense (benefit) for 2008	(20,000)
Current tax expense for 2008 (Income tax payable)	100,000
Income tax expense (total) for 2008	$ 80,000

The **deferred tax benefit** results from the increase in the deferred tax asset from the beginning to the end of the accounting period (similar to the Chelsea example earlier). The deferred tax benefit is a negative component of income tax expense. The total income tax expense of $80,000 on the income statement for 2008 thus consists of two elements—current tax expense of $100,000 and a deferred tax benefit of $20,000. For Hunt, it makes the following journal entry at the end of 2008 to record income tax expense, deferred income taxes, and income tax payable.

Income Tax Expense	80,000	
Deferred Tax Asset	20,000	
Income Tax Payable		100,000

At the end of 2009 (the second year), the difference between the book value and the tax basis of the litigation liability is zero. Therefore, there is no deferred tax asset at this date. Assuming that income tax payable for 2009 is $140,000, Hunt computes income tax expense for 2009 as shown in Illustration 15-17.

Deferred tax asset at the end of 2009	$ –0–
Deferred tax asset at the beginning of 2009	20,000
Deferred tax expense (benefit) for 2009	20,000
Current tax expense for 2009 (Income tax payable)	140,000
Income tax expense (total) for 2009	$160,000

Illustration 15-17
Computation of Income Tax Expense, 2009

The company records income taxes for 2009 as follows.

Income Tax Expense	160,000	
Deferred Tax Asset		20,000
Income Tax Payable		140,000

WHAT'S THE PRINCIPLE?

The elements in the conceptual framework provide support to recognize deferred tax assets and liabilities.

The total income tax expense of $160,000 on the income statement for 2009 thus consists of two elements—current tax expense of $140,000 and deferred tax expense of $20,000. Illustration 15-18 shows the Deferred Tax Asset account at the end of 2009.

Deferred Tax Asset			
2008	20,000	2009	20,000

Illustration 15-18
Deferred Tax Asset Account after Reversals

What do the numbers mean?   Real Assets

A key issue in accounting for income taxes is whether a company should recognize a deferred tax asset in the financial records. Based on the conceptual definition of an asset, a deferred tax asset meets the three main conditions for an item to be recognized as an asset:

1 *It results from a past transaction.* In the Hunt example, the accrual of the loss contingency is the past event that gives rise to a future deductible temporary difference.

2 *It gives rise to a probable benefit in the future.* Taxable income exceeds pretax financial income in the current year (2008). However, in the next year the exact opposite occurs. That is, taxable income is lower than pretax financial income. Because this deductible temporary difference reduces taxes payable in the future, a probable future benefit exists at the end of the current period.

3 *The entity controls access to the benefits.* Hunt can obtain the benefit of existing deductible temporary differences by reducing its taxes payable in the future. Hunt has the exclusive right to that benefit and can control others' access to it.

Market analysts' reaction to the **write-off** of deferred tax assets also supports their treatment as assets. When **Bethlehem Steel** reported a $1 billion charge in a recent year to write off a deferred tax asset, analysts believed that Bethlehem was signaling that it would not realize the future benefits of the tax deductions. Thus, Bethlehem should write down the asset like other assets.

Source: J. Weil and S. Liesman, "Stock Gurus Disregard Most Big Write-Offs But They Often Hold Vital Clues to Outlook," *Wall Street Journal Online* (December 31, 2001).

Beyond the Numbers

Why might a company not realize the future benefits of a tax deduction?

Try it out! The following information is available for Barnes Company for 2007.

1 Deferral, for book purposes, of $30,000 of rent collected in advance. Barnes will earn the rent in 2008.

2 Excess of tax depreciation over book depreciation $60,000. This difference will reverse equally over the years 2008–2010.

3 Pretax financial income $500,000.

4 The enacted tax rate is 35% for 2007 and 40% for 2008–2010.

Instructions

Prepare the journal entries to record income tax expense, deferred income taxes, and income taxes payable for 2007 and 2008. Pretax financial income was $600,000 in 2008.

Solution

2007

Income Tax Expense ($164,500 + $24,000 − $12,000)	176,500	
Deferred Tax Asset ($30,000 × .40)	12,000	
Deferred Tax Liability ($60,000 × .40)		24,000
Income Tax Payable [($500,000 + $30,000 − $60,000) × .35]		164,500

2008

Income Tax Expense ($236,000 + $12,000 − $8,000)	240,000	
Deferred Tax Liability ($60,000/3 × .40)	8,000	
Deferred Tax Asset		12,000
Income Tax Payable [($600,000 − $30,000 + $20,000) × .40]		236,000

Deferred Tax Asset—Valuation Allowance

OBJECTIVE 4

Explain the purpose of a deferred tax asset valuation allowance.

Companies recognize a deferred tax asset for all deductible temporary differences. However, based on available evidence, a company should reduce a deferred tax asset by a **valuation allowance if it is more likely than not** that it **will not realize** some portion or all of the deferred tax asset. "**More likely than not**" means a level of likelihood of at least slightly more than 50 percent.

Assume that Jensen Co. has a deductible temporary difference of $1,000,000 at the end of its first year of operations. Its tax rate is 40 percent, which means it records a deferred tax asset of $400,000 ($1,000,000 × 40%). Assuming $900,000 of income taxes payable, Jensen records income tax expense, the deferred tax asset, and income tax payable as follows.

Income Tax Expense	500,000	
Deferred Tax Asset	400,000	
Income Tax Payable		900,000

WHAT'S THE PRINCIPLE?

The going concern concept assumes that the company can recover the deferred tax assets. However, if the assumption of being able to recover the cost of the investment is not valid, then a company should report a reduction in value.

After careful review of all available evidence, Jensen determines that it is more likely than not that it will not realize $100,000 of this deferred tax asset. Jensen records this reduction in asset value as follows.

Income Tax Expense	100,000	
Allowance to Reduce Deferred Tax Asset		
to Expected Realizable Value		100,000

This journal entry increases income tax expense in the current period because Jensen does not expect to realize a favorable tax benefit for a portion of the deductible temporary difference. Jensen **simultaneously establishes a valuation allowance to recognize the reduction in the carrying amount of the deferred tax asset**. This valuation account is a contra account. Jensen reports it on the financial statements in the following manner.

Deferred tax asset	$400,000
Less: Allowance to reduce deferred tax	
asset to expected realizable value	100,000
Deferred tax asset (net)	$300,000

Illustration 15-19
Balance Sheet
Presentation of Valuation
Allowance Account

Jensen then evaluates this allowance account at the end of each accounting period. If, at the end of the next period, the deferred tax asset is still $400,000, but now it expects to realize $350,000 of this asset, Jensen makes the following entry to adjust the valuation account.

Allowance to Reduce Deferred Tax Asset		
to Expected Realizable Value	50,000	
Income Tax Expense		50,000

Jensen should consider all available evidence, both positive and negative, to determine whether, based on the weight of available evidence, it needs a valuation allowance. For example, if Jensen has been experiencing a series of loss years, it reasonably assumes that these losses will continue. Therefore, Jensen will lose the benefit of the future deductible amounts. We discuss the use of a valuation account under other conditions later in the chapter.

Income Statement Presentation

Circumstances dictate whether a company should add or subtract the change in deferred income taxes to or from income tax payable in computing income tax expense. For example, a company adds an increase in a deferred tax liability to income tax payable. On the other hand, it subtracts an increase in a deferred tax asset from income tax payable. The formula in Illustration 15-20 is used to compute income tax expense (benefit).

OBJECTIVE 5
Describe the presentation of income tax expense in the income statement.

Income Tax Payable or Refundable	±	Change in Deferred Income Taxes	=	Total Income Tax Expense or Benefit

Illustration 15-20
Formula to Compute
Income Tax Expense

In the income statement or in the notes to the financial statements, a company should disclose the significant components of income tax expense attributable to continuing operations. Given the information related to Chelsea in Illustration 15-9 (page 785), Chelsea reports its income statement as follows.

Chelsea Inc.
Income Statement
For the Year Ending December 31, 2008

Revenues		$130,000
Expenses		60,000
Income before income taxes		70,000
Income tax expense		
Current	$16,000	
Deferred	12,000	28,000
Net income		$ 42,000

Illustration 15-21
Income Statement
Presentation of Income
Tax Expense

As illustrated, Chelsea reports both the current portion (amount of income tax payable for the period) and the deferred portion of income tax expense. Another option is to simply report the total income tax expense on the income statement, and then indicate in the notes to the financial statements the current and deferred portions. Income tax expense is often referred to as "Provision for income taxes." Using this terminology, the current provision is $16,000, and the provision for deferred taxes is $12,000.

Specific Differences

<table>
<tr><td>

OBJECTIVE 6

Describe various temporary and permanent differences.

</td><td>

Numerous items create differences between pretax financial income and taxable income. For purposes of accounting recognition, these differences are of two types: (1) temporary, and (2) permanent.

</td></tr>
</table>

Temporary Differences

Taxable temporary differences are temporary differences that will result in taxable amounts in future years when the related assets are recovered. **Deductible temporary differences** are temporary differences that will result in deductible amounts in future years, when the related book liabilities are settled. Taxable temporary differences give rise to recording deferred tax liabilities. Deductible temporary differences give rise to recording deferred tax assets. Illustration 15-22 provides examples of temporary differences.[1]

Illustration 15-22
Examples of Temporary Differences

A. **Revenues or gains are taxable after they are recognized in financial income.**
   An asset (e.g., accounts receivable or investment) may be recognized for revenues or gains that will result in **taxable amounts in future** years when the asset is recovered. Examples:
   1. Sales accounted for on the accrual basis for financial reporting purposes and on the installment (cash) basis for tax purposes.
   2. Contracts accounted for under the percentage-of-completion method for financial reporting purposes and a portion of related gross profit deferred for tax purposes.
   3. Investments accounted for under the equity method for financial reporting purposes and under the cost method for tax purposes.
   4. Gain on involuntary conversion of nonmonetary asset which is recognized for financial reporting purposes but deferred for tax purposes.

B. **Expenses or losses are deductible after they are recognized in financial income.**
   A liability (or contra asset) may be recognized for expenses or losses that will result in **deductible amounts in future years** when the liability is settled. Examples:
   1. Product warranty liabilities.
   2. Estimated liabilities related to discontinued operations or restructurings.
   3. Litigation accruals.
   4. Bad debt expense recognized using the allowance method for financial reporting purposes; direct write-off method used for tax purposes.
   5. Stock-based compensation expense.

C. **Revenues or gains are taxable before they are recognized in financial income.**
   A liability may be recognized for an advance payment for goods or services to be provided in future years. For tax purposes, the advance payment is included in taxable income upon the receipt of cash. Future sacrifices to provide goods or services (or future refunds to those who cancel their orders) that settle the liability will result in **deductible amounts in future years**. Examples:
   1. Subscriptions received in advance.
   2. Advance rental receipts.
   3. Sales and leasebacks for financial reporting purposes (income deferral) but reported as sales for tax purposes.
   4. Prepaid contracts and royalties received in advance.

D. **Expenses or losses are deductible before they are recognized in financial income.**
   The cost of an asset may have been deducted for tax purposes faster than it was expensed for financial reporting purposes. Amounts received upon future recovery of the amount of the asset for financial reporting (through use or sale) will exceed the remaining tax basis of the asset and thereby result in **taxable amounts in future years**. Examples:
   1. Depreciable property, depletable resources, and intangibles.
   2. Deductible pension funding exceeding expense.
   3. Prepaid expenses that are deducted on the tax return in the period paid.

---

[1]*SFAS No. 109* gives more examples of temporary differences. We present the most common types in this chapter.

Determining a company's temporary differences may prove difficult. A company should prepare a balance sheet for tax purposes that it can compare with its GAAP balance sheet. Many of the differences between the two balance sheets are temporary differences.

Originating and Reversing Aspects of Temporary Differences. An **originating temporary difference** is the initial difference between the book basis and the tax basis of an asset or liability, regardless of whether the tax basis of the asset or liability exceeds or is exceeded by the book basis of the asset or liability. A **reversing difference**, on the other hand, occurs when eliminating a temporary difference that originated in prior periods and then removing the related tax effect from the deferred tax account.

For example, assume that Sharp Co. has tax depreciation in excess of book depreciation of $2,000 in 2004, 2005, and 2006. Further, it has an excess of book depreciation over tax depreciation of $3,000 in 2007 and 2008 for the same asset. Assuming a tax rate of 30 percent for all years involved, the Deferred Tax Liability account reflects the following.

	Deferred Tax Liability				
Tax Effects	2007	900	2004	600	Tax Effects
of	2008	900	2005	600	of
Reversing Differences			2006	600	Originating Differences

Illustration 15-23
Tax Effects of Originating and Reversing Differences

The originating differences for Sharp in each of the first three years are $2,000. The related tax effect of each originating difference is $600. The reversing differences in 2007 and 2008 are each $3,000. The related tax effect of each is $900.

Permanent Differences

Some differences between taxable income and pretax financial income are permanent. **Permanent differences** result from items that (1) enter into pretax financial income but **never** into taxable income, or (2) enter into taxable income but **never** into pretax financial income.

Congress has enacted a variety of tax law provisions to attain certain political, economic, and social objectives. Some of these provisions exclude certain revenues from taxation, limit the deductibility of certain expenses, and permit the deduction of certain other expenses in excess of costs incurred. A corporation that has tax-free income, nondeductible expenses, or allowable deductions in excess of cost, has an effective tax rate that differs from its statutory (regular) tax rate.

Since permanent differences affect only the period in which they occur, they do not give rise to future taxable or deductible amounts. As a result, **companies recognize no deferred tax consequences**. Illustration 15-24 shows examples of permanent differences.

A. **Items are recognized for financial reporting purposes but not for tax purposes.**
   Examples:
   1. Interest received on state and municipal obligations.
   2. Expenses incurred in obtaining tax-exempt income.
   3. Proceeds from life insurance carried by the company on key officers or employees.
   4. Premiums paid for life insurance carried by the company on key officers or employees (company is beneficiary).
   5. Fines and expenses resulting from a violation of law.

B. **Items are recognized for tax purposes but not for financial reporting purposes.**
   Examples:
   1. "Percentage depletion" of natural resources in excess of their cost.
   2. The deduction for dividends received from U.S. corporations, generally 70% or 80%.

Illustration 15-24
Examples of Permanent Differences

Examples of Temporary and Permanent Differences

To illustrate the computations used when both temporary and permanent differences exist, assume that Bio-Tech Company reports pretax financial income of $200,000 in each of the years 2006, 2007, and 2008. The company is subject to a 30 percent tax rate, and has the following differences between pretax financial income and taxable income.

1 Bio-Tech reports an installment sale of $18,000 in 2006 for tax purposes over an 18-month period at a constant amount per month beginning January 1, 2007. It recognizes the entire sale for book purposes in 2006.

2 It pays life insurance premiums for its key officers of $5,000 in 2007 and 2008. Although not tax-deductible, Bio-Tech expenses the premiums for book purposes.

The installment sale is a temporary difference, whereas the life insurance premium is a permanent difference. Illustration 15-25 shows the reconciliation of Bio-Tech's pretax financial income to taxable income and the computation of income tax payable.

Illustration 15-25
Reconciliation and Computation of Income Taxes Payable

	2006	2007	2008
Pretax financial income	$200,000	$200,000	$200,000
Permanent difference			
Nondeductible expense		5,000	5,000
Temporary difference			
Installment sale	(18,000)	12,000	6,000
Taxable income	182,000	217,000	211,000
Tax rate	30%	30%	30%
Income tax payable	$ 54,600	$ 65,100	$ 63,300

Note that Bio-Tech **deducts** the installment sales revenue from pretax financial income to arrive at taxable income. The reason: pretax financial income includes the installment sales revenue; taxable income does not. Conversely, it **adds** the $5,000 insurance premium to pretax financial income to arrive at taxable income. The reason: pretax financial income records an expense for this premium, but for tax purposes the premium is not deductible. As a result, pretax financial income is lower than taxable income. Therefore, the life insurance premium must be added back to pretax financial income to reconcile to taxable income.

Bio-Tech records income taxes for 2006, 2007, and 2008 as follows.

December 31, 2006

Income Tax Expense ($54,600 + $5,400)	60,000	
Deferred Tax Liability ($18,000 × 30%)		5,400
Income Tax Payable ($182,000 × 30%)		54,600

December 31, 2007

Income Tax Expense ($65,100 − $3,600)	61,500	
Deferred Tax Liability ($12,000 × 30%)	3,600	
Income Tax Payable ($217,000 × 30%)		65,100

December 31, 2008

Income Tax Expense ($63,300 − $1,800)	61,500	
Deferred Tax Liability ($6,000 × 30%)	1,800	
Income Tax Payable ($211,000 × 30%)		63,300

Bio-Tech has one temporary difference, which originates in 2006 and reverses in 2007 and 2008. It recognizes a deferred tax liability at the end of 2006 because the temporary difference causes future taxable amounts. As the temporary difference reverses, Bio-Tech reduces the deferred tax liability. There is no deferred tax amount associated with the difference caused by the nondeductible insurance expense because it is a permanent difference.

Although an enacted tax rate of 30 percent applies for all three years, the effective rate differs from the enacted rate in 2007 and 2008. Bio-Tech computes the **effective tax rate** by dividing total income tax expense for the period by pretax financial income. The effective rate is 30 percent for 2006 ($60,000 ÷ $200,000 = 30%) and 30.75 percent for 2007 and 2008 ($61,500 ÷ $200,000 = 30.75%).

Tax Rate Considerations

In our previous illustrations, the enacted tax rate did not change from one year to the next. Thus, to compute the deferred income tax amount to report on the balance sheet, a company simply multiplies the cumulative temporary difference by the current tax rate. Using Bio-Tech as an example, it multiplies the cumulative temporary difference of $18,000 by the enacted tax rate, 30 percent in this case, to arrive at a deferred tax liability of $5,400 ($18,000 × 30%) at the end of 2006.

> **OBJECTIVE 7**
>
> **Explain the effect of various tax rates and tax rate changes on deferred income taxes.**

Future Tax Rates

What happens if tax rates are expected to change in the future? In this case, a company should use the **enacted tax rate** expected to apply. Therefore, a company must consider presently enacted changes in the tax rate that become effective for a particular future year(s) when determining the tax rate to apply to existing temporary differences. For example, assume that Warlen Co. at the end of 2005 has the following cumulative temporary difference of $300,000, computed as shown in Illustration 15-26.

Book basis of depreciable assets	$1,000,000
Tax basis of depreciable assets	700,000
Cumulative temporary difference	$ 300,000

Illustration 15-26
Computation of Cumulative Temporary Difference

Furthermore, assume that the $300,000 will reverse and result in taxable amounts in the future, with the enacted tax rates shown in Illustration 15-27.

	2006	2007	2008	2009	2010	Total
Future taxable amounts	$80,000	$70,000	$60,000	$50,000	$40,000	$300,000
Tax rate	40%	40%	35%	30%	30%	
Deferred tax liability	$32,000	$28,000	$21,000	$15,000	$12,000	$108,000

Illustration 15-27
Deferred Tax Liability Based on Future Rates

The total deferred tax liability at the end of 2005 is $108,000. Warlen may only use tax rates other than the current rate when the future tax rates have been enacted, as is the case in this example. **If new rates are not yet enacted for future years, Warlen should use the current rate.**

In determining the appropriate enacted tax rate for a given year, companies must use the **average tax rate**. The Internal Revenue Service and other taxing jurisdictions tax income on a graduated tax basis. For a U.S. corporation, the IRS taxes the first $50,000 of taxable income at 15 percent, the next $25,000 at 25 percent, with higher incremental levels of income at rates as high as 39 percent. In computing deferred income taxes, companies for which graduated tax rates are a significant factor must therefore **determine the average tax rate and use that rate**.

> **WHAT'S THE PRINCIPLE?**
>
> For information to be useful, it must be relevant and reliable. The enacted tax rate is used to record the deferred taxes because it is reliable.

Revision of Future Tax Rates

When a change in the tax rate is enacted, companies should record its effect on the existing deferred income tax accounts immediately. **A company reports the effect as an adjustment to income tax expense in the period of the change.**

Assume that on December 10, 2005, a new income tax act is signed into law that lowers the corporate tax rate from 40 percent to 35 percent, effective January 1, 2007. If Hostel Co. has one temporary difference at the beginning of 2005 related to $3 million of excess tax depreciation, then it has a Deferred Tax Liability account with a balance of $1,200,000 ($3,000,000 × 40%) at January 1, 2005. If taxable amounts related to this difference are scheduled to occur equally in 2006, 2007, and 2008, the deferred tax liability at the end of 2005 is $1,100,000, computed as follows.

Illustration 15-28
Schedule of Future
Taxable Amounts and
Related Tax Rates

	2006	2007	2008	Total
Future taxable amounts	$1,000,000	$1,000,000	$1,000,000	$3,000,000
Tax rate	40%	35%	35%	
Deferred tax liability	$ 400,000	$ 350,000	$ 350,000	$1,100,000

Hostel, therefore, recognizes the decrease of $100,000 ($1,200,000 − $1,100,000) at the end of 2005 in the deferred tax liability as follows.

Deferred Tax Liability	100,000	
Income Tax Expense		100,000

Corporate tax rates do not change often. Therefore, companies usually employ the current rate. However, state and foreign tax rates change more frequently, and they require adjustments in deferred income taxes accordingly.[2]

ACCOUNTING FOR NET OPERATING LOSSES

OBJECTIVE 8

Apply accounting procedures for a loss carryback and a loss carryforward.

Every management hopes its company will be profitable. But hopes and profits may not materialize. For a start-up company, it is common to accumulate operating losses while expanding its customer base but before realizing economies of scale. For an established company, a major event such as a labor strike, rapidly changing regulatory and competitive forces, or a disaster such as 9/11 or Hurricane Katrina can cause expenses to exceed revenues—a net operating loss.

A **net operating loss (NOL)** occurs for tax purposes in a year when tax-deductible expenses exceed taxable revenues. An inequitable tax burden would result if companies were taxed during profitable periods without receiving any tax relief during periods of net operating losses. Under certain circumstances, therefore, the federal tax laws permit taxpayers to use the losses of one year to offset the profits of other years.

Companies accomplish this income-averaging provision through the **carryback and carryforward of net operating losses**. Under this provision, a company pays no income taxes for a year in which it incurs a net operating loss. In addition, it may select one of the two options discussed below and on the following pages.

---

[2]Tax rate changes nearly always will substantially impact income numbers and the reporting of deferred income taxes on the balance sheet. As a result, you can expect to hear an economic consequences argument every time that Congress decides to change the tax rates. For example, when Congress raised the corporate rate from 34 percent to 35 percent in 1993, companies took an additional "hit" to earnings if they were in a deferred tax liability position.

Loss Carryback

Through use of a **loss carryback**, a company may carry the net operating loss back two years and receive refunds for income taxes paid in those years. The company must apply the loss to the earlier year first and then to the second year. It may **carry forward** any loss remaining after the two-year carryback up to 20 years to offset future taxable income. Illustration 15-29 diagrams the loss carryback procedure, assuming a loss in 2008.

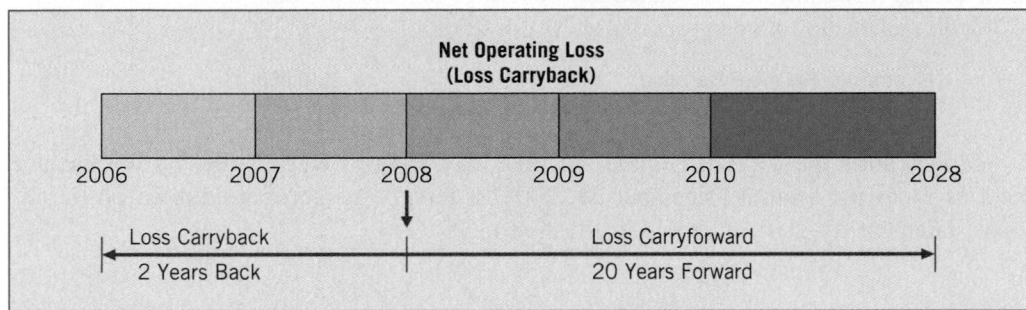

Illustration 15-29
Loss Carryback
Procedure

Loss Carryforward

A company may forgo the loss carryback and use only the **loss carryforward** option, offsetting future taxable income for up to 20 years. Illustration 15-30 shows this approach.

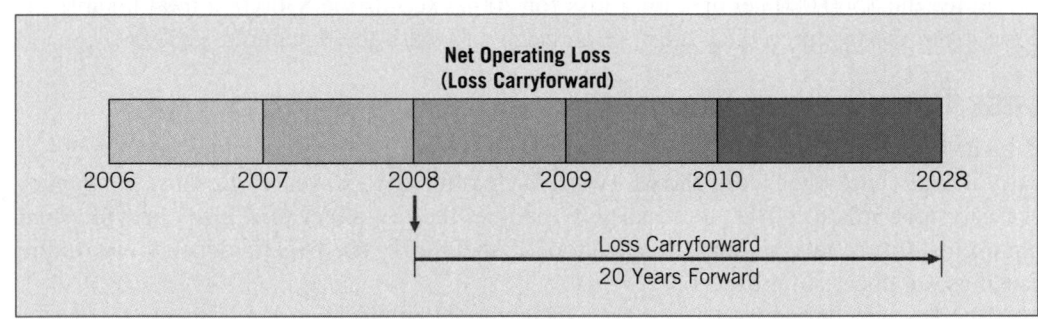

Illustration 15-30
Loss Carryforward
Procedure

Operating losses can be substantial. For example, **Yahoo!** had net operating losses of approximately $5.4 billion at year-end 2004. That amount translates into tax savings of $1.4 billion if Yahoo! is able to generate taxable income before the NOLs expire.

Loss Carryback Example

To illustrate the accounting procedures for a net operating loss carryback, assume that Groh Inc. has no temporary or permanent differences. Groh experiences the following.

Year	Taxable Income or Loss	Tax Rate	Tax Paid
2005	$ 50,000	35%	$17,500
2006	100,000	30%	30,000
2007	200,000	40%	80,000
2008	(500,000)	—	–0–

In 2008, Groh incurs a net operating loss that it decides to carry back. Under the law, Groh must apply the carryback first to the **second year preceding the loss year**. Therefore, it carries the loss back first to 2006. Then, Groh carries back any unused loss to 2007. Accordingly, Groh files amended tax returns for 2006 and 2007, receiving refunds for the $110,000 ($30,000 + $80,000) of taxes paid in those years.

For accounting as well as tax purposes, the $110,000 represents the **tax effect (tax benefit)** of the loss carryback. Groh should recognize this tax effect in 2008, the loss year. Since the tax loss gives rise to a refund that is both measurable and currently realizable, Groh should recognize the associated tax benefit in this loss period.

Groh makes the following journal entry for 2008.

Income Tax Refund Receivable	110,000	
Benefit Due to Loss Carryback (Income Tax Expense)		110,000

Groh reports the account debited, **Income Tax Refund Receivable**, on the balance sheet as a current asset at December 31, 2008. It reports the account credited on the income statement for 2008 as shown in Illustration 15-31.

Illustration 15-31
Recognition of Benefit of the Loss Carryback in the Loss Year

Groh Inc. Income Statement (partial) for 2008	
Operating loss before income taxes	$(500,000)
Income tax benefit	
Benefit due to loss carryback	110,000
Net loss	$(390,000)

Since the $500,000 net operating loss for 2008 exceeds the $300,000 total taxable income from the two preceding years, Groh carries forward the remaining $200,000 loss.

Loss Carryforward Example

If a carryback fails to fully absorb a net operating loss, or if the company decides not to carry the loss back, then it can carry forward the loss for up to 20 years.[3] Because companies use carryforwards to offset future taxable income, the **tax effect of a loss carryforward** represents **future tax savings**. Realization of the future tax benefit depends on future earnings, an uncertain prospect.

The key accounting issue is whether there should be different requirements for recognition of a deferred tax asset for (a) deductible temporary differences, and (b) operating loss carryforwards. The FASB's position is that in substance these items are the same—both are tax-deductible amounts in future years. As a result, the Board concluded that there **should not be different requirements** for recognition of a deferred tax asset from deductible temporary differences and operating loss carryforwards.[4]

Carryforward Without Valuation Allowance

To illustrate the accounting for an operating loss carryforward, return to the Groh example from the preceding section. In 2008 the company records the tax effect of the $200,000 loss carryforward as a deferred tax asset of $80,000 ($200,000 × 40%), assuming that the enacted future tax rate is 40 percent. Groh records the benefits of the carryback and the carryforward in 2008 shown at the top of page 799.

---

[3]The length of the carryforward period has varied. It has increased from 7 years to 20 years over a period of time.

[4]This requirement is controversial because many believe it is inappropriate to recognize deferred tax assets except when assured beyond a reasonable doubt. Others argue that companies should never recognize deferred tax assets for loss carryforwards until realizing the income in the future.

To recognize benefit of loss carryback

Income Tax Refund Receivable	110,000	
Benefit Due to Loss Carryback (Income Tax Expense)		110,000

To recognize benefit of loss carryforward

Deferred Tax Asset	80,000	
Benefit Due to Loss Carryforward (Income Tax Expense)		80,000

Groh realizes the income tax refund receivable of $110,000 immediately as a refund of taxes paid in the past. It establishes a Deferred Tax Asset for the benefits of future tax savings. The two accounts credited are contra income tax expense items, which Groh presents on the 2008 income statement shown in Illustration 15-32.

Illustration 15-32
Recognition of the Benefit of the Loss Carryback and Carryforward in the Loss Year

Groh Inc.
Income Statement (partial) for 2008

Operating loss before income taxes		$(500,000)
Income tax benefit		
Benefit due to loss carryback	$110,000	
Benefit due to loss carryforward	80,000	190,000
Net loss		$(310,000)

The **current tax benefit** of $110,000 is the income tax refundable for the year. Groh determines this amount by applying the carryback provisions of the tax law to the taxable loss for 2008. The $80,000 is the **deferred tax benefit** for the year, which results from an increase in the deferred tax asset.

For 2009, assume that Groh returns to profitable operations and has taxable income of $250,000 (prior to adjustment for the NOL carryforward), subject to a 40 percent tax rate. Groh then realizes the benefits of the carryforward for tax purposes in 2009, which it recognized for accounting purposes in 2008. Groh computes the income tax payable for 2009 as shown in Illustration 15-33.

Illustration 15-33
Computation of Income Tax Payable with Realized Loss Carryforward

Taxable income prior to loss carryforward	$ 250,000
Loss carryforward deduction	(200,000)
Taxable income for 2009	50,000
Tax rate	40%
Income tax payable for 2009	$ 20,000

Groh records income taxes in 2009 as follows.

Income Tax Expense	100,000	
Deferred Tax Asset		80,000
Income Tax Payable		20,000

The benefits of the NOL carryforward, realized in 2009, reduce the Deferred Tax Asset account to zero.

The 2009 income statement that appears in Illustration 15-34 (page 800) does **not report** the tax effects of either the loss carryback or the loss carryforward, because Groh had reported both previously.

Groh Inc. Income Statement (partial) for 2008		
Income before income taxes		$250,000
Income tax expense		
Current	$20,000	
Deferred	80,000	100,000
Net income		$150,000

Carryforward with Valuation Allowance

Let us return to the Groh example. Assume that it is more likely than not that Groh will *not* realize the entire NOL carryforward in future years. In this situation, Groh records the tax benefits of $110,000 associated with the $300,000 NOL carryback, as we previously described. In addition, it records a Deferred Tax Asset of $80,000 ($200,000 × 40%) for the potential benefits related to the loss carryforward, and an allowance to reduce the deferred tax asset by the same amount. Groh makes the following journal entries in 2008.

To recognize benefit of loss carryback

Income Tax Refund Receivable	110,000	
Benefit Due to Loss Carryback (Income Tax Expense)		110,000

To recognize benefit of loss carryforward

Deferred Tax Asset	80,000	
Benefit Due to Loss Carryforward (Income Tax Expense)		80,000

To record allowance amount

Benefit Due to Loss Carryforward (Income Tax Expense)	80,000	
Allowance to Reduce Deferred Tax Asset to Expected Realizable Value		80,000

The latter entry indicates that because positive evidence of sufficient quality and quantity is unavailable to counteract the negative evidence, Groh needs a valuation allowance.

Illustration 15-35 shows Groh's 2008 income statement presentation.

Illustration 15-35
Recognition of Benefit of
Loss Carryback Only

Groh Inc. Income Statement (partial) for 2008	
Operating loss before income taxes	$(500,000)
Income tax benefit	
Benefit due to loss carryback	110,000
Net loss	$(390,000)

In 2009, assuming that Groh has taxable income of $250,000 (before considering the carryforward), subject to a tax rate of 40 percent, it realizes the deferred tax asset. It thus no longer needs the allowance. Groh records the following entries.

To record current and deferred income taxes

Income Tax Expense	100,000	
Deferred Tax Asset		80,000
Income Tax Payable		20,000

To eliminate allowance and recognize loss carryforward

Allowance to Reduce Deferred Tax Asset to Expected Realizable Value	80,000	
Benefit Due to Loss Carryforward (Income Tax Expense)		80,000

Groh reports the $80,000 Benefit Due to the Loss Carryforward on the 2009 income statement. The company did not recognize it in 2008 because it was more likely than not that it would not be realized. Assuming that Groh derives the income for 2009 from continuing operations, it prepares the income statement as shown in Illustration 15-36.

Illustration 15-36
Recognition of Benefit of Loss Carryforward When Realized

Groh Inc. Income Statement (partial) for 2009		
Income before income taxes		$250,000
Income tax expense		
Current	$ 20,000	
Deferred	80,000	
Benefit due to loss carryforward	(80,000)	20,000
Net income		$230,000

Another method is to report only one line for total income tax expense of $20,000 on the face of the income statement and disclose the components of income tax expense in the notes to the financial statements.

Valuation Allowance Revisited

A company should consider all positive and negative information in determining whether it needs a valuation allowance. Whether the company will realize a deferred tax asset depends on whether sufficient taxable income exists or will exist within the carryforward period available under tax law. Illustration 15-37 shows possible sources of taxable income that may be available under the tax law to realize a tax benefit for deductible temporary differences and carryforwards.

Illustration 15-37
Possible Sources of Taxable Income

Taxable Income Sources

a. Future reversals of existing taxable temporary differences
b. Future taxable income exclusive of reversing temporary differences and carryforwards
c. Taxable income in prior carryback year(s) if carryback is permitted under the tax law
d. **Tax-planning strategies** that would, if necessary, be implemented to:
   (1) Accelerate taxable amounts to utilize expiring carryforwards
   (2) Change the character of taxable or deductible amounts from ordinary income or loss to capital gain or loss
   (3) Switch from tax-exempt to taxable investments.[5]

If any one of these sources is sufficient to support a conclusion that a valuation allowance is unnecessary, a company need not consider other sources.

Forming a conclusion that a valuation allowance is not needed is difficult when there is negative evidence such as cumulative losses in recent years. Companies may also cite positive evidence indicating that a valuation allowance is not needed. Illustration 15-38 (page 802) presents examples (not prerequisites) of evidence to consider when determining the need for a valuation allowance.

---

[5]"Accounting for Income Taxes," *Statement of Financial Accounting Standards No. 109* (Norwalk, Conn.: FASB, 1992). Companies implement a tax-planning strategy to realize a tax benefit for an operating loss or tax credit carryforward before it expires. Companies consider tax-planning strategies when assessing the need for and amount of a valuation allowance for deferred tax assets.

Illustration 15-38
Evidence to Consider in
Evaluating the Need for a
Valuation Account

INTERNATIONAL INSIGHT

Under international accounting standards *(IAS 12)*, a company may not recognize a deferred tax asset unless realization is "probable." However, "probable" is not defined in the standard, leading to diversity in the recognition of deferred tax assets.

Negative Evidence

a. A history of operating loss or tax credit carryforwards expiring unused

b. Losses expected in early future years (by a presently profitable entity)

c. Unsettled circumstances that, if unfavorably resolved, would adversely affect future operations and profit levels on a continuing basis in future years

d. A carryback, carryforward period that is so brief that it would limit realization of tax benefits if (1) a significant deductible temporary difference is expected to reverse in a single year or (2) the enterprise operates in a traditionally cyclical business.

Positive Evidence

a. Existing contracts or firm sales backlog that will produce more than enough taxable income to realize the deferred tax asset based on existing sale prices and cost structures

b. An excess of appreciated asset value over the tax basis of the entity's net assets in an amount sufficient to realize the deferred tax asset

c. A strong earnings history exclusive of the loss that created the future deductible amount (tax loss carryforward or deductible temporary difference) coupled with evidence indicating that the loss is an aberration rather than a continuing condition (for example, the result of an unusual, infrequent, or extraordinary item).[6]

The use of a valuation allowance provides a company with an opportunity to manage its earnings. As one accounting expert notes, "The 'more likely than not' provision is perhaps the most judgmental clause in accounting." Some companies may set up a valuation account and then use it to increase income as needed. Others may take the income immediately to increase capital or to offset large negative charges to income.

What do the numbers mean?   Read Those Notes

A recent study of companies' valuation allowances indicates that the allowances are related to the factors identified as positive and negative evidence. And though there is little evidence that companies use the valuation allowance to manage earnings, the press sometimes understates the impact of reversing the deferred tax valuation allowance.

For example, in one year **Verity, Inc.** eliminated its entire valuation allowance of $18.9 million but focused on a net deferred tax gain of $2.9 million in its press release. Why the difference? As revealed in Verity's financial statement notes, other deferred tax expense amounts totaled over $16 million. Thus, the one-time valuation reversal gave an $18.9 million bump to income, not the net $2.9 million reported in the press.

The lesson: After you read the morning paper, read the financial statement notes.

Source: G. S Miller and D. J. Skinner, "Determinants of the Valuation Allowance for Deferred Tax Assets under *SFAS No. 109*," *The Accounting Review* (April 1998).

Beyond the Numbers

Why might a company not want to disclose the reversal of a valuation allowance?

Try it out! Turner Company reported the following pretax income (loss) for both book and tax purposes for 2005-2008.

Year	Pretax Income (Loss)	Tax Rate
2005	$180,000	35%
2006	120,000	35
2007	(420,000)	40
2008	250,000	40

[6]Ibid., pars. 23 and 24.

The tax rates listed were all enacted by the beginning of 2005. Assume the carryback provision is used first for net operating losses.

Instructions

Prepare the journal entries for 2007–2008 to record income tax expense/payable and the tax effects of the loss carryback and carryforward. Assume that at the end of 2007 Turner judges it is more likely than not that one-third of the benefits of the loss carryforward will not be realized.

Solution

2007

Income Tax Refund Receivable [($180,000 + $120,000) × .35]	105,000	
Benefit Due to Loss Carryback		105,000
Deferred Tax Asset [($420,000 − $300,000) × .40]	48,000	
Benefit Due to Loss Carryforward		48,000
Benefit Due to Loss Carryforward ($48,000 × 1/3)	16,000	
Allowance to Reduce Deferred Tax Asset		
to Expected Realizable Value		16,000

2008

Income Tax Expense ($48,000 + $52,000)	100,000	
Deferred Tax Asset		48,000
Income Tax Payable [($250,000 − $120,000) × .40]		52,000
Allowance to Reduce Deferred Tax Asset to		
Expected Realizable Value	16,000	
Benefit Due to Loss Carryforward		16,000

FINANCIAL STATEMENT PRESENTATION

Balance Sheet

Deferred tax accounts are reported on the balance sheet as assets and liabilities. Companies should classify these accounts as a net current amount and a net noncurrent amount. **An individual deferred tax liability or asset is classified as current or noncurrent based on the classification of the related asset or liability for financial reporting purposes.**

> **OBJECTIVE 9**
> Describe the presentation of deferred income taxes in financial statements.

A company considers a deferred tax asset or liability to be related to an asset or liability, if reduction of the asset or liability causes the temporary difference to reverse or turn around. A company should classify a deferred tax liability or asset that is unrelated to an asset or liability for financial reporting, including a deferred tax asset related to a loss carryforward, according to the expected reversal date of the temporary difference.

To illustrate, assume that Morgan Inc. records bad debt expense using the allowance method for accounting purposes and the direct write-off method for tax purposes. It currently has Accounts Receivable and Allowance for Doubtful Accounts balances of $2 million and $100,000, respectively. In addition, given a 40 percent tax rate, Morgan has a debit balance in the Deferred Tax Asset account of $40,000 (40% × $100,000). It considers the $40,000 debit balance in the Deferred Tax Asset account to be related to the Accounts Receivable and the Allowance for Doubtful Accounts balances because collection or write-off of the receivables will cause the temporary difference to reverse. Therefore, Morgan classifies the Deferred Tax Asset account as current, the same as the Accounts Receivable and Allowance for Doubtful Accounts balances.

In practice, most companies engage in a large number of transactions that give rise to deferred taxes. Companies should classify the balances in the deferred tax accounts on the balance sheet in two categories: one for the **net current amount**, and one for the **net non-current amount**. We summarize this procedure as follows.

1 *Classify the amounts as current or noncurrent.* If related to a specific asset or liability, classify the amounts in the same manner as the related asset or liability. If not related, classify them on the basis of the expected reversal date of the temporary difference.

2 *Determine the net current amount* by summing the various deferred tax assets and liabilities classified as current. If the net result is an asset, report it on the balance sheet as a current asset; if a liability, report it as a current liability.

3 *Determine the net noncurrent amount* by summing the various deferred tax assets and liabilities classified as noncurrent. If the net result is an asset, report it on the balance sheet as a noncurrent asset; if a liability, report it as a long-term liability.

To illustrate, assume that K. Scott Company has four deferred tax items at December 31, 2008. Illustration 15-39 shows an analysis of these four temporary differences as current or noncurrent.

Illustration 15-39
Classification of Temporary Differences as Current or Noncurrent

Temporary Difference	Resulting Deferred Tax (Asset)	Resulting Deferred Tax Liability	Related Balance Sheet Account	Classification
1. Rent collected in advance: recognized when earned for accounting purposes and when received for tax purposes.	$(42,000)		Unearned Rent	Current
2. Use of straight-line depreciation for accounting purposes and accelerated depreciation for tax purposes.		$214,000	Equipment	Noncurrent
3. Recognition of profits on installment sales during period of sale for accounting purposes and during period of collection for tax purposes.		45,000	Installment Accounts Receivable	Current
4. Warranty liabilities: recognized for accounting purposes at time of sale; for tax purposes at time paid.	(12,000)		Estimated Liability under Warranties	Current
Totals	$(54,000)	$259,000		

K. Scott classifies as current a deferred tax asset of $9,000 ($42,000 + $12,000 − $45,000). It also reports as noncurrent a deferred tax liability of $214,000. Consequently, K. Scott's December 31, 2008, balance sheet reports deferred income taxes as shown in Illustration 15-40.

Current assets	
Deferred tax asset	$ 9,000
Long-term liabilities	
Deferred tax liability	$214,000

Illustration 15-40
Balance Sheet
Presentation of Deferred
Income Taxes

As we indicated earlier, a deferred tax asset or liability **may not be related** to an asset or liability for financial reporting purposes. One example is an operating loss carryforward. In this case, a company records a deferred tax asset, but there is no related, identifiable asset or liability for financial reporting purposes. In these limited situations, deferred income taxes are classified according to the **expected reversal date** of the temporary difference. That is, a company should report the tax effect of any temporary difference reversing next year as current, and the remainder as noncurrent. If a deferred tax asset is noncurrent, a company should classify it in the "Other assets" section.

The total of all deferred tax liabilities, the total of all deferred tax assets, and the total valuation allowance should be disclosed. In addition, companies should disclose the following: (1) any net change during the year in the total valuation allowance, and (2) the types of temporary differences, carryforwards, or carrybacks that give rise to significant portions of deferred tax liabilities and assets.

Income tax payable is reported as a current liability on the balance sheet. Corporations make estimated tax payments to the Internal Revenue Service quarterly. They record these estimated payments by a debit to Prepaid Income Taxes. As a result, the balance of the Income Tax Payable offsets the balance of the Prepaid Income Taxes account when reporting income taxes on the balance sheet.

Income Statement

Companies should allocate income tax expense (or benefit) to continuing operations, discontinued operations, extraordinary items, and prior period adjustments. This approach is referred to as intraperiod tax allocation.

In addition, companies should disclose the significant components of income tax expense attributable to continuing operations:

**Expanded Discussion of
Intraperiod Tax Allocation**

1   Current tax expense or benefit.

2   Deferred tax expense or benefit, exclusive of other components listed below.

3   Investment tax credits.

4   Government grants (if recognized as a reduction of income tax expense).

5   The benefits of operating loss carryforwards (resulting in a reduction of income tax expense).

6   Tax expense that results from allocating tax benefits either directly to paid-in capital or to reduce goodwill or other noncurrent intangible assets of an acquired entity.

7   Adjustments of a deferred tax liability or asset for enacted changes in tax laws or rates or a change in the tax status of a company.

8   Adjustments of the beginning-of-the-year balance of a valuation allowance because of a change in circumstances that causes a change in judgment about the realizability of the related deferred tax asset in future years.

In the notes, companies must also reconcile (using percentages or dollar amounts) income tax expense attributable to continuing operations with the amount that results from applying domestic federal statutory tax rates to pretax income from continuing operations. Companies should disclose the estimated amount and the nature of each significant reconciling item. Illustration 15-41 (page 807) presents an example from the 2006 annual report of **PepsiCo, Inc.**

These income tax disclosures are required for several reasons:

Additional Examples of Deferred Tax Disclosures

1 *Assessing Quality of Earnings.* Many investors seeking to assess the quality of a company's earnings are interested in the reconciliation of pretax financial income to taxable income. Analysts carefully examine earnings that are enhanced by a favorable tax effect, particularly if the tax effect is nonrecurring. For example, the tax disclosure in Illustration 15-41 indicates that **PepsiCo**'s effective tax rate declined from 36.1 percent in 2005 to 19.3 percent in 2006 (primarily due to settlement of a prior year's tax audit.) The decline translates into a tax savings of $957 million. These savings contributed to PepsiCo's increase in bottom-line income from 2005 to 2006.

2 *Making Better Predictions of Future Cash Flows.* Examination of the deferred portion of income tax expense provides information as to whether taxes payable are likely to be higher or lower in the future. In **PepsiCo**'s case, analysts expect significant future taxable amounts and higher tax payments, due to realization of gains on equity investments, lower depreciation in the future, and higher payments for pension expense. As a result, it may be possible to predict future reductions in deferred tax liabilities leading to a loss of liquidity. Why? Because actual tax payments will be higher than the tax expense reported on the income statement.[7]

3 *Predicting Future Cash Flows from Operating Loss Carryforwards.* Companies should disclose the amounts and expiration dates of any operating loss carryforwards for tax purposes. From this disclosure, analysts determine the amount of income that the company may recognize in the future on which it will pay no income tax. For example, the **PepsiCo** disclosure in Illustration 15-41 indicates that PepsiCo has $6.1 billion in net operating loss carryforwards that it can use to reduce future taxes up to the year 2026 and beyond. However, the valuation allowance indicates that $624 million of the deferred tax asset may not be realized in the future.

Loss carryforwards can be valuable to a potential acquirer. For example, as mentioned earlier, **Yahoo!** has a substantial net operating loss carryforward. A potential acquirer would find Yahoo! more valuable as a result of these carryforwards. That is, the acquirer may be able to use these carryforwards to shield future income. However the acquiring company has to be careful, because the structure of the deal may lead to a situation where the deductions will be severely limited.

Much the same issue arises in companies emerging from bankruptcy. In many cases these companies have large NOLs, but the value of the losses may be limited. This is because any gains related to the cancellation of liabilities in bankruptcy must be offset against the NOLs. For example, when **Kmart Holding Corp.** emerged from bankruptcy in early 2004, it disclosed NOL carryforwards approximating $3.8 billion. At the same time, Kmart disclosed cancellation of debt gains that reduced the value of the NOL carryforward. These reductions soured the merger between Kmart and **Sears** because the cancellation of the indebtedness gains reduced the value of the Kmart carryforwards to the merged company by $3.74 billion.[8]

---

[7]An article by R. P. Weber and J. E. Wheeler, "Using Income Tax Disclosures to Explore Significant Economic Transactions," *Accounting Horizons* (September 1992), discusses how analysts use deferred tax disclosures to assess the quality of earnings and to predict future cash flows.

[8]P. McConnell, J. Pegg, C. Senyak, and D. Mott, "The ABCs of NOLs," *Accounting Issues*, Bear Stearns Equity Research (June 2005). The IRS frowns on acquisitions done solely to obtain operating loss carryforwards. If it determines that the merger is solely tax motivated, the IRS disallows the deductions. But because it is very difficult to determine whether a merger is or is not tax-motivated, the "purchase of operating loss carryforwards" continues.

PEPSICO

PepsiCo, Inc.

(in millions)

Illustration 15-41
Disclosure of Income
Taxes—PepsiCo, Inc.

Note 5: Income Taxes (partial)	2006	2005
Income before income taxes—continuing operations		
U.S.	$3,844	$3,175
Foreign	3,145	3,207
	$6,989	$6,382
Provision for income taxes—continuing operations		
Current: U.S. Federal	$776	$1,638
Foreign	569	426
State	56	118
	1,401	2,182
Deferred: U.S. Federal	(31)	137
Foreign	(16)	(26)
State	(7)	11
	(54)	122
	$1,347	$2,304
Tax rate reconciliation—continuing operations		
U.S. Federal statutory tax rate	35.0%	35.0%
State income tax, net of U.S. Federal tax benefit	0.5	1.4
Taxes on AJCA repatriation	—	7.0
Lower taxes on foreign results	(6.5)	(6.5)
Settlement of prior years' audit	—	—
2006 tax adjustments	(8.6)	—
Other, net	(1.1)	(0.8)
Annual tax rate	19.3%	36.1%
Deferred tax liabilities		
Investments in noncontrolled affiliates	$1,103	$ 993
Property, plant and equipment	784	772
Pension benefits	—	863
Intangible assets other than nondeductible goodwill	169	135
Zero coupon notes	27	35
Other	221	169
Gross deferred tax liabilities	2,304	2,967
Deferred tax assets		
Net carryforwards	667	608
Stock-based compensation	443	426
Retiree medical benefits	541	400
Other employee-related benefits	342	342
Pension benefits	38	—
Other	592	520
Gross deferred tax assets	2,623	2,296
Valuation allowances	(624)	(532)
Deferred tax assets, net	1,999	1,764
Net deferred tax liabilities	$ 305	$1,203
Deferred taxes included within		
Assets:		
Prepaid expenses and other current assets	$ 223	$ 231
Liabilities:		
Deferred income taxes	$ 528	$1,434
Analysis of valuation allowances		
Balance, beginning of year	$ 532	$ 564
Provision/(benefit)	71	(28)
Other additions/(deductions)	21	(4)
Balance, end of year	$ 624	$ 532

(continued on next page)

Illustration 15-41
(continued)

Carryforwards, Credits and Allowances

Operating loss carryforwards totaling $6.1 billion at year-end 2006 are being carried forward in a number of foreign and state jurisdictions where we are permitted to use tax operating losses from prior periods to reduce future taxable income. These operating losses will expire as follows: $0.2 billion in 2007, $5.0 billion between 2008 and 2026 and $0.9 billion may be carried forward indefinitely. In addition, certain tax credits generated in prior periods of approximately $33.9 million are available to reduce certain foreign tax liabilities through 2011. We establish valuation allowances for our deferred tax assets when the amount of expected future taxable income is not likely to support the use of the deduction or credit.

Undistributed International Earnings

The AJCA created a one-time incentive for U.S. corporations to repatriate undistributed international earnings by providing an 85% dividends received deduction. In 2005, we repatriated approximately $7.5 billion in earnings previously considered indefinitely reinvested outside the U.S. and recorded income tax expense of $460 million related to this repatriation.

Reserves

A number of years may elapse before a particular matter, for which we have established a reserve, is audited and finally resolved. The number of years with open tax audits varies depending on the tax jurisdiction. In 2006, we recognized non-cash tax benefits of $602 million, substantially all of which related to the IRS's examination of our consolidated income tax returns for the years 1998 through 2002.

What do the numbers mean?   NOLs: Good News or Bad?

Here are some net operating loss numbers recently reported by several notable companies.

NOLs ($ in millions)

Company	2004 Income (Loss)	Operating Loss Carryforward	Tax Benefit (Deferred Tax Asset)	Comment
Delta Airlines, Inc.	($5,198.00)	$7,500.00	$2,848.00	Begins to expire in 2022. Valuation allowance recorded.
Goodyear	114.80	1,306.60*	457.30	Begins to expire in 2005. Full valuation allowance.
Kodak	556.00	509.00	234.00	Begins to expire in 2005. Valuation allowance on foreign credits only.
Krispy Kreme	57.09	26.40*	9.24	No valuation allowance.
Yahoo! Inc.	42.82	5,400.00	1,443.50	State and federal carryforwards. Begins to expire in 2005. Valuation allowance recorded.

*Not reported; estimated as [(Tax benefit) ÷ 35%].

All of these companies are using the carryforward provisions of the tax code for their NOLs. For many of them, the NOL is an amount far exceeding their reported profits. Why carry forward the loss to get the tax deduction? First, the company may have already used up the carryback provision, which allows only a two-year carryback period. (Carryforwards can be claimed up to 20 years in the future.) In some cases, management expects the tax rates in the future to be higher. This difference in expected rates provides a bigger tax benefit if the losses are carried forward and matched against future income. Is there a downside? To realize the benefits of carryforwards, a company must have future taxable income in the carryforward period in order to claim the NOL deductions. As we learned, if it is more likely than not that a company will not have taxable income, it must record a valuation allowance (and increased tax expense). As the data above indicate, recording a valuation allowance to reflect the uncertainty of realizing the tax benefits has merit. But for some, the NOL benefits begin to expire in the following year, which may be not enough time to generate sufficient taxable income in order to claim the NOL deduction.

Source: Company annual reports.

Beyond the Numbers

What impact do future tax rates have on a company's decision to carry forward rather than carry back its net operating losses?

REVIEW OF THE ASSET-LIABILITY METHOD

The FASB believes that the **asset-liability method** (sometimes referred to as the **liability approach**) is the most consistent method for accounting for income taxes. One objective of this approach is to recognize the amount of taxes payable or refundable for the current year. A second objective is to recognize **deferred tax liabilities and assets** for the **future tax consequences** of events that have been recognized in the financial statements or tax returns.

> OBJECTIVE 10
> **Indicate the basic principles of the asset-liability method.**

To implement the objectives, companies apply some basic principles in accounting for income taxes at the date of the financial statements, as listed in Illustration 15-42.

Basic Principles

a. A current tax liability or asset is recognized for the estimated taxes payable or refundable on the tax return for the current year.
b. A deferred tax liability or asset is recognized for the estimated future tax effects attributable to temporary differences and carryforwards.
c. The measurement of current and deferred tax liabilities and assets is based on provisions of the enacted tax law; the effects of future changes in tax laws or rates are not anticipated.
d. The measurement of deferred tax assets is reduced, if necessary, by the amount of any tax benefits that, based on available evidence, are not expected to be realized.[9]

Illustration 15-42
Basic Principles of the Asset-Liability Method

Discussion of Conceptual Approaches to Interperiod Tax Allocation

Illustration 15-43 (page 810) diagrams the procedures for implementing the asset-liability method.

[9]"Accounting for Income Taxes" (1992), pars. 6 and 8.

Illustration 15-43
Procedures for Computing
and Reporting Deferred
Income Taxes

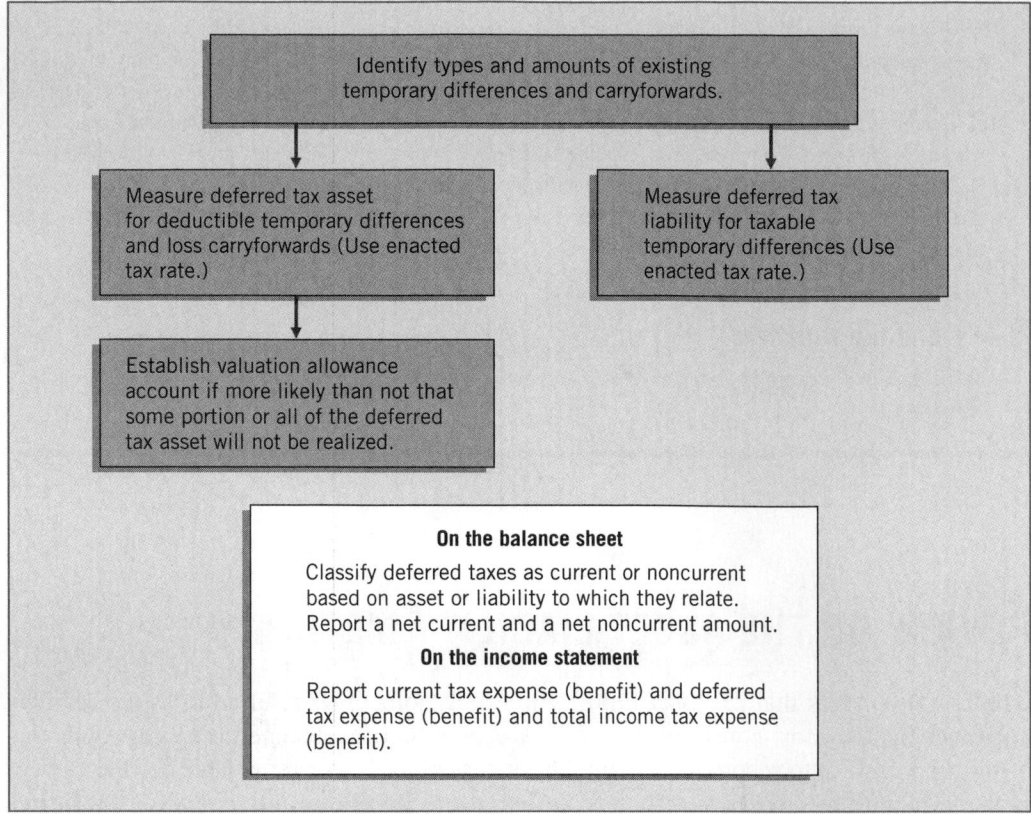

As an aid to understanding deferred income taxes, we provide the following glossary.[10]

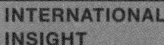

INTERNATIONAL
INSIGHT

iGAAP for income
is based on the same
principles as the U.S.
GAAP—comprehensive
recognition of deferred tax
assets and liabilities.

KEY DEFERRED INCOME TAX TERMS

CARRYBACKS. Deductions or credits that cannot be utilized on the tax return during a year and that may be carried back to reduce taxable income or taxes paid in a prior year. An **operating loss carryback** is an excess of tax deductions over gross income in a year. A **tax credit carryback** is the amount by which tax credits available for utilization exceed statutory limitations.

CARRYFORWARDS. Deductions or credits that cannot be utilized on the tax return during a year and that may be carried forward to reduce taxable income or taxes payable in a future year. An **operating loss carryforward** is an excess of tax deductions over gross income in a year. A **tax credit carryforward** is the amount by which tax credits available for utilization exceed statutory limitations.

CURRENT TAX EXPENSE (BENEFIT). The amount of income taxes paid or payable (or refundable) for a year as determined by applying the provisions of the enacted tax law to the taxable income or excess of deductions over revenues for that year.

DEDUCTIBLE TEMPORARY DIFFERENCE. Temporary differences that result in deductible amounts in future years when recovering or settling the related asset or liability, respectively.

[10]"Accounting for Income Taxes," Appendix E.

DEFERRED TAX ASSET. The deferred tax consequences attributable to deductible temporary differences and carryforwards.

DEFERRED TAX CONSEQUENCES. The future effects on income taxes as measured by the enacted tax rate and provisions of the enacted tax law resulting from temporary differences and carryforwards at the end of the current year.

DEFERRED TAX EXPENSE (BENEFIT). The change during the year in a company's deferred tax liabilities and assets.

DEFERRED TAX LIABILITY. The deferred tax consequences attributable to taxable temporary differences.

INCOME TAXES. Domestic and foreign federal (national), state, and local (including franchise) taxes based on income.

INCOME TAXES CURRENTLY PAYABLE (REFUNDABLE). Refer to current tax expense (benefit).

INCOME TAX EXPENSE (BENEFIT). The sum of current tax expense (benefit) and deferred tax expense (benefit).

TAXABLE INCOME. The excess of taxable revenues over tax deductible expenses and exemptions for the year as defined by the governmental taxing authority.

TAXABLE TEMPORARY DIFFERENCE. Temporary differences that result in taxable amounts in future years when recovering or settling the related asset or liability, respectively.

TAX-PLANNING STRATEGY. An action that meets certain criteria and that a company implements to realize a tax benefit for an operating loss or tax credit carryforward before it expires. Companies consider tax-planning strategies when assessing the need for and amount of a valuation allowance for deferred tax assets.

TEMPORARY DIFFERENCE. A difference between the tax basis of an asset or liability and its reported amount in the financial statements that will result in taxable or deductible amounts in future years when recovering or settling the reported amount of the asset or liability, respectively.

VALUATION ALLOWANCE. The portion of a deferred tax asset for which it is more likely than not that a company will not realize a tax benefit.

You will want to read the CONVERGENCE CORNER on page 814 for discussion of how international convergence efforts relate to income taxes.

ACCOUNTING, ANALYSIS, PRINCIPLES

Allman Company, which began operations at the beginning of 2006, produces various products on a contract basis. Each contract generates a gross profit of $80,000. Some of Allman's contracts provide for the customer to pay on an installment basis. Under these contracts, Allman collects one-fifth of the contract revenue in each of the following four years.

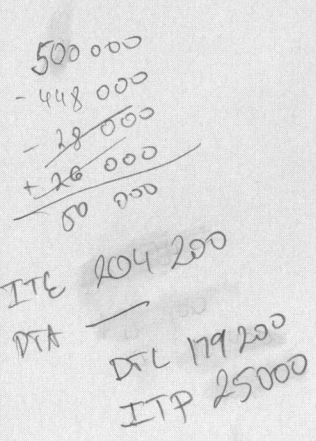

For financial reporting purposes, the company recognizes gross profit in the year of completion (accrual basis); for tax purposes, Allman recognizes gross profit in the year cash is collected (installment basis).

Presented below is information related to Allman's operations for 2008.

1 In 2008, the company completed seven contracts that allow for the customer to pay on an installment basis. Allman recognized the related gross profit of $560,000 for financial reporting purposes. It reported only $112,000 of gross profit on installment sales on the 2008 tax return. The company expects future collections on the related installment receivables to result in taxable amounts of $112,000 in each of the next four years.

2 In 2008 nontaxable municipal bond interest revenue was $28,000.

3 During 2008 nondeductible fines and penalties of $26,000 were paid.

4 Pretax financial income for 2008 amounts to $500,000.

5 Tax rates enacted before the end of 2008 were:

2008	50%
2009 and later years	40%

6 The accounting period is the calendar year.

7 The company is expected to have taxable income in all future years.

Accounting

Prepare the journal entry to record deferred income taxes for 2008.

Analysis

Classify deferred income taxes on the balance sheet at December 31, 2008, and indicate, starting with income before income taxes, how income taxes are reported on the income statement. What is Allman's effective tax rate? Do you believe it will change in the future?

Principles

Explain how the conceptual framework is used as a basis for determining the proper accounting for deferred income taxes.

Solution

Accounting

The first step is to determine Allman Company's income tax payable for 2008 by calculating its taxable income. The computation is as follow.

Pretax financial income for 2008	$500,000
Permanent differences:	
Nontaxable revenue—municipal bond interest	(28,000)
Nondeductible expenses—fines and penalties	26,000
Temporary differences:	
Excess gross profit per books ($560,000 − $112,000)	(448,000)
Taxable income for 2008	$ 50,000

Allman computes income tax payable on taxable income of $50,000 as follows.

Taxable income for 2008	$50,000
Tax rate	50%
Income tax payable (current tax expense) for 2008	$25,000

Allman computes the amounts of deferred income taxes to be reported at the end of 2008 as follows.

Temporary Difference	Future Taxable Amounts	Tax Rate	Deferred Tax (Asset)	Deferred Tax Liability
Installment sales	$448,000	40%		$179,200

Allman records income tax payable, deferred income taxes, and income tax expense as follows.

Income Tax Expense	204,200	
Income Tax Payable		25,000
Deferred Tax Liability		179,200

Analysis

The classification of Allman's deferred tax accounts at the end of 2008 is as follows.

Temporary Difference	Resulting Deferred Tax (Asset)	Liability	Related Balance Sheet Account	Classification
Installment sales		$179,200	Installment Receivable	Current

The balance sheet at the end of 2008 reports the following current liability amounts.

Current liabilities	
Income tax payable	$ 25,000
Deferred tax liability	179,200

Allman's income statement for 2008 reports the following.

Income before income taxes		$500,000
Income tax expense		
Current	$25,000	
Deferred	179,200	204,200
Net income		$295,800

Allman's effective tax rate is 40.8 percent ($204,200 ÷ $500,000). It is likely that Allman's tax rate will increase in the future. The company has a rather large deferred tax liability, which will create taxable amounts in the future. As a result, the company will likely have to increase its taxes paid in the future.

Principles

We can use the conceptual framework to determine that deferred taxes should be reported as assets and liabilities. The conceptual framework provides specific guidance as to how to define assets and liabilities.

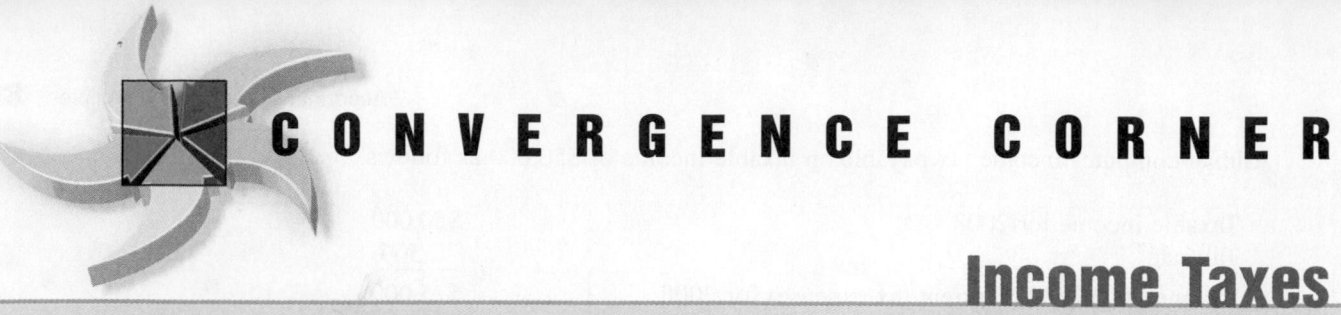

CONVERGENCE CORNER

Income Taxes

The accounting for income taxes in iGAAP is covered in *IAS 12* ("Income Taxes"). Similar to U.S. GAAP, iGAAP uses the asset and liability approach for recording deferred taxes. The differences between iGAAP and U.S. GAAP involve a few exceptions to the asset-liability approach, some minor differences in the recognition, measurement, and disclosure criteria, and differences in implementation guidance

RELEVANT FACTS

• The classification of deferred taxes under iGAAP is always noncurrent. As indicated in the chapter, U.S. GAAP classifies deferred taxes based on the classification of the asset or liability to which it relates.

• Under iGAAP, an affirmative judgment approach is used, by which a deferred tax asset is recognized up to the amount that is probable to be realized. U.S. GAAP uses an impairment approach. In this approach, the deferred tax asset is recognized in full. It is then reduced by a valuation account if it is more likely than not that all or a portion of the deferred tax asset will not be realized.

• iGAAP uses the enacted tax rate or substantially enacted tax rate. ("Substantially enacted" means virtually certain.) For U.S. GAAP, the enacted tax rate must be used.

• The tax effects related to certain items are reported in equity under iGAAP. That is not the case under U.S. GAAP, which charges or credits the tax effects to income.

ABOUT THE NUMBERS

The following schedule taken from the annual report of **Glaxo-SmithKline plc** (which uses iGAAP) indicates the impact of differences in iGAAP and U.S. GAAP for deferred taxes.

Reconciliation to U.S. accounting principles

(e) Deferred taxation (in part):

Total tax expense (in millions of British pounds)

	2006
IFRS:	
Current tax expense	2,710
Deferred tax (credit)/expense	(409)
Total tax expense	2,301
U.S. GAAP:	
Current tax expense	2,735
Deferred tax credit	(685)
Total tax expense	2,050
Total tax expense difference	(251)

Thus, due to the differences highlighted above, Glaxo's income tax expense under iGAAP is 251 million pounds higher than that reported under U.S. GAAP.

ON THE HORIZON

The FASB and the IASB are addressing some of the issues related to convergence in their short-term project on income taxes. For example, it is likely that the term "probable" under iGAAP for recognition of a deferred tax asset will be interpreted to mean "more likely than not." As a result, the reporting for impairments of deferred tax assets will be essentially the same between U.S. GAAP and iGAAP. It is also likely that the IASB will adopt the classification approach used for U.S. GAAP for deferred tax assets and liabilities.

In addition, U.S. GAAP will likely continue to use the enacted tax rate in computing deferred taxes, except in situations where the U.S. taxing jurisdiction is not involved. In that case, companies should use iGAAP which is based on enacted rates or substantially enacted tax rates. Finally, it appears that the allocation of deferred income taxes to equity for certain transactions under iGAAP will be changed to conform to U.S. GAAP, which allocates the effects to income.

Key Terms

asset-liability method, 809
average tax rate, 795
current tax benefit (expense), 785, 799
deductible amounts, 783
deductible temporary difference, 792
deferred tax asset, 787
deferred tax expense (benefit), 785, 788
deferred tax liability, 784
effective tax rate, 795
enacted tax rate, 795
Income Tax Refund Receivable, 798
loss carryback, 797
loss carryforward, 797
more likely than not, 790

net current amount, 804
net noncurrent amount, 804
net operating loss (NOL), 796
originating temporary difference, 793
permanent difference, 793
pretax financial income, 782
reversing difference, 793
taxable amounts, 783
taxable income, 782
taxable temporary difference, 792
tax effect (tax benefit), 798
temporary difference, 783
valuation allowance, 790

Summary of Learning Objectives

1 Identify differences between pretax financial income and taxable income. Companies compute pretax financial income (or income for book purposes) in accordance with generally accepted accounting principles. They compute taxable income (or income for tax purposes) in accordance with prescribed tax regulations. Because tax regulations and GAAP differ in many ways, so frequently do pretax financial income and taxable income. Differences may exist, for example, in the timing of revenue recognition and the timing of expense recognition.

2 Describe a temporary difference that results in future taxable amounts. Revenue recognized for book purposes in the period earned but deferred and reported as revenue for tax purposes when collected results in future taxable amounts. The future taxable amounts will occur in the periods the company recovers the receivable and reports the collections as revenue for tax purposes. This results in a deferred tax liability.

3 Describe a temporary difference that results in future deductible amounts. An accrued warranty expense that a company pays for and deducts for tax purposes, in a period later than the period in which it incurs and recognizes it for book purposes, results in future deductible amounts. The future deductible amounts will occur in the periods during which the company settles the related liability for book purposes. This results in a deferred tax asset.

4 Explain the purpose of a deferred tax asset valuation allowance. A deferred tax asset should be reduced by a valuation allowance if, based on all available

evidence, it is more likely than not (a level of likelihood that is at least slightly more than 50 percent) that it will not realize some portion or all of the deferred tax asset. The company should carefully consider all available evidence, both positive and negative, to determine whether, based on the weight of available evidence, it needs a valuation allowance.

5 Describe the presentation of income tax expense in the income statement. Significant components of income tax expense should be disclosed in the income statement or in the notes to the financial statements. The most commonly encountered components are the current expense (or benefit) and the deferred expense (or benefit).

6 Describe various temporary and permanent differences. Examples of temporary differences are: (1) revenue or gains that are taxable after recognition in financial income; (2) expenses or losses that are deductible after recognition in financial income; (3) revenues or gains that are taxable before recognition in financial income; (4) expenses or losses that are deductible before recognition in financial income. Examples of permanent differences are: (1) items recognized for financial reporting purposes but not for tax purposes, and (2) items recognized for tax purposes but not for financial reporting purposes.

7 Explain the effect of various tax rates and tax rate changes on deferred income taxes. Companies may use tax rates other than the current rate only after enactment of the future tax rates. When a change in the tax rate is enacted, a company should immediately recognize its effect on the deferred income tax accounts. The company reports the effects as an adjustment to income tax expense in the period of the change.

8 Apply accounting procedures for a loss carryback and a loss carryforward. A company may carry a net operating loss back two years and receive refunds for income taxes paid in those years. The loss is applied to the earlier year first and then to the second year. Any loss remaining after the two-year carryback may be carried forward up to 20 years to offset future taxable income. A company may forgo the loss carryback and use the loss carryforward, offsetting future taxable income for up to 20 years.

9 Describe the presentation of deferred income taxes in financial statements. Companies report deferred tax accounts on the balance sheet as assets and liabilities. These deferred tax accounts are classified as a net current and a net noncurrent amount. Companies classify an individual deferred tax liability or asset as current or noncurrent based on the classification of the related asset or liability for financial reporting. A deferred tax liability or asset that is not related to an asset or liability for financial reporting, including a deferred tax asset related to a loss carryforward, is classified according to the expected reversal date of the temporary difference.

10 Indicate the basic principles of the asset-liability method. Companies apply the following basic principles in accounting for income taxes at the date of the financial statements: (1) Recognize a current tax liability or asset for the estimated taxes payable or refundable on the tax return for the current year. (2) Recognize a deferred tax liability or asset for the estimated future tax effects attributable to temporary differences and carryforwards using the enacted tax rate. (3) Base the measurement of current and deferred tax liabilities and assets on provisions of the enacted tax law. (4) Reduce the measurement of deferred tax assets, if necessary, by the amount of any tax benefits that, based on available evidence, companies do not expect to realize.

REVIEW EXERCISE

Johnny Bravo Company began operations in 2008 and has provided the following information.

1 Pretax financial income for 2008 is $100,000.

2 The tax rate enacted for 2008 and future years is 40%.

3 Differences between the 2008 income statement and tax return are listed below.

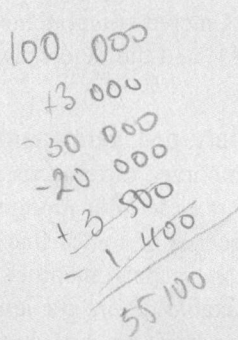

    a Warranty expense accrued for financial reporting purposes amounts to $5,000. Warranty deductions per the tax return amount to $2,000.

    b Gross profit on construction contracts using the percentage-of-completion method for books amounts to $92,000. Gross profit on construction contracts for tax purposes amounts to $62,000.

    c Depreciation of property, plant, and equipment for financial reporting purposes amounts to $60,000. Depreciation of these assets amounts to $80,000 for the tax return.

    d A $3,500 fine paid for violation of pollution laws was deducted in computing pretax financial income.

    e Interest revenue earned on an investment in tax-exempt municipal bonds amounts to $1,400.

    Assume (a) is short-term in nature; assume (b) and (c) are long-term in nature.

4 Taxable income is expected for the next few years.

Instructions

    a Compute taxable income for 2008.

    b Compute the deferred taxes at December 31, 2008, that relate to the temporary differences described above.

c Prepare the journal entry to record income tax expense, deferred taxes, and income taxes payable for 2008.

d Draft the income tax expense section of the income statement beginning with "Income before income taxes."

e Assume that in 2009 Johnny Bravo reported a pretax operating loss of $100,000. There were no other temporary or permanent differences in tax and book income for 2009. Prepare the journal entry to record income tax expense for 2009. Johnny Bravo expects to return to profitability in 2010.

Solution

a

Pretax financial income	$100,000
Permanent differences	
Fine for pollution	3,500
Tax-exempt interest	(1,400)
Originating temporary differences	
Excess warranty expense per books	
($5,000 − $2,000)	3,000
Excess construction profits per books	
($92,000 − $62,000)	(30,000)
Excess depreciation per tax	
($80,000 − $60,000)	(20,000)
Taxable income	$ 55,100

b

Temporary Difference	Future Taxable (Deductible) Amounts	Tax Rate	Deferred Tax (Asset)	Liability
Warranty costs	$ (3,000)	40%	$(1,200)	
Construction contracts	30,000	40%		$12,000
Depreciation	20,000	40%		8,000
Totals	$47,000		$(1,200)	$20,000*

*Because of a flat tax rate, these totals can be reconciled: $47,000 × 40% = $(1,200) + $20,000.

c

Income Tax Expense	40,840	
Deferred Tax Asset	1,200	
Deferred Tax Liability		20,000
Income Tax Payable		22,040

Taxable income for 2008 [from part (a)]	$55,100
Tax rate	40%
Income tax payable for 2008	$22,040
Deferred tax liability at the end of 2008 [from part (b)]	$20,000
Deferred tax liability at the beginning of 2008	–0–
Deferred tax expense for 2008	$20,000
Deferred tax asset at the end of 2008	$ 1,200
Deferred tax asset at the beginning of 2008	–0–
Deferred tax benefit for 2008	$ (1,200)

d	Income before income taxes		$100,000
	Income tax expense		
	Current	$22,040	
	Deferred	18,800	40,840
	Net income		$59,160

e	Income Tax Refund Receivable*	22,040	
	Deferred Tax Asset**	17,960	
	Benefit from Operating Loss Carryback		22,040
	Benefit from Operating Loss Carryforward		17,960

2009 Loss $100,000
*Carryback   (55,100) × 40% = $22,040 refund
**Carryforward $ 44,900 × 40% = $17,960 deferred tax asset

No valuation allowance is needed, since Johnny Bravo is expected to return to profitability in 2010. This is positive evidence that the deferred tax asset will be realized.

Comprehensive Illustration of Interperiod Tax Allocation

Questions

1. Explain the difference between pretax financial income and taxable income.

2. What are the two objectives of accounting for income taxes?

3. Interest on municipal bonds is referred to as a permanent difference when determining the proper amount to report for deferred taxes. Explain the meaning of permanent differences, and give two other examples.

4. Explain the meaning of a temporary difference as it relates to deferred tax computations, and give three examples.

5. Differentiate between an originating temporary difference and a reversing difference.

6. The book basis of depreciable assets for Getty Co. is $900,000, and the tax basis is $700,000 at the end of 2008. The enacted tax rate is 34% for all periods. Determine the amount of deferred taxes to be reported on the balance sheet at the end of 2008.

7. Borg Inc. has a deferred tax liability of $68,000 at the beginning of 2008. At the end of 2008, it reports accounts receivable on the books at $80,000 and the tax basis at zero (its only temporary difference). If the enacted tax rate is 34% for all periods, and income tax payable for the period is $230,000, determine the amount of total income tax expense to report for 2008.

8. What is the difference between a future taxable amount and a future deductible amount? When is it appropriate to record a valuation account for a deferred tax asset?

9. Pretax financial income for Mott Inc. is $300,000, and its taxable income is $100,000 for 2008. Its only temporary difference at the end of the period relates to a $90,000 difference due to excess depreciation for tax purposes. If the tax rate is 40% for all periods, compute the amount of income tax expense to report in 2008. No deferred income taxes existed at the beginning of the year.

10. How are deferred tax assets and deferred tax liabilities reported on the balance sheet?

11. Describe the procedures involved in segregating various deferred tax amounts into current and noncurrent categories.

12. How is it determined whether deferred tax amounts are considered to be "related" to specific asset or liability amounts?

13. At the end of the year, North Carolina Co. has pretax financial income of $550,000. Included in the $550,000 is $70,000 interest income on municipal bonds, $30,000 fine for dumping hazardous waste, and depreciation of $60,000. Depreciation for tax purposes is $45,000. Compute income taxes payable, assuming the tax rate is 30% for all periods.

14. Raleigh Co. has one temporary difference at the beginning of 2008 of $500,000. The deferred tax liability established for this amount is $150,000, based on a tax rate of 30%. The temporary difference will provide the following taxable amounts: $100,000 in 2009; $200,000 in 2010, and $200,000 in 2011. If a new tax rate for 2011 of 25% is enacted into law at the end of 2008, what is the journal entry necessary in 2008 (if any) to adjust deferred taxes?

15 What are some of the reasons that the components of income tax expense should be disclosed and a reconciliation between the effective tax rate and the statutory tax rate be provided?

16 Differentiate between "loss carryback" and "loss carryforward." Which can be accounted for with the greater certainty when it arises? Why?

17 What are the possible treatments for tax purposes of a net operating loss? What are the circumstances that determine the option to be applied? What is the proper treatment of a net operating loss for financial reporting purposes?

18 What controversy relates to the accounting for net operating loss carryforwards?

Brief Exercises

BE15-1 In 2008, Speedy Gonzalez Corporation had pretax financial income of $168,000 and taxable income of $110,000. The difference is due to the use of different depreciation methods for tax and accounting purposes. The effective tax rate is 40%. Compute the amount to be reported as income taxes payable at December 31, 2008.

(LO 1, 2)

BE15-2 Murphy Corporation began operations in 2008 and reported pretax financial income of $225,000 for the year. Murphy's tax depreciation exceeded its book depreciation by $30,000. Murphy's tax rate for 2008 and years thereafter is 30%. In its December 31, 2008, balance sheet, what amount of deferred tax liability should be reported?

(LO 1, 2)

BE15-3 Using the information from BE15-2, assume this is the only difference between Murphy's pretax financial income and taxable income. Prepare the journal entry to record the income tax expense, deferred income taxes, and income tax payable, and show how the deferred tax liability will be classified on the December 31, 2008, balance sheet.

(LO 9)

BE15-4 At December 31, 2007, Yserbius Corporation had a deferred tax liability of $25,000. At December 31, 2008, the deferred tax liability is $42,000. The corporation's 2008 current tax expense is $43,000. What amount should Yserbius report as total 2008 tax expense?

(LO 2, 5)

BE15-5 At December 31, 2008, Deep Space Nine Corporation had an estimated warranty liability of $125,000 for accounting purposes and $0 for tax purposes. (The warranty costs are not deductible until paid.) The effective tax rate is 40%. Compute the amount Deep Space Nine should report as a deferred tax asset at December 31, 2008.

(LO 1, 3)

BE15-6 At December 31, 2007, Next Generation Inc. had a deferred tax asset of $35,000. At December 31, 2008, the deferred tax asset is $59,000. The corporation's 2008 current tax expense is $61,000. What amount should Next Generation report as total 2008 tax expense?

(LO 3, 5)

BE15-7 At December 31, 2008, Stargate Corporation has a deferred tax asset of $200,000. After a careful review of all available evidence, it is determined that it is more likely than not that $80,000 of this deferred tax asset will not be realized. Prepare the necessary journal entry.

(LO 4)

BE15-8 No Doubt Corporation had income before income taxes of $175,000 in 2008. No Doubt's current income tax expense is $40,000, and deferred income tax expense is $30,000. Prepare No Doubt's 2008 income statement, beginning with income before income taxes.

(LO 5)

BE15-9 Tazmania Inc. had pretax financial income of $154,000 in 2008. Included in the computation of that amount is insurance expense of $4,000 which is not deductible for tax purposes. In addition, depreciation for tax purposes exceeds accounting depreciation by $14,000. Prepare Tazmania's journal entry to record 2008 taxes, assuming a tax rate of 45%.

(LO 2, 3)

BE15-10 Terminator Corporation has a cumulative temporary difference related to depreciation of $630,000 at December 31, 2008. This difference will reverse as follows: 2009, $42,000; 2010, $294,000; and 2011, $294,000. Enacted tax rates are 34% for 2009 and 2010, and 40% for 2011. Compute the amount Terminator should report as a deferred tax liability at December 31, 2008.

(LO 2)

BE15-11 At December 31, 2007. Tick Corporation had a deferred tax liability of $680,000, resulting from future taxable amounts of $2,000,000 and an enacted tax rate of 34%. In May 2008, a new income tax act is signed into law that raises the tax rate to 38% for 2008 and future years. Prepare the journal entry for Tick to adjust the deferred tax liability.

(LO 7)

(LO 8) **BE15-12** Valis Corporation had the following tax information.

Year	Taxable Income	Tax Rate	Taxes Paid
2005	$300,000	35%	$105,000
2006	$325,000	30%	$ 97,500
2007	$400,000	30%	$120,000

In 2008 Valis suffered a net operating loss of $450,000, which it elected to carry back. The 2008 enacted tax rate is 29%. Prepare Valis's entry to record the effect of the loss carryback.

(LO 8) **BE15-13** Zoop Inc. incurred a net operating loss of $500,000 in 2008. Combined income for 2006 and 2007 was $400,000. The tax rate for all years is 40%. Zoop elects the carryback option. Prepare the journal entries to record the benefits of the loss carryback and the loss carryforward.

(LO 4, 8) **BE15-14** Use the information for Zoop Inc. given in BE15-13. Assume that it is more likely than not that the entire net operating loss carryforward will not be realized in future years. Prepare all the journal entries necessary at the end of 2008.

(LO 9) **BE15-15** Vectorman Corporation has temporary differences at December 31, 2008, that result in the following deferred taxes.

Deferred tax liability—current	$38,000
Deferred tax asset—current	$(52,000)
Deferred tax liability—noncurrent	$96,000
Deferred tax asset—noncurrent	$(27,000)

Indicate how these balances would be presented in Vectorman's December 31, 2008, balance sheet.

Exercises

(LO 2, 5) **E15-1** **(One Temporary Difference, Future Taxable Amounts, One Rate, No Beginning Deferred Taxes)** South Carolina Corporation has one temporary difference at the end of 2008 that will reverse and cause taxable amounts of $55,000 in 2009, $60,000 in 2010, and $65,000 in 2011. South Carolina's pretax financial income for 2008 is $300,000, and the tax rate is 30% for all years. There are no deferred taxes at the beginning of 2008.

Instructions

(a) Compute taxable income and income taxes payable for 2008. ~~120 000~~ ~~36 000~~

(b) Prepare the journal entry to record income tax expense, deferred income taxes, and income taxes payable for 2008.

(c) Prepare the income tax expense section of the income statement for 2008, beginning with the line "Income before income taxes."

[handwritten margin notes: Income tax expense 90 / Deferred Taxes 54 / Taxes Payable 36]

(LO 2) **E15-2** **(Two Differences, No Beginning Deferred Taxes, Tracked through 2 Years)** The following information is available for Wenger Corporation for 2008.

1. Excess of tax depreciation over book depreciation, $40,000. This $40,000 difference will reverse equally over the years 2009–2012. *~~−40 000~~*

2. Deferral, for book purposes, of $20,000 of rent received in advance. The rent will be earned in 2009. *~~+20 000~~*

3. Pretax financial income, $300,000.

4. Tax rate for all years, 40%.

Instructions

(a) Compute taxable income for 2008. *~~280 000~~*

(b) Prepare the journal entry to record income tax expense, deferred income taxes, and income taxes payable for 2008.

(c) Prepare the journal entry to record income tax expense, deferred income taxes, and income taxes payable for 2009, assuming taxable income of $325,000.

[handwritten margin notes: Inc. T. Expense / Def. T. Asset 8000 / Tax Payable 112 / DTL 16]

(LO 2, 5) **E15-3** **(One Temporary Difference, Future Taxable Amounts, One Rate, Beginning Deferred Taxes)** Bandung Corporation began 2008 with a $92,000 balance in the Deferred Tax Liability account. At the end of 2008, the related cumulative temporary difference amounts to $350,000, and it will reverse evenly over the next 2 years. Pretax accounting income for 2008 is $525,000, the tax rate for all years is 40%, and taxable income for 2008 is $405,000.

Instructions

(a) Compute income taxes payable for 2008.

(b) Prepare the journal entry to record income tax expense, deferred income taxes, and income taxes payable for 2008.

(c) Prepare the income tax expense section of the income statement for 2008 beginning with the line "Income before income taxes."

E15-4 (Three Differences, Compute Taxable Income, Entry for Taxes) Zurich Company reports pretax financial income of $70,000 for 2008. The following items cause taxable income to be different than pretax financial income. **(LO 2, 3, 5, 6)**

1. Depreciation on the tax return is greater than depreciation on the income statement by $16,000.

2. Rent collected on the tax return is greater than rent earned on the income statement by $22,000.

3. Fines for pollution appear as an expense of $11,000 on the income statement.

Zurich's tax rate is 30% for all years, and the company expects to report taxable income in all future years. There are no deferred taxes at the beginning of 2008.

Instructions

(a) Compute taxable income and income taxes payable for 2008.

(b) Prepare the journal entry to record income tax expense, deferred income taxes, and income taxes payable for 2008.

(c) Prepare the income tax expense section of the income statement for 2008, beginning with the line "Income before income taxes."

(d) Compute the effective income tax rate for 2008.

E15-5 (Two Temporary Differences, One Rate, Beginning Deferred Taxes) The following facts relate to Krung Thep Corporation. **(LO 2, 3, 5)**

1. Deferred tax liability, January 1, 2008, $40,000.

2. Deferred tax asset, January 1, 2008, $0.

3. Taxable income for 2008, $95,000.

4. Pretax financial income for 2008, $200,000.

5. Cumulative temporary difference at December 31, 2008, giving rise to future taxable amounts, $240,000.

6. Cumulative temporary difference at December 31, 2008, giving rise to future deductible amounts, $35,000.

7. Tax rate for all years, 40%.

8. The company is expected to operate profitably in the future.

Instructions

(a) Compute income taxes payable for 2008.

(b) Prepare the journal entry to record income tax expense, deferred income taxes, and income taxes payable for 2008.

(c) Prepare the income tax expense section of the income statement for 2008, beginning with the line "Income before income taxes."

E15-6 (Identify Temporary or Permanent Differences) Listed below are items that are commonly accounted for differently for financial reporting purposes than they are for tax purposes. **(LO 6)**

Instructions

For each item below, indicate whether it involves:

1. A temporary difference that will result in future deductible amounts and, therefore, will usually give rise to a deferred income tax asset.

2. A temporary difference that will result in future taxable amounts and, therefore, will usually give rise to a deferred income tax liability.

3. A permanent difference.

Use the appropriate number to indicate your answer for each.

(a) _____ The MACRS depreciation system is used for tax purposes, and the straight-line depreciation method is used for financial reporting purposes for some plant assets.

(b) _____ A landlord collects some rents in advance. Rents received are taxable in the period when they are received.

(c) _____ Expenses are incurred in obtaining tax-exempt income.

(d) _____ Costs of guarantees and warranties are estimated and accrued for financial reporting purposes.

(e) _____ Installment sales of investments are accounted for by the accrual method for financial reporting purposes and the installment method for tax purposes.

(f) _____ For some assets, straight-line depreciation is used for both financial reporting purposes and tax purposes but the assets' lives are shorter for tax purposes.

(g) _____ Interest is received on an investment in tax-exempt municipal obligations.

(h) _____ Proceeds are received from a life insurance company because of the death of a key officer. (The company carries a policy on key officers.)

(i) _____ The tax return reports a deduction for 80% of the dividends received from U.S. corporations. The cost method is used in accounting for the related investments for financial reporting purposes.

(j) _____ Estimated losses on pending lawsuits and claims are accrued for books. These losses are tax deductible in the period(s) when the related liabilities are settled.

(k) _____ Expenses on stock options are accrued for financial reporting purposes.

(LO 2, 3, 4, 6)

E15-7 (Terminology, Relationships, Computations, Entries)

Instructions

Complete the following statements by filling in the blanks.

(a) In a period in which a taxable temporary difference reverses, the reversal will cause taxable income to be _____ (less than, greater than) pretax financial income.

(b) If a $76,000 balance in Deferred Tax Asset was computed by use of a 40% rate, the underlying cumulative temporary difference amounts to $_____.

(c) Deferred taxes _____ (are, are not) recorded to account for permanent differences.

(d) If a taxable temporary difference originates in 2008, it will cause taxable income for 2008 to be _____ (less than, greater than) pretax financial income for 2008.

(e) If total tax expense is $50,000 and deferred tax expense is $65,000, then the current portion of the expense computation is referred to as current tax _____ (expense, benefit) of $_____.

(f) If a corporation's tax return shows taxable income of $100,000 for Year 2 and a tax rate of 40%, how much will appear on the December 31, Year 2, balance sheet for "Income tax payable" if the company has made estimated tax payments of $36,500 for Year 2? $_____.

(g) An increase in the Deferred Tax Liability account on the balance sheet is recorded by a _____ (debit, credit) to the Income Tax Expense account.

(h) An income statement that reports current tax expense of $82,000 and deferred tax benefit of $23,000 will report total income tax expense of $_____.

(i) A valuation account is needed whenever it is judged to be _____ that a portion of a deferred tax asset _____ (will be, will not be) realized.

(j) If the tax return shows total taxes due for the period of $75,000 but the income statement shows total income tax expense of $55,000, the difference of $20,000 is referred to as deferred tax _____ (expense, benefit).

(LO 2, 3, 5, 9)

E15-8 (Two Temporary Differences, One Rate, 3 Years)   Button Company has two temporary differences between its income tax expense and income taxes payable. The information is shown below.

	2008	2009	2010
Pretax financial income	$840,000	$910,000	$945,000
Excess depreciation expense on tax return	(30,000)	(40,000)	(10,000)
Excess warranty expense in financial income	20,000	10,000	8,000
Taxable income	$830,000	$880,000	$943,000

The income tax rate for all years is 40%.

Instructions

(a) Prepare the journal entry to record income tax expense, deferred income taxes, and income tax payable for 2008, 2009, and 2010.

(b) Assuming there were no temporary differences prior to 2008, indicate how deferred taxes will be reported on the 2010 balance sheet. Button's product warranty is for 12 months.

(c) Prepare the income tax expense section of the income statement for 2010, beginning with the line "Pretax financial income."

E15-9 (Carryback and Carryforward of NOL, No Valuation Account, No Temporary Differences) The pretax financial income (or loss) figures for Jenny Spangler Company are as follows. **(LO 8)**

2003	$160,000
2004	250,000
2005	80,000
2006	(160,000)
2007	(380,000)
2008	120,000
2009	100,000

Pretax financial income (or loss) and taxable income (loss) were the same for all years involved. Assume a 45% tax rate for 2003 and 2004 and a 40% tax rate for the remaining years.

Instructions

Prepare the journal entries for the years 2005 to 2009 to record income tax expense and the effects of the net operating loss carrybacks and carryforwards assuming Jenny Spangler Company uses the carryback provision. All income and losses relate to normal operations. (In recording the benefits of a loss carryforward, assume that no valuation account is deemed necessary.)

E15-10 (Two NOLs, No Temporary Differences, No Valuation Account, Entries and Income Statement) Felicia Rashad Corporation has pretax financial income (or loss) equal to taxable income (or loss) from 2000 through 2008 as follows. **(LO 8)**

	Income (Loss)	Tax Rate
2000	$29,000	30%
2001	40,000	30%
2002	17,000	35%
2003	48,000	50%
2004	(150,000)	40%
2005	90,000	40%
2006	30,000	40%
2007	105,000	40%
2008	(60,000)	45%

Pretax financial income (loss) and taxable income (loss) were the same for all years since Rashad has been in business. Assume the carryback provision is employed for net operating losses. In recording the benefits of a loss carryforward, assume that it is more likely than not that the related benefits will be realized.

Instructions

(a) What entry(ies) for income taxes should be recorded for 2004?
(b) Indicate what the income tax expense portion of the income statement for 2004 should look like. Assume all income (loss) relates to continuing operations.
(c) What entry for income taxes should be recorded in 2005?
(d) How should the income tax expense section of the income statement for 2005 appear?
(e) What entry for income taxes should be recorded in 2008?
(f) How should the income tax expense section of the income statement for 2008 appear?

E15-11 (Three Differences, Classify Deferred Taxes) At December 31, 2008, Belmont Company had a net deferred tax liability of $375,000. An explanation of the items that compose this balance is as follows. **(LO 2, 3, 9)**

Temporary Differences	Resulting Balances in Deferred Taxes
1. Excess of tax depreciation over book depreciation	$200,000
2. Accrual, for book purposes, of estimated loss contingency from pending lawsuit that is expected to be settled in 2009. The loss will be deducted on the tax return when paid.	(50,000)
3. Accrual method used for book purposes and installment method used for tax purposes for an isolated installment sale of an investment.	225,000
	$375,000

In analyzing the temporary differences, you find that $30,000 of the depreciation temporary difference will reverse in 2009, and $120,000 of the temporary difference due to the installment sale will reverse in 2009. The tax rate for all years is 40%.

Instructions

Indicate the manner in which deferred taxes should be presented on Belmont Company's December 31, 2008, balance sheet.

(LO 2, 3, 5)

E15-12 (**Two Temporary Differences, One Rate, Beginning Deferred Taxes, Compute Pretax Financial Income**) The following facts relate to Duncan Corporation.

1. Deferred tax liability, January 1, 2008, $60,000.
2. Deferred tax asset, January 1, 2008, $20,000.
3. Taxable income for 2008, $105,000.
4. Cumulative temporary difference at December 31, 2008, giving rise to future taxable amounts, $230,000.
5. Cumulative temporary difference at December 31, 2008, giving rise to future deductible amounts, $95,000.
6. Tax rate for all years, 40%. No permanent differences exist.
7. The company is expected to operate profitably in the future.

Instructions

(a) Compute the amount of pretax financial income for 2008.
(b) Prepare the journal entry to record income tax expense, deferred income taxes, and income taxes payable for 2008.
(c) Prepare the income tax expense section of the income statement for 2008, beginning with the line "Income before income taxes."
(d) Compute the effective tax rate for 2008.

(LO 2, 7)

E15-13 (**One Difference, Multiple Rates, Effect of Beginning Balance versus No Beginning Deferred Taxes**) At the end of 2008, Lucretia McEvil Company has $180,000 of cumulative temporary differences that will result in reporting future taxable amounts as follows.

2009	$ 60,000
2010	50,000
2011	40,000
2012	30,000
	$180,000

Tax rates enacted as of the beginning of 2007 are:

2007 and 2008	40%
2009 and 2010	30%
2011 and later	25%

McEvil's taxable income for 2008 is $320,000. Taxable income is expected in all future years.

Instructions

(a) Prepare the journal entry for McEvil to record income taxes payable, deferred income taxes, and income tax expense for 2008, assuming that there were no deferred taxes at the end of 2007.
(b) Prepare the journal entry for McEvil to record income taxes payable, deferred income taxes, and income tax expense for 2008, assuming that there was a balance of $22,000 in a Deferred Tax Liability account at the end of 2007.

(LO 3, 4)

E15-14 (**Deferred Tax Asset with and without Valuation Account**) Jennifer Capriati Corp. has a deferred tax asset account with a balance of $150,000 at the end of 2007 due to a single cumulative temporary difference of $375,000. At the end of 2008 this same temporary difference has increased to a cumulative amount of $450,000. Taxable income for 2008 is $820,000. The tax rate is 40% for all years. No valuation account related to the deferred tax asset is in existence at the end of 2007.

Instructions

(a) Record income tax expense, deferred income taxes, and income taxes payable for 2008, assuming that it is more likely than not that the deferred tax asset will be realized.

(b) Assuming that it is more likely than not that $30,000 of the deferred tax asset will not be realized, prepare the journal entry at the end of 2008 to record the valuation account.

E15-15 (**Deferred Tax Asset with Previous Valuation Account**) Assume the same information as E15-14, except that at the end of 2007, Jennifer Capriati Corp. had a valuation account related to its deferred tax asset of $45,000. (LO 3, 4, 5)

Instructions

(a) Record income tax expense, deferred income taxes, and income taxes payable for 2008, assuming that it is more likely than not that the deferred tax asset will be realized in full.

(b) Record income tax expense, deferred income taxes, and income taxes payable for 2008, assuming that it is more likely than not that none of the deferred tax asset will be realized.

E15-16 (**Deferred Tax Liability, Change in Tax Rate, Prepare Section of Income Statement**) Novotna Inc.'s only temporary difference at the beginning and end of 2008 is caused by a $3 million deferred gain for tax purposes for an installment sale of a plant asset, and the related receivable (only one-half of which is classified as a current asset) is due in equal installments in 2009 and 2010. The related deferred tax liability at the beginning of the year is $1,200,000. In the third quarter of 2008, a new tax rate of 34% is enacted into law and is scheduled to become effective for 2010. Taxable income for 2008 is $5,000,000, and taxable income is expected in all future years. (LO 2, 5, 7, 9)

Instructions

(a) Determine the amount reported as a deferred tax liability at the end of 2008. Indicate proper classification(s).

(b) Prepare the journal entry (if any) necessary to adjust the deferred tax liability when the new tax rate is enacted into law.

(c) Draft the income tax expense portion of the income statement for 2008. Begin with the line "Income before income taxes." Assume no permanent differences exist.

E15-17 (**Two Temporary Differences, Tracked through 3 Years, Multiple Rates**) Taxable income and pretax financial income would be identical for Huber Co. except for its treatments of gross profit on installment sales and estimated costs of warranties. The following income computations have been prepared. (LO 2, 3, 7)

Taxable income	2007	2008	2009
Excess of revenues over expenses (excluding two temporary differences)	$160,000	$210,000	$90,000
Installment gross profit collected	8,000	8,000	8,000
Expenditures for warranties	(5,000)	(5,000)	(5,000)
Taxable income	$163,000	$213,000	$93,000

Pretax financial income	2007	2008	2009
Excess of revenues over expenses (excluding two temporary differences)	$160,000	$210,000	$90,000
Installment gross profit earned	24,000	–0–	–0–
Estimated cost of warranties	(15,000)	–0–	–0–
Income before taxes	$169,000	$210,000	$90,000

The tax rates in effect are: 2007, 40%; 2008 and 2009, 45%. All tax rates were enacted into law on January 1, 2007. No deferred income taxes existed at the beginning of 2007. Taxable income is expected in all future years.

Instructions

Prepare the journal entry to record income tax expense, deferred income taxes, and income tax payable for 2007, 2008, and 2009.

E15-18 (**Three Differences, Multiple Rates, Future Taxable Income**) During 2008, Kate Holmes Co.'s first year of operations, the company reports pretax financial income at $250,000. Holmes's enacted tax rate is 45% for 2008 and 40% for all later years. Holmes expects to have taxable income in each of the next 5 years. The effects on future tax returns of temporary differences existing at December 31, 2008, are summarized on the following page. (LO 2, 3, 7)

45%   40%. →
250 000 - for. income

| | Future Years | | | | | |
	2009	2010	2011	2012	2013	Total
Future taxable (deductible) amounts:						
Installment sales	$32,000	$32,000	$32,000			$ 96,000
Depreciation	6,000	6,000	6,000	$6,000	$6,000	30,000
Unearned rent	(50,000)	(50,000)				(100,000)

Instructions

(a) Complete the schedule below to compute deferred taxes at December 31, 2008.

(b) Compute taxable income for 2008. 124 000

(c) Prepare the journal entry to record income tax payable, deferred taxes, and income tax expense for 2008.

ITE 111 200
DTA 40 000
  ITP 100 800
   DTL 50 400

| | Future Taxable | | December 31, 2008 | |
| | (Deductible) | Tax | Deferred Tax | |
Temporary Difference	Amounts	Rate	(Asset)	Liability
Installment sales	$ 96,000	40%		
Depreciation	30,000	40%		
Unearned rent	(100,000)	40%		
Totals	$ 26 000		40 000	50 400

(LO 2, 3, 9)

E15-19 (**Two Differences, One Rate, Beginning Deferred Balance, Compute Pretax Financial Income**) Andy McDowell Co. establishes a $100 million liability at the end of 2008 for the estimated site-cleanup costs at two of its manufacturing facilities. All related closing costs will be paid and deducted on the tax return in 2009. Also, at the end of 2008, the company has $50 million of temporary differences due to excess depreciation for tax purposes, $7 million of which will reverse in 2009.

The enacted tax rate for all years is 40%, and the company pays taxes of $64 million on $160 million of taxable income in 2008. McDowell expects to have taxable income in 2009.

DTA 40 0
ITE 44

  ITP 64 4
   DTL 20

+100 - FTA
−50 − FTL
160

Instructions

(a) Determine the deferred taxes to be reported at the end of 2008.

(b) Indicate how the deferred taxes computed in (a) are to be reported on the balance sheet.

(c) Assuming that the only deferred tax account at the beginning of 2008 was a deferred tax liability of $10,000,000, draft the income tax expense portion of the income statement for 2008, beginning with the line "Income before income taxes." (*Hint:* You must first compute (1) the amount of temporary difference underlying the beginning $10,000,000 deferred tax liability, then (2) the amount of temporary differences originating or reversing during the year, then (3) the amount of pretax financial income.)

(LO 2, 3, 9)

E15-20 (**Two Differences, No Beginning Deferred Taxes, Multiple Rates**) Teri Hatcher Inc., in its first year of operations, has the following differences between the book basis and tax basis of its assets and liabilities at the end of 2008.

	Book Basis	Tax Basis
Equipment (net)	$400,000	$340,000
Estimated warranty liability	$200,000	$ –0–

− 60 000
+ 200 000
520 000

It is estimated that the warranty liability will be settled in 2009. The difference in equipment (net) will result in taxable amounts of $20,000 in 2009, $30,000 in 2010, and $10,000 in 2011. The company has taxable income of $520,000 in 2008. As of the beginning of 2008, the enacted tax rate is 34% for 2008–2010, and 30% for 2011. Hatcher expects to report taxable income through 2011.

ITE 128 800
DTA 66 000
  ITP 176 800
   DTL 28 000

Instructions

(a) Prepare the journal entry to record income tax expense, deferred income taxes, and income tax payable for 2008.

(b) Indicate how deferred income taxes will be reported on the balance sheet at the end of 2008.

(LO 2, 3, 7, 9)

E15-21 (**Two Temporary Differences, Multiple Rates, Future Taxable Income**) Nadal Inc. has two temporary differences at the end of 2008. The first difference stems from installment sales, and the second one results from the accrual of a loss contingency. Nadal's accounting department has developed a schedule of future taxable and deductible amounts related to these temporary differences as follows.

[handwritten at top: 34% 38% 38% 58%]

	2009	2010	2011	2012
Taxable amounts	$40,000	$50,000	$60,000	$80,000
Deductible amounts		(15,000)	(19,000)	
	$40,000	$35,000	$41,000	$80,000

[handwritten: +34 000 DTA / −230 000 −DTL / 500 000]

As of the beginning of 2008, the enacted tax rate is 34% for 2008 and 2009, and 38% for 2010–2012. At the beginning of 2008, the company had no deferred income taxes on its balance sheet. Taxable income for 2008 is $500,000. Taxable income is expected in all future years.

[handwritten: ITE 242 880 / DTA 12 920 / ITP 170 000 / DTL 85 800]

Instructions

(a) Prepare the journal entry to record income tax expense, deferred income taxes, and income taxes payable for 2008.

(b) Indicate how deferred income taxes would be classified on the balance sheet at the end of 2008.

E15-22 **(Two Differences, One Rate, First Year)** The differences between the book basis and tax basis of the assets and liabilities of Castle Corporation at the end of 2008 are presented below.

(LO 2, 3, 9)

	Book Basis	Tax Basis
Accounts receivable	$50,000	$-0-
Litigation liability	30,000	-0-

[handwritten: + 30 000 / − 50 000 / 350 000]

It is estimated that the litigation liability will be settled in 2009. The difference in accounts receivable will result in taxable amounts of $30,000 in 2009 and $20,000 in 2010. The company has taxable income of $350,000 in 2008 and is expected to have taxable income in each of the following 2 years. Its enacted tax rate is 34% for all years. This is the company's first year of operations. The operating cycle of the business is 2 years.

[handwritten: ITE 125 800 / DTA 10 200 / ITP 119 000 / DTL 17 000]

Instructions

(a) Prepare the journal entry to record income tax expense, deferred income taxes, and income tax payable for 2008.

(b) Indicate how deferred income taxes will be reported on the balance sheet at the end of 2008.

E15-23 **(NOL Carryback and Carryforward, Valuation Account versus No Valuation Account)** Spamela Hamderson Inc. reports the following pretax income (loss) for both financial reporting purposes and tax purposes. (Assume the carryback provision is used for a net operating loss.)

(LO 4, 7, 8)

Year	Pretax Income (Loss)	Tax Rate
2006	$120,000	34%
2007	90,000	34%
2008	(280,000)	38%
2009	220,000	38%

The tax rates listed were all enacted by the beginning of 2006.

[handwritten: ITE 40 800 / ITP 40 800 / ITE 30 600 / ITP 30 600 / IT Ref Receiv. 71 400 / Benefit due to t.CB 71 400 / DTA 26 600 / Benefit due to LCF 26 600]

[handwritten right: ITE 83 600 / DTA 26 600 / ITP 57 000]

Instructions

(a) Prepare the journal entries for the years 2006–2009 to record income tax expense (benefit) and income tax payable (refundable) and the tax effects of the loss carryback and carryforward, assuming that at the end of 2008 the benefits of the loss carryforward are judged more likely than not to be realized in the future.

(b) Using the assumption in (a), prepare the income tax section of the 2008 income statement beginning with the line "Operating loss before income taxes."

(c) Prepare the journal entries for 2008 and 2009, assuming that based on the weight of available evidence, it is more likely than not that one-fourth of the benefits of the loss carryforward will not be realized.

(d) Using the assumption in (c), prepare the income tax section of the 2008 income statement beginning with the line "Operating loss before income taxes."

[handwritten: OL BIT (280 000) / IT Benefit due LCB 71 400 / due LCF 26 600 / NL 182 000 / → Benefit LCF 6650 / Allowance 6650]

E15-24 **(NOL Carryback and Carryforward, Valuation Account Needed)** Beilman Inc. reports the following pretax income (loss) for both book and tax purposes. (Assume the carryback provision is used where possible for a net operating loss.)

(LO 4, 7, 8)

Year	Pretax Income (Loss)	Tax Rate
2006	$120,000	40%
2007	90,000	40%
2008	(280,000)	45%
2009	120,000	45%

The tax rates listed were all enacted by the beginning of 2006.

[handwritten: ITE 48 000 / ITP 48 000 / ITE 36 000 / ITP 36 000 / IT Ref Recev. 84 000 / Benef due t LCB 84 000 / DTA 31 500 / bought LCF 31 500 / Ben LCF 15 750 / Allowance 15 750]

[handwritten right: ITE 54 000 / DTA 31 500 / ITP 22 500 / Allowan 15 750 / Ben 15 750]

Instructions

(a) Prepare the journal entries for years 2006–2009 to record income tax expense (benefit) and income tax payable (refundable), and the tax effects of the loss carryback and loss carryforward, assuming that based on the weight of available evidence, it is more likely than not that one-half of the benefits of the loss carryforward will not be realized.

(b) Prepare the income tax section of the 2008 income statement beginning with the line "Operating loss before income taxes."

(c) Prepare the income tax section of the 2009 income statement beginning with the line "Income before income taxes."

(LO 4, 7, 8)

E15-25 **(NOL Carryback and Carryforward, Valuation Account Needed)** Meyer reported the following pretax financial income (loss) for the years 2006–2010.

2006	$240,000
2007	350,000
2008	120,000
2009	(570,000)
2010	180,000

Pretax financial income (loss) and taxable income (loss) were the same for all years involved. The enacted tax rate was 34% for 2006 and 2007, and 40% for 2008–2010. Assume the carryback provision is used first for net operating losses.

Instructions

(a) Prepare the journal entries for the years 2008–2010 to record income tax expense, income tax payable (refundable), and the tax effects of the loss carryback and loss carryforward, assuming that based on the weight of available evidence, it is more likely than not that one-fifth of the benefits of the loss carryforward will not be realized.

(b) Prepare the income tax section of the 2009 income statement beginning with the line "Income (loss) before income taxes."

See the book's website, www.wiley.com/college/warfield, for Additional Exercises.

Problems

(LO 2, 3, 5)

P15-1 **(Three Differences, No Beginning Deferred Taxes, Multiple Rates)** The following information is available for Swanson Corporation for 2008.

1. Depreciation reported on the tax return exceeded depreciation reported on the income statement by $100,000. This difference will reverse in equal amounts of $25,000 over the years 2009–2012.

2. Interest received on municipal bonds was $10,000.

3. Rent collected in advance on January 1, 2008, totaled $60,000 for a 3-year period. Of this amount, $40,000 was reported as unearned at December 31, for book purposes.

4. The tax rates are 40% for 2008 and 35% for 2009 and subsequent years.

5. Income taxes of $360,000 are due per the tax return for 2008.

6. No deferred taxes existed at the beginning of 2008.

Instructions

(a) Compute taxable income for 2008.

(b) Compute pretax financial income for 2008.

(c) Prepare the journal entries to record income tax expense, deferred income taxes, and income taxes payable for 2008 and 2009. Assume taxable income was $980,000 in 2009.

(d) Prepare the income tax expense section of the income statement for 2008, beginning with "Income before income taxes."

P15-2 (One Temporary Difference, Tracked for 4 Years, One Permanent Difference, Change in Rate) *(LO 3, 5, 6)*
The pretax financial income of Parker-Gregory Company differs from its taxable income throughout each of 4 years as follows.

Year	Pretax Financial Income	Taxable Income	Tax Rate	
2008	$280,000	$180,000	35%	-70
2009	320,000	225,000	40%	-65
2010	350,000	270,000	40%	-50
2011	420,000	580,000	40%	+190

Pretax financial income for each year includes a nondeductible expense of $30,000 (never deductible for tax purposes). The remainder of the difference between pretax financial income and taxable income in each period is due to one depreciation temporary difference. No deferred income taxes existed at the beginning of 2008.

Instructions

(a) Prepare journal entries to record income taxes in all 4 years. Assume that the change in the tax rate to 40% was not enacted until the beginning of 2009.
(b) Prepare the income statement for 2009, beginning with income before income taxes.

P15-3 (Second Year of Depreciation Difference, Two Differences, Single Rate, Extraordinary Item) The *(LO 2, 5, 6, 9)*
following information has been obtained for the Kerdyk Corporation.

1. Prior to 2007, taxable income and pretax financial income were identical.
2. Pretax financial income is $1,700,000 in 2007 and $1,400,000 in 2008.
3. On January 1, 2007, equipment costing $1,000,000 is purchased. It is to be depreciated on a straight-line basis over 5 years for tax purposes and over 8 years for financial reporting purposes, assuming no salvage value. (*Hint:* Use the half-year convention for tax purposes, see Chapter 10.)
4. Interest of $60,000 was earned on tax-exempt municipal obligations in 2008.
5. Included in 2008 pretax financial income is an extraordinary gain of $200,000, which is fully taxable.
6. The tax rate is 35% for all periods.
7. Taxable income is expected in all future years.

Instructions

(a) Compute taxable income and income tax payable for 2008.
(b) Prepare the journal entry to record 2008 income tax expense, income tax payable, and deferred taxes.
(c) Prepare the bottom portion of Kerdyk's 2008 income statement, beginning with "Income before income taxes and extraordinary item."
(d) Indicate how deferred income taxes should be presented on the December 31, 2008, balance sheet.

P15-4 (Permanent and Temporary Differences, One Rate) The accounting records of Anderson Inc. show *(LO 2, 3, 5,)*
the following data for 2008.

1. Life insurance expense on officers was $9,000.
2. Equipment was acquired in early January for $200,000. Straight-line depreciation over a 5-year life is used, with no salvage value. For tax purposes, Anderson used a 30% rate to calculate depreciation.
3. Interest revenue on State of New York bonds totaled $4,000.
4. Product warranties were estimated to be $60,000 in 2008. Actual repair and labor costs related to the warranties in 2008 were $10,000. The remainder is estimated to be incurred evenly in 2009 and 2010.
5. Sales on an accrual basis were $100,000. For tax purposes, $75,000 was recorded on the installment sales method.
6. Fines incurred for pollution violations were $4,200.
7. Pretax financial income was $850,000. The tax rate is 30%.

Instructions

(a) Prepare a schedule starting with pretax financial income in 2008 and ending with taxable income in 2008.
(b) Prepare the journal entry for 2008 to record income tax payable, income tax expense, and deferred income taxes.

(LO 5, 7, 8, 9)

P15-5 (NOL without Valuation Account) Parnevik Inc. reported the following pretax income (loss) and related tax rates during the years 2004–2010.

	Pretax Income (loss)	Tax Rate
2004	$ 40,000	30%
2005	25,000	30%
2006	60,000	30%
2007	80,000	40%
2008	(200,000)	45%
2009	70,000	40%
2010	90,000	35%

Pretax financial income (loss) and taxable income (loss) were the same for all years since Parnevik began business. The tax rates from 2007–2010 were enacted in 2007.

Instructions

(a) Prepare the journal entries for the years 2008–2010 to record income tax payable (refundable), income tax expense (benefit), and the tax effects of the loss carryback and carryforward. Assume that Parnevik elects the carryback provision where possible and expects to realize the benefits of any loss carryforward in the year that immediately follows the loss year.

(b) Indicate the effect the 2008 entry(ies) has on the December 31, 2008, balance sheet.

(c) Prepare the portion of the income statement, starting with "Operating loss before income taxes," for 2008.

(d) Prepare the portion of the income statement, starting with "Income before income taxes," for 2009.

(LO 2, 3, 9)

P15-6 (Two Differences, Two Rates, Future Income Expected) Presented below are two independent situations related to future taxable and deductible amounts resulting from temporary differences existing at December 31, 2008.

1. Pirates Co. has developed the following schedule of future taxable and deductible amounts.

	2009	2010	2011	2012	2013
Taxable amounts	$300	$300	$300	$ 300	$300
Deductible amount	—	—	—	(1,400)	—

2. Eagles Co. has the following schedule of future taxable and deductible amounts.

	2009	2010	2011	2012
Taxable amounts	$300	$300	$ 300	$300
Deductible amount	—	—	(2,000)	—

Both Pirates Co. and Eagles Co. have taxable income of $3,000 in 2008 and expect to have taxable income in all future years. The tax rates enacted as of the beginning of 2008 are 30% for 2008–2011 and 35% for years thereafter. All of the underlying temporary differences relate to noncurrent assets and liabilities.

Instructions

For each of these two situations, compute the net amount of deferred income taxes to be reported at the end of 2008, and indicate how it should be classified on the balance sheet.

(LO 2, 5, 7)

P15-7 (One Temporary Difference, Tracked 3 Years, Change in Rates, Income Statement Presentation) Gators Corp. sold an investment on an installment basis. The total gain of $60,000 was reported for financial reporting purposes in the period of sale. The company qualifies to use the installment sales method for tax purposes. The installment period is 3 years; one-third of the sale price is collected in the period of sale. The tax rate was 35% in 2007, and 30% in 2008 and 2009. The 30% tax rate was not enacted in law until 2008. The accounting and tax data for the 3 years is shown below.

	Financial Accounting	Tax Return
2007 (35% tax rate)		
Income before temporary difference	$ 70,000	$70,000
Temporary difference	60,000	20,000
Income	$130,000	$90,000

current or long term depends on the underlying A or L

DTL has underlying asset from where the difference comes from

2008 (30% tax rate)

Income before temporary difference	$ 70,000	$70,000
Temporary difference	–0–	20,000
Income	$ 70,000	$90,000

Warranty L = W. Reserve

2009 (30% tax rate)

Income before temporary difference	$ 70,000	$70,000
Temporary difference	–0–	20,000
Income	$ 70,000	$90,000

Loss carry forward is classified current or long term depend on time

Instructions

Depr. is always long term

(a) Prepare the journal entries to record the income tax expense, deferred income taxes, and the income tax payable at the end of each year. No deferred income taxes existed at the beginning of 2007.

(b) Explain how the deferred taxes will appear on the balance sheet at the end of each year. (Assume the Installment Accounts Receivable is classified as a current asset.)

(c) Draft the income tax expense section of the income statement for each year, beginning with "Income before income taxes."

P15-8 **(Two Differences, 2 Years, Compute Taxable Income and Pretax Financial Income)** The following information was disclosed during the audit of Munter Inc.

(LO 2, 3, 5, 9)

1.

Year	Amount Due per Tax Return
2008	$140,000
2009	112,000

2. On January 1, 2008, equipment costing $400,000 is purchased. For financial reporting purposes, the company uses straight-line depreciation, assuming no salvage value, over a 5-year life. For tax purposes, the company uses the elective straight-line method over a 5-year life. (*Hint:* For tax purposes, use the half-year convention; see Chapter 10.)

3. In January 2009, $225,000 is collected in advance rental of a building for a 3-year period. The entire $225,000 is reported as taxable income in 2009, but $150,000 of the $225,000 is reported as unearned revenue in 2009 for financial reporting purposes. The remaining amount of unearned revenue is to be earned equally in 2010 and 2011.

4. The tax rate is 40% in 2008 and all subsequent periods. (*Hint:* To find taxable income in 2008 and 2009 the related income tax payable amounts will have to be "grossed up.")

5. No temporary differences existed at the end of 2007. Munter expects to report taxable income in each of the next 5 years.

Instructions

(a) Determine the amount to report for deferred income taxes at the end of 2008, and indicate how it should be classified on the balance sheet.

(b) Prepare the journal entry to record income taxes for 2008.

(c) Draft the income tax section of the income statement for 2008 beginning with "Income before income taxes." (*Hint:* You must compute taxable income and then combine that with changes in cumulative temporary differences to arrive at pretax financial income.)

(d) Determine the deferred income taxes at the end of 2009, and indicate how they should be classified on the balance sheet.

(e) Prepare the journal entry to record income taxes for 2009.

(f) Draft the income tax section of the income statement for 2009, beginning with "Income before income taxes."

P15-9 **(Five Differences, Compute Taxable Income and Deferred Taxes, Draft Income Statement)** King Company began operations at the beginning of 2008. The following information pertains to this company.

(LO 2, 3, 5, 6, 9)

1. Pretax financial income for 2008 is $100,000.

2. The tax rate enacted for 2008 and future years is 40%

3. Differences between the 2008 income statement and tax return are listed below:

(a) Warranty expense accrued for financial reporting purposes amounts to $5,000. Warranty deductions per the tax return amount to $2,000.

(b) Gross profit on construction contracts using the percentage-of-completion method for books amounts to $92,000. Gross profit on construction contracts for tax purposes amounts to $62,000.

(c) Depreciation of property, plant, and equipment for financial reporting purposes amounts to $60,000. Depreciation of these assets amounts to $80,000 for the tax return.

(d) A $3,500 fine paid for violation of pollution laws was deducted in computing pretax financial income.

(e) Interest revenue earned on an investment in tax-exempt municipal bonds amounts to $1,400. (Assume (a) is short-term in nature; assume (b) and (c) are long-term in nature.)

4. Taxable income is expected for the next few years.

Instructions

(a) Compute taxable income for 2008.

(b) Compute the deferred taxes at December 31, 2008, that relate to the temporary differences described above. Clearly label them as deferred tax asset or liability.

(c) Prepare the journal entry to record income tax expense, deferred taxes, and income taxes payable for 2008.

(d) Draft the income tax expense section of the income statement beginning with "Income before income taxes."

ACCOUNTING IN ACTION

Financial Reporting and Analysis

■ **Financial Reporting Issues: The Procter & Gamble Company**

AIA15-1 The financial statements of **Procter & Gamble (P&G)** can be accessed at the book's website.

Instructions

Refer to P&G's financial statements and the accompanying notes to answer the following questions.

(a) What amounts relative to income taxes does P&G report in its:

    (1) 2006 income statement?

    (2) June 30, 2006, balance sheet?

    (3) 2006 statement of cash flows?

(b) P&G's provision for income taxes in 2004, 2005, and 2006 was computed at what effective tax rates? (See the notes to the financial statements.)

(c) How much of P&G's 2006 total provision for income taxes was current tax expense, and how much was deferred tax expense?

(d) What did P&G report as the significant components (the details) of its June 30, 2006, deferred tax assets and liabilities?

PEPSICO ■ **Comparative Analysis: The Coca-Cola Company and PepsiCo, Inc.**

AIA15-2 The financial statements of **The Coca-Cola Comapany** and **PepsiCo, Inc.** can be accessed at the book's website.

Instructions

Use information found at the book's website to answer the following questions.

(a) What are the amounts of Coca-Cola's and PepsiCo's provision for income taxes for the year 2006? Of each company's 2006 provision for income taxes, what portion is current expense and what portion is deferred expense?

(b) What amount of cash did Coca-Cola and PepsiCo for income taxes pay in 2006?

(c) What was the U.S. federal statutory tax rate in 2006? What was the effective tax rate in 2006 for Coca-Cola and PepsiCo? Why might their effective tax rates differ?

(d) For the year-end 2006, what amounts were reported by Coca-Cola and PepsiCo as (a) gross deferred tax assets and (b) gross deferred tax liabilities?

(e) Do either Coca-Cola or PepsiCo disclose any net operating loss carrybacks and/or carryforwards at year-end 2006? What are the amounts, and when do the carryforwards expire?

■ Financial Statement Analysis

AIA15-3 **Homestake Mining Company** is a 120-year-old international gold mining company with substantial gold mining operations and exploration in the United States, Canada, and Australia. At year-end, Homestake reported the following items related to income taxes (thousands of dollars).

Homestake Mining Company

Total current taxes	$ 26,349
Total deferred taxes	(39,436)
Total income and mining taxes (the provision for taxes per its income statement)	(13,087)
Deferred tax liabilities	$303,050
Deferred tax assets, net of valuation allowance of $207,175	95,275
Net deferred tax liability	$207,775

Note 6: The classification of deferred tax assets and liabilities is based on the related asset or liability creating the deferred tax. Deferred taxes not related to a specific asset or liability are classified based on the estimated period of reversal.

Tax loss carryforwards (U.S., Canada, Australia, and Chile)	$71,151
Tax credit carryforwards	$12,007

Instructions

(a) What is the significance of Homestake's disclosure of "Current taxes" of $26,349 and "Deferred taxes" of $(39,436)?

(b) Explain the concept behind Homestake's disclosure of gross deferred tax liabilities (future taxable amounts) and gross deferred tax assets (future deductible amounts).

(c) Homestake reported tax loss carryforwards of $71,151 and tax credit carryforwards of $12,007. How do the carryback and carryforward provisions affect the reporting of deferred tax assets and deferred tax liabilities?

■ International Reporting Issues

AIA15-4 **Tomkins PLC** is a British company that operates in three business sectors: industrial and automotive, air systems components, and engineering and construction products. Before 2005 Tomkins prepared its accounts in accordance with United Kingdom (U.K.) accounting standards. Like U.S. reporting, U.K. financial reporting is investor-oriented. As a result, British companies report different income amounts for tax and financial reporting purposes. British companies receive different tax treatment for such items as depreciation (capital allowances), and they receive tax credits for operating losses. In 2004 Tomkins reported income of £171.8 million and reported total shareholders' funds of £1,398.7 million at year-end. Tomkins provided the following disclosures related to taxes in its annual report.

If Tomkins had used U.S. GAAP its income would have been higher by £96.1 million in the current year. Stockholders' equity at year-end would have been £764.9 million higher if Tompkins had applied U.S. GAAP.

♦OMKINS

Tomkins PLC

Reconciliation to Accounting Principles Generally Accepted in the United States of America (Unaudited)—Partial

The consolidated financial statements are prepared in conformity with accounting principles generally accepted in the United Kingdom ("U.K. GAAP") which differ in certain respects from accounting principles generally accepted in the United States of America ("U.S. GAAP"). The following is a summary of the material adjustments to profit attributable to shareholders and shareholders' equity determined in accordance with U.K. GAAP, necessary to reconcile to net income and shareholders' equity determined in accordance with U.S. GAAP.

(continued on next page)

Tomkins PLC (continued)
Reconciliation from U.K. GAAP to U.S. GAAP

	3 January 2004 12 months £ million
Profit attributable to shareholders	
Net income under UK GAAP	171.8
U.S. GAAP adjustments:	
Goodwill amortisation	11.9
Goodwill impairment	(30.0)
Reversal of U.K. provision for impairment	51.4
Intangibles amortisation	(1.6)
Valuation of net assets acquired in a business combination	(0.2)
Gain/(loss) on disposal of operations	22.6
Pension costs	3.4
Share options	(4.0)
Capitalised interest	2.2
Deferred income tax	(2.1)
Derivatives	29.5
Restructuring costs	13.0
Net income under U.S. GAAP	267.9

Explanation of the deferred tax difference is as follows:

In Tomkins consolidated financial statements, deferred tax is provided in full on all liabilities. Deferred tax assets are recognised to the extent it is regarded as more likely than not that there will be suitable taxable profits from which the future reversal of the underlying timing differences can be deducted, and for this purpose Tomkins considers only future periods for which forecasts are prepared. Under U.S. GAAP, deferred taxes are provided for all temporary differences on a full asset and liability basis. A valuation allowance is established in respect of those deferred tax assets where it is more likely than not that some portion will not be realised. The look forward period is not limited to the period for which forecasts are prepared.

Instructions

Use the information in the Tomkins disclosure (page 834) to answer the following.

(a) Prepare the journal entry that would be required to reconcile Tomkins' income to U.S. GAAP for the differences in deferred taxes under U.S. and U.K. accounting standards.

(b) In light of the information disclosed, explain why you think Tomkins' equity under U.S. GAAP would be higher at year-end in the current year.

Concepts for Analysis

 **AIA15-5** (**Objectives and Principles for Accounting for Income Taxes**) The amount of income taxes due to the government for a period of time is rarely the amount reported on the income statement for that period as income tax expense.

Instructions

(a) Explain the objectives of accounting for income taxes in general purpose financial statements.

(b) Explain the basic principles that are applied in accounting for income taxes at the date of the financial statements to meet the objectives discussed in (a).

(c) List the steps in the annual computation of deferred tax liabilities and assets.

AIA15-6 **(Basic Accounting for Temporary Differences)** Majoli Company appropriately uses the asset-liability method to record deferred income taxes. Iva Majoli reports depreciation expense for certain machinery purchased this year using the modified accelerated cost recovery system (MACRS) for income tax purposes and the straight-line basis for financial reporting purposes. The tax deduction is the larger amount this year.

Majoli received rent revenues in advance this year. These revenues are included in this year's taxable income. However, for financial reporting purposes, these revenues are reported as unearned revenues, a current liability.

Instructions

(a) What are the principles of the asset-liability approach?
(b) How would Majoli account for the temporary differences?
(c) How should Majoli classify the deferred tax consequences of the temporary differences on its balance sheet?

AIA15-7 **(Identify Temporary Differences and Classification Criteria)** The asset-liability approach for recording deferred income taxes is an integral part of generally accepted accounting principles.

Instructions

(a) Indicate whether each of the following independent situations should be treated as a temporary difference or as a permanent difference and explain why.
  (1) Estimated warranty costs (covering a 3-year warranty) are expensed for financial reporting purposes at the time of sale but deducted for income tax purposes when paid.
  (2) Depreciation for book and income tax purposes differs because of different bases of carrying the related property, which was acquired in a trade-in. The different bases are a result of different rules used for book and tax purposes to compute the basis of property acquired in a trade-in.
  (3) A company properly uses the equity method to account for its 30% investment in another company. The investee pays dividends that are about 10% of its annual earnings.
  (4) A company reports a gain on an involuntary conversion of a nonmonetary asset to a monetary asset. The company elects to replace the property within the statutory period using the total proceeds so the gain is not reported on the current year's tax return.
(b) Discuss the nature of the deferred income tax accounts and possible classifications in a company's balance sheet. Indicate the manner in which these accounts are to be reported.

AIA15-8 **(Accounting and Classification of Deferred Income Taxes)**
Part A
This year Sharapova Company has each of the following items in its income statement.

1. Gross profits on installment sales.

2. Revenues on long-term construction contracts.

3. Estimated costs of product warranty contracts.

4. Premiums on officers' life insurance with Sharapova as beneficiary.

Instructions

(a) Under what conditions would deferred income taxes need to be reported in the financial statements?
(b) Specify when deferred income taxes would need to be recognized for each of the items above, and indicate the rationale for such recognition.
Part B
Sharapova Company's president has heard that deferred income taxes can be classified in different ways in the balance sheet.

Instructions

Identify the conditions under which deferred income taxes would be classified as a noncurrent item in the balance sheet. What justification exists for such classification?

(AICPA adapted)

AIA15-9 **(Explain Computation of Deferred Tax Liability for Multiple Tax Rates)** At December 31, 2008, Hingis Corporation has one temporary difference which will reverse and cause taxable amounts in 2009. In 2008 a new tax act set taxes equal to 45% for 2008, 40% for 2009, and 34% for 2010 and years thereafter.

Instructions

Explain what circumstances would call for Hingis to compute its deferred tax liability at the end of 2008 by multiplying the cumulative temporary difference by:

(a) 45%.
(b) 40%.
(c) 34%.

AIA15-10 **(Explain Future Taxable and Deductible Amounts, How Carryback and Carryforward Affects Deferred Taxes)** Mary Joe Fernandez and Meredith McGrath are discussing accounting for income taxes. They are currently studying a schedule of taxable and deductible amounts that will arise in the future as a result of existing temporary differences. The schedule is as follows.

| | Current Year | Future Years | | | |
	2008	2009	2010	2011	2012
Taxable income	$850,000				
Taxable amounts		$375,000	$375,000	$ 375,000	$375,000
Deductible amounts				(2,400,000)	
Enacted tax rate	50%	45%	40%	35%	30%

Instructions

(a) Explain the concept of future taxable amounts and future deductible amounts as illustrated in the schedule.
(b) How do the carryback and carryforward provisions affect the reporting of deferred tax assets and deferred tax liabilities?

Professional Tools

■ Ethical Decision Making

AIA15-11 **(Deferred Taxes, Income Effects)** Henrietta Aguirre, CPA, is the newly hired director of corporate taxation for Mesa Incorporated, which is a publicly traded corporation. Ms. Aguirre's first job with Mesa was the review of the company's accounting practices on deferred income taxes. In doing her review, she noted differences between tax and book depreciation methods that permitted Mesa to realize a sizable deferred tax liability on its balance sheet. As a result, Mesa paid very little in income taxes at that time.

Aguirre also discovered that Mesa has an explicit policy of selling off plant assets before they reversed in the deferred tax liability account. This policy, coupled with the rapid expansion of its plant asset base, allowed Mesa to "defer" all income taxes payable for several years, even though it always has reported positive earnings and an increasing EPS. Aguirre checked with the legal department and found the policy to be legal, but she's uncomfortable with the ethics of it.

Instructions

Answer the following questions.

(a) Why would Mesa have an explicit policy of selling plant assets before the temporary differences reversed in the deferred tax liability account?
(b) What are the ethical implications of Mesa's "deferral" of income taxes?
(c) Who could be harmed by Mesa's ability to "defer" income taxes payable for several years, despite positive earnings?
(d) In a situation such as this, what are Ms. Aguirre's professional responsibilities as a CPA?

■ Financial Accounting Research (FARS)

AIA15-12 Hallscott Company started operations in 2003, and although it has grown steadily, the company reported accumulated operating losses of $450,000 in its first four years in business. In the most recent year (2007), Hallscott appears to have turned the corner and reported modest taxable income of $30,000. In addition to a deferred tax asset related to its net operating loss, Hallscott has recorded a deferred tax asset related to product warranties and a deferred tax liability related to accelerated depreciation.

Given its past operating results, Hallscott has established a full valuation allowance for its deferred tax assets. However, given its improved performance, Hallscott management wonders whether the company can now reduce or eliminate the valuation allowance. They would like you to conduct some research on the accounting for its valuation allowance.

Instructions

Using the **Financial Accounting Research System (FARS)** database, respond to the following items. (Provide text strings used in your search.)

(a) Briefly explain to Hallscott management the importance of future taxable income as it relates to the valuation allowance for deferred tax assets.

(b) What are the sources of income that may be relied upon to remove the need for a valuation allowance?

(c) What are tax-planning strategies? From the information provided, does it appear that Hallscott could employ a tax-planning strategy to support reducing its valuation allowance?

■ Professional Simulation

AIA15-13 Go to the book's companion website, at **www.wiley.com/college/warfield**, to find an interactive problem that simulates the computerized CPA exam. The professional simulation for this chapter asks you to address questions related to the accounting for taxes.

What do the numbers mean?

Real Liabilities, p. 786

Q: What is the importance of *Statement of Financial Concepts No. 6* to the conceptual framework, and how does it help to resolve various accounting and financial reporting issues?

A: This statement defines many of the key terms used in the financial statements. These terms constitute the language of business. As a consequence, this statement is one of the most important building blocks in developing a conceptual framework.

One of the key definitions relates to a liability. Without a clear definition of a liability, endless debate could take place on whether a deferred tax liability is really a liability. For example, some might argue that deferred tax liabilities are not liabilities because there is no past transaction. Rather, there is only a future transaction related to the payment of the tax. However, as indicated in the discussion, Chelsea performed services for customers in 2007 (the past transaction) that gives rise to taxable income in the future.

Real Assets, p. 789

Q: Why might a company not realize the future benefits of a tax deduction?

A: In some cases, companies take an aggressive stance in regards to certain deductions. It is possible as a result of an IRS audit that the deduction will be disallowed, and therefore the tax benefit will be lost. As indicated in the opening story, companies now have detailed guidelines that require disclosure of these uncertain tax positions. Another situation arises when the company is experiencing substantial losses, which seem likely to continue in the future. As a result, the benefit of the deferred tax asset will be lost.

Read Those Notes, p. 802

Q: Why might a company not want to disclose the reversal of a valuation allowance?

A: Users of financial statements are interested in the concept of earning power. Earning power means the *normal level* of income to be obtained in the future. Earning power differs from actual net income by the amount of irregular revenues, expenses, gains, and losses. Users are interested in earning power because it helps them derive an estimate of future earnings without the "noise" of irregular items. Thus the reversal of a valuation allowance in most cases is an irregular item that increases net income. A company may attempt to gloss over this item in its reporting, hoping that users will believe that it is part of normal earnings and therefore has a high likelihood of continuing in the future. A stable "core earnings" number is generally valued more highly than an irregular item.

(continued on next page)

Guideline Answers to Beyond the Numbers Questions, continued

NOLs: Good News or Bad?, p. 808

Q: What impact do future tax rates have on a company's decision to carry forward rather than carry back its net operating losses?

A: If tax rates will be higher in the future than in the carryback years, the company should consider the carryforward option. However, the company should recognize that if it can carry back, it receives an immediate cash refund. Thus the company must consider whether it will have income in the future, what the tax rate will be, and when will the benefit be received. Once the company determines the cash amount of the benefit received, then it must discount this amount back to the current year in order to assess the carryforward's cash benefit in current dollars.

Remember to check the book's companion website to find additional resources for this chapter.

CHAPTER 16

ACCOUNTING FOR COMPENSATION

Where Have All the Pensions Gone?

Many companies have benefit plans that promise income and other benefits to employees in retirement in exchange for employee services during their working years. However, a shift is on from traditional defined-benefit plans, in which employers bear the risk of meeting the benefit promises, to plans in which employees bear more of the risk. In some cases, employers are dropping retirement plans altogether. Here are some of the reasons for the shift:

- *Competition:* Newer and foreign competitors do not have the same retiree costs that older U.S. companies do. **Southwest Airlines** does not offer a traditional pension plan but **Northwest** and **United** have pension deficits exceeding $100,000 per employee.

- *Cost:* Retirees are living longer, and the costs of retirement are higher. Combined with annual retiree heath care costs, retirements benefits are costing the S&P 500 companies over $25 billion a year and are rising at double-digit rates.

- *Insurance*: Pensions are backed by premiums paid to the **Pension Benefit Guarantee Corp. (PBGC)**. When a company fails, the PBGC takes over the plan. But due to a number of significant company failures, the PBGC is running a deficit, and healthy companies are subsidizing the weak. For example, steel companies pay just 3 percent of PBGC premiums but account for 56 percent of the claims.

- *Accounting:* Accounting rule-makers are considering rules that will require companies to mark their pensions to market to bring U.S. standards in line with international rules. Such a move would increase the reported volatility of the plan and company financial statements. When Britain made this shift, 25 percent of British companies closed their plans to new entrants.

So it is not hard to believe that experts can think of no major company that has instituted a traditional pension plan in the past decade.

Source: Adapted from Nanette Byrnes with David Welch, "The Benefits Trap," BusinessWeek (July 19, 2004), pp. 54–72.

Preview of Chapter 16

As our opening story indicates, the cost of retirement benefits is getting steep. For example, **General Motors'** pension and healthcare costs for retirees in a recent year was $6.2 billion, or approximately $1,784 per vehicle produced. General Motors and many other companies are facing substantial pension and other postretirement expenses and obligations. In this chapter we discuss the accounting issues related to compensation and benefit plans. *The content and organization of the chapter are as follows.*

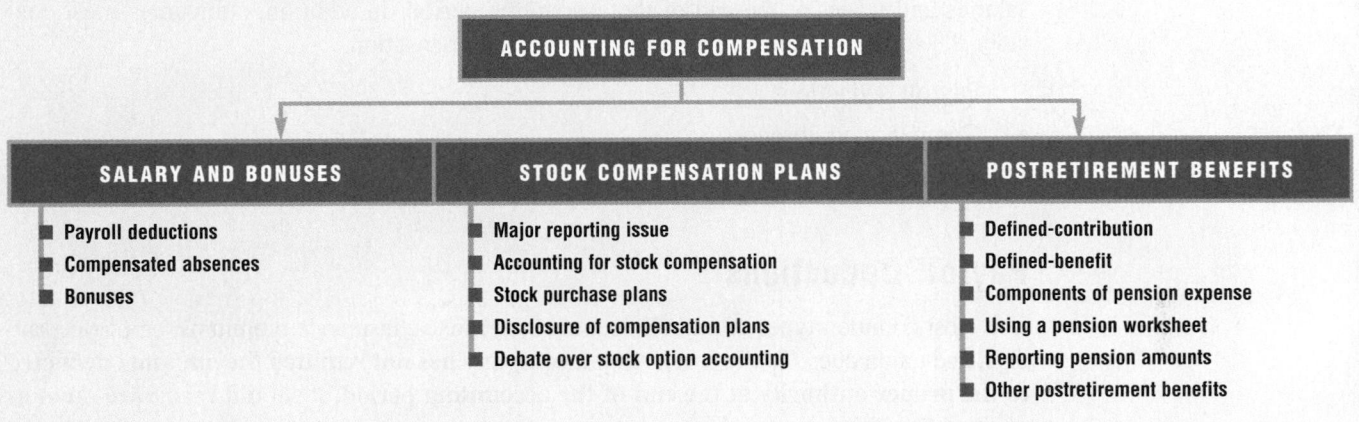

ACCOUNTING FOR COMPENSATION

SALARY AND BONUSES	STOCK COMPENSATION PLANS	POSTRETIREMENT BENEFITS
■ Payroll deductions	■ Major reporting issue	■ Defined-contribution
■ Compensated absences	■ Accounting for stock compensation	■ Defined-benefit
■ Bonuses	■ Stock purchase plans	■ Components of pension expense
	■ Disclosure of compensation plans	■ Using a pension worksheet
	■ Debate over stock option accounting	■ Reporting pension amounts
		■ Other postretirement benefits

Learning Objectives

After studying this chapter, you should be able to:

1. Explain the accounting for salary and bonuses.
2. Describe the accounting for stock compensation plans under generally accepted accounting principles.
3. Discuss the controversy surrounding stock compensation plans.
4. Identify types of pension plans and their characteristics.
5. List the components of pension expense.
6. Utilize a worksheet for employer's pension plan entries.
7. Explain the accounting for prior service cost and gains and losses.
8. Describe the reporting requirements for pension plans in financial statements.

Inside Chapter 16

- **What Do the Numbers Mean?**
  A little honesty goes a long way (p. 849)
  Which plan is right for you? (p. 854)
  Pension costs ups and downs. (p. 861)
  Bailing out. (p. 870)

- **What's the Principle?** (pp. 844, 853, 856, 868, 869)

- **Accounting, Analysis, Principles** (p. 871)
  Record compensation elements.
  Analyze companies with different benefit plans.
  Explain the conceptual basis for recording pension liabilities.

- **Convergence Corner** (p. 873)

Effective compensation programs do the following: (1) motivate employees to high levels of performance, (2) help retain key employees and recruit new talent, (3) base compensation on employee and company performance, (4) maximize the employee's after-tax benefit and minimize the employer's after-tax cost, and (5) use performance criteria that the employer controls. Straight cash compensation plans (salary and perhaps bonus) are an important part of any compensation program.

The accounting for salary (wages) is relatively straightforward. Companies should report as compensation expense the amounts paid to employees for salaries and wages per the employment contract. They report as a current liability amounts owed to employees for salaries and wages at the end of the accounting period. In addition, companies must consider the following items related to employee compensation.

- Payroll deductions
- Compensated absences
- Bonuses

Payroll Deductions

The most common types of payroll deductions are taxes, insurance premiums, employee savings, and union dues. **To the extent that a company has not remitted the amounts deducted to the proper authority at the end of the accounting period, it should recognize them as current liabilities.**

Social Security Taxes

Since January 1, 1937, Social Security legislation has provided federal **Old Age, Survivor, and Disability Insurance (OASDI)** benefits for certain individuals and their families. Funds for these payments come from taxes levied on both the employer and the employee. Employers collect the employee's share of this tax by deducting it from the employee's gross pay and remit it to the government along with their share. The government taxes both the employer and the employee at the same rate, currently 6.2 percent based on the employee's gross pay, up to a $97,500 annual limit. The OASDI tax is usually referred to as **FICA** (the Federal Insurance Contribution Act).

In 1965 Congress passed the first federal health insurance program for the aged—popularly known as **Medicare**. This two-part program alleviates the high cost of medical care for those over age 65. A separate Hospital Insurance tax, paid by both the employee and the employer at the rate of 1.45 percent on the employee's total compensation, finances the Basic Plan, which provides hospital and other institutional services. The Voluntary Plan covers the major part of doctors' bills and other medical and health services. Monthly payments from all who enroll, plus matching funds from the federal government, finance this plan.

The combination of the OASDI tax (FICA) and the federal Hospital Insurance Tax is commonly referred to as the **Social Security tax**. The combined rate for these taxes, 7.65 percent on an employee's wages to $97,500 and 1.45 percent in excess of $97,500, changes intermittently by acts of Congress. **Companies should report as a current liability the amount of unremitted employee and employer Social Security tax on gross wages paid.**

Unemployment Taxes

Another payroll tax levied by the federal government in cooperation with state governments provides a system of unemployment insurance. All employers who meet the following criteria are subject to the Federal Unemployment Tax Act (FUTA): (1) those who paid wages of $1,500 or more during any calendar quarter in the year or preceding year, or (2) those who employed at least one individual on at least one day in each of 20 weeks during the current or preceding calendar year.

Only employers pay the unemployment tax. The rate of this tax is 6.2 percent on the first $7,000 of compensation paid to each employee during the calendar year. The employer receives a tax credit not to exceed 5.4 percent for contributions paid to a state plan for unemployment compensation. Thus, if an employer is subject to a state unemployment tax of 5.4 percent or more, it pays only 0.8 percent tax to the federal government.

State unemployment compensation laws differ both from the federal law and among various states. Therefore, employers must refer to the unemployment tax laws in each state in which they pay wages and salaries. The normal state tax may range from 3 percent to 7 percent or higher. However, all states provide for some form of **merit rating**, which reduces the state contribution rate. Employers who display by their benefit and contribution experience that they provide steady employment may receive this reduction—if the size of the state fund is adequate. In order not to penalize an employer who has earned a reduction in the state contribution rate, federal law allows a credit of 5.4 percent, even when the effective state contribution rate is less than 5.4 percent.

To illustrate, Appliance Repair Co. has a taxable payroll of $100,000. It is subject to a federal rate of 6.2 percent and a state contribution rate of 5.7 percent. However, its stable employment experience reduces the company's state rate to 1 percent. Appliance Repair computes its federal and state unemployment taxes as shown in Illustration 16-1.

State unemployment tax payment (1% × $100,000)	$1,000
Federal unemployment tax [(6.2% − 5.4%) × $100,000]	800
Total federal and state unemployment tax	$1,800

Illustration 16-1
Computation of
Unemployment Taxes

Companies pay federal unemployment tax quarterly and file a tax form annually. Companies also generally pay state contributions quarterly as well. Because both the federal and the state unemployment taxes accrue on earned compensation, companies should record the amount of accrued but unpaid employer contributions **as an operating expense and as a current liability when preparing financial statements at year-end**.

Income Tax Withholding

Federal and some state income tax laws require employers to withhold from each employee's pay the applicable income tax due on those wages. The employer computes the amount of income tax to withhold according to a government-prescribed formula or withholding tax table. That amount depends on the length of the pay period and each employee's taxable wages, marital status, and claimed dependents. If the income tax withheld plus the employee and the employer Social Security taxes exceeds specified amounts per month, the employer must make remittances to the government during the month. Illustration 16-2 summarizes payroll deductions and liabilities.

Item	Who Pays	
Income tax withholding		
FICA taxes—employee share	Employee	
Union dues		Employer reports these amounts as liabilities until remitted.
FICA taxes—employer share		
Federal unemployment	Employer	
State unemployment		

Illustration 16-2
Summary of Payroll
Liabilities

Payroll Deductions Example

Assume a weekly payroll of $10,000 entirely subject to FICA and Medicare (7.65%), federal (0.8%) and state (4%) unemployment taxes, with income tax withholding of $1,320 and union dues of $88 deducted. The company records the wages and salaries paid and the **employee payroll deductions** as follows:

Wages and Salaries Expense	10,000	
Withholding Taxes Payable		1,320
FICA Taxes Payable		765
Union Dues Payable to Local No. 257		88
Cash		7,827

It records the **employer payroll taxes** as follows:

Payroll Tax Expense	1,245	
FICA Taxes Payable		765
Federal Unemployment Tax Payable		80
State Unemployment Tax Payable		400

The employer must remit to the government its share of FICA tax along with the amount of FICA tax deducted from each employee's gross compensation. It should record all unremitted employer FICA taxes as payroll tax expense and payroll tax payable.[1]

Compensated Absences

Compensated absences are paid absences from employment—such as vacation, illness, and holidays. Companies should accrue a liability for the cost of compensation for future absences if **all of the following conditions** exist.[2]

a The employer's obligation relating to employees' rights to receive compensation for future absences is attributable to employees' services **already rendered**.

b The obligation relates to the rights that **vest or accumulate**.

c Payment of the compensation is **probable**.

d The amount can be **reasonably estimated**.[3]

Illustration 16-3 shows an example of an accrual for compensated absences, in an excerpt from the balance sheet of **Clarcor Inc.**

Illustration 16-3
Balance Sheet
Presentation of
Accrual for Compensated
Absences

Clarcor Inc.

Current liabilities	
Accounts payable	$ 6,308
Accrued salaries, wages, and commissions	2,278
Compensated absences	2,271
Accrued pension liabilities	1,023
Other accrued liabilities	4,572
	$16,452

[1]A manufacturing company allocates all of the payroll costs (wages, payroll taxes, and fringe benefits) to appropriate cost accounts such as Direct Labor, Indirect Labor, Sales Salaries, Administrative Salaries, and the like. This abbreviated and somewhat simplified discussion of payroll costs and deductions is not indicative of the volume of records and clerical work that may be involved in maintaining a sound and accurate payroll system.

[2]"Accounting for Compensated Absences," *Statement of Financial Accounting Standards No. 43* (Stamford, Conn.: FASB, 1980), par. 6.

[3]Companies apply these same four conditions to accounting for **postemployment benefits**. Companies provide **postemployment benefits** to past or inactive employees **after employment but prior to retirement**. Examples include salary continuation, supplemental unemployment benefits, severance pay, job training, and continuation of health and life insurance coverage.

If an employer meets conditions (a), (b), and (c) but does not accrue a liability because of a failure to meet condition (d), it should disclose that fact.

Vested rights exist when an employer has an obligation to make payment to an employee even after terminating his or her employment. Thus, vested rights are not contingent on an employee's future service. **Accumulated rights** are those that employees can carry forward to future periods if not used in the period in which earned. For example, assume that you earn four days of vacation pay as of December 31, the end of your employer's fiscal year. Company policy is that you will be paid for this vacation time even if you terminate employment. In this situation, these four days of vacation pay are vested, and your employer must accrue the amount.

Now assume that your vacation days are not vested, but that you can carry the four days over into later periods. Although the rights are not vested, they are accumulated rights for which the employer must make an accrual. However, the amount of the accrual is adjusted to allow for estimated forfeitures due to turnover.

A modification of the general rules relates to the issue of **sick pay**. If sick pay benefits vest, a company must accrue them. If sick pay benefits accumulate but do not vest, a company may choose whether to accrue them. Why this distinction? Companies may administer compensation designated as sick pay in one of two ways. In some companies, employees receive sick pay only if illness causes their absence. Therefore, these companies may or may not accrue a liability because its payment depends on future employee illness. Other companies allow employees to accumulate unused sick pay and take compensated time off from work even when not ill. For this type of sick pay, a company must accrue a liability because the company will pay it, regardless of whether employees become ill.

Companies should recognize the expense and related liability for compensated absences in the year in which the expenses are earned by employees. For example, if new employees receive rights to two weeks' paid vacation at the beginning of their second year of employment, a company considers the vacation pay to be earned during the first year of employment.

What rate should a company use to accrue the compensated absence cost—the current rate or an estimated future rate? *SFAS No. 43* is silent on this subject. Therefore, companies will likely use the current rather than future rate. The future rate is less certain and raises issues concerning the time value of money. To illustrate, assume that Amutron Inc. began operations on January 1, 2008. The company employs 10 individuals and pays each $480 per week. Employees earned 20 unused vacation weeks in 2008. In 2009, the employees used the vacation weeks, but now each earned $540 per week. Amutron accrues the accumulated vacation pay on December 31, 2008, as follows.

Wages Expense	9,600	
Vacation Wages Payable ($480 × 20)		9,600

At December 31, 2008, the company reports on its balance sheet a liability of $9,600. In 2009, it records the vacation pay related to 2008 as follows.

Vacation Wages Payable	9,600	
Wages Expense	1,200	
Cash ($540 × 20)		10,800

In 2009 the use of the vacation weeks extinguishes the liability. Note that Amutron records the difference between the amount of cash paid and the reduction in the liability account as an adjustment to Wages Expense in the period when paid. This difference arises because it accrues the liability account at the rates of pay in effect during the period when employees *earned* the compensated time. The cash paid, however, depends on the rates in effect during the period when employees *used* the compensated time. If Amutron used the future rates of pay to compute the accrual in 2008, then the cash paid in 2009 would equal the liability.[4]

[4]Some companies have obligations for benefits paid to employees after they retire. The accounting and reporting standards for postretirement benefit payments are complex. These standards relate to two different types of **postretirement benefits**: (1) pensions, and (2) postretirement health-care and life insurance benefits. We discuss these issues later in this chapter.

Bonuses

Many companies give a **bonus** to certain or all employees in addition to their regular salaries or wages. Frequently the bonus amount depends on the company's yearly profit. For example, employees at **Ford Motor Company** share in the success of the company's operations on the basis of a complicated formula using net income as its primary basis for computation. A company may consider **bonus payments to employees** as additional wages and should include them as a deduction in determining the net income for the year.

To illustrate the entries for an employee bonus, assume a company shows income for the year 2008 of $100,000. It will pay out bonuses of $10,700 in January 2009. It makes an adjusting entry dated December 31, 2008, to record the bonuses as follows.

Additional Discussion on Bonus Computations

Employees' Bonus Expense	10,700	
Bonus Payable		10,700

In January 2009, when it pays the bonus, the company makes this journal entry:

Bonus Payable	10,700	
Cash		10,700

The company should show the expense account in the income statement as an operating expense. **The liability, Bonus Payable, is usually payable within a short period of time. Companies should include it as a current liability in the balance sheet.**

Try it out! Billips Company's weekly payroll of $46,000 for the week ending December 31, 2008, included FICA taxes withheld of $2,852, federal taxes withheld of $5,980, state taxes withheld of $1,840, and insurance premiums withheld of $500. Billips gives employees a bonus to be paid in the next fiscal year at a rate of 1.5% of net income. Net income for purposes of the bonus for 2008 is $250,000.

Instructions

Prepare the journal entry to record Billips' final payroll expanse and the bonus for 2008.

Solution

Wage Expense	46,000	
FICA Taxes Payable		2,852
Federal Withholding Taxes Payable		5,980
State Withholding Taxes Payable		1,840
Insurance Premiums Payable		500
Cash		34,828
Bonus Expense ($250,000 × 1.5%)	3,750	
Bonus Payable		3,750

STOCK COMPENSATION PLANS

Many companies recognize that they often need a more long-term compensation plan, in addition to a cash component. Long-term compensation plans attempt to develop company loyalty among key employees. An effective way to do so is to give the employees "a piece of

Intrisic value

Marret Prie - E. P

the action"—that is, an equity interest. These plans, generally referred to as **stock compensation plans**, come in many forms. Essentially, they provide the employee with the opportunity to receive stock if the performance of the company (by whatever measure) is satisfactory. Typical performance measures focus on long-term improvements that are readily measurable and that benefit the company as a whole, such as increases in earnings per share, revenues, stock price, or market share.

Stock compensation plans have been a popular way to pay and motivate employees. However, the data reported in Illustration 16-4 indicate that the most popular stock-based compensation plans using stock options may be declining in popularity.

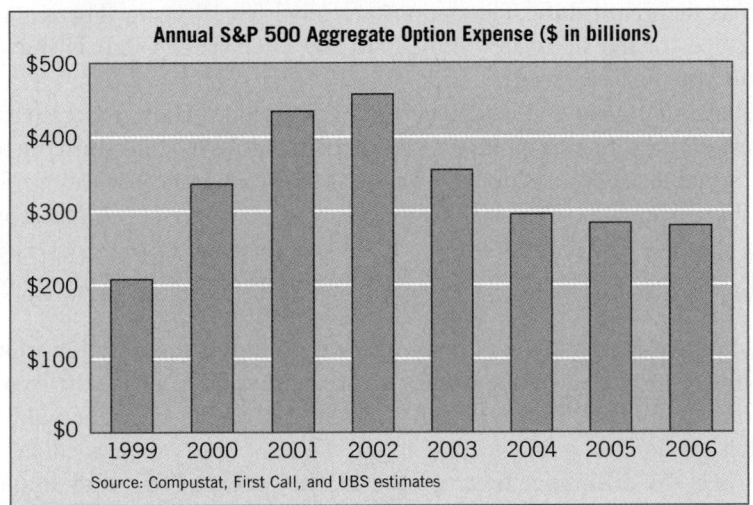

Illustration 16-4
Stock Option
Compensation Expense

Illustration 16-4 indicates that option expense is considerable but peaked in 2002 and now is declining. The major reasons for this decline are two-fold. Critics often cited the indiscriminate use of stock options as a reason why company executives manipulated accounting numbers in an attempt to achieve higher share price. As a result, many responsible companies decided to cut back on the issuance of options, both to avoid such accounting manipulations and to head off investor doubts. In addition, the FASB's new standard in this area will result in companies recording a higher expense when these options are granted.

The data reported in Illustration 16-5 reinforces the point that the design of compensation plans is changing. The study documents the compensation trends of 68 CEOs of companies in the S&P 500 in two recent years.

	Current Year	% Change from Previous Year
Total direct compensation	$7,247,903	8.8%
Salary	908,269	4.1
Bonus	975,000	32.6
Value of stock options	3,217,811	(18.7)
Restricted stock	2,679,435	34.0
Long-term incentive payouts	773,719	72.1

Sources: Compustat, First Call, UBS, Equilar, Inc.

Illustration 16-5
Compensation Elements

What Illustration 16-5 shows is that cash compensation is increasing. In addition, long-term incentives are increasing, but the mix is changing. For example, the use of restricted stock jumped 34 percent but the use of options decreased approximately 19 percent. Yet stock options remain the primary means of compensating these CEOs.

Straight cash compensation plans (salary and perhaps a bonus), though important, are oriented to the short run. As Illustrations 16-4 and 16-5 indicate, stock-based compensation is still a considerable element of employee compensation.

The Major Reporting Issue

Suppose that as an employee for Hurdle Inc., you receive options to purchase 10,000 shares of the firm's common stock as part of your compensation. The date you receive the options is referred to as the **grant date**. The options are good for 10 years. The market price and the exercise price for the stock are both $20 at the grant date. **What is the value of the compensation you just received?**

Some believe that what you have received has no value. They reason that because the difference between the market price and the exercise price is zero, no compensation results. Others argue these options do have value: If the stock price goes above $20 any time in the next 10 years and you exercise the options, you may earn substantial compensation. For example, if at the end of the fourth year, the market price of the stock is $30 and you exercise your options, you earn $100,000 [10,000 options × ($30 − $20)], ignoring income taxes.

The question for Hurdle is how to report the granting of these options. One approach measures compensation cost by the excess of the market price of the stock over its exercise price at the grant date. This approach is referred to as the **intrinsic-value method**. It measures what the holder would receive today if the option was immediately exercised. **Intrinsic value is the difference between the market price of the stock and the exercise price of the options at the grant date**. Using the intrinsic-value method, Hurdle would not recognize any compensation expense related to your options because at the grant date the market price equaled the exercise price. (In the preceding paragraph, those who answered that the options had no value were looking at the question from the intrinsic-value approach.)

The second way to look at the question of how to report the granting of these options bases the cost of employee stock options on the **fair value** of the stock options granted. Under this **fair-value method**, companies use acceptable option-pricing models to value the options at the date of grant. These models take into account the many factors that determine an option's underlying value.[5]

Under previous accounting standards, companies could recognize stock-based compensation using *either* the intrinsic-value method *or* the fair-value method. Given a choice, most companies adopted the intrinsic-value approach because it generally resulted in lower compensation expense. However, in 2002 a number of companies began voluntarily to switch to the fair-value method. By March 2004 over 500 public companies were using the fair-value method. As indicated earlier, a major reason for the change was the desire by companies to show the investing community that they believe in fair and transparent financial reporting, particularly in the aftermath of the many financial reporting scandals.

However, the choice between two methods was not ideal. Some companies included in their income figures the cost of stock-based compensation (the fair-value approach). Others did not. Analysts raised concerns about lack of comparability, and the FASB developed a revised standard for stock-based compensation.

INTERNATIONAL INSIGHT

iGAAP for stock-based compensation (*IFRS 2*) is substantially the same as U.S. GAAP.

---

[5]These factors include the volatility of the underlying stock, the expected life of the options, the risk-free rate during the option life, and expected dividends during the option life.

The new FASB standard requires that companies recognize compensation cost using the fair-value method.[6] The FASB position is that companies should base the accounting for the cost of employee services on the fair value of compensation paid. This amount is presumed to be a measure of the value of the services received. We will discuss more about the politics of this new standard later (see "Debate over Stock Option Accounting" on page 853). Let's first describe the procedures involved.

What do the numbers mean?   A Little Honesty Goes a Long Way

Before adoption of *SFAS No. 123(R)*, companies could choose whether to expense stock-based compensation or simply disclose the estimated costs in the notes to the financial statements. You might think investors would punish companies that decided to expense stock options. After all, most of corporate America has been battling for years to avoid such a fate, worried that accounting for those perks would destroy earnings. And indeed, **Merrill Lynch** estimated that if all S&P 500 companies were to expense options, reported profits would fall by as much as 10 percent.

Yet, as a small but growing band of big-name companies voluntarily made the switch to expensing, investors for the most part showered them with love. With a few exceptions, the stock prices of the "expensers," from **Cinergy** to **The Washington Post**, outpaced the market after they announced the change. And this was at a time when the overall market was in the doldrums.

The few, the brave

Company	Estimated EPS Without options	Estimated EPS With options expensed	% change since announcement Company stock price
Cinergy	$ 2.80	$ 2.77	22.4%
The Washington Post	20.48	20.10	16.4
Computer Associates	−0.46	−0.62	11.1
Fannie Mae	6.15	6.02	6.7
Bank One	2.77	2.61	2.6
General Motors	5.84	5.45	2.6
Procter & Gamble	3.57	3.35	−2.3
Coca-Cola	1.79	1.70	−6.2
General Electric	1.65	1.61	−6.2
Amazon.com	0.04	−0.99	−11.4

Data sources: Merrill Lynch; company reports.

Given the market's general positive reaction to the transparent reporting of stock options, it is puzzling why some companies continued to fight implementation of *SFAS No 123(R)*.

Source: David Stires, "A Little Honesty Goes a Long Way," *Fortune* (September 2, 2002), p. 186. Reprinted by permission. See also Troy Wolverton, "Foes of Expensing Welcome FASB Delay," *TheStreet.com* (October 15, 2004).

Beyond the Numbers

What about companies that did not voluntarily begin expensing options? How do you think the market would respond to their inaction on option expensing?

---

[6]"Accounting for Stock-Based Compensation," *Statement of Financial Accounting Standards No. 123* (Norwalk, Conn: FASB, 1995); and "Share-Based Payment," *Statement of Financial Accounting Standard No. 123(R)* (Norwalk, Conn: FASB, 2004).

Accounting for Stock Compensation

OBJECTIVE 2

Describe the accounting for stock compensation plans under generally accepted accounting principles.

Stock option plans involve two main accounting issues:

1 How to determine compensation expense.

2 Over what periods to allocate compensation expense.

Determining Expense

Under the fair-value method, companies compute total compensation expense based on the fair value of the options expected to vest on the date they grant the options to the employee(s) (i.e., the **grant date**).[7] Public companies estimate fair value by using an option pricing model, with some adjustments for the unique factors of employee stock options. No adjustments occur after the grant date in response to subsequent changes in the stock price—either up or down.

Allocating Compensation Expense

In general, a company recognizes compensation expense in the periods in which its employees perform the service—the **service period**. Unless otherwise specified, the service period is the vesting period—the time between the grant date and the vesting date. Thus, the company determines total compensation cost at the grant date and allocates it to the periods benefited by its employees' services.[8]

Stock Compensation Example

An example will help show the accounting for a stock option plan. Assume that on November 1, 2007, the stockholders of Chen Company approve a plan that grants the company's five executives options to purchase 2,000 shares each of the company's $1 par value common stock. The company grants the options on January 1, 2008. The executives may exercise the options at any time within the next 10 years. The option price per share is $60, and the market price of the stock at the date of grant is $60 per share.

Under the fair-value method, the company computes total compensation expense by applying an acceptable fair value option-pricing model (such as the Black-Scholes option-pricing model). To keep this illustration simple, we assume that the fair-value option-pricing model determines Chen's total compensation expense to be $220,000.

Basic Entries.   Under the fair-value method, a company recognizes the value of the options as an expense in the periods in which the employee performs services. In the case of Chen Company, assume that the expected period of benefit is two years, starting with the grant date. Chen would record the transactions related to this option contract as follows.

At date of grant (January 1, 2008)

No entry.

To record compensation expense for 2008 (December 31, 2008)

Compensation Expense ($220,000 ÷ 2)	110,000	
Paid-in Capital—Stock Options		110,000

To record compensation expense for 2009 (December 31, 2009)

Compensation Expense	110,000	
Paid-in Capital—Stock Options		110,000

[7]"To vest" means "to earn the rights to." An employee's award becomes vested at the date that the employee's right to receive or retain shares of stock or cash under the award is no longer contingent on remaining in the service of the employer.

[8]Note that stock options issued to *non-employees* in exchange for other goods or services must be recognized according to the fair value method in *SFAS 123(R)*.

As indicated, Chen allocates compensation expense evenly over the two-year service period.

Exercise. If Chen's executives exercise 2,000 of the 10,000 options (20 percent of the options) on June 1, 2011 (3 years and 5 months after date of grant), the company records the following journal entry.

June 1, 2011

Cash (2,000 × $60)	120,000	
Paid-in Capital—Stock Options (20% × $220,000)	44,000	
Common Stock (2,000 × $1.00)		2,000
Paid-in Capital in Excess of Par		162,000

Expiration. If Chen's executives fail to exercise the remaining stock options before their expiration date, the company transfers the balance in the Paid-in Capital—Stock Options account to a more properly titled paid-in capital account, such as Paid-in Capital from Expired Stock Options. Chen records this transaction at the date of expiration as follows.

January 1, 2018 (expiration date)

Paid-in Capital—Stock Options	176,000	
Paid-in Capital from Expired Stock Options (80% × $220,000)		176,000

Adjustment. An unexercised stock option does not nullify the need to record the costs of services received from executives and attributable to the stock option plan. Under GAAP, a company therefore does not adjust compensation expense upon expiration of the options.

However, if an employee forfeits a stock option because **the employee fails to satisfy a service requirement** (e.g., leaves employment), the company should adjust the estimate of compensation expense recorded in the current period (as a change in estimate). A company records this change in estimate by debiting Paid-in Capital—Stock Options and crediting Compensation Expense for the amount of cumulative compensation expense recorded to date (and decreasing compensation expense in the period of forfeiture.)

Employee Stock Purchase Plans

Employee stock purchase plans (ESPPs) generally permit all employees to purchase stock at a discounted price for a short period of time. The company often uses such plans to secure equity capital or induce widespread ownership of its common stock among employees. These plans are considered compensatory unless they satisfy *all three* conditions presented below:

1 Substantially all full-time employees may participate on an equitable basis.

2 The discount from market is small. That is, it does not exceed the per share amount of costs avoided by not having to raise cash in a public offering. If the amount of the discount is 5 percent or less, no compensation needs to be recorded.

3 The plan offers no substantive option feature.

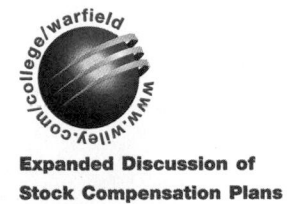

Expanded Discussion of Stock Compensation Plans

For example, Masthead Company's stock purchase plan allowed employees who met minimal employment qualifications to purchase its stock at a 5 percent reduction from market price for a short period of time. The reduction from market price is not considered compensatory. Why? Because the per share amount of the costs avoided by not having to raise the cash in a public offering equals 5 percent.

Companies that offer their employees a compensatory ESPP should record the compensation expense over the service life of the employees. It will be difficult for some companies to claim that their ESPP plans are non-compensatory (and that they need not record compensation expense) unless they change their discount policy, which in the past often was 15 percent. If they change their discount policy to 5 percent, participation in these plans will undoubtedly be lower. As a result, it is likely that some companies will end up dropping these plans.

Disclosure of Compensation Plans

Companies must fully disclose the status of their compensation plans at the end of the periods presented. To meet these objectives, extensive disclosures are required. Specifically, a company with one or more share-based payment arrangements must disclose information that enables users of the financial statements to understand:

1　The nature and terms of such arrangements that existed during the period and the potential effects of those arrangements on shareholders,

2　The effect of compensation cost arising from share-based payment arrangements on the income statement,

3　The method of estimating the fair value of the goods or services received, or the fair value of the equity instruments granted (or offered to grant), during the period,

4　The cash flow effects resulting from share-based payment arrangements.

Illustration 16-6 presents the type of information disclosed for compensation plans.

Illustration 16-6
Stock Option Plan
Disclosure

The Company has a share-based compensation plan. The compensation cost that has been charged against income for the plan was $29.4 million, and $28.7 million for 2008 and 2007, respectively.

　　The Company's 2008 Employee Share Option Plan (the Plan), which is shareholder-approved, permits the grant of share options and shares to its employees for up to 8 million shares of common stock. The Company believes that such awards better align the interests of its employees with those of its shareholders. Option awards are generally granted with an exercise price equal to the market price of the Company's stock at the date of grant; those option awards generally vest based on 5 years of continuous service and have 10-year contractual terms. Share awards generally vest over five years. Certain option and share awards provide for accelerated vesting if there is a change in control (as defined by the Plan).

　　The fair value of each option award is estimated on the date of grant using an option valuation model based on the assumptions noted in the following table.

	2008	2007
Expected volatility	25%–40%	24%–38%
Weighted-average volatility	33%	30%
Expected dividends	1.5%	1.5%
Expected term (in years)	5.3–7.8	5.5–8.0
Risk-free rate	6.3%–11.2%	6.0%–10.0%

　　A summary of option activity under the Plan as of December 31, 2008, and changes during the year then ended are presented below.

Options	Shares (000)	Weighted-Average Exercise Price	Weighted-Average Remaining Contractual Term	Aggregate Intrinsic Value ($000)
Outstanding at January 1, 2008	4,660	42		
Granted	950	60		
Exercised	(800)	36		
Forfeited or expired	(80)	59		
Outstanding at December 31, 2008	4,730	47	6.5	85,140
Exercisable at December 31, 2008	3,159	41	4.0	75,816

　　The weighted-average grant-date fair value of options granted during the years 2008 and 2007 was $19.57 and $17.46, respectively. The total intrinsic value of options exercised during the years ended December 31, 2008 and 2007, was $25.2 million, and $20.9 million, respectively.

　　As of December 31, 2008, there was $25.9 million of total unrecognized compensation cost related to nonvested share-based compensation arrangements granted under the Plan. That cost is expected to be recognized over a weighted-average period of 4.9 years. The total fair value of shares vested during the years ended December 31, 2008 and 2007, was $22.8 million and $21 million, respectively.

Debate over Stock Option Accounting

The FASB faced considerable opposition when it proposed the fair-value method for accounting for stock options. This is not surprising, given that the fair-value method results in greater compensation costs relative to the intrinsic-value model. As the *What Do the Numbers Mean?* box on page 849 indicated, one study documented that, on average, companies in the Standard & Poor's 500 stock index overstated earnings in a recent year by 10 percent through the use of the intrinsic-value method. Nevertheless, some companies such as **Coca-Cola**, **General Electric**, **Wachovia**, **Bank One**, and **The Washington Post**, decided to use the fair-value method. As the CFO of Coca-Cola stated, "There is no doubt that stock options are compensation. If they weren't, none of us would want them."

Yet many in corporate America resisted the fair-value method. Many small high-technology companies are especially vocal in their opposition, arguing that only through offering stock options can they attract top professional management. They contend that recognizing large amounts of compensation expense under these plans places them at a competitive disadvantage against larger companies that can withstand higher compensation charges. As one high-tech executive stated, "If your goal is to attack fat-cat executive compensation in multi-billion dollar firms, then please do so! But not at the expense of the people who are 'running lean and mean,' trying to build businesses and creating jobs in the process."

The stock-option saga is a classic example of the difficulty the FASB faces in issuing an accounting standard. Many powerful interests aligned against the Board. Even some who initially appeared to support the Board's actions later reversed themselves. These efforts undermine the authority of the FASB at a time when it is essential that we restore faith in our financial reporting system.

Transparent financial reporting—including recognition of stock-based expense—should not be criticized because companies will report lower income. We may not like what the financial statements say, but we are always better off when the statements are representationally faithful to the underlying economic substance of transactions.

By leaving stock-based compensation expense out of income, reported income is biased. Biased reporting not only raises concerns about the credibility of companies' reports, but also of financial reporting in general. And even good companies get tainted by biased reporting of a few "bad apples." If we write standards to achieve some social, economic, or public policy goal, financial reporting loses its credibility.

> **OBJECTIVE 3**
> Discuss the controversy involving stock compensation plans.

> **WHAT'S THE PRINCIPLE?**
> The stock option controversy involves economic consequence issues. The FASB believes that companies should follow the neutrality concept. Others disagree, noting that companies should consider factors other than accounting theory.

Try it out! On January 1, 2008, Sloan Company granted 20,000 options to executives. Each option entitles the holder to purchase one share of the company's $10 par value common stock at $30 per share at any time during the next 4 years. The service period for this award is 2 years. Assume the fair-value option pricing model determines that total compensation expense is $450,000. On March 1, 2010, employees exercised 14,000 options when the market price of Sloan's stock was $40 per share.

Instructions

Prepare Sloan's journal entries for January 1, 2008, December 31, 2008, and March 1, 2010.

Solution

January 1, 2008
No entry

December 31, 2008

Compensation Expense ($450,000 ÷ 2 years)	225,000	
Paid-in Capital—Stock Options		225,000

March 1, 2010

Cash (14,000 × $30)	420,000	
Paid-in Capital—Stock Options ($450,000 × 14/20)	315,000	
Common Stock (14,000 × $10)		140,000
Paid-in Capital in Excess of Par		595,000

POSTRETIREMENT BENEFITS

In addition to stock options, other long-term forms of compensation include pensions and other postretirement benefits, such as health care and social-welfare benefits. Many companies have pension plans that provide benefits (payments) to employees after they retire, for services provided while they worked. Pension plans are of two general types:

1 Defined-contribution plans

2 Defined-benefit plans

Defined-Contribution Plan

OBJECTIVE 4

Identify types of pension plans and their characteristics.

In a **defined-contribution plan**, the employer agrees to contribute to a pension trust a certain sum each period, based on a formula. This formula may consider such factors as age, length of employee service, employer's profits, and compensation level. **The plan defines only the employer's contribution**. It makes no promise regarding the ultimate benefits paid out to the employees. A common form of this plan is a **401(k) plan**.

What do the numbers mean?   Which Plan Is Right for You?

Defined-contribution plans, compared to defined-benefit plans, have become much more popular with employers. One reason is that defined-contributions plans are cheaper. It is estimated that defined-contribution plans often cost no more than 3 percent of payroll whereas defined-benefit plans can cost 5 to 6 percent of payroll.

In the late 1970s there were approximately 15 million individuals with defined-contribution plans; today there are over 62 million. This significant change is reflected in the following chart that shows the percentage of companies using various types of plans based on a survey of approximately 150 CFOs and managing corporate directors

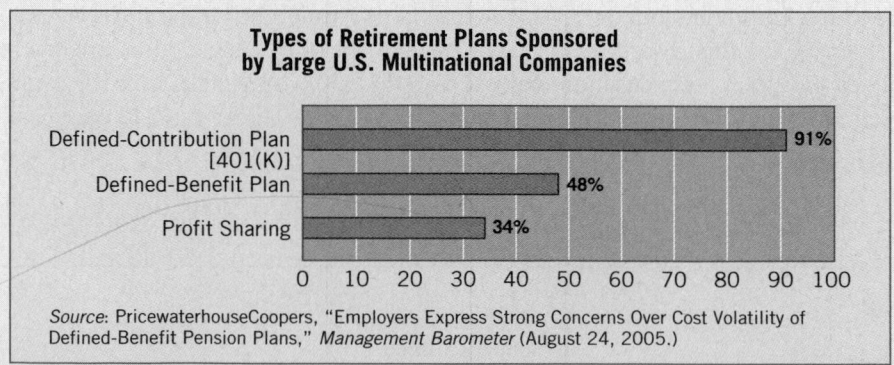

Types of Retirement Plans Sponsored by Large U.S. Multinational Companies

Source: PricewaterhouseCoopers, "Employers Express Strong Concerns Over Cost Volatility of Defined-Benefit Pension Plans," *Management Barometer* (August 24, 2005.)

Although many companies are changing to defined-contribution plans, over 40 million individuals are covered under defined-benefit plans.

Beyond the Numbers

Another recent trend in the labor market is the mobility of workers. Today, workers expect to work for several employers during their careers. This is in contrast to the post-World War II economy in which most employees expected to sign on with one employer for their entire career. Assuming you are a member of this more mobile workforce, which plan would you prefer? Explain.

The size of the pension benefits that the employee finally collects under the plan depends on several factors: the amounts originally contributed to the pension trust, the income accumulated in the trust, and the treatment of forfeitures of funds caused by early terminations of other employees. A company usually turns over to an **independent third-party trustee** the amounts originally contributed. The trustee, acting on behalf of the beneficiaries (the participating employees), assumes ownership of the pension assets and is accountable for their investment and distribution. The trust is separate and distinct from the employer.

The accounting for a defined-contribution plan is straightforward. The employee gets the benefit of gain (or the risk of loss) from the assets contributed to the pension plan. The employer simply contributes each year based on the formula established in the plan. As a result, the employer's annual cost (pension expense) is simply the amount that it is obligated to contribute to the pension trust. The employer reports a liability on its balance sheet only if does not make the contribution in full. The employer reports an asset only if the company contributes more than the required amount.

In addition to pension expense, the employer must disclose the following under a defined-contribution plan: a plan description, including employee groups covered; the basis for determining contributions; and the nature and effect of significant matters affecting comparability from period to period.[9]

Disclosures for Defined-Contribution Plans

Defined-Benefit Plan

A **defined-benefit plan** outlines the benefits that the employee will receive at the time of retirement. These benefits typically are a function of the employee's years of service and the employee's compensation level when he or she nears retirement.

To meet the pension benefit commitments that will arise at retirement, a company must determine what the contribution should be today (a time value of money computation). Companies may use many different contribution approaches. However, the funding method should provide enough money at retirement to meet the benefits defined by the plan.

The employees are the beneficiaries of a defined-contribution trust, but the employer is the beneficiary of a defined-benefit trust. Under a defined-benefit plan, the trust's primary purpose is to safeguard and invest assets so that there will be enough to pay the employer's obligation to the employees. **In form**, the trust is a separate entity. **In substance**, the trust assets and liabilities belong to the employer. That is, **as long as the plan continues, the employer is responsible for the payment of the defined benefits (without regard to what happens in the trust).** The employer must make up any shortfall in the accumulated assets held by the trust. On the other hand, the employer can recapture any excess accumulated in the trust, either through reduced future funding or through a reversion of funds.

Because a defined-benefit plan specifies benefits in terms of uncertain future variables, a company must establish an appropriate funding pattern to ensure the availability of funds at retirement to provide the benefits promised. This funding level depends on a number of factors such as turnover, mortality, length of employee service, compensation levels, and interest earnings.

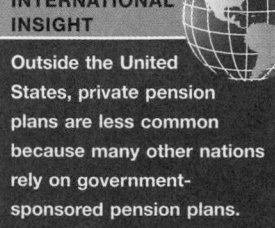

INTERNATIONAL INSIGHT

Outside the United States, private pension plans are less common because many other nations rely on government-sponsored pension plans. Consequently, accounting for defined-benefit pension plans is typically a less important issue elsewhere.

---

[9]"Employers' Accounting for Pension Plans," *Statement of Financial Accounting Standards No. 87* (Stamford, Conn.: FASB, 1985), pars. 63–66.

Employers are at risk with defined-benefit plans because they must contribute enough to meet the cost of benefits that the plan defines. The expense recognized each period is not necessarily equal to the cash contribution. Similarly, the liability is controversial because its measurement and recognition relate to unknown future variables. Thus, the accounting issues related to this type of plan are complex. **Our discussion in the following sections deals primarily with defined-benefit plans.**

Components of Pension Expense

OBJECTIVE **5**

List the components of pension expense.

There is broad agreement that companies should account for pension cost on the **accrual basis**.[10] The profession recognizes that **accounting for pension plans requires measurement of the cost and its identification with the appropriate time periods**. The determination of pension cost, however, is extremely complicated because it is a function of the following components.

1 Service Cost. Service cost is the expense caused by the increase in pension benefits payable—the **projected benefit obligation**—to employees because of their services rendered during the current year. Actuaries[11] compute **service cost** as the present value of the new benefits earned by employees during the year.

2 Interest on the Liability. Because a pension is a deferred compensation arrangement, there is a time value of money factor. As a result, companies record it on a discounted basis. **Interest expense accrues each year on the projected benefit obligation just as it does on any discounted debt.** The actuary helps to select the interest rate, referred to as the **settlement rate**.

WHAT'S THE PRINCIPLE?

The matching concept and the definition of a liability justify accounting for pension cost on the accrual basis. This requires recording an expense when employees earn the future benefits, and recognizing an existing obligation to pay pensions later based on current services received.

3 Return on Plan Assets. The return earned by the accumulated pension fund assets in a particular year is relevant in measuring the net cost to the employer of sponsoring an employee pension plan. Therefore, **a company should adjust annual pension expense for interest and dividends that accumulate within the fund, as well as increases and decreases in the market value of the fund assets**.

4 Amortization of Prior Service Cost. Pension plan amendments (including initiation of a pension plan) often include provisions to increase benefits (or in rare situations, to decrease benefits) for employee service provided in prior years. A company grants plan amendments with the expectation that it will realize economic benefits in future periods. Thus, **it allocates the cost (prior service cost) of providing these retroactive benefits to pension expense in the future, specifically to the remaining service-years of the affected employees**.

5 Gain or Loss. Volatility in pension expense can result from sudden and large changes in the market value of plan assets and by changes in the projected benefit obligation (which changes when actuaries modify assumptions or when actual experience differs from expected experience). Two items comprise this gain or loss: (1) the difference between the actual return and the expected return on plan assets, and (2) amortization of the net gain or loss from previous periods. We will discuss this complex computation later in the chapter.

---

[10]Until the mid-1960s, with few exceptions, companies applied the **cash basis** of accounting to pension plans by recognizing the amount paid in a particular accounting period as the pension expense for the period. The problem was that the amount paid or funded in a fiscal period depended on financial management and was too often discretionary. For example, funding could depend on the availability of cash, the level of earnings, or other factors unrelated to the requirements of the plan. Application of the cash basis made it possible to manipulate the amount of pension expense appearing in the income statement simply by varying the cash paid to the pension fund.

[11]Actuaries train through a long and rigorous certification program to assign probabilities to future events and their financial effects. The insurance industry employs actuaries to assess risks and to advise on the setting of premiums and other aspects of insurance policies. Employers rely heavily on actuaries for assistance in developing, implementing, and funding pension plans.

Illustration 16-7 shows the **components of pension expense** and their effect on total pension expense (increase or decrease).

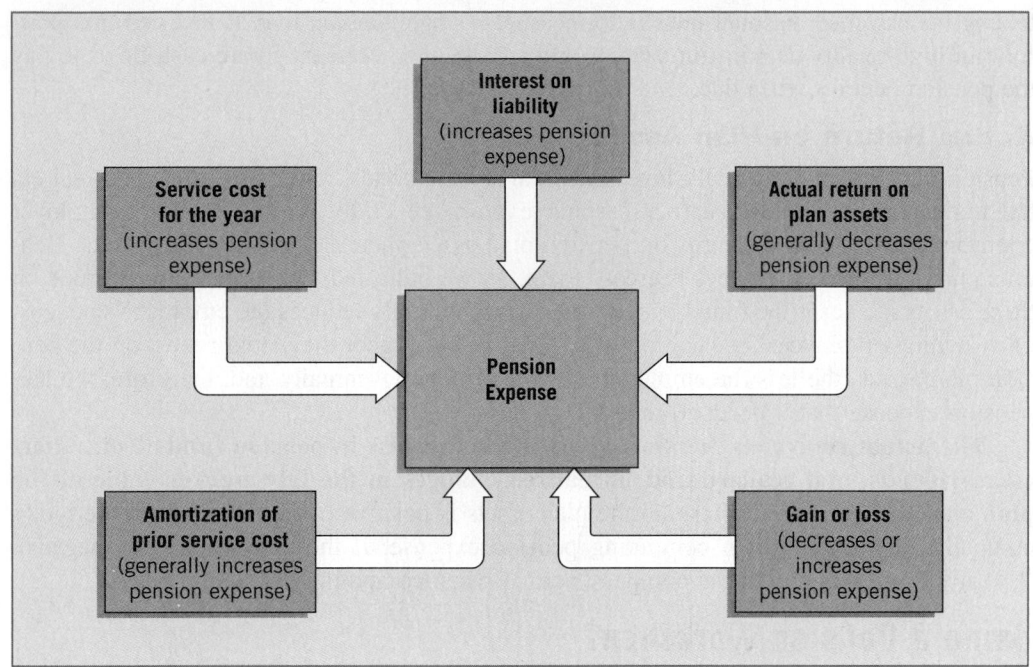

Illustration 16-7
Components of Annual Pension Expense

Service Cost

The **service cost** component recognized in a period is the **actuarial present value of benefits attributed by the pension benefit formula to employee service during the period**. That is, the actuary predicts the additional benefits that an employer must pay under the plan's benefit formula as a result of the employees' current year's service, and then discounts the cost of those future benefits back to their present value.

The Board concluded that **companies must consider future compensation levels in measuring the present obligation and periodic pension expense if the plan benefit formula incorporates them**. In other words, the present obligation resulting from a promise to pay a benefit of 1 percent of an employee's **final pay** differs from the promise to pay 1 percent of **current pay**. To overlook this fact is to ignore an important aspect of pension expense. Thus, FASB adopts the **benefits/years-of-service actuarial method**, which determines pension expense based on future salary levels.

Some object to this determination, arguing that a company should have more freedom to select an expense recognition pattern. Others believe that incorporating future salary increases into current pension expense is accounting for events that have not yet happened. They argue that if a company terminates the plan today, it pays only liabilities for accumulated benefits. **Nevertheless, the FASB indicates that the projected benefit obligation provides a more realistic measure of the employer's obligation under the plan on a going-concern basis and, therefore, companies should use it as the basis for determining service cost.**

Interest on the Liability

The second component of pension expense is **interest on the liability**, or **interest expense**. Because a company defers paying the liability until maturity, the company records it on a discounted basis. The liability then accrues interest over the life of the employee. **The interest component is the interest for the period on the projected benefit obligation outstanding during the period.** The FASB did not address the question of how often to compound the interest cost. To simplify our illustrations and problem materials, we use a simple interest computation, applying it to the beginning-of-the-year balance of the projected benefit liability.

How do companies determine the interest rate to apply to the pension liability? The Board states that the assumed discount rate should **reflect the rates at which companies can**

effectively settle pension benefits. In determining these **settlement rates**, companies should look to rates of return on high quality fixed-income investments currently available, whose cash flows match the timing and amount of expected benefit payments. The objective of selecting the assumed discount rates is to measure a single amount that, if invested in a portfolio of high-quality debt instruments, would provide the necessary future cash flows to pay the pension benefits when due.

Actual Return on Plan Assets

Pension plan assets are usually investments in stocks, bonds, other securities, and real estate that a company holds to earn a reasonable return, generally at minimum risk. Employer contributions and actual returns on pension plan assets increase pension plan assets. Benefits paid to retired employees decrease them. As we indicated, the actual return earned on these assets increases the fund balance and correspondingly reduces the employer's net cost of providing employees' pension benefits. That is, the higher the actual return on the pension plan assets, the less the employer has to contribute eventually and, therefore, the less pension expense that it needs to report.

The actual return on the plan assets is the increase in pension funds from interest, dividends, and realized and unrealized changes in the fair-market value of the plan assets. If the actual return on the plan assets is positive (a gain) during the period, a company subtracts it when computing pension expense. If the actual return is negative (a loss) during the period, the company adds it when computing pension expense.[12]

OBJECTIVE 6

Utilize a worksheet for employer's pension plan entries.

Using a Pension Worksheet

We will now illustrate the basic computation of pension expense using the first three components: service cost, (2) interest on the liability, and (3) actual return on plan assets. We discuss the other pension-expense components (amortization of prior service cost and gains and losses) in later sections. Companies often use a worksheet to record pension-related information. As its name suggests, the worksheet is a working tool. A worksheet is *not* a permanent accounting record: it is neither a journal nor part of the general ledger. The worksheet is merely a device to make it easier to prepare entries and the financial statements.[13] Illustration 16-8 shows the format of the **pension worksheet**.

Illustration 16-8
Basic Format of Pension Worksheet

The "General Journal Entries" columns of the worksheet (middle columns) determine the entries to record in the formal general ledger accounts. The "Memo Record" columns (on the right side) maintain balances in the projected benefit obligation and the plan assets. The difference between the projected benefit obligation and the fair value of the plan assets is the **pension asset/liability**, which is shown in the balance sheet. If the projected benefit obligation is greater than the plan assets, a pension liability occurs. If the projected benefit obligation is less that the plan assets, a pension asset occurs.

---

[12]At this point, we use the actual rate of return. Later, for purposes of computing pension expense, we use the expected rate of return.

[13]The use of this pension entry worksheet is recommended and illustrated by Paul B. W. Miller, "The New Pension Accounting (Part 2)," *Journal of Accountancy* (February 1987), pp. 86–94.

On the first line of the worksheet, a company records the beginning balances (if any). The company records subsequent transactions and events related to the pension plan using debits and credits, and using both sets of columns as if they were one. For each transaction or event, the debits must equal the credits. **The ending balance in the Pension Asset/Liability column should equal the net balance in the memo record.**

2008 Entries and Worksheet

To illustrate the use of a worksheet and how it helps in accounting for a pension plan, assume that on January 1, 2008, Zarle Company adopts a defined-benefit pension plan under *SFAS No. 158*. The following facts apply to the pension plan for the year 2008.

Plan assets, January 1, 2008: $100,000.

Projected benefit obligation, January 1, 2008 is $100,000.

Annual service cost is $9,000.

Settlement rate is 10%.

Actual return on plan assets is $10,000.

Funding contributions are $8,000.

Benefits paid to retirees during the year are $7,000.

Using the data presented above, the worksheet in Illustration 16-9 presents the beginning balances and all of the pension entries recorded by Zarle in 2008. Zarle records the beginning balances for the projected benefit obligation and the pension plan assets on the first line of the worksheet in the memo record. Because the projected benefit obligation and the plan assets are the same at January 1, 2008, the Pension Asset/Liability account has a zero balance at January 1, 2008.

Illustration 16-9

Pension Worksheet—2008

	A	B	C	D	F	G
1		General Journal Entries			Memo Record	
2	Items	Annual Pension Expense	Cash	Pension Asset/ Liability	Projected Benefit Obligation	Plan Assets
3	Balance, Jan. 1, 2008			—	100,000 Cr.	100,000 Dr.
4	(a) Service cost	9,000 Dr.			9,000 Cr.	
5	(b) Interest cost	10,000 Dr.			10,000 Cr.	
6	(c) Actual return	10,000 Cr.				10,000 Dr.
7	(d) Contributions		8,000 Cr.			8,000 Dr.
8	(e) Benefits				7,000 Dr.	7,000 Cr.
9	Journal entry for 2008	9,000 Dr.	8,000 Cr.	1,000 Cr.*		
10	Balance, Dec. 31, 2008			1,000 Cr.**	112,000 Cr.	111,000 Dr.
11						
12	*$9,000 – $8,000 = $1,000					
13	**$112,000 – $111,000 = $1,000					

Entry (a) in Illustration 16-9 records the service cost component, which increases pension expense by $9,000 and increases the liability (projected benefit obligation) by $9,000. Entry (b) accrues the interest expense component, which increases both the liability and the pension expense by $10,000 (the beginning projected benefit obligation multiplied by the settlement rate of 10%). Entry (c) records the actual return on the plan assets, which increases the plan assets and decreases the pension expense. Entry (d) records Zarle's contribution (funding) of assets to the pension fund, thereby decreasing cash by $8,000 and increasing plan assets by $8,000. Entry (e) records the benefit payments made to retirees, which results in equal $7,000 decreases to the plan assets and the projected benefit obligation.

Zarle makes the "formal journal entry" on December 31, which records the pension expense in 2008, as follows.

2008

Pension Expense	9,000	
Cash		8,000
Pension Asset/Liability		1,000

The credit to Pension Asset/Liability for $1,000 represents the difference between the 2008 pension expense of $9,000 and the amount funded of $8,000. Pension Asset/Liability (credit) is a liability because Zarle underfunds the plan by $1,000. The Pension Asset/Liability account balance of $1,000 also equals the net of the balances in the memo accounts. Illustration 16-10 shows that the projected benefit obligation exceeds the plan assets by $1,000, which reconciles to the pension liability reported in the balance sheet.

Illustration 16-10
Pension Reconciliation
Schedule—December 31,
2008

Projected benefit obligation (Credit)	$(112,000)
Plan assets at fair value (Debit)	111,000
Pension asset/liability	$ (1,000)

If the net of the memo record balances is a credit, the reconciling amount in the pension asset/liability column will be a credit equal in amount. If the net of the memo record balances is a debit, the pension asset/liability amount will be a debit equal in amount. The worksheet is designed to produce this reconciling feature, which is useful later in the preparation of the required note disclosures related to pension disclosures.

In this illustration (for 2008), the debit to Pension Expense exceeds the credit to Cash, resulting in a credit to Pension Asset/Liability—the recognition of a liability. If the credit to Cash exceeded the debit to Pension Expense, Zarle would debit Pension Asset/Liability—the recognition of an asset.

Amortization of Prior Service Cost (PSC)

OBJECTIVE 7

Explain the accounting for prior service cost and gains and losses.

When either initiating (adopting) or amending a defined-benefit plan, a company often credits employees for years of service provided before the date of initiation or amendment. As a result of prior service credits, the projected benefit obligation is increased to recognize this additional liability. In many cases, the increase in the projected benefit obligation is substantial.

Should a company report an expense for these **prior service costs (PSC)** at the time it initiates or amends a plan? The FASB says no. The Board's rationale is that the employer would not provide credit for past years of service unless it expects to receive benefits in the future. As a result, a company should not recognize the **retroactive benefits** as pension expense entirely in the year of amendment. **Instead, the employer initially records the prior service cost as an adjustment to other comprehensive income.**[14] **The employer then recognizes the prior service cost as a component of pension expense** during the service periods of those employees who it expects to receive benefits from under the plan.

The cost of the retroactive benefits (including benefits provided to existing retirees) is the increase in the projected benefit obligation at the date of the amendment. An actuary computes the amount of the prior service cost. Amortization of the prior service cost is also an accounting function performed with the assistance of an actuary. The amortization of the prior service cost is based on the average remaining service of employees in the plan (referred to as the **years-of-service method**).

---

[14]"Employers' Accounting for Defined Benefit Pension and Other Postretirement Benefit Plans: An amendment of SFAS Nos. 87, 106, and 132 (R)," *Statement of Financial Accounting Standards No. 158* (Norwalk, Conn.: FASB, 2006). Prior to *SFAS No. 158* prior service costs and unexpected gains and losses (discussed in the next section) were recorded in the Memo Record (off–balance-sheet).

Gain or Loss

Of great concern to companies that have pension plans are the uncontrollable and unexpected swings in pension expense that can result from (1) sudden and large changes in the market value of plan assets, and (2) changes in actuarial assumptions that affect the amount of the projected benefit obligation. If these gains or losses impact fully the financial statements in the period of realization or incurrence, substantial fluctuations in pension expense result.

Therefore, the FASB decided to reduce the volatility associated with pension expense by using **smoothing techniques** that dampen and in some cases fully eliminate the fluctuations.

Smoothing Unexpected Gains and Losses on Plan Assets. One component of pension expense, actual return on plan assets, reduces pension expense (assuming the actual return is positive). A large change in the actual return can substantially affect pension expense for a year. Assume a company has a 40 percent return in the stock market for the year. Should this substantial, and perhaps one-time, event affect current pension expense?

Actuaries ignore current fluctuations when they develop a funding pattern to pay expected benefits in the future. They develop an **expected rate of return** and multiply it by an asset value weighted over a reasonable period of time to arrive at an **expected return on plan assets**. They then use this return to determine its funding pattern.

The FASB adopted the actuary's approach to dampen wide swings that might occur in the actual return. That is, a company includes the **expected return** on the plan assets as a component of pension expense, not the actual return in a given year. To achieve this goal, the company multiplies the expected rate of return by the market-related asset value of the plan assets. The **market-related asset value is either a fair value or a calculated value that recognizes changes in fair value in a systematic and rational manner.**[15]

The difference between the expected return and the actual return is referred to as the **unexpected gain or loss**; the FASB uses the term **asset gains and losses**. **Asset gains** occur when actual return exceeds expected return; **asset losses** occur when actual return is less than expected return.

What do the numbers mean? | Pension Costs Ups And Downs

For some companies, pension plans generated real profits in the late 1990s. The plans not only paid for themselves but also increased earnings. This happens when the expected returns on pension assets exceed the company's annual costs. At **Norfolk Southern**, pension income amounted to 12 percent of operating profit. It tallied 11 percent of such profit at **Lucent Technologies, Coastal Corp.,** and **Unisys Corp.** The issue is important because in these cases management is not driving the operating income— pension income is. And as a result, income can change quickly.

Unfortunately, the stock market stopped booming, substantially increasing pension expense for many companies. The reason: Expected return on a smaller asset base no longer offsets pension service costs and interest on the projected benefit obligation. As a result, many companies are finding it difficult to meet their earnings targets.

Beyond the Numbers

What are some pension asset management strategies that a company could pursue to improve the pension income (return on assets) element of its pension expense?

---

[15]*FASB Statement No. 87,* par. 30. Companies may use different ways of determining the calculated market-related value for different classes of assets. For example, an employer might use fair value for bonds and a five-year-moving-average for equities. But companies should consistently apply the manner of determining market-related value from year to year for each asset class. Throughout our Zarle illustrations, we assume that market-related values based on a calculated value and the fair value of plan assets are equal. *For homework purposes, use the fair value of plan assets as the measure for the market-related value.*

What happens to unexpected gains or losses in the accounting for pensions? Companies record asset gains and asset losses in an account, **Other Comprehensive Income (G/L)**, combining them with gains and losses accumulated in prior years.[16]

Smoothing Unexpected Gains and Losses on the Pension Liability. In estimating the projected benefit obligation (the liability), actuaries make assumptions about such items as mortality rate, retirement rate, turnover rate, disability rate, and salary amounts. Any change in these actuarial assumptions affects the amount of the projected benefit obligation. Seldom does actual experience coincide exactly with actuarial predictions. These unexpected gains or losses from changes in the projected benefit obligation are called **liability gains and losses**.

Companies report liability gains (resulting from unexpected decreases in the liability balance) and liability losses (resulting from unexpected increases) in Other Comprehensive Income (G/L). Companies combine the liability gains and losses in the same Other Comprehensive Income (G/L) account used for asset gains and losses. They accumulate in Accumulated Other Comprehensive Income the asset and liability gains and losses from year to year that are not amortized. This amount is reported on the balance sheet in the stockholders' equity section.

2009 Entries and Worksheet

Continuing the Zarle illustration into 2009, we note that the company amends the pension plan on January 1, 2009, to grant employees prior service benefits with a present value of $80,000. The following facts apply to the pension plan for the year 2009.

Annual service cost is $9,500.

Settlement rate is 10%.

Expected rate of return on pension assets is 9%.

Actual return on plan assets is $11,100.

Annual funding contributions are $20,000.

Benefits paid to retirees during the year are $8,000.

Amortization of prior service cost (PSC) using the years-of-service method: $27,200.

Accumulated other comprehensive income (hereafter referred to as accumulated OCI) on December 31, 2008, is zero.

Illustration 16-11 (page 863) presents a worksheet of all the pension entries and information recorded by Zarle in 2009. We now add two additional columns to the worksheet to record the prior service cost and gains/losses adjustments to other comprehensive income. In addition, as shown in the last two lines of the "Items" column, the other comprehensive income amount related to prior service cost and the gains/losses adjust accumulated other comprehensive income ("Accumulated OCI").

The first line of the worksheet shows the beginning balances of the Pension Asset/ Liability account and the memo accounts. Entry (f) records Zarle's granting of prior service cost, by adding $80,000 to the projected benefit obligation and decreasing other comprehensive income—prior service cost by the same amount. Entries (g), (h), (l), and (m) are similar to the corresponding entries in 2008. To compute the interest cost on the projected benefit obligation for entry (h), we use the beginning projected benefit balance of $192,000, which has been adjusted for the prior service cost amendment on January 1, 2009.

Entries (i) and (j) are related: We illustrated recording the actual return in entry (i) in 2008. Zarle records it similarly in 2009. In 2008 Zarle assumed that the actual return on plan assets equaled the expected return on plan assets. In 2009, the actual return of $11,100 is greater than the expected return of $9,990 (the expected rate of return of 9 percent times

---

[16]"Employers' Accounting for Defined Benefit Pension and Other Postretirement Benefit Plans: An amendment of SFAS Nos. 87, 106, and 132 (R)," *Statement of Financial Accounting Standards No. 158* (Norwalk, Conn.: FASB, 2006).

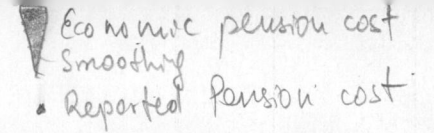
Economic pension cost
Smoothing
• Reported Pension cost

Pension Worksheet–2009

	A	B	C	D	E	F	H	I
1				Other Comprehensive Income			Projected	
2	Items	Annual Pension Expense	Cash	Prior Service Cost	Gains/ Losses	Pension Asset/ Liability	Projected Benefit Obligation	Plan Assets
3	Balance, Dec. 31, 2008			0		1,000 Cr.	112,000 Cr.	111,000 Dr.
4	(f) Prior service cost			80,000 Dr.			80,000 Cr.	0
5								
6	Balance, Jan. 1, 2009						192,000 Cr.	111,000 Dr.
7	(g) Service cost	9,500 Dr.					9,500 Cr.	
8	(h) Interest cost	19,200 Dr.					19,200 Cr.	
9	(i) Actual return	11,100 Cr.						11,100 Dr.
10	(j) Unexpected gain	1,110 Dr.			1,110 Cr.			
11	(k) Amortization of PSC	27,200 Dr.		27,200 Cr.				
12	(l) Contributions		20,000 Cr.					20,000 Dr.
13	(m) Benefits						8,000 Dr.	8,000 Cr.
14								
15	Journal entry for 2009	45,910 Dr.	20,000 Cr.	52,800 Dr.	1,110 Cr.	77,600 Cr.		
16								
17	Accumulated OCI, Dec. 31, 2008			0	0			
18	Balance, Dec. 31, 2009			52,800 Dr.	1,110 Cr.	78,600 Cr.	212,700 Cr.	134,100 Dr.

Sheet1 / Sheet2 / Sheet3

Illustration 16-11
Pension Worksheet—2009

the beginning-of-the-year plan assets balance of $111,000). To smooth pension expense, Zarle defers the unexpected gain of $1,110 ($11,100 − $9,990) by crediting the Other Comprehensive Income (G/L) account and debiting Pension Expense.[17] **As a result of this adjustment, the expected return on the plan assets is the amount actually used to compute pension expense.**

Entry (k) records the 2009 amortization of prior service cost by debiting Pension Expense by $27,200 and crediting the new **Other Comprehensive Income (PSC)** account by the same amount. Entries (l) and (m) are similar to the corresponding entries in 2008.

Zarle makes the following journal entry on December 31 to formally record the 2009 pension expense (the sum of the pension expense column) and related pension information.

2009

Pension Expense	45,910	
Other Comprehensive Income (PSC)	52,800	
Other Comprehensive Income (G/L)		1,110
Cash		20,000
Pension Asset/Liability		77,600

Because the debits to Pension Expense and Other Comprehensive Income (PSC) exceed the funding, Zarle credits the Pension Asset/Liability account for the $77,600 difference. That account is a liability. In 2009, as in 2008, the balance of the Pension Asset/Liability account ($78,600) equals the net of the balances in the memo accounts, as shown in Illustration 16-12.

Projected benefit obligation (Credit)	$(212,700)
Plan assets at fair value (Debit)	134,100
Pension asset/liability	$ (78,600)

Illustration 16-12
Pension Reconciliation Schedule—December 31, 2009

[17]What happens to the gain or loss over time? Because the asset gains and losses can offset the liability gain and losses, the accumulated net gain or loss may not grow very large. But, it is possible that no offsetting will occur, thus allowing the balance in the Net Gain or Loss account to continue to grow. To limit its growth, the FASB has developed approaches to amortize the gain or loss if it gets too large. These approaches are complex and beyond the scope of this text.

The reconciliation is the formula that makes the worksheet work; it relates the components of pension accounting, recorded and unrecorded, to one another.

Reporting Pension Amounts

As you might suspect, a phenomenon as significant and complex as pensions involves extensive reporting and disclosure requirements. We will cover these requirements in two categories: (1) those within the financial statements, and (2) those within the notes to the financial statements.

Within the Financial Statements

Recognition of the Net Funded Status of the Pension Plan.   As required by *SFAS No. 158,* companies recognize on their balance sheet the overfunded or underfunded status of their defined-benefit pension plan. The overfunded or underfunded status—the **net funded status**—is measured as the difference between the fair value of the plan assets and the projected benefit obligation.

The reporting of the funded position of the plan in the balance sheet results because actuarial gains and losses and prior service costs are now recognized in other comprehensive income. Under *SFAS Nos. 87* and *106,* these amounts were not recognized. Under *SFAS No. 158,* actuarial gains and losses and prior service costs will be reflected in the projected benefit obligation and plan assets, with corresponding entries in other comprehensive income.

It should be emphasized that there will be little or no impact on pension expense. This is because the amortization provisions, as articulated in *SFAS Nos. 87* and *106* for actuarial gains and losses and prior service costs, are not changed. In addition, the computation of the other components of pension expense, such as service cost and interest on the projected benefit obligation, still follow the guidelines established in *SFAS Nos. 87* and *106.*

Classification of Pension Asset or Pension Liability.   As indicated, the funded status of the pension plan is reported in the balance sheet. No portion of a pension asset is reported as a current asset. The excess of the fair value of the plan assets over the benefit obligation is classified as a noncurrent asset. The rationale for noncurrent classification is that the pension plan assets are restricted. That is, these assets are used to fund the projected benefit obligation, and therefore noncurrent classification is appropriate.

The current portion of a net pension liability represents the amount of benefit payments to be paid in the next 12 months (or operating cycle, if longer), if that amount cannot be funded from existing plan assets. Otherwise, the pension liability is classified as a noncurrent liability.

Aggregation of Pension Plans.   Some companies have two or more pension plans. In such instances, a question arises as to whether these multiple plans should be combined and shown as one amount on the balance sheet. The Board takes the position that **all overfunded plans should be combined** and shown as a pension asset on the balance sheet. Similarly, if the company has two or more underfunded plans, it combines the **underfunded plans and shows them as one amount** on the balance sheet.

The FASB rejected the alternative of combining *all* plans and representing the net amount as a single net asset or net liability. The rationale: A company does not have the ability to offset excess assets of one plan against underfunded obligations of another plan. Furthermore, netting all plans is inappropriate because offsetting assets and liabilities is not permitted under GAAP unless a right of offset exists.

Actuarial Gains and Losses/Prior Service Costs.   Actuarial gains and losses not recognized as part of pension expense are recognized as increases and decreases in other comprehensive income. The same type of accounting is also used for prior service cost. The Board requires that the prior service cost arising in the year of the amendment (which increases the projected benefit obligation) be recognized by an offsetting debit to other comprehensive income. By recognizing both actuarial gains and losses and prior service cost as part of other comprehensive income, the Board believes that the usefulness of financial statements is enhanced.

To illustrate the presentation of other comprehensive income and related accumulated OCI, assume that Obey Company provides the following information for the year 2008. None of the Accumulated OCI on January 1, 2008, should be amortized in 2008.

Net income for 2008	$100,000
Actuarial liability loss for 2008	60,000
Prior service cost adjustment to provide additional	
benefits in December 2008	15,000
Accumulated OCI, January 1, 2008	40,000

Both the actuarial liability loss and the prior service cost adjustment decrease the funded status of the plan on the balance sheet. This results because the projected benefit obligation increases. However, neither the actuarial liability loss nor the prior service cost adjustment affects pension expense in 2008. In subsequent periods, these items will impact pension expense through amortization. For Obey Company, the computation of "Other comprehensive loss" for 2008 is as follows.

Actuarial liability loss	$60,000
Prior service cost adjustment	15,000
Other comprehensive loss	$75,000

Illustration 16-13
Computation of Other
Comprehensive Loss

The computation of "Comprehensive income" for 2008 is as follows.

Net income	$100,000
Other comprehensive loss	75,000
Comprehensive income	$ 25,000

Illustration 16-14
Computation of
Comprehensive Income

The components of other comprehensive income must be reported in one of three ways: (1) in a second income statement, (2) in a combined statement of comprehensive income, or (3) as a part of the statement of stockholders' equity. Regardless of the format used, net income must be added to other comprehensive income to arrive at comprehensive income. *For homework purposes*, use the second income statement approach unless stated otherwise. Earnings per share information related to comprehensive income is not required.

To illustrate the second income statement approach, assume that Obey Company has reported a traditional income statement. The comprehensive income statement is shown in Illustration 16-15.

Illustration 16-15
Comprehensive Income
Reporting

Obey Company		
Comprehensive Income Statement		
For the Year Ended December 31, 2008		
Net Income		$100,000
Other comprehensive loss		
Actuarial liability loss	$60,000	
Prior service cost	15,000	75,000
Comprehensive income		$ 25,000

The computation of "Accumulated other comprehensive income" as reported in stockholders' equity at December 31, 2008, is as follows.

Illustration 16-16
Computation of
Accumulated Other
Comprehensive Income

Accumulated other comprehensive income, January 1, 2008	$40,000
Other comprehensive loss	75,000
Accumulated other comprehensive loss, December 31, 2008	$35,000

Regardless of the display format for the income statement, the accumulated other comprehensive loss is reported on the stockholders' equity section of the balance sheet of Obey Company as shown in Illustration 16-17. (Illustration 16-17 uses assumed data for the common stock and retained earnings information.)

Illustration 16-17
Reporting of
Accumulated OCI

Obey Company
Balance Sheet
December 31, 2008
(Stockholder's Equity Section)

Stockholders' equity	
Common stock	$100,000
Retained earnings	60,000
Accumulated other comprehensive loss	35,000
Total stockholders' equity	$125,000

By providing information on the components of comprehensive income as well as total accumulated other comprehensive income, the company communicates all changes in net assets. In this illustration, it is assumed that the accumulated other comprehensive income at January 1, 2008, is not adjusted for the amortization of any prior service cost or actuarial gains and losses that would change pension expense. As discussed earlier, these items will be amortized into pension expense in future periods.

Within the Notes to the Financial Statements

Pension plans are frequently important to an understanding of financial position, results of operations, and cash flows of a company. Therefore, a company discloses the following information, either in the body of the financial statements or in the notes. [18]

1 A schedule showing all the major components of pension expense.
Rationale: Information provided about the components of pension expense helps users better understand how a company determines pension expense. It also is useful in forecasting a company's net income.

2 A **reconciliation** showing how the projected benefit obligation and the fair value of the plan assets changed from the beginning to the end of the period.

---

[18]"Employers' Accounting for Defined Benefit Pension and Other Postretirement Benefit Plans: An amendment of SFAS Nos. 87, 106, and 132 (R)," *Statement of Financial Accounting Standards No. 158* (Norwalk, Conn.: FASB, 2006) and "Employers' Disclosure about Pensions and Other Postretirement Benefits," *Statement of Financial Accounting Standards No. 132* (Stamford, Conn.: FASB, 1998). These statements modify the disclosure requirements of *SFAS No. 87*. In our view, these new disclosure requirements improve the transparency of information related to pensions and other post-employment benefits by requiring companies to provide more details about their plan assets, benefit obligations, cash flows, and benefit costs.

Rationale: Disclosing the projected benefit obligation, the fair value of the plan assets, and changes in them should help users understand the economics underlying the obligations and resources of these plans. Explaining the changes in the projected benefit obligation and fair value of plan assets in the form of a reconciliation provides a more complete disclosure and makes the financial statements more understandable.

3 A disclosure of the rates used in measuring the benefit amounts (discount rate, expected return on plan assets, rate of compensation).

Rationale: Disclosure of these rates permits users to determine the reasonableness of the assumptions applied in measuring the pension liability and pension expense.

4 A table indicating the allocation of pension plan assets by category (equity securities, debt securities, real estate, and other assets), and showing the percentage of the fair value to total plan assets. In addition, a company must include a narrative description of investment policies and strategies, including the target allocation percentages (if used by the company).

Rationale: Such information helps financial statement users evaluate the pension plan's exposure to market risk and possible cash flow demands on the company. It also will help users better assess the reasonableness of the company's expected rate of return assumption.

5 The **expected benefit payments** to be paid to current plan participants for each of the next five fiscal years and in the aggregate for the five fiscal years thereafter. Also required is disclosure of a company's best **estimate of expected contributions** to be paid to the plan during the next year.

Rationale: These disclosures provide information related to the cash outflows of the company. With this information, financial statement users can better understand the potential cash outflows related to the pension plan. They can better assess the liquidity and solvency of the company, which helps in assessing the company's overall financial flexibility.

6 The nature and amount of changes in plan assets and benefit obligations recognized in net income and in other comprehensive income of each period.

Rationale: This disclosure provides information on pension elements affecting the projected benefit obligation and plan assets and on whether those amounts have been recognized in income or deferred to future periods.

7 The accumulated amount of changes in plan assets and benefit obligations that have been recognized in other comprehensive income and that will be recycled into net income in future periods.

Rationale: This information indicates the pension-related balances recognized in stockholders' equity, which will affect future income.

8 The amount of estimated net actuarial gains and losses and prior service costs and credits that will be amortized from accumulated other comprehensive income into net income over the next fiscal year.

Rationale: This information helps users predict the impact of deferred pension expense items on next year's income.

In summary, the disclosure requirements are extensive, and purposely so. One factor that has been a challenge for useful pension reporting has been the lack of consistent terminology. Furthermore, a substantial amount of offsetting is inherent in the measurement of pension expense and the pension liability. These disclosures are designed to address these concerns and take some of the mystery out of pension reporting.

Examples of Pension Note Disclosure

In the following sections we provide examples and explain the key pension disclosure elements.

Components of Pension Expense. The FASB requires disclosure of the individual pension expense components (derived from the information in the pension expense worksheet column): (1) service cost, (2) interest cost, (3) expected return on assets, (4) other gains or losses component, and (5) prior service cost component. The purpose of such disclosure is to clarify to more sophisticated readers how companies determine pension expense. Providing information on the components should also be useful in predicting future pension expense.

WHAT'S THE PRINCIPLE?

This represents another compromise between relevance and reliability. The disclosure of the unrecognized items attempts to balance these objectives.

Funded Status of Plan. Having a reconciliation of the changes in the assets and liabilities from the beginning of the year to the end of the year, statement readers can better understand the underlying economics of the plan. In essence, this disclosure (reconciliation) contains the information in the pension worksheet for the projected benefit obligation and plan asset columns.

Illustration 16-18 presents the note disclosure for Zarle's pension plan for 2009, based on the worksheet information in Illustration 16-11. The disclosure indicates the components of pension expense and the elements comprising the funded status of the pension plan. The reconciliation information therein reveals that Zarle underfunds the projected benefit obligation by $78,600. This amount is reported in the balance sheet as a noncurrent liability.

Illustration 16-18
Minimum Note Disclosure of Pension Plan, Zarle Company, 2009

Zarle Company
Notes to the Financial Statements

Note D. The company has a pension plan covering substantially all of its employees. The plan is noncontributory and provides pension benefits that are based on the employee's compensation during the three years immediately preceding retirement. The pension plan's assets consist of cash, stocks, and bonds. The company's funding policy is consistent with the relevant government (ERISA) and tax regulations.

Pension expense for 2009 is comprised of the following components of pension cost.

Service cost	$ 9,500	
Interest on projected benefit obligation	19,200	
Expected return on plan assets	(9,990)	
Amortization of prior service cost	27,200	
Pension expense		$45,910

Other changes in plan assets and benefit obligations recognized in other comprehensive income

Net actuarial loss (gain)	$ (1,110)	
Prior service cost	52,800	
Total recognized in other comprehensive income		51,690
Total recognized in pension expense and other comprehensive income		$97,600

The estimated net actuarial loss and prior service cost for the defined-benefit pension plan that will be amortized from accumulated other comprehensive into pension expense over the next year are estimated to be the same as this year.

The amount recognized as a long-term liability in the balance sheet is as follows:

Noncurrent liability

Pension liability	$78,600

The amount recognized in accumulated other comprehensive income related to pensions consist of:

Net actuarial loss	$ (1,110)
Prior service cost	52,800
Total	$51,690

Change in benefit obligation

Benefit obligation at beginning of year	$112,000
Service cost	9,500
Interest cost	19,200
Amendments (Prior service cost)	80,000
Benefits paid	(8,000)
Benefit obligation at end of year	212,700

Change in plan assets

Fair value of plan assets at beginning of year	111,000
Actual return on plan assets	11,100
Contributions	20,000
Benefits paid	(8,000)
Fair value of plan assets at end of year	134,100
Funded status (liability)	$ (78,600)

The weighted-average discount rate used in determining the 2009 projected benefit obligation was 10 percent. The rate of increase in future compensation levels used in computing the 2009 projected benefit obligation was 4.5 percent. The weighted-average expected long-term rate of return on the plan's assets was 9 percent.

Other Postretirement Benefits

In addition to pensions, companies often provide other types of postretirement benefits as well. These other benefits include life insurance offered outside a pension plan; dental, eye, and medical care; legal and tax services; tuition assistance; day care;, and housing assistance. The costs related to these benefits can be substantial.

Why didn't the FASB cover these other types of postretirement benefits in the earlier pension accounting statement? Because the apparent similarities between the two benefits mask some significant differences, as Illustration 16-19 shows.

> **WHAT'S THE PRINCIPLE?**
>
> Does it make a difference to users of financial statements whether companies recognize pension information in the financial statements or disclose it only in the notes? The FASB was unsure, so in accord with the full disclosure principle, it decided to provide extensive pension plan disclosures.

Item	Pensions	Health-Care Benefits
Funding	Generally funded.	Generally *NOT* funded.
Benefit	Well-defined and level dollar amount.	Generally uncapped and great variability.
Beneficiary	Retiree (maybe some benefit to surviving spouse).	Retiree, spouse, and other dependents.
Benefit payable	Monthly.	As needed and used.
Predictability	Variables are reasonably predictable.	Utilization difficult to predict. Level of cost varies geographically and fluctuates over time.

Illustration 16-19
Differences between Pensions and Postretirement Health-Care Benefits

Expanded Discussion of Other Postretirement Benefits

Two of the differences presented in Illustration 16-19 highlight why measuring the future payments for health-care benefit plans is so much more difficult than for pension plans.

1 Many postretirement plans do not set a limit on health-care benefits. No matter how serious the illness or how long it lasts, the benefits continue to flow. (Even if the employer uses an insurance company plan, the premiums will escalate according to the increased benefits provided.)

2 The level of health-care benefit utilization and health care costs is difficult to predict. The increased longevity and unexpected illnesses (e.g., AIDS), along with new medical technologies (e.g., MRI scans) and cures (e.g., radiation), cause changes in health care utilization.

Examples of Pension and Other Postretirement Benefit Disclosures

Additionally, although the fiduciary and reporting standards for employee benefit funds under government regulations generally cover health-care benefits, the stringent minimum vesting, participation, and funding standards that apply to pensions do not apply to health-care benefits. Nevertheless, many of the basic concepts of pensions, and much of the related accounting terminology and measurement methodology, also apply to other postretirement benefits. As a result, the accounting entries and worksheet treatment are essentially the same as for pensions. Therefore, we omit an illustration for a worksheet for other postretirement benefits.

The disclosures required for other postretirement benefit plans are also similar to, and just as detailed and extensive as, those required for pensions. By recognizing these similarities, under the provisions of *FASB Statement No. 132(R)*, companies can combine pension and other postretirement benefit disclosures.

What do the numbers mean?   Bailing Out

The Pension Benefit Guaranty Corp, (PBGC) recently announced that it would take over responsibility for the pilots' pension plan at **United Airlines** to the tune of $1.4 billion. The federal agency, which acts as an insurer for corporate pension plans, spent much of the past few years securing pension plans for Big Steel, and airlines seem to be next in line. The PBGC became the trustee of **US Airways'** pilot pensions in 2003 and may announce a takeover of that struggling carrier's other three pension plans soon. The grand total at US Air? It's $2.8 billion, chump change next to the $6.4 billion the PBGC will pony up if it has to bail out all four of United's plans. To date the airline industry, which makes up 2 percent of participants in the program, has made 20 percent of claims. The chart below shows how a $6.4 billion bailout would compare with the PBGC's biggest payouts to date.

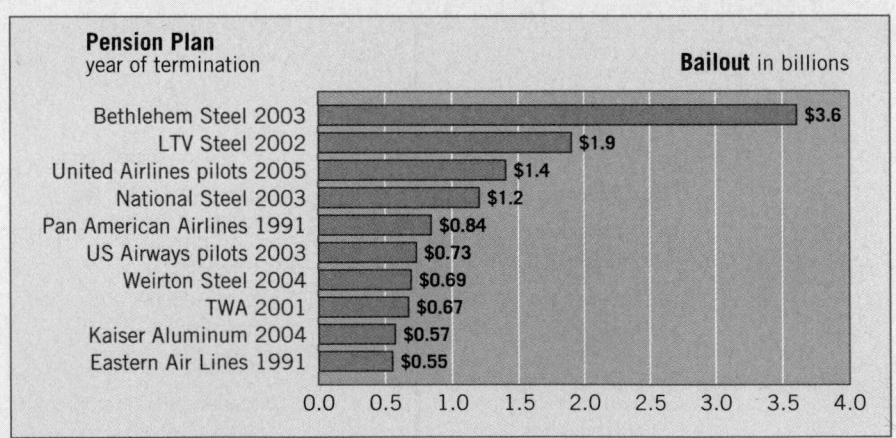

Source: Kate Bonamici, "By the Numbers," *Fortune* (January 24, 2005), p. 24.

Beyond the Numbers

One proposal to deal with the drain on the PBGC would be to increase the premiums the pension plan sponsors pay into the plan. What are the implications of this proposal to the trends in pension plan offerings? (See "Which Plan Is Right for You?" on page 854.)

CONCLUDING REMARKS

Accounting for compensation at one time was relatively straightforward. However, employment agreements have become more complex, making it more difficult to determine the proper expense and related liability. Today, compensation is often in the form of bonuses, stock options, and other noncash forms. These compensation arrangements make it more difficult to determine in what period to report compensation. In addition, the measurement of the related liability becomes more complex. As a result, it is not surprising that much effort is being expended to determine the proper accounting and reporting for these various compensation arrangements.

You will want to read the CONVERGENCE CORNER on page 873 for discussion of how international convergence efforts relate to compensation.

ACCOUNTING, ANALYSIS, PRINCIPLES

The following information is available related to employee salary and benefits of Locksley Corporation for the year 2008.

1 At December 31, 30 junior employees have earned 1 week of paid vacation time, and 10 long-time employees have earned 3 weeks of paid vacation time. The average salary for the junior employees is $600 per week. The more senior employees earn $900 per week.

2 On January 1, 2008, Locksley granted 20,000 options to executives. Each option entitles the holder to purchase one share of the company's $10 par value common stock at $30 per share at any time during the next 4 years. The service period for this award is 2 years. Assume the fair value option-pricing model determines that total compensation expense is $450,000.

3 Locksley received the following information from its actuary related to the company's defined-benefit plan.

Service cost	90,000
Projected benefit obligation, January 1, 2008	700,000
Prior service cost amortization	10,000
Contributions (funding)	140,000
Benefits paid to retirees	60,000
Actual and expected return on plan assets	15,000
Interest/discount rate	9%

Accounting

Prepare the journal entry to record any 2008 expense for (a) the vacation pay, (b) the stock options, and (c) Locksley's contribution to the pension plan in 2008.

Analysis

One of Locksley's competitors does not have a defined-benefit plan but instead provides retirement benefits to its employees through a defined-contribution plan. Briefly discuss the effects of Locksley's defined-benefit plan on common profitability and solvency ratios. Does this affect comparisons to its competitor? Explain.

Principles

The FASB faced considerable opposition when it issued rules related to postretirement benefits. What is the conceptual basis for recording pension assets/liabilities and the related expense in current financial statements?

Solution

Accounting

a Vacation pay:

Wages Expense (30 × 2 × $600)	36,000	
Vacation Wages Payable		36,000

b Stock options:

ABO
– FV of PA
min Pension Liab.

January 1, 2008
No entry

December 31, 2008

Compensation Expense ($450,000 ÷ 2 years)	225,000	
Paid-in Capital-Stock Options		225,000

c Pension plan:

Pension Expense	148,000*	
Cash		140,000
Prepaid/Accrued Pension Cost		8,000

*$90,000 + ($700,000 × .09) + $10,000 − $15,000

Analysis

The primary difference in the accounting effects of a defined-benefit plan relative to the defined-contribution plan is the recognition of a net pension asset or liability on the balance sheet for the defined-benefit plan. This is because the employer bears the risk of meeting the benefits promised to employees at retirement in the defined-benefit plan. Thus, if the assets in the pension plan do not cover the estimated liability, a Pension Liability arises, which increases solvency ratios, such as the debt to assets ratio. Just the reverse happens if the defined benefit plan is overfunded. The income effects of the plans are similar, except that the defined-benefit expense might be relatively more volatile, to the extent the return on assets increases/decreases with movements in the market.

In comparing companies with different pension plans, an analyst must consider all elements of the compensation plan. A company with a defined-contribution plan may need to provide higher levels of other forms of compensation (e.g., salary and bonus) to offset the increased risk that employees bear in the defined-contribution plan.

Principles

In a defined-benefit plan, an employer promises benefits that employees will receive when they retire. While the recognition of the liability is controversial, because its measurement and recognition relate to unknown future variables, these promises meet the definition of a liability. The amounts represent a present obligation, requiring an outflow of assets, as the result of past transactions (employees' work). Employers are at risk with defined-benefit plans because they must contribute enough to meet the cost of benefits that the plan defines. However, by investing in pension assets today to meet the future obligations when they come due, the company may offset the amount of liability reported. In fact, if the assets exceed the estimated liability, the company will report a pension asset.

CONVERGENCE CORNER

P BO
- FV of PA
= V
(PSC)
(Actuarial G/L)

Compensation

The accounting for various forms of compensation plans under iGAAP is found in *IAS 19* ("Employee Benefits") and *IFRS 2* ("Share-Based Payment"). *IAS 19* addresses the accounting for a wide range of compensation elements—wages, bonuses, postretirement benefits, and compensated absences. Both of these standards were recently amended, resulting in significant convergence between iGAAP and U.S. GAAP in this area.

RELEVANT FACTS

• Both iGAAP and U.S.GAAP follow the same model for recognizing stock-based compensation. That is, the fair value of shares and options awarded to employees is recognized over the period to which the employees' services relate.

• Under iGAAP, any payroll taxes arising from share-based payment transactions are recognized over the service period. Under U.S. GAAP, taxes due on employee stock-based compensation are recognized as an expense on the date of the event triggering the measurement and payment of the tax to the taxing authority (generally the exercise date for options and the vesting date for restricted stock).

• iGAAP and U.S. GAAP separate pension plans into defined-contribution plans and defined-benefit plans. The accounting for defined-contribution plans is similar.

• For defined-benefit plans, both iGAAP and U.S. GAAP recognize the net of the pension assets and liabilities on the balance sheet. Unlike U.S. GAAP, which recognizes prior service cost on the balance sheet (as an element of "Accumulated other comprehensive income"), iGAAP does not recognize prior service costs on the balance sheet. Both GAAPs amortize prior service costs into income over the expected service lives of employees.

ABOUT THE NUMBERS

The following schedule taken from the annual report of **Cadbury Schweppes**, which uses iGAAP.

25. Retirement benefit obligations continued (in part)

The market value of the assets and liabilities of the defined-benefit schemes and postretirement medical benefit schemes at 31 December 2006 are as follows:

	UK pension schemes £m	Overseas pension schemes £m	Post-retirement medical benefits £m	Total all schemes £m
Equities	1,002	350	2	1,298
Bonds	763	143	1	907
Property	183	32	-	215
Other	30	34	-	120
	1,978	559	3	2,540
Present value of benefit obligations	(1,988)	(720)	(36)	(2,744)
Recognised in the balance sheet	(10)	(161)	(33)	(204)

The Group's policy is to recognise all actuarial gains and losses immediately. Consequently there are no unrecognized gains or losses.

• Another difference in defined-benefit recognition is that under iGAAP companies have the choice of recognizing actuarial gains and losses in income immediately or amortizing them over the expected remaining working lives of employees. U.S. GAAP does not permit choice; actuarial gains and losses (and prior services costs) are recognized in "Accumulated other comprehensive income" and amortized to income over remaining service lives.

ON THE HORIZON

The FASB and the IASB are working collaboratively on a postretirement benefit project. As discussed in the chapter, the FASB has issued a standard (*SFAS No. 158*) addressing the recognition of benefit plans in financial statements (Phase 1 of its project). The FASB has begun work on the second phase of the project, which will reexamine expense measurement of postretirement benefit plans. The IASB also has added a project in this area, but on a different schedule. The IASB is monitoring the FASB's progress and hopes to issue a converged standard in this area by 2010.

Key Terms

Accumulated rights, 845
Actual return on the plan assets, 858
Actuarial present value, 857
Asset gains and losses, 861
Bonus, 846
Compensated absences, 844
Components of pension expense, 857
Defined-benefit plan, 855
Defined-contribution plan, 854
Expected rate of return, 861
Expected return on plan assets, 861
Fair-value method, 848
Grant date, 848, 850
Interest on the liability/Interest expense, 857
Intrinsic-value method, 848
Liability gains and losses, 862
Net funded status, 864

Other Comprehensive Income (G/L), 862
Other Comprehensive Income (PSC), 863
Pension asset/liability, 858
Pension worksheet, 858
Prior service costs (PSC), 860
Projected benefit obligation, 856
Reconciliation, 866
Retroactive benefits, 860
Service cost, 857
Service period, 850
Settlement rates, 858
Social Security tax, 842
Stock compensation plans, 847
Unexpected gain or loss, 861
Vested rights, 845
Years-of-service method, 860

Summary of Learning Objectives

1 Explain the accounting for salary and bonuses. Companies should report amounts paid to employees for salaries and wages as compensation expense. The most common types of payroll deductions are taxes and miscellaneous items such as insurance premiums, employee savings, and union dues. Companies should recognize any amounts deducted from payroll, but not yet remitted to the proper authority at the end of the accounting period, as current liabilities.

2 Describe the accounting for stock compensation plans under generally accepted accounting principles. Companies must use the fair-value approach to account for stock-based compensation. Under this approach, a company computes total compensation expense based on the fair value of the options that it expects to vest on the grant date. Companies recognize compensation expense in the periods in which the employee performs the services.

3 Discuss the controversy surrounding stock compensation plans. When first proposed, there was considerable opposition to the recognition provisions contained in the fair-value approach. The reason: because that approach could result in substantial, previously unrecognized compensation expense. Corporate America, particularly the high-technology sector, vocally opposed the proposed standard. They believed that the standard would place them at a competitive disadvantage with larger companies that can withstand higher compensation charges. Offsetting such opposition is the need for greater transparency in financial reporting, on which our capital markets depend.

4 Identity types of pension plans and their characteristics. The two most common types of pension arrangements are defined-contribution plans and defined-benefit plans. In *defined-contribution plans,* the employer agrees to contribute to a pension trust a certain sum each period, based on a formula. This formula may consider such factors as age, length of employee service, employer's profits, and compensation level. The plan defines only the employer's contribution; no promise is made regarding the ultimate benefits paid out to the employees. *Defined-benefit plans* specify the benefits that the employee will receive at the time of retirement. These benefits rely on a formula that is a function of the employee's years of service and the employer's compensation level when he or she nears retirement.

5 List the components of pension expense. Pension expense is a function of the following components: (1) service cost, (2) interest on the liability, (3) return on plan assets, (4) amortization of prior service cost, and (5) gain or loss.

6 Utilize a worksheet for employer's pension plan entries. Companies may use a worksheet unique to pension accounting to record both the formal entries and the memo entries to track all the employer's relevant pension plan items and components.

7 Explain the accounting for prior service cost and gains and losses. An actuary computes the amount of the prior service cost and the company records it as an adjustment to the projected benefit obligation and other comprehensive income. The difference between the expected return and the actual return is called asset gains and losses. This component defers the difference between the actual return and expected return on plan assets in computing current-year pension expense.

In estimating the projected benefit obligation (the liability), actuaries make assumptions about such items as mortality rate, retirement rate, turnover rate, disability rate, and salary amounts. Any change in these actuarial assumptions affects the amount of the projected benefit obligation. These unexpected gains or losses from changes in the projected benefit obligation are liability gains and losses. Companies defer recognition of liability gains (resulting from unexpected decreases in the liability balance) and liability losses (resulting from unexpected increases). Instead, companies combine these liability gains and losses in the same Other Comprehensive Income (G/L) account used for asset gains and losses and accumulate them from year to year.

8 **Describe the reporting requirements for pension plans in financial statements.** Currently, companies must disclose the following pension plan information in their financial statements: (1) The components of net periodic pension expense for the period. (2) A schedule showing changes in the benefit obligation and plan assets during the year. (3) A schedule reconciling the funded status of the plan with amounts reported in the employer's statement of financial position. (4) The weighted-average assumed discount rate, the rate of compensation increase used to measure the projected benefit obligation, and the weighted-average expected long-term rate of return on plan assets. (5) A table showing the allocation of pension plan assets by category and the percentage of the fair value to total plan assets. (6) The expected benefit payments for current plan participants for each of the next five fiscal years and for the following five years in aggregate, along with an estimate of expected contributions to the plan during the next year.

REVIEW EXERCISE

Morgan Company provides you with the following information related to its compensation program for its employees.

1 Total payroll for 2008 was $5,000,000, of which $1,400,000 is exempt from Social Security tax because it represent amounts paid in excess of $97,500 to certain employees. The amount paid to employees who earn in excess of $7,000 was $4,200,000. The state unemployment tax is 3.5%, but Morgan Company is allowed a credit of 2.3% by the state for its low unemployment record. Assume the current FICA tax is 7.65% on wages to $97,500 and 1.45% in excess of $97,500. The federal unemployment tax rate is 0.8% after the state credit.

2 On January 2, 2008, Morgan granted options to key executives to purchase 40,000 shares of the company's $1 par value common stock. The option price was set at $40, and the fair value option-pricing model determined total compensation to be $450,000. The market price of the stock at the date of grant was $40. The service period for the award is 2 years. The market price at December 31, 2008, was $62.

3 For the year 2008, Morgan was provided the following pension plan information from its actuary.

Service cost	$ 70,000
Prior service cost amortization	12,000
Contribution to the plan	65,000
Benefits paid	50,000
Projected benefit obligation, January 1, 2008	900,000
Plan assets at January 1, 2008	1,000,000
Actual and expected return on plan assets	90,000
Interest (settlement) rate	8%

a Compute:

   1 The amount of Social Security taxes that Morgan will report as an expense in 2008.

   2 The amount of federal and state unemployment taxes that Morgan will report as expense in 2008.

b Compute the amount, if any, of compensation expense to be reported for the stock option plan for key executives in 2008.

c Compute the amount of pension expense to be reported by Morgan for the year 2008.

Solution

a **1**

Total payroll	$5,000,000
Exempt payroll	1,400,000
	3,600,000
FICA tax rate	7.65%
FICA taxes	$ 275,400
Exempt payroll subject to additional tax	$1,400,000
Hospital insurance tax rate	1.45%
Hospital insurance taxes (HIT)	$ 20,300
FICA taxes	$ 275,400
HIT	20,300
Social Security taxes	$ 295,700

   2

Total payroll	$5,000,000
Exempt payroll	4,200,000
	800,000
Federal employment tax rate	0.8%
Federal employment taxes	$ 6,400
Payroll subject to unemployment taxes	$ 800,000
State unemployment tax rate (3.5% − 2.3%)	1.2%
State unemployment taxes	$ 9,600

b Compensation expense is $225,000 ($450,000 ÷ 2).

c

Service cost	$70,000
Interest on the liability ($900,000 × 8%)	72,000
Expected return on plan assets	(90,000)
Prior service cost amortization	12,000
Pension expense	$64,000

Questions

1 What are compensated absences?

2 Under what conditions must an employer accrue a liability for the cost of compensated absences?

3 Under what conditions is an employer required to accrue a liability for sick pay? Under what conditions is an employer permitted but not required to accrue a liability for sick pay?

4 Caitlin Carter operates a health food store, and she has been the only employee. Her business is growing, and she is considering hiring some additional staff to help her in the store.

Explain to her the various payroll deductions that she will have to account for, including their potential impact on her financial statements, if she hires additional staff.

5 Briefly explain the accounting requirements for stock compensation plans under *Statement of Financial Accounting Standards No. 123(R)*.

6 Weiland Corporation has an employee stock purchase plan which permits all full-time employees to purchase 10 shares of common stock on the third anniversary of their employment and an additional 15 shares on each subsequent anniversary date. The purchase price is set at the market price on the date purchased and no commission is charged. Discuss whether this plan would be considered compensatory.

7 What date or event does the profession believe should be used in determining the value of a stock option? What arguments support this position?

8 Over what period of time should compensation cost of stock options be allocated?

9 How is the compensation expense of stock options computed using the fair value approach?

10 Differentiate between a defined-contribution pension plan and a defined-benefit pension plan. Explain how the employer's obligation differs between the two types of plans.

11 What factors must be considered by the actuary in measuring the amount of pension benefits under a defined-benefit plan?

12 Explain how cash basis accounting for pension plans differs from accrual basis accounting for pension plans. Why is cash basis accounting generally considered unacceptable for pension plan accounting?

13 Identify the five components that comprise pension expense. Briefly explain the nature of each component.

14 What is service cost and what is the basis of its measurement?

15 In computing the interest component of pension expense, what interest rates may be used?

16 Explain the difference between service cost and prior service cost.

17 What is meant by "prior service cost"? When is prior service cost recognized as pension expense?

18 If pension expense recognized in a period exceeds the current amount funded by the employer, what kind of account arises? How should that account be reported in the financial statements? If the reverse occurs—that is, current funding by the employer exceeds the amount recognized as pension expense—what kind of account arises, and how should it be reported?

19 How does an "asset gain or loss" develop in pension accounting? How does a "liability gain or loss" develop in pension accounting?

20 Agar Company reported net income of $25,000 in 2008. It had the following amounts related to its pension plan in 2008: Actuarial liability gain $10,000; Unexpected asset loss $13,000; Accumulated other comprehensive income (G/L) (beginning balance), zero. Determine for 2009 (a) Agar's other comprehensive income, and (b) comprehensive income.

21 Describe the reporting of pension plans for a company with multiple plans, some of which are underfunded and some of which are overfunded.

22 What are postretirement benefits other than pensions?

23 What are the major differences between postretirement health care benefits and pension benefits?

Brief Exercises

BE16-1 Future Zone Corporation's weekly payroll of $23,000 included FICA taxes withheld of $1,426, federal taxes withheld of $2,990, state taxes withheld of $920, and insurance premiums withheld of $250. Prepare the journal entry to record Future Zone's payroll. **(LO 1)**

BE16-2 Tale Spin Inc. provides paid vacations to its employees. At December 31, 2008, 30 employees have each earned 2 weeks of vacation time. The employees' average salary is $600 per week. Prepare Tale Spin's December 31, 2008, adjusting entry. **(LO 1)**

BE16-3 Gargoyle Corporation provides its officers with bonuses based on income. For 2008, the bonuses total $450,000 and are paid on February 15, 2009. Prepare Gargoyle's December 31, 2008, adjusting entry and the February 15, 2009, entry. **(LO 1)**

BE16-4 On January 1, 2008, Johnson Corporation granted 5,000 options to executives. Each option entitles the holder to purchase one share of Johnson's $5 par value common stock at $50 per share at any time during the next 5 years. The market price of the stock is $65 per share on the date of grant. The period of benefit is 2 years. Prepare Johnson's journal entries for January 1, 2008, and December 31, 2008 and 2009, assuming the fair value of the options on the grant date is $75,000. **(LO 2)**

BE16-5 On July 1, 2008, Soriano Corporation granted 10,000 options to executives. Each option entitles the holder to purchase one share of Soriano's $10 par value common stock at $100 per share at any time during the next 5 years. The market price of the stock is $121 per share on the date of grant. The fair value of the options **(LO 2)**

at the grant date is $300,000. The period of benefit is 3 years. Prepare Soriano's journal entries for July 1, 2008, and December 31, 2008 and 2009.

(LO 6)   **BE16-6**   The following information is available for Jack Borke Corporation for 2008.

Service cost	$29,000
Interest on projected benefit obligation	22,000
Return on plan assets	20,000
Amortization of prior service cost	15,200

Compute Borke's 2008 pension expense.

(LO 5, 6)   **BE16-7**   At January 1, 2008, Uddin Company had plan assets of $250,000 and a projected benefit obligation of the same amount. During 2008, service cost was $27,500, the settlement rate was 10%, actual and expected return on plan assets were $25,000, contributions were $20,000, and benefits paid were $17,500. Prepare a pension worksheet for Uddin Company for 2008.

(LO 8)   **BE16-8**   Judy O'Neill Corporation has the following balances at December 31, 2008.

Projected benefit obligation	$2,800,000
Plan assets at fair value	2,000,000
Accumulated OCI (PSC)	1,100,000

How should these balances be reported on O'Neill's balance sheet at December 31, 2008?

(LO 8)   **BE16-9**   DeMent Co. had the following amounts related to its pension plan in 2008.

Actuarial liability loss for 2008	$25,000
Unexpected asset gain for 2008	18,000
Accumulated other comprehensive income (G/L) (beginning balance)	7,000 Cr.

Determine for 2008: DeMent's (a) other comprehensive income and (b) comprehensive income. Net income for 2008 is $26,000; no amortization of gain or loss is necessary in 2008.

(LO 8)   **BE16-10**   At December 31, 2008, Conway Corporation had a projected benefit obligation of $510,000, plan assets of $322,000, accumulated other comprehensive income (PSC) of $127,000, and pension liability of $61,000. Prepare a pension reconciliation schedule for Conway

(LO 8)   **BE16-11**   Caleb Corporation has the following information available concerning its postretirement benefit plan for 2008.

Service cost	$40,000
Interest cost	52,400
Return on plan assets	26,900

Compute Caleb's 2008 postretirement expense.

Exercises

(LO 1)   **E16-1   (Compensated Absences)**   Zero Mostel Company began operations on January 2, 2008. It employs 9 individuals who work 8-hour days and are paid hourly. Each employee earns 10 paid vacation days and 6 paid sick days annually. Vacation days may be taken after January 15 of the year following the year in which they are earned. Sick days may be taken as soon as they are earned; unused sick days accumulate. Additional information is as follows.

Actual Hourly Wage Rate		Vacation Days Used by Each Employee		Sick Days Used by Each Employee	
2008	2009	2008	2009	2008	2009
$10	$11	0	9	4	5

Zero Mostel Company has chosen to accrue the cost of compensated absences at rates of pay in effect during the period when earned and to accrue sick pay when earned.

Instructions

(a) Prepare journal entries to record transactions related to compensated absences during 2008 and 2009.

(b) Compute the amounts of any liability for compensated absences that should be reported on the balance sheet at December 31, 2008 and 2009.

E16-2 **(Compensated Absences)** Assume the facts in the preceding exercise, except that Zero Mostel **(LO 1)** Company has chosen not to accrue paid sick leave until used, and has chosen to accrue vacation time at expected future rates of pay without discounting. The company used the following projected rates to accrue vacation time.

Year in Which Vacation Time Was Earned	Projected Future Pay Rates Used to Accrue Vacation Pay
2008	$10.75
2009	11.60

Instructions

(a) Prepare journal entries to record transactions related to compensated absences during 2008 and 2009.

(b) Compute the amounts of any liability for compensated absences that should be reported on the balance sheet at December 31, 2008, and 2009.

E16-3 **(Payroll Tax Entries)** The total payroll of Rene Auber Company for September 2008 was $480,000, of **(LO 1)** which $110,000 is exempt from FICA tax because it represented amounts paid in excess of $97,500 to certain employees. The amount paid to employees in excess of $7,000 was $400,000. Income taxes in the amount of $90,000 were withheld, as well as $9,000 in union dues. The state unemployment tax is 3.5%, but Auber Company is allowed a credit of 2.3% by the state for its unemployment experience. Also, assume that the current FICA tax is 7.65% on an employee's wages to $97,500 and 1.45% in excess of $97,500. No employee for Auber makes more than $125,000. The federal unemployment tax rate is 0.8% after state credit.

Instructions

Prepare the necessary journal entries if the wages and salaries paid and the employer payroll taxes are recorded separately.

E16-4 **(Payroll Tax Entries)** Green Day Hardware Company's payroll for November 2008 is summarized below. **(LO 1)**

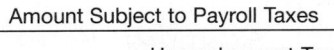

		Amount Subject to Payroll Taxes		
			Unemployment Tax	
Payroll	Wages Due	FICA	Federal	State
Factory	$120,000	$120,000	$40,000	$40,000
Sales	44,000	32,000	4,000	4,000
Administrative	36,000	36,000	—	—
Total	$200,000	$188,000	$44,000	$44,000

At this point in the year some employees have already received wages in excess of those to which payroll taxes apply. Assume that the state unemployment tax is 2.5%. The FICA rate is 7.65% on an employee's wages to $97,500 and 1.45% in excess of $97,500. Of the $188,000 wages subject to FICA tax, $20,000 is in excess of $97,500 related to the sales wages. Federal unemployment tax rate is 0.8% after credits. Income tax withheld amounts to $16,000 for factory, $7,000 for sales, and $6,000 for administrative.

Instructions

(a) Prepare a schedule showing the employer's total cost of wages for November by function. (Round all computations to nearest dollar.)

(b) Prepare the journal entries to record the factory, sales, and administrative payrolls including the employer's payroll taxes.

Compens Expen 225 000
PIC (LO 2) 225 000
Option
x 2

E16-5 **(Issuance and Exercise of Stock Options)** On November 1, 2007, Columbo Company adopted a stock option plan that granted options to key executives to purchase 30,000 shares of the company's $10 par value common stock. The options were granted on January 2, 2008, and were exercisable 2 years after the date of grant if the grantee was still an employee of the company; the options expired 6 years from date of grant. The option price was set at $40, and the fair value option pricing model determines the total compensation expense to be $450,000.

All of the options were exercised during the year 2010: 20,000 on January 3 when the market price was $67, and 10,000 on May 1 when the market price was $77 a share.

Instructions

Prepare journal entries relating to the stock option plan for the years 2008, 2009, and 2010 under the fair value method. Assume that the employees perform services equally in 2008 and 2009.

E16-6 **(Issuance, Exercise, and Termination of Stock Options)** On January 1, 2008, Titania Inc. granted stock options to officers and key employees for the purchase of 20,000 shares of the company's $10 par common

(LO 2) stock at $25 per share. The options were exercisable within a 5-year period beginning January 1, 2010, by grantees still in the employ of the company, and expiring December 31, 2014. The service period for this award is 2 years. Assume that the fair value option-pricing model determines total compensation expense to be $350,000.

On April 1, 2009, 2,000 option shares were terminated when the employees resigned from the company. The market value of the common stock was $35 per share on this date.

On March 31, 2010, 12,000 option shares were exercised when the market value of the common stock was $40 per share.

Instructions

Prepare journal entries using the fair value method to record issuance of the stock options, termination of the stock options, exercise of the stock options, and charges to compensation expense, for the years ended December 31, 2008, 2009, and 2010.

(LO 2) **E16-7** **(Issuance, Exercise, and Termination of Stock Options)** On January 1, 2007, Nichols Corporation granted 10,000 options to key executives. Each option allows the executive to purchase one share of Nichols' $5 par value common stock at a price of $20 per share. The options were exercisable within a 2-year period beginning January 1, 2009, if the grantee is still employed by the company at the time of the exercise. On the grant date, Nichols' stock was trading at $25 per share, and a fair value option-pricing model determines total compensation to be $400,000.

On May 1, 2009, 8,000 options were exercised when the market price of Nichols' stock was $30 per share. The remaining options lapsed in 2011 because executives decided not to exercise their options.

Instructions

Prepare the necessary journal entries related to the stock option plan for the years 2007 through 2011. Nichols uses the fair value approach to account for stock options.

(LO 5) **E16-8** **(Pension Expense, Journal Entries)** The following information is available for the pension plan of Kiley Company for the year 2008.

Actual and expected return on plan assets	$ 12,000
Benefits paid to retirees	40,000
Contributions (funding)	95,000
Interest/discount rate	10%
Prior service cost amortization	8,000
Projected benefit obligation, January 1, 2008	500,000
Service cost	60,000

Instructions

(a) Compute pension expense for the year 2008.

(b) Prepare the journal entry to record pension expense and the employer's contribution to the pension plan in 2008.

(LO 5, 7) **E16-9** **(Computation of Pension Expense)** Rebekah Company provides the following information about its defined-benefit pension plan for the year 2008.

Service cost	$ 90,000
Contribution to the plan	105,000
Prior service cost amortization	10,000
Actual and expected return on plan assets	64,000
Benefits paid	40,000
Pension liability at January 1, 2008	160,000
Plan assets at January 1, 2008	640,000
Projected benefit obligation at January 1, 2008	800,000
Accumulated other comprehensive income (PSC)	
balance at December 31, 2007	150,000
Interest/discount (settlement) rate	10%

Instructions

Compute the pension expense for the year 2008.

(LO 5, 6, 7) **E16-10** **(Preparation of Pension Worksheet)** Using the information in E16-9, prepare a pension worksheet inserting January 1, 2008, balances, showing December 31, 2008, balances and the journal entry recording pension expense.

(LO 5, 6) **E16-11** **(Basic Pension Worksheet)** The following facts apply to the pension plan of Trudy Borke Inc. for the year 2008.

Plan assets, January 1, 2008	$490,000
Projected benefit obligation, January 1, 2008	490,000
Settlement rate	8.5%
Annual pension service cost	40,000
Contributions (funding)	30,000
Actual return on plan assets	49,700
Benefits paid to retirees	33,400

Instructions

Using the preceding data, compute pension expense for the year 2008. As part of your solution, prepare a pension worksheet that shows the journal entry for pension expense for 2008 and the year-end balances in the related pension accounts.

E16-12 **(Basic Pension Worksheet)** The following defined-benefit pension data of Doreen Corp. apply to the year 2008. **(LO 5, 6, 7)**

Projected benefit obligation, January 1, 2008 (before amendment)	$560,000
Plan assets, January 1, 2008	546,200
Pension liability	13,800
On January 1, 2008, Doreen Corp., through plan amendment, grants prior service benefits having a present value of	100,000
Settlement rate	9%
Annual pension service cost	58,000
Contributions (funding)	55,000
Actual return on plan assets	52,280
Benefits paid to retirees	40,000
Prior service cost amortization for 2008	17,000

Instructions

For 2008, prepare a pension worksheet for Doreen Corp. that shows the journal entry for pension expense and the year-end balances in the related pension accounts.

E16-13 **(Disclosures)** Mildred Enterprises provides the following information related to its defined-benefit pension plan. **(LO 8)**

Balances or Values at December 31, 2008	
Projected benefit obligation	$2,737,000
Fair value of plan assets	2,278,329
Accumulated OCI (PSC)	205,000
Accumulated OCI (Net loss) (January 1, 2008, balance, –0–)	45,680
Pension liability	207,991
Other pension plan data:	
Service cost for 2008	$ 94,000
Prior service cost amortization for 2008	45,000
Actual return on plan assets in 2008	130,000
Expected return on plan assets in 2008	175,680
Interest on January 1, 2008, projected benefit obligation	253,000
Contributions to plan in 2008	92,329
Benefits paid	140,000

Instructions

(a) Prepare the note disclosing the components of pension expense for the year 2008.
(b) Determine the amounts of other comprehensive income and comprehensive income for 2008. Net income for 2008 is $35,000.
(c) Compute the amount of accumulated other comprehensive income reported at December 31, 2008.

Problems

WILEY PLUS

(LO 1)

P16-1 (Payroll Tax Entries) Star Wars Company pays its office employee payroll weekly. Below is a partial list of employees and their payroll data for August. Because August is their vacation period, vacation pay is also listed.

Employee	Earnings to July 31	Weekly Pay	Vacation Pay to Be Received in August
Mark Hamill	$4,200	$180	—
Carrie Fisher	3,500	150	$300
Harrison Ford	2,700	110	220
Alec Guinness	7,400	250	—
Peter Cushing	8,000	290	580

Assume that the federal income tax withheld is 10% of wages. Union dues withheld are 2% of wages. Vacations are taken the second and third weeks of August by Fisher, Ford, and Cushing. The state unemployment tax rate is 2.5% and the federal is 0.8%, both on a $7,000 maximum. The FICA rate is 7.65% on employee and employer on a maximum of $97,500 per employee. In addition, a 1.45% rate is charged both employer and employee for an employee's wage in excess of $97,500.

Instructions

Make the journal entries necessary for each of the four August payrolls. The entries for the payroll and for the company's liability are made separately. Also make the entry to record the monthly payment of accrued payroll liabilities.

(LO 1)

P16-2 (Payroll Tax Entries) Below is a payroll sheet for Empire Import Company for the month of September 2004. The company is allowed a 1% unemployment compensation rate by the state; the federal unemployment tax rate is 0.8% and the maximum for both is $7,000. Assume a 10% federal income tax rate for all employees and a 7.65% FICA tax on employee and employer on a maximum of $97,500. In addition, 1.45% is charged both employer and employee for an employee's wage in excess of $97,500 per employee.

Name	Earnings to Aug. 31	September Earnings	Income Tax Withholding	FICA	State U.C.	Federal U.C.
B.D. Williams	$ 6,800	$ 800				
D. Prowse	6,300	700				
K. Baker	7,600	1,100				
F. Oz	13,600	1,900				
A. Daniels	105,000	15,000				
P. Mayhew	112,000	16,000				

Instructions

(a) Complete the payroll sheet and make the necessary entry to record the payment of the payroll.

(b) Make the entry to record the payroll tax expenses of Empire Import Company.

(c) Make the entry to record the payment of the payroll liabilities created. Assume that the company pays all payroll liabilities at the end of each month.

(LO 2)

P16-3 (Stock Option Plan) ISU Company adopted a stock option plan on November 30, 2007, that provided that 70,000 shares of $5 par value stock be designated as available for the granting of options to officers of the corporation at a price of $8 a share. The market value was $12 a share on November 30, 2007.

On January 2, 2008, options to purchase 28,000 shares were granted to president Don Pedro—15,000 for services to be rendered in 2008 and 13,000 for services to be rendered in 2009. Also on that date, options to purchase 14,000 shares were granted to vice president Beatrice Leonato—7,000 for services to be rendered in 2008 and 7,000 for services to be rendered in 2009. The market value of the stock was $14 a share on January 2, 2008. The options were exercisable for a period of one year following the year in which the services were rendered. The fair value of the options on the grant date was $3 per option.

In 2009 neither the president nor the vice president exercised their options because the market price of the stock was below the exercise price. The market value of the stock was $7 a share on December 31, 2009, when the options for 2008 services lapsed.

On December 31, 2010, both president Pedro and vice president Leonato exercised their options for 13,000 and 7,000 shares, respectively, when the market price was $16 a share.

[Handwritten margin notes:]
Content Exp 66 000
PIC stockOp

Compent Exp 60 000
PIC doo 60000

Cash 160 000
PIC stock 60 000
Com stock 100 000
PIC Th 120 000
excess of par

MP − EP = tax difference

Instructions

Prepare the necessary journal entries in 2007 when the stock option plan was adopted, in 2008 when options were granted, in 2009 when options lapsed, and in 2010 when options were exercised.

P16-4 (Two-Year Worksheet) On January 1, 2008, Diana Peter Company has the following defined-benefit pension plan balances. **(LO 5, 6)**

Projected benefit obligation	$4,200,000 *(PBO)*
Fair value of plan assets	4,200,000

The interest (settlement) rate applicable to the plan is 10%. On January 1, 2009, the company amends its pension agreement so that prior service costs of $500,000 are created. Other data related to the pension plan are as follows.

	2008	2009
Service costs	$150,000	$180,000
Prior service costs amortization	–0–	90,000
Contributions (funding) to the plan	140,000	185,000
Benefits paid	200,000	280,000
Actual return on plan assets	252,000	260,000
Expected rate of return on assets	6%	8%

Instructions

(a) Prepare a pension worksheet for the pension plan for 2008 and 2009.
(b) For 2009, prepare the journal entry to record pension-related amounts.

P16-5 (Pension Expense, Journal Entries) Mantle Company sponsors a defined-benefit pension plan. The following information related to the pension plan is available for 2008. **(LO 5)**

	2008
Plan assets (fair value), January 1	$380,000
PV of all earned benefits today — Projected benefit obligation, January 1	600,000
Pension liability, January 1	220,000
Prior service cost, January 1	180,000
Service cost	60,000
Actual and expected return on plan assets	24,000
Amortization of prior service cost	10,000
Contributions (funding)	110,000
Interest/settlement rate	9%

Pension A L   20 000
Pension expense 100,000
*   Cash   110 000*
*   Incon PSC   10 000*

54000↑

Instructions

(a) Compute pension expense for 2008.
(b) Prepare the journal entry(ies) to record the pension expense and the company's funding of the pension plan for 2008.

P16-6 (Comprehensive 2-Year Worksheet) Mount Co. has the following defined-benefit pension plan balances on January 1, 2008. **(LO 5, 6, 7, 8)**

Projected benefit obligation	$4,500,000
Fair value of plan assets	4,500,000

The interest (settlement) rate applicable to the plan is 10%. On January 1, 2009, the company amends its pension agreement so that prior service costs of $600,000 are created. Other data related to the pension plan are as follows.

	2008	2009
Service costs	$150,000	$170,000
Prior service costs amortization	–0–	90,000
Contributions (funding) to the plan	150,000	184,658
Benefits paid	220,000	280,000
Actual return on plan assets	252,000	250,000
Expected rate of return on assets	6%	8%

OCI 510 000
*   142 500*

Components of pension expense — Footnotes
change numbers for OCI
Plan amortiz for next year

Instructions

(a) Prepare a pension worksheet for the pension plan in 2008.
(b) Prepare any journal entry(ies) related to the pension plan that would be needed at December 31, 2008.
(c) Prepare a pension worksheet for 2009 and any journal entry(ies) related to the pension plan as of December 31, 2009.
(d) Indicate the pension-related amounts reported in the 2009 financial statements.

PBO details

ACCOUNTING IN ACTION

Financial Reporting and Analysis

P&G

■ **Financial Reporting Issues: The Procter & Gamble Company**

AIA16-1 The financial statements of **Procter & Gamble (P&G)** can be accessed at the book's website.

Instructions

Refer to P&G's financial statements and the accompanying notes to answer the following questions.

(a) Under P&G's stock-based compensation plan, stock options are granted annually to key managers and directors.
  (1) How many options were granted under the plan during 2006?
  (2) How many options were exercisable at June 30, 2006?
  (3) How many options were exercised in 2006, and what was the average price of those exercised?
  (4) How many years from the grant date do the options expire?
  (5) What was the number of outstanding options at June 30, 2006, and at what average exercise price?

(b) What kind of pension plan does P&G provide its employees in the United States?
(c) What was P&G's pension expense for 2006, 2005, and 2004 for the United States?
(d) What is the impact of P&G's pension plan for 2006 on the company's financial statements?
(e) What information does P&G provide on the target allocation of its pension assets? (Compare the asset allocation for "Pensions" and "Other Retiree Benefits.") How do the allocations relate to the expected returns on these assets?

PEPSICO ■ **Comparative Analysis: The Coca-Cola Company and PepsiCo, Inc.**

AIA16-2 The financial statements of **The Coca-Cola Company** and **PepsiCo, Inc.** can be accessed at the book's website.

Instructions

(a) What employee stock option compensation plans do Coca-Cola and PepsiCo offer?
(b) How many options did Coca-Cola and PepsiCo grant to officers and employees during 2006?
(c) How many options did employees of Coca-Cola and PepsiCo exercise during 2006?
(d) What kind of pension plans do Coca-Cola and PepsiCo provide their employees?
(e) What net periodic pension expense (cost) did Coca-Cola and PepsiCo report in 2006?
(f) What is the year-end 2006 funded status of Coca-Cola's and PepsiCo's U.S. pension plans?
(g) What relevant rates did Coca-Cola and PepsiCo use in computing their pension amounts?

■ Financial Statement Analysis

AIA16-3 Troy Van Beek, assistant controller for Cizek Electric Company, is preparing for a meeting with the loan committee of First City Bank. The loan committee will be reviewing Cizek's financial statements and projections as part of the company's loan-renewal process. Troy expects some questions concerning Cizek's defined-benefit plan. The following year-end information is available ($ in millions) for Cizek.

Projected benefit obligation	$5,285
Pension assets	$4,725
Accumulated OCI (Prior service cost)	$640
Pension expense	$325
Total assets	$21,162

Troy expects the loan committee to ask about the impact of recent changes in the stock and bond capital markets on Cizek' pension plan. For example, one of Cizek's loans has a covenant that is based on the debt to asset ratio.

Instructions

Prepare brief responses to the flowing questions to help Troy prepare for the meeting.

(a) What is the effect of the defined-benefit plan on Cizek's debt to equity ratio?
(b) Recently, market interest rates and returns in the stock market have increased, and similar performance is expected in the next year. What are the implications of these developments for the funded status of Cizek's pension plan and their impact on the debt to total assets ratio?

(c) Troy is also concerned with cost of the pension plan and its drag on earnings. What are some actions that Cizek management could take to decrease the cost of its pension plan?

■ International Reporting Issues

AIA16-4 **Kyowa Hakko Kogyo Co., Ltd.**, is an R&D–based company with special strengths in biotechnology. The company is dedicated to the creation of new value in the life sciences, especially in its two core business segments of pharmaceuticals and biochemicals, and strives to contribute to the health and well-being of people around the world. The company provided the following disclosures related to its retirement benefits in its 2005 annual report.

Kyowa Hakko Kogyo Co., Ltd.

Note 1. Basis of Presenting Consolidated Financial Statements (partial)

Kyowa Hakko Kogyo Co., Ltd. (the "Company") maintains its accounts and records in accordance with the provisions set forth in the Japanese Commercial Code and the Securities and Exchange Law and in conformity with generally accepted accounting principles and practices prevailing in Japan. . . . The Company's fiscal year is from April 1 to March 31. Therefore, "fiscal 2005" begins on April 1, 2004 and ends on March 31, 2005.

Reserve for Retirement Benefits to Employees

A reserve for retirement benefits to employees is provided at an amount equal to the present value of the projected benefit obligation less fair value of the plan assets at the year-end. Unrecognized prior service costs are amortized on a straight-line basis over five years from the year they occur. Unrecognized actuarial differences are amortized on a straight-line basis over ten years from the year after they occur.

Note 8. Reserve for Retirement Benefits to Employees

The Company and its domestic consolidated subsidiaries operate various defined benefit plans, including a corporate pension plan (the so-called cash-balanced plan), a group contributory plan, a tax-qualified pension plan and a severance payment plan.

(a) The reserve for retirement benefits as of March 31, 2005, is analyzed as follows.

	Millions of Yen 2005	Thousands of U.S. Dollars 2005
Projected benefit obligations	¥(63,854)	$(594,599)
Plan assets	31,270	291,182
Unfunded benefit obligations	(32,584)	(303,417)
Unrecognized actuarial differences	7,017	65,341
Unrecognized prior service costs (Note 2)	(5,004)	(46,597)
	¥(30,571)	$(284,673)

(b) The net periodic pension expense related to the retirement benefits for fiscal 2005 is as follows.

	Millions of Yen 2005	Thousands of U.S. Dollars 2005
Service cost	¥2,650	$24,676
Interest cost	1,583	14,741
Expected return on plan assets	(736)	(6,854)
Amortization of unrecognized actuarial differences	1,628	15,160
Amortization of unrecognized prior service costs	(1,431)	(13,325)
	¥3,694	$34,398

(c) Assumptions used in calculation of the above information are as follows.

	2005
Discount rate	2.5%
Expected rate of return	2.8%

Instructions

Use the information on Kyowa to respond to the following requirements.

(a) What are the key differences in accounting for pensions under U.S. and Japanese standards?

(b) Briefly explain how differences in U.S. and Japanese standards for pensions would affect the amounts reported in the financial statements.

(c) In light of the differences identified above, would Kyowa's income and equity be higher or lower under U.S. GAAP compared to Japanese standards? Explain.

Concepts for Analysis

AIA16-5 **(Stock Compensation Plans)** The following two items appeared on the Internet concerning the passage of *SFAS No. 123(R)*.

WASHINGTON, D.C.—February 17, 2005   Congressman David Dreier (R–CA), Chairman of the House Rules Committee, and Congresswoman Anna Eshoo (D–CA) reintroduced legislation today that will preserve broad-based employee stock option plans and give investors critical information they need to understand how employee stock options impact the value of their shares.

"Last year, the U.S. House of Representatives overwhelmingly voted for legislation that would have ensured the continued ability of innovative companies to offer stock options to rank-and-file employees," Dreier stated. "Both the Financial Accounting Standards Board (FASB) and the Securities and Exchange Commission (SEC) continue to ignore our calls to address legitimate concerns about the impact of FASB's new standard on workers' ability to have an ownership stake in the New Economy, and its failure to address the real need of shareholders: accurate and meaningful information about a company's use of stock options."

"In December 2004, FASB issued a stock option expensing standard that will render a huge blow to the 21st century economy," Dreier said. "Their action and the SEC's apparent lack of concern for protecting shareholders, requires us to once again take a firm stand on the side of investors and economic growth. Giving investors the ability to understand how stock options impact the value of their shares is critical. And equally important is preserving the ability of companies to use this innovative tool to attract talented employees."

(*Source: http://dreier.house.gov/releases/pr021705.htm*)

On February 17, Congressman David Dreier (R–CA), and Congresswoman Anna Eshoo (D–CA), officially entered Silicon Valley's bid to gum up the launch of honest reporting of stock option compensation: They co-sponsored a bill to "preserve broad-based employee stock option plans and give investors critical information they need to understand how employee stock options impact the value of their shares." You know what "critical information" they mean: stuff like the stock compensation for the top five officers in a company, with a rigged value set as close to zero as possible. Investors crave this kind of information. Other ways the good Congresspersons want to "help" investors: The bill "also requires the SEC to study the effectiveness of those disclosures over three years, during which time, no new accounting standard related to the treatment of stock options could be recognized. Finally, the bill requires the Secretary of Commerce to conduct a study and report to Congress on the impact of broad-based employee stock option plans on expanding employee corporate ownership, skilled worker recruitment and retention, research and innovation, economic growth, and international competitiveness." . . . It's the old "four corners" basketball strategy: stall, stall, stall. In the meantime, hope for regime change at your opponent, the FASB.

(*Source:* "Here We Go Again!" by Jack Ciesielski, February 21, 2005, *http://www.accountingobserver. com/blog/2005/02/here-we-go-again*)

Instructions

(a) What are the major recommendations of *SFAS No. 123(R)*, "Share-Based Payment"?

(b) How do the provisions of *SFAS No. 123(R)* differ from the bill introduced by members of Congress Dreier and Eshoo, which would require expensing for options issued to only the top five officers in a company? Which approach do you think would result in more useful information? (Focus on comparability.)

(c) The bill in Congress urges the FASB to develop a rule that preserves "the ability of companies to use this innovative tool to attract talented employees." Write a response to these Congress-people explaining the importance of neutrality in financial accounting and reporting.

AIA16-6 **(Pension Terminology)** The following items appear on Hollingsworth Company's financial statements.

1. Under the caption Assets:
Pension asset/liability.

2. Under the caption Liabilities:
   Pension asset/liability.

3. Under the caption Stockholders' Equity:
   Prior service cost as a component of Accumulated Other Comprehensive Income.

4. On the income statement:
   Pension expense.

Instructions

Explain the significance of each of the items above on corporate financial statements. (*Note:* All items set forth above are not necessarily to be found on the statements of a single company.)

AIA16-7 (**Basic Terminology**) In examining the costs of pension plans, Leah Hutcherson, CPA, encounters certain terms. The components of pension costs that the terms represent must be dealt with appropriately if generally accepted accounting principles are to be reflected in the financial statements of entities with pension plans.

Instructions

(a) (1) Discuss the theoretical justification for accrual recognition of pension costs.
    (2) Discuss the relative objectivity of the measurement process of accrual versus cash (pay-as-you-go) accounting for annual pension costs.
(b) Explain the following terms as they apply to accounting for pension plans.
    (1) Market-related asset value.
    (2) Projected benefit obligation.
(c) What information should be disclosed about a company's pension plans in its financial statements and its notes?

(AICPA adapted)

Professional Tools

■ Ethical Decision Making

AIA16-8 (**Pension Termination**) Cardinal Technology recently merged with College Electronix, a computer-graphics manufacturing firm. In performing a comprehensive audit of CE's accounting system, Richard Nye, internal audit manager for Cardinal Technology, discovered that the new subsidiary did not capitalize pension assets and liabilities, subject to the requirements of *FASB Statement No. 87.*

The net present value of CE's pension assets was $15.5 million, the vested benefit obligation was $12.9 million, and the projected benefit obligation was $17.4 million. Nye reported this audit finding to Renée Selma, the newly appointed controller of CE. A few days later Selma called Nye for his advice on what to do. Selma started her conversation by asking, "Can't we eliminate the negative income effect of our pension dilemma simply by terminating the employment of nonvested employees before the end of our fiscal year?"

Instructions

How should Nye respond to Selma's remark about firing nonvested employees?

AIA16-9 (**Postretirement Health-Care Benefits**) Philip Regan, Chief Executive Officer of Relief Dynamics Inc., a large defense contracting firm, is considering ways to improve the company's financial position after several years of sharply declining profitability. One way to do this is to reduce or completely eliminate Relief's commitment to present and future retirees who have full medical and dental benefits coverage. Despite financial problems, the company still is committed to providing excellent pension benefits.

Instructions

Answer the following questions.

(a) What factors should Regan consider before making his decision to cut postretirement health benefits?
(b) Does your answer to the above question change if Relief Dynamics was paying Phil Regan, CEO, a salary of $30 million per year?
(c) In your opinion, how did FASB's *Statement No. 106* influence the commitment of many organizations to its employees?

■ Financial Accounting Research (FARS)

AIA16-10 Richardson Company is contemplating the establishment of a share-based compensation plan to provide long-run incentives for its top management. However, members of the compensation committee of the board of directors have voiced some concerns about adopting these plans, based on news accounts related to a recent accounting standard in this area. They would like you to conduct some research on this recent standard so they can be better informed about the accounting for these plans.

Instructions

Using the **Financial Accounting Research System (FARS)** database, respond to the following items. (Provide text strings used in your search.)

(a) Identify the recent standard governing the accounting for share-based payment compensation plans.

(b) What were the principal reasons for issuing a new standard in this area?

(c) What are the key differences in the measurement of fair value between the new standard and the prior standard?

(d) The Richardson Company board is also considering an employee share-purchase plan, but the board does not want to record expense related to the plan. What criteria must be met to avoid recording expense on an employee stock-purchase plan?

AIA16-11 Jack Kelly Company has grown rapidly since its founding in 2002. To instill loyalty in its employees, Kelly is contemplating establishment of a defined-benefit plan. Kelly knows that lenders and potential investors will pay close attention to the impact of the pension plan on the company's financial statements, particularly any gains or losses that develop in the plan. Kelly has asked you to conduct some research on the accounting for gains and losses in a defined-benefit plan.

Instructions

Using the **Financial Accounting Research System (FARS)** database, respond to the following items. (Provide text strings used in your search.)

(a) Briefly describe how pension gains and losses are accounted for.

(b) Explain the rationale behind the accounting method described in part (a).

(c) Kelly wants to better understand the factors that led to accounting standards for pensions. What environmental factors led to increased regulations over pension cost reporting?

■ Professional Simulation

AIA16-12 Go to the book's companion website, at **www.wiley.com/college/warfield**, to find an interactive problem that simulates the computerized CPA exam. The professional simulation for this chapter asks you to address questions related to the accounting for pensions.

What do the numbers mean?

Guideline Answers to Beyond the Numbers Questions

A Little Honesty Goes a Long Way, p. 849

Q: What about companies that did not voluntarily begin expensing options? How do you think the market would respond to their inaction on option expensing?

A: Some might argue that companies that do not voluntarily expense have something to hide or that they cannot withstand the hit to their earnings when they expense options.

On the other hand, these same companies might respond by cutting back on the use of options when they must account for the expense. This could be viewed by the market as good news, if other compensation methods are more effective while at the same time do not dilute existing shareholders' ownership share. In such a case, non-expensers might also experience positive market reactions.

Which Plan Is Right for You?, p. 854

Q: Another recent trend in the labor market is the mobility of workers. Today, workers expect to work for several employers during their careers. This is in contrast to the post-World War II economy in which most employees expected to sign on with one employer for their entire career. Assuming you are a member of this more mobile workforce, which plan would you prefer? Explain.

A: In a defined-benefit plan, employees generally must stay with an employer for a minimum number of years before their pension benefits vest. Therefore, if an employee

leaves the company before the benefits vest, he or she loses any pension benefits accrued.

Not so with the defined-contribution plan. As indicated, the employee controls the defined-contribution plan assets (and bears the risk associated with the assets.) When employees leave an employer with a defined-contribution plan, they can take their pension savings with them, a feature referred to as "portability." Thus, employees of a mobile workforce, on average, are more likely to prefer a defined-contribution pension plan, because their pension benefits are mobile too.

Pension Costs Ups and Downs, p. 861

Q: What are some pension asset management strategies that a company could pursue to improve the pension income (return on assets) element of its pension expense?

A: Given that the return on assets is a function of the expected rate of return multiplied by the asset balance, the employer can increase the rate of return by increasing the amount invested in pension assets or increase the expected rate of return. That is, simply make bigger contributions to the pension fund or invest in assets that earn higher rates of return.

Companies face a cost-benefit tradeoff in pursuing either of these strategies. First, companies may not receive tax

deductions on excess contributions to their pension fund. These limits are established by the tax code. Furthermore, investing in higher return assets generally will be accompanied by higher risk. Thus, while the returns might be higher, there is also increased risk that some of the investments will do poorly, raising the possibility that the employer will have to make additional contributions to the plan assets to make up for these shortfalls. Note that the required disclosure on the composition of pension assets is designed to provide information that can be used to assess the risk of the pension plan assets.

Bailing Out, p. 870

Q: One proposal to deal with the drain on the PBGC would be to increase the premiums the pension plan sponsors pay into the plan. What are the implications of this proposal to the trends in pension plan offerings? (See "Which Plan Is for You?" on page 854.)

A: Employers (and hence the PBGC, if an employer fails) have a continuing obligation only for a defined-benefit plan.

As a consequence, the proposal to increase the insurance premiums paid to the PBGC will increase the cost for companies that sponsor defined-benefit plans and likely will provide additional incentives for companies to move away from defined-benefit plans.

Remember to check the book's companion website to find additional resources for this chapter.

CHAPTER 17

ACCOUNTING FOR LEASES

More Companies Ask, "Why Buy?"

Leasing has grown tremendously in popularity. Today it is the fastest growing form of capital investment. Instead of borrowing money to buy an airplane, computer, nuclear core, or satellite, a company makes periodic payments to lease these assets. Even gambling casinos lease their slot machines. Of the 600 companies surveyed by the AICPA in 2006, 583 disclosed lease data.[1]

A classic example is the airline industry. Many travelers on airlines such as **United, Delta**, and **Southwest** believe these airlines own the planes on which they are flying. Often, this is not the case. Here are the lease percentages for the major U.S. airlines.

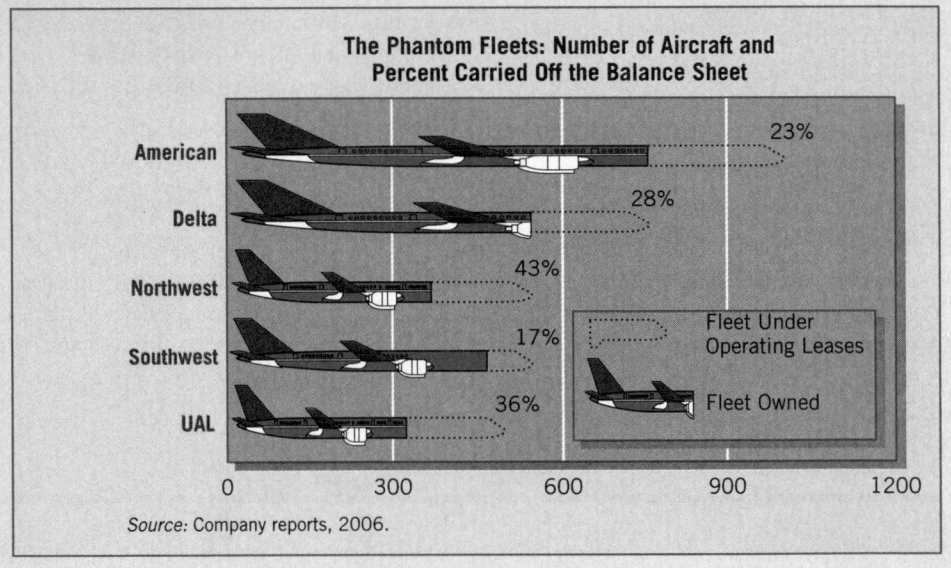

The Phantom Fleets: Number of Aircraft and Percent Carried Off the Balance Sheet

Airline	Percent
American	23%
Delta	28%
Northwest	43%
Southwest	17%
UAL	36%

Fleet Under Operating Leases

Fleet Owned

Source: Company reports, 2006.

As you will learn, airlines lease many of their airplanes due to the favorable accounting treatment they receive if they lease rather than purchase.

[1]AICPA, *Accounting Trends and Techniques—2006.* Eight out of 10 U.S. companies lease all or some of their equipment. Companies that lease tend to be smaller, are high growth, and are in technology-oriented industries (see *www.techlease.com*).

Preview of Chapter 17

Our opening story indicates the increased significance and prevalence of lease arrangements. As a result, the need for uniform accounting and informative reporting of these transactions has intensified. In this chapter we look at the accounting issues related to leasing. *The content and organization of this chapter are as follows.*

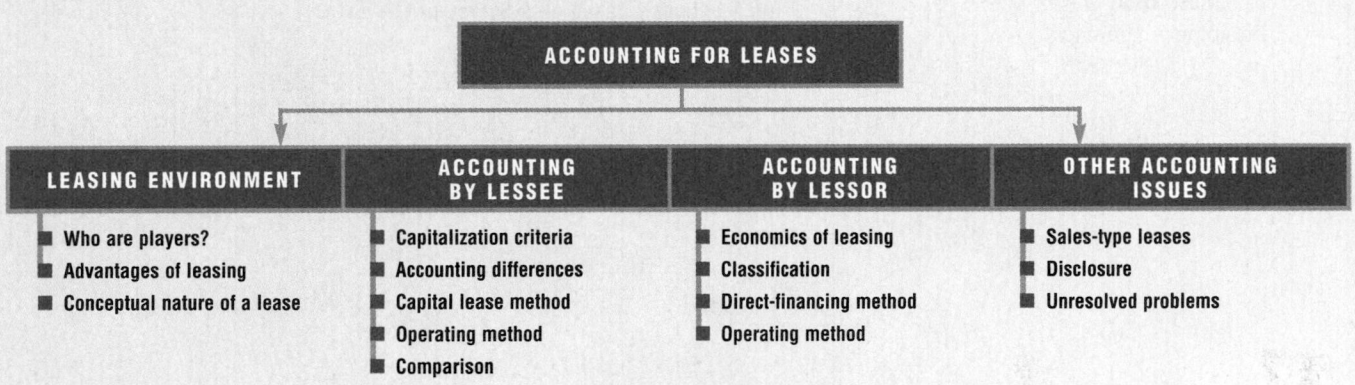

ACCOUNTING FOR LEASES

LEASING ENVIRONMENT	ACCOUNTING BY LESSEE	ACCOUNTING BY LESSOR	OTHER ACCOUNTING ISSUES
■ Who are players? ■ Advantages of leasing ■ Conceptual nature of a lease	■ Capitalization criteria ■ Accounting differences ■ Capital lease method ■ Operating method ■ Comparison	■ Economics of leasing ■ Classification ■ Direct-financing method ■ Operating method	■ Sales-type leases ■ Disclosure ■ Unresolved problems

Learning Objectives

After studying this chapter, you should be able to:

1. Explain the nature, economic substance, and advantages of lease transactions.
2. Describe the accounting criteria and procedures for capitalizing leases by the lessee.
3. Contrast the operating and capitalization methods of recording leases.
4. Identify the classifications of leases for the lessor.
5. Describe the lessor's accounting for direct-financing leases.
6. Describe the lessor's accounting for sales-type leases.
7. List the disclosure requirements for leases.

Inside Chapter 17

- **What Do the Numbers Mean?**
  Off-balance-sheet financing (p. 895)
  Restatements on the menu (p. 904)
  Dollars to doughnuts (p. 906)
  Xerox takes on the SEC (p. 913)
- **What's the Principle?** (pp. 896, 898, 914)
- **Convergence Corner** (p. 918)
- **Accounting, Analysis, Principles** (p. 919)
  Account for a leased asset.
  Discuss the impact of lease accounting on profitability and solvency.
  Explain the reliability attributes of lease capitalization.

THE LEASING ENVIRONMENT

OBJECTIVE 1

Explain the nature, economic substance, and advantages of lease transactions.

Aristotle once said, "Wealth does not lie in ownership but in the use of things"! Clearly, many U.S. companies have decided that Aristotle is right, as they have become heavily involved in leasing assets rather than owning them. For example, Illustration 17-1 shows the growth in leasing transactions from 1990 to 2003.

Illustration 17-1
Equipment Leasing Growth

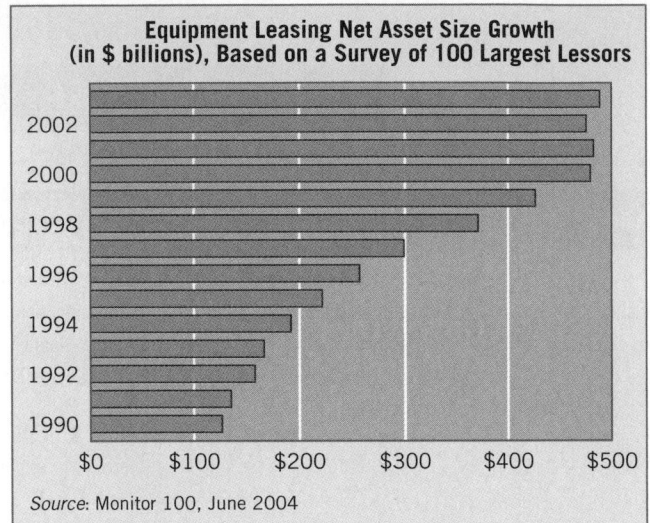

What types of assets are being leased? As the opening story indicated, any type of equipment can be leased, such as railcars, helicopters, bulldozers, barges, CT scanners, computers, and so on. The largest group of leased equipment involves information technology equipment, followed by assets in the transportation area (trucks, aircraft, rail), and then construction and agriculture.

Who Are the Players?

A **lease** is a contractual agreement between a lessor and a lessee. This arrangement gives the **lessee** the right to use specific property, owned by the **lessor**, for a specified period of time. In return for the use of the property, the lessee makes rental payments over the lease term to the lessor.

Who are the lessors that own this property? They generally fall into one of three categories:

1 Banks.

2 Captive leasing companies.

3 Independents.

Banks

Banks are the largest players in the leasing business. They have low-cost funds, which give them the advantage of being able to purchase assets at less cost than their competitors. Banks also have been more aggressive in the leasing markets. They have decided that there is money to be made in leasing, and as a result they have expanded their product lines in this area. Finally, leasing transactions are now more standardized, which gives banks an advantage because they do not have to be as innovative in structuring lease arrangements. Thus banks like **Wells Fargo**, **Chase**, **Citigroup**, and **PNC** have substantial leasing subsidiaries.

892

Captive Leasing Companies

Captive leasing companies are subsidiaries whose primary business is to perform leasing operations for the parent company. Companies like **Caterpillar Financial Services Corp.** (for Caterpillar), **Chrysler Financial** (for Daimler-Chrysler), and **IBM Global Financing** (for IBM) facilitate the sale of products to consumers. For example, suppose that **Sterling Construction Co.** wants to acquire a number of earthmovers from Caterpillar. In this case, Caterpillar Financial Services Corp. will offer to structure the transaction as a lease rather than as a purchase. Thus, Caterpillar Financial provides the financing rather than an outside financial institution.

Captive leasing companies have the point-of-sale advantage in finding leasing customers. That is, as soon as Caterpillar receives a possible order, its leasing subsidiary can quickly develop a lease-financing arrangement. Furthermore, the captive lessor has product knowledge that gives it an advantage when financing the parents' product.

The current trend is for captives to focus primarily on their company's products rather than do general lease financing. For example, **Boeing Capital** and **UPS Capital** are two captives that have left the general finance business to focus exclusively on their parent companies' products.

Independents

Independents are the final category of lessors. Independents have not done well over the last few years. Their market share has dropped fairly dramatically as banks and captive leasing companies have become more aggressive in the lease-financing area. Independents do not have point-of-sale access, nor do they have a low cost of funds advantage. What they *are* often good at is developing innovative contracts for lessees. In addition, they are starting to act as captive finance companies for some companies that do not have a leasing subsidiary.

Illustration 17-2 shows the new business volume by lessor type in a recent five-year period. As the chart shows, both banks and captives have increased business at the expense of the independents.

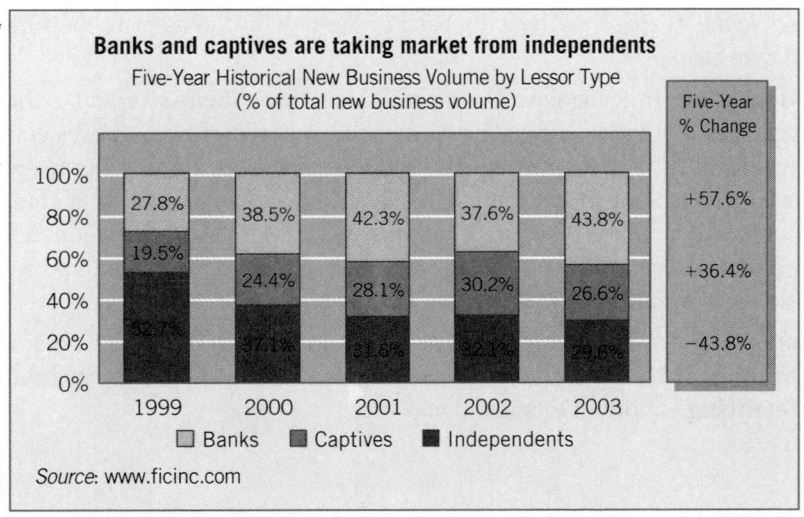

Banks and captives are taking market from independents

Five-Year Historical New Business Volume by Lessor Type
(% of total new business volume)

Illustration 17-2
Lessor Types

Advantages of Leasing

The growth in leasing indicates that it often has some genuine advantages over owning property, such as:

1   **100% Financing at Fixed Rates.** Leases are often signed without requiring any money down from the lessee. This helps the lessee conserve scarce cash—an especially

desirable feature for new and developing companies. In addition, lease payments often remain fixed, which protects the lessee against inflation and increases in the cost of money. The following comment explains why companies choose a lease instead of a conventional loan: "Our local bank finally came up to 80 percent of the purchase price but wouldn't go any higher, and they wanted a floating interest rate. We just couldn't afford the down payment, and we needed to lock in a final payment rate we knew we could live with."

2 **Protection Against Obsolescence.** Leasing equipment reduces risk of obsolescence to the lessee, and in many cases passes the risk of residual value to the lessor. For example, **Merck** (a pharmaceutical maker) leases computers. Under the lease agreement, Merck may turn in an old computer for a new model at any time, canceling the old lease and writing a new one. The lessor adds the cost of the new lease to the balance due on the old lease, less the old computer's trade-in value. As one treasurer remarked, "Our instinct is to purchase." But if a new computer is likely to come along in a short time, "then leasing is just a heck of a lot more convenient than purchasing."

3 **Flexibility.** Lease agreements may contain less restrictive provisions than other debt agreements. Innovative lessors can tailor a lease agreement to the lessee's special needs. For instance, the duration of the lease—the **lease term**— may be anything from a short period of time to the entire expected economic life of the asset. The rental payments may be level from year to year, or they may increase or decrease in amount. The payment amount may be predetermined or may vary with sales, the prime interest rate, the Consumer Price Index, or some other factor. In most cases the rent is set to enable the lessor to recover the cost of the asset plus a fair return over the life of the lease.

4 **Less Costly Financing.** Some companies find leasing cheaper than other forms of financing. For example, start-up companies in depressed industries or companies in low tax brackets may lease to claim tax benefits that they might otherwise lose. Depreciation deductions offer no benefit to companies that have little if any taxable income. Through leasing, the leasing companies or financial institutions use these tax benefits. They can then pass some of these tax benefits back to the user of the asset in the form of lower rental payments.

INTERNATIONAL INSIGHT

Some companies "double dip" on the international level too. The leasing rules of the lessor's and lessee's countries may differ, permitting both parties to own the asset. Thus, both lessor and lessee receive the tax benefits related to depreciation.

5 **Tax Advantages.** In some cases, companies can "have their cake and eat it too" with tax advantages that leases offer. That is, for financial reporting purposes companies do not report an asset or a liability for the lease arrangement. For tax purposes, however, companies can capitalize and depreciate the leased asset. As a result, a company takes deductions earlier rather than later and also reduces its taxes. A common vehicle for this type of transaction is a "synthetic lease" arrangement. (On page 906 we discuss a synthetic lease used by **Krispy Kreme**.)

6 **Off-Balance-Sheet Financing.** Certain leases do not add debt on a balance sheet or affect financial ratios. In fact, they may add to borrowing capacity.[2] Such **off-balance-sheet financing** is critical to some companies.

---

[2]As demonstrated later in this chapter, certain types of lease arrangements are not capitalized on the balance sheet. The liabilities section is thereby relieved of large future lease commitments that, if recorded, would adversely affect the debt to equity ratio. The reluctance to record lease obligations as liabilities is one of the primary reasons some companies resist capitalized lease accounting.

What do the numbers mean?

As shown in our opening story, airlines use lease arrangements extensively. This results in a great deal of off-balance-sheet financing. The following chart indicates that many airlines that lease aircraft understate debt levels by a substantial amount.

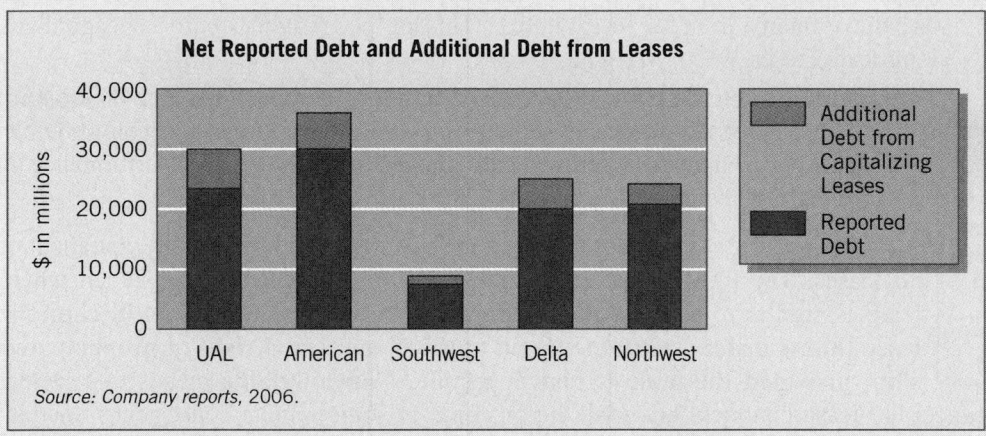

Source: Company reports, 2006.

And airlines are not the only ones playing the off-balance-sheet game. A recent SEC study estimates that for SEC registrants, off-balance-sheet lease obligations total more the $1.3 trillion, or 31 times the amount of on-balance-sheet obligations. (See SEC Off-Balance Sheet report at *www.sec.gov/news/studies/soxoffbalancerpt.pdf.*) Thus, analysts must adjust reported debt levels for the effects of non-capitalized leases. A methodology for making this adjustment is discussed in Eugene A. Imhoff, Jr., Robert C. Lipe, and David W. Wright, "Operating Leases: Impact of Constructive Capitalization," *Accounting Horizons* (March 1991).

Beyond the Numbers

How does noncapitalization of leases affect recorded assets and common ratios based on assets?

Conceptual Nature of a Lease

If **Delta** borrows $47 million on a 10-year note from **Bank of America** to purchase a Boeing 737 jet plane, Delta should clearly report an asset and related liability at that amount on its balance sheet. Similarly, if Delta purchases the 737 for $47 million directly from Boeing through an installment purchase over 10 years, it should obviously report an asset and related liability (i.e., it should "capitalize" the installment transaction).

However, what if Delta **leases** the Boeing 737 for 10 years from **International Lease Finance Corp. (ILFC)**—the world's largest lessor of airplanes—through a noncancelable lease transaction with payments of the same amount as the installment purchase transaction? In that case, opinion differs over how to report this transaction. The various views on **capitalization of leases** are as follows.

1 **Do Not Capitalize Any Leased Assets.** This view considers capitalization inappropriate, because Delta does not own the property. Furthermore, a lease is an **"executory" contract** requiring continuing performance by both parties. Because companies do not currently capitalize other executory contracts (such as purchase commitments and employment contracts), they should not capitalize leases either.

2 **Capitalize Leases That Are Similar to Installment Purchases.** This view holds that companies should report transactions in accordance with their economic substance.

Therefore, if companies capitalize installment purchases, they should also capitalize leases that have similar characteristics. For example, Delta Airlines makes the same payments over a 10-year period for either a lease or an installment purchase. Lessees make rental payments, whereas owners make mortgage payments. Why should the financial statements not report these transactions in the same manner?

3   **Capitalize All Long-Term Leases.** This approach requires only the long-term right to use the property in order to capitalize. This property-rights approach capitalizes all long-term leases.[3]

4   **Capitalize Firm Leases Where the Penalty for Nonperformance Is Substantial.** A final approach advocates capitalizing only "firm" (noncancelable) contractual rights and obligations. "Firm" means that it is unlikely to avoid performance under the lease without a severe penalty.[4]

In short, the various viewpoints range from no capitalization to capitalization of all leases. The FASB apparently agrees with the capitalization approach when the lease is similar to an installment purchase: It notes that Delta **should capitalize a lease that transfers substantially all of the benefits and risks of property ownership, provided the lease is noncancelable**. **Noncancelable** means that Delta can cancel the lease contract only upon the outcome of some remote contingency, or that the cancellation provisions and penalties of the contract are so costly to Delta that cancellation probably will not occur.

This viewpoint leads to three basic conclusions: (1) Companies must identify the characteristics that indicate the transfer of substantially all of the benefits and risks of ownership. (2) The same characteristics should apply consistently to the lessee and the lessor. (3) Those leases that do **not** transfer substantially all the benefits and risks of ownership are operating leases. Companies should not capitalize operating leases. Instead, companies should account for them as rental payments and receipts.

WHAT'S THE PRINCIPLE?

The issue of how to report leases is the classic case of substance versus form. Although legal title does not technically pass in lease transactions, the benefits from the use of the property do transfer.

ACCOUNTING BY THE LESSEE

OBJECTIVE 2

Describe the accounting criteria and procedures for capitalizing leases by the lessee.

If Delta Airlines (the lessee) **capitalizes** a lease, it records an asset and a liability generally equal to the present value of the rental payments. ILFC (the lessor), having transferred substantially all the benefits and risks of ownership, recognizes a sale by removing the asset from the balance sheet and replacing it with a receivable. The typical journal entries for Delta and ILFC, assuming leased and capitalized equipment, appear as shown in Illustration 17-3.

Illustration 17-3
Journal Entries for Capitalized Lease

Delta (Lessee)			ILFC (Lessor)		
Leased Equipment	XXX		Lease Receivable	XXX	
Lease Liability		XXX	Equipment		XXX

---

[3]The property rights approach was originally recommended in a research study by the AICPA: John H. Myers, "Reporting of Leases in Financial Statements," *Accounting Research Study No. 4* (New York: AICPA, 1964), pp. 10–11. Recently, this view has received additional support. See Peter H. Knutson, "Financial Reporting in the 1990s and Beyond," Position Paper (Charlottesville, Va.: AIMR, 1993), and Warren McGregor, "Accounting for Leases: A New Approach," Special Report (Norwalk, Conn.: FASB, 1996).

[4]Yuji Ijiri, *Recognition of Contractual Rights and Obligations,* Research Report (Stamford, Conn.: FASB, 1980).

Having capitalized the asset, Delta records depreciation on the leased asset. Both ILFC and Delta treat the lease rental payments as consisting of interest and principal.

If Delta does not capitalize the lease, it does not record an asset, nor does ILFC remove one from its books. When Delta makes a lease payment, it records rental expense; ILFC recognizes rental revenue.

In order to record a lease as a **capital lease**, the lease must be noncancelable. Further, it must meet one or more of the four criteria listed in Illustration 17-4.

Capitalization Criteria (Lessee)

- The lease transfers ownership of the property to the lessee.
- The lease contains a bargain purchase option.[5]
- The lease term is equal to 75 percent or more of the estimated economic life of the leased property.
- The present value of the minimum lease payments (excluding executory costs) equals or exceeds 90 percent of the fair value of the leased property.[6]

Illustration 17-4
Capitalization Criteria for Lessee

Delta classifies and accounts for leases that **do not meet any of the four criteria** as **operating leases**. Illustration 17-5 shows that a lease meeting any one of the four criteria results in the lessee having a capital lease.

Illustration 17-5
Diagram of Lessee's Criteria for Lease Classification

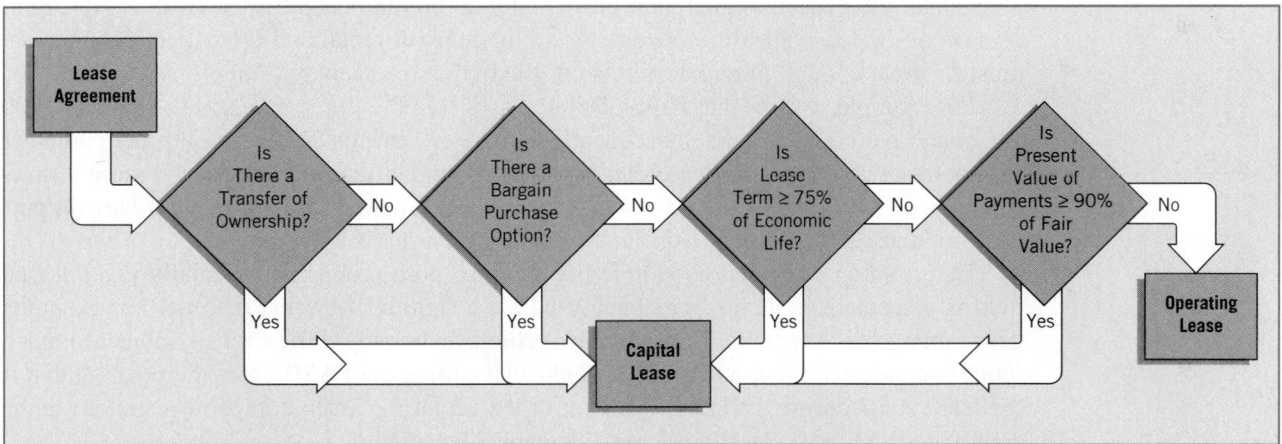

In keeping with the FASB's reasoning that a company consumes a significant portion of the value of the asset in the first 75 percent of its life, the lessee applies neither the third nor the fourth criterion when the inception of the lease occurs during the last 25 percent of the asset's life.

Capitalization Criteria

Three of the four **capitalization criteria** that apply to lessees are controversial and can be difficult to apply in practice. We discuss each of the criteria in detail on the following pages.

Transfer of Ownership Test

If the lease transfers ownership of the asset to the lessee, it is a capital lease. This criterion is not controversial and easily implemented in practice.

---

[5]We define a bargain purchase option in the next section.

[6]"Accounting for Leases," *FASB Statement No. 13* as amended and interpreted through May 1980 (Stamford, Conn.: FASB, 1980), par. 7.

Bargain Purchase Option Test

A **bargain purchase option** allows the lessee to purchase the leased property for a price that is **significantly lower** than the property's expected fair value at the date the option becomes exercisable. At the inception of the lease, the difference between the option price and the expected fair market value must be large enough to make exercise of the option reasonably assured.

For example, assume that Brett's Delivery Service was to lease a Honda Accord for $599 per month for 40 months, with an option to purchase for $100 at the end of the 40-month period. If the estimated fair value of the Honda Accord is $3,000 at the end of the 40 months, the $100 option to purchase is clearly a bargain. Therefore, Brett must capitalize the lease. In other cases, the criterion may not be as easy to apply, and determining *now* that a certain *future* price is a bargain can be difficult.

Economic Life Test (75% Test)

If the lease period equals or exceeds 75 percent of the asset's economic life, the lessor transfers most of the risks and rewards of ownership to the lessee. Capitalization is therefore appropriate. However, determining the lease term and the economic life of the asset can be troublesome.

The **lease term** is generally considered to be the fixed, noncancelable term of the lease. However, a bargain renewal option, if provided in the lease agreement, can extend this period. A **bargain renewal option** allows the lessee to renew the lease for a rental that is lower than the expected fair rental at the date the option becomes exercisable. At the inception of the lease, the difference between the renewal rental and the expected fair rental must be great enough to make exercise of the option to renew reasonably assured.

For example, assume that **Home Depot** leases **Dell** PCs for two years at a rental of $100 per month per computer and subsequently can lease them for $10 per month per computer for another two years. The lease clearly offers a bargain renewal option; the lease term is considered to be four years. However, with bargain renewal options, as with bargain purchase options, it is sometimes difficult to determine what is a bargain.[7]

Determining estimated economic life can also pose problems, especially if the leased item is a specialized item or has been used for a significant period of time. For example, determining the economic life of a nuclear core is extremely difficult. It is subject to much more than normal "wear and tear." As indicated earlier, the FASB takes the position that if the lease starts during the last 25 percent of the life of the asset, companies cannot use the economic life test to classify a lease as a capital lease.

Recovery of Investment Test (90% Test)

If the present value of the minimum lease payments equals or exceeds 90 percent of the fair market value of the asset, then a lessee like Delta should capitalize the leased asset. Why? If the present value of the minimum lease payments is reasonably close to the market price of the aircraft, Delta is effectively purchasing the asset.

Determining the present value of the minimum lease payments involves three important concepts: (1) minimum lease payments, (2) executory costs, and (3) discount rate.

---

[7]The original lease term is also extended for leases having the following: substantial penalties for nonrenewal; periods for which the lessor has the option to renew or extend the lease; renewal periods preceding the date a bargain purchase option becomes exercisable; and renewal periods in which any lessee guarantees of the lessor's debt are expected to be in effect or in which there will be a loan outstanding from the lessee to the lessor. The lease term, however, can never extend beyond the time a bargain purchase option becomes exercisable. "Accounting for Leases: Sale-Leaseback Transactions Involving Real Estate; Sales-Type Leases of Real Estate; Definition of the Lease Term; Initial Direct Costs of Direct Financing Leases," *Statement of Financial Accounting Standards No. 98* (Stamford, Conn.: FASB, 1988).

Minimum Lease Payments. Delta is obligated to make, or expected to make, **minimum lease payments** in connection with the leased property. These payments include the following.

1 **Minimum Rental Payments.** Minimum rental payments are those that Delta must make to ILFC under the lease agreement. In some cases, the minimum rental payments may equal the minimum lease payments. However, the minimum lease payments may also include a guaranteed residual value (if any), penalty for failure to renew, or a bargain purchase option (if any), as we note below.

2 **Guaranteed Residual Value.** The **residual value** is the estimated fair (market) value of the leased property at the end of the lease term. ILFC may transfer the risk of loss to Delta or to a third party by obtaining a guarantee of the estimated residual value. The **guaranteed residual value** is either (1) the certain or determinable amount that Delta will pay ILFC at the end of the lease to purchase the aircraft at the end of the lease, or (2) the amount Delta or the third party guarantees that ILFC will realize if the aircraft is returned. (**Third-party guarantors** are, in essence, insurers who for a fee assume the risk of deficiencies in leased asset residual value.) If not guaranteed in full, the **unguaranteed residual value** is the estimated residual value exclusive of any portion guaranteed.[8]

3 **Penalty for Failure to Renew or Extend the Lease.** The amount Delta must pay if the agreement specifies that it must extend or renew the lease, and it fails to do so.

4 **Bargain Purchase Option.** As we indicated earlier (in item 1), an option given to Delta to purchase the aircraft at the end of the lease term at a price that is fixed sufficiently below the expected fair value, so that, at the inception of the lease, purchase is reasonably assured.

Delta excludes executory costs (defined below) from its computation of the present value of the minimum lease payments.

Executory Costs. Like most assets, leased tangible assets incur insurance, maintenance, and tax expenses—called **executory costs**—during their economic life. If ILFC retains responsibility for the payment of these "ownership-type costs," **it should exclude**, in computing the present value of the minimum lease payments, a portion of each lease payment that represents executory costs. Executory costs do not represent payment on or reduction of the obligation.

Many lease agreements specify that the lessee directly pays executory costs to the appropriate third parties. In these cases, the lessor can use the rental payment **without adjustment** in the present value computation.

Discount Rate. A lessee, like Delta computes the present value of the minimum lease payments using its **incremental borrowing rate**. This rate is defined as: "The rate that, at the inception of the lease, the lessee would have incurred to borrow the funds necessary to buy the leased asset on a secured loan with repayment terms similar to the payment schedule called for in the lease."[9]

To determine whether the present value of these payments is less than 90 percent of the fair market value of the property, Delta discounts the payments using its incremental borrowing rate. Determining the incremental borrowing rate often requires judgment because the lessee bases it on a hypothetical purchase of the property.

However, there is one exception to this rule. If (1) Delta knows the **implicit interest rate computed by ILFC** and (2) it is less than Delta's incremental borrowing rate, then

---

[8]A lease provision requiring the lessee to make up a residual value deficiency that is attributable to damage, extraordinary wear and tear, or excessive usage is not included in the minimum lease payments. Lessees recognize such costs as period costs when incurred. "Lessee Guarantee of the Residual Value of Leased Property," *FASB Interpretation No. 19* (Stamford, Conn.: FASB, 1977), par. 3.

[9]*FASB Statement No. 13,* op. cit., par. 5 (l).

Delta **must use ILFC's implicit rate**. What is the **interest rate implicit in the lease**? It is the discount rate that, when applied to the minimum lease payments and any unguaranteed residual value accruing to the lessor, causes the aggregate present value to equal the fair value of the leased property to the lessor.[10]

The purpose of this exception is twofold. First, **the implicit rate of ILFC is generally a more realistic rate** to use in determining the amount (if any) to report as the asset and related liability for Delta. Second, the guideline ensures that Delta **does not use an artificially high incremental borrowing rate** that would cause the present value of the minimum lease payments to be less than 90 percent of the fair market value of the aircraft. Use of such a rate would thus make it possible to avoid capitalization of the asset and related liability.

Delta may argue that it cannot determine the implicit rate of the lessor and therefore should use the higher rate. However, in most cases, Delta can approximate the implicit rate used by ILFC. The determination of whether or not a reasonable estimate could be made will require judgment, particularly where the result from using the incremental borrowing rate comes close to meeting the 90 percent test. Because Delta **may not capitalize the leased property at more than its fair value** (as we discuss later), it cannot use an excessively low discount rate.

Asset and Liability Accounted for Differently

In a capital lease transaction, Delta uses the lease as a source of financing. ILFC finances the transaction (provides the investment capital) through the leased asset. Delta makes rent payments, which actually are installment payments. Therefore, over the life of the aircraft rented, **the rental payments to ILFC constitute a payment of principal plus interest**.

Asset and Liability Recorded

Under the capital lease method, Delta treats the lease transaction as if it purchases the aircraft in a financing transaction. That is, Delta acquires the aircraft and creates an obligation. Therefore, it records a capital lease as an asset and a liability at the lower of (1) the present value of the minimum lease payments (excluding executory costs) or (2) the fair-market value of the leased asset at the inception of the lease. The rationale for this approach is that companies should not record a leased asset for more than its fair market value.

Depreciation Period

One troublesome aspect of accounting for the depreciation of the capitalized leased asset relates to the period of depreciation. If the lease agreement transfers ownership of the asset to Delta (criterion 1) or contains a bargain purchase option (criterion 2), Delta depreciates the aircraft consistent with its normal depreciation policy for other aircraft, **using the economic life of the asset**.

On the other hand, if the lease does not transfer ownership or does not contain a bargain purchase option, then Delta depreciates it over the **term of the lease**. In this case, the aircraft reverts to ILFC after a certain period of time.

Effective-Interest Method

Throughout the term of the lease, Delta uses the **effective-interest method** to allocate each lease payment between principal and interest. This method produces a periodic interest expense equal to a constant percentage of the carrying value of the lease obligation. When applying the effective-interest method to capital leases, Delta must use the same discount rate that determines the present value of the minimum lease payments.

---

[10]Ibid., par. 5 (k).

Depreciation Concept

Although Delta computes the amounts initially capitalized as an asset and recorded as an obligation at the same present value, the **depreciation of the aircraft and the discharge of the obligation are independent accounting processes** during the term of the lease. It should depreciate the leased asset by applying conventional depreciation methods: straight-line, sum-of-the-years'-digits, declining-balance, units of production, etc. The FASB uses the term "amortization" more frequently than "depreciation" to recognize intangible leased property rights. We prefer "depreciation" to describe the write-off of a tangible asset's expired services.

Capital Lease Method (Lessee)

To illustrate a capital lease, assume that **Caterpillar Financial Services Corp.** (a subsidiary of Caterpillar) and **Sterling Construction Corp.** sign a lease agreement dated January 1, 2008, that calls for Caterpillar to lease a front-end loader to Sterling beginning January 1, 2008. The terms and provisions of the lease agreement, and other pertinent data, are as follows.

- The term of the lease is five years. The lease agreement is noncancelable, requiring equal rental payments of $25,981.62 at the beginning of each year (annuity due basis).
- The loader has a fair value at the inception of the lease of $100,000, an estimated economic life of five years, and no residual value.
- Sterling pays all of the executory costs directly to third parties except for the property taxes of $2,000 per year, which it includes as part of its annual payments to Caterpillar.
- The lease contains no renewal options. The loader reverts to Caterpillar at the termination of the lease.
- Sterling's incremental borrowing rate is 11 percent per year.
- Sterling depreciates, on a straight-line basis, similar equipment that it owns.
- Caterpillar sets the annual rental to earn a rate of return on its investment of 10 percent per year; Sterling knows this fact.[11]

The lease meets the criteria for classification as a capital lease for the following reasons:

1 The lease term of five years, being equal to the equipment's estimated economic life of five years, satisfies the 75 percent test.
2 The present value of the minimum lease payments ($100,000 as computed below) exceeds 90 percent of the fair value of the loader ($100,000).

The minimum lease payments are $119,908.10 ($23,981.62 × 5). Sterling computes the amount capitalized as leased assets as the present value of the minimum lease payments (excluding executory costs—property taxes of $2,000) as shown in Illustration 17-6.

Capitalized amount = ($25,981.62 − $2,000) × Present value of an annuity due of 1 for 5 periods at 10% (Table 5 in Appendix A)
= $23,981.62 × 4.16986
= $100,000

Illustration 17-6
Computation of Capitalized Lease Payments

[11]If Sterling has an incremental borrowing rate of, say, 9 percent (lower than the 10 percent rate used by Caterpillar) and it did not know the rate used by Caterpillar, the present value computation would yield a capitalized amount of $101,675.35 ($23,981.62 × 4.23972). And, because this amount exceeds the $100,000 fair value of the equipment, Sterling would have to capitalize the $100,000 and use 10 percent as its effective rate for amortization of the lease obligation.

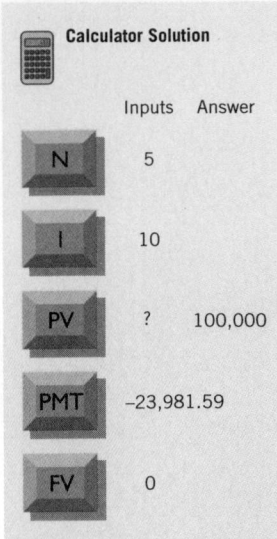

Calculator Solution

	Inputs	Answer
N	5	
I	10	
PV	?	100,000
PMT	−23,981.59	
FV	0	

Sterling uses Caterpillar's implicit interest rate of 10 percent instead of its incremental borrowing rate of 11 percent because (1) it is lower and (2) it knows about it. Sterling records the capital lease on its books on January 1, 2008, as:

Leased Equipment under Capital Leases	100,000	
Lease Liability		100,000

Note that the entry records the obligation at the net amount of $100,000 (the present value of the future rental payments) rather than at the gross amount of $119,908.10 ($23,981.62 × 5).

Sterling records the **first lease payment on January 1, 2008**, as follows:

Property Tax Expense	2,000.00	
Lease Liability	23,981.62	
Cash		25,981.62

Each lease payment of $25,981.62 consists of three elements: (1) a reduction in the lease liability, (2) a financing cost (interest expense), and (3) executory costs (property taxes). The total financing cost (interest expense) over the term of the lease is $19,908.10. This amount is the difference between the present value of the lease payments ($100,000) and the actual cash disbursed, net of executory costs ($119,908.10). Therefore, the annual interest expense, applying the effective-interest method, is a function of the outstanding liability, as Illustration 17-7 shows.

Illustration 17-7
Lease Amortization
Schedule for Lessee—
Annuity-Due Basis

Sterling Construction
Lease Amortization Schedule
(Annuity-due basis)

Date	Annual Lease Payment	Executory Costs	Interest (10%) on Liability	Reduction of Lease Liability	Lease Liability
	(a)	(b)	(c)	(d)	(e)
1/1/08					$100,000.00
1/1/08	$ 25,981.62	$ 2,000	$ −0−	$ 23,981.62	76,018.38
1/1/09	25,981.62	2,000	7,601.84	16,379.78	59,638.60
1/1/10	25,981.62	2,000	5,963.86	18,017.76	41,620.84
1/1/11	25,981.62	2,000	4,162.08	19,819.54	21,801.30
1/1/12	25,981.62	2,000	2,180.32*	21,801.30	−0−
	$129,908.10	$10,000	$19,908.10	$100,000.00	

(a) Lease payment as required by lease.
(b) Executory costs included in rental payment.
(c) 10 percent of the preceding balance of (e) except for 1/1/05; since this is an annuity due, no time has elapsed at the date of the first payment and no interest has accrued.
(d) (a) minus (b) and (c).
(e) Preceding balance minus (d).
*Rounded by 19 cents.

At the end of its fiscal year, December 31, 2008, Sterling records **accrued interest** as follows.

Interest Expense	7,601.84	
Interest Payable		7,601.84

Depreciation of the leased equipment over its five-year lease term, applying Sterling's normal depreciation policy (straight-line method), results in the following entry on December 31, 2008.

Depreciation Expense—Capital Leases	20,000	
Accumulated Depreciation—Capital Leases		20,000
($100,000 ÷ 5 years)		

At December 31, 2008, Sterling separately identifies the assets recorded under capital leases on its balance sheet. Similarly, it separately identifies the related obligations. Sterling classifies the portion due within one year or the operating cycle, whichever is longer, with current liabilities, and the rest with noncurrent liabilities. For example, the current portion of the December 31, 2008, total obligation of $76,018.38 in Sterling's amortization schedule is the amount of the reduction in the obligation in 2009, or $16,379.78. Illustration 17-8 shows the liabilities section as it relates to lease transactions at December 31, 2008.

Current liabilities	
Interest payable	$ 7,601.84
Lease liability	16,379.78
Noncurrent liabilities	
Lease liability	$59,638.60

Illustration 17-8
Reporting Current and Noncurrent Lease Liabilities

Sterling records the lease payment of January 1, 2009, as follows.

Property Tax Expense	2,000.00	
Interest Payable	7,601.84	
Lease Liability	16,379.78	
Cash		25,981.62

Entries through 2012 would follow the pattern above. Sterling records its other executory costs (insurance and maintenance) in a manner similar to how it records any other operating costs incurred on assets it owns.

Upon expiration of the lease, Sterling has fully depreciated the amount capitalized as leased equipment. It also has fully discharged its lease obligation. If Sterling does not purchase the loader, it returns the equipment to Caterpillar. Sterling then removes the leased equipment and related accumulated depreciation accounts from its books.[12]

If Sterling purchases the equipment at termination of the lease, at a price of $5,000 and the estimated life of the equipment changes from five to seven years, it makes the following entry.

Equipment ($100,000 + $5,000)	105,000	
Accumulated Depreciation—Capital Leases	100,000	
Leased Equipment under Capital Leases		100,000
Accumulated Depreciation—Equipment		100,000
Cash		5,000

If the lessee guarantees the residual value, the present value of this residual value should be reported as part of the lease liability. For example, assume that Hogan Co. enters into a three-year lease of machinery on January 1, 2009. The lease requires three annual payments of $20,000, beginning January 1, 2009. In addition, Hogan Co. guarantees the lessor a residual value of $10,000 at the end of the lease. The interest rate used to discount the lease payments is 9 percent. In this case, the present value of the minimum lease payments would be computed as shown in Illustration 17-9 (page 904).

---

[12]If Sterling purchases the front-end loader **during the term of a "capital lease,"** it accounts for it like a renewal or extension of a capital lease. "Any difference between the purchase price and the carrying amount of the lease obligation shall be recorded as an adjustment of the carrying amount of the asset." See "Accounting for Purchase of a Leased Asset by the Lessee During the Term of the Lease," *FASB Interpretation No. 26* (Stamford, Conn.: FASB, 1978), par. 5.

Illustration 17-9
Computation of Present
Value of Minimum Lease
Payments

Rental payment	$ 20,000
Present value of annuity due for 3 years at 9%	× 2.75911
Present value of rental payments	$55,182.20

Present value of guaranteed residual value is $7,721.80 [$10,000 × .77218 ($PVF_{3,9\%}$)]

Present value of rental payments	$55,182.20
Present value of guaranteed residual value	7,721.80
Total present value of minimum lease payments	$62,904.00

If a **bargain purchase option** exists instead of a guaranteed residual value, the lessee should increase the present value of the minimum lease payments by the present value of the option price. In both the guaranteed residual value and the bargain purchase option cases, the lessee is committed to making these payments, and therefore the payments should be reported as an increase to the lease liability and related asset.

Operating Method (Lessee)

Under the **operating method**, rent expense (and the associated liability) accrues day by day to the lessee as it uses the property. **The lessee assigns rent to the periods benefiting from the use of the asset and ignores, in the accounting, any commitments to make future payments.** The lessee makes appropriate accruals or deferrals if the accounting period ends between cash payment dates.

For example, assume that the capital lease illustrated in the previous section did not qualify as a capital lease. Sterling therefore accounts for it as an operating lease. The first-year charge to operations is now $25,981.62, the amount of the rental payment. Sterling records this payment on January 1, 2008, as follows.

Rent Expense	25,981.62	
Cash		25,981.62

Sterling does not report the loader, as well as any long-term liability for future rental payments, on the balance sheet. Sterling reports rent expense on the income statement. And, as discussed later in the chapter, **Sterling must disclose all operating leases that have noncancelable lease terms in excess of one year**.

What do the numbers mean?   Restatements on the Menu

Accounting for operating leases would appear routine, so it is unusual for a bevy of companies in a single industry—restaurants—to get caught up in the accounting rules for operating leases. Getting the accounting right is particularly important for restaurant chains, because they make extensive use of leases for their restaurants and equipment.

The problem stems from the way most property (and equipment) leases cover a specific number of years (the so-called *primary lease term*) as well as renewal periods (sometimes referred to as the *option term*). In some cases, companies were calculating their lease expense for the primary term but depreciating lease-related assets over both the primary and option terms. This practice resulted in understating the total cost of the lease and thus boosted earnings.

For example, the CFO at **CKE Restaurants Inc.**, owner of the Hardee's and Carl's Jr. chains, noted that CKE ran into trouble because it was not consistent in calculating the lease and depreciation expense. Correcting the error at CKE reduced earnings by nine cents a share in fiscal 2002, nine cents a share in fiscal 2003, and 10 cents a share in fiscal 2004. The company now uses the shorter, primary lease terms for calculating both lease expense and depreciation. The change increases depreciation annually, which in turn decreases total assets.

CKE was not alone in improper operating lease accounting. Notable restaurateurs who ran afoul of the lease rules included **Brinker International Inc.,** operator of Chili's; **Darden Restaurants Inc.,** which operates Red Lobster and Olive Garden; and **Jack in the Box**. To correct their operating lease accounting, these restaurants reported restatements that resulted in lower earnings and assets.

Source: Steven D. Jones and Richard Gibson, "Restaurants Serve Up Restatements," *Wall Street Journal* (January 26, 2005). p. C3.

Beyond the Numbers

In some cases companies reported higher earnings and assets upon correcting their lease accounting. Do you think these companies should have to correct their accounting since the prior approach was conservative? Explain based on the qualitative characteristics of accounting information.

Comparison of Capital Lease with Operating Lease

As we indicated, if accounting for the lease as an operating lease, the first-year charge to operations is $25,981.62, the amount of the rental payment. Treating the transaction as a capital lease, however, results in a first-year charge of $29,601.84: depreciation of $20,000 (assuming straight-line), interest expense of $7,601.84 (per Illustration 17-7), and executory costs of $2,000. Illustration 17-10 shows that **while the total charges to operations are the same over the lease term whether accounting for the lease as a capital lease or as an operating lease, under the capital lease treatment the charges are higher in the earlier years and lower in the later years.**[13]

OBJECTIVE 3
Contrast the operating and capitalization methods of recording leases.

Illustration 17-10
Comparison of Charges to Operations—Capital vs. Operating Leases

Sterling Construction
Schedule of Charges to Operations
Capital Lease versus Operating Lease

| Year | Capital Lease | | | | Operating Lease Charge | Difference |
	Depreciation	Executory Costs	Interest	Total Charge		
2008	$ 20,000	$ 2,000	$ 7,601.84	$ 29,601.84	$ 25,981.62	$ 3,620.22
2009	20,000	2,000	5,963.86	27,963.86	25,981.62	1,982.24
2010	20,000	2,000	4,162.08	26,162.08	25,981.62	180.46
2011	20,000	2,000	2,180.32	24,180.32	25,981.62	(1,801.30)
2012	20,000	2,000	—	22,000.00	25,981.62	(3,981.62)
	$100,000	$10,000	$19,908.10	$129,908.10	$129,908.10	$ –0–

If the company uses an accelerated method of depreciation, the differences between the amounts charged to operations under the two methods would be even larger in the earlier and later years.

In addition, using the capital lease approach results in an asset and related liability of $100,000 initially reported on the balance sheet. The lessee would not report any asset or liability under the operating method. Therefore, the following differences occur if using a capital lease instead of an operating lease:

1   An increase in the amount of reported debt (both short-term and long-term).

2   An increase in the amount of total assets (specifically long-lived assets).

3   A lower income early in the life of the lease and, therefore, lower retained earnings.

[13]The higher charges in the early years is one reason lessees are reluctant to adopt the capital lease accounting method. Lessees (especially those of real estate) claim that it is really no more costly to operate the leased asset in the early years than in the later years. Thus, they advocate an even charge similar to that provided by the operating method.

Thus, many companies believe that capital leases negatively impact their financial position: Their debt to total equity ratio increases, and their rate of return on total assets decreases. As a result, the business community resists capitalizing leases.

Whether this resistance is well founded is debatable. From a cash flow point of view, the company is in the same position whether accounting for the lease as an operating or a capital lease. Managers often argue against capitalization for several reasons: First is that capitalization can more easily lead to **violation of loan covenants**. It also can affect the **amount of compensation received by owners** (for example, a stock compensation plan tied to earnings). Finally, capitalization can **lower rates of return** and **increase debt to equity relationships**, making the company less attractive to present and potential investors.[14]

What do the numbers mean?

Dollars to Doughnuts

Krispy Kreme, a chain of some 200 doughnut shops, caught the attention—some good, some bad—of Wall Street. On the good side, investors were impressed by the company's ability to grow rapidly on a relatively small bit of capital. For the first nine months of fiscal 2002, the company's capital expenditures fell to $38 million, from $59 million the year before. Yet Krispy Kreme expanded, along with its customers' waistlines, during the same period: Its earnings rose 73 percent, to $18 million, on sales that were up 27 percent to $277 million.

That's an impressive feat if you care about return on capital. But there was a hole in this doughnut. Amid much hoopla, the company announced in 2001 that it would spend $30 million on a new 187,000 square foot mixing plant and warehouse in Effingham, Illinois. Yet the financial statements failed to disclose the investments and obligations associated with that $30 million.

By financing through a synthetic lease, Krispy Kreme kept the investment and obligation off the books. In a synthetic lease, a financial institution like **Bank of America** set up a *special purpose entity* (SPE) that borrowed money to build the plant and then leased it to Krispy Kreme. For accounting purposes, Krispy Kreme reported an operating lease, but for tax purposes the company was considered the owner of the asset and got depreciation tax deductions.

In response to negative publicity about its use of SPEs Krispy Kreme announced it would change its method of financing construction of its dough-making plant.

Source: Adapted from Seth Lubore and Elizabeth MacDonald, "Debt? Who, Me?" *Forbes* (February 18, 2002), p. 56.

Beyond the Numbers

Krispy Kreme is using different methods for reporting the new plant under GAAP and tax rules. Briefly describe two other situations where tax rules and GAAP differ.

Try it out! On January 1, 2009, Finney Company signed a 6-year noncancelable lease for equipment. The lease requires equal rental payments of $38,796 beginning on January 1, 2009. In addition:

- The equipment has a fair value of $200,000, an estimated useful life of 8 years, and an unguaranteed residual value of $10,000.
- Finney's incremental borrowing rate is 8%, and the lessor's implicit rate is unknown.
- The equipment reverts back to the lessor at the end of the lease term.
- Finney depreciates all of its equipment using the straight-line method.

---

[14]One study indicates that management's behavior did change as a result of *FASB No. 13*. For example, many companies restructure their leases to avoid capitalization. Others increase their purchases of assets instead of leasing. Still others, faced with capitalization, postpone their debt offerings or issue stock instead. However, note that the study found no significant effect on stock or bond prices as a result of capitalization of leases. A. Rashad Abdel-khalik, "The Economic Effects on Lessees of *FASB Statement No. 13,* Accounting for Leases," Research Report (Stamford, Conn.: FASB, 1981).

Instructions

a   Compute the present value of the minimum lease payments.

b   Prepare all necessary journal entries for Finney for 2009.

Solution

a   Present value of minimum lease payments = $38,796 × 4.99271* = $193,697

   *PV of an annuity due of 1 for 6 periods at 8% (Table 5 in Appendix A)

b   **January 1, 2009**

Leased Equipment	193,697	
Cash		38,796
Lease Liability		154,901

This is recorded as a capital lease because the lease meets one of the lease capitalization criteria. In fact, the lease meets both the 90% of fair value test ($193,697 ÷ $200,000 = 97%) and the 75% of useful life test (6 ÷ 8 = 75%).

                              December 31, 2009

Interest Expense ($154,901 × .08)	12,392	
Interest Payable		12,392
Depreciation Expense—Capital Leases ($193,697 ÷ 6)	32,283	
Accumulated Depreciation—Capital Leases		32,283

ACCOUNTING BY THE LESSOR

Earlier in this chapter we discussed leasing's advantages to the lessee. Three important benefits are available to the lessor:

1   **Interest Revenue.** Leasing is a form of financing. Banks, captives, and independent leasing companies find leasing attractive because it provides competitive interest margins.

2   **Tax Incentives.** In many cases, companies that lease cannot use the tax benefit of the asset, but leasing allows them to transfer such tax benefits to another party (the lessor) in return for a lower rental rate on the leased asset. To illustrate, **Boeing Company** might sell one of its 737 jet planes to a wealthy investor who needed only the tax benefit. The investor then leased the plane to a foreign airline, for whom the tax benefit was of no use. Everyone gained. Boeing sold its airplane, the investor received the tax benefit, and the foreign airline cheaply acquired a 737.[15]

3   **High Residual Value.** Another advantage to the lessor is the return of the property at the end of the lease term. Residual values can produce very large profits. **Citigroup** at one time assumed that the commercial aircraft it was leasing to the airline industry would have a residual value of 5 percent of their purchase price. It turned out that they were worth 150 percent of their cost—a handsome profit. However, three years later these same planes slumped to 80 percent of their cost, but still far more than 5 percent.

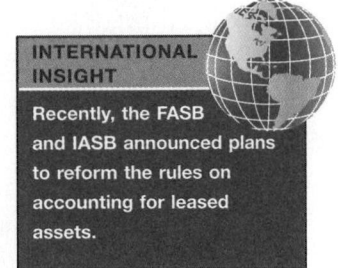

INTERNATIONAL INSIGHT

Recently, the FASB and IASB announced plans to reform the rules on accounting for leased assets.

Economics of Leasing

A lessor, such as Caterpillar Financial in our earlier example, determines the amount of the rental, basing it on the rate of return—the implicit rate—needed to justify leasing the front-end

---

[15]Some would argue that there is a loser—the U.S. government. The tax benefits enable the profitable investor to reduce or eliminate taxable income.

loader. In establishing the rate of return, Caterpillar considers the credit standing of Sterling Construction, the length of the lease, and the status of the residual value (guaranteed versus unguaranteed).

In the Caterpillar/Sterling example on pages 901–904, Caterpillar's implicit rate was 10 percent, the cost of the equipment to Caterpillar was $100,000 (also fair market value), and the estimated residual value was zero. Caterpillar determines the amount of the lease payment as follows.

Illustration 17-11
Computation of Lease
Payments

Fair market value of leased equipment	$100,000.00
Less: Present value of the residual value	–0–
Amount to be recovered by lessor through lease payments	$100,000.00
Five beginning-of-the-year lease payments to yield a 10% return ($100,000 ÷ 4.16986ᵃ)	$ 23,981.62

ᵃPV of an annuity due of 1 for 5 years at 10% (Table 5 in Appendix A)

If a residual value is involved (whether guaranteed or not), Caterpillar would not have to recover as much from the lease payments. Therefore, the lease payments would be less. (Illustration 17-9, on page 904, shows this situation.)

Classification of Leases by the Lessor

OBJECTIVE 4

Identify the classifications of leases for the lessor.

For accounting purposes, the **lessor** may classify leases as one of the following:

1 Operating leases.
2 Direct-financing leases.
3 Sales-type leases.

Illustration 17-12 presents two groups of capitalization criteria for the lessor. If at the date of inception, the lessor agrees to a lease that meets **one or more** of the Group I criteria (1, 2, 3, and 4) and **both** of the Group II criteria (1 and 2), the lessor shall classify and account for the arrangement as a direct-financing lease or as a sales-type lease.[16] (Note that the Group I criteria are identical to the criteria that must be met in order for a lessee to classify a lease as a capital lease, as shown in Illustration 17-4.)

Illustration 17-12
Capitalization Criteria
for Lessor

Capitalization Criteria (Lessor)

Group I
1. The lease transfers ownership of the property to the lessee.
2. The lease contains a bargain purchase option.
3. The lease term is equal to 75 percent or more of the estimated economic life of the leased property.
4. The present value of the minimum lease payments (excluding executory costs) equals or exceeds 90 percent of the fair value of the leased property.

Group II
1. Collectibility of the payments required from the lessee is reasonably predictable.
2. No important uncertainties surround the amount of unreimbursable costs yet to be incurred by the lessor under the lease (lessor's performance is substantially complete or future costs are reasonably predictable).

Why the Group II requirements? The profession wants to ensure that the lessor has really transferred the risks and benefits of ownership. If collectibility of payments is not predictable or if performance by the lessor is incomplete, then the criteria for revenue recognition have not been met. The lessor should therefore account for the lease as an operating lease.

[16]*FASB Statement No. 13,* op. cit., pars. 6, 7, and 8.

For example, computer leasing companies at one time used to buy **IBM** equipment, lease the equipment, and remove the leased assets from their balance sheets. In leasing the assets, the computer lessors stated that they would substitute new IBM equipment if obsolescence occurred. However, when IBM introduced a new computer line, IBM refused to sell it to the computer leasing companies. As a result, a number of the lessors could not meet their contracts with their customers and had to take back the old equipment. The computer leasing companies therefore had to reinstate the assets they had taken off the books. Such a case demonstrates one reason for the Group II requirements.

The distinction for the lessor between a direct-financing lease and a sales-type lease is the presence or absence of a manufacturer's or dealer's profit (or loss): A sales-type lease involves a manufacturer's or dealer's profit, and a direct-financing lease does not. The profit (or loss) to the lessor is evidenced by the difference between the fair value of the leased property at the inception of the lease and the lessor's cost or carrying amount (book value).

Normally, sales-type leases arise when manufacturers or dealers use leasing as a means of marketing their products. For example, a computer manufacturer will lease its computer equipment (possibly through a captive) to businesses and institutions. Direct-financing leases generally result from arrangements with lessors that are primarily engaged in financing operations (e.g., banks). However, a lessor need not be a manufacturer or dealer to recognize a profit (or loss) at the inception of a lease that requires application of sales-type lease accounting.

Lessors classify and account for all leases that do not qualify as direct-financing or sales-type leases as operating leases. Illustration 17-13 shows the circumstances under which a lessor classifies a lease as operating, direct-financing, or sales-type.

INTERNATIONAL INSIGHT

U.S. GAAP is consistent with *International Standard No. 17* (Accounting for Leases). However, the international standard is a relatively simple statement of basic principles, whereas the U.S. rules on leases are more prescriptive and detailed.

Illustration 17-13
Diagram of Lessor's Criteria for Lease Classification

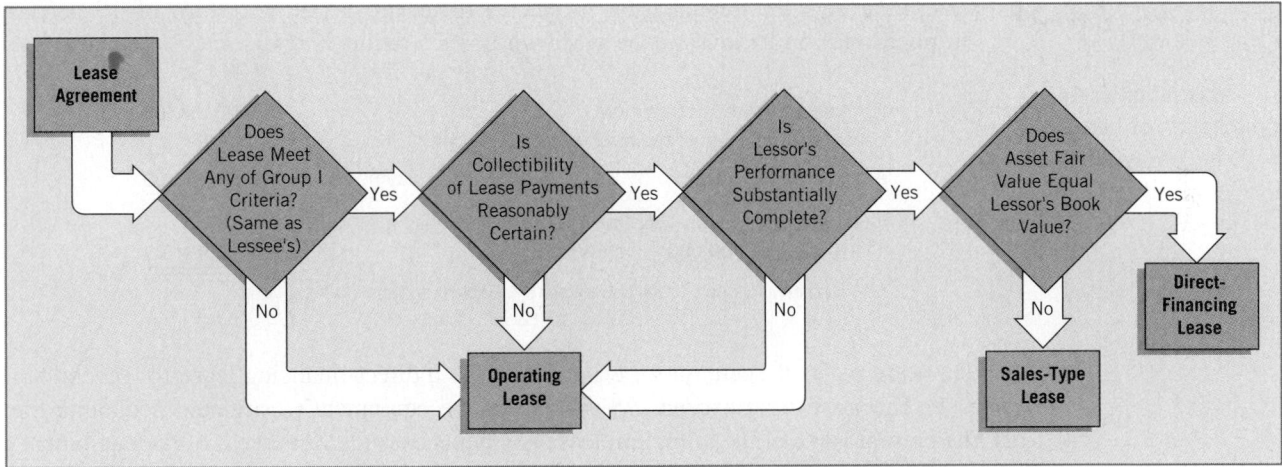

As a consequence of the additional Group II criteria for lessors, a lessor may classify a lease as an **operating** lease but the lessee may classify the same lease as a **capital** lease. In such an event, both the lessor and lessee will carry the asset on their books, and both will depreciate the capitalized asset.

For purposes of comparison with the lessee's accounting, we will illustrate only the operating and direct-financing leases in the following section. We will discuss the more complex sales-type lease later in the chapter.

Direct-Financing Method (Lessor)

Direct-financing leases are in substance the financing of an asset purchase by the lessee. In such a lease, the lessor records a **lease receivable** instead of a leased asset. The lease

OBJECTIVE 5
Describe the lessor's accounting for direct-financing leases.

receivable is the present value of the minimum lease payments plus the present value of the unguaranteed residual value. Remember that "minimum lease payments" include:

1 Rental payments (excluding executory costs).

2 Bargain purchase option (if any).

3 Guaranteed residual value (if any).

4 Penalty for failure to renew (if any).

Thus, the lessor records the residual value, whether guaranteed or not. Also, recall that if the lessor pays any executory costs, then it should reduce the rental payment by that amount in computing minimum lease payments.

The following presentation, using the data from the preceding Caterpillar/Sterling example on pages 901–904, illustrates the accounting treatment for a direct-financing lease. We repeat here the information relevant to Caterpillar in accounting for this lease transaction.

1 The term of the lease is five years beginning January 1, 2008, noncancelable, and requires equal rental payments of $25,981.62 at the beginning of each year. Payments include $2,000 of executory costs (property taxes).

2 The equipment (front-end loader) has a cost of $100,000 to Caterpillar, a fair value at the inception of the lease of $100,000, an estimated economic life of five years, and no residual value.

3 Caterpillar incurred no initial direct costs in negotiating and closing the lease transaction.

4 The lease contains no renewal options. The equipment reverts to Caterpillar at the termination of the lease.

5 Collectibility is reasonably assured and Caterpillar incurs no additional costs (with the exception of the property taxes being collected from Sterling).

6 Caterpillar sets the annual lease payments to ensure a rate of return of 10 percent (implicit rate) on its investment as shown in Illustration 17-14.

Illustration 17-14
Computation of Lease Payments

Fair value of leased equipment	$100,000.00
Less: Present value of residual value	–0–
Amount to be recovered by lessor through lease payments	$100,000.00
Five beginning-of-the-year lease payments to yield a 10% return ($100,000 ÷ 4.16986ᵃ)	$ 23,981.62

ᵃPV of an annuity due of 1 for 5 years at 10% (Table 5 in Appendix A).

The lease meets the criteria for classification as a direct-financing lease for several reasons: (1) The lease term exceeds 75 percent of the equipment's estimated economic life. (2) The present value of the minimum lease payments exceeds 90 percent of the equipment's fair value. (3) Collectibility of the payments is reasonably assured. And (4) Caterpillar incurs no further costs. It is not a sales-type lease because there is no difference between the fair value ($100,000) of the loader and Caterpillar's cost ($100,000).

The Lease Receivable is the present value of the minimum lease payments (excluding executory costs which are property taxes of $2,000). Caterpillar computes it as follows.

Illustration 17-15
Computation of Lease Receivable

Lease receivable = ($25,981.62 − $2,000) × Present value of an annuity due of 1 for 5 periods at 10% (Table 5 in Appendix A)

= $23,981.62 × 4.16986

= $100,000

Caterpillar records the lease of the asset and the resulting receivable on January 1, 2008 (the inception of the lease), as follows.

Lease Receivable	100,000	
Equipment		100,000

Companies often **report** the lease receivable in the balance sheet as "Net investment in capital leases." Companies classify it either as current or noncurrent, depending on when they recover the net investment.[17]

Caterpillar replaces its investment (the leased front-end loader, a cost of $100,000), with a lease receivable. In a manner similar to Sterling's treatment of interest, Caterpillar applies the effective-interest method and recognizes interest revenue as a function of the lease receivable balance, as Illustration 17-16 shows.

Illustration 17-16
Lease Amortization Schedule for Lessor—Annuity-Due Basis

Caterpillar Financial
Lease Amortization Schedule
(Annuity-due basis)

Date	Annual Lease Payment	Executory Costs	Interest (10%) on Lease Receivable	Lease Receivable Recovery	Lease Receivable
	(a)	(b)	(c)	(d)	(e)
1/1/08					$100,000.00
1/1/08	$ 25,981.62	$ 2,000.00	$ –0–	$ 23,981.62	76,018.38
1/1/09	25,981.62	2,000.00	7,601.84	16,379.78	59,638.60
1/1/10	25,981.62	2,000.00	5,963.86	18,017.76	41,620.84
1/1/11	25,981.62	2,000.00	4,162.08	19,819.54	21,801.30
1/1/12	25,981.62	2,000.00	2,180.32*	21,801.30	–0–
	$129,908.10	$10,000.00	$19,908.10	$100,000.00	

(a) Annual rental that provides a 10% return on net investment.
(b) Executory costs included in rental payment.
(c) 10 percent of the preceding balance of (e) except for 1/1/08.
(d) (a) minus (b) and (c).
(e) Preceding balance minus (d).
*Rounded by 19 cents.

On January 1, 2008, Caterpillar records receipt of the first year's lease payment as follows.

Cash	25,981.62	
Lease Receivable		23,981.62
Property Tax Expense/Property Taxes Payable		2,000.00

On December 31, 2008, Caterpillar recognizes the interest revenue earned during the first year through the following entry.

Interest Receivable	7,601.84	
Interest Revenue—Leases		7,601.84

At December 31, 2008, Caterpillar reports the lease receivable in its balance sheet among current assets or noncurrent assets, or both. It classifies the portion due within one year or the operating cycle, whichever is longer, as a current asset, and the rest with noncurrent assets.

Illustration 17-17 shows the assets section as it relates to lease transactions at December 31, 2008.

Illustration 17-17
Reporting Lease Transactions by Lessor

Current assets	
Interest receivable	$ 7,601.84
Lease receivable	16,379.78
Noncurrent assets (investments)	
Lease receivable	$59,638.60

[17]In the notes to the financial statements (see Illustration 17-19, pages 915–916), the lease receivable is reported at its gross amount (minimum lease payments plus the unguaranteed residual value). In addition, the lessor also reports total unearned interest related to the lease. As a result, some lessors record lease receivable on a gross basis and record the unearned interest in a separate account. We illustrate the net approach here because it is consistent with the accounting for the lessee.

The following entries record receipt of the second year's lease payment and recognition of the interest earned.

January 1, 2009

Cash	25,981.62	
Lease Receivable		16,379.78
Interest Receivable		7,601.84
Property Tax Expense/Property Taxes Payable		2,000.00

December 31, 2009

Interest Receivable	5,963.86	
Interest Revenue—Leases		5,963.86

Journal entries through 2012 follow the same pattern except that Caterpillar records no entry in 2012 (the last year) for earned interest. Because it fully collects the receivable by January 1, 2012, no balance (investment) is outstanding during 2012. Caterpillar **recorded no depreciation**. If Sterling buys the loader for $5,000 upon expiration of the lease, Caterpillar recognizes disposition of the equipment as follows.

Cash	5,000	
Gain on Sale of Leased Equipment		5,000

Operating Method (Lessor)

Under the **operating method**, the lessor records each rental receipt as rental revenue. It **depreciates the leased asset in the normal manner**, with the depreciation expense of the period matched against the rental revenue. The amount of revenue recognized in each accounting period is a level amount (straight-line basis) regardless of the lease provisions, unless another systematic and rational basis better represents the time pattern in which the lessor derives benefit from the leased asset.

In addition to the depreciation charge, the lessor expenses maintenance costs and the cost of any other services rendered under the provisions of the lease that pertain to the current accounting period. The lessor **amortizes over the life of the lease** any costs paid to independent third parties, such as appraisal fees, finder's fees, and costs of credit checks, usually on a straight-line basis.

To illustrate the operating method, assume that the direct-financing lease illustrated in the previous section does not qualify as a capital lease. Therefore, Caterpillar accounts for it as an operating lease. It records the cash rental receipt, assuming the $2,000 was for property tax expense, as follows.

Cash	25,981.62	
Rental Revenue		25,981.62

Caterpillar records depreciation as follows (assuming a straight-line method, a cost basis of $100,000, and a five-year life).

Depreciation Expense—Leased Equipment	20,000	
Accumulated Depreciation—Leased Equipment		20,000

If Caterpillar pays property taxes, insurance, maintenance, and other operating costs during the year, it records them as expenses chargeable against the gross rental revenues.

If Caterpillar owns plant assets that it uses in addition to those leased to others, the company **separately classifies the leased equipment and accompanying accumulated depreciation** as Equipment Leased to Others or Investment in Leased Property. If significant in amount or in terms of activity, Caterpillar separates the rental revenues and accompanying expenses in the income statement from sales revenue and cost of goods sold.

OTHER ACCOUNTING ISSUES

We discuss the following three lease accounting issues in this section.

1 Sales-type leases (lessor).

2 Disclosure.

3 Unresolved problems.

Sales-Type Leases (Lessor)

A **sales-type lease** recognizes interest revenue like a direct financing lease. However it also recognizes a manufacturer's or dealer's profit. In a sales-type lease, the lessor records the sale price of the asset, the cost of goods sold and related inventory reduction, and the lease receivable.

OBJECTIVE 6

Describe the lessor's accounting for sales-type leases.

To illustrate, assume that Hartland Co. manufacturers tractors. On January 1, 2008, it leased to Potts Company a tractor that cost $100,000 to manufacture and has a fair value of $140,000. The lease agreement covers the 10-year useful life of the tractor and requires 10 equal payments at the end of each year of $22,784 ($140,000 ÷ $PVF-OA_{10,10\%}$). An interest rate of 10 percent is implicit in the lease agreement. Collectibility of rentals is reasonably assured, and there are no important uncertainties concerning future lessor costs. Given that the conditions for a capital lease are met, the journal entry on the books of the lessor is as follows.

Cost of Goods Sold	100,000	
Lease Receivable	140,000	
Sales Revenue		140,000
Inventory		100,000

The lessor in this case recognizes a gross profit of $40,000 ($140,000 − $100,000) on January 1, 2008. At the end of the year it would also report interest revenue of $14,000 (10% × $140,000).

Many manufactures or dealers of equipment use the sales-type lease because in essence they have sold the product and then finance the sale. Companies that use sales-type leases therefore recognize income earlier than if a direct financing or operating lease is used.

What do the numbers mean?   Xerox Takes on the SEC

Much of **Xerox**'s income is derived from leasing equipment. Reporting such leases as sales leases, Xerox records a lease contract as a sale, with income therefore being recognized immediately. One problem is that each lease receipt is comprised of payments for various items such as supplies, services, financing, and equipment.

The SEC *accused* Xerox of inappropriately allocating lease receipts, which affects the timing of income that is reported. If SEC guidelines were applied, income would be reported in different time periods. Xerox contended that its methods were correct and also noted that when the lease term is up, the bottom line is the same using either the SEC's recommended allocation method or the method used by Xerox.

Although Xerox can refuse to change its method, the SEC has the right to prevent a company from selling stock or bonds to the public if filings of the company have been rejected by the agency.

Apparently, being able to access public markets is very valuable to Xerox. The company agreed to change its accounting according to SEC wishes, and paid a fine of $10 million due to its past accounting practices.

Source: Adapted from "Xerox Takes on the SEC," *Accounting Web* (January 9, 2002), *www.accountingweb.com.*

Beyond the Numbers

To avoid the accounting headaches related to its lease accounting, Xerox could stop selling its equipment through lease arrangements. Do you think this is a good idea? Explain.

Try it out! Peterson Company leased to Martin Corporation a machine that had a cost and fair value of $250,000. The term of the lease is 6 years beginning January 1, 2009, with equal rental payments of $51,128 at the beginning of each year. Martin Corporation assumes direct responsibility for all executory costs. The machine has a 6-year useful life with no salvage value. Peterson's implicit interest rate is 9%. Collectibility of lease payments is reasonably assured with no additional cost to be incurred by Peterson.

Instructions

Prepare Peterson's journal entries for January 1, 2009, December 31, 2009, and January 1, 2010.

Solution

January 1, 2009

Lease Receivable	250,000	
Machine		250,000
Cash	51,128	
Lease Receivable		51,128

This is a capital lease for Peterson because at least one of the Type I and both of the Type II lease capitalization criteria are met. To verify the amount of the lease payments:

$51,128 = $250,000 ÷ 4.88965 (present value of an annuity due for 6 periods at 9%).

December 31, 2009

Interest Receivable [($250,000 − $51,128) × .09]	17,898	
Interest Revenue		17,898

January 1, 2010

Cash	51,128	
Interest Receivable		17,898
Lease Receivable		33,230

OBJECTIVE 7

List the disclosure requirements for leases.

WHAT'S THE PRINCIPLE?

The required disclosures for lessees and lessors are extensive. This is understandable, given the complexity of some lease arrangements, and it is a good illustration of the full disclosure principle.

Disclosing Lease Data

The FASB requires **lessees** and **lessors** to disclose certain information about leases in their financial statements or in the notes. These requirements vary based upon the type of lease (capital or operating) and whether the issuer is the lessor or lessee. These disclosure requirements provide investors with the following information:

- General description of the nature of leasing arrangements.
- The nature, timing, and amount of cash inflows and outflows associated with leases, including payments to be paid or received for each of the five succeeding years.
- The amount of lease revenues and expenses reported in the income statement each period.
- Description and amounts of leased assets by major balance sheet classification and related liabilities.
- Amounts receivable and unearned revenues under lease agreements.[18]

[18]"Accounting for Leases," *FASB Statement No. 13*, as amended and interpreted through May 1980 (Stamford, Conn.: FASB, 1980), par. 16; par. 23.

Illustration 17-18 presents financial statement excerpts from the 2006 annual report of **Tasty Baking Company**. These excerpts represent the statement and note disclosures typical of a lessee having both capital leases and operating leases.

Tasty Baking Company

(dollar amounts in thousands)

Current Liabilities	2006	2005
Current obligations under capital leases	$ 327	$ 534
Noncurrent Liabilities		
Long-term obligations under capital leases, less current portion	208	534

Note 6: Commitments and Contingencies

The company leases certain distribution facilities, machinery, automotive and computer equipment under noncancelable lease agreements. The company expects that in the normal course of business, leases that expire will be renewed or replaced by other leases. . . . Property, plant and equipment relating to capital leases were $2,234 at December 30, 2006, and $2,234 at December 31, 2005, with accumulated amortization of $1,881 and $1,162, respectively. Depreciation and amortization of assets recorded under capital leases was $719 in 2006 and $766 in 2005.

The following is a schedule of future minimum lease payments as of December 30, 2006:

	Capital Leases	Noncancelable Operating Leases
2007	$525	$333
2008	24	293
2009	–	88
2010	–	68
2012	–	59
Later years	–	189
Total minimum lease payments	$549	$1,030
Less interest portion of payments	14	
Present value of future minimum lease payments	$535	

Rental expense was approximately $2,732 in 2006 and $2,792 in 2005.

Handwritten annotations: "interest", "PV of Lease Payments"

Illustration 17-18
Disclosure of Leases
by Lessee

— Description and amount of lease obligations

— General description

— Description and amounts of leased assets

— Nature, timing, and amounts of cash outflows

— Amount of lease rental expense

Illustration 17-19 presents the lease note disclosure from the 2006 annual report of **Hewlett-Packard Company**. The disclosure highlights required lessor disclosures.

Hewlett-Packard Company

invent

Notes to Financial Statements
(in millions)

Note 9: Financing Receivables and Operating Leases (in part)

Financing receivables represent sales-type and direct-financing leases resulting from the marketing of HP's and complementary third-party products. These receivables typically have terms from two to five years and are usually collateralized by a security interest in the underlying assets. Financing receivables also include billed receivables from operating leases. The components of net financing receivables, which are included in financing receivables and long-term financing receivables and other assets, were as follows at October 31:

Continued on next page

Illustration 17-19
Disclosure of Leases
by Lessor

— General description

	2006	2005
	(in millions)	
Minimum lease payments receivable	$ 5,010	$ 5,018
Allowance for doubtful accounts	(80)	(111)
Unguaranteed residual value	289	301
Unearned income	(439)	(411)
Financing receivables, net	4,780	4,797
Less current portion	(2,440)	(2,551)
Amounts due after one year, net	$ 2,340	$ 2,246

Amount receivable and unearned revenues

Scheduled maturities of HP's minimum lease payments receivable are as follows at October 31, 2006:

	2007	2008	2009	2010	2011	Thereafter	Total
Scheduled maturities of minimum	(In millions)						
lease payments receivable	$2,570	$1,413	$661	$221	$86	$59	$5,010

Nature, timing, and amounts of cash inflows

Equipment leased to customers under operating leases was $2.1 billion at October 31, 2006, and $1.9 billion at October 31, 2005, and is included in machinery and equipment. Accumulated depreciation on equipment under lease was $.6 billion at October 31, 2006 and at October 31, 2005. Minimum future rentals on non-cancelable operating leases related to leased equipment are as follows at October 31, 2006:

Description of leased assets

	2007	2008	2009	2010	2011	Thereafter	Total
Minimum future rentals on non-	(In millions)						
cancelable operating leases	$692	$386	$124	$49	$11	$27	$1,289

Amount of future rentals

**Additional Lease
Disclosures**

Lease Accounting—Unresolved Problems

As we indicated at the beginning of this chapter, lease accounting is subject to abuse. Companies make strenuous efforts to circumvent Statement No. 13. In practice, the strong desires of lessees to resist capitalization have rendered the accounting rules for capitalizing leases partially ineffective. Leasing generally involves large dollar amounts that, when capitalized, materially increase reported liabilities and adversely affect the debt-to-equity ratio. Lessees also resist lease capitalization because charges to expense made in the early years of the lease term are higher under the capital lease method than under the operating method, frequently without tax benefit. As a consequence, "let's beat Statement No. 13" is one of the most popular games in town.[19]

To avoid leased asset capitalization, companies design, write, and interpret lease agreements to prevent satisfying any of the four capitalized lease criteria. Companies can easily devise lease agreements in such a way, by meeting the following specifications.

1 Ensure that the lease does not specify the transfer of title of the property to the lessee.

2 Do not write in a bargain purchase option.

3 Set the lease term at something less than 75 percent of the estimated economic life of the leased property.

4 Arrange for the present value of the minimum lease payments to be less than 90 percent of the fair value of the leased property.

The real challenge lies in disqualifying the lease as a capital lease to the lessee, while having the same lease qualify as a capital (sales or financing) lease to the lessor. Unlike lessees, lessors try to avoid having lease arrangements classified as operating leases.[20]

---

[19]Richard Dieter, "Is Lessee Accounting Working?" *CPA Journal* (August 1979), pp. 13–19. This article provides interesting examples of abuses of *Statement No. 13*, discusses the circumstances that led to the current situation, and proposes a solution.

[20]The reason is that most lessors are banks, which are not permitted to hold these assets on their balance sheets except for relatively short periods of time. Furthermore, the capital-lease transaction from the lessor's standpoint provides higher income flows in the earlier periods of the lease life.

Avoiding the first three criteria is relatively simple, but it takes a little ingenuity to avoid the "90 percent recovery test" for the lessee while satisfying it for the lessor. Two of the factors involved in this effort are: (1) the use of the incremental borrowing rate by the lessee when it is higher than the implicit interest rate of the lessor, by making information about the implicit rate unavailable to the lessee; and (2) residual value guarantees.

The lessee's use of the higher interest rate is probably the more popular subterfuge. Lessees are knowledgeable about the fair value of the leased property and, of course, the rental payments. However, they generally are unaware of the estimated residual value used by the lessor. Therefore, the lessee who does not know exactly the lessor's implicit interest rate might use a different (higher) incremental borrowing rate.

The residual-value guarantee is the other unique, yet popular, device used by lessees and lessors. In fact, a whole new industry has emerged to circumvent symmetry between the lessee and the lessor in accounting for leases. The residual-value guarantee has spawned numerous companies whose principal, or even sole, function is to guarantee the residual value of leased assets.

Because the minimum lease payments include the guaranteed residual value for the lessor, this satisfies the 90 percent recovery of fair market value test. The lease is a nonoperating lease to the lessor. **But because a third-party guarantees the residual value, the minimum lease payments of the lessee exclude the guarantee.** Thus, by merely transferring some of the risk to a third party, lessees can alter substantially the accounting treatment by converting what would otherwise be capital leases to operating leases.[21]

The nature of the criteria encourages much of this circumvention, stemming from weaknesses in the basic objective of *Statement No. 13*. Accounting standards-setting bodies continue to have poor experience with arbitrary break points or other size and percentage criteria—such as rules like "90 percent of" and "75 percent of." Some believe that a more workable solution is to require capitalization of all leases that have noncancelable payment terms in excess of one year. Under this approach, lessee acquires an asset (a property right) and a corresponding liability, rather than on the basis that the lease transfers substantially all the risks and rewards of ownership.

Three years after it issued *Statement No. 13,* a majority of the FASB expressed "the tentative view that, if *Statement 13* were to be reconsidered, they would support a property right approach in which all leases are included as 'rights to use property' and as 'lease obligations' in the lessee's balance sheet."[22] The FASB and other international standard setters have issued a report on lease accounting that proposes the capitalization of more leases. This proposal will likely get consideration in the FASB's and IASB's joint project on lease accounting.[23]

You will want to read the CONVERGENCE CORNER on page 918 for discussion of how international convergence efforts relate to lease accounting.

---

[21]As an aside, third-party guarantors have experienced some difficulty. **Lloyd's of London**, at one time, insured the fast-growing U.S. computer-leasing industry in the amount of $2 billion against revenue losses, and losses in residual value, for canceled leases. Because of "overnight" technological improvements and the successive introductions of more efficient and less expensive computers, lessees in abundance canceled their leases. As the market for second-hand computers became flooded, residual values plummeted, and third-party guarantor Lloyd's of London projected a loss of $400 million. The lessees' and lessors' desire to circumvent *FASB Statement No. 13* stimulated much of the third-party guarantee business.

[22]"Is Lessee Accounting Working?" op. cit., p. 19.

[23]H. Nailor and A. Lennard, "Capital Leases: Implementation of a New Approach," *Financial Accounting Series No. 206A* (Norwalk, Conn.: FASB, 2000). Additional detail on the FASB/IASB lease project, which was added to the FASB's technical agenda in July 2006, can be viewed at *http://www.fasb.org/project/leases.shtml.*

CONVERGENCE CORNER

Lease Accounting

Leasing is a global business. Lessors and lessees enter into arrangements with one another without regard to national boundaries. Although U.S. GAAP and iGAAP for leasing are similar, both the FASB and the IASB have decided that the existing accounting does not provide the most useful, transparent, and complete information about leasing transactions that should be provided in the financial statements.

RELEVANT FACTS

• Leasing was on the FASB's initial agenda in 1973 and *SFAS No. 13* was issued in 1976 (before the conceptual framework was developed). *SFAS No. 13* has been the subject of more than 30 interpretations since its issuance.

• The iGAAP leasing standard is *IAS 17*, first issued in 1982. This standard is the subject of only three interpretations. One reason for this small number of interpretations is that iGAAP does not specifically address a number of leasing transactions that are covered by U.S. GAAP. Examples include lease agreements for natural resources, sale-leasebacks, real estate leases, and leveraged leases.

• Both U.S. GAAP and iGAAP share the same objective of recording leases by lessees and lessors according to their economic substance—that is, according to the definitions of assets and liabilities.

• U.S. GAAP for leases is much more "rule-based" with specific bright-line criteria to determine if a lease arrangement transfers the risks and rewards of ownership; iGAAP is more general in its provisions.

ABOUT THE NUMBERS

One illustration of the differences between U.S. GAAP and iGAAP for leases involves disclosure policy. Under U.S. GAAP, extensive disclosure of future noncancelable lease payments is required for the next five years and the years thereafter. Under iGAAP, not as much detail is required, as shown in the sample disclosure below.

---

iGAAP Sample Lease Note Disclosure

Note 38 Leasing arrangements (*in part*) Finance leases relate to manufacturing equipment with lease terms of 5 years. The Group has options to purchase the equipment for a nominal amount at the conclusion of the lease agreements. The Group's obligations under finance leases are secured by the lessors' title to the leased assets.

Finance lease liabilities
(euros, 000,000)

	Minimum lease payments, 31/12/06
No later than 1 year	€ 58
Later than 1 year and not later than 5 years	44
Later than 5 years	—
	102
Less: Future finance charges	13
Present value of minimum lease payments	€ 89

Although some international companies (e.g., Nokia) provide a year-by-year breakout of payments due in years 1 through 5, iGAAP does not require it.

ON THE HORIZON

Lease accounting is one of the areas identified in the IASB/FASB Memorandum of Understanding and also a topic recommended by the SEC in its off-balance-sheet study for standard-setting attention. It was formally added to the agenda of the FASB and IASB as a joint project in 2006. The joint project will be comprehensive. It will address both lessor and lessee accounting. One of the first areas to be studied is, "What are the assets and liabilities to be recognized related to a lease contract?" Should the focus remain on the leased item or the right to use the leased item? This question is tied to the Boards' joint project on the conceptual framework—defining an "asset" and a "liability."

The Boards began deliberations of lease accounting issues in 2007. Those deliberations will result in issuing a discussion paper for public comment, to be published in 2008, that explores those issues and describes the preliminary views of both Boards. You can follow the lease project at either the FASB (*http://www.fasb.org/project/leases.shtml*) or IASB (*http://www.iasb.org/Current+Projects/IASB+Projects/Leases/Leases.htm*) websites.

ACCOUNTING, ANALYSIS, PRINCIPLES

Dell Company is evaluating a lease arrangement being offered by Appleland Company for use of a computer system. The lease is noncancelable, and in no case does Dell receive title to the computers during or at the end of the lease term. The lease starts on January 1, 2008, with the first rental due at the beginning of the year. Additional information related to the lease is as follows.

Yearly rental	$3,557.25
Lease term	3 years
Estimated economic life	5 years
Purchase option	$3,000 at end of 3 years, which approximates fair value
Renewal option	1 year at $1,500; no penalty for nonrenewal; standard renewal clause
Fair value at inception of lease	$10,000
Cost of asset to lessor	$10,000
Residual value	
Guaranteed	–0–
Unguaranteed	$3,000
Incremental borrowing rate of lessee	12%
Executory costs paid by:	*Lessor;* estimated to be $500 per year
Present value of minimum lease payments	
Using incremental borrowing rate of lessee	$8,224.16
Using implicit rate of lessor	Known by lessee, $8,027.48
Estimated fair value at end of lesse	$3,000

Accounting

Analyze the lease capitalization criteria for this lease for Dell Company. Prepare the journal entry for Dell on January 1, 2008.

Analysis

Briefly discuss the impact of the accounting for this lease for two common ratios: return on assets and debt to total assets.

Principles

What element of the reliability (representational faithfulness, verifiability, neutrality) is being addressed when a company like Dell evaluates lease capitalization criteria?

Solution

Accounting

The following is an analysis of Dell's computer lease with Appleland.

1 Transfer of title? No.

2 Bargain purchase option? No.

The option to purchase at the end of 3 years at approximate fair value is clearly not a bargain.

3 Economic life test (75% test): The lease term is 3 years, and no bargain renewal period exists. This is 60% of the estimated economic life.

Therefore the 75% test is not met.

4 Recovery of investment test (90% test):

Fair value	$10,000	Rental payments		$3,557.25
Rate	90%	Less: Executory costs		500.00
90% of fair market value	$ 9,000			3,057.25
		PV of annuity due factor for 3 years at 12%		×2.69005
		PV of minimum lease payments using incremental borrowing rate		$8,224.16

The present value of the minimum lease payments using the incremental borrowing rate is $8,224.16; using the implicit rate, it is $8,027.48. The lessor's implicit rate is therefore higher than the incremental borrowing rate. Given this situation, the lessee uses the $8,224.16 (lower interest rate when discounting) when comparing with the 90% of fair market value. Because the present value of the minimum lease payments is lower than 90% of the fair value, the lease does not meet the recovery of investment test. Note that if the lease payments had been $3,557.25 with no executory costs involved, this lease arrangement would have qualified for capital-lease accounting treatment.

Dell makes the following entry on January 1, 2008, indicating an operating lease.

Rent Expense	3,557.25	
Cash		3,557.25

Analysis

When companies structure leases to avoid capitalization, both the leased asset and the obligation for the noncancelable lease payments are "off-balance-sheet." As a result, the return on assets ratio (ROA = Net income ÷ Average assets) will be overstated, and a company will look more profitable than it really is. The debt to total assets ratio (Total debt ÷ Total assets) will be understated, thereby giving the impression that the company is more solvent than is really the case. If companies capitalize differing percentages of their leases, it will be difficult to compare the companies based on ROAs and debt to total asset ratios.

Principles

The element of reliability that is being addressed is representational faithfulness. The lease criteria are designed to report leases according to their economic substance. Thus, if through a lease arrangement a company controls the risks and rewards of the leased asset, it meets the definition of an asset and should be recognized on the balance sheet. Similarly, the associated liability should be recognized if it represents an unavoidable obligation and thereby meets the definition of a liability. That is, the financial statements faithfully represent (and are more reliable) if they report all assets and liabilities of the company. Of course, structuring a lease to avoid capitalization detracts from representational faithful reporting of the lease arrangement.

Key Terms

bargain purchase option, 898
bargain renewal option, 898
capital lease, 897
capitalization criteria, 897

capitalization of leases, 895
direct-financing lease, 909
effective-interest method, 900
executory costs, 899

Summary of Learning Objectives

1 Explain the nature, economic substance, and advantages of lease transactions. A lease is a contractual agreement between a lessor and a lessee that conveys to the lessee the right to use specific property (real or personal), owned by the lessor, for a specified period of time. In return, the lessee periodically pays cash (rent) to the lessor. The advantages of lease transactions are: (1) 100 percent financing; (2) protection against obsolescence, (3) flexibility, (4) less costly financing, (5) possible tax advantages, and (6) off-balance-sheet financing.

2 Describe the accounting criteria and procedures for capitalizing leases by the lessee. A lease is a capital lease if it meets one or more of the following (Group I) criteria: (1) The lease transfers ownership of the property to the lessee. (2) The lease contains a bargain purchase option. (3) The lease term is equal to 75 percent or more of the estimated economic life of the leased property. (4) The present value of the minimum lease payments (excluding executory costs) equals or exceeds 90 percent of the fair value of the leased property. For a capital lease, the lessee records an asset and a liability at the lower of (1) the present value of the minimum lease payments, or (2) the fair market value of the leased asset at the inception of the lease.

3 Contrast the operating and capitalization methods of recording leases. The total charges to operations are the same over the lease term whether accounting for the lease as a capital lease or as an operating lease. Under the capital lease treatment, the charges are higher in the earlier years and lower in the later years. If using an accelerated method of depreciation, the differences between the amounts charged to operations under the two methods would be even larger in the earlier and later years. If using a capital lease instead of an operating lease, the following occurs: (1) an increase in the amount of reported debt (both short-term and long-term), (2) an increase in the amount of total assets (specifically long-lived assets), and (3) lower income early in the life of the lease and, therefore, lower retained earnings.

4 Identify the classifications of leases for the lessor. A lessor may classify leases for accounting purposes as follows: (1) operating leases, (2) direct-financing leases, (3) sales-type leases. The lessor should classify and account for an arrangement as a direct-financing lease or a sales-type lease if, at the date of the lease agreement, the lease meets one or more of the Group I criteria (as shown in learning objective 2 for lessees) and *both* of the following *Group II* criteria. Group II: (1) Collectibility of the payments required from the lessee is reasonably predictable; and (2) no important uncertainties surround the amount of unreimbursable costs yet to be incurred by the lessor under the lease. The lessor classifies and accounts for all leases that fail to meet the criteria as operating leases.

5 Describe the lessor's accounting for direct-financing leases. Leases that are in substance the financing of an asset purchase by a lessee require the lessor to substitute a "lease receivable" for the leased asset. "Lease receivable" is the present value of the minimum lease payments plus the present value of the unguaranteed residual value. Therefore lessors include the residual value, whether guaranteed or unguaranteed, as part of lease receivable.

6 Describe the lessor's accounting for sales-type leases. A sales-type lease recognizes interest revenue like a direct-financing lease. It also recognizes a manufacturer's or dealer's profit. In a sales-type lease, the lessor records at the inception of the lease the sales price of the asset, the cost of goods sold and related inventory reduction, and the lease receivable.

7 List the disclosure requirements for leases. The disclosure requirements for the lessees and lessors vary based upon the type of lease (capital or operating) and whether the issuer is the lessor or lessee. These disclosure requirements provide investors with the following information: (1) general description of the nature of leasing arrangements, (2) the nature, timing and amount of cash inflows and outflows associated with leases, including payments to be paid or received for each of the five succeeding years, (3) the amount of lease revenues and expenses reported in the income statement each period, (4) description and amounts of leased assets by major balance sheet classification and related liabilities, and (5) amounts receivable and unearned revenues under lease agreements.

Expanded Discussion of Real Estate Leases, Leveraged Leases, and Sale-Leasebacks

REVIEW EXERCISE

Assume that Morgan Bakeries is involved in two different lease situations. Each of these leases is noncancelable, and in no case does Morgan receive title to the properties leased during or at the end of the lease term. All leases start on January 1, 2008, with the first rental due at the beginning of the year. The additional information is shown below.

	Harmon, Inc.	Mendota Truck Co.
Type of property	Cabinets	Truck
Yearly rental	$6,000	$5,582.62
Lease term	20 years	3 years
Estimated economic life	30 years	7 years
Purchase option	None	None
Fair value at inception of lease	$60,000	$20,000
Cost of asset to lessor	$60,000	$15,000
Residual value		
Guaranteed	– 0 –	$7,000
Unguaranteed	$5,000	– 0 –
Incremental borrowing rate of lessee	12%	12%
Executory costs paid by	*Lessee*	*Lessee*
	$300 per year	$500 per year
Present value of minimum lease payments		
Using incremental borrowing rate of lessee	$50,194.68	$20,000
Using implicit rate of lessor	Not known	Not known
Estimated fair value at end of lease	$5,000	Not available

Instructions

a (1) Determine for Morgan Bakeries and Harman Co. whether the lease is a capital or operating lease, and (2) record the journal entries for both the lessee and the lessor on January 1, 2008.

b (1) Determine for Morgan Bakeries and Mendota Truck Co. whether the lease is a capital or operating lease, and (2) record the journal entries for both the lessee and the lessor on January 1, 2008.

Solution

a **(1)** The following is an analysis of the Harmon, Inc. lease.

1 Transfer of title? No.

2 Bargain purchase option? No.

3 Economic life test (75% test). The lease term is 20 years and the estimated economic life is 30 years. Thus it does **not** meet the 75% test.

4 Recovery of investment test (90% test):

Fair value	$60,000	Rental payments	$ 6,000
Rate	90%	PV of annuity due for	
90% of fair market value	$54,000	20 years at 12%	× 8.36578
		PV of rental payments	$50,194.68

Because the present value of the minimum lease payments is less than 90% of the fair value, the 90% test is not met. Both Morgan and Harmon should account for this lease as an operating lease.

(2) The journal entries to record the lease transaction on January 1, 2008, are as follows.

Morgan Bakeries (Lessee)			Harmon, Inc. (Lessor)		
Rent Expense	6,000		Cash	6,000	
Cash		6,000	Rental Revenue		6,000

b **(1)** The following is an analysis of the Mendota Truck Co. lease.

1 Transfer of title? No.

2 Bargain purchase option? No.

3 Economic life test (75% test): The lease term is 3 years and the estimated economic life is 7 years. Thus it does **not** meet the 75% test.

4 Recovery of investment test (90% test):

Fair value	$20,000	Rental payments	$ 5,582.62
Rate	90%	PV of annuity due for	
90% of fair value	$18,000	3 years at 12%	× 2.69005
		PV of rental payments	$15,017.54

(Note: adjusted for $0.01 due to rounding)

PV of guaranteed residual value: $= \$7,000(PVF_{3,12\%}) = \$7,000(.71178) = \$4,982.46$

PV of rental payments	$15,017.54
PV of guaranteed residual value	4,982.46
PV of minimum lease payments	$20,000.00

The present value of the minimum lease payments is greater than 90% of the fair value. Therefore, the 90% test is met. Morgan accounts for the lease as a capital lease, and Mendota has a sales-type lease.

(2) Assuming that Mendota's implicit rate is the same as Morgan's incremental borrowing rate, the following entries are made on January 1, 2008.

Morgan Bakeries (Lessee)			Mendota Truck Co. (Lessor)		
Leased Asset — Truck	20,000		Lease Receivable	20,000	
Lease Liability		20,000	Cost of Goods Sold	15,000	
			Inventory—Truck		15,000
			Sales		20,000

Questions

1 What are the major lessor groups in the United States? What advantage does a captive have in a leasing arrangement?

2 Jackie Remmers Co. is expanding its operations and is in the process of selecting the method of financing this program. After some investigation, the company determines that it may (1) issue bonds and with the proceeds purchase the needed assets, or (2) lease the assets on a long-term basis. Without knowing the comparative costs involved, answer the following questions.

(a) What might be the advantages of leasing the assets instead of owning them?

(b) What might be the disadvantages of leasing the assets instead of owning them?

(c) In what way will the balance sheet be differently affected by leasing the assets as opposed to issuing bonds and purchasing the assets?

3 Identify the two recognized lease accounting methods for lessees, and distinguish between them.

4 Wayne Higley Company rents a warehouse on a month-to-month basis for the storage of its excess inventory. The company periodically must rent space whenever its production greatly exceeds actual sales. For several years the company officials have discussed building their own storage facility, but this enthusiasm wavers when sales increase sufficiently to absorb the excess inventory. What is the nature of this type of lease arrangement, and what accounting treatment should be accorded it?

5 Distinguish between minimum rental payments and minimum lease payments, and indicate what is included in minimum lease payments.

6 Explain the distinction between a direct financing lease and a sales-type lease for a lessor.

7 Outline the accounting procedures involved in applying the operating method by a lessee.

8 Outline the accounting procedures involved in applying the capital lease method by a lessee.

9 Identify the lease classifications for lessors and the criteria that must be met for each classification.

10 Outline the accounting procedures involved in applying the direct financing method.

11 Outline the accounting procedures involved in applying the operating method by a lessor.

12 Joan Elbert Company is a manufacturer and lessor of computer equipment. What should be the nature of its lease arrangements with lessees if the company wishes to account for its lease transactions as sales-type leases?

13 Gordon Graham Corporation's lease arrangements qualify as sales-type leases at the time of entering into the transactions. How should the corporation recognize revenues and costs in these situations?

14 Joann Skabo, M.D. (lessee) has a noncancelable 20-year lease with Countryman Realty, Inc. (lessor) for the use of a medical building. Taxes, insurance, and maintenance are paid by the lessee in addition to the fixed annual payments, of which the present value is equal to the fair market value of the leased property. At the end of the lease period, title becomes the lessee's at a nominal price. Considering the terms of the lease described above, comment on the nature of the lease transaction and the accounting treatment that should be accorded it by the lessee.

15 Describe the effect of a "bargain purchase option" on accounting for a capital lease transaction by a lessee.

16 What disclosures should be made by a lessee if the leased assets and the related obligation are not capitalized?

Brief Exercises

BE17-1 **Callaway Golf Co.** leases telecommunications equipment. Assume the following data for equipment leased from Photon Company. The lease term is 5 years and requires equal rental payments of $30,000 at the beginning of each year. The equipment has a fair value at the inception of the lease of $138,000, an estimated useful life of 8 years, and no residual value. Callaway pays all executory costs directly to third parties. Photon set the annual rental to earn a rate of return of 10%, and this fact is known to Callaway. The lease does not transfer title or contain a bargain purchase option. How should Callaway classify this lease?

(LO 2)

BE17-2 Waterworld Company leased equipment from Costner Company. The lease term is 4 years and requires equal rental payments of $37,283 at the beginning of each year. The equipment has a fair value at the inception of the lease of $130,000, an estimated useful life of 4 years, and no salvage value. Waterworld pays all executory costs directly to third parties. The appropriate interest rate is 10%. Prepare Waterworld's January 1, 2008, journal entries at the inception of the lease.

(LO 2)

BE17-3 Kleckner Corporation recorded a capital lease at $200,000 on January 1, 2008. The interest rate is 12%. Kleckner Corporation made the first lease payment of $35,947 on January 1, 2008. The lease requires eight annual payments. The equipment has a useful life of 8 years with no salvage value. Prepare Kleckner Corporation's December 31, 2008, adjusting entries.

(LO 2)

BE17-4 Use the information for Kleckner Corporation from BE17-3. Assume that at December 31, 2008, Kleckner made an adjusting entry to accrue interest expense of $19,686 on the lease. Prepare Kleckner's January 1, 2009, journal entry to record the second lease payment of $35,947.

(LO 2)

BE17-5 Jana Corporation enters into a lease on January 1, 2008, that does not transfer ownership or contain a bargain purchase option. It covers 3 years of the equipment's 8-year useful life, and the present value of the minimum lease payments is less than 90% of the fair market value of the asset leased. Prepare Jana's journal entry to record its January 1, 2008, annual lease payment of $37,500.

(LO 3)

BE17-6 Assume **IBM** leased equipment that was carried at a cost of $150,000 to Swander Company. The term of the lease is 6 years beginning January 1, 2008, with equal rental payments of $30,677 at the beginning of each year. All executory costs are paid by Swander directly to third parties. The fair value of the equipment at the inception of the lease is $150,000. The equipment has a useful life of 6 years with no salvage value. The lease has an implicit interest rate of 9%, no bargain purchase option, and no transfer of title. Collectibility is reasonably assured with no additional cost to be incurred by IBM. Prepare IBM's January 1, 2008, journal entries at the inception of the lease.

(LO 4, 5)

BE17-7 Use the information for **IBM** from BE17-6. Assume the direct-financing lease was recorded at a present value of $150,000. Prepare IBM's December 31, 2008, entry to record interest.

(LO 4, 5)

BE17-8 Jennifer Brent Corporation owns equipment that cost $72,000 and has a useful life of 8 years with no salvage value. On January 1, 2008, Jennifer Brent leases the equipment to Havaci Inc. for one year with one rental payment of $15,000 on January 1. Prepare Jennifer Brent Corporation's 2008 journal entries.

(LO 4)

BE17-9 Indiana Jones Corporation enters into a 6-year lease of machinery on January 1, 2008, which requires 6 annual payments of $30,000 each, beginning January 1, 2008. In addition, Indiana Jones guarantees the lessor a residual value of $20,000 at lease-end. The machinery has a useful life of 6 years. Prepare Indiana Jones' January 1, 2008, journal entries assuming an interest rate of 10%.

(LO 6, 7)

BE17-10 Starfleet Corporation manufactures replicators. On January 1, 2008, it leased to Ferengi Company a replicator that had cost $110,000 to manufacture. The lease agreement covers the 5-year useful life of the replicator and requires 5 equal annual rentals of $45,400 each. An interest rate of 12% is implicit in the lease agreement. Collectibility of the rentals is reasonably assured, and there are no important uncertainties concerning costs. Prepare Starfleet's January 1, 2008, journal entries.

(LO 6, 7)

Exercises

E17-1 **(Lessee Entries; Capital Lease)** On January 1, 2008, Burke Corporation signed a 5-year noncancelable lease for a machine. The terms of the lease called for Burke to make annual payments of $8,668 at the beginning of each year, starting January 1, 2008. The machine has an estimated useful life of 6 years. The machine reverts back to the lessor at the end of the lease term. Burke uses the straight-line method of

(LO 2)

depreciation for all of its plant assets. Burke's incremental borrowing rate is 10%, and the Lessor's implicit rate is unknown.

Instructions

(a) What type of lease is this? Explain.

(b) Compute the present value of the minimum lease payments.

(c) Prepare all necessary journal entries for Burke for this lease through January 1, 2009.

(LO 2)

E17-2 **(Lessee Computations and Entries; Capital Lease with Guaranteed Residual Value)** Delaney Company leases an automobile with a fair value of $8,725 from John Simon Motors, Inc., on the following terms.

1. Noncancelable term of 50 months.

2. Rental of $200 per month (at end of each month; present value at 1% per month is $7,840).

3. Estimated residual value after 50 months is $1,180. (The present value at 1% per month is $715.) Delaney Company guarantees the residual value of $1,180.

4. Estimated economic life of the automobile is 60 months.

5. Delaney Company's incremental borrowing rate is 12% a year (1% a month). Simon's implicit rate is unknown.

Instructions

(a) What is the nature of this lease to Delaney Company?

(b) What is the present value of the minimum lease payments?

(c) Record the lease on Delaney Company's books at the date of inception.

(d) Record the first month's depreciation on Delaney Company's books. (Assume straight-line.)

(e) Record the first month's lease payment.

(LO 2)

E17-3 **(Lessee Entries; Capital Lease with Executory Costs)** Assume that on January 1, 2008, **Kimberly-Clark Corp.** signs a 10-year noncancelable lease agreement to lease a storage building from Sheffield Storage Company. The following information pertains to this lease agreement.

1. The agreement requires equal rental payments of $72,000 beginning on January 1, 2008.

2. The fair value of the building on January 1, 2008 is $440,000.

3. The building has an estimated economic life of 12 years, with an unguaranteed residual value of $10,000. Kimberly-Clark depreciates similar buildings on the straight-line method.

4. The lease is nonrenewable. At the termination of the lease, the building reverts to the lessor.

5. Kimberly-Clark's incremental borrowing rate is 12% per year. The lessor's implicit rate is not known by Kimberly-Clark.

6. The yearly rental payment includes $2,470.51 of executory costs related to taxes on the property.

Instructions

Prepare the journal entries on the lessee's books to reflect the signing of the lease agreement and to record the payments and expenses related to this lease for the years 2008 and 2009. Kimberly-Clark's corporate year-end is December 31.

(LO 2, 4)

E17-4 **(Type of Lease; Amortization Schedule)** Macinski Leasing Company leases a new machine that has a cost and fair value of $95,000 to Maggie Sharrer Corporation on a 3-year noncancelable contract. Maggie Sharrer Corporation agrees to assume all risks of normal ownership including such costs as insurance, taxes, and maintenance. The machine has a 3-year useful life and no residual value. The lease was signed on January 1, 2008. Macinski Leasing Company expects to earn a 9% return on its investment. The annual rentals are payable on each December 31.

Instructions

(a) Discuss the nature of the lease arrangement and the accounting method that each party to the lease should apply.

(b) Prepare an amortization schedule that would be suitable for both the lessor and the lessee and that covers all the years involved.

(LO 4, 6)

E17-5 **(Lessor Entries; Sales-Type Lease)** Crosley Company, a machinery dealer, leased a machine to Dexter Corporation on January 1, 2008. The lease is for an 8-year period and requires equal annual payments of

PV = 200,001 [handwritten]

$35,013 at the beginning of each year. The first payment is received on January 1, 2008. Crosley had purchased the machine during 2007 for $160,000. Collectibility of lease payments is reasonably predictable, and no important uncertainties surround the amount of costs yet to be incurred by Crosley. Crosley set the annual rental to ensure an 11% rate of return. The machine has an economic life of 10 years with no residual value and reverts to Crosley at the termination of the lease.

[handwritten right margin:
Lease Recev 200001
CGS 160 000
Sales 200 000
Machine 160 000
Cash 35 013
Lease Rec. 35 013

Int. Rec. 18149
Int Revenue 18149]

Instructions

Prepare all necessary journal entries for Crosley for 2008.

(LO 2, 4, 6)

E17-6   (Lessee-Lessor Entries; Sales-Type Lease)   On January 1, 2008, Bensen Company leased equipment to Flynn Corporation. The following information pertains to this lease.

1.   The term of the noncancelable lease is 6 years, with no renewal option. The equipment reverts to the lessor at the termination of the lease.

2.   Equal rental payments are due on January 1 of each year, beginning in 2008.

3.   The fair value of the equipment on January 1, 2008, is $150,000, and its cost is $120,000.

4.   The equipment has an economic life of 8 years. Flynn depreciates all of its equipment on a straight-line basis.

5.   Bensen set the annual rental to ensure an 11% rate of return. Flynn's incremental borrowing rate is 12%, and the implicit rate of the lessor is unknown.

6.   Collectibility of lease payments is reasonably predictable, and no important uncertainties surround the amount of costs yet to be incurred by the lessor.

Instructions

(a)   Discuss the nature of this lease to Bensen and Flynn.
(b)   Calculate the amount of the annual rental payment. *31 943* [handwritten]
(c)   Prepare all the necessary journal entries for Flynn for 2008.
(d)   Prepare all the necessary journal entries for Bensen for 2008.

[handwritten notes:
Sales Type capital   capital
Lease eqp 147 090   Lease L 31943
Lease L 147090   Cash 31943
Depprec. Exp 24 515
Acc Depr. 24 515
Interest Expense 13 818
Int. Payable 13 813

Lease R 150 00
CGS 120 000
Sales 150 000
Inventory 1200
Cash 31 943
Lease R 31943

Int. Receiv. 12986
Int. Rev. 12986]

(LO 4, 5)

E17-7   (Computation of Rental; Journal Entries for Lessor)   Morgan Marie Leasing Company signs an agreement on January 1, 2008, to lease equipment to Cole William Company. The following information relates to this agreement.

1.   The term of the noncancelable lease is 6 years with no renewal option. The equipment has an estimated economic life of 6 years.

2.   The cost of the asset to the lessor is $245,000. The fair value of the asset at January 1, 2008, is $245,000.

3.   The asset will revert to the lessor at the end of the lease term at which time the asset is expected to have a residual value of $43,622, none of which is guaranteed.

4.   Cole William Company assumes direct responsibility for all executory costs.

5.   The agreement requires equal annual rental payments, beginning on January 1, 2008.

6.   Collectibility of the lease payments is reasonably predictable. There are no important uncertainties surrounding the amount of costs yet to be incurred by the lessor.

Instructions

(a)   Assuming the lessor desires a 10% rate of return on its investment, calculate the amount of the annual rental payment required. (*Hint:* Be sure to deduct the present value of the residual value to determine the amount to recover in the lease payments.) Round to the nearest dollar. *46 000* [handwritten]
(b)   Prepare an amortization schedule that would be suitable for the lessor for the lease term.
(c)   Prepare all of the journal entries for the lessor for 2008 and 2009 to record the lease agreement, the receipt of lease payments, and the recognition of income. Assume the lessor's annual accounting period ends on December 31.

[handwritten right margin:
245 000
- 24 624
Interest 19 900   Lease L Recev 245000
Recev 199 000]

(LO 2)

E17-8   (Amortization Schedule and Journal Entries for Lessee)   Laura Leasing Company signs an agreement on January 1, 2008, to lease equipment to Plote Company. The following information relates to this agreement.

1.   The term of the noncancelable lease is 5 years with no renewal option. The equipment has an estimated economic life of 5 years.

2. The fair value of the asset at January 1, 2008, is $80,000.

3. The asset will revert to the lessor at the end of the lease term, at which time the asset is expected to have a residual value of $7,000, none of which is guaranteed.

4. Plote Company assumes direct responsibility for all executory costs, which include the following annual amounts: (1) $900 to Rocky Mountain Insurance Company for insurance, and (2) $1,600 to Laclede County for property taxes.

5. The agreement requires equal annual rental payments of $18,142.95 to the lessor, beginning on January 1, 2008.

6. The lessee's incremental borrowing rate is 12%. The lessor's implicit rate is 10% and is known to the lessee.

7. Plote Company uses the straight-line depreciation method for all equipment.

8. Plote uses reversing entries when appropriate.

Instructions

(Round all numbers to the nearest cent.)

(a) Prepare an amortization schedule that would be suitable for the lessee for the lease term.

(b) Prepare all of the journal entries for the lessee for 2008 and 2009 to record the lease agreement, the lease payments, and all expenses related to this lease. Assume the lessee's annual accounting period ends on December 31.

(LO 2, 4) **E17-9** (**Accounting for an Operating Lease**) On January 1, 2008, Doug Nelson Co. leased a building to Patrick Wise Inc. The relevant information related to the lease is as follows.

1. The lease arrangement is for 10 years.

2. The leased building cost $4,500,000 and was purchased for cash on January 1, 2008.

3. The building is depreciated on a straight-line basis. Its estimated economic life is 50 years.

4. Lease payments are $275,000 per year and are made at the end of the year.

5. Property tax expense of $85,000 and insurance expense of $10,000 on the building were incurred by Nelson in the first year. Payment on these two items was made at the end of the year.

6. Both the lessor and the lessee are on a calendar-year basis.

Instructions

(a) Prepare the journal entries that Nelson Co. should make in 2008.

(b) Prepare the journal entries that Wise Inc. should make in 2008.

(LO 3, 4) **E17-10** (**Accounting for an Operating Lease**) On January 1, 2008, a machine was purchased for $900,000 by Tom Young Co. The machine is expected to have an 8-year life with no salvage value. It is to be depreciated on a straight-line basis. The machine was leased to St. Leger Inc. on January 1, 2008, at an annual rental of $210,000. Other relevant information is as follows.

1. The lease term is for 3 years.

2. Tom Young Co. incurred maintenance and other executory costs of $25,000 in 2008 related to this lease.

3. The machine could have been sold by Tom Young Co. for $940,000 instead of leasing it.

4. St. Leger is required to pay a rent security deposit of $35,000 and to prepay the last month's rent of $17,500.

Instructions

(a) How much should Tom Young Co. report as income before income tax on this lease for 2008?

(b) What amount should St. Leger Inc. report for rent expense for 2008 on this lease?

(LO 3, 4) **E17-11** (**Operating Lease for Lessee and Lessor**) On February 20, 2008, Barbara Brent Inc., purchased a machine for $1,500,000 for the purpose of leasing it. The machine is expected to have a 10-year life, no residual value, and will be depreciated on the straight-line basis. The machine was leased to Chuck Rudy Company on March 1, 2008, for a 4-year period at a monthly rental of $19,500. There is no provision for the renewal of the lease or purchase of the machine by the lessee at the expiration of the lease term. Brent paid $30,000 of commissions associated with negotiating the lease in February 2008.

Instructions

(a) What expense should Chuck Rudy Company record as a result of the facts above for the year ended December 31, 2008? Show supporting computations in good form. *195 000*

(b) What income or loss before income taxes should Brent record as a result of the facts above for the year ended December 31, 2008? (*Hint:* Amortize commissions over the life of the lease.) *63 750*

See the book's companion website, at www.wiley.com/college/warfield, for Additional Exercises.

Problems

P17-1 (**Lessee-Lessor Entries; Operating Lease**) Synergetics Inc. leased a new crane to M. K. Gumowski Construction under a 5-year noncancelable contract starting January 1, 2008. Terms of the lease require payments of $22,000 each January 1, starting January 1, 2008. Synergetics will pay insurance, taxes, and maintenance charges on the crane, which has an estimated life of 12 years, a fair value of $160,000, and a cost to Synergetics of $160,000. The estimated fair value of the crane is expected to be $45,000 at the end of the lease term. No bargain purchase or renewal options are included in the contract. Both Synergetics and Gumowski adjust and close books annually at December 31. Collectibility of the lease payments is reasonably certain, and no uncertainties exist relative to unreimbursable lessor costs. Gumowski's incremental borrowing rate is 10%, and Synergetics' implicit interest rate of 9% is known to Gumowski.

(LO 2, 4)

Instructions

(a) Identify the type of lease involved and give reasons for your classification. Discuss the accounting treatment that should be applied by both the lessee and the lessor. *Oper.*

(b) Prepare all the entries related to the lease contract and leased asset for the year 2008 for the lessee and lessor, assuming:

    (1) Insurance, $500.

    (2) Taxes, $2,000.

    (3) Maintenance, $650.

    (4) Straight-line depreciation and salvage value, $10,000.

(c) Discuss what should be presented in the balance sheet and income statement and related notes of both the lessee and the lessor at December 31, 2008.

P17-2 (**Lessee-Lessor Entries, Balance Sheet Presentation; Sales-Type Lease**) Cascade Industries and Barbara Hardy Inc. enter into an agreement that requires Barbara Hardy Inc. to build three diesel-electric engines to Cascade's specifications. Upon completion of the engines, Cascade has agreed to lease them for a period of 10 years and to assume all costs and risks of ownership. The lease is noncancelable, becomes effective on January 1, 2008, and requires annual rental payments of $620,956 each January 1, starting January 1, 2008.

(LO 2, 4, 6)

Cascade's incremental borrowing rate is 10%, and the implicit interest rate used by Barbara Hardy Inc. and known to Cascade is 8%. The total cost of building the three engines is $3,900,000. The economic life of the engines is estimated to be 10 years with residual value set at zero. Cascade depreciates similar equipment on a straight-line basis. At the end of the lease, Cascade assumes title to the engines. Collectibility of the lease payments is reasonably certain and no uncertainties exist relative to unreimbursable lessor costs.

Instructions

(Round all numbers to the nearest dollar.)

(a) Discuss the nature of this lease transaction from the viewpoints of both lessee and lessor.

(b) Prepare the journal entry or entries to record the transaction on January 1, 2008, on the books of Cascade Industries.

(c) Prepare the journal entry or entries to record the transaction on January 1, 2008, on the books of Barbara Hardy Inc.

(d) Prepare the journal entries for both the lessee and lessor to record the first rental payment on January 1, 2008.

(e) Prepare the journal entries for both the lessee and lessor to record interest expense (revenue) at December 31, 2008. (Prepare a lease amortization schedule for 2 years.)

(f) Show the items and amounts that would be reported on the balance sheet (not notes) at December 31, 2008, for both the lessee and the lessor.

(LO 2, 7)   **P17-3   (Balance Sheet and Income Statement Disclosure—Lessee)**   The following facts pertain to a noncancelable lease agreement between Ben Alschuler Leasing Company and John McKee Electronics, a lessee, for a computer system.

Inception date:	October 1, 2008
Lease term	6 years
Economic life of leased equipment	6 years
Fair value of asset at October 1, 2008	$200,255 ⁼ PV
Residual value at end of lease term	–0–
Lessor's implicit rate	10%
Lessee's incremental borrowing rate	10%
Annual lease payment due at the beginning of each year, beginning with October 1, 2008	$41,800

The collectibility of the lease payments is reasonably predictable, and there are no important uncertainties surrounding the costs yet to be incurred by the lessor. The lessee assumes responsibility for all executory costs, which amount to $5,500 per year and are to be paid each October 1, beginning October 1, 2008. (This $5,500 is not included in the rental payment of $41,800.) The asset will revert to the lessor at the end of the lease term. The straight-line depreciation method is used for all equipment.

The following amortization schedule has been prepared correctly for use by both the lessor and the lessee in accounting for this lease. The lease is to be accounted for properly as a capital lease by the lessee and as a direct financing lease by the lessor.

Date	Annual Lease Payment/ Receipt	Interest (10%) on Lease Liability/ Receivable	Reduction of Lease Liability/ Receivable	Balance of Lease Liability/ Receivable
10/01/08				$200,255
10/01/08	$ 41,800		$ 41,800	158,455
10/01/09	41,800	$15,846	25,954	132,501
10/01/10	41,800	13,250	28,550	103,951
10/01/11	41,800	10,395	31,405	72,546
10/01/12	41,800	7,255	34,545	38,001
10/01/13	41,800	3,799*	38,001	– 0 –
	$250,800	$50,545	$200,255	

*Rounding error is $1.

Instructions

(Round all numbers to the nearest cent.)

(a) Assuming the lessee's accounting period ends on September 30, answer the following questions with respect to this lease agreement.

(1) What items and amounts will appear on the lessee's income statement for the year ending September 30, 2009?

(2) What items and amounts will appear on the lessee's balance sheet at September 30, 2009?

(3) What items and amounts will appear on the lessee's income statement for the year ending September 30, 2010?

(4) What items and amounts will appear on the lessee's balance sheet at September 30, 2010?

(b) Assuming the lessee's accounting period ends on December 31, answer the following questions with respect to this lease agreement.

(1) What items and amounts will appear on the lessee's income statement for the year ending December 31, 2008?

(2) What items and amounts will appear on the lessee's balance sheet at December 31, 2008?

(3) What items and amounts will appear on the lessee's income statement for the year ending December 31, 2009?

(4) What items and amounts will appear on the lessee's balance sheet at December 31, 2009?

P17-4 **(Balance Sheet and Income Statement Disclosure—Lessor)** Assume the same information as in P17-3. **(LO 5, 7)**

Instructions

(Round all numbers to the nearest cent.)

(a) Assuming the lessor's accounting period ends on September 30, answer the following questions with respect to this lease agreement.

(1) What items and amounts will appear on the lessor's income statement for the year ending September 30, 2009?

(2) What items and amounts will appear on the lessor's balance sheet at September 30, 2009?

(3) What items and amounts will appear on the lessor's income statement for the year ending September 30, 2010?

(4) What items and amounts will appear on the lessor's balance sheet at September 30, 2010?

(b) Assuming the lessor's accounting period ends on December 31, answer the following questions with respect to this lease agreement.

(1) What items and amounts will appear on the lessor's income statement for the year ending December 31, 2008?

(2) What items and amounts will appear on the lessor's balance sheet at December 31, 2008?

(3) What items and amounts will appear on the lessor's income statement for the year ending December 31, 2009?

(4) What items and amounts will appear on the lessor's balance sheet at December 31, 2009?

P17-5 **(Lessee Entries and Balance Sheet Presentation; Capital Lease)** Brennan Steel Company as lessee signed a lease agreement for equipment for 5 years, beginning December 31, 2008. Annual rental payments of $32,000 are to be made at the beginning of each lease year (December 31). The taxes, insurance, and the maintenance costs are the obligation of the lessee. The interest rate used by the lessor in setting the payment schedule is 10%; Brennan's incremental borrowing rate is 12%. Brennan is unaware of the rate being used by the lessor. At the end of the lease, Brennan has the option to buy the equipment for $1, considerably below its estimated fair value at that time. The equipment has an estimated useful life of 7 years, and no salvage value has been added. Brennan uses the straight-line method of depreciation on similar owned equipment. **(LO 2, 7)**

Instructions

(Round all numbers to the nearest dollar.)

(a) Prepare the journal entry or entries, with explanations, that should be recorded on December 31, 2008, by Brennan. (Assume no residual value.)

(b) Prepare the journal entry or entries, with explanations, that should be recorded on December 31, 2009, by Brennan. (Prepare the lease amortization schedule for all five payments.)

(c) Prepare the journal entry or entries, with explanations, that should be recorded on December 31, 2010, by Brennan.

(d) What amounts would appear on Brennan's December 31, 2010, balance sheet relative to the lease arrangement?

P17-6 **(Lessee Entries and Balance Sheet Presentation; Capital Lease)** On January 1, 2008, Charlie Doss Company contracts to lease equipment for 5 years, agreeing to make a payment of $94,732 (including the executory costs of $6,000) at the beginning of each year, starting January 1, 2008. The taxes, the insurance, and the maintenance, estimated at $6,000 a year, are the obligations of the lessee. The leased equipment is to be capitalized at $370,000. The asset is to be amortized on a double-declining-balance basis, and the obligation is to be reduced on an effective-interest basis. Doss's incremental borrowing rate is 12%, and the implicit rate in the lease is 10%, which is known by Doss. Title to the equipment transfers to Doss when the lease expires. The asset has an estimated useful life of 5 years and no residual value. **(LO 2, 7)**

Instructions

(Round all numbers to the nearest dollar.)

(a) Explain the probable relationship of the $370,000 amount to the lease arrangement.

(b) Prepare the journal entry or entries that should be recorded on January 1, 2008, by Charlie Doss Company.

(c) Prepare the journal entry to record depreciation of the leased asset for the year 2008.

(d) Prepare the journal entry to record the interest expense for the year 2008.

(e) Prepare the journal entry to record the lease payment of January 1, 2009, assuming reversing entries are not made.

(f) What amounts will appear on the lessee's December 31, 2008, balance sheet relative to the lease contract?

(LO 2, 7)   **P17-7 (Lessee Entries, Capital Lease with Monthly Payments)**   John Roesch Inc. was incorporated in 2007 to operate as a computer software service firm with an accounting fiscal year ending August 31. Roesch's primary product is a sophisticated on-line inventory-control system; its customers pay a fixed fee plus a usage charge for using the system.

Roesch has leased a large, Alpha-3 computer system from the manufacturer. The lease calls for a monthly rental of $50,000 for the 144 months (12 years) of the lease term. The estimated useful life of the computer is 15 years.

Each scheduled monthly rental payment includes $4,000 for full-service maintenance on the computer to be performed by the manufacturer. All rentals are payable on the first day of the month beginning with August 1, 2008, the date the computer was installed and the lease agreement was signed.

The lease is noncancelable for its 12-year term, and it is secured only by the manufacturer's chattel lien on the Alpha-3 system. Roesch can purchase the Alpha-3 system from the manufacturer at the end of the 12-year lease term for 75% of the computer's fair value at that time.

This lease is to be accounted for as a capital lease by Roesch, and it will be depreciated by the straight-line method with no expected salvage value. Borrowed funds for this type of transaction would cost Roesch 12% per year (1% per month). Following is a schedule of the present value of $1 for selected periods discounted at 1% per period when payments are made at the beginning of each period.

Periods (months)	Present Value of $1 per Period Discounted at 1% per Period
1	1.000
2	1.990
3	2.970
143	76.658
144	76.899

Instructions

Prepare, in general journal form, all entries Roesch should have made in its accounting records during August 2008 relating to this lease. Give full explanations and show supporting computations for each entry. Remember, August 31, 2008, is the end of Roesch's fiscal accounting period and it will be preparing financial statements on that date. Do not prepare closing entries.

(AICPA adapted)

(LO 2)   **P17-8 (Basic Lessee Accounting with Difficult PV Calculation)**   In 2006 Judy Yin Trucking Company negotiated and closed a long-term lease contract for newly constructed truck terminals and freight storage facilities. The buildings were erected to the company's specifications on land owned by the company. On January 1, 2007, Judy Yin Trucking Company took possession of the lease properties. On January 1, 2007 and 2008, the company made cash payments of $1,048,000 that were recorded as rental expenses.

Although the terminals have a composite useful life of 40 years, the noncancelable lease runs for 20 years from January 1, 2007, with a bargain purchase option available upon expiration of the lease.

The 20-year lease is effective for the period January 1, 2007, through December 31, 2026. Advance rental payments of $900,000 are payable to the lessor on January 1 of each of the first 10 years of the lease term. Advance rental payments of $320,000 are due on January 1 for each of the last 10 years of the lease. The company has an option to purchase all of these leased facilities for $1 on December 31, 2026. It also must make annual payments to the lessor of $125,000 for property taxes and $23,000 for insurance. The lease was negotiated to assure the lessor a 6% rate of return.

Instructions

(Round all numbers to the nearest dollar.)

(a) Prepare a schedule to compute for Judy Yin Trucking Company the discounted present value of the terminal facilities and related liability at January 1, 2007.

[handwritten top margin: If lesse guarantees than incl (pv residual value) / If lesse does not guarantee do not incl. res. value]

(b) Assuming that the discounted present value of terminal facilities and related liability at January 1, 2007, was $8,400,000, prepare journal entries for Judy Yin Trucking Company to record the following.

(1) Cash payment to the lessor on January 1, 2009.

(2) Amortization of the cost of the leased properties for 2009, using the straight-line method and assuming a zero salvage value.

(3) Accrual of interest expense at December 31, 2009.

Selected present value factors are as follows:

Periods	For an Ordinary Annuity of $1 at 6%	For $1 at 6%
1	.943396	.943396
2	1.833393	.889996
8	6.209794	.627412
9	6.801692	.591898
10	7.360087	.558395
19	11.158117	.830513
20	11.469921	.311805

[handwritten notes scattered around the table: Deprec. Lease Receiv. − residual book value / years to dep / Lessor Equip. / Inter Rev & For Ni / L Equip / Acc Depr / residual Book value / FMV (PV of MLP) DF = Cost / Int. Rev ⟹ Lease Recei Equipment / Lesee Loss on Cap / Acc Depr. / Int. Exp. / Lease L Leased Equip]

(AICPA adapted)

P17-9 **(Operating Lease vs. Capital Lease)** You are auditing the December 31, 2008, financial statements of Sarah Shamess, Inc., manufacturer of novelties and party favors. During your inspection of the company garage, you discovered that a 2007 Shirk automobile not listed in the equipment subsidiary ledger is parked in the company garage. You ask Sally Straub, plant manager, about the vehicle, and she tells you that the company did not list the automobile because the company was only leasing it. The lease agreement was entered into on January 1, 2008, with Jack Hayes New and Used Cars.

(LO 2)

[handwritten right margin: Lessor / FMV or (PV of MLP) > cost / FMV − cost = GP / Interest Rev ? / L Recei FMV / COGS cost / Sales FMV / Inventory Cost]

You decide to review the lease agreement to ensure that the lease should be afforded operating lease treatment, and you discover the following lease terms.

1. Noncancelable term of 50 months.

2. Rental of $180 per month (at the end of each month; present value at 1% per month is $7,055.)

3. Estimated residual value after 50 months is $1,100. (The present value at 1% per month is $699.) Shamess guarantees the residual value of $1,100.

4. Estimated economic life of the automobile is 60 months.

5. Shamess's incremental borrowing rate is 12% per year (1% per month).

Instructions

You are a senior auditor writing a memo to your supervisor, the audit partner in charge of this audit, to discuss the above situation. Be sure to include (a) why you inspected the lease agreement, (b) what you determined about the lease, and (c) how you advised your client to account for this lease. Explain every journal entry that you believe is necessary to record this lease properly on the client's books. (It is also necessary to include the fact that you communicated this information to your client.)

ACCOUNTING IN ACTION

Financial Reporting and Analysis

■ Financial Reporting Issues: The Procter & Gamble Company

AIA17-1 The financial statements of **Procter & Gamble (P&G)** can be accessed at the book's website.

Instructions

Refer to P&G's financial statements, accompanying notes, and management's discussion and analysis to answer the following questions.

(a) What types of leases are used by P&G?

(b) What amount of capital leases was reported by P&G in total and for less than one year?

P&G

(c) What minimum annual rental commitments under all noncancelable leases at June 30, 2006, did P&G disclose?

■ Comparative Analysis: UAL, Inc. and Southwest Airlines

AIA17-2   The financial statements of **UAL, Inc.** and **Southwest Airlines** can be accessed at the book's website.

Instructions

Use information found at the book's website to answer the following questions.

(a) What types of leases are used by Southwest and on what assets are these leases primarily used?

(b) How long-term are some of Southwest's leases? What are some of the characteristics or provisions of Southwest's (as lessee) leases?

(c) What did Southwest report in 2006 as its future minimum annual rental commitments under noncancelable leases?

(d) At year-end 2006, what was the present value of the minimum rental payments under Southwest's capital leases? How much imputed interest was deducted from the future minimum annual rental commitments to arrive at the present value?

(e) What were the amounts and details reported by Southwest for rental expense in 2006, 2005, and 2004?

(f) How does UAL's use of leases compare with Southwest's?

■ Financial Statement Analysis

AIA17-3   The financial statement disclosures from the 2006 annual report of **Tasty Baking Company** are presented in Illustration 17-18.

Instructions

Answer the following questions related to these disclosures.

(a) What is the total obligation under capital leases at December 30, 2006, for Tasty Baking Company?

(b) What is the book value of the assets under capital lease at December 30, 2006, for Tasty Baking Company? Explain why there is a difference between the amounts reported for assets and liabilities under capital leases.

(c) What is the total rental expense reported for leasing activity for the year ended December 30, 2006, for Tasty Baking Company?

(d) Estimate the off-balance-sheet liability due to Tasty Baking's operating leases at fiscal year-end 2006.

AIA17-4   The accounting for operating leases is a controversial issue. Many contend that firms employing operating leases are utilizing significantly more assets and are more highly leveraged than indicated by the balance sheet alone. As a result, analysts often use footnote disclosures to "constructively capitalize" operating lease obligations. One way to do so is to increase a firm's assets and liabilities by the present value of all future minimum rental payments.

Instructions

(a) Obtain the most recent annual report for a firm that relies heavily on operating leases. (Firms in the airline and retail industries are good candidates.) The schedule of future minimum rental payments is usually included in the "Commitments and Contingencies" footnote. Use the schedule to determine the present value of future minimum rental payments, assuming a discount rate of 10%.

(b) Calculate the company's debt-to-total-assets ratio with and without the present value of operating lease payments. Is there a significant difference?

■ International Reporting Issues

AIA17-5   As discussed in the chapter, U.S. GAAP accounting for leases allows companies to use off-balance-sheet financing for the purchase of operating assets. International accounting standards are similar to U.S. GAAP in that under these rules, companies can keep leased assets and obligations off their balance sheets. However, under *International Accounting Standard No. 17 (IAS 17)*, leases are capitalized based on the subjective evaluation of whether the risks and rewards of ownership are transferred in the lease. In Japan, virtually all leases are treated as operating leases. Furthermore, unlike U.S. and IAS standards, the Japanese rules do not require disclosure of future minimum lease payments.

Presented below are recent financial data for three major airlines that lease some part of their aircraft fleet. **American Airlines** prepares its financial statements under U.S. GAAP and leases approximately 27% of its fleet. **KLM Royal Dutch Airlines** and **Japan Airlines (JAL)** present their statements in accordance with their home country GAAP (Netherlands and Japan respectively). KLM leases about 22% of its aircraft, and JAL leases approximately 50% of its fleet.

Financial Statement Data	American Airlines (millions of dollars)	KLM Royal Dutch Airlines (millions of guilders)	Japan Airlines (millions of yen)
As-reported			
Assets	20,915	19,205	2,042,761
Liabilities	14,699	13,837	1,857,800
Income	985	606	4,619
Estimated impact of capitalizing operating leases on:*			
Assets	5,897	1,812	244,063
Liabilities	6,886	1,776	265,103
Income	(143)	24	(9,598)

*Based on *Apples to Apples: Global Airlines: Flight to Quality* (New York: N.Y.: Morgan Stanley Dean Witter, October 1998).

Instructions

(a) Using the as-reported data for each of the airlines, compute the rate of return on assets and the debt to assets ratio. Compare these companies on the basis of this analysis.

(b) Adjust the as-reported numbers of the three companies for the effects of non-capitalization of leases, and then redo the analysis in part (a).

(c) The following statement was overheard in the library: "Non-capitalization of operating leases is not that big a deal for profitability analysis based on rate of return on assets, since the operating lease payments (under operating lease accounting) are about the same as the sum of the interest and depreciation expense under capital lease treatment." Do you agree? Explain.

(d) Since the accounting for leases worldwide is similar, does your analysis above suggest there is a need for an improved accounting standard for leases? (*Hint:* Reflect on comparability of information about these companies' leasing activities, when leasing is more prevalent in one country than in others.)

Concepts for Analysis

AIA17-6 **(Lessee Accounting and Reporting)** On January 1, 2008, Sandy Hayes Company entered into a noncancelable lease for a machine to be used in its manufacturing operations. The lease transfers ownership of the machine to Yen Quach by the end of the lease term. The term of the lease is 8 years. The minimum lease payment made by Yen Quach on January 1, 2008, was one of eight equal annual payments. At the inception of the lease, the criteria established for classification as a capital lease by the lessee were met.

Instructions

(a) What is the theoretical basis for the accounting standard that requires certain long-term leases to be capitalized by the lessee? Do not discuss the specific criteria for classifying a specific lease as a capital lease.

(b) How should Hayes account for this lease at its inception and determine the amount to be recorded?

(c) What expenses related to this lease will Hayes incur during the first year of the lease, and how will they be determined?

(d) How should Hayes report the lease transaction on its December 31, 2008, balance sheet?

AIA17-7 **(Lessor and Lessee Accounting and Disclosure)** Laurie Gocker Inc. entered into a lease arrangement with Nathan Morgan Leasing Corporation for a certain machine. Morgan's primary business is leasing, and it is not a manufacturer or dealer. Gocker will lease the machine for a period of 3 years, which is 50% of the machine's economic life. Morgan will take possession of the machine at the end of the initial 3-year lease and lease it to another, smaller company that does not need the most current version of the machine. Gocker does not guarantee any residual value for the machine and will not purchase the machine at the end of the lease term.

Gocker's incremental borrowing rate is 15%, and the implicit rate in the lease is 14%. Gocker has no way of knowing the implicit rate used by Morgan. Using either rate, the present value of the minimum lease payments is between 90% and 100% of the fair value of the machine at the date of the lease agreement.

Gocker has agreed to pay all executory costs directly and no allowance for these costs is included in the lease payments.

Morgan is reasonably certain that Gocker will pay all lease payments, and because Gocker has agreed to pay all executory costs, there are no important uncertainties regarding costs to be incurred by Morgan. Assume that no indirect costs are involved.

Instructions

(a) With respect to Gocker (the lessee), answer the following.
 (1) What type of lease has been entered into? Explain the reason for your answer.
 (2) How should Gocker compute the appropriate amount to be recorded for the lease or asset acquired?
 (3) What accounts will be created or affected by this transaction and how will the lease or asset and other costs related to the transaction be matched with earnings?
 (4) What disclosures must Gocker make regarding this leased asset?

(b) With respect to Morgan (the lessor), answer the following.
 (1) What type of leasing arrangement has been entered into? Explain the reason for your answer.
 (2) How should this lease be recorded by Morgan, and how are the appropriate amounts determined?
 (3) How should Morgan determine the appropriate amount of earnings to be recognized from each lease payment?
 (4) What disclosures must Morgan make regarding this lease?

(AICPA adapted)

AIA17-8 (Lessee Capitalization Criteria) On January 1, Shinault Company, a lessee, entered into three noncancelable leases for brand-new equipment, Lease L, Lease M, and Lease N. None of the three leases transfers ownership of the equipment to Shinault at the end of the lease term. For each of the three leases, the present value at the beginning of the lease term of the minimum lease payments, excluding that portion of the payments representing executory costs such as insurance, maintenance, and taxes to be paid by the lessor, is 75% of the fair value of the equipment.

The following information is peculiar to each lease.

1. Lease L does not contain a bargain purchase option. The lease term is equal to 80% of the estimated economic life of the equipment.

2. Lease M contains a bargain purchase option. The lease term is equal to 50% of the estimated economic life of the equipment.

3. Lease N does not contain a bargain purchase option. The lease term is equal to 50% of the estimated economic life of the equipment.

Instructions

(a) How should Shinault Company classify each of the three leases above, and why? Discuss the rationale for your answer.
(b) What amount, if any, should Shinault record as a liability at the inception of the lease for each of the three leases above?
(c) Assuming that the minimum lease payments are made on a straight-line basis, how should Shinault record each minimum lease payment for each of the three leases above?

(AICPA adapted)

AIA17-9 (Comparison of Different Types of Accounting by Lessee and Lessor)
Part 1

Capital leases and operating leases are the two classifications of leases described in FASB pronouncements from the standpoint of the **lessee**.

Instructions

(a) Describe how a capital lease would be accounted for by the lessee both at the inception of the lease and during the first year of the lease, assuming the lease transfers ownership of the property to the lessee by the end of the lease.
(b) Describe how an operating lease would be accounted for by the lessee both at the inception of the lease and during the first year of the lease, assuming equal monthly payments are made by the lessee at the beginning of each month of the lease. Describe the change in accounting, if any, when rental payments are not made on a straight-line basis.

Do **not** discuss the criteria for distinguishing between capital leases and operating leases.
Part 2

Sales-type leases and direct-financing leases are two of the classifications of leases described in FASB pronouncements from the standpoint of the **lessor**.

Instructions

Compare and contrast a sales-type lease with a direct-financing lease as follows.

(a) Lease receivable.

(b) Interest revenue.

(c) Manufacturer's or dealer's profit.

Do **not** discuss the criteria for distinguishing between the leases described above and operating leases.

(AICPA adapted)

Professional Tools

■ Ethical Decision Making

AIA17-10 (Lease Capitalization, Bargain Purchase Option) Cuby Corporation entered into a lease agreement for 10 photocopy machines for its corporate headquarters. The lease agreement qualifies as an operating lease in all terms except there is a bargain purchase option. After the 5-year lease term, the corporation can purchase each copier for $1,000, when the anticipated market value is $2,500.

R. Sandberg, the financial vice president, thinks the financial statements must recognize the lease agreement as a capital lease because of the bargain purchase agreement. The controller, J. Girardi, disagrees: "Although I don't know much about the copiers themselves, there is a way to avoid recording the lease liability." She argues that the corporation might claim that copier technology advances rapidly and that by the end of the lease term the machines will most likely not be worth the $1,000 bargain price.

Instructions

Answer the following questions.

(a) What ethical issue is at stake?

(b) Should the controller's argument be accepted if she does not really know much about copier technology? Would it make a difference if the controller were knowledgeable about the pace of change in copier technology?

(c) What should Sandberg do?

■ Financial Accounting Research (FARs)

AIA17-11 Henley Hardware Co. is considering alternative financing arrangements for equipment used in its warehouses. Besides purchasing the equipment outright, Henley is also considering a lease. Accounting for the outright purchase is fairly straightforward, but because Henley has not used equipment leases in the past, the accounting staff is less informed about the specific accounting rules for leases.

The staff is aware of some lease rules related to a "90 percent of fair value," "75 percent of useful life," and "residual value deficiencies," but they are unsure about the meanings of these terms in lease accounting. Henley has asked you to conduct some research on these items related to lease capitalization criteria.

Instructions

Using the **Financial Accounting Research System (FARS)** database, respond to the following items. (Provide text strings used in your search.)

(a) Define "fair value of the leased property." What are some examples of the determination of fair value?

(b) Besides the noncancelable term of the lease, name at least three other considerations in determining the "lease term."

(c) A common issue in the accounting for leases concerns lease requirements that the lessee make up a residual value deficiency that is attributable to damage, extraordinary wear and tear, or excessive usage (e.g., excessive mileage on a leased vehicle). Do these features constitute a lessee guarantee of the residual value such that the estimated residual value of the leased property at the end of the lease term should be included in minimum lease payments?

■ Professional Simulations

AIA17-12 and AIA17-13 Go to the book's companion website, at **www.wiley.com/college/warfield**, to find interactive problems that simulate the computerized CPA exam. The two professional simulations for this chapter ask you to address questions related to the accounting for leases.

What do the numbers mean?

Off-Balance-Sheet Financing, p. 895

Q: How does noncapitalization of leases affect recorded assets and common ratios based on assets?

A: When companies, like airlines, structure leases to avoid capitalization, the leased asset is also "off-balance-sheet." As a result, the denominator of the return on assets ratio (ROA = Net income ÷ Average assets) will be overstated. If companies capitalize differing percentages of their leases, it will be difficult to compare the companies based on ROAs.

Restatements on the Menu, p. 904

Q: In some cases companies reported higher earnings and assets upon correcting their lease accounting. Do you think these companies should have to correct their accounting since the prior approach was conservative? Explain based on the qualitative characteristics of accounting information.

A: Whether the accounting was conservative or aggressive, it is in error and should be corrected. Basing the propriety of accounting on conservatism introduces bias into the reported numbers. Such bias detracts from the neutrality of reporting, which is an element of reliability—one of the primary qualitative characteristics of accounting information.

Dollars to Doughnuts, p. 906

Q: Krispy Kreme is using different methods for reporting the new plant under GAAP and tax rules. Briefly describe two other situations where tax rules and GAAP differ.

A: Here are four types of temporary differences and a couple of examples for each. For a more comprehensive set of examples, see Illustration 15-22.

- Revenues or gains are taxable after they are recognized in financial income. Examples: (1) Sales accounted for on the accrual basis for financial reporting purposes and on the installment (cash) basis for tax purposes. (2) Contracts accounted for under the percentage-of-completion method for financial reporting purposes and a portion of related gross profit deferred for tax purposes.

- Expenses or losses are deductible after they are recognized in financial income. Examples: (1) Product warranty liabilities. (2) Litigation accruals.

- Revenues or gains are taxable before they are recognized in financial income. Examples: (1) Subscriptions received in advance. (2) Advance rental receipts.

- Expenses or losses are deductible before they are recognized in financial income. Examples: (1) Depreciation and amortization of plant and equipment and intangibles. (2) Deductible pension funding exceeding expense.

Xerox Takes on the SEC, p. 913

Q: To avoid the accounting headaches related to its lease accounting, Xerox could stop selling its equipment through lease arrangements. Do you think this is a good idea? Explain.

A: Xerox would be reluctant to abandon leasing in its business. For many lessors, like Xerox, leasing is an important part of its product marketing strategy. Many of Xerox's customers likely expect to be able to purchase Xerox products through lease arrangements. In addition, as discussed in the chapter, Xerox gets the following benefits from leasing: (1) Interest revenue: Leasing provides competitive interest margins. (2) Tax incentives: Companies that lease cannot use the tax benefits of owning assets; leasing allows them to transfer such tax benefits to another party (the lessor) in return for a lower rental rate on the leased asset. (3) Residual value profits: Residual values can produce very large profits when lessors resell leased assets that are returned at the conclusion of the lease.

Remember to check the book's companion website to find additional resources for this chapter.

CHAPTER 18

ADDITIONAL REPORTING ISSUES

So Many Changes

The FASB's conceptual framework describes comparability (including consistency) as one of the qualitative characteristics that contribute to the usefulness of accounting information. Unfortunately, companies are finding it difficult to maintain comparability and consistency due to the numerous changes in accounting principles mandated by the FASB. In addition, a number of companies have faced restatements due to errors in their financial statements. For example, the table below shows types and numbers of accounting changes.

Asset retirement obligations	93	Exchange of nonmonetary assets	24
Taxes	62	Postretirement benefits	12
Stock compensation	36	Other (inventory, impairments, goodwill)	42

The following chart indicates an increasing trend in restatements.

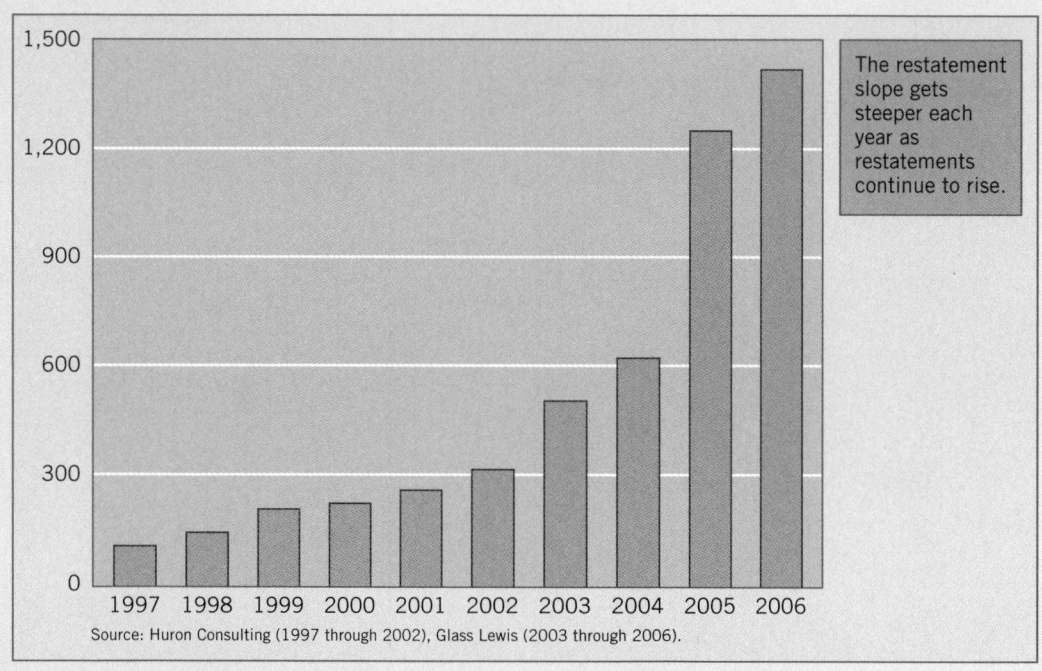

Source: Huron Consulting (1997 through 2002), Glass Lewis (2003 through 2006).

Although the percentage of companies reporting material changes or errors is small, you still must be careful. The reason: The amounts in the financial statements may have changed due to changing accounting principles and/or restatements.

Sources: Accounting change data from *Accounting Trends and Techniques—2006* (New York: AICPA, 2006). Restatement graph from Mark Grothe, "The Errors of Their Ways," *Trend Alert* (February 27, 2007).

Preview of Chapter 18

As our opening story indicates, changes in accounting principles and errors in financial information have increased substantially in recent years. When these changes occur, companies must follow specific accounting and reporting requirements. In addition, to ensure comparability among companies, the FASB has standardized reporting of accounting changes, accounting estimates, error corrections, and related earnings per share information. In this chapter, we discuss these reporting standards, which help investors better understand a company's financial condition. *The content and organization of the chapter are as follows.*

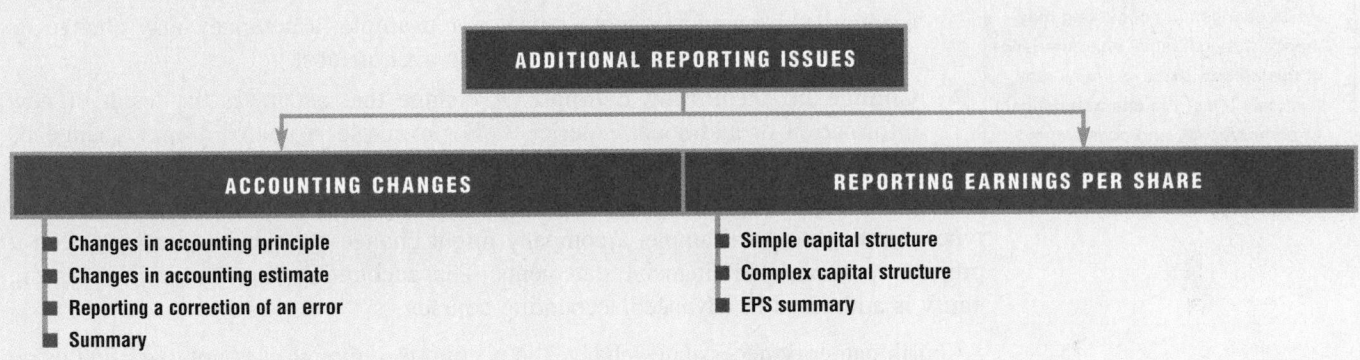

ADDITIONAL REPORTING ISSUES

ACCOUNTING CHANGES	REPORTING EARNINGS PER SHARE
▪ Changes in accounting principle	▪ Simple capital structure
▪ Changes in accounting estimate	▪ Complex capital structure
▪ Reporting a correction of an error	▪ EPS summary
▪ Summary	

Learning Objectives

After studying this chapter, you should be able to:

1. Identify the types of accounting changes.
2. Understand how to account for retrospective accounting changes.
3. Understand how to account for impracticable changes.
4. Describe the accounting for changes in estimates.
5. Describe the accounting for correction of errors.
6. Compute earnings per share in a simple capital structure.
7. Compute earnings per share in a complex capital structure.

Inside Chapter 18

- **What Do the Numbers Mean?**
  Change management (p. 945)
  Can I get my money back? (p. 959)
  Pro forma EPS confusion (p. 965)
  Cuckoo for CoCos (p. 968)

- **What's the Principle?** (pp. 942, 958, 964)

- **Convergence Corner** (p. 974)

- **Accounting, Analysis, Principles** (p. 975)
  Account for an accounting change; compute EPS.
  Discuss the effects of EPS rules on analysis of price-earnings ratios.
  Explain how accounting changes affect relevance and reliability.

ACCOUNTING CHANGES

WHAT'S THE PRINCIPLE?

While changes in accounting may enhance the qualitative characteristic of *usefulness*, these changes may adversely affect the characteristics of *comparability* and *consistency*.

Accounting alternatives diminish the comparability of financial information between periods and between companies; they also obscure useful historical trend data. For example, if **Ford** revises its estimates for equipment useful lives, depreciation expense for the current year will not be comparable to depreciation expense reported by Ford in prior years. Similarly, if **Best Buy** changes to FIFO inventory pricing while **Circuit City** uses LIFO, it will be difficult to compare these companies' reported results. A reporting framework helps preserve comparability when there is an accounting change.

The FASB has established a reporting framework, which involves three types of accounting changes.[1] The three types of accounting changes are:

1 **Change in Accounting Principle.** A change from one generally accepted accounting principle to another one. For example, a company may change its inventory valuation method from LIFO to average cost.

2 **Change in Accounting Estimate.** A change that occurs as the result of new information or additional experience. For example, a company may change its estimate of the useful lives of depreciable assets.

3 **Change in Reporting Entity.** A change from reporting as one type of entity to another type of entity. As an example, a company might change the subsidiaries for which it prepares consolidated financial statements. The accounting for change in reporting entity is addressed in advanced accounting courses.

A fourth category necessitates changes in accounting, though it is not classified as an accounting change.

4 **Errors in Financial Statements.** Errors result from mathematical mistakes, mistakes in applying accounting principles, or oversight or misuse of facts that existed when preparing the financial statements. For example, a company may incorrectly apply the LIFO inventory method for determining its final inventory value.

The FASB classifies changes in these categories because each category involves different methods of recognizing changes in the financial statements. In this section we discuss these classifications. We also explain how to report each item in the accounts and how to disclose the information in comparative statements.

CHANGES IN ACCOUNTING PRINCIPLE

By definition, a **change in accounting principle** involves a **change from one generally accepted accounting principle to another**. For example, a company might change the basis of inventory pricing from average cost to LIFO. Or it might change its method of revenue recognition for long-term construction contracts from the completed-contract to the percentage-of-completion method.

Companies must carefully examine each circumstance to ensure that a change in principle has actually occurred. **Adoption of a new principle** in recognition of events that have occurred for the first time or that were previously immaterial is not an accounting change. For example, a change in accounting principle has not occurred when a company adopts an inventory method (e.g., FIFO) for **newly** acquired items of inventory, even if FIFO differs from that used for **previously recorded** inventory. Another example is certain marketing expenditures that were previously immaterial and expensed in the period incurred. It would not

---

[1]"Accounting Changes and Error Corrections," *Statement of Financial Accounting Standards No. 154* (Stamford, Conn.: FASB, 2005).

be considered a change in accounting principle if they become material and so may be acceptably deferred and amortized.

Finally, what if a company previously followed an accounting principle that was not acceptable? Or what if the company applied a principle incorrectly? In such cases, the profession considers a change to a generally accepted accounting principle a **correction of an error**. For example, a switch from the cash (income tax) basis of accounting to the accrual basis is a correction of an error. Or, if a company deducted salvage value when computing double-declining depreciation on plant assets and later recomputed depreciation without deducting estimated salvage value, it has corrected an error.

A presumption exists that once a company adopts an accounting principle, it should not change. That presumption is understandable, given the idea that consistent use of an accounting principle enhances the usefulness of financial statements. However, the environment continually changes, and companies change in response. Recent standards on such subjects as stock options, exchanges of nonmonetary assets, derivatives, and so on indicate that changes in accounting principle will continue to occur.

Retrospective Accounting Change Approach

When a company changes an accounting principle, it should report the change using retrospective application. **Retrospective application** refers to the application of a different accounting principle to recast previously issued financial statements—**as if the new principle had always been used**. In other words, the company "goes back" and adjusts **prior years' statements** on a basis consistent with the newly adopted principle.[2] In general terms, here is what it must do:

OBJECTIVE 2
Understand how to account for retrospective accounting changes.

1 It adjusts its financial statements for each prior period presented. Thus, financial statement information about prior periods is on the same basis as the new accounting principle.

2 It adjusts the carrying amounts of assets and liabilities as of the beginning of the first year presented. By doing so, these accounts reflect the cumulative effect on periods prior to those presented of the change to the new accounting principle. The company also makes an offsetting adjustment to the opening balance of retained earnings or other appropriate component of stockholders' equity or net assets as of the beginning of the first year presented.

For example, assume that **Target** decides to change its inventory valuation method in 2008 from the retail inventory method (FIFO) to the retail inventory (average cost). It provides comparative information for 2006 and 2007 based on the new method. Target would adjust its assets, liabilities, and retained earnings for periods prior to 2006 and report these amounts in the 2006 financial statements, when it prepares comparative financial statements.

In summary, the FASB requires that companies use the retrospective approach because it provides financial statement users with more useful information. That is, changing the prior statements to be on the same basis as the newly adopted principle results in greater consistency across accounting periods. Users can then better compare results from one period to the next.[3]

---

[2]"Accounting Changes and Error Corrections," *Statement of Financial Accounting Standards No. 154* (Stamford, Conn.: FASB, 2005). This recent standard carries forward many of the provisions in the previous accounting change standard (*APB Opinion No. 20*), including the accounting for errors, changes in estimates, and the disclosures related to accounting changes.

[3]Adoption of the retrospective approach contributes to international accounting convergence. The FASB and the IASB are collaborating on a project in which they have agreed to converge around high-quality solutions to resolve differences between U.S. GAAP and iGAAP. By adopting the retrospective approach, which is the method used in iGAAP, the FASB agreed that this approach is superior to the prior U.S. GAAP approach.

Example of Retrospective Accounting Change

To illustrate the retrospective approach, assume that Denson Company has accounted for its income from long-term construction contracts using the completed-contract method. In 2008 the company changed to the percentage-of-completion method. Management believes this approach provides a more appropriate measure of the income earned. For tax purposes, the company uses the completed-contract method and plans to continue doing so in the future. (We assume a 40 percent enacted tax rate.)

Illustration 18-1 shows portions of two income statements for 2006–2008—for both the completed-contract and percentage-of-completion methods.

Illustration 18-1

Comparative Income Statements for Completed-Contract versus Percentage-of-Completion Methods

Completed-Contract Method
Denson Company
Income Statement (Partial)
For the Years Ended December 31

	2006	2007	2008
Income before income tax	$400,000	$160,000	$190,000
Income tax (40%)	160,000	64,000	76,000
Net income	$240,000	$ 96,000	$114,000

Percentage-of-Completion Method
Denson Company
Income Statement (Partial)
For the Years Ended December 31

	2006	2007	2008
Income before income tax	$600,000	$180,000	$200,000
Income tax (40%)	240,000	72,000	80,000
Net income	$360,000	$108,000	$120,000

To record a change from the completed-contract to the percentage-of-completion method, we analyze the various effects, as Illustration 18-2 shows.

Illustration18-2

Data for Retrospective Change Example

	Pretax Income from		Difference in Income		
Year	Percentage-of-Completion	Completed-Contract	Difference	Tax Effect 40%	Income Effect (net of tax)
Prior to 2007	$600,000	$400,000	$200,000	$80,000	$120,000
In 2007	180,000	160,000	20,000	8,000	12,000
Total at beginning of 2008	$780,000	$560,000	$220,000	$88,000	$132,000
Total in 2008	$200,000	$190,000	$ 10,000	$ 4,000	$ 6,000

The entry to record the change at the beginning of 2008 would be:

Construction in Process	220,000	
Deferred Tax Liability		88,000
Retained Earnings		132,000

The Construction in Process account increases by $220,000 (as indicated in the first column under "Difference in Income" in Illustration 18-2). The credit to Retained Earnings of $132,000 reflects the cumulative income effects prior to 2008 (third column under "Difference in Income" in Illustration 18-2). The company credits Retained Earnings because prior years' income is closed to this account each year. The credit to Deferred Tax Liability represents the adjustment to prior years' tax expense. The company now recognizes that amount, $88,000, as a tax liability for future taxable amounts. That is, in future periods, taxable income will be higher than book income as a result of current temporary differences. Therefore, Denson must report a deferred tax liability in the current year.

What do the numbers mean?

Halliburton offers a case study in the importance of good reporting of an accounting change. Recall from Chapter 7 that Halliburton uses percentage-of-completion accounting for its long-term construction-services contracts. Recently, the SEC questioned the company about its change in accounting for disputed claims.

Prior to 1998 Halliburton took a very conservative approach to its accounting for disputed claims. That is, the company waited until all disputes were resolved before recognizing associated revenues. In contrast, in 1998 the company recognized revenue for disputed claims *before* their resolution, using estimates of amounts expected to be recovered. Such revenue and its related profit are more tentative and subject to possible later adjustment. The accounting method adopted in 1998 is more aggressive than the company's former policy but is within the boundaries of GAAP.

It appears that the problem with Halliburton's accounting stems more from how the company handled its accounting change than from the new method itself. That is, Halliburton did not provide in its 1998 annual report an explicit reference to its change in accounting method. In fact, rather than stating its new policy, the company simply deleted the sentence that described how it accounted for disputed claims. Then later, in its 1999 annual report, the company stated its new accounting policy.

When companies make such changes in accounting, investors need to be informed about the change and about its effects on the financial results. With such information, investors and analysts can compare current results with those of prior periods and can make a more informed assessment about the company's future prospects.

Source: Adapted from "Accounting Ace Charles Mulford Answers Accounting Questions," *Wall Street Journal Online* (June 7, 2002).

Beyond the Numbers

What changes in the environment might Halliburton use to justify the change in its accounting for disputed claims?

Reporting a Change in Principle

The disclosure of accounting changes is particularly important. Users of the financial statements want consistent information from one period to the next. Such consistency ensures the usefulness of financial statements. The major disclosure requirements are as follows.

1 The nature of and reason for the change in accounting principle. This must include an explanation of why the newly adopted accounting principle is preferable.

2 The method of applying the change, and:

a A description of the prior-period information that has been retrospectively adjusted, if any.

b The effect of the change on income from continuing operations, net income (or other appropriate captions of changes in net assets or performance indicators), any other affected line item, and any affected per-share amounts for the current period and for any prior periods retrospectively adjusted.

c The cumulative effect of the change on retained earnings or other components of equity or net assets in the statement of financial position as of the beginning of the earliest period presented.[4]

[4]Presentation of the effect on financial statement subtotals and totals other than income from continuing operations and net income (or other appropriate captions of changes in the applicable net assets or performance indicator) is not required (*SFAS No. 154*, par. 17).

To illustrate, Denson will prepare comparative financial statements for 2007 and 2008 using the percentage-of-completion method (the new-construction accounting method). Illustration 18-3 indicates how Denson presents this information.

Illustration 18-3
Comparative Information Related to Accounting Change (Percentage-of-Completion)

Denson Company
Income Statement (partial)
For the Year Ended

	2008	2007
		As adjusted (Note A)
Income before income tax	$200,000	$180,000
Income tax (40%)	80,000	72,000
Net income	$120,000	$108,000

Note A: Change in Method of Accounting for Long-Term Contracts. The company has accounted for revenue and costs for long-term construction contracts by the percentage-of-completion method in 2008, whereas in all prior years revenue and costs were determined by the completed-contract method. The new method of accounting for long-term contracts was adopted to recognize . . . [state justification for change in accounting principle] . . ., and financial statements of prior years have been restated to apply the new method retrospectively. For income tax purposes, the completed-contract method has been continued. The effect of the accounting change on income of 2008 was an increase of $6,000 net of related taxes and on income of 2007 as previously reported was an increase of $12,000 net of related taxes. The balances of retained earnings for 2007 and 2008 have been adjusted for the effect of applying retroactively the new method of accounting. As a result of the accounting change, retained earnings as of January 1, 2007, increased by $132,000 compared to that reported using the completed-contract method.

As Illustration 18-3 shows, Denson Company reports net income under the newly adopted percentage-of-completion method for both 2007 and 2008. The company retrospectively adjusted the 2007 income statement to report the information on a percentage-of-completion basis. Also, the note to the financial statements indicates the nature of the change, why the company made the change, and the years affected.

In addition, companies are required to provide data on important differences between the amounts reported under percentage-of-completion versus completed-contract. When identifying the significant differences, some companies show the *entire* financial statements and line-by-line differences between percentage-of-completion and completed-contract. However, most companies will show only line-by-line differences. For example, Denson would show the differences in construction in process, retained earnings, gross profit, and net income for 2007 and 2008 under the completed-contract and percentage-of-completion methods.

Retained Earnings Adjustment

As indicated earlier, one of the disclosure requirements is to show the cumulative effect of the change on retained earnings as of the beginning of the earliest period presented. For Denson Company, that date is January 1, 2006. Denson disclosed that information by means of a narrative description (see Note A in Illustration 18-3). Denson also would disclose this information in its retained earnings statement. Assuming a retained earnings balance of $1,360,000 at the beginning of 2006, Illustration 18-4 shows Denson's retained earnings statement under the completed-contract method—that is, before giving effect to the change in accounting principle. (The income information comes from Illustration 18-1.)

Illustration 18-4
Retained Earnings
Statement before
Retrospective Change

Denson Company
Retained Earnings Statement
For the Year Ended

	2008	2007	2006
Retained earnings, January 1	$1,696,000	$1,600,000	$1,360,000
Net income	114,000	96,000	240,000
Retained earnings, December 31	$1,810,000	$1,696,000	$1,600,000

If Denson presents comparative statements for 2007 and 2008 under percentage-of-completion, then it must change the beginning balance of retained earnings at January 1, 2007. The difference between the retained earnings balances under completed-contract and percentage-of-completion is computed as follows.

Retained earnings, January 1, 2007 (percentage-of-completion)	$1,720,000
Retained earnings, January 1, 2007 (completed-contract)	1,600,000
Cumulative effect difference	$ 120,000

The $120,000 difference is the cumulative effect. Illustration 18-5 shows a comparative retained earnings statement for 2007 and 2008, giving effect to the change in accounting principle to percentage-of-completion.

Illustration 18-5
Retained Earnings
Statement after
Retrospective Application

Denson Company
Retained Earnings Statement
For the Year Ended

	2008	2007
Retained earnings, January 1, as reported	—	$1,600,000
Add: Adjustment for the cumulative effect on prior years of applying retrospectively the new method of accounting for construction contracts		120,000
Retained earnings, January 1, as adjusted	$1,828,000	1,720,000
Net income	120,000	108,000
Retained earnings, December 31	$1,948,000	$1,828,000

Denson adjusted the beginning balance of retained earnings on January 1, 2007, for the excess of percentage-of-completion net income over completed-contract net income in 2006. This comparative presentation indicates the type of adjustment that a company needs to make. It follows that this adjustment would be much larger if a number of prior periods were involved.

Direct and Indirect Effects of Changes

Are there other effects that a company should report when it makes a change in accounting principle? For example, what happens when a company like Denson has a bonus plan based on net income and the prior year's net income changes when the company retrospectively applies percentage-of-completion? Should Denson change the reported amount

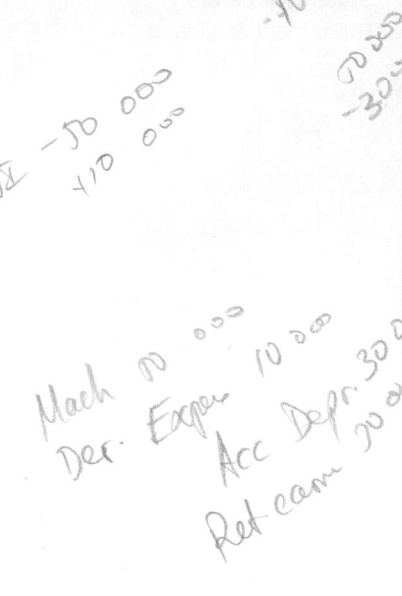

of bonus expense as well? Should Denson adjust net income, given that taxes will be different under the percentage-of-completion and completed-contract methods in prior periods? The answers depend on whether additional effects are direct or indirect.

Direct Effects

The FASB takes the position that companies should retrospectively apply the **direct effects of a change in accounting principle**. An example of a **direct effect** is an adjustment to an inventory balance as a result of a change in the inventory valuation method. For example, as illustrated in our example, Denson Company changed the Construction in Process amounts in prior periods to indicate the change to the percentage-of-completion method. An inventory-related example would be an impairment adjustment resulting from applying the lower-of-cost-or-market test to the adjusted inventory balance. Related changes, such as deferred income tax effects of the impairment adjustment, would also be direct effects.

In addition to recording these direct effects, Denson reports the comparative financial statements as shown in the lower half of Illustration 18-1. These include the new tax amounts. As indicated earlier, companies should record in the current year the direct effect of the change in taxes as a result of the change in accounting principle, and they should present information for prior periods, including changes in taxes, based on the new method.

Indirect Effects

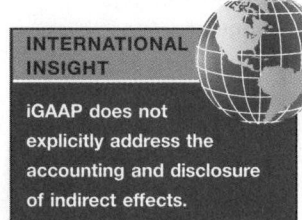

In addition to direct effects, companies can have **indirect effects related to a change in accounting principle**. An **indirect effect** is any change to current or future cash flows of a company that result from making a change in accounting principle that is applied retrospectively. An example of an indirect effect is a change in profit-sharing or royalty payment that is based on a reported amount such as revenue or net income. **Indirect effects do not change prior-period amounts.**

For example, let's assume that Denson Construction has an employee profit-sharing plan based on net income. As Illustration 18-1 showed, Denson would report higher income in 2006 and 2007 if it used the percentage-of-completion method. In addition, let's assume that the profit-sharing plan requires that Denson pay the incremental amount due based on the percentage-of-completion income amounts. In this situation, Denson reports this additional expense **in the current period**; it would not change prior periods for this expense. If the company prepares comparative financial statements, it follows that it does not recast the prior periods for this additional expense.[5]

If the terms of the profit-sharing plan indicate that *no payment is necessary* in the current period due to this change, then the company need not recognize additional profit-sharing expense in the current period. Neither does it change amounts reported for prior periods.

When a company recognizes the indirect effects of a change in accounting principle, it includes in the financial statements a description of the indirect effects. In doing so, it discloses the amounts recognized in the current period and related per share information.

INTERNATIONAL INSIGHT

iGAAP does not explicitly address the accounting and disclosure of indirect effects.

Impracticability

OBJECTIVE 3

Understand how to account for impracticable changes.

It is not always possible for companies to determine how they would have reported prior periods' financial information under retrospective application of an accounting principle change. Retrospective application is considered **impracticable** if a company cannot determine the prior-period effects using every reasonable effort to do so.

---

[5]The rationale for this approach is that companies should recognize, in the period the adoption occurs (not the prior period), the effect on the cash flows that is caused by the adoption of the new accounting principle. That is, the accounting change is a necessary "past event" in the definition of an asset or liability that gives rise to the accounting recognition of the indirect effect in the current period (*SFAS No. 154*, par. B19).

Companies should not use retrospective application if one of the following conditions exists:

1 The company cannot determine the effects of the retrospective application.

2 Retrospective application requires assumptions about management's intent in a prior period.

3 Retrospective application requires significant estimates for a prior period, and the company cannot objectively verify the necessary information to develop these estimates.

If any of the above conditions exists, it is deemed impracticable to apply the retrospective approach. In this case, the company **prospectively applies** the new accounting principle as of the earliest date it is practicable to do so.[6]

For example, assume that Williams Company changed its inventory method from FIFO to LIFO, effective January 1, 2008. Williams prepares statements on a calendar-year basis and has used the FIFO method since its inception. Williams judges it impracticable to retrospectively apply the new method. Determining prior-period effects would require subjective assumptions about the LIFO layers established in prior periods. These assumptions would ordinarily result in the computation of a number of different earnings figures.

As a result, the only adjustment necessary may be to restate the beginning inventory to a cost basis from a lower-of-cost-or-market approach. Williams must disclose only the effect of the change on the results of operations in the period of change. Also, the company should explain the reasons for omitting the computations of the cumulative effect for prior years. Finally, it should disclose the justification for the change to LIFO.[7] Illustration 18-6, from the annual report of **Quaker Oats Company**, shows the type of disclosure needed.

The Quaker Oats Company

Note 1 (In Part): Summary of Significant Accounting Policies

Inventories. Inventories are valued at the lower of cost or market, using various cost methods, and include the cost of raw materials, labor and overhead. The percentage of year-end inventories valued using each of the methods is as follows:

June 30	Current Year	Prior Year
Average quarterly cost	21%	54%
Last-in, first-out (LIFO)	65%	29%
First-in, first-out (FIFO)	14%	17%

Effective July 1, the Company adopted the LIFO cost flow assumption for valuing the majority of remaining U.S. Grocery Products inventories. The Company believes that the use of the LIFO method better matches current costs with current revenues. The cumulative effect of this change on retained earnings at the beginning of the year is not determinable, nor are the pro-forma effects of retroactive application of LIFO to prior years. The effect of this change on current-year fiscal results was to decrease net income by $16.0 million, or $.20 per share.

If the LIFO method of valuing certain inventories were not used, total inventories would have been $60.1 million higher in the current year, and $24.0 million higher in the prior year.

Illustration 18-6
Disclosure of Change to LIFO

[6]*SFAS No. 154*, pars. 8–11.

[7]*SFAS No. 154*, par. 17. In practice, many companies defer the formal adoption of LIFO until year-end. Management thus has an opportunity to assess the impact that a change to LIFO will have on the financial statements and to evaluate the desirability of a change for tax purposes. As indicated in Chapter 9, many companies use LIFO because of the advantages of this inventory valuation method in a period of inflation.

	Barrett Co. decides at the beginning of 2008 to adopt the FIFO method
Try it out!	of inventory valuation. Barrett had used the LIFO method for financial

reporting since its inception on January 1, 2006, and had maintained records adequate to apply the FIFO method retrospectively. Barrett concluded that FIFO is the preferable inventory method because it reflects the current cost of inventory on the balance sheet. The table below presents the effects of the change in accounting principles on inventory and cost of goods sold.

	Inventory Determined by		Cost of Goods Sold Determined by	
Date	LIFO Method	FIFO Method	LIFO Method	FIFO Method
January 1, 2006	$ 0	$ 0	$ 0	$ 0
December 31, 2006	100	80	800	820
December 31, 2007	200	240	1,000	940
December 31, 2008	320	390	1,130	1,100

Other information:

1 For each year presented, sales are $4,500 and operating expenses are $2,500.
2 Barrett provides two years of financial statements. Earnings per share information is not required.

Instructions

(Ignore income taxes.)

a Prepare income statements under LIFO and FIFO for 2006, 2007, and 2008, not considering a change in accounting principle.

b Prepare income statements reflecting the retrospective application of the accounting change from the LIFO method to the FIFO method for 2007 and 2008.

c Prepare the note to the financial statements indicating the financial statement line items for 2008 and 2007 that were affected by the change in accounting principle.

d Prepare comparative retained earnings statements for 2007 and 2008 under FIFO. Retained earnings reported under LIFO are as follows:

	Retained Earnings Balance
December 31, 2006	$1,200
December 31, 2007	2,200
December 31, 2008	3,070

Solution

a

Barrett Co.
Income Statement—LIFO
For the Year Ended December 31

	2006	2007	2008
Sales	$4,500	$4,500	$4,500
Cost of goods sold	800	1,000	1,130
Operating expenses	2,500	2,500	2,500
Net income	$1,200	$1,000	$ 870

Barrett Co.
Income Statement—FIFO
For the Year Ended December 31

	2006	2007	2008
Sales	$4,500	$4,500	$4,500
Cost of goods sold	820	940	1,100
Operating expenses	2,500	2,500	2,500
Net income	$1,180	$1,060	$900

b

Barrett Co.
Income Statement
For the Year Ended December 31

	2008	2007
Sales	$4,500	$4,500
Cost of goods sold	1,100	940
Operating expenses	2,500	2,500
Net income	$ 900	$1,060

c

	2008			2007		
Balance Sheet	LIFO	FIFO	Difference	LIFO	FIFO	Difference
Inventory	$ 320	$ 390	$70	$ 200	$ 240	$40
Retained earnings	3,070	3,140	70	2,200	2,240	40
Income Statement						
Cost of goods sold	$1,130	$1,100	$30	$1,000	$ 940	$60
Net income	870	900	30	1,000	1,060	60

d

	2008	2007
Retained earnings, January 1, as reported		$1,200
Less: Adjustment for cumulative effect of applying new accounting method (FIFO)		20
Retained earnings, January 1, as adjusted	$2,240	1,180
Net income	900	1,060
Retained earnings, December 31	$3,140	$2,240

CHANGES IN ACCOUNTING ESTIMATE

To prepare financial statements, companies must estimate the effects of future conditions and events. For example, the following items require estimates.

OBJECTIVE 4
Describe the accounting for changes in estimates.

1 Uncollectible receivables.

2 Inventory obsolescence.

3 Useful lives and salvage values of assets.

4 Liabilities for warranty costs and income taxes.

5 Change in depreciation methods.

A company cannot perceive future conditions and events and their effects with certainty. Therefore, estimating requires the exercise of judgment. Accounting estimates will change as new events occur, as a company acquires more experience, or as it obtains additional information.

Companies report prospectively changes in accounting estimates. That is, companies should not adjust previously reported results for changes in estimates. Instead, they account for the effects of all changes in estimates in (1) the period of change if the change affects that period only, or (2) the period of change and future periods if the change affects both. The FASB views changes in estimates as **normal recurring corrections and adjustments**, the natural result of the accounting process. It prohibits retrospective treatment.

The circumstances related to a change in estimate differ from those for a change in accounting principle. If companies reported changes in estimates retrospectively, continual adjustments of prior years' income would occur. It seems proper to accept the view that, because new conditions or circumstances exist, the revision fits the new situation (not the old one). Companies should therefore handle such a revision in the current and future periods.

To illustrate, Underwriters Labs Inc. purchased for $300,000 a building that it originally estimated to have a useful life of 15 years and no salvage value. It recorded depreciation for five years on a straight-line basis. On January 1, 2007, Underwriters Labs revises the estimate of the useful life. It now considers the asset to have a total life of 25 years. (Assume that the useful life for financial reporting and tax purposes and depreciation method are the same.) Illustration 18-7 shows the accounts at the beginning of the sixth year.

Illustration 18-7
Book Value after Five
Years' Depreciation

Building	$300,000
Less: Accumulated depreciation—building (5 × $20,000)	100,000
Book value of building	$200,000

Underwriters Labs records depreciation for the year 2007 as follows:

Depreciation Expense	10,000	
Accumulated Depreciation—Building		10,000

The company computes the $10,000 depreciation charge as shown in Illustration 18-8.

Illustration 18-8
Depreciation after
Change in Estimate

$$\text{Depreciation Charge} = \frac{\text{Book Value of Asset}}{\text{Remaining Service Life}} = \frac{\$200,000}{25 \text{ years} - 5 \text{ years}} = \$10,000$$

Companies sometime find it difficult to differentiate between a change in estimate and a change in accounting principle. Is it a change in principle or a change in estimate when a company changes from deferring and amortizing marketing costs to expensing them as incurred because future benefits of these costs have become doubtful? If it is impossible to determine whether a change in principle or a change in estimate has occurred, the rule is this: **Consider the change as a change in estimate.** This is often referred to as a **change in estimate effected by a change in accounting principle**.

Another example of a change in estimate effected by a change in principle is a change in depreciation (as well as amortization or depletion) methods. Because companies change depreciation methods based on changes in estimates about future benefits from long-lived assets, it is not possible to separate the effect of the accounting principle change from that of the estimates. **As a result, companies account for a change in depreciation methods as a change in estimate effected by a change in accounting principle.**[8]

A similar problem occurs in differentiating between a change in estimate and a correction of an error, although here the answer is more clear-cut. How does a company determine whether it overlooked the information in earlier periods (an error), or whether it obtained new information (a change in estimate)? Proper classification is important because the accounting treatment differs for corrections of errors versus changes in estimates. The general rule is this: **Companies should consider careful estimates that later prove to be incorrect as changes in estimate.** Only when a company obviously computed the estimate incorrectly because of lack of expertise or in bad faith should it consider the adjustment an error. There is no clear demarcation line here. Companies must use good judgment in light of all the circumstances.[9]

Disclosures

Illustration 18-9 shows disclosure of a change in estimated useful lives, which appeared in the annual report of **Ampco–Pittsburgh Corporation**.

Ampco–Pittsburgh Corporation

Note 11: Change in Accounting Estimate. The Corporation revised its estimate of the useful lives of certain machinery and equipment. Previously, all machinery and equipment, whether new when placed in use or not, were in one class and depreciated over 15 years. The change principally applies to assets purchased new when placed in use. Those lives are now extended to 20 years. These changes were made to better reflect the estimated periods during which such assets will remain in service. The change had the effect of reducing depreciation expense and increasing net income by approximately $991,000 ($.10 per share).

Illustration 18-9
Disclosure of Change in Estimated Useful Lives

For the most part, companies need not disclose changes in accounting estimate made as part of normal operations, such as bad debt allowances or inventory obsolescence, unless such changes are material. However, for a change in estimate that affects several periods (such as a change in the service lives of depreciable assets), companies should disclose the effect on income from continuing operations and related per-share amounts of the current period. When a company has a change in estimate effected by a change in accounting principle, it must indicate why the new method is preferable. In addition, companies are subject to all other disclosure guidelines established for changes in accounting principle.

REPORTING A CORRECTION OF AN ERROR

No business, large or small, is immune from errors. Unfortunately, as the opening story discussed, the number of errors in financial statements has increased dramatically. Illustration 18-10 indicates significant restatements (error adjustments) over a recent four-year period.

OBJECTIVE 5
Describe the accounting for correction of errors.

[8]*SFAS No. 154*, par. 20.

[9]In evaluating reasonableness, the auditor should use one or a combination of the following approaches.
(a) Review and test the process used by management to develop the estimate.
(b) Develop an independent expectation of the estimate to corroborate the reasonableness of management's estimate.
(c) Review subsequent events or transactions occurring prior to completion of fieldwork.
"Auditing Accounting Estimates," *Statement on Auditing Standards No. 57* (New York: AICPA, 1988).

Illustration 18-10
Restatements: 2003–2006

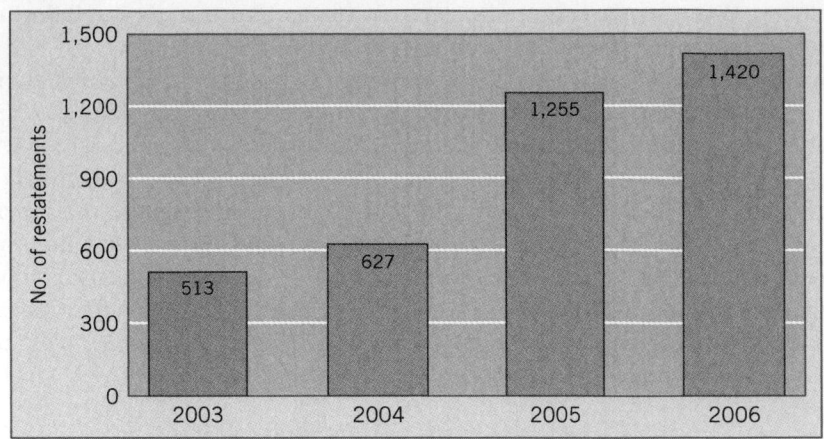

Source: Mark Grothe, "The Errors of Their Ways," *Trend Alert*, Glass Lewis & Co. (February 27, 2007), p. 4.

Certain errors, such as misclassifications of balances within a financial statement, are not as significant to investors as other errors. Significant errors would be those resulting in overstating assets or income, for example. However, investors should know the potential impact of all errors. Even "harmless" misclassifications can affect important ratios. Also, some errors could signal important weaknesses in internal controls that could lead to more significant errors.

In general, accounting errors include the following types:

1 A change from an accounting principle that is **not** generally accepted to an accounting principle that is acceptable. The rationale is that the company incorrectly presented prior periods because of the application of an improper accounting principle. For example, a company may change from the cash (income tax) basis of accounting to the accrual basis.

2 Mathematical mistakes, such as incorrectly totaling the inventory count sheets when computing the inventory value.

3 Changes in estimates that occur because a company did not prepare the estimates in good faith. For example, a company may have adopted a clearly unrealistic depreciation rate.

4 An oversight, such as the failure to accrue or defer certain expenses and revenues at the end of the period.

5 A misuse of facts, such as the failure to use salvage value in computing the depreciation base for the straight-line approach.

6 The incorrect classification of a cost as an expense instead of an asset, and vice versa.

Accounting errors occur for a variety of reasons. Illustration 18-11 (page 955) indicates 11 major categories of accounting errors that drive restatements.

As soon as a company discovers an error, it must correct the error. Companies record **corrections of errors** from prior periods as an adjustment to the beginning balance of retained earnings in the current period. Such corrections are called **prior period adjustments**.[10]

---

[10]"Prior Period Adjustments," *Statement of Financial Accounting Standards No. 16* (Stamford, Conn.: FASB, 1977), p. 5. See Mark L. DeFord and James Jiambalvo, "Incidence and Circumstances of Accounting Errors," *The Accounting Review* (July 1991) for examples of different types of errors and why these errors might have occurred.

Accounting Category	Type of Restatement
Expense recognition	Recording expenses in the incorrect period or for an incorrect amount
Revenue recognition	Improper revenue accounting. This category includes instances in which revenue was improperly recognized, questionable revenues were recognized, or any other number of related errors that led to misreported revenue.
Misclassification	Misclassifying significant accounting items on the balance sheet, income statement, or statement of cash flows. These include restatements due to misclassification of short- or long-term accounts or those that impact cash flows from operations
Equity—other	Improper accounting for EPS, restricted stock, warrants, and other equity instruments
Reserves/Contingencies	Errors involving accounts receivables bad debts, inventory reserves, income tax allowances, and loss contingencies
Long-lived assets	Asset impairments of property, plant, and equipment, goodwill, or other related items.
Taxes	Errors involving correction of tax provision, improper treatment of tax liabilities, and other tax-related items
Equity—other comprehensive income	Improper accounting for comprehensive income equity transactions including foreign currency items, pension adjustments, unrealized gains and losses on certain investments in debt, equity securities, and derivatives.
Inventory	Inventory costing valuations, quantity issues, and cost of sales adjustments
Equity—stock options	Improper accounting for employee stock options
Other	Any restatement not covered by the listed categories including those related to improper accounting for acquisitions or mergers

Source: T. Baldwin and D. Yoo, "Restatements—Traversing Shaky Ground," *Trend Alert,* Glass Lewis & Co. (June 2, 2005), p. 8.

Illustration 18-11
Accounting-Error Types

If it presents comparative statements, a company should restate the prior statements affected, to correct for the error.[11] The company need not repeat the disclosures in the financial statements of subsequent periods.

Example

To illustrate, in 2008 the bookkeeper for Selectric Company discovered an error: In 2007 the company failed to record $20,000 of depreciation expense on a newly constructed building. This building is the only depreciable asset Selectric owns. The company correctly included the depreciation expense in its tax return and correctly reported its income taxes payable. Illustration 18-12 presents Selectric's income statement for 2007 (starting with income before depreciation expense) with and without the error.

Illustration 18-12
Error Correction Comparison

Selectric Company
Income Statement
For the Year Ended, December 31, 2007

		Without Error		With Error
Income before depreciation expense		$100,000		$100,000
Depreciation expense		20,000		0
Income before income tax		80,000		100,000
Current	$32,000		$ 32,000	
Deferred	–0–	32,000	8,000	40,000
Net income		$ 48,000		$ 60,000

[11]The term **"restatement"** is used for the process of revising previously issued financial statements to reflect the correction of an error. This distinguishes an error correction from a change in accounting principle (*SFAS No. 154,* par. 2, j).

Illustration 18-13 shows the entries that Selectric should have made and did make for recording depreciation expense and income taxes.

Illustration 18-13
Error Entries

Entries Company Should Have Made (Without Error)			Entries Company Did Make (With Error)		
Depreciation Expense	20,000		No entry made for depreciation		
Accumulated Depreciation					
—Buildings		20,000			
Income Tax Expense	32,000		Income Tax Expense	40,000	
Income Tax Payable		32,000	Deferred Tax Liability		8,000
			Income Tax Payable		32,000

As Illustration 18-13 indicates, the $20,000 omission error in 2007 results in the following effects.

Income Statement Effects:

Depreciation expense (2007) is understated $20,000.
Income tax expense (2007) is overstated $8,000 ($20,000 × 40%).
Net income (2007) is overstated $12,000 ($20,000 − $8,000).

Balance Sheet Effects:

Accumulated depreciation—buildings is understated $20,000.
Deferred tax liability is overstated $8,000 ($20,000 × 40%).

To make the proper correcting entry in 2008, Selectric should recognize that net income in 2007 is overstated by $12,000, the Deferred Tax Liability is overstated by $8,000, and Accumulated Depreciation—Buildings is understated by $20,000. The entry to correct this error in 2008 is as follows:

Retained Earnings	12,000	
Deferred Tax Liability	8,000	
Accumulated Depreciation—Buildings		20,000

The debit to Retained Earnings results because net income for 2007 is overstated. The debit to the Deferred Tax Liability is made to remove this account, which was caused by the error. The credit to Accumulated Depreciation—Buildings reduces the book value of the building to its proper amount. Selectric will make the same journal entry to record the correction of the error in 2008 whether it prepares single-period (noncomparative) or comparative financial statements.

Single-Period Statements

To demonstrate how to show this information in a single-period statement, assume that Selectric Company has a beginning retained earnings balance at January 1, 2008, of $350,000. The company reports net income of $400,000 in 2008. Illustration 18-14 shows Selectric's retained earnings statement for 2008.

Illustration 18-14
Reporting an Error—
Single-Period Financial
Statement

Selectric Company Retained Earnings Statement For the Year Ended December 31, 2008		
Retained earnings, January 1, as reported		$350,000
Correction of an error (depreciation)	$20,000	
Less: Applicable income tax reduction	8,000	(12,000)
Retained earnings, January 1, as adjusted		338,000
Add: Net income		400,000
Retained earnings, December 31		$738,000

The balance sheet in 2008 would not have any deferred tax liability related to the building, and Accumulated Depreciation—Buildings is now restated at a higher amount. The income statement would not be affected.

Comparative Statements

If preparing comparative financial statements, a company should make adjustments to correct the amounts for all affected accounts reported in the statements for **all periods** reported. The company should restate the data to the correct basis for each year presented. It should **show any catch-up adjustment as a prior period adjustment to retained earnings for the earliest period it reported**. These requirements are essentially the same as those for reporting a change in accounting principle.

For example, in the case of Selectric, the error of omitting the depreciation of $20,000 in 2007, discovered in 2008, results in the restatement of the 2007 financial statements. Illustration 18-15 shows the accounts that Selectric restates in the 2007 financial statements, presented in comparison with those of 2008.

In the balance sheet:	
Accumulated depreciation—buildings	$20,000 increase
Deferred tax liability	$ 8,000 decrease
Retained earnings, ending balance	$12,000 decrease
In the income statement:	
Depreciation expense—buildings	$20,000 increase
Income tax expense	$ 8,000 decrease
Net income	$12,000 decrease
In the retained earnings statement:	
Retained earnings, ending balance (due to lower net income for the period)	$12,000 decrease

Illustration 18-15
Reporting an Error—
Comparative Financial
Statements

Selectric prepares the 2008 financial statements in comparative form with those of 2007 **as if the error had not occurred**. In addition, Selectric must disclose that it has restated its previously issued financial statements, and it describes the nature of the error. Selectric also must disclose the following:

1 The effect of the correction on each financial statement line item and any per-share amounts affected for each prior period presented.

2 The cumulative effect of the change on retained earnings or other appropriate components of equity or net assets in the statement of financial position, as of the beginning of the earliest period presented.[12]

SUMMARY OF ACCOUNTING CHANGES AND CORRECTIONS OF ERRORS

Having guidelines for reporting accounting changes and corrections has helped resolve several significant and long-standing accounting problems. Yet, because of diversity in situations and characteristics of the items encountered in practice, use of professional judgment is of paramount importance. In applying these guidelines, the primary objective is to serve the users of the financial statements. Achieving this objective requires accuracy, full disclosure, and an absence of misleading inferences.

[12]*SFAS No. 154*, par. 26.

Illustration 18-16 summarizes the main distinctions and treatments presented in the discussion in this chapter.

Illustration 18-16
Summary of Guidelines
for Accounting Changes
and Errors

Changes in accounting principle
Employ the retrospective approach by:
a. Changing the financial statements of all prior periods presented.
b. Disclosing in the year of the change the effect on net income and earnings per share for all prior periods presented.
c. Reporting an adjustment to the beginning retained earnings balance in the statement of retained earnings in the earliest year presented.
If impracticable to determine the prior period effect (e.g., change to LIFO):
a. Do not change prior years' income.
b. Use opening inventory in the year the method is adopted as the base-year inventory for all subsequent LIFO computations.
c. Disclose the effect of the change on the current year, and the reasons for omitting the computation of the cumulative effect and pro forma amounts for prior years.

Changes in accounting estimate
Employ the current and prospective approach by:
a. Reporting current and future financial statements on the new basis.
b. Presenting prior period financial statements as previously reported.
c. Making no adjustments to current-period opening balances for the effects in prior periods.

Changes due to error
Employ the restatement approach by:
a. Correcting all prior period statements presented.
b. Restating the beginning balance of retained earnings for the first period presented when the error effects occur in a period prior to that one.

Changes in accounting principle are appropriate **only** when a company demonstrates that the newly adopted generally accepted accounting principle is **preferable** to the existing one. Companies and accountants determine preferability on the basis of whether the new principle constitutes an **improvement in financial reporting**, not on the basis of the income tax effect alone.[13]

But it is not always easy to determine an improvement in financial reporting. **How does one measure preferability or improvement?** Such measurement varies from company to company. **Quaker Oats Company**, for example, argued that a change in accounting principle to LIFO inventory valuation "better matches current costs with current revenues" (see Illustration 18-6, page 949). Conversely, another company might change from LIFO to FIFO because it wishes to report a more realistic ending inventory. How do you determine which is the better of these two arguments? Determining the preferable method requires some "standard" or "objective." Because no universal standard or objective is generally accepted, the problem of determining preferability continues to be difficult.

Initially the SEC took the position that the auditor should indicate whether a change in accounting principle was preferable. The SEC has since modified this approach, noting that greater reliance may be placed on management's judgment in

WHAT'S THE PRINCIPLE?

This is an example of two widely accepted concepts conflicting. Which is more important, matching (emphasis on the income statement) or qualitative characteristic of representational faithfulness (emphasis on the balance sheet)?

---

[13]A change in accounting principle, a change in the reporting entity (special type of change in accounting principle), and a correction of an error require an explanatory paragraph in the auditor's report discussing lack of consistency from one period to the next. A change in accounting estimate does not affect the auditor's opinion relative to consistency; however, if the change in estimate has a material effect on the financial statements, disclosure may still be required. Error correction not involving a change in accounting principle does not require disclosure relative to consistency.

assessing preferability. Even though the preferability criterion is difficult to apply, the general guidelines have acted as a deterrent to capricious changes in accounting principles.[14] **If an FASB standard creates a new principle, expresses preference for, or rejects a specific accounting principle, a change is considered clearly acceptable.**

What do the numbers mean? | Can I Get My Money Back?

When companies report restatements, investors usually lose money. What should investors do if a company misleads them by misstating its financial results? Join other investors in a class-action suit against the company and in some cases, the auditor.

Class-action activity has picked up in recent years, and settlements can be large. To find out about class actions, investors can go online to see if they are eligible to join any class actions. Below are some recent examples.

Company	Settlement Amount	Contact for Claim
Quaker Oats	$ 10,400,000	*www.gilardi.com*
Smart Choice Automotive	$ 2,500,000	*www.gilardi.com*
Sunbeam	$110,000,000	*www.gilardi.com*

The amounts reported are *before* attorney's fees, which can range from 15 to 30 percent of the total. Also, investors may owe taxes if the settlement results in a capital gain on the investment. Thus, investors can get back some of the money they lost due to restatements, but they should be prepared to pay an attorney and the government first.

Source: Adapted from C. Coolidge, "Lost and Found," *Forbes* (October 1, 2001), pp. 124–125.

Beyond the Numbers

Investors with a direct investment in companies like Smart Choice or Sunbeam may recover some of their losses in a class-action suit. What other capital market stakeholders are harmed by restatements? Can these other stakeholders get their money back? Explain.

REPORTING EARNINGS PER SHARE SECTION TWO

Companies commonly report per share amounts for the effects of other items, such as a gain or loss on extraordinary items. The financial press also frequently reports earnings per share data. Further, stockholders and potential investors widely use this data in evaluating the profitability of a company. **Earnings per share** indicates the income earned by each share of common stock. Thus, **companies report earnings per share only for common stock**.

For example, if Oscar Co. has net income of $300,000 and a weighted average of 100,000 shares of common stock outstanding for the year, earnings per share is $3 ($300,000 ÷ 100,000). Because of the importance of earnings per share information, most companies

---

[14]If management has not provided reasonable justification for the change in accounting principle, the auditor should express a qualified opinion. Or, if the effect of the change is sufficiently material, the auditor should express an adverse opinion on the financial statements. "Reports on Audited Financial Statements," *Statement on Auditing Standards No. 58* (New York: AICPA, 1988).

must report this information on the face of the income statement.[15] The exception, due to cost-benefit considerations, is nonpublic companies.[16] Generally, companies report earnings per share information below net income in the income statement. Illustration 18-17 shows Oscar Co.'s income statement presentation of earnings per share.

Illustration 18-17
Income Statement
Presentation of EPS

Net income	$300,000
Earnings per share	$3.00

When the income statement contains intermediate components of income, companies should disclose earnings per share for each component. The presentation in Illustration 18-18 is representative.

These disclosures enable the user of the financial statements to recognize the effects on EPS of income from continuing operations, as distinguished from income or loss from irregular items.[17]

Illustration 18-18
Income Statement
Presentation of EPS
Components

Earnings per share:	
Income from continuing operations	$4.00
Loss from discontinued operations, net of tax	0.60
Income before extraordinary item	3.40
Extraordinary gain, net of tax	1.00
Net income	$4.40

EARNINGS PER SHARE—SIMPLE CAPITAL STRUCTURE

OBJECTIVE 6

Compute earnings per share in a simple capital structure.

A corporation's capital structure is **simple** if it consists only of common stock or includes no **potential common stock** that upon conversion or exercise could dilute earnings per common share. A capital structure is **complex** if it includes securities that could have a dilutive effect on earnings per common share.

The computation of earnings per share for a simple capital structure involves two items (other than net income)—(1) preferred stock dividends and (2) weighted-average number of shares outstanding.

Preferred Stock Dividends

As we indicated earlier, earnings per share relates to earnings per common share. When a company has both common and preferred stock outstanding, **it subtracts the current-year**

[15]"Earnings per Share,"*Statement of Financial Accounting Standards No. 128* (Norwalk, Conn: FASB, 1997). For an article on the usefulness of reported EPS data and the application of the qualitative characteristics of accounting information to EPS data, see Lola W. Dudley, "A Critical Look at EPS,"*Journal of Accountancy* (August 1985), pp. 102–111.

[16]A nonpublic enterprise is an enterprise (1) whose debt or equity securities are not traded in a public market on a foreign or domestic stock exchange or in the over-the-counter market (including securities quoted locally or regionally), or (2) that is not required to file financial statements with the SEC. An enterprise is not considered a nonpublic enterprise when its financial statements are issued in preparation for the sale of any class of securities in a public market.

[17]Companies should present, either on the face of the income statement or in the notes to the financial statements, per share amounts for discontinued operations and extraordinary items.

preferred stock dividend from net income to arrive at income available to common stockholders. Illustration 18-19 shows the formula for computing earnings per share.

$$\text{Earnings Per Share} = \frac{\text{Net Income} - \text{Preferred Dividends}}{\text{Weighted-Average Number of Shares Outstanding}}$$

Illustration 18-19
Formula for Computing Earnings Per Share

In reporting earnings per share information, a company must calculate income available to common stockholders. To do so, the company subtracts dividends on preferred stock from each of the intermediate components of income (income from continuing operations and income before extraordinary items) and finally from net income. If a company declares dividends on preferred stock and a net loss occurs, **the company adds the preferred dividend to the loss** for purposes of computing the loss per share.

If the preferred stock is cumulative and the company declares no dividend in the current year, it subtracts (or adds) **an amount equal to the dividend that it should have declared for the current year only** from net income (or to the loss). The company should have included dividends in arrears for previous years in the previous years' computations.

Weighted-Average Number of Shares Outstanding

In all computations of earnings per share, the **weighted-average number of shares outstanding** during the period constitutes the basis for the per share amounts reported. Shares issued or purchased during the period affect the amount outstanding. Companies must **weight the shares by the fraction of the period they are outstanding.** The rationale for this approach is to find the equivalent number of whole shares outstanding for the year.

To illustrate, assume that Franks Inc. has changes in its common stock shares outstanding for the period as shown in Illustration 18-20.

Date	Share Changes	Shares Outstanding
January 1	Beginning balance	90,000
April 1	Issued 30,000 shares for cash	30,000
		120,000
July 1	Purchased 39,000 shares	39,000
		81,000
November 1	Issued 60,000 shares for cash	60,000
December 31	Ending balance	141,000

Illustration 18-20
Shares Outstanding, Ending Balance— Franks Inc.

Franks computes the weighted-average number of shares outstanding as follows.

Dates Outstanding	(A) Shares Outstanding	(B) Fraction of Year	(C) Weighted Shares (A × B)
Jan. 1–Apr. 1	90,000	3/12	22,500
Apr. 1–July 1	120,000	3/12	30,000
July 1–Nov. 1	81,000	4/12	27,000
Nov. 1–Dec. 31	141,000	2/12	23,500
Weighted-average number of shares outstanding			103,000

Illustration 18-21
Weighted-Average Number of Shares Outstanding

As Illustration 18-21 shows, 90,000 shares were outstanding for three months, which translates to 22,500 whole shares for the entire year. Because Franks issued additional shares on April 1, it must weight these shares for the time outstanding. When the company purchased 39,000 shares on July 1, it reduced the shares outstanding. Therefore from July 1 to November 1, only 81,000 shares were outstanding, which is equivalent to 27,000 shares. The issuance of 60,000 shares increases shares outstanding for the last two months of the year. Franks then makes a new computation to determine the proper weighted shares outstanding.

Stock Dividends and Stock Splits

When **stock dividends** or **stock splits** occur, companies need to restate the shares outstanding before the stock dividend or split, in order to compute the weighted-average number of shares. For example, assume that Vijay Corporation had 100,000 shares outstanding on January 1 and issued a 25 percent stock dividend on June 30. For purposes of computing a weighted-average for the current year, it assumes the additional 25,000 shares outstanding as a result of the stock dividend to be **outstanding since the beginning of the year**. Thus the weighted-average for the year for Vijay is 125,000 shares.

Companies restate for the effects of the issuance of a stock dividend or stock split, but not the issuance or repurchase of stock for cash. Why? Because stock splits and stock dividends do not increase or decrease the net assets of the company. The company merely issues additional shares of stock. Because of the added shares, it must restate the weighted-average shares. Restating allows valid comparisons of earnings per share between periods before and after the stock split or stock dividend. Conversely, the issuance or purchase of stock for cash **changes the amount of net assets**. As a result, the company either earns more or less in the future as a result of this change in net assets. Stated another way, **a stock dividend or split does not change the shareholders' total investment**—it only increases (unless it is a reverse stock split) the number of common shares representing this investment.

To illustrate how a stock dividend affects the computation of the weighted-average number of shares outstanding, assume that Sabrina Company has the following changes in its common stock shares during the year.

Illustration 18-22
Shares Outstanding,
Ending Balance—Sabrina
Company

Date	Share Changes	Shares Outstanding
January 1	Beginning balance	100,000
March 1	Issued 20,000 shares for cash	20,000
		120,000
June 1	60,000 additional shares (50% stock dividend)	60,000
		180,000
November 1	Issued 30,000 shares for cash	30,000
December 31	Ending balance	210,000

Sabrina computes the weighted-average number of shares outstanding as follows.

Illustration 18-23
Weighted-Average
Number of Shares
Outstanding—Stock Issue
and Stock Dividend

Dates Outstanding	(A) Shares Outstanding	(B) Restatement	(C) Fraction of Year	(D) Weighted Shares (A × B × C)
Jan. 1–Mar. 1	100,000	1.50	2/12	25,000
Mar. 1–June 1	120,000	1.50	3/12	45,000
June 1–Nov. 1	180,000		5/12	75,000
Nov. 1–Dec. 31	210,000		2/12	35,000
Weighted-average number of shares outstanding				180,000

Sabrina must restate the shares outstanding prior to the stock dividend. The company adjusts the shares outstanding from January 1 to June 1 for the stock dividend, so that it now states these shares on the same basis as shares issued subsequent to the stock dividend. Sabrina does not restate shares issued after the stock dividend because they are on the new basis. The stock dividend simply restates existing shares. **The same type of treatment applies to a stock split.**

If a stock dividend or stock split occurs after the end of the year, but before issuing the financial statements, a company must restate the weighted-average number of shares outstanding for the year (and any other years presented in comparative form). For example, assume that Hendricks Company computes its weighted-average number of shares as 100,000 for the year ended December 31, 2007. On January 15, 2008, before issuing the financial statements, the company splits its stock 3 for 1. In this case, the weighted-average number of shares used in computing earnings per share for 2007 is now 300,000 shares. If providing earnings per share information for 2006 as comparative information, Hendricks must also adjust it for the stock split.

Comprehensive Example

Let's study a comprehensive example for a simple capital structure. Darin Corporation has income before extraordinary item of $580,000 and an extraordinary gain, net of tax of $240,000. In addition, it has declared preferred dividends of $1 per share on 100,000 shares of preferred stock outstanding. Darin also has the following changes in its common stock shares outstanding during 2008.

Dates	Share Changes	Shares Outstanding
January 1	Beginning balance	180,000
May 1	Purchased 30,000 treasury shares	30,000
		150,000
July 1	300,000 additional shares (3-for-1 stock split)	300,000
		450,000
December 31	Issued 50,000 shares for cash	50,000
December 31	Ending balance	500,000

Illustration 18-24
Shares Outstanding, Ending Balance— Darin Corp.

To compute the earnings per share information, Darin determines the weighted-average number of shares outstanding as follows.

Dates Outstanding	(A) Shares Outstanding	(B) Restatement	(C) Fraction of Year	(D) Weighted Shares (A × B × C)
Jan. 1–May 1	180,000	3	4/12	180,000
May 1–July 1	150,000	3	2/12	75,000
July 1–Dec. 31	450,000		6/12	225,000
Weighted-average number of shares outstanding				480,000

Illustration 18-25
Weighted-Average Number of Shares Outstanding

In computing the weighted-average number of shares, the company ignores the shares sold on December 31, 2008, because they have not been outstanding during the year. Darin then divides the weighted-average number of shares into income before extraordinary item and net income to determine earnings per share. It subtracts its preferred dividends of

$100,000 from income before extraordinary item ($580,000) to arrive at income before extraordinary item available to common stockholders of $480,000 ($580,000 − $100,000).

Deducting the preferred dividends from the income before extraordinary item also reduces net income without affecting the amount of the extraordinary item. The final amount is referred to as **income available to common stockholders**, as shown in Illustration 18-26.

Illustration 18-26
Computation of Income
Available to Common
Stockholders

	(A) Income Information	(B) Weighted Shares	(C) Earnings Per Share (A ÷ B)
Income before extraordinary item available to common stockholders	$480,000*	480,000	$1.00
Extraordinary gain (net of tax)	240,000	480,000	0.50
Income available to common stockholders	$720,000	480,000	$1.50

*$580,000 − $100,000

Darin must disclose the per share amount for the extraordinary item (net of tax) either on the face of the income statement or in the notes to the financial statements. Illustration 18-27 shows the income and per share information reported on the face of Darin's income statement.

Illustration 18-27
Earnings Per Share, with
Extraordinary Item

Income before extraordinary item	$580,000
Extraordinary gain, net of tax	240,000
Net income	$820,000
Earnings per share:	
Income before extraordinary item	$1.00
Extraordinary item, net of tax	0.50
Net income	$1.50

EARNINGS PER SHARE—COMPLEX CAPITAL STRUCTURE

OBJECTIVE 7

Compute earnings per share in a complex capital structure.

WHAT'S THE PRINCIPLE?

By reporting information about possible dilution to common shareholders, diluted EPS provides information about future cash flows (has predictive ability); it illustrates application of the *full disclosure principle*.

The EPS discussion to this point applies to **basic EPS** for a simple capital structure. One problem with a **basic EPS** computation is that it fails to recognize the potential impact of a corporation's dilutive securities. As discussed at the beginning of the chapter, **dilutive securities** are securities that can be converted to common stock.[18] Upon conversion or exercise by the holder, the dilutive securities reduce (dilute) earnings per share. This adverse effect on EPS can be significant and, more importantly, *unexpected* unless financial statements call attention to their potential dilutive effect.

As indicated earlier, a complex capital structure exists when a corporation has convertible securities, options, warrants, or other rights that upon conversion or exercise could dilute earnings per share. When a company has a complex capital structure, **it generally reports both basic and diluted earnings per share**.

Computing **diluted EPS** is similar to computing basic EPS. The difference is that diluted EPS includes the effect of all potential dilutive common shares that were outstanding during the period. The formula in Illustration 18-28 shows the relationship between basic EPS and diluted EPS.

[18]Issuance of these types of securities is typical in mergers and compensation plans.

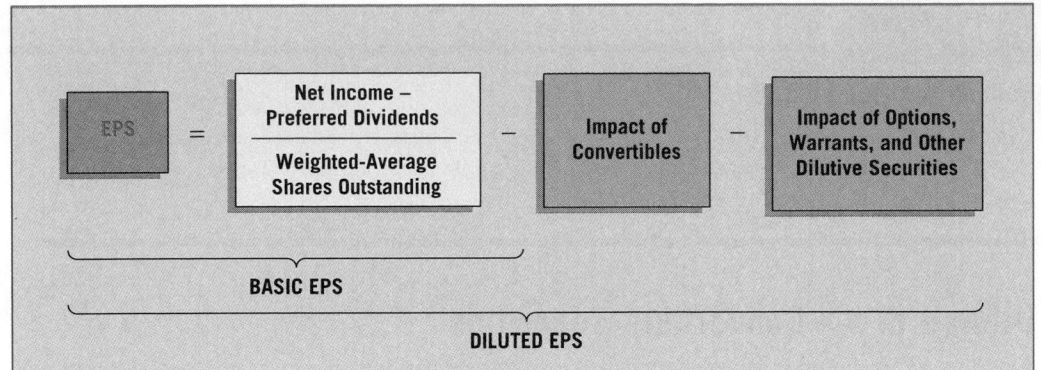

Illustration 18-28
Relation between Basic
and Diluted EPS

Some securities are antidilutive. **Antidilutive securities** are securities that upon conversion or exercise **increase** earnings per share (or reduce the loss per share). Companies with complex capital structures will not report diluted EPS if the securities in their capital structure are antidilutive. The purpose of presenting both basic and diluted EPS is to inform financial statement users of situations that will likely occur (basic EPS) and also to provide "worst case" dilutive situations (dilutive EPS) If the securities are antidilutive, the likelihood of conversion or exercise is considered remote. Thus, companies that have only antidilutive securities must report only the basic EPS number. We illustrated the computation of basic EPS in the prior section. In the following sections, we address the effects of convertible and other dilutive securities on EPS calculations.

INTERNATIONAL INSIGHT

The provisions in U.S. GAAP are substantially the same as those in *International Accounting Standard No. 33*, "Earnings per Share," issued by the IASB.

What do the numbers mean?   Pro Forma EPS Confusion

Many companies are reporting pro forma EPS numbers along with U.S. GAAP-based EPS numbers in the financial information provided to investors. Pro forma earnings generally exceed GAAP earnings because the pro forma numbers exclude such items as restructuring charges, impairments of assets, R&D expenditures, and stock compensation expense. Here are some examples.

Company	U.S. GAAP EPS	Pro Forma EPS
Adaptec	$(0.62)	$ 0.05
Corning	(0.24)	0.09
General Motors	(0.41)	0.85
Honeywell International	(0.38)	0.44
International Paper	(0.57)	0.14
Qualcomm	(0.06)	0.20
Broadcom	(6.36)	(0.13)
Lucent Technologies	(2.16)	(0.27)

Source: Company press releases.

The SEC has expressed concern that pro forma earnings may be misleading. For example, the SEC cited **Trump Hotels & Casino Resorts (DJT)** for abuses related to a recent third-quarter pro forma EPS release. It noted that the firm misrepresented its operating results by excluding a material, one-time $81.4 million charge in its pro forma EPS statement and including an undisclosed nonrecurring gain of $17.2 million. The gain enabled DJT to post a profit in the quarter. The SEC emphasized that DJT's pro forma EPS statement deviated from more conservative U.S. GAAP reporting. Therefore, it was "fraudulent" because it created a "false and misleading impression" that DJT had actually (1) recorded a profit in the third quarter and (2) exceeded consensus earnings expectations by enhancing its operating fundamentals.

As discussed in Chapter 5, SEC Regulation G now requires companies to provide a clear reconciliation between pro forma and GAAP information. And this applies to EPS measures as well.

Sources: See M. Moran, A. J. Cohen, and K. Shaustyuk, "Stock Option Expensing: The Battle Has Been Won; Now Comes the Aftermath,"*Portfolio Strategy/Accounting.* Goldman Sachs (March 17, 2005).

(*continued*)

Beyond the Numbers

What are some situations in which pro forma reporting could make reported accounting numbers, including EPS, more useful? Assume that the pro forma differences are fully disclosed according to Regulation G.

Diluted EPS—Convertible Securities

At conversion, companies exchange convertible securities for common stock. Companies measure the dilutive effects of potential conversion on EPS using the **if-converted method**. This method for a convertible bond assumes: (1) the conversion of the convertible securities at the beginning of the period (or at the time of issuance of the security, if issued during the period), and (2) the elimination of related interest, net of tax. Thus the additional shares assumed issued increase the **denominator**—the weighted-average number of shares outstanding. The amount of interest expense, net of tax associated with those potential common shares, increases the **numerator**—net income.

Comprehensive Example—If-Converted Method

As an example, MayField Corporation has net income of $210,000 for the year and a weighted-average number of common shares outstanding during the period of 100,000 shares. The basic earnings per share is therefore $2.10 ($210,000 ÷ 100,000). The company has two convertible debenture bond issues outstanding. One is a 6 percent issue sold at 100 (total $1,000,000) in a prior year and convertible into 20,000 common shares. The other is a 10 percent issue sold at 100 (total $1,000,000) on April 1 of the current year and convertible into 32,000 common shares. The tax rate is 40 percent.

As Illustration 18-29 shows, to determine the numerator for diluted earnings per share, Mayfield adds back the interest on the if-converted securities, less the related tax effect. Because the if-converted method assumes conversion as of the beginning of the year, May-Field assumes that it pays no interest on the convertibles during the year. The interest on the 6 percent convertibles is $60,000 for the year ($1,000,000 × 6%). The increased tax expense is $24,000 ($60,000 × 0.40). The interest added back net of taxes is $36,000 [$60,000 − $24,000, or simply $60,000 × (1 − 0.40)].

Illustration 18-29
Computation of Adjusted
Net Income

Net income for the year	$210,000
Add: Adjustment for interest (net of tax)	
6% debentures ($60,000 × [1 − .40])	36,000
10% debentures ($100,000 × 9/12 × [1 − .40])	45,000
Adjusted net income	$291,000

Continuing with the information in Illustration 18-29, because Mayfield issues 10 percent convertibles subsequent to the beginning of the year, it weights the shares. In other words, it considers these shares to have been outstanding from April 1 to the end of the year. As a result, the interest adjustment to the numerator for these bonds reflects the interest for only nine months. Thus the interest added back on the 10 percent convertible is $45,000 [$1,000,000 × 10% × 9/12 year × (1 − 0.4)]. The final item in Illustration 18-29 shows the adjusted net income. This amount becomes the numerator for MayField's computation of diluted earnings per share.

MayField then calculates the weighted-average number of shares outstanding, as shown in Illustration 18-30 (next page). This number of shares becomes the denominator for May-Field's computation of diluted earnings per share.

Weighted average number of shares outstanding	100,000
Add: Shares assumed to be issued:	
6% debentures (as of beginning of year)	20,000
10% debentures (as of date of issue, April 1; 9/12 × 32,000)	24,000
Weighted-average number of shares adjusted for dilutive securities	144,000

Illustration 18-30
Computation of Weighted-Average Number of Shares

In its income statement, MayField reports basic and diluted earnings per share.[19] Illustration 18-31 shows this dual presentation.

Net income for the year	$210,000
Earnings Per Share (Note X)	
Basic earnings per share ($210,000 ÷ 100,000)	$2.10
Diluted earnings per share ($291,000 ÷ 144,000)	$2.02

Illustration 18-31
Earnings Per Share Disclosure

Other Factors

The example above assumed that MayField sold its bonds at the face amount. If it instead sold the bonds at a premium or discount, the company must adjust the interest expense each period to account for this occurrence. Therefore, the interest expense reported on the income statement is the amount of interest expense, net of tax, added back to net income. (It is not the interest paid in cash during the period.)

In addition, the conversion rate on a dilutive security may change during the period in which the security is outstanding. For the diluted EPS computation in such a situation, the **company uses the most dilutive conversion rate available**. For example, assume that a company issued a convertible bond on January 1, 2006, with a conversion rate of 10 common shares for each bond starting January 1, 2008. Beginning January 1, 2011, the conversion rate is 12 common shares for each bond, and beginning January 1, 2015, it is 15 common shares for each bond. In computing diluted EPS in 2006, the company uses the conversion rate of 15 shares to one bond.

A final issue relates to preferred stock. For example, assume that MayField's 6 percent convertible debentures were instead 6 percent convertible *preferred stock*. In that case, May-Field considers the convertible preferred as potential common shares. Thus, it includes them in its diluted EPS calculations as shares outstanding. The company does not subtract preferred dividends from net income in computing the numerator. Why not? Because for purposes of computing EPS, it assumes conversion of the convertible preferreds to outstanding common stock. The company uses net income as the numerator—it computes **no tax effect** because preferred dividends generally are not tax-deductible.

Diluted EPS—Options and Warrants

A company includes in diluted earnings per share stock options and warrants outstanding (whether or not presently exercisable), unless they are antidilutive. Companies use the **treasury-stock method** to include options and warrants and their equivalents in EPS computations.

The treasury-stock method assumes that a company exercises the options or warrants at the beginning of the year (or date of issue if later), and that it uses those proceeds to purchase common stock for the treasury. If the exercise price is lower than the market price of the stock, then the proceeds from exercise are insufficient to buy back all the shares. The company then adds the incremental shares remaining to the weighted-average number of shares outstanding for purposes of computing diluted earnings per share.

---

[19]Conversion of bonds is dilutive because EPS with conversion ($2.02) is less than basic EPS ($2.10). Determining dilution when multiple securities are involved is a complex process, which is beyond the scope of this textbook.

For example, if the exercise price of a warrant is $5 and the fair market value of the stock is $15, the treasury-stock method increases the shares outstanding. Exercise of the warrant results in one additional share outstanding, but the $5 received for the one share issued is insufficient to purchase one share in the market at $15. The company needs to exercise three warrants (and issue three additional shares) to produce enough money ($15) to acquire one share in the market. Thus, a net increase of two shares outstanding results.

To see this computation using larger numbers, assume 1,500 options outstanding at an exercise price of $30 for a common share and a common stock market price per share of $50. Through application of the treasury-stock method, the company would have 600 incremental shares outstanding, computed as shown in Illustration 18-32.[20]

Illustration 18-32
Computation of
Incremental Shares

Proceeds from exercise of 1,500 options (1,500 × $30)	$45,000
Shares issued upon exercise of options	1,500
Treasury shares purchasable with proceeds ($45,000 ÷ $50)	900
Incremental shares outstanding (potential common shares)	600

Thus, if the exercise price of the option or warrant is **lower** than the market price of the stock, dilution occurs. An exercise price of the option or warrant **higher** than the market price of the stock reduces common shares. In this case, the options or warrants are **antidilutive** because their assumed exercise leads to an increase in earnings per share.

For both options and warrants, exercise is assumed only if the average market price of the stock exceeds the exercise price during the reported period.[21] As a practical matter, a simple average of the weekly or monthly prices is adequate, so long as the prices do not fluctuate significantly.

What do the numbers mean?   Cuckoo for CoCos

As discussed in the chapter, diluted earnings per share should reflect the potential dilution of all convertible securities, as long as the securities are not antidilutive. However, by exploiting a loophole in the GAAP for EPS, a number of companies issued contingent convertible bonds—called CoCos—that bypassed EPS calculations.

CoCos have additional conditions for conversion that allow companies to avoid revealing how much earnings would be diluted if holders of the bonds exchanged them for stock. In fact, under the rules, companies were able to treat CoCos more like warrants (discussed in the next section); this resulted in the CoCos being antidilutive in EPS calculations. As indicated in the table on the next page, CoCos avoided potential dilution of as much as 15 percent for the following companies:

---

[20]The incremental number of shares may be more simply computed:

$$\frac{\text{Market Price} - \text{Option Price}}{\text{Market Price}} \times \text{Number of Options} = \text{Number of Shares}$$

$$\frac{\$50 - \$30}{\$50} \times 1{,}500 \text{ options} = 600 \text{ shares}$$

[21]Options and warrants have essentially the same assumptions and computational problems, although the warrants may allow or require the tendering of some other security, such as debt, in lieu of cash upon exercise. In such situations, the accounting becomes quite complex. *SFAS No. 128* explains the accounting in this situation.

Company	Potential Dilution
Cephalon	15%
FEI	14
Lattice Semi	13
General Motors	10

From 2000, when the first CoCo was issued, to late 2003, over 300 companies issued CoCos, recording interest expense at lower convertible bond rates and without EPS dilution.

However, the CoCo train may be coming into the station. Due to a ruling by the Emerging Issues Task Force (EITF), companies now must include the shares underlying CoCos in diluted EPS calculations. By late 2004, over 40 companies had modified or redeemed their CoCo bonds to avoid EPS dilution.

Sources: See David Henry, "The Latest Magic in Corporate Finance,"*Business Week* (September 8, 2003), p. 88; and Pat McConnell and Janet Pegg, "Accounting for CoCo Bonds: An Update,"*Equity Research*, Bear Stearns (December 14, 2004). Tabular data are from Bear Stearns.

Beyond the Numbers

Some companies voluntarily redeemed CoCo bonds *before* the final EITF ruling, even though doing so resulted in lower reported EPS. Why might these companies discontinue use of these instruments in advance of the accounting change?

Comprehensive Example—Treasury-Stock Method

To illustrate application of the treasury-stock method, assume that Kubitz Industries, Inc. has net income for the period of $220,000. The average number of shares outstanding for the period was 100,000 shares. Hence, basic EPS—ignoring all dilutive securities—is $2.20. The average number of shares related to options outstanding (although not exercisable at this time), at an option price of $20 per share, is 5,000 shares. The average market price of the common stock during the year was $28. Illustration 18-33 shows the computation of EPS using the treasury-stock method.

	Basic Earnings Per Share	Diluted Earnings Per Share
Average number of shares related to options outstanding:		5,000
Option price per share		× $20
Proceeds upon exercise of options		$100,000
Average market price of common stock		$28
Treasury shares that could be repurchased with proceeds ($100,000 ÷ $28)		3,571
Excess of shares under option over the treasury shares that could be repurchased (5,000 − 3,571)—potential common incremental shares		1,429
Average number of common shares outstanding	100,000	100,000
Total average number of common shares outstanding and potential common shares	100,000 (A)	101,429 (C)
Net income for the year	$220,000 (B)	$220,000 (D)
Earnings per share	$2.20 (B ÷ A)	$2.17 (D ÷ C)

Illustration 18-33
Computation of Earnings Per Share—Treasury Stock Method

Antidilution Revisited

In computing diluted EPS, a company must consider the aggregate of all dilutive securities. But first it must determine which potentially dilutive securities are in fact individually dilutive and which are antidilutive. **A company should exclude any security that is antidilutive**, nor can the company use such a security to offset dilutive securities.

Recall that including antidilutive securities in earnings per share computations increases earnings per share (or reduces net loss per share). With options or warrants, whenever the exercise price exceeds the market price, the security is antidilutive. Convertible debt is antidilutive if the addition to income of the interest (net of tax) causes a greater percentage increase in income (numerator) than conversion of the bonds causes a percentage increase in common and potentially dilutive shares (denominator). In other words, convertible debt is antidilutive if conversion of the security causes common stock earnings to increase by a greater amount per additional common share than earnings per share was before the conversion.

To illustrate, assume that Martin Corporation has a 6 percent, $1,000,000 debt issue that is convertible into 10,000 common shares. Net income for the year is $210,000, the weighted-average number of common shares outstanding is 100,000 shares, and the tax rate is 40 percent. In this case, assumed conversion of the debt into common stock at the beginning of the year requires the following adjustments of net income and the weighted-average number of shares outstanding.

Illustration 18-34
Test for Antidilution

Net income for the year	$210,000	Average number of shares outstanding	100,000
Add: Adjustment for interest (net of tax) on 6% debentures		Add: Shares issued upon assumed conversion of debt	10,000
$60,000 × (1 − .40)	36,000	Average number of common and potential common shares	110,000
Adjusted net income	$246,000		

Basic EPS = $210,000 ÷ 100,000 = $2.10
Diluted EPS = $246,000 ÷ 110,000 = $2.24 = **Antidilutive**

**Expanded Discussion—
EPS Example**

As a shortcut, Martin can also identify the convertible debt as antidilutive by comparing the EPS resulting from conversion, $3.60 ($36,000 additional earnings × 10,000 additional shares), with EPS before inclusion of the convertible debt, $2.10.

Companies should ignore antidilutive securities in all calculations and in computing diluted earnings per share. This approach is reasonable. The profession's intent was to inform the investor of the possible dilution that might occur in reported earnings per share and not to be concerned with securities that, if converted or exercised, would result in an increase in earnings per share.

EPS Presentation and Disclosure

A company with a complex capital structure would present its EPS information as follows.

Illustration 18-35
EPS Presentation—
Complex Capital Structure

Earnings per common share	
Basic earnings per share	$3.30
Diluted earnings per share	$2.70

When the earnings of a period include irregular items, a company should show per share amounts (where applicable) for the following: income from continuing operations, income before extraordinary items, and net income. Companies that report a discontinued operation or an extraordinary item should present per share amounts **for those line items** either on the face of the income statement or in the notes to the financial statements. Illustration 18-36 shows a presentation reporting extraordinary items.

Illustration 18-36
EPS Presentation, with
Extraordinary Item

Basic earnings per share	
Income before extraordinary item	$3.80
Extraordinary item	(0.80)
Net income	$3.00
Diluted earnings per share	
Income before extraordinary item	$3.35
Extraordinary item	(0.65)
Net income	$2.70

A company must show earnings per share amounts for all periods presented. Also, the company should restate all prior period earnings per share amounts presented for stock dividends and stock splits. If it reports diluted EPS data for at least one period, the company should report such data for all periods presented, even if it is the same as basic EPS. When a company restates results of operations of a prior period as a result of an error or a change in accounting principle, it should also restate the earnings per share data shown for the prior periods. Complex capital structures and dual presentation of earnings per share require the following additional disclosures in note form.

1 Description of pertinent rights and privileges of the various securities outstanding.

2 A reconciliation of the numerators and denominators of the basic and diluted per share computations, including individual income and share amount effects of all securities that affect EPS.

3 The effect given preferred dividends in determining income available to common stockholders in computing basic EPS.

4 Securities that could potentially dilute basic EPS in the future that were excluded in the computation because they would be antidilutive.

5 Effect of conversions subsequent to year-end, but before issuing statements.

Illustration 18-37 presents the reconciliation and the related disclosure to meet the requirements of this standard.[22]

Illustration 18-37
Reconciliation for Basic
and Diluted EPS

	Income (Numerator)	Shares (Denominator)	Per Share Amount
For the Year Ended 2008			
Income before extraordinary item	$7,500,000		
Less: Preferred stock dividends	(45,000)		
Basic EPS			
Income available to common stockholders	7,455,000	3,991,666	$1.87
Warrants		30,768	
Convertible preferred stock	45,000	308,333	
4% convertible bonds (net of tax)	60,000	50,000	
Diluted EPS			
Income available to common stockholders + assumed conversions	$7,560,000	4,380,767	$1.73

Stock options to purchase 1,000,000 shares of common stock at $85 per share were outstanding during the second half of 2008 but were not included in the computation of diluted EPS because the options' exercise price was greater than the average market price of the common shares. The options were still outstanding at the end of year 2008 and expire on June 30, 2018.

[22]"Earnings Per Share," *Statement of Financial Accounting Standards No. 128* (Norwalk, Conn.: FASB, 1997). Note that *SFAS No. 123(R)* has specific disclosure requirements regarding stock option plans and earning per share disclosures as well.

Try it out! On January 1, 2008, Reynolds Company issued 10-year, $3,000,000 face value, 8% convertible bonds at par. Each $1,000 bond is convertible into 20 shares of Reynolds common stock. Reynolds' net income in 2008 was $270,000, and its tax rate was 40%. Reynolds had 100,000 shares of common stock outstanding throughout 2008. None of the bonds were converted in 2008.

Instructions

a Compute diluted earnings per share for 2008.

b Compute diluted earnings per share for 2008, assuming the same facts as above except that $1,800,000 of 5% cumulative convertible preferred stock was issued instead of the bonds. Each $100 preferred share is convertible into 3 shares of Reynolds common stock.

Solution

a Earnings per share before assumed bond conversion: $270,000 ÷ 100,000 = $2.70

$$\text{Earnings per share assuming conversion of bonds} = \frac{\$270,000 + [\$3,000,000 \times .08 \times (1 - .40)]}{100,000 + (3,000^* \times 20 \text{ shares})} = \$2.59$$

*$3,000,000 ÷ $1,000

Diluted earnings per share are $2.59 since the assumed conversion of the bonds reduces EPS from $2.70 to $2.59.

b
$$\text{Earnings per share before assumed preferred stock conversion} = \frac{\$270,000 - (\$1,800,000 \times .05)}{100,000} = \$1.80$$

$$\text{Earnings per share assuming preferred stock conversion} = \frac{\$270,000}{100,000 + (18,000^* \times 3)} = \$1.75$$

*$1,800,000 ÷ $100

Diluted earnings per share are $1.75 since the assumed conversion of the preferred stock reduces EPS from $1.80 to $1.75.

SUMMARY OF EPS COMPUTATION

As you can see, computation of earnings per share is a complex issue. It is a controversial area because many securities, although technically not common stock, have many of its basic characteristics. Indeed, some companies have issued these other securities rather than common stock in order to avoid an adverse dilutive effect on earnings per share. Illustrations 18-38 and 18-39 (both on next page) display the elementary points of calculating earnings per share in a simple capital structure and in a complex capital structure.

You will want to read the CONVERGENCE CORNER on page 974 for discussion of how international convergence efforts relate to additional financial reporting issues.

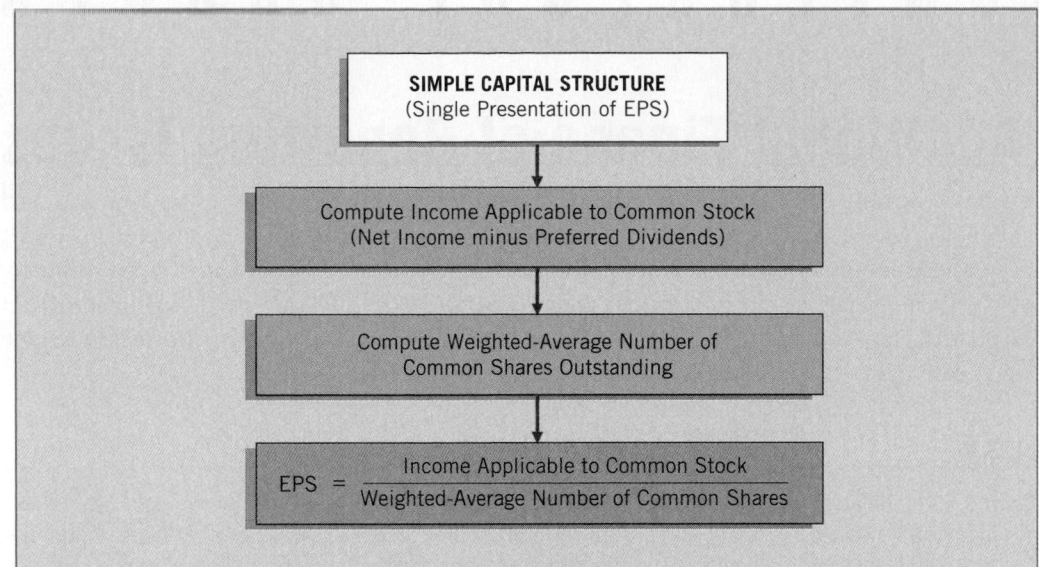

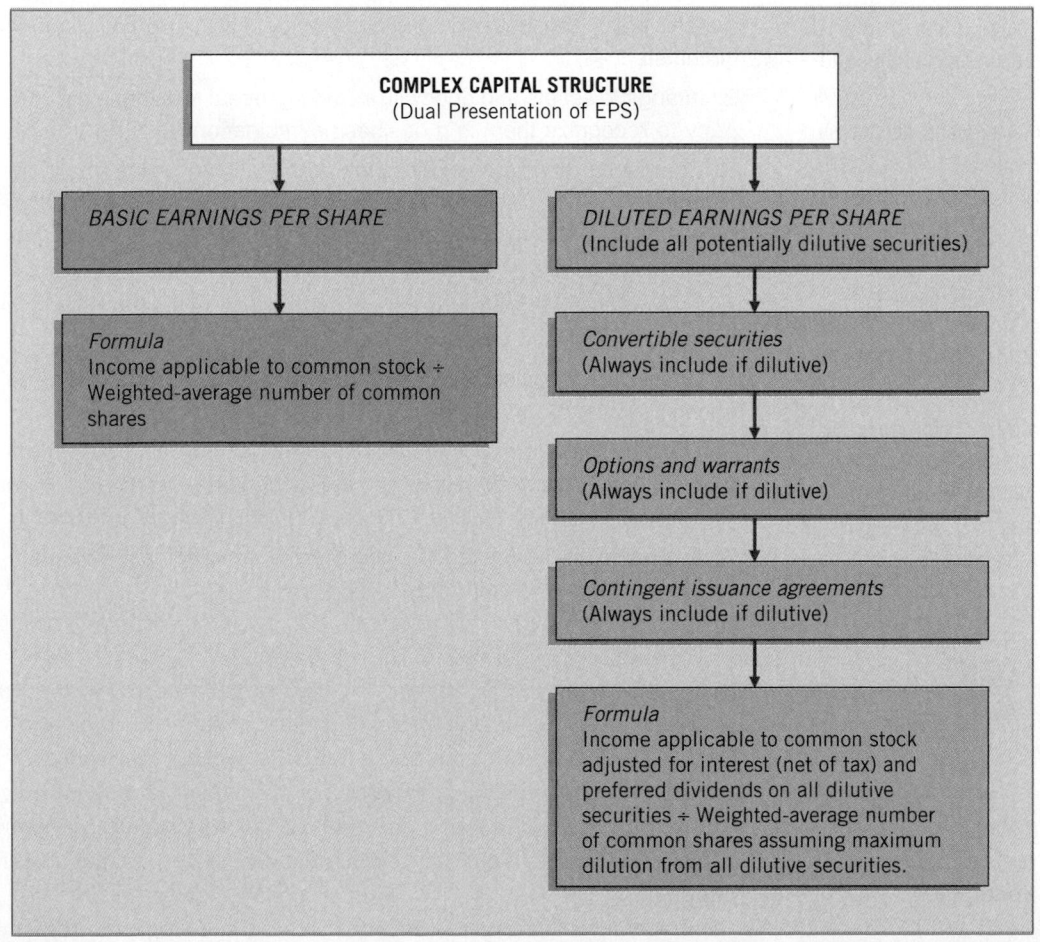

Illustration 18-39
Calculating EPS, Complex
Capital Structure

CONVERGENCE CORNER

Additional Financial Reporting Issues

The iGAAP standard addressing accounting and reporting for changes in accounting principles, changes in estimates, and errors is *IAS 8* ("Accounting Policies, Changes in Accounting Estimates and Errors"). As indicated in the chapter, the FASB issued a standard on changes in accounting principles, changes in estimates, and corrections of errors, which essentially converges U.S. GAAP to *IAS 8*. Earnings per share computations under U.S. GAAP and iGAAP are also similar. *IAS 33* ("Earnings per Share") is the iGAAP standard in this area. The FASB and the IASB have been working together to resolve remaining differences related to earnings per share computations.

RELEVANT FACTS

• One area in which iGAAP and U.S. GAAP differ is the reporting of error corrections in previously issued financial statements. While both GAAPs require restatement, U.S. GAAP is an absolute standard—that is, there is no exception to this rule. Under iGAAP, if restatement is considered impracticable, then a company should report the error in the period in which it believes it practicable to do so, which may be the current period.

• *IAS 8* does not specifically address the accounting and reporting for indirect effects of changes in accounting principles. As indicated in the chapter, U.S. GAAP has detailed guidance on the accounting and reporting of indirect effects.

• Although the calculation of basic and diluted earnings per share is similar between iGAAP and U.S. GAAP, the Boards are working to resolve the few minor differences in EPS reporting. One proposal in the FASB project eliminates the provision allowing companies to rebut the presumption that contracts that can be settled in either cash or shares will be settled in shares. iGAAP requires that share settlement must be used in this situation.

• Other EPS differences relate to (1) the treasury stock method and how the proceeds from extinguishment of a liability should be accounted for, and (2) how to make the computation for the weighted-average of contingently issuable shares.

ABOUT THE NUMBERS

Because iGAAP and U.S. GAAP are quite similar in regard to the accounting and reporting for accounting changes and earnings per share, we provide some observations on the application of iGAAP by foreign companies listing securities in the United States. Recently the staff of the SEC reviewed the iGAAP financial statements of 100 foreign issuers prepared for the first time using iGAAP. The staff did not make any statements regarding the overall quality of the reports but did identify areas where additional questions might be asked. Here are some of the items the staff commented on.

1. Revenue recognition, especially where a company provided generic policy disclosure but did not provide disclosure specific to its circumstances.

2. Intangible assets and goodwill, including the factors that led a company to recognize them in a business combination.

3. Companies' policies for identifying and evaluating impairment, the circumstances resulting in impairment recognition, or the circumstances surrounding impairment reversals of long-lived assets, including goodwill.

4. Leases, including their terms and the future minimum payments under operating and financial leases.

5. Contingent liabilities, including their nature and estimated financial effects.

6. The significant terms of financial instruments, including derivatives, their effects on future cash flow, and the recognition and measurement criteria the company applied in accounting for financial instruments.

7. Additional issues related to income statement and cash flow statement formats and related notes.

ON THE HORIZON

Sir David Tweedie, chair of the IASB, recently stated, "By 2011–2012, U.S. and international accounting should be pretty much the same." There is no question that iGAAP and U.S. GAAP are converging quickly. We have provided the Convergence Corner discussions to help you understand the issues surrounding convergence as they relate to Intermediate Accounting. After reading these discussions, you should realize that iGAAP and U.S. GAAP are very similar in many areas—with differences revolving around some minor technical points. In other situations, the differences are major; for example, iGAAP does not permit LIFO inventory accounting.

Our hope is that the FASB and IASB can quickly complete their convergence efforts, resulting in a single set of high-quality accounting standards for use by companies around the world. For additional insights into the international reporting environment, go to the book's companion website, at **www.wiley.com/college/warfield**.

ACCOUNTING, ANALYSIS, PRINCIPLES

Garner Company began operations on January 1, 2006, and uses the LIFO method of pricing inventory. Management is contemplating a change in inventory methods for 2009. The following information is available for the years 2006–2008. (Ignore all tax effects.)

	Net Income Computed Using	
	FIFO Method	**LIFO Method**
2006	$19,000	$12,000
2007	23,000	14,000
2008	27,000	17,000

On January 1, 2008, Garner issued 10-year, $200,000 face value, 6% bonds, at par. Each $1,000 bond is convertible into 30 shares of Garner common stock. The company has had 10,000 shares outstanding throughout its life. None of the bonds have been exercised as of the end of 2009.

(handwritten: 6000 sh 200,000 × 6% = 12000)

Accounting

(Ignore all tax effects.)

a In 2009, Garner changed to the FIFO method. Prepare the journal entry necessary to record the change in accounting principle.

b Garner's net income in 2009 under the FIFO method was $30,000. Compute basic and diluted earnings per share for Garner Company for 2009.

Analysis

Show how Garner Company will report income and EPS for 2009 and 2008. Briefly discuss the importance of GAAP for EPS computations to analysts evaluating companies based on price-earnings ratios. Consider comparisons for a company over time, as well as comparisons between companies at a point in time.

(handwritten: 300 360)

Principles

Some companies have issued exotic dilutive securities that exploit loopholes in the GAAP related to diluted EPS reporting. (See the discussion of contingently convertible bonds, pages 968–969.) How does the use of these strategies affect the relevance and reliability of reported EPS?

Solution

Accounting

a

Inventory	26,000*	
Retained Earnings		26,000

*($19,000 + $23,000 + $27,000) − ($12,000 + $14,000 + $17,000)

b Computation of EPS:

Basic EPS	**2009**	**2008**
Net income	$30,000	$27,000
Outstanding shares	10,000	10,000
Basic EPS[a]	$3.00	$2.70

[a]2009: $30,000 ÷ 10,000; 2008: $27,000 ÷ 10,000

Diluted EPS

Net income	$30,000	$27,000
Add: Interest savings ($200,000 × 6%)	12,000	12,000
Adjusted net income	$42,000	$39,000
Adjusted net income	$42,000	$39,000
Outstanding shares	10,000	10,000
Shares upon conversion	6,000^b	6,000
Diluted EPS^c	$2.63	$2.44

^b$200,000 ÷ $1,000 = 200 bonds; 200 bonds × 30 = 6,000 shares
^c2009: $42,000 ÷ 16,000; 2008: $39,000 ÷ 16,000

Analysis

EPS Presentation

	2008	2007
Net income	$30,000	$27,000
Basic EPS	$3.00	$2.70
Diluted EPS	$2.63	$2.44

Proper standards for EPS reporting are important to analysts who rely on the reported information in their analysis based on various ratios. In the case of the price-earnings (P-E) ratio, price per share is divided by earnings per share. Analysts use the P-E ratio to evaluate the quality of earnings or to assess a company's growth prospects. However, if companies use different standards to compute EPS, the P-E ratio will not be comparable across companies at a point in time or in comparing a single company from one year to the next. For example, a company with CoCos will have a higher diluted EPS number (and a lower P-E ratio), compared to a similar company that issued non-CoCo convertible bonds. Thus, the P-E ratios are different, but the underlying economics are not, and comparability is lost.

Principles

When companies enter into arrangements with the sole purpose of achieving an accounting result (such as to increase reported EPS), both the reliability and relevance of the information are compromised. With respect to relevance, the *predictive value* of the EPS is affected because the future expected dilution associated with the CoCos is not reflected in the diluted EPS number. What about reliability? The reported EPS for a company using CoCos is not a *faithful representation* of the potential dilution associated with the securities. As discussed in the Analysis response above, this in turn results in lack of comparability between companies.

Key Terms

prior period adjustments, 954
restatement, 955*n*
retrospective application, 943

Summary of Learning Objectives

1 Identify the types of accounting changes. The three different types of accounting changes are: (1) *Change in accounting principle:* a change from one generally accepted accounting principle to another generally accepted accounting principle. (2) *Change in accounting estimate:* a change that occurs as the result of new information or as additional experience is acquired. (3) *Change in reporting entity:* a change from reporting as one type of entity to another type of entity.

2 Understand how to account for retrospective accounting changes. The general requirement for changes in accounting principle is retrospective application. Under retrospective application, companies change prior years' financial statements on a basis consistent with the newly adopted principle. They treat any part of the effect attributable to years prior to those presented as an adjustment of the earliest retained earnings presented.

3 Understand how to account for impracticable changes. Retrospective application is impracticable if the prior period effect cannot be determined using every reasonable effort to do so. For example, in changing to LIFO, the base-year inventory for all subsequent LIFO calculations is generally the opening inventory in the year the company adopts the method. There is no restatement of prior years' income because it is often too impractical to do so.

4 Describe the accounting for changes in estimates. Companies report changes in estimates prospectively. That is, companies should make no changes in previously reported results. They do not adjust opening balances nor change financial statements of prior periods.

5 Describe the accounting for correction of errors. Companies must correct errors as soon as they discover them, by proper entries in the accounts, and report them in the financial statements. The profession requires that a company treat corrections of errors as prior-period adjustments, record them in the year in which it discovered the errors, and report them in the financial statements in the proper periods. If presenting comparative statements, a company should restate the prior statements affected to correct for the errors. The company need not repeat the disclosures in the financial statements of subsequent periods.

6 Compute earnings per share in a simple capital structure. When a company has both common and preferred stock outstanding, it subtracts the current-year preferred stock dividend from net income to arrive at income available to common stockholders. The formula for computing earnings per share is net income less preferred stock dividends, divided by the weighted-average of shares outstanding.

7 Compute earnings per share in a complex capital structure. A complex capital structure requires a dual presentation of earnings per share, each with equal prominence on the face of the income statement. These two presentations are referred to as basic earnings per share and diluted earnings per share. Basic earnings per share relies on the number of weighted-average common shares outstanding (i.e., equivalent to EPS for a simple capital structure). Diluted earnings per share indicates the dilution of earnings per share that will occur if all potential issuances of common stock that would reduce earnings per share takes place. Companies with complex capital structures should exclude antidilutive securities when computing earnings per share.

REVIEW EXERCISE

Tucker Corporation acquired the following assets in January 2006.

Equipment, estimated useful life, 5 years; $30,000 salvage value $350,000
Building, estimated useful life, 40 years; $100,000 salvage value $1,200,000

(handwritten: 200   DDB no salvage)

The equipment has been depreciated using the double-declining-balance method for the first 2 years for financial reporting purposes. In 2008, Tucker decided to change to the straight-line method with no change in the estimated useful life or salvage value. It was also discovered in 2008 that Tucker's bookkeeper had recorded straight-line depreciation on the building each year but had ignored the salvage value.

On January 1, 2008, Tucker issued 10-year, $200,000 face value, 8% bonds, at par. Each $1,000 bond is convertible into 40 shares of Tucker common stock. The company has had 10,000 shares outstanding throughout its life. None of the bonds have been exercised as of the end of 2008.

Instructions

a Prepare Tucker's journal entries in 2008 to account for (1) the change in depreciation methods, and (2) the bookkeeper's error. Assume a 30% tax rate.

b After any adjustments related to part (a), Tucker's income in 2008 was $45,200. Compute basic and diluted earnings per share for Tucker Company for 2008.

Solution

a 1 Double-declining balance depreciation

2006 ($350,000 − 0) × .40 [(1 ÷ 5 yrs.) × 2]	$140,000
2007 ($350,000 − $140,000) × .40	84,000
	$224,000

Cost of equipment	$350,000
Depreciation to date	224,000
Book value (December 31, 2007)	$126,000

Depreciation Expense ($126,000 − $30,000)/3	32,000	
Accumulated Depreciation—Equipment		32,000

2

Building depreciation recorded each year ($1,200,000 ÷ 40)		$30,000
Correct building depreciation/year ($1,200,000 − $100,000) ÷ 40		27,500
Overstated depreciation/year		$ 2,500

Accumulated Depreciation—Building ($2,500 × 2 yrs.)	5,000	
Retained Earnings [$5,000 × (1 − .30)]		3,500
Deferred Tax Liability		1,500

b **Basic EPS**   **2008**

Net income	$45,200
Outstanding shares	10,000
Basic EPS ($45,200 ÷ 10,000)	$4.52

Diluted EPS

Net income	$45,200
Add: Interest savings ($200,000 × 8%)	16,000
Adjusted net income	$61,200

Adjusted net income		$61,200
Outstanding shares	$10,000	
Shares upon conversion	8,000*	18,000
Diluted EPS ($61,200 ÷ 18,000)		$3.40

*$200,000 ÷ $1,000 = 200 bonds; 200 bonds × 40 = 8,000 shares

Questions

1 In recent years, the *Wall Street Journal* has indicated that many companies have changed their accounting principles. What are the major reasons why companies change accounting methods?

2 State how each of the following items is reflected in the financial statements.

(a) Change from FIFO to LIFO method for inventory valuation purposes.

(b) Charge for failure to record depreciation in a previous period.

(c) Litigation won in current year, related to prior period.

(d) Change in the realizability of certain receivables.

(e) Writeoff of receivables.

(f) Change from the percentage-of-completion to the completed-contract method for reporting net income.

3 Discuss briefly the three approaches that have been suggested for reporting changes in accounting principles.

4 Identify and describe the approach the FASB requires for reporting changes in accounting principles.

5 What is the indirect effect of a change in accounting principle? Briefly describe the reporting of the indirect effects of a change in accounting principle.

6 Define a change in estimate and provide an illustration. When is a change in accounting estimate effected by a change in accounting principle?

7 Sandwich State Bank has followed the practice of capitalizing certain marketing costs and amortizing these costs over their expected life. In the current year, the bank determined that the future benefits from these costs were doubtful. Consequently, the bank adopted the policy of expensing these costs as incurred. How should the bank report this accounting change in the comparative financial statements?

8 Indicate how the following items are recorded in the accounting records in the current year of Tami Agler Co.

(a) Impairment of goodwill.

(b) A change in depreciating plant assets from accelerated to the straight-line method.

(c) Large writeoff of inventories because of obsolescence.

(d) Change from the cash basis to accrual basis of accounting.

(e) Change from LIFO to FIFO method for inventory valuation purposes.

(f) Change in the estimate of service lives for plant assets.

9 R. M. Andrews Construction Co. had followed the practice of expensing all materials assigned to a construction job without recognizing any salvage inventory. On December 31, 2008, it was determined that salvage inventory should be valued at $62,000. Of this amount, $29,000 arose during the current year. How does this information affect the financial statements to be prepared at the end of 2008?

10 E. A. Basler Inc. wishes to change from the completed-contract to the percentage-of-completion method for financial reporting purposes. The auditor indicates that a change would be permitted only if it is to a preferable method. What difficulties develop in assessing preferability?

11 Discuss how a change to the LIFO method of inventory valuation is handled when it is impracticable to determine previous LIFO inventory amounts.

12 At December 31, 2008, Amad Company had 600,000 shares of common stock issued and outstanding, 400,000 of which had been issued and outstanding throughout the year and 200,000 of which were issued on October 1, 2008. Net income for 2008 was $3,000,000, and dividends declared on preferred stock were $400,000. Compute Amad's earnings per common share. (Round to the nearest penny.)

13 What effect do stock dividends or stock splits have on the computation of the weighted-average number of shares outstanding?

14 Define the following terms.

(a) Basic earnings per share.

(b) Potentially dilutive security.

(c) Diluted earnings per share.

(d) Complex capital structure.

(e) Potential common stock.

15 What are the computational guidelines for determining whether a convertible security is to be reported as part of diluted earnings per share?

16 Discuss why options and warrants may be considered potentially dilutive common shares for the computation of diluted earnings per share.

17 Explain how convertible securities are determined to be potentially dilutive common shares and how those convertible securities that are not considered to be potentially dilutive common shares enter into the determination of earnings per share data.

18 Explain the treasury stock method as it applies to options and warrants in computing dilutive earnings per share data.

19 Earnings per share can affect market prices of common stock. Can market prices affect earnings per share? Explain.

20 What is meant by the term antidilution? Give an example.

21 What type of earnings per share presentation is required in a complex capital structure?

Brief Exercises

(LO 2) **BE18-1** Beaty Construction Company decided at the beginning of 2008 to change from the completed-contract method to the percentage-of-completion method for financial reporting purposes. The company will continue to use the completed-contract method for tax purposes. For years prior to 2008, pre-tax income under the two methods was as follows: percentage-of-completion $128,000, and completed-contract $80,000. The tax rate is 35%. Prepare Beaty's 2008 journal entry to record the change in accounting principle.

(LO 2) **BE18-2** Refer to the accounting change by Beaty Construction Company in BE18-1. Beaty has a profit-sharing plan, which pays all employees a bonus at year-end based on 1% of pre-tax income. Compute the indirect effect of Beaty's change in accounting principle that will be reported in the 2008 income statement, assuming that the profit-sharing contract explicitly requires adjustment for changes in income numbers.

(LO 2) **BE18-3** Robert Boey, Inc., changed from the LIFO cost flow assumption to the FIFO cost flow assumption in 2008. The increase in the prior year's income before taxes is $1,000,000. The tax rate is 40%. Prepare Boey's 2008 journal entry to record the change in accounting principle.

(LO 4) **BE18-4** Bickner Company changed depreciation methods in 2008 from double-declining-balance to straight-line. Depreciation under double-declining-balance was $90,000, whereas straight-line depreciation prior to 2008 would have been $50,000. Bickner's depreciable assets had a cost of $250,000 with a $50,000 salvage value, and an 8-year remaining useful life at the beginning of 2008. Prepare the 2008 journal entries, if any, related to Bickner's depreciable assets.

(LO 4) **BE18-5** Nancy Castle Company purchased a computer system for $60,000 on January 1, 2006. It was depreciated based on a 7-year life and an $18,000 salvage value. On January 1, 2008, Castle revised these estimates to a total useful life of 4 years and a salvage value of $10,000. Prepare Castle's entry to record 2008 depreciation expense.

(LO 5) **BE18-6** In 2008, John Hiatt Corporation discovered that equipment purchased on January 1, 2006, for $75,000 was expensed at that time. The equipment should have been depreciated over 5 years, with no salvage value. The effective tax rate is 30%. Prepare Hiatt's 2008 journal entry to correct the error.

(LO 5) **BE18-7** At January 1, 2008, William R. Monat Company reported retained earnings of $2,000,000. In 2008, Monat discovered that 2007 depreciation expense was understated by $500,000. In 2008, net income was $900,000 and dividends declared were $250,000. The tax rate is 40%. Prepare a 2008 retained earnings statement for William R. Monat Company.

(LO 6) **BE18-8** Haley Corporation had 2008 net income of $1,200,000. During 2008, Haley paid a dividend of $2 per share on 100,000 shares of preferred stock. During 2008, Haley had outstanding 250,000 shares of common stock. Compute Haley's 2008 earnings per share.

(LO 6) **BE18-9** Barkley Corporation had 120,000 shares of stock outstanding on January 1, 2008. On May 1, 2008, Barkley issued 45,000 shares. On July 1, Barkley purchased 10,000 treasury shares, which were reissued on October 1. Compute Barkley's weighted-average number of shares outstanding for 2008.

(LO 6) **BE18-10** Green Corporation had 200,000 shares of common stock outstanding on January 1, 2008. On May 1, Green issued 30,000 shares. (a) Compute the weighted average number of shares outstanding if the 30,000 shares were issued for cash. (b) Compute the weighted-average number of shares outstanding if the 30,000 shares were issued in a stock dividend.

(LO 7) **BE18-11** Strickland Corporation earned net income of $300,000 in 2008 and had 100,000 shares of common stock outstanding throughout the year. Also outstanding all year was $400,000 of 10% bonds, which are convertible into 16,000 shares of common. Strickland's tax rate is 40 percent. Compute Strickland's 2008 diluted earnings per share.

(LO 7) **BE18-12** Sabonis Corporation reported net income of $400,000 in 2008 and had 50,000 shares of common stock outstanding throughout the year. Also outstanding all year were 5,000 shares of cumulative preferred stock, each convertible into 2 shares of common. The preferred stock pays an annual dividend of $5 per share. Sabonis' tax rate is 40%. Compute Sabonis' 2008 diluted earnings per share.

(LO 7) **BE18-13** Sarunas Corporation reported net income of $300,000 in 2008 and had 200,000 shares of common stock outstanding throughout the year. Also outstanding all year were 30,000 options to purchase common stock at $10 per share. The average market price of the stock during the year was $15. Compute diluted earnings per share.

(LO 6) **BE18-14** The 2008 income statement of Schrempf Corporation showed net income of $480,000 and an extraordinary loss of $120,000. Schrempf had 50,000 shares of common stock outstanding all year. Prepare Schrempf's income statement presentation of earnings per share.

Exercises

E18-1 **(Change in Principle—Long-term Contracts)** Pam Erickson Construction Company changed from the completed-contract to the percentage-of-completion method of accounting for long-term construction contracts during 2008. For tax purposes, the company employs the completed-contract method and will continue this approach in the future. (*Hint:* Adjust all tax consequences through the Deferred Tax Liability account.) The appropriate information related to this change is as follows.

(LO 2)

| | Pretax Income from | | |
	Percentage-of-Completion	Completed-Contract	Difference
2007	$780,000	$590,000	$190,000
2008	700,000	480,000	220,000

Instructions

(a) Assuming that the tax rate is 35%, what is the amount of net income that would be reported in 2008?

(b) What entry(ies) are necessary to adjust the accounting records for the change in accounting principle?

E18-2 **(Change in Principle—Inventory Methods)** Holder-Webb Company began operations on January 1, 2005, and uses the average cost method of pricing inventory. Management is contemplating a change in inventory methods for 2008. The following information is available for the years 2005–2007.

(LO 2, 3)

| | Net Income Computed Using | | |
	Average Cost Method	FIFO Method	LIFO Method
2005	$15,000	$19,000	$12,000
2006	18,000	23,000	14,000
2007	20,000	25,000	17,000

Instructions

(Ignore all tax effects.)

(a) Prepare the journal entry necessary to record a change from the average cost method to the FIFO method in 2008.

(b) Determine net income to be reported for 2005, 2006, and 2007, after giving effect to the change in accounting principle.

(c) Assume Holder-Webb Company used the LIFO method instead of the average cost method during the years 2005–2007. In 2008, Holder-Webb changed to the FIFO method. Prepare the journal entry necessary to record the change in principle.

E18-3 **(Accounting Change)** Taveras Co. decides at the beginning of 2008 to adopt the FIFO method of inventory valuation. Taveras had used the LIFO method for financial reporting since its inception on January 1, 2006, and had maintained records adequate to apply the FIFO method retrospectively. Taveras concluded that FIFO is the preferable inventory method because it reflects the current cost of inventory on the balance sheet. The table below presents the effects of the change in accounting principles on inventory and cost of goods sold.

(LO 2)

| | Inventory Determined by | | Cost of Goods Sold Determined by | |
Date	LIFO Method	FIFO Method	LIFO Method	FIFO Method
January 1, 2006	$ 0	$ 0	$ 0	$ 0
December 31, 2006	100	80	800	820
December 31, 2007	200	240	1,000	940
December 31, 2008	320	390	1,130	1,100

Other information:

1. For each year presented, sales are $3,000 and operating expenses are $1,000.

2. Taveras provides two years of financial statements. Earnings per share information is not required.

Instructions

(a) Prepare income statements under LIFO and FIFO for 2006, 2007, and 2008.

(b) Prepare income statements reflecting the retrospective application of the accounting change from the LIFO method to the FIFO method for 2008 and 2007.

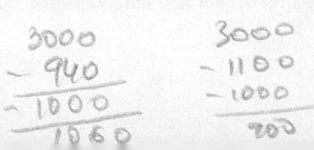

(c) Prepare the note to the financial statements describing the change in method of inventory valuation. In the note, indicate the income statement line items for 2008 and 2007 that were affected by the change in accounting principle.

(d) Prepare comparative retained earnings statements for 2007 and 2008 under FIFO. Retained earnings reported under LIFO are as follows:

	Retained Earnings Balance
December 31, 2006	$1,200
December 31, 2007	2,200
December 31, 2008	3,070

(LO 2)

E18-4 **(Accounting Change)** Gordon Company started operations on January 1, 2002, and has used the FIFO method of inventory valuation since its inception. In 2008, it decides to switch to the average-cost method. You are provided with the following information.

	Net Income		Retained Earnings (Ending balance)
	Under FIFO	Under Average-Cost	Under FIFO
2002	$100,000	$ 90,000	$100,000
2003	70,000	65,000	160,000
2004	90,000	80,000	235,000
2005	120,000	130,000	340,000
2006	300,000	290,000	590,000
2007	305,000	310,000	780,000

Instructions

(a) What is the beginning retained earnings balance at January 1, 2004, if Gordon prepares comparative financial statements starting in 2004?

(b) What is the beginning retained earnings balance at January 1, 2007, if Gordon prepares comparative financial statements starting in 2007?

(c) What is the beginning retained earnings balance at January 1, 2008, if Gordon prepares single-period financial statements for 2008?

(d) What is the net income reported by Gordon in the 2007 income statement if it prepares comparative financial statements starting with 2005?

(LO 2)

E18-5 **(Accounting Change)** Presented below are income statements prepared on a LIFO and FIFO basis for Kenseth Company, which started operations on January 1, 2007. The company presently uses the LIFO method of pricing its inventory and has decided to switch to the FIFO method in 2008. The FIFO income statement is computed in accordance with the requirements of *SFAS No. 154*. Kenseth's profit-sharing agreement with its employees indicates that the company will pay employees 10% of income before profit sharing. Income taxes are ignored.

	LIFO Basis		FIFO Basis	
	2008	2007	2008	2007
Sales	$3,000	$3,000	$3,000	$3,000
Cost of goods sold	1,130	1,000	1,100	940
Operating expenses	1,000	1,000	1,000	1,000
Income before profit sharing	870	1,000	900	1,060
Profit sharing expense	87	100	96	100
Net income	$ 783	$ 900	$ 804	$ 960

Instructions

Answer the following questions.

(a) If comparative income statements are prepared, what net income should Kenseth report in 2007 and 2008?

(b) Explain why, under the FIFO basis, Kenseth reports $100 in 2007 and $96 in 2008 for its profit-sharing expense.

(c) Assume that Kenseth has a beginning balance of retained earnings at January 1, 2008, of $8,000 using the LIFO method. The company declared and paid dividends of $2,000 in 2008. Prepare the retained earnings statement for 2008, assuming that Kenseth has switched to the FIFO method.

(LO 4)

E18-6 **(Accounting Changes—Depreciation)** Kathleen Cole Inc. acquired the following assets in January of 2005.

Equipment, estimated service life, 5 years; salvage value, $15,000	$525,000
Building, estimated service life, 30 years; no salvage value	$693,000

The equipment has been depreciated using the sum-of-the-years'-digits method for the first 3 years for financial reporting purposes. In 2008, the company decided to change the method of computing depreciation to the straight-line method for the equipment, but no change was made in the estimated service life or salvage value. It was also decided to change the total estimated service life of the building from 30 years to 40 years, with no change in the estimated salvage value. The building is depreciated on the straight-line method.

Instructions

(a) Prepare the general journal entry to record depreciation expense for the equipment in 2008.

(b) Prepare the journal entry to record depreciation expense for the building in 2008. (Round all computations to two decimal places.)

E18-7 (**Change in Estimate and Error; Financial Statements**) Presented below are the comparative income statements for Denise Habbe Inc. for the years 2007 and 2008.

(LO 4, 5)

	2008	2007
Sales	$340,000	$270,000
Cost of sales	200,000	142,000
Gross profit	140,000	128,000
Expenses	88,000	50,000
Net income	$ 52,000	$ 78,000
Retained earnings (Jan. 1)	$ 125,000	$ 72,000
Net income	52,000	78,000
Dividends	(30,000)	(25,000)
Retained earnings (Dec. 31)	$147,000	$125,000

The following additional information is provided:

1. In 2008, Denise Habbe Inc. decided to switch its depreciation method from sum-of-the-years'-digits to the straight-line method. The assets were purchased at the beginning of 2007 for $100,000 with an estimated useful life of 4 years and no salvage value. (The 2008 income statement contains depreciation expense of $30,000 on the assets purchased at the beginning of 2007.)

2. In 2008, the company discovered that the ending inventory for 2007 was overstated by $24,000; ending inventory for 2008 is correctly stated.

Instructions

Prepare the revised retained earnings statement for 2007 and 2008, assuming comparative statements. (Ignore income taxes.)

E18-8 (**Accounting Changes and Errors**) Listed below are various types of accounting changes and errors.

(LO 4, 5)

_____ 1. Change in a plant asset's salvage value.

_____ 2. Change due to overstatement of inventory.

_____ 3. Change from sum-of-the-years'-digits to straight-line method of depreciation.

_____ 4. Change from presenting unconsolidated to consolidated financial statements.

_____ 5. Change from LIFO to FIFO inventory method.

_____ 6. Change in the rate used to compute warranty costs.

_____ 7. Change from an unacceptable accounting principle to an acceptable accounting principle.

_____ 8. Change in a patent's amortization period.

_____ 9. Change from completed-contract to percentage-of-completion method on construction contracts.

_____ 10. Change from FIFO to average-cost inventory method.

Instructions

For each change or error, indicate how it would be accounted for using the following code letters:

(a) Accounted for prospectively.

(b) Accounted for retrospectively.

(c) Neither of the above.

E18-9 (**Error and Change in Estimate—Depreciation**) Joy Cunningham Co. purchased a machine on January 1, 2005, for $550,000. At that time it was estimated that the machine would have a 10-year life and no

(LO 4, 5)

salvage value. On December 31, 2008, the firm's accountant found that the entry for depreciation expense had been omitted in 2006. In addition, management has informed the accountant that the company plans to switch to straight-line depreciation, starting with the year 2008. At present, the company uses the sum-of-the-years'-digits method for depreciating equipment.

Instructions

Prepare the general journal entries that should be made at December 31, 2008 to record these events. (Ignore tax effects.)

(LO 4) **E18-10 (Depreciation Changes)** On January 1, 2004, Jackson Company purchased a building and equipment that have the following useful lives, salvage values, and costs.

> Building, 40-year estimated useful life, $50,000 salvage value, $800,000 cost
> Equipment, 12-year estimated useful life, $10,000 salvage value, $100,000 cost

The building has been depreciated under the double-declining balance method through 2007. In 2008, the company decided to switch to the straight-line method of depreciation. Jackson also decided to change the total useful life of the equipment to 9 years, with a salvage value of $5,000 at the end of that time. The equipment is depreciated using the straight-line method.

Instructions

(a) Prepare the journal entry(ies) necessary to record the depreciation expense on the building in 2008.
(b) Compute depreciation expense on the equipment for 2008.

(LO 4) **E18-11 (Change in Estimate—Depreciation)** Peter M. Dell Co. purchased equipment for $510,000 which was estimated to have a useful life of 10 years with a salvage value of $10,000 at the end of that time. Depreciation has been entered for 7 years on a straight-line basis. In 2008, it is determined that the total estimated life should be 15 years with a salvage value of $5,000 at the end of that time.

Instructions

(a) Prepare the entry (if any) to correct the prior years' depreciation.
(b) Prepare the entry to record depreciation for 2008.

(LO 4) **E18-12 (Change in Estimate—Depreciation)** Gerald Englehart Industries changed from the double-declining balance to the straight-line method in 2008 on all its plant assets. There was no change in the assets' salvage values or useful lives. Plant assets, acquired on January 2, 2005, had an original cost of $1,600,000, with a $100,000 salvage value and an 8-year estimated useful life. Income before depreciation expense was $270,000 in 2007 and $300,000 in 2008.

Instructions

(a) Prepare the journal entry(ies) to record the change in depreciation method in 2008.
(b) Starting with income before depreciation expense, prepare the remaining portion of the income statement for 2007 and 2008.

(LO 2) **E18-13 (Change in Principle—Long-term Contracts)** Cullen Construction Company changed from the completed-contract to the percentage-of-completion method of accounting for long-term construction contracts during 2008. For tax purposes, the company employs the completed-contract method and will continue this approach in the future. The appropriate information related to this change is as follows.

	Pretax Income from		
	Percentage-of-Completion	Completed-Contract	Difference
2007	$980,000	$690,000	$290,000
2008	900,000	480,000	420,000

Instructions

(a) Assuming that the tax rate is 40%, what is the amount of net income that would be reported in 2008?
(b) What entry(ies) are necessary to adjust the accounting records for the change in accounting principle?

(LO 2) **E18-14 (Various Changes in Principle—Inventory Methods)** On the next page is the net income of Anita Ferreri Instrument Co., a private corporation, computed under the three inventory methods using a periodic system.

	FIFO	Average-Cost	LIFO
2005	$26,000	$24,000	$20,000
2006	30,000	25,000	21,000
2007	28,000	27,000	24,000
2008	34,000	30,000	26,000

Instructions

(Ignore tax considerations.)

(a) Assume that in 2008 Ferreri decided to change from the FIFO method to the average-cost method of pricing inventories. Prepare the journal entry necessary for the change that took place during 2008, and show net income reported for 2005, 2006, 2007, and 2008.

(b) Assume that in 2008 Ferreri, which had been using the LIFO method since incorporation in 2005, changed to the FIFO method of pricing inventories. Prepare the journal entry necessary to record the change in 2008 and show net income reported for 2005, 2006, 2007, and 2008.

E18-15 **(Weighted-Average Number of Shares)** Newton Inc. uses a calendar year for financial reporting. The company is authorized to issue 9,000,000 shares of $10 par common stock. At no time has Newton issued any potentially dilutive securities. Listed below is a summary of Newton's common stock activities. **(LO 6)**

1.	Number of common shares issued and outstanding at December 31, 2005	2,000,000
2.	Shares issued as a result of a 10% stock dividend on September 30, 2006	200,000
3.	Shares issued for cash on March 31, 2007	2,000,000
	Number of common shares issued and outstanding at December 31, 2007	4,200,000
4.	A 2-for-1 stock split of Newton's common stock took place on March 31, 2008.	

Instructions

(a) Compute the weighted-average number of common shares used in computing earnings per common share for 2006 on the 2007 comparative income statement.

(b) Compute the weighted-average number of common shares used in computing earnings per common share for 2007 on the 2007 comparative income statement.

(c) Compute the weighted-average number of common shares to be used in computing earnings per common share for 2007 on the 2008 comparative income statement.

(d) Compute the weighted-average number of common shares to be used in computing earnings per common share for 2008 on the 2008 comparative income statement.

E18-16 **(EPS: Simple Capital Structure)** On January 1, 2008, Wilke Corp. had 480,000 shares of common stock outstanding. During 2008, it had the following transactions that affected the common stock account. **(LO 6)**

February 1	Issued 120,000 shares
March 1	Issued a 10% stock dividend
May 1	Acquired 100,000 shares of treasury stock
June 1	Issued a 3-for-1 stock split
October 1	Reissued 60,000 shares of treasury stock

Instructions

(a) Determine the weighted-average number of shares outstanding as of December 31, 2008.

(b) Assume that Wilke Corp. earned net income of $3,456,000 during 2008. In addition, it had 100,000 shares of 9%, $100 par nonconvertible, noncumulative preferred stock outstanding for the entire year. Because of liquidity considerations, however, the company did not declare and pay a preferred dividend in 2008. Compute earnings per share for 2008, using the weighted-average number of shares determined in part (a).

(c) Assume the same facts as in part (b), except that the preferred stock was cumulative. Compute earnings per share for 2008.

(d) Assume the same facts as in part (b), except that net income included an extraordinary gain of $864,000 and a loss from discontinued operations of $432,000. Both items are net of applicable income taxes. Compute earnings per share for 2008.

E18-17 **(EPS: Simple Capital Structure)** Ace Company had 200,000 shares of common stock outstanding on December 31, 2008. During the year 2009 the company issued 8,000 shares on May 1 and retired 14,000 shares on October 31. For the year 2009 Ace Company reported net income of $249,690 after a casualty loss of $40,600 (net of tax). **(LO 6)**

Instructions

What earnings per share data should be reported at the bottom of its income statement, assuming that the casualty loss is extraordinary?

(LO 6)   **E18-18** **(EPS: Simple Capital Structure)** Flagstad Inc. presented the following data.

Net income	$2,500,000 — 400 000
Preferred stock: 50,000 shares outstanding, $100 par, 8% cumulative, not convertible	5,000,000
Common stock: Shares outstanding 1/1	750,000 × 4/12 ×2 500
Issued for cash, 5/1	300,000 1050 × 3/12 ×2 525
Acquired treasury stock for cash, 8/1	150,000 900 × 2/12 ×2 300
2-for-1 stock split, 10/1	1800 3/12 450
	1775

Instructions

Compute earnings per share.

(LO 6)   **E18-19** **(EPS: Simple Capital Structure)** A portion of the combined statement of income and retained earnings of Seminole Inc. for the current year follows.

Income before extraordinary item		$15,000,000 — 300 000
Extraordinary loss, net of applicable income tax (Note 1)		1,340,000
Net income		13,660,000
Retained earnings at the beginning of the year		83,250,000
		96,910,000
Dividends declared:		
On preferred stock—$6.00 per share	$ 300,000	
On common stock—$1.75 per share	14,875,000	15,175,000
Retained earnings at the end of the year		$81,735,000

Note 1. During the year, Seminole Inc. suffered a major casualty loss of $1,340,000 after applicable income tax reduction of $1,200,000.

At the end of the current year, Seminole Inc. has outstanding 8,500,000 shares of $10 par common stock and 50,000 shares of 6% preferred.

On April 1 of the current year, Seminole Inc. issued 1,000,000 shares of common stock for $32 per share to help finance the casualty.

7 800 000 ×3/12   1875
8 800 000 .9/12   6 375/8 250

Instructions

Compute the earnings per share on common stock for the current year as it should be reported to stockholders.

(LO 6)   **E18-20** **(EPS: Simple Capital Structure)** On January 1, 2008, Lennon Industries had stock outstanding as follows.

6% Cumulative preferred stock, $100 par value, issued and outstanding 10,000 shares	$1,000,000 60 000
Common stock, $10 par value, issued and outstanding 200,000 shares	2,000,000

To acquire the net assets of three smaller companies, Lennon authorized the issuance of an additional 160,000 common shares. The acquisitions took place as shown below.

Date of Acquisition	Shares Issued	
Company A April 1, 2008	50,000	200 × 3/12 50
Company B July 1, 2008	80,000	250 × 3/12 62.5
Company C October 1, 2008	30,000	330 × 3/12 82.5
		360 × 3/12 90
		285

On May 14, 2008, Lennon realized a $90,000 (before taxes) insurance gain on the expropriation of investments originally purchased in 1994.

On December 31, 2008, Lennon recorded net income of $300,000 before tax and exclusive of the gain.

Instructions

Assuming a 50% tax rate, compute the earnings per share data that should appear on the financial statements of Lennon Industries as of December 31, 2008. Assume that the expropriation is extraordinary.

E18-21 (EPS: Simple Capital Structure) At January 1, 2008, Langley Company's outstanding shares included the following.

> 280,000 shares of $50 par value, 7% cumulative preferred stock
> 900,000 shares of $1 par value common stock

Net income for 2008 was $2,530,000. No cash dividends were declared or paid during 2008. On February 15, 2009, however, all preferred dividends in arrears were paid, together with a 5% stock dividend on common shares. There were no dividends in arrears prior to 2008.

On April 1, 2008, 450,000 shares of common stock were sold for $10 per share, and on October 1, 2008, 110,000 shares of common stock were purchased for $20 per share and held as treasury stock.

Instructions

Compute earnings per share for 2008. Assume that financial statements for 2008 were issued in March 2009.

E18-22 (EPS with Convertible Bonds, Various Situations) In 2007 Chirac Enterprises issued, at par, 60 $1,000, 8% bonds, each convertible into 100 shares of common stock. Chirac had revenues of $17,500 and expenses other than interest and taxes of $8,400 for 2008. (Assume that the tax rate is 40%.) Throughout 2008, 2,000 shares of common stock were outstanding; none of the bonds was converted or redeemed.

Instructions

(a) Compute diluted earnings per share for 2008.
(b) Assume the same facts as those assumed for part (a), except that the 60 bonds were issued on September 1, 2008 (rather than in 2007), and none have been converted or redeemed.
(c) Assume the same facts as assumed for part (a), except that 20 of the 60 bonds were actually converted on July 1, 2008.

E18-23 (EPS with Convertible Bonds and Preferred Stock) On January 1, 2008, Crocker Company issued 10-year, $2,000,000 face value, 6% bonds, at par. Each $1,000 bond is convertible into 15 shares of Crocker common stock. Crocker's net income in 2008 was $300,000, and its tax rate was 40%. The company had 100,000 shares of common stock outstanding throughout 2008. None of the bonds were converted in 2008.

Instructions

(a) Compute diluted earnings per share for 2008.
(b) Compute diluted earnings per share for 2008, assuming the same facts as above, except that $1,000,000 of 6% convertible preferred stock was issued instead of the bonds. Each $100 preferred share is convertible into 5 shares of Crocker common stock.

E18-24 (EPS with Options, Various Situations) Venzuela Company's net income for 2008 is $50,000. The only potentially dilutive securities outstanding were 1,000 options issued during 2007, each exercisable for one share at $6. None has been exercised, and 10,000 shares of common were outstanding during 2008. The average market price of Venzuela's stock during 2008 was $20.

Instructions

(a) Compute diluted earnings per share. (Round to nearest cent.)
(b) Assume the same facts as those assumed for part (a), except that the 1,000 options were issued on October 1, 2008 (rather than in 2007). The average market price during the last 3 months of 2008 was $20.

E18-25 (EPS with Convertible Bonds and Preferred Stock) Simon Corporation issued 10-year, $5,000,000 par, 7% callable convertible subordinated debentures on January 2, 2008. The bonds have a par value of $1,000, with interest payable annually. The current conversion ratio is 14 : 1, and in 2 years it will increase to 18 : 1. At the date of issue, the bonds were sold at 98. Bond discount is amortized on a straight-line basis. Simon's effective tax was 35%. Net income in 2008 was $9,500,000, and the company had 2,000,000 shares outstanding during the entire year.

Instructions

(a) Prepare a schedule to compute both basic and diluted earnings per share.
(b) Discuss how the schedule would differ if the security was convertible preferred stock.

(LO 7)

E18-26 **(EPS with Warrants)** Howat Corporation earned $360,000 during a period when it had an average of 100,000 shares of common stock outstanding. The common stock sold at an average market price of $15 per share during the period. Also outstanding were 15,000 warrants that could be exercised to purchase one share of common stock for $10 for each warrant exercised.

Instructions

(a) Are the warrants dilutive?
(b) Compute basic earnings per share.
(c) Compute diluted earnings per share.

$$\frac{360000}{100\,000 + 5000}$$

See the book's companion website, at www.wiley.com/college/warfield, for Additional Exercises.

$$\frac{5 \cdot 15000}{15}$$

Problems

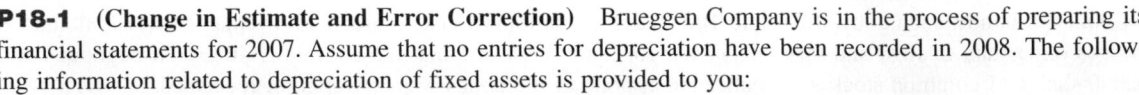

(LO 4, 5)

P18-1 **(Change in Estimate and Error Correction)** Brueggen Company is in the process of preparing its financial statements for 2007. Assume that no entries for depreciation have been recorded in 2008. The following information related to depreciation of fixed assets is provided to you:

1. Brueggen purchased equipment on January 2, 2005, for $65,000. At that time, the equipment had an estimated useful life of 10 years with a $5,000 salvage value. The equipment is depreciated on a straight-line basis. On January 2, 2008, as a result of additional information, the company determined that the equipment has a remaining useful life of 4 years with a $3,000 salvage value.

2. During 2008 Brueggen changed from the double-declining balance method for its building to the straight-line method. The building originally cost $300,000. It had a useful life of 10 years and a salvage value of $30,000. The following computations present depreciation on both bases for 2006 and 2007.

	2007	2006
Straight-line	$27,000	$27,000
Declining-balance	48,000	60,000

3. Brueggen purchased a machine on July 1, 2006, at a cost of $80,000. The machine has a salvage value of $8,000 and a useful life of 8 years. Brueggen's bookkeeper recorded straight-line depreciation in 2006 and 2007 but failed to consider the salvage value.

Instructions

(a) Prepare the journal entries to record depreciation expense for 2008 and correct any errors made to date related to the information provided. (Round all computations to two decimal places.)
(b) Show comparative net income for 2007 and 2008. Income before depreciation expense was $300,000 in 2008, and was $310,000 in 2007. Ignore taxes.

(LO 2, 4, 5)

P18-2 **(Comprehensive Accounting Change and Error Analysis Problem)** Larry Kingston Inc. was organized in late 2005 to manufacture and sell hosiery. At the end of its fourth year of operation, the company has been fairly successful, as indicated by the following reported net incomes.

2005	$140,000[a]	2007	$205,000
2006	160,000[b]	2008	276,000

[a]Includes a $12,000 increase because of change in bad debt experience rate.
[b]Includes extraordinary gain of $40,000.

The company has decided to expand operations and has applied for a sizable bank loan. The bank officer has indicated that the records should be audited and presented in comparative statements to facilitate analysis by the bank. Larry Kingston Inc. therefore hired the auditing firm of Check & Doublecheck Co. and has provided the following additional information.

1. In early 2006, Larry Kingston Inc. changed its estimate from 2% to 1% on the amount of bad debt expense to be charged to operations. Bad debt expense for 2005, if a 1% rate had been used, would have been $12,000. The company therefore restated its net income for 2005.

2. In 2008, the auditor discovered that the company had changed its method of inventory pricing from LIFO to FIFO. The effect on the income statements for the previous years is as follows.

	2005	2006	2007	2008
Net income unadjusted—LIFO basis	$140,000	$160,000	$205,000	$276,000
Net income unadjusted—FIFO basis	155,000	165,000	215,000	260,000
	$ 15,000	$ 5,000	$ 10,000	($ 16,000)

3. In 2008 the auditor discovered that:
   a. The company incorrectly overstated the ending inventory by $11,000 in 2007.
   b. A dispute developed in 2006 with the Internal Revenue Service over the deductibility of entertainment expenses. In 2005, the company was not permitted these deductions, but a tax settlement was reached in 2008 that allowed these expenses. As a result of the court's finding, tax expenses in 2008 were reduced by $60,000.

Instructions

(a) Indicate how each of these changes or corrections should be handled in the accounting records. Ignore income tax considerations.

(b) Present comparative income statements for the years 2005 to 2008, starting with income before extraordinary items. Ignore income tax considerations.

P18-3 **(Accounting Changes)** Plato Corporation performs year-end planning in November of each year before their calendar year ends in December. The preliminary estimated net income is $3 million. The CFO, Mary Sheets, meets with the company president, S. A. Plato, to review the projected numbers. She presents the following projected information.

(LO 5)

Plato Corporation
Projected Income Statement
For the Year Ended December 31, 2008

Sales		$29,000,000
Cost of goods sold	$14,000,000	
Depreciation	2,600,000	
Operating expenses	6,400,000	23,000,000
Income before income tax		6,000,000
Income tax		3,000,000
Net income		$ 3,000,000

Plato Corporation
Selected Balance Sheet Information
At December 31, 2008

Estimated cash balance	$ 5,000,000
Available-for-sale securities (at cost)	10,000,000
Security fair value adjustment account (1/1/08)	200,000

Estimated market value at December 31, 2008:

Security	Cost	Estimated Market
A	$ 2,000,000	$ 2,200,000
B	4,000,000	3,900,000
C	3,000,000	3,000,000
D	1,000,000	2,800,000
Total	$10,000,000	$11,900,000

Other information at December 31, 2008:

Equipment	$ 3,000,000
Accumulated depreciation (5-year SL)	1,200,000
New robotic equipment (purchased 1/1/08)	5,000,000
Accumulated depreciation (5-year DDB)	2,000,000

The corporation has never used robatic equipment before, and Sheets assumed an accelerated method because of the rapidly changing technology in robotic equipment. The company normally uses straight-line depreciation for production equipment.

Plato explains to Sheets that it is important for the corporation to show an $8,000,000 net income before taxes because Plato receives a $1,000,000 bonus if the income before taxes and bonus reaches $8,000,000. Plato also does not want the company to pay more than $3,000,000 in income taxes to the government.

Instructions

(a) What can Sheets do within GAAP to accommodate the president's wishes to achieve $8,000,000 in income before taxes and bonus? Present the revised income statement based on your decision.

(b) Are the actions ethical? Who are the stakeholders in this decision, and what effect do Sheets's actions have on their interests?

(LO 4) **P18-4** **(Change in Principle—LIFO to Average-Cost—Periodic)** The management of Kreiter Instrument Company had concluded, with the concurrence of its independent auditors, that results of operations would be more fairly presented if Kreiter changed its method of pricing inventory from last-in, first-out (LIFO) to average-cost in 2008. Given below is the 5-year summary of income under LIFO and a schedule of what the inventories would be if stated on the average-cost method.

Kreiter Instrument Company
Statement of Income and Retained Earnings
For the Years Ended May 31

	2004	2005	2006	2007	2008
Sales—net	$13,964	$15,506	$16,673	$18,221	$18,898
Cost of goods sold					
Beginning inventory	1,000	1,100	1,000	1,115	1,237
Purchases	13,000	13,900	15,000	15,900	17,100
Ending inventory	(1,100)	(1,000)	(1,115)	(1,237)	(1,369)
Total	12,900	14,000	14,885	15,778	16,968
Gross profit	1,064	1,506	1,788	2,443	1,930
Administrative expenses	700	763	832	907	989
Income before taxes	364	743	956	1,536	941
Income taxes (50%)	182	372	478	768	471
Net income	182	371	478	768	470
Retained earnings—beginning	1,206	1,388	1,759	2,237	3,005
Retained earnings—ending	$ 1,388	$ 1,759	$ 2,237	$ 3,005	$ 3,475
Earnings per share	$1.82	$3.71	$4.78	$7.68	$4.70

Schedule of Inventory Balances Using Average-Cost Method
For the Years Ended May 31

2003	2004	2005	2006	2007	2008
$950	$1,124	$1,091	$1,270	$1,480	$1,699

Instructions

Prepare comparative statements for the 5 years, assuming that Kreiter changed its method of inventory pricing to average-cost. Indicate the effects on net income and earnings per share for the years involved. Kreiter Instruments started business in 2003. (All amounts except EPS are rounded up to the nearest dollar.)

P18-5 (Accounting Change and Error Analysis) On December 31, 2008, before the books were closed, the management and accountants of Keltner Inc. made the following determinations about three depreciable assets.

1. Depreciable asset A was purchased January 2, 2005. It originally cost $495,000 and, for depreciation purposes, the straight-line method was originally chosen. The asset was originally expected to be useful for 10 years and have a zero salvage value. In 2008, the decision was made to change the depreciation method from straight-line to sum-of-the-years'-digits, and the estimates relating to useful life and salvage value remained unchanged.

2. Depreciable asset B was purchased January 3, 2004. It originally cost $120,000 and, for depreciation purposes, the straight-line method was chosen. The asset was originally expected to be useful for 15 years and have a zero salvage value. In 2008, the decision was made to shorten the total life of this asset to 9 years and to estimate the salvage value at $3,000.

3. Depreciable asset C was purchased January 5, 2004. The asset's original cost was $140,000, and this amount was entirely expensed in 2004. This particular asset has a 10-year useful life and no salvage value. The straight-line method was chosen for depreciation purposes.

Additional data:

1. Income in 2008 before depreciation expense amounted to $400,000.

2. Depreciation expense on assets other than A, B, and C totaled $55,000 in 2008.

3. Income in 2007 was reported at $370,000.

4. Ignore all income tax effects.

5. 100,000 shares of common stock were outstanding in 2007 and 2008.

Instructions

(a) Prepare all necessary entries in 2008 to record these determinations.

(b) Prepare comparative retained earnings statements for Eloise Keltner Inc. for 2007 and 2008. The company had retained earnings of $200,000 at December 31, 2006.

P18-6 (EPS with Complex Capital Structure) Diane Leto, controller at Dewey Yaeger Pharmaceutical Industries, a public company, is currently preparing the calculation for basic and diluted earnings per share and the related disclosure for Yaeger's external financial statements. Below is selected financial information for the fiscal year ended June 30, 2008.

Dewey Yaeger Pharmaceutical Industries		
Selected Statement of		
Financial Position Information		
June 30, 2008		
Long-term debt		
Notes payable, 10%		$ 1,000,000
7% convertible bonds payable		5,000,000
10% bonds payable		6,000,000
Total long-term debt		$12,000,000
Shareholders' equity		
Preferred stock, 8.5% cumulative, $50 par value,		
100,000 shares authorized, 25,000 shares issued		
and outstanding		$ 1,250,000
Common stock, $1 par, 10,000,000 shares authorized,		
1,000,000 shares issued and outstanding		1,000,000
Additional paid-in capital		4,000,000
Retained earnings		6,000,000
Total shareholders' equity		$12,250,000

The following transactions have also occurred at Yaeger.

1. Options were granted in 2006 to purchase 100,000 shares at $15 per share. Although no options were exercised during 2008, the average price per common share during fiscal year 2008 was $20 per share.

2. Each bond was issued at face value. The 7% convertible debenture will convert into common stock at 50 shares per $1,000 bond. It is exercisable after 5 years and was issued in 2007.

3. The 8.5% preferred stock was issued in 2006.

4. There are no preferred dividends in arrears; however, preferred dividends were not declared in fiscal year 2008.

5. The 1,000,000 shares of common stock were outstanding for the entire 2008 fiscal year.

6. Net income for fiscal year 2008 was $1,500,000, and the average income tax rate is 40%.

Instructions

For the fiscal year ended June 30, 2008, calculate the following for Dewey Yaeger Pharmaceutical Industries.

(a) Basic earnings per share.

(b) Diluted earnings per share.

(LO 6)

P18-7 (Basic EPS: Two-Year Presentation) Hillel Corporation is preparing the comparative financial statements for the annual report to its shareholders for fiscal years ended May 31, 2007, and May 31, 2008. The income from operations for each year was $1,800,000 and $2,500,000, respectively. In both years, the company incurred a 10% interest expense on $2,400,000 of debt, an obligation that requires interest-only payments for 5 years. The company experienced a loss of $500,000 from a fire in its Scotsland facility in February 2008, which was determined to be an extraordinary loss. The company uses a 40% effective tax rate for income taxes.

The capital structure of Hillel Corporation on June 1, 2006, consisted of 2 million shares of common stock outstanding and 20,000 shares of $50 par value, 8%, cumulative preferred stock. There were no preferred dividends in arrears, and the company had not issued any convertible securities, options, or warrants.

On October 1, 2006, Hillel sold an additional 500,000 shares of the common stock at $20 per share. Hillel distributed a 20% stock dividend on the common shares outstanding on January 1, 2007. On December 1, 2007, Hillel was able to sell an additional 800,000 shares of the common stock at $22 per share. These were the only common stock transactions that occurred during the two fiscal years.

Instructions

(a) Identify whether the capital structure at Hillel Corporation is a simple or complex capital structure, and explain why.

(b) Determine the weighted-average number of shares that Hillel Corporation would use in calculating earnings per share for the fiscal year ended
   (1) May 31, 2007.
   (2) May 31, 2008.

(c) Prepare, in good form, a comparative income statement, beginning with income from operations, for Hillel Corporation for the fiscal years ended May 31, 2007, and May 31, 2008. This statement will be included in Hillel's annual report and should display the appropriate earnings per share presentations.

(CMA adapted)

(LO 7)

P18-8 (EPS Computation of Basic and Diluted EPS) Edmund Halvor of the controller's office of East Aurora Corporation was given the assignment of determining the basic and diluted earnings per share values for the year ending December 31, 2008. Halvor has compiled the information listed below.

1. The company is authorized to issue 8,000,000 shares of $10 par value common stock. As of December 31, 2007, 3,000,000 shares had been issued and were outstanding.

2. The per share market prices of the common stock on selected dates were as follows.

	Price Per Share
July 1, 2007	$20.00
January 1, 2008	21.00
April 1, 2008	25.00
July 1, 2008	11.00
August 1, 2008	10.50
November 1, 2008	9.00
December 31, 2008	10.00

3. A total of 700,000 shares of an authorized 1,200,000 shares of convertible preferred stock had been issued on July 1, 2007. The stock was issued at its par value of $25, and it has a cumulative dividend of $3 per share. The stock is convertible into common stock at the rate of one share of convertible preferred for one share of common. The rate of conversion is to be automatically adjusted for stock splits and stock dividends. Dividends are paid quarterly on September 30, December 31, March 31, and June 30.

4. East Aurora Corporation is subject to a 40% income tax rate.

5. The after-tax net income for the year ended December 31, 2008 was $13,550,000.

The following specific activities took place during 2008.

1. January 1—A 5% common stock dividend was issued. The dividend had been declared on December 1, 2007, to all stockholders of record on December 29, 2007.

2. April 1—A total of 200,000 shares of the $3 convertible preferred stock was converted into common stock. The company issued new common stock and retired the preferred stock. This was the only conversion of the preferred stock during 2008.

3. July 1—A 2-for-1 split of the common stock became effective on this date. The board of directors had authorized the split on June 1.

4. August 1—A total of 300,000 shares of common stock were issued to acquire a factory building.

5. November 1—A total of 24,000 shares of common stock were purchased on the open market at $9 per share. These shares were to be held as treasury stock and were still in the treasury as of December 31, 2008.

6. Common stock cash dividends—Cash dividends to common stockholders were declared and paid as follows.

   April 15—$0.30 per share
   October 15—$0.20 per share

7. Preferred stock cash dividends—Cash dividends to preferred stockholders were declared and paid as scheduled.

Instructions

(a) Determine the number of shares used to compute basic earnings per share for the year ended December 31, 2008.

(b) Determine the number of shares used to compute diluted earnings per share for the year ended December 31, 2008.

(c) Compute the adjusted net income to be used as the numerator in the basic earnings per share calculation for the year ended December 31, 2008.

P18-9 (Computation of Basic and Diluted EPS) The information below pertains to Prancer Company for 2008. **(LO 7)**

Net income for the year	$1,200,000
8% convertible bonds issued at par ($1,000 per bond). Each bond is convertible into 40 shares of common stock.	2,000,000
6% convertible, cumulative preferred stock, $100 par value. Each share is convertible into 3 shares of common stock.	3,000,000
Common stock, $10 par value	6,000,000
Common stock options (granted in a prior year) to purchase 50,000 shares of common stock at $20 per share	500,000
Tax rate for 2008	40%
Average market price of common stock	$25 per share

There were no changes during 2008 in the number of common shares, preferred shares, or convertible bonds outstanding. There is no treasury stock.

Instructions

(a) Compute basic earnings per share for 2008.
(b) Compute diluted earnings per share for 2008.

ACCOUNTING IN ACTION

Financial Reporting and Analysis

■ Financial Reporting Issues: The Procter & Gamble Company

P&G

AIA18-1 The financial statements of **Procter & Gamble (P&G)** can be accessed at the book's website.

Instructions

Refer to P&G's financial statements and the accompanying notes to answer the following questions.

(a) Were there changes in accounting principles reported by P&G during the three years covered by its income statements (2004–2006)? If so, describe the nature of the change and the year of change.

(b) What use did P&G make of estimates in 2006?

(c) What were the basic and diluted earnings per share for P&G in 2004–2006? What are the securities that give rise to P&G's complex capital structure?

PEPSICO ■ Comparative Analysis: The Coca-Cola Company and PepsiCo, Inc.

AIA18-2 The financial statements of **The Coca-Cola Company** and **PepsiCo, Inc.** can be accessed at the book's website.

Instructions

Use information found at the book's website to answer the following questions.

(a) Identify the changes in accounting principles reported by Coca-Cola and Pepsico during the 3 years covered by its income statements (2004–2006). Describe the nature of the change and the year of change.

(b) What are the weighted-average number of shares used by Coca-Cola and PepsiCo in 2006, 2005, and 2004 to compute diluted earnings per share?

(c) What was the diluted net income per share for Coca-Cola and PepsiCo for 2006, 2005, and 2004?

■ Financial Statement Analysis

AIA18-3 Twin Ricky Inc. (TRI) manufactures a variety of consumer products. The company's founders have run the company for 30 years and now are interested in retiring. They are seeking a purchaser who will continue the company's operations. A group of investors, Donna Inc., is looking into the acquisition of TRI.

To evaluate its financial stability and operating efficiency, Donna Inc. requested that TRI provide the latest financial statements and selected financial ratios. Summary information provided by TRI is presented below.

TRI
Statement of Income
For the Year Ended November 30, 2008
(in thousands)

Sales (net)	$30,500
Interest income	500
Total revenue	31,000
Costs and expenses	
Cost of goods sold	17,600
Selling and administrative expense	3,550
Depreciation and amortization expense	1,890
Interest expense	900
Total costs and expenses	23,940
Income before taxes	7,060
Income taxes	2,900
Net income	$ 4,160

TRI
Statement of Financial Position
As of November 30
(in thousands)

	2008	2007
Cash	$ 400	$ 500
Marketable securities (at cost)	500	200
Accounts receivable (net)	3,200	2,900
Inventory	5,800	5,400
Total current assets	9,900	9,000
Property, plant, & equipment (net)	7,100	7,000
Total assets	$17,000	$16,000

Accounts payable	$ 3,700	$ 3,400
Income taxes payable	900	800
Accrued expenses	1,700	1,400
Total current liabilities	6,300	5,600
Long-term debt	2,000	1,800
Total liabilities	8,300	7,400
Common stock ($1 par value)	2,700	2,700
Paid-in capital in excess of par	1,000	1,000
Retained earnings	5,000	4,900
Total shareholders' equity	8,700	8,600
Total liabilities and shareholders' equity	$17,000	$16,000

Selected Financial Ratios

	TRI		Current Industry Average
	2006	2007	
Current ratio	1.62	1.61	1.63
Acid-test ratio	.63	.64	.68
Times interest earned	8.50	8.55	8.45
Net profit margin	12.1%	13.2%	13.0%
Total debt to net worth	1.02	.86	1.03
Total asset turnover	1.83	1.84	1.84
Inventory turnover	3.21	3.17	3.18

Instructions

(a) Calculate a new set of ratios for the fiscal year 2008 for TRI based on the financial statements presented.

(b) Explain the analytical use of each of the seven ratios presented, describing what the investors can learn about TRI's financial stability and operating efficiency.

(c) Identify two limitations of ratio analysis.

(CMA adapted)

Concepts for Analysis

AIA18-4 **(Analysis of Various Accounting Changes and Errors)** Erin Kramer Inc. has recently hired a new independent auditor, Jodie Larson, who says she wants "to get everything straightened out." Consequently, she has proposed the following accounting changes in connection with Erin Kramer Inc.'s 2008 financial statements.

1. At December 31, 2008, the client had a receivable of $820,000 from Holly Michael Inc. on its balance sheet. Holly Michael Inc. has gone bankrupt, and no recovery is expected. The client proposes to write off the receivable as a prior period item.

2. The client proposes the following changes in depreciation policies.

   (a) For office furniture and fixtures it proposes to change from a 10-year useful life to an 8-year life. If this change had been made in prior years, retained earnings at December 31, 2008, would have been $250,000 less. The effect of the change on 2008 income alone is a reduction of $60,000.

   (b) For its equipment in the leasing division the client proposes to adopt the sum-of-the-years'-digits depreciation method. The client had never used SYD before. The first year the client operated a leasing division was 2009. If straight-line depreciation were used, 2009 income would be $110,000 greater.

3. In preparing its 2008 statements, one of the client's bookkeepers overstated ending inventory by $235,000 because of a mathematical error. The client proposes to treat this item as a prior period adjustment.

4. In the past, the client has spread preproduction costs in its furniture division over 5 years. Because its latest furniture is of the "fad" type, it appears that the largest volume of sales will occur during the first 2 years after introduction. Consequently, the client proposes to amortize preproduction costs on a per-unit basis, which will result in expensing most of such costs during the first 2 years after the furniture's introduction. If the new accounting method had been used prior to 2008, retained earnings at December 31, 2007, would have been $375,000 less.

5. For the nursery division the client proposes to switch from FIFO to LIFO inventories because it believes that LIFO will provide a better matching of current costs with revenues. The effect of making this change on 2009 earnings will be an increase of $320,000. The client says that the effect of the change on December 31, 2008, retained earnings cannot be determined.

6. To achieve a better matching of revenues and expenses in its building construction division, the client proposes to switch from the completed-contract method of accounting to the percentage-of-completion method. Had the percentage-of-completion method been employed in all prior years, retained earnings at December 31, 2008, would have been $1,175,000 greater.

Instructions

(a) For each of the changes described above decide whether:
   (1) The change involves an accounting principle, accounting estimate, or correction of an error.
   (2) Restatement of opening retained earnings is required.
(b) What would be the proper adjustment to the December 31, 2008, retained earnings?

AIA18-5 (Analysis of Various Accounting Changes and Errors) Various types of accounting changes can affect the financial statements of a business enterprise differently. Assume that the following list describes changes that have a material effect on the financial statements for the current year of your business enterprise.

1. A change from the completed-contract method to the percentage-of-completion method of accounting for long-term construction-type contracts.
2. A change in the estimated useful life of previously recorded fixed assets as a result of newly acquired information.
3. A change from deferring and amortizing preproduction costs to recording such costs as an expense when incurred because future benefits of the costs have become doubtful. The new accounting method was adopted in recognition of the change in estimated future benefits.
4. A change from including the employer share of FICA taxes with Payroll Tax Expenses to including it with "Retirement benefits" on the income statement.
5. Correction of a mathematical error in inventory pricing made in a prior period.
6. A change from presentation of statements of individual companies to presentation of consolidated statements.
7. A change in the method of accounting for leases for tax purposes to conform with the financial accounting method. As a result, both deferred and current taxes payable changed substantially.
8. A change from the FIFO method of inventory pricing to the LIFO method of inventory pricing.

Instructions

Identify the type of change that is described in each item above and indicate whether the prior year's financial statements should be retrospectively applied or restated when presented in comparative form with the current year's statements.

AIA18-6 (Analysis of Three Accounting Changes and Errors) Listed below are three independent, unrelated sets of facts relating to accounting changes.

Situation 1

Penelope Millhouse Company is in the process of having its first audit. The company has used the cash basis of accounting for revenue recognition. Millhouse president, A. G. Shumway, is willing to change to the accrual method of revenue recognition.

Situation 2

Cheri Nestor Co. decides in January 2008 to change from FIFO to weighted-average pricing for its inventories.

Situation 3

Laura Osmund Co. determined that the depreciable lives of its fixed assets are too long at present to fairly match the cost of the fixed assets with the revenue produced. The company decided at the beginning of the current year to reduce the depreciable lives of all of its existing fixed assets by 5 years.

Instructions

For each of the situations described, provide the information indicated below.

(a) Type of accounting change.
(b) Manner of reporting the change under current generally accepted accounting principles including a discussion, where applicable, of how amounts are computed.
(c) Effect of the change on the balance sheet and income statement.

AIA18-7 (Change in Principle, Estimate) As a certified public accountant, you have been contacted by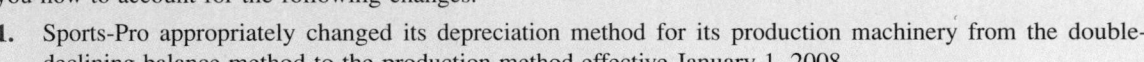
Ben Thinken, CEO of Sports-Pro Athletics, Inc., a manufacturer of a variety of athletic equipment. He has asked
you how to account for the following changes.

1. Sports-Pro appropriately changed its depreciation method for its production machinery from the double-
    declining balance method to the production method effective January 1, 2008.

2. Effective January 1, 2008, Sports-Pro appropriately changed the salvage values used in computing depreci-
    ation for its office equipment.

3. On December 31, 2008, Sports-Pro appropriately changed the specific subsidiaries constituting the group of
    companies for which consolidated financial statements are presented.

Instructions

Write a 1 to 1½ page letter to Ben Thinken explaining how each of the above changes should be presented in
the December 31, 2008, financial statements.

AIA18-8 (EPS: Preferred Dividends, Options, and Convertible Debt) "Earnings per share" (EPS) is
the most featured single financial statistic about modern corporations. Daily published quotations of stock
prices have recently been expanded to include for many securities a "times earnings" figure that is based on EPS.
Stock analysts often focus their discussions on the EPS of the corporations they study.

Instructions

(a) Explain how dividends or dividend requirements on any class of preferred stock that may be outstanding
    affect the computation of EPS.

(b) One of the technical procedures applicable in EPS computations is the "treasury stock method." Briefly
    describe the circumstances under which it might be appropriate to apply the treasury stock method.

(c) Convertible debentures are considered potentially dilutive common shares. Explain how convertible
    debentures are handled for purposes of EPS computations.

(AICPA adapted)

AIA18-9 (EPS Concepts and Effect of Transactions on EPS) Fernandez Corporation, a new audit client
of yours, has not reported earnings per share data in its annual reports to stockholders in the past. The treasurer, Angelo Balthazar, requested that you furnish information about the reporting of earnings per share data in
the current year's annual report in accordance with generally accepted accounting principles.

Instructions

(a) Define the term "earnings per share" as it applies to a corporation with a capitalization structure com-
    posed of only one class of common stock. Explain how earnings per share should be computed and how
    the information should be disclosed in the corporation's financial statements.

(b) Discuss the treatment, if any, that should be given to each of the following items in computing earnings per
    share of common stock for financial statement reporting.

  (1) Outstanding preferred stock issued at a premium with a par value liquidation right.

  (2) The exercise at a price below market value but above book value of a common stock option issued dur-
      ing the current fiscal year to officers of the corporation.

  (3) The replacement of a machine immediately prior to the close of the current fiscal year at a cost 20%
      above the original cost of the replaced machine. The new machine will perform the same function as
      the old machine that was sold for its book value.

  (4) The declaration of current dividends on cumulative preferred stock.

  (5) The acquisition of some of the corporation's outstanding common stock during the current fiscal year.
      The stock was classified as treasury stock.

  (6) A 2-for-1 stock split of common stock during the current fiscal year.

  (7) A provision created out of retained earnings for a contingent liability from a possible lawsuit.

AIA18-10 (EPS, Antidilution) Matt Kacskos, a stockholder of Howat Corporation, has asked you, the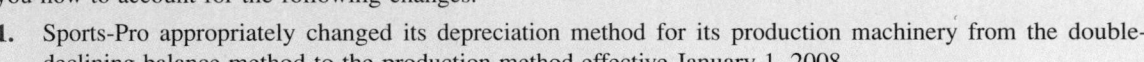
firm's accountant, to explain why his stock warrants were not included in diluted EPS. In order to explain
this situation, you must briefly explain what dilutive securities are, why they are included in the EPS calculation, and why some securities are antidilutive and thus not included in this calculation.

Instructions

Write Mr. Kacskos a 1 to 1½ page letter explaining why the warrants are not included in the calculation. Use
the following data to help you explain this situation.

Howat Corporation earned $228,000 during the period, when it had an average of 100,000 shares of common stock outstanding. The common stock sold at an average market price of $25 per share during the period. Also outstanding were 15,000 warrants that could be exercised to purchase one share of common stock at $30 per warrant.

Professional Tools

■ Ethical Decision Making

AIA18-11 **(Change in Estimates)** Andy Frain is an audit senior of a large public accounting firm who has just been assigned to the Usher Corporation's annual audit engagement. Usher has been a client of Frain's firm for many years. Usher is a fast-growing business in the commercial construction industry. In reviewing the fixed asset ledger, Frain discovered a series of unusual accounting changes, in which the useful lives of assets, depreciated using the straight-line method, were substantially lowered near the midpoint of the original estimate. For example, the useful life of one dump truck was changed from 10 to 6 years during its fifth year of service. Upon further investigation, Andy was told by Vince Lloyd, Usher's accounting manager, "I don't really see your problem. After all, it's perfectly legal to change an accounting estimate. Besides, our CEO likes to see big earnings!"

Instructions
Answer the following questions.

(a) What are the ethical issues concerning Usher's practice of changing the useful lives of fixed assets?
(b) Who could be harmed by Usher's unusual accounting changes?
(c) What should Frain do in this situation?

■ Financial Accounting Research (FARS)

AIA18-12 As part of the year-end accounting process and review of operating policies, Konerko Co. is considering a change in the accounting for its equipment from the straight-line method to an accelerated method. Your supervisor wonders how the company will report this change in principle. He read in a newspaper article that the FASB has issued a standard in this area and has changed GAAP for a "change in estimate that is effected by a change in accounting principle." (Thus, the accounting may be different from that he learned in intermediate accounting.) Your supervisor wants you to research the authoritative guidance on a change in accounting principle related to depreciation methods.

Instructions
Using the **Financial Accounting Research System (FARS)** database, respond to the following items. (Provide text strings used in your search.)

(a) What are the accounting and reporting guidelines for a change in accounting principle related to depreciation methods?
(b) What are the conditions that justify a change in depreciation method, as contemplated by Konerko Co?
(c) What was the FASB's reasoning for changing the accounting guidance for accounting principle changes related to depreciation?

■ Professional Simulations

AIA18-13 and AIA 18-14 Go to the book's companion website, at **www.wiley.com/college/warfield**, to find interactive problems that simulate the computerized CPA exam. The professional simulations for this chapter ask you to address questions related to changes in accounting principle and to EPS computations.

What do the numbers mean?

Change Management, p. 945

Q: What changes in the environment might Halliburton use to justify the change in its accounting for disputed claims?

A: Two related sources of change seem most likely. First, Halliburton's customer base may be changing such that it can more reliably estimate amounts to be paid upon resolution of claims. The new mix of customers could have bet-ter payment track records, or they may be purchasing services that are less uncertain as to any disputes that might arise. Second, Halliburton may have developed better information systems internally that it can use to better estimate the amounts to be received under its range of contracts.

Can I Get My Money Back?, p.959

Q: Investors with a direct investment in companies like Smart Choice or Sunbeam may recover some of their losses in a class-action suit. What other capital market stakeholders are harmed by restatements? Can these other stakeholders get their money back? Explain.

A: Restatements raise questions not only about the companies that report the restatements but also about the general reliability of information in the capital markets. As a result, investors and creditors may levy an information risk premium when deciding whether to invest in stocks or lend money. Thus, even companies with good accounting may pay a higher cost of capital. Investors, in turn, may have fewer investment opportunities if companies stay out of the market due to the higher costs. Thus, everyone loses when the quality of accounting is, or is perceived to be, in decline.

Pro Forma EPS Confusion, p. 965

Q: What are some situations in which pro forma reporting could make reported accounting numbers, including EPS, more useful? Assume that the pro forma differences are fully disclosed according to Regulation G.

A: Pro forma reporting can be useful, and even desirable, in situations in which reported accounting numbers are not representative of the underlying economics of the business and may not be predictive of future performance. For example, an infrequent or unusual event (e.g., a strike or a storm loss) may affect the reported results in the current period but is less relevant for predicting future results. Also, certain industry practices may affect the comparability of reports to other companies not affected by those practices. For example, companies in the pharmaceutical industry may provide pro forma reports for contingencies arising from lawsuits related to their drugs. This could make their reports more comparable to other companies not so exposed to litigation. In both of these situations, pro forma reports can provide useful information, if they are fully disclosed.

Cuckoo for CoCos, p. 968

Q: Some companies voluntarily redeemed CoCo bonds *before* the final EITF ruling, even though doing so resulted in lower reported EPS. Why might these companies discontinue use of these instruments in advance of the accounting change?

A: These companies may have redeemed their CoCos earlier than required simply because they "saw the writing on the wall" that the CoCo loophole would be closed. Alternatively, or in addition, companies may have been motivated by bad publicity related to the use of CoCos. While there could be legitimate reasons to issue a CoCo versus a plain-vanilla convertible bond, it is difficult to convince the market that the main motivation was not to get the boost in EPS. By winding down their CoCos, companies can avoid the increase in their cost of capital associated with questionable accounting practices.

Remember to check the book's companion website to find additional resources for this chapter.

APPENDIX A

ACCOUNTING AND THE TIME VALUE OF MONEY

In accounting (and finance), the phrase **time value of money** indicates a relationship between time and money—that a dollar received today is worth more than a dollar promised at some time in the future. Why? Because of the opportunity to invest today's dollar and receive interest on the investment. Yet, when deciding among investment or borrowing alternatives, it is essential to be able to compare today's dollar and tomorrow's dollar on the same footing—to "compare apples to apples." Investors do that by using the concept of **present value**, which has many applications in accounting.

Learning Objectives

After studying this appendix, you should be able to:

1. Identify accounting topics where the time value of money is relevant.
2. Distinguish between simple and compound interest.
3. Use appropriate compound interest tables.
4. Identify variables fundamental to solving interest problems.
5. Solve future and present value of 1 problems.
6. Solve future value of ordinary and annuity due problems.
7. Solve present value of ordinary and annuity due problems.
8. Solve present value problems related to deferred annuities and bonds.
9. Apply expected cash flows to present value measurement.

Inside Appendix A

■ **What Do the Numbers Mean?**
A pretty good start (p. 1004)
Up in smoke (p. 1020)
Fed watching (p. 1028)

APPLICATIONS OF TIME VALUE CONCEPTS

OBJECTIVE 1

Identify accounting topics where the time value of money is relevant.

Financial reporting uses different measurements in different situations—historical cost for equipment, net realizable value for some inventories, fair value for investments. As we discussed in Chapter 2, the FASB increasingly is requiring the use of fair values in the measurement of assets and liabilities. According to the FASB's recent standard on fair value measurements, the most useful fair value measures are based on prices established in active markets. However, for many assets and liabilities, market-based fair value information is not readily available. In these cases, fair value can be estimated based on the expected future cash flows related to the asset or liability. Using present value techniques, these future cash flows then can be converted into present values.[1]

Because of the increased use of present values in this and other contexts, it is important to understand present value techniques.[2] We list some of the applications of present value-based measurements to accounting topics below; we discuss many of these in the following chapters.

PRESENT VALUE-BASED ACCOUNTING MEASUREMENTS

1 **NOTES.** Valuing noncurrent receivables and payables that carry no stated interest rate or a lower than market interest rate.

2 **LEASES.** Valuing assets and obligations to be capitalized under long-term leases and measuring the amount of the lease payments and annual leasehold amortization.

3 **PENSIONS AND OTHER POSTRETIREMENT BENEFITS.** Measuring service cost components of employers' postretirement benefits expense and postretirement benefits obligation.

4 **LONG-TERM ASSETS.** Evaluating alternative long-term investments by discounting future cash flows. Determining the value of assets acquired under deferred payment contracts. Measuring impairments of assets.

5 **SINKING FUNDS.** Determining the contributions necessary to accumulate a fund for debt retirements.

6 **BUSINESS COMBINATIONS.** Determining the value of receivables, payables, liabilities, accruals, and commitments acquired or assumed in a "purchase."

7 **DISCLOSURES.** Measuring the value of future cash flows from oil and gas reserves for disclosure in supplementary information.

8 **INSTALLMENT CONTRACTS.** Measuring periodic payments on long-term purchase contracts.

In addition to accounting and business applications, compound interest, annuity, and present value concepts apply to personal finance and investment decisions. In purchasing a home or car, planning for retirement, and evaluating alternative investments, you will need to understand time value of money concepts.

The Nature of Interest

Interest is payment for the use of money. It is the excess cash received or repaid over and above the amount lent or borrowed (**principal**). For example, Corner Bank lends Hillfarm Company $10,000 with the understanding that it will repay $11,500. The excess over $10,000, or $1,500, represents interest expense.

The lender generally states the amount of interest as a rate over a specific period of time. For example, if Hillfarm borrowed $10,000 for one year before repaying $11,500, the rate of interest is 15 percent per year ($1,500 ÷ $10,000). The custom of expressing

---

[1]"Fair Value Measurement," *Statement of Financial Accounting Standards No. 157* (Norwalk, Conn.: FASB, September 2006).

[2]Many recent standards, such as *FASB Statements No. 106, 107, 113, 114, 141, 142, 144, 155,* and *157,* have addressed the issue of present value in the pronouncement or related basis for conclusions.

interest as a percentage rate is an established business practice.[3] In fact, business managers make investing and borrowing decisions on the basis of the rate of interest involved, rather than on the actual dollar amount of interest to be received or paid.

How is the interest rate determined? One important factor is the level of credit risk (risk of nonpayment) involved. Other factors being equal, the higher the credit risk, the higher the interest rate. Low-risk borrowers like **Microsoft** or **Intel** can probably obtain a loan at or slightly below the going market rate of interest. However, a bank would probably charge the neighborhood delicatessen several percentage points above the market rate, if granting the loan at all.

The amount of interest involved in any financing transaction is a function of three variables:

VARIABLES IN INTEREST COMPUTATION

1 PRINCIPAL. The amount borrowed or invested.

2 INTEREST RATE. A percentage of the outstanding principal.

3 TIME. The number of years or fractional portion of a year that the principal is outstanding.

Thus, the following three relationships apply:

- The larger the principal amount, the larger the dollar amount of interest.
- The higher the interest rate, the larger the dollar amount of interest.
- The longer the time period, the larger the dollar amount of interest.

Simple Interest

OBJECTIVE 2

Distinguish between simple and compound interest.

Companies compute **simple interest** on the amount of the principal only. It is the return on (or growth of) the principal for one time period. The following equation expresses simple interest.[4]

$$\text{Interest} = p \times i \times n$$

where

p = principal
i = rate of interest for a single period
n = number of periods

To illustrate, Barstow Electric Inc. borrows $10,000 for three years with a simple interest rate of 8% per year. It computes the total interest it will pay as follows.

$$\begin{aligned}\text{Interest} &= p \times i \times n \\ &= \$10,000 \times .08 \times 3 \\ &= \$2,400\end{aligned}$$

[3]Federal law requires the disclosure of interest rates on an **annual basis** in all contracts. That is, instead of stating the rate as "1% per month," contracts must state the rate as "12% per year" if it is simple interest or "12.68% per year" if it is compounded monthly.

[4]Business mathematics and business finance textbooks traditionally state simple interest as: I(interest) = P(principal) $\times$ R(rate) $\times$ T(time).

If Barstow borrows \$10,000 for three months at 8%, the interest is \$200, computed as follows.

$$\text{Interest} = \$10{,}000 \times .08 \times 3/12$$
$$= \$200$$

Compound Interest

John Maynard Keynes, the legendary English economist, supposedly called it magic. Mayer Rothschild, the founder of the famous European banking firm, proclaimed it the eighth wonder of the world. Today, people continue to extol its wonder and its power. The object of their affection? Compound interest.

We compute **compound interest** on principal **and** on any interest earned that has not been paid or withdrawn. It is the return on (or growth of) the principal for two or more time periods. Compounding computes interest not only on the principal but also on the interest earned to date on that principal, assuming the interest is left on deposit.

To illustrate the difference between simple and compound interest, assume that Vasquez Company deposits \$10,000 in the Last National Bank, where it will earn simple interest of 9% per year. It deposits another \$10,000 in the First State Bank, where it will earn compound interest of 9% per year compounded annually. In both cases, Vasquez will not withdraw any interest until three years from the date of deposit. Illustration A-1 shows the computation of interest Vasquez will receive, as well as its accumulated year-end balance.

Illustration A-1
Simple vs. Compound Interest

Last National Bank

Simple Interest Calculation	Simple Interest	Accumulated Year-end Balance
Year 1 \$10,000.00 × 9%	\$ 900.00	\$10,900.00
Year 2 \$10,000.00 × 9%	900.00	\$11,800.00
Year 3 \$10,000.00 × 9%	900.00	\$12,700.00
	\$2,700	

First State Bank

Compound Interest Calculation	Compound Interest	Accumulated Year-end Balance
Year 1 \$10,000.00 × 9%	\$ 900.00	\$10,900.00
Year 2 \$10,900.00 × 9%	981.00	\$11,881.00
Year 3 \$11,881.00 × 9%	1,069.29	\$12,950.29
	\$2,950.29	

\$250.29 Difference

Note in the illustration above that simple interest uses the initial principal of \$10,000 to compute the interest in all three years. **Compound interest uses the accumulated balance (principal plus interest to date) at each year-end to compute interest in the succeeding year.** This explains the larger balance in the compound interest account.

Obviously, any rational investor would choose compound interest, if available, over simple interest. In the example above, compounding provides \$250.29 of additional interest revenue. For practical purposes, compounding assumes that unpaid interest earned becomes a part of the principal. Furthermore, the accumulated balance at the end of each year becomes the new principal sum on which interest is earned during the next year.

Compound interest is the typical interest computation applied in business situations. This occurs particularly in our economy, where companies use and finance large amounts of long-lived assets over long periods of time. Financial managers view and evaluate their investment opportunities in terms of a series of periodic returns, each of which they can reinvest to yield additional returns. Simple interest usually applies only to short-term investments and debts that involve a time span of one year or less.

The current debate on Social Security reform provides a great context to illustrate the power of compounding. One proposed idea is for the government to give $1,000 to every citizen at birth. This gift would be deposited in an account that would earn interest tax-free until the citizen retires. Assuming the account earns a modest 5% annual return until retirement at age 65, the $1,000 would grow to $23,839. With monthly compounding, the $1,000 deposited at birth would grow to $25,617.

Why start so early? If the government waited until age 18 to deposit the money, it would grow to only $9,906 with annual compounding. That is, reducing the time invested by a third results in more than a 50% reduction in retirement money. The example illustrates the importance of starting early when the power of compounding is involved.

Compound Interest Tables (see pages 1040–1041)

OBJECTIVE 3

Use appropriate compound interest tables.

We present five different types of compound interest tables at the end of this chapter. These tables should help you study this chapter as well as solve other problems involving interest.

INTEREST TABLES AND THEIR CONTENTS

1 **FUTURE VALUE OF 1 TABLE.** Contains the amounts to which 1 will accumulate if deposited now at a specified rate and left for a specified number of periods. (Table 1)

2 **PRESENT VALUE OF 1 TABLE.** Contains the amounts that must be deposited now at a specified rate of interest to equal 1 at the end of a specified number of periods. (Table 2)

3 **FUTURE VALUE OF AN ORDINARY ANNUITY OF 1 TABLE.** Contains the amounts to which periodic rents of 1 will accumulate if the payments (rents) are invested at the **end** of each period at a specified rate of interest for a specified number of periods. (Table 3)

4 **PRESENT VALUE OF AN ORDINARY ANNUITY OF 1 TABLE.** Contains the amounts that must be deposited now at a specified rate of interest to permit withdrawals of 1 at the **end** of regular periodic intervals for the specified number of periods. (Table 4)

5 **PRESENT VALUE OF AN ANNUITY DUE OF 1 TABLE.** Contains the amounts that must be deposited now at a specified rate of interest to permit withdrawals of 1 at the **beginning** of regular periodic intervals for the specified number of periods. (Table 5)

Illustration A-2 lists the general format and content of these tables. It shows how much principal plus interest a dollar accumulates to at the end of each of five periods, at three different rates of compound interest.

Illustration A-2
Excerpt from Table 1

Future Value of 1 At Compound Interest
(Excerpt from Table 1, page 1041)

Period	9%	10%	11%
1	1.09000	1.10000	1.11000
2	1.18810	1.21000	1.23210
3	1.29503	1.33100	1.36763
4	1.41158	1.46410	1.51807
5	1.53862	1.61051	1.68506

The compound tables rely on basic formulas. For example, the formula to determine the future value factor (*FVF*) for 1 is:

$$FVF_{n,i} = (1 + i)^n$$

where

$FVF_{n,i}$ = future value factor for *n* periods at *i* interest

n = number of periods

i = rate of interest for a single period

Financial calculators include preprogrammed $FVF_{n,i}$ and other time value of money formulas. We illustrate the use of these tools to solve time value of money problems in Appendix C at the book's companion website.

To illustrate the use of interest tables to calculate compound amounts, assume an interest rate of 9%. Illustration A-3 shows the future value to which 1 accumulates (the future value factor).

Period	Beginning-of-Period Amount	×	Multiplier (1 + i)	=	End-of-Period Amount*	Formula $(1 + i)^n$
1	1.00000		1.09		1.09000	$(1.09)^1$
2	1.09000		1.09		1.18810	$(1.09)^2$
3	1.18810		1.09		1.29503	$(1.09)^3$

*Note that these amounts appear in Table 1 in the 9% column.

Illustration A-3
Accumulation of Compound Amounts

Throughout our discussion of compound interest tables, note the intentional use of the term **periods** instead of **years**. Interest is generally expressed in terms of an annual rate. However, many business circumstances dictate a compounding period of less than one year. In such circumstances, a company must convert the annual interest rate to correspond to the length of the period. To convert the "annual interest rate" into the "compounding period interest rate," a company **divides the annual rate by the number of compounding periods per year**.

In addition, companies determine the number of periods by **multiplying the number of years involved by the number of compounding periods per year**. To illustrate, assume an investment of $1 for six years at 8% annual interest compounded **quarterly**. Using Table 1, page 1040, read the factor that appears in the 2% column on the 24th row—six years × four compounding periods per year, namely 1.60844, or approximately $1.61. Thus, all compound interest tables use the term **periods**, not **years**, to express the quantity of *n*. Illustration A-4 shows how to determine (1) the interest rate per compounding period and (2) the number of compounding periods in four situations of differing compounding frequency.[5]

12% Annual Interest Rate over 5 Years Compounded	Interest Rate per Compounding Period	Number of Compounding Periods
Annually (1)	.12 ÷ 1 = .12	5 years × 1 compounding per year = 5 periods
Semiannually (2)	.12 ÷ 2 = .06	5 years × 2 compoundings per year = 10 periods
Quarterly (4)	.12 ÷ 4 = .03	5 years × 4 compoundings per year = 20 periods
Monthly (12)	.12 ÷ 12 = .01	5 years × 12 compoundings per year = 60 periods

Illustration A-4
Frequency of Compounding

[5]Because interest is theoretically earned (accruing) every second of every day, it is possible to calculate interest that is **compounded continuously**. Using the natural, or Napierian, system of logarithms facilitates computations involving continuous compounding. As a practical matter, however, most business transactions assume interest to be compounded no more frequently than daily.

How often interest is compounded can substantially affect the rate of return. For example, a 9% annual interest compounded **daily** provides a 9.42% yield, or a difference of 0.42%. The 9.42% is the **effective yield**.[6] The annual interest rate (9%) is the **stated, nominal,** or **face rate**. When the compounding frequency is greater than once a year, the effective interest rate will always exceed the stated rate.

Illustration A-5 shows how compounding for five different time periods affects the effective yield and the amount earned by an investment of $10,000 for one year.

Illustration A-5
Comparison of Different
Compounding Periods

Interest Rate	Compounding Periods				
	Annually	Semiannually	Quarterly	Monthly	Daily
8%	8.00%	8.16%	8.24%	8.30%	8.33%
	$800	$816	$824	$830	$833
9%	9.00%	9.20%	9.31%	9.38%	9.42%
	$900	$920	$931	$938	$942
10%	10.00%	10.25%	10.38%	10.47%	10.52%
	$1,000	$1,025	$1,038	$1,047	$1,052

Fundamental Variables

OBJECTIVE 4

**Identify variables
fundamental to
solving interest
problems.**

The following four variables are fundamental to all compound interest problems.

FUNDAMENTAL VARIABLES

1 **RATE OF INTEREST.** This rate, unless otherwise stated, is an annual rate that must be adjusted to reflect the length of the compounding period if less than a year.

2 **NUMBER OF TIME PERIODS.** This is the number of compounding periods. (A period may be equal to or less than a year.)

3 **FUTURE VALUE.** The value at a future date of a given sum or sums invested assuming compound interest.

4 **PRESENT VALUE.** The value now (present time) of a future sum or sums discounted assuming compound interest.

Illustration A-6 depicts the relationship of these four fundamental variables in a **time diagram**.

[6]The formula for calculating the **effective rate**, in situations where the compounding frequency (n) is greater than once a year, is as follows.

$$\text{Effective rate} = (1 + i)^n - 1$$

To illustrate, if the stated annual rate is 8% compounded quarterly (or 2% per quarter), the effective annual rate is:

$$\begin{aligned} \text{Effective rate} &= (1 + .02)^4 - 1 \\ &= (1.02)^4 - 1 \\ &= 1.0824 - 1 \\ &= .0824 \\ &= 8.24\% \end{aligned}$$

In some cases, all four of these variables are known. However, at least one variable is unknown in many business situations. To better understand and solve the problems in this chapter, we encourage you to sketch compound interest problems in the form of the preceding time diagram.

SINGLE-SUM PROBLEMS

Many business and investment decisions involve a single amount of money that either exists now or will in the future. Single-sum problems are generally classified into one of the following two categories.

1 Computing the **unknown future value** of a known single sum of money that is invested now for a certain number of periods at a certain interest rate.

2 Computing the **unknown present value** of a known single sum of money in the future that is discounted for a certain number of periods at a certain interest rate.

When analyzing the information provided, determine first whether the problem involves a future value or a present value. Then apply the following general rules, depending on the situation:

- **If solving for a future value**, *accumulate* all cash flows to a future point. In this instance, interest increases the amounts or values over time so that the future value exceeds the present value.

- **If solving for a present value**, *discount* all cash flows from the future to the present. In this case, **discounting** reduces the amounts or values, so that the present value is less than the future amount.

Preparation of time diagrams aids in identifying the unknown as an item in the future or the present. Sometimes the problem involves neither a future value nor a present value. Instead, the unknown is the interest or discount rate, or the number of compounding or discounting periods.

Future Value of a Single Sum

To determine the **future value** of a single sum, multiply the future value factor by its present value (principal), as follows.

$$FV = PV \ (FVF_{n,i})$$

where

$$FV = \text{future value}$$
$$PV = \text{present value (principal or single sum)}$$
$$FVF_{n,i} = \text{future value factor for } n \text{ periods at } i \text{ interest}$$

To illustrate, Bruegger Co. wants to determine the future value of $50,000 invested for five years compounded annually at an interest rate of 11%. Illustration A-7 (page 1008) shows this investment situation in time-diagram form.

OBJECTIVE **5**
Solve future and present value of 1 problems.

Illustration A-7
Future Value
Time Diagram
($n = 5$, $i = 11\%$)

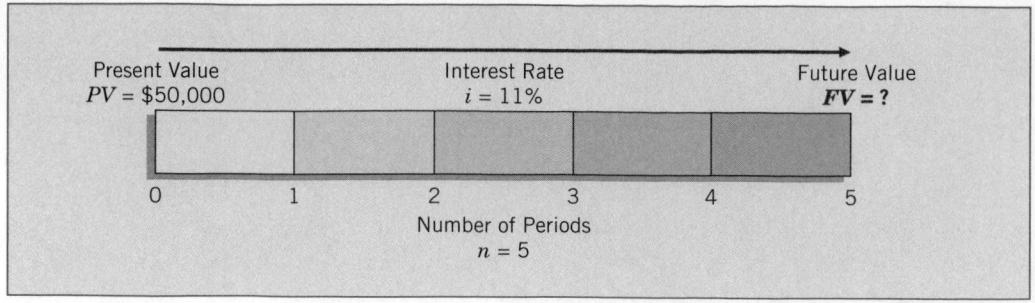

Using the future value formula, Bruegger solves this investment problem as follows.

$$
\begin{aligned}
\text{Future value} &= PV \ (FVF_{n,i}) \\
&= \$50{,}000 \ (FVF_{5,11\%}) \\
&= \$50{,}000 \ (1 + .11)^5 \\
&= \$50{,}000 \ (1.68506) \\
&= \$84{,}253
\end{aligned}
$$

To determine the future value factor of 1.68506 in the formula above, Bruegger uses a financial calculator or reads the appropriate table, in this case Table 1 (11% column and the 5-period row).

Companies can apply this time diagram and formula approach to routine business situations. To illustrate, assume that **Commonwealth Edison Company** deposited \$250 million in an escrow account with **Northern Trust Company** at the beginning of 2008 as a commitment toward a power plant to be completed December 31, 2011. How much will the company have on deposit at the end of four years if interest is 10%, compounded semiannually?

With a known present value of \$250 million, a total of eight compounding periods (4 × 2), and an interest rate of 5% per compounding period (.10 ÷ 2), the company can time-diagram this problem and determine the future value as shown in Illustration A-8.

Illustration A-8
Future Value
Time Diagram
($n = 8$, $i = 5\%$)

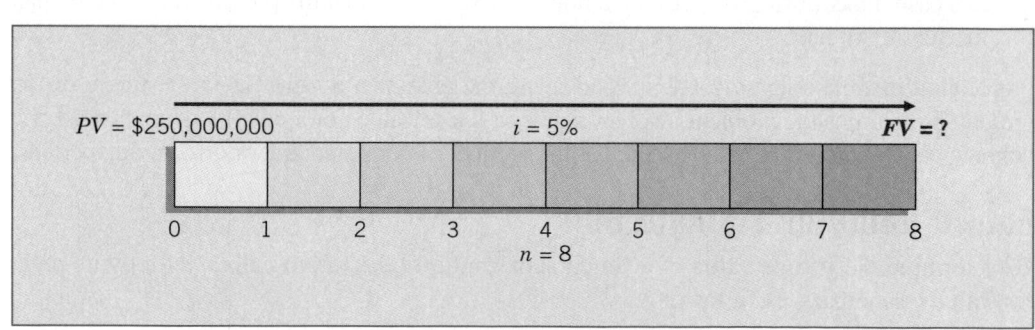

$$
\begin{aligned}
\text{Future value} &= \$250{,}000{,}000 \ (FVF_{8,5\%}) \\
&= \$250{,}000{,}000 \ (1 + .05)^8 \\
&= \$250{,}000{,}000 \ (1.47746) \\
&= \$369{,}365{,}000
\end{aligned}
$$

Using a future value factor found in Table 1 (5% column, 8-period row), we find that the deposit of \$250 million will accumulate to \$369,365,000 by December 31, 2011.

Present Value of a Single Sum

The Bruegger example on pages 1007–1008 showed that $50,000 invested at an annually compounded interest rate of 11% will equal $84,253 at the end of five years. It follows, then, that $84,253, five years in the future, is worth $50,000 now. That is, $50,000 is the present value of $84,253. The **present value** is the amount needed to invest now, to produce a known future value.

The present value is always a smaller amount than the known future value, due to earned and accumulated interest. In determining the future value, a company moves forward in time using a process of **accumulation**. In determining present value, it moves backward in time using a process of **discounting**.

As indicated earlier, a "present value of 1 table" appears at the end of this chapter as Table 2. Illustration A-9 demonstrates the nature of such a table. It shows the present value of 1 for five different periods at three different rates of interest.

Present Value of 1 at Compound Interest
(Excerpt from Table 2, page 1043)

Period	9%	10%	11%
1	0.91743	0.90909	0.90090
2	0.84168	0.82645	0.81162
3	0.77218	0.75132	0.73119
4	0.70843	0.68301	0.65873
5	0.64993	0.62092	0.59345

Illustration A-9
Excerpt from Table 2

The following formula is used to determine the present value of 1 (present value factor):

$$PVF_{n,i} = \frac{1}{(1 + i)^n}$$

where

$$PVF_{n,i} = \text{present value factor for } n \text{ periods at } i \text{ interest}$$

To illustrate, assuming an interest rate of 9%, the present value of 1 discounted for three different periods is as shown in Illustration A-10.

Discount Periods	1	$\div$ $(1 + i)^n$	= Present Value*	Formula $1/(1 + i)^n$
1	1.00000	1.09	.91743	$1/(1.09)^1$
2	1.00000	$(1.09)^2$	.84168	$1/(1.09)^2$
3	1.00000	$(1.09)^3$	.77218	$1/(1.09)^3$

*Note that these amounts appear in Table 2 in the 9% column.

Illustration A-10
Present Value of $1 Discounted at 9% for Three Periods

The present value of any single sum (future value), then, is as follows.

$$PV = FV\ (PVF_{n,i})$$

where

$$PV = \text{present value}$$
$$FV = \text{future value}$$
$$PVF_{n,i} = \text{present value factor for } n \text{ periods at } i \text{ interest}$$

To illustrate, what is the present value of $84,253 to be received or paid in five years discounted at 11% compounded annually? Illustration A-11 (page 1010) shows this problem as a time diagram.

Illustration A-11
Present Value
Time Diagram
($n = 5, i = 11\%$)

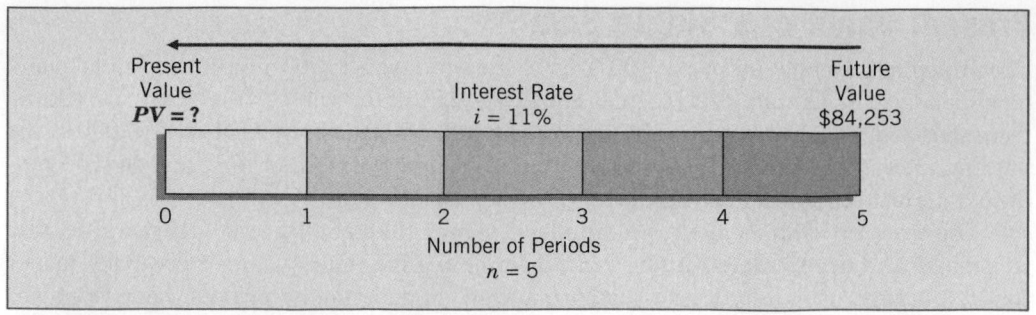

Using the formula, we solve this problem as follows.

$$\text{Present value} = FV\ (PVF_{n,i})$$
$$= \$84,253\ (PVF_{5,11\%})$$
$$= \$84,253 \left(\frac{1}{(1 + .11)^5} \right)$$
$$= \$84,253\ (.59345)$$
$$= \$50,000$$

To determine the present value factor of 0.59345, use a financial calculator or read the present value of a single sum in Table 2 (11% column, 5-period row).

The time diagram and formula approach can be applied in a variety of situations. For example, assume that your rich uncle decides to give you $2,000 for a trip to Europe when you graduate from college three years from now. He proposes to finance the trip by investing a sum of money now at 8% compound interest that will provide you with $2,000 upon your graduation. The only conditions are that you graduate and that you tell him how much to invest now.

To impress your uncle, you set up the time diagram in Illustration A-12 and solve this problem as follows.

Illustration A-12
Present Value
Time Diagram
($n = 3, i = 8\%$)

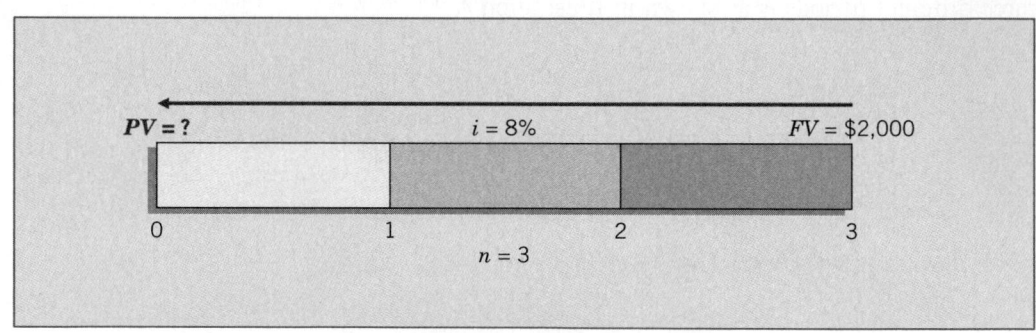

$$\text{Present value} = \$2,000\ (PVF_{3,8\%})$$
$$= \$2,000 \left(\frac{1}{(1 + .08)^3} \right)$$
$$= \$2,000\ (.79383)$$
$$= \$1,587.66$$

Advise your uncle to invest $1,587.66 now to provide you with $2,000 upon graduation. To satisfy your uncle's other condition, you must pass this course (and many more).

Solving for Other Unknowns in Single-Sum Problems

In computing either the future value or the present value in the previous single-sum illustrations, both the number of periods and the interest rate were known. In many business situations, both the future value and the present value are known, but the number of periods or the interest rate is unknown. The following two examples are single-sum problems (future value and present value) with either an unknown number of periods (n) or an unknown interest rate (i). These examples, and the accompanying solutions, demonstrate that knowing any three of the four values (future value, FV; present value, PV; number of periods, n; interest rate, i) allows you to derive the remaining unknown variable.

Example—Computation of the Number of Periods

The Village of Somonauk wants to accumulate $70,000 for the construction of a veterans monument in the town square. At the beginning of the current year, the Village deposited $47,811 in a memorial fund that earns 10% interest compounded annually. How many years will it take to accumulate $70,000 in the memorial fund?

In this illustration, the Village knows both the present value ($47,811) and the future value ($70,000), along with the interest rate of 10%. Illustration A-13 depicts this investment problem as a time diagram.

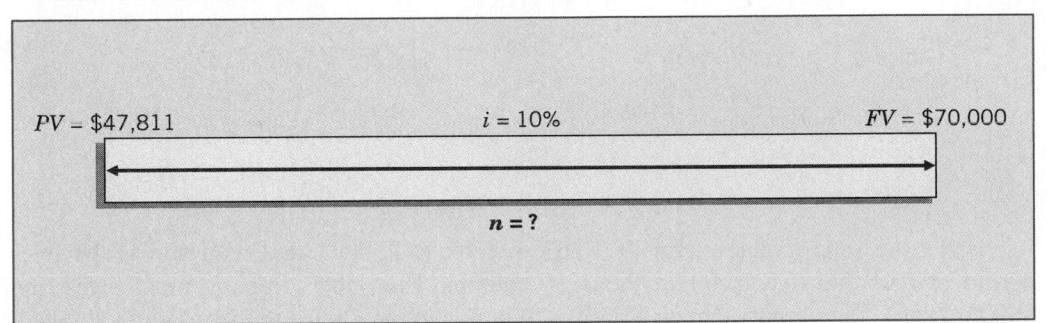

Illustration A-13
Time Diagram to Solve for Unknown Number of Periods

Knowing both the present value and the future value allows the Village to solve for the unknown number of periods. It may use either the future value or the present value formulas, as shown in Illustration A-14.

Future Value Approach	Present Value Approach
$FV = PV\,(FVF_{n,10\%})$	$PV = FV\,(PVF_{n,10\%})$
$\$70{,}000 = \$47{,}811\,(FVF_{n,10\%})$	$\$47{,}811 = \$70{,}000\,(PVF_{n,10\%})$
$FVF_{n,10\%} = \dfrac{\$70{,}000}{\$47{,}811} = 1.46410$	$PVF_{n,10\%} = \dfrac{\$47{,}811}{\$70{,}000} = .68301$

Illustration A-14
Solving for Unknown Number of Periods

Using the future value factor of 1.46410, refer to Table 1 and read down the 10% column to find that factor in the four-period row. Thus, it will take four years for the $47,811 to accumulate to $70,000 if invested at 10% interest compounded annually. Or, using the present value factor of 0.68301, refer to Table 2 and read down the 10% column to find that factor in the four-period row.

Example—Computation of the Interest Rate

Advanced Design, Inc. needs $1,409,870 for basic research five years from now. The company currently has $800,000 to invest for that purpose. At what rate of interest must it invest the $800,000 to fund basic research projects of $1,409,870, five years from now?

The time diagram in Illustration A-15 depicts this investment situation.

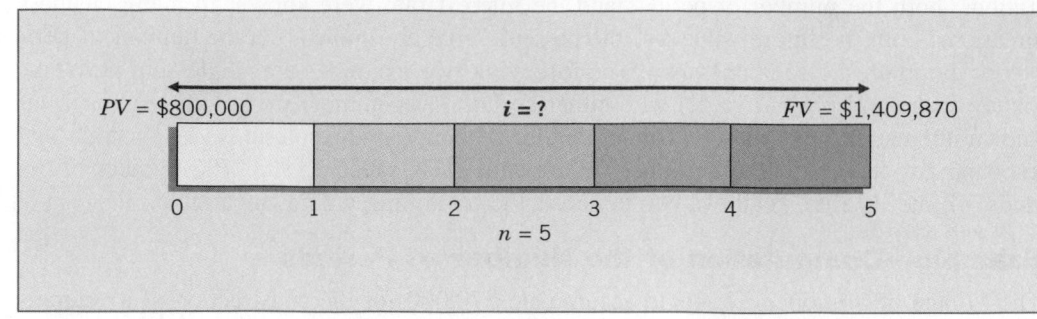

Advanced Design may determine the unknown interest rate from either the future value approach or the present value approach, as Illustration A-16 shows.

Future Value Approach	Present Value Approach
$FV = PV (FVF_{5,i})$	$PV = FV (PVF_{5,i})$
$\$1,409,870 = \$800,000 (FVF_{5,i})$	$\$800,000 = \$1,409,870 (PVF_{5,i})$
$FVF_{5,i} = \dfrac{\$1,409,870}{\$800,000} = 1.76234$	$PVF_{5,i} = \dfrac{\$800,000}{\$1,409,870} = .56743$

Using the future value factor of 1.76234, refer to Table 1 and read across the five-period row to find that factor in the 12% column. Thus, the company must invest the $800,000 at 12% to accumulate to $1,409,870 in five years. Or, using the present value factor of .56743 and Table 2, again find that factor at the juncture of the five-period row and the 12% column.

ANNUITIES

The preceding discussion involved only the accumulation or discounting of a single principal sum. However, many situations arise in which a series of dollar amounts are paid or received periodically, such as installment loans or sales; regular, partially recovered invested funds; or a series of realized cost savings.

For example, a life insurance contract involves a series of equal payments made at equal intervals of time. Such a process of periodic payment represents the accumulation of a sum of money through an annuity. An **annuity**, by definition, requires the following: (1) periodic payments or receipts (called **rents**) of the same amount, (2) the same-length interval between such rents, and (3) compounding of **interest** once each interval. The **future value of an annuity** is the sum of all the rents plus the accumulated compound interest on them.

Note that the rents may occur at either the beginning or the end of the periods. If the rents occur at the end of each period, an annuity is classified as an **ordinary annuity**. If the rents occur at the beginning of each period, an annuity is classified as an **annuity due**.

Future Value of an Ordinary Annuity

One approach to determining the future value of an annuity computes the value to which **each** of the rents in the series will accumulate, and then totals their individual future values.

For example, assume that $1 is deposited at the **end** of each of five years (an ordinary annuity) and earns 12% interest compounded annually. Illustration A-17 shows the computation of the future value, using the "future value of 1" table (Table 1) for each of the five $1 rents.

End of Period in Which $1.00 Is to be Invested						Value at End of Year 5
Present	1	2	3	4	5	
	$1.00 →					$1.57352
		$1.00 →				1.40493
			$1.00 →			1.25440
				$1.00 →		1.12000
					$1.00	1.00000
Total (future value of an ordinary annuity of $1.00 for 5 periods at 12%)						$6.35285

Illustration A-17
Solving for the Future Value of an Ordinary Annuity

Because an ordinary annuity consists of rents deposited at the end of the period, those rents earn no interest during the period. For example, the third rent earns interest for only two periods (periods four and five). It earns no interest for the third period since it is not deposited until the end of the third period. When computing the future value of an ordinary annuity, the number of compounding periods will always be **one less than the number of rents**.

The foregoing procedure for computing the future value of an ordinary annuity always produces the correct answer. However, it can become cumbersome if the number of rents is large. A formula provides a more efficient way of expressing the future value of an ordinary annuity of 1. This formula sums the individual rents plus the compound interest, as follows:

$$FVF\text{-}OA_{n,i} = \frac{(1+i)^n - 1}{i}$$

where

$$FVF\text{-}OA_{n,i} = \text{future value factor of an ordinary annuity}$$
$$i = \text{rate of interest per period}$$
$$n = \text{number of compounding periods}$$

For example, $FVF\text{-}OA_{5,12\%}$ refers to the value to which an ordinary annuity of 1 will accumulate in five periods at 12% interest.

Using the formula above has resulted in the development of tables, similar to those used for the "future value of 1" and the "present value of 1" for both an ordinary annuity and an annuity due. Illustration A-18 provides an excerpt from the "future value of an ordinary annuity of 1" table.

Future Value of an Ordinary Annuity of 1 (Excerpt from Table 3, page 1045)			
Period	10%	11%	12%
1	1.00000	1.00000	1.00000
2	2.10000	2.11000	2.12000
3	3.31000	3.34210	3.37440
4	4.64100	4.70973	4.77933
5	6.10510	6.22780	6.35285*

Illustration A-18
Excerpt from Table 3

*Note that this annuity table factor is the same as the sum of the future values of 1 factors shown in Illustration A-17.

Interpreting the table, if $1 is invested at the end of each year for four years at 11% interest compounded annually, the value of the annuity at the end of the fourth year is $4.71 (4.70973 × $1.00). Now, multiply the factor from the appropriate line and column of the table by the dollar amount of **one rent** involved in an ordinary annuity. The result: the accumulated sum of the rents and the compound interest to the date of the last rent.

The following formula computes the future value of an ordinary annuity.

$$\text{Future value of an ordinary annuity} = R \ (FVF\text{-}OA_{n,i})$$

where

$$R = \text{periodic rent}$$
$$FVF\text{-}OA_{n,i} = \text{future value of an ordinary annuity factor}$$
$$\text{for } n \text{ periods at } i \text{ interest}$$

To illustrate, what is the future value of five $5,000 deposits made at the end of each of the next five years, earning interest of 12%? Illustration A-19 depicts this problem as a time diagram.

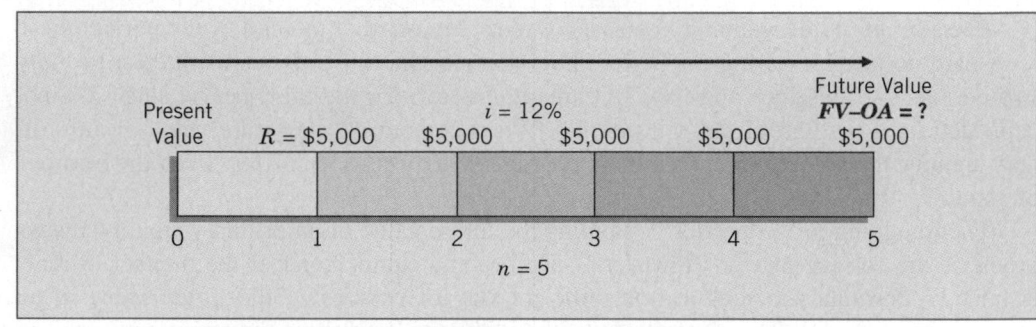

Use of the formula solves this investment problem as follows.

$$\text{Future value of an ordinary annuity} = R \ (FVF\text{-}OA_{n,i})$$
$$= \$5,000 \ (FVF\text{-}OA_{5,12\%})$$
$$= \$5,000 \left(\frac{(1 + .12)^5 - 1}{.12} \right)$$
$$= \$5,000 \ (6.35285)$$
$$= \$31,764.25$$

To determine the future value of an ordinary annuity factor of 6.35285 in the formula above, use a financial calculator or read the appropriate table, in this case, Table 3 (12% column and the 5-period row).

To illustrate these computations in a business situation, assume that Hightown Electronics deposits $75,000 at the end of each six-month period for the next three years, to accumulate enough money to meet debts that mature in three years. What is the future value that the company will have on deposit at the end of three years if the annual interest rate is 10%? The time diagram in Illustration A-20 depicts this situation.

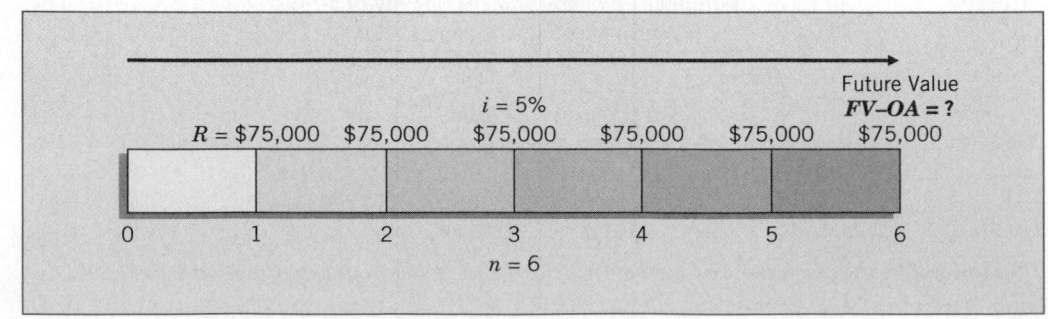

The formula solution for the Hightown Electronics situation is as follows.

$$\text{Future value of an ordinary annuity} = R \ (FVF\text{-}OA_{n,i})$$
$$= \$75,000 \ (FVF\text{-}OA_{6,5\%})$$
$$= \$75,000 \left(\frac{(1 + .05)^6 - 1}{.05} \right)$$
$$= \$75,000 \ (6.80191)$$
$$= \$510,143.25$$

Thus, six six-month deposits of \$75,000 earning 5% per period will grow to \$510,143.25.

Future Value of an Annuity Due

The preceding analysis of an ordinary annuity assumed that the periodic rents occur at the **end** of each period. Recall that an **annuity due** assumes periodic rents occur at the **beginning** of each period. This means an annuity due will accumulate interest during the first period (in contrast to an ordinary annuity rent, which will not). In other words, the two types of annuities differ in the number of interest accumulation periods involved.

If rents occur at the end of a period (ordinary annuity), in determining the **future value of an annuity** there will be one less interest period than if the rents occur at the beginning of the period (annuity due). Illustration A-21 shows this distinction.

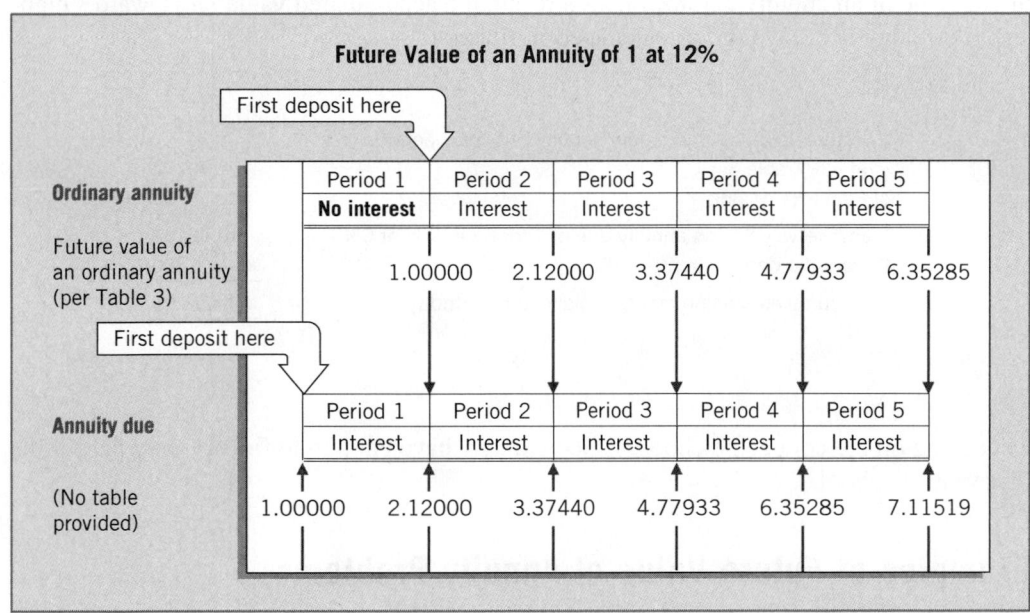

Illustration A-21
Comparison of the Future Value of an Ordinary Annuity with an Annuity Due

In this example, the cash flows from the annuity due come exactly one period earlier than for an ordinary annuity. As a result, the future value of the annuity due factor is exactly 12% higher than the ordinary annuity factor. For example, the value of an ordinary annuity factor at the end of period one at 12% is 1.00000, whereas for an annuity due it is 1.12000.

To find the future value of an annuity due factor, multiply the future value of an ordinary annuity factor by 1 plus the interest rate. For example, to determine the future value of an annuity due interest factor for five periods at 12% compound interest, simply multiply the future value of an ordinary annuity interest factor for five periods (6.35285), by one plus the interest rate (1 + .12), to arrive at 7.11519 (6.35285 × 1.12).

To illustrate the use of the ordinary annuity tables in converting to an annuity due, assume that Sue Lotadough plans to deposit \$800 a year on each birthday of her son Howard.

She makes the first deposit on his tenth birthday, at 6% interest compounded annually. Sue wants to know the amount she will have accumulated for college expenses by her son's eighteenth birthday.

If the first deposit occurs on Howard's tenth birthday, Sue will make a total of eight deposits over the life of the annuity (assume no deposit on the eighteenth birthday), as shown in Illustration A-22. Because all the deposits are made at the beginning of the periods, they represent an annuity due.

Illustration A-22
Annuity Due Time
Diagram

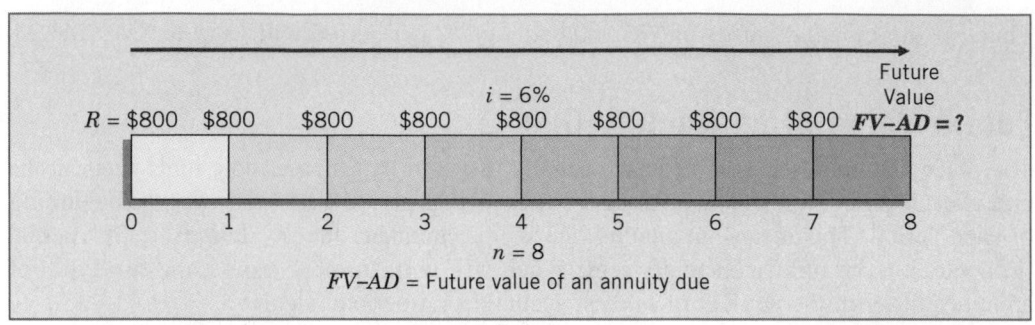

Referring to the "future value of an ordinary annuity of 1" table for eight periods at 6%, Sue finds a factor of 9.89747. She then multiplies this factor by (1 + .06) to arrive at the future value of an annuity due factor. As a result, the accumulated value on Howard's eighteenth birthday is $8,393.05, as calculated in Illustration A-23.

Illustration A-23
Computation of
Accumulated Value of
Annuity Due

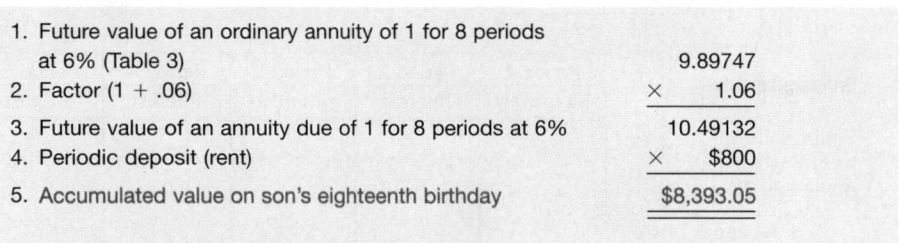

Depending on the college he chooses, Howard may have enough to finance only part of his first year of school.

Examples of Future Value of Annuity Problems

The foregoing annuity examples relied on three known values—amount of each rent, interest rate, and number of periods. Using these values enables us to determine the unknown fourth value, future value.

The first two future value problems we present illustrate the computations of (1) the amount of the rents and (2) the number of rents. The third problem illustrates the computation of the future value of an annuity due.

Computation of Rent

Assume that you plan to accumulate $14,000 for a down payment on a condominium apartment five years from now. For the next five years, you earn an annual return of 8% compounded semiannually. How much should you deposit at the end of each six-month period?

The $14,000 is the future value of 10 (5 × 2) semiannual end-of-period payments of an unknown amount, at an interest rate of 4% (8% ÷ 2). Illustration A-24 depicts this problem as a time diagram.

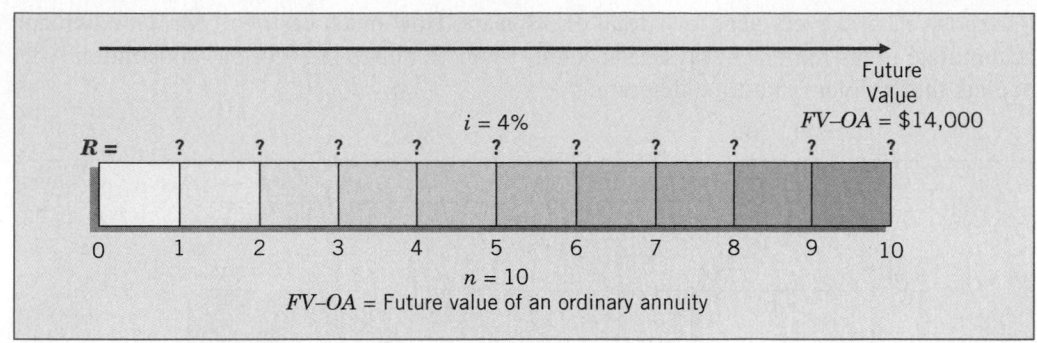

Illustration A-24
Future Value of Ordinary
Annuity Time Diagram
(n = 10, i = 4%)

Using the formula for the future value of an ordinary annuity, you determine the amount of each rent as follows.

$$\text{Future value of an ordinary annuity} = R\ (FVF\text{-}OA_{n,i})$$

$$\$14{,}000 = R\ (FVF\text{-}OA_{10,4\%})$$

$$\$14{,}000 = R(12.00611)$$

$$R = \$1{,}166.07$$

Thus, you must make 10 semiannual deposits of $1,166.07 each in order to accumulate $14,000 for your down payment.

Computation of the Number of Periodic Rents

Suppose that a company's goal is to accumulate $117,332 by making periodic deposits of $20,000 at the end of each year, which will earn 8% compounded annually while accumulating. How many deposits must it make?

The $117,332 represents the future value of (n = ?) $20,000 deposits, at an 8% annual rate of interest. Illustration A-25 depicts this problem in a time diagram.

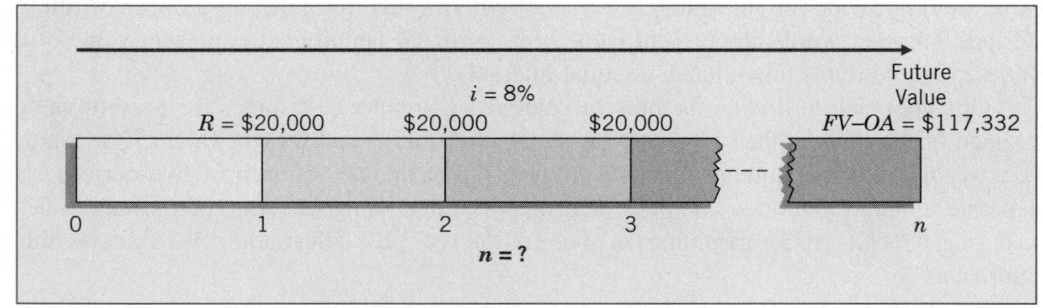

Illustration A-25
Future Value of Ordinary
Annuity Time Diagram, to
Solve for Unknown
Number of Periods

Using the future value of an ordinary annuity formula, the company obtains the following factor.

$$\text{Future value of an ordinary annuity} = R\ (FVF\text{-}OA_{n,i})$$

$$\$117{,}332 = \$20{,}000\ (FVF\text{-}OA_{n,8\%})$$

$$FVF\text{-}OA_{n,8\%} = \frac{\$117{,}332}{\$20{,}000} = 5.86660$$

Use Table 3 and read down the 8% column to find 5.86660 in the five-period row. Thus, the company must make five deposits of $20,000 each.

Computation of the Future Value

To create his retirement fund, Walter Goodwrench, a mechanic, now works weekends. Mr. Goodwrench deposits $2,500 today in a savings account that earns 9% interest. He plans to deposit $2,500 every year for a total of 30 years. How much cash will Mr. Goodwrench accumulate in his retirement savings account, when he retires in 30 years? Illustration A-26 depicts this problem in a time diagram.

Illustration A-26
Future Value Annuity
Due Time Diagram
($n = 30$, $i = 9\%$)

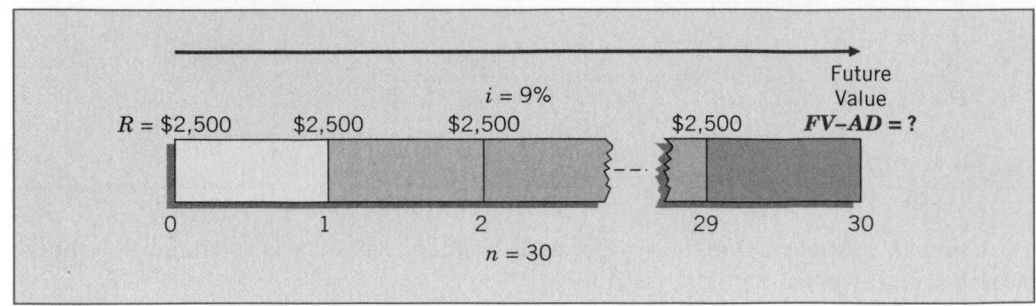

Using the "future value of an ordinary annuity of 1" table, Mr. Goodwrench computes the solution as shown in Illustration A-27.

Illustration A-27
Computation of
Accumulated Value of an
Annuity Due

1. Future value of an ordinary annuity of 1 for 30 periods at 9%	136.30754
2. Factor (1 + .09)	× 1.09
3. Future value of an annuity due of 1 for 30 periods at 9%	148.57522
4. Periodic rent	× $2,500
5. Accumulated value at end of 30 years	$371,438

Present Value of an Ordinary Annuity

OBJECTIVE 7

Solve present value of ordinary and annuity due problems.

The present value of an annuity is **the single sum** that, if invested at compound interest now, would provide for an annuity (a series of withdrawals) for a certain number of future periods. In other words, the present value of an ordinary annuity is the present value of a series of equal rents, to withdraw at equal intervals.

One approach to finding the present value of an annuity determines the present value of each of the rents in the series and then totals their individual present values. For example, we may view an annuity of $1, to be received at the **end** of each of five periods, as separate amounts. We then compute each present value using the table of present values (see pages 1042–1043), assuming an interest rate of 12%. Illustration A-28 shows this approach.

Illustration A-28
Solving for the Present
Value of an Ordinary
Annuity

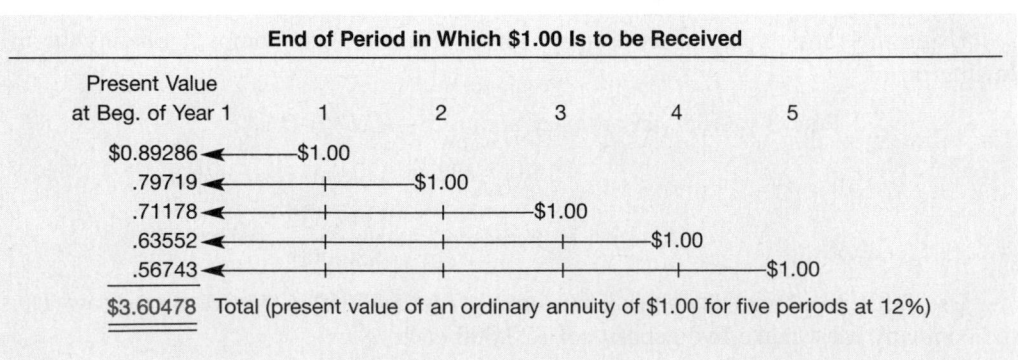

This computation tells us that if we invest the single sum of $3.60 today at 12% interest for five periods, we will be able to withdraw $1 at the end of each period for five periods. We can summarize this cumbersome procedure by the following formula.

$$PVF\text{-}OA_{n,i} = \frac{1 - \dfrac{1}{(1+i)^n}}{i}$$

The expression $PVF\text{-}OA_{n,i}$ refers to the present value of an ordinary annuity of 1 factor for n periods at i interest. Ordinary annuity tables base present values on this formula. Illustration A-29 shows an excerpt from such a table.

Illustration A-29
Excerpt from Table 4

Present Value of an Ordinary Annuity of 1
(Excerpt from Table 4, page 1047)

Period	10%	11%	12%
1	0.90909	0.90090	0.89286
2	1.73554	1.71252	1.69005
3	2.48685	2.44371	2.40183
4	3.16986	3.10245	3.03735
5	3.79079	3.69590	3.60478*

*Note that this annuity table factor is equal to the sum of the present value of 1 factors shown in Illustration A-28.

The general formula for the present value of any ordinary annuity is as follows.

Present value of an ordinary annuity = R ($PVF\text{-}OA_{n,i}$)

where

$$R = \text{periodic rent (ordinary annuity)}$$
$$PVF\text{-}OA_{n,i} = \text{present value of an ordinary annuity of 1}$$
$$\text{for } n \text{ periods at } i \text{ interest}$$

To illustrate with an example, what is the present value of rental receipts of $6,000 each, to be received at the end of each of the next five years when discounted at 12%? This problem may be time-diagrammed and solved as shown in Illustration A-30.

Illustration A-30
Present Value of Ordinary
Annuity Time Diagram

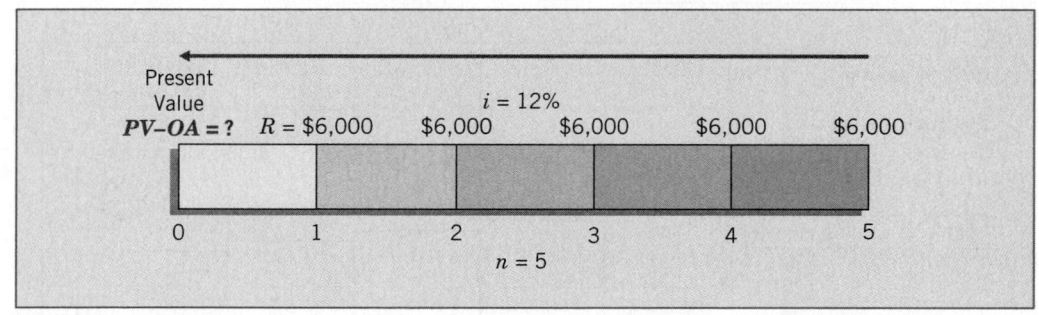

The formula for this calculation is as shown below.

$$\text{Present value of an ordinary annuity} = R\ (PVF\text{-}OA_{n,i})$$
$$= \$6,000\ (PVF\text{-}OA_{5,12\%})$$
$$= \$6,000\ (3.60478)$$
$$= \$21,628.68$$

The present value of the five ordinary annuity rental receipts of $6,000 each is $21,628.68. To determine the present value of the ordinary annuity factor 3.60478, use a financial calculator or read the appropriate table, in this case Table 4 (12% column and 5-period row).

Time value of money concepts also can be relevant to public policy debates. For example, several states had to determine how to receive the payments from tobacco companies as settlement for a national lawsuit against the companies for the healthcare costs of smoking.

The **State of Wisconsin** was due to collect 25 years of payments totaling $5.6 billion. The state could wait to collect the payments, or it could sell the payments to an investment bank (a process called *securitization*). If it were to sell the payments, it would receive a lump-sum payment today of $1.26 billion. Is this a good deal for the state? Assuming a discount rate of 8% and that the payments will be received in equal amounts (e.g., an annuity), the present value of the tobacco payment is:

$$\$5.6 \text{ billion} \div 25 = \$224 \text{ million} \times 10.67478^* = \$2.39 \text{ billion}$$
$$^*PV\text{-}OA_{(i = 8\%, n = 25)}$$

Why would some in the state be willing to take just $1.26 billion today for an annuity whose present value is almost twice that amount? One reason is that Wisconsin was facing a hole in its budget that could be plugged in part by the lump-sum payment. Also, some believed that the risk of not getting paid by the tobacco companies in the future makes it prudent to get the money earlier.

If this latter reason has merit, then the present value computation above should have been based on a higher interest rate. Assuming a discount rate of 15%, the present value of the annuity is $1.448 billion ($5.6 billion ÷ 25 = $224 million; $224 million × 6.46415), which is much closer to the lump-sum payment offered to the State of Wisconsin.

Present Value of an Annuity Due

In our discussion of the present value of an ordinary annuity, we discounted the final rent based on the number of rent periods. In determining the present value of an annuity due, there is always one fewer discount period. Illustration A-31 shows this distinction.

Illustration A-31
Comparison of Present Value of an Ordinary Annuity with an Annuity Due

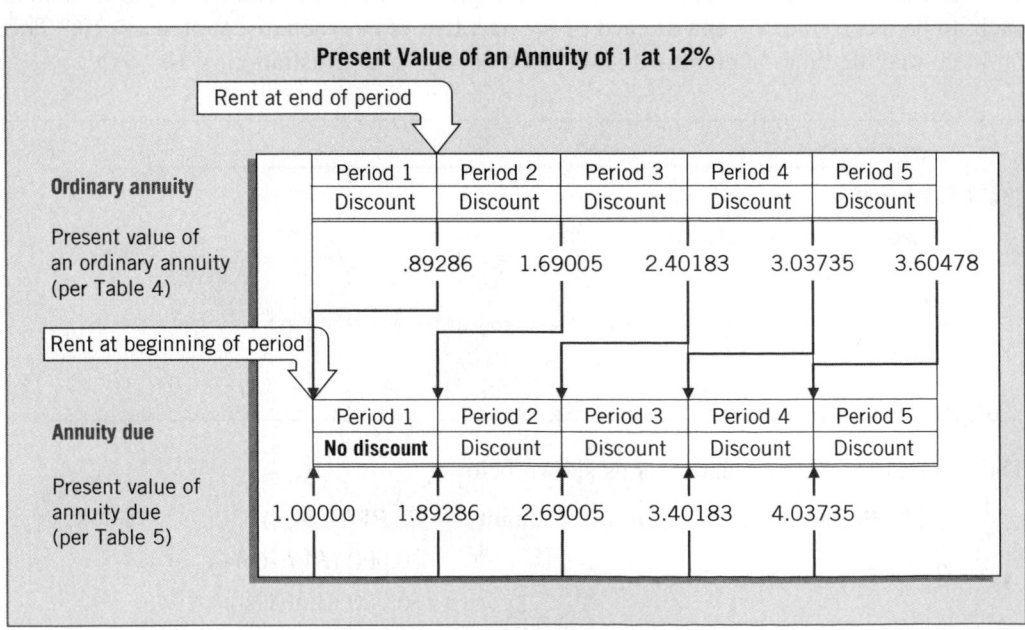

Because each cash flow comes exactly one period sooner in the present value of the annuity due, the present value of the cash flows is exactly 12% higher than the present value of an ordinary annuity. Thus, **to find the present value of an annuity due factor,**

multiply the present value of an ordinary annuity factor by 1 plus the interest rate (that is, $1 + i$).

To determine the present value of an annuity due interest factor for five periods at 12% interest, take the present value of an ordinary annuity for five periods at 12% interest (3.60478) and multiply it by 1.12 to arrive at the present value of an annuity due, 4.03735 (3.60478 × 1.12). We provide present value of annuity due factors in Table 5.

To illustrate, Space Odyssey, Inc., rents a communications satellite for four years with annual rental payments of $4.8 million to be made at the beginning of each year. If the relevant annual interest rate is 11%, what is the present value of the rental obligations? Illustration A-32 shows the company's time diagram for this problem.

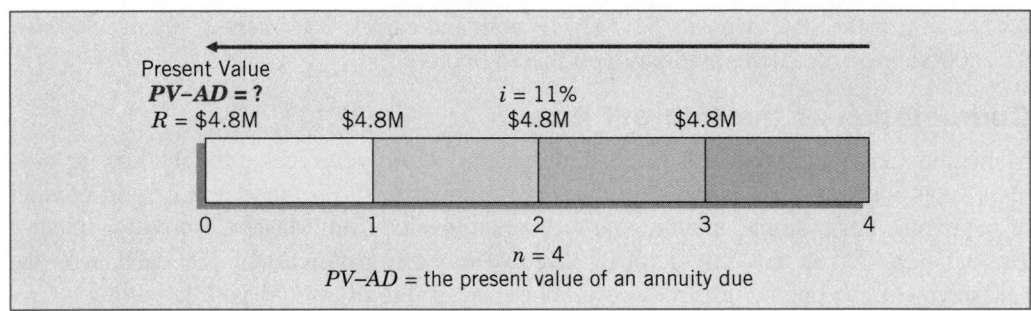

Illustration A-32
Present Value of Annuity Due Time Diagram ($n = 4$, $i = 11\%$)

Illustration A-33 shows the computations to solve this problem.

1. Present value of an ordinary annuity of 1 for 4 periods at 11% (Table 4)	3.10245
2. Factor (1 + .11)	× 1.11
3. Present value of an annuity due of 1 for 4 periods at 11%	3.44372
4. Periodic deposit (rent)	× $4,800,000
5. Present value of payments	$16,529,856

Illustration A-33
Computation of Present Value of an Annuity Due

Using Table 5 also locates the desired factor 3.44371 and computes the present value of the lease payments to be $16,529,808. (The difference in computations is due to rounding.)

Examples of Present Value of Annuity Problems

In the following three examples, we demonstrate the computation of (1) the present value, (2) the interest rate, and (3) the amount of each rent.

Computation of the Present Value of an Ordinary Annuity

You have just won a lottery totaling $4,000,000. You learn that you will receive a check in the amount of $200,000 at the end of each of the next 20 years. What amount have you really won? That is, what is the present value of the $200,000 checks you will receive over the next 20 years? Illustration A-34 (page 1022) shows a time diagram of this enviable situation (assuming an appropriate interest rate of 10%).

You calculate the present value as follows:

$$\text{Present value of an ordinary annuity} = R \ (PVF\text{-}OA_{n,i})$$
$$= \$200,000 \ (PVF\text{-}OA_{20,10\%})$$
$$= \$200,000 \ (8.51356)$$
$$= \$1,702,712$$

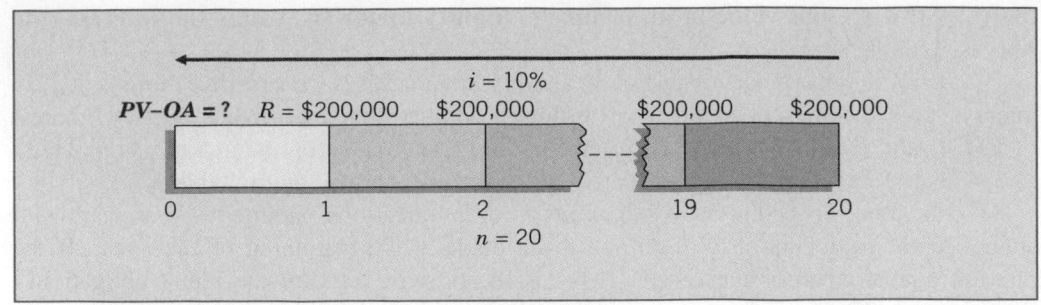

As a result, if the state deposits $1,702,712 now and earns 10% interest, it can withdraw $200,000 a year for 20 years to pay you the $4,000,000.

Computation of the Interest Rate

Many shoppers use credit cards to make purchases. When you receive the invoice for payment, you may pay the total amount due or you may pay the balance in a certain number of payments. For example, assume you receive an invoice from MasterCard with a balance due of $528.77. You may pay it off in 12 equal monthly payments of $50 each, with the first payment due one month from now. What rate of interest would you be paying?

The $528.77 represents the present value of the 12 payments of $50 each at an unknown rate of interest. The time diagram in Illustration A-35 depicts this situation.

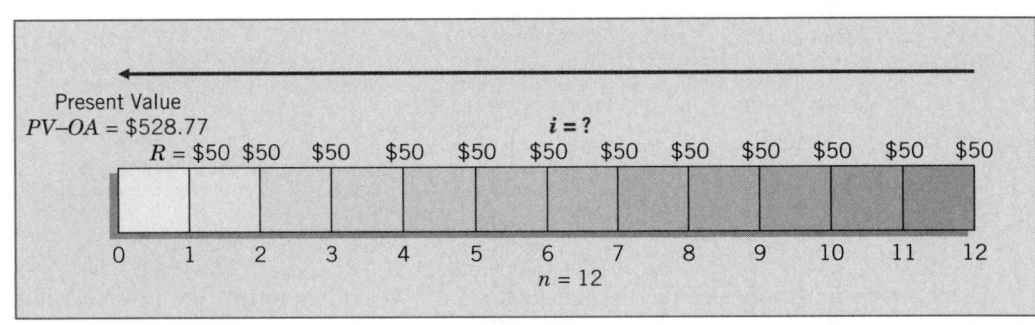

You calculate the rate as follows.

$$\text{Present value of an ordinary annuity} = R \, (PVF\text{-}OA_{n,i})$$

$$\$528.77 = \$50 \, (PVF\text{-}OA_{12,i})$$

$$(PVF\text{-}OA_{12,i}) = \frac{\$528.77}{\$50} = 10.57540$$

Referring to Table 4 and reading across the 12-period row, you find 10.57534 in the 2% column. Since 2% is a monthly rate, the nominal annual rate of interest is 24% (12 × 2%). The effective annual rate is 26.82413% $[(1 + .02)^{12} - 1]$. Obviously, you are better off paying the entire bill now if possible.

Computation of a Periodic Rent

Norm and Jackie Remmers have saved $36,000 to finance their daughter Dawna's college education. They deposited the money in the Bloomington Savings and Loan Association, where it earns 4% interest compounded semiannually. What equal amounts can their daughter withdraw at the end of every six months during her four college years, without exhausting the fund? Illustration A-36 shows a time diagram of this situation.

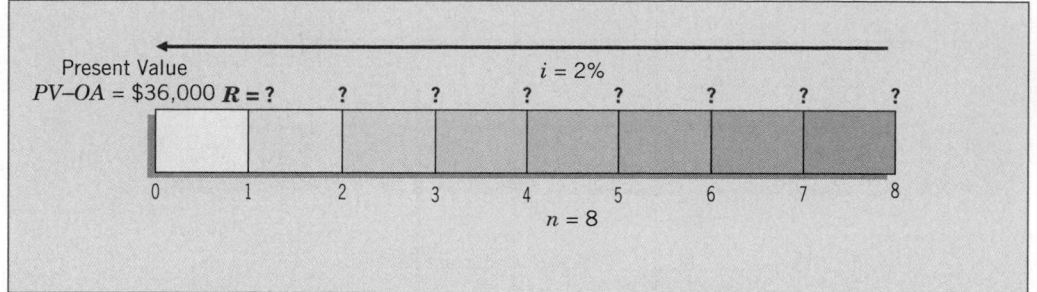

Determining the answer by simply dividing $36,000 by eight withdrawals is wrong. Why? Because that ignores the interest earned on the money remaining on deposit. Dawna must consider that interest is compounded semiannually at 2% (4% ÷ 2) for eight periods (4 years × 2). Thus, using the same present value of an ordinary annuity formula, she determines the amount of each withdrawal that she can make as follows.

$$\text{Present value of an ordinary annuity} = R\ (PVF\text{-}OA_{n,i})$$
$$\$36,000 = R\ (PVF\text{-}OA_{8,2\%})$$
$$\$36,000 = R\ (7.32548)$$
$$R = \$4,914.35$$

MORE COMPLEX SITUATIONS

Solving time value problems often requires using more than one table. For example, a business problem may need computations of both present value of a single sum and present value of an annuity. Two such common situations are:

1 Deferred annuities.
2 Bond problems.

> **OBJECTIVE 8**
> **Solve present value problems related to deferred annuities and bonds.**

Deferred Annuities

A **deferred annuity** is an annuity in which the rents begin after a specified number of periods. A deferred annuity does not begin to produce rents until two or more periods have expired. For example, "an **ordinary annuity** of six annual rents deferred 4 years" means that no rents will occur during the first 4 years, and that the first of the six rents will occur at the end of the fifth year. "An **annuity due** of six annual rents deferred four years" means that no rents will occur during the first four years, and that the first of six rents will occur at the beginning of the fifth year.

Future Value of a Deferred Annuity

Computing the future value of a deferred annuity is relatively straightforward. Because there is no accumulation or investment on which interest may accrue, the future value of a deferred annuity is the same as the future value of an annuity not deferred. That is, computing the future value simply ignores the deferred period.

To illustrate, assume that Sutton Corporation plans to purchase a land site in six years for the construction of its new corporate headquarters. Because of cash flow problems, Sutton budgets deposits of $80,000, on which it expects to earn 5% annually, only at the end of the fourth, fifth, and sixth periods. What future value will Sutton have accumulated at the end of the sixth year? Illustration A-37 (page 1024) shows a time diagram of this situation.

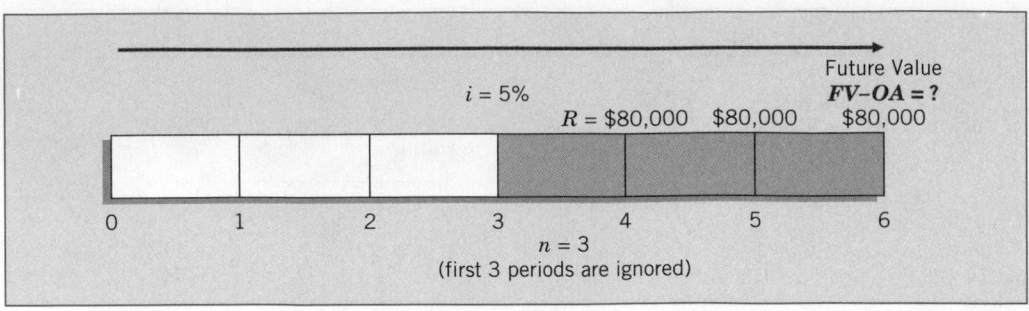

Sutton determines the value accumulated by using the standard formula for the future value of an ordinary annuity:

$$\text{Future value of an ordinary annuity} = R \, (FVF\text{-}OA_{n,i})$$
$$= \$80,000 \, (FVF\text{-}OA_{3,5\%})$$
$$= \$80,000 \, (3.15250)$$
$$= \$252,200$$

Present Value of a Deferred Annuity

Computing the present value of a deferred annuity must recognize the interest that accrues on the original investment during the deferral period.

To compute the present value of a deferred annuity, we compute the present value of an ordinary annuity of 1 as if the rents had occurred for the entire period. We then subtract the present value of rents that were not received during the deferral period. We are left with the present value of the rents actually received subsequent to the deferral period.

To illustrate, Tom Bytehead has developed and copyrighted tutorial software for students in advanced accounting. He agrees to sell the copyright to Campus Micro Systems for six annual payments of $5,000 each. The payments will begin five years from today. Given an annual interest rate of 8%, what is the present value of the six payments?

This situation is an ordinary annuity of six payments deferred four periods. The time diagram in Illustration A-38 depicts this sales agreement.

Illustration A-38
Time Diagram for Present
Value of Deferred Annuity

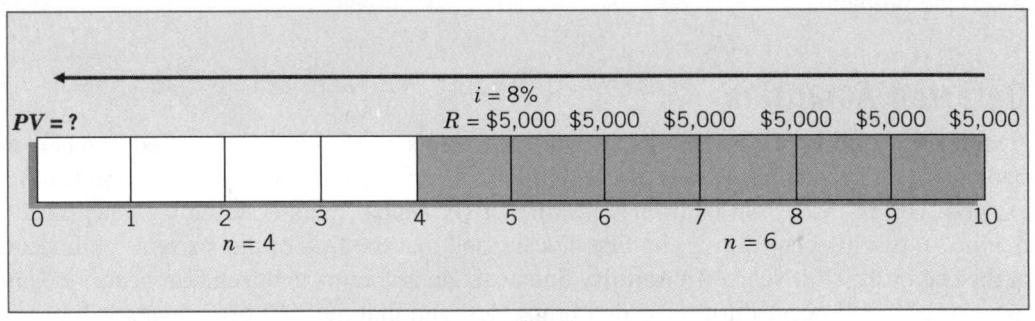

Two options are available to solve this problem. The first is to use only Table 4, as shown in Illustration A-39.

Illustration A-39
Computation of the
Present Value of a
Deferred Annuity

1. Each periodic rent		$5,000
2. Present value of an ordinary annuity of 1 for total periods (10) [number of rents (6) plus number of deferred periods (4)] at 8%	6.71008	
3. Less: Present value of an ordinary annuity of 1 for the number of deferred periods (4) at 8%	−3.31213	
4. Difference		× 3.39795
5. Present value of 6 rents of $5,000 deferred 4 periods		$16,989.75

The subtraction of the present value of an annuity of 1 for the deferred periods eliminates the nonexistent rents during the deferral period. It converts the present value of an ordinary annuity of $1.00 for 10 periods to the present value of six rents of $1.00, deferred 4 periods.

Alternatively, Bytehead can use both Table 2 and Table 4 to compute the present value of the 6 rents. He can first discount the annuity six periods. However, because the annuity is deferred four periods, he must treat the present value of the annuity as a future amount to be discounted another four periods. The time diagram in Illustration A-40 depicts this two-step process.

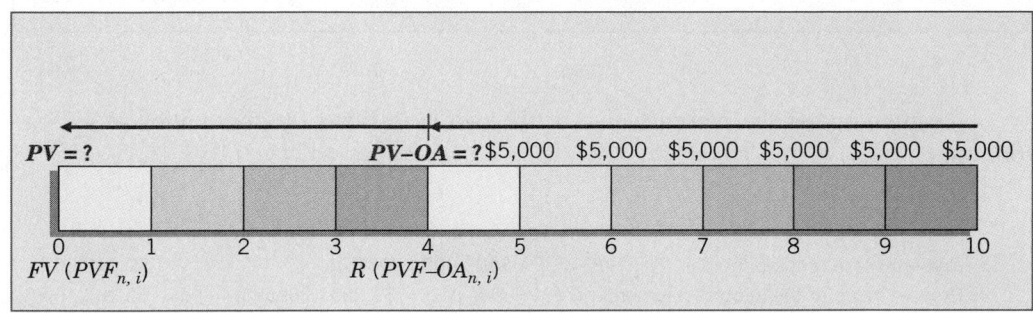

Illustration A-40
Time Diagram for Present Value of Deferred Annuity (Two-Step Process)

Calculation using formulas would be done in two steps, as follows.

Step 1: Present value of
an ordinary annuity $= R \ (PVF\text{-}OA_{n,i})$
$= \$5,000 \ (PVF\text{-}OA_{6,8\%})$
$= \$5,000 \ (4.62288)$
(Table 4, Present value of an ordinary annuity)
$= \$23,114.40$

Step 2: Present value of
a single sum $= FV \ (PVF_{n,i})$
$= \$23,114.40 \ (PVF_{4,8\%})$
$= \$23,114.40 \ (.73503)$
(Table 2, Present value of a single sum)
$= \$16,989.78$

The present value of $16,989.78 computed above is the same as in Illustration A-39, although computed differently. (The $0.03 difference is due to rounding.)

Valuation of Long-Term Bonds

A long-term bond produces two cash flows: (1) periodic interest payments during the life of the bond, and (2) the principal (face value) paid at maturity. At the date of issue, bond buyers determine the present value of these two cash flows using the market rate of interest.

The periodic interest payments represent an annuity. The principal represents a single-sum problem. The current market value of the bonds is the combined present values of the interest annuity and the principal amount.

To illustrate, Alltech Corporation on January 1, 2008, issues $100,000 of 9% bonds due in five years with interest payable annually at year-end. The current market rate of interest for bonds of similar risk is 11%. What will the buyers pay for this bond issue?

The time diagram in Illustration A-41 depicts both cash flows.

Illustration A-41
Time Diagram to Solve
for Bond Valuation

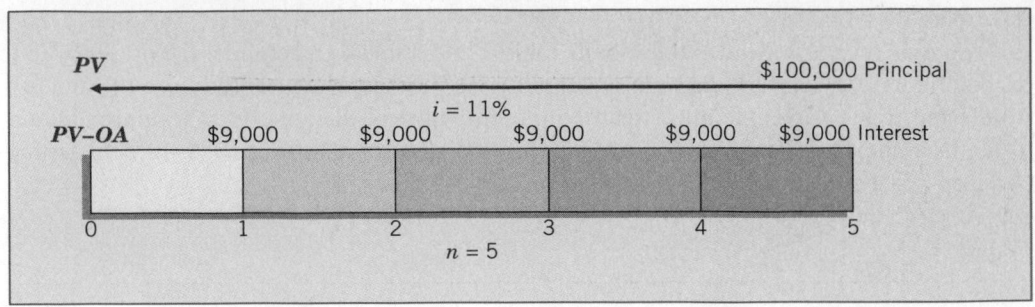

Alltech computes the present value of the two cash flows by discounting at 11% as follows.

Illustration A-42
Computation of the
Present Value of an
Interest-Bearing Bond

1. Present value of the principal: $FV (PVF_{5,11\%})$ = $100,000 (.59345)	$59,345.00
2. Present value of the interest payments: $R (PVF\text{-}OA_{5,11\%})$ = $9,000 (3.69590)	33,263.10
3. Combined present value (market price)—carrying value of bonds	$92,608.10

By paying $92,608.10 at date of issue, the buyers of the bonds will realize an effective yield of 11% over the five-year term of the bonds. This is true because Alltech discounted the cash flows at 11%.

Effective-Interest Method of Amortization of Bond Discount or Premium

In the previous example (Illustration A-42), Alltech Corporation issued bonds at a discount, computed as follows.

Illustration A-43
Computation of Bond
Discount

Maturity value (face amount) of bonds		$100,000.00
Present value of the principal	$59,345.00	
Present value of the interest	33,263.10	
Proceeds (present value and cash received)		92,608.10
Discount on bonds issued		$ 7,391.90

Alltech amortizes (writes off to interest expense) the amount of this discount over the life of the bond issue.

The preferred procedure for amortization of a discount or premium is the **effective-interest method**. Under the effective-interest method:

1 The company issuing the bond first computes bond interest expense by multiplying the carrying value of the bonds at the beginning of the period by the effective interest rate.

2 The company then determines the bond discount or premium amortization by comparing the bond interest expense with the interest to be paid.

Illustration A-44 depicts the computation of bond amortization.

**Use of Spreadsheets
to Calculate Bond
Amortization**

Bond Interest Expense	Bond Interest Paid	
$\left(\begin{array}{c}\text{Carrying Value}\\\text{of Bonds at}\\\text{Beginning of Period}\end{array}\times\begin{array}{c}\text{Effective}\\\text{Interest}\\\text{Rate}\end{array}\right)$	$-\left(\begin{array}{c}\text{Face Amount}\\\text{of Bonds}\end{array}\times\begin{array}{c}\text{Stated}\\\text{Interest}\\\text{Rate}\end{array}\right)=$	**Amortization Amount**

The effective-interest method produces a periodic interest expense equal to **a constant percentage of the carrying value of the bonds**. Since the percentage used is the effective rate of interest incurred by the borrower at the time of issuance, the effective-interest method results in matching expenses with revenues.

We can use the data from the Alltech Corporation example to illustrate the effective-interest method of amortization. Alltech issued $100,000 face value of bonds at a discount of $7,391.90, resulting in a carrying value of $92,608.10. Illustration A-45 shows the effective-interest amortization schedule for Alltech's bonds.

Schedule of Bond Discount Amortization
5-Year, 9% Bonds Sold to Yield 11%

Date	Cash Interest Paid	Interest Expense	Bond Discount Amortization	Carrying Value of Bonds
1/1/08				$92,608.10
12/31/08	$9,000[a]	$10,186.89[b]	$1,186.89[c]	93,794.99[d]
12/31/09	9,000	10,317.45	1,317.45	95,112.44
12/31/10	9,000	10,462.37	1,462.37	96,574.81
12/31/11	9,000	10,623.23	1,623.23	98,198.04
12/31/12	9,000	10,801.96	1,801.96	100,000.00
	$45,000	$52,391.90	$7,391.90	

[a]$100,000 ×.09 = $9,000 [c]$10,186.89 − $9,000 = $1,186.89
[b]$92,608.10 ×.11 = $10,186.89 [d]$92,608.10 + $1,186.89 = $93,794.99

We use the amortization schedule illustrated above for note and bond transactions in Chapters 8 and 12.

PRESENT VALUE MEASUREMENT

In the past, most accounting calculations of present value relied on the most likely cash flow amount. *Concepts Statement No. 7* introduces an **expected cash flow approach**.[7] It uses a range of cash flows and incorporates the probabilities of those cash flows to provide a more relevant measurement of present value.

To illustrate the expected cash flow model, assume that there is a 30% probability that future cash flows will be $100, a 50% probability that they will be $200, and a 20% probability that they will be $300. In this case, the expected cash flow would be $190 [($100 × 0.3) + ($200 × 0.5) + ($300 × 0.2)]. Traditional present value approaches would use the most likely estimate ($200). However, that estimate fails to consider the different probabilities of the possible cash flows.

OBJECTIVE 9

Apply expected cash flows to present value measurement.

[7]"Using Cash Flow Information and Present Value in Accounting Measurements," *Statement of Financial Accounting Concepts No. 7* (Norwalk, Conn.: FASB, 2000).

A popular pastime in today's financial markets is "Fed watching." Why is the practice of following the policy decisions of the Federal Reserve Bank and its chair, Alan Greenspan (now Ben Bernanke), of interest? Through a number of policy options, the Fed has the ability to move interest rates up or down—and these rate changes can affect the wealth of all market participants. For example, if the Fed wants to raise rates (because the overall economy is getting overheated), it can raise the discount rate, which is the rate banks pay to borrow money from the Fed. This rate increase will factor into the rates banks and other creditors use to lend money. As a result, companies will think twice about borrowing money to expand their businesses. The result will be a slowing economy. A rate cut does just the opposite: It makes borrowing cheaper, and can help the economy expand as more companies borrow to expand their operations.

But what is good for the borrowers may not be so good for lenders. Banks earn interest on loans and investments and pay interest to depositors, and recently, with long-term rates remaining at nearly all-time lows, some banks are now at risk if interest rates rise. This is because the banks get squeezed when they make long-term loans at fixed rates (e.g., 30-year mortgage loans) but pay depositors variable rates on shorter-term deposits (e.g., 6-month certificates of deposit). The banks lose if the Fed raises rates because they will continue to earn lower returns on their long-term loans but pay higher interest on deposits.

Some banks—**Fifth-Third Bank** and **New York Community Bancorp**—recently incurred significant charges to change the balance of their assets and liabilities to guard against higher interest rates. So it is not surprising that all companies, whether borrowers or lenders, are Fed watchers.

Source: Adapted from David Franecki, "Thanks, Alan: These Stock Groups Stand to Gain from Fed Rate Cuts," *Barrons Online* (January 22, 2001); and A. C. Puwaslki; "Banks Exposed to a Flattening Yield Curve and Rising Interest Rates," *Industry Analysis: Regional Banks and Thrifts,* Center for Financial Research and Analysis (February 23, 2005).

Choosing an Appropriate Interest Rate

After determining expected cash flows, a company must then use the proper interest rate to discount the cash flows. The interest rate used for this purpose has three components:

THREE COMPONENTS OF INTEREST

1 PURE RATE OF INTEREST (2%–4%). This would be the amount a lender would charge if there were no possibilities of default and no expectation of inflation.

2 EXPECTED INFLATION RATE OF INTEREST (0%–?). Lenders recognize that in an inflationary economy, they are being paid back with less valuable dollars. As a result, they increase their interest rate to compensate for this loss in purchasing power. When inflationary expectations are high, interest rates are high.

3 CREDIT RISK RATE OF INTEREST (0%–5%). The government has little or no credit risk (i.e., risk of nonpayment) when it issues bonds. A business enterprise, however, depending upon its financial stability, profitability, etc., can have a low or a high credit risk.

The FASB takes the position that after computing the expected cash flows, a company should discount those cash flows by the **risk-free rate of return**. That rate is defined as **the pure rate of return plus the expected inflation rate**. The Board notes that the expected cash flow framework adjusts for credit risk because it incorporates the probability of receipt or payment into the computation of expected cash flows. Therefore, the rate used to discount the expected cash flows should consider only the pure rate of interest and the inflation rate.

Example of Expected Cash Flow

To illustrate, assume that Al's Appliance Outlet offers a two-year warranty on all products sold. In 2008 Al's Appliance sold $250,000 of a particular type of clothes dryer. Al's Appliance entered into an agreement with Ralph's Repair to provide all warranty service on the dryers sold in 2008. To determine the warranty expense to record in 2008 and the amount of warranty liability to record on the December 31, 2008, balance sheet, Al's Appliance must measure the fair value of the agreement. Since there is not a ready market for these warranty contracts, Al's Appliance uses expected cash flow techniques to value the warranty obligation.

Based on prior warranty experience, Al's Appliance estimates the expected cash outflows associated with the dryers sold in 2008, as shown in Illustration A-46.

Year	Cash Flow Estimate	×	Probability Assessment	=	Expected Cash Flow
2009	$3,800		20%		$ 760
	6,300		50%		3,150
	7,500		30%		2,250
			Total		$6,160
2010	$5,400		30%		$1,620
	7,200		50%		3,600
	8,400		20%		1,680
			Total		$6,900

Illustration A-46
Expected Cash Outflows—Warranties

Applying expected cash flow concepts to these data, Al's Appliance estimates warranty cash outflows of $6,160 in 2009 and $6,900 in 2010.

Illustration A-47 shows the present value of these cash flows, assuming a risk-free rate of 5% and cash flows occurring at the end of the year.

Year	Expected Cash Flow	×	PV Factor, $i = 5\%$	=	Present Value
2009	$6,160		0.95238		$ 5,866.66
2010	6,900		0.90703		6,258.51
			Total		$12,125.17

Illustration A-47
Present Value of Cash Flows

Key Terms

Summary of Learning Objectives

1 Identify accounting topics where the time value of money is relevant. Some of the applications of present value–based measurements to accounting topics are: (1) notes, (2) leases, (3) pensions and other postretirement benefits, (4) long-term assets, (5) sinking funds, (6) business combinations, (7) disclosures, and (8) installment contracts.

2 Distinguish between simple and compound interest. See items 1 and 2 in the Fundamental Concepts on page 1031.

3 Use appropriate compound interest tables. In order to identify which of the five compound interest tables to use, determine whether you are solving for (1) the future value of a single sum, (2) the present value of a single sum, (3) the future value of a series of sums (an annuity), or (4) the present value of a series of sums (an annuity). In addition, when a series of sums (an annuity) is involved, identify whether these sums are received or paid (1) at the beginning of each period (annuity due) or (2) at the end of each period (ordinary annuity).

4 Identify variables fundamental to solving interest problems. The following four variables are fundamental to all compound interest problems: (1) *Rate of interest:* unless otherwise stated, an annual rate, adjusted to reflect the length of the compounding period if less than a year. (2) *Number of time periods:* the number of compounding periods (a period may be equal to or less than a year). (3) *Future value:* the value at a future date of a given sum or sums invested assuming compound interest. (4) *Present value:* the value now

(present time) of a future sum or sums discounted assuming compound interest.

5 Solve future and present value of 1 problems. See items 5(a) and 6(a) in the Fundamental Concepts on page 1031.

6 Solve future value of ordinary and annuity due problems. See item 5(b) in the Fundamental Concepts on page 1031.

7 Solve present value of ordinary and annuity due problems. See item 6(b) in the Fundamental Concepts on page 1031.

8 Solve present value problems related to deferred annuities and bonds. Deferred annuities are annuities in which rents begin after a specified number of periods. The future value of a deferred annuity is computed the same as the future value of an annuity not deferred. To find the present value of a deferred annuity, compute the present value of an ordinary annuity of 1 as if the rents had occurred for the entire period, and then subtract the present value of rents not received during the deferral period. The current market value of bonds combines the present values of the interest annuity and the principal amount.

9 Apply expected cash flows to present value measurement. The expected cash flow approach uses a range of cash flows and the probabilities of those cash flows to provide the most likely estimate of expected cash flows. The proper interest rate used to discount the cash flows is the risk-free rate of return.

FUNDAMENTAL CONCEPTS

1 SIMPLE INTEREST. Interest on principal only, regardless of interest that may have accrued in the past.

2 COMPOUND INTEREST. Interest accrues on the unpaid interest of past periods as well as on the principal.

3 RATE OF INTEREST. Interest is usually expressed as an annual rate, but when the compounding period is shorter than one year, the interest rate for the shorter period must be determined.

4 ANNUITY. A series of payments or receipts (called rents) that occur at equal intervals of time. Types of annuities:

(a) Ordinary Annuity. Each rent is payable (receivable) at the end of the period.

(b) Annuity Due. Each rent is payable (receivable) at the beginning of the period.

5 FUTURE VALUE. Value at a later date of a single sum that is invested at compound interest.

(a) Future Value of 1 (or value of a single sum). The future value of $1 (or a single given sum), FV, at the end of n periods at i compound interest rate (Table 1).

(b) Future Value of an Annuity. The future value of a series of rents invested at compound interest. In other words, the accumulated total that results from a series of equal deposits at regular intervals invested at compound interest. Both deposits and interest increase the accumulation.

(1) Future Value of an Ordinary Annuity. The future value on the date of the last rent (Table 3).

(2) Future Value of an Annuity Due. The future value one period after the date of the last rent. When an annuity due table is not available, use Table 3 with the following formula.

$$\text{Value of annuity due of 1 for } n \text{ rents} = \text{(Value of ordinary annuity for } n \text{ rents)} \times (1 + \text{interest rate})$$

6 PRESENT VALUE. The value at an earlier date (usually now) of a given future sum discounted at compound interest.

(a) Present Value of 1 (or present value of a single sum). The present value (worth) of $1 (or a given sum), due n periods hence, discounted at i compound interest (Table 2).

(b) Present Value of an Annuity. The present value (worth) of a series of rents discounted at compound interest. In other words, it is the sum when invested at compound interest that will permit a series of equal withdrawals at regular intervals.

(1) Present Value of an Ordinary Annuity. The value now of $1 to be received or paid at the end of each period (rents) for n periods, discounted at i compound interest (Table 4).

(2) Present Value of an Annuity Due. The value now of $1 to be received or paid at the beginning of each period (rents) for n periods, discounted at i compound interest (Table 5). To use Table 4 for an annuity due, apply this formula.

$$\text{Present value of annuity due of 1 for } n \text{ rents} = \text{(Present value of an ordinary annuity of } n \text{ rents} \times (1 + \text{interest rate})$$

Exercises

(Interest rates are per annum unless otherwise indicated.)

(LO 3)   **EA-1   (Using Interest Tables)**   For each of the following cases, indicate (a) to what rate columns, and (b) to what number of periods you would refer in looking up the interest factor.

1.   In a future value of 1 table

	Annual Rate	Number of Years Invested	Compounded
a.	9%	9	Annually
b.	12%	5	Quarterly
c.	10%	15	Semiannually

2.   In a present value of an annuity of 1 table

	Annual Rate	Number of Years Involved	Number of Rents Involved	Frequency of Rents
a.	9%	25	25	Annually
b.	10%	15	30	Semiannually
c.	12%	7	28	Quarterly

(LO 2, 5)   **EA-2   (Simple and Compound Interest Computations)**   Alan Jackson invests $20,000 at 8% annual interest, leaving the money invested without withdrawing any of the interest for 8 years. At the end of the 8 years, Alan withdrew the accumulated amount of money.

Instructions

(a)   Compute the amount Alan would withdraw assuming the investment earns simple interest.

(b)   Compute the amount Alan would withdraw assuming the investment earns interest compounded annually.

(c)   Compute the amount Alan would withdraw assuming the investment earns interest compounded semiannually.

(LO 5, 6, 7)   **EA-3   (Computation of Future Values and Present Values)**   Using the appropriate interest table, answer each of the following questions. (Each case is independent of the others.)

(a)   What is the future value of $7,000 at the end of 5 periods at 8% compounded interest?

(b)   What is the present value of $7,000 due 8 periods hence, discounted at 11%?

(c)   What is the future value of 15 periodic payments of $7,000 each made at the end of each period and compounded at 10%?

(d)   What is the present value of $7,000 to be received at the end of each of 20 periods, discounted at 5% compound interest?

(LO 6, 7)   **EA-4   (Computation of Future Values and Present Values)**   Using the appropriate interest table, answer the following questions. (Each case is independent of the others).

(a)   What is the future value of 20 periodic payments of $4,000 each made at the beginning of each period and compounded at 8%?

(b)   What is the present value of $2,500 to be received at the beginning of each of 30 periods, discounted at 10% compound interest?

(c)   What is the future value of 15 deposits of $2,000 each made at the beginning of each period and compounded at 10%? (Future value as of the end of the fifteenth period.)

(d)   What is the present value of six receipts of $1,000 each received at the beginning of each period, discounted at 9% compounded interest?

(LO 6, 7)   **EA-5   (Computation of Present Value)**   Using the appropriate interest table, compute the present values of the following periodic amounts due at the end of the designated periods.

(a) $30,000 receivable at the end of each period for 8 periods compounded at 12%.

(b) $30,000 payments to be made at the end of each period for 16 periods at 9%.

(c) $30,000 payable at the end of the seventh, eighth, ninth, and tenth periods at 12%.

(LO 5, 6, 7)   **EA-6   (Future Value and Present Value Problems)**   Presented below are three unrelated situations.

(a)   Dwayne Wade Company recently signed a lease for a new office building, for a lease period of 10 years. Under the lease agreement, a security deposit of $12,000 is made, with the deposit to be returned at the expiration of the lease, with interest compounded at 10% per year. What amount will the company receive at the time the lease expires?

(b) Serena Williams Corporation, having recently issued a $20 million, 15-year bond issue, is committed to make annual sinking fund deposits of $600,000. The deposits are made on the last day of each year and yield a return of 10%. Will the fund at the end of 15 years be sufficient to retire the bonds? If not, what will the deficiency be?

(c) Under the terms of his salary agreement, president Rex Walters has an option of receiving either an immediate bonus of $40,000, or a deferred bonus of $70,000 payable in 10 years. Ignoring tax considerations, and assuming a relevant interest rate of 8%, which form of settlement should Walters accept?

EA-7 (Computation of Bond Prices)   What would you pay for a $50,000 debenture bond that matures in 15 years and pays $5,000 a year in interest if you wanted to earn a yield of: **(LO 8)**

(a) 8%?   **(b)** 10%?   **(c)** 12%?

EA-8 (Computations for a Retirement Fund)   Clarence Weatherspoon, a super salesman contemplating retirement on his fifty-fifth birthday, decides to create a fund on an 8% basis that will enable him to withdraw $20,000 per year on June 30, beginning in 2014 and continuing through 2017. To develop this fund, Clarence intends to make equal contributions on June 30 of each of the years 2010–2013.   **(LO 8)**

Instructions

(a) How much must the balance of the fund equal on June 30, 2013, in order for Clarence Weatherspoon to satisfy his objective?

(b) What are each of Clarence's contributions to the fund?

EA-9 (Unknown Rate)   LEW Company purchased a machine at a price of $100,000 by signing a note payable, which requires a single payment of $123,210 in 2 years. Assuming annual compounding of interest, what rate of interest is being paid on the loan?   **(LO 5)**

EA-10 (Unknown Periods and Unknown Interest Rate)   Consider the following independent situations.   **(LO 5)**

(a) Mike Finley wishes to become a millionaire. His money market fund has a balance of $92,296 and has a guaranteed interest rate of 10%. How many years must Mike leave that balance in the fund in order to get his desired $1,000,000?

(b) Assume that Serena Williams desires to accumulate $1 million in 15 years using her money market fund balance of $182,696. At what interest rate must Serena's investment compound annually?

EA-11 (Evaluation of Purchase Options)   Sosa Excavating Inc. is purchasing a bulldozer. The equipment has a price of $100,000. The manufacturer has offered a payment plan that would allow Sosa to make 10 equal annual payments of $16,274.53, with the first payment due one year after the purchase.   **(LO 7)**

Instructions

(a) How much total interest will Sosa pay on this payment plan?

(b) Sosa could borrow $100,000 from its bank to finance the purchase at an annual rate of 9%. Should Sosa borrow from the bank or use the manufacturer's payment plan to pay for the equipment?

EA-12 (Analysis of Alternatives)   The Black Knights Inc., a manufacturer of high-sugar, low-sodium, low-cholesterol TV dinners, would like to increase its market share in the Sunbelt. In order to do so, Black Knights has decided to locate a new factory in the Panama City area. Black Knights will either buy or lease a site depending upon which is more advantageous. The site location committee has narrowed down the available sites to the following three buildings.   **(LO 5, 6, 7)**

Building A: Purchase for a cash price of $600,000, useful life 25 years.

Building B: Lease for 25 years with annual lease payments of $69,000 being made at the beginning of the year.

Building C: Purchase for $650,000 cash. This building is larger than needed; however, the excess space can be sublet for 25 years at a net annual rental of $7,000. Rental payments will be received at the end of each year. The Black Knights Inc. has no aversion to being a landlord.

Instructions

In which building would you recommend that The Black Knights Inc. locate, assuming a 12% cost of funds?

EA-13 (Computation of Bond Liability)   Lance Armstrong Inc. manufactures cycling equipment. Recently the vice president of operations of the company has requested construction of a new plant to meet the increasing demand for the company's bikes. After a careful evaluation of the request, the board of directors has decided to raise funds for the new plant by issuing $2,000,000 of 11% term corporate bonds on March 1, 2007, due on   **(LO 8)**

March 1, 2022, with interest payable each March 1 and September 1. At the time of issuance, the market interest rate for similar financial instruments is 10%.

Instructions

As the controller of the company, determine the selling price of the bonds.

(LO 8) **EA-14 (Computation of Pension Liability)** Nerwin, Inc. is a furniture manufacturing company with 50 employees. Recently, after a long negotiation with the local labor union, the company decided to initiate a pension plan as a part of its compensation plan. The plan will start on January 1, 2008. Each employee covered by the plan is entitled to a pension payment each year after retirement. As required by accounting standards, the controller of the company needs to report the pension obligation (liability). On the basis of a discussion with the supervisor of the Personnel Department and an actuary from an insurance company, the controller develops the following information related to the pension plan.

Average length of time to retirement	15 years
Expected life duration after retirement	10 years
Total pension payment expected each year after retirement for all employees. Payment made at the end of the year.	$700,000 per year

The interest rate to be used is 8%.

Instructions

On the basis of the information above, determine the present value of the pension obligation (liability).

(LO 5, 6) **EA-15 (Investment Decision)** Andrew Bogut just received a signing bonus of $1,000,000. His plan is to invest this payment in a fund that will earn 8%, compounded annually.

Instructions

(a) If Bogut plans to establish the AB Foundation once the fund grows to $1,999,000, how many years until he can establish the foundation?

(b) Instead of investing the entire $1,000,000, Bogut invests $300,000 today and plans to make 9 equal annual investments into the fund beginning one year from today. What amount should the payments be if Bogut plans to establish the $1,999,000 foundation at the end of 9 years?

(LO 6, 7) **EA-16 (Retirement of Debt)** Jesper Parnevik borrowed $70,000 on March 1, 2006. This amount plus accrued interest at 12% compounded semiannually is to be repaid March 1, 2016. To retire this debt, Jesper plans to contribute to a debt retirement fund five equal amounts starting on March 1, 2011, and for the next 4 years. The fund is expected to earn 10% per annum.

Instructions

How much must be contributed each year by Jesper Parnevik to provide a fund sufficient to retire the debt on March 1, 2016?

(LO 7) **EA-17 (Computation of Amount of Rentals)** Your client, Ron Santo Leasing Company, is preparing a contract to lease a machine to Souvenirs Corporation for a period of 25 years. Santo has an investment cost of $365,755 in the machine, which has a useful life of 25 years and no salvage value at the end of that time. Your client is interested in earning an 11% return on its investment and has agreed to accept 25 equal rental payments at the end of each of the next 25 years.

Instructions

You are requested to provide Santo with the amount of each of the 25 rental payments that will yield an 11% return on investment.

(LO 5, 7) **EA-18 (Least-Costly Payoff)** Assume that **Sonic Foundry Corporation** has a contractual debt outstanding. Sonic has available two means of settlement: It can either make immediate payment of $2,600,000, or it can make annual payments of $300,000 for 15 years, each payment due on the last day of the year.

Instructions

Which method of payment do you recommend, assuming an expected effective interest rate of 8% during the future period?

(LO 5, 7) **EA-19 (Least-Costly Payoff)** Assuming the same facts as those in EA-18 except that the payments must begin now and be made on the first day of each of the 15 years, what payment method would you recommend?

EA-20 **(Expected Cash Flows)** For each of the following, determine the expected cash flows. (LO 9)

	Cash Flow Estimate	Probability Assessment
(a)	$ 3,800	20%
	6,300	50%
	7,500	30%
(b)	$ 5,400	30%
	7,200	50%
	8,400	20%
(c)	$(1,000)	10%
	2,000	80%
	5,000	10%

EA-21 **(Expected Cash Flows and Present Value)** Andrew Kelly is trying to determine the amount to set (LO 9) aside so that he will have enough money on hand in 2 years to overhaul the engine on his vintage used car. While there is some uncertainty about the cost of engine overhauls in 2 years, by conducting some research online, Andrew has developed the following estimates.

Engine Overhaul Estimated Cash Outflow	Probability Assessment
$200	10%
450	30%
550	50%
750	10%

Instructions

How much should Andrew Kelly deposit today in an account earning 6%, compounded annually, so that he will have enough money on hand in 2 years to pay for the overhaul?

See the book's companion website, www.wiley.com/college/warfield, for Additional Exercises.

Problems

(Interest rates are per annum unless otherwise indicated.)

PA-1 **(Various Time Value Situations)** Answer each of these unrelated questions. (LO 5, 6, 7)

(a) On January 1, 2008, Aaron Brown Corporation sold a building that cost $250,000 and that had accumulated depreciation of $100,000 on the date of sale. Brown received as consideration a $275,000 zero-interest-bearing note due on January 1, 2011. There was no established exchange price for the building, and the note had no ready market. The prevailing rate of interest for a note of this type on January 1, 2008, was 9%. At what amount should the gain from the sale of the building be reported?

(b) On January 1, 2008, Aaron Brown Corporation purchased 200 of the $1,000 face value, 9%, 10-year bonds of Walters Inc. The bonds mature on January 1, 2018, and pay interest annually beginning January 1, 2009. Brown purchased the bonds to yield 11%. How much did Brown pay for the bonds?

(c) Aaron Brown Corporation bought a new machine and agreed to pay for it in equal annual installments of $4,000 at the end of each of the next 10 years. Assuming that a prevailing interest rate of 8% applies to this contract, how much should Brown record as the cost of the machine?

(d) Aaron Brown Corporation purchased a special tractor on December 31, 2008. The purchase agreement stipulated that Brown should pay $20,000 at the time of purchase and $5,000 at the end of each of the next 8 years. The tractor should be recorded on December 31, 2008, at what amount, assuming an appropriate interest rate of 12%?

(e) Aaron Brown Corporation wants to withdraw $100,000 (including principal) from an investment fund at the end of each year for 9 years. What should be the required initial investment at the beginning of the first year if the fund earns 11%?

(LO 5, 6, 7)

PA-2 **(Various Time Value Situations)** Using the appropriate interest table, provide the solution to each of the following four questions by computing the unknowns.

(a) What is the amount of the payments that Tom Brokaw must make at the end of each of 8 years to accumulate a fund of $70,000 by the end of the eighth year, if the fund earns 8% interest, compounded annually?

(b) Anderson Cooper is 40 years old today and he wishes to accumulate $500,000 by his sixty-fifth birthday so he can retire to his summer place on Lake Hopatcong. He wishes to accumulate this amount by making equal deposits on his fortieth through his sixty-fourth birthdays. What annual deposit must Anderson make if the fund will earn 12% interest compounded annually?

(c) Jane Pauley has $20,000 to invest today at 9% to pay a debt of $56,253. How many years will it take her to accumulate enough to liquidate the debt?

(d) Maria Shriver has a $27,600 debt that she wishes to repay 4 years from today; she has $18,181 that she intends to invest for the 4 years. What rate of interest will she need to earn annually in order to accumulate enough to pay the debt?

(LO 5, 6, 7)

PA-3 **(Analysis of Alternatives)** Assume that **Wal-Mart, Inc.** has decided to surface and maintain for 10 years a vacant lot next to one of its discount-retail outlets to serve as a parking lot for customers. Management is considering the following bids involving two different qualities of surfacing for a parking area of 12,000 square yards.

Bid A: A surface that costs $5.25 per square yard to install. This surface will have to be replaced at the end of 5 years. The annual maintenance cost on this surface is estimated at 20 cents per square yard for each year except the last year of its service. The replacement surface will be similar to the initial surface.

Bid B: A surface that costs $9.50 per square yard to install. This surface has a probable useful life of 10 years and will require annual maintenance in each year except the last year, at an estimated cost of 9 cents per square yard.

Instructions

Prepare computations showing which bid should be accepted by Wal-Mart, Inc. You may assume that the cost of capital is 9%, that the annual maintenance expenditures are incurred at the end of each year, and that prices are not expected to change during the next 10 years.

(LO 6, 7)

PA-4 **(Evaluating Payment Alternatives)** Terry O'Malley has just learned he has won a $900,000 prize in the lottery. The lottery has given him two options for receiving the payments: (1) If Terry takes all the money today, the state and federal governments will deduct taxes at a rate of 46% immediately. (2) Alternatively, the lottery offers Terry a payout of 20 equal payments of $62,000 with the first payment occurring when Terry turns in the winning ticket. Terry will be taxed on each of these payments at a rate of 25%.

Instructions

Assuming Terry can earn an 8% rate of return (compounded annually) on any money invested during this period, which pay-out option should he choose?

(LO 5, 6, 7)

PA-5 **(Analysis of Alternatives)** Sally Brown died, leaving to her husband Linus an insurance policy contract that provides that the beneficiary (Linus) can choose any one of the following four options.

(a) $55,000 immediate cash.

(b) $3,700 every 3 months payable at the end of each quarter for 5 years.

(c) $18,000 immediate cash and $1,600 every 3 months for 10 years, payable at the beginning of each 3-month period.

(d) $4,000 every 3 months for 3 years and $1,200 each quarter for the following 25 quarters, all payments payable at the end of each quarter.

Instructions

Assuming an interest rate of 2½% per quarter, compounded quarterly, which option would you recommend that Linus exercise?

(LO 8)

PA-6 **(Purchase Price of a Business)** During the past year, Nicole Bobek planted a new vineyard on 150 acres of land that she leases for $27,000 a year. She has asked you as her accountant to assist her in determining the value of her vineyard operation. The vineyard will bear no grapes for the first 5 years (1–5). In the next 5 years (6–10), Nicole estimates that the vines will bear grapes that can be sold for $60,000 each year. For the next 20 years (11–30), she expects the harvest will provide annual revenues of $100,000. But during the last 10 years (31–40) of the vineyard's life, she estimates that revenues will decline to $80,000 per year.

During the first 5 years the annual cost of pruning, fertilizing, and caring for the vineyard is estimated at $9,000; during the years of production, 6–40, these costs will rise to $10,000 per year. The relevant market rate of interest for the entire period is 12%. Assume that all receipts and payments are made at the end of each year.

Instructions

Dick Button has offered to buy Nicole's vineyard business by assuming the 40-year lease. On the basis of the current value of the business, what is the minimum price Nicole should accept?

PA-7 **(Time Value Concepts Applied to Solve Business Problems)** Answer the following questions related to Derek Lee Inc.

(a) Derek Lee Inc. has $572,000 to invest. The company is trying to decide between two alternative uses of the funds. One alternative provides $80,000 at the end of each year for 12 years, and the other is to receive a single lump sum payment of $1,900,000 at the end of the 12 years. Which alternative should Lee select? Assume the interest rate is constant over the entire investment.

(b) Derek Lee Inc. has completed the purchase of new Dell computers. The fair market value of the equipment is $824,150. The purchase agreement specifies an immediate down payment of $200,000 and semiannual payments of $76,952 beginning at the end of 6 months for 5 years. What is the interest rate, to the nearest percent, used in discounting this purchase transaction?

(c) Derek Lee Inc. loans money to John Kruk Corporation in the amount of $600,000. Lee accepts an 8% note due in 7 years with interest payable semiannually. After 2 years (and receipt of interest for 2 years), Lee needs money and therefore sells the note to Chicago National Bank, which demands interest on the note of 10% compounded semiannually. What is the amount Lee will receive on the sale of the note?

(d) Derek Lee Inc. wishes to accumulate $1,300,000 by December 31, 2018, to retire bonds outstanding. The company deposits $300,000 on December 31, 2008, which will earn interest at 10% compounded quarterly, to help in the retirement of this debt. In addition, the company wants to know how much should be deposited at the end of each quarter for 10 years to ensure that $1,300,000 is available at the end of 2018. (The quarterly deposits will also earn at a rate of 10%, compounded quarterly.) (Round to even dollars.)

PA-8 **(Analysis of Alternatives)** Homer Simpson Inc., a manufacturer of steel school lockers, plans to purchase a new punch press for use in its manufacturing process. After contacting the appropriate vendors, the purchasing department received differing terms and options from each vendor. The Engineering Department has determined that each vendor's punch press is substantially identical and each has a useful life of 20 years. In addition, Engineering has estimated that required year-end maintenance costs will be $1,000 per year for the first 5 years, $2,000 per year for the next 10 years, and $3,000 per year for the last 5 years. Following is each vendor's sale package.

Vendor A: $45,000 cash at time of delivery and 10 year-end payments of $15,000 each. Vendor A offers all its customers the right to purchase at the time of sale a separate 20-year maintenance service contract, under which Vendor A will perform all year-end maintenance at a one-time initial cost of $10,000.

Vendor B: Forty semiannual payments of $8,000 each, with the first installment due upon delivery. Vendor B will perform all year-end maintenance for the next 20 years at no extra charge.

Vendor C: Full cash price of $125,000 will be due upon delivery.

Instructions

Assuming that both Vendor A and B will be able to perform the required year-end maintenance, that Simpson's cost of funds is 10%, and the machine will be purchased on January 1, from which vendor should the press be purchased?

PA-9 **(Analysis of Business Problems)** Jean-Luc is a financial executive with Starship Enterprises. Although Jean-Luc has not had any formal training in finance or accounting, he has a "good sense" for numbers and has helped the company grow from a very small company ($500,000 sales) to a large operation ($45 million in sales). With the business growing steadily, however, the company needs to make a number of difficult financial decisions in which Jean-Luc feels a little "over his head." He therefore has decided to hire a new employee with "numbers" expertise to help him. As a basis for determining whom to employ, he has decided to ask each prospective employee to prepare answers to questions relating to the following situations he has encountered recently. Here are the questions.

(a) In 2006, Starship Enterprises negotiated and closed a long-term lease contract for newly constructed truck terminals and freight storage facilities. The buildings were constructed on land owned by the company. On January 1, 2007, Starship took possession of the leased property. The 20-year lease is effective for the period January 1, 2007, through December 31, 2026. Advance rental payments of $800,000 are payable to the lessor (owner of facilities) on January 1 of each of the first 10 years of the lease term. Advance payments of $300,000 are due on January 1 for each of the last 10 years of the lease term. Starship has an option to purchase all the leased facilities for $1 on December 31, 2026. At the time the lease was negotiated, the fair value of the truck terminals and freight storage facilities was approximately $7,200,000. If the company had borrowed the money to purchase the facilities, it would have had to pay 10% interest. Should the company have purchased rather than leased the facilities?

(b) Last year the company exchanged a piece of land for a zero-interest-bearing note. The note is to be paid at the rate of $12,000 per year for 9 years, beginning one year from the date of disposal of the land.

Margin notes: (LO 5, 6, 7) — PA-7; (LO 6, 7) — PA-8; (LO 5, 6, 7) — PA-9

An appropriate rate of interest for the note was 11%. At the time the land was originally purchased, it cost $90,000. What is the fair value of the note?

(c) The company has always followed the policy to take any cash discounts on goods purchased. Recently the company purchased a large amount of raw materials at a price of $800,000 with terms 2/10, n/30 on which it took the discount. Starship has recently estimated its cost of funds at 10%. Should Starship continue this policy of always taking the cash discount?

(LO 5, 6, 7)   **PA-10   (Analysis of Lease vs. Purchase)**   Jose Rijo Inc. owns and operates a number of hardware stores in the New England region. Recently the company has decided to locate another store in a rapidly growing area of Maryland. The company is trying to decide whether to purchase or lease the building and related facilities.

Purchase: The company can purchase the site, construct the building, and purchase all store fixtures. The cost would be $1,650,000. An immediate down payment of $400,000 is required, and the remaining $1,250,000 would be paid off over 5 years at $300,000 per year (including interest). The property is expected to have a useful life of 12 years, and then it will be sold for $500,000. As the owner of the property, the company will have the following out-of-pocket expenses each period.

Property taxes (to be paid at the end of each year)	$40,000
Insurance (to be paid at the beginning of each year)	27,000
Other (primarily maintenance which occurs at the end of each year)	16,000
	$83,000

Lease: First National Bank has agreed to purchase the site, construct the building, and install the appropriate fixtures for Rijo Inc. if Rijo will lease the completed facility for 12 years. The annual costs for the lease would be $240,000. Rijo would have no responsibility related to the facility over the 12 years. The terms of the lease are that Rijo would be required to make 12 annual payments (the first payment to be made at the time the store opens and then each following year). In addition, a deposit of $100,000 is required when the store is opened. This deposit will be returned at the end of the twelfth year, assuming no unusual damage to the building structure or fixtures.

Currently the cost of funds for Rijo Inc. is 10%.

Instructions

Which of the two approaches should Rijo Inc. follow?

(LO 8)   **PA-11   (Pension Funding)**   You have been hired as a benefit consultant by Maugarite Alomar, the owner of Attic Angels. She wants to establish a retirement plan for herself and her three employees. Maugarite has provided the following information: The retirement plan is to be based upon annual salary for the last year before retirement and is to provide 50% of Maugarite's last-year annual salary and 40% of the last-year annual salary for each employee. The plan will make annual payments at the beginning of each year for 20 years from the date of retirement. Maugarite wishes to fund the plan by making 15 annual deposits beginning January 1, 2008. Invested funds will earn 12% compounded annually. Information about plan participants as of January 1, 2008, is as follows.

Maugarite Alomar, owner: Current annual salary of $40,000; estimated retirement date January 1, 2033.

Kenny Rogers, flower arranger: Current annual salary of $30,000; estimated retirement date January 1, 2038.

Anita Baker, sales clerk: Current annual salary of $15,000; estimated retirement date January 1, 2028.

Willie Nelson, part-time bookkeeper: Current annual salary of $15,000; estimated retirement date January 1, 2023.

In the past, Maugarite has given herself and each employee a year-end salary increase of 4%. Maugarite plans to continue this policy in the future.

Instructions

(a) Based upon the above information, what will be the annual retirement benefit for each plan participant? (Round to the nearest dollar.) (*Hint:* Maugarite will receive raises for 24 years.)

(b) What amount must be on deposit at the end of 15 years to ensure that all benefits will be paid? (Round to the nearest dollar.)

(c) What is the amount of each annual deposit Maugarite must make to the retirement plan?

(LO 8)    **PA-12   (Pension Funding)**   James Qualls, newly appointed controller of KBS, is considering ways to reduce his company's expenditures on annual pension costs. One way to do this is to switch KBS's pension fund assets from First Security to NET Life. KBS is a very well-respected computer manufacturer that recently has experienced a sharp decline in its financial performance for the first time in its 25-year history. Despite financial problems, KBS still is committed to providing its employees with good pension and postretirement health benefits.

Under its present plan with First Security, KBS is obligated to pay $43 million to meet the expected value of future pension benefits that are payable to employees as an annuity upon their retirement from the company. On the other hand, NET Life requires KBS to pay only $35 million for identical future pension benefits. First Security is one of the oldest and most reputable insurance companies in North America. NET Life has a much weaker reputation in the insurance industry. In pondering the significant difference in annual pension costs, Qualls asks himself, "Is this too good to be true?"

Instructions

Answer the following questions.

(a) Why might NET Life's pension cost requirement be $8 million less than First Security's requirement for the same future value?

(b) What ethical issues should James Qualls consider before switching KBS's pension fund assets?

(c) Who are the stakeholders that could be affected by Qualls's decision?

PA-13 (Expected Cash Flows and Present Value) Larry's Lawn Equipment sells high-quality lawn mow- **(LO 7, 9)** ers and offers a 3-year warranty on all new lawn mowers sold. In 2008, Larry sold $300,000 of new specialty mowers for golf greens for which Larry's service department does not have the equipment to do the service. Larry has entered into an agreement with Mower Mavens to provide all warranty service on the special mowers sold in 2008. Larry wishes to measure the fair value of the agreement to determine the warranty liability for sales made in 2008. The controller for Larry's Lawn Equipment estimates the following expected warranty cash outflows associated with the mowers sold in 2008.

Year	Cash Flow Estimate	Probability Assessment
2009	$2,000	20%
	4,000	60%
	5,000	20%
2010	$2,500	30%
	5,000	50%
	6,000	20%
2011	$3,000	30%
	6,000	40%
	7,000	30%

Instructions

Using expected cash flow and present value techniques, determine the value of the warranty liability for the 2008 sales. Use an annual discount rate of 5%. Assume all cash flows occur at the end of the year.

PA-14 (Expected Cash Flows and Present Value) At the end of 2008, Richards Company is conducting an **(LO 7, 9)** impairment test and needs to develop a fair value estimate for machinery used in its manufacturing operations. Given the nature of Richard's production process, the equipment is for special use. (No second-hand market values are available.) The equipment will be obsolete in 2 years, and Richard's accountants have developed the following cash flow information for the equipment.

Year	Net Cash Flow Estimate	Probability Assessment
2009	$6,000	40%
	8,000	60%
2010	$ (500)	20%
	2,000	60%
	3,000	20%
	Scrap value	
2010	$ 500	50%
	700	50%

Instructions

Using expected cash flow and present value techniques, determine the fair value of the machinery at the end of 2008. Use a 6% discount rate. Assume all cash flows occur at the end of the year.

Table 1 Future Value of 1 (Future Value of a Single Sum)

$$FVF_{n,i} = (1 + i)^n$$

(n) Periods	2%	2½%	3%	4%	5%	6%
1	1.02000	1.02500	1.03000	1.04000	1.05000	1.06000
2	1.04040	1.05063	1.06090	1.08160	1.10250	1.12360
3	1.06121	1.07689	1.09273	1.12486	1.15763	1.19102
4	1.08243	1.10381	1.12551	1.16986	1.21551	1.26248
5	1.10408	1.13141	1.15927	1.21665	1.27628	1.33823
6	1.12616	1.15969	1.19405	1.26532	1.34010	1.41852
7	1.14869	1.18869	1.22987	1.31593	1.40710	1.50363
8	1.17166	1.21840	1.26677	1.36857	1.47746	1.59385
9	1.19509	1.24886	1.30477	1.42331	1.55133	1.68948
10	1.21899	1.28008	1.34392	1.48024	1.62889	1.79085
11	1.24337	1.31209	1.38423	1.53945	1.71034	1.89830
12	1.26824	1.34489	1.42576	1.60103	1.79586	2.01220
13	1.29361	1.37851	1.46853	1.66507	1.88565	2.13293
14	1.31948	1.41297	1.51259	1.73168	1.97993	2.26090
15	1.34587	1.44830	1.55797	1.80094	2.07893	2.39656
16	1.37279	1.48451	1.60471	1.87298	2.18287	2.54035
17	1.40024	1.52162	1.65285	1.94790	2.29202	2.69277
18	1.42825	1.55966	1.70243	2.02582	2.40662	2.85434
19	1.45681	1.59865	1.75351	2.10685	2.52695	3.02560
20	1.48595	1.63862	1.80611	2.19112	2.65330	3.20714
21	1.51567	1.67958	1.86029	2.27877	2.78596	3.39956
22	1.54598	1.72157	1.91610	2.36992	2.92526	3.60354
23	1.57690	1.76461	1.97359	2.46472	3.07152	3.81975
24	1.60844	1.80873	2.03279	2.56330	3.22510	4.04893
25	1.64061	1.85394	2.09378	2.66584	3.38635	4.29187
26	1.67342	1.90029	2.15659	2.77247	3.55567	4.54938
27	1.70689	1.94780	2.22129	2.88337	3.73346	4.82235
28	1.74102	1.99650	2.28793	2.99870	3.92013	5.11169
29	1.77584	2.04641	2.35657	3.11865	4.11614	5.41839
30	1.81136	2.09757	2.42726	3.24340	4.32194	5.74349
31	1.84759	2.15001	2.50008	3.37313	4.53804	6.08810
32	1.88454	2.20376	2.57508	3.50806	4.76494	6.45339
33	1.92223	2.25885	2.65234	3.64838	5.00319	6.84059
34	1.96068	2.31532	2.73191	3.79432	5.25335	7.25103
35	1.99989	2.37321	2.81386	3.94609	5.51602	7.68609
36	2.03989	2.43254	2.89828	4.10393	5.79182	8.14725
37	2.08069	2.49335	2.98523	4.26809	6.08141	8.63609
38	2.12230	2.55568	3.07478	4.43881	6.38548	9.15425
39	2.16474	2.61957	3.16703	4.61637	6.70475	9.70351
40	2.20804	2.68506	3.26204	4.80102	7.03999	10.28572

Table 1 Future Value of 1

8%	9%	10%	11%	12%	15%	(n) Periods
1.08000	1.09000	1.10000	1.11000	1.12000	1.15000	1
1.16640	1.18810	1.21000	1.23210	1.25440	1.32250	2
1.25971	1.29503	1.33100	1.36763	1.40493	1.52088	3
1.36049	1.41158	1.46410	1.51807	1.57352	1.74901	4
1.46933	1.53862	1.61051	1.68506	1.76234	2.01136	5
1.58687	1.67710	1.77156	1.87041	1.97382	2.31306	6
1.71382	1.82804	1.94872	2.07616	2.21068	2.66002	7
1.85093	1.99256	2.14359	2.30454	2.47596	3.05902	8
1.99900	2.17189	2.35795	2.55803	2.77308	3.51788	9
2.15892	2.36736	2.59374	2.83942	3.10585	4.04556	10
2.33164	2.58043	2.85312	3.15176	3.47855	4.65239	11
2.51817	2.81267	3.13843	3.49845	3.89598	5.35025	12
2.71962	3.06581	3.45227	3.88328	4.36349	6.15279	13
2.93719	3.34173	3.79750	4.31044	4.88711	7.07571	14
3.17217	3.64248	4.17725	4.78459	5.47357	8.13706	15
3.42594	3.97031	4.59497	5.31089	6.13039	9.35762	16
3.70002	4.32763	5.05447	5.89509	6.86604	10.76126	17
3.99602	4.71712	5.55992	6.54355	7.68997	12.37545	18
4.31570	5.14166	6.11591	7.26334	8.61276	14.23177	19
4.66096	5.60441	6.72750	8.06231	9.64629	16.36654	20
5.03383	6.10881	7.40025	8.94917	10.80385	18.82152	21
5.43654	6.65860	8.14028	9.93357	12.10031	21.64475	22
5.87146	7.25787	8.95430	11.02627	13.55235	24.89146	23
6.34118	7.91108	9.84973	12.23916	15.17863	28.62518	24
6.84847	8.62308	10.83471	13.58546	17.00000	32.91895	25
7.39635	9.39916	11.91818	15.07986	19.04007	37.85680	26
7.98806	10.24508	13.10999	16.73865	21.32488	43.53532	27
8.62711	11.16714	14.42099	18.57990	23.88387	50.06561	28
9.31727	12.17218	15.86309	20.62369	26.74993	57.57545	29
10.06266	13.26768	17.44940	22.89230	29.95992	66.21177	30
10.86767	14.46177	19.19434	25.41045	33.55511	76.14354	31
11.73708	15.76333	21.11378	28.20560	37.58173	87.56507	32
12.67605	17.18203	23.22515	31.30821	42.09153	100.69983	33
13.69013	18.72841	25.54767	34.75212	47.14252	115.80480	34
14.78534	20.41397	28.10244	38.57485	52.79962	133.17552	35
15.96817	22.25123	30.91268	42.81808	59.13557	153.15185	36
17.24563	24.25384	34.00395	47.52807	66.23184	176.12463	37
18.62528	26.43668	37.40434	52.75616	74.17966	202.54332	38
20.11530	28.81598	41.14479	58.55934	83.08122	232.92482	39
21.72452	31.40942	45.25926	65.00087	93.05097	267.86355	40

Table 2 Present Value of 1 (Present Value of a Single Sum)

$$\text{PVF}_{n,i} = \frac{1}{(1 + i)^n} = (1 + i)^{-n}$$

(n) Periods	2%	2½%	3%	4%	5%	6%
1	.98039	.97561	.97087	.96154	.95238	.94340
2	.96117	.95181	.94260	.92456	.90703	.89000
3	.94232	.92860	.91514	.88900	.86384	.83962
4	.92385	.90595	.88849	.85480	.82270	.79209
5	.90573	.88385	.86261	.82193	.78353	.74726
6	.88797	.86230	.83748	.79031	.74622	.70496
7	.87056	.84127	.81309	.75992	.71068	.66506
8	.85349	.82075	.78941	.73069	.67684	.62741
9	.83676	.80073	.76642	.70259	.64461	.59190
10	.82035	.78120	.74409	.67556	.61391	.55839
11	.80426	.76214	.72242	.64958	.58468	.52679
12	.78849	.74356	.70138	.62460	.55684	.49697
13	.77303	.72542	.68095	.60057	.53032	.46884
14	.75788	.70773	.66112	.57748	.50507	.44230
15	.74301	.69047	.64186	.55526	.48102	.41727
16	.72845	.67362	.62317	.53391	.45811	.39365
17	.71416	.65720	.60502	.51337	.43630	.37136
18	.70016	.64117	.58739	.49363	.41552	.35034
19	.68643	.62553	.57029	.47464	.39573	.33051
20	.67297	.61027	.55368	.45639	.37689	.31180
21	.65978	.59539	.53755	.43883	.35894	.29416
22	.64684	.58086	.52189	.42196	.34185	.22751
23	.63416	.56670	.50669	.40573	.32557	.26180
24	.62172	.55288	.49193	.39012	.31007	.24698
25	.60953	.53939	.47761	.37512	.29530	.23300
26	.59758	.52623	.46369	.36069	.28124	.21981
27	.58586	.51340	.45019	.34682	.26785	.20737
28	.57437	.50088	.43708	.33348	.25509	.19563
29	.56311	.48866	.42435	.32065	.24295	.18456
30	.55207	.47674	.41199	.30832	.23138	.17411
31	.54125	.46511	.39999	.29646	.22036	.16425
32	.53063	.45377	.38834	.28506	.20987	.15496
33	.52023	.44270	.37703	.27409	.19987	.14619
34	.51003	.43191	.36604	.26355	.19035	.13791
35	.50003	.42137	.35538	.25342	.18129	.13011
36	.49022	.41109	.34503	.24367	.17266	.12274
37	.48061	.40107	.33498	.23430	.16444	.11579
38	.47119	.39128	.32523	.22529	.15661	.10924
39	.46195	.38174	.31575	.21662	.14915	.10306
40	.45289	.37243	.30656	.20829	.14205	.09722

Table 2 Present Value of 1

8%	9%	10%	11%	12%	15%	(n) Periods
.92593	.91743	.90909	.90090	.89286	.86957	1
.85734	.84168	.82645	.81162	.79719	.75614	2
.79383	.77218	.75132	.73119	.71178	.65752	3
.73503	.70843	.68301	.65873	.63552	.57175	4
.68058	.64993	.62092	.59345	.56743	.49718	5
.63017	.59627	.56447	.53464	.50663	.43233	6
.58349	.54703	.51316	.48166	.45235	.37594	7
.54027	.50187	.46651	.43393	.40388	.32690	8
.50025	.46043	.42410	.39092	.36061	.28426	9
.46319	.42241	.38554	.35218	.32197	.24719	10
.42888	.38753	.35049	.31728	.28748	.21494	11
.39711	.35554	.31863	.28584	.25668	.18691	12
.36770	.32618	.28966	.25751	.22917	.16253	13
.34046	.29925	.26333	.23199	.20462	.14133	14
.31524	.27454	.23939	.20900	.18270	.12289	15
.29189	.25187	.21763	.18829	.16312	.10687	16
.27027	.23107	.19785	.16963	.14564	.09293	17
.25025	.21199	.17986	.15282	.13004	.08081	18
.23171	.19449	.16351	.13768	.11611	.07027	19
.21455	.17843	.14864	.12403	.10367	.06110	20
.19866	.16370	.13513	.11174	.09256	.05313	21
.18394	.15018	.12285	.10067	.08264	.04620	22
.17032	.13778	.11168	.09069	.07379	.04017	23
.15770	.12641	.10153	.08170	.06588	.03493	24
.14602	.11597	.09230	.07361	.05882	.03038	25
.13520	.10639	.08391	.06631	.05252	.02642	26
.12519	.09761	.07628	.05974	.04689	.02297	27
.11591	.08955	.06934	.05382	.04187	.01997	28
.10733	.08216	.06304	.04849	.03738	.01737	29
.09938	.07537	.05731	.04368	.03338	.01510	30
.09202	.06915	.05210	.03935	.02980	.01313	31
.08520	.06344	.04736	.03545	.02661	.01142	32
.07889	.05820	.04306	.03194	.02376	.00993	33
.07305	.05340	.03914	.02878	.02121	.00864	34
.06763	.04899	.03558	.02592	.01894	.00751	35
.06262	.04494	.03235	.02335	.01691	.00653	36
.05799	.04123	.02941	.02104	.01510	.00568	37
.05369	.03783	.02674	.01896	.01348	.00494	38
.04971	.03470	.02430	.01708	.01204	.00429	39
.04603	.03184	.02210	.01538	.01075	.00373	40

Table 3 Future Value of an Ordinary Annuity of 1

$$\text{FVF-OA}_{n,i} = \frac{(1 + i)^n - 1}{i}$$

(n) Periods	2%	2½%	3%	4%	5%	6%
1	1.00000	1.00000	1.00000	1.00000	1.00000	1.00000
2	2.02000	2.02500	2.03000	2.04000	2.05000	2.06000
3	3.06040	3.07563	3.09090	3.12160	3.15250	3.18360
4	4.12161	4.15252	4.18363	4.24646	4.31013	4.37462
5	5.20404	5.25633	5.30914	5.41632	5.52563	5.63709
6	6.30812	6.38774	6.46841	6.63298	6.80191	6.97532
7	7.43428	7.54743	7.66246	7.89829	8.14201	8.39384
8	8.58297	8.73612	8.89234	9.21423	9.54911	9.89747
9	9.75463	9.95452	10.15911	10.58280	11.02656	11.49132
10	10.94972	11.20338	11.46338	12.00611	12.57789	13.18079
11	12.16872	12.48347	12.80780	13.48635	14.20679	14.97164
12	13.41209	13.79555	14.19203	15.02581	15.91713	16.86994
13	14.68033	15.14044	15.61779	16.62684	17.71298	18.88214
14	15.97394	16.51895	17.08632	18.29191	19.59863	21.01507
15	17.29342	17.93193	18.59891	20.02359	21.57856	23.27597
16	18.63929	19.38022	20.15688	21.82453	23.65749	25.67253
17	20.01207	20.86473	21.76159	23.69751	25.84037	28.21288
18	21.41231	22.38635	23.41444	25.64541	28.13238	30.90565
19	22.84056	23.94601	25.11687	27.67123	30.53900	33.75999
20	24.29737	25.54466	26.87037	29.77808	33.06595	36.78559
21	25.78332	27.18327	28.67649	31.96920	35.71925	39.99273
22	27.29898	28.86286	30.53678	34.24797	38.50521	43.39229
23	28.84496	30.58443	32.45288	36.61789	41.43048	46.99583
24	30.42186	32.34904	34.42647	39.08260	44.50200	50.81558
25	32.03030	34.15776	36.45926	41.64591	47.72710	54.86451
26	33.67091	36.01171	38.55304	44.31174	51.11345	59.15638
27	35.34432	37.91200	40.70963	47.08421	54.66913	63.70577
28	37.05121	39.85980	42.93092	49.96758	58.40258	68.52811
29	38.79223	41.85630	45.21885	52.96629	62.32271	73.63980
30	40.56808	43.90270	47.57542	56.08494	66.43885	79.05819
31	42.37944	46.00027	50.00268	59.32834	70.76079	84.80168
32	44.22703	48.15028	52.50276	62.70147	75.29883	90.88978
33	46.11157	50.35403	55.07784	66.20953	80.06377	97.34316
34	48.03380	52.61289	57.73018	69.85791	85.06696	104.18376
35	49.99448	54.92821	60.46208	73.65222	90.32031	111.43478
36	51.99437	57.30141	63.27594	77.59831	95.83632	119.12087
37	54.03425	59.73395	66.17422	81.70225	101.62814	127.26812
38	56.11494	62.22730	69.15945	85.97034	107.70955	135.90421
39	58.23724	64.78298	72.23423	90.40915	114.09502	145.05846
40	60.40198	67.40255	75.40126	95.02552	120.79977	154.76197

Table 3 Future Value of an Ordinary Annuity of 1

8%	9%	10%	11%	12%	15%	(n) Periods
1.00000	1.00000	1.00000	1.00000	1.00000	1.00000	1
2.08000	2.09000	2.10000	2.11000	2.12000	2.15000	2
3.24640	3.27810	3.31000	3.34210	3.37440	3.47250	3
4.50611	4.57313	4.64100	4.70973	4.77933	4.99338	4
5.86660	5.98471	6.10510	6.22780	6.35285	6.74238	5
7.33592	7.52334	7.71561	7.91286	8.11519	8.75374	6
8.92280	9.20044	9.48717	9.78327	10.08901	11.06680	7
10.63663	11.02847	11.43589	11.85943	12.29969	13.72682	8
12.48756	13.02104	13.57948	14.16397	14.77566	16.78584	9
14.48656	15.19293	15.93743	16.72201	17.54874	20.30372	10
16.64549	17.56029	18.53117	19.56143	20.65458	24.34928	11
18.97713	20.14072	21.38428	22.71319	24.13313	29.00167	12
21.49530	22.95339	24.52271	26.21164	28.02911	34.35192	13
24.21492	26.01919	27.97498	30.09492	32.39260	40.50471	14
27.15211	29.36092	31.77248	34.40536	37.27972	47.58041	15
30.32428	33.00340	35.94973	39.18995	42.75328	55.71747	16
33.75023	36.97371	40.54470	44.50084	48.88367	65.07509	17
37.45024	41.30134	45.59917	50.39593	55.74972	75.83636	18
41.44626	46.01846	51.15909	56.93949	63.43968	88.21181	19
45.76196	51.16012	57.27500	64.20283	72.05244	102.44358	20
50.42292	56.76453	64.00250	72.26514	81.69874	118.81012	21
55.45676	62.87334	71.40275	81.21431	92.50258	137.63164	22
60.89330	69.53194	79.54302	91.14788	104.60289	159.27638	23
66.76476	76.78981	88.49733	102.17415	118.15524	184.16784	24
73.10594	84.70090	98.34706	114.41331	133.33387	212.79302	25
79.95442	93.32398	109.18177	127.99877	150.33393	245.71197	26
87.35077	102.72314	121.09994	143.07864	169.37401	283.56877	27
95.33883	112.96822	134.20994	159.81729	190.69889	327.10408	28
103.96594	124.13536	148.63093	178.39719	214.58275	377.16969	29
113.28321	136.30754	164.49402	199.02088	241.33268	434.74515	30
123.34587	149.57522	181.94343	221.91317	271.29261	500.95692	31
134.21354	164.03699	201.13777	247.32362	304.84772	577.10046	32
145.95062	179.80032	222.25154	275.52922	342.42945	644.66553	33
158.62667	196.98234	245.47670	306.83744	384.52098	765.36535	34
172.31680	215.71076	271.02437	341.58955	431.66350	881.17016	35
187.10215	236.12472	299.12681	380.16441	484.46312	1014.34568	36
203.07032	258.37595	330.03949	422.98249	543.59869	1167.49753	37
220.31595	282.62978	364.04343	470.51056	609.83053	1343.62216	38
238.94122	309.06646	401.44778	523.26673	684.01020	1546.16549	39
259.05652	337.88245	442.59256	581.82607	767.09142	1779.09031	40

Table 4 Present Value of an Ordinary Annuity of 1

$$PVF\text{-}OA_{n,i} = \frac{1 - \dfrac{1}{(1+i)^n}}{i}$$

(n) Periods	2%	2½%	3%	4%	5%	6%
1	.98039	.97561	.97087	.96154	.95238	.94340
2	1.94156	1.92742	1.91347	1.88609	1.85941	1.83339
3	2.88388	2.85602	2.82861	2.77509	2.72325	2.67301
4	3.80773	3.76197	3.71710	3.62990	3.54595	3.46511
5	4.71346	4.64583	4.57971	4.45182	4.32948	4.21236
6	5.60143	5.50813	5.41719	5.24214	5.07569	4.91732
7	6.47199	6.34939	6.23028	6.00205	5.78637	5.58238
8	7.32548	7.17014	7.01969	6.73274	6.46321	6.20979
9	8.16224	7.97087	7.78611	7.43533	7.10782	6.80169
10	8.98259	8.75206	8.53020	8.11090	7.72173	7.36009
11	9.78685	9.51421	9.25262	8.76048	8.30641	7.88687
12	10.57534	10.25776	9.95400	9.38507	8.86325	8.38384
13	11.34837	10.98319	10.63496	9.98565	9.39357	8.85268
14	12.10625	11.69091	11.29607	10.56312	9.89864	9.29498
15	12.84926	12.38138	11.93794	11.11839	10.37966	9.71225
16	13.57771	13.05500	12.56110	11.65230	10.83777	10.10590
17	14.29187	13.71220	13.16612	12.16567	11.27407	10.47726
18	14.99203	14.35336	13.75351	12.65930	11.68959	10.82760
19	15.67846	14.97889	14.32380	13.13394	12.08532	11.15812
20	16.35143	15.58916	14.87747	13.59033	12.46221	11.46992
21	17.01121	16.18455	15.41502	14.02916	12.82115	11.76408
22	17.65805	16.76541	15.93692	14.45112	13.16300	12.04158
23	18.29220	17.33211	16.44361	14.85684	13.48857	12.30338
24	18.91393	17.88499	16.93554	15.24696	13.79864	12.55036
25	19.52346	18.42438	17.41315	15.62208	14.09394	12.78336
26	20.12104	18.95061	17.87684	15.98277	14.37519	13.00317
27	20.70690	19.46401	18.32703	16.32959	14.64303	13.21053
28	21.28127	19.96489	18.76411	16.66306	14.89813	13.40616
29	21.84438	20.45355	19.18845	16.98371	15.14107	13.59072
30	22.39646	20.93029	19.60044	17.29203	15.37245	13.76483
31	22.93770	21.39541	20.00043	17.58849	15.59281	13.92909
32	23.46833	21.84918	20.38877	17.87355	15.80268	14.08404
33	23.98856	22.29188	20.76579	18.14765	16.00255	14.23023
34	24.49859	22.72379	21.13184	18.41120	16.19290	14.36814
35	24.99862	23.14516	21.48722	18.66461	16.37419	14.49825
36	25.48884	23.55625	21.83225	18.90828	16.54685	14.62099
37	25.96945	23.95732	22.16724	19.14258	16.71129	14.73678
38	26.44064	24.34860	22.49246	19.36786	16.86789	14.84602
39	26.90259	24.73034	22.80822	19.58448	17.01704	14.94907
40	27.35548	25.10278	23.11477	19.79277	17.15909	15.04630

Table 4   Present Value of an Ordinary Annuity of 1

8%	9%	10%	11%	12%	15%	(n) Periods
.92593	.91743	.90909	.90090	.89286	.86957	1
1.78326	1.75911	1.73554	1.71252	1.69005	1.62571	2
2.57710	2.53130	2.48685	2.44371	2.40183	2.28323	3
3.31213	3.23972	3.16986	3.10245	3.03735	2.85498	4
3.99271	3.88965	3.79079	3.69590	3.60478	3.35216	5
4.62288	4.48592	4.35526	4.23054	4.11141	3.78448	6
5.20637	5.03295	4.86842	4.71220	4.56376	4.16042	7
5.74664	5.53482	5.33493	5.14612	4.96764	4.48732	8
6.24689	5.99525	5.75902	5.53705	5.32825	4.77158	9
6.71008	6.41766	6.14457	5.88923	5.65022	5.01877	10
7.13896	6.80519	6.49506	6.20652	5.93770	5.23371	11
7.53608	7.16073	6.81369	6.49236	6.19437	5.42062	12
7.90378	7.48690	7.10336	6.74987	6.42355	5.58315	13
8.24424	7.78615	7.36669	6.98187	6.62817	5.72448	14
8.55948	8.06069	7.60608	7.19087	6.81086	5.84737	15
8.85137	8.31256	7.82371	7.37916	6.97399	5.95424	16
9.12164	8.54363	8.02155	7.54879	7.11963	6.04716	17
9.37189	8.75563	8.20141	7.70162	7.24967	6.12797	18
9.60360	8.95012	8.36492	7.83929	7.36578	6.19823	19
9.81815	9.12855	8.51356	7.96333	7.46944	6.25933	20
10.01680	9.29224	8.64869	8.07507	7.56200	6.31246	21
10.20074	9.44243	8.77154	8.17574	7.64465	6.35866	22
10.37106	9.58021	8.88322	8.26643	7.71843	6.39884	23
10.52876	9.70661	8.98474	8.34814	7.78432	6.43377	24
10.67478	9.82258	9.07704	8.42174	7.84314	6.46415	25
10.80998	9.92897	9.16095	8.48806	7.89566	6.49056	26
10.93516	10.02658	9.23722	8.54780	7.94255	6.51353	27
11.05108	10.11613	9.30657	8.60162	7.98442	6.53351	28
11.15841	10.19828	9.36961	8.65011	8.02181	6.55088	29
11.25778	10.27365	9.42691	8.69379	8.05518	6.56598	30
11.34980	10.34280	9.47901	8.73315	8.08499	6.57911	31
11.43500	10.40624	9.52638	8.76860	8.11159	6.59053	32
11.51389	10.46444	9.56943	8.80054	8.13535	6.60046	33
11.58693	10.51784	9.60858	8.82932	8.15656	6.60910	34
11.65457	10.56682	9.64416	8.85524	8.17550	6.61661	35
11.71719	10.61176	9.67651	8.87859	8.19241	6.62314	36
11.77518	10.65299	9.70592	8.89963	8.20751	6.62882	37
11.82887	10.69082	9.73265	8.91859	8.22099	6.63375	38
11.87858	10.72552	9.75697	8.93567	8.23303	6.63805	39
11.92461	10.75736	9.77905	8.95105	8.24378	6.64178	40

Table 5   Present Value of an Annuity Due of 1

$$PVF\text{-}AD_{n,i} = 1 + \frac{1 - \dfrac{1}{(1 + i)^{n-1}}}{i}$$

(n) Periods	2%	2½%	3%	4%	5%	6%
1	1.00000	1.00000	1.00000	1.00000	1.00000	1.00000
2	1.98039	1.97561	1.97087	1.96154	1.95238	1.94340
3	2.94156	2.92742	2.91347	2.88609	2.85941	2.83339
4	3.88388	3.85602	3.82861	3.77509	3.72325	3.67301
5	4.80773	4.76197	4.71710	4.62990	4.54595	4.46511
6	5.71346	5.64583	5.57971	5.45182	5.32948	5.21236
7	6.60143	6.50813	6.41719	6.24214	6.07569	5.91732
8	7.47199	7.34939	7.23028	7.00205	6.78637	6.58238
9	8.32548	8.17014	8.01969	7.73274	7.46321	7.20979
10	9.16224	8.97087	8.78611	8.43533	8.10782	7.80169
11	9.98259	9.75206	9.53020	9.11090	8.72173	8.36009
12	10.78685	10.51421	10.25262	9.76048	9.30641	8.88687
13	11.57534	11.25776	10.95400	10.38507	9.86325	9.38384
14	12.34837	11.98319	11.63496	10.98565	10.39357	9.85268
15	13.10625	12.69091	12.29607	11.56312	10.89864	10.29498
16	13.84926	13.38138	12.93794	12.11839	11.37966	10.71225
17	14.57771	14.05500	13.56110	12.65230	11.83777	11.10590
18	15.29187	14.71220	14.16612	13.16567	12.27407	11.47726
19	15.99203	15.35336	14.75351	13.65930	12.68959	11.82760
20	16.67846	15.97889	15.32380	14.13394	13.08532	12.15812
21	17.35143	16.58916	15.87747	14.59033	13.46221	12.46992
22	18.01121	17.18455	16.41502	15.02916	13.82115	12.76408
23	18.65805	17.76541	16.93692	15.45112	14.16300	13.04158
24	19.29220	18.33211	17.44361	15.85684	14.48857	13.30338
25	19.91393	18.88499	17.93554	16.24696	14.79864	13.55036
26	20.52346	19.42438	18.41315	16.62208	15.09394	13.78336
27	21.12104	19.95061	18.87684	16.98277	15.37519	14.00317
28	21.70690	20.46401	19.32703	17.32959	15.64303	14.21053
29	22.28127	20.96489	19.76411	17.66306	15.89813	14.40616
30	22.84438	21.45355	20.18845	17.98371	16.14107	14.59072
31	23.39646	21.93029	20.60044	18.29203	16.37245	14.76483
32	23.93770	22.39541	21.00043	18.58849	16.59281	14.92909
33	24.46833	22.84918	21.38877	18.87355	16.80268	15.08404
34	24.98856	23.29188	21.76579	19.14765	17.00255	15.23023
35	25.49859	23.72379	22.13184	19.41120	17.19290	15.36814
36	25.99862	24.14516	22.48722	19.66461	17.37419	15.49825
37	26.48884	24.55625	22.83225	19.90828	17.54685	15.62099
38	26.96945	24.95732	23.16724	20.14258	17.71129	15.73678
39	27.44064	25.34860	23.49246	20.36786	17.86789	15.84602
40	27.90259	25.73034	23.80822	20.58448	18.01704	15.94907

Table 5   Present Value of an Annuity Due of 1

8%	9%	10%	11%	12%	15%	(n) Periods
1.00000	1.00000	1.00000	1.00000	1.00000	1.00000	1
1.92593	1.91743	1.90909	1.90090	1.89286	1.86957	2
2.78326	2.75911	2.73554	2.71252	2.69005	2.62571	3
3.57710	3.53130	3.48685	3.44371	3.40183	3.28323	4
4.31213	4.23972	4.16986	4.10245	4.03735	3.85498	5
4.99271	4.88965	4.79079	4.69590	4.60478	4.35216	6
5.62288	5.48592	5.35526	5.23054	5.11141	4.78448	7
6.20637	6.03295	5.86842	5.71220	5.56376	5.16042	8
6.74664	6.53482	6.33493	6.14612	5.96764	5.48732	9
7.24689	6.99525	6.75902	6.53705	6.32825	5.77158	10
7.71008	7.41766	7.14457	6.88923	6.65022	6.01877	11
8.13896	7.80519	7.49506	7.20652	6.93770	6.23371	12
8.53608	8.16073	7.81369	7.49236	7.19437	6.42062	13
8.90378	8.48690	8.10336	7.74987	7.42355	6.58315	14
9.24424	8.78615	8.36669	7.98187	7.62817	6.72448	15
9.55948	9.06069	8.60608	8.19087	7.81086	6.84737	16
9.85137	9.31256	8.82371	8.37916	7.97399	6.95424	17
10.12164	9.54363	9.02155	8.54879	8.11963	7.04716	18
10.37189	9.75563	9.20141	8.70162	8.24967	7.12797	19
10.60360	9.95012	9.36492	8.83929	8.36578	7.19823	20
10.81815	10.12855	9.51356	8.96333	8.46944	7.25933	21
11.01680	10.29224	9.64869	9.07507	8.56200	7.31246	22
11.20074	10.44243	9.77154	9.17574	8.64465	7.35866	23
11.37106.	10.58021	9.88322	9.26643	8.71843	7.39884	24
11.52876	10.70661	9.98474	9.34814	8.78432	7.43377	25
11.67478	10.82258	10.07704	9.42174	8.84314	7.46415	26
11.80998	10.92897	10.16095	9.48806	8.89566	7.49056	27
11.93518	11.02658	10.23722	9.54780	8.94255	7.51353	28
12.05108	11.11613	10.30657	9.60162	8.98442	7.53351	29
12.15841	11.19828	10.36961	9.65011	9.02181	7.55088	30
12.25778	11.27365	10.42691	9.69379	9.05518	7.56598	31
12.34980	11.34280	10.47901	9.73315	9.08499	7.57911	32
12.43500	11.40624	10.52638	9.76860	9.11159	7.59053	33
12.51389	11.46444	10.56943	9.80054	9.13535	7.60046	34
12.58693	11.51784	10.60858	9.82932	9.15656	7.60910	35
12.65457	11.56682	10.64416	9.85524	9.17550	7.61661	36
12.71719	11.61176	10.67651	9.87859	9.19241	7.62314	37
12.77518	11.65299	10.70592	9.89963	9.20751	7.62882	38
12.82887	11.69082	10.73265	9.91859	9.22099	7.63375	39
12.87858	11.72552	10.75697	9.93567	9.23303	7.63805	40

APPENDIX B

REPORTING CASH FLOWS

In Chapter 6 we learned that the primary purpose of the statement of cash flows is to provide information about an entity's cash receipts and cash payments during a period. A secondary objective is to provide information on a cash basis about its operating, investing, and financing activities. **The statement of cash flows therefore reports cash receipts, cash payments, and net change in cash resulting from operating, investing, and financing activities of a company during a period, in a format that reconciles the beginning and ending cash balances.**

In this appendix we review the structure of the statement of cash flows and examine some complexities in its preparation.

Learning Objectives

After studying this appendix, you should be able to:

1. Identify sources of information for a statement of cash flows.
2. Prepare a statement of cash flows.
3. Discuss special problems in preparing a statement of cash flows.
4. Understand the direct method of calculating net cash flow from operating activities.

Inside Appendix B

■ **What Do the Numbers Mean?**
Not what it seems (p. 1066)

■ **What's the Principle? (p. 1059)**

SECTION ONE   INDIRECT METHOD

OBJECTIVE 1

Identify sources of information for a statement of cash flows.

Before we review the steps in preparing the statement of cash flows, here are some important points to remember related to the sources of information for the statement of cash flows.

1. Comparative balance sheets provide the basic information from which to prepare the report. Additional information obtained from analyses of specific accounts is also included.

2. An analysis of the Retained Earnings account is necessary. The net increase or decrease in Retained Earnings without any explanation is a meaningless amount in the statement. Without explanation, it might represent the effect of net income, dividends declared, or prior period adjustments.

3. The statement includes all changes that have passed through cash or have resulted in an increase or decrease in cash.

4 Writedowns, amortization charges, and similar "book" entries, such as depreciation of plant assets, represent neither inflows nor outflows of cash, because they have no effect on cash. To the extent that they have entered into the determination of net income, however, the company must add them back to or subtract them from net income, to arrive at net cash provided by operating activities.

PREPARING THE STATEMENT OF CASH FLOWS

To review the steps in the preparation of the statement of cash flows, we use data covering the 2008 operations of Tax Consultants Inc. Tax Consultants Inc. had a good year in 2008. It expanded its operations to include the sale of computer software used in tax-return preparation and tax planning. Thus, inventory is a new asset appearing in the company's December 31, 2008, balance sheet. Illustrations B-1 and B-2 show Tax Consultants' comparative balance sheets, its income statement, and additional information for 2008. The company uses the indirect method to compute and present net cash flow from operating activities.

Tax Consultants Inc.
Comparative Balance Sheets
As of December 31

Assets	2008	2007	Change Increase/Decrease
Cash	$ 54,000	$ 37,000	$ 17,000 Increase
Accounts receivable	68,000	26,000	42,000 Increase
Inventories	54,000	–0–	54,000 Increase
Prepaid expenses	4,000	6,000	2,000 Decrease
Land	45,000	70,000	25,000 Decrease
Buildings	200,000	200,000	–0–
Accumulated depreciation—buildings	(21,000)	(11,000)	10,000 Increase
Equipment	193,000	68,000	125,000 Increase
Accumulated depreciation—equipment	(28,000)	(10,000)	18,000 Increase
Totals	$569,000	$386,000	
Liabilities and Stockholders' Equity			
Accounts payable	$ 33,000	$ 40,000	$ 7,000 Decrease
Bonds payable	110,000	150,000	40,000 Decrease
Common stock ($1 par)	220,000	60,000	160,000 Increase
Retained earnings	206,000	136,000	70,000 Increase
Totals	$569,000	$386,000	

Illustration B-1
Comparative Balance Sheets for Tax Consultants Inc.

Tax Consultants Inc.
Income Statement
For the Year Ended December 31, 2008

Revenues		$890,000
Cost of goods sold	$465,000	
Operating expenses	221,000	
Interest expense	12,000	
Loss on sale of equipment	2,000	700,000
Income from operations		190,000
Income tax expense		65,000
Net income		$125,000

Illustration B-2
Income Statement for Tax Consultants Inc.

Illustration B-2
(continued)

Additional Information

(a) Operating expenses include depreciation expense of $33,000 and amortization of prepaid expenses of $2,000.

(b) Land was sold at its book value for cash.

(c) Cash dividends of $55,000 were declared and paid.

(d) Interest expense of $12,000 was paid in cash.

(e) Equipment with a cost of $166,000 was purchased for cash. Equipment with a cost of $41,000 and a book value of $36,000 was sold for $34,000 cash.

(f) Bonds were redeemed at their book value for cash.

(g) Common stock ($1 par) was issued for cash.

OBJECTIVE 2

Prepare a statement of cash flows.

Using the information in Illustrations B-1 and B-2, let's review the steps in preparing the statement of cash flows.

Step 1: Determining the Net Increase/Decrease in Cash

The first step in the preparation of the statement of cash flows is to determine the change in cash. As the comparative balance sheets show, cash increased $17,000 in 2008.

Step 2: Determining Net Cash Flow Provided/Used by Operating Activities

We explain the adjustments to net income of $125,000 as follows.

Increase in Accounts Receivable. The increase in accounts receivable of $42,000 represents accrual-basis revenues in excess of cash collections in 2008. The company deducts this increase from net income to convert from the accrual basis to the cash basis.

Increase in Inventories. The $54,000 increase in inventories represents an operating use of cash, not an expense. Tax Consultants therefore deducts this amount from net income, to arrive at net cash flow from operations. In other words, when inventory purchased exceeds inventory sold during a period, cost of goods sold on an accrual basis is lower than on a cash basis.

Decrease in Prepaid Expenses. The $2,000 decrease in prepaid expenses represents a charge to the income statement for which Tax Consultants made no cash payment in the current period. The company adds back the decrease to net income, to arrive at net cash flow from operating activities.

Decrease in Accounts Payable. When accounts payable decrease during the year, cost of goods sold and expenses on a cash basis are higher than they are on an accrual basis. To convert net income to net cash flow from operating activities, the company must deduct the $7,000 in accounts payable from net income.

Depreciation Expense (Increase in Accumulated Depreciation). Accumulated Depreciation—Buildings increased $10,000 ($21,000 − $11,000). The Buildings account did not change during the period, which means that Tax Consultants recorded depreciation expense of $10,000 in 2008.

Accumulated Depreciation—Equipment increased by $18,000 ($28,000 − $10,000) during the year. But Accumulated Depreciation—Equipment decreased by $5,000 as a result of the sale during the year. Thus, depreciation for the year was $23,000. The company reconciled Accumulated Depreciation—Equipment as follows.

Beginning balance	$10,000
Add: Depreciation for 2008	23,000
	33,000
Deduct: Sale of equipment	5,000
Ending balance	$28,000

The company must add back to net income the total depreciation of $33,000 ($10,000 + $23,000) charged to the income statement, to determine net cash flow from operating activities.

Loss on Sale of Equipment. Tax Consultants Inc. sold for $34,000 equipment that cost $41,000 and had a book value of $36,000. As a result, the company reported a loss of $2,000 on its sale. To arrive at net cash flow from operating activities, it must add back to net income the loss on the sale of the equipment. The reason is that the loss is a noncash charge to the income statement. The loss did not reduce cash, but it did reduce net income.

From the foregoing items, the company prepares the operating activities section of the statement of cash flows, as shown in Illustration B-3.

Cash flows from operating activities		
Net income		$125,000
Adjustments to reconcile net income to		
net cash provided by operating activities:		
Depreciation expense	$33,000	
Loss on sale of equipment	2,000	
Increase in accounts receivable	(42,000)	
Increase in inventories	(54,000)	
Decrease in prepaid expenses	2,000	
Decrease in accounts payable	(7,000)	(66,000)
Net cash provided by operating activities		59,000

Illustration B-3
Operating Activities
Section of Cash Flows
Statement

Step 3: Determining Net Cash Provided/Used by Investing and Financing Activities

By analyzing the remaining changes in the balance sheet accounts, Tax Consultants identifies cash flows from investing and financing activities.

Land. Land decreased $25,000 during the period. As indicated from the information presented, the company sold land for cash at its book value. This transaction is an investing activity, reported as a $25,000 source of cash.

Equipment. An analysis of the equipment account indicates the following.

Beginning balance	$ 68,000
Purchase of equipment	166,000
	234,000
Sale of equipment	41,000
Ending balance	$193,000

The company used cash to purchase equipment with a fair value of $166,000—an investing transaction reported as a cash outflow. The sale of the equipment for $34,000 is also an investing activity, but one that generates a cash inflow.

Bonds Payable. Bonds payable decreased $40,000 during the year. As indicated from the additional information, the company redeemed the bonds at their book value. This financing transaction used $40,000 of cash.

Common Stock. The common stock account increased $160,000 during the year. As indicated from the additional information, Tax Consultants issued common stock of $160,000 at par. This financing transaction provided cash of $160,000.

Retained Earnings. Retained earnings changed $70,000 ($206,000 − $136,000) during the year. The $70,000 change in retained earnings results from net income of $125,000 from operations and the financing activity of paying cash dividends of $55,000.

$2800 = 10000 - 3000 \times X$

Statement of Cash Flows—2008

Tax Consultants Inc. combines the foregoing items to prepare the statement of cash flows shown in Illustration B-4.

Illustration B-4
Statement of Cash Flows
for Tax Consultants Inc.

Tax Consultants Inc. Statement of Cash Flows For the Year Ended December 31, 2008 Increase (Decrease) in Cash		
Cash flows from operating activities		
Net income		$125,000
Adjustments to reconcile net income to net cash provided by operating activities:		
Depreciation expense	$ 33,000	
Loss on sale of equipment	2,000	
Increase in accounts receivable	(42,000)	
Increase in inventories	(54,000)	
Decrease in prepaid expenses	2,000	
Decrease in accounts payable	(7,000)	(66,000)
Net cash provided by operating activities		59,000
Cash flows from investing activities		
Sale of land	25,000	
Sale of equipment	34,000	
Purchase of equipment	(166,000)	
Net cash used by investing activities		(107,000)
Cash flows from financing activities		
Redemption of bonds	(40,000)	
Sale of common stock	160,000	
Payment of dividends	(55,000)	
Net cash provided by financing activities		65,000
Net increase in cash		17,000
Cash, January 1, 2008		37,000
Cash, December 31, 2008		$ 54,000

SPECIAL PROBLEMS IN STATEMENT PREPARATION

OBJECTIVE 3

Discuss special problems in preparing a statement of cash flows.

We discussed some of the special problems related to preparing the statement of cash flows in connection with the preceding illustrations. Other problems that arise with some frequency in the preparation of this statement include the following.

1 Adjustments similar to depreciation.

2 Accounts receivable (net).

3 Other working capital changes.

4 Net losses.

5 Gains/losses.

6 Stock options.

7 Postretirement benefit cost.

8 Extraordinary items.

9 Significant noncash transactions.

Adjustments Similar to Depreciation

Depreciation expense is the most common adjustment to net income that companies make to arrive at net cash flow from operating activities. But there are numerous other noncash expense or revenue items. Examples of expense items that companies must add back to net income are the **amortization of limited-life intangible assets** such as patents, and the **amortization of deferred costs** such as bond issue costs. These charges to expense involve expenditures made in prior periods that a company amortizes currently. These charges reduce net income without affecting cash in the current period.

Also, **amortization of bond discount or premium** on long-term bonds payable affects the amount of interest expense. However, neither changes cash. As a result, a company should add back discount amortization and subtract premium amortization from net income to arrive at net cash flow from operating activities.

In a similar manner, **changes in deferred income taxes** affect net income but have no effect on cash. For example, **Delta Airlines** reported an increase in its liability for deferred taxes of approximately $1.2 billion. This change in the liability increased tax expense and decreased net income, but did not affect cash. Therefore, Delta added back $1.2 billion to net income on its statement of cash flows.

Another common adjustment to net income is **a change related to an investment in common stock** when recording income or loss under the equity method. Recall that under the equity method, the investor (1) debits the investment account and credits revenue for its share of the investee's net income, and (2) credits dividends received to the investment account. Therefore, the net increase in the investment account does not affect cash flow. A company must deduct the net increase from net income to arrive at net cash flow from operating activities.

To illustrate, assume that Victor Co. owns 40 percent of Milo Inc. During the year Milo reports net income of $100,000 and pays a cash dividend of $30,000. Victor reports this in its statement of cash flows as a deduction from net income in the following manner— Equity in earnings of Milo, net of dividends, $28,000 [($100,000 − $30,000) × 40%].

If Victor Co. does not exercise significant influence over Milo, it cannot use the equity method. Instead, it uses the fair-value method. Under the fair-value method, Victor does not recognize any of Milo's net income. Further, it records any cash dividend received as revenue. As a result, the company makes no adjustment to net income in the statement of cash flows because cash dividends received are included in income.

Accounts Receivable (Net)

Up to this point, we assumed no allowance for doubtful accounts—a contra account—to offset accounts receivable. However, if a company needs an allowance for doubtful accounts, how does that allowance affect the company's determination of net cash flow from operating activities? For example, assume that Redmark Co. reports net income of $40,000. It has the accounts receivable balances as shown in Illustration B-5.

	2008	2007	Change Increase/Decrease
Accounts receivable	$105,000	$90,000	$15,000 Increase
Allowance for doubtful accounts	(10,000)	(4,000)	6,000 Increase
Accounts receivable (net)	$ 95,000	$86,000	9,000 Increase

Illustration B-5
Accounts Receivable Balances, Redmark Co.

Because an increase in the Allowance for Doubtful Accounts results from a charge to bad debts expense, a company should add back an increase in the Allowance for Doubtful Accounts to net income to arrive at net cash flow from operating activities. Illustration B-6 (page 1056) shows one method for presenting this information in a statement of cash flows.

Redmark Co.
Statement of Cash Flows (partial)
For the Year 2008

Cash flows from operating activities		
Net income		$40,000
Adjustments to reconcile net income to net		
cash provided by operating activities:		
Increase in accounts receivable	$(15,000)	
Increase in allowance for doubtful accounts	6,000	(9,000)
		$31,000

Instead of separately analyzing the allowance account, a short-cut approach is to net the allowance balance against the receivable balance and compare the change in accounts receivable on a net basis. Illustration B-7 shows this presentation.

Redmark Co.
Statement of Cash Flows (partial)
For the Year 2008

Cash flows from operating activities	
Net income	$40,000
Adjustments to reconcile net income to	
net cash provided by operating activities:	
Increase in accounts receivable (net)	(9,000)
	$31,000

This short-cut procedure works also if the change in the allowance account results from a writeoff of accounts receivable. This reduces both the Accounts Receivable and the Allowance for Doubtful Accounts. No effect on cash flows occurs. Because of its simplicity, *use the net approach for your homework assignments.*

Other Working Capital Changes

Up to this point, we showed how companies handled all of the changes in working capital items (current asset and current liability items) as adjustments to net income in determining net cash flow from operating activities. You must be careful, however, because **some changes in working capital**, **although they affect cash**, **do not affect net income**. Generally, these are investing or financing activities of a current nature.

One activity is the purchase of **short-term available-for-sale securities**. For example, the purchase of short-term available-for-sale securities for $50,000 cash has no effect on net income but it does cause a $50,000 decrease in cash.[1] A company reports this transaction as a cash flow from investing activities as follows.[2]

Cash flows from investing activities	
Purchase of short-term available-for-sale securities	$(50,000)

[1]If the basis of the statement of cash flows is **cash and cash equivalents** and the short-term investment is considered a cash equivalent, then a company reports nothing in the statement because the transaction does not affect the balance of cash and cash equivalents. The Board notes that cash purchases of short term investments generally are part of the company's cash management activities rather than part of its operating, investing, or financing activities.

[2]"Accounting for Certain Investments in Debt and Equity Securities," *Statement of Financial Accounting Standards No. 115* (Norwalk, Conn.: 1993), par. 118.

What about **trading securities**? Because companies hold these investments principally for the purpose of selling them in the near term, companies should classify the cash flows from purchases and sales of trading securities as cash flows from **operating activities**.[3]

Another example is the issuance of a **short-term nontrade note payable** for cash. This change in a working capital item has no effect on income from operations but it increases cash by the amount of the note payable. For example, a company reports the issuance of a $10,000 short-term note payable for cash in the statement of cash flows as follows.

Cash flows from financing activities	
Issuance of short-term note	$10,000

Another change in a working capital item that has no effect on income from operations or on cash is a **cash dividend payable**. Although a company will report the cash dividends when paid as a financing activity, it does not report the declared but unpaid dividend on the statement of cash flows.

Net Losses

If a company reports a net loss instead of a net income, it must adjust the net loss for those items that do not result in a cash inflow or outflow. The net loss, after adjusting for the charges or credits not affecting cash, may result in a negative or a positive cash flow from operating activities.

For example, if the net loss is $50,000 and the total amount of charges to add back is $60,000, then net cash provided by operating activities is $10,000. Illustration B-8 shows this computation.

Net loss		$(50,000)
Adjustments to reconcile net income to net		
cash provided by operating activities:		
Depreciation expense	$55,000	
Amortization of patents	5,000	60,000
Net cash provided by operating activities		$ 10,000

Illustration B-8
Computation of Net Cash Flow from Operating Activities—Cash Inflow

If the company experiences a net loss of $80,000 and the total amount of the charges to add back is $25,000, the presentation appears as follows.

Net loss	$(80,000)	
Adjustments to reconcile net income to		
net cash used by operating activities:		
Depreciation expense	25,000	
Net cash used by operating activities	$(55,000)	

Illustration B-9
Computation of Net Cash Flow from Operating Activities—Cash Outflow

Although not illustrated in this appendix, a negative cash flow may result even if the company reports a net income.

Gains/Losses

In the illustration for Tax Consultants, the company experienced a loss of $2,000 from the sale of equipment. The company added this loss to net income to compute net cash flow from operating activities because **the loss is a noncash charge in the income statement**.

If Tax Consultants experiences a **gain** from a sale of equipment it too requires an adjustment to net income. Because a company reports the gain in the statement of cash flows

[3]Ibid., par. 118.

1058 Appendix B ■ Reporting Cash Flows

as part of the cash proceeds from the sale of equipment under investing activities, **it deducts the gain from net income to avoid double counting**—once as part of net income, and again as part of the cash proceeds from the sale.

Similarly, if a company recognizes in income the gains and losses on the sale of investments, these gains or losses are deducted or added back, respectively, in computing net cash flow from operating activities. Note that this treatment is applicable to trading securities and any investments accounted for under the fair value option for both realized and unrealized gain or losses. *Unrealized* holding gains or losses on available-for-sale investments are not adjusted in the computation of net cash flow from operating activities. This is because these gains or losses are recorded in stockholders' equity, not income.

Stock Options

Recall for share-based compensation plans that companies are required to use the fair-value method to determine total compensation cost. The compensation cost is then recognized as an expense in the periods in which the employee provides services. When Compensation Expense is debited, Paid-in Capital—Stock Options is often credited. Cash is not affected by recording the expense. **Therefore, the company must increase net income by the amount of compensation expense from stock options in computing net cash flow from operating activities.**

To illustrate how this information should be reported on a statement of cash flows, assume that First Wave Inc. grants 5,000 options to its CEO, Ann Johnson. Each option entitles Johnson to purchase one share of First Wave's $1 par value common stock at $50 per share at any time in the next two years (the service period). The fair value of the options is $200,000. First Wave records compensation expense in the first year as follows:

Compensation Expense ($200,000 ÷ 2)	100,000	
Paid-in Capital—Stock Options		100,000

In addition, if we assume that First Wave has a 35 percent tax rate, it would recognize a deferred tax asset of $35,000 ($100,000 × 35%) in the first year as follows:

Deferred Tax Asset	35,000	
Income Tax Expense		35,000

Therefore on the statement of cash flows for the first year, First Wave reports the following (assuming a net income of $600,000).

Net income	$600,000
Adjustments to reconcile net income to net cash provided by operating activities:	
Share-based compensation expense	100,000
Increase in deferred tax asset	(35,000)

As shown in First Wave's statement of cash flows, it adds the share-based compensation expense to net income because it is a non-cash expense. The increase in the deferred tax asset and the related reduction in income tax expense increase net income. Although the negative income tax expense increases net income, it does not increase cash. Therefore it should be deducted.

Subsequently, if Ann Johnson exercises her options, Third Wave reports "Cash provided by exercise of stock options" in the financing section of the statement of cash flows.[4]

---

[4]Companies receive a tax deduction related to share-based compensation plans at the time employees exercise their options. The amount of the deduction is equal to the difference between the market price of the stock and the exercise price at the date the employee purchases the stock, which in most cases, is much larger than the total compensation expense recorded. When the tax deduction exceeds the total compensation recorded, this provides an additional cash inflow to the company. For example, in a recent year **Cisco Systems** reported an additional cash inflow related to its stock option plans equal to $537 million. Under the provisions of *SFAS No. 123(R)*, this tax-related cash inflow is reported in the financing section of the statement of cash flows. See "Share-Based Payment," *Statement of Financial Accounting Standard No. 123(R)* (Norwalk, Conn.: FASB, 2004) par. 68.

Postretirement Benefit Costs

If a company has postretirement costs such as an employee pension plan, chances are that the pension expense recorded during a period will either be higher or lower than the cash funded. When the expense is higher or lower than the cash paid, **the company must adjust net income by the difference between cash paid and the expense reported** in computing net cash flow from operating activities.

Extraordinary Items

Companies should report **either as investing activities or as financing activities** cash flows from extraordinary transactions and other events whose effects are included in net income, but which are not related to operations.

For example, assume that Tax Consultants had land with a carrying value of $200,000, which was condemned by the state of Maine for a highway project. The condemnation proceeds received were $205,000, resulting in a gain of $5,000 less $2,000 of taxes. In the statement of cash flows (indirect method), the company would deduct the $5,000 gain from net income in the operating activities section. It would report the $205,000 cash inflow from the condemnation as an investing activity, as follows.

Cash flows from investing activities	
Condemnation of land	$205,000

Note that Tax Consultants handles the gain at its **gross** amount ($5,000), not net of tax. The company reports the cash received in the condemnation as an investing activity at $205,000, also exclusive of the tax effect.

The FASB requires companies to classify **all income taxes paid as operating cash outflows**. Some suggested that income taxes paid be allocated to investing and financing transactions. But the Board decided that allocation of income taxes paid to operating, investing, and financing activities would be so complex and arbitrary that the benefits, if any, would not justify the costs involved. Under both the direct method and the indirect method, companies must disclose the total amount of income taxes paid.[5]

WHAT'S THE PRINCIPLE?

By rejecting the requirement to allocate taxes to the various activities, the Board invoked the cost-benefit constraint. The information would be beneficial, but the cost of providing such information would exceed the benefits of providing it.

Significant Noncash Transactions

Because the statement of cash flows reports only the effects of operating, investing, and financing activities in terms of cash flows, it omits some **significant noncash transactions** and other events that are investing or financing activities. Among the more common of these noncash transactions that a company should report or disclose in some manner are the following.

Examples of Cash Flow Statements

1   Acquisition of assets by assuming liabilities (including capital lease obligations) or by issuing equity securities.

2   Exchanges of nonmonetary assets.

3   Refinancing of long-term debt.

---

[5]For an insightful article on some weaknesses and limitations in the statement of cash flows caused by implementation of *FASB Statement No. 95*, see Hugo Nurnberg, "Inconsistencies and Ambiguities in Cash Flow Statements Under *FASB Statement No. 95*," *Accounting Horizons* (June 1993), pp. 60–73. Nurnberg identifies the inconsistencies caused by the three-way classification of all cash receipts and cash payments, gross versus net of tax, the ambiguous disclosure requirements for noncash investing and financing transactions, and the ambiguous presentation of third-party financing transactions. See also Paul B. W. Miller, and Bruce P. Budge, "Nonarticulation in Cash Flow Statements and Implications for Education, Research, and Practice," *Accounting Horizons* (December 1996), pp. 1–15; and Charles Mulford and Michael Ely, "Calculating Sustainable Cash Flow: A Study of the S&P 100," *Georgia Tech Financial Analysis Lab* (October 2004).

4 Conversion of debt or preferred stock to common stock.

5 Issuance of equity securities to retire debt.

A company does not incorporate these noncash items in the statement of cash flows. If material in amount, these disclosures may be either narrative or summarized in a separate schedule at the bottom of the statement, or they may appear in a separate note or supplementary schedule to the financial statements.[6] Illustration B-10 shows the presentation of these significant noncash transactions or other events in a separate schedule at the bottom of the statement of cash flows.

Illustration B-10
Schedule Presentation of Noncash Investing and Financing Activities

Net increase in cash	$3,717,000
Cash at beginning of year	5,208,000
Cash at end of year	$8,925,000
Noncash investing and financing activities	
Purchase of land and building through issuance of 250,000 shares of	
common stock	$1,750,000
Exchange of Steadfast, NY, land for Bedford, PA, land	$2,000,000
Conversion of 12% bonds to 50,000 shares of common stock	$ 500,000

Or, companies may present these noncash transactions in a separate note, as shown in Illustration B-11.

Illustration B-11
Note Presentation of Noncash Investing and Financing Activities

Note G: Significant noncash transactions. During the year the company engaged in the following significant noncash investing and financing transactions:	
Issued 250,000 shares of common stock to purchase land and building	$1,750,000
Exchanged land in Steadfast, NY, for land in Bedford, PA	$2,000,000
Converted 12% bonds due 2007 to 50,000 shares of common stock	$ 500,000

DIRECT METHOD

OBJECTIVE 4

Understand the direct method of calculating net cash flow from operating activities.

There are two different methods available to adjust income from operations on an accrual basis to net cash flow from operating activities: the indirect (reconciliation) method and the direct (income statement) method.

The FASB encourages use of the direct method and permits use of the indirect method. Yet, if the direct method is used, the Board requires that companies provide in a separate schedule a reconciliation of net income to net cash flow from operating activities. Therefore, under either method, companies must prepare and report information from the indirect (reconciliation) method.

---

[6]Some noncash investing and financing activities are part cash and part noncash. Companies should report only the cash portion on the statement of cash flows. The noncash component should be reported at the bottom of the statement or in a separate note.

Companies do not generally report certain other significant noncash transactions or other events in conjunction with the statement of cash flows. Examples of these types of transactions are **stock dividends, stock splits, and restrictions on retained earnings**. Companies generally report these items, neither financing nor investing activities, in conjunction with the statement of stockholders' equity or in schedules and notes pertaining to changes in stockholders' equity accounts.

INDIRECT METHOD

For consistency and comparability and because it is the most widely used method in practice, we used the indirect method in the examples just presented. We determined net cash flows from operating activities by adding back to or deducting from net income those items that had no effect on cash. Illustration B-12 presents more completely the common types of adjustments that companies make to net income to arrive at net cash flow from operating activities.

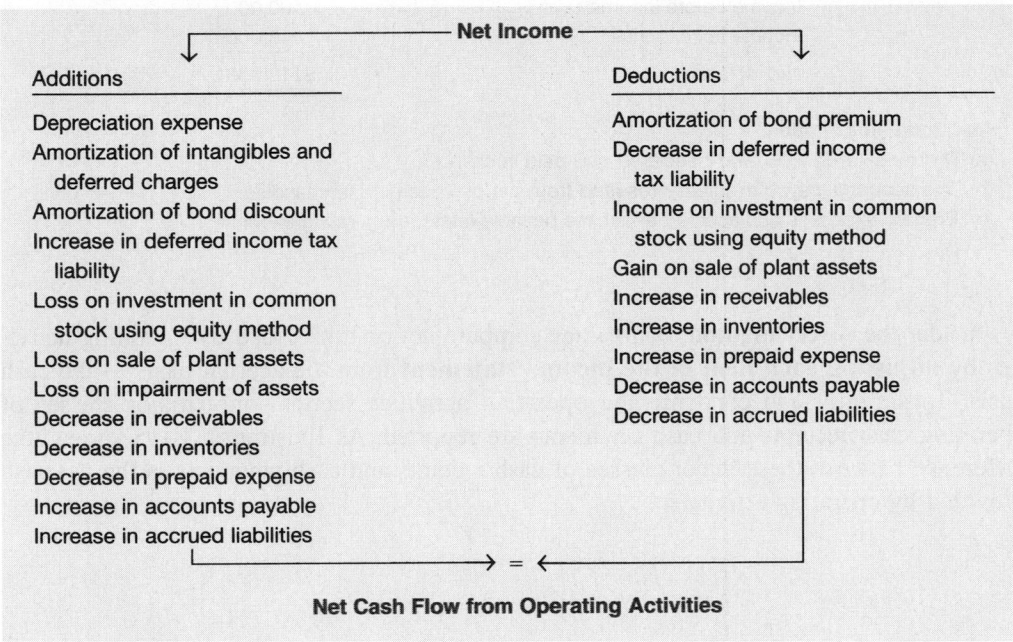

Illustration B-12
Adjustments Needed to Determine Net Cash Flow from Operating Activities—Indirect Method

The additions and deductions listed above reconcile net income to net cash flow from operating activities, illustrating why the indirect method is also called the reconciliation method.

DIRECT METHOD—AN EXAMPLE

Under the direct method the statement of cash flows reports net cash flow from operating activities as major classes of *operating cash receipts* (e.g., cash collected from customers and cash received from interest and dividends) and *cash disbursements* (e.g., cash paid to suppliers for goods, to employees for services, to creditors for interest, and to government authorities for taxes).

We illustrate the direct method here in more detail to help you understand the difference between accrual-based income and net cash flow from operating activities. This example also illustrates the data needed to apply the direct method. Emig Company, which began business on January 1, 2008, has the following selected balance sheet information.

	December 31 2008	2007
Cash	$159,000	–0–
Accounts receivable	15,000	–0–
Inventory	160,000	–0–
Prepaid expenses	8,000	–0–
Property, plant, and equipment (net)	90,000	–0–
Accounts payable	60,000	–0–
Accrued expenses payable	20,000	–0–

Illustration B-13
Balance Sheet Accounts for Emig Co.

Emig Company's December 31, 2008, income statement and additional information are as follows.

Illustration B-14
Income Statement for
Emig Co.

Revenues from sales		$780,000
Cost of goods sold		450,000
Gross profit		330,000
Operating expenses	$160,000	
Depreciation	10,000	170,000
Income before income taxes		160,000
Income tax expense		48,000
Net income		$112,000

Additional Information:
(a) Dividends of $70,000 were declared and paid in cash.
(b) The accounts payable increase resulted from the purchase of merchandise.
(c) Prepaid expenses and accrued expenses payable relate to operating expenses.

Under the **direct method**, companies compute net cash provided by operating activities by **adjusting each item in the income statement** from the accrual basis to the cash basis. To simplify and condense the operating activities section, only major classes of operating cash receipts and cash payments are reported. As Illustration B-15 shows, the difference between these major classes of cash receipts and cash payments is the net cash provided by operating activities.

Illustration B-15
Major Classes of Cash
Receipts and Payments

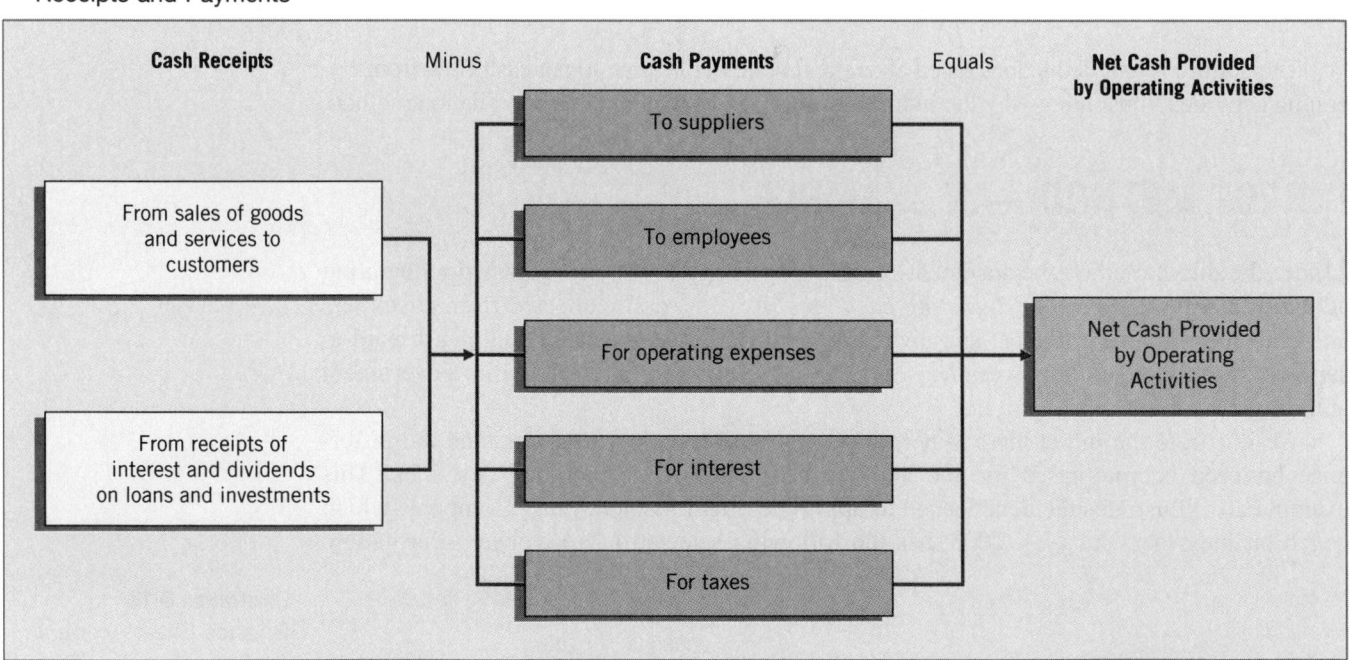

An efficient way to apply the direct method is to analyze the revenues and expenses reported in the income statement in the order in which they are listed. The company then determines cash receipts and cash payments related to these revenues and expenses. In the following sections, we present the direct method adjustments for Emig Company in 2008, to determine net cash provided by operating activities.

Cash Receipts from Customers. The income statement for Emig Company reported revenues from customers of $780,000. To determine cash receipts from customers, the company considers the change in accounts receivable during the year.

When accounts receivable increase during the year, revenues on an accrual basis are higher than cash receipts from customers. In other words, operations led to increased revenues, but not all of these revenues resulted in cash receipts. To determine the amount of increase in cash receipts, deduct the amount of the increase in accounts receivable from the total sales revenues. Conversely, a decrease in accounts receivable is added to sales revenues, because cash receipts from customers then exceed sales revenues.

For Emig Company, accounts receivable increased $15,000. Thus, cash receipts from customers were $765,000, computed as follows.

Revenues from sales	$780,000
Deduct: Increase in accounts receivable	15,000
Cash receipts from customers	$765,000

Emig could also determine cash receipts from customers by analyzing the Accounts Receivable account as shown below.

Accounts Receivable

1/1/08	Balance	–0–	Receipts from customers	765,000
	Revenues from sales	780,000		
12/31/08	Balance	15,000		

Illustration B-16 shows the relationships between cash receipts from customers, revenues from sales, and changes in accounts receivable.

Cash Receipts from Customers	=	Revenues from Sales	{ + Decrease in Accounts Receivable or – Increase in Accounts Receivable

Illustration B-16
Formula to Compute Cash Receipts from Customers

Cash Payments to Suppliers. Emig Company reported cost of goods sold on its income statement of $450,000. To determine cash payments to suppliers, the company first finds purchases for the year, by adjusting cost of goods sold for the change in inventory. When inventory increases during the year, purchases this year exceed cost of goods sold. As a result, the company adds the increase in inventory to cost of goods sold, to arrive at purchases.

In 2008, Emig Company's inventory increased $160,000. The company computes purchases as follows.

Cost of goods sold	$450,000
Add: Increase in inventory	160,000
Purchases	$610,000

After computing purchases, Emig determines cash payments to suppliers by adjusting purchases for the change in accounts payable. When accounts payable increase during the year, purchases on an accrual basis are higher than they are on a cash basis. As a result, it deducts from purchases the increase in accounts payable to arrive at cash payments to suppliers. Conversely, if cash payments to suppliers exceed purchases, Emig adds to purchases the decrease in accounts payable. Cash payments to suppliers were $550,000, computed as follows.

Purchases	$610,000
Deduct: Increase in accounts payable	60,000
Cash payments to suppliers	$550,000

Emig also can determine cash payments to suppliers by analyzing Accounts Payable, as shown below.

	Accounts Payable			
Payments to suppliers	550,000	1/1/08	Balance	–0–
			Purchases	610,000
		12/31/08	Balance	60,000

Illustration B-17 shows the relationships between cash payments to suppliers, cost of goods sold, changes in inventory, and changes in accounts payable.

Illustration B-17
Formula to Compute
Cash Payments to
Suppliers

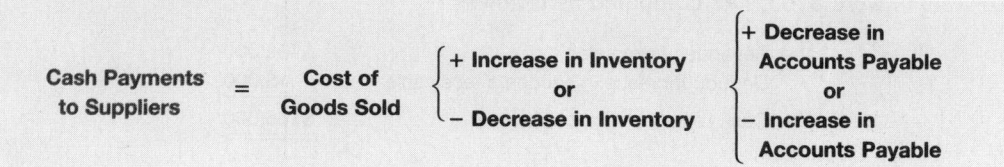

Cash Payments for Operating Expenses. Emig reported operating expenses of $160,000 on its income statement. To determine the cash paid for operating expenses, it must adjust this amount for any changes in prepaid expenses and accrued expenses payable.

For example, when prepaid expenses increased $8,000 during the year, cash paid for operating expenses was $8,000 higher than operating expenses reported on the income statement. To convert operating expenses to cash payments for operating expenses, the company adds to operating expenses the increase of $8,000. Conversely, if prepaid expenses decrease during the year, it deducts from operating expenses the amount of the decrease.

Emig also must adjust operating expenses for changes in accrued expenses payable. When accrued expenses payable increase during the year, operating expenses on an accrual basis are higher than they are on a cash basis. As a result, the company deducts from operating expenses an increase in accrued expenses payable, to arrive at cash payments for operating expenses. Conversely, it adds to operating expenses a decrease in accrued expenses payable, because cash payments exceed operating expenses.

Emig Company's cash payments for operating expenses were $148,000, computed as follows.

Operating expenses	$160,000
Add: Increase in prepaid expenses	8,000
Deduct: Increase in accrued expenses payable	(20,000)
Cash payments for operating expenses	$148,000

The relationships among cash payments for operating expenses, changes in prepaid expenses, and changes in accrued expenses payable are shown in Illustration B-18.

Illustration B-18
Formula to Compute
Cash Payments for
Operating Expenses

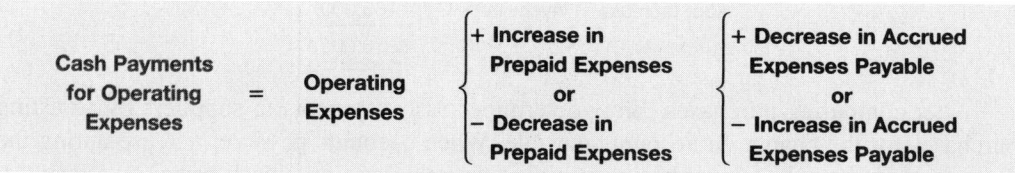

Note that the company did not consider depreciation expense, because it is a noncash charge.

Cash Payments for Income Taxes. The income statement for Emig shows income tax expense of $48,000. This amount equals the cash paid. How do we know that? Because the comparative balance sheet indicated no income taxes payable at either the beginning or end of the year.

Summary of Net Cash Flow from Operating Activities— Direct Method

The following schedule summarizes the computations illustrated above.

Illustration B-19
Accrual Basis to Cash Basis

Accrual Basis		Adjustment	Add (Subtract)	Cash Basis
Revenues from sales	$780,000 −	Increase in accounts receivable	$(15,000)	$765,000
Cost of goods sold	450,000 +	Increase in inventory	160,000	
	−	Increase in accounts payable	(60,000)	550,000
Operating expenses	160,000 +	Increase in prepaid expenses	8,000	
	−	Increase in accrued expenses payable	(20,000)	148,000
Depreciation expense	10,000 −	Depreciation expense	(10,000)	–0–
Income tax expense	48,000			48,000
Total expense	668,000			746,000
Net income	$112,000	Net cash provided by operating activities		$ 19,000

Illustration B-20 shows the presentation of the direct method for reporting net cash flow from operating activities for the Emig Company illustration.

Illustration B-20
Operating Activities Section—Direct Method, 2008

Emig Company
Statement of Cash Flows (partial)

Cash flows from operating activities		
Cash received from customers		$765,000
Cash payments:		
To suppliers	$ 550,000	
For operating expenses	148,000	
For income taxes	48,000	746,000
Net cash provided by operating activities		$ 19,000

If Emig Company uses the direct method to present the net cash flows from operating activities, it must provide in a separate schedule the reconciliation of net income to net cash provided by operating activities. The reconciliation assumes the identical form and content of the indirect method of presentation, as shown below.

Illustration B-21
Reconciliation of Net Income to Net Cash Provided by Operating Activities

Emig Company
Reconciliation

Net income		$112,000
Adjustments to reconcile net income to net cash provided by operating activities:		
Depreciation expense	$ 10,000	
Increase in accounts receivable	(15,000)	
Increase in inventory	(160,000)	
Increase in prepaid expenses	(8,000)	
Increase in accounts payable	60,000	
Increase in accrued expense payable	20,000	(93,000)
Net cash provided by operating activities		$ 19,000

When the direct method is used, the company may present this reconciliation at the bottom of the statement of cash flows or in a separate schedule.

What do the numbers mean?

Recent events highlight the importance that the market attributes to operating cash flow. By showing an improving cash flow, a company can give a favorable impression of its ongoing operations. For example, **WorldCom** concealed declines in its operations by capitalizing certain operating expenses—to the tune of $3.8 billion! This practice not only "juiced up" income but also made it possible to report the cash payments in the investing section of the cash flow statement rather than as a deduction from operating cash flow.

The SEC recently addressed a similar cash flow classification issue with automakers like **Ford**, **GM**, and **Daimler-Chrysler**. For years, automakers classified lease receivables and other dealer-financing arrangements as investment cash flows. Thus, they reported an increase in lease or loan receivables from cars sold as a use of cash in the investing section of the statement of cash flows. The SEC objected and now requires automakers to report these receivables as operating cash flows, since the leases and loans are used to facilitate car sales. At GM, these reclassifications reduced its operating cash flows from $7.6 billion to $3 billion in the year before the change. So while the overall cash flow—from operations, investing, and financing—remained the same, operating cash flow at these companies looked better than it really was.

Source: Peter Elstrom, "How to Hide $3.8 Billion in Expenses," *BusinessWeek Online* (July 8, 2002); and Judith Burns, "SEC Tells US Automakers to Retool Cash-Flow Accounting," *Wall Street Journal Online* (February 28, 2005).

Key Terms

significant noncash transactions, 1059
statement of cash flows, 1050

Summary of Learning Objectives

1 Identify sources of information for a statement of cash flows. The information to prepare the statement usually comes from three sources: (1) *Comparative balance sheets*. Information in these statements indicates the amount of the changes in assets, liabilities, and equities during the period. (2) *Current income statement*. Information in this statement is used in determining the cash provided by operations during the period. (3) *Selected transaction data*. These data from the general ledger provide additional detailed information needed to determine how cash was provided or used during the period.

2 Prepare a statement of cash flows. Preparing the statement involves three major steps: (1) Determine the change in cash. This is the difference between the beginning and the ending cash balance shown on the comparative balance sheets. (2) Determine the net cash flow from operating activities. This procedure is complex; it involves analyzing not only the current year's income statement but also the comparative balance sheets and the selected transaction data. (3) Determine

cash flows from investing and financing activities. Analyze all other changes in the balance sheet accounts to determine the effects on cash.

3 Discuss special problems in preparing a statement of cash flows. These special problems are: (1) adjustments similar to depreciation; (2) accounts receivable (net); (3) other working capital changes; (4) net losses; (5) gains/losses; (6) stock options; (7) postretirement benefit costs; (8) extraordinary items; and (9) significant noncash transactions.

4 Understand the direct method of calculating net cash flow from operating activities. Under the direct approach, companies calculate the major classes of operating cash receipts and cash disbursements. Companies summarize the computations in a schedule of changes from the accrual to the cash basis income statement. Presentation of the direct approach of reporting net cash flow from operating activities takes the form of a condensed cash-basis income statement.

Exercises

EB-1 **(Preparation of Operating Activities Section—Indirect Method, Periodic Inventory)** The income statement of Vince Gill Company is shown below.

(LO 2, 3)

Vince Gill Company		
Income Statement		
For the Year Ended December 31, 2008		
Sales		$6,900,000
Cost of goods sold		
Beginning inventory	$1,900,000	
Purchases	4,400,000	
Goods available for sale	6,300,000	
Ending inventory	1,600,000	
Cost of goods sold		4,700,000
Gross profit		2,200,000
Operating expenses		
Selling expenses	450,000	
Administrative expenses	700,000	1,150,000
Net income		$1,050,000

Additional information:

1. Accounts receivable decreased $360,000 during the year.
2. Prepaid expenses increased $170,000 during the year.
3. Accounts payable to suppliers of merchandise decreased $275,000 during the year.
4. Accrued expenses payable decreased $100,000 during the year.
5. Administrative expenses include depreciation expense of $60,000.

Instructions

Prepare the operating activities section of the statement of cash flows for the year ended December 31, 2008, for Vince Gill Company, using the indirect method.

EB-2 **(Schedule of Net Cash Flow from Operating Activities—Indirect Method)** Ballard Co. reported $145,000 of net income for 2008. The accountant, in preparing the statement of cash flows, noted several items occurring during 2008 that might affect cash flows from operating activities.

(LO 3, 4)

1. Ballard purchased 100 shares of treasury stock at a cost of $20 per share. The company resold these shares at $25 per share.
2. Ballard sold 100 shares of IBM common at $200 per share. The acquisition cost of these shares was $145 per share. This investment was shown on Ballard's December 31, 2007, balance sheet as an available-for-sale security.
3. Ballard revised its estimate for bad debts. Before 2008, Ballard's bad debt expense was 1% of its net sales. In 2008, this percentage was increased to 2%. Net sales for 2008 were $500,000, and net accounts receivable decreased by $12,000 during 2008.
4. Ballard issued 500 shares of its $10 par common stock for a patent. The market value of the shares on the date of the transation was $23 per share.
5. Depreciation expense is $39,000.
6. Ballard Co. holds 40% of the Nirvana Company's common stock as a long-term investment. Nirvana Company reported $27,000 of net income for 2008.
7. Nirvana Company paid a total of $2,000 of cash dividends to all investees in 2008.
8. Ballard declared a 10% stock dividend. One thousand shares of $10 par common stock were distributed. The market price at date of issuance was $20 per share.

Instructions

Prepare a schedule that shows the net cash flow from operating activities using the indirect method. Assume no items other than those listed above affected the computation of 2008 net cash flow from operating activities.

(LO 3, 4)   **EB-3** **(SCF—Indirect Method)**   Condensed financial data of Pat Metheny Company for 2008 and 2007 are presented below.

Pat Metheny Company
Comparative Balance Sheet
As of December 31, 2008 and 2007

	2008	2007
Cash	$1,800	$1,150
Receivables	1,750	1,300
Inventory	1,600	1,900
Plant assets	1,900	1,700
Accumulated depreciation	(1,200)	(1,170)
Long-term investments (Held-to-maturity)	1,300	1,420
	$7,150	$6,300
Accounts payable	$1,200	$ 900
Accrued liabilities	200	250
Bonds payable	1,400	1,550
Capital stock	1,900	1,700
Retained earnings	2,450	1,900
	$7,150	$6,300

Pat Metheny Company
Income Statement
For the Year Ended December 31, 2008

Sales	$6,900
Cost of goods sold	4,700
Gross margin	2,200
Selling and administrative expense	930
Income from operations	1,270
Other revenues and gains	
Gain on sale of investments	80
Income before income tax	1,350
Income tax expense	540
Net income	810
Cash dividends	260
Income retained in business	$ 550

Additional information:

During the year, $70 of common stock was issued in exchange for plant assets. No plant assets were sold in 2008.

Instructions

Prepare a statement of cash flows using the indirect method.

(LO 3, 4)   **EB-4** **(SCF—Direct Method)**   Data for Pat Metheny Company are presented in EB-3.

Instructions

Prepare a statement of cash flows using the direct method. (Do not prepare a reconciliation schedule.)

(LO 2, 3)   **EB-5** **(Classification of Transactions)**   Following are selected balance sheet accounts of Allman Bros. Corp. at December 31, 2008 and 2007, and the increases or decreases in each account from 2007 to 2008. Also presented is selected income statement information for the year ended December 31, 2008, and additional information.

Selected balance sheet accounts	2008	2007	Increase (Decrease)
Assets			
Accounts receivable	$ 34,000	$ 24,000	$ 10,000
Property, plant, and equipment	277,000	247,000	30,000
Accumulated depreciation	(178,000)	(167,000)	(11,000)

	2008	2007	Increase
Liabilities and stockholders' equity			
Bonds payable	$ 49,000	$46,000	$ 3,000
Dividends payable	8,000	5,000	3,000
Common stock, $1 par	22,000	19,000	3,000
Additional paid-in capital	9,000	3,000	6,000
Retained earnings	104,000	91,000	13,000

Selected income statement information for the year ended December 31, 2008

Sales revenue	$155,000
Depreciation	33,000
Gain on sale of equipment	14,500
Net income	31,000

Additional information:

1. During 2008, equipment costing $45,000 was sold for cash.
2. Accounts receivable relate to sales of merchandise.
3. During 2008, $20,000 of bonds payable were issued in exchange for property, plant, and equipment. There was no amortization of bond discount or premium.

Instructions

Determine the category (operating, investing, or financing) and the amount that should be reported in the statement of cash flows for the following items.

1. Payments for purchase of property, plant, and equipment.
2. Proceeds from the sale of equipment.
3. Cash dividends paid.
4. Redemption of bonds payable.

EB-6 (SCF Theory and Analysis of Transactions) John Lee Hooker Company is a young and growing producer of electronic measuring instruments and technical equipment. You have been retained by Hooker to advise it in the preparation of a statement of cash flows using the indirect method. For the fiscal year ended October 31, 2008, you have obtained the following information concerning certain events and transactions of Hooker.

1. The amount of reported earnings for the fiscal year was $800,000, which included a deduction for an extraordinary loss of $110,000 (see item 5 below).
2. Depreciation expense of $315,000 was included in the income statement.
3. Uncollectible accounts receivable of $40,000 were written off against the allowance for doubtful accounts. Also, $51,000 of bad debt expense was included in determining income for the fiscal year, and the same amount was added to the allowance for doubtful accounts.
4. A gain of $9,000 was realized on the sale of a machine. It originally cost $75,000, of which $30,000 was undepreciated on the date of sale.
5. On April 1, 2008, lightning caused an uninsured building loss of $110,000 ($180,000 loss, less reduction in income taxes of $70,000). This extraordinary loss was included in determining income as indicated in 1 above.
6. On July 3, 2008, building and land were purchased for $700,000. Hooker gave in payment $75,000 cash, $200,000 market value of its unissued common stock, and signed a $425,000 mortgage note payable.
7. On August 3, 2008, $800,000 face value of Hooker's 10% convertible debentures were converted into $150,000 par value of its common stock. The bonds were originally issued at face value.

Instructions

Explain whether each of the seven numbered items above is an inflow or an outflow of cash, and explain how it should be disclosed in John Lee Hooker's statement of cash flows for the fiscal year ended October 31, 2008. If any item is neither an inflow nor an outflow of cash, explain why it is not, and indicate the disclosure, if any, that should be made of the item in John Lee Hooker's statement of cash flows for the fiscal year ended October 31, 2008.

EB-7 (Analysis of Transactions' Effect on SCF) Each of the following items must be considered in preparing a statement of cash flows for Sage Fashions Inc. for the year ended December 31, 2008.

1. Fixed assets that had cost $20,000 6½ years before and were being depreciated on a 10-year basis, with no estimated scrap value, were sold for $5,250.

2. During the year, goodwill of $15,000 was considered impaired and was completely written off to expense.
3. During the year, 500 shares of common stock with a stated value of $25 a share were issued for $34 a share.
4. The company sustained a net loss for the year of $2,100. Depreciation amounted to $2,000 and patent amortization was $400.
5. Uncollectible accounts receivable in the amount of $2,000 were written off against the Allowance for Doubtful Accounts.
6. Investments (available-for-sale) that cost $12,000 when purchased 4 years earlier were sold for $10,600. The loss was considered ordinary.
7. Bonds payable with a par value of $24,000 on which there was an unamortized bond premium of $2,000 were redeemed at 103. The gain was credited to ordinary income.

Instructions

For each item, state where it is to be shown in the statement and then how you would present the necessary information, including the amount. Consider each item to be independent of the others. Assume that correct entries were made for all transactions as they took place.

(LO 3, 4)   **EB-8** **(Preparation of Operating Activities Section—Direct Method)**   Data for the Vince Gill Company are presented in EB-1.

Instructions

Prepare the operating activities section of the statement of cash flows using the direct method.

(LO 3, 4)   **EB-9** **(Preparation of Operating Activities Section—Direct Method)**   Krauss Company's income statement for the year ended December 31, 2008, contained the following condensed information.

Revenue from fees		$840,000
Operating expenses (excluding depreciation)	$624,000	
Depreciation expense	60,000	
Loss on sale of equipment	26,000	710,000
Income before income taxes		130,000
Income tax expense		40,000
Net income		$ 90,000

Krauss's balance sheet contained the following comparative data at December 31.

	2008	2007
Accounts receivable	$37,000	$54,000
Accounts payable	41,000	31,000
Income taxes payable	4,000	8,500

(Accounts payable pertains to operating expenses.)

Instructions

Prepare the operating activities section of the statement of cash flows using the direct method.

(LO 2, 3)   **EB-10** **(Preparation of Operating Activities Section—Indirect Method)**   Data for Krauss Company are presented in EB-9.

Instructions

Prepare the operating activities section of the statement of cash flows using the indirect method.

(LO 3, 4)   **EB-11** **(Computation of Operating Activities—Direct Method)**   Presented below are two independent situations.

Situation A:
Annie Lennox Co. reports revenues of $200,000 and operating expenses of $110,000 in its first year of operations, 2008. Accounts receivable and accounts payable at year-end were $71,000 and $29,000, respectively. Assume that the accounts payable related to operating expenses. Ignore income taxes.

Instructions

Using the direct method, compute net cash provided by operating activities.

Situation B:

The income statement for Blues Traveler Company shows cost of goods sold of $310,000 and operating expenses (exclusive of depreciation) of $230,000. The comparative balance sheet for the year shows that inventory increased $26,000, prepaid expenses decreased $8,000, accounts payable (related to merchandise) decreased $17,000, and accrued expenses payable increased $11,000.

Instructions

Compute (a) cash payments to suppliers and (b) cash payments for operating expenses.

EB-12 (SCF—Direct Method) Los Lobos Corp. uses the direct method to prepare its statement of cash flows. Los Lobos's trial balances at December 31, 2008 and 2007, are as follows. **(LO 3, 4)**

	December 31	
	2008	2007
Debits		
Cash	$ 35,000	$ 32,000
Accounts receivable	33,000	30,000
Inventory	31,000	47,000
Property, plant, & equipment	100,000	95,000
Unamortized bond discount	4,500	5,000
Cost of goods sold	250,000	380,000
Selling expenses	141,500	172,000
General and administrative expenses	137,000	151,300
Interest expense	4,300	2,600
Income tax expense	20,400	61,200
	$756,700	$976,100
Credits		
Allowance for doubtful accounts	$ 1,300	$ 1,100
Accumulated depreciation	16,500	15,000
Trade accounts payable	25,000	15,500
Income taxes payable	21,000	29,100
Deferred income taxes	5,300	4,600
8% callable bonds payable	45,000	20,000
Common stock	50,000	40,000
Additional paid-in capital	9,100	7,500
Retained earnings	44,700	64,600
Sales	538,800	778,700
	$756,700	$976,100

Additional information:

1. Los Lobos purchased $5,000 in equipment during 2008.
2. Los Lobos allocated one-third of its depreciation expense to selling expenses and the remainder to general and administrative expenses.
3. Bad debt expense for 2008 was $5,000, and writeoffs of uncollectible accounts totaled $4,800.

Instructions

Determine what amounts Los Lobos should report in its statement of cash flows for the year ended December 31, 2008, for the following items.

1. Cash collected from customers.
2. Cash paid to suppliers.
3. Cash paid for interest.
4. Cash paid for income taxes.
5. Cash paid for selling expenses.

See the book's companion website, at www.wiley.com/college/warfield, for Additional Exercises.

Problems

(LO 2, 3)   **PB-1 (SCF—Indirect Method)** The following is Blue Man Corp.'s comparative balance sheet accounts at December 31, 2008 and 2007, with a column showing the increase (decrease) from 2007 to 2008.

Comparative Balance Sheets			
	2008	2007	Increase (Decrease)
Cash	$ 807,500	$ 700,000	$107,500
Accounts receivable	1,128,000	1,168,000	(40,000)
Inventories	1,850,000	1,715,000	135,000
Property, plant and equipment	3,307,000	2,967,000	340,000
Accumulated depreciation	(1,165,000)	(1,040,000)	(125,000)
Investment in Blige Co.	305,000	275,000	30,000
Loan receivable	262,500	—	262,500
Total assets	$6,495,000	$5,785,000	$710,000
Accounts payable	$1,015,000	$ 955,000	$ 60,000
Income taxes payable	30,000	50,000	(20,000)
Dividends payable	80,000	100,000	(20,000)
Capital lease obligation	400,000	—	400,000
Capital stock, common, $1 par	500,000	500,000	—
Additional paid-in capital	1,500,000	1,500,000	—
Retained earnings	2,970,000	2,680,000	290,000
Total liabilities and stockholders' equity	$6,495,000	$5,785,000	$710,000

Additional information:

1. On December 31, 2007, Blue Man acquired 25% of Blige Co.'s common stock for $275,000. On that date, the carrying value of Blige's assets and liabilities, which approximated their fair values, was $1,100,000. Blige reported income of $120,000 for the year ended December 31, 2008. No dividend was paid on Blige's common stock during the year.
2. During 2008, Blue Man loaned $300,000 to TLC Co., an unrelated company. TLC made the first semi-annual principal repayment of $37,500, plus interest at 10%, on December 31, 2008.
3. On January 2, 2008, Blue Man sold equipment costing $60,000, with a carrying amount of $35,000, for $40,000 cash.
4. On December 31, 2008, Blue Man entered into a capital lease for an office building. The present value of the annual rental payments is $400,000, which equals the fair value of the building. Blue Man made the first rental payment of $60,000 when due on January 2, 2009.
5. Net income for 2008 was $370,000.
6. Blue Man declared and paid cash dividends for 2008 and 2007 as shown below.

	2008	2007
Declared	December 15, 2008	December 15, 2007
Paid	February 28, 2009	February 28, 2008
Amount	$80,000	$100,000

Instructions

Prepare a statement of cash flows for Blue Man Corp. for the year ended December 31, 2008, using the indirect method.

(AICPA adapted)

(LO 2, 3)   **PB-2 (SCF—Indirect Method)** The comparative balance sheets for Shenandoah Corporation show the following information.

	December 31	
	2008	2007
Cash	$ 38,500	$13,000
Accounts receivable	12,250	10,000
Inventory	12,000	9,000
Investments	–0–	3,000
Building	–0–	29,750
Equipment	40,000	20,000
Patent	5,000	6,250
	$107,750	$91,000
Allowance for doubtful accounts	3,000	4,500
Accumulated depreciation on equipment	2,000	4,500
Accumulated depreciation on building	–0–	6,000
Accounts payable	5,000	3,000
Dividends payable	–0–	5,000
Notes payable, short-term (nontrade)	3,000	4,000
Long-term notes payable	31,000	25,000
Common stock	43,000	33,000
Retained earnings	20,750	6,000
	$107,750	$91,000

Additional data related to 2008 are as follows.

1. Equipment that had cost $11,000 and was 30% depreciated at time of disposal was sold for $2,500.
2. $10,000 of the long-term note payable was paid by issuing common stock.
3. Cash dividends paid were $5,000.
4. On January 1, 2008, the building was completely destroyed by a flood. Insurance proceeds on the building were $30,000 (net of $2,000 taxes).
5. Investments (available-for-sale) were sold at $3,700 above their cost. The company has made similar sales and investments in the past.
6. Cash of $15,000 was paid for the acquisition of equipment.
7. A long-term note for $16,000 was issued for the acquisition of equipment.
8. Interest of $2,000 and income taxes of $6,500 were paid in cash.

Instructions

Prepare a statement of cash flows using the indirect method. Flood damage is unusual and infrequent in that part of the country.

PB-3 (SCF—Indirect Method, and Net Cash Flow from Operating Activities) Comparative balance sheet accounts of Secada Inc. are presented below.

(LO 2, 3)

Secada Inc.		
Comparative Balance Sheet Accounts		
As of December 31, 2008 and 2007		
	December 31	
Debit Accounts	2008	2007
Cash	$ 45,000	$ 33,750
Accounts Receivable	67,500	60,000
Merchandise Inventory	30,000	24,000
Investments (available-for-sale)	22,250	38,500
Machinery	30,000	18,750
Buildings	67,500	56,250
Land	7,500	7,500
	$269,750	$238,750

Credit Accounts	2008	2007
Allowance for Doubtful Accounts	$ 2,250	$ 1,500
Accumulated Depreciation—Machinery	5,625	2,250
Accumulated Depreciation—Buildings	13,500	9,000
Accounts Payable	30,000	24,750
Accrued Payables	3,375	2,625
Long-Term Note Payable	26,000	31,000
Common Stock, no par	150,000	125,000
Retained Earnings	39,000	42,625
	$269,750	$238,750

Additional data (ignoring taxes):

1. Net income for the year was $42,500.
2. Cash dividends declared during the year were $21,125.
3. A 20% stock dividend was declared during the year. $25,000 of retained earnings was capitalized.
4. Investments that cost $20,000 were sold during the year for $23,750.
5. Machinery that cost $3,750, on which $750 of depreciation had accumulated, was sold for $2,200.

Secada's 2008 income statement follows (ignoring taxes).

Sales		$540,000
Less: Cost of goods sold		380,000
Gross margin		160,000
Less: Operating expenses (includes $8,625 depreciation and $5,400 bad debts)		120,450
Income from operations		39,550
Other: Gain on sale of investments	$3,750	
Loss on sale of machinery	(800)	2,950
Net income		$ 42,500

Instructions

Prepare a statement of cash flows using the indirect method.

(LO 2, 3)   **PB-4 (Indirect SCF)** Seneca Corporation has contracted with you to prepare a statement of cash flows. The controller has provided the following information.

	December 31 2008	December 31 2007
Cash	$ 43,500	$13,000
Accounts receivable	12,250	10,000
Inventory	12,000	10,000
Investments	–0–	3,000
Building	–0–	29,750
Equipment	35,000	20,000
Copyright	5,000	5,250
Totals	$107,750	$91,000
Allowance for doubtful accounts	$ 3,000	$ 4,500
Accumulated depreciation on equipment	2,000	4,500
Accumulated depreciation on building	–0–	6,000
Accounts payable	5,000	4,000
Dividends payable	–0–	5,000
Notes payable, short-term (nontrade)	3,000	4,000
Long-term notes payable	36,000	25,000
Common stock	38,000	33,000
Retained earnings	20,750	5,000
	$107,750	$91,000

Additional data related to 2008 are as follows.

1. Equipment that had cost $11,000 and was 40% depreciated at time of disposal was sold for $2,500.
2. $5,000 of the long-term note payable was paid by issuing common stock.
3. Cash dividends paid were $5,000.
4. On January 1, 2008, the building was completely destroyed by a flood. Insurance proceeds on the building were $33,000 (net of $4,000 taxes).
5. Investments (available-for-sale) were sold at $2,500 above their cost. The company has made similar sales and investments in the past.
6. Cash of $10,000 was paid for the acquisition of equipment.
7. A long-term note for $16,000 was issued for the acquisition of equipment.
8. Interest of $2,000 and income taxes of $5,000 were paid in cash.

Instructions

(a) Use the indirect method to analyze the above information and prepare a statement of cash flows for Seneca. Flood damage is unusual and infrequent in that part of the country.

(b) What would you expect to observe in the operating, investing, and financing sections of a statement of cash flows of:
 (1) a severely financially troubled firm?
 (2) a recently formed firm which is experiencing rapid growth?

PB-5 (**SCF—Direct and Indirect Methods from Comparative Financial Statements**) George Winston Company, a major retailer of bicycles and accessories, operates several stores and is a publicly traded company. The comparative statement of financial position and income statement for Winston as of May 31, 2008, are shown below and on the next page. **(LO 3, 4)**

George Winston Company
Comparative Statement of Financial Position
As of May 31

	2008	2007
Current assets		
Cash	$ 33,250	$ 20,000
Accounts receivable	80,000	58,000
Merchandise inventory	210,000	250,000
Prepaid expenses	9,000	7,000
Total current assets	332,250	335,000
Plant assets		
Plant assets	600,000	502,000
Less: Accumulated depreciation	150,000	125,000
Net plant assets	450,000	377,000
Total assets	$782,250	$712,000
Current liabilities		
Accounts payable	$123,000	$115,000
Salaries payable	47,250	72,000
Interest payable	27,000	25,000
Total current liabilities	197,250	212,000
Long-term debt		
Bonds payable	70,000	100,000
Total liabilities	267,250	312,000
Shareholders' equity		
Common stock, $10 par	370,000	280,000
Retained earnings	145,000	120,000
Total shareholders' equity	515,000	400,000
Total liabilities and shareholders' equity	$782,250	$712,000

George Winston Company
Income Statement
For the Year Ended May 31, 2008

Sales	$1,255,250
Cost of merchandise sold	722,000
Gross profit	533,250
Expenses	
Salary expense	252,100
Interest expense	75,000
Other expenses	8,150
Depreciation expense	25,000
Total expenses	360,250
Operating income	173,000
Income tax expense	43,000
Net income	$ 130,000

The following is additional information concerning Winston's transactions during the year ended May 31, 2008.

1. All sales during the year were made on account.
2. All merchandise was purchased on account, comprising the total accounts payable account.
3. Plant assets costing $98,000 were purchased by paying $48,000 in cash and issuing 5,000 shares of stock.
4. The "other expenses" are related to prepaid items.
5. All income taxes incurred during the year were paid during the year.
6. In order to supplement its cash, Winston issued 4,000 shares of common stock at par value.
7. Bonds were called at face value.
8. Cash dividends of $105,000 were declared and paid at the end of the fiscal year.

Instructions

(a) Compare and contrast the direct method and the indirect method for reporting cash flows from operating activities.

(b) Prepare a statement of cash flows for Winston Company for the year ended May 31, 2008, using the direct method. Be sure to support the statement with appropriate calculations. (A reconciliation of net income to net cash provided is not required.)

(c) Using the indirect method, calculate only the net cash flow from operating activities for Winston Company for the year ended May 31, 2008.

(LO 2, 3, 4)   **PB-6** (SCF—Direct and Indirect Methods)   Comparative balance sheet accounts of Jensen Company are presented below.

Jensen Company
Comparative Balance Sheet Accounts
As of December 31

Debit Balances	2008	2007
Cash	$ 80,000	$ 51,000
Accounts Receivable	145,000	130,000
Merchandise Inventory	75,000	61,000
Investments (Available-for-sale)	55,000	85,000
Equipment	70,000	48,000
Buildings	145,000	145,000
Land	40,000	25,000
Totals	$610,000	$545,000

Credit Balances

Allowance for Doubtful Accounts	$ 10,000	$ 8,000
Accumulated Depreciation—Equipment	21,000	14,000
Accumulated Depreciation—Building	37,000	28,000
Accounts Payable	70,000	60,000
Income Taxes Payable	12,000	10,000
Long-Term Notes Payable	62,000	70,000
Common Stock	310,000	260,000
Retained Earnings	88,000	95,000
Totals	$610,000	$545,000

Additional data:

1. Equipment that cost $10,000 and was 40% depreciated was sold in 2008.
2. Cash dividends were declared and paid during the year.
3. Common stock was issued in exchange for land.
4. Investments that cost $35,000 were sold during the year.
5. There were no write-offs of uncollectible accounts during the year.

Jensen's 2008 income statement is as follows.

Sales	$950,000
Less: Cost of goods sold	600,000
Gross profit	350,000
Less: Operating expenses (includes depreciation expense and bad debt expense)	250,000
Income from operations	100,000
Other revenues and expenses	
Gain on sale of investments $15,000	
Loss on sale of equipment (3,000)	12,000
Income before taxes	112,000
Income taxes	45,000
Net income	$ 67,000

Instructions

(a) Compute net cash provided by operating activities under the direct method.
(b) Prepare a statement of cash flows using the indirect method.

PB-7 (SCF—Direct Method) Mardi Gras Company has not yet prepared a formal statement of cash flows for the 2008 fiscal year. Comparative balance sheets as of December 31, 2007 and 2008, and a statement of income and retained earnings for the year ended December 31, 2008, are presented below and on page 1078. **(LO 4)**

Mardi Gras Company
Statement of Income and Retained Earnings
For the Year Ended December 31, 2008
($000 omitted)

Sales		$3,800
Expenses		
Cost of goods sold	$1,200	
Salaries and benefits	725	
Heat, light, and power	75	
Depreciation	80	
Property taxes	19	
Patent amortization	25	
Miscellaneous expenses	10	
Interest	30	2,164

Income before income taxes		1,636
Income taxes		818
Net income		818
Retained earnings—Jan. 1, 2008		310
		1,128
Stock dividend declared and issued		600
Retained earnings—Dec. 31, 2008		$ 528

Mardi Gras Company
Comparative Balance Sheets
As of December 31
($000 omitted)

Assets	2008	2007
Current assets		
Cash	$ 383	$ 100
U.S. Treasury notes (Available-for-sale)	–0–	50
Accounts receivable	740	500
Inventory	720	560
Total current assets	1,843	1,210
Long-term assets		
Land	150	70
Buildings and equipment	910	600
Accumulated depreciation	(200)	(120)
Patents (less amortization)	105	130
Total long-term assets	965	680
Total assets	$2,808	$1,890
Liabilities and Stockholders' Equity		
Current liabilities		
Accounts payable	$ 420	$ 340
Income taxes payable	40	20
Notes payable	320	320
Total current liabilities	780	680
Long-term notes payable—due 2010	200	200
Total liabilities	980	880
Stockholders' equity		
Common stock	1,300	700
Retained earnings	528	310
Total stockholders' equity	1,828	1,010
Total liabilities and stockholders' equity	$2,808	$1,890

Instructions

Prepare a statement of cash flows using the direct method. Changes in accounts receivable and accounts payable relate to sales and cost of goods sold. Do not prepare a reconciliation schedule.

(CMA adapted)

(LO 3, 4)   **PB-8** (**SCF—Direct Method**)   Cleveland Company had the following information available at the end of 2008.

Cleveland Company
Comparative Balance Sheets
As of December 31, 2008 and 2007

	2008	2007
Cash	$ 15,000	$ 4,000
Accounts receivable	17,500	12,950
Short-term investments	20,000	30,000

Inventory	42,000	35,000
Prepaid rent	3,000	12,000
Prepaid insurance	2,100	900
Office supplies	1,000	750
Land	125,000	175,000
Building	350,000	350,000
Accumulated depreciation	(105,000)	(87,500)
Equipment	525,000	400,000
Accumulated depreciation	(130,000)	(112,000)
Patent	45,000	50,000
Total assets	$910,600	$871,100
Accounts payable	$ 27,000	$ 32,000
Taxes payable	5,000	4,000
Wages payable	5,000	3,000
Short-term notes payable	10,000	10,000
Long-term notes payable	60,000	70,000
Bonds payable	400,000	400,000
Premium on bonds payable	20,303	25,853
Common stock	240,000	220,000
Paid-in capital in excess of par	20,000	17,500
Retained earnings	123,297	88,747
Total liabilities and stockholders' equity	$910,600	$871,100

Cleveland Company
Income Statement
For the Year Ended December 31, 2008

Sales revenue		$1,160,000
Cost of goods sold		(748,000)
		412,000
Gross margin		
Operating expenses		
Selling expenses	$ 79,200	
Administrative expenses	156,700	
Depreciation/Amortization expense	40,500	
Total operating expenses		(276,400)
Income from operations		135,600
Other revenues/expenses		
Gain on sale of land	8,000	
Gain on sale of short-term investment	4,000	
Dividend revenue	2,400	
Interest expense	(51,750)	(37,350)
Income before taxes		98,250
Income tax expense		(39,400)
Net income		58,850
Dividends to common stockholders		(24,300)
To retained earnings		$ 34,550

Instructions

Prepare a statement of cash flows for Cleveland Company using the direct method accompanied by a reconciliation schedule. Assume the short-term investments are available-for-sale securities.

COMPANY INDEX

OFFICIAL ACCOUNTING PRONOUNCEMENTS

The following list of official accounting pronouncements constitutes the major part of *generally accepted accounting principles* (GAAP) and represents the authoritative source documents for much of the discussion contained in this book.

Date Issued		No.	Title
			Accounting Research Bulletins (ARB's), Committee on Accounting Procedures, AICPA (1953–1959)
June	1953	No. 43	Restatement and Revision of *Accounting Research Bulletins Nos. 1–42*, and *Accounting Terminology Bulletin No. 1* (originally issued 1939–1953) (amended)
Oct.	1954	No. 44	Declining-Balance Depreciation; Revised July, 1958 (amended)
Oct.	1955	No. 45	Long-term Construction-type Contracts (unchanged)
Feb.	1956	No. 46	Discontinuance of Dating Earned Surplus (unchanged)
Sept.	1956	No. 47	Accounting for Costs of Pension Plans (superseded)
Jan.	1957	No. 48	Business Combinations (superseded)
April	1958	No. 49	Earnings Per Share (superseded)
Oct.	1958	No. 50	Contingencies (superseded)
Aug.	1959	No. 51	Consolidated Financial Statements (amended and partially superseded)
			Accounting Terminology Bulletins, Committee on Terminology, AICPA
Aug.	1953	No. 1	Review and Résumé (of the eight original terminology bulletins) (amended)
Mar.	1955	No. 2	Proceeds, Revenue, Income, Profit, and Earnings (amended)
Aug.	1956	No. 3	Book Value (unchanged)
July	1957	No. 4	Cost, Expense, and Loss (amended)
			Accounting Principles Board (APB) Opinions, AICPA (1962–1973)
Nov.	1962	No. 1	New Depreciation Guidelines and Rules (amended)
Dec.	1962	No. 2	Accounting for the "Investment Credit" (amended)
Oct.	1963	No. 3	The Statement of Source and Application of Funds (superseded)
Mar.	1964	No. 4	Accounting for the "Investment Credit" (amending No. 2)
Sept.	1964	No. 5	Reporting of Leases in Financial Statements of Lessee (superseded)
Oct.	1965	No. 6	Status of Accounting Research Bulletins (partially superseded)
May	1966	No. 7	Accounting for Leases in Financial Statements of Lessors (superseded)
Nov.	1966	No. 8	Accounting for the Cost of Pension Plans (superseded)
Dec.	1966	No. 9	Reporting the Results of Operations (amended and partially superseded)
Dec.	1966	No. 10	Omnibus Opinion—1966 (amended and partially superseded)
Dec.	1967	No. 11	Accounting for Income Taxes (superseded)
Dec.	1967	No. 12	Omnibus Opinion—1967 (partially superseded)
Mar.	1969	No. 13	Amending Paragraph 6 of *APB Opinion No. 9*, Application to Commercial Banks (unchanged)
Mar.	1969	No. 14	Accounting for Convertible Debt and Debt Issued with Stock Purchase Warrants (unchanged)
May	1969	No. 15	Earnings per Share (superseded)
Aug.	1970	No. 16	Business Combinations (superseded)
Aug.	1970	No. 17	Intangible Assets (superseded)
Mar.	1971	No. 18	The Equity Method of Accounting for Investments in Common Stock (amended)
Mar.	1971	No. 19	Reporting Changes in Financial Position (amended)
July	1971	No. 20	Accounting Changes (superseded)
Aug.	1971	No. 21	Interest on Receivables and Payables (amended and partially superseded)
April	1972	No. 22	Disclosure of Accounting Policies (amended)
April	1972	No. 23	Accounting for Income Taxes—Special Areas (superseded)
April	1972	No. 24	Accounting for Income Taxes—Equity Method Investments (unchanged)
Oct.	1972	No. 25	Accounting for Stock Issued to Employees (unchanged)
Oct.	1972	No. 26	Early Extinguishment of Debt (amended)
Nov.	1972	No. 27	Accounting for Lease Transactions by Manufacturer or Dealer Lessors (superseded)
May	1973	No. 28	Interim Financial Reporting (amended and partially superseded)
May	1973	No. 29	Accounting for Nonmonetary Transactions (amended)
June	1973	No. 30	Reporting the Results of Operations (amended)
June	1973	No. 31	Disclosure of Lease Commitments by Lessees (superseded)
			Financial Accounting Standards Board (FASB), Statements of Financial Accounting Standards (1973–2007)
Dec.	1973	No. 1	Disclosure of Foreign Currency Translation Information (superseded)
Oct.	1974	No. 2	Accounting for Research and Development Costs (amended)
Dec.	1974	No. 3	Reporting Accounting Changes in Interim Financial Statements (superseded)
Mar.	1975	No. 4	Reporting Gains and Losses from Extinguishment of Debt (superseded)
Mar.	1975	No. 5	Accounting for Contingencies (amended)
May	1975	No. 6	Classification of Short-term Obligations Expected to be Refinanced
June	1975	No. 7	Accounting and Reporting by Development Stage Enterprises
Oct.	1975	No. 8	Accounting for the Translation of Foreign Currency Transactions and Foreign Financial Statements (superseded)

Date Issued		No.	Title
Oct.	1975	No. 9	Accounting for Income Taxes—Oil and Gas Producing Companies (superseded)
Oct.	1975	No. 10	Extension of "Grandfather" Provisions for Business Combinations (superseded)
Dec.	1975	No. 11	Accounting for Contingencies—Transition Method
Dec.	1975	No. 12	Accounting for Certain Marketable Securities (superseded)
Nov.	1976	No. 13	Accounting for Leases (amended, interpreted, and partially superseded)
Dec.	1976	No. 14	Financial Reporting for Segments of a Business Enterprise (amended)
June	1977	No. 15	Accounting by Debtors and Creditors for Troubled Debt Restructurings (amended)
June	1977	No. 16	Prior Period Adjustments (amended)
Nov.	1977	No. 17	Accounting for Leases—Initial Direct Costs
Nov.	1977	No. 18	Financial Reporting for Segments of a Business Enterprise—Interim Financial Statements
Dec.	1977	No. 19	Financial Accounting and Reporting by Oil and Gas Producing Companies (amended)
Dec.	1977	No. 20	Accounting for Forward Exchange Contracts (superseded)
April	1978	No. 21	Suspension of the Reporting of Earnings per Share and Segment Information by Nonpublic Enterprises (amended)
June	1978	No. 22	Changes in the Provisions of Lease Agreements Resulting from Refundings of Tax-Exempt Debt (amended)
Aug.	1978	No. 23	Inception of the Lease
Dec.	1978	No. 24	Reporting Segment Information in Financial Statements That Are Presented in Another Enterprise's Financial Report
Feb.	1979	No. 25	Suspension of Certain Accounting Requirements for Oil and Gas Producing Companies
April	1979	No. 26	Profit Recognition on Sales-Type Leases of Real Estate
May	1979	No. 27	Classification of Renewals or Extensions of Existing Sales-Type or Direct Financing Leases
May	1979	No. 28	Accounting for Sales with Leasebacks
June	1979	No. 29	Determining Contingent Rentals
Aug.	1979	No. 30	Disclosure of Information about Major Customers
Sept.	1979	No. 31	Accounting for Tax Benefits Related to U.K. Tax Legislation Concerning Stock Relief
Sept.	1979	No. 32	Specialized Accounting and Reporting Principles and Practices in AICPA Statements of Position and Guides on Accounting and Auditing Matters (amended and partially superseded)
Sept.	1979	No. 33	Financial Reporting and Changing Prices (amended and partially superseded)
Oct.	1979	No. 34	Capitalization of Interest Cost (amended)
Mar.	1980	No. 35	Accounting and Reporting by Defined Benefit Pension Plans (amended)
May	1980	No. 36	Disclosure of Pension Information (superseded)
July	1980	No. 37	Balance Sheet Classification of Deferred Income Taxes (amended)
Sept.	1980	No. 38	Accounting for Preacquisition Contingencies of Purchased Enterprises (superseded)
Oct.	1980	No. 39	Financial Reporting and Changing Prices: Specialized Assets—Mining and Oil and Gas
Nov.	1980	No. 40	Financial Reporting and Changing Prices: Specialized Assets—Timberlands and Growing Timber
Nov.	1980	No. 41	Financial Reporting and Changing Prices: Specialized Assets—Income-Producing Real Estate
Nov.	1980	No. 42	Determining Materiality for Capitalization of Interest Cost
Nov.	1980	No. 43	Accounting for Compensated Absences (amended)
Dec.	1980	No. 44	Accounting for Intangible Assets of Motor Carriers (superseded)
Mar.	1981	No. 45	Accounting for Franchise Fee Revenue (amended)
Mar.	1981	No. 46	Financial Reporting and Changing Prices: Motion Picture Films
Mar.	1981	No. 47	Disclosure of Long-Term Obligations (amended)
June	1981	No. 48	Revenue Recognition When Right of Return Exists
June	1981	No. 49	Accounting for Product Financing Arrangements
Nov.	1981	No. 50	Financial Reporting in the Record and Music Industry
Nov.	1981	No. 51	Financial Reporting by Cable Television Companies (amended)
Dec.	1981	No. 52	Foreign Currency Translation (amended)
Dec.	1981	No. 53	Financial Reporting by Producers and Distributors of Motion Picture Films (superseded)
Jan.	1982	No. 54	Financial Reporting and Changing Prices: Investment Companies (superseded)
Feb.	1982	No. 55	Determining Whether a Convertible Security is a Common Stock Equivalent (superseded)
Feb.	1982	No. 56	Designation of AICPA Guide and SOP 81-1 on Contractor Accounting and SOP 81-2 on Hospital-Related Organizations as Preferable for Applying *APB Opinion 20* (superseded)
Mar.	1982	No. 57	Related Party Disclosures (amended)
April	1982	No. 58	Capitalization of Interest Cost in Financial Statements that Include Investments Accounted for by the Equity Method
April	1982	No. 59	Deferral of the Effective Date of Certain Accounting Requirements for Revision Plans of State and Local Governmental Units
June	1982	No. 60	Accounting and Reporting by Insurance Enterprises (amended)
June	1982	No. 61	Accounting for Title Plant (amended)
June	1982	No. 62	Capitalization of Interest Cost in Situations Involving Certain Tax-Exempt Borrowings and Certain Gifts and Grants
June	1982	No. 63	Financial Reporting by Broadcasters (amended)

Date Issued		No.	Title
Sept.	1982	No. 64	Extinguishment of Debt Made to Satisfy Sinking-Fund Requirements (superseded)
Sept.	1982	No. 65	Accounting for Certain Mortgage Bank Activities (amended)
Oct.	1982	No. 66	Accounting for Sales of Real Estate (amended)
Oct.	1982	No. 67	Accounting for Costs and Initial Rental Operations of Real Estate Projects (amended)
Oct.	1982	No. 68	Research and Development Arrangements (amended)
Nov.	1982	No. 69	Disclosures about Oil and Gas Producing Activities
Dec.	1982	No. 70	Financial Reporting and Changing Prices: Foreign Currency Translation
Dec.	1982	No. 71	Accounting for the Effects of Certain Types of Regulation (amended)
Feb.	1983	No. 72	Accounting for Certain Acquisitions of Banking or Thrift Institutions (amended)
Aug.	1983	No. 73	Reporting a Change in Accounting for Railroad Track Structures
Aug.	1983	No. 74	Accounting for Special Termination Benefits Paid to Employees
Nov.	1983	No. 75	Deferral of the Effective Date of Certain Accounting Requirements for Pension Plans of State and Local Governmental Units (superseded)
Nov.	1983	No. 76	Extinguishment of Debt (superseded)
Dec.	1983	No. 77	Reporting by Transferors for Transfers of Receivables with Recourse (superseded)
Dec.	1983	No. 78	Classifications of Obligations that Are Callable by the Creditor
Feb.	1984	No. 79	Elimination of Certain Disclosures for Business Combinations by Nonpublic Enterprises (superseded)
Aug.	1984	No. 80	Accounting for Futures Contracts (superseded)
Nov.	1984	No. 81	Disclosure of Postretirement Health Care and Life Insurance Benefits
Nov.	1984	No. 82	Financial Reporting and Changing Prices: Elimination of Certain Disclosures
Mar.	1985	No. 83	Designation of AICPA Guides and Statement of Position on Accounting by Brokers and Dealers in Securities, by Employee Benefit Plans, and by Banks as Preferable for Purposes of Applying *APB Opinion 20*
Mar.	1985	No. 84	Induced Conversions of Convertible Debt
Mar.	1985	No. 85	Yield Test for Determining Whether a Convertible Security Is a Common Stock Equivalent (superseded)
Aug.	1985	No. 86	Accounting for the Costs of Computer Software to be Sold, Leased, or Otherwise Marketed
Dec.	1985	No. 87	Employers' Accounting for Pensions (amended)
Dec.	1985	No. 88	Employers' Accounting for Settlements and Curtailments of Defined Benefit Pension Plans and for Termination Benefits (amended and partially superseded)
Dec.	1986	No. 89	Financial Reporting and Changing Prices (amended)
Dec.	1986	No. 90	Regulated Enterprises—Accounting for Abandonments and Disallowances of Plant Costs
Dec.	1986	No. 91	Accounting for Nonrefundable Fees and Costs Associated with Originating or Acquiring Loans and Initial Direct Costs of Leases
Aug.	1987	No. 92	Regulated Enterprises—Accounting for Phase-in Plans
Aug.	1987	No. 93	Recognition of Depreciation by Not-for-Profit Organizations
Oct.	1987	No. 94	Consolidation of All Majority-Owned Subsidiaries
Nov.	1987	No. 95	Statement of Cash Flows (amended)
Dec.	1987	No. 96	Accounting for Income Taxes (superseded)
Dec.	1987	No. 97	Accounting and Reporting by Insurance Enterprises for Certain Long-Duration Contracts and for Realized Gains and Losses from the Sale of Investments
June	1988	No. 98	Accounting for Leases; Sale-Leaseback Transactions Involving Real Estate; Sales-Type Leases of Real Estate; Definition of the Lease Term; Initial Direct Costs of Direct Financing Leases
Sept.	1988	No. 99	Deferral of the Effective Date of Recognition of Depreciation by Not-for-Profit Organizations
Dec.	1988	No. 100	Accounting for Income Taxes—Deferral of the Effective Date of *FASB Statement No. 96*
Dec.	1988	No. 101	Regulated Enterprises—Accounting for the Discontinuation of Application of *FASB Statement No. 71* (amended)
Feb.	1989	No. 102	Statement of Cash Flows—Exemption of Certain Enterprises and Classification of Cash Flows from Certain Securities Acquired for Resale (amended)
Dec.	1989	No. 103	Accounting for Income Taxes—Deferral of the Effective Date of *FASB Statement No. 96*
Dec.	1989	No. 104	Statement of Cash Flows—Net Reporting of Certain Cash Receipts and Cash Payments and Classification of Cash Flows from Hedging Transactions
Mar.	1990	No. 105	Disclosure of Information About Financial Instruments with Off-Balance-Sheet Risk and Financial Instruments with Concentrations of Credit Risk (superseded)
Dec.	1990	No. 106	Employers' Accounting for Postretirement Benefits Other Than Pensions (amended and partially superseded)
Dec.	1991	No. 107	Disclosures about Fair Value of Financial Instruments (amended)
Dec.	1991	No. 108	Accounting for Income Taxes—Deferral of the Effective Date of *FASB Statement No. 96*
Feb.	1992	No. 109	Accounting for Income Taxes (amended and partially superseded)
Aug.	1992	No. 110	Reporting by Defined Benefit Pension Plans of Investment Contracts
Nov.	1992	No. 111	Rescission of *FASB Statement No. 32* and Technical Corrections
Nov.	1992	No. 112	Employers' Accounting for Postemployment Benefits
Dec.	1992	No. 113	Accounting and Reporting for Reinsurance of Short-Duration and Long-Duration Contracts
May	1993	No. 114	Accounting by Creditors for Impairment of a Loan (amended)
May	1993	No. 115	Accounting for Certain Investments in Debt and Equity Securities (amended and partially superseded)

Date Issued		No.	Title
June	1993	No. 116	Accounting for Contributions Received and Contributions Made (amended and partially superseded)
June	1993	No. 117	Financial Statements of Not-for-Profit Organizations (amended)
Oct.	1994	No. 118	Accounting by Creditors for Impairments of a Loan—Income Recognition and Disclosures
Oct.	1994	No. 119	Disclosure about Derivative Financial Instruments and Fair Value of Financial Instruments (superseded)
Jan.	1995	No. 120	Accounting and Reporting by Mutual Life Insurance Enterprises
Mar.	1995	No. 121	Accounting for the Impairment of Long-Lived Assets (superseded)
May	1995	No. 122	Accounting for Mortgage Servicing Rights (superseded)
Oct.	1995	No. 123	Accounting for Stock-Based Compensation (revised)
Nov.	1995	No. 124	Accounting for Certain Investments Held by Not-for-Profit Organizations (amended and partially superseded)
June	1996	No. 125	Accounting for Transfers and Servicing of Financial Assets and Extinguishment of Liabilities (superseded)
Dec.	1996	No. 126	Exemption from Certain Required Disclosures about Financial Instruments for Certain Nonpublic Entities
Dec.	1996	No. 127	Deferral of the Effective Date of Certain Provisions of *FASB Statement No. 125*
Feb.	1997	No. 128	Earnings per Share (amended)
Feb.	1997	No. 129	Disclosure of Information about Capital Structure
June	1997	No. 130	Reporting Comprehensive Income (amended and partially superseded)
June	1997	No. 131	Reporting Disaggregated Information about a Business Enterprise
Feb.	1998	No. 132	Employers' Disclosures about Pensions and Other Postretirement Benefits – an amendment of *FASB Statements No. 87, 88,* and *106* (revised) (amended and partially superseded)
June	1998	No. 133	Accounting for Derivative Instruments and Hedging Activities (amended and partially superseded)
Oct.	1998	No. 134	Accounting for Mortgage-Backed Securities Retained after the Securitization of Mortgage Loans Held for Sale by a Mortgage Banking Enterprise (an amendment of *FASB Statement No. 65*)
Feb.	1999	No. 135	Rescission of *FASB Statement No. 75* and Technical Corrections (amended)
June	1999	No. 136	Transfers of Assets to a Not-for-Profit Organization or Charitable Trust That Raises or Holds Contributions for Others (amended)
June	1999	No. 137	Accounting for Derivative Instruments and Hedging Activities—Deferral of the Effective Date for *FASB Statement No. 133* (an amendment of *Statement No. 133*)
June	2000	No. 138	Accounting for Certain Derivative Instruments and Certain Hedging Activities (an amendment of *FASB Statement No. 133*)
June	2000	No. 139	Rescission of *FASB Statement No. 53* and amendments to *FASB Statements No. 63, 89,* and *121*
Sept.	2000	No. 140	Accounting for Transfers and Servicing of Financial Assets and Extinguishments of Liabilities (a replacement of *FASB Statement 125*) (amended and partially superseded)
June	2001	No. 141	Business Combinations (amended)
June	2001	No. 142	Goodwill and Other Intangible Assets (amended and partially superseded)
June	2001	No. 143	Accounting for Asset Retirement Obligations (amended and partially superseded)
Aug.	2001	No. 144	Accounting for the Impairment or Disposal of Long-Lived Assets (amended and partially superseded)
April	2002	No. 145	Rescission of *FASB Statements No. 4, 44,* and *64,* Amendment of *FASB Statement No. 13,* and Technical Corrections
June	2002	No. 146	Accounting for Costs Associated with Exit or Disposal Activities (amended and partially superseded)
Oct.	2002	No. 147	Acquisitions of Certain Financial Institutions, an Amendment of *FASB Statements No. 72* and *144* and *FASB Interpretation No. 9*
Dec.	2002	No. 148	Accounting for Stock-Based Compensation—Transition and Disclosure
April	2003	No. 149	Amendment of *Statement 133* on Derivative Instruments and Hedging Activities
May	2003	No. 150	Accounting for Certain Financial Instruments with Characteristics of Both Liabilities and Equity (amended)
Nov.	2004	No. 151	Inventory Costs – an amendment of *ARB No. 43*, Chapter 4
Dec.	2004	No. 152	Accounting for Real Estate Time-Sharing Transactions
Dec.	2004	No. 153	Exchanges on Non-Monetary Assets – an amendment of *APB Opinion No. 29*
May	2005	No. 154	Accounting Changes and Error Corrections – a replacement of *APB Opinion No. 20* and *FASB Statement No. 3*
Feb.	2006	No. 155	Accounting for Certain Hybrid Financial Instruments—an amendment of *FASB Statements No. 133* and *140*
Mar.	2006	No. 156	Accounting for Servicing of Financial Assets—an amendment of *FASB Statement No. 140* (amended)
Sept.	2006	No. 157	Fair Value Measurements
Sept.	2006	No. 158	Employers' Accounting for Defined Benefit Pension and Other Postretirement Plans—an amendment of *FASB Statements No. 87, 88, 106,* and *132R*
Feb.	2007	No. 159	The Fair Value Option for Financial Assets and Financial Liabilities—Including an amendment of *FASB Statement No. 115*

Date Issued		No.	Title

**Financial Accounting Standards Board (FASB),
Interpretations (1974–2006)**

Date Issued		No.	Title
June	1974	No. 1	Accounting Changes Related to the Cost of Inventory (*APB Opinion No. 20*)
June	1974	No. 2	Imputing Interest on Debt Arrangements Made Under the Federal Bankruptcy Act (*APB Opinion No. 21*) (superseded)
Dec.	1974	No. 3	Accounting for the Cost of Pension Plans Subject to the Employee Retirement Income Security Act of 1974 (*APB Opinion No. 8*)
Feb.	1975	No. 4	Applicability of *FASB Statement No. 2* to Purchase Business Combinations (amended)
Feb.	1975	No. 5	Applicability of *FASB Statement No. 2* to Development Stage Enterprises (superseded)
Feb.	1975	No. 6	Applicability of *FASB Statement No. 2* to Computer Software
Oct.	1975	No. 7	Applying *FASB Statement No. 7* in Statements of Established Enterprises
Jan.	1976	No. 8	Classification of a Short-Term Obligation Repaid Prior to Being Replaced by a Long-Term Security (*FASB Statement No. 6*)
Feb.	1976	No. 9	Applying *APB Opinion No. 16* and *17* when a Savings and Loan or Similar Institution is Acquired in a Purchase Business Combination (*APB Op. No. 16 & 17*) (amended)
Sept.	1976	No. 10	Application of *FASB Statement No. 12* to Personal Financial Statements (*FASB Statement No. 12*)
Sept.	1976	No. 11	Changes in Market Value after the Balance Sheet Date (*FASB Statement No. 12*)
Sept.	1976	No. 12	Accounting for Previously Established Allowance Accounts (*FASB Statement No. 12*)
Sept.	1976	No. 13	Consolidation of a Parent and Its Subsidiaries Having Different Balance Sheet Dates (*FASB Statement No. 12*)
Sept.	1976	No. 14	Reasonable Estimation of the Amount of a Loss (*FASB Statement No. 5*)
Sept.	1976	No. 15	Translation of Unamortized Policy Acquisition Costs by Stock Life Insurance Company (*FASB Statement No. 8*) (amended and partially superseded)
Feb.	1977	No. 16	Clarification of Definitions and Accounting for Marketable Equity Securities That Become Nonmarketable (*FASB Statement No. 12*)
Feb.	1977	No. 17	Applying the Lower of Cost or Market Rule in Translated Financial Statements (*FASB Statement No. 8*) (superseded)
Mar.	1977	No. 18	Accounting for Income Taxes in Interim Periods (*APB Op. No. 28*) (amended)
Oct.	1977	No. 19	Lessee Guarantee of the Residual Value of Leased Property (*FASB Statement No. 13*)
Nov.	1977	No. 20	Reporting Accounting Changes under AICPA Statements of Position (*APB Op. No. 20*)
April	1978	No. 21	Accounting for Leases in a Business Combination (*FASB Statement No. 13*) (amended)
April	1978	No. 22	Applicability of Indefinite Reversal Criteria to Timing Differences (*APB Op. No. 11* and *23*)
Aug.	1978	No. 23	Leases of Certain Property Owned by a Governmental Unit or Authority (*FASB Statement No. 13*)
Sept.	1978	No. 24	Leases Involving Only Part of a Building (*FASB Statement No. 13*)
Sept.	1978	No. 25	Accounting for an Unused Investment Tax Credit (*APB Op. No. 2, 4, 11, and 16*)
Sept.	1978	No. 26	Accounting for Purchase of a Leased Asset by the Lessee During the Term of the Lease (*FASB Statement No. 13*)
Nov.	1978	No. 27	Accounting for a Loss on a Sublease (*FASB Statement No. 13* and *APB Op. No. 30*) (amended)
Dec.	1978	No. 28	Accounting for Stock Appreciation Rights and Other Variable Stock Option or Award Plans (*APB Op. No. 15* and *25*) (amended)
Feb.	1979	No. 29	Reporting Tax Benefits Realized on Disposition of Investments in Certain Subsidiaries and Other Investees (*APB Op. No. 23* and *24*)
Sept.	1979	No. 30	Accounting for Involuntary Conversions of Nonmonetary Assets to Monetary Assets (*APB Op. No. 29*)
Feb.	1980	No. 31	Treatment of Stock Compensation Plans in EPS Computations (*APB Op. No. 15* and *Interp. 28*) (superseded)
Mar.	1980	No. 32	Application of Percentage Limitations in Recognizing Investment Tax Credit (*APB Op. No. 2, 4, and 11*)
Aug.	1980	No. 33	Applying FASB Statement No. 34 to Oil and Gas Producing Operations (*FASB Statement No. 34*)
Mar.	1981	No. 34	Disclosure of Indirect Guarantees of Indebtedness of Others (*FASB Statement No. 5*)
May	1981	No. 35	Criteria for Applying the Equity Method of Accounting for Investments in Common Stock (*APB Op. No. 18*)
Oct.	1981	No. 36	Accounting for Exploratory Wells in Progress at the End of a Period
July	1983	No. 37	Accounting for Translation Adjustments upon Sale of Part of an Investment in a Foreign Entity (Interprets *FASB Statement No. 52*)
Aug.	1984	No. 38	Determining the Measurement Date for Stock Option, Purchase, and Award Plans Involving Junior Stock (Interprets *APB Opinion No. 25*)
Mar.	1992	No. 39	Offsetting of Amounts Related to Certain Contracts (Interprets *APB Opinion No. 10* and *FASB Statement No. 105*) (amended)
Apr.	1993	No. 40	Applicability of Generally Accepted Accounting Principles to Mutual Life Insurance and Other Enterprises (Interprets *FASB Statements No. 12, 60, 97, and 113*)

Date Issued		No.	Title
Dec.	1994	No. 41	Offsetting of Amounts Related to Certain Repurchase and Reverse Repurchase Agreements
Sept.	1996	No. 42	Accounting for Transfers of Assets in Which a Not-for-Profit Organization is Granted Variance Power
June	1999	No. 43	Real Estate Sales (Interprets FASB Statement No. 66) (amended)
		No. 44	Accounting for Certain Transactions involving Stock Compensation (an interpretation of *APB Opinion No. 25*) (amended)
Nov.	2002	No. 45	Guarantor's Accounting and Disclosure Requirements for Guarantees, Including Indirect Guarantees of Indebtedness of Others (amended)
Jan.	2003	No. 46	Consolidation of Variable Interest Entities (an interpretation of *ARB No. 51*, revised) (amended)
March	2005	No. 47	Accounting for Conditional Asset Retirement Obligations – an interpretation of *FASB Statement No. 143*
June	2006	No. 48	Accounting for Uncertainty in Income Taxes—an interpretation of *FASB Statement No. 109*

Financial Accounting Standards Board (FASB), Technical Bulletins (1979–2002)

Date Issued		No.	Title
Dec.	1979	No. 79-1	Purpose and Scope of FASB Technical Bulletins and Procedures for Issuance (revised)
Dec.	1979	No. 79-2	Computer Software Costs
Dec.	1979	No. 79-3	Subjective Acceleration Clauses in Long-Term Debt Agreements
Dec.	1979	No. 79-4	Segment Reporting of Puerto Rican Operations
Dec.	1979	No. 79-5	Meaning of the Term 'Customer' as it Applies to Health Care Facilities under *FASB Statement No. 14*
Dec.	1979	No. 79-6	Valuation Allowances Following Debt Restructuring
Dec.	1979	No. 79-7	Recoveries of a Previous Writedown under a Troubled Debt Restructuring Involving a Modification of Terms
Dec.	1979	No. 79-8	Applicability of *FASB Statements 21* and *33* to Certain Brokers and Dealers in Securities
Dec.	1979	No. 79-9	Accounting in Interim Periods for Changes in Income Tax Rates
Dec.	1979	No. 79-10	Fiscal Funding Clauses in Lease Agreements
Dec.	1979	No. 79-11	Effect of a Penalty on the Term of a Lease
Dec.	1979	No. 79-12	Interest Rate Used in Calculating the Present Value of Minimum Lease Payments
Dec.	1979	No. 79-13	Applicability of *FASB Statement No. 13* to Current Value Financial Statements
Dec.	1979	No. 79-14	Upward Adjustment of Guaranteed Residual Values
Dec.	1979	No. 79-15	Accounting for Loss on a Sublease Not Involving the Disposal of a Segment
Dec.	1979	No. 79-16	Effect on a Change in Income Tax Rate on the Accounting for Leveraged Leases (revised)
Dec.	1979	No. 79-17	Reporting Cumulative Effect Adjustment from Retroactive Application of *FASB No. 13*
Dec.	1979	No. 79-18	Transition Requirements of Certain FASB Amendments and Interpretations of *FASB Statement No. 13*
Dec.	1979	No. 79-19	Investor's Accounting for Unrealized Losses on Marketable Securities Owned by an Equity Method Investee
Dec.	1980	No. 80-1	Early Extinguishment of Debt through Exchange for Common or Preferred Stock (amended)
Dec.	1980	No. 80-2	Classification of Debt Restructuring by Debtors and Creditors
Feb.	1981	No. 81-1	Disclosure of Interest Rate Futures Contracts and Forward and Standby Contracts
Feb.	1981	No. 81-2	Accounting for Unused Investment Tax Credits Acquired in a Business Combination Accounted for by the Purchase Method
Feb.	1981	No. 81-3	Multiemployer Pension Plan Amendments Act of 1980
Feb.	1981	No. 81-4	Classification as Monetary or Nonmonetary Items
Feb.	1981	No. 81-5	Offsetting Interest Cost to be Capitalized with Interest Income
Nov.	1981	No. 81-6	Applicability of Statement 15 to Debtors in Bankruptcy Situations
Jan.	1982	No. 82-1	Disclosure of the Sale or Purchase of Tax Benefits through Tax Leases (amended)
Mar.	1982	No. 82-2	Accounting for the Conversion of Stock Options into Incentive Stock Options as a Result of the Economic Recovery Tax Act of 1981
July	1983	No. 83-1	Accounting for the Reduction in the Tax Basis of an Asset Caused by the Investment Tax Credit (ITC)
Mar.	1984	No. 84-1	Accounting for Stock Issued to Acquire the Results of a Research and Development Arrangement (amended)
Sept.	1984	No. 84-2	Accounting for the Effects of the Tax Reform Act of 1984 on Deferred Income Taxes Relating to Domestic International Sales Corporations
Sept.	1984	No. 84-3	Accounting for the Effects of the Tax Reform Act of 1984 on Deferred Income Taxes of Stock Life Insurance Enterprises
Oct.	1984	No. 84-4	In-Substance Defeasance of Debt
Mar.	1985	No. 85-1	Accounting for the Receipt of Federal Home Loan Mortgage Corporation Participating Preferred Stock
Mar.	1985	No. 85-2	Accounting for Collateralized Mortgage Obligations (CMOs) (superseded)

Date Issued		No.	Title
Nov.	1985	No. 85-3	Accounting for Operating Leases with Scheduled Rent Increases
Nov.	1985	No. 85-4	Accounting for Purchases of Life Insurance (superseded)
Dec.	1985	No. 85-5	Issues Relating to Accounting for Business Combinations (amended)
Dec.	1985	No. 85-6	Accounting for a Purchase of Treasury Shares
Oct.	1986	No. 86-1	Accounting for Certain Effects of the Tax Reform Act of 1986
Dec.	1986	No. 86-2	Accounting for an Interest in the Residual Value of a Leased Asset (amended)
April	1987	No. 87-1	Accounting for a Change in Method of Accounting for Certain Postretirement Benefits
Dec.	1987	No. 87-2	Computation of a Loss on an Abandonment
Dec.	1987	No. 87-3	Accounting for Mortgage Servicing Fees and Rights (amended)
Dec.	1988	No. 88-1	Issues Relating to Accounting for Leases
Dec.	1988	No. 88-2	Definition of a Right of Setoff
Dec.	1990	No. 90-1	Accounting for Separately Priced Extended Warranty and Product Maintenance Contracts
Apr.	1994	No. 94-1	Application of Statement 115 to Debt Securities Restructured in a Troubled Debt Restructuring
Dec.	1997	No. 97-1	Accounting under Statement 123 for Certain Employee Stock Purchase Plans with a Look-Back Option
July	2001	No. 01-1	Effective Date for Certain Financial Institutions of Certain Provisions of Statement No. 140 Related to the Isolation of Transferred Financial Assets

Financial Accounting Standards Board (FASB), Statements of Financial Accounting Concepts (1978–2006)

Nov.	1978	No. 1	Objectives of Financial Reporting by Business Enterprises
May	1980	No. 2	Qualitative Characteristics of Accounting Information
Dec.	1980	No. 3	Elements of Financial Statements of Business Enterprises
Dec.	1980	No. 4	Objectives of Financial Reporting by Nonbusiness Organizations
Dec.	1984	No. 5	Recognition and Measurement in Financial Statements of Business Enterprises
Dec.	1985	No. 6	Elements of Financial Statements
Feb.	2000	No. 7	Using Cash Flow Information and Present Value in Accounting Measurements

NATIONAL ACCOUNTING BOARDS AND ORGANIZATIONS

American Accounting Association (AAA)
5717 Bessie Drive
Sarasota, FL 34233-2399
(941) 921-7747
www.aaahq.org

American Institute of Certified Public Accountants (AICPA)
1211 Avenue of the Americas
New York, NY 10036-8775
(212) 596-6200
www.aicpa.org

Association of Government Accountants (AGA)
2208 Mount Vernon Ave.
Alexandria, VA 22301-1314
(703) 684-6931
www.agacgfm.org

Financial Accounting Standards Board (FASB)
401 Merritt 7
P.O. Box 5116
Norwalk, CT 06856-5116
(203) 847-0700
www.fasb.org

Financial Executives International (FEI)
200 Campus Drive
Florham Park, NJ 07932-0674
(973) 765-1000
www.fei.org

Governmental Accounting Standards Board (GASB)
401 Merritt 7
P.O. Box 5116
Norwalk, CT 06856-5116
(203) 847-0700
www.gasb.org

International Accounting Standards Board (IASB)
30 Cannon Street
London EC4M 6XH, United Kingdom
Telephone: +44 (0)20 7246 6410
www.iasb.org

Institute of Internal Auditors (IIA)
247 Maitland Avenue
Altamonte Springs, FL 32701-4201
(407) 937-1100
www.theiia.org

Institute of Management Accountants (IMA)
10 Paragon Drive
Montvale, NJ 07645-1718
(201) 573-9000
www.imanet.org

Securities and Exchange Commission (SEC)
100 F Street, NE
Washington, DC 20549
(202) 551-6551
www.sec.gov